PSYCHOLOGY: A STUDY OF A SCIENCE

THE SERIES

STUDY I. CONCEPTUAL AND SYSTEMATIC

Volume 1. **Sensory, Perceptual, and Physiological Formulations**

CONTRIBUTORS: *Albert A. Blank, James J. Gibson, C. H. Graham, D. O. Hebb, Harry Helson, J. C. R. Licklider, Clifford T. Morgan, Kenneth N. Ogle, M. H. Pirenne and F. H. C. Marriott, Leo Postman and Edward C. Tolman, W. C. H. Prentice*

Volume 2. **General Systematic Formulations, Learning, and Special Processes**

CONTRIBUTORS: *Dorwin Cartwright, Douglas G. Ellson, W. K. Estes, F. C. Frick, Edwin R. Guthrie, Harry F. Harlow, R. A. Hinde, Arthur L. Irion, Frank A. Logan, Neal E. Miller, B. F. Skinner, Edward C. Tolman*

Volume 3. **Formulations of the Person and the Social Context**

CONTRIBUTORS: *Solomon E. Asch, Raymond B. Cattell, Franz J. Kallmann, Daniel Katz and Ezra Stotland, Paul F. Lazarsfeld, Henry A. Murray, Theodore M. Newcomb, Talcott Parsons, David Rapaport, Carl R. Rogers, Herbert A. Thelen*

Psychology: A Study of a Science

STUDY II. EMPIRICAL SUBSTRUCTURE
AND RELATIONS WITH OTHER SCIENCES

Volume 5. The Process Areas, the Person,

and Some Applied Fields:

Their Place in Psychology and in Science

STUDY II. EMPIRICAL SUBSTRUCTURE AND RELATIONS WITH OTHER SCIENCES

Volume 4. **Biologically Oriented Fields: Their Place in Psychology and in Biological Science**

CONTRIBUTORS: *Fred Attneave, Paul R. David and Laurence H. Snyder, R. C. Davis, I. T. Diamond and K. L. Chow, C. H. Graham and Philburn Ratoosh, William H. Ittelson, Robert B. Livingston, Carl Pfaffmann, Karl H. Pribram, Floyd Ratliff, W. A. Rosenblith and Eda B. Vidale, Burton S. Rosner, Gerhardt von Bonin, Karl Zener and Mercedes Gaffron*

Volume 5. **The Process Areas, the Person, and Some Applied Fields: Their Place in Psychology and in Science**

CONTRIBUTORS: *D. E. Berlyne, Irvin L. Child, Paul M. Fitts, Norman Guttman, Ernest R. Hilgard, Douglas H. Lawrence, Robert W. Leeper, Daniel R. Miller, Leo Postman, Eliot H. Rodnick, Julian B. Rotter, Nevitt Sanford, W. N. Schoenfeld and W. W. Cumming, Franklin V. Taylor*

Volume 6. **Investigations of Man as Socius: Their Place in Psychology and the Social Sciences**

CONTRIBUTORS: *Kenneth J. Arrow, Donald T. Campbell, David French, A. Irving Hallowell, Alex Inkeles, George Katona, William W. Lambert, Robert E. Lane, F. G. Lounsbury, Charles E. Osgood, Muzafer Sherif, Herbert A. Simon, George and Louise Spindler, James Tobin and F. Trenery Dolbear, Jr.*

POSTSCRIPT TO THE STUDY

(This title in preparation)

Volume 7. **Psychology and the Human Agent** *(by Sigmund Koch)*

Psychology: A Study of a Science

STUDY II. EMPIRICAL SUBSTRUCTURE
AND RELATIONS WITH OTHER SCIENCES

Volume 5. The Process Areas, the Person,

and Some Applied Fields:

Their Place in Psychology and in Science

Edited by Sigmund Koch

DUKE UNIVERSITY

McGRAW-HILL BOOK COMPANY, INC.

New York   San Francisco   Toronto   London

PSYCHOLOGY: A STUDY OF A SCIENCE was made possible by funds granted by the National Science Foundation to the American Psychological Association, and carried out under the sponsorship of the latter organization. Neither agency, however, is to be construed as endorsing any of the published findings or conclusions of the Study.

PREFACE

When one looks back over the history of science, the successes are likely to be stressed and the failures forgotten. Thus one tends to see science as starting with a sure sense of direction and progressing neatly to its present form: or so it is for the older and well-established branches of science, but not for psychology. Psychology has not one sure sense of direction but several quite unsure directions. Growth is erratic, and there is much casting about for the most crucial problems and the most powerful methods. These apparent differences between psychology and the older branches of science may result from the difficulty of developing a science of man; it is perhaps significant that many of the problems of psychology were not attacked by the methods of science until so late a date in history. Or the differences may be an illusion resulting from the much closer view we have of the beginning struggles to develop a science of psychology than we now have of the beginning efforts in the older sciences.

Certainly psychology has its problems, and they are not easy. Nevertheless, knowledge has grown rapidly in the short history of man's efforts to develop a science of behavior, and the time seems appropriate for a major effort to examine the progress that has been made in attempting to find a way, or ways, to the attainment of the explanatory power that we like to think of as characteristic of science. A growing body of empirical information, a serious concern over methodological issues, and a variety of efforts to bring a selected body of fact into the organizing framework of theory all emphasize the need for that line of questioning—always going on in science—which explores the shape of knowledge, the range and inner connections of the ideas through which it has been developed and organized, the changing substructures of empirical data, and their emerging relations to each other and to the findings of other sciences. The seven volumes of *Psychology: A Study of a Science* are a response to this need.

The first three volumes, which bear the collective title *Study I. Conceptual and Systematic,* are concerned with many of the systematic formulations of recent and current influence which psychologists have developed to account for the phenomena in which they are interested.

09484

Each systematic position is analyzed by its originator, or a person connected with its development, in a way which gives attention to the problems it seeks to solve, the empirical basis on which it rests, its degree of success, and its relations to other formulations.

A second set of three volumes, collectively called *Study II. Empirical Substructure and Relations with Other Sciences,* inquires, again through the efforts of creatively active investigators, into the organization of various fields of empirical knowledge, the relations of one to another, and to work going forward in other sciences. It also examines such problems in reverse through the participation of social and biological scientists who consider the relations of their own special fields to various parts of psychology.

Volume 7—*Psychology and the Human Agent*—will present the Study Director's view of certain problems of psychological inquiry in the light of the findings of the project.

Primary credit for the initiation of these studies goes to the Association's Policy and Planning Board, which decided in 1952 that the time had come for a thorough and critical examination of the status and development of psychology. The National Science Foundation agreed upon the desirability of such an undertaking and has generously supported the effort. When funds from the National Science Foundation were found to be insufficient for all of the expenses of the studies, the American Psychological Association provided the supplementary funds necessary to complete the work.

From the beginning, the study was divided into two parts. One part dealt with the education of psychologists and the factors conducive to research productivity in psychology. That part was directed by Professor Kenneth Clark of the University of Minnesota—now Dean Clark of the University of Colorado—who has reported the findings in *America's Psychologists: A Survey of a Growing Profession,* published by the American Psychological Association in 1957.

The other part, the part with which the present series of volumes is concerned, has dealt with the substance of psychological thought and data. Professor Sigmund Koch of Duke University has been responsible for this part of the study. Working closely with him has been a panel of consultants consisting of Lyle H. Lanier, Howard H. Kendler, Conrad G. Mueller, and Karl E. Zener. These men, but chiefly Dr. Koch, have planned, organized, interpreted and edited the work, and successfully enlisted the cooperation of the approximately eighty authors whose original papers constitute the basic material of the series.

In the background—at a safe distance from the labors that have sometimes engulfed Dr. Koch, his panel of consultants, and the primary authors—has been a steering committee on which I had the pleasure of serving as chairman, and having as colleagues Clarence H. Graham, Lyle H. Lanier, Robert B. MacLeod, Eliot H. Rodnick, M. Brewster Smith, and Robert L. Thorndike. The steering committee helped to make administrative arrangements and helped to decide on the scope of the studies, but takes no credit for their successful completion.

In the preface to *America's Psychologists* we have already acknowledged our gratitude to Kenneth Clark and his collaborators who helped to produce that volume. It is our final pleasant duty to express our thanks to Duke University for making Dr. Koch's time available; to the National Science Foundation for its necessary and generous financial support and for the counsel and support of John T. Wilson, Assistant Director for the Biological Sciences; to Lyle H. Lanier, Howard H. Kendler, Conrad G. Mueller, and Karl E. Zener for their critical and devoted help; to all the authors whose names appear on the title pages for their original contributions; and—most of all—to Sigmund Koch for directing and driving through to completion what we hope will be an oft-consulted aid to the scholars and research workers who are striving to increase the rigor and further the development of scientific psychology.

Dael Wolfle, CHAIRMAN
STEERING COMMITTEE
POLICY AND PLANNING BOARD

CONTENTS

Preface vii
Dael Wolfle

Introduction to Study II 1
Sigmund Koch

Perception and Learning 30
Leo Postman

Laws of Behavior and Facts of Perception 114
Norman Guttman

**The Nature of a Stimulus: Some Relationships between
Learning and Perception** 179
Douglas H. Lawrence

Behavior and Perception 213
W. N. Schoenfeld and W. W. Cumming

Motivation in Learning Theory 253
Ernest R. Hilgard

**Motivational Problems Raised by Exploratory and
Epistemic Behavior** 284
D. E. Berlyne

**Learning and the Fields of Perception, Motivation,
and Personality** 365
Robert W. Leeper

Personality: Its Place in Psychology 488
Nevitt Sanford

**Problems of Personality and Some Relations to An-
thropology and Sociology** 593
Irvin L. Child

The Study of Social Relationships: Situation, Identity,
and Social Interaction 639
Daniel R. Miller

Clinical Psychology, Psychopathology, and Research
on Schizophrenia 738
Eliot H. Rodnick

A Historical and Theoretical Analysis of Some Broad
Trends in Clinical Psychology 780
Julian B. Rotter

Human Engineering and Psychology 831
Franklin V. Taylor

Engineering Psychology 908
Paul M. Fitts

Name Index 935

Subject Index 953

INTRODUCTION TO STUDY II

Psychology: A Study of a Science is a report of the inquiries of many men into the status and tendency of psychological science. There were two major contexts of inquiry: *Study I* sought analytic understanding of many systematic formulations of current influence, while *Study II* sought insight into the structure, mutual interrelations, and associations with other sciences of the main empirical areas in which psychological research proceeds. The findings of *Study I. Conceptual and Systematic* have already been published as the first three volumes of *Psychology: A Study of a Science*. This fifth volume, along with the fourth and sixth, comprise *Study II. Empirical Substructure and Relations with Other Sciences*. A postscript volume by the Study Director completes the series.

Many motives can bring—and apparently have brought—readers to the series. It can be approached as a group of handbooks, textbooks, or as an encyclopedia; as a complement to the education of the student and a supplement to that of the advanced worker; as a repository of remedial reading for the repentant specialist or the overdiffuse generalist; as a guide to the recent history of the science; as a source work for the comparative analysis and assessment of theory, method, research strategies; as a detailed index to the emerging structure of the science; as data for the mapping of research within special fields and of cross-field interrelations; as an aid to inferences concerning the achievements, shortcomings, trends, prospects of our science. There is much in this Study that can nourish all such motives, as indeed many others. But first and foremost the Study is a *study* with its own milieu of aims, values, methods, questions—its own biography. Most of that biography was set forth in Volume 1, which contains the General Introduction to the Series (pages 1–18) and an Introduction to Study I (pages 19–40). The present Introduction to Study II will complete the story—happily with some dispatch because of the availability of the material just cited.

Each *study, volume, essay* is a self-contained unit which may be read with profit. But a nice appreciation of any of the units demands that it be seen in relation to the total Study. Study II, for instance, differs in problematic incidence from Study I, but it is animated by similar values and is not without overlap in subject matter, the difference be-

1

tween the "systematic" and the "empirical" being, after all, something less than absolute. Moreover, the two studies were designed so as to complement each other in certain respects—some of them obvious and some perhaps not immediately apparent. For instance, substantive areas thinly sampled in Study I were somewhat more fully represented in Study II. Again, systematic influence—necessarily one of the stronger selective criteria for contributors to Study I—resulted in a high proportion of senior contributors; the differing incidence of Study II made it possible to invite a larger proportion of younger investigators (though we make no claim to the satisfaction of "New-Frontier" standards). Points such as these are easily clarified in the present introduction. But if the reader is fully to realize any of the varied aims which may bring him to this Study, it is well that he see it in the first instance *as* a study, bearing its full burden of identity. For *that,* the reader must see this Introduction to Study II in relation to the introductions in Volume 1.

In this introduction, we consider briefly (1) the plan of the over-all Study, (2) the history and rationale of Study II, (3) the factors determining the composition of the contributor group and the coverage of this study, and (4) certain anticipations concerning the character of the findings.

RÉSUMÉ OF DESIGN OF "PSYCHOLOGY: A STUDY OF A SCIENCE"

For the immediate orientation of the reader, the next few paragraphs are given over to a résumé of the Study's plan.

Study I. Conceptual and Systematic

This study involved the intensive analysis of thirty-four "systematic formulations" of widely varying type and subject-matter reference, and all of established influence in recent psychology. A systematic formulation was defined quite generally as "any set of sentences formulated as a tool for ordering knowledge with respect to some specified domain of events, or furthering the discovery of such knowledge": in applying this definition, care was taken that no formulation be precluded by nonconformity to standardized conceptions of the nature of "theory." Since each systematic formulation is the end product of a human effort to see and state order in a given domain, each analysis was made either by the originator(s) of the formulation in question or (in a few cases) by individuals creatively associated with the *development* of formulations of which they were not the primary authors.

Each systematist was invited to approach his work with certain common *themes of analysis* in mind. These were designed to invite a convergence of insight on problems of systematization which had emerged from the practice of the past three decades, more or less. Some of the suggested problems had been conspicuous in previous "metasystematic" discussion, but required, in our opinion, exposure to a wider range of systematically schooled sensibilities. Others were problems that seemed critically posed by recent systematic work, yet ones which had received little or no explicit attention.

The dominating hope was for analyses that might illumine the relations between the creative *processes* of systematizing and their publicly expressed *products*. It was thus hoped that the atmosphere of the study might encourage as much concern with background influences, orienting presuppositions, and working methods as with conceptual content, research achievements, and prospects. It was felt that analysis of this order could itself have creative consequences; reflective scrutiny of the extent and depth envisaged means *rethinking*. The primary intent of the discussion themes (and indeed, the constant aim of editorial effort) was to realize an atmosphere that might invite such emphases. Authors were requested to make explicit reference to the themes in their writing only to an extent they deemed appropriate or congenial. The use of the themes for facilitating the collation of findings was thus a secondary, if still important, aim. As matters turned out, most authors adhered to them sufficiently to give the reader an excellent purchase for the detection of similarities and differences on key issues.

The grounds for the selection of the thirty-four formulations included in Study I are given in Volume 1 (pages 21–27). The aim was a reasonably balanced diversification of formulations (as judged by many consultants) with respect to (1) subject-matter reference, and (2) conceptual and methodological "type." Many significant formulations that we would have wished to represent in the original list were excluded by spatial and other arbitrary restrictions. Nor was it possible to include in the final domain all formulations originally chosen. Though the proportion of inclusions is remarkable, there were some individuals who could not participate. We do not, then, claim "representativeness" even in an informal and impressionistic sense. We do, however, claim sufficient diversity to extend markedly the range of formulations which in recent years have been given sustained analytic attention.

Study II. Empirical Substructure and Relations with Other Sciences

This study seeks increased understanding of the internal structure of psychological science and its place in the matrix of scientific activity. A large number of distinguished investigators in psychology proper and in related biological and social sciences were invited to write papers which examine the organization of empirical knowledge within subareas of these disciplines and chart their cross-connections. Psychologist contributors were asked to consider the relations between their own fields of special competence and the rest of psychology and, if they wished, to inquire also into relations with relevant segments of other sciences. Social and biological scientists were asked to examine the relations between their own fields and psychology.

All who were invited are individuals whose research interests have bridged conventionally discriminated fields of knowledge. Each was asked to place special emphasis on those "bridging problems" which had been central in his own research experience. As in the case of Study I, certain common themes of analysis were proposed. The "themes" for Study II comprise a detailed breakdown of the senses in which questions of "mapping" subject-matter structure and exploring field interrelations might be entertained. The analytic themes were intended to play rather different roles in the two studies. Because in Study I the analytic unit was typically a circumscribed "systematic formulation," it was reasonable to encourage adherence to the themes in some degree. In Study II, the scope of the topics made it impossible for any author to embark on more than a few of the many analytic directions that could be pursued in considering subject-matter interrelations. The analytic themes were thus offered primarily as an illustrative check list in the hope that concrete and differentiated questioning might be encouraged, and that certain perhaps promising modes of analysis of a sort not often carried out be at least considered.

Though the topography of a science is too vast and labile for comprehensive or final mapping, this very fact makes it more important to assay the contours of knowledge as best we can. Study II exploits the only resource available in such problems—individual vision. It assumes that a pool of expert, specialized minds can give insight of a sort not ordinarily available into the emerging structure of a science. Forty-two essays have been contributed by fifty authors (counting collaborators) whose interests have signally spanned subdivisions of psychology, or of social or biological science on the one hand, and psychology on the other. Just as in the case of Study I, contributors and topics are not meant to be "representative"—whatever that can mean—of their respective populations: the intention is to extend the range of areas which have been considered from a perspective like that of Study II, the range of sensibilities which have been trained on such interrelational questions, and the range of analytic approaches that have been made. The hope is that the study will not only extend knowledge of the developing structure of our science, but will highlight the importance of explicit questioning concerning the articulation of knowledge and recommend to the reader, by the rhetoric of its insights, the habit of such questioning.

Psychology and the Human Agent

This volume is a postscript to the Study, representing certain views formed by the director in its course. The book (1) records those attitudes toward *a* science and science which necessarily color the spirit of the Study, (2) constructs trends from the massive findings of the two group studies, and (3) considers, in the light of the Study's premises and apparent trends, certain problems of psychological inquiry suggested by the practice of the past several decades.

HISTORY AND RATIONALE OF STUDY II

Psychology: A Study of a Science is the result of a project sponsored by the American Psychological Association and subsidized jointly by the National Science Foundation and the sponsoring organization. The project, known as "Project A of the APA Study of the Status and Development of Psychology," was inaugurated in the fall of 1952. It, and a separately administered sister project ("Project B") had their origin in proposals of the Association's Policy and Planning Board concerning the desirability of a series of investigations into psychological knowledge and the institutional and occupational arrangements which had evolved in its pursuit. It was the Board's energetic advocacy of such a program (especially under the chairmanship of Lyle H. Lanier in 1951–1952) that eventuated in the constitution of the two projects: Project A to be concerned with the "methodological, theoretical, and empirical status of psychological science," and Project B with "occupational, educational, and institutional problems."

Kenneth Clark served as Director of Project B (and has already reported its results in his book, *America's Psychologists*[1]). The present editor served as Director of Project A. Both projects profited from the counsel of an advisory committee under the chairmanship of Dael Wolfle. Each director also had the advice of a panel of consultants. Dr. Wolfle has described the relations of these groups to the project in his *Preface*.

Certain of the stages in the process of translating the general mandate for the project into the detailed plan for *Psychology: A Study of a Science* have been described in the General Introduction to the series (Volume 1, pages 6–14). Let it suffice here to reduce an intricate story to a few words.

From the beginning it was decided to proceed gradually: to set no plan into action until it was clear that it could stir a reasonable community of imaginations, and until there was at least some evidence for its practicability. After a lengthy planning process involving an intricate

---

[1] K. E. Clark, *America's Psychologists: A Survey of a Growing Profession*, Washington, American Psychological Association, 1957.

give-and-take between the director, the committee, panel, and selected consultants, the investigation that was to become *Study I. Conceptual and Systematic* was launched in the fall of 1953. Further planning concerning Study II and, to some extent, the more slender venture of the director's book continued through October, 1954. The present study was initiated at that time.

In planning, it was felt important to arrive at relatively limited, if still challenging, objects of study: to avoid the kind of grandiosity on which group investigations can so easily founder. Moreover, objects of inquiry were sought which might most profit from the circumstances of group inquiry. If grandiosity was thus held under control, exuberance was another matter! Many such objects suggested themselves during the planning, too many. Their range is barely suggested in the discussion of "rationale" given in the Volume 1 general introduction (pages 7–14). The ideas for the present study (as those for Study I) thus represent a selection from a wide array of possibilities.

Among the many types of questions that can be asked about a science, none could well be more important than those concerning the relations among its chief fields of inquiry and its interpenetrations with other disciplines concerned with overlapping objects of study. Yet in psychology few questions have been pursued with less vigor. It has long been a platitude to lament the growing specialism and insulation of research areas in our science. But the lament has occasioned not much more than discomfort and perhaps not enough of that.

Nevertheless, the investigator who wishes to environ his work with meaning has necessarily held certain beliefs about such matters. These, however, have often been so thin as to be tantamount to a brushing aside of the type of problem they address. Thus, for instance, it has been fairly fashionable to assume that the traditional, so to say, "process fields" of psychology (as e.g., perception, learning, motivation) are essentially chapter headings, having no systematic significance. The frequent corollary is that whatever is viable in the various fields will somehow be integrated in some future theory. But whether a theory can integrate research in diverse and largely insulated fields without the theorist keeping carefully in view from an early stage the detailed relations which obtain among them is not often considered. Certainly those theorists of the recent past who assumed that all significant problems of psychology could be solved via postulates local to a single research area have not in the results of their work increased confidence in such a position.

The relatively superficial concern with interrelationship issues often reflects a judgment that such problems cannot be solved within the terms given by the state of psychology. It is held that the main areas distinguished by convention are essentially distinctions of investigative convenience and with this it is usual to presume that analysis would show each such field to be a loose congeries of research findings having little rational coherence. But since the analysis is almost never made, it is impossible to test the *coherence* of field boundaries and thus arrive at more significant organizations. *Psychology: A Study of a Science* has constantly emphasized a view which sees most things in science as an uneven compound of the rational and extrarational, but certainly the relative proportion may be made to vary.

There is no way out of it. Even were the "field" distinctions wholly ones of "convenience," it would be well to know whether and to what extent they *are* convenient. But one can doubt the story to be that simple. The rather crassly defined fields into which convention parcels psychological knowledge could be distinctions of convenience, yet not of *mere* convenience. Certainly if we trace fields like perception, learning, cognition, motivation, emotion, into the history of psychology, near or remote, it becomes clear that such fields were premised on analyses of psychological phenomena meant to have systematic and even a crude ontological significance. The late nineteenth-century psychologists who talked about cognition, conation, and affection, for instance, thought they were talking about dimensions of analysis which in some sense fitted psychological phenomena and were adequate to them. The conventionalist and nominalist sensibility of recent psychology prefers to see its subareas as collections of functional relationships among characteristic (but often not character*ized*) classes of variables. It is perhaps this nominalism which, at some level in the inquirer's personality, has supported the rather nonchalant attitude toward interrelational problems. But, whether these collections of functional relationships are seen as having "functional," systematic, or even ontological force or not, their relation must be taken seriously if we are to have a meaningful science. Plural inquiries must stand in some kind of relationship if we are to have a science. If they stand in none, we have no science.

Despite such tendencies to evade interrelational problems, they have not been bypassed. They cannot be. They are constantly thrust upon us by the exigencies of research planning, pedagogy, and administration. The upshot is that we are content with superficial levels of analysis and cognitively thin stereotypes. For example, it has not in recent memory been rare for a theorist to champion either a "purely behavioral" or a "physiological" frame of reference for his concepts and translate this preference into the grain of an ambitious theory *before* essaying detailed analysis of actual and possible relations between physiology and psychology. Indeed, there have been cases when, say, a dogmatic "empty organism" approach has become an embarrassment after the "purely be-

havioral" theory begins to generate psychophysiological analyses and research.

To pursue the area of this illustration a bit further: For a long time
in recent history, consideration of relations between psychology and
physiology was left pretty much to philosophers of science, a group not
eminently qualified in either field. The philosophers proceeded from a
context established by the traditional "mind-body problem." For a period
—coinciding with the hegemony of positivism—of some twenty-five
years, it was something of a fashion to show that this problem becomes
meaningful only upon translation into questions concerning the relations
between the "language systems" of psychology and physiology. But actual
analysis of these relations, if not eschewed, was approached in a way that
could yield little of value to the empirical scientist. In effect, the philosophers called for an analysis they did not make, while the psychologists
posited stereotypes (e.g., "All explanations must come from physiology,"
"No explanations can come from physiology," "Psychological laws are
derivable in principle from physiology but psychology must first develop
at its own level") for which they did not even *invite* analysis. In the
course of what discussion took place, the issue was addressed in hopelessly global form: e.g., *prescriptions* recommending some desirable future
relationship between the two disciplines were not distinguished from *description* of extant relations, or either of these from *prediction,* based on
apparent trends, of probable future relations. Again, much of the discussion seemed to presume that the relations of psychology to the biological
sciences *in general* would be established once the matter was got straight
for physiology: that specific relations with other biological disciplines
need not be considered.

The century has seen considerably more attention given to relations
of psychology and the social sciences than to its relations with the biological sciences. Much of this has come from within the social sciences where,
for obvious historical reasons, the need to establish identity is great and
where psychology is readily seen as some kind of base line against which
a *persona* may be traced. And social psychology, a specifically twentieth-
century product, has perforce faced the same problem in reverse. But
here, too, thinking has tended to be dominated by stereotype. For instance, it is often claimed that psychology and sociology deal with behavior at different levels of abstraction, independently of efforts to specify
the formal or contentual characteristics of the abstractive levels in question. Assumptions may be made to the effect that it *is* or *is not* legitimate
to transfer concepts from a psychological to a sociological (or political-
science, or anthropological) context, or vice versa, with little clear analysis of the grounds for the one belief or the other. Again, much enthusiasm has gone into programs toward the "interdisciplinary" integra-

tion of psychology and the social sciences, with little prior exploration of the nature and degree of integration of the relevant sciences taken separately.

But questions concerning interrelations among the *subparts of psychology* have been slighted even more than those concerning relations with its bordering sciences. Conventionally discriminated areas of psychological science are variously held to be supplementary, independent, reducible one to the other, related according to one or another set of "bridging laws" or improperly subdivided, but such positions are rarely backed up by intensive analyses of the areas in question. Not seldom, workers in a given field are victims of an irresistible tendency to see their specialty as embracing the entire science; in the embrace, the rest of the science is often squeezed to death. Students of sensory process have been known to see no room for perceptual process; of learning, no room for either; of all, none for personality; of personality, none for all: men are easily drugged by the grandeur of their solipsisms. And in each such area there are subareas and sub-subareas within which solipsisms of descending magnitude may be achieved.

Crosscutting such substantive areas, discriminations such as the "pure" versus the "applied" figure with increasing importance in recent history, especially with the growth of vast professional groupings like the clinical. Here again it can be said that though many dogmas exist with regard to interrelations—of knowledge, training, professional roles, etc.— these dogmas have not often been backed by sustained and differentiated analysis.

The preceding account of certain of the circumstances which invite a study like this may impress the reader as rather more bleak than it need be. For instance, especially over the last ten or fifteen years, a number of research clusters which relate variables usually assigned to discrete fields have become conspicuous. There was the "new look" in perception and, more generally, the cluster of concerns with relations between motivational and perceptual variables. Another cluster has involved relations between perception and personality. Perhaps most conspicuous has been a massive concentration of interest—heavily documented in the present study but certainly evident outside it—in relations between perception and learning. This increase of interstitial interest no doubt announces a changing atmosphere and is certainly encouraging. But the depth of the earlier neglect and the thinness *still* of the present interest could not well be better documented than by the *character* of the newer interstitial research. The research that has been done on the relations of motivational and perceptual variables, or perceptual and so-called "personality variables," however valuable, has by and large involved narrow and adventitiously selected sets of variables and has been correlated with few far-reaching or searching examinations of relations between the fields from which they derive. As for the present interest in learning-perception relations, this admirable development, it must be recalled, occurred only after the field of perception itself had been all but legislated out of existence (at least in this country) for a period of roughly thirty years. Learning had *preempted* perception during the hegemony of behaviorism and neobehaviorism; neo-neobehaviorism, in willing peception back to life, is at the same time drawing attention to what can happen in the history of a science as a result of piecemeal viewing.

Words like "fields," "areas," "research clusters," "disciplines," are deceptive. The terms in which we talk about the architecture of knowledge inevitably suggest knowledge to be more architectonic than it is. Study II supposes that more explicit and intensive interest in the emerging structure of psychology is desirable. But it is well that an investigation into the "structure" of knowledge commence with a profound appreciation of the limits upon any such enterprise.

The study does not, for instance, suppose that everything that has been or is being done in psychology can fall into place, or in some way be "salvaged," in the terms of some happy and even-tempered interrelational scheme. Far from it—much that happens in a science is expendable (would that we knew precisely what!); much that is not expendable may fall at a given time into no orderly relations with any consistent map. The study does not presume that what is currently called psychology is best regarded as a single cohesive field of knowledge; rather, it stresses the importance of asking at all times penetrating questions about the degree of integration or fractionation of the field relative to prevailing definitions. The study does not even suppose that all *significant* knowledge need now or ever fall into one systematic or rational pattern; nothing says that differing universes of discourse, or even disparate "levels" of analysis must be commensurable. The study does not suppose that there is any privileged route to the conquest of interrelational problems or any special methodological gimmickry that can either enhance or replace individual vision. Though the units of study are units of "empirical" subject matter, it sees no absolute distinction between what is called the "theoretical" and the "empirical," and it is as eager to encourage exploration of interrelations via theoretical integrations or realignments as it is to encourage attempts at charting relations among empirical variables approached in a systematically more neutral way.

The study, of course, supposes that any single study addressed to the problems at issue can make only modest progress and that the progress is to be measured more in terms of the habits of thinking it recommends to its readers than its particular findings. It does not pretend to address every field of psychology distinguished by current convention or even every important field. Though it has assembled the views of many creative and knowledgeable men, it has no intention of fusing them into some single "standard" view of the structure and associations of our science. On the contrary, it has sought to ensure against the emergence of an "official" map by arranging that most sectors of the terrain of study be inspected by a plurality of viewers. In the end, what matters to this study is that the individual reader enrich his *own* view of the science, in his own way. If the study provides materials which in any degree will enable this, its purpose will have been well accomplished.

COVERAGE, CONTRIBUTOR GROUP, AND WORKING ATMOSPHERE

In planning the study, we sought to ensure far-ranging coverage of subject matter and to encourage concrete and differentiated analysis, but to allow the specific representation of cross-field topics and analytic questions to be determined by the authors' predilections. The pattern of this study is thus very largely a pattern of its authors' sensibilities playing, each in its own mode, upon problems that interest them.

The units of subject matter available to the study for the initiation of its inquiries can, of course, be no more "rationally" bounded than the "fields" distinguished by current convention. The purpose, after all, is to explore, not prejudge, the structure of the science. Inclusion of a field implied no commitment as to its *actual* degree of coherence—whether in respect to the character of its empirical variables, its problems, its methods, its role in the systematic analysis of behavior or experience, or any other attribute. In establishing the general framework of coverage, it was felt best to select subject-matter areas of relatively broad scope (say, "learning," rather than "conditioning" or "verbal learning") or, in the case of cross-science relations, entire disciplines. These units were meant to set the framework for the inclusion of contributors; as will be seen, the role of contributors was not necessarily to consider the cross-field problems raised by the *entire* (crassly defined) area they represented, but rather to stress *specific* bridging problems in the line of their primary interests and research. In the choice of "intra-psychological" fields, it was felt wisest to concentrate on areas conventionally allocated to *fundamental* psychology but, because of the importance of stimulating more explicit interest in the relations between pure and applied psychology, to include as well at least two applied fields.

Against such a background, the "fields" ultimately arrived at for consideration in their relationships were (1) from within *psychology*—

sensory psychology, perception, physiological psychology, learning, motivation, personality, social psychology, psycholinguistics, clinical psychology, and human engineering; (2) from within *biological science*—aspects of physiology, neuroanatomy, and genetics; and (3) from within *social science*—aspects of sociology, anthropology, linguistics, economics, and political science. It need hardly be added that the study does not regard this list of fields as exhausting its domain; even for psychology per se, there are obviously so many incidences from which crosscutting and overlapping breakdowns can be derived that it is not possible to say what "exhaustiveness" could mean in such a connection.

The design of Study II called for individuals whose primary professional background was in some one of the "fields" indicated above to consider its relations to some one or combination of the others. In the terminology of the study, the field which the analyst represents, by virtue of professional affiliation, is the "field of primary reference"; the "field(s) of secondary reference" is the domain(s) whose relationship to his "own" field the analyst proposes to explore. The *specific* bounding, for purposes of the analysis, of *both* fields of reference is of course the option of the analyst, an option always influenced by his particular cross-field research history. Though each author was asked to place special emphasis on those "bridging problems" which had been central in his own research experience, he was encouraged also to reach out from this core and bound his field of concern as generally as he might wish.

A *plurality* of individuals of differing background, systematic predilection, or specialized cross-area interest, was invited to "represent" *each* field of primary reference. The hope was that—depending on the breadth and density of the given field—it might be represented by between two and five individuals. For most of the fields of primary reference, this hope was realized.

It should be emphasized that though a contributor was always invited to "represent" a given field of primary reference, his field(s) of secondary reference was never specified. Rather, he was asked to pursue the analysis of cross-field relations in whatever directions he might wish. Thus the pattern of specific cross-field relationships considered in the study was largely *author-determined*. Any attempt to compose the domain of study by some arbitrary combination and permutation of the fields of reference would have been close to meaningless. The chances of nontrivial knowledge about cross-field relations being won by an analyst who had not already established intimate interests in the relevant problems would be very slight. A major strength of the present study is precisely that it taps the knowledge and insight of authors in the *particular* contexts in which they are in fact most knowledgeable and insightful.

It will be noted also that the way in which the study's coverage was planned makes it possible for two (or more) authors to elect the same primary and secondary reference-field combination. Such overlap, when it occurs, is often more apparent than real, in that the meaning of "same" in such a context can be markedly qualified by the different perceptions that two analysts may have of their fields of reference. Be this as it may, provision for overlaps of this sort was considered another strength of the plan. The play of differing scientific sensibilities on the same substantive issues (be they *really* the same or only nominally so) can be highly illuminating. Moreover, patterns of convergence on given cross-field combinations and on given fields of secondary reference would to some extent be diagnostic of the distribution of interest in interstitial problems of the field at large; any clusterings of interest would mean clusterings of analysis at precisely those points which require maximum attention if a just picture of the status of the science is to be derived. In administering the study, it was standard policy to advise authors to plan their essays without regard to the possibility of overlaps with the topics of their colleagues.

A few words are now in order about the arduous process of converting these framework decisions into the *actual* coverage of the study. The initial step was to begin—with the help of the Project A panel and many consultants, each expert in some field of the study—a list of contributor candidates. A few months of intensive thought and interchange produced a list of imposing architecture. Like all such lists, it never did become fully stable: it required frequent adjustments to the exigencies of the study.

The more obvious criteria of election to the list were research distinction in the field of primary reference, significant evidence of scholarly and analytic ability, and established interest—preferably as realized in a long-range research program—in problems of a cross-field or cross-discipline nature. Among the more subtle criteria was a preference for men of especially self-determining cast.

In the background were a number of considerations of a more special sort. One was the hope that a number of men known to have original and stimulating ideas but not noted for their readiness to appear in the literature might be persuaded to participate. Others were addressed as much to the interests of the project as a whole as to those of Study II. Thus, because Study I had been populated by a high proportion of contributors in the "elder-statesman" category, it was hoped that the balance might be redressed by including a reasonable number of younger, if still mature, contributors in Study II. Another such consideration had much to do with the relative number of candidates sought to represent each area. This was the desire to represent more fully in the present study certain of the areas (e.g., physiological psychology) that had been only thinly sampled in Study I. Contrariwise, one of the fields especially widely covered in the first study (learning) was represented in the second by rather fewer contributors than might otherwise have been appropriate.

The numbers of contributors ultimately representing each of the study's fields of primary reference were conditioned by many factors, some planned and some outside our control. As already mentioned, it was envisaged at the outset that each field should be represented by between two and five contributors. Within these limits, efforts were made to represent subfields of fundamental psychology in a density roughly reflecting their extent and current importance. For each of the two applied fields (clinical psychology and human engineering), two contributors were to be sought. There were to be between two and three contributors for each of the biological and social sciences included as primary reference fields —this for a number of pragmatic reasons, such as the need to limit the study's size and the expected difficulty of enlisting nonpsychologist contributors.

Reference to the tables of contents will show that in a rough way these framework requirements were satisfied in the final distribution of contributors. The main disappointments were the failure to obtain plural representation of the three biological sciences included as fields of primary reference and of sociology. To some extent this is compensated for by the very large number of biologically oriented *psychologists* who consider relations with biological science, and the fairly large number of personality and social psychologists who entertain questions of relationship with sociology.

For areas having multiple representation, the constant effort was to achieve *diversified groups* of contributors—men who, by virtue of differences in systematic approach, research background, or scientific temperament, would be likely to see their problems in different ways. Obviously, for groups of the size involved and characteristics of the subtlety at issue, there could be no thought of some principle of diversification. If, however, inferences can be made from the essays to characteristics of their authors, it is fairly evident that this aspect of the planning was not frustrated.

So much for the *planning* of the representation. The final roster was not, of course, uninfluenced by the availability (and in a few cases the pertinacity) of authors. About as many people refused to participate as the number who ultimately did. This 50 per cent rate of refusals is, we think, fairly modest for a study of the present character, and was not out of line with expectation. In Study I, there had been a markedly lower rate. But in Study I the unit of analysis had been given systematic formulations and the men approached were in most instances their owners. Not only a vested interest in the objects of analysis but an expectation (not always borne out) that they need not go far afield in the preparation of their analysis, worked toward acceptance. In the present study, equally overcommitted people were being asked to take on a task which, though in the line of their interest, could not call on identifications of comparable power and which, moreover, was of a sort that often required extensive scholarly preparation. Despite these circumstances, relatively few of the Study II refusals came from the psychologist candidates. By far the largest number came from the "related" disciplines and, among these, most from the biologists.

These reality conditions of the present study are significant for understanding the character of the final domain but are instructive, too, as positive findings relative to the problems broached by the study. Thus, for instance, the almost standard pattern of the refusals from the biological scientists and, to a lesser extent, the social scientists, was to express enthusiasm for the aims of the study but to plead an almost total lack of knowledge concerning the area of secondary reference (psychology). If the editor is any judge of correspondence, he can report that these protestations were characteristically of the most sincere sort, even if it be supposed that their authors could sometimes have discovered supplementary grounds for refusing. When it is realized that each of these candidates was a distinguished investigator, known largely for work which had bridged over into psychology, and further, that the group as a whole (especially the biologists) represented a large proportion of those in their fields known at the time to be doing such interrelational work, a number of conclusions become fairly compelling. It becomes fairly evident that those committed to interdisciplinary work are not in general combining plural disciplines into single skulls (as the slogan of interdisciplinary training executives would have it) but tend to be crossing field boundaries rather adventitiously in the pursuit of problems originating in the home territory. One gets little impression of a concern with a broader environment of interrelationships which might condition the significance of the specific cross-field variables under study. Whether this state of affairs is regrettable is not here the issue. What *is* the issue is that we have here an important descriptive fact concerning the status of interdisciplinary thinking—one which can give pause to confidence in the imminence of sweeping interdisciplinary "integrations" and lend realism to interdisciplinary training schemes. But more appropriate to the immediate purpose, the reader approaching Study II may derive from the present finding some useful perspective. Questions of field and discipline relationships *have* been neglected, neglected even by many of those whose work is by way of erecting those relationships. These problems are *not* easy. Vision can and must be trained on them but will not readily come to focus.

The story of our working methods is the story of an *atmosphere* of work. For such tasks as are addressed by the study there are no secret weapons: there is only the hope of inviting the play of specialized, creative minds on the objects and issues which they most prize. The hope was to realize an atmosphere that invited self-determination, freshness, spontaneity, *and* intellectual craftsmanship.

As is already evident, a central awareness of the study was the desirability of a more differentiated attack on interrelationship issues than had been usual. To a large extent the design of the study guarantees this, in that the main basis for bounding topics is the authors' more or less specialized cross-field research interests. But it was hoped that a set toward differentiated questioning could be sharpened by working out a detailed breakdown of the *types* of analytic questions that can be asked about the relations between any two fields of knowledge. These "themes of analysis" were among the materials explaining the study that were sent to all authors before their work began. They were offered essentially as an illustrative check list of the *range* of questions that might be asked. It was made clear that the themes had no legislative intent, that in the analyses they could be responded to selectively or not at all.

The themes of analysis discriminate a large number of highly specified questions which fall into six categories: (1) "mapping," in terms of definitive variable-constellations and in other ways, the fields of primary and secondary reference; (2) realignments, resulting from the analyses of 1, of conventional "field" boundaries; (3) "bridging laws" (i.e., cross-area functional dependencies) and formal relationships; (4) interrelations of methods, both research and systematic; (5) knowledge overlaps, including transpositions *and* duplications of findings, as between the areas of primary and secondary reference; (6) collaborative, administrative, and educational mechanisms as these have affected or promise to affect the interrelations of the fields under analysis.

The problem addressed by such a breakdown is not, of course, the sort that has a unique solution. What can be claimed for the breakdown arrived at is that it separates issues which heretofore have often been considered in deceptively global form into constituent *particular* questions. It strives also to ask a sufficient range of questions to do some degree of justice to the many different things that can be meant by a "field" or "area" of a science. A field, after all, can be approached as a body of formulated knowledge, the totality of the inquiring action that has generated that knowledge, the methods—empirical and formal—that are definitive, or the institutional, ideological, and material arrangements that in some way may be characteristic. The field may be approached as a collection of lawful or lawlike functional relationships, as a characteristic family or constellation of *empirical* variables, as a group of *systematic* variables assigned some general common property or function in a theory, as the collectivity of all systematic variables discriminated by all theories addressed to a cluster of empirical problems believed in some sense cohesive, as a class of processes, phenomena, or empirical problems believed unified by a relatively cohesive set of empirical laws, as a class of processes having some relatively independent causal influence on organismic functioning, etc. In characterizing a field, or a relationship between fields as defined in any of these ways, one can raise questions of history, of present status, or of indicated trend for the future. One can raise *descriptive* questions, or *normative* ones concerning *desirable* future status or relationship.

The *nature* of the relations that may be asserted or explored as between any of the given units that result from the above multifarious criteria may itself be looked into from quite different incidences. One might, for instance, look into primarily *formal* relationships (as, e.g., independence, deducibility, subsumability, translatability, etc.)—a type of consideration, incidentally, which in too many earlier analyses tended to preempt other more useful lines of approach. Again, one can try to discern, or perhaps hypothesize, empirical, or for that matter, systematic, laws which bridge between variables in the one domain and the other. Or one can inquire into "methodic" relations (in several senses of the methodic) between any two areas, even when these are not *defined* against a methodic criterion. One can entertain questions about interrelations (as e.g., influence lines) between the institutional, ideological, or administrative factors which environ inquiry in the fields under analysis. And many other questions.

Not all such questions are equally significant but more than a few are quite significant. *None* are at all significant unless posed in at least fairly clear independence of the others. The themes of analysis are a selection from among such contexts of questioning as are implicit in the above illustrations. The items are formulated with some explicitness and often supplemented with rather full explanation. The result is a not unformidable document. It appears as an appendix to Volume 6 and is offered to the reader in the same spirit it was to the authors—as a device for encouraging differentiated thinking about questions of structure and relationship, if not in these particular terms, at least in some *particular* terms.

To ensure that the themes be considered with a certain high seriousness, they were submitted to authors as a kind of ideal discussion outline which—we were quick to point out—"no . . . analyst can hope fully to satisfy." The items were in fact developed and sequenced in such a way as to set the terms of something pretty close to an "ideal" analysis, given infinite time, intelligence, and indefatigability of soul. Since the relata of analysis were sizable fields of knowledge, it was not, of course, expected that any given one of the items was susceptible to full answer, let alone any marked number of them. It was emphasized in the introduction to the outline that the task defined was "in any literal sense, impossible," and that "the condition of psychological knowledge is such that only modest increments of insight into issues of the sort here envisaged are attainable." Other escape exits were lushly distributed throughout the themes of analysis, and even more so in the letter of invitation and ensuing correspondence with contributors. Moreover, unlike the practice in Study I, where the themes of analysis played a somewhat different role, no editorial response to Study II manuscripts was ever directed toward increasing, or even encouraging, adherence to the themes. That the escape exits were effective is fairly evident from the fact that the architecture of the outline is visible in precisely none of the essays.

The themes did, we think, play pretty much the role expected of them. At the most general level, the earnestness of their intent elicited earnestness in return. Again, the atmosphere of the themes certainly has encouraged *intensive* analysis—short of which few considerations of inter-relationship issues can achieve much more than the circulation of stereotype. And finally, the evidence of the essays argues the probability that a wider range of questions, and more highly specified ones, have been asked than has characterized the *genre* of interrelational analyses in the past.

Did the themes have a "grooving effect"? The evidence says "No," while the range of the themes, and the variety of ways they comprehend of looking at the structure of the science, is such that they could hardly have constricted thinking.

But the themes should not detain us. What is important is not the questions men can raise but those they do raise, especially the questions that most recommend themselves to committed men at the frontiers of their fields. Whatever force this study has is gathered from the willingness of many such men searchingly to look *across* these frontiers at approximately the same time in history in directions set by their own curiosities. The emerging shape of a science is the emerging shape of what such men do and of what they see. If there has been anything happy about the study's conduct, this has been its disposition to hem in vision as little as possible, to depend on "mechanism" to a minimum, and to employ what mechanism it does for liberating ends.

The atmosphere of the study was the fifty atmospheres of the relationships, long-continued ones, with the individual authors. If any generalizations can be made about these, the main thing of note was the gallantry and forbearance of those on the productive side of the relationships. All gave the work their best effort and for most this meant exceedingly strenuous and long-continued effort. Many—however they approached their topic—found that the demands of such structural or interrelational problems as they were addressing were rather crueller than they had anticipated. Yet they pushed on without complaint. Virtually all were issue-centered, amiable, even appreciative, when editorial suggestions were made, no matter how obsessive the latter. The universal quantifier must, we fear, be dropped when it comes to the matter of promptness in meeting deadlines. A few men were model, a fair number finished within the secret timetable that most editors perforce sew in the lining of their Inverness, but not inconsiderable numbers worked agonizingly through their sixth, eighth, and even dozenth deadlines. This may sound like the kind of secret to which all editors are privy, but the present one doubts that extrapolation from normal editorial experience can give a sense of what can happen when there are fifty authors working on tasks so challenging as those posed by this study. Whatever the elements of anguish in these thoughts, it is by way of further praise of the authors that we mention them. For the rather considerable scatter in the receipt of manuscripts made it desirable to suggest that those received earlier be brought up to date. Of the many men thus penalized for their own virtue, almost all gave their uncomplaining cooperation.

At the editorial end of these fifty relationships, the main consistency was that such problems as the study was engaging could only be advanced by a pluralism of the widest excursion, by an utterly free play of the contributors' sensibilities within the quite general frame of the study's objectives. No goal or analytic direction that an author wished to pursue was ever discouraged. Whether the author wished to approach his topic via a theoretical or pretheoretical integration of the fields at issue, or primarily by empirical survey; whether he wished to stress one type of relationship question or many; whether he chose one field of secondary reference or several, or indeed, to train attention on the structure of the field of primary reference per se—all such matters were entirely his own option. Length of manuscript (short of flagrant indecency relative to the size of the volumes) was always his option, though we did, of course, uniformly express a preference for *detailed* analysis. In editing manuscripts, the editor's conception of his role was that of putting himself at the service of the particular objectives which the contributor had set. His suggestions were addressed to such ends as clarity, sound scholarship, consistency, occasionally style, and most generally, how best to strengthen or develop the author's argument.

A few *technical* injunctions were fairly consistently, though not inflexibly, asserted. Mention of these may give the reader some useful fore-knowledge about the character of the essays. One was that essays be written at a level which, though not necessarily nontechnical, would be clear to nonspecialized readers. Along with this went a constant concern that essays be written in a self-contained way and not lean too heavily on mere citations of the literature, especially literature not likely to be known to the nonspecialist. A related concern was that authors describe in at least a little detail empirical studies on which exposition or argument hinged in any important way. Finally, since almost all of the essays perform in part the function of a review article, authors were urged to prepare generous and careful bibliographies. As a result, whatever utility the study may have for handbook purposes—and it is a not inconsiderable one—has been maximized.

SOME ANTICIPATIONS

The value of the essays is in their detail—details of analysis, creative thinking, and scholarship, which are best left unblurred by synoptic survey or the manufacture of some synthetic pattern. Volume 7, the postscript volume of *Psychology: A Study of a Science,* will consider findings from various of the essays and even trends suggested by certain groupings of them, but with no disposition toward the manufacture of a "total pattern." Here we consider a miscellany of matters which may in some measure prepare the reader for navigating among the findings.

First, a few words about the grouping of the essays into the three volumes. The intention of the tripartite bounding is clear enough. Volume 4 is meant to embrace the essays of the biologists and those psychologists whose fields of primary reference are in most intimate contact with the biological sciences. Volume 5 demarcates those essays in which the primary fields of reference belong more strictly to "psychological psychology"; this does not imply that these areas are *unrelated* to biological science (or social science for that matter), either in principle or as seen by the authors of the essays. The final volume is of course meant to comprehend essays in which social psychology is taken as the primary reference field and those in which aspects of social science play this role. Here again, there is no implication that these fields are independent of the other groupings.

If there is an element of arbitrariness in the tripartite-volume breakdown, there is a greater one in the assignment of certain of the essays to given volumes. For instance, of the four essays in which perception is the field of primary reference, three appear in Volume 4; one (Postman's) in Volume 5. It is not at all clear that Postman's treatment of perception and learning is any further from biology than, say, Ittelson's presentation of perception and transactional psychology, but it was appropriate to put Postman's essay in Volume 5 because it forms a natural cluster with the essays in which learning is field of primary reference. Again, the essays in which personality is field of primary reference (especially Miller's, Sanford's, Child's) could have clustered about as well with the essays of Volume 6 as they do with those of Volume 5, where they are situated, but there were considerations of balancing the size of volumes. Nor, it may be added, is it an unrefreshing idea to interrupt the customary wedlock between personality and social psychology and assign one of the cowering partners to a volume which will come under the gaze of fundamental psychologists.

What is mainly to be emphasized *re* the "packaging" of the essays is that the unit of planning was the total study, not the individual volume. Indeed, a necessary consequence of the interrelational objectives is that the contents of each volume range freely (if with variable bias) over the entire breadth of psychology and related sciences. The fields of *secondary reference* were, it will be recalled, taken in any directions the authors wished to pursue. Thus, for instance, the geneticists David and Snyder (Volume 4) look toward personality, abnormal psychology, and individual differences, among other directions. The physiological psychologists Diamond and Chow (Volume 4) look largely toward learning. An essay by the anthropologist A. Irving Hallowell (Volume 6) is as firmly rooted in biological science as any of the papers in Volume 4. Another anthropologist, David French (Volume 6) looks toward perception and cognition. Donald T. Campbell (Volume 6), with social psychology as field of primary reference, pursues relationships with learning, perception, and certain developments in the neurological area. Psychology *as a whole* is inescapable in each of these volumes and the purity of the reader's specialism is nowhere without risk of violation.

The fact that fields of secondary reference were spontaneously chosen by the authors affords an instructive opportunity to gauge—from the distribution of choices—the directions in which bridging interests are going in the field at large. Though we do not argue that as the study goes, so goes the science, it is hardly likely that the choices of a group of authors so large, so influential, and so varied in field of primary affiliation would not, in some appreciable degree, be diagnostic of the general situation. In this connection, one of the most impressive general findings of the study is the convergence of bridging interests toward *perception*. Every author who took learning as field of primary reference (Guttman, Lawrence, Leeper, and Schoenfeld and Cumming in Volume 5) chose to consider relations with perception. One author, Postman (also in Volume 5), who was expected to take learning as his field of primary reference decided instead to put perception in its place and transpose learning to the secondary field. And the choice of perception as the main, or one of the main, fields of secondary reference by authors representing areas as diverse as neurophysiology, physiological psychology, sensory psychology, personality, human engineering, social psychology, anthropology, and linguistics will not of course escape the reader's notice. That the last several years have seen a quickening of interest in perception is evident from the general literature. What this study suggests is that perception is by way of becoming the "basic" field of psychological interest and the foundation field of its conceptualizations—indeed, that it has by now almost certainly supplanted learning in these respects.

An interesting by-product of the concentration of author interest on perception is that the reader can look forward to what amounts to a virtual subanthology on the topic of extending learning and behavior theories to this empirical domain. This is not only Postman's, Guttman's, Lawrence's, and Schoenfeld and Cumming's major theme, but it is conspicuously addressed also by Graham and Ratoosh, Ratliff, and Attneave (Volume 4), and Campbell and Osgood (Volume 6), and, in rather different spirit, by Zener and Gaffron, and Ittelson (Volume 4), and Leeper (Volume 5). Such a subanthology should have for the reader not only the drama of timeliness, but more substantial values. After all, agreement now seems general that among the things a psychologist cannot avoid coming to terms with are the problems and phenomena of perception. Moreover, no psychologist, especially if he be an American one, can avoid coming to terms with behaviorism. And the distinctive mark of the *present phase* of behaviorism—the "neo-neobehaviorism" that began to emerge in the early fifties—is in fact the concern with perceptual, and more generally, central process. It is well, then, that the particular intersection of theoretical and problematic interests at issue be viewed with utmost care and from many angles. It is well, also, that it be viewed both in celebrant mood (there is much to celebrate at the return of the repressed) *and* critically. Precisely such viewing is afforded by the study, though, because of the fortuities of representation, the volume of celebration exceeds that of the criticism. To compensate for this imbalance, may the editor suggest that such critical consideration of the rationale of behavioristic analyses of perception as exemplified, say, in the methodological section of the Zener-Gaffron paper, be given especial attention by the reader.

Turning now to the individual papers, the happiest generalization that can be made is that few can be made. The papers are widely varied in character but each in its own way realizes such qualities as we have seen to be definitive of the study's atmosphere. Some of them give primary emphasis to theoretical ideas intended to integrate or reveal the relatedness of discrete fields; others give the main concern to tracing cross-field relations among empirical variables. Some of the analyses are process-centered, some focus on the organization of extant clusters of knowledge, others are method-centered. Some papers accent emerging substantive and formal relationships as between fields at different levels of analysis; others focus on interstitial *problems* upon which a plurality of fields may bear in complementary fashion; still others concentrate on the structure of single large areas (e.g., personality) on the assumption that extrafield relations will be most naturally revealed when structure lines are drawn with sufficient fineness. Some of the papers approach their topics historically; others in terms of current status, or indeed, *sub species aeternitatis*. Some of the essays adopt the strategy of detailed analysis of "samples" of the literature in the areas under consideration; others are developed in a somewhat less Baconian fashion. In each, a man is speaking for himself, addressing his own problems in his own accents.

Though length and scope of the essays vary, even the shorter of them do not frustrate the hope for detailed and sustained analysis. That the essays raise far more differentiated structural and interrelational questions than has been customary in discussions of this sort is obvious. That such differentiated inquiry is important to our science and should be among its continuing responsibilities is made plain, if only from the complexities, the sometimes unsuspected moot alternatives, that emerge when *specific* questioning is pursued. Readers, say, of Volume 4, will find any of the textbook slogans concerning the "nature" or "role" of physiological psychology they may bring with them evaporating into a degree of triviality worse than emptiness before completing a few dozen pages. And, taking the study as a whole, similar claims might be made with respect to the time-worn textbook slogans concerning relations between perception and motivation, personality and perception, motivation and learning, social psychology and psychology, given social sciences and psychology, applied and pure psychology, etc.

Perhaps the major dimension of variation in authors' conceptions of their tasks had to do with whether they aimed primarily toward a theoretical integration of the fields comprising the relata of analysis, or a systematically more neutral survey of empirical structure or relations. This, it should be noted, is no simple continuum—especially if it be recognized that even the grouping of *empirical* variables local to specific studies into more general classes is a theory-like process. And, of course, there is no metric for the "degree of the theoretical," or decision rule which neatly separates "theory" and "pretheory." Whatever continuum such qualifications permit to exist is populated in virtually every segment by the essays of the present study.

Closest to that extreme which marks empirical survey as the method of preference are Lambert's paper on social psychology (Volume 6) and

Davis' on physiological psychology (Volume 4). Both of these men make an intensive effort to explore the structure and associations of their fields by reconstructing from characteristic samples of the relevant literature the chief empirical variable-classes that have set the terms of research. Comparable to such an approach are those parts of Rosner's essay on psychophysics and neurophysiology (Volume 4) in which he seeks to reconstruct the chief empirical and systematic variables characteristic of both fields of reference. Other articles, which focus primarily (but certainly not exclusively) on empirical interrelations, may be exemplified by David and Snyder's discussion of psychology and genetics, Diamond and Chow's of biological psychology (Volume 4); Berlyne's essay on exploratory behavior, Taylor's and Fitts' on human engineering (Volume 5); Sherif's essay on social psychology, French's and the Spindlers' essays on the relations between psychology and anthropology, Katona's on relations with economics (Volume 6).

By far the most typical approach is one which gives approximately equal weight to theoretical analysis and empirical survey. Good examples might be as follows: Volume 4—Rosner's paper (taken as a whole), Ratliff on joint relations of physics, physiology, and psychology for vision, Graham and Ratoosh on sensory psychology and perception, Livingston on psychology and neurophysiology, von Bonin on neuroanatomy and psychology, Zener and Gaffron on perception, Ittelson on perception and transactional psychology; Volume 5—Postman on perception and learning, Hilgard on motivation and learning, Leeper on learning, perception, and personality, Sanford on personality, Child on personality in relation to anthropology and sociology; Volume 6—Osgood on psycholinguistics, Inkeles on sociology and psychology, Hallowell on personality, culture, and society in behavioral evolution, Lane on political science and psychology, Simon on economics and psychology.

Finally, we have essays which in high (but varying) degree stress theoretical modes of analysis. Among the purest cases—though none are uncontaminated with the empirical—are Attneave's consideration of perception and related areas (Volume 4); Lawrence on learning and perception, Schoenfeld and Cumming on behavior and perception, and Miller on social aspects of motivation (Volume 5); Campbell on social attitudes and acquired behavioral dispositions, and Arrow on utility in economic behavior (Volume 6).

It is to be emphasized that both theoretical and (relatively speaking) "theoretically neutral" modes of analysis have their place in considering problems of field structure and relationships. "Theoretical integration" impresses one as the *mode par excellence*—especially if the analysis can disclose meaningful relations between fields, or parts thereof, which previously seemed discrete. But if it be the most dashing mode, it is not always feasible; still less often is it the mode of choice in the present state of the science. There are stages before theoretical integration (in any strong sense of "theory") is possible, at which analysis of cross-field relations at relatively empirical levels is a necessary condition to meaningful theoretical advance.

From the typing of the essays just offered, it should be clear that there are important continuities between Study I and Study II. In Study I, the unit of analysis was the individual theory ("systematic formulation," in our preferred phrase); in Study II, it is the research area(s). The body psychological being finite, these disparate cuts will overlap. Almost every essay of Study II makes reference—usually extensive reference—to theoretical materials, and some develop theoretical ideas in a focal way. Contrariwise, few of the analyses of Study I neglect considering the bearing of the systematic formulation at issue on a plurality of empirical domains, and thus on cross-field relations. Efficient use of the series requires that the reader keep in mind this complementarity of the two studies. With respect to *either* of the major types of question posed by the different studies, both taken together will give far fuller and better-balanced coverage than will the study of primary relevance per se.

In an earlier part of this introduction, it was indicated that though the conventionalized field distinctions are in many ways adventitious and arbitrary, certain of them derive historically from analyses which in some sense were considered ontologically significant. To put this in the most vulgarly direct terms, there was a time when perception or learning or motivation or emotion was unembarrassedly considered as in the first instance a real part-process (not, of course, an independent or self-subsistent one) within the process flux mediating real actions and even real experiences of a real organism in a real world. As the present century progressed, such uncouth ontologizing was displaced by the sophisticated and hygienic imagery of variables and functions, data languages and construct languages, along with the presumption that only fools could find the confines of the linguacentric predicament chafing. During this nominalist and conventionalist deflection in the recent history of our epistemology, it became almost a matter of course to ask questions not about subject matter, but about collectivities of sentences that the "literature" had deposited concerning subject matter. Or perhaps one *did* ask first-order questions, but the object of inquiry was so filmy and assumptional—so much a fiction based on an illegitimate inference—that one did not much care *what* questions.

Against this background, it is most refreshing to note in the present study a tendency to take *process,* and more generally, the *objects* of psychological knowledge seriously. In discussing field structure or interrelations, most of our authors are not merely revising or creating filing systems for indifferent units of knowledge, but are in fact looking beyond the bits and pieces of research that have emerged in the academic workshop toward a psychological universe to which research must be adequate. That universe is once more acknowledged, and desire to render it intelligible seems burgeoning. Such changes are not evident in all essays in the same degree, but in some degree they are evident in all.

This new serious concern with process is perhaps most evident in Volume 4. By and large, the physiological psychologists represented in this study seem to have a compelling feeling that the brain (and to some extent the rest of the organism) is *there*. Our three biologists express this feeling perhaps even more uninhibitedly (some going so far as to speculate about the relation between brain and mind, brain and consciousness, mind and body), but for biologists who always *were* "naïve," this is no departure. A similar concern for process, however, can be seen in many ways among the other contributors, the more strictly "psychological" psychologists. There is, for instance, virtually not a single empty-organism position expressed in the study: Learning theorists and even personality and social psychologists all not only acknowledge the organism in some general way, but often lean rather heavily on the recent advances in the neurological and neurophysiological disciplines. Again, the already noted interest in perception on the part of S-R and learning theorists seems another acknowledgement that a universe of actual problems exists.

Important among the developments here at issue is the tendency of not a few of the authors to approach their topics not first and foremost in terms of the exploration or realignment of extant bodies of knowledge, but in what might be characterized as "process-centered" terms. Thus, for instance, Zener and Gaffron (Volume 4) ask as their main question: What specifically is perception as a process phase in the economy of the organism—an organism which experiences in a significant sense, which acts, and which does both relative to a world and to itself? This is an ancient kind of question but one which we have too long been too "sophisticated" to re-raise. In raising it anew, the authors are led to certain methodic suggestions, theoretical vistas, and empirical observations, all far from old. From a quite different perspective, Attneave (also Volume 4) addresses perception in a process-centered way, in this case performing the remarkable feat of saying many things which seem substantively apt or plausible about the real organism in terms largely of *information theory*. Other largely process-centered analyses are Ittelson's on perception and transactional psychology (Volume 4); Berlyne's on exploratory behavior, and Leeper's on learning-perception relations (Volume 5); Campbell's on acquired behavioral dispositions, Hallowell's on personality, culture, and society, Lounsbury's on linguistics and psychology, Katona's on economics and psychology (Volume 6)—to mention but a sample.

The authors of Study II—as of Study I—are not merely recording history; they are extending history. Analysis of the shape and relational texture of knowledge as conceived by the study is not "mere" analysis. To see knowledge in new ways, to test the knowledge in a field against the objects of that field, to realign knowledge, is to *create* new knowledge. Those already acquainted in any degree with *Psychology: A Study of a Science* will know that one of its fondest aims has been to advance a conception of analysis which sees it as a joint analytico-creative task. This objective is well realized by the essays of Study II.

Few of the authors were left unchanged by the practice of such analysis: for the reader this means that he can expect something fresh in virtually every essay. In the course of their analyses, many of the authors make important theoretical and methodological contributions which had not before seen the light of day. Examples are to be seen in the papers by Rosner, Rosenblith and Vidale, Zener and Gaffron, Attneave (Volume 4); Guttman, Lawrence, Schoenfeld and Cumming, Leeper, Miller (Volume 5); Campbell, Hallowell, and Lane (Volume 6). In other cases, positions previously established are significantly extended or brought to bear on new ranges of subject matter. Conspicuous examples are the papers of Pfaffmann and of Graham and Ratoosh (Volume 4); Postman, Berlyne, Child, Rodnick (Volume 5); Sherif, Osgood, Inkeles, Katona, and Arrow (Volume 6). In still other cases, we get an essentially new way of viewing the content and organization of an interstitial area: e.g., the papers of Pribram and Davis (Volume 4); of Sanford and of Rotter (Volume 5); of Lambert, French, and Simon (Volume 6). Again, certain of the papers are unique in that they address interrelational topics which have never before been considered in any direct or extensive way: cases in point are Ratliff's consideration of physics, physiology (especially single-receptor physiology), and psychology relative to vision (Volume 4); the extended discussions in Volume 5 of the relations between human engineering and general psychology by Taylor and by Fitts; the evolutionary consideration of relations among personality, culture, and society in the mode of Hallowell, or the Spindlers' consideration of the specific problems of culture change in relation to psychology (Volume 6). These sources of creative novelty are not, of course, mutually exclusive: many, indeed most, of the papers present them in combination.

In these paragraphs we have been trying to anticipate certain of the qualities of the findings, yet protect the reader's freshness of vision by not constructing trends upon the findings. In minor violation of this restraint, may we raise an issue which the reader very probably already has in mind. What of psychology's current classification of "fields" (i.e., fields as defined at the level of generality of perception, learning, and the other "primary" reference areas of this study)? Does the study suggest some new and super-rational breakdown—a comfortable and tidy geography in which everything will find its place?

The study does not. Indeed, the study would tend to suggest that the perennial and poignant thirst of psychologists for a set of new-fangled field breakdowns is doomed to perennial and poignant frustration. The editor doubts that the findings of this study are a necessary condition to the verdict, but they are certainly confirmatory.

Field names are labels, variably applied, to what is seen by men as related clusters of inquiry. The flux of history, the variability of individual vision, and the unsystematic variety of senses in which a field itself can be defined, inevitably makes these labels highly ambiguous. Different men will—and *should*—continue to see fields differently relative to their own systematic beliefs and options.

Any new classification arrived at must be an organization dictated by the terms of some systematic view or theory. Until a "theory" sufficiently compelling to command general acceptance comes along, there can be no breakdown of fields any more serviceable than the present one. A theory of the requisite scope, analytic power, and adequacy to *warrant* any extensive realignment of fields is not exactly imminent and, indeed, may be unachievable in principle.

Whatever the degree of theoretical integration psychology ultimately achieves, it is well to recognize that certain of the fields currently demarcated cut into events from different incidences—incidences dictated by different universes of discourse. Different universes of discourse are not necessarily different "levels"; they *can* be just different—unsystematically so. This lugubrious circumstance is, we think, made evident, explicitly or implicitly, in many of the essays in these volumes. Given problematic ends in view—in life as in science—*are* often incommensurable; they require incommensurable concepts, methods, and will inevitably beget incommensurable answers. Much of what is comprehended, say, in social psychology, personality, or psychopathology, will probably not fall into the grain of any single conceptual language that might unite, say, aspects of sensory psychology, perception, and learning. Psychology will progress more rapidly toward whatever "rationality" of organization or conceptual integration may be possible, if such framework limits are clearly acknowledged and understood.

There are other (and not unrelated) expectations which, when carried into investigations of the shape and texture of knowledge, can work toward a trivial, if not illusory, outcome. An obvious one is the assumption that there are necessarily vast submerged riches in our attained backlog of research which, if only extracted by some felicitous culling, could lift us to a new level of knowledge. About such a hope we need perspective. There may indeed be in the history of our science hidden leads—even findings—of great value. But the history of our science also tells us that only a narrow and adventitiously chosen range of questions has been asked. This is not to our discredit. After all, we have had the courage to address a subject matter having the most awesome amplitude of any in the history of institutionalized knowledge-seeking.

The *realistic* likelihood is that the truly important advances in our science will come from new knowledge, based on new problematic sensitivities, and new ways of addressing questions. To this, a necessary condition is ceaselessly to look at past knowledge in a way at once faithful yet unconstrained, critical yet creative—by constant attention, that is, to some such questions of structure and relationship as have been raised in the present study. It is this consideration which defines the significance of the pursuits posed by Study II. The best use that the reader can make of the study is to approach it for such an end.

Recently the editor has had occasion to indulge his penchant for neologism by discriminating a syndrome called "ameaningful thinking." Ameaningful thought or inquiry "regards knowledge as the result of 'processing' rather than discovery; it presumes that knowledge is an almost automatic result of a gimmickry, an assembly line, a 'methodology'; it assumes that inquiring behavior is so rigidly and fully regulated by *rule,* that in its conception of inquiry it sometimes allows the rules totally to displace their human users. Presuming as it does that knowledge is 'generated' by processing, its conception of knowledge is fictionalistic, conventionalistic, 'a-ontological.' So strongly does it see knowledge under such aspects that it sometimes seems to suppose that the object of inquiry is an ungainly and annoying irrelevance, that knowledge can be created by fiat."

Ameaningful thinking is a specific yet highly complex syndrome, which requires far more subtle and extended description than can be given here. But psychologists will already have noted that such a trend is pervasive in the culture at large and, if they be heroically honest, that it is not unknown in the recent history of that subculture formed by "psychology." Perhaps the most direct and telling way to convey the special hope of a study like the present one is that it might serve, however modestly, *as a counterforce to ameaning in our science*. The tendency in past decades to raise questions concerning the shape of knowledge only intermittently and halfheartedly can be seen as related to an ameaningful habit of inquiry. For, in considering questions of structure and relationship, what are we doing other than setting local inquiry into a broader environment of meanings? And what *can* we be doing as inquirers if we do not at least try to do *that?*

PERCEPTION AND LEARNING

LEO POSTMAN
Department of Psychology
University of California

Introduction 31
Definitions of Perception. 31
  Phenomenology 32
  Stimulus-response analysis of discrimination 35
  Converging operations in the determination of perceptual functions . . 37
  Psychophysical correspondence 43
  Perception as inference 45
    Probabilistic functionalism 45
    Transactional functionalism 46
    Perceptual "hypotheses" 47
  Summary: independent and dependent variables in the definition of perception. 48
    Data language 48
    Independent variables 49
    Dependent variables 51
    Intervening variables and constructs 51
Definition of Learning 54
Conceptualizations of Perceptual Learning 57
  Phenomenology 57
    Logical analysis 57
    Empirical implications 59
  Stimulus-response analysis 60
    Response-produced cues 60
    Differentiation of response-produced cues. 61
  Psychophysical correspondence 63
    Specificity theory 63
    Specificity theory versus association theory 64
Experimental Designs in the Study of Perceptual Learning 66
  The effects of past experience on the perception of form 66
    Differential-training experiments 67
    Gottschaldt's experiments 67
    Identification of incomplete and ambiguous figures 71

The effect of differential reinforcement on figure-ground perception . . 72
Interpretation of differential-training experiments 72
Control of perceptual development 74
Evaluation of assumed effects of past experience 76
Studies of sensory deprivation 79
Improvement in perceptual judgments 82
Summary of empirical findings 83
Acquisition of judgment scales 84
Probabilistic learning of perceptual judgments 89
Developmental studies of the constancies 89
Differentiation of naïve and analytic attitudes 89
Conditioning of judgments in constancy experiments 90
Conditioning of judgments to cues of limited validity 90
Perceptual Learning and the Recognition of Words 91
Methodological status of studies of word recognition 91
The measurement of recognition thresholds 91
Relationship to measures of retention 93
Systematic significance of measures of word recognition 95
The role of response processes 95
Recognition as a function of stimulus variables 98
Stimulus-response relationships in recognition 99
"Bridging Laws" between perception and learning 101
References 103

INTRODUCTION

There are two substantive issues which arise in the study of the relationship between perception and learning: (1) to what extent perception is learned or modified by learning and (2) to what extent learning can be understood as perceptual change. The present chapter will focus on the first of these questions. We shall begin with a discussion of the definitions of the two areas of reference. It will become clear that historical cleavages concerning the definition and delimitation of the concept of perception continue to dominate current theoretical debates. These cleavages are necessarily reflected in the theoretical approaches to the problem of perceptual learning. In the second part of the chapter we shall consider the methodology of experiments on perceptual learning and review some of the major issues on which empirical research and theoretical analysis have centered.

DEFINITIONS OF PERCEPTION

There is notable lack of agreement on the definition of the term *perception* and the operations appropriate to its investigation. Disagreements on usage have assumed major importance in the analysis of the effects of past experience and motivation on perception. Thus, there have been recurrent attempts to dismiss experimental demonstrations of perceptual learning as not being concerned with perception as such but with judgment or inference. A brief survey of current trends in the definition and classification of perceptual data will help to locate some of the sources of disagreement about the relationship between perception and learning.

Five major emphases can be detected in the definitions of perception accepted explicitly or implicitly by various contemporary writers: (1) phenomenology, (2) stimulus-response analysis of discrimination, (3) identification of perceptual dispositions by converging operations, (4) psychophysical correspondence, and (5) perception as an inferential process. Each of these emphases will be illustrated by reference to general theoretical discussions which have appeared during the last few years.

Phenomenology

For gestalt psychologists, and those influenced by them, the basic data of perception are given in phenomenological description. The phenomenological method is considered essential for the discovery of the configurational laws of perception. According to the principle of isomorphism, phenomenal experience also provides an important source of hypotheses about the neurological basis of perceptual organization [113, 114, 115]. Ideally, phenomenological observation should be "naïve," and the categories of response used by the subject must not be restricted.

Conceptually, experience is separated sharply from response, and the phenomenologist is anxious not to confuse the percept with the action occasioned by the percept. How, then, is another's percept to be determined? The problem is, indeed, a timeworn one, but the fact is that phenomenologists have often failed to face up to it and as yet have not provided a satisfactory answer. A one-to-one correspondence between experience and report appears to be assumed in many experiments, but this assumption is abandoned when the investigator wishes to make distinctions between perception on the one hand and judgment, inference, and interpretation on the other. The phenomenologist then finds himself in a methodological impasse. He wishes to defend perceptual experiences as a class of events *sui generis,* but he cannot specify the rules for identifying and describing these events. At that point, he is apt to abandon objective methodology and to appeal to his own experiences and those of others in judging the validity of perceptual reports. The difficulties which an exponent of the phenomenological approach faces in attempting an objective definition of perception are clearly illustrated in a recent discussion by Prentice [155]. In considering the relationship between percept (experience) and overt behavior, Prentice offers the following definition: "By perceiving we normally *mean* something by nature private, confined to the perceiver. . . . In its usual sense, the term 'perception' applies to that hypothetical event, directly reportable (if at all) only by the subject himself, an event that may or may not modify any behavior observable to others" (*sic!*) [155, pp. 31f.]. The retreat into a private world is undoubtedly prompted by the investigator's conviction that he himself has perceptual experiences that have no observable consequences. Since perceptions are inherently private, the best we can do, according to Prentice, is to make approximate inferences about them. Prentice cannot state any precise rules for such inferences but suggests that " . . . we infer that our subject has perceived a particular stimulus pattern in a particular way only if his behavior [verbal reports, discriminations, etc.] makes any other explanation too improbable to accept. In the last analysis, each of us must (and does) decide for himself whether to be convinced" [155, p. 31]. In short, the inference of a perception requires the proof of the null hypothesis for all other alternative explanations, and the point at which the inference becomes legitimate is a matter of individual conviction. The requirement that *all* possible alternative explanations be eliminated and the reference to the investigator's personal convictions prepare a position from which data at variance with the theorist's own experiences and expectations can be dismissed as not truly perceptual. That is, in fact, what Prentice proceeds to do in reviewing evidence on the effects of learning and motivation on perception.

When subjective criteria are used in the definition of perception, the door is opened to the inclusion and exclusion of data for purposes of making a theoretical position invulnerable to experimental disproof. An example of the resulting confusion between classification and interpretation of data is provided in a recent review of the role of past experience in visual perception by Zuckerman and Rock [200], who appear to be writing in defense of the gestalt position on this issue. Their paper is of interest because it provides a particularly clear illustration of the ways in which arbitrary classifications of perceptual experience have been used for a priori support of a theoretical argument.

Zuckerman and Rock propose a set of restrictions on the term *perception* which make it a foregone conclusion that almost any evidence for the effects of past experience can be rejected as irrelevant. They argue that perception must, first of all, be differentiated from recognition. Recognition implies a "feeling of familiarity" and hence, by definition, is dependent on past experience, and specifically on the "communication" between a perceptual process and memory traces. In investigations of the role of past experience the effects on the "percept qua form" must be evaluated rather than the effects on recognition. If this distinction is to be taken seriously, one of two conclusions follows: (1) perception can be investigated only with forms that have never been experienced before, or (2) subjects must be led to differentiate the "purely" perceptual components of their experiences from those constituting the feeling of recognition. The first alternative is patently absurd; the second calls for an unlikely feat of introspective analysis which certainly should not be expected in the context of naïve phenomenological description. For the present at least, the distinction appears to be operationally empty; it becomes mischievous when it is used, after the fact, to dispose of experiments in which the effects of past experience were evaluated by other criteria.

A second distinction is made between form perception per se and the discriminated identity of complex patterns. It is acknowledged that the differentiation of complex forms increases as a function of experience. The writers take it for granted that such improvement in discrimination is attributable to the action of memory traces aroused by an unchanged percept. Hence, they conclude, changes in the discriminability of complex forms are not a matter of form *perception!* No hint is given as to how one might distinguish operationally between a change in form perception per se and a change in discriminability mediated by trace arousal. Similar difficulties attach to the third distinction, viz., between perception and interpretation, i.e., between pure form and meaning. The writers acknowledge that it is difficult for an observer to make this distinction: "Usually, we do not first experience a pure form percept and then become aware of its meaning" [200, p. 281]. Nevertheless, it is urged that "functionally" the two processes must be distinguished. If the distinction makes no difference in reportable experience (or response), it is hard to understand what is meant by a "functional" separation of the two processes. The discussion strongly suggests that those features of experience which are not an exclusive function of the stimulus pattern are to be regarded as products of interpretation. When descriptive classification and theoretical interpretation are confounded, it is not surprising to find experience fractionated by fiat to conform to the demands of theory. Shades of Würzburg!

The use of question-begging definitions is, of course, not a necessary consequence of concern with the subject's phenomenal experience. Such usage is bound to develop, however, when phenomenal experience is used selectively and without operational restraints in support of a particular theory of perception. The basic weakness of such practices lies in the failure to recognize the essential distinction, emphasized by Bergmann and Spence [10], between the subject's object language and the experimenter's metalanguage. A fundamental requirement of any theory of perception is bypassed, viz., the specification of precise rules for the classification and analytic treatment of the subject's responses. Graham has put the matter clearly: " . . . the problem of analysis and classification of response does not involve accepting them as understandable conversation, but is one of formulating their uniformities and rules in a system where they are taken *as* behavior. . . . Conversation is not viewed as such but is considered in terms of other words or symbols—that is, scientific description that formulates the rules of the subject's conversation" [77, p. 66].

To the extent that these requirements are met, there is no methodological objection to any terms or constructs merely on the grounds that they are "mentalistic" or "introspectionistic" [10, p. 2]. Thus, the analysis of phenomenal experience could be a legitimate problem for perceptual theory, provided that there were accepted procedures for the classification of phenomenological observations and rules for making inferences from observed stimulus-response correlations to the properties of "experience." Thus far, exponents of the phenomenological method have failed to provide such rules.

Stimulus-Response Analysis of Discrimination

The domain of perception need not lose its identity in a behavioristic psychology. In an objective psychology, the term *perception* denotes a class of stimulus-response relationships. While the formal requirements for the manipulation of stimuli and the measurement of responses are continuous with those applied to other problems of behavior analysis, the domain of perception derives its distinctive status from the range of stimuli manipulated, the restrictions on the responses measured, and the nature of the variables held constant in the experimental situation. In a series of important papers Graham [74, 75, 76, 77, 78] has outlined the concepts and methods of a behavioristic approach to perception. While his analysis is most readily applied to the procedures of psychophysics, it can in principle be extended to other kinds of experimental situations as well.

According to Graham, the basic program of behavior analysis is embodied in the general equation $R = f(a, b, c \ldots n \ldots t \ldots x, y, z)$; i.e., in any given situation response is a function of a number of variables which have been manipulated or held constant in the experimental situation. "In particular, the first letters of the alphabet (a, b, c) refer to properly specified aspects of stimuli; the last letters $(\ldots x, y, z)$ to properly specified conditions of the subject (physiological and inferred, including the effects of instruction stimuli); R to response; n to number of presentations; and t to time. The terms are not always independent of each other" [76, p. 62]. In a psychophysical experiment, e.g., in the determination of the absolute threshold by the method of constant stimuli, some characteristic of the physical stimulus (a) is varied systematically, and the condition of the organism is manipulated by means of an instruction stimulus (x_1). While the threshold for a is being measured, other aspects of the stimulus (b, c) are held constant. As for conditions of the organism, the instruction stimulus (x_1) is explicitly specified as constant, and other parameters (y, z) are assumed to be at constant or limiting values. Among the latter, past reinforcements of the critical response (R) is of especial significance. The analysis of the stimulus-response relationships proceeds on the assumption that the observed variations do not reflect changes in the strength of association between different values of the controlling stimulus parameter and R. Specifically, the verbal responses by which the subject communicates his discriminations are assumed to have reached asymptotic strength. The function determined in the psychophysical experiment thus reduces to a special case of the general equation, viz., $R = F(a, x_1)$, with all other variables held constant. From this function critical values of the stimulus (a_c) required for the attainment of a particular response criterion, such as 50 or 75 per cent correct responses, can be specified; i.e., thresholds can be determined.

The above analysis applies to single psychophysical functions. The next step is to derive what Graham calls a perceptual function. The critical value a_c is measured successively at different values of another parameter, say, b. It is then possible to determine the function relating a_c to b, e.g., $\Delta I/I$ as a function of I. This is a "stimulus-stimulus function," with response constant. Formally, in terms of the general equation $a_c = \Phi(b, x_1, R_1)$, i.e., in the statement of the perceptual function the instruction stimulus (x_1), the nature of the response (R_1) as well as the other parameters listed in the general equation are assumed to be constant. It is equally possible, of course, to study a_c as a function of parameters defining a condition of the organism, i.e., to determine $a_c = \Phi(x_1, z, R_1)$. In an experiment investigating the effects of practice on a differential threshold, for example, the parameter z may refer to the number of practice trials.

Graham's analysis not only translates the procedures of classical psychophysics into the systematic language of stimulus and response but also serves to highlight the essential differences between the phenomenological and the behavioristic approach to perception. The functions described by Graham can be determined if, and only if, both the independent and the dependent variables are restricted to specified classes and are capable of measurement. The critical methodological problem arises, of course, in connection with the specification and measurement of responses. For purposes of measurement, responses must be restricted to clearly defined alternatives which can be scaled along quantitative continua, e.g., in terms of probability of occurrence. It is this requirement which phenomenological observation does not even begin to meet. Graham suggests that we can order psychological experimentation along a continuum according to the degree of stimulus and response restriction. Phenomenological report and the psychophysical experiment define the extremes of this continuum.

This formulation makes it possible to make a sharp distinction between the object language of the subject and the pragmatic metalanguage of the experimenter. When the words descriptive of some characteristic of the stimulus, e.g., *brightness, hue,* or *saturation,* are used in the instructions or in the subject's reports, these terms are part of the social language shared by experimenter and subject. When these words are applied to a dimension of discrimination inferred from observed stimulus-response relationships, they are part of the experimenter's metalanguage. Under the term *perception* is subsumed the class of stimulus-response functions from which inferences about discrimination are made. Hence, " . . . we should not expect to hypothesize about a generic *process* of perception as we might about a specific component process" [77, p. 74]. The concept of perception, then, refers not to a process *sui generis* but to a class of functions based on the same variables and having the same general form as other analytic statements about behavior. The distinctive characteristic of this class is the measurement of responses as a function of systematic changes in the stimulus at specified constant or limiting conditions of the organism.

Converging Operations in the Determination of Perceptual Functions

One of the persistent objections to a stimulus-response analysis of perceptual discrimination stems from the apprehension that measures of discrimination are confounded by response variables. A failure of discrimination may be due to the lack of appropriately differentiated responses; constant errors may reflect the subject's biases in favor of some reports rather than others, etc. There is substantial experimental evidence for the operation of response biases in perceptual experiments [e.g., 16, 67, 184]. It is clear that response parameters may have a significant effect on measures of discrimination, but the recognition of this fact does not in any sense point away from a positivistic and operational approach to the analysis of perception. The operational procedures which are required to make the inferred properties of the perceptual system independent of specific response parameters have been spelled out clearly by Garner, Hake, and Eriksen [54]. The main points of their discussion will now be summarized.

An apparent difficulty arises when the term *perception* is treated as synonymous with "discriminatory response" on the ground that a concept is defined fully by the operations on which it is based. If perception is equated to response, it is, of course, impossible to distinguish between the properties of perceptual processes and the properties of response processes. Such a flat identification of the concept of perception with response is, however, not a necessary and, indeed, not a proper application of operational procedures. An adequate definition of a concept cannot be based on a single experimental procedure; instead, a theoretically useful concept must be anchored to a set of operations. The writers call attention to Bridgman's statement: "Operational definitions, in spite of their precision, are in application without significance unless the situations to which they are applied are sufficiently developed so that at least two methods are known of getting to the terminus" [20, p. 248].

In an operational analysis of perceptual processes, the measurement of discriminatory responses is a necessary first step. No inferences about perceptual processes can be made unless responses can be shown to vary systematically with the conditions of stimulation. Evidence for discrimination is not, however, sufficient in itself for precise inferences about the perceptual process. Additional operations are required which serve to separate effects attributable to the response system from those attributable to the perceptual process. Thus, inferences about perceptual processes, like inferences about any intervening processes, must be based on *converging operations*. Converging operations are described as " . . . any set of two or more experimental operations which allow the selection or elimination of alternative hypotheses or concepts which could explain an experimental result" [54, pp. 150f.]. To serve this purpose, converging operations must be less than perfectly correlated; in general, the more independent the operations, the more efficient they are in supporting a decision between alternative hypotheses. A similar argument was advanced by the present author [145] in introducing the concept of *perceptual response disposition*. Such a disposition is inferred when two (or more) methods of measurement lead to consistent conclusions concerning the subject's discrimination of a set of stimuli. If the results of the different methods of measurement do not agree, " . . . the analytic problem is to divide the observed systematic variance in responses into two major components: that due to the common perceptual disposition and that contributed by the availability or probability of the specific responses used" [145, p. 65].

The purpose of converging operations, then, is to delimit the properties of a hypothetical perceptual process from those of the response system. Take response differentiation, for example. Clearly, the precision of discrimination may depend on the number of response categories available to the subject. Strictly speaking, no conclusions about the inferred perceptual process per se can be drawn on the basis of a single experiment using a particular set of response categories. Only if and when the critical values of the stimulus determined in successive experiments are independent of the number of response categories are such inferences justified. Garner, Hake, and Eriksen discuss several examples of the potential use of converging operations for the clarification of current problems in which the distinction between perceptual and response effects is at issue.

Among the areas of application which are suggested one of the most significant is that of sensory scaling. When subjects express their judgments in numerical form, as in fractionation or direct estimation of magnitudes, it is hazardous to assume that the scale of numbers accurately reflects the quantitative relations among the perceptual events. "The question is not whether they can use the *number* scale correctly, when using it as an abstract scale, but rather whether they use it in such a way as to reflect a metric property of the perceptual system" [54, p. 156]. Numerical responses are used widely in the identification and ordering of stimulus objects. The fact that subjects can use this well-differentiated and highly available system of responses consistently under a given instruction does not endow the resulting sensory scales with validity [52]. The assumption of one-to-one correspondence between numerical values and perceived magnitudes must be checked by additional psychophysical procedures in which a different system of responses is used to determine the relationships among the perceptual magnitudes. Such a converging operation gains in power if it does not use numerical responses of any kind, since different numerical scales may merely represent transforms of the same underlying response system.

An important example of such an analysis is provided in a study by Garner [53], who found that scales of loudness constructed by the method of fractionation and equisection do not coincide. (In the method of fractionation the subject adjusted variable tones until they seemed half as loud as the standards; in the method of equisection the subject adjusted the intensities of a series of tones so as to divide a given loudness range into equal intervals.) Although the two sets of values initially did not agree, it was possible to achieve convergence to a single loudness scale which was derived from the interrelation of the two independent scales. Specifically, Garner assumed (1) that the method of fractionation yields judgments of a constant ratio and generates a scale with a true zero point but that the verbalized ratio is not necessarily the correct one and (2) that the method of equisection produces a scale of equal intervals with an unknown zero point. Thus, there are two loudness functions in each of which one of the constants necessary for a true ratio scale is missing. On the further assumption that both scales are related to the true loudness function, a method is then developed for determining those values of the constants (zero point and value of the judged ratio) which best fit the entire set of points. In this instance, the corrected ratio for the fractionation function was 1 : 1.70, whereas a ratio of 1 : 2 had been verbalized. Garner was able to show that the derived scale was valid for individual subjects, served to reduce the variability among the loudness scales of different subjects, and agreed well with other data on equal-loudness intervals. The values of the derived scale are more likely than the immediately verbalized values to reflect the quantitative relationships among the perceptual magnitudes. In his conclusion Garner suggests that it may be useful to consider the loudness function as a hypothetical construct which must be inferred rather than determined by direct observation [53, p. 87].

Although not always explicitly labeled as such, converging operations have played a significant role in the critical analysis of experiments concerned with the effects of motivation on perception. Thus, the application of operational analysis serves to throw grave doubt on the concept of subception introduced by Lazarus and McCleary [124]. A process of subception, i.e., unconscious discrimination, was postulated by these investigators to account for the fact that unverbalized responses such as the GSR may discriminate among motivationally significant stimuli when verbal responses do not. As Garner, Hake, and Eriksen point out, this finding may be described as a partial correlation between the stimulus and GSR, with verbal response held constant (see also the analysis by Eriksen [43]). Such a partial correlation can be a function of differences between the two response systems; for example, all-or-none verbal responses are less well differentiated than a continuous measure of GSR. In order to justify the assumption of a process of unconscious perception, it becomes necessary to show that (1) the first-order correlation between stimuli and discriminative responses is greater for the nonverbal than the verbal responses and (2) the use of a particular limited set of responses does not depress the latter correlation. The second of these requirements calls for the use of converging operations. Bricker and Chapanis [19] have, in fact, already shown that the discriminative efficiency of verbal responses increases when subjects are not limited to a single response in the presence of the stimulus.

Analysis by converging operations has also called into question the assumption of a process of perceptual defense to explain the difference in recognition thresholds between emotional and "neutral" words [131]. In an early critique of this concept, Howes and Solomon [96] suggested that the observed differences in thresholds may be a function, at least in part, of the subjects' disposition to withhold the reports of socially taboo responses. Thus, even with word frequency held constant, there are two alternative explanations of any differences between thresholds—differential sensitivity to emotional and neutral stimuli versus response inhibition. Converging operations were required to decide between these alternatives; i.e., the two explanations had to be pitted against each other. For verbal stimuli at least, the evidence favors the hypothesis of response inhibition: the difference between the thresholds can be reduced or increased by manipulation of the subject's readiness to report socially objectionable words [e.g., 118, 148].

The alternatives among which we must decide by converging operations are suggested by observation and theory. However, the convergence on a specific set of properties of a perceptual system is never definitive. The point is worth emphasizing in view of the tendency to reify "pure perception" in disregard of the fact that a construct based on a limited set of observations can be described only approximately and tentatively. In practice, the results of converging operations are often assumed rather than determined explicitly. Thus, in the determination of a function of the form $R = F(a, x_1)$, i.e., with an aspect a of the stimulus varied and the instruction stimulus specified as x_1, it is assumed that other properties of the stimulus and the conditions of the organism are at constant or limiting values. In short, it is taken for granted that the response differentiation is adequate to reveal the discriminatory capacity of the organism. If there is reason to question this assumption, the nature of the criterion response can be varied and the effect of the response parameter on the functional relationship can be assessed. The assumption about the "constant or limiting value" of the conditions of the organism is subject to experimental check. The degree of discrimination inferred from a single psychophysical experiment is, therefore, based on assumed converging operations.

The term *perceptual*, then, denotes a disposition or process inferred on the basis of observed stimulus-response relationships. The classification of *single* responses as perceptual or nonperceptual has no adequate operational basis. Nevertheless, there are persisting attempts to establish criteria for separating perceptual from nonperceptual *responses*. The inevitable difficulties attendant upon such attempts are clearly exhibited in two recent proposals for the definition of perceptual responses. According to Hochberg [90], a discriminatory response should be classified as perceptual if and only if it requires the presence of a stimulus and the resulting excitation of neural processes. In this way, perceptions can presumably be separated from judgments or memories. Such a definition fails in its purpose for two reasons: (1) it presupposes full information about stimulus-response contingencies, i.e., the functional relationship from which perceptual dispositions must be inferred is assumed to be given; (2) responses characteristically used in the determination of psychophysical relationships, e.g., reports of "present" and "absent," would not qualify as discriminatory responses, since they are not specific to any stimulus pattern. On the other hand, responses such as reflexes would have to be considered perceptual—an extension of the term which would certainly be inconsistent with Hochberg's emphasis on phenomenal experience.

It appears that single responses can be classified as perceptual or nonperceptual only if one is willing to introduce assumptions about the determinants of perception into the definition itself. A further illustration of this difficulty, which seems to be inevitable, is provided by the definition of perception offered in Bartley's textbook [7]. In order to be classified as perceptual, a reaction must satisfy two criteria: it must be immediate as well as discriminatory. Quite apart from the fact that any sharp dividing line between immediate and nonimmediate behavior must be arbitrary, close examination shows that the definition cannot be applied to any single instance of behavior unless certain theoretical suppositions are taken for granted. Immediacy refers to the speed with which a reaction develops in the organism, not to the latency of the overt response. Thus, the investigator would have to make a judgment based on theoretical considerations whether or not a response is immediate. In a similar vein, Bartley defines discriminatory responses as " . . . behavior that involves cerebral cortical participation" [7, p. 26]. Again, the decision as to whether or not this property is present depends on theory and not on operational criteria. Such difficulties are avoided when it is recognized that the term *perceptual* cannot be appropriately applied to either stimuli or responses but only to a construct inferred from stimulus-response relationships.

Throughout this section we have, in agreement with Garner, Hake, and Eriksen, emphasized the distinction between the *perceptual system* and the *response system*. The perceptual system designates a class of constructs inferred from observed psychophysical functions (correlations between stimulus attributes and discriminative responses). The term *response system* refers to the properties of the responses which are used as the dependent variables in the measurement of discrimination. For example, in any given psychophysical experiment the prescribed responses may vary with respect to availability, differentiation, the extent to which they are subject to sequential biases, etc. The variance attributable to the response system must be partialled out when inferences are made about the perceptual system. This operational distinction between two systems is fully consistent with a theoretical position which attributes properties of responses to the inferred perceptual processes themselves. The conceptualization of perception as a class of cue-producing responses is a case in point [e.g., 37]. Within the framework of such a theoretical position, it remains necessary to make a distinction between the properties of overt discriminative responses and of inferred perceptual responses.

Psychophysical Correspondence

In the preceding sections we have considered methodological criteria for the definition and delimitation of perceptual data. Cutting across the operational problems is the question of the range of facts which must be encompassed in an orderly investigation of the domain of perception. The answer to this question has significant implications for the choice of stimulus and response variables in perceptual experiments. The historical doctrine of the dependence of perception on sensation has, of course, largely determined the range of problems investigated in perceptual research and the basic methods of attack used both by adherents to this doctrine and by their opponents. Sensation was assumed to be precisely determined by stimulation. Perceptions develop around a basic sensory core to which other elements such as images are added through experience. It follows that the stimulus variables which are effective in perception are identical with those known to determine sensation, viz., energy changes at the receptor. Experience changes, however, as a context accrues to the basic sensory core. Thus, strict psychophysical laws hold for sensation but not for perception, and the discriminatory capacities of the organism and the processes mediating it must be determined through the psychophysics of sensation.

The doctrine of sensation was challenged by gestalt psychology, but in some fundamental ways the departure from traditional structuralism was not as great as it might at first appear. The emphasis on unitary forms substituted large elements for small ones, and sensory organization took the place of the associative compounding of sensations and images. The basic conception of proximal stimulation remained, however, fundamentally unchanged. "There is no organization among these [retinal] stimuli; the formation of specific units occurs in neural function. Nonetheless, in some respects the results of organization may tell us more about the world around us than the light waves are apt to do" [115, p. 160]. For structuralists and gestaltists alike, the proximal stimuli formed an "indifferent mosaic" upon which organization was imposed—through compounding of sensations and images, or through the operation of field forces in the brain. Neither approach admitted of one-to-one correspondence between the characteristics of proximal stimulation and perceptual experience. The traditional assumptions about the relationship, or rather lack of relationship, between proximal stimulation and the characteristics of perception have been challenged by Gibson [61, 62, 63, 64]. His psychophysical theory calls for a radical reformulation of the functional relationships in perception. At the same time, Gibson argues for an extension of the traditional boundaries of the domain of perception. Thus, the development of this theory has served to raise some major new questions concerning the relationship between perception and learning.

It is Gibson's thesis that all properties of the phenomenal world are in strict one-to-one correspondence with variables of stimulation (energy flux at the receptors). The functional relationships between stimulation and perceptual experience can be stated as strict psychophysical laws, and the methods of psychophysics are directly applicable to the study of perception. This programmatic assertion reflects a logical and experimental reexamination of the independent and dependent variables in perceptual experiments. The characteristics of stimulation are not limited to such variables of low order as frequency and intensity, which have been traditionally manipulated in psychophysical experiments. The organism is also sensitive to variables of high order, e.g., ratios, gradients, and rates. The high-order variables can be measured in the energy flow at the receptors and brought under experimental control. It is these high-order variables which correspond to the properties of surfaces and objects in the environment and to which perception is in strict psychophysical correspondence. As for perceptual experience, we must conceive of it as discriminative and ordered along phenomenal dimensions. The psychophysical laws of perception relate these discriminative dimensions of experience to the high-order variables of stimulation. Gibson has successfully applied such psychophysical analysis to the perception of such properties of the "visual world" as surfaces, edges, and slants, and to the perception of motion.

For a discussion of the relationship between perception and learning it is of especial significance that Gibson has extended the hypothesis of psychophysical correspondence to the perception of events, meanings, and values. All such perceptions, like those of objects in space, are dependent on patterns of physical stimulation at the receptors. To the extent that there is one-to-one correspondence between stimulus patterns and perceptions or responses, the functional relationship is essentially the same as that revealed in psychophysical investigations of classical perceptual phenomena. Thus, for Gibson the domain of perception includes all those experiences (or responses) for which strict dependence on stimulus variables of a low or high order can be demonstrated.

Gibson has recognized that the psychophysical laws established under strictly controlled conditions of observation may not fully apply under other circumstances, e.g., when stimulation is equivocal or impoverished. Things and events which serve as cues to action in a rapidly changing environment may often have to be recognized and identified under difficult and reduced conditions conducive to constant errors and misperceptions. The occurrence of systematic errors does not, however, constitute evidence which is fundamentally at variance with the doctrine of psychophysical correspondence. Instead, two kinds of perception must be distinguished—literal and schematic. In literal perception, which is studied by the psychophysical methods under optimal conditions of observation, the discriminative capacities of the organism are maximized. Literal observation yields a " . . . phenomenal world composed of all the properties that can be discriminated" [62, p. 102]. Under difficult conditions perception becomes schematic, i.e., selective and simplified: observation and report may be influenced significantly by motivation and expectation. Schematic perception, nonetheless, is a function of physical variables of stimulation, but the specific variables on which it is dependent comprise only a fraction of the total array effective in literal perception. The continuity between literal and schematic perception is evident from the fact that schematic observation becomes literal when precise discrimination is required.

Perception as Inference

Probabilistic functionalism. In asserting that perceptual discrimination is in one-to-one correspondence with proximal stimulation, Gibson breaks sharply with the classical conception of the role of stimulation in perception. An equally radical departure from the classical tradition but taking, as it were, the opposite direction is represented by Brunswik's probabilistic functionalism [27, 29, 30]. From the functionalist point of view, the critical relationship is between the *distal* value of the stimulus (measured in physical units) and the perceptual response. Perception is treated as an achievement of the organism, and the degree of achievement is measured by the correlation between the perceptual judgment and the distal value of the stimulus. This correlation defines the *functional validity* of the perceptual judgment.

Proximal stimuli provide the organism with cues on the basis of which the distal properties of objects can be estimated. The relationship between distal properties and proximal effects is probable rather than certain. A given value of a distal variable may give rise to a variety of patterns of proximal stimulation. Conversely, the presence of a particular pattern of proximal stimulation does not signify the presence of a unique distal property. There may be varying degrees of correlation between proximal cues and distal properties; the correlation measures the *ecological validity* of the cue with respect to the distal property. Under normal environmental conditions ecological validities are less than perfect.

Success in estimating ("attaining") the distal properties of objects thus depends on the utilization of patterns of proximal cues each of which has only limited validity. Since the association between distal properties and proximal effects is variable and undependable, the organism must learn to use different patterns of cues interchangeably and to weight each cue in accordance with its validity. The uncertainty of object-cue relationships, however, makes errorless perceptual judgment impossible in principle. The environment limits the organism to inferences about probable events [see also 89, pp. 111–117].

The treatment of perceptual judgments as estimates based on probabilistic cues represents a modern version of Helmholtz's theory of unconscious inference. There are, however, important differences between the classical and modern accounts of perceptual inference. Helmholtz assumed that the inferential process leading to a perceptual judgment is initially conscious but becomes automatized through experience; i.e., "unconscious" connotes "no longer conscious." In contemporary analyses, such as Brunswik's, a sequence of steps akin to inferential reasoning constitutes a conceptual model for the interpretation of the perceptual process [28]. In the application of the model deviations from the norms of inferential reasoning—what Brunswik called the "stupidity of perception" [25, pp. 119f.]—are emphasized along with the congruities between perceptual judgment and rational inference. There is no assumption that a conscious inferential activity occurs initially or is present later in vestigial form [for a detailed discussion of this position see 152].

Transactional functionalism. The inferential nature of the perceptual process is also central to the theoretical position of Ames [2] and other exponents of the "transactionalist" point of view [32, 99, 100, 109]. Apart from a series of ingenious demonstrations illustrating ambiguous cue-object relationships, little seems to have been added to the central idea that perceptual judgment may be likened to a process of inference which takes account of past environmental contingencies. To be sure, a new terminology is employed. Perceptions are described as the "apprehending of probable significances" and "prognostive directives for action." The individual is said to " . . . make sense out of the intrinsically meaningless sensory impingements by assessing their significance in terms of his assumptive world" [99]. While the vocabulary used in the labeling of hypothetical processes may be a matter of taste, the language of the transactionalists seems to offer few if any advantages over the terminology employed by Brunswik. The latter was developed through detailed analyses of the perceptual constancies and has largely remained tied to the variables manipulated in constancy experiments. Thus, concepts like ecological validity and functional validity are given precise quantitative meaning by correlations between variables measurable in investigations of the constancies. The concepts used in the theorizing of the transactionalists have not been given a comparable degree of precision.

Perceptual "hypotheses." A complete theory of perceptual inference must include consideration of the processes which constitute the "utilization of cues," i.e., the responses which lead to what appears to be an inferential judgment. Brunswik dismissed this problem as a matter of "process detail," emphasizing the fact that any given perceptual achievement could result from a variety of alternative and equivalent processes of mediation. As a functional theorist, he was concerned almost exclusively with the exploration of the conditions which allow the organism to obtain correct information about the environment. For those concerned with the relationship between perception and learning, the inferential behavior itself becomes a focus of interest. The construct of perceptual hypothesis [21, 144] was proposed in an attempt to conceptualize the sequence of events that issues in a perceptual judgment in the presence of a given pattern of proximal cues. Hypotheses were described as ence of a given pattern of proximal cues. Hypotheses were described as "predispositions of the organism" to respond to the information carried by proximal cues. Perceptual hypotheses have the status of mediating responses. The variables of which the strength of hypotheses is a function —frequency of past confirmation, number of competing hypotheses and motivational consequences—parallel those governing habits in general. While perceptual hypotheses may be regarded as a class of mediating responses, they are not assumed to be synonymous with any specific effector activity. It is primarily in this last respect that the concept of perceptual hypothesis appears to diverge from that of a cue-producing response which has been invoked as a mediator of perceptual judgments. As a matter of fact, however, recent analyses no longer equate cue-producing responses with specific effector activities [37, 135]. In spite of differences in terminology, the systematic status and empirical implications of perceptual hypotheses and cue-producing responses converge closely.

The term "hypothesis" was designed to emphasize the assumption that in any given situation perceptual judgments are subject to change by environmental reinforcement. The relation between hypothesis and information provided by proximal cues was described as cyclical in nature, with a continuous process of trial and check, trial and check [cf. 197] until confirmation has occurred. The amount of trial and check— as indicated, for example, by the cumulative number of receptor-exposure acts—will vary with the context in which the perceptual judgment is made as well as with the initial strength of the hypothesis [144, p. 251].

The essential feature of treatments of perception as an inferential process is the assumption that the final judgment or discrimination is mediated by learned responses to proximal cues. Such treatments take it for granted that certain stimuli function as cues; i.e., they are concerned with the sequence of events that is initiated by the receptive processes. Inasmuch as they do not deal with the question of how stimuli come to function as cues [cf. 64, p. 34], they are not comprehensive theories of perception. Rather, the analyses discussed in this section may be viewed as theories of perceptual judgment. In fact, in the context of these analyses the terms *discrimination, judgment,* and *categorization* [cf. 22] tend to be used interchangeably. It is no accident that theories of perceptual inference have found their primary application in situations in which there is less than perfect correlation between proximal and distal stimulus values, e.g., constancy experiments and investigations using reduced or impoverished conditions of stimulation. Learned mediators are invoked to account for the fact that in spite of this lack of correlation judgments of distal properties show considerable consistency and validity. The necessity of assuming such intervening processes has, of course, remained a focus of controversy. In the case of the constancies, for example, Gibson has taken the position that they are in no way an exception to the principle of strict psychophysical correspondence [61, pp. 186f.]. Similarly, Pratt [154] has argued that the facts of constancy can be subsumed under the general laws of psychophysics. As for conditions of reduced stimulation, there has been a disposition to consider them as unrepresentative of perception in general or, indeed, as conditions of "controlled misperception" [62, p. 96]. It would be difficult, however, to maintain a sharp distinction between conditions of stimulation which are and which are not impoverished or to agree on a sense in which one or the other situation provides a more valid method for determining the basic laws of perception. A general theory of perception must be applicable to the total range of conditions under which a significant amount of discrimination can be shown to occur.

Summary: Independent and Dependent Variables in the Definition of Perception

The divergencies among current definitions of perception may be examined with respect to (1) data language, (2) independent variables, (3) dependent variables, and (4) the relation of intervening variables and concepts to independent and dependent variables.

Data language. It is apparent that there is a continuing rift between those who insist that the data of perceptual experiments must, in principle, be reducible to the physical thing language and those for whom the possibility of such reduction is of secondary importance. The division centers, as we have seen, around the status accorded to phenomenological observation. Emphasis on phenomenology has led to a stubborn neglect of the distinction between the language of the subject and the language of the experimenter. As a result (1) the immediate data language of many perceptual experiments has remained ambiguous, and (2) observations in the data language (records of subject's reports and introspections) are often arbitrarily put in direct correspondence with properties of inferred constructs (percepts). Such practices have persisted because operational definitions of such critical theoretical terms as *percept* and *experience* are lacking or remain equivocal.

Independent variables. The systematic independent variables of perceptual experiments have historically fallen into two broad classes: (1) variables of proximal stimulation conceived as energy changes at the receptor and (2) conditions of the organism, especially those constituting a "set" for discriminating selected characteristics of the stimulus. The coordinated experimental independent variables have been (1) manipulations of physical stimuli designed to produce changes in proximal stimulation and (2) manipulations of the organism, notably by the use of instruction stimuli to human subjects.

There have been two significant departures from the traditional definition of the proximal stimulus as a major independent variable in the analysis of perceptual functions. The first is represented by Gibson's position that the stimulus should not be defined as energy change at a single receptor—a definition entailed by the distinction between sensation and perception—but rather in terms of distributions or patterns of energy, i.e., higher-order variables. The projection on the retinas represents, although it may not literally duplicate, the external pattern, and the strict laws of psychophysical correspondence can be determined in relation to either specification of the stimulus.

The second shift in the traditional definition of stimulus conditions is represented by an emphasis on distal stimulus as distinguished from proximal variables. The relative weight of distal and proximal variables as determiners of the perceptual response is assessed in the constancy experiment. In a functionalist analysis such as Brunswik's the correlation between the distal value of the stimulus and the perceptual response provides a measure of the organism's ability to maintain a stable perceptual environment in spite of continuous changes in the proximal pattern of stimulation.

The experimental manipulations of the stimulus conditions reflect, of course, the investigator's conceptualization of his independent variables. When the relationship between proximal stimulation and discrimination is to be determined, precise control and measurement of the physical dimensions of the stimulus are essential. This is true whether low-order or high-order variables of proximal stimulation are assumed to be in correspondence with the subject's discrimination. When the discrimination of distal properties is in question, the degree to which proximal stimulation is manipulated and controlled depends on the purpose of the experimenter. A high degree of control is required when the role of specific proximal mediators in constancy is investigated [e.g., 92]. On the other hand, control of proximal stimulation may be deliberately neglected for purposes of demonstrating the situational generality of constancy [26].

Let us turn now to the second type of independent variable, i.e., manipulation of the organism, represented by the instruction stimulus which is a necessary part of the antecedent conditions in any perceptual experiment. The systematic independent variable at issue here is the readiness to respond selectively ("set") induced in the subject prior to the presentation of the stimuli. The choice of a particular instruction stimulus reflects a basic decision about the kind of data on which inferences about perceptual processes must be based. The point becomes clear when one considers the nature of the instruction stimulus in a classical introspectionist experiment, a phenomenological study, and a modern psychophysical experiment. Results obtained with the different instruction stimuli would be incommensurable.

The fact that manipulation of the subject's attitude by means of instruction stimuli can produce major variations in psychophysical judgments has been clearly demonstrated in studies of the perceptual constancies [e.g., 91, 111]. A naïve-realistic attitude favors perceptual constancy, whereas an analytic attitude shifts the judgment away from the distal toward the proximal value of the stimulus object. It has generally been assumed that object constancy prevails under "natural" perceptual attitudes whereas judgments of proximal values can be obtained only under artificial attitudes established through elaborate training. This assumption has recently been challenged by Gilinsky [66] on the basis of her study of the effects of observational attitudes on size constancy. She suggests that the judgments obtained under the analytic attitude exemplify immediate sense perception and that the perceptual constancies achieved under the naïve-realistic attitude are dependent on a complex learned process of estimation. The hypothesis that the learning of observational attitudes plays a major role in perceptual development is worthy of serious consideration and emphasizes the potential importance of the instruction stimulus as a systematic independent variable.

Manipulation of the instruction stimulus has been traditionally used as a method for investigating the effects of preparatory set on perceptual discrimination. Ever since Külpe's classical demonstration [117], evidence has been accumulating that discrimination can be increased by instructions preparing the subject for the classes of objects or attributes on which he will be required to report [e.g., 33, 79, 116, 127, 128, 149, 156, 199]. An important unresolved question is, however, whether preparatory instructions influence perceptual discrimination per se or improve accuracy by increasing immediate memory and by restricting the range of the subject's responses. In an important series of experiments Lawrence and his associates [122, 123] have shown that instructions given immediately after the presentation of a complex stimulus may be as effective as instructions given prior to exposure in improving identification or discrimination of selected attributes. The procedure of manipulating the temporal position of the instruction stimulus (instructions after exposure versus instructions before and after) was also used in a recent series of studies by Long et al. [127, 128, 156]. The results suggest that a preparatory set may facilitate perceptual discrimination as distinct from retention and response selection under highly restricted conditions, viz., when the number of alternatives among which the subject must choose is small and the total stimulus pattern contains distinctive elements.

The problem raised by the studies on preparatory set again illustrates the importance of the distinction between the perceptual system and the response system. Experiments such as those of Lawrence exemplify the use of converging operations for purposes of distinguishing between the effect of preparatory set on the two systems. Regardless of the locus of its action, however, the instruction stimulus cannot be neglected as a major systematic variable in perceptual experiments.[1]

Dependent variables.   As we have emphasized, one of the most serious sources of confusion in current discussions of perception is the frequent lack of clarity about the systematic status of the dependent variables in empirical investigations. In stimulus-response analyses of perception the systematic dependent variable is some parameter of discriminatory response, e.g., the probability of occurrence of one of a set of alternative responses. It is difficult, on the other hand, to specify the nature of the dependent variable in phenomenological investigations. Empirically, the dependent variable is the subject's verbal report, but there are no rules for the classification and quantitative treatment of such responses.

Intervening variables and constructs.   Quite apart from the systematic status of the independent and dependent variables and the logic of inference, fundamental divergencies in the construct language of per-

---

[1] In a recent study Epstein and Rock [42] present evidence purporting to show that preparatory set has no significant effects on perceptual recognition. In their experiments expectations induced by verbal instructions did not influence the identification of ambiguous forms when pitted against opposing effects of frequency and/or recency. The results merely show, of course, that under certain conditions recency and frequency are more effective than instructional sets. The difficulties inherent in this type of design are discussed below in connection with Gottschaldt's experiments pitting frequency against structural factors. Experiments avoiding these difficulties yield clear evidence for the effectiveness of preparatory set [e.g., 127, 128, 156].

ceptual theorists are readily apparent. The purpose of phenomenological analysis is to reconstruct the nature of the subject's experience. In this context "experience" refers to unobserved and unobservable events rather than to abstract formal relationships. By contrast, inferences about perceptual processes may be intervening variables in the narrower technical sense, i.e., quantities derived from the manipulation of empirical variables and without explicit or implicit references to unobservable events. Finally, the inferences may embody assertions about physiological events which are in principle observable; i.e., they may take the form of hypothetical constructs in the sense of MacCorquodale and Meehl [130]. The reconstruction of experience and the abstraction of empirical relationships by means of intervening variables are essentially incompatible approaches to a theory of perception, and it is doubtful that they can be combined in a pragmatic integration as Allport has suggested [1, p. 56].

One of the major sources of conceptual confusion in contemporary perceptual theory has been the vague and inconsistent usage of the terms *whole* and *configuration*. These concepts are, of course, at the core of gestalt theory as opposed to "elementaristic" and "mechanistic" approaches. Bergmann [8, 9] has presented a penetrating and closely reasoned critical analysis of the semantic obscurities and logical contradictions surrounding the configurational doctrine; the confusions stem in no small measure from persistent failure to distinguish between descriptive and explanatory usage. Some parts of Bergmann's critique which are especially relevant to the present discussion will now be briefly summarized.

The descriptive usage of *configuration* may be considered first. Bergmann points out that the description of a configuration is always a conjunction of statements. Among the constituents of the conjunction there usually is an "atomic" relational statement, e.g., one specifying relative spatial positions. The inclusion of relational statements is, of course, a commonplace in scientific description and not an innovation of gestalt theory. Nevertheless, it is the presence of relational properties which has led gestaltists to object to the analytic treatment of configurations as connected parts (*Undverbindungen*). The irrelevancy of the objection is incisively pointed out by Bergmann as follows: "The description of a configuration is indeed always an and-connection; but to say that the configuration itself is one is simply nonsense, just as it would be nonsense to say that a chair is a noun because, as it happens, 'chair' is a noun: for patently it makes no sense to ascribe linguistic (syntactical) properties to things nonlinguistic. Thus, since the indictment makes no sense, the so-called 'elementarists' could not possibly be guilty" [9, pp. 149f.].

In its explanatory usage the concept of configuration focuses on the interaction among parts, as exemplified by the assertions that the whole is more than the sum of its parts and that the whole determines the nature of its parts. In analyzing such assertions, Bergmann shows that some of their implications are by no means peculiar to *gestalten* and can be adequately translated into positivistic terms whereas other implications are either untenable or reflect a confusion between description and explanation. (1) It is generally true that when we know the laws governing two individual systems, these laws do not enable us to specify the interaction of these two systems. In order to do so, a theory must generate "composition rules" which are empirical laws. Once this state of affairs is recognized, it is clear that there is no contradiction between analysis into part processes and the occurrence of interaction among such part processes, unless one wishes to deny in principle the possibility of composition laws. (2) It is possible that within a given system the value of any one variable is a function of all other relevant variables. Recognition of this possibility does not constitute an objection to the search for relatively autonomous systems of variables. What Bergmann calls "the dogma of total dynamic interdependence" [8, p. 451] is a poor substitute for analysis. (3) It is true that the response to a given physical stimulus may change as a function of the context of other stimuli in which it is presented. It is fallacious to conclude, however, that the stimulus changes as a function of its context and that the whole thus determines the nature of its constituent parts. This fallacy represents a confusion between description and explanation. What changes, of course, is the response to a constant stimulus. The reasons for the change are a matter of process analysis.

The difficulties attaching to the concept of configuration are compounded when an isomorphism between brain processes and phenomenal experience is asserted. The same relational statements are said to apply to two classes of configurations—the neural and the phenomenal. The hypothesis is, of course, an instance of the doctrine of psychophysical parallelism. Thus, all the hoary conceptual burdens of dualism fall upon the hypothesis, and it has neither plausibility nor promise as an explanatory tool. As Boring [17] has pointed out, the dualism implied in the doctrine of isomorphism may be either metaphysical or epistemological. If it is metaphysical, there is no reason to expect two noncomparable systems to have the same relational properties. If the dualism is epistemological, it is again unlikely that two systems of knowledge will generate the same relational properties. Boring concludes: "The presumption is strongly against isomorphism in a dualism, and, since *psychoneural isomorphism* describes a dualistic relation, the presumption must lie against it" [17, pp. 579f.]. The inescapable difficulties that confront any operational test of psychoneural isomorphism have also been spelled out by Boring [18]. Even if it were possible to obtain reliable evidence for isomorphic relationships, a problem would remain that is as old as it is intractable—that of specifying the nature of the communication or interaction between the two isomorphic systems.

The doctrine of configuration and its derivatives have had a persistent and pervasive influence on perceptual theory. Their dominance reflects the fact that gestalt theory was the major articulate approach to perception after the decline of structuralism. Yet, as we have tried to show, the philosophical and methodological contexts in which configurationism developed are essentially alien to the positivistic and operational emphases of much of American behavior theory. It is not surprising that today there is agreement neither on the data language of perceptual experiments nor on the rules by which recorded observations are placed in correspondence with theoretical constructs. The logical and semantic difficulties have not only impeded the development of perceptual theory but have also loomed large as obstacles to the orderly appraisal of the relationship between perception and learning.

DEFINITION OF LEARNING

A precise and comprehensive definition of learning is difficult to achieve. In contrast to what we have found to be true in the case of perception, however, there is little disagreement among learning theorists about the classification of experimental facts as instances of learning. The disagreements center around the necessary and sufficient conditions of learning and the interpretation of the learning process. Thus, few investigators are likely to object to the definition offered by Hilgard: "Learning is a process by which an activity originates or is changed through training procedures (whether in the laboratory or in the natural environment) as distinguished from changes by factors not attributable to training" [88, p. 4]. Admittedly, there are difficulties in translating this definition into operations which clearly distinguish the facts attributable to learning from those due to maturation and work decrement. As Hilgard has suggested, the ambiguity in such cases is often one of fact, not definition [88, p. 5].

The fact that the definition of learning has not been a major theoretical issue reflects a considerable amount of agreement on the *empirical* independent and dependent variables that define an experiment on learning. The need for the restriction and orderly classification of responses has been more generally recognized in experiments on learning than in investigations of perception. Hence the problem of separating responses which should and should not be classified as instances of learned behavior has not been nearly as troublesome as the parallel problem of classifying response functions as perceptual and nonperceptual. There is, of course, the problem of separating the effects of training from those of work decrement and maturation, to which we have already alluded. Theoretical analysis has also led to the important distinction between learning and performance which parallels that between perception and judgment in so far as an analytic separation is made between the responses of which the organism is potentially capable and the responses which actually occur in a given test situation. The distinction between learning and performance has been translated into experimental designs which make it possible to assess whether an observed change in behavior is attributable to one or the other. As we have seen, it has proved difficult to give clear operational meaning to the difference between perception and judgment.

A discussion of the systematic status of independent and dependent variables in learning experiments will not be attempted here. It is important to note, however, that the psychophysical relationships established in experiments on perception are often taken for granted in the specification of the conditions of learning. In stimulus-response analyses of learning, when an object is described as a cue to which responses are associated, it is assumed that the critical cue is discriminable from other cues along certain psychophysical dimensions and that such discrimination remains constant from trial to trial. The treatment of psychophysical relationships as constant parameters in learning experiments is illustrated in studies of generalization in which response strength is plotted against scaled sensory magnitudes, e.g., the number of just noticeable differences of pitch and loudness [93, 94].

In studies of generalization the assumption is made that the test stimuli are discriminable from the standard. This assumption was tested empirically in a study by Kalish [107] which makes an important methodological contribution. With human subjects Kalish was able to demonstrate close correspondence between the discriminability function for wavelength of light and the shape of the generalization gradient along that dimension. Specifically, the shape of the gradient corresponded to the slope of the discriminability function in the region of the standard. No such correspondence between generalization and discriminability was found with pigeons. Kalish suggests that the essential difference between generalization and discrimination lies in the fact that the latter develops under differential reinforcement. This difference in operations may have varying effects from species to species. With human subjects the two sets of operations yield parallel functions, at least for the continuum of wavelength.

In experiments on choice discrimination, the investigator must make certain assumptions about the positions of positive and negative cues along a psychophysical continuum in order to assess the difficulty of the

subject's task. The same assumptions must also be made for purposes of
analyzing such aspects of discrimination learning as continuity and transposition. As Riley [161] has recently shown for transposition, an incomplete or faulty analysis of the variables of stimulation determining the
discriminability of the cues may be an important source of error in the
interpretation of experimental results. It is true, of course, that stimulus-
response theories such as Hull's include discriminative processes in the
chain of constructs mediating between stimulus and response—the concept of afferent neural interaction [98] is a case in point. In practice,
however, psychophysical relationships continue to be treated as fixed
parameters of the experimental situation.

Gibson has been especially critical of learning theorists for their failure to concern themselves with the question of how specific stimulus patterns come to function as cues. "Energies do not have cue properties unless and until the differences in energy have correspondingly different
effects in perception. The total range of physical stimulation is very rich
in complex variables and these are theoretically capable of becoming
cues and constituting information. This is just where learning comes in"
[64, p. 35]. The point is essentially that perceptual learning must often
precede instrumental learning; i.e., the organism must learn to identify
the objects which are to serve as cues in the acquisition of new habits.
The investigation of cue-response learning is, however, in no sense in-
validated by a recognition of the fact that the acquisition of identifying
responses may be an essential condition for the establishment of instrumental habits.

Cognitive theorists who consider learning as a process of perceptual
organization or reorganization must equally make assumptions about the
validity of psychophysical correspondences established in perceptual experiments. Exposure to the features of a learning situation, e.g., to
choice point, maze path, and goal, are assumed to produce a sequence
of perceptual events which in turn result in the permanent changes
(memories, expectancies) that constitute learning. For such theories the
psychophysical laws governing the perception of environmental features
are obviously of central significance. In practice cognitive learning
theorists have, however, been inclined to accept current assumptions
about perceptual processes, e.g., the so-called gestalt laws, and to focus
predominantly on the relationship between the hypothetical perceptual
events and performance. In general, then, learning theorists of all per-
suasions have been disposed to take a body of perceptual facts for granted
in specifying the conditions of acquisition and performance. Such an
attitude has considerable pragmatic justification as long as assumptions
about perceptual functions are critically reexamined whenever the evidence appears inconsistent with them. Since learning theorists have

usually treated perceptual functions as fixed parameters, it is not surprising that they have shown relatively little concern with perceptual learning in the narrower sense, i.e., changes in perceptual functions resulting from practice. It is to a consideration of perceptual learning in this sense that we turn next.

CONCEPTUALIZATIONS OF PERCEPTUAL LEARNING

Our concern in the next sections will be with the conceptualization of perceptual learning and with the experimental methods brought to bear on this problem. No detailed review of the empirical evidence will be attempted, but selected studies of general theoretical or methodological significance will be considered in some detail.

The question at issue is as old as the study of perception itself. What are the effects of "past experience"—training in the natural environment and the laboratory—on perception? As compared to the volume of theoretical debate, the facts bearing on the question are relatively scant and controversial. Our discussion of the problems of definition has pointed to a basic source of difficulty in the experimental and theoretical analysis of perceptual learning. The lack of consensus on the operational definition of the constructs of perceptual theory has (1) led to wide divergencies in experimental procedures and methods of measurement and (2) been conducive to theoretically inspired disagreements about the significance of empirical findings. Conceptualizations of the process of perceptual learning reflect the same basic emphases that we discerned in the definitions of perception. What one means by perceptual learning depends, of course, on what he means by perception and what kinds of data he is willing to accept as a basis of inference about perceptual processes. A basic cleavage again exists between the phenomenological approach and stimulus-response analysis of discrimination.

Phenomenology

Logical analysis. When the basic data of perception are those of phenomenological description, perceptual learning means a change in phenomenal appearance which is attributable to past experience or training. In general, gestalt psychologists have tended to deprecate the scope and importance of such learning. The reasons for this attitude are partly historical and partly inherent in the theory. In opposing sensationism and elementarism, gestalt theory perforce included in its attack the context theory of meaning and the doctrine of unconscious inference [115]. Both of these build perceptions out of sensations through a process of associative learning. In arguing against sensationism, therefore, gestalt psychologists found it necessary to attack empiricism on both logical and factual grounds [113], apparently on the assumption that these two points of view were necessarily linked. It is now clear, especially from Hebb's analysis [84], that such a linkage is by no means inevitable. The positive argument for the importance of sensory organization and brain dynamics made it equally important to minimize empiricistic explanations of the laws of perception.

With the structuralist account of perception ruled out, gestalt psychologists equated perceptual learning to the determination of sensory organization by memory traces. Once the question has been posed in this way, formidable logical difficulties appear to arise against the hypothesis that past experience can modify perception, and especially form perception. The traditional arguments [113, 115] have been restated by Zuckerman and Rock [200]. In analyzing the implications of the statement that past experience with a form will influence perception of that form, they ask: " . . . how can a memory trace left by an unorganized mass of sensory data create a shaped visual object in the present field?" [200, p. 278]. If the initial perception of a form is unorganized, so is its memory trace. Consequently past experience as represented in memory traces cannot account for present perceptual organization. Closely related is the "Höffding problem" emphasized by Köhler [114]. When the perception of a form has left an organized memory trace, subsequent perceptions can be modified only if that particular trace is aroused upon recurrence of the stimulus. Such selective trace arousal must be based on formal similarities between the ongoing perceptual process and the trace rather than the activation of specific neural pathways since the recognition of familiar forms is largely independent of retinal location [e.g., 50]. But if the communication between process and trace depends on their formal similarity, then the perceptual process must be organized before it can serve to arouse the appropriate trace [cf. also 188]. Thus, sensory organization is in principle independent of past experience although the possibility is left open that a trace, once aroused, may modify or "reorganize" an ongoing perceptual process.

These "logical" arguments represent a subtle form of *petitio principii*. It is taken as axiomatic that (1) past experience modifies perception through the agency of trace-process communication and (2) the trace is to be conceived as a simulacrum of the perception, varying along the same dimensions as the phenomenal percept itself. These suppositions are, of course, no more than hypotheses of gestalt theory and cannot legitimately be used as premises in a demonstration of the *logical* difficulties alleged to be "inherent" [200, p. 277] in the empiricistic view of perception. Hebb's analysis [84] has shown that it is at least possible to *conceive* of a process of neural development in which the perception of form emerges gradually through the cumulative effects of experience. Neither the assumption of trace-process communication nor the conception of trace as a shadowy likeness of the percept is inevitable. While there may be disagreement about the adequacy of Hebb's theory, it does not appear open to the criticism of logical contradictions. The allegation that an empiricist view of form perception is untenable on logical grounds is without merit.

Empirical implications. The experimental attack on the empiricist position has typically taken the form of pitting past experience against present sensory organization. The difficulties which arise in the interpretation of these experiments will be discussed below (see pp. 66–82). The avowed purpose of such investigations was not to show that past experience never influences perception but rather that immediate processes of sensory organization can override the effects of training. Apologists for the gestalt position, such as Luchins [129], have objected heatedly to the allegation that gestalt theory denies the possibility of perceptual learning. The defense is documented by references to statements of gestalt theorists, e.g., Wertheimer's inclusion of past experience as a determiner of perceptual grouping [190]. The fact remains, however, that perceptual learning, in the sense of gradual development of perceptual organization, is inconsistent with the basic tenets of gestalt theory. The logical arguments which we discussed in the preceding paragraph do, in fact, cast doubt on the possibility of such learning if one accepts the basic premises of gestalt theory. On the other hand, the hypothesis that the arousal of traces may serve to reorganize an ongoing process of perceptual organization is consistent with the assumptions of the theory. Such an explanation is offered, for example, for the perceptual changes produced in experiments on the kinetic depth effect [189]. A stationary form which is initially perceived as two-dimensional is seen as three-dimensional following a rotation which imparts depth to the figure by means of the kinetic depth effect. It is assumed that the perceptual process corresponding to the stationary form "communicates" with the three-dimensional trace laid down during rotation, and the interaction of process and trace produces a perception in depth. Similarly, the perception of meaning can be attributed to the arousal of traces associated with perceptual units. Such units form segregated wholes, not by virtue of their meaning, but in accordance with the laws of sensory organization. Meaning is added to these units, presumably as a result of trace-process communication. "Gestalt psychology claims that it is precisely the original segregation of circumscribed wholes which makes it possible for the sensory world to appear so utterly imbued with meaning to the adult; for, in its gradual entrance into the sensory field meaning follows the lines drawn by natural organization; it usually enters into segregated wholes" [115, p. 139]. It is noteworthy, and indeed not devoid of irony, that this statement represents essentially a context theory of meaning—meaning accrues to a "natural" sensory core. The only difference from the traditional Titchenerian view is that sensory organization has been substituted for sensation. We conclude that the conceptualization of perceptual learning in gestalt theory is essentially continuous with that of structuralism and represents what the Gibsons [64] call an "enrichment" hypothesis.

Stimulus-Response Analysis

When inferences about perception are based on stimulus-response functions, perceptual learning is defined by changes in such functions which are attributable to training. It will be useful at this point to refer back briefly to Graham's formal statement of psychophysical relationships. The statement that perceptual learning has occurred would take the form $a_c = \Phi(x_1, n, R_1)$, where a_c is a critical value of the stimulus such as a threshold derived from a psychophysical experiment, x_1 is the instruction stimulus, R_1 is the restricted class of responses measured in the psychophysical experiment, and n is a variable specifying the conditions of training, e.g., the number of practice trials (see p. 35f. above). The pragmatic value of a stimulus-response analysis of perceptual functions becomes apparent here. When inferences about perceptual discrimination are based on *restricted* measures of stimuli and responses, there is no difficulty in specifying and *measuring* the changes in behavior that define perceptual learning. Unless the responses measured in the perceptual experiment are restricted, the course of perceptual learning cannot be determined reliably.

Response-produced cues. The systematic status of perceptual learning in a stimulus-response theory of behavior has been receiving increasing attention in recent years. If the perceptual process can be modified by learning, it becomes appropriate to assign the functional characteristics of a response to this process. Thus, Dollard and Miller define perception as a response-produced cue [37, pp. 178f.]. The conditions determining the acquisition of the cue-producing responses are the same as those which apply to other responses studied explicitly in learning experiments. The cue-producing response need not be conceived as a glandular or muscular effector activity; response can be defined more broadly as any reaction which can " . . . become functionally connected with an antecedent event through learning."

The functional rather than anatomical definition of stimulus and response makes it possible to carry the analysis of response-produced cues beyond proprioception to central events. Such an extension is discussed explicitly by Miller in his contribution to an earlier volume of this study: "Adding to the peripheral responses, the possibility of images and other central responses made possible by the myriad potential connections in the brain greatly increases the number of different distinctive cue-producing responses that are available and that do not interfere with overt activity" [135, p. 243]. The shift to functional definitions also permits the consideration within the framework of S-R theory of "flexible cybernetic behavior" [pp. 248ff.] involving relational responses to relational stimuli with guidance by feedback. An earlier analysis of "copying" behavior by Miller and Dollard [136, pp. 152–164] had, in fact, been built on the assumption that relational responses to relational cues can be established and refined by differential reinforcement. Miller recognizes that the broadened definitions of stimulus and response imply a convergence of S-R theory and cognitive theory on common concepts and problems. One important difference remains, however, between the two points of view. Even in a "liberalized" S-R formulation, the basic principles of learning and performance are assumed to be the same for all stimulus-response associations, whether the processes be peripheral or central. Cognitive theories have not been disposed to attribute response properties to central processes.

An extension of S-R laws to central processes is also found in an analysis by Berlyne [11], who suggests that phase sequences in the associative areas of the cortex may be interpreted as having the function of both stimuli and responses: "They come to be evoked *through learning* by antecedent activity in the sensory cortex, and they come to stimulate *through learning* the firing of further groups of neurons, including ultimately those of the motor nerves" [pp. 139f.]. Berlyne lists a number of experimental facts which are consistent with this interpretation, e.g., the effects of experience on absolute and differential thresholds, stimulus generalization and discrimination in perception, sensory conditioning and preconditioning. He also points to the parallel between stimulus satiation and reactive inhibition and suggests that images may be regarded as anticipatory fractional components of the perceptual response. Finally, he conceptualizes attention as the momentary effective reaction potential (sE_R) of the perceptual response. The analysis is of interest in showing one way in which perceptual learning can be conceptualized within the existing framework of stimulus-response theory. Analyses showing that the development of selective perceptual responses can be predicted from the postulates of S-R reinforcement theory have also been presented by Spence [178] and Wickens [196].

Differentiation of response-produced cues. The perceptual response, then, can be conceived as a mediator or identifying response which produces cues to which instrumental responses can be associated. It is the instrumental response which changes the environmental conditions of the organism and which directly precedes differential reinforcement. The identifying response, which occurs earlier in the sequence, is less subject to modification by reinforcement than the instrumental response [108]. In an analysis of the two-phase process initiated by sensory stimulation—differential identifying response to the sensory input and performance of the instrumental response—Kanfer [108] points out that experimental studies of perception usually focus on one of these phases to the exclusion of the other. In psychophysical investigations the identifying response is made explicit, or, more exactly, the experimental arrangements are such as to support inferences about the cue-producing responses which usually remain implicit. Thus, the conditions of reinforcement for the overt verbal or motor responses are assumed to be constant during the determination of a psychophysical function (cf. p. 36 above). In studies of discrimination learning, especially with animal subjects, the emphasis is on the acquisition of an instrumental response. Under these circumstances, inferences about mediating perceptual responses become more hazardous. Once an instrumental response is activated, it may persist even after the identifying response has changed. Moreover, after an instrumental response has been associated with a specific response-produced cue, it may generalize to a wide range of other cues. The performance of instrumental responses is also significantly influenced by conditions of motivation and incentive. The general point is an extremely important one, since the ability to acquire instrumental responses to specific stimulus patterns has frequently been used to test the effects of past experience on perception.

When instrumental responses are associated with response-produced cues, the distinctiveness of these cues [120, 121] becomes a significant determinant of transfer and generalization. The arousal of a common mediator serves to make external stimuli equivalent, and differentiation of mediators favors discrimination. It follows that the distinctiveness of cues should be capable of experimental manipulation; i.e., attachment of different identifying responses to a set of stimuli should facilitate discrimination among them. Considerable experimental effort and theoretical interest have recently focused on the problem of stimulus predifferentiation [3, 4, 6, 51, 69, 70, 71, 166, 183]. The typical experimental procedure consists of attaching verbal labels to a set of stimuli and then testing for transfer from such pretraining to subsequent discrimination among the stimuli. While there is substantial evidence for positive transfer, the hypothesis that discrimination learning depends on the distinctiveness of response-produced cues has received only partial support. Thus, the specificity of the verbal labels does not significantly influence the amount of transfer [81, 82, 162]. Effectiveness of the predifferentiation training is also a function of the "appropriateness" of the label, where appropriateness is measured by the consistency with which untrained subjects apply the label to the stimulus pattern [143]. This finding indicates that the preexperimental meaning of the pattern may influence the amount of differentiation produced by the attachment of new labels. As for the effects of predifferentiation on discriminability, there is no evidence that preliminary training changes the differential threshold, even though there are significant effects on delayed recognition [3]. While the results must, therefore, be interpreted with caution, the investigations are important in representing an experimental attack on the role of response-produced cues in discrimination.

Psychophysical Correspondence

Specificity theory. A central assumption of the position which we have been discussing is that perceptual (cue-producing) responses follow the same general laws as do other responses. From this point of view, perceptual learning consists of the elaboration and differentiation of responses evoked by external stimulus patterns. Discrimination among a series of stimuli improves as the responses evoked by each member of the series become more specific and the response-produced cues more distinctive. In emphasizing the contribution of associative learning to perceptual discrimination, such a view is continuous with the classical theory of context: it is not possible to account for perceptual discrimination entirely in terms of the variables of proximal stimulation; the history of the subject's past responses to any given stimulus pattern must be considered as well. This conception of perceptual learning is at variance with the doctrine of strict psychophysical correspondence, and for this reason it is not surprising to find it explicitly challenged by Gibson and Gibson [64]. In an important theoretical paper the Gibsons contrast the classical associationistic view of perceptual learning, which they designate as *enrichment theory,* with an interpretation derived from the hypothesis of psychophysical correspondence, to which they refer as the *specificity theory.*

An associationistic theory of perceptual learning must assume that as a result of experience the sensory effects of stimulation are "enriched" by a context of associations. This basic assumption is present regardless of whether the associations are conceived as images, memories, or response-produced cues. According to the Gibsons, this position confronts two major difficulties: (1) it accepts the distinction between sensation and perception, i.e., between sensory core and associative context—a distinction which has proved intractable to experimental analysis; (2) it implies that as a result of learning, perception comes to be in decreasing correspondence with stimulation. As the associative context becomes richer and more diversified, the sensory input accounts for less and less of the total variance in perceptual discrimination. Thus, there appears to be a contradiction between the assumed effects of perceptual learning and the observed improvements in discrimination as a function of experience.

By contrast, the specificity theory assumes that at all stages of perceptual development discrimination is in strict correspondence to the variables of proximal stimulation. Practice improves discrimination by making it possible for the organism to respond to more subtle and more complex variables of stimulation. "Perceptual learning, then, consists of responding to variables of stimulation not previously responded to" [64, p. 34]. New qualities, features, and dimensions of variation are elaborated as a function of experience, and to the extent that discrimination is thus refined, perception comes to be in *increasing* rather than decreasing correspondence with stimulation. In such a description of perceptual learning, there is no need to distinguish between sensation and perception. Psychophysical correspondence is the rule from the outset and remains the principle governing perceptual discrimination. " . . . perceptual experience even at the outset consists of a world, not of sensation, . . . and the world gets more and more properties as the objects in it get more distinctive . . . the phenomenal properties and the phenomenal objects correspond to physical properties and physical objects in the environment *whenever learning is successful*" [64, p. 34]. While the statement is cast in phenomenological terms, it can be given a stimulus-response formulation. Thus, perceptual learning can be described as an increase in the specificity of responses to stimuli, " . . . accompanied by an increase in the ability to respond differentially to the dimensional variables of the stimuli" [65, p. 447].

Specificity theory versus association theory. In emphasizing the importance of differential responses as mediators of perceptual learning, the Gibsons agree with the associationistic position. The source of disagreement lies in the insistence that perceptual learning is restricted, *by definition,* to those cases in which the subject acquires differential responses to variables of stimulation not previously responded to. Thus, again by definition, perceptual learning results in improved discrimination and an increase in the degree of psychophysical correspondence. However, if learning is to be defined as a change in behavior under conditions of practice, the restriction that the change always be in the direction of increased psychophysical correspondence can be questioned [146]. If a subject is trained to make a certain kind of constant error, it is not immediately apparent that such training should not be considered as perceptual learning. The fact that our training procedures are usually aimed at improving discrimination and frequently succeed in doing so does not detract from the systematic significance of the problem of definition.

In any event, one may question the assertion that according to association theory, perceptual learning necessarily results in a progressive decrease of correspondence between response and stimulation. The argument was developed with reference to the structuralist theory which assumed that an imaginal fringe accrues to the sensory core, and that the context of imagery " . . . puts more in the perception than the sensory stimuli can account for" [180, p. 115]. Contemporary association theory is not concerned with the analysis of the givens of consciousness but rather with the sequence of events from sensory stimulation to instrumental response. According to the analysis of Dollard and Miller, cited above, perceptual learning consists of the acquisition of cue-producing responses to external stimuli. Instrumental responses elicited by response-produced cues are subject to differential reinforcement. The effects of such reinforcements will influence, to some extent at least, the antecedent perceptual responses as well (cf. p. 62 above). Thus, cue-producing responses which mediate fine discriminations and lead to successful manipulation and locomotion will be favored over those resulting in failures of discrimination. An associationistic theory of perceptual learning does not entail the conclusion that perception comes to be in decreasing correspondence with stimulation.

It is not sufficient simply to assert that the organism comes to respond to new variables of stimulation and to elaborate new qualities, for these are the very facts that a theory of perceptual learning must explain. The term *respond* must be given systematic status. In discussions of perceptual learning, "response to stimulation" has carried at least three different meanings: (1) receptor adjustments favoring exposure to stimulation [e.g., 39, 198], (2) reactions of the central nervous system initiated by stimulation, and (3) discriminatory or identifying responses. It is only in the second sense that perceptual learning can in principle be described as a nonassociative process, and we must presume that it is in that sense that specificity theory conceives of the changes produced by practice. The question remains of how changes in the central effects of stimulation issue into appropriate discriminatory or identifying responses. Thus, the process of perceptual learning inevitably includes an associative component. This fact is brought home most clearly when the perception of signs and symbols is considered. An object acquires sign properties by virtue of sequential dependencies among environmental events. Hence the discrimination of sign properties depends on the organism's commerce with environmental sequences and is of necessity an associative process. Similarly, marks and sounds which are initially undifferentiated come to serve as symbols by virtue of their consistent appearance and usage in sequences and contexts prescribed by convention. Again the discrimination of symbols must be seen as an associative process. A theory of perceptual learning which neglects or takes for granted the changes in stimulus-response functions which result from practice is incomplete and is apt to neglect the behavioral context in which perceptual differentiations are developed.

EXPERIMENTAL DESIGNS IN THE STUDY OF PERCEPTUAL LEARNING

The experimental questions asked in studies of perceptual learning and the designs used to answer them reflect the conceptual differences on which we have focused in the preceding sections. Concern with sensory organization led to studies of the effects of past experience on the perception of form. It is primarily in such studies that support for nativistic and empiricist theories of perception has been sought. An altogether different tradition is represented by the large volume of work on the improvement of perceptual judgment as a function of practice [55]. Much of that work was not explicitly related to general theories of perceptual learning, but the problem of improved discrimination readily lends itself to a stimulus-response analysis. It then becomes a question of major theoretical significance whether improvement in perceptual judgment is a function of the same variables as is the acquisition of verbal and motor responses in conventional learning experiments. From a functionalist point of view, perceptual learning improves the utilization of proximal cues to distal objects. As a result of experience, the array of effective cues increases, and the organism comes to weight different cues in accordance with their validity. The conditions determining such utilization of cues have been studied primarily in experiments on the perceptual constancies.

The Effects of Past Experience on the Perception of Form

The question of whether past experience influences perceptual organization is of central importance for gestalt theory. Although it is true that gestalt theory does not logically entail a strictly nativistic theory of perception, the principles of brain dynamics used to account for perceptual organization fail to provide for the cumulative effects of past experience. The systematic attack on elementarism, moreover, extended to the hypothesis that perceptual configurations were the result of associative learning. This systematic background is reflected in the experimental procedures which have been used in testing the empiricist hypothesis, viz., situations in which the effects of past experience are *pitted against* the laws of organization. The major experimental designs used for this purpose may be classified as follows: (1) differential-training experiments; (2) evaluation of assumed effects of past experience; and (3) studies of sensory deprivation. The methodological problems presented by each of these procedures will now be considered.

Differential-training experiments. The reference experiment which has provided a landmark in discussions of perceptual learning is the well-known study by Gottschaldt [72, 73]. An analysis of this experiment will serve to exhibit the limitations of differential-training experiments in assessing the effects of past experience on sensory organization.

Gottschaldt's experiments. In the first major part of Gottschaldt's experiment five simple geometric figures (*a*-figures) were exposed to subjects with widely different frequency. To one group of (three) subjects each of the *a*-figures was shown 3 times; to a second group of (nine) subjects each of the *a*-figures was shown 520 times. During training, each exposure lasted for one second. In the critical test after the end of training, complex *b*-figures were exposed for three seconds; the *a*-figures were a geometrical part of the *b*-figures. The instructions to the subjects were to *describe* the *b*-figures; they were explicitly requested to describe any feature by which their attention was attracted. The reports were ranged along a continuum, defined at one extreme by those cases in which " . . . the *a*-figure instantly stood out from *b* without any assistance from the subject," and at the other, by those cases in which " . . . no trace of *a* was perceived or suspected—the *b*-figure was described *as such* without reference to *a*" [41, pp. 111f.]. When the various types of reports were grouped into positive ones, i.e., those judged to show an influence of past experience, and negative ones, there was no difference as a function of the frequency of exposures during training.

In the second part of this experiment the same subjects were given additional exposures to the *a*-figures (two and twenty respectively for the two groups) and instructed to search actively for the *a*-figures during the presentation of the *b*-figures. While such instructions served to increase the number of positive reports, the increases were independent of the amount of prior training. In a series of further experiments Gottschaldt manipulated the subject's set, i.e., the degree of expectancy for the presence of *a*-figures at the time of presentation of the *b*-figures. He concluded that " . . . as soon . . . as the *b*-figure was exposed in a situation which directed the subject toward the perception of *a*, there resulted (quite apart from the number of earlier presentations) a tendency to see the *b*-complex in a manner given by this vector" [41, p. 113].

These findings have been considered an experimental disproof of empiricistic theory [113, p. 155] and continue to be cited as conclusive evidence for the " . . . victory of grouping factors over past experience" (*sic!*) [200, p. 283]. In view of the significance attached to Gottschaldt's results, it becomes important to point to several serious flaws both in method and in logic which make it difficult to draw any firm conclusions from this investigation and related studies. Consider the strictly logical difficulties first. The purpose of the study was to prove the null hypothesis, viz., that at least for some figures repetition has no effect on the perception of components. Clearly the failure to find a significant difference under a selected set of conditions does not support any general conclusion about repetition unless the occurrence of a difference is unequivocally predicted from theory. Such a prediction cannot be made from "empiricist theory" for the particular conditions used by Gottschaldt. The past history of exposures is not known for either the a-figures, the total b-figures, or components of the b-figures. Arbitrary judgments about their relative familiarity [113, pp. 155f.] are scarcely compelling. The rate at which the discrimination of the component figures should develop cannot be predicted. The basic units of which both training and test figures are constructed—lines and angles—have been experienced by the subject for a total lifetime prior to the experiment. How much differential training is required to modify habits with respect to the specific patterns used in the experiment it is simply impossible to say. The basic point here is, of course, quite simple: in the absence of precise quantitative deductions based on theory, negative results cannot be adequately interpreted.

The methodological uncertainties of the experiment are equally serious. The basic data consisted of "spontaneous" descriptions of the complex figures. If the subject failed to make reference to the a-figure, it was concluded that a was not discriminable. Such an assumption is, of course, completely untenable. All that can be legitimately concluded from such records is that discriminatory responses to a were weaker than those to other parts of the test figure. Certainly a flat assertion that "a was not seen" [200, p. 283] is not warranted. It is quite possible that another measure of discrimination—e.g., using the a-figures as conditioned stimuli and using the b-figures in tests of generalization—would have yielded positive results. There are few cases in the history of perceptual experimentation in which the need for converging operations (cf. pp. 37–43) is as clearly illustrated as in the Gottschaldt experiments. It is not reasonable to take it for granted that appropriate descriptive responses to the a-figures had been fully differentiated and were at asymptotic strength when the subject was confronted with the complex b-figures. Gottschaldt himself showed that the ability to discover hidden a-figures improved with practice [41, pp. 114f.]. Similar results were obtained by Hanawalt [83], who also found general transfer effects, i.e., improvement in the ability to discover a specific a-figure in a variety of test patterns generalized to the discrimination of new designs. Such transfer effects persisted over a considerable period of time. The single series of tests used by Gottschaldt does not warrant the conclusion that the a-figures were "psychologically not present" [41, p. 114].

Even if one accepts Gottschaldt's measures at their face value, the total pattern of results does not permit clear-cut conclusions about the influence of prior training on the discrimination of component figures. When a strong set for *a*-figures was established, subjects achieved considerable success in discriminating the familiar units. Gottschaldt chose to treat set or expectancy as "situational forces" which are independent of past experience. Such a strict separation of set from habit is not, however, tenable. In order to be activated or facilitated by instructions, a discriminatory response must first be learned. A "situational force" could hardly produce any results unless the *a*-figure had, indeed, been made familiar by training and the *b*-figure was subject to analysis, "autochthonous gestalt factors" to the contrary notwithstanding. Once it has been shown that under certain conditions of training and instruction the familiar components can be discriminated in the "cohesive" test figures, any sweeping generalizations about the ineffectiveness of past experience are out of order. There remains the argument that the influence of repetition is not "automatic" [115, pp. 190f.]; i.e., it is not independent of the subject's set at the time of the test. It would be difficult to point to a theory of learning which would predict practice effects that remain invariant with the conditions of testing. The distinction between learning and performance is, of course, clearly recognized, and at any given moment the probability of a response depends not only on the strength of a habit but also on the conditions prevailing at the time of observation, including set. The fact that discrimination varies as a function of set is hardly evidence for the prevalence of sensory dynamics over learning.

Gottschaldt's conclusions were challenged by the results of later investigations, notably that of Djang [36]. Here the frequency with which the hidden test figure was discriminated varied significantly with the amount of prior practice. It is true that Djang's materials and procedure differed from those of Gottschaldt. During practice, the subjects learned to associate a nonsense syllable with each of the *a*-figures. Both the simple and complex figures were composed of dots, and the degree of camouflage tended to be less complete than in Gottschaldt's designs. As in the earlier study, the ease with which the hidden figure could be unmasked varied from one set of stimulus materials to the next. To argue that the differences in method and materials vitiate the relevance of Djang's findings to Gottschaldt's general thesis [200, pp. 284f.] obscures the theoretical issue, viz., whether or not the discrimination of form is significantly influenced by training. Gottschaldt's particular figures are no more essential for testing this hypothesis than any other arbitrarily selected set of materials. It is equally pointless and operationally meaningless to argue that results such as Djang's do not prove that " . . . there is a difference in frequency of *perception* of the simple form but only that there is a difference in the *utilization* of this form based on recognition" [200, p. 285]. If such an argument had any merit at all—and it is difficult to see how the assertion could be adequately tested—it would apply with equal force to Gottschaldt's own finding: the subjects' failure to report on the presence of the *a*-figure would not justify the conclusion that these figures had not been perceived. There merely may have been no " . . . utilization of the form based on recognition!" Such *ad hoc* reinterpretations underline the fact that the question of whether training enhances the "real" perception of the masked figures cannot be answered by conventional indices of discrimination. Both positive and negative results are interpreted as consistent with the null hypothesis, and the experiment becomes a futile exercise in self-fulfilling prophecy.

A study by Schwartz [169] shows that significant effects of training can be obtained even with Gottschaldt's original figures when well-differentiated and available responses are used in the identification of the *a*-figures. During the preliminary training Schwartz's experimental groups associated each of the five *a*-figures with a familiar verbal response (a color name). The control subjects learned to associate each of five outline faces with a familiar first name. On the critical test of recognition of the embedded figures, the control group and one of the experimental groups were provided with a key showing the five *a*-figures and their associated labels. A second experimental group was tested without a key. All subjects identified the camouflaged *a*-figure by means of its associated verbal response. Both experimental groups, who had received preliminary training with the *a*-figures, significantly surpassed the control group. A comparison between the two experimental groups showed that the effects of training were independent of the use of a key during the tests. A supplementary experiment eliminated the possibility that subjects made their identifications on the basis of the irrelevant cue of relative size. Finally, comparisons of tests immediately after the end of training and after an interval of forty-eight hours showed no decline in the effects of practice.

We conclude that in spite of its "classical" status the Gottschaldt experiment does not constitute a theoretically reasonable or methodologically sound procedure for investigating the effects of training on form perception. To summarize our discussion, there are three major reasons why it is impossible to conclude from such an experiment that form perception is independent of past training: (1) The dependent variable—something like spontaneous phenomenal emergence of the masked figure during presentation of the complex test figure—has not been given adequate operational definition. Significant effects of practice are found when other measures of discrimination or other materials are used. However, negative results have been accepted at face value, whereas positive findings have been questioned freely as not satisfying the criteria of truly perceptual changes. (2) In the critical tests of the effects of training the nature and strength of competing preexperimental habits are left uncontrolled and remain unknown. Formally, this is tantamount to testing transfer effects without taking account of the initial strength of responses to the stimuli in the transfer task. (3) Support for a theoretical position is based on acceptance of the null hypothesis. Such an argument is untenable in principle, especially when the hypothesis under attack does not generate precise predictions for the specific conditions of the experiment. The same strictures apply, of course, to the many demonstrations scattered through treatises on gestalt psychology [113, 115, 190] purporting to show that perceptual organization does *not* conform to the alleged expectations of an "empiricist" theory.

Identification of incomplete and ambiguous figures. When initial responses to the test stimuli are variable and appropriate identifying responses are readily available to the subject, controlled training may produce major improvements in form discrimination. Thus, preliminary training selectively strengthens one of the alternative identifying responses. Consider, for example, Leeper's study [125] of the "development of sensory organization." In his first experiment Leeper investigated the effects of prior exposure to incomplete figures, supplemented by verbal descriptions, upon subsequent identification of these figures. The stimulus materials were fragmentary drawings such as those used in Street's Gestalt Completion Test [179], which can be perceived as schematic representations of conventional objects. The experimental groups practiced recognition of the figures on two successive days. The training consisted of visual exposures of the figures, supplemented by verbal descriptions. More than three weeks after the original training, the critical figures as well as some new nonsense figures were presented tachistoscopically to the experimental groups as well as to a control group which had received no prior training. The experimental subjects were considerably more successful than the control subjects in recognizing the incomplete figures. The frequency of incorrect identifications was very low, so that the observed improvement could not be simply attributed to an increase in the probability of the appropriate verbal responses. The possibility cannot be ruled out, however, that associations between some parts or distinctive features of the figures and verbal responses were established during the original training. This ambiguity in the results is serious, since Leeper is concerned with the effects of training on sensory organization. In his interpretation he appears to assume a one-to-one correspondence between sensory organization (phenomenal appearance) and verbal report. This assumption is hazardous, and it remains to be shown that in a situation such as Leeper's the identifying responses on the test of retention were not mediated by fragmentary cues.

In Leeper's second experiment the stimulus materials were two ambiguous figures (Boring's "My wife and my mother-in-law" and the "pirate-rabbit" figure devised by Leeper). A control group was exposed to the figures without any prior treatment. One experimental group was prepared verbally for one or the other of the possible organizations. For a second experimental group the preparation was "perceptual"; i.e., a drawing emphasizing one of the alternative organizations was presented before the critical test. Perceptual preparation was highly effective in determining the response to both ambiguous figures, whereas verbal preparation was effective with only one figure, viz., the one to which the response was in general relatively slow (pirate-rabbit). Again it is difficult to say to what extent generalization of verbal responses from the preliminary procedures to the test trials contributed to these results.

The effect of differential reinforcement on figure-ground perception. Similar difficulties attach to the interpretation of experiments, initiated by the well-known study of Schafer and Murphy [168] in which attempts are made to modify figure-ground relationships by differential reward and punishment [101, 138, 163, 177]. In these experiments, two pairs of profiles are presented during the preliminary training period, and a name is learned for each profile. During the training, the members of each pair are given differential reinforcement. The effects of the training are assessed in test trials in which the pairs of profiles are combined into a reversible figure and the subject is required to name the face which he has recognized. The results are not consistent. In any event, this method of testing makes it impossible to determine to what extent preference for rewarded figures or avoidance of punished figures reflects a differential readiness to report names associated with reward and punishment. This difficulty is pointed up by the finding of Smith and Hochberg [174] that under appropriate instructions a large proportion of subjects is able to report correctly both of the alternative figures. Under these circumstances, the distribution of choices may well be largely a matter of response bias. The uncertainty in the existing data can probably be removed by the use of appropriate converging operations. In the meantime, the experiments have not provided firm evidence for the effects of differential training on figure-ground segregation. Conclusions derived from these data concerning the "autistic" determination of perceptual learning appear to be premature.

Interpretation of differential-training experiments. Experiments using the method of differential training with adult human subjects are not likely to produce conclusive results concerning the role of learning in the development of form perception. At the time of such an investigation, the basic perceptual habits determining the recognition of familiar items and the discrimination of relatively new forms have been fully established and thoroughly practiced. No experimental pattern can, of course, be considered new in the full sense of the term, since it is bound to be composed of elements—lines, angles, curves—which appear continually in the individual's environment and which are apt to evoke perceptual habits that are highly resistant to modification. When the organism's perceptual history has not been controlled, the failure of differential training does not permit any conclusions about the relative importance of sensory dynamics and learning. When positive results are obtained, as in some of the studies discussed above, it is equally hazardous to extend the conclusions to the development of form perception in general. The most plausible interpretation is that controlled practice allows the individual to apply old perceptual habits to a new situation and, in doing so, to attach differential identifying responses to the critical stimulus patterns used in the training. The findings of both Djang and Leeper can be understood on this basis. An experiment by Gibson and Gibson [64] provides a clear-cut example of the acquisition of a differential identifying response based on preexperimental perceptual habits. Subjects were presented with a nonsense form and required to differentiate it from a series of test items of varying degrees of similarity to the critical item. Adult subjects reached the criterion of errorless identification in as few as three trials; for children the specificity of the identifying response increased more slowly. Success in recognition was accompanied by an increase in verbal descriptions reflecting the differences between the critical items and the other forms in the test series. The subjects learned to identify the critical item because they were able to categorize it along dimensions which had been thoroughly established prior to the experiment. As the extremely rapid learning by adult subjects indicates, frequency of exposure as such was probably of little significance. Success in recognition depended on the availability of the appropriate identifying responses. Experiments of this kind are not concerned with the establishment of the relevant dimensions of discrimination. They do show how practiced discriminations are generalized to new instances.

The basic point which we wish to emphasize is that differential-training experiments with adult subjects cannot be used to arbitrate between nativistic and empiricistic theories of form perception. In relation to that problem, the Gottschaldt experiments, the *experimenta crucis* of the gestaltists, and the discussions built around these are altogether futile. The important distinction between early learning and adult learning has been emphasized by Hebb. "Learning at maturity concerns patterns and events whose parts at least are familiar and which already have a number of other associations. . . . It seems always to involve a recombination of familiar perceptions and familiar patterns of movement" [84, p. 127]. The situation is parallel in verbal learning. The rote learning of a series of unfamiliar items, such as nonsense syllables or consonant syllables, does not yield direct information about the acquisition of basic language habits. Rather, we try to understand the subject's performance in the rote-learning situation with reference to preexperimental language habits, e.g., the frequency of usage of different letter sequences and the association value of the component items. Language habits may facilitate or interfere with the learning and retention of a series of unfamiliar verbal items. Similarly, preexperimental perceptual habits may aid or hinder the performance of the task required of the subject in a differential-training experiment. This is not in any way to deprecate the study of perceptual learning in adults but merely to point to its essential inadequacy as tests of the "empiricist" theory.

Control of perceptual development. Control of the perceptual history of the organism calls for the use of animal subjects. In an interesting series of experiments Gibson, Walk, and their associates have investigated the influence of early exposure to specific forms on subsequent discrimination learning in rats. Considered as a whole, the results are not conclusive, but the sequence of experiments makes an important methodological contribution and exhibits the complex problems of control and interpretation that arise in the analysis of the effects of early experience. In the first of these studies [57], an experimental group and a control group were raised from birth in well-illuminated cages surrounded by white cardboard. On the walls of the cages of the experimental animals metal forms—equilateral triangles and circles—were mounted. The forms were present from birth throughout the duration of the study and constituted the critical difference between the otherwise identical visual environments of the experimental and control groups. Painted versions of the two forms were used as the stimuli in a discrimination task which both groups of animals learned at the age of approximately ninety days. It should be noted that the cage forms continued to be displayed during the period of discrimination learning. For half the animals in each group the circle was correct, and for the other half the triangle. Significant differences between the two groups were found in the discrimination task: the experimental group reached criterion faster and made fewer errors than did the control group. Since the visual forms had not been associated with reward prior to the experiment, the writers concluded that the results " . . . seem to demonstrate clearly the positive transfer from experience in viewing the test stimuli without the complications introduced by specific application of reinforcement" [57, p. 241].

The next experiments in the series [186] confirmed the conclusion that the beneficial effects of early visual experience are independent of reinforcement. Thus, when animals were exposed to only one form during growth, those experimental subjects for which the familiar stimulus was made negative in the discrimination task performed slightly better than those for which it was made positive. Both experimental groups surpassed the control groups which had not been exposed to any visual form. In another test of the effects of early reinforcement, subjects were fed for ten weeks from a replica of the apparatus used in the subsequent discrimination task. One group was fed consistently from a stimulus holder showing the same (painted) form, and this form was later made positive for half the subjects and negative for the other half. Another group received 50 per cent reinforcements with each of the forms. There were no differences in performance on the discrimination task as a function of the prior conditions of reinforcement. In this case, none of the experimental groups surpassed the control group which had no early experience with the forms.

Further experimental analyses showed that beneficial effects of early exposure to visual patterns must be interpreted with great caution and do not necessarily imply the gradual development of form perception through repeated stimulation. (1) It is not clear whether and to what extent the facilitating effects are specific to the forms used during the exposure period. While generalization from the cage forms was limited to similar test patterns, a group given early exposure to the test forms did not differ significantly from a group exposed to irregularly formed pieces of rock [59]. (2) Early exposure had no beneficial effects if it occurred only prior to the discrimination test or only during the discrimination test. Moreover, rats reared in the dark performed the tasks as well as animals growing up in a normal visual environment [60]. (3) The beneficial effects disappeared when the forms exposed during the prediscrimination period were painted on a surface rather than cut out of metal [60, 186]. The investigators concluded, therefore, that the results " . . . add no support to the theory that perceptual discrimination of a form is an achievement resulting from an integration process of the neural elements involved" [60, p. 80]. They suggested, instead, that the forms cut out of metal, which have depth at their edges, cause the subject to respond to such distinctive features as can serve as effective cues in the discrimination task.

A method similar to that of Gibson and Walk has been used by Forgus to investigate the influence of visual exposure on subsequent discrimination learning. In Forgus's first study [47], test performance benefited more from early than late experience—a finding that was not repeated by Gibson et al. in the experiment mentioned above. In a later study [48], Forgus advanced the hypothesis that contrasts between the forms used in early exposure and on the discrimination test sensitize the animals to distinctive features of the latter. The critical test required discrimination between a circle and a triangle, with the triangle positive. Three sets of stimuli were used in a fifty-two-day period of prior visual exposure: a circle and an intact triangle, a circle and a triangle with broken sides, a circle and a cornerless triangle. The information transmitted from a triangle is assumed to be concentrated at the angles; hence greater effects were expected from omission of the corners than from the discontinuity of the sides. While all experimental groups surpassed a control group, exposure to the cornerless triangle resulted in by far the best performance on the discrimination test. Like the final conclusion of Gibson and Walk, Forgus's interpretation stresses sensitization to distinctive cues rather than a process of neural integration.

The methodological value of the studies of early visual exposure should be emphasized. In these experiments the subject's perceptual history is controlled, and the nature of his experience with the specific critical stimuli used in the discrimination task is known. Controlled differential training during growth has distinct advantage over sensory deprivation, or at least provides an important supplement to it, since questions of organic deterioration and general performance decrements do not arise. These studies constitute an important step in the analysis of the development of form discrimination.

Evaluation of assumed effects of past experience. With adult human subjects the possibilities of controlled manipulation of visual experience are extremely limited. In relation to the opportunities for perceptual learning in the subject's daily environment, the amount of differential training that can be achieved in laboratory experiments is negligible. For this reason, investigations of perceptual learning have sought to utilize differences in visual experience produced outside the laboratory. In such studies, discrimination is measured for stimuli which clearly have occurred with widely different frequencies in the past history of the subject. An investigation by Henle [85] may be used as a reference experiment. In an attempt to assess the effects of past experience on form perception, Henle compared the discrimination of letters and digits and their mirror reversals under conditions of reduced stimulation (peripheral presentation and tachistoscopic exposure). No one would question the assumption that the obverse forms of letters or digits are encountered with vastly higher frequency than are the reverse forms. The use of forms which differ only in orientation largely controls for structural differences between the familiar and unfamiliar items. In the main experiments the critical items were interspersed in a series of nonsense forms in order to minimize the subjects' set for letters and digits. Under these conditions the obverse forms were discriminated with significantly greater frequency than were the reverse forms. However, when preliminary series were used to establish a set for letters, the discrimination of the reverse forms improved considerably, and the difference in favor of the more familiar forms was greatly reduced. This convergence occurred regardless of whether the preliminary set-inducing series consisted of obverse or reverse forms.

The experiment demonstrates the influence of extraexperimental learning on the discrimination of form. At the same time the study clearly exhibits the problems of interpretation that may arise in the evaluation of the effects of extraexperimental learning. In her analysis, Henle appears to regard amount of prior visual exposure as the single critical variable in her experiment. Variations in the probability of occurrence of a form are, however, likely to have another important consequence. The more frequently a form occurs in the environment, the stronger and more readily evoked will be the identifying responses associated with that form. Common forms are not only encountered frequently but also named and reproduced frequently. The relative strength of identifying responses becomes a critical factor when discrimination is measured under conditions of reduced stimulation. (Unless reduced stimulation is used, 100 per cent discrimination is likely, and the differences among the forms become indeterminate.) The subject must respond to discriminated fragments of the stimulus, and the stronger the identifying response associated with the total form, the more likely it is to generalize to parts of the form. Identifying responses to obverse letters must be assumed to have a much higher initial probability than responses to reverse letters, and this fact may be sufficient to account for the differences in accuracy of recognition obtained in Henle's main experiments.

Henle offers some complex speculations about the conditions of "trace-process communication" to account for the reduction in difference between the two kinds of form when subjects are given a set for letters. It is at least equally plausible to attribute this result to the development of transfer between response systems. Responses to obverse and reverse letters are parts of the same habit hierarchy. Once the subject begins to anticipate the occurrence of letters, there is rapid transfer from one system of identifying responses to the other. The anticipation of letters ("set") serves to mediate such transfer. The situation may be compared to that in Wickens's experiments [192, 193, 194, 195] in which transfer between responses in the same habit hierarchy was shown to occur readily without additional training. There is internal evidence in Henle's data consistent with this interpretation. The difference between obverse and reverse forms was reduced not only by the introduction of a set for letters but also diminished in the course of the main experimental series, i.e., as a function of the prior presentation of letters and digits. The progressive improvement in the discrimination of reverse forms can be attributed to cumulative response transfer.

In any event, experiments in which the independent variable is simply characterized as "past experience" are not likely to throw much light on the mechanisms of perceptual learning. At best, the exclusive determination of perceived form by innate sensory dynamics can be called in question. Only as detailed theories of perceptual learning replace the synthetic "empiricist" position can specific hypotheses about the effects of preexperimental learning be formulated and tested. A series of studies [46, 137, 140] designed to test a specific implication of Hebb's theory of perceptual learning exemplifies such a development. The experimental hypotheses were derived from Hebb's assumption that " . . . a particular perception depends on the action of particular neural cells, assembled slowly by the repeated stimulation of a specific receptor matrix" [137, p. 43]. Different parts of a receptor surface must be individually trained and will be functionally equivalent only if they have received equal amounts of training. Reading English text should not train all parts of the retina to an equal degree, since the reader invariably progresses from left to right; i.e., while one word is in central vision, the next word appears in the right field. The experiments demonstrated that habitual readers of English recognize words to the right of the fixation point significantly better than words to the left of the fixation point. This difference becomes apparent, however, only after about six years of schooling. Subjects whose first language is Yiddish, in which reading is from right to left, recognize more Yiddish words to the left than to the right of fixation. These results were obtained even when subjects were unable to predict from trial to trial where the next word would be exposed and from which language it was to be drawn. It should be noted that control experiments eliminated a number of alternative explanations, such as differences in visual acuity, lateral cerebral dominance, and anisotropy of visual space. The control experiments illustrate the use of converging operations in inferring the properties of a perceptual system. A recent study by Heron [86] showed, however, that the difference in favor of the right field is obtained only if the letters are exposed in one field at a time. If letters are exposed simultaneously on both sides of the fixation point, recognition is higher in the *left* field. Heron interprets his findings as evidence for an attentional process which develops in the fluent reader. There is (1) a set to attend to the right and (2) a post-exposure process which produces tendencies to fixate near the beginning of the line and then to move the eyes from left to right.[2] With single ex-

---

[2] Heron assumes that attentional processes are effective after exposure of the stimulus, since the neural activity involved in perception continues for some time after the end of the exposure. It is interesting to recall in this connection the finding of Lawrence and his associates [122, 123] that instructions given after exposure were as effective in improving recognition as were instructions given prior to exposure.

posures in the right field the two postexposure tendencies act together and recognition is maximized. With single exposure in the left field, and with simultaneous exposures in both fields, the tendency to move the eyes to the beginning of the line becomes dominant. This analysis moves away from the earlier assumption of a more efficient organization in the left projection area. The results can, however, be interpreted within the framework of Hebb's theory, with emphasis on eye movements as determiners of the sequence of excitatory processes.

Studies of sensory deprivation. Investigations concerned with the effects of sensory deprivation on perception are complementary to studies using the method of differential training. Does a subject deprived of early visual experience show a decrement in form discrimination? In some of the early studies, in which animals were reared in total darkness [157, 158], permanent physiological damage to the visual system could have resulted. Recent studies have avoided or greatly reduced this difficulty by allowing the animal to be stimulated by diffuse light during the deprivation period while eliminating all pattern vision [159, 159a, 172, 173]. The critical experimental tests consist of discrimination problems in which differential reinforcement is contingent upon response to visual form. Control animals reared in a normal visual environment typically surpass the experimental animals in the speed of instrumental learning [159, 172] as well as in interocular transfer [34, 160, 173]. The performance of the experimental animals tends, however, to be variable, and the differences from the controls are not always consistent.

These results present serious problems of interpretation. The difficulties center around the validity of inferences about perceptual capacity based on the animals' performance in the instrumental learning task. Such inferences are valid only on the assumption that the effects of sensory deprivation are specific to pattern discrimination and do not produce general performance decrements. The argument that a major change in visual environment may interfere with the acquisition of instrumental responses to any visual stimuli cannot be readily met with the existing data [cf. 134]. In the two-stage analysis of discrimination learning discussed earlier (pp. 61–62 above), it was pointed out that inferences from instrumental responses to mediating perceptual processes are hazardous, because the occurrence of appropriate identifying responses is only one of a number of conditions governing the performance of instrumental responses. Thus, it is not possible to assume a priori a one-to-one correspondence between identifying responses and instrumental responses. At this point we also recall Graham's insistence that in the determination of perceptual functions past reinforcements of the critical response (R) be at a constant or limiting value (pp. 35–36). When the critical response is an instrumental act which is being established and reinforced during the test of discrimination, this condition clearly is not met.

Studies of sensory deprivation gain in power if it is possible to specify differential preferences or errors of discrimination which are predicted by the nativistic and empiricist hypotheses and which can be measured in a standard situation without acquisition of new instrumental acts. Two examples of such studies will now be considered, both of which are concerned with depth perception rather than pattern discrimination. In the experiments on the "visual cliff" by Gibson and Walk [58, 185a, 187], the *preference between two responses requiring equal amounts of instrumental skill* is used to determine the subject's capacity for depth perception. In Hess's experiments [87] on pecking in chicks the *direction of the subject's errors* is used to test for the presence of binocular vision.

In the studies of the visual cliff the subject is confronted with two patterns of stimulation one of which is characteristic of a near surface and the other of a far surface. The apparatus consists of a large sheet of heavy glass elevated a foot or more above the floor. A center board divides the sheet into two surfaces. Patterned material is placed flush under one side of the glass, whereas the same material is placed on the floor under the other side to simulate a far surface (visual cliff). The subject is placed on the center board, and the frequency of crossings to the two sides is measured. The tests can be made as soon as the subject is capable of independent locomotion. Human infants, as well as the young of other species (chicks, lambs, pigs, kittens, and dogs), prefer the shallow side with marked consistency. The specific responses on the test reflect the degree to which the organism relies on visual cues in its normal habitat. Thus, the rat which is a nocturnal animal and makes heavy use of tactual cues, shows relatively little preference for the shallow side so long as it can explore the surface with its vibrissae. When the center board is elevated so that the tactual contact is lost, rats show a degree of preference comparable to that of the other species.

The method of sensory deprivation was used to test whether the depth perception responsible for the avoidance of the visual cliff was innately determined. An experimental group of rats reared in the dark until the age of ninety days was compared with a matched control group raised under normal visual conditions. Both groups alike avoided the deep side, and the hypothesis of innate determination appeared to be supported. These findings were recently confirmed by Nealey and Edwards [139].

Systematic manipulation of the conditions of stimulation had indicated that motion parallax rather than the gradient of pattern density provided the critical cue for the discrimination of depth. What appears to be given innately, therefore, is depth perception based on motion parallax, whereas discrimination based on pattern density probably requires a period of training. Comparisons between the dark-reared and light-reared subjects supported this interpretation. Both groups preferred the shallow side when pattern density was held constant and motion parallax provided the major cue of depth. When motion parallax was eliminated, variations in pattern density produced the usual preference in the light-reared but not in the dark-reared animals.[3]

It is instructive to compare this investigation with the earlier study of Lashley and Russell [119] using the method of sensory deprivation to test the hypothesis that depth perception in rats is innately determined. In the critical experimental test, animals reared in the dark to 100 days of age were required to jump from one platform to another across varying distances. The dark-reared subjects could not, however, perform this task without a period of training in the light. After preliminary training, the force with which they jumped tended to be proportionate to the size of the gap, just as it was for the light-reared subjects in another study [167]. While the results were consistent with the nativistic hypothesis, they remained inconclusive because of the unknown effects of the preliminary training. By contrast, in the studies of Gibson and Walk both groups enter the test situation with the instrumental skills essential for determining their response preferences.

The question under investigation in Hess's [87] experiment was whether binocular vision in chickens is a matter of innate organization or learning. For a period of two to three months after hatching, a group of chickens was deprived of all opportunity to use binocular vision. The birds wore hoods which had openings for only one eye; openings for the right and left eye were alternated from day to day. The accuracy of the pecking response was used as an index of discrimination. For the critical test the birds were fitted with binocular prisms. The nature of the errors now depended on whether the bird used monocular or binocular vision. If monocular cues were used, the chicken would hit the surface on which the grain was exposed but miss to the side away from the exposed eye, i.e., strike to the right or to the left of the target. If binocular cues were used, the target would be localized nearer than it actually was, and the chickens would peck short of the grain. The latter result was obtained, and Hess concluded that the use of binocular cues was not dependent on learning. For purposes of the present discussion we wish to emphasize the efficiency of the experimental design in which the direction rather than the sheer number of errors is used to assess the effects of deprivation.

In the case of human subjects, evidence concerning the effects of sensory deprivation comes from studies of the congenitally blind to whom

---

[3] Dark-reared kittens initially showed no differential response to depth. After a week in the light, which was sufficient for normal visual maturation, they consistently preferred the shallow side.

sight has been restored. A large number of case reports summarized by Von Senden [185] has been used as the basis of theoretical discussions, notably by Hebb [84]. The validity of the evidence has been questioned [191], since the reports include anecdotal observations and often lack adequate controls. The usual objection has been raised that the analyses of the observations fail to distinguish "between perceptual and interpretative processes" [200, p. 286]. That is, the patients may have perceived the forms but were unable to name them. The total pattern of results does not support such an explanation of all the observed deficiencies in visual function. Especially notable is the patients' inability to generalize identifying responses to visual forms; i.e., even after the appropriate name of a form was clearly available, identification broke down when the stimulus context was changed. Since such generalization eventually becomes possible, a gradual process of perceptual learning is indicated. Explanations in terms of performance variables do not appear to handle the data adequately. While the clinical observations clearly do not meet the requirements of crucial experiments, they offer strong indirect support to Hebb's conclusion that " . . . the course of perceptual learning in man is gradual, proceeding from a dominance of color, through a period of separate attention to each part of a figure, to a gradually arrived at identification of the whole as a whole: an apparently simultaneous instead of serial apprehension" [84, p. 32].

The experiments discussed in this section are concerned with opposing theories of form perception and bear primarily upon the problem of "sensory organization." The question at issue is how visual forms acquire "identity" [84, p. 26]. Typically, the controlled or assumed conditions of training are different from the conditions of testing. Psychophysical procedures are used to assess the effects of past training. The question of whether the type of judgment required of the subject improves with practice is usually not central to the purpose of these investigations. There is considerable evidence that discriminative judgments of visual form do, indeed, improve with practice [e.g., 13, 49, 171]. In experiments concerned with the relative importance of sensory organization and learning this fact points to a potential source of uncontrolled variance. Discontinuity between the conditions of training and testing complicates the interpretation of the experimental results but is inevitable when the effects of extraexperimental learning are under study.

Improvement in Perceptual Judgments

We now turn to experimental investigations which are concerned explicitly with the improvement in perceptual judgments as a function of practice. The distinguishing feature of such experiments is that a class of perceptual judgments is practiced under controlled conditions, and the changes in the accuracy of these judgments are evaluated as a function of the conditions of practice. In terms of Graham's formal analysis, the experiments are concerned with the determination of $a_c = \Phi(x_1, n, R_1)$; i.e., a critical stimulus value such as a threshold is related to the conditions of practice with instruction stimulus and response parameters held constant (see pp. 35–36).

These experiments are important in the analysis of the relationship between perception and learning. The formal characteristics of the experimental design parallel those conventionally employed in other studies of learning. Thus it becomes possible to make direct comparisons between the conditions determining the acquisition, transfer, and retention of perceptual judgments on the one hand and of verbal and motor habits on the other. If the same principles can be shown to apply in both areas of investigation, a major step will have been taken toward the conceptual integration of perception and learning.

Summary of empirical findings. The experimental work on improvement in perceptual judgments has been fully reviewed by Eleanor J. Gibson [55]. Her survey presents an impressive amount of evidence for the effectiveness of practice in producing increased accuracy of discrimination. Such improvement has been demonstrated for many different dimensions of discrimination and for both absolute and relative judgments. The fact that perceptual judgments improve under many conditions as a function of practice may, then, be considered established. The question remains whether the functional relationships in perceptual learning parallel those in verbal and motor learning. This question in turn leads to the broader problem of the application to these data of existing concepts of learning theory.

Gibson's review supports a number of generalizations about the conditions and characteristics of perceptual learning: (1) Accuracy of discrimination is an increasing function of the amount of practice. With few exceptions, the evidence indicates that improvement is greater in the early than in the late stages of practice; i.e., the learning curve usually is negatively accelerated. (2) Explicit reinforcement, whether by correction or reward, does not appear to be a necessary condition of learning. In some cases, the possibility of self-reinforcement cannot be ruled out. Gibson cites several cases, however, in which improvement did occur but there was no apparent opportunity for self-reinforcement. The reduction in the differential threshold for weight without knowledge of results is a case in point. (3) Comparisons of practice with and without reinforcement consistently show the former to be more effective. The most common form of reinforcement consists of correction or knowledge of results. Gibson suggests that the beneficial effects of reinforcement may vary with the amount of information given to the subject. (4) Studies of transfer provide little evidence of general improvement in perceptual skill after practice of a specific discrimination. Thus, tachistoscopic training appears to transfer " . . . only insofar as the test and training tasks are similar" [55, p. 418]. There is firm evidence for transfer from one area of a sensory surface to another, and notably for bilateral transfer in vision and touch. Thus far, there is only scattered information on the theoretically important question of dimensional transfer, i.e., the transfer that is obtained when the test stimuli are shifted along the stimulus continuum. There are indications that the improvement produced by practice may spread to new stimuli not presented during training. (5) Retention of perceptual learning has not been studied systematically. The available data indicate, however, that perceptual skills suffer long-term forgetting and are subject to retroactive inhibition.

Acquisition of judgment scales. These facts are consistent with the view that the variables governing the acquisition and performance of verbal and motor habits apply to perceptual skills as well. Two major problems arise, however, in the treatment of perceptual learning as a special case of habit formation. First, the operations of psychophysical measurement often make it difficult to describe the effects of practice as changes in the strength of specific stimulus-response connections. The subject uses a restricted number of responses in judging a series of stimuli. "The correspondence is not usually between any particular response and any particular stimulus, but rather between a system—more precisely, a scale—of responses and a distribution of stimuli" [106, p. 342]. Thus, practice will produce improvement not only when the number of differential responses is equal to the number of test stimuli but also when the number of stimuli exceeds the number of available responses. When there is transfer along a dimension, it is clear that the effects of practice are not limited to the strengthening of specific stimulus-response connections. Second, the finding that practice without reinforcement may increase the accuracy of discrimination, i.e., produce *systematic changes* in the distribution of responses, is not consistent with most current interpretations of learning. Even theories which do not include a principle of effect assume that systematic changes in behavior are a function of the consequences which follow the organism's responses. Thus, in Guthrie's contiguity theory rewards serve to change the stimulus situation and thereby protect the successful response from being unlearned [80]. In a cognitive theory learning is equated to the acquisition of information about sign-significate relationships [181]. In short, there is agreement on the empirical law of effect if not on the principle of reinforcement. Theoretical analyses of perceptual learning must now take account of the apparent failures of the empirical law of effect. The facts can be made consistent with the principle of effect if one assumes that there is a drive

to perceive [197] and that reduction of this drive differentially reinforces effective receptor-exposure acts.[4] The operational definition of a
drive to perceive offers formidable difficulties, however, although the
studies of stimulus deprivation in human subjects [14] appear to give
some support to the concept.

In the face of these problems conceptualizations of perceptual learning have placed heavy reliance on the principles of stimulus generalization and differentiation. In such analyses, the stimuli are assumed to vary
along a single continuum, and the categories of response are arranged as
an ordered series. A theory developed by Johnson [102, 103, 104, 105,
106] shows how the principle of stimulus generalization can be used to
account for the acquisition of a judgment scale. Johnson starts with the

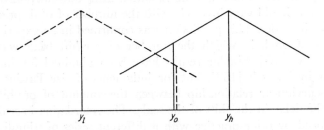

FIG. 1. Generalization of the effects of stimulation along a
perceptual continuum. y_l designates the central effects of a
stimulus which has been judged *low,* and y_h the central
effects of a stimulus judged *high.* The judgment of a new
intermediate stimulus depends on the relative heights of the
two generalization gradients at y_o. [From Johnson, D. M. *The
psychology of thought and judgment.* New York: Harper,
1955, p. 344. Reproduced by permission.]

assumption that any given physical stimulus x produces a central effect y
which is " . . . functionally related to that aspect or dimension of the
stimulus which the organism is prepared to perceive" [106, p. 343]. Thus,
variations in wavelength of sounds produce changes in perceived pitch.
Figure 1 illustrates how generalization of the central effects results in the
formation of a two-category scale. The subject is presented with two
stimuli, x_l and x_h, and instructed to call each *low* or *high.* Symmetrical
and linear gradients of generalization around the central effects y_l and y_h
are assumed. The judgment of a new stimulus x_o will depend on the
distance of y_o from y_l and y_h. The mean of the central effects thus defines
the midpoint of the scale at which the probabilities of the two responses
are equal. This midpoint (category limen) can be estimated on the basis

[4] For a comprehensive review of research on the orienting response see Berlyne's
recent book [12, especially chap. 4].

of an assumed relationship between the value of the physical stimulus x and the central effect y. In the case of the pitch function, for example, this relationship is taken to be logarithmic, and the midpoint of the scale is at the geometric mean of the stimulus frequencies. Johnson has found good agreement between predicted and obtained limens for two-category judgments of both pitch [104] and weight [102]. The argument is readily extended to cases in which the number of stimuli and/or responses is larger than two.

Johnson assumes that each judgment of a stimulus can be treated as a unit of practice. All practice units enter into the determination of the mean stimulus value defining the midpoint of the scale, i.e., stimuli must be weighted according to their frequency of occurrence. It also follows that the speed with which a scale is shifted after introduction of a new set of stimuli should vary inversely with the number of trials prior to the change in the series. This prediction was confirmed in an experiment on judgments of pitch in which the number of preshift trials was varied systematically [105]. Similar results have been obtained for judgments of weight by Tresselt [182], but for judgments of size Parducci [142] found a curvilinear relationship between the amount of preshift training and the delay in the shift of the scale. The retardation in scale learning produced by prior practice with a different series of stimuli may be likened to associative inhibition. In general, the acquisition of a scale conforms to the paradigm of paired-associate learning except that (1) the stimulus terms are continuously variable and (2) the number of responses available to the subject may be smaller than the number of stimuli presented for judgment. Under these circumstances each response must necessarily be generalized over a range of stimulus values.

After a given amount of training, the degree of correspondence between the distribution of stimuli and the categories of response will depend on the amount of overlap among the gradients of generalization along the stimulus continuum. The more extensive the overlap, the larger will be the variable error. Gibson [55, pp. 422f.] has suggested that the decrease in variable error with practice may be described as the reduction in the gradients of generalization around successive points on the stimulus continuum. As Fig. 2 indicates, practice has the effect of increasing stimulus-response specificity. Theoretical analysis is thus focused on the process of progressive differentiation which appears to occur both with and without differential reinforcement. Gibson suggests that " . . . a quality hitherto not responded to in isolation is being differentiated from the total stimulus input and utilized as a cue variable" [55, p. 423]. That is, repeated exposures allow the subject to discover, and to respond to, higher-order variables of stimulation [64, p. 40]. As we have pointed out earlier, such an interpretation constitutes a hypothesis about the final results of practice; it does not specify the mechanism of learning responsible for the discovery of, and responsiveness to, high-order variables of stimulation. A question which may deserve especial attention is whether improvement in such cases results from the acquisition of increasingly efficient receptor-exposure acts. The nature of these instrumental acts is likely to influence the speed and confidence of the subject's judgments, and the latter may serve as sources of differential reinforcement. Thus, some of the improvement with practice may not be

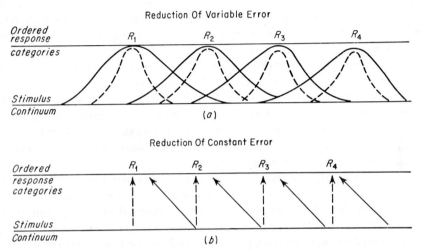

Fig. 2. An analysis of the processes mediating improvement of perceptual judgment as a function of practice. (*a*) Each solid distribution indicates the range of stimuli which might elicit a given response before training; each broken one indicates the range which might elicit the response after a hypothetical process of differentiation produced by training. (*b*) The solid arrows indicate an S-R relationship which might exist before training; the broken arrows, a relationship which might exist after hypothetical correction of a constant error. From Gibson [55, p. 424].

specific to any given scale of judgments. Just as a subject practicing successive rote series "learns to learn," so a subject in an experiment on perceptual judgment may learn to look or to listen.

A decrease in *variable* error implies a reduction in stimulus generalization. Decreases in *constant* errors may occur independently of any change in stimulus-response specificity (cf. Fig. 2). Consistent over- or underestimation is eliminated as the subject is led (1) to shift *all* his responses upward or downward or (2) to revise the definition of the unit in terms of which he categorizes the test stimuli. In the latter case there is a correction in what Gibson calls the judge's conceptual scale [55, p. 481]. The rapid elimination of constant errors produced by the revision of a conceptual scale is illustrated in a study by Gibson and Bergman [56] in which subjects were trained to make absolute estimates of distances in yards. The training was conducted with shifting targets under conditions which made it impossible for the subject to learn a limited number of verbal responses to specific cues. Constant errors of over- and underestimation were significantly reduced, if not eliminated altogether, by a few trials with correction; in fact, much of the improvement occurred after only one training trial. The subjects readily changed their definition of a yard to compensate for the bias revealed in their initial judgments. Without the correction provided in training, a control group showed no reduction in constant error. When the criterion of accuracy is applied to perceptual judgments, reduction in constant errors can produce major improvements. Such improvements appear to be largely determined by changes in the response system per se and should be distinguished from those reflecting a reduction in stimulus generalization. Gibson and Bergman recognize this distinction when they ascribe the decrease in variable error obtained in their experiment to the differentiation of a *perceptual* scale and the elimination of constant error to the learning of a *conceptual* scale.

In general, the theoretical analysis of perceptual learning has been designed to account for increases in accuracy of discrimination as a function of practice. Accuracy is, of course, an external evaluative criterion applied to the effects of practice. Strictly speaking, any systematic change in stimulus-response relationships produced under controlled conditions of practice satisfies the definition of learning whether or not it is accompanied by " . . . a closer approximation of discriminative responses to differential stimulation" [55, p. 422]. The theoretically most comprehensive definition of perceptual learning would, therefore, not include the criterion of increased accuracy. In the vast majority of cases, perceptual learning is, indeed, in the direction of increased psychophysical correspondence. When differential reinforcement or correction is given, the situation is explicitly designed to strengthen correct discriminative responses selectively. When discriminative responses produce cues to instrumental activity, accuracy of discrimination leads to successful locomotions and manipulations. Hence environmental reinforcements will also favor progressive improvements in discrimination (see pp. 61–62 above). There are cases, however, in which practice without reinforcement leads to greater consistency but not accuracy of judgments [38, 170]. Furthermore, systematic errors of judgment may be produced by reinforcement of a bias [31, 126]. To the extent that constant errors reflect the characteristics of a conceptual scale, such errors should be readily enhanced by misleading information just as they are easily eliminated by correct information. The general point is of systematic though only of minor practical importance. The task of theory is to account for progressive *changes* in judgment as a function of practice rather than for progressive *improvement*. The fact that practice leads almost invariably to improvement reflects the conditions under which perceptual learning typically occurs and does not necessarily point to an essential characteristic of the learning process itself.

Probabilistic Learning of Perceptual Judgments

From a functionalist point of view, accuracy of judgment is a measure of the organism's achievement in estimating distal values on the basis of proximal cues [29, 30]. As we have seen earlier (pp. 45–46), the accuracy of perceptual judgments is assumed to be a function of the organism's ability to combine and weight a variety of proximal cues so as to maximize the likelihood of a correct inference. Perceptual learning consists of the acquisition of dispositions to utilize proximal cues in accordance with their "ecological validity," i.e., in accordance with the degree of their association with distal properties of the object. The experiments on perceptual learning conducted by Brunswik and his associates were concerned with the conditions determining increased efficiency in the utilization of cues. The experiments have been summarized in detail elsewhere in these volumes [153, pp. 547–551]. We shall limit ourselves, therefore, to a brief summary of the types of experimental design employed in these studies.

Developmental studies of the constancies. The perceptual constancies provided Brunswik with the basic paradigm for the analysis of the organism's ability to estimate the distal value of the stimulus from a multiplicity of fallible proximal cues. Developmental studies of the classical constancies—size [15], shape [112], and brightness [24]—were designed to chart the development of this ability as a function of past experience. In each case, degree of constancy at first increased with age and then showed a decline with the approach of maturity. The terminal reversals were ascribed to the development of an analytic attitude which interferes with constancy.

Differentiation of naïve and analytic attitudes. The degree of constancy varies with the subject's attitude. A naïve-realistic attitude favors constancy, whereas an analytic attitude increases the correspondence between the judgment and the proximal value of the stimulus. In general, a naïve-realistic attitude can be adopted more readily and functions more effectively than an analytic one. It is assumed that the requirements of locomotion and manipulation early establish and maintain an orientation toward the distal properties of objects; at a later stage of development competing analytic attitudes are acquired. Since attitudes are regarded as learned dispositions, they should be subject to modification by training. Progressive differentiation of attitudes under conditions of controlled practice has been demonstrated [111]; i.e., as a result of training, judgments made under the two attitudes show increasing divergence (see also p. 50 above).

Conditioning of judgments in constancy experiments. It is assumed that perceptual judgments are based on proximal cues which the subject has learned to combine and weight in accordance with their validity. Manipulation of the relationship between cues and distal properties should, therefore, produce systematic shifts in perceptual judgments. When an initially ineffective cue is consistently paired with a particular distal property, the perceptual judgment should become conditioned to the cue. Such conditioning of perceptual judgments was demonstrated in several experiments [40, 44, 45, 91] in which degree of constancy was caused to vary systematically as a function of specific contextual cues. Although it was possible to establish effective new cues under controlled conditions of training, the process of acquisition was found to be slow and extinction extremely rapid.

Conditioning of judgments to cues of limited validity. One of the fundamental tenets of Brunswik's analysis concerns the probabilistic relationship between distal features and proximal cues. No one proximal cue or combination of cues is invariably associated with a particular distal property; the association is only more or less probable. Thus, perceptual responses to cues of limited validity are characteristic of the conditions of daily life. For this reason Brunswik attached considerable importance to experiments on perceptual learning in which the critical object-cue relationship was reinforced intermittently rather than continuously. Significant perceptual learning occurred under conditions of partial reinforcement [31, 126] and was shown to be independent of the subject's ability to verbalize the contingency between the environmental events.

These experiments add to the weight of the evidence for the modification of perceptual judgments under controlled conditions of training. Brunswik's emphasis was on the utilization of proximal cues to distal features of the environment. Thus, the criteria of *improvement* as a function of practice differ systematically from those typically employed in the studies of perceptual learning which were reviewed in the previous section. In the experiments on constancy, proximal and distal variables are varied independently, and improvement consists in increasing correspondence between judgment and distal properties which obtains in spite of variations in the proximal conditions of stimulation. In psychophysical studies of sensitivity, on the other hand, the distal and proximal values of stimuli typically vary together, and improvement denotes increasing correspondence between judgments and both characteristics of stimulation. Another difference concerns the control over extraneous cues. In conventional psychophysical experiments, conditions other than the physical value of the test stimulus are carefully held constant; the experimenter's aim is to isolate the function relating the physical values of the stimulus to the distribution of discriminatory responses. Thus, improvement, if it occurs, is necessarily synonymous with increasing psychophysical correspondence. The functionalist, on the other hand, is concerned with the total range of conditions which contribute to the discrimination of the distal value of the stimulus, including contextual cues and nonrandom sequences of events. In one of the experiments cited earlier [31], for example, subjects were deliberately taught a positional bias in judging differences between weights. Judgments in accordance with the bias increased the probability of a correct response. From a functionalist point of view acquisition of the bias is an instance of perceptual learning. It would not be so regarded by E. J. Gibson [55], who equates perceptual learning with increasing stimulus-response specificity. The divergence in interpretation emphasizes the point that improvement is an evaluative criterion. It will be more difficult to achieve agreement on such a criterion than on a more general definition of perceptual learning in terms of systematic *changes* in stimulus-response relationships as a function of practice.

PERCEPTUAL LEARNING AND THE RECOGNITION OF WORDS

In the final section of this paper we shall consider a strategic area of contact between perception and learning, more specifically verbal learning. In the study of word recognition experimental operations and theoretical concepts show important continuities with both traditional disciplines. The interpretation of these experiments brings into relief the methodological problems that arise when one attempts to distinguish sharply between characteristics of the perceptual system and the response system.

Methodological Status of Studies of Word Recognition

The measurement of recognition thresholds. Adaptations of the classical psychophysical methods, notably the methods of limits and constant stimuli, are used in the determination of recognition thresholds for words. There is one critical feature, however, which distinguishes the word-recognition experiment from other psychophysical procedures: the threshold of discrimination is defined by the value of the stimulus at which the subject's verbal response corresponds to the test item, e.g., when the subject speaks or writes the word to which he is being exposed. Thus, the subject's responses characteristically change from trial to trial until the correct item has been produced. Under these conditions the subject's linguistic habits inevitably influence his performance in the discrimination task. By contrast, other psychophysical procedures, e.g., those used in the determination of sensory thresholds, use a limited set of responses ("yes" or "no," "higher" or "lower," etc.) which are assumed to be equally probable and available at all stages of the experiment. Although sequential dependencies among such judgments have been demonstrated (cf. p. 37 above), it is reasonable to assume that the subject's verbal habits have only limited effects on the measures of discrimination when the choices are restricted to a few well-learned responses. As we enlarge the number of alternative responses among which the subject must decide on each trial, the influence of verbal (or motor) habits and response sets on the measure of discrimination inevitably increases. The word-recognition experiment may, therefore, be regarded as the extreme point on a continuum of psychophysical situations arranged according to the degree to which verbal habits can contribute to the observed measure of discrimination.

Examination of the experimental procedures in studies of word recognition clearly points to the importance of verbal habits and response sets as determinants of the threshold of recognition. A series of words is presented under conditions of reduced stimulation or interference, e.g., tachistoscopically for visual recognition or in the presence of a masking noise for auditory recognition. On any given trial, therefore, the subject may discriminate only a fragment of the stimulus. Uusally the subject's task is to give a written or spoken reproduction of the stimulus word. The number and sequence of responses elicited by the fragmentary cues will depend on (1) the subject's linguistic repertoire and (2) the reduction of alternative responses produced by whatever information he has about the composition of the list. A second procedure consists of providing the subject with the list of possible choices and requiring him to make a decision among them on every trial. This method largely eliminates the influence of linguistic habits but makes it possible to assess directly the effects upon discrimination of variations in the number of alternatives. The larger the number of alternatives among which the subject must choose on any given trial, the higher is the threshold of recognition [23, 133].

Viewed as a psychophysical procedure, the typical experiment on word recognition clearly *does not* satisfy the requirement that the class of responses used for measuring discrimination be at a constant level of strength (cf. p. 35 above). With stimulus conditions held constant, the probability of a correct discriminatory response will vary from word to word according to the position of the test item in the verbal hierarchy of the subject. Relative probabilities of occurrence are adequately predicted by measures of the frequency of usage of the words [95, 97, 132, 147, 152, 164, 175]. The probability of a correct discriminatory response will also change in the course of an experiment to the extent that information about the series serves to restrict the number of alternative responses.

Relationship to measures of retention. The experimental operations used in the determination of recognition thresholds for words exhibit important continuities with the methods of measuring retention. Consider two major measures of retention, viz., recall and recognition. These methods differ from each other with respect to two essential characteristics: (1) the presence or absence of the test item as a stimulus during the test and (2) the specific response required of the subject. In recall the test item is absent, and the subject must reproduce it without specific cues other than those provided by the situational context (and possibly by other items which he has already succeeded in reproducing). In a test of recognition memory the item is present, and the subject must classify it as correct or incorrect. When discrimination is measured by written or spoken reproduction of the stimulus word, the subject's responses are like those in a test of recall. In the second type of experiment on word recognition, in which the subject must choose among fixed alternatives, the responses are like those in a test of recognition memory, because a classification of the item rather than active reproduction is required. (The classification, to be sure, is more precise than in a standard test of recognition memory and requires matching rather than mere designation as correct or incorrect.) With respect to stimulus conditions, the experiment on word recognition occupies a position intermediate between the two tests of retention. The correct item is present, but it is exposed under impoverished rather than above-threshold conditions of stimulation; i.e., the subject is provided with a fragmentary cue to reproduction or identification.

Tests of recall and recognition memory differ substantially in their sensitivity to the results of past learning precisely because the correct items are not presented as stimuli in the former and are fully reinstated in the latter. In the experiment on word recognition an intermediate degree of "stimulus support" is given, and it may be reasonable to expect an intermediate degree of sensitivity to the effects of past training. In a test of word recognition we usually measure retention not for a specific practice series but for verbal habits of long standing acquired outside the experimental situation (response probability). When the test of word recognition is given after pretraining on a series of verbal items, as, for example, in some experiments concerned with the effects of frequency of exercise [5, 110, 151, 176], the convergence of the perceptual situation and of standard tests of memory becomes explicit.

A clear demonstration of the continuity between tests of word recognition and conventional tests of retention is found in a study by Cohn [35]. Since the results of this experiment have a central bearing on the present discussion, they will be considered in some detail. The training procedure consisted of the presentation of nonsense words under conditions of incidental learning. Both the frequency of exercise and the consequences associated with the words were varied systematically. Frequencies of 1, 5, 10, and 25 presentations were used. At each frequency, there were two words followed by reward, two words followed by punishment, and two "neutral" words which were neither rewarded nor punished. The effects of training were measured by four methods: (1) free recall, (2) a conventional test of recognition, (3) a tachistoscopic test

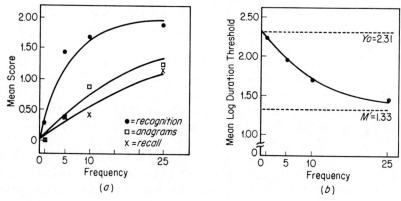

Fig. 3a and b. The effects of different frequencies of prior exposure on recognition thresholds and various measures of retention. From Cohn [35, p. 293].

of recognition in which thresholds were measured by the duration of exposure required for correct report, and (4) an anagram-reconstruction test in which the practiced words were presented in scrambled form and had to be reconstructed within a limited time.

Figure 3 shows the mean scores on the four tests as a function of frequency of exercise. The thresholds of recognition vary inversely with frequency, whereas the other scores increase with frequency. In all cases the relationship between frequency of exercise and test scores is adequately described by a growth function of the same form. Cohn concludes that " . . . regardless of the test used to measure memory, frequency of prior exposure has a homologous effect on what is manifestly remembered" [35, p. 293]. The rate at which the functions approach their asymptotes varies, however, from test to test. The rate of approach to the asymptote limits the range of frequencies to which a given test can be differentially sensitive. Thus, conventional recognition scores rise steeply with early increases in frequency and then level off. Free-recall scores, on the other hand, rise quite gradually and continue to discriminate among high frequencies of exercise long after conventional recognition scores have leveled off. The rate at which the threshold function approaches its asymptote is intermediate between those for recall and conventional recognition. Hence the threshold measure has a range of effectiveness which is intermediate between those of the standard tests of memory. The results show that it is important to distinguish between the general form of the frequency function and the sensitivity of a test to differences in a given range of frequencies. The situation is similar to that in psychophysical measurement where psychometric functions of the same general form differ in precision.

Cohn also found that recall scores varied significantly as a function of consequence, whereas conventional recognition scores did not. With tachistoscopic presentation, very short exposures produced results identical with those of the recall test; i.e., there were significant differences as a function of consequence. With very long exposures the results corresponded closely to those obtained by the conventional method of recognition, i.e., consequence during training had no significant effect on performance. "Therefore, the tachistoscopic procedure produced data which behaved as though it were proceeding from recall to recognition memory. It is interesting that some writers have labeled the procedure a perceptual test, whereas here it appears entirely reasonable to talk about it as a learning measure" [35, p. 295].

Systematic Significance of Measures of Word Recognition

The role of response processes.　Word recognition under conditions of reduced stimulation provides an example par excellence of a set of relationships which bridges the traditional distinction between perception and learning. The experimental operations are those of psychophysical measurement; the probability of a correct discriminatory response is a function not only of the conditions of presentation but also of the subject's verbal habits and response sets. The significant correlation between response probabilities and recognition thresholds leads to the question of whether the thresholds can in any sense be regarded as measures of perceptual discrimination. This problem has created considerable confusion, because the question has been asked in either-or terms, viz., whether recognition thresholds measure the properties of response systems *or* perceptual sensitivity. No decision between these alternatives is possible, because the sequence of responses is determined *both* by the conditions of physical stimulation and by the subject's verbal habits. The point becomes clear when we consider (1) the determination of the threshold for a single word and (2) the variation in thresholds for a series of words. When we restrict our analysis to a single word (or a class of equated words), response probability is held constant. Accuracy of recognition then varies directly with the intensity or duration of the stimulus. Frequency of correct responses plotted against the stimulus variable yields a typical psychometric function [164]. The threshold is a measure of discriminability, and the effectiveness of different conditions of exposure can be appropriately evaluated by this measure.

Now consider variations in threshold from word to word. With conditions of presentation held constant, differences in threshold are a function of response probability; i.e., the variation *among words* measures a property of the verbal response system.[5] The possibility need not be ruled out that frequency of past exposure also influences sensory integration [141]. The operations of the word-recognition experiment make it difficult, however, to demonstrate such effects over and above those of response probability. In the case of letter sequences at least, sheer frequency of exposure uncorrelated with response frequency does not appear to influence recognition thresholds [150]. In summary, when a series of different words is presented at changing intensities or durations of exposure, both the discriminability of the cues (letters, phonemes) and the verbal habits of the subjects will determine the distribution of responses. The contribution of each of these factors can be demonstrated with the other held constant. When both are varied simultaneously, they work together to determine the values of recognition thresholds.

The interpretation of word recognition is obscured rather than clarified by the recent analysis of a *"Vexierversuch"* published by Goldiamond and Hawkins [68]. These writers address themselves to the question of whether the data obtained in studies of word recognition " . . . are to be given a perceptual interpretation *or* a response interpretation" [68, p. 457; italics ours]. The first part of the experiment consisted of a training session in which subjects practiced a series of nonsense syllables. The frequency with which syllables were repeated varied between one and twenty-five presentations. Training was followed by a recognition session in which subjects were informed that the practiced syllables would be exposed subliminally; actually blank slides were exposed. When the scoring procedure of the ascending method of limits was applied to the subjects' responses, the usual inverse relationship was obtained between log frequency of exercise and the mock thresholds of recognition. "The similarity between these results, which cannot be ascribed to perception, and the data obtained from similar experiments where a stimulus has been presented, was interpreted as challenging a perceptual interpretation of the word-frequency-recognition relationship, where similar pro-

---

[5] It is assumed that the words will not differ with respect to the average discriminability of the units (letters, phonemes) of which they are composed.

cedures are utilized" [68, p. 462]. As far as the empirical finding is concerned, Goldiamond and Hawkins simply rediscovered a well-known fact, viz., that response probability is a function of frequency of usage. In a conventional recognition experiment, the subjects' responses are a joint function of the conditions (intensity or duration) of stimulation and response probabilities. When stimulus conditions are eliminated as an effective variable, the relative strengths of the associations established during training entirely determine the sequence of the subjects' responses, and hence the mock thresholds. The relationship between a conventional threshold experiment and the *Vexierversuch* is analogous to that between a test of recognition memory and a test of recall: differences in associative strength can be detected both in the presence and absence of the correct item. This does not mean, of course, that recognition is a special case of recall, or vice versa.

It is misleading, therefore, to use the *Vexierversuch* as a paradigm of recognition behavior and to reconstruct what happens in response to sensory stimulation from what happens in the absence of stimulation. It would be absurd to assert that the visual or auditory exposure of the stimulus word does not influence the subject's responses. Mock thresholds are, of course, bound to be considerably higher than recognition thresholds, even though the relationship to frequency of usage is parallel in the two cases.[6] If a random sample of English words were used instead of a short list of practiced nonsense syllables, the difference is likely to be extremely great. In fact, it is doubtful that mock thresholds could be determined for more than an occasional word. The better the discrimination of stimulus fragments, the more restriction there is on the number of alternative responses, and therefore the greater the probability of success is on any given trial. The stimulus intensity or duration required to narrow the alternatives down to the correct response provides one measure of the associative strength of that response; relative frequency of occurrence in a series of random guesses (as in the experiment of Goldiamond and Hawkins) provides another measure. The difference between the two measures is not removed by the fact that some random guessing undoubtedly occurs in the conventional recognition situation. As long as conventional thresholds and mock thresholds are of a different order of magnitude, the two measures are simply not equivalent. When two distributions of measures have the same general *shape*, it does not follow that they reflect identical psychological processes. The absolute level of performance cannot be ignored. There is no justification for the conclusion that the threshold functions obtained in experiments on visual and

---

[6] In mimicking the ascending method of limits, Goldiamond and Hawkins gave twenty-five "exposures" per word. Only about half the items were "recognized," although the subjects' choices were restricted to a pool of ten items.

auditory word recognition are " . . . an artifact of coupling an ascending energy series to sequential progression of a series" [68, p. 462].

Recognition as a function of stimulus variables. The joint dependence of recognition responses on specific variables of stimulation and on prior verbal training is brought out clearly when transfer of training across sensory modalities is considered. In an experiment by Rosenzweig and the author [151] subjects were given either visual or auditory practice on a series of nonsense trigrams. Following the preliminary training, recognition for these items was tested in either a visual or an auditory test. The four possible combinations of practice and testing were used. All tests yielded an inverse relationship between frequency of exercise and recognition thresholds but the degree of this relationship varied significantly with the particular combination of training and test conditions. (1) The differential effects of practice are greater when the same sense modality is used in the training and the test than when there is a change in modality. The sensitivity of the test to the effects of training depends on the similarity of the stimulus cues in the two situations. The similarity of cues is, of course, greater in single-modality than in dual-modality conditions. (2) The transfer effects from visual training to auditory test were greater than in the opposite direction. An explanation of this asymmetry of transfer effects may again be sought through an analysis of the specific cues which elicit the practiced responses on the recognition test. It is probable that during visual training the subject tends to repeat the stimulus words subvocally (reports of the subjects confirm this supposition). Subvocal responses during visual training produce cues which can readily generalize to an auditory test. There do not appear to be any reactions during auditory training which similarly facilitate the performance of the practiced responses during the visual test. The asymmetry of the transfer effects was reflected in the frequency with which practiced items appeared as incorrect responses (intrusion errors) prior to recognition. There were more intrusions in the auditory test after visual training than in the converse transfer situation. We may note in passing that on all tests the frequency of intrusions first increased and then decreased as a function of stimulus intensity. This systematic trend in the frequency of intrusions indicates that the rate at which practiced items were reproduced was contingent upon the discriminability of stimulus fragments. (3) In general, the effects of training were more pronounced in auditory than in visual recognition. This difference between modalities was associated with a strikingly greater frequency of complete (three-letter) responses to auditory than to visual stimuli. The results clearly show that the response probabilities established by practice interact in an orderly and reliable manner with the particular stimulus conditions under which recognition is tested.

Evidence from other studies [95, 132, 147, 165] provides a further example of interaction between stimulus conditions and response probabilities. The inverse relationship between frequency of usage and recognition thresholds obtains in both vision and audition. The variable of word *length* has, however, opposite effects in the two modalities, and the interaction of word length with frequency takes different forms in visual and auditory experiments. Refer to Fig. 4, which shows the joint effects of frequency and length on the visual and auditory recognition thresholds for words. With visual presentation, thresholds *increase* as a function of word length. The detrimental influence of length is greatest at low frequencies of usage; when frequency is high, the effects of length are negligible. With auditory presentation, on the other hand, recognition thresholds *decrease* as a function of length at all levels of frequency. The differential effects of word length could not be predicted on the basis of response probabilities, since the distributions of frequencies and lengths were the same in the two experiments. The divergence of results in the two situations becomes understandable on the assumption that responses are elicited by discriminated fragments of stimulation. In the visual experiment words of different lengths were compared at fixed durations of exposure. The larger the number of letters in a word, the more rapidly must each be discriminated when the exposure is too short to permit shifts in fixation. Thus, increases in word length lead to a reduction in the proportion of letters that can be discriminated during a single exposure. The lower the response probability, the more sensitive the thresholds of recognition are to changes in the discriminability of single units. In masked auditory presentation, on the other hand, all words were pronounced at a normal rate, and the duration of exposure was proportional to the length of the word. The opportunities for an effective reduction in the number of alternatives therefore increased with the length of the word. The tendency, already noted, to give more complete responses to auditory than to visual stimuli probably contributed to the results shown in Fig. 4: with reduced stimulation, a long word requires a larger amount of completion than a short word. It is likely that more complete responses are given in the auditory situation because subjects find it harder to reproduce phonetic fragments than to record single letters or groups of letters discriminated visually. The instrumental responses available to the subject are more favorable to stimulus-response specificity in the visual than in the auditory situation.

Stimulus-response relationships in recognition. The analysis of word recognition brings into relief a problem of interpretation that exists to some extent whenever identifying responses are used to measure discrimination. The degree of measured discrimination always depends on both the conditions of stimulation and the probability of the appropriate

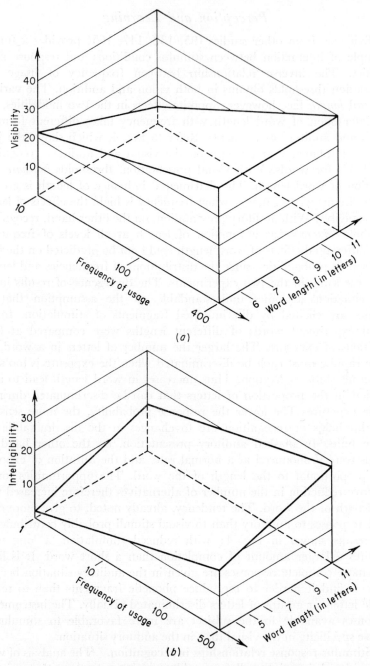

FIG. 4a and b. Visual and auditory recognition thresholds as a joint function of frequency of usage and word length. The visual data are from Postman and Adis-Castro [147]; the auditory data are from Howes [95]. From Rosenzweig and Postman [165]. Reprinted from *Science* by permission.

100

identifying responses. Varying some aspect of the stimulus, we draw conclusions about perceptual processes from the distribution of identifying responses on the assumption that the probabilities of alternative responses are equal (cf. Graham's analysis discussed above, pp. 35–37). Whenever the range of identifying responses is less restricted than it is in the classical psychophysical situations, the assumption of equal response probabilities is likely not to be met. In so far as word recognition reflects both the conditions of stimulation and the availability of appropriate responses, it is typical of many, if not most, situations in which the identification of objects is required. It is clearly improper to describe identifying *responses* as perceptual or nonperceptual. Identification cannot occur in the absence of discriminable cues and hence is dependent on perceptual processes; nor can discrimination be observed unless the appropriate differentiating responses are in the subject's repertoire. When the probabilities of alternative responses are held constant, inferences about perceptual processes become possible. When discriminability is held constant, differences in the strengths of identifying responses can be assessed. As the purpose of the investigator shifts from the determination of perceptual functions to the measurement of habit strength, it is not the classes of stimuli and responses that change but rather the controlling parameters that are isolated by means of the experimental operations.

"Bridging Laws" between Perception and Learning

In conclusion, we may raise the question of whether the existing empirical evidence justifies the formulation of "bridging laws" between perception and learning. To give an affirmative answer would be to confuse promising possibilities with accomplished facts. As our discussion has shown, the methodology and analytic language of the two traditional disciplines have been converging only slowly and painfully. The analysis of perceptual processes, and of the interrelations between perception and learning in particular, continues to be retarded by the explicit or implicit intrusion of phenomenological biases. The basic difficulty stems not so much from the concern with "subjective" experience but from the failure of the phenomenologists to specify either the systematic or the empirical dependent variables of perceptual experiments. The resulting confusion between data language and construct language has made it exceedingly difficult to state and examine functional relationships between variables from the two fields of reference. What is more, the lack of objective criteria in the classification of phenomenological data has been used to render a priori assumptions about interrelations between perception and learning invulnerable to experimental disproof.

In spite of wide theoretical divergencies, there is substantial consensus on the nature and specification of empirical variables in the study of learning. The empirical independent variables can usually be specified in terms of the number and temporal pattern of presentations of selected classes of stimuli (including those which have the systematic status of reinforcers). The empirical dependent variables are parameters of restricted classes of responses. Graham has spelled out with precision and rigor the ways in which the variables of perceptual experiments can be stated in the same stimulus-response language (see pp. 35–37). It is our conviction that Graham's analysis provides a firm methodological foundation for the experimental analysis of the interrelations between perception and learning.

The closest approximation to bridging laws can, in fact, be found in that area of research in which a deliberate attempt has been made to coordinate the definitions of the variables drawn from the two fields of inquiry. We are referring here to the experiments on changes in perceptual judgment under controlled conditions of practice (pp. 82–91). The experiments are concerned with changes in selected classes of stimulus-response relationships as a function of practice. With the problem stated in this way, systematic concepts of learning theory, notably those of stimulus generalization and differentiation, have been effectively applied to the analysis of the data and have permitted the formulation of testable hypotheses about the conditions and characteristics of perceptual learning. The empirical evidence is still scattered and not free from contradictions, but it may not be premature to conclude that some of the major variables governing the acquisition and performance of verbal and motor skills apply to perceptual learning as well. With the continued exploration of the effects of practice on judgment, a body of bridging laws may indeed emerge.

In other substantive areas of inquiry, notably that concerned with the role of learning in form discrimination, the formulation of bridging laws has been retarded not only by inadequate measures of discrimination but also by loose and vague specifications of the independent variables defining practice. Investigators have addressed themselves to the question of whether "past experience" influences form discrimination. The empirical translation of the variable of past experience has been capricious. Experimental manipulation of the frequency of exposures has alternated with comparison among stimuli assumed to have different degrees of familiarity. There have been frequent failures to take account of the effects of extraexperimental learning, with regard to both frequency of past exposures and availability of appropriate differentiating responses. In any event, "past experience" has no systematic status as an independent variable. In the absence of explicit theories of perceptual learning critical tests of the effects of past experience have often been arbitrary and therefore have remained inconclusive. There have, to be sure, been experiments demonstrating significant effects of past experience defined in one way or another, but such sporadic findings do not generate bridging laws except in the most superficial sense.

Our main concern in this paper has been with perceptual learning in the sense of changes in perceptual discrimination produced by practice. The bridging laws we have discussed are those concerned with this particular relationship between perception and learning. There is, of course, another class of possible bridging laws, viz., those embodying functional relationships between the conditions of perceptual discrimination and the acquisition and performance of verbal and motor responses. An example of such a law would be one relating the shape of the gradient of generalization to psychophysically scaled variations in the stimulus. As we pointed out, learning theorists have tended to take certain psychophysical relationships for granted, and it is primarily in studies of choice discrimination that the relationship between perceptual discrimination and the acquisition of instrumental responses has been an explicit focus of interest. Finally, in studies of human learning and memory a long controversy has centered around the gestalt hypothesis that the laws of perceptual organization determine the course of learning and retention. This hypothesis states not so much a bridging law as a superordinate law which reduces the facts of perception, learning, and retention to special manifestations of a more fundamental process. This controversy is outside the scope of our present inquiry. Suffice it to say that the methodological difficulties which have bedeviled empirical tests of the gestalt principles of perceptual organization become multiplied when these laws are applied to problems of learning and retention. Thus, the hypothesis has had little or no firm empirical support.

We conclude that there are few if any firmly established bridging laws between perception and learning at the present time. The prospects for the establishment of a coherent body of such laws appear to be bright once the methodological requirements and the conceptual language of the two disciplines are brought into closer correspondence than they are today. Some important steps in this direction have already been taken.

REFERENCES

1. Allport, F. H. *Theories of perception and the concept of structure.* New York: Wiley, 1955.
2. Ames, A. Visual perception and the rotating trapezoidal window. *Psychol. Monogr.,* 1951, **65**, No. 7 (Whole No. 234).
3. Arnoult, M. D. Transfer of predifferentiation training in simple and multiple shape discrimination. *J. exp. Psychol.,* 1953, **45**, 401–409.
4. Arnoult, M. D. Stimulus predifferentiation: some generalizations and hypotheses. *Psychol. Bull.,* 1957, **54**, 339–350.

5. Baker, Katherine E., & Feldman, H. Threshold-luminance for recognition in relation to frequency of prior exposure. *Amer. J. Psychol.*, 1956, **69**, 278–280.

6. Baker, Katherine E., & Wylie, Ruth C. Transfer of verbal training to a motor task. *J. exp. Psychol.*, 1950, **40**, 632–638.

7. Bartley, S. H. *Principles of perception.* New York: Harper, 1958.

8. Bergmann, G. Theoretical psychology. *Annu. Rev. Psychol.*, 1953, **4**, 435–458.

9. Bergmann, G. *Philosophy of science.* Madison, Wis.: Univer. of Wis. Press, 1957.

10. Bergmann, G., & Spence, K. W. The logic of psychological measurement. *Psychol. Rev.*, 1944, **51**, 1–24.

11. Berlyne, D. E. Attention, perception and behavior theory. *Psychol. Rev.*, 1951, **58**, 137–146.

12. Berlyne, D. E. *Conflict, arousal, and curiosity.* New York: McGraw-Hill, 1960.

13. Bevan, W., & Zener, K. Some influences of past experience upon the perceptual thresholds of visual form. *Amer. J. Psychol.*, 1952, **65**, 434–442.

14. Bexton, W. A., Heron, W., & Scott, T. H. Effects of decreased variation in the sensory environment. *Canad. J. Psychol.*, 1954, **8**, 70–76.

15. Beyrl, F. Über die Grössenauffassung bei Kindern. *Z. Psychol.*, 1926, **100**, 344–371.

16. Blackwell, H. R. Psychophysical thresholds: experimental studies of methods of measurement. *Engng Res. Bull.*, Univer. of Michigan, 1953, 36.

17. Boring, E. G. Psychophysiological systems and isomorphic relations. *Psychol. Rev.*, 1936, **43**, 565–587.

18. Boring, E. G. A psychological function is the relation of successive differentiations of events in the organism. *Psychol. Rev.*, 1937, **44**, 445–461.

19. Bricker, P. D., & Chapanis, A. Do incorrectly perceived tachistoscopic stimuli convey some information? *Psychol. Rev.*, 1953, **60**, 181–188.

20. Bridgman, P. W. Some general principles of operational analysis. *Psychol. Rev.*, 1945, **52**, 246–249.

21. Bruner, J. S. Personality dynamics and the process of perceiving. In R. R. Blake & G. V. Ramsey (Eds.), *Perception: an approach to personality.* New York: Ronald, 1951. Pp. 121–147.

22. Bruner, J. S. On perceptual readiness. *Psychol. Rev.*, 1957, **64**, 123–152.

23. Bruner, J. S., Miller, G. A., & Zimmerman, Claire. Discriminative skill and discriminative matching in perceptual recognition. *J. exp. Psychol.*, 1955, **49**, 187–192.

24. Brunswik, E. Zur Entwicklung der Albedowahrnehmung. *Z. Psychol.*, 1928, **109**, 40–115.

25. Brunswik, E. *Wahrnehmung und Gegenstandswelt.* Vienna: Deuticke, 1934.

26. Brunswik, E. Distal focusing of perception: Size constancy in a repre-

sentative sample of situations. *Psychol. Monogr.*, 1944, **56**, No. 1 (Whole No. 254).

27. Brunswik, E. The conceptual framework of psychology. *Int. Encycl. unif. Sci.*, 1, no. 10. Chicago: Univer. of Chicago Press, 1952.

28. Brunswik, E. "Ratiomorphic" models of perception and thinking. In N. Mailloux (Ed.), *Proc. 14th Int. Congr. Psychol.*, Montreal, 1954.

29. Brunswik, E. Representative design and probabilistic theory in a functional psychology. *Psychol. Rev.*, 1955, **63**, 193–217.

30. Brunswik, E. *Perception and the representative design of psychological experiments.* Berkeley, Calif.: Univer. of Calif. Press, 1956.

31. Brunswik, E., & Herma, H. Probability learning of perceptual cues in the establishment of a weight illusion. *J. exp. Psychol.*, 1951, **41**, 281–289.

32. Cantril, H., Ames, A., Hastorf, A. H., & Ittelson, W. H. Psychology and scientific research. *Science*, 1949, **110**, 461–464, 491–497, 517–522.

33. Chapman, D. W. Relative effects of determinate and indeterminate aufgaben. *Amer. J. Psychol.*, 1932, **44**, 163–174.

34. Chow, K. L., & Nissen, H. W. Interocular transfer of learning in visually naive and experienced infant chimpanzees. *J. comp. physiol. Psychol.*, 1955, **48**, 229–237.

35. Cohn, Barbara N. Projective methods and verbal learning. *J. abnorm. soc. Psychol.*, 1954, **49**, 290–297.

36. Djang, Siao-Sung. The role of past experience in the visual apprehension of masked forms. *J. exp. Psychol.*, 1937, **20**, 29–59.

37. Dollard, J., & Miller, N. E. *Personality and psychotherapy.* New York: McGraw-Hill, 1950.

38. Drury, M. B. Progressive changes in non-foveal perception of line patterns. *Amer. J. Psychol.*, 1933, **45**, 628–646.

39. Ehrenfreund, D. An experimental test of the continuity theory of discrimination learning with pattern vision. *J. comp. Psychol.*, 1948, **41**, 408–422.

40. Eissler, K. Die Gestaltkonstanz der Sehdinge. *Arch. ges. Psychol.*, 1933, **88**, 487–550.

41. Ellis, W. D. *A source book of Gestalt psychology.* London: Routledge & Kegan Paul, 1938.

42. Epstein, W., & Rock, I. Perceptual set as an artifact of recency. *Amer. J. Psychol.*, 1960, **73**, 214–228.

43. Eriksen, C. W. Subception: fact or artifact? *Psychol. Rev.*, 1956, **63**, 74–80.

44. Fieandt, K. v. Dressurversuche an der Farbenwahrnehmung. *Arch. ges. Psychol.*, 1936, **96**, 467–495.

45. Fieandt, K. v. *Über Sehen von Tiefengebilden bei wechselnder Beleuchtungsrichtung.* Helsinki: Psychol. Institute, Univer. Helsinki, 1938.

46. Forgays, D. G. The development of differential word recognition. *J. exp. Psychol.*, 1953, **45**, 165–168.

47. Forgus, R. H. Advantage of early over late perceptual experience in improving form discrimination. *Canad. J. Psychol.*, 1956, **10**, 147–155.

48. Forgus, R. H. The effect of different kinds of form pre-exposure on form discrimination learning. *J. comp. physiol. Psychol.*, 1958, **51**, 75–78.

49. Franz, S. I., & Layman, J. D. Studies in cerebral function. I. Peripheral retinal learning and practice transfer. *Publ. Univer. Calif. Los Angeles, Educ., Phil., Psychol.*, 1933, **1**, 65–78.

50. Franz, S. I., & Morgan, R. C. Studies in cerebral function. III. Transfer of effects of learning from one retinal area to other retinal areas. *Publ. Univer. Calif. Los Angeles, Educ., Phil., Psychol.*, 1933, **1**, 99–105.

51. Gagné, R. M., & Baker, Katherine E. Stimulus pre-differentiation as a factor in transfer of training. *J. exp. Psychol.*, 1950, **40**, 439–451.

52. Garner, W. R. Context effects and the validity of loudness scales. *J. exp. Psychol.*, 1954, **48**, 218–224.

53. Garner, W. R. Technique and a scale for loudness measurement. *J. acoust. Soc. Amer.*, 1954, **26**, 73–88.

54. Garner, W. R., Hake, H. W., & Eriksen, C. W. Operationism and the concept of perception. *Psychol. Rev.*, 1956, **63**, 149–159.

55. Gibson, Eleanor J. Improvement in perceptual judgments as a function of controlled practice or training. *Psychol. Bull.*, 1953, **50**, 401–431.

56. Gibson, Eleanor J., & Bergman, R. The effect of training on absolute estimation of distance over the ground. *J. exp. Psychol.*, 1954, **48**, 473–482.

57. Gibson, Eleanor J., & Walk, R. D. The effect of prolonged exposure to visually presented patterns on learning to discriminate them. *J. comp. physiol. Psychol.*, 1956, **49**, 239–242.

58. Gibson, Eleanor J., & Walk, R. D. The "visual cliff." *Scient. Amer.*, 1960, **202**, 64–71.

59. Gibson, Eleanor J., Walk, R. D., Pick, H. L., Jr., & Tighe, T. J. The effect of prolonged exposure to visual patterns on learning to discriminate similar and different patterns. *J. comp. physiol. Psychol.*, 1958, **51**, 584–587.

60. Gibson, Eleanor J., Walk, R. D., & Tighe, T. J. Enhancement and deprivation of visual stimulation during rearing as factors in visual discrimination learning. *J. comp. physiol. Psychol.*, 1959, **52**, 74–81.

61. Gibson, J. J. *The perception of the visual world.* Boston: Houghton Mifflin, 1950.

62. Gibson, J. J. Theories in perception. In W. Dennis (Ed.), *Current trends in psychological theory.* Pittsburgh: Univer. of Pittsburgh Press, 1951.

63. Gibson, J. J. Perception as a function of stimulation. In S. Koch (Ed.), *Psychology: a study of a science.* Vol. 1. New York: McGraw-Hill, 1959. Pp. 456–501.

64. Gibson, J. J., & Gibson, Eleanor J. Perceptual learning: differentiation or enrichment? *Psychol. Rev.*, 1955, **62**, 32–41.

65. Gibson, J. J., & Gibson, Eleanor J. What is learned in perceptual learning? A reply to Professor Postman. *Psychol. Rev.*, 1955, **62**, 447–450.

66. Gilinsky, Alberta S. The effect of attitude upon the perception of size. *Amer. J. Psychol.*, 1955, **68**, 173–192.
67. Goldiamond, I. Indicators of perception: I. Subliminal perception, subception, unconscious perception: an analysis in terms of psychophysical indicator methodology. *Psychol. Bull.*, 1958, **55**, 373–411.
68. Goldiamond, I., & Hawkins, W. F. Vexierversuch: the log relationship between word-frequency and recognition obtained in the absence of stimulus words. *J. exp. Psychol.*, 1958, **56**, 457–463.
69. Goss, A. E. Transfer as a function of type and amount of preliminary experience with the task stimuli. *J. exp. Psychol.*, 1953, **46**, 419–428.
70. Goss, A. E. A stimulus-response analysis of the interaction of cue-producing and instrumental responses. *Psychol. Rev.*, 1955, **62**, 20–31.
71. Goss, A. E., & Greenfeld, N. Transfer to a motor task as influenced by conditions and degree of prior discrimination training. *J. exp. Psychol.*, 1958, **55**, 258–269.
72. Gottschaldt, K. Über den Einfluss der Erfahrung auf die Wahrnehmung von Figuren, I. *Psychol. Forsch.*, 1926, **8**, 261–317.
73. Gottschaldt, K. Über den Einfluss der Erfahrung auf die Wahrnehmung von Figuren, II. *Psychol. Forsch.*, 1929, **12**, 1–87.
74. Graham, C. H. Psychophysics and behavior. *J. gen. Psychol.*, 1934, **10**, 299–310.
75. Graham, C. H. Behavior, perception and the psychophysical methods. *Psychol. Rev.*, 1950, **57**, 108–120.
76. Graham, C. H. Behavior and the psychophysical methods: an analysis of some recent experiments. *Psychol. Rev.*, 1952, **59**, 62–70.
77. Graham, C. H. Sensation and perception in an objective psychology. *Psychol. Rev.*, 1958, **65**, 65–76.
78. Graham, C. H., & Ratoosh, P. Notes on some interrelations of sensory psychology, perception, and behavior. In S. Koch (Ed.), *Psychology: a study of a science.* Vol. 4. New York: McGraw-Hill, 1962.
79. Green, B. F., & Anderson, L. K. Color coding in a visual search task. *J. exp. Psychol.*, 1956, **51**, 19–24.
80. Guthrie, E. R. *The psychology of learning.* (Rev. Ed.) New York: Harper, 1952.
81. Hake, H. W., & Eriksen, C. W. Effect of number of permissible response categories on learning of a constant number of visual stimuli. *J. exp. Psychol.*, 1955, **50**, 161–167.
82. Hake, H. W., & Eriksen, C. W. Role of response variables in recognition and identification of complex visual forms. *J. exp. Psychol.*, 1956, **52**, 235–243.
83. Hanawalt, N. G. The effect of practice upon perception of simple designs masked by complex designs. *J. exp. Psychol.*, 1942, **31**, 134–148.
84. Hebb, D. O. *The organization of behavior.* New York: Wiley, 1949.
85. Henle, Mary. An experimental investigation of past experience as a determinant of visual form perception. *J. exp. Psychol.*, 1942, **30**, 1–22.
86. Heron, W. Perception as a function of retinal locus. *Amer. J. Psychol.*, 1957, **70**, 38–48.

87. Hess, E. H. Space perception in the chick. *Scient. Amer.*, 1956, **195**, 71–80.

88. Hilgard, E. R. *Theories of learning.* New York: Appleton-Century-Crofts, 1948.

89. Hilgard, E. R. The role of learning in perception. In R. R. Blake & G. V. Ramsey (Eds.), *Perception: an approach to personality.* New York: Ronald, 1951.

90. Hochberg, J. E. Perception: toward the recovery of a definition. *Psychol. Rev.*, 1956, **63**, 400–405.

91. Holaday, B. E. Die Grossenkonstanz der Sehdinge. *Arch. ges. Psychol.*, 1933, **88**, 419–486.

92. Holway, A. H., & Boring, E. G. Determinants of apparent visual size with distance variant. *Amer. J. Psychol.*, 1941, **54**, 21–37.

93. Hovland, C. I. The generalization of conditioned responses. I. The sensory generalization of conditioned responses with varying frequencies of tone. *J. gen. Psychol.*, 1937, **17**, 125–148.

94. Hovland, C. I. The generalization of conditioned responses. II. The sensory generalization of conditioned responses with varying intensities of tone. *J. genet. Psychol.*, 1937, **51**, 279–291.

95. Howes, D. H. On the relation between the intelligibility and frequency of occurrence of English words. *J. acoust. Soc. Amer.*, 1957, **29**, 296–305.

96. Howes, D. H., & Solomon, R. L. A note on McGinnies' "Emotionality and perceptual defense." *Psychol. Rev.*, 1950, **57**, 229–234.

97. Howes, D. H., & Solomon, R. L. Visual duration threshold as a function of word probability. *J. exp. Psychol.*, 1951, **41**, 401–410.

98. Hull, C. L. *Principles of behavior.* New York: Appleton-Century Crofts, 1943.

99. Ittelson, W. H. The constancies in perceptual theory. *Psychol. Rev.*, 1951, **58**, 285–294.

100. Ittelson, W. H. Perception and transactional psychology. In S. Koch (Ed.), *Psychology: a study of a science.* Vol. 4. New York: McGraw-Hill, 1962.

101. Jackson, D. N. A further examination of the role of autism in a visual figure-ground relationship. *J. Psychol.*, 1954, **38**, 339–357.

102. Johnson, D. M. Generalization of a scale of values by the averaging of practice effects. *J. exp. Psychol.*, 1944, **34**, 425–436.

103. Johnson, D. M. How a person establishes a scale for evaluating his performance. *J. exp. Psychol.*, 1946, **36**, 25–34.

104. Johnson, D. M. Generalization of a reference scale for judging pitch. *J. exp. Psychol.*, 1949, **39**, 316–321.

105. Johnson, D. M. Learning function for a change in the scale of judgment. *J. exp. Psychol.*, 1949, **39**, 851–860.

106. Johnson, D. M. *The psychology of thought and judgment.* New York: Harper, 1955.

107. Kalish, H. I. The relationship between discriminability and generalization: a re-evaluation. *J. exp. Psychol.*, 1958, **55**, 637–644.

108. Kanfer, F. H. Perception: identification and instrumental activity. *Psychol. Rev.*, 1956, **63**, 317–329.

109. Kilpatrick, F. P. (Ed.) *Human behavior from the transactional point of view.* Hanover, N. H.: Inst. for Associated Research, 1952.

110. King-Ellison, P., & Jenkins, J. J. The durational threshold of visual recognition as a function of word-frequency. *Amer. J. Psychol.*, 1954, **67**, 700–703.

111. Klimpfinger, S. Ueber den Einfluss von intentionaler Einstellung und Uebung auf die Gestaltkonstanz. *Arch. ges. Psychol.*, 1933, **88**, 551–598.

112. Klimpfinger, S. Die Entwicklung der Gestaltkonstanz vom Kind zum Erwachsenen. *Arch. ges. Psychol.*, 1933, **88**, 599–628.

113. Koffka, K. *Principles of Gestalt psychology.* New York: Harcourt, 1935.

114. Köhler, W. *Dynamics in psychology.* New York: Liveright, 1940.

115. Köhler, W. *Gestalt psychology.* New York: Liveright, 1947.

116. Krulee, G. K., Podell, J. E., & Ronco, P. G. Effect of number of alternatives and set on the visual discrimination of numerals. *J. exp. Psychol.*, 1954, **48**, 75–80.

117. Külpe, O. Versuche über Abstraktion. *Ber. I. Kongr. exp. Psychol.*, 1904, 56–68.

118. Lacey, O. W., Lewinger, H., & Adamson, J. F. Foreknowledge as a factor affecting perceptual defense and alertness. *J. exp. Psychol.*, 1953, **45**, 169–174.

119. Lashley, K. S., & Russell, J. T. The mechanism of vision: XI. A preliminary test of innate organization. *J. genet. Psychol.*, 1934, **45**, 136–144.

120. Lawrence, D. H. Acquired distinctiveness of cues: I. Transfer between discriminations on the basis of familiarity with the stimulus. *J. exp. Psychol.*, 1949, **39**, 770–784.

121. Lawrence, D. H. Acquired distinctiveness of cues: II. Selective association in a constant stimulus situation. *J. exp. Psychol.*, 1950, **40**, 175–188.

122. Lawrence, D. H., & Coles, D. R. Accuracy of recognition with alternatives before and after the stimulus. *J. exp. Psychol.*, 1954, **47**, 208–214.

123. Lawrence, D. H., & LaBerge, D. L. Relationship between recognition accuracy and order of reporting stimulus dimensions. *J. exp. Psychol.*, 1956, **51**, 12–18.

124. Lazarus, R. S., & McCleary, R. A. Autonomic discrimination without awareness: a study of subception. *Psychol. Rev.*, 1951, **58**, 113–122.

125. Leeper, R. A study of a neglected portion of the field of learning—the development of sensory organization. *J. genet. Psychol.*, 1935, **46**, 41–75.

126. Levin, M. M. Inconsistent cues in the establishment of perceptual illusions. *Amer. J. Psychol.*, 1952, **65**, 517–532.

127. Long, E. R., Henneman, R. H., & Garvey, W. D. An experimental

analysis of set: the role of sense-modality. *Amer. J. Psychol.*, 1960, **73**, 563–567.

128. Long, E. R., Reid, L. S., & Henneman, R. H. An experimental analysis of set: variables influencing the identification of ambiguous visual stimulus-objects. *Amer. J. Psychol.*, 1960, **73**, 553–562.

129. Luchins, A. S. An evaluation of some current criticisms of Gestalt psychological work on perception. *Psychol. Rev.*, 1951, **58**, 69–95.

130. MacCorquodale, K., & Meehl, P. E. On a distinction between hypothetical constructs and intervening variables. *Psychol. Rev.*, 1948, **55**, 95–107.

131. McGinnies, E. Emotionality and perceptual defense. *Psychol. Rev.*, 1949, **56**, 244–251.

132. McGinnies, E., Comer, P. B., & Lacey, O. L. Visual recognition thresholds as a function of word length and word frequency. *J. exp. Psychol.*, 1952, **44**, 65–69.

133. Miller, G. A., Heise, G. A., & Lichten, D. The intelligibility of speech as a function of the context of the test materials. *J. exp. Psychol.*, 1951, **41**, 329–335.

134. Miller, M. Observation of initial visual experience in rats. *J. Psychol.*, 1948, **26**, 223–228.

135. Miller, N. E. Liberalization of basic S-R concepts: extensions to conflict behavior, motivation and social learning. In S. Koch (Ed.), *Psychology: a study of a science.* Vol. 2. New York: McGraw-Hill, 1959. Pp. 196–292.

136. Miller, N. E., & Dollard, J. *Social learning and imitation.* New Haven: Yale Univer. Press, 1941.

137. Mishkin, M., & Forgays, D. G. Word recognition as a function of retinal locus. *J. exp. Psychol.*, 1952, **43**, 43–48.

138. Murphy, G. Affect and perceptual learning. *Psychol. Rev.*, 1956, **64**, 1–15.

139. Nealey, S. M., & Edwards, B. J. "Depth perception" in rats without pattern-vision experience. *J. comp. physiol. Psychol.*, 1960, **53**, 468–469.

140. Orbach, J. Retinal locus as a factor in the recognition of visually perceived words. *Amer. J. Psychol.*, 1952, **65**, 555–562.

141. Osgood, C. E. Motivational dynamics of language behavior. In M. R. Jones (Ed.), *Nebraska symposium on motivation.* Lincoln, Nebr.: Univer. of Nebr. Press, 1957. Pp. 348–424.

142. Parducci, A. Direction of shift in the judgment of single stimuli. *J. exp. Psychol.*, 1956, **51**, 169–178.

143. Pfafflin, Sheila M. Stimulus meaning and stimulus predifferentiation. *J. exp. Psychol.*, 1960, **59**, 269–274.

144. Postman, L. Toward a general theory of cognition. In J. H. Rohrer & M. Sherif (Eds.), *Social psychology at the crossroads.* New York: Harper, 1951. Pp. 242–272.

145. Postman, L. The experimental analysis of motivational factors in per-

ception. In *Current theory and research in motivation*. Lincoln, Nebr.: Univer. of Neb. Press, 1953. Pp. 59–108.

146. Postman, L. Association theory and perceptual learning. *Psychol. Rev.*, 1955, **62**, 438–446.

147. Postman, L., & Adis-Castro, G. Psychophysical methods in the study of word recognition. *Science*, 1957, **125**, 193–194.

148. Postman, L., Bronson, Wanda C., & Gropper, G. L. Is there a mechanism of perceptual defense? *J. abnorm. soc. Psychol.*, 1953, **48**, 215–224.

149. Postman, L., & Bruner, J. S. Multiplicity of set as a determinant of perceptual behavior. *J. exp. Psychol.*, 1949, **39**, 369–377.

150. Postman, L., & Conger, Beverly. Verbal habits and the visual recognition of words. *Science*, 1954, **119**, 671–673.

151. Postman, L., & Rosenzweig, M. R. Practice and transfer in the visual and auditory recognition of verbal stimuli. *Amer. J. Psychol.*, 1956, **69**, 209–226.

152. Postman, L., & Schneider, B. M. Personal values, visual recognition and recall. *Psychol. Rev.*, 1951, **58**, 271–284.

153. Postman, L., & Tolman, E. C. Brunswik's probabilistic functionalism. In S. Koch (Ed.), *Psychology: a study of a science*. Vol. 1. New York: McGraw-Hill, 1959. Pp. 502–564.

154. Pratt, C. C. The role of past experience in perception. *J. Psychol.*, 1950, **30**, 85–107.

155. Prentice, W. C. H. "Functionalism" in perception. *Psychol. Rev.*, 1956, **63**, 29–38.

156. Reid, L. S., Henneman, R. H., & Long, E. R. An experimental analysis of set: the effect of categorical restriction. *Amer. J. Psychol.*, 1960, **73**, 568–572.

157. Riesen, A. H. The development of visual perception in man and chimpanzee. *Science*, 1947, **106**, 107–108.

158. Riesen, A. H. Arrested vision. *Scient. Amer.*, 1950, **183**, 16–19.

159. Riesen, A. H. Plasticity of behavior: psychological aspects. In H. F. Harlow & C. N. Woolsey (Eds.), *Symposium on biological and biochemical bases of behavior*. Madison, Wis.: Univer. of Wis. Press, 1958.

159a.Riesen, A. H. Effects of stimulus deprivation on the development and atrophy of the visual sensory system. *Amer. J. Orthopsychiatry*, 1960, **30**, 23–36.

160. Riesen, A. H., Kurke, M. I., & Mellinger, Jeanne C. Interocular transfer of habits learned monocularly in visually naive and visually experienced cats. *J. comp. physiol. Psychol.*, 1953, **46**, 166–172.

161. Riley, D. A. The nature of the effective stimulus in animal discrimination learning: transposition reconsidered. *Psychol. Rev.*, 1958, **65**, 1–7.

162. Robinson, J. S. The effect of learning verbal labels for stimuli on their later discrimination. *J. exp. Psychol.*, 1955, **49**, 112–115.

163. Rock, I., & Fleck, F. S. A re-examination of the effect of monetary reward and punishment in figure-ground perception. *J. exp. Psychol.*, 1950, **40**, 766–776.

164. Rosenzweig, M. R., & Postman, L. Intelligibility as a function of frequency of usage. *J. exp. Psychol.*, 1957, **54**, 412–422.
165. Rosenzweig, M. R., & Postman, L. Frequency of usage in the perception of words. *Science*, 1958, **127**, 263–266.
166. Rossman, I. L., & Goss, A. E. The acquired distinctiveness of cues: the role of discriminative verbal response in facilitating the acquisition of discriminative motor responses. *J. exp. Psychol.*, 1951, **42**, 173–182.
167. Russell, J. T. Depth discrimination in the rat. *J. genet. Psychol.*, 1932, **40**, 136–161.
168. Schafer, R., & Murphy, G. The role of autism in a figure-ground relationship. *J. exp. Psychol.*, 1943, **32**, 335–343.
169. Schwartz, Carol B. Visual discrimination of camouflaged figures. Unpublished doctoral dissertation, Univer. of Calif. Berkeley, 1961.
170. Seashore, H., & Bavelas, A. The functioning of knowledge of results in Thorndike's line-drawing experiment. *Psychol. Rev.*, 1941, **48**, 155–164.
171. Seward, J. P. The effect of practice on the visual perception of form. *Arch. Psychol.*, 1931, **20**, No. 130.
172. Siegel, A. I. Deprivation of visual form definition in the ring dove: I. Discriminatory learning. *J. comp. physiol. Psychol.*, 1953, **46**, 115–119.
173. Siegel, A. I. Deprivation of visual form definition in the ring dove. II. Perceptual-motor transfer. *J. comp. physiol., Psychol.*, 1953, **46**, 249–252.
174. Smith, D. E., & Hochberg, J. E. The effect of "punishment" (electric shock) on figure-ground perception. *J. Psychol.*, 1954, **38**, 83–87.
175. Solomon, R. L., & Howes, D. H. Word frequency, personal values, and visual duration thresholds. *Psychol. Rev.*, 1951, **58**, 256–270.
176. Solomon, R. L., & Postman, L. Frequency of usage as a determinant of recognition thresholds for words. *J. exp. Psychol.*, 1952, **43**, 195–201.
177. Sommer, R. Perception and monetary reinforcement: II. The effects of rewards and punishments in the visual modality. *J. Psychol.*, 1956, **42**, 143–148.
178. Spence, K. W. Cognitive versus stimulus-response theories of learning. *Psychol. Rev.*, 1950, **57**, 159–172.
179. Street, R. F. *A Gestalt completion test: a study of a cross section of intellect.* New York: Bur. Publ. Teach. Coll., 1931.
180. Titchener, E. B. *A beginner's psychology.* New York: Macmillan, 1915.
181. Tolman, E. C. *Purposive behavior in animals and men.* New York: Century, 1932.
182. Tresselt, Margaret E. The influence of amount of practice upon the formation of a scale of judgment. *J. exp. Psychol.*, 1947, **37**, 251–260.
183. Vanderplas, J. M. Transfer of training and its relation to perceptual learning and recognition. *Psychol. Rev.*, 1958, **65**, 375–385.
184. Verplanck, W. S., Collier, G. H., & Cotton, J. W. Nonindependence of successive responses in measurements of the visual threshold. *J. exp. Psychol.*, 1952, **44**, 273–282.

185. Von Senden, M. *Raum und Gestaltauffassung bei operierten Blind-geborenen vor und nach der Operation.* Leipzig: Barth, 1932.
185a. Walk, R. D., & Gibson, Eleanor J. A comparative and analytical study of visual depth perception. *Psychol. Monogr.,* 1961, **75,** No. 15.
186. Walk, R. D., Gibson, Eleanor J., Pick, H. L., Jr., & Tighe, T. J. Further experiments on prolonged exposure to visual forms: the effect of single stimuli and prior reinforcement. *J. comp. physiol. Psychol.,* 1958, **51,** 483–487.
187. Walk, R. D., Gibson, Eleanor J., & Tighe, T. J. Behavior of light- and dark-raised rats on a visual cliff. *Science,* 1957, **126,** 80–81.
188. Wallach, H. Some considerations concerning the relation between perception and cognition. *J. Pers.,* 1949, **18,** 6–13.
189. Wallach, H., O'Connell, D. N., & Neisser, U. The memory effect of visual perception of three-dimensional form. *J. exp. Psychol.,* 1953, **45,** 360–368.
190. Wertheimer, Max. Untersuchungen zur Lehre von der Gestalt, II. *Psychol. Forsch.,* 1923, **4,** 301–350.
191. Wertheimer, Michael. Hebb and Senden on the role of learning in perception. *Amer. J. Psychol.,* 1951, **64,** 133–137.
192. Wickens, D. D. The transference of conditioned excitation and conditioned inhibition from one muscle group to the antagonistic muscle group. *J. exp. Psychol.,* 1938, **22,** 101–123.
193. Wickens, D. D. The simultaneous transfer of conditioned excitation and conditioned inhibition. *J. exp. Psychol.,* 1939, **24,** 332–338.
194. Wickens, D. D. Studies of response generalization in conditioning. I. Stimulus generalization during response generalization. *J. exp. Psychol.,* 1943, **33,** 221–227.
195. Wickens, D. D. Studies of response generalization in conditioning. II. The comparative strength of the transferred and non-transferred responses. *J. exp. Psychol.,* 1943, **33,** 330–332.
196. Wickens, D. D. Stimulus-response theory as applied to perception. In *Learning theory, personality theory and clinical research.* New York, Wiley, 1954. Pp. 22–35.
197. Woodworth, R. S. Reinforcement of perception. *Amer. J. Psychol.,* 1947, **60,** 119–124.
198. Wyckoff, L. B., Jr. The role of observing responses in discrimination learning. Part I. *Psychol. Rev.,* 1952, **59,** 431–442.
199. Yokoyama, M., as reported by E. G. Boring. Attribute and sensation. *Amer. J. Psychol.,* 1924, **35,** 301–304.
200. Zuckerman, C. B., & Rock, R. A reappraisal of the roles of past experience and innate organizing processes in visual perception. *Psychol. Bull.,* 1957, **54,** 269–296.

LAWS OF BEHAVIOR AND FACTS OF PERCEPTION[1]

NORMAN GUTTMAN
Department of Psychology
Duke University

Introduction 114
   Personal and background factors determining the present views 121
An Encounter with Laws of Reinforcement 123
   Some introspection on the internal conduct of science. 130
   Steady states versus transients. 132
Behavior Kinetics and Behavior Structure. 134
An Encounter with Stimulus Generalization 136
The Primary Generalization Gradient: The Inverse Hypothesis. 139
Sensory Order and Generalization 144
Further Problems of Generalization and Experiments 148
   Summation of generalization 148
   Generalization, preference, and choice 152
Basic Concepts of Conditioning Theory 157
   The elements of discrimination formation 157
   Conditioning and event perception 161
   Attention and generalization 163
   On the observability of the stimulus 165
   On the response 166
Behavior Theory as a General Outlook 170
Reprise. 173
References. 174

INTRODUCTION

The aim of this essay is to present certain ideas on the relationships between the psychology of behavior ("learning theory") and the psy-

[1] Work on this paper, and some of the research it describes, was supported by Grants M-631, M-1002, and M-3917 from the National Institutes of Health, Public Health Service, and by grants from the Duke University Research Council. The writing was begun under a fellowship from the John Simon Guggenheim Memorial Foundation. I gratefully acknowledge these sources of support, and I wish to thank the colleagues, teachers, and students who have helped me in innumerable ways toward the present product. My debt to each of them is very great.

chology of the afferent processes (sensation, sensory integration, perception). I begin with the recognition that we may at least define for ourselves two psychological disciplines whose participants have different concerns and somewhat distinguishable outlooks. Much could be said about each discipline and its outlook, and about each subject matter and the principles which pertain to it. A great many contrasts and comparisons are possible. However, I am aware that I must lay a considerable amount of groundwork before I can approach the difficult questions of relationship even in a general way with any hope of achieving success or cogency.

In order to be productive, a discussion of the relationships between the topics of perception and behavior must be conducted at an elementary level, for the treatment must deal with concepts which are each at the starting point of psychological inquiry. The questions which are called up by juxtaposition of the terms *perception* and *behavior* are already implied by those passages in elementary textbooks where psychology is defined for the beginning student as the science of "behavior and experience." It is instructive that here, in a paper in an advanced treatment of psychology as a science, where we are concerned with the relationships between various branches of current psychology, we should again find *behavior* and *perception* juxtaposed and again find ourselves pondering their relationships. The persistent questions in psychology are those which are evident to a beginner. I suspect that if we stray too far from the answers he may give (or if we put the questions in a non-elementary way), we are in danger of being entirely lost. To him it is evident, as it must be to us, that the psychophysical problem stands as the indissoluble background of our puzzlements, and of such inquiries as this. I regret to refer so soon to that philosophical dilemma, since it is supposed to have been ejected once and for all from empirical science; I shall try to atone a little for this sudden reference by promising not to discuss the psychophysical problem baldly as a topic in its own right. Yet I do not want to start somewhere beyond the beginning, and I do not wish to reach that stage of practiced disregard from which a return look toward philosophical origins cannot be endured. Psychological outlooks and strategies may well be characterized by categories in the language of the philosophers (monistic, dualistic, naïvely realistic, etc.), and we need never deprive ourselves of the chance to use these terms.

Ultimately this essay will comment on the contemporary scene in systematic psychology and come up with an outlook on general psychological approaches. Perhaps it can suggest directions in which to look for further knowledge, and it is only if this is accomplished that the whole undertaking may be justified. A premise, as I see it, of methodological discourse (and a reasonable source of qualms about the undertaking) is that one should try to say just those things which may conceivably enhance the fruitfulness and scope of concrete inquiries. Such an aim is easy to avow but so very hard to execute that many workers in psychology abjure theoretical discourse entirely; they trustfully allow investigation to run as it will, modestly permitting their fine works and products to stand on their own merits without benefit of a visible, articulate structure of larger premises and implications. This style of operation implies that outright efforts to make framework things exceedingly bold and clear are in the net gratuitous or, in the worst instances, quite misleading. I confess I cannot fully answer this attitude, having for some time taken just this course. I must admit that when—at the end of the long contest between the simpleton and the philosopher—Candide commands Pangloss to cultivate the garden, I am somewhat moved to obey. Why prolong the colloquy?

Despite these misgivings, I have come to feel that there may be something to be gained by making a statement that is as simple as possible regarding the very knotty and divisive issues which surround behavior as one thing and perception, sensation, etc., as another. The attitude to be revealed is one which emerges from cultivating a certain garden, and what I come out with as a general attitude and an attitude for research is not startling and not new. I arrive at the non-Promethean outcome of the *status quo,* or something very much like it: a reiteration of the sheer reality of two psychological enterprises or subdisciplines and of two or several or how many psychological subject matters which must, at least at the start, be treated as distinct and cultivated with separate zeal. Yet this basic acknowledgment contains a further major implication: that one may always seek by constructive steps to discover whatever linkages there are between the elements in the two domains of behavior and perception. The view I present proceeds by stages: it accepts the two domains of psychological events and provides that each domain be allowed room and time for full development; then it advises the continuing quest for relationships. I put aside any possibility of an instantaneous dialectical fusion of perception and behavior or of events of perception and events of behavior (and certainly of the sum of our knowledge of the two), but I would recommend that the development of psychological knowledge is very much contingent upon the working out of such relationships *in extenso.* This view represents a kind of methodological pluralism of the sort which has much been practiced and sometimes articulated without much appeal. It is consistent with the continuing task of psychology from the beginning, which I see as the objectification of realities known at the outset not to be very substantial in the ordinary sense. Perhaps we may understand psychology as a whole to be a working out of the psychophysical situation *in extenso.* I have no capability and hence no intention of going beyond the elements of the topic as it originally presents itself, and therefore I do not offer anything beyond a rather conventional set of views.

Expressed as doctrines, these views do not come out in the simplest terms, but they start with the simplest outlook on the world. Although I have not always done so in the course of my own thinking, I also start with the premise that descriptions or denotations of psychological events mean exactly what they appear to mean. For example, when a person sees a purple flash, the statement that he does so refers to his seeing the purple flash. When he recoils in terror, the statement that he does so refers to this recoiling. The analysis of *classes* of events such as seeing purple flashes and recoiling in terror is extremely complex, and the conditions for the occurrence of such events are, of course, incompletely specifiable. But the laws of color refer to what colors will be seen and what changes in color will be seen under certain conditions, not to anything quite different. The laws of behavior refer to the conditions under which recoiling and similar events are likely to occur. Now it may be that a person will recoil when he sees purple flashes. Thus, if I wish to predict when he will recoil, I will first have to predict when he will see purple flashes. It will be helpful in carrying out this prediction if I know the laws of vision, including those of color. Generally, then, the prediction of behavior from a knowledge of physical circumstances will be aided by, if it is not inevitably dependent upon, knowledge of perception and upon such laws as we can find. This, as I see it, is quite simply the main relation between the psychology of the afferent processes and that of behavior.

My view is that of a student of behavior engaged primarily in investigating the stimulus control of operant behavior in animals. In this context one encounters at every turn the psychology of the afferent processes; one is thrust against the facts, the concepts, the theories, the problems, and the modes of thought of those classical branches of psychology which may conveniently and accurately be called "sensation and perception." Under the circumstances of such a line of inquiry, one can scarcely afford a view which is negative toward the extant psychology of afferent processes or neglectful of this domain. Neither can one afford what is much the same thing: the definition of psychology which is preeminently or exclusively the psychology of behavior and which thus proposes to incorporate from the start under one monolithic heading all the facts, events, and relationships which are not prima facie—and not upon analysis, either—strict matters of behavior. A less strenuous view is empirically and heuristically more efficient, and it is also philosophically unburdening.

I shall in the further course of this paper try to state the ground rules and guidelines one relies upon in studying the sensory control of behavior. These are not the ideas which may be most appropriate when one is embarking on the study of behavior at an earlier stage. It is probably evident that my manner of approach to the main questions before us is not the modal one found among students of conditioning and learning. For this reason, I shall have to try to explain or to suggest quite generally how I view the psychology of learning and behavior. As to many topics and questions and strategies in this field, my opinions are not coincident with contemporary viewpoints, and I have to accept the necessity of making many negative statements in a methodological essay, since some methods and outlooks are contestably bad. My only comfort as I face this prospect, and the perhaps more uncomfortable prospect of telling in quite autobiographical terms how I have reached my contrary opinions, is that the positions I differ from are in themselves negative and exclusive in their effects and inhibiting to inquiry. The chief conceptual and methodological problem for the study of behavior, as I see it, is to reach a statement of the premises of this discipline which makes *maximally accessible* the contributions of other branches of psychology and of adjacent sciences.

The more I ponder my present viewpoint on perception and behavior, according to which actions and percepts are accepted as unqualified realities, the more it becomes plausible to me that the very erection of stimulus-response learning theory and its employment as a general psychological outlook have been dependent upon the denial of the reality of experiential events. It appears to me now that many radical behaviorists are currently attempting to maneuver perception back into a "legitimate" place in the psychological world by the use of the terms and concepts whose development and elaboration and currency stemmed from such a denial in the first place. Is this not the case when we hear the terms *operant seeing* or *perceptual response?* Are these not awkward and unnecessary mixtures of terms, and might we not be better off using plain language? Surely a perception is a response in the sense that it is contingent upon stimulation, but surely it is not a response in the same sense that an operant is and could not be subject to the same descriptions and laws. When we encounter the phrase *conditioned seeing,* we must sense a conceptual strain, because the term *conditioning* was invented and elaborated in the service of an "objective" approach which was designed to eliminate reference to such things as seeing from the beginning. Then which term offers a better grasp of the psychological episode described by such a phrase: *conditioned response* or *seeing?*

I feel that both terms will be of help under circumstances appropriate to each, provided that we are willing to concede that the words in the language of behavior do not have a priority under all circumstances. The language of learning and behavior is a new one, as new as the discipline which studies behavior. The language of experiential events is an old one. It is the language of common sense and is the platform upon which the science of afferent processes is erected. Because it is old, we must know that it evolved to serve in the identification of psychological processes and events known for a very long time as part of the reality about human beings. As this language comes to us in science, it does not tell us what we should like to know about perceptual events, and especially it tells us very little about processes and laws of perception. Yet its very existence as a language contains facts of a broad sort which are not made use of by the attempt to substitute a complete different language over-all in psychology. The reasons which are offered for the initial discard of this language are to me no longer cogent, and the recent history of this attempt convinces me that it leads to such confusion that it must be completely abandoned. The effort to speak the language of behavior *only* is just inefficient, and to do so leads to bad experiments on perception, to a truncated set of laws of behavior, and to wide misinterpretations as to what our current knowledge of behavioral laws portends, theoretically and practically.

In the statement of the ground rules for studying behavior offered by Skinner [71], the main reason presented for not dealing with "units of behavior," such as seeing or hearing, is that they imply conceptual schemes deterrent to a fresh approach to psychology considered as the science of observable behavior. In a sense, this argument is true; it is true because the whole implication is true. If *P*, then *Q*. If we wish to have a science of just observable behavior, then we will be deterred by getting mixed up with all that reference to "seeing" entails. The implication statement is true because the laws which a science of behavior yields will not apply in certain clear respects to perceptual events. These events have dimensions and modes of identification quite different from those that are appropriate to instances of action, to which the laws of behavior indeed apply.

The dimensions of events of perception (and other experiences) are different from those of actions, no matter how we approach them. The attributes are different whether (1) the class of subjective events is recognized primitively, which is to say phenomenally, or (2) perceptions are dealt with as states of organisms entering into a prediction of their actions (intervening variables)[2] [see 19]. But because radical behavior-

[2] We must note that the primitive recognition of perceptions as a class, the recognition of the subjectivity of such a class of events, comes about from a primitive acquaintance with the laws of physics or from a more sophisticated knowledge of the causal theory of perception. It is important to clarify that the subjective character of the class is a matter of inference, not introspection, though we may "introspectively" (directly) describe the properties of particular events.

ism has wished to deny perception or experience in the phenomenal sense (sense 1), it has not taken advantage of perception in sense 2, the manner in which it must absolutely enter systems of laws of behavior which attempt to predict motor events from physical stimulation. The reluctance to do the latter is compounded by the hazard that if internal states and their changes are admitted, the claims of a molar behavioral system to make predictions are much reduced, or at least slowed for practical purposes. The strategy which has been employed has typically been to use the language of perception to describe "stimuli," and to do so unawares, which then makes invisible the task of a physical description of stimulation.

The laws of behavior consist of such statements as: "The rate of food-reinforced operant is a function of the antecedent deprivation schedule." While this principle may apply to the frequency with which I will hallucinate rainbows when aesthetically deprived, there are no possible laws of behavior which account for what happens when I project my hallucination (or my afterimage) on a colored screen. A science of behavior, of course, makes no pretense of making such predictions, since it is not a science of stimulation (to use this word in the broadest possible meaning), but then it cannot make itself out to be an in-principle-complete psychology and get along without a direct reference, or a reference by construction, to such states consequent upon stimulation as are investigated by the classical disciplines of sensation and perception. When we have to speak of a hallucination, I can see no advantage in speaking of a "hallucinatory response" but rather many grave disadvantages which are hardly countered by the appending of the shallowly invidious word *response* because this term seems to imply something palpable and external. But I am naïve enough to believe that most of the occurrences of real consequence to psychology are in a rough but important sense *internal* to organisms and subject to investigation only by the most tedious and inferential means. One of the consequences of radical behaviorism as general outlook has been to imply, in a rather willy-nilly way, that psychological phenomena are quite open to view, that they are easily investigated, and that virtually any changes which can be found in behavior are significant as such. For this reason, among others, our journals are crowded with findings, but not with information. Radical behaviorism may no longer be popular as an explicit doctrine, but its investigative consequences are a persistent part of the scene. Psychology is just about as hard to study as it has always been, and perhaps it is made slightly harder by current implications that it is easy.

Thus far I have implied an outlook on the study of behavior and the study of afferent processes which gives them equal weight at the outset. When these weights depart from equality, the departure is in the direction implied by the title of this essay, for it appears to me that in many instances our knowledge about perceptual processes is more secure, sometimes more precise, than our knowledge about the behavioral relationships (expressed as laws) to which such facts are in closest correspondence. It is not wholly misleading to aver that we know more about, let us say, color vision than about how colors function as conditioned stimuli, more about space perception than about spatial learning. For this reason I have chosen to speak of facts in the one instance, and laws—of more tentative character—in the other. The distinction is not invidious; it does not imply a choice between subject matters, because perceptions are ingredients in behaviors, the latter being larger things and necessarily harder to understand, to regularize. In so far as there is a choice implied, it is a choice of perspective as regards our state of knowledge.

In beginning to present my opinions, I have stated a difference between my view on the definition of psychology and that presented by Skinner, who, as one of the major spokesmen for radical behaviorism, has been extremely influential upon the field of psychology in recent years in doctrinal and substantive ways. His influence upon me was very great, since I was happily apprenticed to him at an early age and was his student. Subsequently, I became the student of others, both in the behavioral and sensory-perceptual traditions of psychology, and my ideas and evaluations have reflected these later influences and experiences. In order to explicate my views, I shall have to resort to a kind of autobiography strewn with opinions. I am grateful to the Editor of this series for inviting the inclusion of autobiographical materials, since the invitation reopens the opportunity to use the first-person style and thus allows the easy identification of elements of personal commitment and opinion. A psychological theory contains a great deal which is not objective and, therefore, may well include references to the theorist. A theory, which is to say a viewpoint, cannot exist without a viewer, who may enter the scene at his liberty whenever the objects of interest are hard to make out, as is typically the case in psychology.

Personal and Background Factors Determining the Present Views

While the story I shall tell of the evolution of my opinions is faithful to my own history, I should not be surprised if it were to describe many other recent psychological careers in a general way. From a start as a student of behavior (the term "learning theorist" is too decorous for all of us in this profession), I have seen my interests move in a number of directions. My earliest interest, and still my predominant vocation, is bound up with conditioning, especially operant conditioning along the lines formulated and elucidated by Skinner. This concern has been built upon, and fused with, some knowledge (though insufficient) of receptor processes, first in gustation and then in vision. An infatuation with more complex processes of visual perception has been superimposed upon this second endearment. And though I began with no acquaintance with biology, I have found my thinking becoming progressively more physiological in whatever halting way it could.

These have, perhaps, been unlikely progressions for a student of molar behavior, but not so unlikely if one accepts the naturalness of any progression from an initial level of psychological analysis and an initial set of materials, and if one grants the divagations of any investigator. If you start with some knowledge of episodes of action in animals (which is where I started in psychology) you can do three things, which the reader can easily anticipate as constituting the whole range of possibilities: you can go up, toward man, since he is presumably higher; you can go down, toward simpler creatures and systems than you already know about; or you can stay at about the same level and try to find out more things at that level. I have really done mostly the last, but ever gravitated in my thoughts by more microscopic imaginings and speculations. I have tended toward explanations of behavior, and of the simple kinds of behavioral change I first encountered in operant conditioning, and all the while I have tried to describe this behavior change a little better. I think I have found whatever I could learn about afferent processes and physiology helpful in this pursuit.

When one surveys these cognitive alternatives (leaving aside the practical alternative of just using certain knowledge instead of using it to get more knowledge), one need not be concerned with the abstract or absolute value of any of them or how one should, in an ultimate sense, balance among them. Seldom, of course, does one choose a single further direction when coming upon any intellectual heritage, e.g., psychoanalysis. But one may well be interested in considering the things which are contingent upon the various possibilities: further development of behavioral relationships at their own level or going from these toward higher or lower levels. I hope to clarify what these levels mean, and what empirical and theoretical activities seem to be involved in "going up" and "going down." First and at length I shall talk about what I have seemed to myself to have done, going across and looking down, and much later I shall consider upward extensions. However, I must say that when I began, it was not at all clear to me that there was much question of levels to be considered, for I was swayed by circumstantial and temperamental factors of an unconscious sort, and I had no effective notions about the generality of the knowledge I started with. Nor had I quite come to see, as I do now with conviction, that if any extension of laws of behavior is undertaken (sideward, upward, or downward) with the anticipation that existing laws and concepts are not going to be changed

—but only their power proved—then this anticipation involves a *complete* misunderstanding of science. My present feeling is that we may look more for an improvement of concepts than a refinement of laws; at an intermediate stage of receptivity I saw without much doctrinal strain than an improvement of laws and relationships per se was not only possible but intriguing. A student of Skinner must surely come to possess as much empirical catholicity as his own temperament will allow, and this advantage will in turn promote the activity of molding and reshaping of concepts. The initial yield of an experiment may be a relationship, but the more important product of a sequence of experiments along some line of inquiry is a redefinition and expansion of the meaning of the terms which have entered our initial hypotheses and empirical laws.

AN ENCOUNTER WITH LAWS OF REINFORCEMENT

At any rate, the first chance I had to do more than transmit and ponder the information I had about behavioral processes took place at Indiana University in association with W. K. Estes around 1947. Both of us had been in various capacities students and colleagues of B. F. Skinner before the war and had been privileged to follow him to Indiana. We were also privileged to have been able to encounter the power, the clarity, and the possibilities of Skinner's approach to the description and analysis of behavior. His scheme and his language afforded, as it must to any student, a firm and convincing grasp upon the experimental phenomena of behavior, and we had seen his approach put to an impossible but successful test in the development, during the war, of methods for training pigeons to guide bombs [74]. And we were infused with another enthusiasm which came both out of what we had seen of the manifest orderliness of behavior in the operant conditioning situation and out of the publication of Hull's *Principles of behavior.* This was an enthusiasm for laws of behavior in quantitative form. Estes and I are both analytically minded (more and less, respectively). Turning then toward an intensive study of what we knew best, we took up the tools for getting better quantitative laws of instrumental behavior than were available.

Our first step was to build four operant-conditioning apparatuses. (The reader may verify this point at least by consulting Estes' paper [15] in Study I, Volume 2, of the present work.) As the result of further steps, which I will trace in detail, I encountered a law of sensation (Fechner's law) along the way. This impressed me very greatly, but Estes less so, and I began to find that I was interested in sensation, and was becoming a physiological psychologist unawares. Why I must so often bring Estes' name into this account is that, besides our collaboration as student and teacher, the story contains a point of divergence between his interests and mine, and upon this departure of interests and views I shall later base some of my discussion of learning theory.

In our quest for quantitative, empirical laws of learning the first trouble we encountered was with the apparatus, not with the laws. Although we wanted to get conditioning data for both hunger and thirst drives, the reinforcement magazines which we had intended to serve us in two ways delivered uniform quantities of water but were no good when it came to dry food. They brought up quite variable quantities of the ground Purina Chow we first tried. In looking for a more uniformly pulverized material, we tried granulated sugar, but this material did not work either, so poor was the apparatus. The only thing to do was to compromise with versatility, to give up for the moment the attack on general laws for hunger and thirst, and to dissolve the sugar in the water. This "solution" worked excellently in the apparatus and was a very effective reinforcer. The rats conditioned and performed nicely if we were generous with the sugar and not so nicely if we were stingy.

The possibility of varying concentration of sugar solution in order to vary magnitude of reinforcement resulted in a thesis [25] for me and put me off on quite a different line of inquiry, into the sensory mechanisms of reinforcement. The results of these experiments will bear less discussion than the implications I wish to draw from the results and the method of analysis in regard to tactics for the study of behavior and the strategy for obtaining its various kinds of laws. There was, however, a critical finding: the rate of bar pressing of rats reinforced by sucrose solution was a nearly logarithmic function of the concentration of sucrose. This relationship appeared when the reinforcement was delivered periodically rather than uniformly with each response, so that the drinking of the solution did not compete seriously with the reinforced act of bar pressing. The log relationship appeared also when extinction tests were carried out following reinforcement with various concentrations. Thanks to Estes' tutelage in the method of least squares, I was able to fit an equation to the points relating rate of bar pressing to concentration (Fig. 1). A semilogarithmic function fitted very well. Why? I began to ponder this fact.

The instigation for pondering was the drive-reduction theory of Hull, which was much in the air at the time. To me this was an unconvincing hypothesis, a too teleological one, a hypothesis which had unclear experimental consequences. It did not coincide even grossly with the obvious rapidity of operant conditioning; how could the almost instantaneous activation of behavior seen after reinforcement wait until some metabolic changes resulting from food intake had wended their way into the nervous system? The notion of "conditioned drive reduction" was a less concrete and less believable idea, and too obviously a verbal ploy.

But the requirement for a more satisfactory stab at explanation could not be ejected from the atmosphere. The bad hypothesis was a spur, and it made one face a realm of ignorance. I must specify that my ponderings made little inroad into the question of the *instantaneity* of the activation seen after reinforcement; my guesses pertained just to the *degree* of

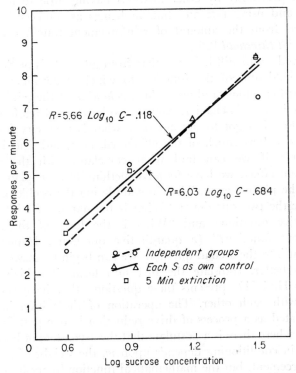

Fig. 1. Semilogarithmic relationship between rate of bar pressing and sucrose concentration used as reinforcement, for (*a*) four independent groups of rats, (*b*) *S*s tested repeatedly with various concentrations, (*c*) *S*s extinguished after reinforcement with single concentrations [25].

activation observed and left the problem of the speed of the change untouched.

In contemplating the good fit of a logarithmic function to the rate of responding versus concentration data, the Fechner law for intensity of sensation suggested itself. Perhaps the effectiveness of the sucrose as reinforcement was proportional to the *effective* magnitude of stimulation it produced. Perhaps then the minimally effective stimulus to obtain a reinforcement effect would be at or near the absolute threshold. One test of both hypotheses was to extrapolate the empirical rate-concentration function back to the origin of the curve to the value of near-zero behavioral effectiveness (i.e., the unconditioned operant rate) and see what value of sucrose corresponded to this hypothetical stimulus. The value found (about 1 per cent) was very close to the value (0.5 per cent) determined previously by other methods having little to do with reinforcement and using rats and human beings as subjects. The number extrapolated from the amount of reinforcement function I called the *reinforcement threshold* [26].

I believed—and still believe—that from an analysis of the reinforcement threshold and of the function to which it pertained, one could obtain a further understanding of the *mechanism* of the reinforcing stimulus qua activator of behavior. Now an explanation of reinforcement (or anything else) has got to say not only what is necessary for getting it going but also how much of the effect will be found. Put it the other way around: if we can find what correlates with the amount-of-reinforcement effect, we have found something of an explanation of the nature of the phenomenon. Thus in considering the problem, I came to tie together the two questions: "What is the nature of reinforcement?" (a qualitative question) and "What is the form of the amount-of-reinforcement function?" (a quantitative question). If one can gain some insight into the second question, we can begin to answer the first— or perhaps better, translate the first into terms in which it can be studied. As Hull [47] presents these questions, they have very little relationship with each other. The operation of the reinforcing stimulus is simply stated as a process of drive reduction in one postulate and left at that; elsewhere there is a postulate that the asymptote of habit strength established in conditioning depends upon w, the weight of food used at each reinforcement, but the mathematical function by means of which w enters is arbitrary. The function is exponential, but it could just as well be, say, sigmoid; and the empirical measure w, and what w means, is not seen as having a bearing on the presumed form of the curve. However, if we postulate that drive reduction is the qualitative "essence" of reinforcement, we should be further willing to say that the amount of drive reduction should determine the amount of reinforcing effect and—more specifically—that different amounts of food should produce different quantities of reinforcement in proportion to the extent that they produce a decrease in drive. In such regards, Hull's scheme was loose and undeveloped, though, as I said, it served me as a positive stimulus in so far as it suggested questions and as a negative stimulus in so far as it provided both unbelievable hypotheses and ways of framing hypotheses.

Behind the alternative approach lay certain general notions of scientific explanation and certain specific ones taken from the discipline of psychophysics, which also operates in terms of the general ideas. In vision, the explanation of the visibility curve comes about by *matching* another curve (absorption) to this function. Explanations must be quantitative to be cogent; a measurable aspect of a phenomenon must be linked up to something already known and measured. The whole phenomenon cannot be derived, at least not any biological phenomenon as a whole. Psychophysics teaches that an approach to finding the necessary conditions under which a phenomenon will occur is to find the minimal conditions, and here is where the notion of a threshold enters with enormous utility. In vision, the Bunsen-Roscoe law ($I \times t = c$) gives us the dimensions of the threshold. Thus we know that the fundamental process at the receptor is photochemical absorption, and we shall not get vision started until we get a certain amount of energy absorbed. But we have thereby obtained a key to a physical explanation of the very first part of this first stage in vision. The reinforcement threshold is constructed by analogy to the foregoing.

Next, from the first finding and hypothesis, that for sucrose the amount of reinforcement obtained α the logarithm of concentration α the amount of sensory effect α the intensity of sensation of sweetness, a more direct test of the notions later suggested itself. Coming across the previous determinations [58] of the relative sweetnesses of various sugars (isosweetness functions for human beings), I predicted that if rats were reinforced with different concentrations of both sucrose and glucose, equally sweet concentrations of the two substances would yield equal rates of bar pressing, which is to say equal amounts of activation by the reinforcing stimulus. This prediction (about the only one I have ever made) was confirmed [27], and the findings (Fig. 2) have been replicated by other workers [12, 69]. The quantitative prediction being borne out depends, however, less upon the analysis than upon the morphological and physiological similarities between man and rat, especially as to their taste mechanisms.

Are we here in possession of a quantitative theory of reinforcement? In a sense yes, but in many senses no, because the formulation is only a poor and partial one, for it does not pertain to whole classes of situations and it says only a few things about the situations to which it pertains. It does not say, for example, much about release from pain as a reward. (Campbell [10] has developed similar notions for escape from shock, but there is no very well-worked-out psychophysics of pain to quantify his development.) In the situations I studied, only a small part of the relationships obtained are accounted for by the surrounding analysis. The analysis does not say that the relationship between concentration and rate of bar pressing is an increasing function or that sugar will be reinforcing for rats at all. It does not predict the numerical slope of the rate versus concentration function for any set of conditions. These are empirical facts and determinations. Given these and many other facts, the analysis says something about the relationships between two (or more) performance curves of arbitrary slope and of a form to be determined by psychophysical methods.[3]

Without the analysis, however, the whole series of experiments yields

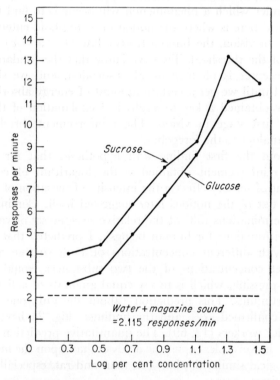

FIG. 2. Rate of bar pressing for rats reinforced with various concentrations of sucrose and glucose solution. On linear portions of curves, equally sweet solutions yield equal rates of operant activity [27].

very little that is not immediately evident to common sense. With the analysis, there may be some insight into the workings of the organism (and perhaps many species) in the systematic terms of the analysis of behavior *and* of antecedent sciences. Before I was in a position to do any

[3] I can only mention here that a much more general analysis of the conditions under which a reinforcing stimulus will be effective has been developed by Premack [63] on the basis of the notion of response prepotency. Premack's conception is quite similar to the principle presented by Wyckoff [82] and other elicitation theorists. Premack offers the generalization that a stimulus will be a positive reinforcer when it leads to a response of higher rate (I think he means, more generally,

analysis, a visitor to the laboratory asked me what I was doing. Since he was a sophisticated psychologist, he asked me to describe the work in terms I could tell my mother. I could tell him only about rats working harder for more sugar, but this is something anyone could have said had the question been posed. I have subsequently tried to employ the frame of mind adopted by this interviewer to guide my appraisal of experiments. Psychological questions start with matters of common sense, but they have simply got to go beyond common-sense answers to be worth pursuing. One way they can do so is to find contact with theoretical traditions which are properly more arcane. This cannot get started unless there is an intent to give a descriptive study some ultimate explanatory flexure, however small.

Let me now try to elicit whatever methodological lessons came to me out of the experimental and theoretical episode I have so far sketched.

It is good to describe behavior, but it is better to explain it.

It is necessary to have a good description before trying to explain.

The better the measurements of behavior, the better the description.

The operant-conditioning situation is an excellent one for getting measurements of behavior.

The rate of occurrence of a free operant is an excellent measure, and the freer the operant, the better.

Rate of responding is a meaningful measure, because ten responses per minute mean twice as much behavioral effect as do five per minute.

Here it is essential to understand that in these experiments, if latency, for example, had been used, either no analysis would have been possible or a very weak one. Two seconds of latency do not mean half of what four seconds do. But if we *count events,* that is another thing. Two responses, as nearly as two responses can be alike (and they can be alike if highly practiced), are physically twice one. This is the essential of the operant method if one is studying activity. Moreover, a reinforcement threshold in terms of latency would be very difficult to specify, since the unconditioned latency is a very shadowy thing to try to extrapolate to, in a way that the unconditioned rate of responding is not.

"strength") than the stimulus for the response in progress at the time of presentation of the possibly reinforcing stimulus. This conception is one in which I would concur, and the picture I have presented in terms of stimulation intensity assumes a momentarily fixed hierarchy of response organization as to strength. It assumes that any of the sapid stimuli which elicit drinking are prepotent over the stimuli eliciting bar pressing specifically. My analysis may be considered as a special case of Premack's, focusing upon the variations in the strength of drinking responses which are allied to variation of eliciting stimulation and ignoring the variations in strength resulting from other operations. The elicitation hypothesis is more extensive than the present one, much more powerful as to the range of conditions it covers, and—though undeveloped in this respect—highly suggestive as to the whole internal mechanism involved in instrumental conditioning.

As to stimuli, the more precise the conditions of stimulus control, the better the measurements of behavior. (The size of a piece of banana cannot easily be controlled as a psychological stimulus.)

The more closely the measurement and control of stimulation in one experiment parallel the conditions of stimulus control in other experiments, the better are your chances of interpreting it, assuming the other experiments are informative.

Psychophysics and such disciplines contain a great deal of information. (But there are no psychophysics of bananas.)

Behavioral experiments sometimes yield results interpretable by means of psychophysical relationships.

An explanation consists of matching a functional relationship with one previously known but not applied to the case you have in hand in quite the same way in which you will show it to be applicable.

It is good to try to explain your findings, to interpret. Unless you can make an explanation of a pretty obvious fact, you may not have much to say.

You will be lucky to explain anything, but if you do not try, you may not be able to say anything new. Whatever you can say which is new will make sense *especially* in its relationship to existing systematic knowledge.

Some Introspection on the Internal Conduct of Science

Apart from these homilies and articulate realizations as the result of first experiments, I was able to discover that an integral part of my own thinking (though the observations may not apply to anyone else) was pictorial. I was picturing what was possibly going on in the rat as he endured or savored the experimental arrangement. First, there was the gross picture of the sugar solution washing over the rat's tongue, then the film of liquid streaming over its area and invading at a microscopic and then a molecular level the rat's organs and cells of taste, arousing a larger and then a tapering barrage of impulses which would cause his prepared little licking to increase and then subside. And there were imaginings all the while of the shape and size and dwindling goodness of this taste in his mouth. Were these overdrawn empathies and pictures? Not more, I think, than are necessary for an attempt to understand psychological processes or for an interest in them. The activation of imagination, pictorial or empathic, the liberation of its play over the physical and subjective aspects of the events which interest us, its dance from one level of detail to another, the widening of the field of imaginative view as one's eye moves from small objects to large—these seem to me essential processes in the "context of discovery" and the conduct of inquiry. Only the results of imagination and disciplined analysis can be recorded. The free exercise of imagination cannot be directly taught; it is not a part of any set of methodological rules. It is incommunicable in the distinct sense that imagination is an activity, and rules and precepts are stimuli which can be passed from one person to another. But there are methodological communications which encourage or discourage the exercise of imagination. The notion of the empty organism contends with this useful process, whatever are the other salutary consequences of this purifying precept, and all these consequences must be weighed together. In balance I would weigh speculations over rigor, because there is so much yet to be imagined about. From my own experience, which is much a history of taking precepts too seriously, I would judge that it is important not to advise the search for empty correlations between S and R, for the meaning of these concepts is physical in the first instance, and their meaning becomes greater as they comprehend more physical detail and intervening physical detail. And a consequence of remaining in principle at the level of molar S and molar R is dissuasion from delving into those facts of physiology, of general biology and physics, which furnish the materials and the little pictures for insertion into the imaginative mill. (This educational consequence has almost been realized in the curriculum of certain institutions, where it is believed that psychology can be taught independently of other sciences, except—perhaps—mathematics.)

It may thus be seen that I became in the manner of my thinking and beliefs, a physiological psychologist of a sort. However, I was unable to accept this title until the occurrence of a personal episode I shall relate. After depositing my thesis with the librarian of Indiana University, I revisited the library, and, for reasons which were no doubt vainglorious, I looked up the entry in the card catalogue. I found to my shock that the librarian had stamped the card in purple letters: "PHYSIOLOGICAL PSYCHOLOGY." The shock was not color shock but doctrinal. Surely I had cut up no rats and peered into their innards—I had just studied the effects of amount of reinforcement on operant behavior—it was a straight problem in learning. It took me some time to realize that the librarian was right and I was wrong. She had read only the title of my study, I could be sure, but with the good naïveté of a Descartes or a La Mettrie (who would have made the same classification) she had understood that I had studied the effect of one variable with quite physical dimensions (sucrose concentration) upon another pertaining to the functioning of an organism (rate of responding), which also had physical dimensions. Here was the essence of physiology; my study of the beating of the rat against the bar in the box was not in principle different from a study of the beating of the heart in its cavity. The two systems of rat and heart are different in size and complexity, but the methods and concepts which pertain are much the same. Physiological studies in psychology are of the same genre whether one is looking at the skin or looking inside it. The distinctions between the kind of psychology I was doing and what I could recognize as clearly "physiological" then became arbitrary and pragmatic, not a matter of principle, and not worth any effort to maintain. Undoubtedly Skinner's influential arguments for a study of behavior as a discipline independent of neurology (and physiology in the narrower sense) were, as framed initially, just pragmatic arguments, and subject to pragmatic flexion. All studies of the behavior of organisms, by the very definition of behavior, are physiological. Then they must draw upon the same materials and be conducted in the same mood.

It took no prolonged reflections on the meaning of physiological psychology to convince me that my first gropings for a general quantitative expression for the amount-of-reinforcement function were foredoomed. No biologist would have attempted such a thing in the first place, but whatever credence I might have had in the possibility was quickly dissipated by the specificity of the facts and relationships. It may be momentarily inspiring to look for a general law, but there is seldom any reason to expect one. For every stimulus there is a law, but not necessarily the same law—in fact, necessarily not the same. For every system of organism, stimulus, and response we can arrange there will be lawfulness of all sorts. It is good to study such systems intensively—the more intensively, the better. The more our knowledge of a system, the better and more precise will be the laws of the system. But the more precise the laws of the system, the more nearly they will be the laws of that system, and not other systems. From an intensive study of many systems, we will obtain a notion of how to analyze all sorts of systems and what to look for, but not what will be found in any detail.

Steady States versus Transients

The experiments which led me to begin to think in a sensory and physiological direction contained of course many other findings of a systematic sort which afforded no such possibility. Each animal which was conditioned in the apparatus Estes and I made gave a conditioning curve, and some of the curves were extremely regular in form. Considering conditioning curves with various amounts of reinforcement, when high concentrations were used, the rate of responding increased reinforcement by reinforcement with strikingly continuous regularity. For such "learning curves" and subsequently for many others, Estes developed a mathematical formulation which generated functions which provided remarkably good fits. The explanatory task which Estes undertook was enormously more difficult than anything I have mentioned so far by way of explanation. Estes undertook with vigor and success one of the classical tasks of learning theory and carried its development to the highest stage so far attained. The initial and basic task of quantitative learning theory was seen by him, as by the workers who preceded him with less acumen and talent, to be that of providing a rational account of learning curves.

I had dealt only with "steady states," not with "transients," not with the observed changes in performance with time or trials. This theoretical task Estes saw to be valuable *only* if it has a rational base and if it resulted in more than the fitting of arbitrary *empirical* equations to data. This guiding evaluation must be concurred with, but when I contemplated the obstacles which were presented to me by the data in my possession and by the limitations of my own mathematical talents, I quickly became convinced that I should never be able to do anything very satisfactory along these lines. One thing which stopped me was that not all the curves of operant conditioning I saw were smooth and regular, and especially when smaller amounts of reinforcement were used, the rate of responding increased haltingly and irregularly. It would take a weakly reinforced rat hours of sporadic and oscillating performance to reach a stable level of bar pressing, whereas a generously reinforced rat would in a few minutes produce a cumulative record which looked as though it had been traced by a short segment of a French curve. An account which would satisfactorily cover the range of actual cases seemed to me beyond my personal powers, and there it currently remains, beyond mine and anyone else's.

In the course of later reflection, which I hope included only a small amount of rationalization, I began to feel that the enterprise itself was of questionable value. I am sure that formulations of the sequence of performance changes which will give quite satisfactory fits to empirical curves are technically possible; with the application of computer methods they will probably come about in the next years. In principle such formulations cannot be denied, but the efforts to realize this in-principle possibility are premised on views of the learning processes and of the unfinished tasks of behavior theory which have seemed to me less and less inviting. An explanation of these reservations will require some time to develop, but I shall begin with one notion concerning an inherent limitation of abstract mathematical accounts of behavior which relates to matters already discussed.

If we refer just to the steady-state data of operant performance so much gone into, it would seem in principle necessary that an account of performance curves which included mention of asymptotic performance (steady state) would have to rely on psychophysical determinations to furnish these numbers. If the mathematical system were indeed powerful enough to deduce these numbers, then it would be powerful enough to deduce a great deal of psychophysics as well. There is of course no way to predict, say, equal-sweetness functions on purely physiological grounds, but it would seem natural to look for such a possibility in a future physiology of taste, based upon physical chemistry. Suppose a more abstract and general quantitative account of behavior could do the same.

Then a part of such an abstract system would be logically equivalent to a part of physiology. There cannot be two mathematical accounts of one relationship which do not in part have the same substantive reference. Now the abstract treatment may relinquish the task of predicting a psychophysical relationship and accept the fact as a given from outside the system. Such a course would be sound and, I further believe, necessary. This type of limitation of any quantitative theory of behavior has, however, more grave consequences for the prospects of the approach than my little example would so far appear to imply, for it means to me that a great many behavioral consequences of stimulus manipulation will yield data outside the bounds of an abstract system detached from other sciences.

BEHAVIOR KINETICS AND BEHAVIOR STRUCTURE

Apart from the limitations of mathematical treatments of behavior and how they treat the problems they undertake, my reservations concerning the *whole* approach of theoretical schemes which start from the learning curve derive from a skepticism as to whether accounts of the *sequence* of behavior and of sequential changes in behavior or learning are central to the phenomena. I judge that *time* is a terribly overestimated sort of variable in our view of psychological processes. We are deceived about its importance because behavior is typically repeated in learning experiments and behavioral experiments not having to do with learning. I think there is a whole major division of thinking about behavior (and about psychology) between those who are impressed with the way time enters into behavior—the learning curve of performance versus time, trials, reinforcements; the temporal distribution of practice; the repetition of stimulation; the learning about sequences of events (CS, *then* UCS; response, *then* reinforcing stimulus)—and those who are hardly concerned with time at all. The first view is the temporal, or kinetic, outlook on behavior, the second I shall call *structural*. In the second view, the emphasis is on *organization* in all its senses and aspects. The first view was firmly endeared to me when I began, but as the result of changes in my structure, which have taken a long time, I am more firmly convinced of the value of holding and professing the second. In the kinetic view, the structure of behavior is taken very much for granted. Units of behavior are assumed; they are experimentally given or easily produced, and the focus of attention is upon the course of manifestation of behavior and the factors which determine this course. The variables which appear most prominent are those which produce the largest changes in activation, and among these factors drive states and reinforcers naturally come to the fore. In the structural view, the interest is upon the internal constitution of behavior and upon its definition, even though one may profitably employ changes in activation to answer questions of structure. The laws of behavior kinetics, which no doubt exist, currently have less appeal for me than the laws of behavior *structure,* which are little known. In a structural view, the generic questions are: "What is a stimulus?"; "What is a response?"; "What is learned?"; "What is learning?"; "What sorts of psychological organizations and reorganizations are there, and what are their bases?"[4] If one feels he can provide relatively satisfactory answers to such questions, he is detached from structural and substantive questions. I am at a loss to answer these questions, though I have some suggestions to offer, and I shall now tell how these questions became important for me and displaced the problems of behavior and learning which once seemed so compelling. I came therewith to take a querulous view of available laws of conditioning as satisfactory laws of learning, because they appeared to be not very satisfactory laws of phenomena of conditioning. Because the laws of conditioning appeared to me qualitatively ineffectual and nondescriptive, I became a fortiori less concerned with their quantitative elaboration in terms of any formal system. Ultimately I came also to require a less simple philosophical view of the psychological enterprise and to voice the sentiments expressed in the first pages of this paper.

All these peregrinations and little heresies began as the result of studying stimulus generalization, a stock and sensible item of anybody's learning theory. I judge that this experience was a necessary condition, not just because necessity must be ascribed to any biographical episode which has consequences, but because without studying stimuli very particularly and in certain ways one need never run into their complexities. In most studies of conditioning, either classical or instrumental, the stimuli are maintained constant, physically constant. The learning curve pertains precisely to the condition that the environment is held as fixed as possible and its possibilities exploited. In one whole line of behavioral inquiry, when stimuli are manipulated, as indeed they must be to study such problems as interstimulus interval in classical conditioning or delay of rein-

---

[4] The structural view is typified by such writers as Lashley, Krechevsky, and Hebb [40], by the explicit "morphopsychology" of Klüver [52], by the concerns illustrated in Hayek's essay on the sensory order [38], and, of course, by virtually the entire gestalt school. The views of Campbell [11] and Smedslund [75] on the problem of "what-is-learned" center on questions which are here called "structural" and are highly consonant with the present outlook. Among associationists Restle especially has devoted attention to delineation of the stimulus in spatial learning [65] and of the changing stimuli in learning-set formation [66]. However, I must agree with Dodwell's critique of the abstractness of the stochastic-model treatment of stimulation [13] and with his position that accounts of the stimulus in, for example, learning of shape discriminations, must rely upon more concrete facts of form perception.

forcement in operant conditioning or backward conditioning or schedules of reinforcement, *it is only the arrangement of stimulations which is altered*. The paradigms and laws of conditioning pertain mostly to such situations and their variations. The arrangements may pertain to the temporal structure of stimulations relative to each other, or relative to actions, or relative to both other stimulations and actions. But this is a quite different sort of thing from variation of the properties of stimulation per se. I cannot emphasize too much the distinction between manipulation of arrangement and manipulation of properties. What happens in the latter case is alluded to by the phenomenon of stimulus generalization, by such terms as transfer, irradiation, induction, stimulus equivalence, transposition, and the like. For such phenomena we have only some suggestive terms, but no adequate set of concepts and little we should wish to call laws.

AN ENCOUNTER WITH STIMULUS GENERALIZATION

My involvement with the empirical phenomenon of stimulus generalization resulted from a conjunction of ideas and methods invented by B. F. Skinner, a hypothesis or several developed by C. L. Hull and other theorists, some psychophysical ideas for ferment, and a colleague, H. I. Kalish. I shall discuss all but the last of these in turn.

By 1950 or before, Skinner demonstrated [73] that one could study which stimuli were effective in controlling a conditioned operant by (1) bringing the operant to a high and stable rate by the use of aperiodic (variable interval) reinforcement and (2) submitting the operant to extinction, which would then be quite prolonged, and testing the rate of responding in the presence of a variety of briefly introduced stimuli. This convenient method was a manifestation of ideas immanent in Skinner's analysis of behavior from its fertile outset. In his paper on *The generic nature of the concepts of stimulus and response* [70], Skinner showed that the word *stimulus* as it appears in the systematic languages of both reflexology and conditioning refers to a class of items, the same being logically paralled by *response*. It is not possible to state in a few words the importance and fertility of this analysis, to trace the developments which have been predicated upon these notions, which have virtually been incorporated in all of systematic behavior theory, not to mention the many instances where a clarification of thought and issues may be realized if this analysis is taken into serious account. The development of the remainder of this essay is predicated upon the generic nature of the stimulus concept and will not cohere as a development without a prior understanding of what this concept entails. I am not in a position to reproduce Skinner's analysis here, but the experiments I shall describe are to be understood chiefly as attempts to obtain an empirical specification of the effective class of stimulation for selected examples of conditioned responses.

I shall use Skinner's term *stimulus class* (S-C) when we speak of "what" (meaning the S-C) the animal has been conditioned to and his term stimulus instance (S-I) when we must speak of such events as: "The S-I on the third trial was a 1,000-cps tone." S-I's are specific stimulations, dated events when they have occurred and events with possible dates when we speak of their possible occurrences. S-C's are constructions or concepts. Their composition may be known only by means of the application of S-I's, although a mere listing of effective S-I's is not sufficient to describe a given S-C. An S-C is developed or altered in the process of conditioning, which comes about through the application of some small number of S-I's.

The problem of stimulus generalization is to learn about the S-C. I would suggest that it may be more efficient to conceptualize the S-C as a *state* rather than a class. When the organism is in such-and-such a state, a certain class of stimuli have such-and-such an effectiveness. The S-C is an attribution of the organism, and the S-I an actual or possible effect from the environment on the organism. I believe that the use of some such terminology is well-nigh indispensable for the formulation of certain theoretical and empirical problems, and for the description of the methods for exploring them.[5]

[5] The case I present for the understanding of certain topics in these terms I would like to offer independently of the philosophical ideas previously suggested, which argue for a dualism of psychological subject matters. The core of the latter viewpoint, as the reader may well anticipate, is that the language of perception is used to denote stimuli (the bird was conditioned to a red spot) and should be recognized as such. "Red" is not a proper description of the S-I, which must be in physical terms. Neither is "red" an especially informative description of the S-C, which must be quantitatively specified through experiments, or the language of perception gainfully employed, or *both,* as I would dualistically recommend. Dealing with this problem, Skinner states: "The reinforcement of the response 'red,' for example, is contingent upon the presence of a red object. . . . A red object then becomes a discriminative stimulus, an 'occasion' for the successful emission of the response 'red'" [72]. The main psychological problem Skinner sees here is the prediction of verbal behavior. So do I, but I cannot regard as scientifically satisfactory or complete a law of the "red-saying" reflex in which the independent variable is "any red object." Such a law does not carry us beyond common sense, and if the common-sense account of the matter implies that "red" is indeed an object property, common sense (naïve realism) is in this regard completely wrong; it cannot be relied upon in the study of the stimulational variables which control behavior and in the statement of whatever quantitative laws we can find. On these grounds I reach a dualistic philosophy and methodology. Whether Skinner ultimately does or not is difficult to assess, but I should predict that in dealing with *exactly* the same experimental problems as are discussed in this essay, anyone would have to become quite explicitly dualistic. A prediction can be based upon an extrapolation of the histories of those who have become involved in psychophysics; this aspect of human scientific behavior is highly predictable.

In Skinner's formulation of the problem of the S-C, the membership class is left entirely open as a general thing. What the S-C is after conditioning is an entirely empirical matter. The S-C is an ellipsis to be filled in, as is the R-C. I believe that such an approach is exactly appropriate to the state of our knowledge of such matters on the whole. In general I do not believe that we have any but the crudest and most intuitive ways of predicting which S-I's other than the identical ones employed in conditioning will be responded to or to what degree. In textbooks we frequently find the statement that a conditioned response will generalize to a range of similar stimuli and to an extent which decreases as similarity decreases. This is offered as a law of "stimulus generalization." Such a statement is a useless tautology as it stands. In any more exact meaning, as I shall show, it has not yet been shown to be true. In simplest form, the law does not cover the case which is typical rather than exceptional for individual subjects, that some S-I *other than* the conditioned S-I is responded to *more* strongly than the conditioned S-I.

We must amend our position of ignorance in one respect, however, if we start at the beginning. If the S-I has been specified in the first instance in physical terms, there are cases where we can predict what will happen as we alter it by depending on the laws of the receptive processes. To choose an unlikely example, if our CS has been a threshold light with dimensions, ignoring area $I_j \cdot t_k = C$, we can obviously predict that any stimulation with the same C will show complete transfer. This is of course *sensory identity,* and one dimension of the S-C for this example would have to define a sensory-identity class of stimuli of equal effectiveness. But a physicalistic psychology, such as we all desire, must speak of this case or make clear that the case is out of bounds in relation to the phenomena of greater interest, which are those of associative equivalence, identity, and similarity. Of course we can come to such distinctions only if we start from the broadest point of view and start by treating the variations in stimulation from the vantage points afforded by the sciences of stimulation. Only to a small extent, I think, has the "learning-theory" treatment of the whole matter made such an effort, because it ignored these disciplines from the start or took advantage of their concepts in the most halting and piecemeal and unconscious way. It is of advantage just to begin with to have the possibility of considering sensory similarity, perceptual similarity, associative similarity, and the like, for these categories denote levels of processing of stimulation and levels of organization of afferent input. These levels of organization and process will be of value to consider in dealing with what is a problem of organization to begin with.

But I did not begin with all these theoretical considerations when I started to work with stimulus generalization. In teaching a course on operant conditioning to undergraduates, I had regularly used pigeons as subjects and had set up the key-pecking apparatus with a row of colored gelatin filters behind the key so that the students could train their birds to peck at a shocking-fuschia key and obtain generalization of the response to dark blue, light blue, and green and to purplish red, orange, and yellow. The filters were theatrical gelatins lifted from the drama workshop next door, but this did not entirely account for the dramatic and satisfactory results. Skinner's findings were reproduced by the group of pigeons and students with great ease and uniformity. It was very interesting that in arranging the seven filters in a line of similarity to my eye and in accordance with my knowledge of the color circle, I had put them in the order in which the pigeons generally arranged them to either side of color number 4 (shocking fuchsia) in the middle. The arrangement by the pigeons was of course not spatial but an order in terms of the number of responses produced in extinction while the various colors were being presented in random sequence.

These classroom findings and this method were seen by H. I. Kalish to invite a systematic attack (in which I joined) upon the theoretical problems around the phenomenon of stimulus generalization. With the aid of better endowed colleagues, we were able to buy an optical monochromator, and out of our own funds some pigeons and plywood. The monochromator had to be substituted for the theatrical gelatins; better control of stimulation was a necessity for possibly interpretable results, for any psychophysics. I shall discuss now some results we obtained in working with the system of the pigeon and the spectrum, some theoretical questions we examined, and a few of the broader issues to which these questions pertain.

THE PRIMARY GENERALIZATION GRADIENT: THE INVERSE HYPOTHESIS

The first theoretical problem had to do with the form of the generalization gradient, the primary generalization gradient after conditioning to a single stimulus. As to this problem and others, the postulates of Hull's system were brought to bear upon our thinking by Kalish, who was a student of Spence. Hull, like Spence, supposes that one clue to the form of the stimulus-generalization function is a scaling of the physical stimulus dimension in JND units, in terms of psychophysical units of stimulus spacing. This supposition was common to Hovland [46], to Schlosberg and Solomon [67], and to others who had considered this problem systematically. The hypothesis is that generalization from the conditioned stimulus occurs inversely to psychological distance measured in JND units. Whether this hypothesis is true, I do not know to this day. At this writing, the basic rule of the generalization gradient still occupies me, and all one can say is that the matter is considerably more involved than this obvious and reasonable hypothesis suggests. One does not know when the efforts of all who have worked on this first quantitative problem of stimulus generalization will yield a coherent rule, or a manner of thinking which may, for individual systems of stimulus-response-and-organism, yield whatever several coherent rules there may be.

Kalish and I tested the "inverse hypothesis" (as it was later called by Leo Ganz) by training different groups of pigeons to respond to conditioned stimuli selected from different points in the spectrum [30]. The inverse hypothesis states in essence that generalization is the inverse of sensory discrimination, that a response will generalize to the extent that the organism does not discriminate stimulus differences. The hypothesis is a formal way of saying that generalization depends upon similarity, and this notion seems so reasonable that it is difficult to imagine that it could not be true or easily verified. In more formal terms, we can say:

The generalization curve may be considered as a set of decrements from an established value of activity to the conditioned stimulus. The decrement in responding (generalization decrement = GD) per unit stimulus change is the slope of the generalization curve. If we consider the GD as having the dimensions of a probability difference, then

$$\text{Slope of generalization curve} = \frac{GD}{\Delta S} = \frac{\Delta p(R)}{\Delta S}$$

But we know that the psychophysical difference threshold (JND) is really also a slope measure of the psychometric function. It tells how rapidly the probability of detecting a difference changes with change in stimulation, i.e.,

$$JND = \text{slope of psychometric function} = \frac{\Delta S}{\Delta p(R)}$$

If, as a psychophysical procedure, one has used one of the constant methods and two judgment categories, the conventional and fixed value of $\Delta p(R)$ is the interval from $p(R) = 0.50$ to $p(R) = 0.75$, but this is arbitrary, and the choice of interval only determines the absolute size of the JND. Clearly the absolute value of any JND is not a very meaningful number, but for the purpose of testing the inverse hypothesis, all that matters is the correlation between slopes of generalization curves and slopes of psychometric curves in the same continuum. From the foregoing, we should expect just by comparing the dimensions of the two concepts,

$$\text{Slope of generalization curve} \; \alpha \; \frac{1}{JND}$$

The inverse hypothesis makes no statements as to the over-all form of the curve of generalization. It does not state that the generalization gradient is concave or convex, or of some particular shape, such as exponential. A large literature [e.g., 68] deals with the question of the "shape of the generalization gradient"; the question does not begin to have meaning until the units for the measurement of R and of S are specified, and even then all sorts of transformation of units and scales are possible. Discussions of the shapes of generalizations curves in such abstract terms as are often employed are quite vacuous, but we may observe that the problem of the discriminability and generalization is a legitimate and approachable problem (1) whenever one can obtain generalization curves of whatever form for several conditioned stimuli in a dimension where discriminability varies from region to region and (2) where one knows the *relative* values of discriminability (difference thresholds, JND's, or sensory distances) in the continuum.

For the spectrum, we expected that we would obtain relatively narrow generalization gradients for such regions as around 580 mμ (yellow) JND's are relatively small, and somewhat broader curves for CS's at 550 or 530 mμ (greens) selected from regions where JND's are considerably larger. For man, the curve of $\Delta\lambda$ versus λ is well known; for the pigeon, Hamilton and Coleman [32] found that this function has approximately the same configuration. But in our study, to our unresolved surprise, we were unable to find any variations of generalization slope which corresponded to differences in the discriminability of spectrum lights (See Figs. 3 and 4). Indeed the simplest though least satisfactory rule one could state was that the slope of generalization curve for this case was independent of the position of the CS in the spectrum. Our experiment contained many flaws, and the tentative conclusion to which it led was based upon the failure to reject the null hypothesis, which is always dangerous. Technically there was the flaw that we had no proper control over luminosity, but when this was corrected in a better-controlled study by Blough [4], the inverse hypothesis was still not borne out.

To say that this problem "requires more study" is somewhat more than an apologetic cliché. To date there does not exist information which offers any clear picture of the relationship between generalization and discriminability (sensory distance, similarity) or any other independently determined measures on sensory continua. Psychophysical facts and associative relations have not been tied together in what would seem to be an obvious respect. Perhaps there are different sets of relationships for the two classes of continua which Stevens [77] has distinguished as prothetic and metathetic.

Perhaps the entire supposition of the "inverse hypothesis" is wrong, in so far as it may be a mistake to consider as equivalent the change in probability of response of the psychometric curve and the changes in rate

or activation of behavior seen in generalization curves. The latter measures contain a component of sheer response elicitation, corresponding
to what distinguishes the situation of just behaving from the situation of
judging. The latter situation is more complex in that two or more response categories are involved and less complex in the sense that response

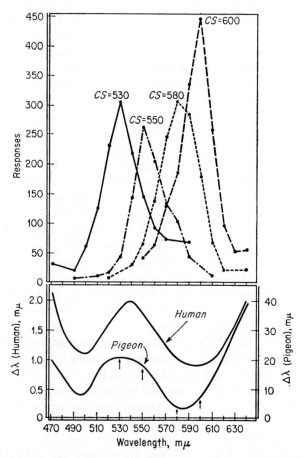

Fig. 3. Generalization gradients for groups of pigeons
trained to various wavelengths. Below, spectrum discriminability functions for man and pigeon [30, 32].

production of some sort is guaranteed and stabilized by the surrounding
conditions of the judgment experiment.

Empirically, it is suggestive that there appears to be a high within-
groups and within-subjects variability of the modes of gradients when the
CS is yellow, a region of high discriminability. Presumably at this region
there is a fine balance between the green and red sensory components,

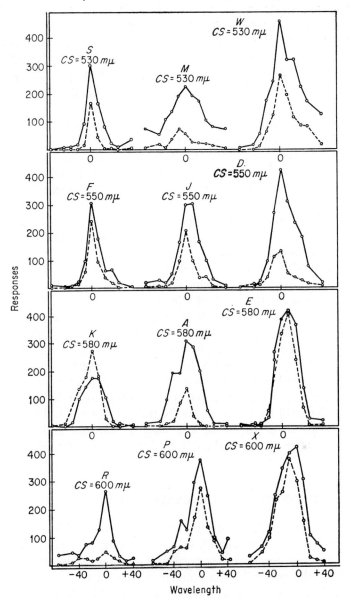

FIG. 4. Spectrum generalization gradients for individual pigeons trained with indicated wavelengths. Solid line represents first test; dashed line, second test [30].

and there is a rapid change in the relative degrees of sensory activation as one moves out of this region in either direction. Suppose that the association is made to these components separately; thus it may swing unstably in either direction, as the result of random factors within or between subjects. The experimental suggestion which comes out of these meager speculations is that the variability of generalization curves, not their slope, is an inverse function of $\Delta\lambda$, or generally ΔS.

But the whole question is open qualitatively and quantitatively. There is available no more than a set of guesses as to how large a range of stimuli will activate a conditioned response and how much each of them will activate the response. In effect we have no quantitative or semi-quantitative law of stimulus generalization, no statement—nor yet the data for essaying a statement—which carries us much beyond our initial tautology that some stimuli somehow similar to the conditioned stimulus will also evoke behavior. We know only that the conditioned S-I is a member of a class of some sort.

Our condition of ignorance relative to the previous matter will not, however, keep me from discussing a whole range of problems and topics present to view in the field of stimulus generalization. I shall discuss some further quantitative problems, some experiments, and some matters which go far afield from the immediate descriptive problems and enter into questions of mechanism. The experiments will be a rather local selection, depending too much upon those which have been done by colleagues and students, and upon those systems of behavior most familiar to me. I hope these will be representative of problems of more than local interest and that they will lead us in generally fruitful directions. Thus I may be able to drop out of the scene and serve as narrator and opiner, with opinions to offer on more than the substantial matters with which we begin.

SENSORY ORDER AND GENERALIZATION

I shall continue these infirmly based discussions with the mention of a topic which is to me, though in a vague way, of supervening importance to the one we have discussed and just put aside. The significant thing about the generalization gradient for the pigeon and the spectrum is that it should be orderly at all. The same could be said of any gradient of generalization. The pigeon knows the spectrum, in an important sense of the word "know." After training to one wavelength, the pigeon's degree of activation to different wavelengths varies in accord with the *order* of physical wavelengths. The curve of generalization is not just an "error curve" (in the statistical sense) but a curve of errors systematically regulated and distributed in a nice relation to physical facts. Everything the subject does except respond to the conditioned S-I's is an error, but the errors have a pattern and a sense, and they reveal a structure. The animal has a "color-space" which is in part a map of the measurable (by us) attributes of the various stimulations. This color space, if I may speak henceforth metaphorically, is the structure, the system, the organization, within which the stimulus class is determined. When we have conditioned the pigeon to a wavelength, we have produced a kind of motoric flexure in this space. The space is flexed upwards toward the production of behavior if we have reinforced the behavior; the kink is centered at or about the conditioned stimulus, but a whole region is affected by the conditioning experience. We can make the bend sharper, by further training [36], put in several kinks by using several stimuli [49], make the bend go down rather than up by inhibitory training [44], and surely all sorts of other strange things. But in every case the conditioned stimulus, in the sense of the S-C, is not some physical event or object but a range within a preordained continuum. The continuum must exist, so to speak, before the conditioning process can be meaningfully regarded to have taken hold.

I do not know how to allude to the color space of the pigeon except in terms of my phenomenology of colors and their similarities, or by references to such graphic devices as chromaticity diagrams wherein the continuousness of the space is invisibly assumed. But we are forced into the inference of a space or a system of some sort when we are struck with the ordering of the animal's operant behavior production. The mere fact of this ordering, this structuredness relative to stimulation, strikes me as a more fundamental thing than any behavioral relationship which corresponds to a part of it or any accident of training which makes it manifest. The possibility of such stimulational orderings, whatever they are or however they may be developed, lies behind all incidents of learning and laws of learning. What do we come upon here, if we do not take for granted the very character of our behavioral observations? Sensory continua, dimensions of experience, something like a sensorium, some animal analogue of Kant's phenomenal categories? The questions and the answers, which are not sufficient answers, are meant as rhetorical. But we cannot escape that we have encountered just the edge of the domain of afferent processes, a juncture where we can expect further connections between the domains of sensation and learning. If I were able, I would indicate some plausible pathways to follow from where we stand, just having glimpsed a problem, but I can continue only to grope in possible directions.

In so far as anything is clear, association of behavior to something appears to be a matter of association to a dimension (or to ranges on multiple dimensions). If the level of motivation of a pigeon is greatly heightened after training, virtually the whole spectrum elicits behavior, according to available data [80]. If we raise the ontogenetic question, I do not believe that the pigeon "learns" the spectral order, or any sensory order. This is a sheer guess, but for the rhesus monkey, Ganz has determined that orderly spectrum generalization exists in animals raised in darkness from birth [17, 18]. Surely there must be some stimulational structures biologically given which can be built upon and combined with others. Beyond such sensory orders as hues and pitches, we must recognize the possibility of orderings at higher levels—perceptual and cognitive, to employ descriptive though crude terms. At what level, and under what conditions, biological and experiential, will we find effective the ordering of visible facial patterns, from impassivity to joy, from impassivity to threat or scorn? What does it take to make us respond to the numerical order among counted subjects? To the continuum of densities of materials? To what animals, and under what circumstances, can it matter whether a visible object is parallel to another, whether one object encloses or partly encloses another, whether the path or speed of an object has such-and-such characteristics, referred to a domain of similar characteristics?

Faced with problems such as these, which can be problems of stimulus generalization and explored by its methods, but which are more patently problems of sensation and sensory organization, of perception and perceptual organization, of perceptual development, of learning in a broad ontogenetic sense, and also questions of comparative psychology, one may wish to retreat somewhat from one's initial impression that the main question of generalization is to come upon the equation for generalization curves. The latter is always a legitimate question, but it lies within a larger context. From this point of view there appears to be less reason to assume that there will be a general equation even to cover those cases where we have been able to isolate the natural and proper dimensionality of the stimulus class, where we have found the aspects of stimulation and its further processing which have become pertinent to a given association. From a larger point of view, the situation becomes one of great and almost terrifying specificity, and somewhat beyond the pale of learning theory as currently conceived in abstract form.

The problem of the dimensionality of the stimulus class bears some reflection. What do we mean by a sensory dimension? It is a case where the order of an association can be revealed by manipulation of the simpler physical dimensions of stimulation and where, furthermore, we are not obliged to consider stimulation to more than one receptive system and what may happen within this system for more than a brief time. We may stay within a modality and can characterize the order by using units which are descriptive of spatially and temporally confined "proximal stimulation." The wavelength generalization dimension for the pigeon is of this type, and the fact that the curve assumes order when the wavelength is the abscissa of the curve betokens and confirms this. The color process can be generated by quite minimal stimulation, and goes no further, as far as its associative possibilities are concerned, by prolongation of stimulation. This is not so if we consider the case of visual form in the two-dimensional sense, and still less the case when we come to three-dimensional form and object formation as a process requiring time and most likely a series of consequent actions of receptive surfaces and samplings of the "optic array" [21]. Quite clearly, certain dimensions of association such as the number series require very explicit action systems to be initiated and carried through (counting) in order that this cognitive series become effective. Clearly the "properties" of "stimuli" become properties only upon the sequential execution of organizing processes and actions. Only a "naïve realist" would think otherwise, and with more than a little passion, I would aver that the grappling of molar behavior theory with such questions as we are considering has revealed such an attitude and an incognizance of what complexities must be considered if we are to move toward a reasonably physicalistic psychology and a differentiated treatment of stimulation.

What do we mean, roughly speaking, by a perceptual dimension, admitting that the distinctions we are exploring are not firm? It is such a one as object size, where two or several attributes and sequelae of simpler stimulations (like retinal extent and distance cues) must combine, as a ratio or some other function, to yield a new quantity or process capable of entering into association. When conditions permit the perception of object size and the stabilization of this percept, the principal effect need not be considered the generation of an associative possibility vis-à-vis size, but rather the generation of certain more immediate motor possibilities. When an object has been perceived as having a given size and shape and spatial disposition, it becomes "graspable" or "walk-aroundable," etc. But the conditions for these motor dispositions are part of the conditions for the association to size or spatial location as dimensions of generalization.

The general point I should suggest is that whatever becomes associated to, as a stimulus class and therefore a dimension of generalization, will be that consequence of stimulation which has been permitted to reach development under the circumstances, and the association will attach to that segment of internal processing which has reached the highest level, so to speak, of development. If the stimulus is a printed word, I will associate to the brightness of the page if the stimulus is very brief, to a form if I can see a form, to the word if I am permitted to read, to the meaning if I understand the language, or to the sound if I can just pronounce it. By this example, I allude to the question of the dimensionality of the stimulus class. The facts and concepts of sensation and perception are integral to carrying the exploration beyond the point we must leave it, for the terms of analysis these disciplines employ are correct and are confirmed in the detailed study of behavior. The study of behavior can, however, greatly supplement the information these disciplines supply; it can make some of the phenomena of common interest more tangible and approachable, and can even put more convenient cast upon certain classical problems of description and explanation in the field of psychological organization.

FURTHER PROBLEMS OF GENERALIZATION AND EXPERIMENTS

Summation of Generalization

The intriguing and convenient system of the pigeon and the spectral continuum has lent itself to the exploration of a number of more complex cases and aspects of sensory generalization. Following our attempt to discern the features of generalization after conditioning to a single stimulus, Kalish and I studied the pattern of generalization produced after conditioning to two wavelengths [49] and after conditioning to three wavelengths [50]. Hull postulates a summation of the effects of different conditioned stimuli with quantitatively different values in the same continuum. The notion which underlies this hypothesis is, I believe, Pavlov's picture of a spread of excitation across the sensory cortex, starting from the point of the conditioned stimulus as a focus [62]. Such a neural mechanism is absent from Hull's theory, but its functional counterpart survives as a postulate. In conjunction with further postulates, the Hullian postulate of summation makes what are at first sight quite definite predictions about the results to be expected for conditioning to several stimuli given that one knows (1) the generalization curve for each of them independently and (2) how each *curve* would change as the level of activation changes. Our handling of the matter was quite inferential in some respects, but we had some prior information on the shape of single-stimulus gradients and some fairly good evidence that the form of the curve remained quite constant but was altered multiplicatively as its absolute level went from high to low in the course of extinction. (The latter is quite interesting, in that it indicates that one can describe extinction just as a change of activation of a constant state, or pattern of associations, quite apart from the time course of arriving at a such-and-such level of this state. This would be a time-independent description of extinction.) But we assumed that the same multiplicative course would be characteristic of the increase in level during training.

For several cases of equal amounts of variable-interval reinforcement training to two alternated wavelengths, the generalization curves (Fig. 5) were not such as to enable us to make a decisive conclusion between hypothesis of summation, à la Hull and the opposite hypothesis that the curve for the two stimuli would not summate at all. That is to say, by a

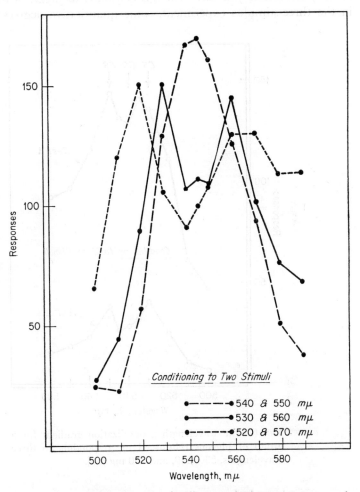

FIG. 5. Generalization gradients for three groups of pigeons, each group having been given equal training on a certain pair of wavelengths [49].

proper selection of the activity-level constants attributed to each of two smaller, underlying hypothetical curves, we could use Hull's rules to generate the proper "summated" curve obtained empirically. Give or take a little, it was about as good a picture as could be provided by the

alternative of just superimposing two single-stimulus curves at the obtained peak levels and drawing around their upper outline, assuming
that the overlap played no role. Quantitative psychological theories can
explain a great deal (even what may not be true), and they are extremely flexible if you have enough constants to juggle with. However,
in the three-stimulus experiment, some quantitative degrees of freedom

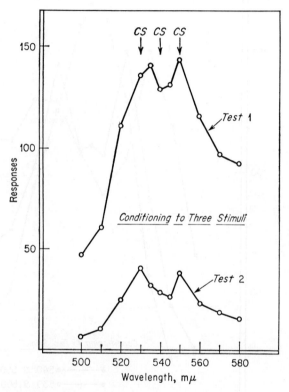

Fig. 6. The wavelength generalization gradient for a
group of pigeons reinforced for responding to three
wavelengths, 530, 540, and 550 mμ [50].

are removed, and the qualitative results are more determining of the
picture. Here we were not able to find the center of three stimuli strengthened by its spectral neighbors (Fig. 6). Now I do not wish to make out that
our results are more than fragmentary in relation to the whole problem.
But I am dubious as to the existence of summation of generalization,
either in manifest behavior [2] or in the substrate of generalization,
whatever the substrate may be. Because I am dubious about the historical

picture of the latter and because there I think some very real problems lie —in relation to which behavioral experiments can be directed—I am especially querulous of the summation hypothesis.

We can well speculate about the substrate, in the absence of guiding data of any sort. It is notable that in Pavlov's picture, the sensory continua taken as prototypal, are those such as somesthesis or pitch, where there may be found a topographic projection of receptive elements upon the cortex in higher animals. This spatial neural array is taken to be linked with some sensory continuum. Such a prototype and the behavioral hypothesis to which it leads may be doubted if only because innumerable sensory continua and more complex continua of stimulus generalization could hardly have counterparts which are so simply or crudely spatial. What place could correspond to the rate of flashing of a light, or to any continuum involving time? What to intensive variations of stimuli? Is there a locus for a given intensity and an adjacent loci for adjacent intensities? What of qualities, and really what of perceptual and higher-order continua such as apparent size? Pavlov's notion is no more preposterous than any other structural hypothesis which anyone could now frame, because the problem is so opaque and enormous, but the Pavlovian ideas in structural or functional form are therefore no better a guide to behavioral results than any other.

Secondly, we may notice that the spread of excitation which Pavlov discusses is by no means to be mistaken for the effect we wish to understand, namely, the state of *excitability* of a rather permanent sort which is established in learning. Clearly the central structural problem of learning is how *excitation* results in changes in *excitability*. The curve of generalization more or less depicts this state of excitability, or accessibility to stimulation. Thus the problems of learning, generalization, and memory are interfused at the structural level. At this level, I find it hard to think that there is more than one sort of problem, though we cannot know how many types of mechanism are capable of displaying the foregoing triad of functions. These functions may be subsumed under the heading of the engram. In so far as there are fundamental scientific problems in psychology, those which have a direct connection with the material of other sciences, we should have to regard the engram as the principal one of these. As always, it stands most prominent in the minds of general scientists who are naïve about psychology, who are happily acquainted with just its grossest facts, and who have none of our local fads and squabbles to surmount. The solution is not much nearer than it has ever been. When Guthrie, in one of his last statements [24], indicates that we know little more about association than Aristotle did, I prefer to think that he meant the structural basis of association. The responsibility and service which falls to psychology within this problem is to state its facts in such a clear way that the functional requirements for the mechanism can be seen without impediment or shallowness, and to state its theories so as not to preempt the possibility of more fundamental ones. In the matter of summation, the question is not whose rule is right, and not even what is the rule, but what, at last, does the rule mean.

It is easy to fall into the habit of thinking that what is depicted by a curve of generalization is some active but graded force which can then interact with some other force of different peripheral origin. But the curve denotes the *effects* of previous stimulation; it defines the dependent variable affected in the course of previous stimulation; it depicts more of the effect than we would have known about had we not probed with a set of new stimuli. Generalization is not a special process different from association itself, but a state pertaining to associations. We can quite safely leave stimulus generalization, I think, on the dependent variable side of the ledger, although (as I shall show) we may use the generalization curve for making a great many predictions of an R-R sort.

It is equally easy and mistaken to consider that stimulus generalization is an "explanation" of transfer of training generally or of any instance of behavior where a response occurs under altered environmental circumstances. *Generalization* is not a process but the name of a category of phenomena for which the word *transfer* could be used with equal accuracy. If cortical irradiation were a fact, it would explain both generalization and transfer.

Generalization, Preference, and Choice

In an informative series of experiments [43], W. K. Honig has shown that from a known wavelength generalization gradient one can predict not only the level of activation produced by various stimulations but also the pattern of preferences and choices between stimuli. The findings support in essential respects one of the hypotheses developed by Spence [76] in his analysis of transposition. Spence assumes that, given the separate and independent absolute activation levels for each of two stimuli, the choices manifested when these stimuli are presented together reflects the order of absolute strengths. Honig tested this principle in the simplest case when only one wavelength has been reinforced and also after several versions of discrimination training. For simple conditioning, pigeons were trained to peck at one wavelength of light in a box containing two keys. Sometimes the light was on one key, sometimes on the other, sometimes on both, but equally reinforced under all circumstances. In testing (Fig. 7), each subject was repeatedly exposed to eleven wavelengths $(a, b, c, \ldots k)$, including the CS, f, and also to ten pairs (a with b, b

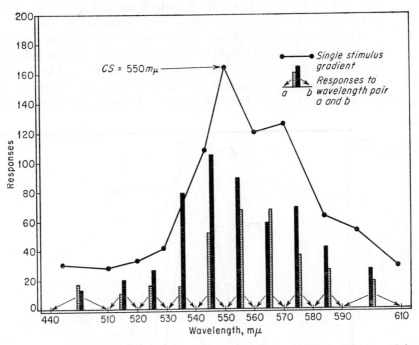

Fɪɢ. 7. Generalization gradient and pattern of preferences obtained from training to 550 mμ and testing with wavelengths from 490 to 610 mμ singly and also in the designated pairs. Honig [43].

with c, etc.). Each wavelength singly produced a given rate of responding. Each pair produced a certain rate of responding, proportional to the activation yielded by the more active member, but the responses were distributed in such ratios as, for the pair (a, b),

$$\text{The proportion to } a = \frac{a \text{ rate alone}}{a \text{ rate alone} + b \text{ rate alone}}$$

and

$$\text{The proportion to } b = \frac{b \text{ rate alone}}{\text{the same denominator}}$$

The same rule could be applied to all pairs, (b, c), (c, d), etc. The predictions which can be made as to choice behavior from generalization data are (1) how many choices will be made and (2) how many responses each stimulus will receive, and thus of course the preference ratio. This analysis is extremely powerful, although we do not know at present whether it will apply to other systems. The analysis holds when the choice pairs are such as (b, j) or (e, h) which are not physically "adjacent" and not chosen from the same side of the generalization curve.[6]

Honig's experiment shows that a conditioned operant may be considered to consist of an infinitely numerous class of separate reflexes (with respect to such a number of separate generalized S-I's). The operant may be decomposed experimentally into these systems, and the systems may be pitted against one another. The process of conditioning produces such a

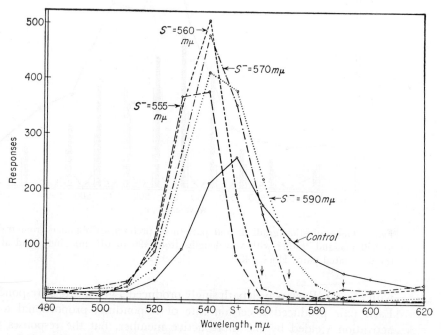

FIG. 8. Generalization gradients for groups of pigeons trained to discriminate between 550 mμ as S+ and various negative stimuli (indicated S− values). Control group was trained to 550 mμ only. Following discrimination training, with training stimuli presented successively, maximally effective wavelengths are displaced away from S−. Data from Hanson [35].

hierarchy of possible behaviors of ordered strengths, as well as strengthening the manifested response itself. The state resulting from conditioning is extremely intricate, though some of its rules may be quite simple, and the state can be manifested by an indefinitely large number of operations.

[6] It may be observed that in this analysis, response probabilities (relative frequencies of responding) are derived from activation measures (rates). A given rate ratio uniquely determines a probability, but to a given probability there may correspond an infinite number of pairs of absolute rates. The relation is one-many in the one case, many-one in the other. For this reason, it may be well to consider rate of occurrence a more "fundamental" measure than probability in the quantification of behavior.

Honig showed that the rules of choice characteristic of a simple conditioned operant could be applied with a few qualifications to the state resulting from discrimination training, i.e., reinforcement of one wavelength and extinction of another. In one experiment the positive and negative stimuli were presented in succession during training, and in another they were presented side by side. The states produced by the two procedures were quite different. After successive training Honig found the generalization pattern to duplicate what had previously been found by

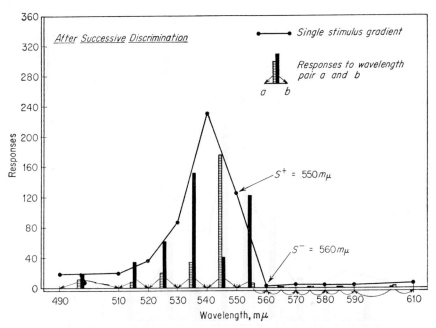

Fig. 9. Generalization gradient and pattern of preferences obtained after training to discriminate between 500 mμ as S+ and 560 mμ as S—, presented in succession during training. Honig [43].

H. M. Hanson in an experiment on the effects of discrimination training upon generalization [34, 35]. Hanson determined that if responses to a generalized stimulus are extinguished, the resulting curve of generalization (Fig. 8) shows "peak shift." That is, if a, b, and c, are wavelengths, if b is reinforced and c extinguished, then the maximally effective stimulus will be some stimulus a more remote on the continuum from c than is b. Such a finding was qualitatively predicted by Spence, although certain of quantitative features of Spence's analysis are not supported by Hanson's data. When Honig repeated this experiment and tested both for generalization and choice, he confirmed that there were "supernormal" activating stimuli such as a and that a was chosen over all other stimuli (Fig. 9). The previous choice relationships held for the whole generalization range. However, if *b* and *c* had been presented together during training, there was no peak shift, no drastic change in the form of the generalization curve, no drastic change in the over-all preference pattern (Fig. 10). Stimulus *b* was preferred over *c* when a choice was allowed, but nothing was preferred over *b*. When *c* was presented singly, *c* was not greatly suppressed. It would appear that the weakness of the negative stimulus (*c*) was contingent on the

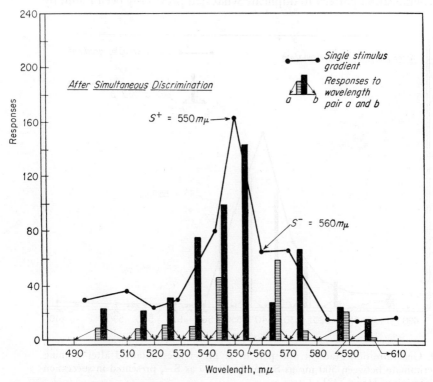

FIG. 10. Generalization gradient and pattern of preferences obtained after training to discriminate between 550 mμ as S+ and 560 mμ as S—, presented simultaneously during training. Honig [43].

presence of the positive (*b*) and that simultaneous training results in a special relationship between these stimuli. I shall not further detail these findings, and the reader may consult the reports for a view of the recent state of the problems. Over-all, however, these experiments yield a revealing picture of some of the structure of habits learned under various arrangements. The studies supplement the recent important findings of Bitterman and his colleagues [e.g., 3] on the nature of behavioral organization in discrimination learning, and the very great number of other and earlier analyses in this field. I may merely allude to the beginning efforts that have been made to explore the organization of multidimensional generalization and discrimination [8] and of conditional discrimination [5]. The concept of generalization is a tool for the exploration of such phenomena, not an explanation of their nature, for we hardly are in a position to glimpse the main features of even simpler processes.

BASIC CONCEPTS OF CONDITIONING THEORY

The Elements of Discrimination Formation

Looking through the lens of the generalization experiment, we may yet observe aspects of basic learning processes which were otherwise less apparent. For example, we may ask about discrimination learning what procedural ingredients are required to produce a differential activation to two stimuli. Conventionally it is assumed that response to one stimulus must be reinforced and response to the other not reinforced (punishment would be an added but inessential feature). In one departure from this procedure [29], pigeons were reinforced at one level (once per minute) in the presence of one wavelength and in other periods also reinforced but at a lower level (once per five minutes) in the presence of another wavelength. The rates to both stimuli increased but, of course, differentially. Then the pattern of wavelength generalization was determined (Fig. 11). It appeared as virtually the same pattern we would have found had the pigeons been rewarded for one and extinguished for the other; the state which resulted was like that Hanson had found after successive discrimination, but this time with a shift of peak away from the relatively weakly reinforced stimulus. If properly extinguished stimuli may be regarded as negative, then a less well-reinforced stimulus may be also regarded as functionally negative. This study supplies another reason for regarding the determination of the values of stimuli (their algebraic signs, so to speak) as being determined on a relational, contextual basis. We did not find a small amount of excitation for the somewhat-reinforced stimulus and a larger for the somewhat more reinforced, as we would have found had their effects been independent. This general sort of finding can be obtained without testing generalization. In an experiment with M. Siskel (unpublished data), rats were tested on two reinforcement ranges, in the one case 5, 10, 20, and 40 per cent solutions of sucrose and in another case 0, 2.5, 5, and 10 per cent. The rate versus concentration functions were semilogarithmic for both ranges, but the curve for the lower range had a much higher slope, so high, in fact, that the rate for 10 per cent in the low context exceeded that for 40 per cent in the high context. This type of determining relationship argues strongly for taking frame-of-reference and adaptation-level [42] considerations into account in any experiment where more than one stimulus is presented. Here is an explicit principle of perception which makes itself felt in the detailed study of behavior.

Looking again at the ingredients of discrimination formation, an experiment by Honig, Thomas, and the author [45] asked this question: If

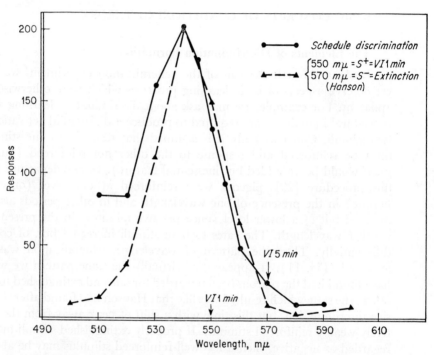

Fig. 11. Pattern of generalization after reinforcement of 550 mμ on a once-per-minute schedule (VI1) and 570 mμ on a once-per-five-minute schedule (VI5). The pattern may be compared with the result found by Hanson for reinforcement and extinction of these stimuli [29].

one reinforced one stimulus and then independently and later extinguished a generalization stimulus, would one necessarily form a discrimination? Pigeons were reinforced first in the presence of 550 mμ, on a subsequent day extinguished in the presence of 570 mμ to a low level, and on the following day tested for generalization. The pattern of generalization which resulted from this procedure was, however, what one would expect had there been instituted no extinction to a *specific* generalized stimulus. The curve of activity was lower over-all, but there was no decrement specific to the region of the extinguished stimulus, no peak shift such as we take as the sign of the formation of a successive discrimination. When these subjects were subsequently given successive-discrimination training involving the Pavlovian "method of contrasts," the discrimination was easily formed, and the typically warped pattern of generalization was found. Whether the successful discrimination was then formed more readily we do not know, but there is sufficient evidence to emphasize the importance of the conventional method of contrasts in the formation of discrimination. Reinforcement and extinction do not, as temporally unrelated ingredients, add up to a discrimination. If we seek for whatever else is required or facilitative under the heading of "opportunity to observe contrasts" or "to perceive differences," or to carry out a temporal integration of stimulation, we shall be looking in the right direction. These headings will not explain, but they are of indispensible heuristic import.

A significant experiment by Terrace [78] has shown that a discrimination may be established without the manifestation and extinction of responding to the negative stimulus. In Terrace's "errorless" discrimination procedure, the pigeon is trained to a light of one color and then another color is substituted so briefly at first and with such a low intensity that a peck is not made. Nor is any peck made on later trials as the negative stimulus is gradually brought in with full intensity and indefinite duration. Possible behavior to the negative stimulus is delicately habituated. Then a second discrimination may be superimposed upon the first, again without errors, by fading in a pattern on the positive color—while fading it out—and bringing a second pattern on the negative color and making that color disappear. If an error is induced by mistake, the pattern of behavior becomes disorganized.

From many considerations I conjecture that the development of differential behavior levels to two stimuli requires some ingredient I should call "discriminative inhibition." This tendency I believe to be central not only to discrimination learning but more importantly to extinction itself. I feel it may be more fruitful to consider the extinction process secondary to discrimination in a very broad sense, to discriminative inhibition specifically, than to consider extinction as itself the basis for discrimination learning. A mere physical difference between two stimuli, given differential reinforcement, is not sufficient to produce differential activation; we know that the difference in stimuli must exceed some value. If the physical difference is very small and the difference in reinforcement conditions very small, the animal may, as shown by Hanson [33], at first manifest stronger behavior to the unreinforced stimulus, then weaker behavior, and may go through several such cycles of "misidentification" before ultimately achieving the discrimination. I do not look upon extinction as the "passive, automatic" outcome of nonreinforcement but as something akin to the perception of a difference. A study by Armus [1] has shown that extinction in a runway is more rapid after large amounts of reinforcement (many food pellets) than after small amounts (one or few). This result is not compatible with the idea that extinction is the exhaustion of a response tendency, but it agrees with the conception that extinction is more likely when a change of situational conditions is more perceptible. King et al. [51] have found that beyond a certain ordinal number of reinforced trials, resistance to extinction decreases. Resistance to extinction is a *nonmonotonic* function of number of reinforcements. The greater the number of reinforcements, the greater is the "push," but the longer the string of reinforcements has been, the easier it is to detect that the string has been broken.

The nonmonotonic relation between number of reinforcements and resistance to extinction which was shown very clearly by King and his associates has actually been available in the literature for a long time. The finding was first demonstrated by Finger [16], then by Mote [60], and more recently by North and Stimmel [61]. Lawrence and Miller [55] considered Finger's results artifactual and ascribed them to "a source of confusion." The source of confusion that they removed in their experiment which yielded opposite results (they used differentiated start and goal boxes in a runway) was also not present in subsequent experiments which have yielded results like Finger's. The finding that reinforcement does not simply add excitation and that extinction does not simply subtract it has little effect on the general conception of the reinforcement and extinction phenomena, nor has it determined in any fundamental way the formal treatments of conditioning in such theories as Hull's, Spence's, or Estes'. Yet this finding goes to the core of the Pavlovian view of learning. Personally, I did not see the significance of these awkward results until I was able to question the fundamentalness and uniqueness of Pavlovian concepts quite generally.

Technically, these findings indicate that one cannot predict the rate of change of performance during extinction from measures of performance while reinforcement is being administered. The dynamics of extinction cannot be predicted from the statics of prior performance. This type of unpredictability is shown in an experiment by Thomas [79], which attempted to correlate measures of the rate of formation of a discrimination between two wavelengths with prior measures of the generalization decrement between these wavelengths. First wavelength *a* was reinforced and the generalization to *b* obtained. Then a discrimination was formed between *a* and *b*. Across individual subjects there was no significant correlation between the rate of formation of the discrimination and the previously determined generalization decrement.

Theoretically speaking, one may well regard the following phenomena as of a single type:

1. The rapid extinction of a conditioned response after prolonged reinforcement

2. The rapidity of extinction following repeated conditionings and extinctions [7]

3. The positive effect of overlearning upon discrimination reversal [64]

4. The achievement of one-trial discrimination reversal after repeated reversals [14]

5. The achievement of learning-set performance after the the the solution of numerous problems [37]

In all cases, the rapidity of extinction (discriminative suppression) is revealed after prolonged experience in a stabilized environment. I would suggest that the essentials of extinction are more clearly manifested under these asymptotic conditions when few extraneous factors are operating rather than when one is dealing with a relatively naïve subject undergoing the first experimental extinction experience. In all five phenomena listed, the conditions maximize the possibility that the change of sequence presented (old stimulus–old response–new consequence) will be noticed and hence effective in changing the behavior of the organism.

The foregoing characterizations of the extinction phenomenon in cognitive, perceptual terms are not intended as explanations, and not intended as operational definitions for the experimental recognition of the phenomenon. They are characterizations directed at obtaining perspective, and I believe they have some heuristic value. My immediately following discussion of conditioning will be conducted in the same vein. All that I am saying about these fundamental and revered phenomena is to illustrate the value of using common-sense intuitions concerning their nature and determining circumstances, rather than relying entirely upon experimentally derived concepts the factual status of which is less secure and which, without modulation by an ordinary understanding of psychology, will lead to a radical and bizarre picture of learning and behavioral change. Common sense cannot predict numbers, but it can typically predict the gross shape of common and simple phenomena. This is so because the types of observation we make in the learning laboratory are not radically different from those we make in a thousand other situations. Therefore, what such experimental observations yield cannot be in a gross sense absolutely new but only more refined and analytic in comparison with knowledge based upon ordinary experience.

Conditioning and Event Perception

The episode which in the language of conditioning we describe as the strengthening of an operant following reinforcement would be described by the layman as learning to press the bar in order to get a pellet, or to peck the key in order to get some grain. If we ask the layman for an explanation of how this learning took place, he might say (if he were not focused on the purposive aspects of the episode, the "in-order-to" or the "wanting") that the animal, once he had done it, saw that bar pressing was followed by the food's dropping in. I do not think that the layman would be altogether wrong in talking about the sequence the animal perceived and came to know about, the sequence of action and environmental consequence. For the conditions under which this sequence, as a consecutive pair of stimulations, can come to have an influence upon the animal's disposition are just about the conditions which are required for any sequence of events to be, in the ordinary sense, perceived, and the elements which can function as cue, response, and reward are just about of the same dimensions as those which could function as a signal in any context where discrimination of sequence was specifically required. I believe that the latter is a principle which has some experimental consequences and, indeed, that it is used implicitly as a guide to designing the experimental environment so that it will be appropriate to the animal and result in successful conditioning.

If we once look at conditioning as temporal integration (and this would apply to both classical and instrumental conditioning), we may see that the stimulational elements which may function as units and the temporal fusions which are formed of these units have a characteristic size for any species or individual organism. Naturally, and commonsensically, if I listen to a boring lecture and thereafter find that my behavior at the supper table is unseemly and unsatisfactory to my family and myself, I may as a consequence avoid going to boring lectures before supper. This adaptive consequence may be predicated upon some insight, some verbalization, and the proper hierarchy of values, but it is the whole thing of the lecture and the whole thing of the supper which typically have a relationship to each other, and not the stepping out of the lecture hall and the opening of the door to my house. The situation would be somewhat different for a lower organism, but quantitatively different. The functional units would be, I believe, quite different in size for the two species, but within a species and within an individual at a given stage or state, there would be consistencies and correlations between unit sizes, and there might well be consistencies between the sizes of stimulus units and response units. I am in possession of no data which might support such a way of looking at the problem, but I must ask the reader to grant that the notion has some gross plausibility. One will be interested in the problem if one is concerned with the concrete description of stimulus and response, and one may then be inclined to consider that temporal-unit formation and conditioning (which is by definition a matter of sequence) do not lie within entirely different psychological contexts.

Now not only are the experimental situations we work with when we use animals such as to contain appropriate ingredients for temporal integration, but also the general conditions under which we expect conditioning to transpire are of a characteristic sort. The experimental space is quiet and not visually various: the animal is awake, healthy, and alert. If we are skillful experimenters, the animal is not frantic and not oblivious to casual changes in the environment which we introduce. These changes are introduced upon a background of steady or of adapted stimulation. Even so we may *not* get conditioning if we introduce a sequence of stimuli (classical conditioning) or if a change we introduce follows one made by the animal in the course of movement (instrumental conditioning). But when the happy effect takes place, it takes place very quickly and suddenly, as quickly as a perception transpires. And it must, because the stimulations themselves do not last very long, and if the mechanism for the change of behavioral state were not swift, it would long since have been discarded in the experiments of evolution.

Attention and Generalization

Having established a habit in a certain environmental surrounding, we may vary aspects of the stimulation one or several at a time in order to discover which continua yield orderly behavioral functions. For certain variations of the environment after behavior has been established, we will find the response quite unaffected. For other and more informative variations we will find clues to the structure of the behavior which has been developed and modified. One class of ineffective variations will be those which do not affect receptors at all. Another category will be those which may affect receptors and, in the instance in hand, actually do yet which participate minimally in the response system of interest. As to the latter, an interesting example may be drawn from the comparison between (1) variation of wavelength when pigeons have been reinforced in the presence of a given monochromatic light, and (2) variation of auditory frequency when pigeons have been reinforced in the presence of a given audible tone. For the auditory case, Jenkins and Harrison [48] found little or no generalization decrement with frequency, in marked contrast to case 1. Jenkins noted that complete elimination of the tone made no difference. From a comparison of the two situations, Jenkins develops the important principle that only such sources of stimulation as are immediately involved in the elicitation, control, or guidance of behavior will yield, upon variation, orderly generalization curves. A continuously maintained spot of light of some color guides the pigeon's spatial coordination in pecking. A continuously maintained tone does not, and there is no corresponding frequency generalization curve, even though the response is reinforced always in the accompaniment of this stimulation. However, when a tone-on–tone-off discrimination is established, there is an orderly generalization function as to frequency (and presumably other auditory dimensions as well). In line with this sort of reasoning, Heinemann and Rudolph have shown that the smaller the diameter of a circle which surrounds the pigeon's pecking key, the sharper will be the generalization gradient when luminance of the circle is varied. The smaller the circle, the more guidance it affords to responding, and the more its properties come to control behavior [41].

Thus, prior to studying the quantitative character of an association which has been formed, we must separate those features of the environment which have qualitatively entered the association from those which have not. At this point we have identified partially what the subject is and has been "attending to." Certain stimulus instances from certain modalities and certain sequelae of these enter the stimulus class of a given piece of behavior and some do not. Those which do are "stimuli" in the typical psychological sense, and to make the functional difference clear we should not blush to use the term "attention" to describe the function. Skinner has very explicitly noted that "attention" may be thought of as that relationship which subsists between discriminative stimuli and the operant behavior which these events occasion. We must note that in Hull's formal treatment of stimulus generalization, there is little taking account of attention. The equation for the stimulus-generalization function is primarily centered on *one* independent variable, the number of JND's of stimulus change. Only if there is a prior assumption (which there may be, but implicitly) that the formulation will apply only to certain features of stimulation (which may then be called stimuli) will the system begin to work. A central aspect of Lashley's critique [54] of Hull is a demand for a qualification of this sort. But there is more than a semantic issue here: there is a difference in perspective, which has to do with a cognizance or incognizance of the enormous complexity of the processing of stimulation before behavior transpires. Of these events, attention is a gross part.

A recent and excellent experiment on stimulus generalization [39] may be selected from many examples to illustrate the foregoing. Monkeys were trained to perform two acts, one for food, one to avoid shock, concurrently in the presence of a light of a given intensity. When the intensity of light was varied, there was decreasing food-rewarded behavior but no change in the level of avoidance behavior. The hypothesis is offered that avoidance behavior generalizes more broadly than approach. This interpretation is the only feature of the experiment of which I am dubious, though I can just voice but not support an alternative view. I suggest that the light was not conditioned to the avoidance behavior here at all, not in control of such responding, not being attended to. Suppose one had varied the character of the grill floor from which shock had been received, changing its texture or spacing. It is not unreasonable that such changes in stimulation would have produced an opposite general conclusion.

On the Observability of the Stimulus

In every experimental arrangement, the relevant and controlling stimulation has to be discovered, and its properties can be described only at the end of a long chain of inferences. When we speak of "the stimulus," we are not referring to a directly observable entity. It has been the custom of some students of behavior to proclaim the objectivity of the enterprise by asserting that both stimuli and responses are directly observable. By not qualifying this assertion they have not fully identified a difficulty in all psychological experiments. If we mean by "the stimulus" the stimulus class, this is by definition a construct, a state of an organism with respect to an in-principle infinitely numerous collection of stimulations. The state of susceptibility to stimulation may be perfectly definite, it may remain the same over a great time, it may be describable by a mathematical function which affords good predictions, but the state, nonetheless, remains a construct, a disposition whose character we should like to delineate and possibly explain. If, now, we turn to instances of stimulation and their immediate sequelae, their accompanying response instances, we are prohibited by physical considerations from more than inferring what these physical events were, since, for example, if a given stimulation is absorbed in the retina, it cannot be absorbed anywhere else. This sort of physical singularity of S-I's is associated with the so-called "egocentric predicament." Two persons may observe the same object, by means of different S-I's, and we may infer whether in general they see the same things (e.g., have the same laws of color vision or pattern vision), but whether the instances of seeing are the same, we are "prohibited from observing," and for much the same reasons that we must infer the nature of S-I's, in the study of behavior. Only objects are observable.

The value of recognizing the stimulus in every sense as a matter of inference is to induce us to understand that we may be mistaken about it in regard to any situation. If we have some bland notion that stimuli are "directly observable," we shall not be terribly interested in making correct inferences about S-C's and S-I's. We may assume, for example, that when a rat is proceeding down a maze, one step is cueing off the next, and we may ignore what may indeed be happening, that the determiners of his pathway are to be found in his visual field and are indeed the result of some rather subtle aspects of things going on there. Some of these retinal determiners are invitingly discussed by Gibson [20].

It may be thought that to a very great extent the course of understanding of spatial learning in animals has been obstructed by wrong notions about the organization of lomotor behavior. Those, like Tolman, who believed that rats had effective visual stimulation when their eyes were open were able to show that a great deal of behavioral reorganization could be established merely by allowing rats to wander in mazes. Even more pertinently, Caldwell [9], Gleitman [22], and McNamara et al. [59] have demonstrated that rats transported through mazes can learn the pathways without walking at all.

The inconvenient aspect of these experiments is that rats were used as subjects and vision in the rat is not the predominant mode of behavioral organization or the readiest source of its organization. It is also slightly regrettable that the more informative experiments in this area were done recently rather than early in the game, for had it been otherwise, the conspicuous issues of modern learning theory would be quite different. One's notions about the effective stimuli for a given item of behavior are enormously influential in shaping one's notions about the basic principles of learning. I see the difference between so-called reinforcement theories and nonreinforcement theories more as a difference between two conceptions of the organization of locomotor behavior than as a difference between two hypotheses concerning the role of terminal reinforcement. It would be even more correct to say that reinforcement views have had a weak or nonexistent conception of the behavior in question and the latent-learning people have had another which determined the kind of experiments they did but not the grounds on which they were led to argue for their position. The more relevant position which may be taken by the perceptionist may well be to ask his opponent to reflect on what happens during the first reinforced maze trial *prior* to reinforcement. The sequence of stimulations and changes in stimulation which are undergone at this time are the obvious precondition of any effect of the reinforcement being felt by the second trial. The learning which goes on prior to the first reinforcement is as latent as any which may go on if the reinforcement is delayed until the tenth "trial." The thesis implied here will not be further developed in the rather deceptive terms of the latent-learning literature. The substantial question may instead be regarded as one more nearly of space perception within a novel spatial arrangement, of the development of an orientation, and of effective locomotor behavior via visual stimulation, via locomotion and receptor orientation, and via the two combined. It would best be studied with other species than the rat, not including the earthworm.

On the Response

What I have just said about the stimulus as a construct may be transposed *mutatis mutandis* to the response instance and class. Just above I have naturally slipped over some questions of response organization. It is hardly worthwhile to exert much effort to maintain a distinction between the stimulus class and the response class, since the distinction between measurements of stimulation and measurements of action is experimentally patent. The immediate sequelae of stimulation are temporally continuous with the antecedents and course of motor activity. Any action which occupies a sizable span of time is regulated by the contingent changes in stimulation. Typically, changes in stimulation are consequent upon action, rather than the reverse, at least in nonsessile animals, and to the extent that we may at all fix a temporal origin in the stream of activity. And if one may conjecture on phenomenology, the conscious state in man reflects events we should call motor no less than those which are sensory, and, even though changes in perception are typically occasioned by changes in peripheral stimulation, the subjective character of these changes is allied no less to changes in motoric disposition than to changes in more immediately afferent systems [57, 83].

In the study of behavior, the identification of the pattern of action to which a given instance belongs and the identification of the pattern which is affected when, in the course of learning, an episode of action is manifested—these are prime problems of experimental inference within the fields of the description of behavior as such and of learning. These questions are discussed by Skinner vis-à-vis the classification of reflexes as the first step toward his sytematization. The criterion Skinner offers is functional: all the various topographies of action which are strengthened when one is elicited and strengthened are members of a class, just as all the stimulations whose possible effects are concurrently potentiated are members of a stimulus class. This formulation is extremely useful for experimental purposes, but it is again an ellipsis. It says that there will be some class but offers only implicit clues as to what the membership of the class will be. For the most part this approach takes for granted the existence of organized episodes of behavior and the organization of these behaviors into functional groupings. It assumes all the facts of motor organization, those corresponding facts of perceptual organization directly related to movement, and whatever else in the organism which makes patterns of movement functionally cohere. This approach, which begins at the level of the organized response class, at approximately the level of an organized manipulatory response specifically, begins to ask its questions in terms of the fate of such units following certain arrangements of the environment. The premises give rise to the study of the kinetics of behavior units—what I have earlier called the kinetic approach. In principle this approach is not the only possible outcome of the foregoing analysis, since one may also try to fill in the ellipsis of the response class and seek the basis of its membership. It is somewhat a matter of taste as to which to do. However, it is quite the case that our knowledge of the organization of action is quite meager, at both the descriptive and structural levels, and that it often is customary to proceed as though the suggestions implicit in the present research on animal behavior and reinforcement as one organizing variable were quite a satisfactory and general account of the matter.

The implicit notion about the organization of behavior conveyed by reinforcement studies is that the class of behavior modified by reinforcement consists generally of those action patterns which bear a rather close topographical resemblance to the manifested and reinforced instances of movement. Generally this is less and less the case as one moves up to higher species. From an observation of behaviors reinforced in a wide range of animals, some thirty species, Breland and Breland [6] conclude that an important limiting factor on the development of new response systems through reinforcement is the tendency of strongly reinforced behaviors to regress toward species-specific behaviors containing components irrelevant to the reinforcement contingency. Implicit in many behavioral studies is the assumption that the action pattern recognized by the experimenter and used by him as the basis for the reinforcement contingency is representative of the temporal span and form of the action systems at work in the subject and affected by the reinforcing events. It is not possible here to discuss the numerous studies which are less than fully meaningful because insufficient attention was devoted to an accurate delineation of the response class or classes involved, but we may refer on the positive side to such analyses as have been made recently by Goodnow and her associates [e.g., 23] of the probability-learning situation in terms of hypotheses or strategies and also to Levine's development [56] of a system for the quantitative description and assessment of performance in the learning-set situation in terms of outcome-dependent and outcome-independent hypotheses at a more complex level of organization than the single movement and reward. It may only serve as a weak corrective to less sophisticated approaches to reemphasize the logical point that the response class is always a matter of inference rather than of direct observation.

The problem of the response *itself* is the permanent problem of the science of behavior, and the question of the delineation of behavior is always a part of any study of behavior. The tasks of behavior description and the search for behavioral mechanisms are at the outset somewhat distinct, but they cannot remain so for long. To pursue as we should the topic of the organization of responses and response systems would carry us beyond the topic of this essay, even though such a pursuit would point in the direction of the main business of behavioral science. A substantive treatment might start with elementary reflexes at or about the level of anatomical simplicity called segmental, e.g., the myotatic reflexes which concern single receptive and motor units. We would next proceed to intersegmental units which show more topographical variation, which implicate several types and loci of efferent and afferent elements, and which contain more functional possibilities. We should then consider suprasegmental systems which regulate posture, which accommodate the locomotor patterns, and which, in conjunction with higher levels of visceral reflex organization, determine the whole tonic substrate of behavior. Ultimately we should be in a position to discuss the composition and function of those more unstable and variable reflexes we call operant activities. These represent the interplay of virtually all receptive systems, but most especially the distance receptors and the internal sensors of body state (the "motivational" receptors). The variability and apparent spontaneity of operants presumably depend upon the sheer number of receptive systems they implicate and the number of stimulational components which must be achieved before action is ready. The drawn-out actions we call operant, which can command any available sector of the motoric, may well be considered reflexes of the distance receptors, for they come about principally under the influence of specialized exteroceptors, and the termini of these extensive actions coincide with the achievement of complex exteroceptive states. During their occurrence operants are regulated by exteroceptive changes and external feedback loops (or by proprioceptive patterns isomorphic with visual states or changes). The future readiness of operants and their future forms are also regulated by exteroceptive consequences (reinforcements). In ourselves the stimulational conditions an operant in progress may satisfy are represented to us as an image—a moving image or a stationary one, an image with visceral components if we are eager and confident or an image with only mood components if we are fantasying. The image[7] betokens the organization of the operant, but we cannot render any more substantial picture of its organizations as to space or time or quality, since we can hardly go beyond the level of the myotatic reflex in substantial terms. "We know a little about the elementary effects of stimulation on the sense-organs of our subjects; we observe their responsive behavior when it becomes overt. But between these terms there is more *terra incognita* than there was on the map of Africa sixty years ago" [53]. So observed Köhler in 1929, and his appraisal is essentially correct at this moment. Perhaps we are in a somewhat better position now to

---

[7] A parallel and a dependence should be noted between these allusions to the image and the concepts of Von Holst [81], especially his notion of the "efference copy," or "image." Furthermore, the reference above to such behavior patterns as strategies or hypotheses should be taken to allow the possibility of more complex "efference copies" which can be matched by sequential stimulations achieved in the course of more complex behaviors. These strategic images might have to include logical properties, whatever such may be.

grasp the functional requirements for behavior mechanisms, and this has resulted from advances in the description both of behavior and of perception, but the enormous matters which remain—at the level of simple actions and level of more elaborate organizations—remain as common problems for the psychology of behavior and the psychology of the afferent processes.

BEHAVIOR THEORY AS A GENERAL OUTLOOK

The comments I have offered so far pertain to the conceptual and theoretical aspects of the psychology of behavior in relation to these aspects of the psychology of the afferent processes. But there is one further thing to consider: systems of behavior, theories of learning, comprise more than sets of laws which pertain to experimental phenomena; typically they are efforts toward general psychologies. They may offer perspectives on nonexperimental phenomena, as well as on experimental phenomena beyond their initial purviews. They may lend themselves as guides to practical action. These functions and aims of behavior theory are so plain that any observer of the recent scene could name dozens of extensions and applications of behavioral principles. The "learning-theory" approach is virtually the keynote of the last few decades in American psychology; neobehaviorism partakes of the impetus and popularity and appeal which attached to behaviorism a few decades earlier.

The appeal must be accepted as a matter of fact and understood, not contested or denied. The appeal has two sources: practical and cognitive. Nothing can be more practical than a science of practices, and the appeal of a science of behavior in this regard can necessarily never be matched by, for example, a psychology of afferent processes exclusively. The cognitive appeal of behavior is virtually a matter of cognitive necessity as long as there is a resistive subject matter of behavior to be understood. In many formulations, however, behavior theory has not shown itself to be very clear about the distinctions between theoretical and practical science, and to some extent has not wished to make the distinction clear, since its self-concept has included a devotion to practical virtues and necessities. To a very large extent, I should judge, the distance which has separated theories of behavior from the science of afferent processes has been determined by the unwillingness of students of behavior to be deterred by an involvement in things of no overwhelming practical import. This unwillingness cannot be sustained in any attempt to make a detailed analysis of stimulus and response and to obtain refined experimental laws of behavior. In this pursuit, practical considerations can play no role.

As a general outlook, the learning-theory approach must be understood to contain the following main elements: First, the approach contains the attitude that from the start psychological processes must be regarded as intimately associated with action and as determined at some level by their adaptive significance. (This is the functionalist, Darwinian, naturalistic attitude.) Second, the approach seeks lawful relationships and promotes the application of causal analysis to psychological events. Third, the approach affords a set of categories in terms of which the analysis may be performed for specific cases and extended to as yet unanalyzed cases.

We must refer to all these elements if we are to understand the appeal and extensibility of learning theories. The theories have in a sense been constructed just so as to make possible the extensions that we may note on every hand, and it has been customary for those who employ them (1) to support these conceptions on the basis of their extensibility and (2) to suggest that the sole reason the theories contained the possibility of extension is that they are composites of veridical principles. That a learning theory is extensible and applicable to a wide range of situations because of its laws is a notion which is neither wholly correct nor incorrect, and an answer in terms of the veridicality of laws is not wholly pertinent.

The initial and pervasive appeal of learning theory, and an important source of its extensibility, is the fact that the approach furnishes a set of terms which enables us to make sense of the psychological world. It provides a set of categories, such as stimulus, response, drive, and reinforcement, which afford the possibility of a cognitive order. Given these categories, every verb denotes a response, every noun a stimulus. Every wish, desire, need, craving, or aspiration becomes a drive; every reward, goal, incentive, satisfaction, fulfillment, or success becomes a reinforcement. The chaos and accidental variety of the psychological domain now becomes laid out along certain straight lines, and events find their places within a system of coordinates. The achievement of this much order is no mean achievement, and the order attained is, thus far considered, no incorrect order, for the categories identified by learning theory denote certain of the main ingredients of virtually every psychological episode.

As to the function of categorization, the power of learning theory depends upon the systematic employment of a set of terms. These terms are abstract, necessarily general, and yet—if properly applied—somewhat more functional and definite than the terms of common sense, for the categories are linked also to a set of propositions which are at least, and at most, qualitatively general. Without doubt, it is typically the case that responses are somehow determined by the number of prior reinforcements, without doubt somehow by the contemporary drive state. I wish to stress that the functional relationships which are the substance of learning theory are qualitative in nature, even though in any experimental instance these relationships can be represented by numerical data. Although these relationships parallel the obvervations of common sense they go somewhat beyond, and they go beyond chiefly in the respect that they are expressed as functional relationships. Thus, as we have indicated, an important part of the learning-theory approach is the intent and the practice of thinking about psychological subject matter in terms of functional relations, the employment of the logical categories of independent variable and dependent variable.

I think it affords some understanding to identify the approach of learning theory with these ingredients, especially the employment of a systematic language and the application of certain formats of scientific thinking to psychological subject matter. But the possession of the latter is hardly the exclusive franchise of one branch of psychology, even though the manifested self-concept of behavior theory has often revealed such an implicit conviction. Too frequently the retrospective defense of a set of behavioral principles has strongly and implicitly depended upon an argument for science itself, for the elements of the logic of science, for empiricism, and even for the hopefulness of the scientific attitude. Upon these common denominators, the differences among the various major learning theories become quite small. They have about equal possibilities for extension, and these are collectively about equal to the opportunities which are opened by the application of scientific methods, quite generally, to psychological events.

The opportunities afforded by the learning-theory approach to the analysis and manipulation of nonexperimental phenomena of psychology are not inherently greater or smaller than the opportunities opened by any causal analysis, and the limitations and conditions which apply to these opportunities apply irrespectively of doctrine. The utility of a set of analytical categories, when extended to some new and resistant phenomenon, depends chiefly upon two factors: the skill and intuition of the analyzer and the opacity and complexity of the phenomenon. The opportunities for control of a phenomenon, once some understanding has been achieved, depend upon the degree to which the control of independent variables lie within the grasp of the controller and the extent to which such variables are intrinsically effective. All these limiting factors are factual and particulate and even personal. With respect to these limiting factors, the learning-theory approach is not inherently more powerful than any other, and indeed there are tendencies associated with this approach which impose special limits. For whatever reasons, it is sometimes believed that the sheer application of the categorizing language constitutes a sufficient analysis. For example, in the treatment of

ychoanalytic phenomena, the substitution of "drive" for "libido" is
ken as a gain. The reverse is I think the case, since the problem of
derstanding such aspects of human behavior is not defined by the sub-
tution of more abstract terms for more particular ones. The substitu-
n blurs the distinctions between drives which are germane to an
derstanding and simultaneously takes out of the picture the systematic
servations made by Freud and his school of the special operations of
e sexual drive in man in contemporary society. Learning theory can
ply no observations of comparable relevance and differentiation; if
were to put itself in position to do so, it would have to resort to much
: same observational base as has been used by psychoanalysis itself.
e richness of psychoanalytic conceptions can easily be lost in the act
such subsumings, and the general content of such learning-theory
tions as drive, reinforcement, and conditioning (qua association) is
eady presupposed by psychoanalysis, which then proceeds to more
mplex functions and phenomena. The observations upon which our
alitative laws of learning are based are of such an obvious sort that
t they could hardly have been missed, though left unexpressed, in the
rse of more detailed inquiries of psychoanalysis. Past this primitive
nt we encounter phenomena and processes, like fantasy and identifica-
n and hysterical-symptom formation, beyond the level which the de-
ed development of learning theory has thus far reached and also quite
ond the range of its categories.

REPRISE

Let me make the briefest reprise, with no intention of summary or
clusions. I have attempted to offer a general attitude and a working
tude toward the development of psychological knowledge which ex-
an effort toward the use of both the behavioral and sensory-per-
tual traditions. I see the distinctive philosophical attitude which has
wn up around the study of behavior as unnecessary and impeding,
l to make use of the materials of the classical traditions, another
tude seems to me to be required, the methodological dualism which I
e expressed at the beginning of this paper. The use of a dualistic or
ralistic dogma is just this: to make us free to use and ponder the
cepts about psychological events which come to us in languages which
not the accustomed language of behavior.

I do not see how the psychology of behavior can proceed, and in
ctice I think it does not proceed, without infusion from informal con-
ts of common sense, of intuition, of introspection, of sensation and
ception. The continuing aim of behavioral inquiry, as I see it, is the
elopment of theoretical concepts at a level superior to common sense.

This aim is dependent upon the discovery of informative quantitative relationships, which pertain on the one hand to the activation of behavior and on the other hand to the constitution of behavioral episodes. The elaboration of quantitative relationships for their own sake or for inclusion in a separate formal system of behavior is not taken here as a proximal or ultimate goal. Toward the understanding of behavioral structure and mechanisms, a scientific treatment must be allied with the extant psychology of afferent processes and in turn contribute, by it own methods, to this discipline. A psychology of afferent processes moves from the vernacular to a systematic language ultimately in intimate and analytical contact with the language of general science. I cannot imagine a psychological treatment which is not pervaded by theoretical intent or a theoretical intent which does not seek contact with the materials and relationships of more analytical disciplines. In relation to the treatment of stimulation typically practiced by the study of behavior—which has inherently a more complex subject matter—the treatments of stimulation which may be found elsewhere are more analytical and considerably more sophisticated.

I have tried to illustrate in a number of instances the substantial relevance of sensory and perceptual concepts and relationships in the development of laws of behavior. I have not in any systematic way surveyed the enormous content of these classical fields, and because I have had to start with quite primitive considerations, with impeding philosophical retrenchments, I have dealt with only a scattered few of the materials of sensation and perception which were available long ago. Thus, I have not touched upon the more recent developments in these fields, nor have I mentioned many late technical and theoretical items to which I could not well serve as a guide, but which strike me as enormously important and suggestive.

The last thing I should wish to intimate is that our present knowledge of afferent processes provides a touchstone to the understanding of behavior. I avoid this as I should avoid the implication, which I am sure will not be drawn, of the sufficiency of extant behavioral principles themselves. Yet what may come out of an open approach to the understanding of psychological events by the application of all scientific resources, and by what directions, not I nor anyone may foresee.

REFERENCES

1. Armus, H. L. Effect of magnitude of reinforcement on acquisition and extinction of a running response. *J. exp. Psychol.*, 1959, **58**, 61–63.
2. Bilodeau, E. A., Brown, J. S., & Meryman, J. J. The summation of generalized reactive tendencies. *J. exp. Psychol.*, 1956, **51**, 293–298.

3. Bitterman, M. E., & Wodinsky, J. Simultaneous and successive discrimination. *Psychol. Rev.*, 1953, **60**, 371–376.

4. Blough, D. The shape of some wavelength generalization gradients. *J. exp. anal. Behavior.*, 1961, **4**, 31–40.

5. Boneau, C. A. Conditional discrimination and positive and negative generalization gradients. Paper read at Eastern Psychol. Ass., Philadelphia, 1961.

6. Breland, K., & Breland, M. The misbehavior of organisms. *Amer. Psychologist*, 1961, **16**, 681–684.

7. Bullock, D. H., & Smith, W. C. An effect of repeated conditioning and extinction upon operant strength. *J. exp. Psychol.*, 1953, **46**, 349–352.

8. Butter, C. M. Stimulus generalization and discrimination along the dimensions of wavelength and angular orientation. Unpublished doctoral dissertation, Duke Univer., 1959.

9. Caldwell, W. E., & McCracken, W. I. The effects of visual orientation on the maze learning ability of the white rat. *J. genet. Psychol.*, 1955, **86**, 69–77.

10. Campbell, B. A. The fractional reduction in noxious stimulation required to produce "just noticeable" learning. *J. comp. physiol. Psychol.*, 1955, **48**, 141–148.

11. Campbell, D. T. Operational delineation of "What is learned" via the transposition experiment. *Psychol. Rev.*, 1954, **61**, 167–174.

12. Collier, G. H. Regulation of intake and magnitude of reinforcement. Paper read at A.A.A.S. meetings, Denver, 1961.

13. Dodwell, P. C. Coding and learning in shape discrimination. *Psychol. Rev.*, 1961, **68**, 373–382.

14. Dufort, R. H., Guttman, N., & Kimble, G. A. One-trial discrimination reversal in the white rat. *J. comp. physiol. Psychol.*, 1954, **47**, 248–249.

15. Estes, W. K. The statistical approach to learning theory. In S. Koch (Ed.), *Psychology: a study of a science.* Vol. 2. New York: McGraw-Hill, 1959. Pp. 380–491.

16. Finger, F. W. The effect of varying conditions of reinforcement upon a simple running response. *J. exp. Psychol.*, 1942, **30**, 53–68.

17. Ganz, L. Stimulus generalization and the behavioral analysis of perceptual organization. Unpublished doctoral dissertation, Univer. of Chicago, 1959.

18. Ganz, L., & Riesen, A. H. Stimulus generalization to hue in the dark-reared macaque. *J. comp. physiol. Psychol.*, 1962, **55**, 92–99.

19. Garner, W. R., Hake, H. W., & Eriksen, C. W. Operationism and the concept of perception. *Psychol. Rev.*, 1956, **63**, 149–159.

20. Gibson, J. J. Visually controlled locomotion and visual orientation in animals. *Brit. J. Psychol.*, 1958, **49**, 182–194.

21. Gibson, J. J. Perception as a function of stimulation. In S. Koch (Ed.), *Psychology: a study of a science.* Vol. 1. New York: McGraw-Hill, 1959. Pp. 456–501.

22. Gleitman, H. Place learning without previous performance. *J. comp. physiol. Psychol.*, 1955, **48**, 77–79.

23. Goodnow, Jacqueline J., & Pettigrew, T. F. Effect of prior patterns experience upon strategies and learning sets. *J. exp. Psychol.*, 1955, 381–389.

24. Guthrie, E. R. Association by contiguity. In S. Koch, (Ed.), *P chology: a study of a science.* Vol. 2. New York: McGraw-Hill, 19 Pp. 158–195.

25. Guttman, N. Operant conditioning, extinction, and periodic reinfor ment in relation to concentration of sucrose used as reinforcing age *J. exp. Psychol.*, 1953, 46, 213–224.

26. Guttman, N. Theories of reinforcement and the reinforcement thresh Amer. *Psychologist,* 1953, 8, 360–361. (Abstract of paper read at An Psychol. Ass., Cleveland, Ohio, 1953.)

27. Guttman, N. Equal-reinforcement values for sucrose and glucose s tions compared with equal-sweetness values. *J. comp. physiol. Psych* 1954, 47, 358–361.

28. Guttman, N. The pigeon and the spectrum and other perplexi *Psychol. Rep.*, 1956, 2, 449–460.

29. Guttman, N. Generalization gradients around stimuli associated v different reinforcement schedules. *J. exp. Psychol.*, 1959, 58, 335–34(

30. Guttman, N., & Kalish, H. I. Discriminability and stimulus general tion. *J. exp. Psychol.*, 1956, 51, 79–88.

31. Guttman, N., & Kalish, H. I. Experiments on discrimination. *Sci Amer.*, 1958, 198, 77–82.

32. Hamilton. W. F., & Coleman, T. B. Trichromatic vision in the pig as illustrated by the spectral hue discrimination curve. *J. comp. Psyc* 1933, 15, 183–191.

33. Hanson, H. M. The effects of discrimination training on stimulus eralization. Unpublished doctoral dissertation, Duke Univer., 1956.

34. Hanson. H. M. Discrimination training effect upon stimulus genera tion gradient for spectrum stimuli. *Science,* 1957, 125, 888–889.

35. Hanson, H. M. Effects of discrimination training on stimulus genera tion. *J. exp. Psychol.*, 1959, 58, 321–334.

36. Hanson, H. M. Stimulus generalization following three-stimulus crimination training. *J. comp. physiol. Psychol.*, 1961, 54, 181–185.

37. Harlow, H. F. The formation of learning sets. *Psychol. Rev.*, 1949. 51–65.

38. Hayek, F. A. *The sensory order.* Chicago: Univer. of Chicago P 1952.

39. Hearst, E. Stimulus generalization gradients for appetitive and aver behavior. *Science,* 1960, 132, 1769–1770.

40. Hebb, D. O. *The organization of behavior: a neuropsychological the* New York: Wiley, 1949.

41. Heinemann, E., & Rudolph, R. L. The effect of discrimination trai on stimulus generalization. *Amer. J. Psychol.*, in press.

42. Helson, H. Adaptation-level as a basis for a quantitative theory of fra of reference. *Psychol. Rev.*, 1948. 55, 297–313.

43. Honig, W. K. Prediction of preference, transposition, and transposi

reversal from the generalization gradient. Unpublished doctoral dissertation, Duke Univer., 1958.

Honig, W. K. Generalization of extinction on the spectral continuum. *Psychol. Record,* 1961, **11,** 269–278.

Honig, W. K., Thomas, D. R., & Guttman, N. Differential effects of massed extinction and discrimination training on the generalization gradient. *J. exp. Psychol.,* 1959, **58,** 145–152.

Hovland, C. I. The generalization of conditioned responses: I. The sensory generalization of conditioned responses with varying frequencies of tone. *J. gen. Psychol.,* 1937, **17,** 125–148.

Hull, C. L. *Principles of behavior.* New York: Appleton-Century-Crofts, 1943.

Jenkins, H. M., & Harrison, R. H. Effect of discrimination training on auditory generalization. *J. exp. Psychol.,* 1960, **59,** 246–253.

Kalish, H. I., & Guttman, N. Stimulus generalization after equal training on two stimuli. *J. exp. Psychol.,* 1957, **53,** 139–144.

Kalish, H. I., & Guttman, N. Stimulus generalization after training on three stimuli: a test of the summation hypothesis. *J. exp. Psychol.,* 1959, **57,** 268–272.

King, R. A., Wood, P., & Butcher, J. Decreased resistance to extinction as a function of reinforcement. *Amer. Psychologist,* 1961, **16,** 468. (Abstract of paper read at Amer. Psychol. Ass., New York, 1961.)

Klüver, H. *Behavior mechanisms in monkeys.* Chicago: Univer. of Chicago Press, 1933.

Köhler, W. *Gestalt psychology.* New York: Liveright, 1929.

Lashley, K. S., & Wade, M. The Pavlovian theory of generalization. *Psychol. Rev.,* 1946, **53,** 72–87.

Lawrence, D. H., & Miller, N. E. A positive relationship between reinforcement and resistance to extinction produced by removing a source of confusion from a technique that had produced opposite results. *J. exp. Psychol.,* 1947, **37,** 494–509.

Levine, M. A model of hypothesis behavior in discrimination learning set. *Psychol. Rev.,* 1959, **66,** 353–366.

Mach, E. *The analysis of sensations.* Chicago: Open Court Publishing, 1914.

MacLeod, S. The construction and attempted validation of sensory sweetness scales. *J. exp. Psychol.,* 1952, **44,** 316–323.

McNamara, H. J., Long, J. B., & Wike, E. L. Place learning without performance. *J. comp. physiol. Psychol.,* 1956, **49,** 478–479.

Mote, F. A. The effect of different amounts of reinforcement upon the acquisition and extinction of a simple running response. *J. exp. Psychol.* 1944, **34,** 216–226.

North, A. J., & Stimmel, D. T. Extinction of an instrumental response following a large number of reinforcements. *Psychol. Rep.,* 1960, **6,** 227–233.

Pavlov, I. P. *Conditioning reflexes.* G. V. Anrep (Trans.). London: Oxford Univer. Press, 1927.

63. Premack, D. Toward empirical behavior laws: I. Positive reinforcement. *Psychol. Rev.,* 1959, **66,** 219–233.

64. Reid, L. S. The development of noncontinuity behavior through continuity learning. *J. Psychol.,* 1953, **46,** 107–112.

65. Restle, F. Discrimination of cues in mazes: a resolution of the "place-vs.-response" question. *Psychol. Rev.* 1957, **64,** 217–228.

66. Restle, F. Toward a quantitative description of learning set data. *Psychol. Rev.,* 1958, **65,** 77–91.

67. Schlosberg, H., & Solomon, R. L. Latency of response in a choice discrimination. *J. exp. Psychol.,* 1943, **33,** 22–39.

68. Shephard, R. N. Stimulus and response generalization: deduction of the generalization gradient from a trace model. *Psychol. Rev.,* 1958, **65,** 242–256.

69. Shuford, E. H., Jr. Palatability and osmotic pressure of glucose and sucrose as determinants of intake. *J. comp. physiol. Psychol.,* 1959, **52,** 150–153.

70. Skinner, B. F. The generic nature of the concepts of stimulus and response. *J. gen. Psychol.,* 1935, **12,** 40–65.

71. Skinner, B. F. *The behavior of organisms.* New York: Appleton-Century-Crofts, 1938.

72. Skinner, B. F. The operational analysis of psychological terms. *Psychol. Rev.,* 1945, **52,** 270–277.

73. Skinner, B. F. Are theories of learning necessary? *Psychol. Rev.,* 1950, **57,** 193–216.

74. Skinner, B. F. Pigeons in a pelican. *Amer. Psychologist,* 1960, **15,** 28–37.

75. Smedslund, J. The problem of "What is learned?" *Psychol. Rev.,* 1953, **60,** 157–158.

76. Spence, K. W. The differential response in animals to stimuli varying within a single dimension. *Psychol. Rev.,* 1937, **44,** 430–444.

77. Stevens, S. S. On the psychophysical law. *Psychol. Rev.,* 1957, **64,** 153–181.

78. Terrace, H. S. Discrimination learning with and without "errors." Unpublished doctoral dissertation, Harvard Univer., 1961.

79. Thomas, D. R. Operant discrimination and generalization as a function of motivation. Unpublished doctoral dissertation, Duke Univer., 1961.

80. Thomas, D. R., & King, R. A. Stimulus generalization as a function of level of motivation. *J. exp. Psychol.,* 1959, **57,** 323–328.

81. Von Holst, E. Relations between the central nervous system and the peripheral organs. *Brit. J. Anim. Behav.,* 1954, **2,** 89–94.

82. Wyckoff, L. B., Jr. A mathematical model and an electronic model for learning. *Psychol. Rev.,* 1954, **61,** 89–97.

83. Zener, K. E., & Gaffron, Mercedes. Perceptual experience: an analysis of its relations to the external world through internal processings. In S. Koch (Ed.), *Psychology: a study of a science.* Vol. 4. New York: McGraw-Hill, 1962.

THE NATURE OF A STIMULUS: SOME RELATIONSHIPS BETWEEN LEARNING AND PERCEPTION

DOUGLAS H. LAWRENCE
Department of Psychology
Stanford University

Introduction 179
Psychophysics and Learning. 180
    Psychophysical assumptions 180
    Learning-theory assumptions 183
Learning-theory Approaches to Set. 183
    Receptor-adjustment behaviors 184
    Additive hypothesis 185
    Substitute-stimulus hypothesis 186
Coding-response Hypothesis. 187
    Coding and coding operations 187
    Coding responses 189
    Selection of coding responses 190
    Shifts in S-R correlations 191
Implications of Coding Hypothesis 192
    Coding systems and physical dimensions. 193
    Attributes 195
    Organizations of coding responses 197
Applications to Experimental Problems 198
    Perceptual problems 198
    Continuity in learning 200
    Relational responding. 202
    Conditional responding 203
    Similarity and generalization. 205
    Transfer. 209
References. 211

INTRODUCTION

This chapter deals with a limited aspect of the relationship between perception and learning, especially with those common problems that are

traditionally assigned to the influence of set, instructions, attitudes, a
like factors. Although these problems are common to the two fields, lit
progress has been made in finding a common solution for them. This
not due to any lack of similarity in the methodological approaches us
in learning and in perception. As Graham [12, 13] and others ha
pointed out, both fit a stimulus-response formulation. In each some
ternal event called a stimulus is manipulated, and the correspondi
changes in behavior are noted. In this sense each establishes a corre
tion or association between these two types of variables. The lack
agreement in accounting for the influences of sets, instructions, attitud
and like factors seems to stem more from a lack of a common langua
or a common set of concepts.

In keeping with the bias of the author, the present attempt at rec
ciliation employs concepts derived primarily from learning theory. B
cally the approach is one of translating these old problems into a n
language. Such translations can be misleading if their results are ta
as an explanation rather than a restatement. On the other hand, t
can be helpful if they suggest new relationships between problems a
new approaches to their solution. As a background for the pres
formulation, some of the implicit assumptions underlying the psyc
physical method are first reviewed. Secondly, some of the previous
tempts by learning theory to handle the problems of set and instructi
are briefly outlined. These two surveys made possible a comparison a
contrast with the present development.

PSYCHOPHYSICS AND LEARNING

Psychophysical Assumptions

The logic of the perceptual, or more specifically the psychophysi
method centers about the concept of correlation. The observer is
sented with a wide variety of stimulus events to each of which he re
with one of a set of responses. As there are usually more stimulus ev
than response categories, each response is elicited by more than on
the stimulus events. These latter are a class of equivalent stimuli
respect to a given response. Having established this correspondence
correlation, between stimulus classes and response categories, the psy
physicist then looks at the physical characteristics of the stimuli, e.g.,
frequency and intensity aspects of a group of tones. He determines
relative weight each of these characteristics has in the total correlat
If in the case of tones he can demonstrate two things, first, that inte
tends to differentiate between the stimulus classes but not within t

and, secondly, that other characteristics such as frequency tend to differentiate within but not between stimulus classes, then he is willing to speak of a stimulus dimension, or attribute, such as loudness.

This correlation is clearly an abstraction, both at the stimulus and at the response end. If all the behavior of the subject at the time, including his posture, his orientation, etc., and all the stimuli controlling this behavior, including kinesthetic, tactual, etc., are considered, it is clear that the psychophysicist is concerned only with changes in the stimulus situation that are correlated with changes in that limited set of responses he has selected for study. He implicitly assumes that the total sensory input can be divided into two functional parts: the static stimuli that maintain and continue ongoing activity and the phasic stimuli correlated with limited changes in behavior. Only the phasic stimuli are of primary interest to him. The role of the static stimuli in perception and learning is rarely given explicit recognition except in the work of Freeman [5] and a few others.

A second implicit assumption determining the nature of the correlations obtained hinges on the psychophysicist's choice of the physical variables used to describe the stimulus events. For instance, physicists have found that the most valuable description of a set of tones is in terms of frequency and intensity spectra. Knowing these they are able to reconstruct the tones. In this sense these spectra are "basic" descriptions. Perhaps for this reason the psychophysicist has tended to retrict his stimulus-response correlations to these "basic" variables. It is clear, however, that a very large number of variables can be defined that will order and partially describe any given set of stimulus events. These will be derived measures in the sense of being ratios, differences, sums, and like patterns of relationships between the parts of a complex stimulus event. These may not be the most useful descriptions from the physicist's point of view, but they may greatly simplify the psychophysical correlations that are obtained. It is always theoretically possible that a derived measure of this type can be defined that will give a simpler functional relation between stimuli and responses than obtains when "basic" physical measures are used [cf. 8, 9].

A third implicit assumption made by the psychophysicist undoubtedly stems from his use of mature and highly trained subjects who give stimulus-response correlations that are stable with time. Consequently he is little concerned with the genesis of these correlations. He admits that learning and past experience are involved to some extent. The fact that one tone is called loud and the other soft or that one color is called blue and the other red obviously depends upon learning. Nevertheless, the implied assumption of psychophysics, or at least sensationalistic psychology, seems to be that the correlations are basically innate and unlearned. These approaches assume that any learning observed is an artifact of the measurement process. The implication is that with the proper physiological techniques, it would be possible to demonstrate that from the first each stimulus class gives rise to a specific though covert reaction. In this sense there are "true," a priori, innate correlations between stimulus and response. But in lieu of these physiological techniques, it is necessary through learning to substitute overt, measurable responses for these covert reactions. Consequently, any systematic changes in the psychophysical correlations probably stem from this indirect nature of our present measuring procedures. Basically it seems to be this type of argument that permits the psychophysicist to ignore the extensive empirical findings which show that these correlations do change considerably during repeated experience with the stimulus material [7].

Finally it should be noted that there is one important variable in all psychophysical studies which the experimenter uses but to which he rarely gives explicit recognition in his theoretical formulations. This is the role played by sets, instructions, attitudes, and like variables in determining the nature of the correlation obtained. For instance, suppose that the stimuli consist of tones generated by the random pairing of intensity and frequency. If the subject is instructed to respond to loudness but to ignore pitch, his responses are highly correlated with intensity but only to a minor extent with frequency. If now he is instructed to respond to pitch but to ignore loudness, this correlation suddenly shifts so that frequency carries most of the weight and intensity very little. In this illustration it is true that the response terms as well as the correlation between stimuli and responses vary with these changes in instructions. In the first instance the subject says loud-soft and in the second high-low. This is irrelevant, however, for in each case exactly the same overt behavior, such as saying the numbers one through ten, can be employed. Then even though the set of stimuli and the set of responses are unchanged, a change in instructions completely modifies the nature of the correlation between them.

This influence of instructions is highly convenient for the psychophysicist. It provides him with a method for determining the range of psychological attributes involved for any given set of stimuli. At the same time it poses a difficult problem. All our theories about behavior tend to assume a direct association between the stimulus and the response. In so far as this association has been established through learning, it has a relatively long history of practice and reinforcement. It can only be modified in a like manner, i.e., by continued practice of the new association. There is little if any allowance in our theories for sudden and immediate changes brought about by instructions or like factors.

Learning-theory Assumptions

Learning theory like psychophysics tends to formulate its problems in terms of stimulus-response correlations. There are two major ways, however, in which these fields differ: The learning theorist is interested primarily in the genesis and development of the stimulus-response correlations. He is only secondarily interested in the nature of this function once it has stabilized. His concepts of reinforcement, extinction, habit strength, and the like are concerned with the conditions necessary for the strengthening and weakening of such associations. But while he stresses changes in these correlations as the result of experience and practice, his formulations are concerned primarily with quantitative changes in them, not with qualitative changes. He is interested in showing that through reinforcement priorly existing associations that were too weak to be elicited become strong enough to have measurable influences on performance. He is much less interested in the possibility that there may be a qualitative shift in these correlations with experience; i.e., responses that originally were dependent on one characteristic of the stimuli later become dependent on a different one.

A second difference between the learning approach and psychophysics is in the analysis of the stimulus event. The learning theorist tends to take the stimulus as a given, easily defined and manipulated unit. He is satisfied with a relatively global description of it as a light or a tone. It is only in his concept of stimulus generalization that he explicitly recognizes the possibility of analyzing it in terms of dimensions or characteristics.

Despite the learning theorist's tendency to take stimuli as unanalyzed units, he can account readily for the psychophysical type of correlation by treating it as a form of discrimination. If the correlation is primarily between the intensity of a group of tones as stimuli and verbal labels as responses, this implies that frequency and other stimulus characteristics have been randomly paired with intensity during training. As a consequence the various intensities become differentially associated with the responses as the result of reinforcement, but the frequencies were equally associated with each response, because this aspect of the stimulus event has been equally reinforced in the conjunction with each of the responses. This formulation in terms of discrimination training readily fits any psychophysical correlation that is established.

LEARNING-THEORY APPROACHES TO SET

The major problem confronting learning theory is to account for any sudden shifts in these correlations as the result of instructions, sets, attitudes, or like factors. As indicated above, a correlation based primarily on intensity is only possible if the various frequencies involved have been equally associated with each response. But if the various frequencies have been equally associated with each response, then these frequencies cannot be the basis for a psychophysical correlation regardless of additional instructions that are given. These frequencies can become correlated with the responses only if further training is given during which the correlation on the basis of the intensities is lost. Only one such correlation can exist at a given time for a given set of tones. Thus learning theory is faced with a difficult problem in explanation whenever the correlation shifts suddenly from primary dependency on one physical aspect of the stimuli to another.

Receptor-adjustment Behaviors

Learning theory has attempted to cope with this problem of set in a variety of ways. The most frequent approach has been to postulate changes in the proximal-stimulus event even though the distal stimulus remains constant. The presumed mechanism has been that of orientation behavior or receptor-adjustment acts. Included here are more complex forms of response that might be called stimulus-application behaviors. For example, the proximal stimulus from contact with a piece of sandpaper will vary greatly depending upon whether the finger is placed on it or drawn rapidly across it. Again in taste the proximal stimulus from a given substance will be very different depending upon how the subject controls his breathing, distributes the substance over his tongue, and the like. In each of these instances the correlation between the distal-stimulus characteristics and the responses changes because the proximal stimulus that mediates this correlation is varying as the result of the subject's behavior. There can be little doubt that these behaviors can and do play an important part in determining the nature of the psychophysical correlations found and the sudden shifts in them that are observed.

Discussions of these orientation, receptor-adjustment, and stimulus-application behaviors, however, usually have overlooked one of the most important implications of this type of formulation. If such behaviors are to account for sudden shifts in correlation, they must be under control of stimulus events that are relatively independent of those determining the overt behaviors being measured. If the presentation of a visual stimulus, for example, fully determined both the receptor-adjustment behavior and the overt response measured, the correlation between the stimulus and the response would be exactly the same on all occasions. Under such circumstances the distal stimulus would have fully determined the proximal stimulus when it determined the receptor-adjustment behavior. Shifts in correlation can occur only if the receptor-adjustment behavior, and thus the proximal stimulus, varies independently of the distal stimulus being judged. As long as it relies on this receptor-orientation type of mechanism, learning theory like psychophysics must make a distinction between two roles played by the total sensory input. Functionally part of it must be eliciting the changes in overt behavior that are being measured, and part of it must be controlling the receptor-adjustment and other continuing behaviors.

In addition to the above difficulty, there are many situations in which it is probable that these orientation, receptor-adjustment, and stimulus-application behaviors cannot account for the sudden shifts in correlation that are found. In the case of auditory stimuli, visual stimuli presented tachistoscopically, and the like, there is every reason for believing that the proximal stimulus is constant or nearly so. Nevertheless, shifts in correlation are observed. To account for these learning theory has resorted to a variety of postulated mechanisms intervening between the proximal stimulus and the response. These attempted solutions can be grouped in two general though overlapping types.

Additive Hypothesis

The first of these is the additive hypothesis. This attempts to explain the correlations observed by assuming that the "true" stimulus for overt behavior is a complex composed of external stimulus components plus covert components contributed by memory and past experience. Common examples are the sour taste associated with the sight of lemons and the feeling of coldness aroused by the sight of ice. There are difficulties with this type of formulation, however, as it applies to shifts in correlation between stimuli and responses. It assumes that any shifts in correlation are due to a change in the complex, i.e., that the component contributed by past experience or memory changes while the external component remains constant. There is, however, no theoretical basis for this functional independence of the two components. The covert component is presumably tied to the external one as the result of learning, so that given the latter, the former is determined.

In some instances an attempt has been made to provide independent control over the two stimulus components. Nevertheless, the additive hypothesis continues to have difficulty. This is most readily apparent in its account of conditional reactions of the type studied by Lashley [17]. In these studies the additive hypothesis assumes that the external stimulus situation can be analyzed into two components, the critical stimulus, such as the black-white cards in a jumping apparatus, and a surround, or context, stimulus. Each of these can be manipulated independently. When context A is present, the animal jumps to the black card, and when context B is present, it jumps to the white card. It is assumed that the animal is responding to a complex, the critical stimulus plus a surround. Consequently, when the surround changes, so does the complex. The result is a corresponding change in the correlation between the critical stimulus and the response.

The difficulties experienced by the additive hypothesis in explaining conditional reactions are not readily apparent in the simple example given above. But they are obvious enough when the set of stimuli and responses become larger. Suppose there are four different objects. When context A is present, the animal must associate each of these objects with a different response as represented by the pairings S1-R1, S2-R2, S3-R3, and S4-R4. When context B is present the same four responses are involved, but the stimulus-response pairings are represented by S1-R4, S2-R3, S3-R2, and S4-R1. Now if the complex for each reaction is the additive influence of the context stimulus plus the object stimulus, this becomes an impossible problem. Each context stimulus is equally associated with each of the four responses. Consequently, neither, when taken alone, has any tendency differentially to evoke the four responses, and, therefore, shifting from one context to the other cannot have any influence on the order in which the responses are evoked. This leaves only the object stimuli. But each of these has been equally associated with two different conflicting responses. Consequently, if the influence of a complex consists of the additive sum of the response-evoking tendencies of the context stimulus plus those of the object stimulus, there is no basis for either of the above correlations, let alone a shift from one to another.

Hull, recognizing this general difficulty, amended the additive hypothesis with the principle of afferent neural interaction [15]. This merely states that when S1 is combined with context A it is a different stimulus than when combined with context B, and that context A is a different stimulus when combined with S1 than when combined with S2. If this is the case, conditional reactions of this sort are feasible. However, this principle only states the desired solution to the problem. It does not indicate how such interactions between components of a complex are possible.

Substitute-stimulus Hypothesis

The second general approach used by Hullian learning theory to account for shifts in correlation is the substitute stimulus hypothesis. In the work of Dollard and Miller [4, 23] and others, it is assumed that each association between a proximal stimulus and a response is mediated. The proximal stimulus gives rise to an implicit, or covert, response which in turn produces an implicit, or covert, stimulus. It is this latter response-produced stimulus that elicits the overt behavior. The characteristics of this implicit response, and thus the characteristics of the response-produced stimulus, depend upon the conditions of training. Thus as the training varies, it is possible for these implicit responses, and the resulting implicit stimuli, to become modified until they are more discriminable, more distinctive, than were the initial implicit reactions to the proximal stimuli. Once this association between a proximal stimulus and an implicit reaction is established, it is relatively durable. It tends to be aroused in any new situation containing the proximal stimulus. The result is that new overt behaviors can be learned more rapidly in this new situation than is possible when this mediation process has not been established by past experience. Thus this formulation makes possible transfer between situations involving the same proximal stimuli that cannot be accounted for in the absence of these mediators [cf. 18]. It is as though familiarity with a set of proximal stimuli modifies them in such a way that new behaviors can be associated more rapidly with them than is possible in the absence of such familiarity.

This stimulus-substitution hypothesis, however, cannot account for sudden shifts in correlation between stimuli and responses. There is no basis for independent control of the proximal and response-produced stimuli. The latter are a direct function of the former. As a consequence, it has exactly the same difficulty as the additive hypothesis in attempting to explain how sets, instructions, attitudes, and like factors can shift the correlation.

CODING-RESPONSE HYPOTHESIS

The substitution hypothesis, however, does suggest a possible "conceptual" mechanism that accounts for these sudden shifts in correlation. The following is an attempt to show the logical possibilities of this mechanism and to indicate some of its implications for problems in perception and learning. Again it should be emphasized that this involves basically a translation of these problems into a new language based on learning-theory concepts. It is a way of conceptualizing these problems, not an empirically grounded explanation of them. The approach is analogous to recent formulations by Hebb and Gibson in that it divides the usual stimulus-response association into two parts with learning occurring within the perceptual, or "sensory," component and within the response, or motor, component.

Coding and Coding Operations

It is first assumed that all stimulus-response correlations are mediated; i.e., the correlation between the response and the proximal stimulus is never direct but always depends upon an intervening event. The conceptual device used to describe this intervening, or mediating, event is similar to the idea of coding. By coding the following is meant: If there is a set of objects or events and to each of them a different label is assigned, then the labels code these objects or events. More generally whenever a one-to-one correspondence between two sets of events is established, either set of events can be taken as a code representing the other set. Nothing more than this is implied by the term coding as used in the present context.

In the above illustration, however, the correspondence between a set of events and its code is arbitrarily determined. Any one of the labels can be associated with any one of the events. In most actual instances of coding, this arbitrariness is reduced. In these a set of rules, which will be called the coding operation, is established. Given these rules and the set of events to be coded, it then is fully determined as to which item of the code is associated with a given event. It is in this sense that numbers in statistics are said to be coded when a constant is subtracted from each. These code items are different from the original data but yet contain all the information necessary for certain computations. The use of the term coding can be extended to include cases in which the original data consists of pairs of numbers. If the differences or ratios of these pairs are computed, then these are code items representing aspects of the original data. In such cases it is the relationships within that data that are coded. Thus whenever a constant operation or transformation is made on a set of quantities, the result of such an operation is a coding system.

The concept of coding is equally applicable to the interactions between physical objects and events. It is only in a proleptic sense that one can speak of the weights and heights of a set of physical objects. These weights and heights are potentialities of the objects, but they are actualized only by some operation of weighing or measuring. In this case the operations depend upon physical interactions, not mathematical transformations, but nonetheless they can be thought of as coding operations in that they assign code items, the actual weights and heights, to each object.

These operations may involve quite directly forms of overt behavior on the part of individuals. Again it is only in a proleptic sense that one can speak of the vibration rates of a set of wires of different lengths, masses, and tensions. First some operation, such as plucking the strings, must be performed before these potentialities can be realized. This behavior is a coding operation, because as a result of this interaction with the objects a code item, the vibration rate, is assigned to each.

These illustrations emphasize the following characteristics of a coding process: The same operation applied to a set of different objects produces a series of code items, i.e., a coding system. This operation can be a naturalistic interaction between physical events and may involve overt behavior on the part of an individual. The resulting code item need correlate with, or represent, only limited aspects of the original event, not the event in its entirety; e.g., length and height are correlated with the areal extent of objects but not necessarily with the mass. Furthermore, these code items may at times represent relationships between characteristics of the object; e.g., the vibration rate of a string varies directly with its tension but inversely with its length and mass. In such cases the same coding operation performed on two different objects may result in the same code item. Finally it should be emphasized that in all instances the factors determining the selection of a coding operation tend to be independent of the factors determining the presence or absence of the event to be coded. An event rarely if ever dictates the coding operation; this latter depends upon the problem to be solved, the social context in which it occurs, and like factors. Consequently, in so far as much of our everyday behavior is determined by code items rather than directly by the events with which the items are associated, i.e., we react more to our symbolic representation of things than to the things per se, it is necessary to consider both the factors that determine the event and the factors that determine the coding operation if we wish to predict the resulting behavior.

Coding Responses

It is this general schema that is to be applied to the sensory input of the organism. The sensory input as represented by the proximal stimulus corresponds to the physical objects in the above examples. But in its role as an elicitor of behavior, its properties are unspecified until a coding operation is determined. Corresponding to the coding operation in the above examples, it is assumed that the subject makes an implicit, covert response. Calling it a response is somewhat misleading, because normally a response is thought of as something elicited by the stimulus event. The assumption here, however, is that this implicit response is aroused by factors other than the sensory input under discussion. Nonetheless, it is to be thought of as a form of instrumental behavior. The reason for calling it an instrumental response is that such behavior interacts with environmental events to produce new stimuli, as when the bar pressing of a rat in the Skinner box produces the click of the food-release mechanism. Similarly this assumed implicit response operates on the sensory input. It is called a coding response because in interaction with the sensory input it produces a new event or code item which then represents the stimulus. This new event is the "stimulus-as-coded" or "stimuli-as-coded" (s-a-c). It is this s-a-c that is directly associated with, and elicits, the overt behavior being measured.

Thus the general schema is as follows: there is a sensory input; this is acted upon by the coding response, an implicit reaction that is controlled by factors other than the proximal stimulus; the consequence of this interaction is the s-a-c; and it is this latter that is directly associated with the overt behavior.

The plausibility of this formulation hinges to a large extent on what is assumed about the establishment, maintenance, and modification of the coding response. Here it is assumed that the form taken by this response is in most instances the result of learning. The qualification "in most instances" is used advisedly so as to reserve the possibility that in some cases motivational, endocrineal, emotional, and like factors may innately determine the coding response, especially in lower animals. This would permit the formulation to be integrated with some of the findings of the ethologists. The emphasis in this paper, however, is on the establishment and modification of the coding response through training and past experience.

Selection of Coding Responses

In the present formulation learning tends to involve the establishment of two habits simultaneously. Through essentially a trial-and-error process, the organism must determine an appropriate coding response and at the same time develop an association between the resulting s-a-c and the overt response. The feasibility of such learning can be illustrated best by a simplified example.

Assume that at the choice point of a T maze an animal is confronted with either a circle or a square. Each of these can be either black or white, and each can be either large or small. The problem is so arranged that when the stimulus object is black, irrespective of its size or shape, the animal must turn to the right in order to be rewarded, and when it is white, he must turn to the left. It is assumed that when the animal is first introduced to this situation he has a limited repertory of coding responses that are elicited by this T-maze context. These are rc-1, a coding response such that it produces s-a-c primarily correlated with the brightness aspects of the input but not with the shape or size characteristics; rc-2, which produces s-a-c primarily correlated with size; and rc-3, which produces s-a-c primarily correlated with shape. If initially rc-2 is elicited, for whatever reason, it is clear that the problem cannot be solved, because the s-a-c it produces have no consistent relationship to the rewards in the situation. In common-sense terms the animal is reacting to size, not brightness. Consequently, no amount of trial and error in his overt behavior will lead to consistent reinforcement as long as this coding response is elicited at each trial. It is assumed that the consequence of this inconsistent reinforcement is a change in the coding response. The next one elicited may well be rc-1, which produces s-a-c primarily correlated with brightness. Now trial and error in his overt behavior can lead to the discovery of the correct response for each stimulus event.

Thus the learning of a naïve animal in this situation involves a two-stage process. At the "sensory" end an appropriate coding response must first be elicited, i.e., one which produces s-a-c which are correlated with the same aspects of the sensory input as are the reinforcements in the situation. Once such a coding response is elicited, the "motor" association between the resulting s-a-c and overt responses can be established. The entire process, however, takes place simultaneously much in the manner now postulated for the serial chaining of behaviors. Consequently, the learning curve in the naïve animal would still exhibit gradual and continuous improvement.

It should be emphasized that once the appropriate coding response is elicited and consistently followed by reinforcement, it would tend to become associated with the contextual or unchanging aspects of the test situation, e.g., aspects of the maze stem, spatial cues, drive states, and the like. Consequently, during this learning process the total sensory input is being divided into two functional parts: the stable and unchanging aspects that elicit the appropriate coding response and the critical or changing aspects that through their interaction with the coding response control the overt behavior.

In the above example the impression is given that the set of possible coding responses is very limited and that each produces a system of s-a-c correlated with only limited aspects of the critical stimuli. A more realistic conception is to assume that the range of possible coding responses in this situation is practically unlimited. Many of these are similar in the sense that each produces s-a-c correlated in part with the brightness aspects of the critical stimulus but also dependent upon other irrelevant aspects of the situation such as spatial, tactual, and auditory characteristics. In so far as the s-a-c resulting from any of these are correlated with brightness, any one of these coding responses is adequate for solving the problem. Nonetheless, because their s-a-c are also dependent upon irrelevant chance aspects of the situation, it is difficult to set up an entirely consistent discrimination on the basis of such a coding response. This being the case, any further modification of the coding response that would produce s-a-c more strictly correlated with brightness and less dependent upon irrelevant aspects leads to more consistent reinforcement. Allowing for this possibility, it is clear that part of the continued improvement in discrimination may result from modifications in the coding response rather than from the continued strengthening of already established associations.

Shifts in S-R Correlations

This schematic account of the learning of a coding response must be extended, however, in order to account for any sudden shifts in the stimulus-response correlations. A paridigm for such shifts in correlation, based upon the previous example, is the following: Assume that in T-maze A, the animal is to be taught to respond to the brightness character-istics of the critical stimuli at the choice point, turning right to black and left to white. However, in T-maze B, where the stimulus characteristics of the stem and other stable features of the situation are different from those in A, the animal is to be taught to turn left for large stimulus ob-jects and right for small ones, irrespective of their brightness or shape. If the animal masters both these problems, then there is an obvious shift in the stimulus-response correlations between maze A and maze B even though the critical stimuli and the overt responses are exactly the same in each.

To account for this type of learning, it is assumed that the animal has solved maze A in the manner previously described. He is then intro-duced to maze B. In so far as the stable, contextual aspects of this maze have some similarity to those in maze A, they tend as the result of gen-eralization to elicit the coding response appropriate to maze A. But as this produces s-a-c correlated with brightness rather than size, the result is some degree of negative transfer. Consistent reinforcement cannot be obtained as long as this coding response persists. Consequently, the gen-eralized association between this coding response and the contextual cues in maze B extinguishes, and a new coding response is elicited. If this lat-ter is one that produces s-a-c which are dependent, at least in part, upon size variables, the new problem can be mastered. The resulting con-sistent reinforcement establishes an association between this new cod-ing response and those contextual aspects specific to maze B. At this stage of training, the animal reacts to brightness in maze A and to size in maze B. The basis for this selective reaction is the fact that one coding re-sponse is elicited by the contextual aspects specific to maze A and a different coding response by those contextual aspects characteristic of maze B.

IMPLICATIONS OF CODING HYPOTHESIS

Phrased in this way, this proposed coding mechanism, it is ap-parent, stems from the same general conception that gave rise to emphasis on receptor-adjustment and substitute-stimulus hypotheses. In each the stimulus-response correlation is mediated. In the case of receptor-adjust-ment behavior the intervening event is the proximal stimulus that varies as the receptor adjustment changes; in the substitute-stimulus hypoth-esis it is the response-produced stimulus that varies as the result of learn-ing; and in the coding-response formulation it is the s-a-c that are con-trolled by changes in the coding response. Despite this similarity, however, the present formulation goes beyond the other two in its implications.

The most obvious of these implications is the wide range of values and forms it permits the s-a-c to take. With a fixed sensory input it assumes that each different coding response produces a new s-a-c. Thus, there is a whole family of potential code items corresponding to each proximal stimulus event. On the other hand when the coding response is constant, each new sensory input produces a different s-a-c. But under these circumstances the set of s-a-c produced by a given coding response tends to form a system, i.e., to be ordered in the same sense that a mathematical function orders a set of values.

Perhaps these conceptions are somewhat clearer when phrased in the following way: Given a set of proximal stimuli, such as tones, a physicist can specify certain of their properties. This he does by applying any one of a number of operations to the proximal stimulus. One such operation codes it with respect to its intensity, a second with respect to frequency, and so on. Each of these operations produces a "physical" coding system that orders the stimulus events with respect to a given dimension. In the same sense, each organism is assumed to operate by means of implicit coding responses on the proximal stimulus. The result of this interaction between the coding response and the stimulus event is a code item, called an s-a-c. All the s-a-c resulting from a given coding response form a "psychological" coding system which orders the stimulus events with respect to some attribute. The nature of this ordering can be determined indirectly. The necessary methodology is that found in studies on psychological scaling. Once this ordering is determined, moreover, it is possible to correlate this psychological coding system with various physical ones, as when tonal volume is correlated with intensity and frequency.

Coding Systems and Physical Dimensions

The nature of the relationship between the physical and psychological coding systems for any given set of sensory inputs may take a variety of forms. In many instances the s-a-c may correlate highly with some physical aspects of the stimulus and not with others. This tends to be the case in loudness judgments. A physical description of the tone involves the specification of both intensity and frequency. Nonetheless, the system of s-a-c corresponding to loudness is correlated primarily with intensity and only secondarily with frequency. The same is often true in the case of visual stimuli. An adequate physical description involves specification of wavelength, intensity, areal extent, and so on. But depending upon the nature of the coding response employed by the individual, the resulting system of s-a-c may have sizable correlations with only one or two of these physical dimensions. Thus in many instances the functional stimulus, or s-a-c, to which the individual reacts may be related to only a selected aspect of the sensory input as this is defined physically.

In most instances the relationships between the physical and psychological coding systems will be of a highly complex nature. This presumably results in large part from the different criteria used in developing these coding systems. The physical system has been developed so as to facilitate the prediction of interactions between physical events. By specifying the energy and frequency spectra of a tone, the physicist is then able to predict how this event will interact with some other physical system, such as a mechanical one. On the other hand, the criteria for determining whether or not a given individual can interact with his environment successfully may be of a very different nature. These criteria often center about object discrimination and identification. When the subject sees a light on the highway at night, the important question for him is whether it is a motorcycle, an automobile, or a street lamp. Perhaps such discriminations are most efficiently made when based on a coding system correlated with a variety of aspects of the situation and their interrelationships rather than with the coding systems traditionally employed by the physicist. That is, the code items may depend upon ratios or other relational aspects of the input rather than its absolute properties. Consequently, the two coding systems, that employed by the physicist and that resulting from a given coding response, need not be related in any simple way. But there is always the possibility that the physicist can define a new operation that will produce a coding system directly related to the one produced by a given coding response. To achieve this, he frequently may have to resort to the use of "derived," i.e., relational-type, measures rather than "basic" measures in the description of the physical stimuli. Thus, the present formulation permits the establishment of stimuli-response correlations, but these are likely to be more complex than those sought previously in the history of psychophysics.

Another difference frequently found between the physical and psychological coding systems is in terms of their relative degrees of broadness. It is usual in psychophysics to use a rather narrow definition of the proximal stimulus. The psychophysicist tends to take a selected aspect of the total sensory input as the proximal stimulus to investigate, and frequently this selected aspect is limited to a given sensory modality. In investigating audition, for instance, he takes the intensity and frequency spectra of the tone as an adequate description of the stimulus event, ignoring all the visual, tactual, and kinesthetic input occurring at the same time. This limited description is adequate for his purposes within the bounds of the laboratory, for here the other aspects of the input are more or less held constant. But in many real-life situations, this restricted definition of the proximal stimulus to a given sensory modality is inadequate. Keeping in mind that the criteria for efficient interaction with the environment requires such things as valid object discrimination and recognition, it is apparent that the necessary coding must be related to the sensory input from a variety of sensory modalities. For instance, if the discrimination and identification of a wine depends upon its "dryness," the most efficient coding response would be one that produced a system of s-a-c that related to gustatory, olfactory, and tactual aspects of the sensory input. The argument is not that the psychophysicist is unable to give a physical coding to all these aspects of the sensory input and relate them to the judgmental behavior of the subject; rather, that he rarely does so. On the other hand, the present thesis is that many of the coding responses used by the individual may produce systems of s-a-c that correlate with aspects from several sensory modalities. When this occurs, as possibly in the case of the "dryness" of wines, the resulting system of s-a-c form a psychological attribute in exactly the same sense as does "loudness." But it is an attribute that is broadly based on a wide range of aspects of the sensory input.

Previous emphasis on sensory modalities in classifying psychophysical relationships has led to some confusion. The definition of a sensory modality is based largely on extrapsychological considerations. It is defined in terms of the specific group of receptors that are activated on any occasion. Once the distinction is made on these grounds, however, it is implicitly carried over into discussions of behavior. It is assumed that any time two such groups of receptors are simultaneously activated, there then must be two distinct and independent factors controlling behavior. For instance, if an individual has experienced a train blowing its whistle, there is a strong tendency to formulate his experience of this event in terms of a visual and an auditory image as though these must of necessity be distinct and segregated experiences. The forced nature of this distinction becomes clear in other situations such as everyday taste discriminations. To be consistent with the above, it is necessary to say that each such discrimination involves a gustatory, olfactory, tactual, and temperature image, even though the individual is unaware of them and cannot distinguish between their contributions. In such instances it seems much more natural to formulate the result as a single stimulus-response correlation rather than as a collection of them. To do so, however, implies that the stimulus unit involved need have little relationship to the conventional modality distinctions.

Attributes

In the present formulation any given response tends to be elicited by a single s-a-c. This latter is the "effective" stimulus for overt behavior.

It is always a member of a coding system, i.e., that set of resultants from the interaction between a single coding response and a variety of sensory inputs. Such a system corresponds most closely to what traditionally has been called an attribute. There is no implication, however, that the code items, the s-a-c, in such a system must correlate only with physical dimensions of stimuli in a single modality. If the dryness of wines is a system dependent upon a single coding response, it is an attribute even though the s-a-c in the system are correlated jointly with gustatory, olfactory, and tactual components.

Again, if only those coding systems are considered whose s-a-c are exclusively correlated with physical dimensions in a single modality, there are many more of them than has been traditionally asserted. Many of them are joint functions of several "basic" dimensions, i.e., correlated with "derived" measures in the sense that volume in audition is considered to be a joint function of frequency and intensity. Such an assumption is necessary if one is to account for the sixteen or more visual attributes listed by Helsen [14].

Finally each of these coding systems, irrespective of the aspects of the physical input with which its s-a-c are correlated, has the same logical status as any other. This gets rid of the ambiguity in the usual use of the term "quality." At times this refers to the distinction between modalities, such as in the difference between pitch and color, and at times to the specific values within an attribute, such as in the differences between blue and red. In the present formulation pitch and color represent two different coding systems, whereas colors are probably items within a given system. On the other hand, if the difference between color and pitch is to be described as qualitative, then the difference between loudness and pitch is equally qualitative.

Once it is granted that coding systems can vary as widely as this, then the Gibsons [10] are justified in considering much of learning to be a matter of discovering new aspects of the stimulus situation rather than the building up of associations. These discoveries are a matter of developing new coding responses. As each coding response actualizes some of the potentialities in the sensory input, each additional one "discovers" something new in the proximal stimulus. The two-point tactual threshold may be such a case. Initially, for instance, the subject's discrimination may be based on s-a-c correlated primarily with pressure components of the stimulus. For a given separation of the points, the s-a-c produced might be highly similar to that produced by a single point. If now a new coding response is brought into play that produces s-a-c correlated with the tactual stimuli from skin deformation, it is conceivable that the same spatial separation of the points produces an s-a-c that is clearly distinguished from that due to a single point. Such a process gives continued improvement in the differential threshold, but this is not due to improved discrimination within a single attribute. Rather, the subject has discovered a new attribute that permits more efficient discrimination.

Organizations of Coding Responses

If the coding system based on a single coding response is taken as the basic unit of analysis, it is clear that these can become organized into a variety of complex groupings. This occurs as the result of learning. In everyday situations many successful reactions depend only on the discrimination of the presence or absence of some event. This is the case in conditioning experiments where the identification is merely of the presence or absence of the conditioned stimulus, such as a tone. As a consequence, any coding system whose s-a-c are correlated with aspects of the auditory stimulus, either in whole or in part, can be the basis for this discrimination. Or in more complex instances such as the identification of the presence or absence of a blast from a steam whistle, coding systems that produce s-a-c correlated with either the characteristics of the auditory, the visual, or some joint function of these two modalities would provide the basis for the discrimination. In each of these illustrations, the coding responses underlying these systems form a group of equivalent behaviors. Assuming that they have been elicited successively on the same occasion or even on different occasions but in the same context, they can form a habit family in the Hullian sense [16]. Thus they become more interrelated and interdependent than do any two randomly chosen coding responses, at least within that context. Within such a family of coding responses each member has an implicative relationship with every other. If the individual's experience is appropriate whenever one of these coding responses occurs, i.e., whenever it produces s-a-c on the basis of which a discrimination can be made, then the other coding responses also are appropriate. This is not true for members from different families.

More complex organizations of these families of coding responses are possible because of the inclusion of coding systems that are jointly correlated with several modalities. These organizations are analogous to the part-whole relationship. Suppose the dryness of wines is such a coding system, its s-a-c being jointly determined by gustatory, olfactory, and tactual components. In addition to this coding response, there can be three families of coding responses, one corresponding to each of the three modalities. Consequently, any time the coding system for dryness is appropriate, it implies that each of these families is also appropriate. In its absence, however, no one of these families implies the other, nor does any of them imply the coding response for dryness. Thus while the relationships between coding responses within a family are transitive and symmetrical, this is not true for the present type of organization. It is a hierarchical ordering. The relationship between the coding system for dryness and the families is asymmetrical, and there is no implicative relationships between the three families.

It must be emphasized that in this discussion the relationships are between coding responses, not between the specific s-a-c each produces. In any sense of the term, the s-a-c corresponding to dryness are as qualitatively different from those corresponding to the gustatory component as are the latter from those corresponding to the tactual component. The first does not contain the other two as units or parts. These relationships must be thought of as analogous to those among a hierarchy of concepts. When an object is classified as a "house," it implies that a number of subordinate characteristics are determinable, such as floors, windows, and walls. It does not specify the determinant value of any of these, i.e., that the walls are brick, stucco, or wood. Similarly, one coding response can imply a second, but it does not entail any specific value for the s-a-c produced.

APPLICATIONS TO EXPERIMENTAL PROBLEMS

The postulation of coding responses and the assumption of various forms of organization between them permits a reinterpretation of a number of problems in perception and learning. One of these problems is that of "restructuring" the sensory input. If an individual is reacting on the basis of a coding response whose s-a-c are correlated with stimulus characteristics of several modalities or several characteristics of a given modality, theoretically it is always possible for him to develop new coding responses dependent upon only subsets of these components or characteristics. Thus where there formerly was a single functional stimulus, there now are two or more. Conversely, if the individual has several coding responses, each dependent upon a different set of characteristics, theoretically it is always possible for him to establish a new coding response that is dependent upon the combined sets. Thus as judged by an individual's discriminations, restructuring can take the form of either analysis or integration.

Perceptual Problems

These possibilities underlie an individual's ability to report several characteristics of a stimulus object, such as its color, form, and brightness, after a brief exposure to it as in a tachistoscopic experiment. Suppose that he uses a coding response that is jointly dependent upon these three characteristics. This produces but a single s-a-c. There is no mechanism postulated that permits this to be broken down into specific values, one for each of the three characteristics involved. Instead it must be assumed that such a coding response permits him to identify the object and then from memory to specify its characteristics.

The implications of such an indirect procedure fit in well with the results from studies employing incongruous objects, e.g., a black six of hearts [cf. 2]. In this situation a coding response dependent upon the joint characteristics would produce a single s-a-c. This would be similar to two or more others that were associated with definite verbal responses, e.g., the black six of spades and the red six of hearts. At the same time it would be sufficiently different from them to mark it as unfamiliar. This should lead to conflict and an increase in recognition time. On the other hand, if the coding response used was dependent upon a more limited set of the object's characteristics, this would lead to immediate though incorrect identification of it as a familiar object. But in the reconstruction of its components from memory there would be a falsification of some of the object's true characteristics. These seem to be two of the more common types of reaction found in such situations.

Coding responses of the above class, which depend upon multiple characteristics of the stimulus object, are not feasible in the Külpe type of experiment. Here the values of color, form, and brightness are combined randomly and in a way that does not lead to object identification. Nevertheless, the individual is able to report with some degree of accuracy on each of these characteristics. In the present formulation it is necessary to assume that three different and successive coding responses are involved. In so far as these occur successively, it implies the additional assumptions of a stimulus or memory trace and that this is not destroyed by the application of any of the coding responses. But as this trace can be assumed to fade or change with time, the expectation is that the accuracy of report on the first characteristic will be greater than on the second and that this will be more accurate than on the third. Furthermore, if the individual is "set" by instructions for one of these characteristics but not for the others, his accuracy of report on the anticipated characteristic should be greater than on the others. The set ensures not only the elicitation of that coding response but also that it will occur first. Without a specific set the elicitation of the other two is less probable, for it depends upon the context of the task and the degree of organization among the three coding responses. It is not crucial, however, whether this set is given before or immediately after the stimulus presentation. In both cases the proximal stimulus and its trace must be available before the coding responses can operate. These implications concerning the Külpe type of experiment fit in well with recent experimental findings [20, 21].

The converse of this situation arises when there is a set of objects to be discriminated but each object can be defined only as a combination of physical characteristics. This is the case with four lights consisting of the four combinations of two colors and two brightnesses. In such instances two alternative accounts are possible: Correct discrimination can be the resultant of two successive coding responses, one for color and the other for brightness; the identification of the object is then a reconstruction from these two s-a-c. Alternatively, there can be a single coding response producing s-a-c correlated with a joint function of the two characteristics; each response then elicits a single s-a-c that permits identification. These are not conflicting alternatives, as each may occur under some circumstances. In the majority of instances the second seemingly is favored, however, as suggested by the frequency with which objects can be correctly identified without the individual's being able to report accurately on specific characteristics.

A similar problem arises in information theory with the attempt to define redundancy at the psychological level. If there are four lights each differing in brightness and in color, there is logical redundancy in that the lights can be distinguished by either characteristic alone. Consequently, it has been anticipated that discrimination would be increasingly accurate with increasing redundancy. The empirical findings, however, have been conflicting. Sometimes there is improvement and sometimes not. This is to be expected in terms of the present formulation, because there are basically four ways in which the individual can make these discriminations, only one of which makes use of the redundancy involved. The individual can use (1) a coding response dependent upon a joint function of the two characteristics, (2) one based on color alone, (3) one based on brightness alone, or (4) the latter two used in succession. There is no a priori reason why the sets of s-a-c produced by each of the first three should be different in discriminability. Only in the fourth case is improved identification anticipated. In that instance failure to discriminate for any reason on the basis of the first coding response can be corrected by the second. Thus the search for rules governing psychological redundancy cannot be restricted to variables in the physical stimulus. It must include factors controlling the coding responses used by the individual and the interaction of these with the characterisics of the stimulus.

Continuity in Learning

Perhaps of more general interest are the implications of this formulation for the continuity-noncontinuity controversy in learning theory. Two different questions are involved. The first is whether the establishment of associations is a continuous and gradual process or an all-or-none affair, and the second is whether all aspects of the stimulus situation become associated with the response or only selected ones. The main empirical evidence on this controversy has come from discrimination-reversal studies. These tend to show that if the pairing of reinforcement and critical cue in the discrimination is reversed during the early stages of training, i.e., before the subject is responding with better than chance accuracy, this retards the rate of mastery of the reversed discrimination. This finding has been interpreted as supporting both the idea of continuous learning and the idea that all aspects of the stimulus are associated with the response [3, 24].

It is apparent that the present formulation also favors the first assumption of the continuity hypothesis, i.e., of gradual increases in habit strength. Both the association between the s-a-c and the overt response and the establishment of the appropriate coding response are assumed to be continuous processes. On the other hand, it supports the contention that as a rule only selected aspects of the proximal stimulus are correlated with the s-a-c.

Two different implications follow from this assumption of selective responding. First, if the individual is responding on the basis of a coding response that is dependent upon only a limited set of the proximal stimulus characteristics, the other characteristics cannot become associated with the response even though they are physically present. Secondly, if the individual shifts to a new coding response that is dependent upon characteristics of the proximal stimulus other than the original ones, the first association established becomes nonfunctional. It is nonfunctional in the sense that it is neither strengthened nor weakened by additional training in the presence of the original set of stimulus characteristics.

Discrimination reversal studies have little direct bearing on either of these points. If in these studies the individual's coding response produces s-a-c that are in any way dependent upon the critical cues, irrespective of which other stimulus characteristics are involved, any reversal of the discrimination should retard learning. It is quite probable in most instances that such a coding response is present, because the design of the apparatus and the pretraining given is sufficient to ensure it. Thus the individual can be responding to selected characteristics of the proximal stimulus and yet show the results predicted by the continuity theory. Only if the system of s-a-c involved is in no way dependent upon the critical-stimulus characteristics does it follow that the rate of mastery of the discrimination should be unaffected by the reversal.

Data relevant to the second of the implications, i.e., that an association can become nonfunctional, comes from an experiment by Goodwin and Lawrence [11]. It employed two sets of cues, black-white alleys and high-low hurdles, randomly paired on successive trials in a simultaneous discrimination. Rats were first trained to the high hurdle as positive irrespective of whether it was black or white. The assumption was that during this training a coding response dependent on hurdles but independent of brightness was established, because the former were consistently but the latter only randomly reinforced. Without any change in the physical stimulus the reinforcement was then correlated with white irrespective of the hurdle with which it was paired. The assumption was that during this second discrimination a new coding response dependent upon brightness but independent of hurdles was established. As a test of these assumptions the reinforcement was again paired with the hurdle cues. For half the subjects the high hurdle was again positive just as on the first discrimination. For the other half the low hurdle was the positive cue. This had been the negative cue on the first discrimination.

If the assumption is correct that the associations based on hurdles were nonfunctional during the learning of the second, or black-white, discrimination, then the first group had only to revert in a consistent way to its previous coding response based on hurdles. Once this occurred, the discrimination would be mastered, for then the previously learned associations were available. The second not only had to revert to its previous coding response, but having done so it must reverse its former associations. This should greatly retard mastery of the third discrimination. If, on the other hand, the assumptions of the continuity theorists are correct, i.e., that all characteristics of the proximal stimulus become equally associated with the response, then there should be no difference between the two groups. The associations with the hurdle cues would have been erased during the training on the black-white discrimination because of the equal reinforcement and nonreinforcement each of the hurdle cues received. The results showed a marked difference between the two groups favoring the present formulation. This was true irrespective of the amount of overlearning given on the black-white discrimination. While not conclusive, this suggests that associations established under one coding response can become nonfunctional when there is a marked change in that coding response.

Relational Responding

Any attempt to formulate the nature of stimulus units must face the problem of relational responding. A discussion of this issue usually is confused by two different usages of the term relational. In one sense it implies that the correlations between behavior and sensory input often are more readily described in terms of differences, ratios, and like derived measures of the sensory input than in terms of absolute measures. If, for instance, an individual's behavior is most directly predicted from the ratio of two light intensities, this is taken as evidence for relational responding. The second usage of the term implies that an individual's reaction to a given unit in the sensory input varies as a function of the context in which that unit occurs. The question here is not whether the behavior is best predicted from derived measures of the stimulus. Rather, there is the implicit assumption that in some indirect way the context can modify the correlation between the unit and the response.

The first usage of the term relational presents no great difficulties for the present formulation. In analogy to null instruments it is easy to conceive of a coding response depending upon the relationship between two or more characteristics of the stimulus rather than upon their absolute values. Presumably many of the psychophysical studies on differential thresholds and experiments on frame of reference effects involve correlations of this type. The judgments involved frequently are of the "greater than" or "less than" type without any specification of exact values. But it should be noted that the present formulation does not give a priori preference to either relational responding or to responding in terms of the absolute properties of the stimulus. Either is possible. The one used in a given situation depends in part upon the past training of the individual and the present arrangement and demands of the task.

In many discussions of this problem it has been suggested that correlations based on derived measures of the stimulus imply a comparison process. But the usage of the term comparison process is ambiguous. In its restricted usage comparison implies that two logically distinct units or characteristics of the stimulus must be present simultaneously before the individual can respond to the relationship between them. This, however, merely says that there are alternative ways in which the sensory input can be described. The behavioral question is whether there is one process controlling the response or whether there are two. In the present formulation it is a question of whether there is one s-a-c correlated with some joint function of the two logically distinct units in the stimulus or whether there are two, one for each of the units. The broader usage of the comparison idea implies the latter with the further stipulation that the individual reacts to the relationships between them. If behavior is controlled in this way, it falls outside the present formulation. It demands a mechanism for interrelating distinct s-a-c that is not allowed for in this account.

Conditional Responding

The second usage of the term relational centers about the fact that the correlation between a given unit of the stimulus and the response changes as a function of changes in the context of that unit. The implication seems to be that a logical analysis of the sensory input has been made into a unit and its context. This unit is further analyzed into parts or characteristics. In context A the correlation between the unit and the response is dependent primarily upon one set of these characteristics, but then it shifts to dependency upon a different set in context B. For instance, if the logically designated unit is a tone, the individual reacts primarily to its loudness in one context but to its pitch in a second. In this sense his responses depend upon some relationship between the unit and its context.

As previously indicated most situations of this type can be formulated in terms of the paradigm for conditional reactions. To reiterate, assume that there are four tones, $T1$, $T2$, $T3$, and $T4$, each differing from the others in frequency and intensity. In addition, there are two context stimuli, A and B, and four overt responses, R1, R2, R3, and R4. When context A is present, the individual pairs the tones and responses in the order $T1$-R1, $T2$-R2, $T3$-R3, and $T4$-R4. When context B is present, he pairs them in the order $T1$-R3, $T2$-R4, $T3$-R1, and $T4$-R2. This is a conditional reaction in the sense that the correlation involved is conditional on the context. In the present formulation this type of reaction is possible if each context calls out an appropriate but different coding response, e.g., one that produces s-a-c primarily correlated with intensity and a second that produces s-a-c primarily correlated with frequency. The tones then are coded in two different systems each of which can be associated with the overt responses. The fundamental assumption is that the total sensory input can become separated during training into two functional parts, the context and the critical stimuli, and that each can play a different role in the resulting behavior. The context controls the coding response evoked, and the critical stimuli in interaction with these coding responses produces s-a-c that elicit the overt behaviors. The feasibility of this functional separation of the sensory input was demonstrated earlier.

A number of testable implications follow from this formulation. There should be differential effects on behavior depending upon whether changes are made in the critical stimuli or the context. If a fifth tone is added to the series that is intermediate with respect to the others in intensity and frequency, there should be conflict between two of the overt responses, such as R2 and R3, when context A is present, and between two different ones, such as R1 and R4, when context B is present. If, on the other hand, the contexts are modified, the conflict should be between the two overt responses paired with a given tone such as R1 and R3. Furthermore, the two stimulus-response orderings should be relatively independent. Changes in the associations between s-a-c and overt responses when context A is present should have relatively little transfer effect to the context-B situation even though the same set of critical stimuli are involved on both occasions.

Having demonstrated that the sensory input can be divided into two functional parts as the result of learning, it is not difficult to extend the analysis so as to incorporate the stimulus components from drive and emotional states into the context. This suggests a reinterpretation of the influence these states have on guiding behavior as contrasted to energizing it. Their influence in many instances would be through their control of the coding response, not through the addition of stimulus components to the critical stimuli. It would be related to Tolman's concept of the "breadth of learning," where this is interpreted to mean that drive and emotional states influence the range and type of stimulus characteristics that become associated with the overt behavior [1, 26]. The formulation can be extended to include the influence of verbal instructions and like variables. They would have the same role as the context stimuli in the above example.

There are, however, difficulties in applying this conditional-reaction paradigm to sequential behaviors in which there are obvious shifts in correlation but no apparent changes in the accompanying stimulus situation. One possibility is that the sensory feedback from making an overt response can provide part of the components of the context for the next coding response. Basically this is the idea that the movements made in striking a match provide part of the context in preparing for a visual stimulus. Another possibility is in terms of the associations within families of coding responses such as those discussed previously. In familiar situations each would elicit another in fixed order as the result of past learning. This organization of coding responses could have an influence on the number of discriminations made in a unit time. The difference between a novice and an expert in appraising an object with a microscope undoubtedly depends in part upon the range of coding responses each has developed. But assuming that each has the same repertory, there can be differences in the rate at which each assimilates relevant information depending upon the degree of organization among the coding responses. If each tends to elicit the next, this can lead to a rapid survey of the object as contrasted to the case in which such associations are absent. Because it is an organization of coding responses and not of specific s-a-c, this would be true even though there were no way of anticipating the exact values on each characteristic or of the relations between them.

Similarity and Generalization

Another class of problems that any attempt to define a stimulus unit must deal with centers around the concept of stimulus similarity. At the formal level it is always possible to state innumerable ways in which two events are alike and an equal number in which they are unlike. Unless one of these is taken as a criterion, no determinate answer to the degree of similarity between two events can be given. The criterion adopted in psychology always has been the extent to which stimuli can be substituted for each other in eliciting a given response. If after training to one stimulus the individual responds in the same way to others without further training, these are taken as a set of similar stimuli. At this level it is an empirical question as to whether or not two stimuli are similar. Consequently, the search has been for some defining property that will predict, independently of observed behavior, which stimuli form a similarity set.

Two general approaches have been taken to this problem. The most frequent one has sought a defining property that is independent of the individual's behavior. This leads to either the common-element or the dimensional formulation. The common-element approach assumes that a set of stimuli can be analyzed into parts or characteristics and that any two having a number of these characteristics in common can be substituted for each other. This reduces the concept of similarity to that of identity. The dimensional approach orders stimuli along physically defined continua such as intensity and frequency. It then assumes that the probability that one stimulus may be substituted for a second increases as the distance between them decreases in this multidimensional space. Both approaches further assume that once a set of similar stimuli have been defined in these ways, they can be substituted for one another irrespective of which new behaviors or tasks are involved.

The main difficulty with either the common-element or the dimensional formulation is apparent whenever the role of instructions, sets, or attitudes is considered. Tones that are not too different in intensity but which differ widely in frequency may act as a set of similar stimuli when the subject is making loudness judgments. This is the whole basis for establishing loudness contours. On the other hand, they cannot be substituted for one and another when the subject is making pitch judgments. Thus whether or not a given set of stimuli form a similarity set depends upon factors that fall outside the definitions. Until these factors are incorporated into a definition of similarity, the problem is not much advanced over a purely empirical procedure.

A second approach has been to make similarity a function of past learning. It is assumed that every stimulus-response correlation is mediated. Intervening between the stimulus and the response there is an implicit reaction that gives rise to a response-produced stimulus. This latter is the direct elicitor of the overt behavior. Consequently, through training it is possible to associate several stimuli with this implicit reaction. They then have acquired similarity [4] in the sense that each can be substituted for the other in giving rise to the implicit reaction and thereby eliciting the common overt response. The main advantage of this approach is that it accounts for similarity, as defined by the substitution criterion, between two stimuli when this would not be predicted by either the common-element or the dimensional formulation. Its main disadvantages are the following: First of all, it does not allow for any independent control of the mediating reaction; this is directly tied to the external stimulus. Consequently, it cannot account for the sudden changes in similarity such as were illustrated in the above example with the tones. Secondly, it makes no allowance for the influence of physically defined similarities among the stimuli. Presumably any randomly selected group of stimuli can acquire similarity in this sense with the proper training procedures.

The concept of similarity in the present formulation is basically a compromise between these two approaches. Each coding response produces a system of s-a-c, the direct elicitors of overt behavior. Consequently, the concept of similarity centers about the question of the extent to which one s-a-c can be substituted for another. Each coding response determines a correlation between certain characteristics of the stimulus situation and the s-a-c. If it is applied to two sensory inputs identical in these characteristics but differing widely in others, there is still but a single s-a-c. In some instances even though the two inputs differ in absolute value on each definable characteristic, they may produce the same s-a-c if the correlation involved is dependent upon a relationship between these characteristics. In this sense the present formulation allows for similarity based on the concept of identity or common elements in the various stimuli. When the same coding response is applied to a series of inputs, it produces s-a-c all within the same coding system. It is assumed that all items within such a system are ordered. The ordering involved is analogous to that produced by a mathematical function. As the coding response imposes a transformation on each input, the resultants, i.e., the system of s-a-c, form an ordered series because of their common derivation. Consequently, whether one s-a-c can be substituted for another depends upon their juxtaposition in this series. In this sense the present formulation allows for the dimensional concept of similarity. Finally it is evident that the definition of similarity takes into account the individual's behavior and past learning. Whether or not a given group of stimuli form a similarity set cannot be determined solely in terms of the physical characteristics of the stimuli. The nature of the coding response must always be considered.

This formulation demands a reconsideration of the concept of generalization gradients. The aspect of this concept that is most difficult to accept, especially as it applies to human beings, is the following: If an individual is tested for pitch discrimination by any of the standard psychophysical methods, the range of substitutible frequencies is quite limited; i.e., the generalization gradient goes to zero in short order. On the other hand, if the individual is first conditioned to one tone and then others varying in frequency are substituted for it, the resulting generalization gradient is relatively flat and includes a large number of frequencies. This latter gradient, however, is taken by most learning theorists as the truer picture of the spread of habit strength along the dimension of frequency. Then in order to account for the psychophysical results, they find it necessary to assume that this steep gradient is the resultant of discrimination training. It is the algebraic sum of two gradients of the type found in conditioning, one of positive habit strength established about a given tone through reinforcement and a second of negative habit strength established about another tone through nonreinforcement.

The anomalous feature in this learning-theory account is the absence of any transfer effect. Even though the individual has established the psychophysical discrimination prior to any conditioning training, he still gives a flat generalization gradient in the conditioning situation. If this result is taken at face value, it must be assumed that each time the individual associates a new response with a given stimulus, say a manipulative rather than a verbal one, the conditioning type of gradient reestablishes itself. Discrimination training must be reinstated once again. This total lack of transfer of a discrimination from one set of overt behaviors to another is contrary to everyday expectations.

In the present formulation the difference between the generalization gradients in the psychophysical and the conditioning situations is not a contrast between a derived gradient and a primary one. It stems primarily from a difference in the coding responses involved. In conditioning the individual is required to make a discrimination between the presence and the absence of a tone. Consequently, any one of a number of different coding responses is appropriate in this situation. It is conceivable that the one employed produces s-a-c correlated with many aspects of the situation. The frequency aspect alone may carry relatively little weight in producing changes in the s-a-c. When test tones are presented that differ from the training one only in frequency, the changes in behavior may be small and difficult to see. On the other hand, the individual is not required to make a discrimination between the presence and the absence of a tone in the psychophysical situation. Instead it is a discrimination between two tones that differ only in frequency. As a consequence successful discrimination implies a coding response whose s-a-c are almost exclusively correlated with frequency. Thus any change in this characteristic results in relatively large changes in the s-a-c.

The implicit assumption in this argument is that the coding system for any given coding response contains roughly the same number of discriminable clusters of s-a-c. If the generalization gradients in the conditioning and psychophysical situations were expressed in terms of this quantity, they would show equal slopes. But when expressed as a function of the frequency, the conditioning one is flat, because this characteristic has little weight in the correlation, whereas the psychophysical one is steep, because here this characteristic carries most of the weight. In so far as there is a "true" generalization gradient for frequency alone, it is more nearly approximated by the psychophysical than by the conditioning study.

The above interpretation implies that all learning is a form of discrimination. It involves a trial-and-error period during which one coding response is substituted for another until eventually one is hit upon that produces a system of s-a-c that permit consistent reinforcement. As each new coding response brings into play a different coding system, there is a series of generalization gradients characteristic of different stages of learning. However, from the empirical point of view this series can be characterized as a single gradient. In this case there should be continuing changes in the slope of that gradient with continued training. It should become steeper with respect to those stimulus characteristics that carry increasing weight in the correlation and less steep with respect to those that carry decreasing weight.

Transfer

This formulation also accounts for the results of studies on the transfer of a discrimination along a continuum [19]. It has been found that the discrimination between two slightly different figures, brightnesses, or tones is most rapidly established if the individual is first trained on stimuli that differ widely in this respect and then these are slowly transformed into the test stimuli. In the present formulation this implies that successful discrimination on the test stimuli, those differing only in a few characteristics, permits a relatively limited number of coding responses, i.e., those whose s-a-c are correlated exclusively with sets of these characteristics. This is analogous to saying that the situation demands a very precise and limited set of instrumental behaviors in order to ensure consistent reinforcement. But as these are only a limited set of those likely to be elicited from a naïve subject, they are established slowly if at all. On the other hand, a much larger set of coding responses permits successful discrimination when the discrimination is started with stimuli differing widely on these same characteristics. Any one dependent in part on these characteristics, even though they carry little weight in the correlation, produce s-a-c different enough to permit consistent reinforcement. By gradually transforming these stimuli into the test ones, a gradual shift in the coding response is forced so that it approximates more and more closely to the ones necessary for successful discrimination on the test stimuli. It is essentially a form of learning by approximation so successfully employed by Skinner [25]. In this case, however, it operates on the coding response rather than on the overt behavior.

Perhaps the most general implication of this formulation in terms of coding responses concerns the range and type of transfer effects it makes possible. There is considerable experimental evidence indicating that individuals deprived of the use of a given sensory modality during early life show slow and unstable learning to stimuli in that modality when its use is later restored to them. But with continued practice their rate of learning approximates that of normal individuals. Similarly there is experimental evidence indicating that if an individual is given additional, uncontrolled experience with stimuli in a given modality early in life, his rate of learning to such stimuli is faster than for normals when tested at a later age. Both types of study lend themselves to an interpretation in terms of coding responses. Initial experience with stimuli in any modality demands both the establishment of appropriate coding responses and the association of the resulting s-a-c with overt behaviors. This makes for relatively slow learning. Once families of coding responses have become associated with context stimuli, verbal instructions, drive states, and the like, they can be brought into play in new situations whenever the context stimuli are present. Under these circumstances learning is relatively rapid, because only the associations between the s-a-c and the new overt behaviors have to be established. Unfortunately, in most of these studies the transfer effects observed are so gross and unanalyzed that it is impossible to say whether they are due to this or to any one of a number of other possible factors.

There are a number of controlled studies, such as those on stimulus predifferentiation and the acquired distinctiveness of cues [6, 18], clearly indicating that such transfer effects can occur in terms of previous familiarity with the stimulus conditions independently of any carry-over of specific overt behaviors. These studies frequently employ a discrimination in which two or more characteristics of the stimuli are randomly paired on successive trials. The individual, however, must discriminate on the basis of one of these characteristics. This tends to ensure that a coding response is acquired that produces s-a-c correlated with this dimension but not with the randomly varying one. After this training the individuals are given a second task involving this same random pairing of stimulus characteristics. Now, however, the overt responses demanded are very different from those in the first task. This makes it impossible for the stimulus-response associations to transfer from the training to the test situation. Half the individuals are trained to the same stimulus characteristic as in the first task and the rest to the other stimulus characteristic. The first group that is discriminating on the basis of the familiar stimulus learns more rapidly than does the second. This indicates that the previous discrimination has transferred to the new task even though new overt behaviors must be learned. This is the result expected if learning is a two-stage process, one involving the establishment of a coding response and the other an association between its s-a-c and overt behaviors. Thus it is possible that much of an individual's early learning consists of developing coding responses appropriate to a wide variety of stimulus situations. In so far as these are readily brought into play in new situations, there is positive transfer even though new overt behaviors are being learned.

A final aspect of this transfer problem concerns negative transfer effects. If learned associations between stimulus and response involved all characteristics of the stimulus, it is to be anticipated that each time a new response is associated with that stimulus, there should be frequent signs of conflict and negative tranfer. The old association has to be extinguished before the new one can be established. Such negative transfer effects, however, are hard to demonstrate in the sophisticated individual. He becomes "mazewise" in the sense that successive problems in the same situation tend to show positive transfer effects even though they involve the learning of antagonistic responses to the same stimuli. There are two ways that this surprising lack of negative transfer effects can be accounted for in the present formulation. The first is in terms of the positive transfer from problem to problem once the appropriate coding responses are established. This masks any negative transfer effect resulting from the extinction of previous associations between overt responses and the s-a-c. Secondly, it can stem from the fact that groups of stimulus-response associations can be thrown in and out of "gear" by changes in the coding response. Even though the same stimulus object occurs in two successive tasks, it is conceivable that the individual shifts from one coding response to another. If the new one is dependent upon a different set of stimulus characteristics than was the original, then all the associations between the original system of s-a-c and overt behaviors become nonfunctional. New learning then can occur without the need for extinguishing the previous associations. The change in coding responses implies, however, that new context stimuli, drive states, or instructions have been introduced into the situation. This interpretation fits well with the results from studies on matching behavior and with the rapid shifts from one characteristic to another in a constant stimulus situation [22].

REFERENCES

1. Bruner, J. S., Matter, J., & Papanek, M. L. Breadth of learning as a function of drive level and mechanization. *Psychol. Rev.,* 1955, **62**, 1–10.
2. Bruner, J. S., & Postman, L. Perception of incongruity: a paradigm. *J. Pers.,* 1949–1950. **18**, 206–223.
3. Deese, J. *The psychology of learning.* New York: McGraw-Hill, 1952.
4. Dollard, J., & Miller, N. E. *Personality and psychotherapy.* New York: McGraw-Hill, 1950. Chap. 6, Introduction to higher mental processes: effect on transfer and discrimination.
5. Freeman, G. L. *The energetics of human behavior.* Ithaca, N.Y.: Cornell Univer. Press, 1948.

6. Gagne, R. M., & Baker, K. E. Stimulus pre-differentiation as a factor in transfer of training. *J. exp. Psychol.*, 1950, **40**, 439–451.

7. Gibson, Eleanor J. Improvement in perceptual judgments as a function of controlled practice or training. *Psychol. Bull.*, 1953, **50**, 401–431.

8. Gibson, J. J. *The perception of the visual world.* New York: Houghton Mifflin, 1950.

9. Gibson, J. J. Perception as a function of stimulation. In S. Koch (Ed.), *Psychology: a study of a science.* Vol. 1. New York: McGraw-Hill, 1959.

10. Gibson, J. J., & Gibson, Eleanor J. Perceptual learning—differentiation or enrichment? *Psychol. Rev.*, 1955, **62**, 32–41.

11. Goodwin, W. R., & Lawrence, D. H. The functional independence of two discrimination habits associated with a constant stimulus situation. *J. comp. physiol. Psychol.*, 1955, **48**, 437–443.

12. Graham, C. H. Behavior and the psychophysical methods: an analysis of some recent experiments. *Psychol. Rev.*, 1952, **59**, 62–70.

13. Graham, C. H., & Ratoosh, P. Notes on some interrelations of sensory psychology, perception, and behavior. In S. Koch (Ed.), *Psychology: a study of a science.* Vol. 4. New York: McGraw-Hill, 1962.

14. Helsen, H. (Ed.) *Theoretical foundations of psychology.* New York: Van Nostrand, 1951.

15. Hull, C. L. *Principles of behavior.* New York: Appleton-Century-Crofts, 1943.

16. Hull, C. L. *A behavior system.* New Haven, Conn.: Yale Univer. Press, 1952.

17. Lashley, K. S. Conditional reactions in the rat. *J. Psychol.*, 1938, **6**, 311–324.

18. Lawrence, D. H. Acquired distinctiveness of cues: II. Selective association in a constant stimulus situation. *J. exp. Psychol.*, 1950, **40**, 175–188.

19. Lawrence, D. H. The transfer of a discrimination along a continuum. *J. comp. physiol. Psychol.*, 1952, **45**, 511–516.

20. Lawrence, D. H., & Coles, G. R. Accuracy of recognition with alternatives before and after the stimulus. *J. exp. Psychol.*, 1954, **47**, 208–214.

21. Lawrence, D. H., & Laberge, D. Relationship between recognition accuracy and order of reporting stimulus dimensions. *J. exp. Psychol.*, 1956, **51**, 12–18.

22. Lawrence, D. H., & Mason, W. A. Systematic behavior during discrimination reversal and change of dimensions. *J. comp. physiol. Psychol.*, 1955, **48**, 267–271.

23. Miller, N. E. Liberalization of basic S-R concepts: extensions to conflict behavior, motivation, and social learning. In S. Koch (Ed.), *Psychology: a study of a science.* Vol. 2. New York: McGraw-Hill, 1959.

24. Osgood, C. E. *Method and theory in experimental psychology.* New York: Oxford Univer. Press, 1953.

25. Skinner, B. F. *The behavior of organisms.* New York: Appleton-Century-Crofts, Inc., 1938. Chap. 8, The differentiation of a response.

26. Tolman, E. C. Cognitive maps in rats and men. *Psychol. Rev.*, 1948, **55**, 189–208.

BEHAVIOR AND PERCEPTION[1]

W. N. SCHOENFELD AND W. W. CUMMING
Department of Psychology
Columbia University

Introduction 214
The Problem of Perception 214
    Delimiting the area 214
    Conditions of use of the term perception 216
The Simple Paradigm: $S \rightarrow R$ 220
    The definition of stimulus 220
    The definition of response 222
    Conditioning and stimulus discrimination 224
    Psychophysics 227
        Absolute and difference limens 227
        The psychophysical response 230
        Stimulus presentation procedures 231
        Response latency 231
        The "instruction variable" 231
        Animal psychophysics 232
The Advanced Paradigm: $S \rightarrow R_1 \cdot R_2$ 233
    The sequential response dependency 233
    The "perceptual response" 233
    Some questions regarding $R_1 \cdot R_2$ 235
    "Instructions": reprise 237
    The reporting response 240
    Paradigms for mediated generalization 241
Assessment of Some Representative Perceptions 244
    Illusions, relations, and the constancies 245
    Figure-ground phenomena 247
Summary 249
References 250

[1] Since this paper was submitted to the Study, a number of writings consonant with our argument have appeared. Among the more recent is one which serves to bring the discussion closer to date by I. Goldiamond in *Experimental foundations of clinical psychology*. A. J. Bachrach (Ed.), New York: Basic Books, 1962.

INTRODUCTION

Today's reader of psychological literature can scarcely fail to be impressed by the spate of material he encounters dealing with problems labeled perceptual. He might, indeed, be tempted at first to suppose that the topic of perception is one of the broadest in the entire field of psychology, only to realize finally that such a conclusion is traceable primarily to definitions which leave the boundaries of perception indeterminate. It is our purpose here to inquire into the meaning of the term *perception,* and to put it in touch with modern behavior theory. To this end, we shall indicate along the way, for a few well-known examples of perception, the direction that a behavior analysis might take.

In pursuing our purpose, we shall not attempt a review of the perceptual literature, partly because others have already done a goodly portion of that task. Nor are we mainly interested in criticizing the work of perceptual theorists. We shall seek an account of perception that is consonant with behavior theory, and aim more to show that the dress is appropriate to the climate than that all other costumes are inappropriate. Finally, we shall have no novel theory of perception to advocate, nor any terminology to introduce which differs in any substantial way from language systems now in common use. We believe that there is no such thing as a "theory of perception" divorced from a general theory of behavior. With the topic of perception in hand, our line of thought will simply display our disposition to approach behavioral phenomena in particular ways. To those of similar attitude [e.g., 19, 28], the outcome may appear obvious; others, of different mind, may find it irrelevant.

THE PROBLEM OF PERCEPTION

Delimiting the Area

It seems necessary, before proceeding farther, to delimit the area we propose to treat. Definitions of perception are many, varied, and frequently implicit rather than explicit. Representatively, Allport [1] writes that perception is concerned with " . . . our awareness of the objects or conditions around us. It is the way things look to us, or the way they sound, feel, taste, or smell." Yet he does not seem to intend that all sensory data are to be classified as perceptual.

Historically, the area of perception has often been delineated through contrast with the area of sensation. Thus, Woodworth [58] says, "*Sensation* points to the sense organs with their nerves and nerve centers as the object of study. . . . In a sensation experiment we apply stimuli that are quite restricted and typically simple. . . . In a sensation experiment we are interested in the correlation of (the subject's) report with the stimulus. . . ." On the other hand, it is held that *"Perception* points to the objects of the world which we know through the senses. . . . In a perception experiment we are interested in the correlation of [the subject's] report with a certain objective fact." In another place, Woodworth draws the same distinction in the following terms: "Experiments requiring the subject to report the stimulus are abundant in the study of the senses and are often called experiments on sensation, while experiments calling for a report of the object, or objective fact, indicated by a stimulus belong in the study of perception." Thus, the distinction between sensation and perception was drawn along two lines: (1) the stimulus-object distinction, and (2) differences in the behavior of the experimenter either in his instructions to the subject, or in his treatment of the data, or in his reasons for performing the experiment.

The real difficulties in circumscribing the area to be dealt with here do not arise when the word *perception* is used to denote a class of experiments or experimental procedures, but rather when it is used to denote a class of experiences. Allport [1] certainly makes this transformation: "A phenomenological experience of an object, that is to say, the way some object or situation appears to the subject as dependent upon his own organism, as observer-involved, non-denotive and 'private,' is called a *percept."* At worst, this reduces to a solipsism which excludes all scientific investigation; at best, it stakes out the area as a preserve for those who do not believe that "whatever exists, exists in some amount, and can be measured."

Many writers have insisted that perception is an activity and ought to be treated as a verb. It is not often clear, however, what the dimensions of this activity might be. Given action properties, we might subsume perception under "response," but it is doubtful that perceptual theorists ever meant to assign a response's quantifiable properties to a perception. Rather, perception appears to be something independent, concurrent with other activities or interacting with them, a something within the organism which may be the basis for a "report." In such a usage, perception has some of the logical properties of a stimulus in that it exercises control over the "report."

Whatever the word perception may or may not mean, one thing must be true if it is to be of any use whatever to a natural science of behavior: it must show up, or evidence itself, in observable behavior. To hold that perception has an independent noncorporeal existence, either in itself or as a cause of behavior, puts the matter into metaphysics; to hold that perception exists corporeally but has no effect on behavior both contradicts the asserted importance of perception and makes it irrelevant to the science; to hold that perception is a hypothetical construction for purposes of behavior theory is to agree, apart from the debatable merits of such a construction, that behavior is the initial datum of reference.

Conditions of Use of the Term Perception

Because behavior is the final touchstone of the presence or functioning of perception, we might ask: What characteristics of an organism's response lead an onlooker to assert that the behavior is perceptual? If, as is the case, we are not offered any satisfactory explicit objective criteria by which we may ourselves recognize the presence of perception, then we must fall back upon the following alternative: to take as our datum the behavior of one professing to detect the presence of perception. What are the cues with which his profession is correlated? In thus changing our target from perception itself to the behavior of a person responding with the word *perception,* we do more than simply seek the speaker's implicit definition of his word. In fact, we leave open two possibilities: (1) that the response "perception" has no referent at all, or too universal a referent, in the behavior of the organism he is looking at, and that the response has its determinants in the speaker, or in his environment, exclusive of the organism looked at, and (2) that the signs which lead the onlooker to speak of perception are really in the behavior looked at, but are unknown to the speaker or are different from what he might claim them to be, so that, after identification, those signs prove to be the same as those used by behavior science as explicit *definientia* for terms other than perception. If (1), then perception poses no special problem for behavior science; if (2), the same conclusion follows, since the term is subsumable under already established classificatory rubrics. The problem of perception affords an example of how much may sometimes be won by a shift of attention away from a presumed behavioral problem to the response of that performing organism, the scientist himself.

To our question about the aspects of any response which lead to the onlooker's designation of that response as evidencing perception, an answer may be quickly given, though it will need some elaboration. We hold that belief in "perception" is based on complexities in the $S \rightarrow R$ relation, or on ignorance concerning that relation. Starting with the general basic formula

$$R = f(S)$$

where R is the response (dependent variable) and S is a controlling independent variable (usually a stimulus operation), perception is alleged to be present whenever either or both of the following are true:

1. $f(S)$ *is not a simple relation and is either partly or wholly unknown.* While the complexity of the relation may be the cause of ignorance concerning it, the complexity is often the result of an inability to

specify the stimulus in any simple way. Classical examples of this are found in what gestaltists called closure and *prägnanz* and the like, and more lately in some of the Ames demonstrations where functional analyses of the stimulus determinants have not been adequately carried out. When such analyses are done, as recently begun with figural aftereffects, they tend to dissipate the mystery that calls up in an onlooker the idea of an inner organizing perception. Where the stimulus is specifiable, but $f(S)$ is complex, the dissipation of mystery begins when $f(S)$ begins to be known. This has occurred, for example, with the octave cycle in pitch discrimination, and with color-naming responses plotted as the hue-discrimination function. When the complex relations between light stimuli and color-naming responses are worked out, even the experiential mystery which surrounds color vision will disappear, and the topic will lose its perceptual disguise. When $f(S)$ is wholly unknown, of course, it is impossible to say whether it is complex, but the history of experimental psychology offers many instances of once-suspected complexity where relatively simple stimulus functions were eventually found. Thus, the Purkinje shift was finally subsumed under the relation between intensity and the relative-visibility curves. Sometimes, sets of comparatively simple interacting functions have turned up, as in depth perception. In short, as $f(S)$ becomes clearer, the dependent variable R is freed from bondage to our ignorance and comes out from perception's yoke.

The complexity of $f(S)$ may reside in its parameters, some of which may be partly or wholly unknown. This means that the expression $R = f(S)$ needs to be expanded [e.g., 21, 22, 23] into

$$R = f(a, b, c, \ldots)$$

to indicate that an adequate specification of S may involve many variables operating in combination. Inadequate specification of S was the basis of much prolonged controversy over perceptual phenomena like the constancies and Koffka's slanted telegraph poles [33]. In many such cases, $f(S)$ has parameters once unknown, later roughly limned, and today more clearly understood. The size-weight illusion exemplifies an $f(S)$ where the volume of the weight being judged has long been known as a crucial parameter and a set of functions is readily obtainable; in contrast, perception of the vertical still has parameters to be discovered and so appears as the mysterious product of the "perceiver." Given multiple parameters, our ignorance may concern the existence and mode of their operation rather than the basic mathematical form of $f(S)$. Some, moreover, may involve more than just a better specification of the stimulus, extending to the condition of the organism at the time $f(S)$ is being measured. The latter cases fall into several classes, each of which may require complex specification: (*a*) the conditioning history of the response with respect to the stimulus parameters or aspects; the fact that organisms accumulate a reinforcement biography with respect to a response is exemplified by the Bruner-Goodman experiment with coins [9], Hanawalt's study of the partial recall of figures [25], gestalt closure, the work of Riesen [45] and Senden [47], experiments on social norms, and others; (*b*) the motivation level existing at the time that $R = f(a, b, c, . . .)$ is under measurement [e.g., 35]; (*c*) other states and conditions of the organism such as brain injury, drugs, fatigue, anoxia, and so on; (*d*) the genetic constitution of the organism; and (*e*) the maturational stage of the organism.

2. *R is relatively complex, with either identifiable component responses having individual conditioning histories more clearly known than R itself, or with conditional probabilities among component responses arising from special circumstances of reinforcement.* Ofttimes, an R that is alleged to be perceptual is a composite of many responses. This is certainly true of, but not limited to, human verbal behavior like words or sentences or phrases. Moreover, in many instances of verbal and other forms of behavior, alternate forms of response are available in the organism's repertory, making it appear that any particular one is unimportant because there is some underlying permanent perception that is the referent, or master, of R. Such R equivalents are established, of course, through biographies in which a class or set of R's have received equivalent reinforcement treatment. Yet it is easier to see how a word is learned than a sentence, and how word synonyms are taught than sentence equivalents. The comparative difficulty makes it appear that the large composite R, more than any component response, reflects control by an underlying reality.

Such considerations aside, however, the components of complex R's may be linked by certain probability relations among themselves. That is to say, the response complexity involved in chaining [32], which arises from special circumstances of reinforcement history, is that of conditional probabilities among responses: if a stimulus heightens the probability of a given response, the latter's occurrence, when it transpires, heightens the probability of occurrence of a second given response. Thus, if one part of a chained R is probed out, later parts may follow. This is especially apparent with verbal chains like clichés, colloquialisms, conventional phrases, and the like, but it shows up also in the case of stereotypes where, for example, if a person is identified with a nationality tag he is also likely to be responded to with (perceived as describable by) a set of adjectival words. Conditional probabilities underlie a range of behavior phenomena extending from the free association technique of psychoanalysis to span-of-apprehension tests where the ability correctly to perceive (respond to) whole words or sentences, as so-called higher units, almost matches that for separate letters or digits [38].

The existence of R equivalents produces a measured variability in R, but variability in R may also be the result of the way R starts, or of which R starts [27]. It must be recognized, furthermore, that an R, or series of R's, in progress may make their own stimulus contributions, and thus produce modifications in later R's through new complexities in $R = f(a, b, c, \ldots)$. This latter possibility finds expression in research on intraverbal dependencies [20, 37, 46]; in Guthrie's [24] concept of movement-produced stimuli; in Skinner's [53] view that a rate of response can be reinforced, and in his view regarding the operation of verbal autoclitics; and in Kantor's [31] interbehaviorism.

As said earlier, in addition to the sequential complexity of response chains, complexity can exist in the size or spread of an R, as measured by the number of smaller component responses occurring, or tending to occur, close together in time that make up the observed R. When a stimulus tends to evoke incompatible components, the category broadens to include response conflict. Such conflicts are exemplified in verbal behavior by blends [56], and by the psychophysical responses of "equal" or "bisection." The problems of "stimulus registration" and "perceptual defense" also enter here, since, as we urge, perceiving is responding and the question of whether or not a stimulus is registered or defended against is referable to the reinforcement history of incompatible responses (perceptions) with respect to that stimulus.

In summary, the belief that perception is a necessary concept in a science of behavior takes strength from complexities in the S → R relation, and from ignorance concerning that relation. From those complexities, and from that ignorance, comes the notion of "perception dependent upon the perceiver." It is as if one were saying that, beyond stimulus control, responding is somehow directed by an inner process which is the personal psychic contribution of the perceiver. If $R = f(S)$ were a 1:1 relation, or a simply proportional one, or even a higher-order but well-understood one, the felt need for the term perception would vanish. An onlooker would then more likely think in terms of sensory physiology or response-mechanism physiology in a manner analogous to the way the laws of reflex action were once viewed, and there would never have arisen such historical distinctions as those of sensation versus perception, or inner versus outer psychophysics, which represented attempts to deal with S → R complexity.

The issue becomes all the sharper when R is verbal, because the experimenter may choose to treat verbal behavior as a special sort of datum. If he takes it as referentially introspective, then he becomes the captive of his subject's verbal reinforcement history and must accept his subject's perceptual lexicon. This is, however, not the only course open to the scientist and was not the one taken in operational psychophysics, or in the early papers of men like J. B. Watson and W. S. Hunter and H. M. Johnson, or in the language analyses of Kantor [29, 30] and Skinner [53]. This second course is to proceed on the view that verbal responses are not privileged data exempted from the treatment given any other behavior. It is this view which is taken here.

As seen, we can exhaust the categorical sources of complexity in the $R = f(S)$ paradigm. They are not different from those already met with in behavior theory, and they do not include perception. For behavior theory, any alleged instance of perception must be referable to these already established categories, after which perception as an explanatory, or even descriptive, term may be abandoned.

Perhaps a final question is in order. If these categories are exhaustive, what remains of the gestalt view that there are certain natural correspondences between responses (or perceptions) and their generating stimuli which, even if complex, are independent of conditioning history? The question is unanswerable because of its indefiniteness and because the problem was never properly stated in the first place. To be sure, much of an organism's behavior is determined by its body structure and therefore is under genetic control in part. But the arguments derived by gestalt theorists from their demonstrations were of a scholastic character. While they were classifying perceptual phenomena, they were insulating them by the doctrine of isomorphism. Experimental parametric analysis of "natural" correspondences was neglected, while *Gestalttheorie* busied itself with phenomenological description.

THE SIMPLE PARADIGM: S → R

What has been said thus far points to a treatment of perception that rests on the terms stimulus and response. Since this course is not without its pitfalls, it is perhaps wise to expose first some of the denotations of these terms.

The Definition of Stimulus

The definition of *stimulus* is to be sought among the independent variables and parameters of a behavioral experiment; of these, stimulus designates only an arbitrarily limited class, the communality of which is usually referred to the sense organs and to the doctrine of specific nerve energies. Stimulus entered behavior science as the causative term in the concept of the reflex, but its meaning expanded and changed somewhat as the reflex concept was emancipated from sole connection with *in vitro* studies, tropisms, animal preparations, and the like. Given modern behavior theory's emphasis on intact organisms, stimulus has become coordinated with experimental independent variables affecting behavior.

The essential point to be noticed is that, in an empirical behavior science, stimulus must be defined in the language of the physical sciences.

Recognition of the necessity for defining stimulus physically has been slowed throughout the history of psychology by the intrusion of several supplementary invalid ideas. Among these, for example, are the notions of proximal versus distal stimulus, potential versus actual stimulus, stimulus as energy impinging on a receptor, and stimulus as energy change that produces behavior changes. Such diversions, which ultimately destroy the value of the term stimulus and leave it sterile [39], are attempts to deal with two facts which, though seemingly irreconcilable, are really simple matters of conventional interest and usage among behavior scientists. First, stimulus stands for a class of physical changes in an organism's environment introduced as independent variables in an experiment; second, of those physical changes only certain ones, or degrees of them, produce behavioral effects. To take an absurdly extreme case, suppose that the experimenter introduces an auditory signal in London for an organism under study in Chicago and observes no effect on the organism's behavior. Was the signal a "stimulus" or not? Indeed, it was. The seeming absurdity arises only because we are usually interested in that class of stimuli which can be shown to have some significant behavioral correlates. That interest, however, does not compromise the definition of stimulus in any way, nor should it mislead us to think of stimuli as only those physical environment changes which produce behavior changes. The definition of stimulus is a perfectly general one, but, by way of shorthand convenience rather than logical necessity, we most often use the term for those classes of independent variables which affect sense organs and produce correlated behavior changes. This is conventional usage, however, not a rational delimitation.

While the physical definition of stimulus is not troublesome to an experimenter, it is sometimes extended by theorists in a confusing manner. These extensions include states of the organism, motives, emotions, or pure constructions. We shall not ourselves take such license, since it (1) makes stimulus a matter of enumeration only, removing all defining class properties and even divesting it of any physical referent whatever, or (2) gives stimulus meaning only in terms of the particular role assigned to it in the system of the individual theorist. In the first case, the word loses whatever generality it possessed; in the second, it not only loses generality but may be taken completely out of the realm of empirical science (e.g., Lewin).

These considerations regarding stimulus have implications for an understanding of perception. As said earlier, the stimulus-object distinction is sometimes used to separate perception from sensation. The distinction, however, cannot remove perception from stimulus-response hegemony but only directs us to consider stimulus complexity again. Few, if any, would wish to defend the proposition that a sense organ is affected according to different principles depending on whether it is impinged upon by energy from a stimulus or from an object. With stimulus properly viewed, to distinguish it from object is to traffic in distinctions without differences. A line, a chair, or a color do not require specifications which remove them from the context of sense-organ activity. The stimulus-object distinction becomes interesting only as it brings into focus those modes of stimulus complexity which lead an onlooker to respond with the word *object*.

The physical parameters, or aspects, of a stimulus include form, size, locus of stimulation, wavelength, energy, etc., all or any of which may be called upon when we operationally denote a stimulus. The term might, indeed, be *stimulus complex* to celebrate the fact that many physical variables are involved in a complete depiction. In the typical sensation experiment, the psychophysicist may independently manipulate any of the dimensions of the S complex which he chooses and specify $R = f(S)$ with any combination of its parameters. With such manipulation of an S complex (only one aspect of the complex being changed at a time), changes in response strength are observed which may be correlated with the simple changes in the stimulus, and there is no need to introduce the special concept "object." In ordinary experience, however, aspects or dimensions of many S complexes are often nonindependent in the sense that several physical measures of the complex tend to vary concomitantly. While such S complexes are in no fundamental way different from the complexes presented in a sensation experiment, the concomitant variation of aspects provides these complexes with a special character by virtue of the subject's discriminative history with respect to them. Thus, behavior may be controlled by aspects of the complex normally covariant with the one selected for measurement and manipulation in a sensation experiment. Evidence for such behavioral control leads an onlooker to speak of the "object-character" of the complex and to relegate the behavioral effects to one or another type of perception.

The Definition of Response

Our comments on stimulus in the preceding section find parallels in the case of *response*. The definition of response is to be sought among the dependent variables of a behavior experiment; of these, response designates an arbitrarily limited class of events, the communality of which is usually referred to the smooth or striate musculature and, occasionally, to duct glands. Response is defined in the language of physical science with particular reference to muscular contraction. Such reference has sometimes been historically diluted, for example, by speaking of the "response" of a neuron or "responses" of sense organs, but these dilutions and their sources need not detain us since they are merely figures of speech based on equating response to "effect" in a broad and wholly uninformative way. We shall also ignore uses of the term which leave the operations of measurement completely unspecified, as in "response to therapy," "response to treatment," and "response to stress," since these usages only serve to weaken whatever precision the term may otherwise have. Because the term response belongs among the dependent variables of behavior science, it is measured rather than directly manipulated. Such measurements represent consequences of muscular contraction. There is no intention, however, to restrict the range of consequences in which we may be interested. Often the response may be covert, which means that the consequences may only be measured by electromyographic equipment. In the casual case, the response may be manifested only through effects registered upon other behavior of the organism itself as measuring instrument, as with introspection and the "reporting response" (see below, pp. 240 ff.), but the theorist is not thereby excused from ultimate reference to the musculature.

The physical definition of response implies physical measurement. Since any R belongs to a generic class [50], the frequency of occurrence of R-class members is, in single organisms, available as a datum, as is probability of occurrence (relative populational probability) in groups of subjects or in groups of trials with single subjects, while single R's, considered as all-or-none events, may be measured in magnitude, duration, time course, topography, or distributions of these measures. In addition, the whole S → R correlation gives rise to the measurement categories of latency and threshold. At least one of these measures, or some derived one, must appear as the dependent variable in every behavior experiment. In this sense, the class of variables labeled response exhausts the dependent variables of psychology. It will not escape attention that threshold is properly included as an R measure, although it is a derived one; reports of S measures as thresholds are valid only because they are referable to some conventionally accepted probability of R evocation.

Neither the "meaning" of R, nor its significance, its social value, its survival value, its aggressiveness, is a legitimate measure of R. An R is a physical event, and it is measured as such; the uses, goals, interpretations, and other value judgments regarding R events are matters apart from their physical measurement. Nor does the response have the dimensions of a stimulus, even though such dimensions may be used for shorthand convenience in measuring R. Thus, although the response "green" may be produced by stimulating with light of a given wavelength, color names must be treated as response occurrences rather than in terms of their lexical content. The R"four", obtained by the method of single stimuli or a rating scale, cannot be added to the R$_{\text{"two"}}$ and averaged to obtain the number 3.00 to be treated as if the subject had emitted R$_{\text{"three"}}$. Rather, R$_{\text{"four"}}$ and R$_{\text{"two"}}$ may be recorded as having occurred once each with measurable latencies, magnitudes, and the like.

In part, the stimulus-object distinction, mentioned earlier, springs not only from the stimulus complexity involved in an object but from the choice of the R to be measured and the experimenter's interpretation of that R. In much of what has been said so far, we have chosen examples where the responses involved were verbal. Experiments with human subjects need not, of course, use verbal R's, or even nonverbal R's that are under the experimenter's verbal instructional control; but verbal R's are the rule, and it is from them that the transition is made by the onlooker from sensation to perception. To put the case: when the verbal R is not one correlated, as the psychophysical R$_{\text{"yes"}}$ is, with the presence of whole S, but instead is one like color naming or shape naming or object naming, certain complications of analysis arise. These complications stem from the special reinforcement history of the latter responses as well as from the experimenter's lexical interpretation of the response. His interpretation, of course, is based on the experimenter's membership in the same verbal community to which his subject belongs. Titchener, when on the trail of "sensation," called such responses "object error" (*Kundgabe*), but he found them acceptable for "perception." In the latter case, he exemplified the object error with respect to his own behavior as stimulus. In like manner, much of psychophysical scaling depends upon the experimenter's interpretation of the subject's response. The fact that lawful relations may be uncovered does not alter the conclusion that the difference between sensation and perception lies not in the subject's behavior but rather in that of the experimenter reacting to his subject's behavior.

Conditioning and Stimulus Discrimination

A science of behavior takes its data and its principles at the level of stimulus-response correlation. It is in this context that the notation $S \rightarrow R$ designates a behavioral paradigm, with the notation $R = f(S)$ simply paraphrasing the idea of covariation. Collaterally, it is recognized that S and R are generic terms and that the bounds of the S class and the R class are subject to such experimental restriction as will yield a lawful relation between them [49, 50]. We shall speak of the $S \rightarrow R$ paradigm as *simple* when the correlation sought or found involves (parameters aside) one S and one R; later in the discussion, an *advanced* paradigm will be introduced in which attention will be focused on two R's in sequence, the first of which covaries with S, while the second R covaries with the first R.

Experimental procedures called *conditioning* are those which establish or maintain an S → R correlation where none, or a different one, existed before. Procedures to accomplish this are empirically discovered, and respecting them there is wide agreement among behavior scientists. In dealing with those procedures, modern reinforcement vocabulary recommends itself because it can be used with least encumbrance by false theoretical issues; accordingly, that vocabulary will be employed here when necessary.

Our topic of perception makes entry into behavior science via that aspect of conditioning called *stimulus discrimination*. Discrimination is evidenced by an organism in its responding. Regardless of the response under scrutiny and the R measure employed, two stimuli must produce a difference in the response measure if they are to be considered as discriminated. Thus, as Skinner pointed out long ago, the prototypical discriminative case is that involving one response and two stimuli, and these considerations hold true as much for human psychophysics and verbal behavior as for the nonverbal discriminations of animals.

The conditioning of a stimulus-response relation also increases the correlation between that same response and other stimuli having properties in common with the conditioned stimulus. This is the well-known phenomenon called *stimulus generalization*. Because the amount of generalization is a function of the degree of communality of elements of stimulus complexes, a generalization function is obtainable for stimuli graded along a physical continuum. The experimentally conditioned S, and any other stimulus on a physical-property continuum with it, are said to generalize to the extent that they overlap in capacity to evoke R; to the extent that they differ in evocative capacity, they are said to be discriminated. Thus, some degree of discrimination is inherent in any original generalization gradient of nonzero slope. But customary usage intends by discrimination the outcome of special training which augments the response difference to conditioned S and generalizing S beyond that produced merely by the latter's position, more or less remote, on the physical continuum containing the former. Such augmentation is achieved by a selective reinforcement procedure, involving an interspersed presentation (Pavlov's method of contrasts) of the two stimuli in which the operation (reinforcement) imparting strength to R in relation to the one stimulus (positive stimulus or CS^+, or S^D) is not carried out in relation to the other stimulus (negative stimulus or CS^-, or S). Discriminative training by selective reinforcement, in short, is a combination of conditioning and extinction. Each stimulus, the one correlated with reinforcement and the one not so correlated, gives rise to its own generalization gradient, the former a conditioning gradient and the latter an extinction gradient; the interaction of the two gradients and the accumulation of small differences in evocative strength between the two stimuli as a result of continued selective reinforcement lead to the resultant differences between $CS^+ \to R$ and $CS^- \to R$, or between $S^D \to R$ and $S \to R$.

These matters, routinely known, impinge more intimately on perception when human verbal behavior is considered. Here, Skinner [53] has pointed out a basic identity between discrimination and that important class of verbal response which he labels the *tact* (verb: to tact). The tact is a verbal response under the discriminative control of an S^D. A speaker, making a tact response to a stimulus, is, in effect, "naming" the stimulus. The response is the one provided by the lexicon of his verbal community, since the form of a tact is an arbitrary phonemic selection assigned by a language to a given S^D. Tact responses encompass that part of the language which is engaged in identification and naming, such as nouns, verbs, adjectives, the semanticist's "signs," Fries's [20] classes I, II, and III, and so on. To ensure the correlation of a tact with its proper S^D, a verbal community supplies the speaker with a variety of reinforcers, usually secondary or generalized, because otherwise hearers could suspect that the tact in question is under the control of drive and of the particular reinforcer being used, rather than of the appropriate S^D. When training a discriminative response in an animal, using so-called primary reinforcers, special precautions are needed [5, 44] because the mere occurrence of the response does not permit us to say whether it is naming the S^D or "manding" [53] the reinforcer. The difficulty arises because the two functional controls of the response are not differentiable in this case. The fundamental character of a tact could be approximated with an animal by employing a variety of reinforcers, including generalized ones (i.e., irrelevant to the specific drive prevailing).

Any tact, as a discriminative response within the precinct of verbal behavior, can itself be tacted (named, described, or identified) by other members of the verbal community who hear it. The latter will tact it in such ways as they themselves have been conditioned to do. Thus, if in the visual presence of a certain object a speaker says "table," his hearers can themselves speak of that $S^D \to R_{tact}$ correlation in whatever conventional ways they have been taught. They might, for example, say the speaker "sees" the table, or "perceives" the table, or "perceptually organizes" the table, and so on. Any case of a tact response can lead to the ascription or substitution by onlookers of the terms "perception" or "perceptual organization" for that tact, but this always involves mistaking the datum. The datum in verbal behavior is the verbal response itself, and never the supposed referent of the response, or its lexical meaning, or its alleged subjective content. Tacts do have referents of a sort by virtue of the way they are trained, those referents being the controlling S^D's.

Whatever regularities in behavior are derived from treating verbal responses as identical with their S^D's are incidental by-products of the reinforcement history of the responses with respect to their controlling S^D's. It is through the abandonment of the response as datum that such areas as semantic symbolism, or subjective magnitude scales in psychophysics, engender their difficulties. In the end, such an abandonment can lead to renouncing the science of behavior in favor of metaphysics.

Psychophysics

Our topic, as an area of scientific investigation, may be said to have had its beginning with early *psychophysics,* which was created by men who were interested in relating features of the physical world to the way in which that world is perceived. With a certain naïveté, they wished to determine how the world is "seen" by correlating the verbal responses of a psychophysical observer with the stimuli in his environment. Where the correlations uncovered have in turn been related to the physiology of sense organs, they have been relegated to sensation. Nevertheless, a commentary on perception also must include some attention to psychophysics and the psychophysical methods. Although operationally all the psychophysical methods involve correlation of response with stimulus and are diagrammable as cases of the simple S → R paradigm, discussion of some of the problems they raise must be postponed to a later point.

It may be noted here that the following discussion bypasses the argument that absolute thresholds in psychophysics are a special variety of difference threshold. The correctness of this view is not a matter of logic but rather of empirical considerations regarding the types of response required of the subject, his conditioning history with respect to stimulus reporting, the instructions to him during the experiment, and so on. Certain adjustments of these variables would, indeed, make absolute thresholds a variety of *DL* for that subject. Nonetheless, in customary psychophysical procedures, differences in the response bases of the two limens are not to be overlooked.

Absolute and difference limens. Pyschophysical methods used to determine an absolute threshold are marked by: (1) R is conditioned to the presence of whole S, or S complex, with no special discriminative training as regards any particular aspect or property of S, and (2) the S operation required to yield any desired value of the R measure can be specified to the necessary degree of refinement. Thus, the determination of an absolute threshold involves only observation of the relative frequency with which the response conditioned to the particular stimulus occurs as a function of variation in some property of that stimulus (for example, intensity). The psychophysical methods of limits and constant stimuli use this relative frequency measure of R occurrences to define a threshold value of S, and the required S can be specified precisely for any desired probability of R. The absolute threshold has traditionally been stated as some arbitrary point on this function, since the transition from an S value yielding an R probability of zero to an S value yielding an R probability of unity is not abrupt or discontinuous. Complete specification of an absolute threshold requires (1) criteria for identification of R, (2) the arbitrary threshold-defining value of R probability, (3) the S value yielding the threshold R probability, and (4) additional specifications of S in terms of its nonvaried parameters (including instructions). To this last we should add, of course, the training given R in the presence of S, although this is assumed, in the usual case, on the basis of the subject's membership in a particular reinforcement community in which certain kinds of conditioning are likely.

Although R probability has been used in illustration, it should not be concluded that it represents the only R measure which may be used in specification of a threshold. R magnitude or R latency, as well as others, can be put to such service. No change in the fundamental definition of an absolute threshold is required thereby, although the specification of the threshold will be changed accordingly.

The terms *supraliminal* and *subliminal* in the vocabulary of psychophysicists must be understood in the context of the conditions, outlined above, in which these terms are legitimately employed. Since the threshold is defined by an arbitrary value of the R measure, other values of the R measure may be observed in the presence of so-called subliminal stimuli [e.g., 36]. In addition, the rationale of psychophysics does not require that R's with different identification criteria have the same threshold; in fact, such is not the case. To determine the limen for a specified R, to observe that a different R occurs to stimuli below that limen, and to apply the term subliminal in connection with the latter observation, is to mistake the nature and logic of the psychophysical methods. A similar error is made when stimulus parameters (e.g., duration or frequency) other than the one varied to yield a threshold (e.g., intensity) are altered to produce responding to assertedly "subliminal" cues.

When psychophysical methods are employed to determine a difference threshold, they require more complex analysis than when used to determine an absolute threshold. While the response "different" can be conditioned to whole S complexes, permitting the difference threshold to be treated in the same terms as used here for the absolute threshold, this treatment would ignore certain features of the usual procedures for determining difference thresholds. The determination of a difference threshold requires, among other things, the presentation of at least two S complexes. The conditioning of the R"different" presumes that the observer has already been trained to respond to each of these S complexes. The R"different" is a tact of the simultaneous presence of two topographically different R's, namely, the R conditioned to each of the S complexes presented. The R"different" requires discriminative training with respect to the presence of different R's. For this reason, psychophysical methods for determining difference thresholds are discussed later under the advanced paradigm. We note here, however, that the difference threshold is similar to the absolute threshold in that the S operation required to yield any desired value of the R measure can be specified to the necessary degree of refinement. The problems of R identification, of criterion R measure for defining the threshold, and of S specification remain the same.

The problem of the difference threshold is related to the topic of stimulus-generalization gradients, in that both ask how much difference there must be between stimuli in order to produce differences in R measures, or even different R's. In the fundamental case, generalization is evidenced when an R conditioned in the presence of an S complex is evocable despite changes in some aspect or property of the complex. The amount of difference in R measure acceptable as evidencing lowered generalization is arbitrary, but no more so than, and in exactly the same sense as, the criterion R-measure values in the psychophysical methods are arbitrary. Generalization and absolute thresholds also are clearly related, in that a single S is presented and a single R recorded. The absolute threshold and generalization are measured with what comparative psychologists call "successive discrimination" and can be treated with the simple paradigm, S → R. On the other hand, the difference threshold is the product of "simultaneous discrimination" and needs to be treated with an advanced paradigm.

In the latter case, the behavior of the observer is an instance of R conflict where one response is reinforced and the other extinguished. Even a small difference in the strengths of the responses can lead to an immediate choice. Since, when two incompatible R's conflict, only one R is possible and its occurrence not only adds to its measured probability but automatically decreases the measured likelihood of the alternative, such simultaneous discriminations may appear to be quite precise in comparison with successive discriminations.

When a difference threshold is being measured in a simultaneous discrimination situation, the response of record is not evoked by either of the presented stimuli alone. That response is, rather, controlled by the responses made to the individual stimuli. The simultaneous nature of the discrimination is sometimes obscured by the fact that the stimuli may be presented successively. Successive presentation of stimuli gives rise to the "time error," in consequence of the intervening responses on which the $R_{\text{"different"}}$ or the $R_{\text{"same"}}$ must be based.

The psychophysical response.   In the determination of the absolute threshold, two "categories of judgment" (response) are customarily allowed. The subject is told, for example, to say "yes" if he sees the stimulus and "no" if he does not. A third category, "doubtful," when retained, must also be allied to the more complex paradigm in consort with "equal" and "different." In fact, only one R is needed for absolute thresholds, the occurrence or nonoccurrence of that R being the dependent variable of the experiment. The "yes" response can be used, without provision for "no," since the latter can be replaced by nonoccurrence of the former. In this form, the method is closer to the fundamental discriminative case illustrated by Skinner's S^D-$S^\triangle$ procedure. When the method of limits is modified for special purposes, such as determining the temporal course of dark adaptation, thresholds may be taken on the basis of a single R occurrence rather than per cent frequency, but the foregoing general considerations continue to apply.

It may be taken from what has been said that the psychophysical response "yes" is a special case of the tact relation mentioned earlier. This R may be termed a *generalized tact* to signify that it has been reinforced in the presence of many different S complexes and extinguished when none is present. It is, therefore, an indicator of the presence of a complex, naming the complex as other tacts do, but having the advantage that it can be transferred, as a general indicator, to any stimulus complex which the experimenter may use. We will not here stop to consider the interpretation that "yes" really tacts the presence of some more specific response to the stimulus, but the fact that other generalized tacts ("equal," "different," etc.) require such an interpretation suggests that it may be required here also.

The method of single stimuli in some forms differs from other psychophysical methods in that it allows and records several discriminative responses instead of concentrating all experimental attention on a single response. The concurrent measurement of many responses should not obscure the fundamental point that each R in such an experiment has a separate discriminative history and has its own generalization gradient. The stimulus complex for each response overlaps with those for the alternative responses, and the procedure is aimed at securing thresholds for each of the conflicting alternatives. The experiment is, in reality, studying the conditions necessary for the emission of each R. The effect of overlapping stimulus complexes for different R's is complicated in some cases by conditional probability relations between the R's. Thus, many responses are covariant to the extent that they exist as members of the same R chain. The response "yes" has the added advantage of not being chained to other responses.

Stimulus presentation procedures. One of the characteristics which distinguish the various psychophysical methods is the procedure of S presentation. Determination of the absolute threshold requires the presentation of a single stimulus and the measurement of some response to that stimulus. Two of the classical methods, constant stimuli and limits, are designed to do this and differ only in the order in which stimuli are presented. These two methods stand on the same theoretical foundation, save that data obtained by the two methods are complicated by sequential response dependencies, possibly different in the two cases.

Response latency. It was said earlier that response latency is another measure available in psychophysics for specifying a threshold, and we may exemplify it by Cattell's "reaction time" method. Here, stimuli or stimulus differences to which latencies are equal, are defined as equally discriminable. The method approaches the threshold value of S via a different rationale; for example, if the whole Latency = f(stimulus intensity) function were obtained, threshold S might be defined as that value lying midway between the function's limits, in a manner analogous to the half-life of radioactive elements.

Again, as said earlier, when a stimulus value (or range) has once been specified as subliminal with one psychophysical method, it is possible through varying other parameters to determine a different kind of threshold for that stimulus by some other method. Illustrative is the Postman-Bruner-McGinnies procedure [42]. The experimental method in these studies involves, first, choosing an S value which will elicit a given ("correct") response with a percentage frequency below that conventionally accepted as defining a threshold, and second, giving repeated successive presentations of that S or increasing the duration of S, or both. The number of S repetitions or the increased duration of S, needed before the subject correctly names the stimulus, is taken as the datum from which a sort of threshold is derived. This threshold, of course, requires no more than an S → R description. However, as this method is usually employed (e.g., in "perceptual defense"), the response of record is not correlated with the presence of whole S but rather, as in the method of single stimuli, with some particular aspect or property of S, so that the analogy to the psychophysical "yes" becomes attenuated. A later section has relevance to studies relying on this method.

The "instruction variable." Among the verbal aspects of human psychophysical studies, the so-called "instruction variable" figures importantly. Instructions to human subjects have several roles. For one thing, they serve the function of shortening the experiment if the long period of language training that precedes the experiment is not reckoned. In animal experiments, the work may need to begin at an earlier point to provide the equivalent to instructions. Still, human subjects have been known to misunderstand instructions, to resist serving, to fail to give "good" data, and never to overcome the "object error." Where instructions are effective, it is their conditioning history which makes them so.

Animal psychophysics. While we may choose for present purposes to treat human studies as being most germane to perception, it ought not be overlooked that animal parallels can be drawn at every step. The warrant for drawing such parallels is given by the theoretical attitude that verbal reports have no special status exempting them from treatment in the same manner as any other responding. Animal experiments may be of value in exposing the conditioning histories necessary for certain kinds of discriminative responding. Such studies, using both autonomic and partially restricted operant responses, have long been used to measure thresholds both absolute and differential. The methods used have often not had much formal procedural similarity to the psychophysical methods, although this is not difficult to achieve. The recent work of Ratliff and Blough [3, 4, 5, 43, 44] on the dark adaptation function in the pigeon has shown the possibility of devising new procedures approximating the psychophysical methods for the free operant situation.

The format of Skinner's free-operant discriminative experiments is readily applicable to both the definition and the measurement of thresholds. An absolute limen is the lowest value S^D can take before, in its pairing with an S^Δ of value zero, the differential in response rates to S^D and S^Δ disappears and responding assumes the characteristics it would have under a schedule of partial reinforcement in which the same temporal features and reinforcement contingencies prevail as during the prior S^D-S^Δ schedule. A difference limen is given by the nearest that S^Δ can approach S^D before, were S^Δ to approach any closer, the differential in response rates to S^D and S^Δ disappears and responding assumes the characteristics it would have under a schedule of partial reinforcement in which the same temporal features and reinforcement contingencies prevail as during the prior S^D-S^Δ schedule. How much difference in response rate (or response probability) we wish to accept as defining the threshold is again arbitrary but no more troublesome than the arbitrariness involved in the psychophysical methods. From a behavioral viewpoint, absolute and difference limens in a free operant situation are fundamentally related.

Animal experiments do not, of course, feature verbal reports, yet perception is often ascribed to animals. Here again, the reasons are to be found in the obscurity of the $R = f(S)$ function, and of the response's history and complexity. The verbal reports in human experiments do not make those experiments different in kind from animal ones but only heighten the difficulty of analysis and the likelihood that the human examples will be taken as perceptual.

THE ADVANCED PARADIGM: $S \to R_1 \cdot R_2$

The Sequential Response Dependency

Many behaviors dubbed perceptual are not adequately described by the simple $S \to R$ paradigm to which we have appealed up to this point, and for these we shall need to use a more intricate schema. This new paradigm may be written $S \to R_1 \cdot R_2$, in which R_1 is an initial response to S, and R_2 is a second response whose correlation with S is only through R_1; that is, R_2 is conditional upon the occurrence of R_1. Indeed, it was possible to assign some of our earlier behavioral examples to the simple $S \to R$ formula only because, as with the "yes" response of psychophysical experiments, the regularity of the data permits ignoring R_1. Nevertheless, that assignment was made with some loss of understanding. For our analysis of perception to proceed, the more advanced paradigm becomes necessary. We may now turn to behaviors which, though often regular enough to permit ignoring R_1, still would be misconceived were the existence of R_1, and the dependence of R_2 upon it, not explicitly acknowledged.

To introduce the paradigm $S \to R_1 \cdot R_2$ is to multiply complexities. Yet the behavior to be explained is complex, and it is not surprising that the simple formulation reaches the end of its utility. Two of these added complexities may be recognized at the outset: (1) Where before we had $R = f(S)$, we now have $R_1 = f(S)$ and $R_2 = f(R_1)$. Earlier, we held that the term perception is used by an onlooker when certain things were true of the behavior under inspection. The field of play for our onlooker's perceptual vocabulary is at least doubled by the introduction of the statement, $R_2 = f(R_1)$. (2) The very existence of R_1 may be unsuspected, so that the quasi correlation between S and R_2 is the source of behavior variability. The challenging and somewhat unpredictable observations sometimes made by perception theorists arise from the neglect of R_1's role as mediator. Consideration of the advanced paradigm makes it possible to extend the range of our discussion.

The "Perceptual Response"

The role of R_1 in the advanced paradigm may perhaps be clarified by an example. Imagine a person across whose visual field there flies a bird; to the query, "Did you see that bird?" he responds, "I saw it," and the simple $S \to R$ paradigm apparently covers the case well enough. But were the reply, instead, "No, I did not see it," the perceptual theorist might be inclined to say that our observer was "inattentive" or "lost in thought," or whatever, and therefore did not "perceive" or "register" the bird. It seems necessary to introduce between S (bird) and R ("see" or "not see") another term which is f(S), whose presence or absence is the basis of the *reporting response*. Now, to call this inserted term "perception" helps not at all. The insertion must be explicated as more than a hypothetical construction; that is, it must be coordinated with a real event, consequent to S but antecedent to R_2. To this event, the report R_2 can be attached by training. When an observer says "did see" or "did not see," he is not making a verbal R to S, since the latter may be retinally present in both cases. He is reporting something other than S. This other-than-S must be something real, not a fiction, since his report is conditioned to it. We have chosen to write this intervening event as R_1, partly in deference to its being a consequence of S and partly because we can deal with it in response terms. We emerge with what, in general form, once might have been called a motor theory of perception. But now it is not, however, perception which is motorially explained. Rather, the account deals with the conditioning basis of, or referent for, reporting responses.

When writing $R_2 = f(R_1)$, we express no prejudice for or against the view that by R_1 is really meant the stimulus accompaniments of R_1 or some parametric condition of the organism. While each of the latter ideas may be more acceptable formally from certain theoretical standpoints, the formula as written is more meaningful to other theorists. If stimulus accompaniments of the intervening event are conceived to be the conditioners of the R_2 report, the advanced paradigm would be written $S_1 \rightarrow \begin{bmatrix} R_1 \\ S_2 \end{bmatrix} \cdot R_2$. Still another conception would avoid the use of an intervening term altogether and cleave to the simple $S \rightarrow R$ formula by making S a complex consisting, in our example, not only of "bird" but also of all the parameters of S exposure, and also, possibly, making R a complex of which only one component, the report, is experimentally recorded. In such an S complex are all the stimuli, including instructions, operating upon the observer at the time "bird" was presented to his eye; in the R complex are all the observer's ongoing responses to the S complex which serve as parameters, interfering or facilitating, of the occurrence of the report we record as his response. At any rate, the intervening event we have been talking about must be some combination of stimuli and responses, since no other terms—such as emotion or state or drive or structure—will fit the role this middle term must play.

The necessity for inserting R_1 into the simple $S \rightarrow R$ paradigm is felt in many quarters. One reads of "conditioning a perception," "acquiring a perception," "reinforcing a perception," "extinguishing a perception," "distorting a perception," and so on, and experimental data allegedly supporting such phrases are offered in the literature. Almost always, of course, the data are actually R_2 measures, while the allegations are about "perception." Still, it would be curious if the conditioning vocabulary were being invoked for nothing more than a hypothetical fiction. Moreover, the experimental reality of R_1 is implied by research like that of Davis [15], and by studies of the response basis of "thoughts" and "images." On all scores, the two-response sequence of our advanced paradigm forces itself upon our attention.

Some Questions regarding $R_1 \cdot R_2$

Many considerations may be raised respecting the responses of the sequence $R_1 \cdot R_2$ which bear on the topic of perception. Only a few of these are selected for mention here. We begin with concern for R_1.

An initial question regarding R_1 is that of its relation to S, namely, whether it is an unconditioned or conditioned response and, if the latter, how its reinforcement history may be conceived. For some organisms, including human beings, at birth and for some period thereafter, a multiplicity of stimuli, singly or in combination, indiscriminately produce a multiplicity of responses, giving James's adult's eye view of an infant's eye view of the world as blooming, buzzing confusion. At that stage, when even in the terms of perception theory nothing is perceived, we may think of responding as unconditioned and nondiscriminative, the organism being literally blind, deaf, and so on, in the sense of having neither differential responses to stimuli nor any R_2 for reporting $S \to R$. In short, stimuli have no meaning for the organism [52]. Upon responses in, and differentiable from, this pool of behavior, selective reinforcement is brought to bear, by society or nature, in correlation with the presence or absence of relevant stimuli. The shaping of behavior by the accumulating history of selective reinforcement gives specificity of response to one sensory modality as against another, and within any one modality to stimulus properties like intensity, movement, and form. Our earlier discussion of perception depended only on this simple discrimination training, and on the unmediated correlation of responses with stimulus cues. A treatment of perception, however, need not concern itself with the original acquisition of conditioned R_1. Only a child-developmental approach to perception ever needs to start where the initial response to S is unconditioned. Unconditioned and diffuse responses to S may continue to be evocable indefinitely, as suggested by myographic data [13]. To date, however, perception theory has not been concerned with these responses, and we may lay them aside.

The conditioning history of R_1 often results in reducing the response below casual detectability, as in silent reading, attending, listening, delayed responding, and the like. This reduction occurs both in response magnitude and in topographical range of the responses. It can be carried to the point where the presence of R_1 in human subjects is unsuspected. R_1 may even be undescribable by the "perceiver" himself, let alone an onlooker, and special training must be given if the perceiver is to be able reliably to report it (as, "I saw the bird"). Even so, the fact that the reporting response is conditioned to R_1 does not automatically guarantee that further verbal responding will accurately describe R_1. While R_2 has many of the properties of "consciousness" or "awareness," the subject may attribute his awareness not to R_1 but to S itself. Thus, after saying "I saw it," the observer of our bird may deny, on questioning, that his report was occasioned by a response (R_1) at all, and deliver himself of a discourse regarding perception and seeing. His discourse is itself, however, under the control of conditioners other than R_1. In short, he misapprehends or does not appropriately verbalize the actual referent of his report "saw" [32]. Doubtless, further special discriminative training, perhaps reminiscent of Titchener, could bring his report under the control of the actual properties of R_1, so that he could tact his seeing behavior.

It is, perhaps, not altogether a digression to note that the conditioned relation $S \rightarrow R_1$ establishes S as a sufficient but not a necessary antecedent for R_1. Involved here are some old textbook evasions, for example, that light is the adequate stimulus for vision, the word *adequate* serving as the reason for not accepting pressure on the eyeball as a visual stimulus or, at least, not accepting it as a perceptual-visual stimulus even if it is accepted as a sensational-visual one. That a stimulus other than light could be the basis of a visual report seemed far-fetched in an approach to vision that used the $S \rightarrow - \cdot R_2$ ("I see") relation and ignored an intervening response. The presence of a bird is only the optimal condition for seeing a bird. In fact, it is commonplace that a response may be multiply caused, and this should at least take away the flavor of unnaturalness from "seeing" responses made to nonlight stimuli. The recognition of multiple causation removes the need for speaking of light and eyeball pressure as generalizing stimuli and preserves generalization for physical continua of stimulus properties.

Since R_2 may also be multiply caused, R_1 is a sufficient but not necessary condition for R_2, just as S is for R_1. The *Vexirversuche,* or catch tests, of psychophysical experiments are designed, in the experimental context, to make S both sufficient and necessary for R_1, and also R_1 both sufficient and necessary for R_2. Only by fulfilling the requirements of both sufficiency and necessity can psychophysical verbal responses of human subjects, which are R_2 measures, be depended on to yield stimulus-response lawfulness. It turns out that the double requirement can actually be met quite well, which is the reason for the fruitfulness of psychophysics and its utility for theories of sensory physiology. For the same reason, one can treat a good portion of psychophysics under the simple $S \rightarrow R$ paradigm. The regularity of the data, arising from the sufficiency-necessity achievement, permits ignoring R_1.

One may report "I saw" without R_1's having occurred, and indeed without S. On such occasions the observer might be regarded as "lying" or being deviously motivated. But if a way is found to activate or reinstate R_1, even in the absence of S, R_2 ("I saw") becomes more trustworthy, although it might be relegated to the categories of "recall" or "visual imagery." There are known ways of reinstating R_1 in the absence of S, such as using a more remote stimulus to begin a chain of responses in which R_1 is embedded (e.g., visualizing mother by visiting her old home, or looking at her favorite chair; or, recalling a race by bending down to the starting line of a track). If R_1 in the absence of S lacks some of the properties of R_1 as originally conditioned to S, then the R_2 report may be qualified as being vague, less intense, and the other usual things said of memories and images. Slight additional stimulation by low intensity values of S, together with otherwise produced activation of R_1, may summatively lead to particularly sharp imagination [41]. The most remarkable part of all this is how much we trust another person's R_2 when we have only the slim grounds of our verbal instructions: "Shut your eyes and think of an orange." In the absence of S, the reinstatement of R_1 under socially unacceptable circumstances is often dealt with as "hallucination," or "catharsis," etc.

Our insistence upon the reality of R_1 may lead some to inquire about its locus, that is, just what the response is, or what effector segment is involved in seeing or hearing. We must admit to immense, but not total, ignorance on this score. Naked-eye data are usually inadequate because of the reduced character of R_1. In this area, myographic studies loom as guideposts. But the question of R_1 locus is not important to the principle of our argument. It would not matter which response out of the primitive behavior pool is adventitiously, or by social or natural design, selected for conditioning as the initial perceptual response to S. Nor does it matter whether such selection is in part determined by species-genetic factors which might make some responses more likely as unconditioned responses to an S or perhaps more easily conditionable. It is sufficient that *some* R_1 be so conditioned. Our argument is that some R_1 *is* so conditioned and that an understanding of perception must take it into account.

"Instructions": Reprise

The advanced paradigm $S \rightarrow R_1 \cdot R_2$ permits us to treat in increased detail the "instruction," the "instruction variable," the "instruction stimulus," and *"Einstellung,"* or "determining tendency." Although instructions to the subject have been an almost universal part of psychophysical and perceptual experiments, they are sometimes overlooked in systematic treatments.

Instructions in psychological experiments are of three varieties:

1. Instructions which direct the subject to orient his receptors, or to suspend certain activities while getting ready to perform others. Thus, the subject is told to "Look into the aperture," or "You will hear a series of tones through the earphones," or "Get ready." The efficacy of such instructions depends on a verbal conditioning history. In lower organisms, as Wyckoff [59] has pointed out, such "observing responses" must often be explicitly trained in connection with any one experiment.

2. Instructions which direct or restrict the response which the subject is to make, as "Press the telegraph key," or "Say either 'yes,' 'no,' or 'not sure.' " Occasionally, instructions may be a combination of the first two kinds, as, "Tell me if the second weight is heavier or lighter than the first," "If you see one of these lights come on, press the key," or "Adjust this middle light so that it is just halfway between the other two lights in brightness." In animal experimentation, directive or restrictive instruction is replaced by the conditioning of the response to be measured.

3. Instructions intended to motivate the subject or to tap existing motivations, as, "Respond as fast as you can," "Do as well as you can, because your score will be compared with the scores of others," or "Be very careful not to respond if both lights come on." Again, because of the complex nature of verbal behavior, this third type of instruction is often blended with the first two, as, "All you need do is to adjust the length of this line until it is as long as the comparison line."

Instructions pose a special problem for several reasons. It is not clear that they have the status of stimuli at any point in the experiment other than at the time when they are actually given by the experimenter. Even at that time, there may be no clearly observable response to them. After the experiment is begun, they are frequently not repeated again, and it may be questioned whether a stimulus given before an experiment is, in any ordinary sense, acting as a stimulus in the later stages of the experiment. Moreover, only very infrequently is the subject's specific conditioning history with respect to the instructions known at all. In some studies, the experimenter may give a few "practice trials" to make sure that the subject "understands the instructions," but often even this step is omitted.

In terms of our paradigm, we will assume that the instruction stimulus initiates an R_1 [12]. This R_1 differs from those discussed earlier only in that it is perseverative rather than transient. It might be demarcated as a special variety of R_1 by calling it the "instruction response" R_i. This R_i is present throughout the experiment, and on each trial it modifies the stimulus complex present on that trial. The traditional problem of set or determining tendency falls within the scope of the R_i variable. Such a perseverative instruction response plays a role comparable to that of the postural orientations sometimes observed in delayed-reaction experiments with lower organisms. In higher organisms, the instruction response may not be sufficiently overt to be observable, and the R_i may consist simply of heightened tension in some response system, or of a subvocal verbal chain. Thus, when told to "cancel all words that contain both the letters e and s," the human adult may need to present these instructions to himself repeatedly while performing the task, until the complex discrimination is sufficiently well trained to short-circuit self-instruction in this form. A task for human subjects may be greatly complicated by changing the instructions on each trial. Even simple alternation of instructions may initially produce chaotic behavioral consequences [e.g., 11]. Eventually, the suitable R_i is conditioned to the distinctive stimuli which are presented on the trial or sequence of trials, and relatively rapid alternation of instruction stimuli produce rapid alternation of appropriate instructed responses. Harlow's work [26] on "learning sets" exemplifies the same phenomenon in animals, where nonreinforcement apparently serves a function akin to an instruction stimulus, weakening the currently perseverating R_i and strengthening the competing R_i. Eventually, the first trial "instructs" the subject on the appropriate R_i to maintain on that set of trials.

Because the instruction response is frequently not observable to the naked eye while its existence yet seems necessary, researchers have attempted by various means to locate the perceptual needle in the motor haystack. There may be, however, no optimal location in which to look. Often the particular response conditioned as a perseverating R_i is selected by happenstance, particularly in higher organisms with their immense motor repertory.

The ability to learn and make use of such persistent, covert instruction responses obviously demands several things of an organism. First, a large response repertory is required if the instruction stimuli are to be of help in a variety of rapidly shifting situations. Second, instruction responses must occasionally persist for long periods of time and must, therefore, be relatively effortless. Third, and especially often in the human case, several instruction stimuli may be blended on any trial, which means that several instruction responses must be made simultaneously. Any incompatibility among R_i's would preclude their service as multiple controllers on any trial.

As child educators and animal trainers well know, the persistence of an instruction response requires training. It is probable that instruction responses are established as whatever R_i's chance to be present when a particular R_2 is reinforced. These R_i's become extended in time, so that, even when S has been withdrawn, R_2 may be conditional upon them. That is to say, the opportunity for R_2 to procure reinforcement is not coincident with S presence. The time gap between S and R_2 is bridged by R_i. Even in higher organisms, the reinforcement contingency producing this second-order discrimination may take a long time to be effective. Lower organisms lend themselves to the study of instruction responses, since, first, their response repertory is sufficiently limited to permit the identification of R_i; second, unless special training is given, R_i may not become covert; third, the experimenter is less likely to take for granted the ability of the subject to make R_i; and, fourth, the subject is less likely to have already learned R_i's to particular stimuli. Indeed, the tendency of a human subject to give interfering "self-instruction" on the basis of an extensive history of previous reinforcement may override the effects of the independent variable being employed at the moment by the experimenter. When this happens, the experimenter must reverse or extinguish a previously learned discrimination. Sometimes, such self-instructions and their R_i products are referred to as *hypotheses,* and it is no cause for surprise that such hypotheses may be conditioned, extinguished, given intermittent reinforcement, and otherwise manipulated.

The Reporting Response

In our advanced paradigm, perceptual response has been suggested as the term for R_1. Perhaps a fitting name for R_2 would be reporting response, and we have already used this several times. With a human observer, R_2 is either overtly vocal or is verbally mediated, and the whole problem of perception thus falls, with its own idiosyncratic content, into the general area of verbal behavior. As a reporting response, R_2 is a tact, its discriminative stimulus or referent being R_1. Because R_1 is characteristically reduced in magnitude, it shares the privacy of interoceptive stimuli, and perceptual reports have accordingly been thought of as "introspective." R_1 itself, however, has some tact properties, since in its conditioning it comes under the discriminative control of S. In line with this, R_2 may be said to have some features of Skinner's [53] secondary verbal behavior, in that it has a discriminated response, albeit not necessarily a verbal one, as its controlling event.

As said in an earlier section, the control of S over R_1 and of R_1 over R_2 is marked by the relation of sufficiency but not necessity, and by multiple causality. An example of these controls is afforded by an experiment[2] designed to answer this question: If an auditory stimulus which is ordinarily perceptible is presented to a hypnotized subject while that sub-

    [2] W. N. Schoenfeld. Unpublished study, 1950. The cooperation of R. C. Davis, and his kindness in permitting use of his laboratory, are acknowledged.

ject is under trance instructions "not to hear" and if, thereafter, the subject is questioned as to whether he heard anything and replies "I did not," what conclusion can be drawn about the presence or absence of a "perception"? In the study, myographic records from subjects in trance were taken on stimulus presentation prior to the "do not hear" phase of the experiment. These were compared to records taken during that phase when subjects, questioned while still in trance, reported not having heard the stimulus. Although not conclusive, the data suggested that the usual muscular response to the stimulus, as measured before the "do not hear" instructions, was maintained with perhaps some lowering of magnitude during the instructed-deafness phase. What, then, did the subject's denial of hearing indicate? At what level of behavior did the denial take place? Apparently, the subjects did "hear" to the extent that R_1, the myographic response, still occurred; but R_2, the reporting response, was now under the experimenter's instructional control "do not hear," rather than under the customary waking control exercised by R_1.

In the area of psychophysics, there are instances in which R_2 must be considered to be based upon a complex of R_1's. One such instance is that of the "equal" response in the method of adjustment. Another is in the methods of limits and constant stimuli when a third judgment category is permitted. The response "equal" is surely not directly tied to the stimuli under comparison, since equality is not a stimulus property to which a tacting response can be conditioned. We have no receptor for equality, as we do for intensity or frequency of stimulus. The problem, then, is what an observer is reporting when, under instructions to make a comparative judgment, he says that two stimuli are "equal." By force, we must regard his "equal" as referring to two $S \rightarrow R_1$ connections in which the two R_1's are responses to the two S complexes being presented. The observer matches not the stimuli but his R_1's to those stimuli. It is the response conflict between R_1's which, for some range around its maximum, is tacted as "equality."

Paradigms for Mediated Generalization

In the advanced paradigm, the control by R_1 over R_2 leads us to turn some attention to mediated effects in conditioning, or, as they are usually called, mediated generalizations.

Two experimental formulae make up the core of mediational phenomena in conditioning. In simplest form, these are:

$$(\alpha)$$

where R represents any experimentally chosen response, and S_a and S_b represent two different stimuli each separately conditioned to R.

$$S \begin{cases} \nearrow R_a \\ \searrow R_b \end{cases} \tag{β}$$

where S represents a stimulus having a conditioning history with respect to each of two different responses, R_a and R_b. Once these paradigmed situations have been established experimentally, mediated generalization may be demonstrated along two lines, that of mediated extinction effects and that of mediated strengthening effects.

Mediated extinction with paradigm (α) involves extinction of the $S_a \rightarrow R$ correlation, and the observation that $S_b \rightarrow R$ is thereby weakened. A related special case is that of "stimulus patterning," in which the response is extinguished to part of a conditioned stimulus complex and the evocative efficiency of other parts of the complex is found to have diminished. With paradigm (β), mediation is tested by experimentally extinguishing $S \rightarrow R_a$ and observing the consequent effect on $S \rightarrow R_b$. The order in which $S \rightarrow R_a$ and $S \rightarrow R_b$ are conditioned will determine which response will play the greater role as mediator in extinction. We might presume that if $S \rightarrow R_a$ has the prior history, R_a will occur in some reduced form during the conditioning of $S \rightarrow R_b$ and thus form a portion of the conditioners of R_b. In other words, this conditioning history assures that R_a and R_b will form a functional unit to some degree. It is possible that the extent of the mediation obtainable with paradigm (β) would be related in some way to the number of topographic properties held in common by R_a and R_b.

Mediated strengthening begins with the same two core paradigms. Proceeding from (β), a second stimulus is conditioned to one of the responses, and the mediation is measured by the extent to which this second stimulus assumes control over the other response. Thus, given

$$\begin{matrix} & \nearrow R_a \\ S_a & \\ & \searrow R_b \\ & \nearrow \\ S_b & \end{matrix} \tag{γ}$$

the question is whether, and to what degree, $S_b \rightarrow R_a$ subsequently appears. Necessary experimental safeguards, of course, are to measure the preexperimental degree of generalization of S_a and S_b, and also to show that any effects obtained are not due to sensitization by S_b. Mediated acquisition of the sort discussed here is probably explicable by the fact that there is some tendency for R_a to occur while R_b is being conditioned (where R_a is the response with the prior conditioning history). In this way, R_a functions in the manner of our previously discussed R_1. If this is correct, it would mean that neither R_a nor R_b is in pure form during either the conditioning of $S_b \rightarrow R_b$ or the testing of $S_b \rightarrow R_a$.

Where the foregoing case begins with paradigm (β) and adds (α), the second possibility of mediated acquisition begins with the paradigm (α) and adds (β). Thus, given paradigm (α) already experimentally established, a second response is conditioned to one of the stimuli, and the mediation is measured by the extent to which control over this second response is assumed by the other stimulus. Thus, given

$$(\delta)$$

the question is whether, and to what degree, $S_a \rightarrow R_b$ appears.

The order of addition of paradigms (α) and (β), despite the similarity in the final diagrams, has significant consequences, one of which is that the second order described by paradigm (δ) is much more likely to produce mediated acquisition than (γ). This greater effectiveness of the second order of addition arises from the fact that R_a is evoked by S_b while that stimulus is being conditioned to R_b, so that the later measure of $S_a \rightarrow R_b$ strength as an index of mediation does not start from a true zero of $S_a \rightarrow R_b$ strength, but rather from some positive value accruing from R_a's mediation function.

The operation of mediated generalization in various perceptual phenomena is illustrated by such cases as conditioned seeing, synesthesia, and sensory preconditioning. Conditioned seeing has been given reality by experiments like that of Bruner and Postman [10], Baker and Mackintosh [2], Leuba [34], and Ellson [16, 17, 18]. Akin to conditioned seeing is synesthesia, which can result from conditioning several of an object's stimulus properties, as part of a stimulus complex, to a common response. Thus, if a certain shape-color-taste of a novel fruit has been conditioned to the response "persimmon" and if later the taste is conditioned to the response "tart," then, afterward, similar shapes and colors may produce the response ("feeling") of "tart taste," or, conversely, a tart taste may be "colored." Co-stimulation is characteristic also of sensory preconditioning experiments [6, 7, 8], where S_a and S_b may be presented together even in advance of $S_a \rightarrow R_a$ or $S_b \rightarrow R_a$ conditioning, with the subsequent mediation arising from some unmeasured and perhaps unknown responses to those stimuli. Sensory preconditioning may appear to be closer to paradigm (α), and to arise from a novel sort of pure stimulus generalization created by co-stimulation, but this appearance derives from neglecting to measure responses during the initial co-stimulation phase of the experiment [57]. This same criticism can be made of the view that co-stimulation by shape-color-taste suffices to cause simple generalization of these stimuli without appeal to response mediation. That co-stimulation alone is not the key to synesthesia, conditioned seeing, and sensory preconditioning—and that it is not was implied by those researchers who early adopted the term mediated generalization—is urged by several considerations, among them the fact that the same effects may be produced even if S_a and S_b are at separate times and never conjunctively conditioned to a common response. When co-stimulation experiments fail to yield positive results (as in latent learning, on occasion), the failure is sometimes ascribed to the organism's "inattention" to the stimuli, or to its "selective reception." But there is no meaning in such phrases that is not inferred from responding. Although it may seem remote from the actual experimental operations of the researcher, prudence would endorse the conclusion that mediated extinction and acquisition have a response foundation and are not the result of simple co-stimulation alone.

ASSESSMENT OF SOME REPRESENTATIVE PERCEPTIONS

Our glance at mediated generalization was meant mainly to illustrate how a behavioral science might begin its analysis of a perceptual problem. Before closing, we may perhaps say something about a few other examples drawn from a miscellany at hand which figure prominently in the field of perception. As always, we proceed by asking first what the responses are which enter the phenomenon to be explained. Although a complete or correct identification may be beyond our reach, we can at least rough out the variables to which we would look for explanation. When the responses are identified, the question of how they can be evoked remains, which is to say, what the independent variables are which control them. These are the sole questions, and they are recognizable at once as defining again the $S \rightarrow R$ principle. Our examples are chosen to include some in which the response involved may be taken as known, and the question is how to evoke it. "Illusions," "relations," and "constancy" are of this sort. We also include some examples, namely, figure-ground phenomena, where it is necessary to identify the actual response, while the controlling variables may be presumed known.

Illusions, Relations, and the Constancies

The experimentally measured responses in illusions, relations, and constancy may be verbal ("this one is longer," "reddish," "six feet tall," etc.) or nonverbal (pointing, adjusting, myographic spikes, etc.). In any instance, our concern is with how the given response is controlled, or why it is evoked under specified conditions. Although illusions, relations, and the constancies are often regarded as different in kind, upon reflection it seems more likely true that they are kin one to the other. Is not a constancy an illusion, and a relation a constancy? The three terms together designate behavioral phenomena in which our attention is called to special types of control exercised by stimulus complexes and by discriminative histories that are usually forgotten in our bemusement over the phenomena themselves.

Some illusions are produced by a discriminative history in which parts of a stimulus complex vary concomitantly. It is commonplace that we may produce a given response by presenting an S complex which does not contain the relevant stimulus aspect, or degree, that is usually required. Thus, if in an organism's experience S_x and S_y have varied concomitantly as parts of an S complex, we may evoke R_x, relevant to S_x, by presenting an S complex containing an appropriate value of S_y but an inappropriate value of S_x. When observed within a single sense modality, such illusions verge on the classical problem of stimulus generalization, and even on sensory physiology (as when a subject gives different color names for a fixed wavelength of light when intensity is changed). But rather more glamour attaches to illusory phenomena when cross-sense control is involved. This is true of the size-weight illusion as studied by the psychophysical methods of constant stimuli or of single stimuli. The latter method provides perhaps the simpler instance of manipulating an "inappropriate" aspect of the stimulus in order to get out a given response. If we present a subject with a container of a certain weight, we may ask what size it must be visually to prompt the response "one pound." The environment has frequently in the past required such judgments (responses) on the basis of visual size. Some such judgments are nonverbal. Before an adequate lifting response is made, some prior response occurs on the basis of visual cues. Lifting responses of inappropriate magnitude have been extinguished in the past, producing a visual weight discrimination, in effect. As size and weight are correlated in the visual discriminative history, illusions can be produced by manipulating size alone and calling for a weight response. There is nothing inappropriate about the stimulus aspect of size. Yet, because it does not recommend itself to the layman's common notion of what weight should be judged by, we can amaze him by demonstrating the "illusion." Similar phenomena, produced experimentally, can easily be cited.

The Müller-Lyer effect falls within this same type. The response is known ("This one is longer," or pointing, or adjusting to equality). Our question is, how lines winged in such-and-such fashion come to evoke the same responses as lines varied in linear extent only. We may compare the over-all length of a complex form embedding a line $A, \rangle\!\!-\!\!-\!\!-\!\!\langle$, with that of another complex form embedding line $A, \langle\!\!-\!\!-\!\!-\!\!\rangle$, and look to the conditioning history of the subject for an explanation of the "illusion" which leads him to call A longer in its former context. A subject's judgments of length before coming to the laboratory have demanded that over-all length be taken into account. Common behaviors of putting things into boxes or envelopes or shoes have required it. A subject brings his discriminative history to the laboratory with him, and he "sees" one A as longer. Now, if we experimentally dissociate the line length from the over-all form length, reinforcing only judgments that are correct as to length of A, the so-called illusion disappears, and the subject "sees" the two A's as equal. Some may wish to speak of "reinforcing a perception," but it is sufficient to speak of reinforcing a response.

A striking instance of manipulating perception by reinforcing a response is found in Sherif's [48] work on the autokinetic effect. It may be that the response "moving" is produced by eliminating cues that control the response "stationary." The response "stationary" itself depends on many cues other than motion on a receptor surface, since the environment is constantly in movement when the receptors are moved. (So, the response "stationary" was one of the last to reappear in Stratton's [55] and Snyder and Pronko's [54] inverted vision experiments.) The absence of cues for "stationary" produces "seen" movement. Thereafter, responses of direction and amount of the "seen" movement may be directly controlled by the subject's reinforcing community.

Perception of relations, including transposition, also involves known responses, and the problem again is how to evoke them. Relations are an important part of object discrimination, where reinforcement is seldom contingent on the absolute magnitudes of the several stimulus aspects presented. As an organism moves about in space, the absolute magnitudes of the several components of an S complex are always undergoing change, but the changes are correlated as amongst the various components [51]. Relations among certain components of different S complexes, however, are maintained. It is not surprising that the organism learns to respond to the relation rather than absolute magnitudes, since his reinforcement contingencies may depend on those invariant relations. As Guthrie [24] once remarked, the physical relation among parts of a stimulus complex is as much a part of the complex as the parts themselves. It is the nature of the common environment, of the organism moving about in it, and of the reinforcement contingencies afforded which together produce relational responding. An environment in which S complexes remained constant and gave the organism no experience of fixed relations among stimulus components varying in absolute magnitude would yield an organism with no "perception of relations" beyond, possibly, some generalization gradients of small interest to perceptual theory.

The constancies, wherein again the responses are known and the discriminative cues are sought, provide our last example of behavioral control by S complexes and reinforcement history. When the response "white" is conditioned to a piece of paper, it is reinforced no matter what absolute and relative amounts of incident and reflected light may prevail on any given occasion. Later on, differential reinforcement of "white" may be given only under certain ranges of those absolute and relative values. The point is that the response "white" comes under the control of many portions of the S complex, not the least of which are those aspects associated with the paper. Other stimulus variables share control of the response "white," and the paper is "seen" as white under many different magnitudes of those variables. Similarly, an S complex may be "seen" as a man regardless of retinal image size. Many stimulus or R_1 aspects, such as cues of distance, or familiarity, can control the response "man." When an S complex is sufficiently changed in the values of its controlling cues, the looked-for response becomes less probable, and "constancy breaks down."

The central point of our treatment of illusions, relations, and constancies lies in an insistence upon consideration of the conditioning history of the R_1 upon which the observed R_2 (reporting response, tact) is based. In a complex world the assumption of a complex history for R_1 can hardly be a matter of debate. The answers to many perceptual questions are to be sought not only in developmental, psychophysical, and physiological-genetic studies, but also in studies in which original perceptual illusions, relations, and constancies are manufactured and manipulated in the refined world of the laboratory.

Figure-ground Phenomena

The figure-ground phenomenon, sometimes set forth as a perceptual case invulnerable to S → R analysis, is almost unique in its lack of specificity. One cannot even be sure of just what the phenomenon is, or just what the responses are which supposedly reveal the presence of a figure-ground relation. Its alleged universality and pervasiveness are, of course, the companions of its nonspecificity. Consider what is done when a naïve subject is presented, let us say, with a common visual S complex and is asked to indicate which part is the figure and which the ground. He is likely to be puzzled by the question and request to have the words explained. There then follow leading descriptions, circumlocutions, synonyms, hints, appeals, and instructions, after which the subject points to one part, announcing that that is the figure, the rest the ground. Having been told how to make the identification, he makes it. In the subsequent interrogation, he makes other responses to such questions as: How does it look? Is the figure in front of the ground? Is it nearer to him? Set off from the ground? Is it contoured? Is the ground continuous behind it? His answers satisfy the questioner that he really perceives the thing as he should. In fact, this means that he sees it as the questioner believes it should be seen, and as the questioner sees it and has told him it should be seen. In short, he presently agrees with the questioner in his "perception." Much of the perceptual case rests upon personal validation. Where the subject has incorporated in his own repertory the R_2's that were the experimenter's rationale for performing the experiment, who is to trust the result?

Now, this is plainly a very complicated business. Not only is the figure-ground character of the subject's perception a matter of response inference, and not only has he been prompted to give certain responses, but we are far from dealing with his actual responses, and we do not know specifically which of his responses we ought to concern ourselves with. How shall we deal with a response like "This is in front, and the rest is continuous behind it"? A subject's reinforcement history gives ample basis for a conditional probability between "in front of" and "nearer to me," and between "in front of" and "continuous behind it," since that is the way physical objects are usually encountered, hence, usually "seen" or responded to. How shall we deal behaviorally with "It has a shape, this is its contour" (after we grant the interest that such responses have for the visual psychophysiologist as being relevant to stimulus gradients of wavelength or intensity which fractionate visual fields)? And what are we to say if, after presenting a picture of a uniform field with a keyhole through which the subject may see some objects, he reports that the distant objects and the keyhole are both figures while the uniform field is the ground? Is he wrong, and if so by what token?

With the figure-ground problem we must at the outset decide what response we shall examine and thereafter hold fast to it, whether it be the subject's pointing and tracing, or his words or sentences, or some combination of these. It is a wholly arbitrary matter that we assign to a selected response, or set of responses, the reference "figure" and to others "ground." Moreover, an appropriately arranged discriminative history will determine to which part of a presented S complex the subject will make our criterion response. The part he responds to in a particular way *is* the figure, and the rest *is* ground, by definition and not by some inherent and mystical correctness. The very existence of reversible figures shows this to be true, though ironically enough they are often supposed to exhibit the contrary. Indeed, were they not already known, the creatability of reversible figures would be predictable from a behavior analysis.

The occurrence of a predesignated response makes clear which part of an S complex is figure and which ground. The fact that in the human case the response may serve as cue for additional reporting responses ("introspections") should not confuse the issue. Where Osgood [40] thinks Koffka is artful in asking why we see things and not the holes between them, we may challenge the observation and reply that one may in fact see either. Our seeing lies in our responding, and we respond in criterion fashion to any part of an S complex in conformity with our discriminative training and the controlling variables present.

SUMMARY

This paper takes its start from the view that there is no "theory of perception" divorced from a general theory of behavior. Indeterminacies have resulted from attempts to define perception independently of behavior and especially to distinguish it from sensation. Perception remains closely allied to the continually developing behavioral theory of discrimination, including psychophysics. It is suggested that if current usages of the term perception are to be understood, it may be necessary to look for the term's referent in the verbal habits of onlookers who assert of any given instance of behavior that it is perceptual. When this is done, it appears that the word perception is evoked by certain types of complexity in behavioral functions. These complexities are examined, and examples are analyzed in the vocabulary of reinforcement theory.

The treatment of perception in discriminative terms requires two general paradigms: first, the simple $S \rightarrow R$ formula and, second, a more advanced schema, $S \rightarrow R_1 \cdot R_2$. In the latter, which is characteristic of so-called perceptual behavior in human beings, R_2 is conditional upon the prior R_1. If R_1 may be termed the perceptual response, it is suggested that R_2 be called the reporting response, and the relation of R_2 to the area of verbal behavior is pointed out. Examples are cited to show how the reduction of perception to stimulus-response concepts might proceed. By force, the analyst's attention is drawn to the response terms in the paradigms, since perceiving must finally evidence itself in responding if it is to be treatable at all in a natural science of behavior.

REFERENCES

1. Allport, F. H. *Theories of perception and the concept of structure.* New York: Wiley, 1955.
2. Baker, K. E., & Mackintosh, I. The influence of past associations upon attributive color judgments. *J. exp. Psychol.*, 1955, 49, 281–286.
3. Blough, D. S. A method for tracing dark adaptation in the pigeon. *Science*, 1955, 121, 703–704.
4. Blough, D. S. Dark adaptation in the pigeon. *J. comp. physiol. Psychol.*, 1956, 49, 425–430.
5. Blough, D. S., A method for obtaining psychophysical thresholds from the pigeon. *J. exp. anal. Beh.*, 1958, 1, 31–43.
6. Brogden, W. J. Sensory pre-conditioning. *J. exp. Psychol.*, 1939, 25, 323–332.
7. Brogden, W. J. Tests of sensory pre-conditioning with human subjects. *J. exp. Psychol.*, 1942, 31, 505–517.
8. Brogden, W. J., & Gregg, L. W. Studies of sensory conditioning measured by the facilitation of auditory acuity. *J. exp. Psychol.*, 1951, 42, 384–389.
9. Bruner, J. S., & Goodman, C. C. Value and need as organizing factors in perception. *J. abnorm. soc. Psychol.*, 1947, 42, 33–44.
10. Bruner, J. S., & Postman, L. On the perception of incongruity: a paradigm. *J. Pers.*, 1949, 18, 206–223.
11. Culler, A. J. Interference and adaptability. *Arch. Psychol.*, 1912, No. 24.
12. Davis, R. C. Set and muscular tension. *Indiana Univer. Publ. Sci. Ser.*, 1940, No. 10.
13. Davis, R. C. Motor effects of strong auditory stimuli. *J. exp. Psychol.*, 1948, 38, 257–275.
14. Davis, R. C. Motor responses to auditory stimuli above and below threshold. *J. exp. Psychol.*, 1950, 40, 107–120.
15. Davis, R. C. The stimulus trace in effectors and its relation to judgment responses. *J. exp. Psychol.*, 1952, 44, 377–390.
16. Ellson, D. G. Hallucinations produced by sensory conditioning. *J. exp. Psychol.*, 1941, 28, 1–20.
17. Ellson, D. G. Experimental extinction of an hallucination produced by sensory conditioning. *J. exp. Psychol.*, 1941, 28, 350–361.
18. Ellson, D. G. Critical conditions influencing sensory conditioning. *J. exp. Psychol.*, 1942, 31, 333–338.
19. Eriksen, C. W., & Browne, C. T. An experimental and theoretical analysis of perceptual defense. *J. abnorm. soc. Psychol.*, 1956, 52, 224–230.
20. Fries, C. C. *The structure of English.* New York: Harcourt, Brace, 1952.
21. Graham, C. H. Psychophysics and behavior. *J. gen. Psychol.*, 1934, 10, 299–310.
22. Graham, C. H. Behavior, perception and the psychophysical methods. *Psychol. Rev.*, 1950, 57, 108–120.
23. Graham, C. H. Behavior and the psychophysical methods: an analysis of some recent experiments. *Psychol. Rev.*, 1952, 59, 62–70.

24. Guthrie, E. R. *The psychology of learning.* New York: Harper, 1935.

25 Hanawalt, N. G. Memory trace for figures in recall and recognition. *Arch. Psychol.,* 1937, No. 216.

26. Harlow, H. F. The formation of learning sets. *Psychol. Rev.,* 1949, **56,** 51–65.

27. Howes, D., & Osgood, C. E. On the combination of associative probabilities in linguistic contexts. *Amer. J. Psychol.,* 1954, **67,** 241–258.

28. Kanfer, F. H. Perception: identification and instrumental activity. *Psychol. Rev.,* 1956, **63,** 317–329.

29. Kantor, J. R. *An objective psychology of grammar.* Bloomington, Ind.: Indiana Univer. Press, 1936.

30. Kantor, J. R. *Psychology and logic.* Bloomington, Ind.: Principia Press, 1945.

31. Kantor, J. R. *Principles of psychology.* (Rev. ed.) Bloomington, Ind.: Principia Press, 1949 (1st ed., 1924).

32. Keller, F. S., & Schoenfeld, W. N. *Principles of psychology.* New York: Appleton-Century-Crofts, 1950.

33. Koffka, K. *Principles of gestalt psychology.* New York: Harcourt, Brace, 1935.

34. Leuba, C. Images as conditioned sensations. *J. exp. Psychol.,* 1940, **26,** 345–351.

35. Levine, R., Chein, I., & Murphy, G. The relation of the intensity of a need to the amount of perceptual distortion: a preliminary report. *J. Psychol.,* 1942, **13,** 283–293.

36. McCleary, R. A., & Lazarus, R. S. Autonomic discrimination without awareness: an interim report. *J. Pers.,* 1949, **18,** 171–179.

37. Miller, G. A., & Selfridge, J. A. Verbal context and the recall of meaningful material. *Amer. J. Psychol.,* 1950, **63,** 176–185.

38. Miller, G. A., Bruner, J. S., & Postman, L. Familiarity of letter sequences and tachistoscopic identification. *J. gen. Psychol.,* 1954, **50,** 129–139.

39. Mueller, C. G., & Schoenfeld, W. N. Edwin R. Guthrie. In W. K. Estes, et al. *Modern learning theory.* New York: Appleton-Century Crofts, 1954. Pp. 345–379.

40. Osgood, C. E. *Method and theory in experimental psychology.* New York: Oxford Univer. Press, 1953.

41. Perky, C. W. An experimental study of imagination. *Amer. J. Psychol.,* 1910, **21,** 422–452.

42. Postman, L., Bruner, J. S., & McGinnies, E. M. Personal values as selective factors in perception. *J. abnorm. soc. Psychol.,* 1948, **43,** 142–154.

43. Ratliff, F. Some interrelations among physics, physiology, and psychology in the study of vision. In S. Koch (Ed.), *Psychology: a study of a science.* Vol. 4. New York: McGraw-Hill, 1962.

44. Ratliff, F., & Blough, D. S. Behavioral studies of visual processes in the pigeon. USN, ONR, Tech. Report, 1954 (Contract N5 ori-07663, Project NR140-072).

45. Riesen, A. H. The development of visual perception in man and chimpanzee. *Science,* 1947, **106,** 107–108.

46. Schoenfeld, W. N., & Cumming, W. W. Verbal dependencies in the analysis of language behavior. Unpublished research report, Council on Research in the Social Sciences, Columbia Univer., 1953.
47. Senden, M. von. *Raum- und Gestaltauffassung bei operierten Blindgeborenen vor und nach der Operation.* Leipzig: Barth, 1932.
48. Sherif, M. A study of some social factors in perception. *Arch. Psychol.,* 1935, No. 187.
49. Skinner, B. F. The concept of the reflex in the description of behavior. *J. gen. Psychol.,* 1931, **5,** 427–458.
50. Skinner, B. F. The generic nature of the concepts of stimulus and response. *J. gen. Psychol.,* 1935, **12,** 40–65.
51. Skinner, B. F. *Science and human behavior.* New York: Macmillan, 1953.
52. Skinner, B. F. What is psychotic behavior? In *Theory and treatment of the psychoses.* St. Louis: Washington Univer. Stud., 1956.
53. Skinner, B. F. *Verbal behavior.* New York: Appleton-Century-Crofts, 1957.
54. Snyder, F. W., & Pronko, N. H. *Vision with spatial inversion.* Wichita, Kansas: Univer. of Wichita Press, 1952.
55. Stratton, G. M. Vision without inversion of the retinal image. *Psychol. Rev.,* 1897, **4,** 341–360.
56. Sturtevant, E. H. *An introduction to linguistic science.* New Haven: Yale Univer. Press, 1947.
57. Wickens, D. D., & Briggs, G. E. Mediated stimulus generalization as a factor in sensory pre-conditioning. *J. exp. Psychol.,* 1951, **42,** 197–200.
58. Woodworth, R. S. *Experimental psychology.* New York: Holt, 1938.
59. Wyckoff, L. B. The role of observing responses in discrimination learning. Part I. *Psychol. Rev.,* 1952, **59,** 431–442.

MOTIVATION IN LEARNING THEORY[1]

ERNEST R. HILGARD
Department of Psychology
Stanford University

Introduction 253
Some Needed Revisions in Hullian Aversive-drive Theory 255
   Needs and aversive drives. 255
   The arousal aspect of drive 257
   Drive enhancement through perceived incentives 258
   Neglected drives 258
   Frustration-induced drives 259
Some Problems of Primary and Secondary Reinforcement 260
   Intermittent reinforcement as critical of secondary reinforcement . . . 262
Neohedonism: Affective Arousal as the Core of Motivation 263
Other Sources of Motivational Psychology. 268
   Influence of Freud, Lewin, and others 268
   Three classes of motivational psychology 269
   Some possibilities with respect to the organization of motives. . . . 277
      Value properties not goal-oriented 277
      Short motivated-behavior sequences 278
      Behavior systems. 278
      Personality syndromes 278
References. 279

INTRODUCTION

In order to take a fresh look at learning as the field of primary inquiry and at motivation as the secondary field, we do well to begin with

[1] This chapter was originally prepared while the author was a fellow at the Center for Advanced Study in the Behavioral Sciences, on leave from Stanford University. Some of the concepts considered here show the results of discussion at the Center with other behavioral scientists in residence, particularly (but not exclusively) with Daniel E. Berlyne, David A. Hamburg, William W. Lambert, André M. Weitzenhoffer, John M. W. Whiting, and Joseph Wolpe. I wish to acknowledge the assistance of Mrs. Barbara Anderson in the preparation of the material on which Table 3 is based.

Hull's system, widely influential among American learning experimenters at mid-century. Hull succeeded in expressing clearly the distinction between associative factors (learning or habit) and nonassociative factors (drive and other performance variables), while proposing a quantitative system for their interaction. Although the system is vulnerable to attack, it is a major achievement, and Hull was fully aware that it was merely a step along the road to better formulations.

The input variables in Hull's system, with the intervening variables directly associated with them, are listed in Table 1. The input variables are those features within the organism and the environment that have to be understood before the process of response evocation (as output) can be accounted for.

TABLE 1. INPUT VARIABLES AND INTERVENING VARIABLES DIRECTLY ASSOCIATED WITH THEM IN HULL'S FINAL SYSTEM [35]

Input variable		Intervening variable	
N	Number of prior reinforcements	$_sH_R$	Habit strength
$_{s'}H_R$	Generalized habit, based on same response conditioned to another stimulus	$_{s'}H_R$	Generalized habit strength from related habit
C_D	Drive condition (deprivation, noxious stimulation)	D	Drive
		S_D	Drive stimulus
S	Intensity of evocative stimulus	V	Stimulus-intensity dynamism
w	Amount (weight) of goal object (food reward)	K	Incentive motivation
W	Work required in responding	I_R	Reactive inhibition
		$_sI_R$	Conditioned inhibition

We note immediately that there are three associative factors among the intervening variables (habit strength, generalized habit strength, and conditioned inhibition) and five nonassociative performance factors (drive, drive stimulus, stimulus-intensity dynamism, incentive motivation, and reactive inhibition). We are now confronted with a problem of definition. All associative factors can be classified as learning. Can all nonassociative factors be classified as motivational? If by motive we mean anything that affects the strength at which associative factors are manifested in behavior, then all the nonassociative factors are motivational: they are inciters to behavior, goads, or brakes upon behavior. They all affect the utilization of habit. Unless some quality of goal directedness is added to our definition of motivation, all nonassociative factors are motivational. Because Hull does not explicitly include goal directedness in his definition of drive, we may without violating his system say that drive is but one of five motivational components that he recognized. (It is more usual to confine the discussion of motivation to drive, but precedent for the broader usage is found in the inclusion of K, named by Hull as incentive motivation, and entering his system parallel to all the other nonassociative factors.) For our purposes we shall call all nonassociative performance factors motivational and proceed to consider Hull's system from this standpoint.

Hull assigned three roles to drive:

1. Drive is a necessary condition for the occurrence of primary reinforcement and for the origination and continuation of the effectiveness of secondary reinforcement. In this role drive is unique among the nonassociative performance factors, for only it (or its correlative S_D) serves reinforcement.

2. Drive is a necessary condition for habits to manifest themselves in behavior. Drive activates habit strength into reaction potential, which (if suprathreshold) leads to overt performance. This characteristic of drive is shared by the other multipliers of habit strength (especially V and K). An important feature of this aspect of D (in Hull's system) is that the role is indiscriminate, that is, that D arises from all drives that are active and can multiply any habit on the verge of being activated. We shall return to this point.

3. Specific drives furnish distinctive stimuli (S_D), so that the organism can learn to turn one way when hungry and another when thirsty, even though external stimuli are unchanged. These distinctive stimuli also serve, through conditioning, to integrate long sequences, or chains, of responses. This discriminative role of drive is not, strictly speaking, motivational; however, S_D will contribute its share to the stimulus dynamism (V), so that it has some motivational role. The S_D function is systematically that of any other persistent stimulus, such as a white line drawn on the floor of the maze marking the true path.

To Hull, all drives were aversive; that is, *escape* from the drive is adaptive. All drives follow the paradigm of food deprivation, water deprivation, or painful stimulation. Hence in referring to Hull's drive conception I shall hereafter use the expression *aversive drive*, to distinguish between his theory and the possibility that there are also appetitive drives.

SOME NEEDED REVISIONS IN HULLIAN AVERSIVE-DRIVE THEORY

In this section I intend to remain somewhat within the framework of Hullian theory but to call attention to the points at issue among those with theories close to Hull's.

Needs and Aversive Drives

The first point to be made is that there is more ambiguity about the drive state than at first appears. At first the conception appears simple enough: a thirsty horse will drink, while one not thirsty will not. Hence the thirst drive is aroused in the first horse and not in the second.

There are two main classes of primary aversive drives: (1) those based on deprivation (e.g., hunger and thirst) and (2) those based on noxious stimulation (e.g., pain, fear). The former arise through internal conditions of the organism and have some periodicity, while the latter are contingent upon specific external stimulation.[2] Hull equated the two by using as his paradigm for painful drive the continuous exposure to an electrically charged grid, escape from which was equivalent to escaping from continuing hunger pangs. Studies of approach-avoidance conflict [e.g., Miller, 52, 55] show quite different gradients for responses controlled by the two kinds of drive, and it is quite possible that some distinction should be made between them. The distinction between these two classes of aversive drives is then the first improvement to be made in Hullian theory.

A second problem (not unrelated) arises over the question of drive as *state* versus drive as *stimulus*. Drive can be conceived as stimulus in the case of pain (the "state" of tissue injury not really entering into the analysis), and hunger can be accounted for (partially, at least) on the basis of stimuli from stomach contractions. Hence the activation of habit into performance by way of drive may be by way of massive stimulation, not unlike stimulus dynamism (V). But drive also acts as a *state*, such as can be produced by hormones and drugs, enhancing or reducing reaction. We can move from state to stimulus if we think of the drive as modifying *thresholds* rather than as producing stimuli [e.g., Campbell and Sheffield, 15].[3] Referring to the previous paragraph, we may note that the deprivation drives are likely to operate via both states and stimuli, the pain drives through stimuli alone. Hence the unequal effects of a drug, such as alcohol, upon the approach and avoidance reactions, make sense if we think of the drug as reducing the *stimulus* aspect of hunger and pain drives while leaving the influence of the *hunger state* unmodified. Thus it was found that a rat that would not approach food and eat it because of a conflict between hunger and pain avoidance would risk the shock and approach the food under alcohol [Conger, 17]. I do not wish to jump ahead to guess the full answers to what are very

[2] The possible importance of the distinction between the internal, periodic drives and those dependent upon specific stimulation was called to my attention strongly by John M. W. Whiting.

[3] The reader unfamiliar with Hull's writings may gather from secondary accounts that he was far more dogmatic than in fact he was. He recognized, for example, that drives might alter thresholds [34, p. 241]. Drive as a "state" seemed to him incomplete unless drive stimuli were aroused. Thus, on the page referred to, he writes of caffeine as a pseudodrive substance because it produces nothing corresponding to a drive stimulus.

complex problems. Surely more careful analysis of the drive problem will have to deal with the problems of stimulus aspects of drive, hormonal and other general changes in state, and the problems of threshold changes. Some of the complexities have been pointed out by Miller [54].

The Arousal Aspect of Drive

Drive as a general multiplier (D) is supposed to depend upon all drives that are operative and to act upon all habit strengths. The basic formula for Hull is

$$_sE_R = {}_sH_R \times D$$

While rather ingenious experiments have been performed to study this relationship, and even to determine whether or not some measure (e.g., manifest anxiety) should be treated as D, the notion of the arousal mechanism as a simple function of D is probably faulty.

The time is ripe to reexamine the specificity of the drive-habit inter-action. It is not necessary to make drive altogether specific or altogether general. It is quite possible that some drives (e.g., anxiety) may strengthen a wide variety of behaviors while others (e.g., sexual arousal in the male) may be much more specific. There are almost surely con-flicting drives as well as conflicting habits. Although Hull allowed for these problems through his distinction between D and S_D, the differentiat-ing aspects of drive became overshadowed in his system by the more generalized D, which he compared with Freud's libido [34, p. 252].

There is a puzzling paradox in systematic science. By setting bound-ary conditions carefully enough, experiments and limited theories come into close agreement. Then the experimenter supports his theory by ruling out those circumstances which do not conform. For example, Farber [20] in a very thoughful review of the role of motivation in verbal learn-ing and performance accepts manifest anxiety as a motivational variable, because it follows the rules attributed to D, but he argues against achieve-ment motivation, because *eagerness* as a general habit does not conform completely to the rules defining D within the system. Anyone outside the system would see eagerness as also a motivational influence; the fact that it has an associative history does not make it less motivational than *apprehensiveness*, which also has an associative history, such that it can be measured on a verbal anxiety scale. In fairness to the systematist, he is free to follow the restricted rules that he announces; in fairness to the critic, however, he is also free to point out the artificialities that creep in when the boundary conditions are set too narrowly.

Careful study will probably show *degrees* of generality to be attributed to drive states. It is well known, for example, that the sympathetic nervous system acts somewhat more diffusely than the parasympathetic. It is possible that aversive drives share the diffuseness of sympathetic action, while drives more closely tied to parasympathetic response might be more specific. The whole field requires careful study, not enforcement of the dogma that there is a general drive state D that is independent of the source of drive, multiplying all habits indiscriminately.

Drive Enhancement through Perceived Incentives

The incentive-motivation factor K that is a multiplier of habit strength (for Hull) or a fraction to be added to the multiplier D (for Spence) is a consequence of the incentive on the *preceding* trial. Thus an animal fed in the food box at the end of a maze on one trial may run *faster* on the second trial as a consequence of this incentive motivation.

Neither Hull nor Spence includes the role of *perceived* incentives in the basic system (although they are, of course, aware of the problem and have things to say about them in derivations). While, again, the experimenter can play what game he wishes, the drive aspects of perceived incentives have long been known to be exceedingly important. The example of the male dog aroused by the odor and sight of the bitch in heat is so familiar as to require no experimental demonstration that the perceived incentive arouses the drive. The old experiments of Bayer [6], in which food-satiated hens would eat again when a new supply of food appeared, supported Katz's two-component theory of motivation, one component being the need, the other component the external circumstances [37]. Later, Anderson [4] stressed the externalization of drive. Hence one amendment to the theory is an incentive-motivation component based on the *perceived* incentive in addition to the previously experienced one that gives rise to the present K. This component is so commonly present among animals with distance receptors that it is artificial to ignore it.

Neglected Drives

Hull's experimental results were based almost entirely upon three drives: hunger, thirst, and pain. The hunger drive was so preeminent that in his postulate systems he introduced such a variable as w, whose only quantification was the weight of food used as reward. Because he had a quantitative program to develop, he can be excused for so limiting himself. But now that the system is under examination, it is important that some of the elementary principles be tested upon other drives to determine whether or not the original paradigms are applicable.

The sex drive, for example, has qualities differing somewhat from the others. There is a sex difference that cannot be ignored. Consider only the male. Deprivation alone does not arouse the male sex drive, although there is of course a deprivation-satisfaction effect. The perceived incentive (a receptive female) is very important, although some inappropriate objects may be made the objects of sexual attempts. Furthermore, the preparatory activity in the presence of the goal object (not only in the approach to the presence of the object) has motivational importance; the goal response is incompletely described by the final response that brings tension release. When the whole cycle of activity is taken seriously it also calls attention to neglected aspects of the motivational cycle under other familiar drives. For example, a careful study of food-related activity would also show the transporting and hoarding of food, establishing food preferences, etc., along with the ingestion of food. Perhaps these neglected responses are also motivationally relevant, even at a fairly primitive level of analysis.

The study of other neglected drives has helped point up weakness in the coverage of the Hullian system, although, of course, efforts can be made to incorporate them within the system. Harlow [28] has made the studies that he and his students and collaborators engaged in on manipulation and exploration the occasion for a violent attack on the aversive-drive theory. Related work, not necessarily leading to the same conclusions, has been undertaken by others, e.g., on exploratory drive [Montgomery, 57], on curiosity [Berlyne, 8], on activity [Hill, 32]. In arguing for more (rather than fewer) innate drives, Nissen [62] stressed, among others, the drive to perceive or to know, based on the principle that capacity is its own motivation.

The upshot is that these neglected drives must be taken seriously. It may be that Murphy's [60] classification into visceral, sensory, and activity drives will prove helpful and that these will not all enter into learning and performance in exactly the same way.

Frustration-induced Drives

Another class of drives, as consequences of frustration, has lately come in for considerable discussion. The conception was implicit in the writings of the Yale group who took up the notion from Freud that frustration tends to instigate aggression [Dollard et al., 18] and in the writings of Lewin (see, for example, French [23]), but it was stated in accordance with Hullian learning theory by Brown and Farber [14] and, with some differences, by Amsel and Roussel [3] and Lambert and Solomon [40]. The problem has been carefully reviewed by Marx [47].

If frustration arouses emotion (e.g., anger), the high-tension state may act as a drive similar to the high-tension states of fear or anxiety which have been interpreted as drives for many years.

Once one is called upon to explain a complex situation resulting from the blocking of activity already under way and motivated by a relevant drive, the possibility of an irrelevant drive (frustration-induced) adds variations that only careful experimentation will be able to resolve. Perhaps the simplest case is that of intermittent reinforcement, with the nonreinforced trials interpreted as mildly frustrating. Even this simple case is known to be quite complex; it is suggested that one of the effects of intermittent reinforcement is upon drive (rather than upon habit), thus accounting in part for the effectiveness of such reinforcement [Sears, Whiting, Nowlis, and Sears, 70].

In summary, it is suggested that revisions of Hull's theory of drive will have to be more specific about the problems of drive state, drive stimulus, and the possibility of several classes of drives; that the problem of drive generality will have to be broken down into consideration of degrees of generality, possibly varying for the several drive classes; that the drive-enhancement value of perceived incentives must be added to the incentive-motivation based on prior trials; that neglected drives will have to be taken seriously; that the problems raised by the class of frustration-induced drives will have to be resolved.

SOME PROBLEMS OF PRIMARY AND SECONDARY REINFORCEMENT

The clearest paradigm of reinforcement through drive reduction (the classical form of reinforcement in Hull's aversive-drive theory) is that of the rat moving from a charged grid to an uncharged one on the other side of a hurdle. The aversive state produced by the electric charge continues if the rat stays on the original side; the aversive state is terminated by jumping the hurdle and going to the "safe" side; hence, through reinforcement, the rat "learns" to jump over the hurdle when the grid is charged. The drive-reduction theory of reinforcement asserts the generality of this pattern of events. It is assumed that reinforcement by way of food is really escape from hunger pangs, just as safety is escape from painful shock.

Various considerations have led to the abandonment of the drive-reduction theory as an exclusive interpretation of reinforcement. The facts of secondary reinforcement early led to difficulties for Hull. Although need reduction was necessary for primary reinforcement, it was not necessary for secondary reinforcement; yet Hull believed that primary and secondary reinforcement were at bottom one [34, pp. 99–101]. Experiments on the reward value of nonnutritive saccharin and of copulation without ejaculation were also critical [e.g., Sheffield and Roby, 72; Sheffield, Wulff, and Backer, 74]. While some of the fistula experiments show that food in the stomach may be reinforcing [Miller and

Kessen, 56], we now know enough not to expect need satisfaction to be the sole basis for reinforcement.[4]

What alternatives are there? Learning may take place through one or more of the following events:

1. Drive-reduction through satisfying a need. (This is the classical theory, now known to be insufficient.)
2. Drive-stimulus reduction. Events that do not replenish deprivation may nevertheless reduce the drive stimulus (S_D).
3. Some type of response at the goal may be reinforcing, not necessarily with any specific influence directly upon D or S_D. There are several possibilities here:
   a. Mere change of conditions may not prevent primary associations from remaining intact [Guthrie, 25, 26].
   b. The occurrence of a prepotent response may be reinforcing [Sheffield, Roby, and Campbell, 73].
   c. Some kind of relaxing response as the culmination of goal activity may be reinforcing [Miller, 53].
   d. Some kind of affective response may be reinforcing (Thorndike's satisfying aftereffect).
   e. Some kind of response related to the total motivational sequence may be reinforcing (fulfilling an anticipation; Thorndike's "OK" response, etc.).
4. Learning may take place through stimulus substitution (classical conditioning), the only importance of reinforcement being the production of the unconditioned response [Pavlov, 66].
5. Learning may be due to the formation of cognitive structures (association of ideas, latent learning) with a negligible contribution from reinforcement [Tolman, 80, 81].

The prevalence of secondary reinforcement means that the classical theory (the first one above) can be maintained only if some sort of secondary drive is produced that a secondary reinforcer can reduce. The best candidate (for aversive drives) has been fear or anxiety. A threatened punishment may arouse fear as a secondary drive; a run to safety will then reduce the fear and thus be reinforcing.[5] Here the drive is secondary, but the reinforcement is primary. Perhaps all driven behavior has its anxiety components (being hungry can be as frightening as being shocked); in that case, a secondary reinforcer such as a white food box

---

[4] A good appraisal of the drive-reduction hypothesis and alternatives to it can be found in Bindra [10, pp. 118–139].

[5] An excellent historical review of learning under anxiety and aversion is that by Solomon and Brush [75].

can reduce food anxiety because of its association with anxiety reduction when food was present. This is close to Mowrer's current interpretation of secondary reinforcement as providing "hope" [Mowrer, 58, 59]. If the classical theory is to be saved, the simplest way to do it is to allow an anxiety component for all drives. This is not implausible, because (within the theory) all drives are aversive and the organism is seeking to be rid of them. As long as they are active, the organism is in a disturbed state.

The various alternatives under 3 (p. 261) can be used to account for secondary reinforcement, because the reinforcing events in question can all occur without drive satisfaction. The distinction between primary and secondary is irrelevant in 4 and 5 (p. 261).

The weakening of the drive-reduction theory of reinforcement has left the field open for new attacks on the nature of reinforcing events. The possibilities are many: a unified theory, stressing one or the other major interpretation, a two-factor theory, or a multifactor theory.

It should be noted in passing that the *quantitative* importance of drive in relation to reinforcement was eliminated from Hull's final system. All that was needed for sH_R to develop at full strength was some unspecified minimum of drive reduction. It is evident that such an unspecified minimum can have no real systematic meaning. Hence we might say that Hull left the problem of reinforcement wide open.

Intermittent Reinforcement as Critical of Secondary Reinforcement

The assumption that secondary reinforcement is based on the association of stimuli near the goal with primary reinforcement has received searching criticism through the experiments on rat learning by Lawrence and Festinger [40a]. In their experiments they show that limiting the number of trials on which rewards are given, producing delay prior to reward, or requiring more effort to receive reward, all increase resistance to extinction, although the opposite effects would be predicted from a simple secondary reinforcement explanation, in which with more reward stronger secondary reinforcement would be expected. After reviewing and rejecting the theories of intermittent reinforcement of Humphreys, Sheffield, Estes, Logan, and Amsel, they offer a theory of their own, resting basically on Festinger's theory of cognitive dissonance originally proposed to account for human behavior [Festinger, 22]. The secondary reward aspects of a situation with insufficient reward are said to depend, not on the usual interpretation of secondary reinforcement, but on the "extra attractions" that are used to reduce dissonance when an activity is performed with minimal or intermittent reward or with excessive effort. These "extra attractions" increase resistance to extinction when the reward is absent altogether. A cognitive interpretation of this kind is more in the tradition of Tolman and Lewin than that of Hull.

NEOHEDONISM: AFFECTIVE AROUSAL AS THE CORE OF MOTIVATION

The many problems raised within the aversive-drive theory of motivation and within the drive-reduction theory of reinforcement have led to fresh looks at the whole problem.

There were all along those who were uncomfortable with the Hullian theory. Even the near neighbors, all behaviorists of one sort or another, found much to criticize: Guthrie, Tolman, Skinner. There were others who approached motivation in other ways, e.g., McDougall, Allport, Murphy, Murray, Lewin, Young. The turning of the tide could come only when those within the S-R camp became sufficiently dissatisfied with their own accepted framework that they would look aside, returning to the richness (and confusion) of the phenomenal world. Such a return is disturbing, because to the person who sees in it the collapse of a neat system it appears to be a step backward. It is, instead, more like the outbreeding of a line of race horses that has been too long inbred. The achievements of Hullian theory will not be lost when the effort is made to enrich thinking about motivation through bringing back some of the facts that were set aside while the theory was under construction. The relationships discovered because the system was precise enough to call for a search for them will continue to hold. These very facts and relationships will provide a means for testing novel theories as they emerge. This furnishing of tested relationships is itself an important contribution of precise, if limited, theories.

Pleasure-pain theories are age-old and have never been relinquished. Yet at the height of the popularity of the aversive-drive theory the pleasurable end of the dimension tended to drop out, and the painful end of the dimension tended to be treated nonaffectively (e.g., as sensory pain, tension, avoidance responses). As late as 1955 a strong defense was made of the drive-reduction theory, its author regarding as superfluous any additional principles to account for pleasure-seeking behavior, though considerable ingenuity had to be exercised to save drive-reduction where the evidence showed highly energetic goal response [Brown, 12].

The importance of an affective component to motivation was stressed over twenty years ago in the standard textbook on the facts and theories of motivation [Young, 86], but the time was not yet ripe for learning theorists to pay attention; they are much readier to listen now to the experimentally buttressed version of the theory [Young, 87, 88].

The beginning of the renewed interest in affective arousal as the core of motivation can be attributed to McClelland [42], who, with his collaborators, elaborated the position a little later [45]. I am calling his position *neohedonism* to indicate that it has a resemblance to older views and at the same time is new. McClelland's theory came at the time when there was readiness for it. He directly challenged the alternative views (with which, as a Yale Ph.D. in the field of learning, he was well familiar), and support came quickly from an unexpected source: electrical stimulation of the brains of rats [Olds and Milner, 64]. Hence the pendulum began to swing, and one may now go along with Young [87, 88] in expecting in the decade ahead more serious attention to affectivity as a factor in motivation.

McClelland [42] defined a motive as " . . . a strong affective association, characterized by an anticipatory goal reaction and based on past association of certain cues with pleasure or pain."

McClelland's position has much in common with Spence's version of the drive-reinforcement position [76] except for two important differences:

1. Motive is a term broader than drive, for it includes the associative aspects of learned performance implied in the anticipatory goal reaction, as well as the energizing aspect of drive.

2. The energizing aspect is based upon cues associated with pleasure and pain. Thus pleasure and pain, rather than drive reduction or something else, define the reinforcing state of affairs. Because of this emphasis upon pleasure and pain, McClelland has stated the law of effect in more nearly its original form as a law of affect.

Most of what the drive-reduction theory handles well can be treated according to the master motive of *anxiety*, which bears negative affective connotations. Other behavior according to McClelland, particularly that studied under the "neglected drives," is better treated by accepting a broad class of *appetitive* motives assigned positive affective connotations.

McClelland attempted to develop a quantitative theory of affective arousal, *slight* changes in intensity of stimulation producing pleasant affect, *extreme* changes unpleasant affect [45]. It is of historical interest that Fechner [21] wrote along the same lines as early as 1873 and was quoted favorably by Freud [24]. This quantitative theory has not been pushed very far, however, and it does not play a central role in the studies of motivation carried out later by McClelland and his followers. All the same, the experiments by Alpert [2] and Haber [27] show that it is possible to do objective experimentation in general agreement with McClelland's quantitative theory. They suffice to show that if affective processes come to take a more central place an objective, quantitative interpretation is at least conceivable. The studies by Young and his students [87, 88] lead to the same interpretation; we need have no fear that neohedonism means the abandonment of gains in objectivity over the recent years.

To return now to consider what learning theory would look like if affective arousal were made an important aspect of motivation, we note, first of all, that many issues would remain exactly where they stand, for the translation from drive reduction to satisfaction of curiosity, to confirming an expectation, to affective arousal often does not lead to any contradiction. A position on a theoretical issue can often be shifted markedly without abandoning the major presuppositions. As the facts become clearer, it becomes increasingly difficult to find an issue between the alternative theories [e.g., Seward, 71].

An illustration of shifting ground without shifting commitment is provided by the history of the controversy over latent learning. At first the issue is ignored [Hull, 34]; then the existence of latent learning is seriously questioned [Reynolds, 68], Spence and Lippitt, [77]; finally, when the evidence for latent learning becomes increasingly clear, it is *derived* from S-R reinforcement theory, and, to crown it all, Hull [35] uses the early Tolman and Honzik experiment [83] as a confirmation of his prediction from his S-R reinforcement theory! The specific circumstances under which latent learning is or is not found will have to be determined experimentally at the present stage of theorizing, whatever one's commitment; the theory of affective arousal can be made as applicable as, but probably no more so than, other prevailing theories.

Without expecting any revolutionary gains through the introduction of affective arousal, one may at the same time expect some problems to be viewed from a fresh standpoint, and, because of the fresh look, one may expect the subject matter of experiments on learning and motivation to be somewhat extended.

The following general considerations provide the raw materials out of which an affective theory of motivation in relation to learning can be constructed:

1. Aversive drives, whether due to deprivation or noxious stimulation, are characterized by negative affect (unpleasantness, pain, avoidance responses, fear, anxiety, anger). Their alleviation (drive reduction) is characterized by positive affect (pleasantness, relaxation, gratification). Therefore whenever a drive-reduction interpretation of reinforcement is applicable, the principle of affective change will also be applicable. These considerations apply as well to the secondary aversive drives (fear, anxiety) as to the primary ones. The drive-reduction principle may then be translated into some form of affective modification in the direction from negative to positive, or perhaps from more negative to less negative or from less positive to more positive. The basic principle is *change in the direction of positive affect*.

2. A change in the direction of positive affect can be produced by responses that are highly energized as well as by those that are relaxing.

The greatest amount of sophistry is required by the drive-reduction theorists to make highly excited responses drive-reducing; the great advantage of the affective-arousal theory is that it does not require these mental gymnastics. Here is the point at which careful experimentation is likely to produce a genuine issue as between the theories. Sheffield's prepotent-response theory of reinforcement can be reinterpreted according to affective arousal. That is, drinking saccharin and copulating can be interpreted as providing heightened pleasure, even though they are not drive-reducing. Hence the affective theory is here more parsimonious than the theories that require an explanation for highly energized responses that is different from that for responses marked by relaxation.

On the basis of ordinary everyday experience this is the point of greatest appeal of the affective-arousal theory over the tension-reduction theory. People seek occasions for laughter, for excitement, for thrill, for strenuous activity. To be sure, they may be resolving conflicts, letting off steam, or in other ways getting rid of some sort of psychic tension, but this assertion does not answer the scientific question. We need to know, on the basis of careful experimentation, whether there is any genuine contradiction between some instances of pleasure seeking and tension reduction.

This is the kind of issue in which sophistry often takes precedence over experimentation, for it is almost impossible to assert, even with heightened tension, that there is not some reciprocal reduction in tension elsewhere, and this may be enough to "save" a tension-reduction theory. As some wag has put it, scientific laws, like political laws, are sometimes "enforced" as well as "discovered." In the long run, however, we need to state our laws in such a way that they can be "repealed" on the basis of evidence, if they are no longer found to be sound.

3. Affect may attach, as McDougall thought, to striving toward goals, to overcoming obstacles along the way. The problem of the persistence of motivated behavior has to be faced along with the problem of reinforcement [Peak, 67]. The affective-arousal theory must allow for an influence of *affective accompaniments of goal-directed behavior* prior to the perception of the goal and prior to its achievement. Here we meet the problem in two aspects: First there is the problem of the role of intensified negative affect (anger) as obstacles delay progress toward the goal, and, second, there is the problem of positive affect (delight) as subgoals are passed.

The notion of *frustration-induced drives* has become a plausible supplement to the drive-reduction theory. It can be incorporated in the affective-arousal theory on the assumption that negative affect is energizing. It is equally plausible that positive affect is energizing and that a class of *success-induced drives* will be called for by the affective-arousal theory. Certainly the joy of successful accomplishment affects the later choice of similar activities. ("Nothing succeeds like success.")

The satisfactory working out of an affective-arousal theory will be no easy task, and my glib mention of success-induced motives, for example, must not be understood as a step in theory construction. It is merely an instance of how a fresh look, based on the principle of affective arousal, tends to open up for examination neglected aspects of motivational sequences.

4. Purely cognitive theories [e.g., Tolman, 80, 81] will be rejected unless a role is assigned to affectivity. In order for the theory to be consistent, the assumption will have to be made that perceived relationships will be learned (i.e., retained as associations or cognitive structures) only if their contiguous or patterned relationship was perceived with some sort of affective emphasis. Thus it may be pleasant to clear up ambiguities and to achieve clarity in perception; dangerous or threatening stimuli can be expected to arouse negative affect. Tolman had, of course, a principle of emphasis within his theory [82], though in his quarrel with S-R reinforcement theory and in defense of latent learning he tended to lose sight of it. (In his final statement of his position, he again acknowledged it [81].) The affective-arousal theory would bring back emphasis as a factor in association and would insist that emphasis is always (in part, at least) affective.

It may be noted that affective processes are being used in three ways: (1) affective change in the direction of positive affect is said to be the equivalent of drive reduction in reinforcement and to account for energetic as well as relaxing consummatory activity; (2) affectivity, whether positive or negative, is said to be energizing (in sustaining motivated-behavior sequences); and (3) affective processes are said to be emphatic (in forming associations). Drive is also used in these several ways (i.e., drive reduction, activity enhancement, emphasis via S_D or r_g-s_g). Those who are made unhappy by the several different uses of drive in relation to learning sometimes propose two-factor theories of learning [e.g., Mowrer, 58, 59, Solomon and Brush, 75]. These attempt to account, on the one hand, for contiguous associations (here attributed in part to "emphasis" by affective arousal) and, on the other hand, for the sustaining, strengthening, and directing of sequences of acts which lead toward, and are given, a unitary character by some sort of goal response or end state (here referred to as "enhancing positive affect"). Thus the difficult issue of the number of kinds of learning will not be resolved by an appeal to affectivity, for the differentiating features of the processes are not a matter of the quality of affectivity but of the kinds of perceptual-motor processes or instrumental acts that enter into association. If affectivity is assigned a role throughout motivated learning, the possibility of a unified theory appears (intuitively) more likely than if affectivity is assigned to one kind of learning and not to other kinds.

Mowrer's third version of the two-factor theory [59, p. 213] abandons the distinction between sign learning and solution learning (the second version) in favor of a distinction between incremental reinforcement (punishment, fear, disappointment) and decremental reinforcement (reward, relief, hope). This sounds rather like an affective-arousal theory, with the distinction one between pleasant and unpleasant affect. Mowrer discusses the relationship between his views and those of Young and Mc-Clelland at some length. He concludes that both hedonism and homeostasis (i.e., drive reduction) are important, but " . . . in the broad evolutionary scheme of things, pleasure is important, i.e., has survival value, *only if* it is correlated with homeostatic adjustment" [59, p. 276]. It is not at all clear that this conclusion is a necessary one: the whole argument is really on this point. Some insist that primary drives and their reduction are at base what all other motivation ("secondary reinforcement") is based upon; others insist that too much that is in reality primary is called secondary just because it is not known to be drive-reducing. The affective-arousal side of the argument is that palatability without hunger, the contact between the infant and the mother, curiosity, and many other goal activities, can be sustained by their affective arousal without necessary relation to any prior "primary" reinforcement.

OTHER SOURCES OF MOTIVATIONAL PSYCHOLOGY

The psychology of learning does not have to rest exclusively on either the drive theory or the affective-arousal theory as its source of ideas about motivation. Other suggestions come from human motivation, particularly as studied in the clinic and in social behavior.

Influence of Freud, Lewin, and Others

A preeminent influence is of course that of Sigmund Freud. His influence has been felt strongly within S-R reinforcement theory through such writers as Dollard and Miller, Mowrer, Sears, and Whiting and Child, and even Hull devoted a paper to psychoanalysis [33]. It so happened that the ideas of anxiety and conflict were translatable into the language of drive, and psychosexual stages of development (oral, anal, etc.) lent themselves also to drive interpretation. Despite a congeniality between psychoanalysis and behaviorism that has been in evidence for many years [30], the use of psychoanalytic ideas in learning theory has been very selective, in part because of the preoccupation of the learning experimenters with food, water, and electric shock. The reverse process (using learning theory to account for psychoanalytic facts) has tended to go farther afield. But some features at the heart of the Freudian conception of motivation—e.g., wish fulfillment in dreams, the newer ego psychology—have had little influence upon learning theory.

Another influential figure was Lewin. Some of his interpretations have found a permanent place in motivational and learning literature, but they are so unassimilated to the prevailing theories that a reviewer of Lewin's contributions felt free to write that the verdict of the laboratory was a negative one [Estes, 19]. Yet some of the things he pointed out and set his students to work on, such as the degree of policing required in threatened punishment versus that required in reward, the basic types of conflict and their resolution, ego involvement and level of aspiration, memory for completed and uncompleted tasks, psychological satiation, are repeatedly referred to and have been the occasions for numerous followup experiments.

From social psychology there come various leads, some of which seem so remote from the standard treatments of motivation as to seem scarcely motivationally relevant, such as Mead's self-psychology [50] and Parson's theory of action [65]. More obviously relevant is Festinger's theory of dissonance [22].

Festinger's theory of cognitive dissonance has come into relationship with learning theory very directly through the series of experiments on the effects of intermittent reinforcement on rat learning reported by Lawrence and Festinger [40a], and described earlier (page 262).

Three Classes of Motivational Psychology

There exists a certain amount of selective inattention, whereby psychologists working in one field tend to read the things related to that field, or at least assimilate only those materials that come within their working frame of reference. This is probably a necessary part of the division of labor in science. If one attempted to read everything relevant, he could do nothing else and would even have to give up on that. Hence no adverse value judgment upon any individual is involved in pointing out the fact of such inattention, even though it may cause some gaps within the orderly development of a field of science. I have attempted to examine the possibility that motivational psychology may be divided into several classes by reviewing the contributions to the published volumes of the *Nebraska symposium on motivation* [61]. Granted that the writers are chosen by a local group at one university and may not be representative, and that all those who are invited do not come, the fact remains that the spectrum of choice is wide, and the writers are reputable and distinguished. The editor, M. R. Jones, assures me that the refusals have been very few. The symposium is a psychological one; there have been no psychiatrists or humanists within it; the only sociologist has written jointly with a psychologist, and the one anthropologist (Whiting) is noted for his collaboration with psychologists. With all its limitations as a sample of contemporary thinking about motivation, it serves my purposes reasonably well. I have assumed that participation in such a symposium places a little social pressure on the participant to relate his ideas to those who express similar viewpoints, or to pay attention to viewpoints that appear antagonistic to his own. The participants in the symposium have not reacted uniformly to this social pressure. Some have cited very few references (as few as 11) and others have given a thorough review of the literature on their topics (one citing 173 references). Despite these variations, it seemed illuminating to find the sources most frequently cited—and to note the omissions—by participants with different orientations. When the study was originally undertaken, only the first four volumes were available. A preliminary classification, based on a knowledge of the writer rather than a study of his lecture, permitted the classification of the articles into three groups according to the orientation of the writer or writers (Table 2). Because of the small number of physiological articles, these were ignored in the first analysis.

TABLE 2. CLASSIFICATION OF WRITERS ACCORDING TO ORIENTATION, NEBRASKA SYMPOSIUM ON MOTIVATION, 1953–1956

Orientation	Number of lectures
Learning theory and experimentation:	
Brown, Farber, Harlow, Koch, Marx, Mowrer, Nissen, Postman, Ritchie, Seward, Solomon, and Brush	11
Physiology of motivation:	
Beach, Olds, and Young	3
Personality and social psychology:	
Atkinson, Festinger, Klein, McClelland, Maslow, Miller and Swanson, Newcomb, Nowlis, Peak, and Rotter	10
Total	24

For comparative purposes it was decided to select ten of the learning lectures for study alongside the ten prepared by those with clinical, personality, and social orientation. This called for omitting one writer from among the learning theorists. Convenience dictated that Mowrer be omitted, because the volume of lectures at hand was defective in not having his bibliography. This is perhaps unfortunate, because of the group he is the learning writer most interested in the clinical implications. Nevertheless, no conclusion to be drawn would be changed had he been substituted for one of the other writers.

Some illustrative differences between the references cited by those with learning orientations and the others are given in Table 3.

TABLE 3. PREFERRED WRITERS AMONG THOSE WITH LEARNING ORIENTATION AND AMONG THOSE WITH PERSONALITY-SOCIAL ORIENTATION, NEBRASKA SYMPOSIUM ON MOTIVATION, 1953–1956

	Number of lectures in which named writer is cited	
Writer cited	Learning orientation (10 lectures)	Personality-social orientation (10 lectures)
Writers cited with approximately equal frequency:		
Harlow....................	5	5
Farber....................	4	4
Hebb.....................	4	4
Meehl....................	3	3
MacCorquodale............	2	3
Sears, R. R...............	3	2
Young....................	2	3
Klein....................	2	2
Mean per chapter..........	2.5	2.6
Writers cited by more of those with learning orientation:		
Hull.....................	8	1
Miller, N. E..............	8	3
Brown, J. S..............	7	4
Spence...................	6	0
Mowrer..................	6	2
Tolman..................	6	3
Estes....................	4	0
Nissen...................	4	1
Sheffield, F. D...........	4	1
Woodworth...............	4	1
Mean per chapter..........	5.7	1.6
Writers cited by more of those with personality-social orientation:		
Atkinson.................	2	6
McClelland...............	2	5
Freud....................	0	4
Murray..................	0	4
Bergmann................	0	3
Postman.................	2	4
Bruner..................	1	3
Mean per chapter..........	0.7	2.9

Those who know the background will be able to interpret Table 3 rather easily, despite the numerous reservations that would have to be stated regarding its exact quantities. There is, first of all, considerable overlap, which is as it should be in a symposium of this kind. The fact that among the writers cited with equal frequency none was cited by more than half of each orientation is unimportant. The total frequency is limited by the lack of congruence among the personality-social writers, among whom the most frequently cited writer (Atkinson) was cited by only one more than Harlow, who was cited equally often by the learning-orientation group.

The learning orientation shows the expected pattern of domination by the Hullian background. The five writers most frequently cited by this group all fall within the Yale tradition; the remainder are recognizable as experimental psychologists with closely related positions, even though critical of Hull's views.

The personality-social orientation group shows the expected interest in projective tests as the dominant approach to motivation, the first four writers falling within this group (if we count Freud, whose "depth psychology" lies behind the interest in projection). The citation of Bergmann seems out of place, but his article in the *Annual Review of Psychology* [7] attacked the Meehl and MacCorquodale position, which we noted also interested these writers. The Bruner-Postman interest follows their introduction of the work on need as a factor in perception.

The lack of mutual influence of these dominant interests points to what I have designated as selective inattention. Despite Hull's prominence in the learning-orientation group, only one of the personality-social–orientation lecturers found occasion to mention him, and none mentions Spence. Even Miller and Mowrer, who, with their collaborators, have written influential books on personality and psychotherapy, seem to have made but little dent on those who start with other presuppositions.

Correspondingly, only two of the learning-orientation group recognized the writings of McClelland and Atkinson, and none found occasion to cite either Freud or Murray, despite their importance for other writers on motivation.

The conclusion to be drawn is that the learning-theory approach has not yet incorporated the data from the personality studies, nor has learning theory given the specific direction to personality and social investigations that the learning theorists themselves propose. The influence of the learning theory approach upon the field of personality and social psychology appears to be limited to the small group taught to believe that learning theory is the guide to all the problems of psychology.

The results of the analysis in Table 3 permit some other generalizations. For example, it is clear that there is less coherence among the positions labeled personality-social than among those labeled learning orientation. While two writers are cited by eight of the ten with learning orientation, only one writer is cited by as many as six of the personality-social group. In fact, the raw tabulations from which the table was derived showed that the learning writer who cited the fewest from those listed in Table 3 mentioned five of the twenty-five, while the personality-social theorist most discordant from his fellows cited none of them, and two others cited but one and two of the twenty-five. It is apparent that there is no motivation theory dominant among the personality-social group comparable to the Hullian drive theory among the learning group. This is true despite the prevalence of psychoanalytic thinking among both groups.

As a check on the foregoing three more volumes in the *Nebraska symposium on motivation* were examined to find out if the generalizations based on the first four volumes continue to hold. The writers seem to fall into four groups (Table 4). These are the three groups indicated earlier

TABLE 4. CLASSIFICATION OF WRITERS ACCORDING TO ORIENTATION, NEBRASKA SYMPOSIUM ON MOTIVATION, 1957–1959

Orientation	Number of lectures
Learning theory and experimentation:	
Bolles, Estes, Spence	3
Biological and physiological orientation:	
Hess, Lindsley, Malmo, Morgan, Schneirla	5
Learning and personality orientation:	
Littman, Osgood, Whiting, Wittenborn	4
Personality and social psychology:	
Cattell, Ericksen, Janis, Levin and Baldwin, Rodnick and Garmezy, Pauline S. Sears	6
Total	18

plus a group with learning and personality orientation, who have made a serious effort to examine the claims of the Hullian type of learning theory in its broader applications to problems of child development, language, personality, and social behavior.

The new lectures have been studied for their bibliographic citations of the writers preferred in the 1953-to-1956 lectures (from Table 3) with the results shown in Table 5. The same general trends are repeated. That is, those with a learning orientation have a favorite set of authors to whom they refer, and these authors are cited by few of those with a personality-social orientation. While as before there is less agreement among the personality-social group as to the authors whom they prefer, these authors are cited almost never by the learning group. The biological group also ignores the personality-social favorites, while recognizing a few of the preferred learning-theory authors. The separately classified learning-personality group of lecturers spread their references more broadly, as might be anticipated, with greater agreement on authors preferred by the learning group than on those preferred by the personality-social group.

While there are many accidental factors leading to the results found in Tables 2 to 5, the suggestion is a strong one that we have three classes of motivation theory:[6]

1. A learning-theory orientation, dominated by the Hull-Spence tradition, in which drive is the key concept and physiological specification of events is subordinated to behavioral relationships.

2. A biological-physiological orientation, in which physiological, anatomical, and evolutionary-naturalistic considerations prevent at present a close integration with the learning-theory approach. There is, of course, a congeniality between these approaches, as represented, for example, by the physiological program undertaken by N. E. Miller [55] and his associates.

---

[6] That these conclusions are not dependent upon the exigencies of the *Nebraska symposium* but reflect genuine rifts in the contemporary psychology of motivation is shown clearly by examining the emphasis of recent books with motivation in their titles. Thus Bindra [10], in a well-documented book of 361 pages, devotes but 6 pages to human motivation, while a number of other books are concerned exclusively with human motivation [Atkinson, 5; Lindzey, 41; Stacey, 78].

A number of other books have appeared since this chapter was first prepared, and their neglect is regretted. These include a systematic review of motivation theories by Madsen [46], whose book is remarkably complete in coverage, except for the omission of Freudian concepts; a clear statement of the Hull multiplicative drive theory, with reservations, and with extensions to human behavior, by Brown [13]; a review of the problem of curiosity in animals and man, including a modified form of drive-reduction theory and some neurophysiological speculation, by Berlyne [9]. The book by Olds [63] is difficult to classify; its conjectures probably do not represent the writer's present thinking. Hall [27a] writes in the experimental-physiological tradition. Logan [41a] deals with some very specific aspects of reinforcement as they affect rat learning and performance.

For another classification of motivation, according to twenty-seven topics, including their representation in the *Nebraska symposium* volumes, see Cofer [16]. Because of the scatter of interest, Cofer despairs of finding any unity and concludes: " . . . if present trends continue, motivation as a distinct concept, coordinate to other psychological concepts, may well disappear." Irwin [36] refutes this despairing conclusion by pointing out that *preference* is a fundamental motivational concept coordinate with *discrimination* as a fundamental perceptual concept. My own opinion is that *any* psychological category, including perception, learning, and emotion, has a loosely defined boundary, because it is abstracted from a whole matrix of events. It is because these categories are convenient, rather than because they are precise, that they survive.

TABLE 5. CITATIONS IN 1957–1959 OF WRITERS PREFERRED IN 1953–1956,
NEBRASKA SYMPOSIUM ON MOTIVATION

Writer cited	Learning orientation (3 lectures)	Biological orientation (5 lectures)	Learning-personality orientation (4 lectures)	Personality-social orientation (6 lectures)
Writers cited with equal frequency by different orientations in 1953–1956:				
Harlow....................	0	4	2	1
Farber....................	1	0	2	0
Hebb.....................	2	3	3	0
Meehl....................	0	0	0	0
MacCorquodale............	1	0	0	0
Sears, R. R...............	0	1	1	3
Young....................	2	2	2	0
Klein.....................	0	0	0	1
Mean per chapter.........	2.0	2.0	2.5	0.8
Writers cited by more with learning orientation in 1953–1956:				
Hull......................	3	2	2	2
Miller, N. E...............	2	3	2	3
Brown, J. S...............	1	1	2	0
Spence....................	3	1	2	0
Mowrer...................	1	1	1	0
Tolman...................	2	0	1	0
Estes.....................	2	0	1	0
Nissen....................	0	2	2	0
Sheffield, F. D............	2	2	1	0
Woodworth...............	2	1	2	0
Mean per chapter.........	6.0	2.6	4.0	0.8
Writers cited by more with personality-social orientation in 1953–1956:				
Atkinson..................	0	0	1	2
McClelland................	0	0	1	2
Freud....................	0	0	0	3
Murray...................	0	0	0	0
Bergmann.................	1	0	1	0
Postman..................	0	0	3	2
Bruner...................	0	0	2	1
Mean per chapter.........	0.3	0.0	2.0	1.7

3. A personality-social approach, which, unlike the first two approaches, tends to emphasize human motivation instead of animal motivation. This third approach has not achieved any internal unity, and this lack of unity requires some interpretation. There are several recognizable strands, with some degree of overlap:

a. One group has been occupied largely with giving specificity to developmental problems to which Freud called attention, by studying these problems according to principles of stimulus-response learning. The names of Child, Dollard, Miller, Mowrer, Sears, and Whiting suggest this approach. Although they have been productive in the personality-social field for many years and their views are widely known, the analysis of the *Nebraska symposium* volumes suggests that their work is quoted (in the theoretical context of motivation) primarily by those who take the same point of departure, that is, who start with learning theory and see where they can go with it. Those who start with projective tests, perceptual defense, and interpersonal relationships variously conceived do not seem to find a need for the relationships uncovered by the learning theorists.

b. Another group, also influenced by Freudian conceptions, has worked its way into the motivational problems by way of cognition. Thus the cognitive styles of Klein [38] become related to problems of perceptual defense. The projective tests, such as Blum's Blacky Test [11], are often used in the specific test of psychoanalytic hypotheses, while projective tests in general (e.g., Rorschach and TAT) carry a large psychoanalytic background. It is probably because the S-R learning theory has been so weak on the cognitive side that there is little use made of learning theory by those who start with cognition.

c. Still another group shows an influence of the work of Lewin, especially the work on level of aspiration and Zeigarnik effect. The two most identifiable modern forms of this are the study of the achievement motive (McClelland, Atkinson, P. S. Sears) and the study of cognitive dissonance (Festinger). Because of the cognitive features in this work its relationships to the standard S-R learning theory have also been slight, although a bridge is provided by Lawrence and Festinger [40a].

Perhaps a fourth type of motivational psychology might be added, one emphasizing values and life's meaning, as stressed in humanistic writings, religion, and existentialism. This is not directly represented in the *Nebraska symposium*.

The purpose of this chapter is to relate motivation to learning, so that the above characterizations of nonlearning theories of motivation are left in sketchy form. If the analysis is correct, one real weakness of contemporary learning theory, especially as it applies to human motivation, is its skimpy treatment of problems of cognition and value.

Some Possibilities with Respect to the Organization of Motives

I have had occasion elsewhere to call attention to the desirability of a conception of the self as a background for human motivation [29]. The main point is that motivational systems have some sort of organization that endures through time, and when motives are related to this organization, we can think of the maintenance of self-esteem, self-fulfillment, self-actualization, and the avoidance of self-deprecation as background factors determining what specific activities and consequences have motivational significance. There are many contemporary expressions of this kind of motivation, as in the writings of Maslow [48], Rogers [69], and White [84]. Our learning theories have been particularly weak in dealing with hierarchies of value, with overlapping motives (of both short-range and long-range significance), the kinds of motives that characterize the human individual with continuous memories, with the capacity to bind the past through the present with the future.

Let us now examine some of the possibilities with respect to the organization of motives as they have been suggested by various writers:

Value properties not goal-oriented. Koch [39] has attempted to show that we have been somewhat misled by seeing all motivation as end-oriented, as under the control of extrinsic determiners. While in more practical accounts of motivation the distinction has often been made between intrinsic and extrinsic motivation [e.g., 31], it is Koch's contention that we have not taken seriously the "value-properties" that intrinsically determine whether or not a given process is abient or adient. Thus the enjoyment of a painting need not rest on anxiety reduction, identification, or anything else that the painting does or leads to: the subject looks at the painting because of something intrinsic in the very act of looking. This "something" is the "value-property."

This emphasis on intrinsic "value-properties" represents an extreme reaction to the prevailing emphasis on a behavior sequence leading to some sort of extrinsic goal. It appears that there is a family resemblance to affective-arousal theories, although Koch denies that his theory is a form of neohedonism, because the process that has intrinsic value need not give pleasure. Perhaps intrinsic hedonic satisfaction is a special case of value property: the special case that happens to be pleasurable. Again, the enjoyment of something "for itself" has been part of certain aesthetic theories, and the appreciation of the intrinsic meaning of the moment is one of the teachings of some forms of Buddhism. While Koch has not proposed any such extension of his theory, the theory is more than a corrective to the emphasis on extrinsic motivation, and when the theory is developed, it will probably be found to have kinship with other historical theories of human motivation. The existentialists, for example, are offended at the prevailing separation of subject and object, implied in all extrinsic theories. Theirs is, in this respect, another form of "intrinsic" theory [49].

Short motivated-behavior sequences. The standard fare of the learning experimenters and theorists has been the short sequence of motivated activity, typified by the hungry rat's running through the maze to be fed at the end. This becomes a very natural unit of behavior for analysis in S-R terms, or in terms of behavior routes to be confirmed by the reaching of expected goals.

This short sequence is not to be taken lightly. It may turn out to be the most convenient unit to be used in the sampling of more complex and longer enduring motives. For example, McClelland, in the analysis of a TAT story to measure a persisting motive, such as an achievement motive, analyzes the story in essentially the short-sequence manner: a starting point, some obstacle to be overcome on the way, and some resolution or outcome, with its attendant affective consequences [45]. Likewise, Miller, Galanter, and Pribram [51], in their search for a unit of behavior to describe planned activity, hit upon the TOTE (test, operate, test, exist) as their unit, essentially a short segment. Here the short segment does not define the interest of these writers; it is instead a methodological convenience by which to sample motivated behavior that is relevant to longer-enduring and personality-relevant behavior.

Behavior systems. Whiting and Child [85] have made good use of what they call behavior systems, that is, a set of habits built upon a common drive originating in early childhood. The systems are near relatives to the Freudian character structures (anal, oral, etc.), but they are reinterpreted in S-R reinforcement terms. The derivative behavior may include new motives (secondary drives, frustration-induced drives) as well as new habits learned on top of old ones. For example, the adult interpretation of illness is found to be related to kinds of child-rearing practices that produce anxiety in one or another of the behavior systems based on a given drive. The concept of behavior system goes beyond that of the motivated behavior sequence in that the life history of the motivated behavior comes under examination.

Personality syndromes. If one of the Whiting-Child behavior systems dominates the individual, it may be said to characterize his personality. Thus the personality structures of the compulsive personality, the authoritarian personality, or the Icarus syndrome may emerge as "personality types" producing underlying similarities among a number of persons.

A truly dynamic conception of personality is one accounting for adult personality on the basis of inherited individual differences and social learning via the common experiences in the social environment and the individual experiences due to the special roles and special accidents of individual development. Any fundamental description of this resulting personality will include a statement about motivation, and this statement will point out *how* the individual learns, as well as *what* he learns. The personality-social psychologists have not yet agreed on a way of describing motivational organization that proves very useful to the learning theorist. Until they do, it is not surprising that the learning theorist goes about his business on a scale within which he can be precise. That he is ready to use what the personality psychologist provides is evident in the popularity of Taylor's anxiety scale [79] and in other attempts to relate personality variables to laboratory learning [Farber, 20].

These problems of motivational organization go beyond the drive theory and the affective-arousal theory. They require attention to specific content of motives, as emphasized by McClelland [43], and the settling of other disputes among those who study motivation in relation to personality [Allport, 1].

REFERENCES

1. Allport, G. W. The trend in motivational theory. *Amer. J. Orthopsychiat.*, 1953, **23**, 107–119.
2. Alpert, R. Perceptual determinants of affect. Unpublished master's thesis, Wesleyan University, 1953. Cited in McClelland et al. [45, page 51].
3. Amsel, A., & Roussel, J. Motivational properties of frustration: I. Effect on a running response of the addition of frustration to the motivational complex. *J. exp. Psychol.*, 1952, **43**, 363–368.
4. Anderson, E. E. The externalization of drive. I. Theoretical considerations. *Psychol. Rev.*, 1941, **48**, 204–224.
5. Atkinson, J. W. (Ed.) *Motives in fantasy, action, and society.* Princeton, N.J.: Van Nostrand, 1958.
6. Bayer, E. Beiträge zur Zweikomponenten Theorie des Hungers. *Z. Psychol.*, 1929, **112**, 1–54.
7. Bergmann, G. Theoretical psychology. *Annu. Rev. Psychol.*, 1953, **4**, 435–458.
8. Berlyne, D. E. The arousal and satiation of perceptual curiosity in the rat. *J. comp. physiol. Psychol.* 1955, **48**, 238–246.
9. Berlyne, D. E. *Conflict, arousal, and curiosity.* New York: McGraw-Hill, 1960.
10. Bindra, D. *Motivation, a systematic reinterpretation.* New York: Ronald, 1959.
11. Blum, G. S. A study of the psychoanalytic theory of psychosexual development. *Genet. Psychol. Monogr.*, 1949, **39**, 3–99.
12. Brown, J. S. Pleasure seeking behavior and the drive-reduction hypothesis. *Psychol. Rev.*, 1955, **62**, 169–179.
13. Brown, J. S. *The motivation of behavior.* New York: McGraw-Hill, 1961.
14. Brown, J. S., & Farber, I. E. Emotions conceptualized as intervening

variables—with suggestions toward a theory of frustration. *Psychol. Bull.*, 1951, **48**, 465–496.

15. Campbell, B. A., & Sheffield, F. D. Relation of random activity to food deprivation. *J. comp. physiol. Psychol.*, 1953, **46**, 320–322.
16. Cofer, C. N. Motivation. *Annu. Rev. Psychol.*, 1959, **10**, 173–202.
17. Conger, J. J. The effects of alcohol on conflict behavior in the albino rat. *Quart. J. Stud. Alcohol*, 1951, **12**, 1–29.
18. Dollard, J., Doob, L. W., Miller, N. E., Mowrer, O. H., Sears, R. R., et al. *Frustration and aggression.* New Haven: Yale Univer. Press, 1939.
19. Estes, W. K. Kurt Lewin. In W. K. Estes et al., *Modern learning theory.* New York: Appleton-Century-Crofts, 1954. Pp. 317–344.
20. Farber, I. E. The role of motivation in verbal learning and performance. *Psychol. Bull.*, 1955, **52**, 311–327.
21. Fechner, G. T. *Einige Ideen zur Schöpfungs- und Entwicklunggeschichte der Organismen.* Leipzig: Breitkopf & Härtel, 1873.
22. Festinger, L. *A theory of cognitive dissonance.* Evanston, Ill.: Row, Peterson, 1957.
23. French, J. R. P., Jr. Organized and unorganized groups under fear and frustration. *Univer. Iowa Stud. Child Welf.*, 1944, **20**, 231–307.
24. Freud, S. *Beyond the pleasure principle.* J. Strachey (Trans.) New York: Liveright, 1950.
25. Guthrie, E. R. *The psychology of learning.* New York: Harper, 1935. Rev. ed., 1952.
26. Guthrie, E. R. Association by contiguity. In S. Koch (Ed.), *Psychology: a study of a science.* Vol. 2. New York: McGraw-Hill, 1959. Pp. 158–194.
27. Haber, R. N. Discrepancy from adaptation level as a source of affect. *J. exp. Psychol.*, 1958, **56**, 370–375.
27a. Hall, J. F. *Psychology of motivation.* Chicago: Lippincott, 1961.
28. Harlow, H. F. Mice, monkeys, men, and motives. *Psychol. Rev.*, 1953, **60**, 23–32.
29. Hilgard, E. R. Human motives and the concept of the self. *Amer. Psychologist*, 1949, **4**, 374–382.
30. Hilgard, E. R. Freud and experimental psychology. *Behav. Sci.*, 1957, **2**, 74–79.
31. Hilgard, E. R., & Russell, D. H. Motivation in school learning. In *Learning and instruction.* Chicago: Forty-ninth Yearbook, National Society for the Study of Education, 1950. Pp. 36–68.
32. Hill, W. F. Activity as an autonomous drive. *J. comp. physiol. Psychol.*, 1956, **49**, 15–19.
33. Hull, C. L. Modern behaviorism and psychoanalysis. *Trans. N. Y. Acad. Sci.*, Ser. II, 1939, **1**, 79–82.
34. Hull, C. L. *Principles of behavior.* New York: Appleton-Century-Crofts, 1943.
35. Hull, C. L. *A behavior system.* New Haven: Yale Univer. Press, 1952.
36. Irwin, F. W. Motivation and performance. *Annu. Rev. Psychol.*, 1961, **12**, 217–242.

37. Katz, D. *Animals and men.* New York: Longmans, Green, 1937.
38. Klein, G. S. Need and regulation. In M. R. Jones (Ed.), *Nebraska symposium on motivation.* Lincoln, Nebr: Univer. of Nebr. Press, 1954. Pp. 224–274.
39. Koch, S. Behavior as "intrinsically" regulated: work notes toward a pre-theory of phenomena called "motivational." In M. R. Jones (Ed.), *Nebraska symposium on motivation.* Lincoln, Nebr: Univer. of Nebr. Press, 1956. Pp. 42–87.
40. Lambert, W. W., & Solomon, R. L. Extinction of a running response as a function of distance of block point from the goal. *J. comp. physiol. Psychol.*, 1952, **45**, 269–279.
40a. Lawrence, D. H., & Festinger, L. *Deterrents and reinforcement: the psychology of insufficient reward.* Stanford, Calif.: Stanford Univer. Press, 1962.
41. Lindzey, G. (Ed.) *Assessment of human motives.* New York: Holt, Rinehart & Winston, 1958.
41a. Logan, F. A. *Incentive: how the conditions of reinforcement affect the performance of rats.* New Haven: Yale Univer. Press, 1960.
42. McClelland, D. C. *Personality.* New York: Sloane, 1951.
43. McClelland, D. C. Some social consequences of achievement motivation. In M. R. Jones (Ed.), *Nebraska symposium on motivation.* Lincoln, Nebr.: Univer. of Nebr. Press, 1955. Pp. 41–69.
44. McClelland, D. C. (Ed.) *Studies in motivation.* New York: Appleton-Century-Crofts, 1955.
45. McClelland, D. C., Atkinson, J. W., Clark, R. A., & Lowell, E. L. *The achievement motive.* New York: Appleton-Century-Crofts, 1953.
46. Madsen, K. B. *Theories of motivation.* Copenhagen: Munksgaard, 1959.
47. Marx, M. H. Some relations between frustration and drive. In M. R. Jones (Ed.), *Nebraska symposium on motivation.* Lincoln, Nebr.: Univer. of Nebr. Press, 1956. Pp. 92–130.
48. Maslow, A. H. *Motivation and personality.* New York: Harper, 1954.
49. May, R. The nature of creativity. In H. H. Anderson (Ed.), *Creativity and its cultivation.* New York: Harper, 1959. Pp. 55–68.
50. Mead, G. H. *Mind, self and society.* Chicago: Univer. of Chicago Press, 1934.
51. Miller, G. A., Galanter, E., & Pribram, K. H. *Plans and the structure of behavior.* New York: Holt-Dryden, 1960.
52. Miller, N. E. Comments on theoretical models illustrated by the development of a theory of conflict behavior. *J. Pers.*, 1951, **20**, 82–100.
53. Miller, N. E. Learnable drives and rewards. In S. S. Stevens (Ed.), *Handbook of experimental psychology.* New York: Wiley, 1951. Pp. 435–472.
54. Miller, N. E. Effects of drugs on motivation: the value of using a variety of measures. *Ann. N. Y. Acad. Sci.*, 1956, **65**, 318–333.
55. Miller, N. E. Liberalization of basic S-R concepts: extensions to conflict behavior, motivation, and social learning. In S. Koch (Ed.), *Psychology:*

a study of a science. Vol. 2. New York: McGraw-Hill, 1959. Pp. 196–292.

56. Miller, N. E., & Kessen, Marion L. Reward effects of food via stomach fistula compared with those of food via mouth. *J. comp. physiol. Psychol.,* 1952, **45**, 555–564.

57. Montgomery, K. C. The role of the exploratory drive in learning. *J. comp. physiol. Psychol.,* 1954, **47**, 60–64.

58. Mowrer, O. H. Two-factor learning theory reconsidered, with special reference to secondary reinforcement and the concept of habit. *Psychol. Rev.,* 1956, **63**, 114–128.

59. Mowrer, O. H. *Learning theory and behavior.* New York: Wiley, 1960.

60. Murphy, G. *Personality.* New York: Harper, 1947.

61. *Nebraska symposium on motivation* M. R. Jones, (Ed.). Lincoln, Nebr.: Univer. of Nebr. Press, 1953, 1954, 1955, 1956, 1957, 1958, 1959.

62. Nissen, H. W. The nature of the drive as innate determinant of behavioral organization. In M. R. Jones (Ed.), *Nebraska symposium on motivation.* Lincoln, Nebr.: Univer. of Nebr. Press, 1954. Pp. 281–321.

63. Olds, J. *The growth and structure of motives.* Glencoe, Ill.: Free Press, 1956.

64. Olds, J., & Milner, P. Positive reinforcement produced by electrical stimulation of septal area and other regions of rat brain. *J. comp. physiol. Psychol.,* 1954, **47**, 419–427.

65. Parsons, T. *The structure of social action.* New York: McGraw-Hill, 1937.

66. Pavlov, I. P. *Conditioned reflexes.* London: Oxford Univer. Press, 1927.

67. Peak, Helen. Attitude and motivation. In M. R. Jones (Ed.), *Nebraska symposium on motivation.* Lincoln, Nebr.: Univer. of Nebr. Press, 1955. Pp. 149–189.

68. Reynolds, B. A repetition of the Blodgett experiment on "Latent learning." *J. exp. Psychol.,* 1945, **35**, 504–516.

69. Rogers, C. R. A theory of therapy, personality, and interpersonal relationships, as developed in the client-centered framework. In S. Koch (Ed.), *Psychology: a study of a science.* Vol. 3. New York: McGraw-Hill, 1959. Pp. 184–256.

70. Sears, R. R., Whiting, J. W. M., Nowlis, V., & Sears, Pauline S. Some child-rearing antecedents of aggression and dependency in young children. *Genet. Psychol. Monogr.,* 1953, **47**, 135–234.

71. Seward, J. P. Reinforcement and expectancy: two theories in search of a controversy. *Psychol. Rev.,* 1956, **63**, 105–113.

72. Sheffield, F. D., & Roby, T. B. Reward value of a non-nutritive sweet taste. *J. comp. physiol. Psychol.,* 1950, **43**, 471–481.

73. Sheffield, F. D., Roby, T. B., & Campbell, B. A. Drive reduction versus consummatory behavior as determinants of reinforcement. *J. comp. physiol. Psychol.,* 1954, **47**, 349–354.

74. Sheffield, F. D., Wulff, J. J., & Backer, R. Reward value of copulation without sex drive reduction. *J. comp. physiol. Psychol.,* 1951, **44**, 3–8.

75. Solomon, R. L., & Brush, Elinor S. Experimentally derived conceptions

of anxiety and aversion. In M. R. Jones (Ed.), *Nebraska symposium on motivation.* Lincoln Nebr.: Univer. of Nebr. Press, 1956. Pp. 212–305.

76. Spence, K. W. *Behavior theory and conditioning.* New Haven: Yale Univer. Press, 1956.

77. Spence K. W., & Lippitt, R. An experimental test of the sign-gestalt theory of trial and error learning. *J. exp. Psychol.,* 1946, **36,** 491–502.

78. Stacey, C. L., & De Martino, M. F. (Eds.). *Understanding human motivation.* Cleveland, O.: Howard Allen, 1958.

79. Taylor, J. A. A personality scale of manifest anxiety. *J. abnorm. soc. Psychol.,* 1953, **48,** 285–290.

80. Tolman, E. C. *Purposive behavior in animals and men.* New York: Appleton-Century-Crofts, 1932. (Reprinted, Univer. of California Press, 1949.)

81. Tolman, E. C. Principles of purposive behavior. In S. Koch (Ed.), *Psychology: a study of a science.* Vol. 2. New York: McGraw-Hill, 1959. Pp. 92–157.

82. Tolman, E. C., Hall, C. S., & Bretnall, E. Pearl. A disproof of the law of effect and a substitution of the laws of emphasis, motivation, and disruption. *J. exp. Psychol.,* 1932, **15,** 601–614.

83. Tolman, E. C., & Honzik, C. H. Introduction and removal of reward and maze performance in rats. *Univer. Calif. Publ. Psychol.,* 1930, **4,** 257–275.

84. White, R. W. Motivation reconsidered: the concept of competence. *Psychol. Rev.,* 1959, **66,** 297–333.

85. Whiting, J. M. W., & Child, I. L. *Child training and personality.* New Haven: Yale Univer. Press, 1953.

86. Young, P. T. *Motivation of behavior.* New York: Wiley, 1936.

87. Young, P. T. The role of hedonic processes in motivation. In M. R. Jones (Ed.), *Nebraska symposium on motivation.* Lincoln, Nebr.: Univer. of Nebr. Press, 1955. Pp. 193–238.

88. Young, P. T. The role of affective processes in learning and motivation. *Psychol. Rev.,* 1959, **66,** 104–125.

MOTIVATIONAL PROBLEMS RAISED BY EXPLORATORY AND EPISTEMIC BEHAVIOR[1]

D. E. BERLYNE

Department of Psychology
University of Toronto

Introduction 285
The Nature and Determinants of Exploratory Behavior 286
Definition of exploratory behavior 286
Classification of exploratory behavior 288
Determinants of exploratory behavior 290
Collative properties 290
Two hypotheses 293
Arguments favoring the conflict hypothesis 294
The Question of Exploratory Drives 295
Alternatives to exploratory-drive explanations 296
Reasons for drive concepts 298
The appropriateness of exploratory-drive concepts 300
Criterion 1 301
Criterion 2 301
Criterion 3 302
Concluding comment 306
Arousal 306
Arousal and drive 307
Arousal and activity level 307
Arousal and efficiency 308
Drive conditions and arousal 308
Arousal and selectivity 308
Arousal as an aversive condition 310
Arousal and exploratory behavior 310
The orientation reaction 311
Effects of collative variables on arousal 313

[1] This paper was written while the author was affiliated with Boston University. Its preparation and some of the research described in it were facilitated by a grant-in-aid from the Behavioral Sciences Division of the Ford Foundation and by research grant M-4495 from the National Institute of Mental Health, U.S. Public Health Service.

Conflict reduction and reward 315
Collative Motivation 316
Epistemic Behavior 322
The motivation of epistemic behavior 323
Experimental data relevant to epistemic curiosity 326
Exploratory Behavior, Collative Motivation, and Learning 329
Classical and instrumental conditioning and verbal learning 329
Learning and attention 331
Latent and incidental learning 332
Voluntary behavior 335
Conclusions 336
Extensions to Other Areas 338
Perceptual and intellectual development in the child 338
Origins of social attachments 341
Individual differences 344
Variations in arousal processes 344
Lát's dimension of "excitability" 345
Personality traits 346
Cultural differences 347
Humor 347
Aesthetics 348
Relations between art and science 349
A Final Word 351
References 353

INTRODUCTION

The recent history of research on exploratory and related behavior illustrates one way in which interrelations between diverse psychological phenomena can come to light. Some specific forms of behavior, which current theories have tended to overlook, begin to receive concentrated study. This study draws attention to new problems, new factors, and new principles, which are found to have a wider and wider scope as their investigation proceeds. Consequently, what began as a modest and circumscribed inquiry leads the investigator, willy-nilly, far beyond his initial area of interest and forces him to view an extensive panorama from a new vantage point. The panorama encompasses not only phenomena that established theories have failed to assimilate but even some of those from which they have drawn the bulk of their sustenance.

The kinds of behavior that are placed under headings such as "curiosity," "entertainment," and "play" received no more than perfunctory consideration for many years. This was partly because it was difficult to make biological sense of them and partly because their apparent frivolity made other matters seem more urgent. But once their investigation began in earnest, in the early 1950s, their ramifications turned out to be far-reaching. The failure of existing theories to account for them appeared as a grave blemish and even cast doubt on the adequacy of these theories to the phenomena that they purported to reflect most faithfully.

We shall start out with an examination of exploratory behavior, and we shall then allow the issues that arise out of this examination to carry us farther and farther afield.

The first problems to demand our attention will be those of defining and classifying exploratory behavior. We shall next consider the principal factors that have so far been shown to determine the strength and direction of exploratory behavior. Prominent among them we shall find a peculiar group of stimulus properties that we shall call *collative properties,* and the special questions that they raise will call for some discussion. The need to relate the facts about exploratory behavior to prevalent theories of motivation will then oblige us to discuss the nature and legitimacy of the concept of "exploratory drive."

Having come so far, we shall turn to recent neurophysiological research on the reticular formation, arousal processes, and the orientation reaction, which puts the whole notion of "drive," both in its general aspects and as related to exploratory behavior particularly, in a new light. Under the heading of *Collative Motivation,* we shall attempt to synthesize some of the implications for motivation theory of the facts reviewed up to this point.

We shall then look at epistemic, or knowledge-seeking, behavior, which, although it overlaps with exploratory behavior in human subjects and seems to have much in common with it, requires a separate analysis at this stage.

Finally, we shall point to a variety of current lines of inquiry, both theoretical and experimental, suggesting a far wider range for the concepts and principles that our discussion has brought to the fore. Research guided by these concepts and principles may, it will appear, not merely increase our understanding of exploratory and epistemic behavior but illuminate fresh aspects of some of the most basic questions in psychology.

THE NATURE AND DETERMINANTS OF EXPLORATORY BEHAVIOR

Definition of Exploratory Behavior

It is not at all easy to define exploratory behavior and to distinguish it sharply from other behavior. Exploratory responses have the function of altering the stimulus field. They modify stimulation from sources that are already represented in the stimulus field, and they introduce stimulation from sources that were not hitherto represented.

When we say that X "is the function of" a class of responses, we may mean any of at least three different things:

1. In so far as the responses depend on inherited mechanisms, we may mean that the ability to bring about X helped to give these mechanisms a selective advantage and thus to establish them as part of the innate equipment of the species.

2. In so far as the responses have been acquired through instrumental conditioning, we may mean that their being followed by X is what provided reinforcement for their original learning and that they would extinguish if they ceased to be followed by X.

3. We may be referring to a positive feedback process in the performance of the responses. We may mean that the responses will continue as long as X occurs, whereas they will cease or change their form if X ceases.

Yet, all responses change the stimulus field in some way, and one might very well claim that any response must have the production of a change in the stimulus field as part of its function in the senses outlined above. A food-seeking response produces a change from a stimulus field in which food is absent to one in which food is present and perceptible. An escape response changes the stimulus field from one including a painful stimulus to one without it. But the essential point seems to be that the stimulus changes introduced by nonexploratory behavior are accompanied by biologically important effects on tissues other than the sense organs and the nervous system, and this is not true of the changes due to exploration.

One way out might be to suppose that exploratory responses serve to provide information, and their function is concerned only with such stimulus changes as yield information. But in the light of present evidence, this does not seem to be quite true. Exploratory behavior is apparently affected by other properties of stimuli than those that can be described in information-theoretic language.

Alternatively, it might be supposed that exploratory behavior introduces cue stimuli whereas other responses introduce stimuli with drive-inducing or rewarding properties. There is something to this, but it also is unlikely to be adequate. As we shall see, the stimuli introduced by exploratory responses, while they often have properties that enable stimuli to serve as effective cues, e.g., distinctiveness, may be said to have important drive-inducing and rewarding aspects as well.

Perhaps the real source of difficulty is the fact that virtually all responses have an exploratory function to some degree. Since they all have effects on the stimulus field, at least by producing proprioceptive stimulation and usually by producing visual, auditory, and other stimulation as well, their consequences may not merely remove disturbances in nonneural tissues but also serve to guide subsequent behavior or furnish satisfactions of an aesthetic or curiosity-relieving nature.

This duality of function has provoked disputes, particularly with regard to discrimination-learning experiments in animals and to verbal-learning experiments in human beings in which words like "right" and "wrong" are used as reinforcers. When an animal chooses to approach one of the stimulus objects in a discrimination situation, he is doing something that might secure the reward, and at the same time he is obtaining information about the consequences of making a particular sort of choice which can guide future choices. Some writers have laid stress on the one function, and others have stressed the other [154]. In human verbal learning, there have been disputes about how far the word "right" acts as a reward and how far it is a means of informing the subject how well he is doing.

The early functionalists, e.g., Dewey [55] and William James [98], argued that the stimulus-response unit can be a misleading abstraction if taken out of its context. They pointed out that a stimulus must itself be the result of an earlier response, if only the response of attending to the stimulus. Similarly, the response of a stimulus-response unit must in its turn give rise to stimuli that influence the next step in behavior. From this point of view, exploratory behavior might be thought of as behavior with the sole function of changing the stimulus field, whereas the stimulus-introducing function is present in other kinds of behavior but secondary to other biological consequences.

Classification of Exploratory Behavior

The term *exploratory behavior* is now used to cover an extremely wide assortment of phenomena with nothing very tangible to hold them together apart from our failure to recognize a specific biological function that can be associated with them. It is more than likely that future research will show us in some cases to have been grouping together phenomena that do not have too much in common and show some of the distinctions that now seem essential to be trivial. But in the meantime, we must make such classifications as seem expedient, while bearing in mind how provisional they must be. This is not for the sake of a pedantic delight in drawing distinctions but because distinguishable kinds of exploratory behavior, which have been lumped together in the literature, may well be governed by different principles, and even the principles common to them may not work in the same way when applied to all of them.

First of all, we can divide up exploratory behavior according to the form it takes. We have *receptor-adjusting* responses, consisting of changes in the orientation of sense organs and of physicochemical processes within sense organs affecting their sensitivity. Then we have *locomotor exploration,* which consists of changes in the location of the whole body. And finally, we have the residual category of *investigatory* responses, mostly manipulative, which alter stimulation by acting either on objects in which stimuli originate or on objects intervening between potential sources of stimulation and receptors.

At present, it is impossible to say with any certainty what essential distinctions correspond to these superficial boundary lines. We can, however, mark out some other divisions which cut across these and which we can already see the dangers of overlooking.

There is, for example, the distinction between *extrinsic* and *intrinsic* exploration, or, to be more precise, between responses with primarily extrinsic and intrinsic exploratory functions. Exploration may be said to have an extrinsic function if it introduces cues to guide a subsequent response with its own source of reinforcement. This is the kind of exploration that an animal engages in when he is looking for food or that a dentist engages in when he is examining a new patient's teeth. If exploration is extrinsic, we can attribute the strength of the exploratory response at least partly to the secondary reward value of the cues resulting from it, derived from their association with the reinforcement following the next response. Intrinsic exploration, on the other hand, raises more difficult and more interesting problems. This is the kind of exploration that introduces stimuli that can be said to be rewarding in themselves, regardless of any instrumental activity that they may evoke.

Although extrinsic and intrinsic exploratory functions ought to be sharply distinguished, it is not so easy to separate extrinsic from intrinsic exploratory responses absolutely. Even when exploration is primarily aimed at information to guide subsequent behavior, intrinsically rewarding stimulus properties are likely to play some part. This is borne out by an experiment by Weiner [192], in which subjects were set to watch for white spots on a screen and to respond by pressing a key as soon as a white spot was seen. Looking for white spots was therefore a clear example of extrinsic exploration. But Weiner found that the rate of key pressing increased if red spots, for which no overt response was required, were presented from time to time. The red spots must evidently have provided some kind of intrinsic reinforcement that added to the extrinsic reinforcement value of the white spots.

Then, there is the distinction between *specific* and *diversive* exploration, which has certainly not received as much notice in the literature as it deserves. Specific exploration has the function of providing stimulation from a definite source. No other source will do instead. It is the kind of behavior that we perform when we are said to be "looking for" or "taking a closer look at" something in particular. Diversive exploration is what in human life goes by such names as "recreation," "entertainment," or "seeking a change." In this case, the function is to secure stimulation with certain structural properties compatible with a large range of content. The source or content of the stimulation does not matter at all as long as it provides the right degree of "interest."

Determinants of Exploratory Behavior

The probability, vigor, and direction of exploratory responses evidently come under the control of a large number of factors, including the state of the organism and properties of external stimuli. Among the properties of external stimuli that have proved to be important are many that are known to play an important part in other areas of behavior. They include, for example, stimulus intensity and affective value, by which we mean association with biologically beneficial or noxious stimuli. But there is one group of stimulus properties that stands out among others as supremely influential with regard to exploratory behavior and suggestive of a host of problems that cry out for research on several fronts.

Collative properties. These stimulus properties of outstanding importance are what, for want of a better term, we may call *collative* properties, since they all depend on the collation, or comparison, of information from different sources. It may be a matter of comparing the stimulus in question with others accompanying it, or it may be a matter of comparing a present stimulus with others encountered in the past. Collative properties are properties such as *novelty, surprisingness, change, ambiguity, incongruity, blurredness,* and power to induce *uncertainty.*

They are interesting for at least four groups of reasons:

1. Their logical analysis raises some difficult questions from the start. It will be seen that, although it is convenient and usual to talk of them as properties of stimulus patterns, they may just as well be regarded as properties of the organism's reactions to these stimulus patterns. Better still, they may be thought of as relations between properties of the stimulus field and properties of the organism. The value of these variables—how much novelty, complexity, etc., a given stimulus pattern has—will clearly vary from one individual organism to another and from time to time within the same organism, so that, to evaluate them, we must not only examine the stimulus patterns themselves but also look at what is happening inside the organism that is exposed to them.

If we consider the terms that are used to refer to collative stimulus properties, many of them can be seen to cover a number of logically quite distinct entities. There are, for example, a number of quite different senses in which something can be "novel" [25]. Something can be novel because one has never seen anything quite like it before or because one has never seen anything like it in the last ten minutes. It may be novel even though one has both frequently and recently seen elements resembling all of those that are present, because one has never seen them in anything like the present combination.

The word "complexity" is associated with an even greater number of distinguishable concepts. For example, in an experiment by the author [22], visual figures were exposed side by side on a screen, and how long subjects spent looking at each of them was recorded. It was found that a greater proportion of time was devoted to inspecting a figure with elements in a less regular or symmetrical spatial arrangement, a figure containing more material, a figure made up of more heterogeneous material, or a figure with a less regular shape. In a somewhat similar experiment with three- to nine-months-old infants, it was found that a first fixation was more likely to be attracted to a figure with more internal contour [23].

All these variables might be referred to as degrees of "complexity." They are all opposites of properties of the kind that the Gestalt school associated with "goodness of configuration" [106]. Yet they are not by any means identical. A figure might possess a high degree of one together with a low degree of any of the others.

Furthermore, distinct collative properties often occur in correlation with one another in natural, everyday situations. Objects that are novel tend to be surprising, and vice versa, although they can be one without the other. Objects that are complex often produce uncertainty: a subject may wonder what to call them, and a partial view of them may make him wonder what the rest will be like.

So there is a great deal of overlap among the denotations of these collative words, although their connotations are distinct. We do not have a one-to-one correspondence between the words and the concepts.

2. All the collative properties are eminently quantitative. They can all exist in varying degrees, and we shall have to find ways of measuring them and allotting numerical values to them before research can go much farther. But the task of measuring them lands us in all kinds of perplexities from the outset. Some of these perplexities are, no doubt, connected with the difficulty, mentioned above, of knowing to what extent we ought to be looking more closely at the stimulus patterns and to what extent we ought to be looking more closely at the subject's reactions, or indeed of knowing what exactly we ought to be looking at in both.

Information theory seems likely to be of some help in our approach to these problems. There is one collative variable, namely, power to induce uncertainty, that information theory has already given us a precise way of handling. *Uncertainty,* otherwise known as "entropy," is, of course, the basic notion of statistical information theory [168], and the formula $-\sum_i p_i \log_2 p_i$ can be used to assign a value to it whenever certain conditions are fulfilled, i.e., that we can draw up a list of alternative possibilities and associate a probability with each of them. Moreover, the collative variable of "surprisingness" comes very close to the information-theoretic concept of "amount of information" [165]. Yet it is highly doubtful whether the language of information theory suffices for everything that needs to be said about collative variables [21].

Precise and usable measures of *complexity* have been offered for highly specific classes of stimuli, e.g., geometrical shapes [7, 156], patterns of dots [172], polygons and lines of poetry [31], musical passages [47, 107]. But what we need is some way of measuring complexity that can be applied indifferently to all stimulus patterns, including patterns belonging to different sensory modes. There are indications that complexity can be related to information-theoretic variables like "redundancy" and "information content" [6, 25, 92], but a great deal of further research will have to be done before this approach can yield measuring techniques of practical utility.

3. Collative properties can evidently give stimulus patterns the power to elicit other forms of behavior besides exploration. Some of these other forms of behavior will be discussed later in this paper. The task of identifying the factors that determine what behavior will actually prevail offers a vast field for investigation, which is so far largely uncharted.

One particularly perplexing fact is that unusually novel, surprising, or incongruous stimulus patterns may in some circumstances evoke extreme fear [85], which leads, of course, to withdrawal, the diametrical opposite of exploratory approach. So far, all we can do is speculate about the conditions in which such patterns attract and the conditions in which they repel.

It seems to be at least partly a matter of the *degree* of novelty, surprisingness, and complexity. Several experiments with animals show that novel environments may induce fear at first, i.e., while they are extremely novel, but induce exploration a little later when the novelty has time to diminish somewhat. Human experience indicates that, while an unduly monotonous and hackneyed environment can be tryingly vapid, an environment that overloads us with unfamiliar details may occasion a great deal of stress; what we welcome and seek is an environment with just the right intermediate influx of novelty and complexity, sufficiently rich to be interesting but not dense enough to be bewildering.

4. If all the collative variables have similar motivational effects, giving rise to both exploratory and other forms of behavior—and this seems to be the case—one essential question that arises is what they all have in common to give them these effects. The answers to this question that emerge from the literature of the last ten years or so are of two types.

Two hypotheses.   One type of answer is derivable from what we may call the *discrepancy* hypothesis. According to this hypothesis, an organism is sensitive to discrepancies between the kind of stimulus that it receives and the kind of stimulus that it is set to receive, and the size of a discrepancy determines whether the organism continues with its present behavior or is motivated to alter it.

For some versions of the discrepancy hypothesis, what the organism is set to receive means what it *wants*. This is the case, for example, with motivational theories inspired by cybernetics: the degree of correspondence or disparity between goal conditions and perceived conditions determines whether positive or negative feedback will obtain and thus whether the organism will persist in, or desist from, what it is doing.

For other versions, what the organism is set to receive is rather what it is *expecting*. According to Voronin and Sokolov [190], exploratory behavior is elicited whenever an incoming stimulus fails to coincide with a "nervous model" of the kind of stimulation that has been experienced in the recent past.

Finally, there are versions that incorporate both these views. In the theory put forward by McClelland and associates [122], positivity or negativity of "affect" depends on how far an incoming stimulus departs from the organism's "adaptation level," a concept that seems to combine the connotations of what is wanted and what is expected. And in Anokhin's [1] theory, which enjoys widespread influence in the U.S.S.R., a mechanism called the "action acceptor" monitors, through "reverse afferentation," the stimulus patterns that result from actions. As long as these patterns agree with the anticipatory excitation embodied in the action acceptor, a response will be preserved. But if there is "discordance," a " . . . biologically negative reaction, a reaction of dissatisfaction, which I. P. Pavlov designated a 'difficult condition,' " will exist [2, p. 148]. Pavlov's "difficult condition" is, of course, identifiable with what Western writers would call "high drive," "high arousal," or an "aversive condition." According to Anokhin, it gives rise to exploratory activity in the first instance, and subsequently to the learning of a different response. The nature of the anticipatory excitation may depend on expectations generated by previous experience, on motivational states, and, in human subjects, on verbal instructions.

The second kind of hypothesis attributes the common motivational effects of collative variables to *conflict,* by which is meant the simultaneous instigation of incompatible responses. The conflict hypothesis has been developed theoretically and experimentally in several directions by the writer [16, 17, 20, 21, 25, 26, 27].

Another version of it has recently been advocated by Polezhaev [149, 150, 151, 152]. Like many Russian psychologists and physiologists, Polezhaev does not use motivational terms, but he contends that the acquisition of new responses and the exploratory behavior that precedes it result from conflict between antagonistic "reflexes." This contention is supported by his conditioning experiments with dogs and constitutes an extension of some of Anokhin's ideas.

Hebb [85], while not referring specifically to exploratory behavior, mentions "conflict" as a condition that can cause "emotional disturbance." The underlying "disruption of cortical organization" may result from "the occurrence of incompatible phase sequences" [85, p. 148] in the brain, but he discusses most thoroughly the case " . . . when an expectancy fails to get sensory reinforcement" [85, p. 87]. An earlier writer who linked "emotion" with conflict was Darrow [50].

Arguments favoring the conflict hypothesis. The conflict hypothesis has the advantage over the discrepancy hypothesis of being more comprehensive, covering everything that the discrepancy hypothesis covers and more. A case can be built up for the view that all the collative variables involve conflict [25]. For example, a stimulus pattern that is novel must bear some resemblance to a number of familiar stimulus patterns, say x, y, and z, and yet not be quite like any of them. This means that responses associated with x, y, and z will be instigated by stimulus generalization, and yet, since x, y, and z are distinct, there must be some degree of incompatibility between these responses. Furthermore, the fact that the novel stimulus pattern is discriminable from x, y, z will make for some inhibition of these responses, and this will conflict with their excitation. When a stimulus pattern is surprising, we can expect a conflict between a response called forth by the actual nature of what is perceived and a response held in readiness for the stimulus pattern that was expected. Similarly, it is likely that complex stimulus patterns evoke a number of disparate identifying or classifying or predictive responses.

Relations between the concept of uncertainty and the concept of conflict seem to be particularly close when we consider the properties that a degree-of-conflict measure, as a function of response strength, ought to fulfill [21, 25, 34, 130]. Degree of conflict should surely be higher, (1) the greater the number of competing response tendencies, (2) the greater their total absolute strength, and (3) the nearer they come to being equally strong. In areas of behavior where we have responses that may be partially incompatible with one another, we have to introduce (4) degree of incompatibility, as a further determinant.

The information-theoretic variable, uncertainty or entropy, fulfills most of these requirements but not all of them [21; 25, chap. 2]. It increases as the number of alternatives increases and also as the alternatives approach equiprobability, which, as far as responses are concerned, means equality of strength. But uncertainty does not reflect differences in absolute strength, and it can, of course, be applied only to situations in which alternatives are altogether mutually exclusive.

A subject is said to have a certain degree of uncertainty when he is awaiting an event that may belong to any of a number of alternative classes, each having its probability. He will then presumably have mobilized a number of responses, corresponding to the various kinds of stimuli that might eventuate and with relative strengths corresponding to their probabilities. But as long as the alternative event classes are distinct, there must be some incompatibility and thus some competition among the responses that are being held in readiness.

One particular limitation of the relation of discrepancy, as it figures in the various forms of discrepancy hypothesis, is its essentially dyadic nature. The notion of a degree-of-conflict measure, on the other hand, allows for the possibility of conflict among more than two response tendencies, and three or more mutually exclusive responses must often be instigated simultaneously.

THE QUESTION OF EXPLORATORY DRIVES

As relations between antecedent variables, whether properties of external stimuli or states of the organism, and consequent variables in the field of exploratory behavior have been worked out or adumbrated, the need has inevitably been felt for unifying concepts around which theories could be built. Among those writers who have not contented themselves with recording empirical findings, the favorite nucleus of crystallization has been the notion of "curiosity" or "exploratory drive."

Exploratory drives were freely invoked to explain the sporadic observations of exploratory activity that occurred in the United States in the 1930s and 1940s [e.g., 138, 140]. When intensive work in exploration burgeoned in the early 1950s, the claim that mammals have exploratory and manipulatory drives which are not simply offshoots of other, more familiar drives was voiced with enthusiasm and emphasis [e.g., 80]. More recently, exploratory drives have come under attack [e.g., 30, 105]. It is sometimes felt that such notions encourage pseudo-explanations and that those who resort to them are eluding the problems of a little-understood form of behavior by a procedure akin to the irresponsible listing of instincts that incurred the ridicule of Holt [93].

Yet the implications, the utility, and the drawbacks of the concept of an exploratory drive have rarely received the careful scrutiny that they warrant, either from those who have warmly embraced such a concept or from those who have bitterly inveighed against it.

Alternatives to Exploratory-drive Explanations

So far, there have been two principal alternatives to analyzing exploratory behavior with the help of a drive concept.

The first of these simply attributes variations in the strength of exploratory responses to variations in the power of particular stimuli to evoke them. It is illustrated by the practice, prevalent in the Soviet Union, of attributing exploration to "orienting" or "orienting-investigatory reflexes," innate in some cases and conditioned in others. The role of novelty is explained in terms of a diminution in the power of a particular stimulus pattern to evoke an orienting reflex with massed presentation, which is analogous to what happens with many recognized inherited reflexes [see 82, 91] and with conditioned responses, even when they continue to be reinforced [143].

A related treatment is Bindra's analysis [30] of exploratory responses as "directed acts" whose occurrence depends jointly on external stimulus conditions, including novelty, and internal conditions, such as level of arousal and blood chemistry. However, his acknowledgment of the role of internal conditions brings him a little nearer to those who have used exploratory-drive concepts.

Another variant appears in formulations that attribute changes in the direction of exploration to Glanzer's [72] "stimulus satiation," i.e., to a postulated decline in the power of a stimulus to evoke any response as exposure to it is prolonged.

The most serious difficulties for these treatments arise when the stimulus that is most clearly responsible for the strength and form of exploratory behavior, the stimulus with the important collative properties, does not occur until an exploratory response has been completed. In such instances, the exploratory response has to be regarded as a product of instrumental conditioning and calls for the same sort of theoretical analysis as other instrumental conditioned responses. We have to identify the consequences that are responsible for the reinforcement of these responses or give some comparable analysis in terms of expectations [186] or backward connections [145].

This brings us to the second kind of alternative to analyses that introduce exploratory drives. Koch [105], for example, reminds us that a "rather surprising fraction" of our daily round is

. . . spent in such ways as "doodling," tapping out rhythms, being the owners of perseverating melodies, nonsense rhymes, "irrelevant" memory episodes; noting the attractiveness of a woman, the fetching quality of a small child, the charm of a shadow pattern on the wall, the loveliness of a familiar object in a particular distribution of light; looking at the picture over our desk, or out of the window; feeling disturbed at someone's tie, repelled by a face, entranced by a voice; telling jokes, idly conversing, reading a novel, playing the piano, adjusting the wrong position of a picture or a vase, gardening.

Although he does not speak of them in this way, all these activities either fit the category of exploratory behavior as we have conceived it or represent the kinds of affective reaction that underlie exploratory behavior. Koch declares that reference to exploratory drives and the like makes him "wince." He prefers to assume that a human being is attracted to a certain action " . . . because it produces a process characterized by certain value-determining properties."

However, when one looks closely at exploratory activities (including the occupations that Koch enumerates) together with their sensory consequences, the first thing one notices is that values, in Koch's sense, are apt to fluctuate widely and rapidly. What is irresistibly alluring at one moment will in all likelihood be utterly indifferent a little later and may even become sickeningly distasteful before long. The attractiveness of an activity or a stimulus pattern is especially apt to collapse after a few repetitions in close succession. So we cannot go very far in the discussion of value properties without recognizing that values vary with the state of the organism. And the necessity of taking account of changes in the state of the organism is precisely what has prompted the introduction of drive concepts, both in connection with exploration and in motivation theory generally.

Other treatments that make the strength of exploratory responses depend on the attractiveness of resulting stimulation have been proposed by Dember and Earl [54] and by Fiske and Maddi [62]. They single out novelty and complexity as qualities determining the degree of attractiveness, and they emphasize that what forms of stimulation are most acceptable must vary with the state of the organism. The question thus arises: Do the states of the organism that affect exploratory behavior qualify for categorization as drive states?

Whatever the answer, not all "exploratory-drive" notions can be equally defensible. To assert that an organism throughout its life has a "need for stimulation" or a "drive to explore" is not spectacularly helpful, especially with something as exquisitely selective as exploration and as subject to competition from other forms of behavior. Individuals may have differing probabilities over their lifetimes of engaging in exploration in particular situations, and if this is so, we are entitled to speak of an exploratory *disposition*. But this notion must be differentiated from that of an exploratory *drive*, which serves to describe intraindividual variations.

The notion of an exploratory drive will be useful and legitimate only as long we can distinguish occasions within the life of an individual organism when the drive is more or less strong and as long as we can distinguish between drives for different kinds of stimulation.

Reasons for Drive Concepts

Before we consider the advisability of speaking about drives in relation to exploratory behavior, and as a preliminary to the more general motivational discussions to which this will lead us later, let us review the principal reasons why psychologists have found it difficult to do without drive concepts in other contexts.

1. A drive concept is necessary if one recognizes an intensity dimension in behavior. In that case, one notes that certain conditions change an inactive animal into a restless and mobile one and that this state of restlessness and mobility continues until a condition that restores quiescence is reached. Their marked effects on activity level call for identification of certain situations as drive-inducing or drive-increasing and others as drive-reducing.

Some writers, on the other hand, think of a behavior space simply partitioned into classes, so that what an animal is doing falls into one class or another at any particular moment. This treatment is, for example, usual among constructors of mathematical learning models [38, 39], who, as they admit [39, p. 330], have so far failed to find a place for response amplitude in their systems. In a similar way, many Russian writers picture an animal as coming under the sway of one reflex after another. For example, if an animal is obstreperous in an experimental harness, it is showing the "reflex of freedom," a term originated by Pavlov [144], whereas if it stands quietly, it is performing a "postural reflex" [152].

For those who dispense with an intensity dimension, the descriptions given by McDougall [123, 124] and others of an animal galvanized into activity by some internal or external source of disturbance and then relapsing into relative immobility when its goal has been achieved mean simply that there are conditions in which an animal will turn from behavior of class A to behavior of class B and that there are other conditions in which it will give up class B either to pass on to class C or to return to class A. In these terms, it does not seem to be a fact worthy of much note.

But for those who recognize that there are wide and often abrupt variations in an animal's general level of activity and that those variations are of paramount importance for psychological inquiry, the notion of a drive level, fluctuating with internal and external conditions, is difficult to forgo. The more recent psychophysiological notion of "arousal," as we shall see later, lends more weight to the claim that it is a variable of consequence and permits us to characterize it a little more precisely.

2. Another reason for drive concepts is the fact that behavior is not completely determined by the external stimulus situation. An individual animal will perform markedly different responses in the same stimulus situation on different occasions. We thus have to ascertain both the nature of the external stimuli that are acting and the nature of the organism's state if we are to predict behavior. Variables referring to the organism's state have to be evaluated from a knowledge of its previous history or from tests of its behavior in other situations. Since different states bring different kinds of reaction to the fore, we have to recognize "drives" in the plural.

Brown [33] has recommended that we speak not of "drives" but of "sources of drive," which simply become associatively linked with corresponding kinds of behavior. This recommendation has a good deal of merit, but there are differences that we cannot afford to neglect between the associative functions of factors that are classed as "motivational" and those of other stimuli, external or internal.

Factors inside the organism that make certain responses more probable than others are considered motivational if, for one thing, they strengthen broad classes of responses and if, for another, they act for periods of minutes or hours. On the one hand, this distinguishes them from other internal factors, like thoughts or precisely localized interoceptive stimuli, which give preponderant probability to at most a few highly specific responses and are usually present for only a few seconds. On the other hand, they differ from habits or personality traits, which certainly influence the probabilities of different classes of behavior but endure for a large part of an individual's life.

3. The remaining reason for introducing drive concepts relates to the reinforcement of instrumental learning. Motor responses become stronger when their performance is closely followed by certain conditions, which we call "rewards," but few, if any, of the rewards that have been identified maintain a constant effectiveness. Something that is potently reinforcing in one set of circumstances may have no effect or may even possess a punishing quality in other circumstances, especially after being repeatedly applied.

The appearance of food will reinforce a response in an animal that has not eaten for twenty-four hours, but an animal that is satiated may very well be unaffected by it. A response that carries an animal to a safe part of a box after experiencing electric shocks from a grid covering the floor will be intensely reinforced, but there is nothing rewarding about finding oneself free from pain if one has not been in pain or in fear of pain within the last few seconds.

It is of course partly a matter of how one defines a reinforcing condition. If one defines it as "ingesting food," one can say that this condition is invariably rewarding but will just not take place in an animal that has been crammed with food. Likewise "termination of electric shock" may be considered invariably rewarding, but this condition is impossible to realize in an animal that is not being subjected to shock.

Be that as it may, it must be admitted that whether or not a particular consequence of a response will strengthen the response, and if so how much, cannot generally be predicted without knowing something about the subject's state and, in particular, something about its recent history.

Most of the cases in point are ones in which there is a so-called "aversive" condition. This is a condition whose termination is rewarding and therefore a condition heightening the reward value of a particular state of affairs, namely, its own absence.

The Appropriateness of Exploratory-drive Concepts

We find ourselves, then, with three criteria for the appropriateness of drive concepts, viz., that we can recognize conditions that alter the organism's level of over-all activity and the vigor of whatever behavior happens to be uppermost, that we can recognize conditions lasting minutes or hours that alter the relative strengths of different response classes and make certain broad kinds of behavior more likely to be uppermost, and that we can recognize conditions that alter the reward value of particular states of affairs.

There should, it would seem, be three distinct kinds of drive concept corresponding to these three criteria. But the fact that the drive conditions that are most commonly discussed and studied, e.g., hunger and pain, appear to fulfill all three of them has brought a unitary conception of drive into general use. How interdependent the three criteria actually are must, however, still be considered an open question. There will presumably be a connection between the second and third criteria, since a condition that increases the effectiveness of a particular kind of reward will generally be a condition in which responses leading to that kind of reward are especially strong. This can be expected to come about through learning, although there is also evidence for innate associations between some physiological states and responses that are adaptive in those states [184].

In judging the applicability of drive concepts to exploratory behavior, we must distinguish cases where exploratory responses are *unlearned*, cases where they are due to *classical conditioning*, and cases where they are due to *instrumental conditioning*.

There are presumably unlearned exploratory responses, although we are far from being in a position as yet to identify them with any certainty. Ocular pursuit movements are widely believed to depend on an innate reflex, but the fact that they normally take a week or two to become perfected after birth, the exact period varying widely from infant to infant, and the fact that they are farther advanced in premature babies than in term babies of the same age since conception [69, 153] argue that they are at least in part a product of learning. Locomotor responses seem largely to be a product of maturation, and they can subserve exploratory among other functions.

It is, however, amply demonstrated that exploratory responses can be evoked through classical conditioning. Russian experimenters, in particular, have shown repeatedly with dogs and human children that a signal that habitually precedes another stimulus will elicit anticipatory receptor adjustments. They generally take the form of turning the head and eyes in the direction from which the anticipated stimulus usually comes. Even without special experimental arrangements, conditioned exploratory responses appear unmistakably as infants look round on hearing footsteps a few months after birth or as they look for an object that an adult names or points to, about a year later.

Criterion 1. We can expect both unlearned and classically conditioned exploratory responses to be affected by any conditions that heighten over-all activity. Hunger appears to be such a condition, and Zimbardo and Miller [199] cite data from an experiment on locomotor exploration in the rat to support the view that hunger will strengthen a clearly prepotent exploratory response. Likewise, in an experiment by Jones [101], human subjects were confined for eight hours in a dark room with an opportunity to make patterns of lights appear on the ceiling by pressing a key, and both periodic electric shocks and fourteen hours of prior abstinence from food increased the proportion of investigatory responses made during the first half of the session.

The relations between exploration and conditions of general activation will come up for further elaboration later when we consider the psychophysiological concept of "arousal."

Criterion 2. To turn to the second criterion, the frequency of exploratory responses and their power to oust competing responses certainly undergo variations in a constant stimulus situation that must be attributed to changes in the state of the organism. When an object or environment is first encountered by a rat or a monkey or a child, any tendency to explore may well be overshadowed by flight or frightened immobility [25]. And after an object or environment has elicited intensive exploration, exploratory responses will generally wane and give way to other activities or to relaxed inactivity, despite the unvarying presence of the same external stimuli. These facts are, of course, connected with the large influence that collative stimulus properties have in determining the duration of exploratory behavior, and as we have mentioned, collative properties depend not only on the physicochemical nature of a stimulus pattern but also on the state of the organism and, in particular, on the nature of the traces left in the nervous system by past experiences of similar patterns.

Criterion 3.   We must finally discuss the applicability of the third criterion and the more specific question of whether there are aversive conditions that make exploratory responses likely and give a high reward value to the consequences of exploratory responses. This means, of course, concentrating on exploratory responses that are acquired through instrumental conditioning. For this discussion, two variations need to be distinguished:

a. Common human experience and observation of animals indicate that a state of unrest and distress, at times quite severe, can be brought on by perceiving something under unfavorable conditions, such that the small amount of information received from the object in question leaves considerable uncertainty regarding the object's characteristics. These conditions may obtain, for example, when the object is too far away, when the subject's view of it is blurred as a result of some medium separating him from it, when it is seen in peripheral vision, when it is glimpsed too briefly, or when it is seen in poor illumination. Noise injected by a medium of transmission, brevity, distance, or insufficient intensity could similarly restrict the inflow of information through distance receptors other than those serving vision. When such is the case, animals and human beings are frequently prompted to engage in exploratory activities, which may take the form of receptor adjustments, of locomotion or of investigatory responses acting on the object or on the transmitting medium, and if these expedients are able to make available enough supplementary information, the state of unrest or distress is eventually assuaged. The exploration in question is, of course, *specific* exploration, in the sense explained earlier, since only stimulation from the object responsible for the disturbance in the first place can help to remove the disturbance.

When these conditions are realized, we can see that the reward value of the information resulting from exploratory behavior depends on the uncomfortable state produced by the earlier deficiency of information. So we can then regard the initial perception of the object as productive of an aversive state, or state of drive, such as we usually call curiosity. This kind of curiosity, which we may call *perceptual curiosity,* may evidently be brought on by uncertainty, which, in line with our previous discussion, we can interpret as a form of conflict. A similar state of affairs can clearly be realized if an object perceived in favorable conditions is novel or complex. Copious information may then be coming from the aspects of the object that are in view, but the subject does not have a readily available prepotent response to make, and so several disparate responses are called out at once.

The resulting conflict can then be resolved by exploration, (1) if it secures access to information from hidden aspects of the object, favoring one competing response over another, (2) if it intensifies or prolongs stimulation, so that the disturbance can be removed through habituation, or (3) if it gives the subject time to work out a new prepotent response that can be attached to the disturbing stimulus pattern, thus mitigating the effects of its novelty or complexity.

Although everyday observation of ourselves and of other animal organisms convinces us that these kinds of responses occur, experimental evidence is surprisingly lacking. Perhaps the most directly relevant technique is one devised by Lindsley [117]. The image on a television screen remains clearly visible as long as a certain minimum rate of switch pressing is maintained, but it grows dimmer whenever the rate of responding sinks below the minimum. The restoration of adequate visibility proves to be an extremely effective source of reinforcement for human subjects.

A finding of the author's [19] might likewise be interpreted in terms of curiosity arousal and curiosity reduction but cannot be said to demand such an interpretation unequivocally. Subjects were allowed to give themselves as many tachistoscopic exposures of each of a series of visual figures as they pleased by pressing a key. It was found that the number of exposures per figure was larger when figures were surprising or incongruous or more complex or more highly laden with information. The subjects went through a succession of experiments of this kind using different material, the order being counterbalanced among them, and the average number of responses per picture rose from experiment to experiment. This finding is consistent with the supposition that later exposures of a figure relieved the curiosity induced by the initial exposures, which had left doubts about what had been seen, and thus reinforced the investigatory key-pressing response.

b. Quite a different picture is presented by instrumentally conditioned exploratory responses of a *diversive* character. These are responses, usually investigatory, that can be reinforced by any stimulus pattern that is sufficiently "interesting" or "entertaining," i.e., that has suitable intensity, color, and collative properties.

For example, mice will learn to jump on to a platform that clicks and sinks slightly [104], rats will learn to press a bar if this leads to an increase in illumination [71, 88, 95], monkeys confined in a box will learn to open a door if this enables them to see what is going on outside [40], and human beings confined in a dark room will learn to press a key that causes colored lights to be projected on the ceiling [102].

In situations of this sort, the response is not preceded by a state that can be construed as "wanting" contact with a particular stimulus object, and stimuli emanating from more or less any stimulus object could have the attributes on which reinforcement of the response depends. We have thus no grounds here for invoking a *curiosity* drive, but it might be thought that a *boredom* drive is operating.

There have been several experiments in which a given pattern of sights or sounds has been found to reinforce a diversive investigatory response more effectively, the more time a subject spends deprived of stimulation before being given a chance to perform the response. Such is the case when rats [155] or monkeys [63] press a lever to see a light go on, when monkeys open a door to look out [41], and when human subjects press keys to see patterns of light on the ceiling [102].

It would appear, therefore, that we have here a reinforcing agent whose reward value varies with the state of the organism, but this time it is a state that depends on stimulus deprivation rather than on incomplete, uncertainty-inducing perception. We must, however, proceed cautiously with this assumption for a number of reasons.

For one thing, experiments by Premack and Collier [155] showed the number of light-reinforced bar pressings per experimental session to increase with the length of the intersession interval even when this interval was spent in a busy colony room that was constantly illuminated. And in fact, whatever the intersession interval, rats that were taken from the colony room performed more bar-pressing responses than rats taken from a dark and empty box. This latter result seems likely to be due to differences in activity level, since the rats taken from the dark box "appeared to be sluggish," and since a similar depression of response rate was found in stimulus-deprived rats when the bar-pressing response did not turn on a light.

It is, in fact, often difficult to tell how far the frequency of an investigatory response reflects the reward value of its consequence and how far it reflects the level of general activity. A number of ways of surmounting this problem, often ingenious, have been tried. But the most conclusive way is to study the strength of the response after the consequence whose reward value is in question has been withdrawn, since reward value means, by definition, power to promote learning and learning implies an enduring rise in response strength. This method has been used by Crowder and associates [48, 49], who gave rats a fifteen-minute extinction period one day after the training session. It was found, in some but not in all conditions, that the frequency with which a bar was pressed during the extinction session was increased if the pressing of the bar had resulted in the appearance of a dim light the day before.

This technique has not been used to find out whether the extent to which an investigatory response is reinforced by a given consequence varies with the length of time spent in an impoverished environment before the training session. Such an experiment might possibly vindicate the notion of a boredom drive.

In human life, there are certainly times when, without seeming to be either curious or bored, we do something that brings us into contact with an unexpected "interesting" experience. Although we were not expecting it or wanting it, we welcome it, and we may very well be induced to repeat the action that led to it. Similarly, in experiments on investigatory behavior in animals, the stimuli consequent on an investigatory response often have some reward value even when there is no prior period of stimulus deprivation.

In cases of this kind, the criteria for appropriateness of drive concepts are not manifestly fulfilled. But we can assimilate them to other cases where a drive concept is justified by assuming that the unexpected and unlooked-for stimulus first raises and then reduces drive, the two processes taking place in such close succession that they are not sharply distinguishable. This is what we have elsewhere [25] called the mechanism of the *arousal jag*. We must wait until we come to discuss the "orientation reaction" and other psychophysiological processes connected with exploratory behavior before we can make this hypothesis seem less farfetched and strained.

The effectiveness of diversive rewards may evidently increase with their novelty. This is shown by the regular finding that the rate of responding declines within an experimental session. A different sort of evidence comes from the experiment, already mentioned, by Crowder, Morris, Dyer, and Robinson [48], who compared groups of rats that had light onset contingent on bar pressing with control groups that experienced equal numbers of light onsets that were independent of their behavior. Experimental subjects that were allowed to perform ten reinforced responses showed a greater response rate than the corresponding control subjects during a test session without light the next day, but the difference between experimental and control subjects did not appear when there were thirty or ninety reinforcements. This finding fits the assumption that light onset loses its reward value when it has been experienced a great number of times in close succession, so that the response leading to it, ceasing to be reinforced, undergoes some extinction by the end of the training session. In other words, a rat that has received many reinforcements of this kind is in a different drive state from one that has received few, by our third criterion.

Sometimes, however, an animal will perform a diversive investigatory response more or less indefatigably. Monkeys may persist in opening a door for as long as nineteen hours at a time [42]. When this is the case, we may surmise, pending further experimentation, that a boredom drive mounts in the interval between successive responses and is then relieved by the stimulation consequent on a response, only to start mounting again. This is, of course, most plausible when the stimulus field undergoes a transient alteration after each investigatory response and then quickly reverts to its initial state.

Concluding comment. The strongest reasons for linking exploratory behavior with the concept of "drive" come, however, not from observations of exploratory behavior itself but from quite a different source, namely research on the psychophysiological dimension of arousal, which we shall consider next.

AROUSAL

The psychophysiological measures that have been studied since 1950 as indices of "arousal" have, in most cases, been on the scene for quite some time.

There are, for example, the various changes associated with activation of the autonomic nervous system, e.g., circulatory, respiratory, and skin-conductance changes, whose existence has been recognized since the nineteenth century and which received particularly intensive study during the 1920s and the 1930s. They were then usually regarded as indices of "emotion" and reviewed in a chapter with that heading in the standard textbooks of the period, although there were at times quite acrimonious disputes about the precise meaning of "emotion" and what role it played in behavior.

Other indices of arousal belong to electroencephalography (EEG). That oscillating electrical potentials can be recorded from the cerebral cortex was discovered by Caton in 1874, but the modern technique of electroencephalography was initiated by Berger [12] about 1930. The best-known and most intensively investigated EEG phenomenon is, of course, the one known variously as the "arousal pattern," the "activation pattern," "desynchronization," or "alpha blocking"—the replacement of alpha waves, which normally predominate when a subject is awake but relaxed and inattentive, by more irregular, low-voltage, high-frequency activity. This phenomenon can be provoked by an almost bewildering variety of conditions, e.g., anxiety, the appearance of a stimulus that commands attention, instructions to engage in thinking. There is the problem of deciding what all these conditions have in common, since that must be the essential determinant of the blocking, but, whatever it is, words like "alertness" and "attentiveness" seem to fit it.

In 1935, Darrow [51] described an autonomic process, the galvanic skin response (GSR), as an index of "attention," while Lindsley [115] argued for the recognition of the EEG activation pattern as an indication of "emotion." So it was becoming evident that EEG desynchronization and autonomic, particularly sympathetic, processes did not have sharply distinguishable roles, and a junction was formed between the concepts of "attentiveness" and "emotion" by associating each of them with both sets of physiological phenomena.

Experiments by Bonvallet, Dell, and Hiebel [32] demonstrated that signs of autonomic activation and of EEG activation occur together, both spontaneously and in response to stimulation. So, although the correlations between these various processes are far from perfect, they seem in large measure to represent elements of a unitary pattern.

An important step forward took place in 1949 when Moruzzi and Magoun [137] published the first of a succession of studies by many investigators linking the EEG arousal pattern with the reticular formation of the brain stem. Subsequent work confirmed and amplified the view that the reticular formation (now often called the *reticular arousal system,* or RAS) is the portion of the nervous system most intimately concerned with how vigilant, attentive, or wide-awake the organism is, although it has become increasingly evident that the collaboration between this structure and other, neighboring parts of the brain is of decisive importance also. These include the cerebral cortex, which not only receives excitatory influences from the reticular formation but also sends facilitatory and inhibitory impulses down to it, the areas in the hypothalamus and central gray matter of the brain stem whose stimulation activates the autonomic nervous system, and the areas in the palaeocortex and brain stem whose stimulation has been found to have rewarding or punishing effects [131, 142].

The final stage in the evolution of the concept of "arousal" occurred when allusions to an "arousal pattern" or "arousal reaction," which was either present or not present and thus acted in an all-or-none manner, began to give way to the concept of a level or dimension of "arousal" or "activation" [25, 56, 86, 116, 127, 134]. From this point of view, level of arousal is a continuous variable, fluctuating between the extremes of deep sleep and frenzied excitement, and constitutes an essential feature of the psychophysiological state of an organism at a particular moment.

The relevance of work on arousal to our present inquiry depends on considerations of two kinds, namely, those that link the concept of "arousal" with the concept of "drive" and those that link the concept of "arousal" with exploratory behavior.

Arousal and Drive

There are three kinds of consideration that link arousal with drive:

1. Arousal and activity level. An animal in a state of high arousal conforms in many respects to the accepted picture of an animal in a state of high drive. In conditions where no response is called forth predominantly, e.g., when a hungry animal finds himself in an unfamiliar environment with no source of food in sight, high arousal or high drive means a high level of diffuse bodily activity. If an animal is confronted with a stimulus that evokes a clear-cut response, whether learned or unlearned, a rise in arousal (produced, for example, by direct stimulation of the reticular formation), like an increase in drive, enhances the vigor and the readiness with which the response is executed.

2. Arousal and efficiency.   It has often been observed that "overmotivation" can have a deleterious effect on performance; it can disrupt coordination and even leave an animal virtually paralyzed. And there are comparable data [56, 62, 86, 128, 180] suggesting that maximum efficiency in a task that requires delicate sensorimotor coordination and optimal use of information taken from the environment occurs at intermediate levels of arousal; both too little and too much arousal prevent efficiency from reaching its peak.

3. Drive conditions and arousal.   More and more of the conditions that are recognized to involve increases in drive, e.g., sexual receptiveness, excess of carbon dioxide [53], hunger [11], thirst [10], and lack of sleep [5, 128] appear, in the light of accumulating experimental data, to precipitate rises in arousal, as shown either by direct probes of the activity of the reticular formation or by EEG and autonomic indices of arousal.

Facts like these have persuaded several writers [e.g., 86, 116, 127, 134] to equate the concepts of "arousal" and "drive." This step may not be unduly audacious as long as we are thinking of the first criterion for the appropriateness of drive concepts, since a higher level of arousal means a higher level of general activity. But with regard to the other criteria, the equation of arousal and drive poses suggestive but as yet unsettled questions.

Arousal and Selectivity

Is a state of high arousal a state in which a particular broad class of behavior comes to the fore?

There appear to be times when high arousal is signaled by diffuse restlessness or aimless action, although these are generally times when arousal is extraordinarily high (e.g., panic or mania) or when prepotent responses are frustrated.

The reticular formation, the structure on which level of arousal is held to depend most directly, has been widely represented as an indiscriminate agent which responds alike to excitation from differing sources and produces identical effects no matter how it has been activated.

Nevertheless, we must note, first, that high arousal can evidently be induced by a variety of external and internal conditions, each of which will normally embody its characteristic stimuli, associated with specific classes of overt behavior.

Secondly, activation of the reticular formation must usually be accompanied by activation of adjoining structures, with which it is known to be connected. These include the hypothalamus and the palaeocortex, in both of which structures areas controlling particular groups of activities, corresponding to particular biological needs and particular drive states, have been identified [15, 89, 125].

Lastly, the celebrated mass action of the RAS is now being questioned. It has been recognized for some time that a division of labor must exist between the brain stem reticular formation and the nonspecific thalamic nuclei which have often been held to constitute the anterior portion of the RAS. There have, however, been two sharply differing views regarding the relations between them.

Jasper [99] concluded that, while the lower parts of the RAS activate the cortex as a whole, the thalamic parts may be able to activate particular cortical areas separately. This suggestion has been utilized by Sokolov [176] and by Fessard and Gastaut [61] to account for the phases of widespread and spatially restricted activation of the cortex that appear in succession as a stimulus is repeated.

According to the other view, advocated by Tissot and Monnier [185] and by the Tbilisi school [13, 162], the thalamic reticular system and the mesencephalic, pontine, and bulbar RAS have antagonistic effects, the former being deactivating and inhibitory while the latter are activating and excitatory.

These two views may, of course, not be completely irreconcilable with each other. The thalamic reticular nuclei could be selectively exciting particular centers while checking potentially interfering activity in the greater part of the brain.

Anokhin [3, 4] has recently expressed doubts about the nonspecificity of even the brain stem reticular formation. He has shown that different chemical substances will block the normal reticular reaction to some kinds of stimuli while leaving the potency of other stimuli unaffected. For example, chlorpromazine blocks EEG desynchronization to noxious stimuli only, whereas urethane leaves an animal in a drowsy condition, insensitive to most stimuli but still capable of being awakened by pain. Anokhin concludes from these and other facts that " . . . qualitatively different biological reactions (orienting reaction, defensive reaction and alimentary reaction) excite in the reticular formation different complexes of neural elements which are specific to them. These neural elements, in their turn, exert a specific activating influence on the cerebral cortex mobilizing in it intracortical connections adequate to the given reaction."

There may, therefore be different forms of high arousal, each tending to coincide with a corresponding form of overt activity. If this is so, we have grounds for equating arousal with the concept of drive derived from our second criterion.

Arousal as an Aversive Condition

With respect to our third criterion, there would seem at first glance to be good reasons for linking arousal with the concept of drive as a condition affecting reward value. States of high arousal can certainly be distinctly aversive, and their alleviation is frequently welcomed. Most recognized rewarding agents bring about relaxation and quiescence, which we suppose to represent decreases in arousal. But we are certainly not yet entitled to assert firmly that reduction of arousal is invariably rewarding.

One group of facts, in particular, seems to stand in the way of this assertion, namely, the evidence that boredom, a condition resulting from a deficiency in the kinds of stimulation that elevate arousal, can be extremely distressing and that the termination of boredom by a renewed influx of such stimulation can be potently rewarding.

The author has elsewhere [25, chap. 7] put forward the somewhat paradoxical hypothesis that lack of stimulation or monotony is unpleasant, when it is, because it produces a rise rather than a fall in arousal. This hypothesis was offered rather reticently, but a few scraps of experimental evidence and some speculations, derived from neurophysiological findings on the relations between the cerebral cortex and the reticular formation, were offered in support. It was also pointed out that drowsiness or sleep, i.e., low arousal, is usually experienced as agreeable, the exceptions being cases where some undesirable consequence of loss of alertness is to be anticipated. To say that something is agreeable is, of course, not the same as to say that it is rewarding, since the latter, in our sense, implies power to reinforce an instrumental response. But there certainly seems to be a high degree of coincidence between conditions reported as agreeable and reinforcing conditions.

Since then, further pertinent data have become available. Davis [52] found that reduction of exteroceptive stimulation below normal levels occasion rises in muscular and circulatory activity accompanied by slower breathing. A number of experiments reviewed by Kubzanzky [108] reveal that, while sensory deprivation is not always experienced as uncomfortable, electrocutaneous, EEG, and circulatory changes indicative of high arousal are apt to appear during periods when motor and verbal signs of emotional disturbance are present.

Arousal and Exploratory Behavior

We must now examine two sets of reasons for linking exploratory behavior with increases in arousal.

1. The orientation reaction. Some early observations of Zeleny [198] in Pavlov's laboratory caused Pavlov [143] to recognize what he called at various times the "orientational reflex," "the investigatory reflex," "the what-is-it? reflex," and the "adjusting reflex." The reflex was manifested by such overt responses as turning the eyes, head, and trunk toward a source of stimulation and pricking up the ears. It was elicited from animals by the "slightest change in the world around them."

A new phase of intensive Soviet research on the orientation reflex, or orientation reaction, dates from the start of the 1950s. Much of its impetus appears to have come from Gershuni's [68] finding that auditory stimuli such as evoke overt receptor-adjusting responses also elicit EEG desynchronization and the GSR and that these phenomena coincide with a fall in sensory thresholds. At about the same time, Robinson and Gantt [161] in the United States showed motor aspects of the orientation reaction to be accompanied by autonomic processes in dogs.

Since then, a copious stream of studies, most of them coming from the U.S.S.R. [176] but some of them coming from other parts of the world [e.g., 57, 67, 126], have justified a broadened conception of the orientation reaction as a pervasive complex of physiological changes, involving virtually the whole organism and elicitable by any stimulus that has not been a constant or recurrent feature of the environment during the last few minutes.

The complex includes (*a*) overt receptor-adjusting responses, (*b*) the EEG arousal pattern, (*c*) vegetative processes (circulatory, respiratory, electrocutaneous, and pupillary), (*d*) physicochemical and muscular processes within sense organs that affect their sensitivity and resolving power, and (*e*) increased tension in the skeletal musculature. These, it will be noted, include processes that equip the organism to perceive the precipitating stimulus more clearly and cull more information from it, as well as processes preparing for drastic emergency action. They also include the EEG and autonomic indices of heightened arousal, so that the orientation action can be seen to embody a transient rise in the level of arousal, although long-term upward adjustments of the base line of arousal may also occur if alerting stimuli succeed one another at short intervals.

Work on the orientation reaction has shown, then, that some forms of exploratory activity, notably receptor-adjusting responses, are accompanied by an increase, usually temporary, in arousal, or, if we accept the view equating arousal with drive, in drive. The corresponding fact has not been demonstrated directly with other forms of exploratory behavior, except in an experiment by Fox [63], who found prolonged desynchronization in the brains of his monkeys while they were performing manual investigatory responses at a high rate. Nevertheless, it would seem highly plausible that exploratory behavior in general is associated with increases in arousal, since receptor-adjusting, locomotor, and investigatory exploration seem to be governed by similar properties of external stimuli, particularly collative properties, and since other forms of exploration generally terminate with receptor-adjusting responses.

We must, however, beware of oversimplification as we attempt to extract the main import of research on the orientation reaction for the general theory of motivation. Before going any farther, we must note how investigators of the orientation reaction, having been initially impressed with the global, integrated nature of the phenomenon, are now paying attention to the different forms, phases, and aspects that it presents. We have already discussed the parallel development in the investigation of arousal.

It may, for one thing, make a great difference whether an animal receives a stimulus that does not evoke a specific adaptive response immediately, either because the stimulus has not yet been identified or because it is novel, or whether it receives a stimulus that has, in the past, often heralded an event of biological importance [75, 150]. In the first case exploratory behavior will take the form of a general alertness and looking about, as distinct from looking at, or for, something in particular, while in the second case the animal will probably be looking fixedly in the direction of the heralded stimulus. Moreover, in the first case the animal will typically suspend activity and remain still until it is assured that nothing untoward is in the offing, whereas in the second case it will be mobilized for prompt action.

In any case, when an animal in his natural habitat is confronted with the kind of situation that provokes an orientation reaction, his behavior is likely to go through a phase of keeping relatively motionless while gathering as much information as possible, followed by a phase of taking vigorous action. To quote Pavlov [cited by Lát, 111]:

As [an animal] begins to familiarize itself with a new environment, it has to wait a while after each stimulus, regardless of the receptors the latter affects, i.e. it must abstain from further motion, suppress its momentary activity, since it does not know the demands that the new situation will impose on its organism: painful, pleasant, or indifferent. Only gradually, as the animal becomes familiar with the environment, does this reflex slowly change to a new type of special exploratory reflex, or, following the latter, into other corresponding reflexes.

Madlafousek [126] proposes that, just as the earlier, nonspecific phase was called that "what-is-it? reflex" by Pavlov, the later phase of seeking a particular stimulus be called the "where-is-it? reflex."

Some of the components of the orientation reaction, e.g., processes affecting sense organs and the "arrest reaction" associated with the stimulation of the thalamic reticular system, will, we must assume, be especially concerned with the former phase, and others, including tensing of the musculature and the GSR in the palms and soles (apparently due to perspiration, which, as Darrow [51] pointed out, facilitates gripping), with the second phase.

Many of the processes preparing the organism for the more active second phase can, without doubt, be brought into play and held in readiness during the cautious first phase. But from this point of view, it is interesting to note that changes in heart rate, blood flow and respiration, which must have opposite directions according to whether activity or inactivity is to be promoted, have regularly been recorded by both American [e.g., 57, 161] and East European [e.g., 146, 179] experimenters to behave in a more variable way than other changes recognized as components of the orientation reaction and not always to occur in concomitance with them. Circulatory and respiratory changes may take opposite directions with different subjects, with stimuli belonging to different modalities, or with earlier and later presentations of the same stimulus. Something of this sort might be expected if the circulatory and respiratory systems were indeed caught between the contradictory tasks of facilitating immobilization and mobilization.

2. Effects of collative variables on arousal. The second kind of evidence for a link between exploratory behavior and arousal processes comes from demonstrations that collative stimulus properties, the major determinants of the strength and direction of exploratory behavior, affect the level of arousal.

Manifestations of high arousal have often been shown to be influenced by collative properties of stimulus patterns, but the experiments in question have usually confounded several collative properties, making it impossible to tell which was the effective factor or whether they all played some part.

For example, after a tone of a certain pitch is sounded a number of times in close succession, the various components of the orientation reaction usually weaken and finally disappear, but the unexpected introduction of a tone of a different pitch will revive them. The new tone is, of course, both novel and surprising, and so it is difficult to assess the separate effects of these properties.

Other experiments have used the kind of design exemplified by the experiments of Hovland and Sears [94], who required their subjects to move a pencil in one direction on seeing a red light and in another direction on seeing a green light. After a number of trials of this sort, lights of both colors appeared at once, and various signs of disruption and disturbance ensued. The appearance of both lights together was, however, not only conflict-inducing but also novel, surprising, and greater in total luminous intensity, than a single light would have been.

In an experiment by the author [27] the effects of degree of conflict on one component of the orientation reaction, namely the GSR, were sampled in isolation from other collative properties. The apparatus consisted of a vertical panel bearing eight lights arranged in the shape of a diamond, two at each corner, and a key that could be pressed in any of four directions corresponding to the corners of the diamond. Low-conflict trials, for which two lights at one corner of the diamond were illuminated together and the subject had to press the key in the corresponding direction, were interspersed with high-conflict trials, for which two lights at different corners were illuminated and subjects had to press the key in either, but not both, of the corresponding directions.

Differences in luminous intensity were excluded by using two lights in both cases, while differences in novelty and surprisingness were excluded by telling the subject in advance what was going to happen and mingling the two kinds of trial in a random order. There was also a preliminary phase, in which no overt response was required, to control for possible effects of intrinsic differences, e.g., in complexity, between the two kinds of stimulus pattern.

The stimuli were on for ten seconds, and during the phase requiring an overt key-pressing response the response had to be made as soon as the stimuli terminated, so that the GSR elicited by stimulus onset was free from contamination by the motor process. It was found, in fact, that high-conflict trials produced significantly larger stimulus-onset GSRs than low-conflict trials and that this difference did not appear in the preliminary phase, so that variables other than degree of conflict can be discounted.

This finding that an arbitrary form of conflict, segregated as far as possible from other collative variables, affects the magnitude of the orientation reaction is in line with the hypothesis attributing the motivational effects of collative variables to conflict and thus provides some corroboration for that hypothesis. Further corroboration came in a second experiment of the same series, in which a word-association situation was used. It was found that high-uncertainty stimulus words (i.e., those that produce a large range of different responses with about equal frequency in different subjects) produced larger GSRs than low-uncertainty stimulus words (i.e., words that evoke one response predominantly in most subjects). The words were taken from the list compiled by Laffal [109], and it was assumed in accordance with his arguments that intersubject uncertainty gives an estimate of intrasubject uncertainty, since most responses are culturally determined, and intrasubject response uncertainty was taken as equivalent to degree of conflict.

The next task was clearly to take, one by one, the various collative variables, which we may now with more confidence regard as special forms of conflict, and ascertain whether they influence the magnitude of the orientation reaction, or in other words, the degree of change in the level of arousal. The requisite demonstration has already been achieved several times in the case of novelty. Many experimenters [see 25, p. 175] have found autonomic and EEG components of the orientation reaction to decline with successive presentations of an identical stimulus. Sharpless and Jasper [169] found the same effect when they sounded the activity of the reticular formation through implanted electrodes. In such experiments, the first presentation of the stimulus may possess both surprisingness and novelty, but, as presentations follow one another, any surprise will soon disappear, and later presentations will differ from their forerunners only in being less novel.

A third experiment by the author [21] showed the GSR to be greater for surprising than for nonsurprising stimulus patterns, with degree of surprisingness isolated from degree of novelty. The stimulus patterns consisted of pairs of lights, resembling those used for low-conflict trials in the first experiment, appearing either at the upper corner of the diamond (A) or at the right-hand corner (B). Surprise without novelty was contrived by telling subjects that lights would appear at corners A and B in alternation but actually using sequences such as: *AB AB AB AB AB AB AB AA AB AB.* The A in the sixteenth position is here surprising, since its occurrence contradicts expectations built up both by the verbal instructions and by the previous course of the sequence. But it was not novel, since lights at corner A had already occurred eight times and the immediately previous stimulus pattern appeared at A. The surprising patterns produced greater GSRs, whether they had a key-pressing response attached to them or not.

Vigor of motor activity, being one of the indices of arousal, should increase with degree of conflict if conflict is an arousal-inducing condition. In a series of experiments with rats, Lowell [119] verified that speed of running can be raised by approach-approach conflict, induced by placing a rat midway between two lights of a kind that has recently marked the location of food. But not all the predictions from the hypothesis were confirmed. More recently, Worrell and Castaneda [194] gave human subjects the task of deciding which of two visual stimuli was more intense and recording the decision by grasping one of two dynamometers. The smaller the difference in intensity between the stimuli to be compared, the greater the pressure that was exerted on the dynamometer, and we can assume that the greater the similarity between the stimuli to be discriminated, the greater the degree of conflict.

Conflict Reduction and Reward

If collative variables mean differences in degree of conflict, as we have hypothesized, and if arousal or drive increases with conflict, a crucial question is whether reduction of conflict acts as a reward. This bears on the question of whether collative variables can induce aversive states and thus be held to influence drive according to our third criterion.

An experiment by Wyckoff [195] may represent an illustration of such an effect. Wyckoff's pigeons could perform a pedal-pressing response which caused a white panel to turn green or red. The rate of performing this response was found to rise, provided that the resulting color indicated whether or not food was obtainable by pecking at the panel. One would suppose that the sight of the white panel, being associated with both successful and futile pecking responses, engendered conflict and that the appearance of green or red reduced conflict by causing either the performance or the withholding of the response to prevail. The findings are, however, amenable to other interpretations, and Wyckoff himself offered an explanation in terms of secondary reinforcement.

Two similar sets of experiments, by Hearst and Sidman [84] and by Egger and Miller [58], have been aimed directly at the question. In both of them, there was a stimulus condition (a light or a tone or the absence of a light or a tone) associated with conflict; when this stimulus condition was presented, an instrumental motor response resulted in the delivery of food and also in the administration of electric shock. There was also a second motor response which for some animals or in one phase of the experiment removed the stimulus situation associated with conflict while for other animals or in another phase of the experiment it did not have this effect. It was performed more frequently when it did.

These findings are highly suggestive but, unfortunately, not quite conclusive. In the experiment by Hearst and Sidman, about half of the subjects showed unmistakable learning of the conflict-reducing response but the other half did not. Moreover, as Egger and Miller state, there are a large number of factors that might affect the performance of the second response, and the reward value of conflict reduction has not yet been demonstrated with adequate controls for all of these. In any case, the conflict generated by training an animal to use a motor response as a means of obtaining food and later introducing noxious stimuli while the response is being performed is of rather a special kind and perhaps not ideally suitable for testing the reward value of conflict reduction in general.

COLLATIVE MOTIVATION

Putting together the data yielded by these various lines of research, we can offer a first approximation to a theory of *collative motivation,* i.e., motivation dependent on collative variables.

But first of all, we must draw a distinction between *arousal* and *arousal potential.* By arousal potential we mean all those variables, including collative properties of stimuli, with which arousal, in most conditions, increases. But although arousal seems on the whole to vary directly with these properties, the actual relation between arousal and arousal potential is likely to be curvilinear. We have already reviewed reasons for believing that arousal will mount when arousal potential falls inordinately low, as in conditions of monotony or sensory deprivation. Arousal may also go up as stimuli of decreasing intensity begin to approach the absolute threshold [189]. At the other extreme, too much arousal potential may be responsible for a drop in arousal, a phenomenon of the kind Pavlov called "supramaximal inhibition." It is well known that a sudden deluge of bad news, of exciting events, or even of causes for rejoicing can leave a person in a daze, reminiscent of Pavlov's descriptions of dogs in "hypnotic phases" brought on by conditions that "overstrain" the nervous system.

It looks as if there were, at any moment, a minimum of arousal of which the organism is capable. Where the minimum lies will vary with external and internal conditions. After deprivation of sleep, fatigue, or time spent in a dull environment, the minimum may be quite low, and after a prolonged succession of alarming or novel experiences it may become unusually high. In a healthy, waking subject, we can suppose that the minimum will generally be quite some distance above the lower extreme but that it will never approach the upper extreme.

When arousal stands above its possible minimum, we assume that there will be an aversive state and that anything that serves to bring it down toward its possible minimum will have a reward value. Maintaining the level of arousal near its possible minimum will mean seeking just the right intermediate influx of arousal potential and escaping from environments where arousal potential is too high or too low.

This view of the interrelations of arousal potential, level of arousal, and affective tone (drive level, degree of discomfort) contrasts with the view that has been most common [e.g., 62, 86]. The prevalent theory, which we may call Theory I, assumes an increasing monotonic relation between arousal and arousal potential, and an inverted U-shaped relation between the attractiveness of a situation and the arousal that it generates (see Fig. 1*a*). Fiske and Maddi maintain that " . . . positive affect is associated with shifts of activation toward normal level." They adopt the hypothesis that the normal or optimal level of activation (corresponding to what we are calling arousal) is an intermediate level, and they state that " . . . an organism's level of activation varies directly over time with the total impact of current stimulation" (corresponding to what we are calling arousal potential). Hebb, similarly, supposes that the level of arousal will increase with the amount of sensory "bombardment" and that the organism will be attracted to conditions that maintain arousal at an optimal (i.e., intermediate) level.

The view that we are favoring may be called Theory II (see Fig. 1*b*). It postulates a U-shaped relation between arousal and arousal potential (with the possibility of a decline at the upper extreme of arousal potential due to supramaximal inhibition) and a decreasing monotonic

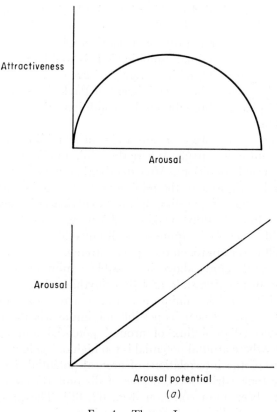

Attractiveness

Arousal

Arousal

Arousal potential

(*a*)

Fig. 1*a*. Theory I.

relation between the attractiveness of a situation and the arousal resulting from it.

Either the two curves in Fig. 1*a* or the two curves in Fig. 1*b* will, when put together, yield a relation between attractiveness and arousal potential of the kind depicted in Fig. 2. In other words, according to both theories, a moderate degree of arousal potential will be most attractive, and this is amply borne out by empirical evidence.

So there is no way of distinguishing between the two theories as long as we consider solely the relations between affective tone and arousal potential. We can distinguish between them, however, if we have some means of assessing arousal independently of its effects on affective tone. Such means are provided by psychophysiological measures, and at least two kinds of experiment using these methods have tended to support Theory II over Theory I.

First, there are the experiments, considered earlier, in which signs

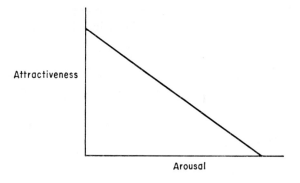

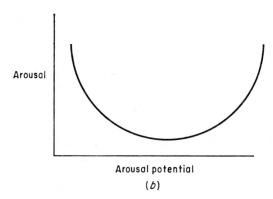

Fig. 1*b*. Theory II.

of high arousal appear when subjects are subjected to sensory deprivation, i.e., to an environment where arousal potential is extremely scanty. Secondly, there are experiments in which a simple stimulus pattern, whether it be a tone or a flash of light combined with a passive arm movement, is applied repeatedly for a long period [176]. Such monotonous stimulation will be highly novel at first, then go through a stage of intermediate novelty, and end by being the very reverse of novel. The experiments have demonstrated that, as repetitions of the stimulation succeed one another, the magnitude of the orientation reaction and the subject's over-all level of arousal gradually sink and then undergo a resurgence.

When an organism has some choice with respect to the environment it enters, it will, we may expect, prefer to place itself in one with just the right collative properties and to leave one that is either too dull or too exciting. A human being may give his environment the right collative properties by surrounding himself with artifacts designed for this purpose—works of art, decorations, means of entertainment. But there will be times when an organism, human or infrahuman, will find itself

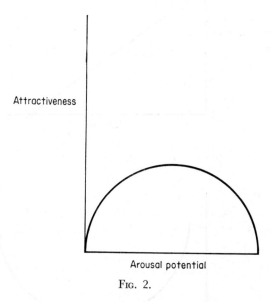

Fig. 2.

caught in an environment that is too rich or too poor in arousal potential, independently of its own actions. Then various remedies may be open.

When the trouble is a deficiency in arousal potential, the optimum can be restored only by gaining access to more intensive or more varied external stimulation or, if this is impossible, by providing oneself with internal stimulation, e.g., imagery or thoughts, to substitute for it. But when the influx of arousal potential is excessive, more numerous alternatives offer themselves.

Reactions may occur that we should regard as indicative of fear; the organism may run away or remain in a cowering, motionless posture. A human being may be able to handle the situation with distorted perception, such as those that are said to characterize persons with high "intolerance of ambiguity" [65].

But in the long run, the only effective remedy consists of approaching the intrusive stimulus source and tolerating the excess of arousal potential long enough to absorb more stimulation and information, e.g., through exploratory behavior. Prolonged and intensified exposure to a disturbing stimulus can reduce arousal potential in various ways. It can reduce novelty by bringing about habituation, and it can reduce complexity by enabling the subject to learn how to organize a stimulus pattern. It can reduce conflict if the new information that accrues from it serves to strengthen one response tendency at the expense of its competitors, to generate a new response that crowds out those responses that are in conflict, or to cancel incompatibilities due to previous learning.

Although it means postponing relief from highly arousing stimulation and even suffering an intensification of it before it ceases to disturb (cf. Freud's reality principle), exploration is likely to prove more advisable in the long run than any other course of action. This is both because overarousing stimulus situations are apt to recur, so that only exploration can blunt their future impact, and because the capacity for symbolic representation that is so pronounced in the human nervous system means that the memory or thought of something puzzling, strange, or conflict-inducing may continue to disturb until the problem has been faced and definitively disposed of.

It must of course be stressed that this is merely a provisional picture of what happens, pending further advances on both psychological and physiological fronts. It is, for example, quite possible that, in some conditions, rises in arousal are accompanied by rewarding effects. For example, Soltysik [178] finds, in experiments on alimentary instrumental conditioning in the dog, that a conditioned stimulus that has regularly preceded the appearance of food provokes a rise in one index of arousal, namely heart rate, and that heart rate remains high when the food appears, showing no abrupt drop such as could account for the reward value of receipt of food. If a conditioned inhibitor, e.g., a buzzer, is introduced a few seconds after the onset of the conditioned stimulus, the combination never having been accompanied by food, heart rate drops sharply. This state of affairs evidently does not act as a reward, however, as the motor response (a movement of the foreleg) is then withheld.

We need, of course, much more information on the relations between the "reward centers" that have been discovered in the lower parts of the brain [142] and the dimension of arousal. All we know is that such centers in the limbic system and hypothalamus have neural connections with the reticular formation and that some of the points whose brief (0.5 second) stimulation is rewarding actually fall within its boundaries [73]. Unfortunately, when stimulation lasting 1 second or less is found to reinforce an instrumental response, we have no way of separating the roles of stimulus onset and stimulus termination. Malmo [128] found that a 0.5-sec shock to the rat's septal area, an area outside the reticular formation whose brief stimulation powerfully reinforces a bar-pressing response, is followed by a drop in heart rate, a sign of lowered arousal.

EPISTEMIC BEHAVIOR

The term *epistemic behavior* refers to behavior whose function, in the senses discussed at the start of this paper, is to equip the organism with *knowledge*, by which we mean structures of symbolic responses [16, 25, chap. 10]. These structures remain with the organism as part of the fruits of learning, and their possession can be practically useful or intrinsically satisfying on future occasions, since they embody information about stimulus events that may then no longer be directly accessible. In this respect, epistemic behavior differs from exploratory behavior, whose function is to provide stimuli that will be immediately useful or satisfying. But in practice, especially in human beings, the two forms of behavior will often coincide, since a response that introduces something new into the stimulus field will usually also leave an enduring trace in the symbolic structures that constitute knowledge.

Epistemic behavior can be divided into three categories, namely, epistemic *observation,* which includes the experimental and other observational techniques of science, *consultation,* which includes asking other people questions or consulting reference books, and *directed thinking.* Directed thinking, like autistic thinking, consists of chains of symbolic responses, but it differs from the latter in its epistemic function, since autistic thinking aims rather at the nonepistemic enjoyment of internal stimulation, whether akin to the enjoyment received from exploratory behavior or acting as a substitute for organic gratification. Directed thinking has a special status among the three kinds of epistemic behavior, since the other two generally occur in conjunction with it and since the knowledge that comes from any of the three kinds of epistemic behavior must ultimately be utilized, e.g., for the guidance of overt behavior, through its participation in directed thinking.

It has already been mentioned that many responses have both an instrumental and an exploratory function. We can go farther, and note that most skeletal responses of higher animals yield both immediate effects of biological importance and stored information that can influence future behavior. Successive trials in any trial-and-error situation constitute not only attempts to secure a reward that may be needed for the relief of a pressing drive but also means of securing information about the probable consequences of performing similar responses in future. Stored information resulting from learning will not be knowledge, in our restricted sense of the word, unless the effects on future behavior are exerted through symbolic responses, representing the external stimulus events from which they derive. In human behavior, this will often be the case; the subject will subsequently be able to remember, or think about, the consequences of a response that he has performed.

If a response is to be executed for its informative function alone, this function can often be fulfilled by a curtailed version of it. For example, we do not have to ingest a mouthful of a substance to tell whether or not it is palatable; a slight lick will be sufficient. We do not have to plunge into the sea to find out whether the temperature is right for swimming; an immersion of the big toe of one foot will answer the question. A mildly threatening gesture will usually be enough to tell us what effect aggressive or truculent behavior would have on somebody whose behavior we wish to control.

And if we need to recall and anticipate the consequence of a response that we have performed in the past, an even more curtailed form of response will suffice, provided that a representation of the response together with a representation of the situation in which the response is performed will lead to a representation of the consequences. When these conditions hold, an internal or implicit response is all that is required, and such are the responses on which directed thinking depends. These implicit symbolic responses form structures whose properties are discussed elsewhere [26]. Epistemic behavior both utilizes these structures, once they have been organized, and contributes to their growth and renovation.

The Motivation of Epistemic Behavior

We have already gone into the reasons for concluding that some exploratory behavior, but by no means all, is propelled by a state of discomfort or high drive or high arousal, to which the term *perceptual curiosity* may be appropriate. The strength of perceptual curiosity is evidently dependent on such collative properties of external stimulus situations as novelty, surprisingness, and complexity, although internal conditions must also play their part. And we have reviewed arguments for the conclusion that collative properties involve conflict.

Epistemic behavior would seem to follow the discomfort-relief or drive-and-drive-reduction pattern, if anything, more regularly than exploratory behavior. There are, it seems, conditions in which exploratory responses result from inborn reflexes and others in which they are evoked through classical conditioning. Even when exploratory responses result from instrumental conditioning, they can evidently be reinforced by "interesting" consequent stimulus patterns, which are rewarding without being preceded by any discomfort or, in other words, without in any sense being sought.

But epistemic responses can hardly occur innately or as classically conditioned responses. There may be times when "interesting" items of knowledge are unforeseeably gained through a particular form of behavior, e.g., browsing through a particular kind of book or conversing with a particular person, and they are rewarding enough to make for repetitions of that form of behavior. This must, however, be relatively rare.

Epistemic behavior must generally be initiated by a specific dissatisfaction, and knowledge, which marks the successful completion of epistemic behavior and supplies its reinforcement, can hardly be rewarding, or even be identifiable, apart from its power to assuage the original dissatisfaction. It is doubtful, as we have noted, whether exploratory behavior can be regarded solely as a collection of devices for procuring information, since other properties of stimuli than information-theoretic ones seem to have some influence in instigating and reinforcing exploratory responses. But epistemic behavior yields knowledge, i.e., structures of symbolic responses, and these have no readily apparent function apart from an informative one. Other properties of symbolic content may be important for autistic thinking, but not for directed thinking or other kinds of epistemic behavior.

According to information theory, there can be no receipt of information without initial uncertainty or entropy. In order to specify the amount of information embodied in an observed event, we must have been able beforehand to enumerate alternative events that might have occurred and to assign to each of them a probability. And, having noted the close relation between the information-theoretic concept of uncertainty and the psychological concept of conflict, we can suppose that the corresponding psychological fact is equally valid: that the receipt of information cannot be rewarding without some initial conflict, since the psychological function of information is to reduce conflict.

The extrinsic-intrinsic dichotomy can be applied to epistemic behavior, as to exploratory behavior. In the extrinsic case, knowledge is welcomed for the sake of its contribution to the attainment of a practical goal, whereas, in the intrinsic case, knowledge is welcomed for the satisfaction that it yields in itself and especially, if we are right, for its power to relieve conflict.

But once again, there will be a great deal of overlap, and both kinds of motivation will probably be at work to some extent in all epistemic endeavors. Even when one is attacking a concrete practical problem, the problem will generally be broken down into subproblems, each of which must receive a solution in turn. Each subproblem, until a solution has been found for it, is a source of uncertainty and hence conflict. Each subproblem will thus have its corresponding motivation to seek a solution, stemming from conflict and akin to the motivation that underlies intrinsic epistemic behavior. Contrariwise, the possibility of some practical application or personal gain looms over the purest science, and it may be difficult to demonstrate that it carries no weight at all with the scientist.

The kind of conflict that underlies epistemic curiosity must be *conceptual conflict,* i.e., conflict between symbolic response tendencies [17, 25, chap. 11]. Conflicts of one kind and another are inseparable from the very essence of thinking, as a number of considerations make clear.

As many writers have said, and as our earlier discussion indicated, thinking consists of processes that would lead to overt action if they were not cut short before the motor system is brought into play, and this state of affairs must necessarily mean conflict. There must be some factor that initiated the process in the first place and would cause it to complete itself if it were acting alone, and there must be another factor that interrupts the process and prevents it from going any farther. These two factors will thus be making contradictory demands on the nervous system. As Thurstone [183] puts it, " . . . the basic relation, when there is no conflict or deliberation, is that of an idea which issues forthwith into the action that corresponds with the idea . . . it is only when there is a conflict between two unfinished or proposed actions, two conflicting ideas, that the effect of ideomotor action is withheld."

And conflict is likewise implied by quite another essential characteristic of thinking, also well expressed by Thurstone. "To think with superior intelligence," he says, "is to render focal our purposes when they have acquired only the few attributes which are sufficient to point towards types of adjustment rather than specified adjustments." In other words, intelligence means handling highly abstract concepts in thought, concepts that require more detail to be added to them before they can point to a definite overt response.

To quote Thurstone further, "To think is to add new attributes to that which we are thinking about." This evidently means that the objects of thought must become gradually less and less abstract. We begin with elements that specify a few properties and leave many possibilities open for the remaining properties. Then more and more details are supplied, so that the area of vagueness is narrowed down.

What this implies in information-theoretic language is that thinking begins with a high degree of uncertainty and uncertainty is diminished step by step. But psychologically, uncertainty means conflict. In the initial stages, when we have thoughts that could lead to any of a wide variety of actions and the action that is to be sanctioned has not yet been identified, we have a high degree of conflict, since many alternative and hence incompatible responses will be held in readiness. Then this conflict together, presumably, with the curiosity that results from it will be progressively lessened until one line of behavior is left with such a predominance over its rivals that it can be embarked on without inhibition or hesitation.

Experimental Data Relevant to Epistemic Curiosity

One special case of epistemic behavior that has received some attention from decision theorists is that of "sequential decision making" [191], in which the subject goes through a series of choices between making his terminal decision and postponing it so as to secure more information. The additional information will generally involve a cost, but it may improve the chances of making a good decision to an extent that outweighs the cost. Whether the subject elects to obtain more information or not will, we might expect, depend partly on what he stands to lose if he makes a wrong decision but also partly on his degree of uncertainty or conflict. And experiments by Irwin and Smith [96] and Becker [9] suggest that this is the case, which implies that the factors that we are associating with epistemic curiosity play a part even when knowledge is sought as a means to a mercenary end.

When, as is usual in experiments on perception and thinking, a subject is instructed by an experimenter to seek the answer to a question, it is not easy to say how far the terms "extrinsic" and "intrinsic" are pertinent. But however that may be, an experiment by Zajonc and Morrissette [196] shows how receptiveness to offered information may vary with degree of uncertainty. The subjects were shown photographs in a tachistoscope and were required to estimate how many bomb craters were visible in them. Some groups were given what purported to be estimates made by pilots. Verbal reports supplied measures of the subjects' feelings of uncertainty with respect to their own answers, and those subjects who were more uncertain showed more of a tendency to change their estimates in the direction of those attributed to the pilots.

In an experiment by the author [18], high school students were exposed to written material about invertebrate animals. There was an experimental group, which had a fore-questionnaire, then a series of statements including answers to the questions in the fore-questionnaire, and finally an after-questionnaire repeating the same questions. A control group underwent the same procedure, except that the fore-questionnaire was omitted. It was found that the experimental group gave significantly more correct answers to the after-questionnaire, a result ascribed to the arousal of epistemic curiosity by the fore-questionnaire.

But there was also an attempt to test the effects of the determinants of degree of conflict by comparing the curiosity-inducing effects of different classes of questions. This was done by means of two devices, i.e., by asking subjects to indicate questions whose answers they would most like to know (the "marking test") and by noting which questions were answered correctly in the after-questionnaire (the "retention test"). More curiosity was, it turned out, induced by questions about more familiar animals, according to both tests, and questions about more familiar animals can be assumed to arouse stronger and more numerous competing response tendencies. According to the marking test, more curiosity was induced by questions that surprised the subjects and by questions that were judged to couple the name of an animal with a predicate that seemed unlikely to apply to it, findings which confirm the role of degree of incompatibility.

So, in this experiment, one of the determinants of degree of conflict, namely, degree of incompatibility, received a fair test, and two others, namely, number and absolute strength of competing response tendencies, received an indirect and moderately satisfactory test through an assumed relation with familiarity of subject matter. The remaining determinant, namely, nearness to equality of strength of competing response tendencies, was not tested.

A more recent experiment [29] was accordingly carried out in order to test this last factor and also to supply a more direct test of the hypothesis that epistemic curiosity will increase the number of alternative responses. The material consisted of quotations, each of which was followed by the names of two or three possible authors. The subjects were told that the quotations had been shown to a group of 100 high school teachers who had been asked to guess in each case who the true author was. Each of the names of possible authors under each quotation was coupled with a number, purporting to represent how many teachers selected it. The task was to indicate the twelve quotations whose true authors the subject would most like to know and then to rank-order the questions so marked according to the degree of curiosity induced.

Findings confirmed the expectation that quotations coupled with three possible authors' names would induce more curiosity than those coupled with the names of two. There was also some confirmation for the expectation that quotations with even distributions of guesses would induce more curiosity than quotations with guesses predominantly allotted to one author. The design of the experiment dissociated these factors from the content of the quotations, so that by now there is some evidence for an effect of all four determinants of degree of conflict on epistemic curiosity.

Next, we may mention Morozova's work on "interest" in children

[135, 136, and personal communication]. Interest, as she conceives it, implies (1) directedness of activity, (2) emotional involvement, and (3) activity that is self-motivated. The intensity and direction of interest are judged from (1) motor activity, (2) questions spontaneously asked by the child, and (3) the child's replies to questions such as, "What else would you like to know?" It seems, therefore, that Morozova means by "interest" much the same as we mean by "intrinsic epistemic curiosity."

Her principal conclusion is that interest is induced most effectively when a child is presented with a situation that can be seen to entail "struggle" or apparent "contradiction," i.e., conceptual conflict. He may be told of a plant that can grow without sunlight or of Spartacus who was a popular hero and yet refused to take part in a war against the patricians. He may be confronted with the mutually discrepant requirements of a practical task, such as finding the latitude and longitude of a particular place.

The youngest subjects of school age need to identify themselves with a hero who is embroiled in the conflicting demands of a concrete problem. At a later stage, it is sufficient if the hero is faced with a conflict-ridden theoretical problem, and finally, at about the age of thirteen, the conflictful features of a situation can be appreciated without reference to a hero.

The pedagogical implications of all this stress on conceptual conflict may be of some importance. Even since Herbart, educationists have recommended that new material should be presented in a way which relates it harmoniously to the "apperceptive mass" that the child's previous learning has deposited. This will, no doubt, facilitate the process of assimilation. But it may be that the opposite condition—a head-on clash between new material and prior experience—is best able to motivate intellectual inquiry and accomplishment in the first instance.

With some subject matter, such as mathematics, this technique is often not applicable, perhaps because school children do not possess a rich enough fund of established beliefs for a new experience to challenge. But there have been several recent attempts to find ways of improving the teaching of mathematics, and some of them have succeeded quite spectacularly in drawing enthusiasm for abstract algebraic or geometrical principles from quite young children. The most successful methods (e.g., those devised by G. Polya of Stanford University and by D. L. Page of the University of Illinois) work by inducing conflict between belief and disbelief. The child is first introduced to a few cases in which the principle is seen to hold. This makes the child eager to find out whether it holds in other cases too, and then, when it is becoming evident that it does, his doubts and puzzlement are definitively eliminated by showing him why it must hold in all cases.

Finally, we may cite a pedagogical experiment by Bruner [35]. Instead of learning geography in the usual way, some sixth-grade children were invited to work out the probable locations of cities from a knowledge of the physical features and natural resources of a region. They were later permitted to compare the results of their deductions with the actual locations. This novel method of instruction evidently induced much more zeal and, one would imagine, better retention and a more complete grasp of the operative principles than the usual method of simply presenting facts. We can attribute this to epistemic curiosity, engendered, in the first place, by conflict among the various possibilities suggested by the physical and economic background information and, secondly, by doubts about how near the inferences would come to the truth.

EXPLORATORY BEHAVIOR, COLLATIVE MOTIVATION, AND LEARNING

The sheer quantity of time and energy that the higher animals devote to exploratory behavior should suffice to give its investigation a high priority and to make its earlier neglect regrettable. Yet indications of an even wider significance are steadily accumulating.

In the remainder of this chapter, we shall look at a variety of psychological problems and at reasons, drawn from recent research, why exploratory behavior and the processes associated with it may have an important bearing on them. We shall begin with the superlatively fundamental topic of learning, proceeding from its most primitive to its most elaborate forms.

Classical and Instrumental Conditioning and Verbal Learning

In all the standard classical-conditioning and instrumental-conditioning situations, there is one stimulus that can be expected to embody appreciable arousal potential, namely, the so-called "reinforcing agent." This is the unconditioned stimulus in the case of classical conditioning and the rewarding stimulus or goal-object stimulus in the case of instrumental conditioning. It may be a stimulus emanating from an event with important effects on nonneural tissues, or it may be a stimulus that has frequently been contiguous with an event of this kind, as in the situations grouped under "secondary reinforcement" and "higher-order conditioning." The presence of such a stimulus is commonly regarded as a necessary condition for the change in response strength that betokens learning.

There are, however, other stimuli involved, namely, the so-called "conditioned stimuli" or "discriminative stimuli," whose associations with the response are being strengthened or weakened. The fact that practically any indifferent stimulus belonging to any sensory mode can function in this capacity has obscured the likelihood that the nature of these stimuli also may have some say in determining how effective learning can be.

Razran [157, 158], summing up findings in Russian laboratories, has stated that a conditioned response will become attached to a stimulus only if the stimulus is such as to evoke a moderately strong orientation reaction. One of the properties that determines the magnitude of the orientation reaction is intensity, and Razran's summary of Russian work suggests that conditioned stimuli will be ineffective if they are extremely intense or extremely weak. But apart from intensity, there are other factors, including attitudinal factors within the subject, to which Razran refers collectively as "attensity," asserting that, all things being equal, moderate attensity will make for optimal conditioning.

As the researches of Pavlov and his pupils have shown, the evocation of an extremely marked orientation reaction may suppress any other response that might have been performed. This may prevent the formation of a new conditioned response, and a similar mechanism is believed to produce the external inhibition that prevents an already established conditioned response from appearing when its conditioned stimulus is accompanied by a distracting extraneous stimulus. Toward the end of his life, Pavlov [144] attributed external inhibition explicitly to negative induction from the orientation reaction that is evoked by the extraneous stimulus. It will be remembered from our neurophysiological discussion that the orientation reaction often includes an inhibitory phase, possibly connected with activation of the thalamic reticular system, and there is fragmentary evidence to suggest that this phase will be particularly prominent when the evoking stimulus is exceptionally impressive.

When the conditioned stimulus is intense, or otherwise disturbing, to an exceedingly high degree, conditioned behavior may succumb to "supramaximal inhibition." This seems, however, to be a process that prevents the stimulus from producing an orientation reaction. Certainly, when a comparable phenomenon occurs in human beings, it is generally accompanied by decreased awareness.

More recently, it has been demonstrated that an indifferent stimulus may lose some or all of its power to become associated with a conditioned response if its power to evoke an orientation reaction has been diminished. This can happen, for example, if a stimulus is robbed of novelty by repeated presentation before being paired with a reinforcing agent.

Russian experiments [177, 187] show that if a subject is exposed to a conditioned stimulus a number of times before the conditioning process is started, conditioning may fail altogether in circumstances where it would otherwise have been attained quite easily. It will occur in some subjects, but when it does so, either the orientation reaction to the conditioned stimulus will revive as soon as the reinforcing agent is introduced or the conditioned response will be of an unusually automatic, mechanical nature. In the latter case, the subject is likely to report that he did not realize that he was performing the response or that he was not aware of the connection between his response and the conditioned stimulus.

The importance of the arousal value, and especially the collative properties, of a conditioned stimulus is likewise attested by at least one American experiment: Lubow and Moore [120] found that a conditioned leg-withdrawal response in the goat was harder to establish when the auditory conditioned stimulus had been presented a number of times before conditioning trials and thus made less novel.

That the appearance of classical conditioned responses goes hand in hand with changes in arousal is amply demonstrated by the literature on physiological correlates of conditioning that has become quite profuse since World War II [37, 61, 66]. Modifications of arousal processes have also been shown to play a part in instrumental conditioning [83] and in verbal learning [141].

The orientation reaction is especially pronounced when learned responses are in the process of becoming established, dropping out when these responses are fully mastered and automatic. Obrist, for example, found EEG desynchronization and the GSR to be most strongly evoked by a nonsense syllable when the syllable had just begun to show signs of being learned [141]. John and Killam [100], studying avoidance conditioning in the cat with implanted electrodes and with a rhythmically flashing light as conditioned stimulus, found nonspecific subcortical structures, including the reticular formation, to be implicated during the early stages of training but not once the response had been fully acquired.

Further confirmation that the structures associated with arousal processes play an essential role in acquisition, but not in retention, comes from some experiments by Cardo [44]. He found lesions of the mesencephalic reticular formation to prevent the acquisition of an instrumental avoidance response in the rat and to retard the acquisition of an instrumental food-seeking response. But similar lesions had no effect whatever on these responses if they had already been mastered before the operation.

Learning and Attention

How crucial the properties, especially the collative properties, of conditioned stimuli can be becomes most evident when we recall that in practice stimulus-response associations are rarely mobilized in isolation. In laboratory situations, one stimulus, or a small number of stimuli, in which the experimenter is particularly interested may be acting in virtual isolation; background stimuli are deliberately given little intensity, novelty, complexity, etc., and thus such a low arousal value that any effects that they might have are by far outweighed. But in a natural environment, an animal or human being will invariably be surrounded by a mass of stimuli with which distinct unlearned or learned responses are associated. In the case of human beings there will, for example, be at least a verbal response and a manipulatory response associated with every stimulus present, as well as a locomotor response that would bring the subject into contact with each stimulus object.

But only the responses corresponding to one, or at most a circumscribed number, of the stimuli that are present can actually be performed. There will, in other words, be many stimuli competing for "attention in performance" [25, chap. 3], and which stimuli will prevail in this contest for control over behavior must depend on many factors. They will include factors inside the organism brought on by instructions to pay attention to this or that, by internal stimuli connected with motivational states, or, through previous conditioning, by signals that herald the advent of a particular stimulus. But attributes of external stimuli, affective value and collative properties, will also be of some consequence.

To turn to a different but cognate question, a number of conditioned stimuli may be present at the time of reinforcement, but if these stimuli are later applied separately, the conditioned response will generally turn out to be evoked by some of them but not by others. And even if several stimuli have simultaneously acquired an increment of association with the response, the size of the increment is apt to vary widely from one to another [193]. Exactly the same finding appears when an instrumental response has been performed and reinforced in the presence of a stimulus pattern and the components of the pattern are presented one by one [121, 159].

All these phenomena must result partly from central attentive processes [25, chap. 3], which appear to be strongly influenced by collative variables among others, and partly from receptor-adjusting responses, which intensify the impact of certain environmental features while muffling the impact of others. The obvious dependence of all forms of discrimination learning on the acquisition of appropriate attentive and receptor-adjusting processes, focused on the crucial aspects of the stimulus objects, has been receiving more and more recognition of late from both experimenters and builders of theoretical models.

Latent and Incidental Learning

The task of identifying the properties of indifferent stimuli that can affect the likelihood and effectiveness of learning becomes especially urgent when we come to situations where learning results from conjunctions of indifferent stimuli alone, with no biologically beneficial or noxious stimuli clearly present. Such learning is generally termed *latent learning* when infrahuman animals are concerned. Much human remembering is, however, of the same kind, and the parallels between latent learning in animals and human remembering become most evident when we consider what has come to be called *incidental remembering,* i.e., remembering that has no manifest practical value and is devoid of any intention to commit something to memory.

When human beings remember, they are making use of internalized symbolic responses representing external stimulus events. These symbolic responses can be made to occur overtly and can thus be opened up to objective study, by asking the subject to communicate them by speaking, writing, drawing, acting, etc. Animals are said to manifest latent learning when, having once had an opportunity to experience certain combinations or successions of external events, they show by their overt behavior on a later occasion that they have acquired and retained some information from this early phase of familiarization. But the response that occurs during the test phase as a manifestation of latent learning either did not occur at all during the familiarization phase or, if it occurred, it did so together with others and not in conditions that would have led to its differential strengthening.

So we have to assume that what was actually acquired was a set of "expectations" corresponding to the external events experienced during the familiarization phase and that the evocation of these expectations during the test phase accounts for the adaptive behavior that then appeared. These expectations might be regarded as rudimentary symbolic responses, although we have no way of identifying them by making them overt as we have in the case of human beings.

Latent learning has raised a number of embarrassing problems for learning theorists. The first of these problems is whether or not it actually occurs in animals like the rat. By now the answer that it does seems clearly warranted [167, 182], and quite astonishing capacities for it in the cat and the dog have been demonstrated by Beritov [14]. In any case, this particular problem is of relatively minor interest, since processes classifiable as latent learning occur beyond any question in human beings.

The second problem arises from the fact that, both in the rat and in man, latent or incidental learning is often rather flimsy and unpredictable. If in some conditions it is clearly in evidence, it may be conspicuously absent at times when there has been ample opportunity to acquire it and when it could have been put to good use.

The third problem, which has been of special concern to those who seek to fit latent learning and incidental remembering into a conception of learning derived from classical-conditioning and instrumental-conditioning experiments, is how latent learning is reinforced. This last problem does not, of course, arise for those who are content to accept latent learning as something radically different from either kind of conditioning or for those who, like Tolman [186], tend to see latent learning as the prototype of which classical and instrumental conditioning are specialized variants.

It seems likely that collative motivation may hold the key to the last two problems. Human experience indicates that, capricious though our powers of recall may seem to be, we tend to find ourselves remembering events that drew attention. They might have drawn attention because of their biological significance and consequent affective value, but when this is not so, they are usually found to have collative properties like novelty, or surprisingness, or puzzlingness, which, as we have seen, have a special hold over arousal processes. The events in question are, in other words, ones that could be presumed to evoke powerful orientation reactions, and the drop in arousal that succeeds the transient rise represented by an orientation reaction might well have a reward value that could explain how latent learning is reinforced. The mechanism is apparently the one that we have called the arousal jag and discussed in connection with investigatory behavior [25].

Tolman, in discussing learning in general, put forward his "law of emphasis," according to which some of the stimuli that animals encounter will stand out, with the result that "expectancies" or "cognitions" in which they figure will be built up more easily than others. But for one thing Tolman did not work out this law in detail, and for another he seems to have been thinking particularly of affective, i.e., rewarding and punishing, value rather than of the other stimulus properties that govern attention and arousal.

Some writers [e.g., 181] have conjectured that reduction of curiosity or exploratory drive might supply the reinforcement for latent learning. But as long as little research had been done on curiosity and its determinants, little could be done to test this hypothesis. Now that we have a stock of at least tentative conclusions about exploratory behavior and about arousal processes, it would seem worthwhile to take up the study of latent and incidental learning anew, and it would seem likely that collative properties of stimuli will have a considerable say in determining when this kind of learning will take place, how effective it will be, and which of the multitudinous stimuli to which a subject is exposed on any one occasion will be represented in it.

Some corroboration for these suppositions comes from an observation that has frequently been reported by Russian experimenters [e.g., 114, 163], with reference to the form of latent learning known in the West as *sensory preconditioning*. Sensory preconditioning is said to occur when two stimuli, S_1 and S_2, have been paired a number of times and a response that later becomes associated with S_1 is found to have acquired an association also with S_2 as a result of the initial pairing of the two stimuli. The significant observation is that, when sensory preconditioning is obtained, S_1 will generally be found to evoke conditioned receptor-adjusting responses, aimed in the direction of S_2.

Voluntary Behavior

Even since the beginnings of systematic experimental work on learning, the relations between the lower, more automatic forms of behavior and the higher, more rational forms of behavior have been recognized as a source of interesting but contentious problems. Some have refused to acknowledge any essential difference between the two and have insisted that both are products of the same basic principles of learning, differing only in degree of complexity. Others have maintained that the two kinds of behavior form completely nonoverlapping realms and that the principles worked out from studies of conditioned responses have no applicability whatever to the most characteristically human psychological processes.

It is noteworthy that more and more psychologists in both Western countries and Eastern European countries are now striving to clarify the problem from an intermediate position, which acknowledges the profundity of the differences between higher and lower behavior but holds that these differences cannot be understood unless they are related to basic principles and concepts with a bearing on all behavior.

American writers [e.g., 90, chap. 11; 173] have dealt with the kinds of behavior that we call "voluntary," "rational," and "conscious" by stressing the regulatory role of verbal response-produced stimuli. The developmental investigations of Luria [121] and his associates on the acquisition of voluntary control over behavior have carried this line of inquiry some distance farther.

But a new facet of the problem has been accentuated by Zaporozhets [197]. According to this writer, the most important distinctions between voluntary and involuntary behavior depend on the role of feedback stimulation. The most primitive forms of behavior are guided simply by feedback from the end result; the subject engages in trial and error, and at the end of each trial he receives information about whether or not the goal has been reached, whereupon he either persists in what he is doing or tries out a different kind of behavior. But voluntary behavior is behavior that is monitored throughout its course; the subject receives feedback throughout his passage between the start and the goal, so that he is constantly informed whether or not he is on the right track and passing through the necessary way stations. Any correction that might be necessary can thus be introduced while the reaction is in full swing. This continuous monitoring accounts for the unique flexibility of voluntary behavior, which can be stopped or transformed if unexpected conditions are encountered at any point. It requires the development of a repertoire of attentive processes and exploratory responses directed toward both key external cues and proprioceptive feedback stimuli.

Zaporozhets cites, in support of his view, an experiment by Lisina [118], who gave subjects voluntary control over a normally involuntary vasomotor response by directing their attention to stimuli indicative of their own vasodilatations and vasoconstrictions. The criterion for voluntary control was the ability to produce vasodilatation in a finger while undergoing electric shock, a response opposite to the normal unconditioned reflex. Success was attained with some subjects by providing artificial feedback stimuli with properties that varied with the degree of distension of the blood vessels—a tone of varying pitch, the sight of a moving oscillograph pen, varying pressure applied to the hand. The most universally and completely effective technique consisted in training subjects to discriminate the forms of natural feedback stimulation that result from vasodilatation and vasoconstriction.

These procedures depended on learning to use appropriate "orientation reactions" in the wide sense that Russian writers give the term, i.e., to cover all kinds of attentive processes. They will presumably have involved both central attentive processes and orienting responses in the more restricted sense of receptor adjustments.

Zaporozhets also cites a sizable mass of experiments from his own laboratory which show that children will learn most effectively to perform complex activities in response to verbal instruction or by imitation if they are first trained to attend both to critical external landmarks and to proprioceptive stimulation from their own actions. Other experiments show how their spontaneous receptor-adjusting responses help them to organize and plan their activities, as soon as they reach the requisite degree of maturity.

Conclusions

It is clear from the studies that we have just cited and from others that learning of all varieties takes place most readily when something has occurred to jolt arousal above its normal level and when the subject is bringing all his exploratory resources to bear on significant stimulus events. Excessively high arousal and excessively pronounced orientation reactions may impede learning by disrupting the coordination of behavior or by suppressing all nonexploratory activities. But generally speaking, the orientation reaction marks periods of maximum plasticity

[188]. The organism finds itself faced with the unprecedented demands of a new environmental situation and left in the lurch by established ways of behaving. New forms of adaptation have to be worked out, which lends overriding urgency to the extraction of information.

Russian writers, in particular, are tending to assume that, if a stimulus is to affect behavior, it must, in general, not only undergo "analyzing" processes (i.e., processes in sense organs, specific afferent pathways, and sensory cortical areas that discriminate stimulus properties) but also evoke an orientation reaction, i.e., become a focus of attention. The only exceptions they appear to recognize are some of the more mechanical forms of behavior that depend on subcortical structures and can thus go on outside the subject's awareness. Western neurophysiologists have been veering toward a rather similar view in concluding that external stimuli must excite the cortex through both specific and diffuse (i.e., reticular) pathways if they are to lead to cortically controlled motor processes.

The orientation reaction entails a transient rise in arousal, and repeated elicitation of phasic orientation reactions is likely to be accompanied by a gradual upward swing in the base-line level of arousal. Now, states of heightened arousal that are generated by novelty or surprise or uncertainty or conflict and that occasion exploratory responses constitute what we have called perceptual curiosity. It seems, therefore, that the role of curiosity in motivating learned changes in behavior may be more widespread than has hitherto been suspected.

An even more inviting field for speculation and subsequent research is offered by the role of drops in arousal. There is, first, the tendency of the various component processes of the orientation reaction to decline soon after the initial impact of a stimulus, as the nervous system recovers from its momentary disequilibrium. In addition, there is generally a downward drift in the base line of arousal, coinciding with the progressive extinction of the orientation reaction, in response to prolonged or recurrent encounters with an indifferent stimulus.

The disappearance of the orientation reaction and the return of arousal to its normal level may be followed by relaxation and relative immobility. This will usually be the case when the continued or repeated stimulus is harmless and has no special biological significance. At other times, there is identification of a familiar stimulus and performance of a habitual response associated with it. At yet other times, when an animal is going through a learning process, arousal processes drop out when a new behavior pattern has become solidly entrenched.

The arousal system apparently retires into the background when the influx of information and the consequent reduction of conflict have gone far enough for a course of action or inaction to be selected. It is noteworthy that the orientation reaction persists at full strength and the arousal system remains keyed up whenever a series of difficult discriminations is imposed on an organism.

If our previous line of thought is valid, a reduction in arousal is a reduction in drive, and the hypothesis that reductions in drive reinforce responses and thus determine which responses will be retained has played a leading role on the psychological scene for some time. Here, it offers itself for consideration in a new guise.

EXTENSIONS TO OTHER AREAS

We shall end, apart from a final word, with excursions into a few areas of psychological research that may seem remote from those that have concerned us so far. They are, nevertheless, highly animated areas and include some of the most vital problems of psychology within their limits.

We shall look at ideas that have been advanced by some of the most active specialists in these areas, and it will be apparent that, despite differences in terminology, they are talking about processes akin to those that have dominated our earlier discussion. And we shall look at research data confirming the relevance of these processes to a broad assortment of phenomena. Sometimes, there will be evidence that exploratory responses are performing special functions. At other times, major roles for arousal processes, collative variables, and conflict in particular will be discernable.

Perceptual and Intellectual Development in the Child

Piaget [147] has made the rather startling assertion that maturation of unlearned mechanisms, learning due to experience of external events, and social influence transmitted through the medium of language do not suffice to account for the progressive organization of perceptual and intellectual activities in the child. There is, he believes, an additional factor making for change in the direction of superior "adaptiveness" or "intelligence," and he calls it "equilibration." It consists of an autonomous tendency for these activities to achieve more and more complete "equilibrium."

"Disequilibrium" and "equilibrium" are properties of the structures in which responses are coordinated and depend on the interrelations of the responses that result from these structures. So Piaget seems to be accepting a conclusion to which our consideration of other problems has led us, namely, that changes in behavior can be impelled not only by visceral disturbances and external irritations but also by inharmonious relations between the organism's own responses or, as we have called it, *conflict.* Piaget's "equilibration" seems to be a kind of instrumental learning motivated by conflict and reinforced by conflict reduction. This interpretation is supported by Piaget's explanation that better equilibrium means more "prediction" and "security," i.e., less uncertainty and less liability to surprise.

The implications of the notion of "equilibration" with reference to perception have been worked out in considerable detail [148]. The "error of the standard," the tendency for those parts of the stimulus field on which attention is focused to appear relatively larger, gives rise to illusions, since some parts of a visual figure will receive a disproportionate number of "centerings," i.e., acts of attention, and consequently undergo a net overestimation with respect to size. Moreover, the relative dimensions of parts of a figure will appear to change as attention wanders from one point to another, and this will sooner or later be experienced as a confusing and intolerable inconsistency.

In the older child and the adult, these imperfections of perception are partially offset by "perceptual activities." They include systematic reorganizations of receptor-adjusting responses, so that appearances from different fixation points are adequately sampled and collated, and mechanisms whereby perception is jointly determined by information received from the present visual field and stored information from earlier experiences. Evidence that the extent of visual illusions depends on attention comes from tachistoscopic experiments, in which fixation points are prescribed, and from cinematographic studies of eye movements. The focus of attention will, of course, not always coincide with the focus of fixation [64], but it will usually do so.

Other data from Piaget's laboratory show that illusions weaken as the length of a tachistoscopic exposure is increased, as exposures to a figure succeed one another without any knowledge of results, or simply as subjects grow older. These data suggest that, given enough time, a subject comes to mitigate the shortcomings of perception. This is presumably achieved through a systematization of attentive processes and a fuller sampling of the information derivable from them. If so, such systematization must have an endogenous source of reinforcement, and conflict reduction is one obvious candidate for this role.

Our ability to make use of logical thinking saves us from the hazards of relying exclusively on perception. In early years, the child makes inferences that an adult would recognize as fallacious. But more and more powerful and comprehensive logical structures appear, one after another, until early adolescence sees the attainment of those that make the highest accomplishments of mathematics and science possible.

Studies by Piaget and his associates [74, 78, 133] exhibit the striking differences between a child who is persuaded to accept a simple truth about some natural or mathematical phenomenon by dint of exposure to instances of it and the older child who can "understand" why it has to be so. The latter child justifies his acceptance, not by reference to what he has been shown, but by deduction from general principles. He can gauge how wide the range of application of the proposition in question must be, and, in contrast with the younger child who has not yet acquired the relevant logical structure, his belief in the proposition is unshakeable.

The firmness of his conviction may, of course, be regarded simply as different in degree from that of the younger child who has nothing but empirical demonstration to go on, and it may be pointed out that the wrong-headed convictions of a child or an adult who reasons illogically are often equally unshakeable. Nevertheless, these differences between kinds of behavior appearing at different ages are dramatic and require explanation. There are evidently ways in which symbolic behavior patterns can draw much more effective reinforcement from their own interrelations than from external stimulus events, and here again, some kind of conflict reduction may well be the essential factor.

Some support for the suggestion that conflict motivates the adoption of new logical structures comes from a series of experiments by Smedslund [174]. In what Piaget calls the "stage of intuitive thought," i.e., roughly between the ages of four and seven years, children typically believe that a mass of plasticine will either increase or decrease in quantity when its shape is changed from a ball to a sausage. Smedslund tried out a great variety of techniques in the hope of accelerating the appearance of a conviction that quantity remains constant despite changes in shape. One technique was incomparably more successful than any of the others, converting eight out of fifteen subjects to judgments of equality. It used procedures such as elongating one of two masses of plasticine and then breaking off a piece before asking the subject to compare it with the unchanged mass.

The tendency to believe that quantity increases when something becomes longer presumably conflicted with the tendency to believe that quantity decreases when part of something is subtracted. The new belief that elongation leaves quantity unchanged was presumably discovered in the course of a search for a way out of the impasse and reinforced by its conflict-relieving consequences.

Piaget's notion of "equilibrium" involves a balance between the two requirements of "assimilation" and "accommodation." The multiplicity of processes that Piaget puts under these two headings makes their interpretation a little hazardous and thus inevitably a little subjective. But it seems that "accommodation" refers to the need for a reaction to fit the characteristics of external stimulus events, and "assimilation" refers to the need for the reaction called forth by an external stimulus to fit what is already in the organism, either as a result of prior experience or constitutionally.

If accommodation is insufficient, the subject will be liable to conflict from surprise (since there will be discrepancies between inferred stimulus properties and actual stimulus properties) or, when external rewards or punishments are at stake, to frustration. If assimilation is insufficient, the subject will be liable to conflict from novelty (since the external stimuli that he encounters may belong to categories to which no appropriate response is allotted), to uncertainty (inability to form any firm expectation), or to occlusion (overstepping of information-processing capacity).

An ideal structure of thought, which is approximated within restricted fields by the most successful branches of mathematics and science, would be proof against failures of either accommodation or assimilation. It could come up against no external phenomenon that it was unable to account for or predict in advance. It would possess to an ultimate degree what Piaget calls "mobile equilibrium," which embodies maximum consistency with maximum flexibility.

Origins of Social Attachments

To turn to the affective side of development, evidence that collative motivation forms one of the major roots of socialization seems to be accumulating from the most scattered and unexpected sources.

Whether the emotional bond between a human child and his parents could be due to anything like the "imprinting" that has been observed in lower animals, especially birds, is a question that we are not yet in a position to answer categorically. Since the human infant, unlike the young of most other animals, is incapable of locomotion for some time after birth [77], human imprinting could not consist of a tendency to follow the parent about but would rather take the form of smiling, vocalization, and directing movements of head and eyes toward the parent.

Data reviewed by Moltz [132] lead him to identify the stimulus properties that induce imprinting with those that draw attention. The one that has been most widely discussed in connection with imprinting is movement; the animal in question is said to follow the first moving object that it encounters after it has been hatched or born. But other attention-drawing properties can also be influential. The object of imprinting is generally so large that it dominates the visual field, and James [97] has shown that a flickering light will be approached by chicks in preference to a steady light. It seems, therefore, that the original following about of the object of imprinting may be a kind of locomotor exploration, since not only the response but also the evoking stimulus conditions resemble those that have figured in studies of exploratory activity.

Moltz notes further that, as several studies have shown, both lower animals and human infants are apt to be afraid of strange situations and objects, but this fear takes some time to develop after the start of life. Our earlier discussions suggest that this fear is due to conflict stemming from novelty or surprise, and the subject cannot recognize deviations until he has had time to develop responses corresponding to familiar stimulus patterns. The object of imprinting will thus have been originally encountered and kept in view at a time when the subject was relatively free from fear. The stimuli characterizing the object will consequently have become conditioned to a state of low fear, or as we may be inclined to put it, low arousal.

When at a later age the subject is frightened by finding himself in a strange situation or for some other reason, contact with the object of imprinting may serve as a means of reducing fear, and Moltz cites experimental results obtained by himself and others that tally with the view that imprinting has this function. There are, however, several other and less devious ways in which the proximity of a parent could become associated with fear reduction [see 103].

Gewirtz [70] and Rheingold [160] have both raised the question of what makes human beings stand out among the objects perceived by a human infant. They both conclude, in answer to this question, that human beings must stand out initially as exceptionally rich foci of "interesting" stimulation. In comparison with most objects in the infant's surroundings, they move about more, they give rise to a more extensive assortment of stimulus patterns in all modalities, they undergo more frequent changes, and they possess more internal contour, the last property being especially potent in attracting an infant's gaze [23]. These are all properties that can be expected to exert a dominant influence on processes of attention, including the orientation reaction. They are properties that appear to make indifferent stimuli particularly effective as conditioned stimuli, and they are also properties that can reinforce investigatory behavior.

Rheingold [160] mentions, as an incidental observation, that infants will often vocalize and smile at inanimate objects, such as a wallpaper pattern or a rattle, which may be comparable to human beings in their collative properties.

During succeeding months and years, the child learns not only to seek human company and to be emotionally affected by it but also to respond to the outward signs of attitudes and feelings that others harbor toward him. He comes to be rewarded by signs of approval, esteem, affection, and deference, and to be disturbed by signs of their opposites.

The prevalent hypothesis among learning theorists has been that stimuli denoting favorable attitudes acquire secondary reward value through association with primary rewards, while stimuli associated with unfavorable attitudes become fear-inducing through their association with physical discomforts. Skinner [173], for example, describes the former as "generalized reinforcers," implying that they have all accompanied a variety of primary rewards. Provision of food and relief of pain have generally loomed largest among the primary rewards assumed to underlie social reinforcement, but Harlow's experiments [81] recommend that "contact comfort," i.e., tactual and thermal stimuli from physical contact, should be inserted near the head of the list.

We may wonder whether more consideration ought to be given to collative factors here also. There are certainly families both in our society and in others in which a child is physically ill-treated whenever he is not in good grace with his parents and in which he is fed and cared for only when they are well disposed toward him. But in many households, physical comfort and gratification bear little relation to whether a child has incurred pleasure or displeasure.

Might it not rather be that when a child is on good terms with those about him, things follow a smooth, accustomed course, whereas when he does something that is deemed improper, he does not know what is likely to happen? His parents are then apt to behave in some unprecedented way, so that the child is subjected to uncertainty before they have reacted and to surprise afterward.

Protection against unbearable intrusions of novelty, surprisingness, complexity, uncertainty, or indecision may, as Hebb and Thompson [87] contend, be one of the principal advantages of living in an organized society with set patterns of behavior, offering repetitive sequences of stimuli, prescribing set reactions for common contingencies and thus set expectations regarding the reactions of other persons to one's own deeds.

Perhaps the main reason why people exclude from most of their acquaintances thoughts and revelations about themselves that they may make available to a psychotherapist is not the fear that the average layman would hear them with disapproval but rather the fact of not knowing how he would react, since society does not lay down a stock way of behaving in such circumstances. And perhaps the therapist is so prolific of solace because the patient knows that the same unruffled demeanor and bland "Hm, hm" will be forthcoming whatever he dares to say.

It has become almost a truism among social psychologists [e.g., 43, 170] that social norms serve to reduce uncertainty not only about human behavior but about other matters as well. Every society has a stock of beliefs answering a high proportion of the questions that its members may be inclined to ask and thus effectively satisfying or staving off the epistemic curiosity of most of its members most of the time. It provides techniques and standards by which novel experiences can readily be judged and categorized, and if its established techniques and standards are for once found wanting, it readily fills the gap with new ones. It is only at times of exceptional crisis, when established beliefs break down irrevocably under a deluge of unparalleled events, that the group is discredited as a source of wisdom and its members are ready to embrace any radically new cultural system that seems to offer an explanation of what is going on and a plausible description of what will happen next.

Even when social life is proceeding normally, it seems, in the light of experimental findings gathered by Schachter [166], that a desire for "cognitive clarity" can be one of the principal forces that incite human beings to associate with one another. In Schachter's experiments, subjects were given to understand that they would soon be undergoing some rather painful electric shocks for the sake of scientific research, and they were given the choice of spending the waiting period alone or with others in a similar predicament.

Most subjects wanted to be with others, and the data suggested that this was largely because they found it difficult to evaluate their own feelings and behavior and hoped that an opportunity to compare their own reactions with those of others would reveal, for example, whether they were being unduly and exceptionally cowardly in wanting to escape from this situation or unduly and exceptionally docile in putting up with it. Human beings have, Schachter concludes, an inveterate tendency to wonder how "correct" their feelings and beliefs are, and interaction with others is often the only way in which criteria of normality can be set up to allay this uncertainty.

Individual Differences

Some contemporary lines of research on individual differences have paid attention to variations in exploratory behavior and arousal processes, seeking to relate them to other aspects of psychological variability. Others with very different starting points have found themselves obliged sooner or later to take account of differences in degree and mode of responsiveness to collative variables.

This work illustrates further the wide range of topics with which the problems raised by exploratory behavior make contact and the way in which a growing number of contrasting approaches are converging toward them.

Variations in arousal processes. There are clearly many ways in which the working of arousal processes can differ from individual to individual. There can be differences in the mean magnitude of the orientation reaction to a given kind of stimulus, in how many presentations of the stimulus occur before the orientation reaction extinguishes, in the average duration of the orientation reaction to a particular stimulus. In addition, there can be differences in the prevailing level of arousal and in the extent of spontaneous fluctuations in the level of arousal that do not depend on external stimulation. As for motivational aspects, we can expect differences in the minimal level of arousal that can be achieved and in the influx of arousal potential that is needed to keep the subject as near this level as possible. Finally, there can be differences in the relative prominence of various components of the orientation reaction.

Most of these psychophysiological differences have been studied by experimenters at one time or another, and some of them have been linked with personality traits. But unfortunately, those who have studied the physiological processes have rarely been conversant with standardized methods of measuring personality or even standardized schemes for describing and classifying it. So it is difficult to know what to make of the terms used to characterize the personalities that go together with certain peculiarities in the working of arousal, let alone to relate them to well-authenticated dimensions of personality. And little has been done to find out what correlations exist among the psychophysiological variations that we have enumerated.

One of the few exceptions is the work of the group headed by Teplov in Moscow. This group has been studying human individual differences in the light of Pavlov's latest classificatory scheme, which recognized three dimensions: strength of nervous system, degree of equilibrium between excitatory and inhibitory processes, and mobility. It was once generally believed that both the magnitude of the orientation reaction and its resistance to extinction were indices of the strength dimension. But a factor-analytic study [164] included among its variables the magnitude and resistance to extinction of the vasomotor component of the orientation reaction to visual and auditory stimuli and found these to have no significant loading on the strength factor. A subsequent study [139] showed, however, that the duration and resistance to extinction of EEG desynchronization, evoked either by flashes of light or by tones, possess fairly high negative correlations with the extinction rate of a nonreinforced conditioned response and with the speed of acquiring differential inhibition, both of which are accepted as indices of the equilibrium dimension.

Lát's dimension of "excitability." Lát [110, 111] has found it possible to classify rats along a unitary dimension of "excitability" with strength of exploratory behavior among its indices and with offshoots reaching into the fields of metabolism and anatomy.

In one study, rats were subjected to an instrumental-reward-conditioning situation, in which they could obtain food by pressing a bar on receiving a particular visual or auditory stimulus, and an instrumental-avoidance-conditioning situation, in which they could avert an electric shock by jumping onto a vertical grating on receiving a particular visual or auditory signal. Individual differences in excitability were revealed by speed of conditioning in the two situations, number of "spontaneous" responses between presentations of the discriminatory stimulus, and amount of exploratory behavior, measured both by frequency of the rearing response and by amount of locomotion. All these were positively intercorrelated.

It is significant that, although rate of conditioning as such increased with excitability, performance in a task requiring discrimination—bar pressing was rewarded with food when a steady light was on but not when an intermittent light was on—was curvilinearly related to excitability. The difference between the rates of responding in the presence of the positive and negative stimuli was at a maximum in animals that were moderately excitable [personal communication].

Excitability increased linearly with rate of growth and with food intake (calories ingested per unit of body surface). More excitable rats preferred diets rich in carbohydrates and poor in proteins and fats, while less excitable ones had the opposite preferences. Excitability could also be manipulated by controlling carbohydrate, fat, and protein intake. Rats with an intermediate degree of excitability had the largest body rates when fully grown and the smallest adrenal glands [112].

Personality traits. On a very different level of analysis, a number of motivational dispositions affecting exploratory and epistemic behavior have been shown to vary in prevailing strength from person to person and to possess some degree of generality. These are the "exploration (curiosity) erg" [45], "sensitivity to problems" [79], and "need for cognition" [46]. The tests by which these traits are defined seem particularly pertinent to epistemic curiosity, although Cattell's "exploration erg" seems to have something to do with aesthetic interests too.

Since about 1950, personality theorists have become preoccupied with a number of dimensions that seem to reflect differences in reaction to collative motivation. There is, for example, "intolerance of ambiguity" [65], involving a tendency to avoid stimulus patterns that do not fall neatly into familiar categories or to refuse to recognize their anomalies when they are encountered. Then, there is the "simplicity-complexity" dimension of aesthetic preferences [8, 59]. And finally, there is the distinction between "repressers" and "intellectualizers" [113].

All these dimensions of personality appear primarily to reflect preferences for particular ways of dealing with collative conflict. One kind of reaction depends on selective attention; it works by making behavior depend on one aspect of a stimulus pattern, perhaps on a distorted perception of it, and refusing to take account of other features that might have different implications for behavior. Related reactions consist simply of withdrawing from, or avoiding, stimulus situations that involve the subject in conflict. These seem to be the reactions favored by those with high "intolerance of ambiguity," by those whose preferences tend toward "simplicity," and by "repressers."

The other kind of reaction makes use of exploratory or epistemic behavior. The subject can approach the disturbing stimulus in order to extract more information from it or in order to become habituated to it, or he can work out an appropriate way of treating it through directed thinking or some other kind of epistemic activity. Such seem to be the favorite recourses of those with low "intolerance of ambiguity," of those who prefer "complexity," and of "intellectualizers."

Some direct corroboration of our interpretation, linking these traits with exploratory behavior, comes from Smock and Holt [175]. In a variant of an experiment cited earlier [19], they allowed six-year-old children to give themselves as many $\frac{1}{4}$-second exposures to each of a series of visual figures as they wished. The children, like the adult subjects of the other experiment, performed more investigatory responses to see more complex or more incongruous figures. Smock and Holt later administered the Blum Transition Test, which they describe as a test of "rigidity," although it has often been regarded as a test of "intolerance of ambiguity." The number by which investigatory responses exposing more complex or incongruous figures exceeded investigatory responses exposing simpler or nonincongruous figures varied inversely with intolerance of ambiguity.

Cultural differences. It is clear that there must also be variations from one society to another with respect to the region of the arousal continuum that is preferred, the means that are used to keep arousal within this region, and the extent to which arousal is affected by particular kinds of experiences [28].

Humor

In many instances of humor, an audience member goes through two clearly separable phases in succession. The first is a phase in which he is surprised, puzzled, baffled, and perhaps even offended. Then follows a phase in which he becomes aware of aspects of the situation that put an end to his discomfiture; he may see that the joke makes sense in a different way than he was anticipating, or he may realize that it was not meant seriously.

These two phases can be plausibly identified as a phase of arousal and a phase of arousal reduction, and some of the same collative variables that we have been constantly encountering in other contexts must be playing their part here also [25, chap. 9].

At other times, there is not such a clear-cut division into a phase of being taken aback and a phase of "catching on." But there will usually be clearly specifiable aspects of the joke that introduce incongruity, ambiguity, or some other variety of conceptual conflict, and other aspects that are calculated to relieve conflict and to reassure. We may speculate that, in cases of this sort, the phases of arousal and of arousal reduction succeed each other so rapidly that they defy separation. The mechanism would then be an instance of the arousal jag which we have invoked to explain the reinforcing effects of novel, surprising, or complex stimuli in other contexts.

Aesthetics

What we have been calling collative variables coincide in large measure with the factors that have been discussed for centuries by aestheticians under the headings of "form," "structure," and "composition." It is generally agreed that a work of art may please through its form as well as through its content, although the relative weight placed on these two factors differs from one style to another. And in attempting to analyze the elusive nature of "formal beauty," writers have generally found themselves detecting two requirements that are in a sense opposite, since the structural properties that subserve the one make the other more difficult to satisfy, and yet in a sense complementary, since each presupposes the other [25, chap. 9].

The first of these requirements is described variously by phrases such as "maintaining interest," "holding the attention," "presenting a challenge." It seems to be a matter of preventing arousal from dropping below a desirable minimum or at least preventing it from dropping below this minimum for long. And the devices that are employed by creative artists to fulfill this requirement are those that we should expect to find employed in the light of our previous discussions: variety, ambiguity, deviation from stylistic norms, failure to confirm expectations induced by material in one part of the work regarding material in another part.

The other requirement is "making sense," "having a definite structure," "being coherent," and this apparently pertains to moderating or relieving arousal. It also is achieved by means whose manner of working will by now be familiar to us: conforming to a standardized form sanctioned by a particular style, obeying rules that restrict the range of permissible patterns and thus cut down uncertainty, introducing a sequence of patterns that share some quality even though they may differ in other respects.

Creative artistry is revealed in the skill with which these two divergent trends are mixed, balanced, set against each other, and in fact made congruent with each other despite their potential opposition. The outcome is one of "unity in variety" or "uniformity in diversity." A lucid whole is formed out of a patchwork of heterogeneous details. The meaning of each element becomes clear as the organizing principles of the work reveal its relations to other elements.

The sequence of arousal-increasing and arousal-decreasing devices and the psychological nature of the interaction between them are most evident in the temporal arts of music and literature, and the most thoroughgoing attempts to analyze them have been applied to music in particular [47, 107, 129]. But there are obvious isomorphisms between the principles of composition and structural artifices that are found in the temporal arts and those that are found in the spatially organized visual arts. In any case, it is not possible to differentiate temporal and spatial art organization absolutely. Spatially contiguous elements must generally be registered in succession, while the plan of a temporal pattern is generally apprehended as whole and often represented by a spatial form after it is completed.

So the arousal-sustaining and the arousal-mitigating aspects of visual art objects have been distinguished and painstakingly analyzed by several writers [e.g., 31, 60, 76, 156]. But the drive-inducing role of the former and the drive-reducing role of the latter are more readily recognizable when, for example, a later incident explains a puzzling earlier incident in a novel or when a chromatic note is shown by what follows to denote an entry into a new key.

Relations between Art and Science

The boundary lines between art and science have always presented problems, at least to those who have sought to delimit them theoretically. Artists commonly claim to be communicating truth, which sounds like an encroachment on the prerogatives of science. It has often been said that the pure mathematician is aiming at aesthetic satisfaction, and the most successful scientific achievements certainly yield aesthetic pleasure. The way in which creative artists describe their own work is strikingly reminiscent of some aspects of scientific activity. An artist often "experiments"; he may try out a new "idea" or a new technique to find out what kind of effect it will produce. He sets himself a "problem" and struggles until he has "solved" it. He is uncomfortable and continues to modify his work as long as it fails to fit what he has to "express" or to fulfill some ideal of "significant form" that he has set before himself, and he declares himself content when his work has reached a form that relieves his discomfort.

Nevertheless, the yardsticks by which the products of art and science are evaluated are reasonably distinct in practice, and there is certainly no mistaking the differences between their orders of priority. Art may depict the findings of science as a subsidiary function, and scientific research may be conducted and reported in an artistic fashion. Aesthetic and scientific aims may be combined and even reinforce each other up to a point, but beyond that point one or the other of them must be subordinated.

Science, like art, is caught between two divergent requirements, and an examination of these, such as Bunge [36] has attempted, may help us to understand both the affinities and the disparities between the two domains. The two requirements of science are "simplicity," long recognized as a touchstone for deciding among otherwise equally valid theories, and what Bunge calls "complexity," or "accuracy." Simplicity, which has a number of forms that Bunge distinguishes, involves economy of one sort or another. It makes a theory psychologically manageable. It prevents overstrain of the limited information-processing capacity of the nervous system. Complexity, on the other hand, means ability to reflect natural phenomena precisely and correctly. The inadequacies of a simple theory become apparent when new facts are discovered that it does not fit. The theory must then be modified to take account of these new facts, and that will inevitably mean that the theory must become less tidy.

At first sight, these two requirements may seem to correspond to the arousal-inducing and the arousal-reducing aspects of aesthetic form. But they are actually not quite the same. Both the "simplicity" and the "complexity" of science have a conflict-reducing and thus arousal-reducing function, the one minimizing conflict due to occlusion, inconsistency, and uncertainty, the other minimizing conflict due to surprise. They correspond, in fact, to Piaget's "assimilation" and "accommodation" respectively, in terms of our earlier interpretation. They reflect, respectively, the coherence and the flexibility that define the most advanced structures of thought.

Simplicity must certainly be one aim of science. Otherwise, a set of propositions describing particular localized facts would be sufficient, and no summary or explanatory schemes would be called for. But, as Bunge argues, simplicity has sometimes been overstressed. The adoption of truth as the target of science means that the aim of complexity, in the sense of maximum conformity to facts, must have overriding precedence. This is one way in which science and art differ. Another is that while art must draw both its motivating conflicts as well as its rewarding alleviations of conflict from its own structure, science derives enough impetus from confrontations with natural phenomena, so that its formal properties can be concentrated on relieving conflict.

A FINAL WORD

The upshot of our far-ranging survey is not to dispute anything that established theories of motivation have asserted so much as to map out extensions that should be built on to them.

Our conceptions of motivation bear the imprint of Darwin's evolutionary theory, sharpened by Cannon's notion of homeostasis. We see animal life as a ceaseless struggle to forestall threats to well-being or to eliminate them as soon as possible after their initial impact. Disturbances that prompt corrective action will originate from within when stocks of essential substances like nutriment or water are low or when concentrations of troublesome substances like carbon dioxide or sex hormones are high. They can originate from the external environment when it contains injurious conditions or events that heredity or learning has marked out as ominous. A human being devotes much of his time and capacity for disquiet to threats to his social standing and to his interpersonal ties.

The various lines of research that we have reviewed indicate some additions that must be made to the conditions that can provoke disturbance, distress, high drive, high arousal, and therefore to the behavior patterns that an animal must have available if his adaptation is not to break down. These added sources of discomfort appear to stem from the complexity of the nervous systems of high animals. On the one hand, the most advanced nervous systems are multipartite enough for many processes to be initiated in them at once. On the other hand, they appear to be so constructed that every unit can act, directly or indirectly, on every other. Conflict, the simultaneous initiation of processes that cannot all reach fruition and that therefore impede one another, must be occurring all the time. An animal organism could scarcely function at all if it did not have resources for coping with conflict. The nervous system evidently possesses mechanisms of reciprocal inhibition that overpower competing processes when a prepotent process is under way [2, 15, 171]. But these mechanisms will often not suffice, especially when no process is able to achieve prepotency immediately. Then other resources must come into play, including the ones that have figured in our review.

How much conflict there will be at any particular time depends largely, we may surmise, on the collative properties of the stimuli that are acting on the organism. So we can state some of the additional needs that we must recognize with reference to them.

The human organism at least is apparently adapted to an environment with a moderately high influx of stimulation, information, or, to use the comprehensive term that we have judged it best to use, arousal potential. If it is placed in an abnormally uneventful environment, its functioning is impaired, its tranquillity is upset, and it must strive to restore arousal potential to an adequate level.

Extremely high arousal potential generally means uncertainty about what will follow, an aggravation of the conflict to which neural processes are continually subject, and thus a need for information to adjudicate among the divergent response tendencies that the situation has stirred up. When this happens, many recourses are possible, but exploratory and epistemic behavior are among the most consistently effective.

The susceptibility of the human organism to surprise, uncertainty, and conflict is increased immeasurably by its capacity for symbolization. Images and words, memories and thoughts, cause anticipations of impending events and representations of hidden stimulus properties to proliferate. Each of these must mobilize one or more response tendencies, and a multiplicity of response tendencies means a multiplicity of opportunities for conflict.

Yet, the human being is equipped with a much richer assortment of devices for overcoming conflict than any other species. Resolution of conflict is evidently so gratifying that we deliberately seek out conditions in which mystifications and clarifications, disconcertions and reassurances, aggravations and alleviations of conflict, are suitably apportioned. This is, of course, especially so whenever the immediate requirements of survival cease to be pressing. It must account in part, but certainly not entirely, for such recreational outlets as playing games, traveling, attempting puzzles, and attending circuses, as well as for such highly esteemed pursuits as scholarship, the sciences, the arts, and wit.

We are still far from the time when we shall be able to frame a precise theory of all these phenomena. The main obstacle, besides the complexity of some of the processes in question and the short time for which they have been seriously investigated, is the lack of measuring techniques for collative variables. As we have recognized, stimulus patterns can be more or less novel, surprising, complex, incongruous, indistinct, or unintelligible, and enormous differences in behavior can turn on subtle differences in the values that these variables assume.

We can easily gauge how critical their quantitative properties are by looking at either extreme of the gamut of phenomena that we have surveyed. At one extreme, an animal confronted with a strange object seems to be wavering between exploration, flight, frightened immobility, aggressiveness, and maybe sexual or alimentary behavior. He may try out several of them in succession or in alternation, and which will prevail depends on the interrelations between his state and the degree to which his environment possesses collative properties. At the opposite extreme, we all know how the slightest increase or decrease in novelty, complexity, clarity, etc., can turn a highly appreciated work of art or joke into one that falls flat.

Much experimental and theoretical work will be needed before we can hope to have the necessary measuring techniques at our disposal. Until they are available, we can do little more than point to factors that are likely to make a difference and thus to repay investigation in many areas of psychology, but we cannot always predict exactly what difference they will make.

Since our theoretical analysis of exploratory, epistemic, and related behavior has not led us to repudiate established theories but to propose extensions and modifications, our approach has some bearing on questions of theoretical strategy.

Virtually every few months, a book or a journal article contains what amounts to an invitation to cast aside everything that psychologists have done so far and to rebuild psychology anew after some pattern furnished by the writer. Flaws in existing conceptualizations are tellingly pointed out, and a new scheme is put forward that is free from these particular flaws. The innovator shows that his new scheme can do a few things that an established theoretical scheme cannot do, but he usually does not show that his new scheme can do the many things that the old scheme can do. So the net gain is not evident, and the psychologist finds himself in a position not unlike that of the miller, his son, and the donkey, in Aesop's fable.

The lines of research that we have reviewed show how it is possible to recognize serious deficiencies in existing theories and yet to overcome these deficiencies by renovating theoretical fabrics that have given good wear. The renovations that are required may have radical implications, but it should be possible to effect them without unraveling the whole texture. This will not only be economical; it will also enable new areas of research to be integrated smoothly and firmly with old areas. The method of obtaining a new sock by darning an old sock until none of the original wool remains has served other sciences well and may have advantages for psychology also. If the sock grows more capacious or even turns into a sweater in the process, so much the better.

REFERENCES

Note: Coverage of the literature relevant to exploratory and epistemic behavior that appeared before the end of 1959 was attempted in Reference 25. This literature is therefore not included in full in the following bibliography, which should be consulted in conjunction with that of the earlier work by readers seeking comprehensive documentation.

1. Anokhin, P. K. [Peculiarities of the afferent apparatus of the conditioned reflex and its significance for psychology.] *Vop. Psikhol.*, 1955, 1, (6), 16–38.

2. Anokhin, P. K. *Vnutrennee tormozhenie kak problema fiziologii.* [Internal inhibition as a physiological problem.] Moscow: Medgiz, 1958.

3. Anokhin, P. K. [New data on the functional heterogeneity of the reticular formation of the brain stem.] *Zh. Vys. Nerv. Deiat.,* 1959, **9,** 489–499.

4. Anokhin, P. K. On the specific action of the reticular formation on the cerebral cortex. *EEG clin. Neurophysiol.,* 1960 (Suppl. 13), 257–267. Amsterdam: Elsevier Publishing Company.

5. Armington, J. E., & Mitnick, L. L. Electroencephalogram and sleep deprivation. *J. appl. Physiol.,* 1959, **14,** 247–250.

6. Attneave, F. Some informational aspects of visual perception. *Psychol. Rev.,* 1954, **6,** 183–193.

7. Attneave, F. Physical determinants of the judged complexity of shapes. *J. exp. Psychol.,* 1957, **53,** 221–227.

8. Barron, F., & Welsh, G. S. Perception as a possible factor in personality style: its measurement by a figure preference test. *J. Psychol.,* 1952, **33,** 199–207.

9. Becker, G. M. Sequential decision making: Wald's model and estimates of parameters. *J. exp. Psychol.,* 1958, **55,** 628–636.

10. Bélanger, D. Les relations entre la fréquence cardiaque du rat et les niveaux de tendance et d'activation. Unpublished doctoral dissertation, Univer. of Montreal, 1959.

11. Bélanger, D., & Tétreau, B. L'influence d'une motivation inappropriée sur le comportement du rat et sa fréquence cardiaque. *Canad. J. Psychol.,* 1961, **15,** 6–14.

12. Berger, H. Über das Elektrenkephalogramm des Menschen. II. *J. Physiol. Neurol., Leipzig,* 1930, **40,** 160–179.

13. Beritov, I. S. [Morphological and physiological bases of temporary connections in the cerebral cortex.] *Trudy Inst. Fiziol. Beritashvili,* 1956, **10,** 3–72.

14. Beritov, I. S. *O nervnykh mekhanizmakh prostranstvennoi orientatsii vysshikh pozvonochnykh zhivotnykh.* [On the neural mechanisms of spatial orientation in higher vertebrates.] Tbilisi: Acad. Sci. Georgian SSR, 1959.

15. Beritov, I. S. *Nervnye mekhanizmy povedeniia vysshikh pozvonochnykh zhivotnykh.* [Neural mechanisms of the behavior of higher vertebrates.] Moscow: Acad. Sci. USSR, 1961.

16. Berlyne, D. E. Knowledge and stimulus-response psychology. *Psychol. Rev.,* 1954, **61,** 245–254.

17. Berlyne, D. E. A theory of human curiosity. *Brit. J. Psychol.,* 1954, **45,** 180–191.

18. Berlyne, D. E. An experimental study of human curiosity. *Brit. J. Psychol.,* 1954, **45,** 256–265.

19. Berlyne, D. E. Conflict and information-theory variables as determinants of human perceptual curiosity. *J. exp. Psychol.,* 1957, **53,** 399–404.

20. Berlyne, D. E. Conflict and choice time. *Brit. J. Psychol.,* 1957, **48,** 106–118.
21. Berlyne, D. E. Uncertainty and conflict: a point of contact between information-theory and behavior-theory concepts. *Psychol. Rev.,* 1957, **64,** 329–339.
22. Berlyne, D. E. The influence of complexity and novelty in visual figures on orienting responses. *J. exp. Psychol.,* 1958, **55,** 289–296.
23. Berlyne, D. E. The influence on the albedo and complexity of stimuli on visual fixation in the human infant. *Brit. J. Psychol.,* 1958, **49,** 315–318.
24. Berlyne, D. E. Supplementary report: complexity and orienting responses with longer exposures. *J. exp. Psychol.,* 1958, **56,** 183.
25. Berlyne, D. E. *Conflict, arousal, and curiosity.* New York: McGraw-Hill, 1960.
26. Berlyne, D. E. Les équivalences psychologiques et les notions quantitatives. In D. E. Berlyne & J. Piaget, *Théorie du comportement et opérations. (Etudes d'Epistémologie Génétique,* XII.) Paris: Presses Universitaires de France, 1960.
27. Berlyne, D. E. Conflict and the orientation reaction. *J. exp. Psychol.,* 1961, **62,** 476–483.
28. Berlyne, D. E. New paths in motivation theory. In T. Gladwin & W. C. Sturtevant (Eds.), *Anthropology and human behavior.* Washington, D.C.: Anthropological Society of Washington, 1962.
29. Berlyne, D. E. Uncertainty and epistemic curiosity. *Brit. J. Psychol.,* 1962, **53,** 27–34.
30. Bindra, D. *Motivation—a systematic reinterpretation.* New York: Ronald, 1959.
31. Birkhoff, G. *Aesthetic measure.* Cambridge, Mass.: Harvard Univer. Press, 1933.
32. Bonvallet, M., Dell, P., & Hiebel, G. Tonus sympathique et activité électrique corticale. *EEG clin. Neurophysiol.,* 1954, **6,** 119–144.
33. Brown, J. S. *The motivation of behavior.* New York: McGraw-Hill, 1960.
34. Brown, J. S., & Farber, J. E. Emotions conceptualized as intervening variables—with suggestions toward a theory of frustration. *Psychol. Bull.,* 1951, **48,** 465–495.
35. Bruner, J. S. *The process of education.* Cambridge, Mass.: Harvard Univer. Press, 1961.
36. Bunge, M. The weight of simplicity in the construction and assaying of scientific theory. *Phil. Sci.,* 1961, **28,** 120–149.
37. Buser, P., & Roger, A. J. Interprétation du conditionnement sur la base des données électroencéphalographiques. *Proc. 1st. Int. Cong. Neurol. Sci.,* 1957, 417–444.
38. Bush, R. R., & Estes, W. K. *Studies in mathematical learning theory.* Stanford, Cal.: Stanford Univer. Press, 1959.
39. Bush, R. R., & Mosteller, F. *Stochastic models for learning.* New York: Wiley, 1955.

40. Butler, R. A. Discrimination learning by rhesus monkeys to visual-exploration motivation. *J. comp. physiol. Psychol.* 1953, **46**, 95–98.

41. Butler, R. A. The effect of deprivation of visual incentives on visual exploration motivation in monkeys. *J. comp. physiol. Psychol.*, 1957, **50**, 177–179.

42. Butler, R. A., & Harlow, H. F. Persistence of visual exploration in monkeys. *J. comp. physiol. Psychol.*, 1954, **47**, 258–263.

43. Cantril, H. *The psychology of social movements.* New York: Wiley, 1941.

44. Cardo, B. Rapports entre le niveau de vigilance et le conditionnement chez l'animal. Etude pharmacologique et neurologique. *J. Physiol., Paris*, 1961, **53**, 5–212.

45. Cattell, R. G. *Personality and motivation structure and measurement.* Yonkers, N.Y.: World, 1957.

46. Cohen, A. R., Stotland, E., & Wolf, M. An experimental investigation of need for cognition. *J. abnorm. soc. Psychol.*, 1955, **51**, 291–297.

47. Coons, E., & Kraehenbuehl, D. Information as a measure of structure in music. *J. Music Theory*, 1958, **2**, 127–161.

48. Crowder, W. F., Morris, J. B., Dyer, W. R., & Robinson, J. V. Resistance to extinction and number of weak-light reinforcements. *J. Psychol.*, 1961, **51**, 361–364.

49. Crowder, W. F., Wilkes, W. P., & Crowder, T. H. Weak-light reinforcement with and without control for response facilitation. *J. Psychol.*, 1960, **49**, 181–184.

50. Darrow, C. W. Emotion as functional decortication: the role of conflict. *Psychol. Rev.*, 1935, **42**, 566–578.

51. Darrow, C. W. The galvanic skin reflex (sweating) and blood pressure as preparatory and facilitative functions. *Psychol. Bull.*, 1936, **33**, 73–94.

52. Davis, R. C. Somatic activity under reduced stimulation. *J. comp. physiol. Psychol.*, 1959, **52**, 304–314.

53. Dell, P. C. Some basic mechanisms of the translation of bodily needs into behavior. In *Ciba Foundation symposium on the neurological bases of behavior.* Boston: Little, Brown, 1958.

54. Dember, W. N., & Earl, R. W. Analysis of exploratory, manipulatory and curiosity behaviors. *Psychol. Rev.*, 1957, **64**, 91–96.

55. Dewey, J. The reflex arc concept in psychology. *Psychol. Rev.*, 1896, **3**, 357–370.

56. Duffy, E. The psychological significance of the concept of "arousal" or "activation." *Psychol. Rev.*, 1957, **64**, 265–275.

57. Dykman, R. A., Reese, W. G., Galbrecht, C. R., & Thomasson, P. J. Psychophysiological reactions to novel stimuli: measurement, adaptation, and relationship of psychological variables in the normal human. *Ann. N. Y. Acad. Sci.*, 1959, **79**, 43–107.

58. Egger, M., & Miller, N. E. Will rats work to escape from conflict? *Amer. Psychologist*, 1960, **15**, 174.

59. Eysenck, H. J. *Dimensions of personality.* London: Kegan Paul, 1947.

60. Fechner, G. T. *Vorschule der Ästhetik.* Leipzig: Breitkopf & Härtel, 1876.

61. Fessard, M. A., & Gastaut, M. Corrélations physiologiques de la formation des réflexes conditionnés. In M. A. Fessard, M. Gastaut, A. N., Leontiev, G. de Montpellier, & H. Piéron, *Le conditionnement et l'apprentissage.* Paris: Presses Universitaires de France, 1958.

62. Fiske, D. W., & Maddi, S. R. (Eds.) *Functions of varied experience.* Homewood, Ill.: Dorsey Press, 1961.

63. Fox, S. S. Maintained sensory input and sensory deprivation in monkeys: behavioral and neuropharmacological study. Unpublished doctoral dissertation, Univer. of Michigan, 1959.

64. Fraisse, P., Ehrlich, S., & Vurpillot, E. Etudes de la centration perceptive par la méthode tachistoscopique. *Arch. Psychol.,* Geneva, 1956, **35,** 193–214.

65. Frenkel-Brunswik, Else. Intolerance of ambiguity as an emotional and perceptual personality variable. *J. Pers.,* 1949, **18,** 108–143.

66. Galambos, R. The neural basis of learning. In *Handbook of physiology.* Section 1. (Neurophysiology), Vol. 3. Baltimore: Williams & Wilkins, 1961.

67. Gastaut, H., & Roger, A. Les mécanismes de l'activité nerveuse supérieure envisagés au niveau des grandes structures fonctionnelles du cerveau. *EEG clin. Neurophysiol.,* 1960 (Suppl. 13), 13–32. Amsterdam: Elsevier Publishing Company.

68. Gershuni, G. V. [Reflex reactions under the action of external stimuli.] *Fiziol. Zh. SSSR,* 1959, **35,** No. 5.

69. Gesell, A., & Amatruda, S. *The embryology of behavior.* New York & London: Harper, 1945.

70. Gewirtz, J. L. A learning analysis of the effects of normal stimulation, privation and deprivation on the acquisition of social motivation and attachments. In B. M. Foss (Ed.), *Determinants of infant behaviour.* London: Methuen; New York: Wiley, 1961.

71. Girdner, J. B. An experiment analysis of the behavioral effects of a perceptual consequence unrelated to organic drive states. *Amer. Psychologist,* 1953, **8,** 354–355.

72. Glanzer, M. Stimulus satiation: an explanation of spontaneous alternation and related phenomena. *Psychol. Rev.,* 1953, **60,** 257–268.

73. Glickman, S. E. Reinforcing properties of arousal. *J. comp. physiol. Psychol.,* 1960, **53,** 68–71.

74. Goustard, M., Gréco, P., Matalon, B., & Piaget, J. *La logique des apprentissages.* (*Etudes d'Epistémologie Génétique,* XI.) Paris: Presses Universitaires de France, 1959.

75. Grastyán, E., Lissák, K., Madarász, I., & Dunhoffer, H. Hippocampal electrical activity during the development of conditioned reflexes. *EEG clin. Neurophysiol.,* 1959, **11,** 409–430.

76. Graves, M. E. *The art of color and design.* New York: McGraw-Hill, 1951.

77. Gray, P. H. Theory and evidence of imprinting in human infants. *J. Psychol.*, 1958, **46**, 155–166.

78. Gréco, P., & Piaget, J. *Apprentissage et connaissance.* (*Etudes d'Epistémologie Génétique, VII.*) Paris: Presses Universitaires de France, 1959.

79. Guilford, J. The structure of intellect. *Psychol. Bull.*, 1956, **53**, 267–293.

80. Harlow, H. F. Mice, monkeys, men, and motives. *Psychol. Rev.*, 1953, **50**, 23–32.

81. Harlow, H. F., & Zimmermann, E. R. The development of affectional responses in infant monkeys. *Proc. Amer. Phil. Soc.*, 1958, **102**, 501–509.

82. Harris, J. D. Habituatory response decrement in the intact organism. *Psychol. Bull.*, 1943, **40**, 385–422.

83. Hearst, E., Beer, B., Sheatz, G., & Galambos, R. Some electrophysiological correlates of conditioning in the monkey. *EEG clin. Neurophysiol.*, 1960, **12**, 137–152.

84. Hearst, E., & Sidman, M. Some behavioral effects of a concurrently positive and negative stimulus. *J. exp. Anal. Behav.*, 1961, **4**, 251–256.

85. Hebb, D. O. *The organization of behavior.* New York: Wiley, 1949.

86. Hebb, D. O. Drives and the CNS (conceptual nervous system). *Psychol. Rev.*, 1955, **62**, 243–254.

87. Hebb, D. O., & Thompson, W. R. The social significance of animal studies. In G. Lindzey (Ed.), *Handbook of social psychology.* Cambridge, Mass.: Addison-Wesley, 1954.

88. Henderson, R. L. Stimulus intensity dynamism and secondary reinforcement. Unpublished doctoral dissertation, Univer. of Missouri, 1953.

89. Hess, W. R. Das Zwischenhirn als Koordinationsorgan. *Helv. Physiol. Acta*, 1943, **1**, 549–565.

90. Hilgard, E. R., & Marquis, D. G. *Conditioning and learning.* New York: Appleton-Century, 1940.

91. Hinde, R. A. Changes in responsiveness to a constant stimulus. *Brit. J. Anim. Behav.*, 1954, **2**, 41–55.

92. Hochberg, J., & McAlister, E. A quantitative approach to figural "goodness." *J. exp. Psychol.*, 1953, **46**, 361–364.

93. Holt, E. B. *Animal drive and the learning process.* New York: Holt, 1931.

94. Hovland, C. I., & Sears, R. R. Experiments on motor conflict: I. Types of conflict and their modes of resolution. *J. exp. Psychol.*, 1938, **23**, 477–493.

95. Hurwitz, H. M. B. Conditioned responses in rats reinforced by light. *Brit. J. Anim. Behav.*, 1956, **4**, 31–33.

96. Irwin, F., & Smith, W. A. S. Value cost and information as determiners of decision. *J. exp. Psychol.*, 1957, **56**, 229–232.

97. James, H. Flicker: an unconditioned stimulus for imprinting. *Canad. J. Psychol.*, 1959, **13**, 59–67.

98. James, W. *The principles of psychology.* New York: Holt, 1890.
99. Jasper, H. H. Functional properties of the thalamic reticular system. In J. F. Delafresnaye (Ed.), *Brain mechanisms and consciousness.* Oxford: Blackwell, 1954.
100. John, E. R., & Killam, K. F. Electrophysiological correlates of avoidance conditioning in the cat. *J. Pharmacol. exp. Ther.,* 1959, **125,** 252–274.
101. Jones, A. Supplementary report: information deprivation and irrelevant drive as determiners of instrumental responses. *J. exp. Psychol.,* 1961, **62,** 310–311.
102. Jones, A., Wilkinson, H. J., & Braden, I. Information deprivation as a motivational variable. *J. exp. Psychol.,* 1961, **62,** 126–137.
103. Kessen, W., & Mandler, G. Anxiety, pain, and the inhibition of distress. *Psychol. Rev.,* 1961, **68,** 396–404.
104. Kish, G. B., & Antonitis, J. J. Unconditioned operant behavior in two homozygous strains of mice. *J. genet. Psychol.,* 1956, **88,** 121–124.
105. Koch, S. Psychological science versus the science-humanism antinomy: intimations of a significant science of man. *Amer. Psychologist,* 1961, **16,** 629–639.
106. Koffka, K. *Principles of Gestalt psychology.* New York: Harcourt Brace, 1935.
107. Kraehenbuehl, D., & Coons, E. Information as a measure of the experience of music. *J. Aesthet. art Crit.,* 1959, **17,** 510–522.
108. Kubzansky, P. E. The effects of reduced environmental stimulation on human behavior: a review. In A. D. Biderman & H. Zimmer, *The manipulation of human behavior.* New York: Wiley, 1961. Pp. 51–95.
109. Laffal, J. Response faults in word association as a function of response entropy. *J. abnorm. soc. Psychol.,* 1955, **50,** 265–270.
110. Lát, J. The relationship of the individual differences in the regulation of food intake, growth and excitability of the central nervous system. *Physiol. Bohemoslovenica,* 1956, **5,** 38–42.
111. Lát, J. [The problematics of the study of the higher nervous activity of freely moving animals and research into so-called spontaneous reactions.] *Česk. Psychol.,* 1957, **1,** 25–38.
112. Lát, J., & Weisz, P. [On the relation between individual differences in the excitability of the central nervous system and adrenal activity.] *Česk. Fysiol.,* 1958, **7,** 293–294.
113. Lazarus, R. S., Eriksen, C. W., & Fonda, C. P. Personality dynamics and auditory perceptual recognition. *J. Pers.,* 1951, **19,** 471–482.
114. Lebedinskaia, E. I. [On the interrelation of conditioned orienting and conditioned motor reflexes in the formation of temporary connections between two indifferent stimuli.] In L. G. Voronin et al. (Eds.), *Orientirovochny refleks i orientirovochno-issledovatel 'skaia deiatelnost'.* [The orienting reflex and exploratory behavior.] Moscow: Acad. Pedag. Sci., 1958.
115. Lindsley, D. B. Emotion. In S. S. Stevens (Ed.), *Handbook of experimental psychology.* New York: Wiley, 1951.

360   D. E. BERLYNE

116. Lindsley, D. B. Psychophysiology and motivation. In M. R. Jones (Ed.), *Nebraska symposium on motivation*. Lincoln: Univer. of Neb. Press, 1957.

117. Lindsley, O. R. Conjugate reinforcement schedules. Paper read at Amer. Psychol. Ass., New York, September, 1961.

118. Lisina, M. I. [The role of orientation in the conversion of involuntary into voluntary reactions.] In L. G. Voronin et al. (Eds.), *Orientirovochny refleks i orienitirovochno-issledovatel'skaia deiatelnost'*. [The orienting reflex and exploratory behavior.] Moscow: Acad. Pedag. Sci., 1958.

119. Lowell, E. L. The effect of conflict on motivation. Unpublished doctoral dissertation, Harvard Univer., 1952.

120. Lubow, R. E., & Moore, A. U. Latent inhibition: the effect of nonreinforced pre-exposure to the conditional stimulus. *J. comp. physiol. Psychol.*, 1959, **52**, 415–419.

121. Luria, A. R. *The role of speech in the regulation of normal and abnormal behavior*. New York: Liveright, 1961.

122. McClelland, D. C., Atkinson, J. W., Clark, R. A., & Lowell, E. L. *The achievement motive*. New York: Appleton-Century-Crofts, 1953.

123. McDougall, W. *An introduction to social psychology*. Boston: Luce; London: Methuen, 1908.

124. McDougall, W. *An outline of psychology*. London: Methuen; New York: Scribner, 1923.

125. MacLean, P. D. Psychosomatic disease and the "visceral brain." *Psychosom. Med.*, 1950, **11**, 338–353.

126. Madlafousek, J. [The orientation reaction as a preliminary component of the protective and adaptive apparatus of the organism.] *Česk. Psychol.*, 1957, **1**, 39–44.

127. Malmo, R. B. Activation: a neuropsychological dimension. *Psychol. Rev.*, 1959, **66**, 367–386.

128. Malmo, R. B. Slowing of heart rate following septal stimulation in rats. *Science*, 1961, **133**, 1128–1130.

129. Meyer, L. B. *Emotion and meaning in music*. Chicago: Univer. of Chicago Press, 1956.

130. Miller, N. E. Experimental studies in conflict. In J. McV. Hunt (Ed.), *Personality and the behavior disorders*. New York: Ronald, 1944.

131. Miller, N. E. Central stimulation and other new approaches to motivation and reward. *Amer. Psychologist*, 1958, **13**, 100–108.

132. Moltz, H. Imprinting: empirical basis and theoretical significance. *Psychol. Bull.*, 1960, **57**, 291–314.

133. Morf, A., Smedslund, J., Vinh-Bang, & Wohlwill, J. F. *L'Apprentissage des structures logiques*. (*Etudes d'Epistémologie Génétique*, IX.) Paris: Presses Universitaires de France, 1959.

134. Morgan, C. T. Physiological mechanisms of motivation. In M. R. Jones (Ed.), *Nebraska symposium an motivation*. Lincoln: Univer. of Nebr. Press, 1957.

135. Morozova, Nataliia G. [The psychological conditions for the arousal and

modification of interest in children in the process of reading popular scientific literature.] *Izvestiia Akad. Pedag. Nauk RSFSR,* 1955, **73,** 100–149.

136. Morozova, Nataliia G. *Vospitanie ponznavatel'nykh interesov u detei v sem'e.* [The education of cognitive interests in children in the family.] Moscow: Acad. Pedag. Sci., 1961.

137. Moruzzi, G., & Magoun, H. W. Brain stem reticular formation and the activation of the EEG. *EEG clin. Neurophysiol.,* 1949, **1,** 455–473.

138. Mote, F. A., & Finger, F. W. Exploratory drive and secondary reinforcement in the acquisition and extinction of a simple running response. *J. exp. Psychol.,* 1942, **31,** 57–68.

139. Nebylitsyn, V. D. [Some electroencephalographic indices of the equilibrium of neural processes.] *Doklady Akad. Pedag. Nauk,* 1961, No. 2, 115–120.

140. Nissen, H. W. A study of exploratory behavior in the white rat by means of the obstruction method. *J. genet. Psychol.,* 1930, **37,** 361–376.

141. Obrist, W. D. Skin resistance and electroencephalographic changes associated with learning. Unpublished doctoral dissertation, Northwestern Univer., 1950.

142. Olds, J. Physiological mechanisms of reward. In M. R. Jones (Ed.), *Nebraska symposium on motivation.* Lincoln: Univer. of Nebr. Press, 1955.

143. Pavlov, I. P. *Conditioned reflexes.* Oxford: Oxford Univer. Press, 1927.

144. Pavlov, I. P. *Lectures on conditioned reflexes.* New York: Liveright, 1928.

145. Pavlov, I. P. The reply of a physiologist to psychologists. *Psychol. Rev.,* 1932, **39,** 91–127.

146. Petelina, V. V. [The vegetative component of the orienting reaction of the vestibular, visual and auditory analyzers.] In L. G. Voronin, et al. (Eds.), *Orientirovochny refleks i orientirovochno-issledovatel'skaia deiatelnost'.* [The orienting reflex and exploratory behavior.] Moscow: Acad. Pedag. Sci., 1958.

147. Piaget, J. Logique et équilibre dans les comportements du sujet. In L. Apostel, B. Mandelbrot, & J. Piaget, *Logique et équilibre. (Etudes d'Epistémologie Génétique,* II.) Paris: Presses Universitaires de France, 1956.

148. Piaget, J. *Les mécanismes perceptifs.* Paris: Presses Universitaires de France, 1961.

149. Polezhaev, E. F. [On cortical co-ordination during the transition between sleep and wakefulness.] *Doklady Akad. Nauk. SSSR,* 1959, **126,** 1149–1152.

150. Polezhaev, E. F. [Novelty as a stimulus for special reactions.] *Byull. Eksptl. Biol. i Med.,* 1959, **2,** 9–14.

151. Polezhaev, E. F. [Concerning the physiological conditions of closing connections.] *Doklady Akad. Nauk. SSSR,* 1960, **130,** 469–472.

152. Polezhaev, E. F. [Phase changes in EEG as indications of the formation of cortical co-ordination.] *Fiziol. Zh. SSSR,* 1960, **46,** 26–36.

153. Polikanina, R. I., & Probatova, L. E. [The stabilization of the orientation reaction in premature infants.] In L. G. Voronin, et al. *Orientirovochny refleks i orientirovochno-issledovatel'skaia deiatelnost'.* [The orienting reflex and exploratory behavior.] Moscow: Acad. Pedag. Sci., 1958.

154. Postman, L. The history and present status of the law of effect. *Psychol. Bull.,* 1947, **44,** 489–563.

155. Premack, D., & Collier, G. Analysis of nonreinforcement variables affecting response probability. *Psychol. Monogr.,* 1962, **76,** No. 5 (Whole No. 524).

156. Rashevski, N. Contributions to the mathematical biophysics of visual perception with special reference to the theory of aesthetic values of geometrical patterns. *Psychometrika,* 1938, **3,** 253–271.

157. Razran, G. The dominance-contiguity theory of the acquisition of classical conditioning. *Psychol. Bull.,* 1957, **54,** 1–46.

158. Razran, G. The observable unconscious and the inferable conscious in current Soviet psychophysiology. *Psychol. Rev.,* 1961, **68,** 81–147.

159. Reynolds, G. S. Attention in the pigeon. *J. exp. Anal. Behav.,* 1961, **4,** 203–208.

160. Rheingold, H. L. The effect of environmental stimulation upon social and exploratory behavior in the human infant. In B. M. Foss (Ed.), *Determinants of infant behaviour.* London: Methuen; New York: Wiley, 1961.

161. Robinson, J., & Gantt, H. The orienting reflex (questioning reaction): cardiac, respiratory, salivary and motor components. *Johns Hopk. Hosp. Bull.,* 1947, **80,** 231–253.

162. Roitbak, A. I. [Electrical phenomena in the focus of a conditioned stimulus.] *Trudy Inst. Fiziol. Beritashvili,* 1958, **11,** 121–156.

163. Rokotova, N. A. [The formation of temporary connections in the cerebral cortex under the action of several indifferent stimuli.] *Zh. vys. nerv. deiat.,* 1952, **2,** 753–759.

164. Rozhdestvanskaia, V. I., Nebylitsyn, V. D., Borisova, M. N., & Ermolaeva-Tomina, L. B. [A comparative study of different indices of strength of nervous system in man.] *Vop. Psikhol.,* 1960, **6,** (5), 41–56.

165. Samson, E. W. *Fundamental natural concepts of information theory.* Cambridge, Mass.: Air Force Cambridge Research Center, 1951.

166. Schachter, S. *The psychology of affiliation.* Minneapolis: Univer. of Minn. Press, 1959.

167. Seward, J. P. An experimental analysis of latent learning. *J. exp. Psychol.,* 1949, **39,** 177–186.

168. Shannon, C. E., & Weaver, W. *Mathematical theory of communication.* Urbana: Univer. of Ill. Press, 1949.

169. Sharpless, S., & Jasper, H. Habituation of the arousal reaction. *Brain,* 1956, **79,** 655–680.

170. Sherif, M. *An outline of social psychology.* New York: Harper, 1948.

171. Sherrington, C. S. *The integrative action of the nervous system.* London: Constable, 1906.

172. Sickles, W. R. Probability, perception, and form. Unpublished doctoral dissertation, Univer. of Calif., 1955.

173. Skinner, B. F. *Science and human behavior.* New York: Macmillan, 1953.

174. Smedslund, J. The acquisition of conservation of substance and weight in children. V. Practice in conflict situations without external reinforcement. *Scand. J. Psychol.,* 1962 (in press).

175. Smock, C. D., & Holt, B. G. Children's reactions to novelty: an experimental study of curiosity motivation. Paper read at Soc. Res. Child Devel., University Park, Pa., 1961.

176. Sokolov, E. N. *Vospriiate i uslovny refleks.* [Perception and the conditioned reflex.] Moscow: Moscow Univer. Press, 1958.

177. Sokolov, E. N., & Paramanova, N. B. [On the role of the orientation reflex in the formation of motor conditioned reactions in man.] *Zh. vys. nerv. deiat.,* 1956, 6, 702–709.

178. Soltysik, S. Studies on avoidance conditioning: III. Alimentary conditioned reflex model of the avoidance reflex. *Acta Biol. Exp.,* 1960, 20, 183–192.

179. Soltysik, S., Jaworska, K., Kowalska, M., & Radom, S. Cardiac responses to simple acoustic stimuli in dogs. *Acta Biol. Exp.,* 1961, 21, 235–252.

180. Stennett, R. A. The relationship of performance level to level of arousal. *J. exp. Psychol.,* 1957, 56, 54–61.

181. Taylor, J. G. Behavior oscillation and the growth of preferences. *Psychol. Rev.,* 1949, 56, 77–87.

182. Thistlethwaite, D. A critical review of latent learning and related experiments. *Psychol. Bull.,* 1951, 48, 97–129.

183. Thurstone, L. L. *The nature of intelligence.* London: Kegan Paul; New York: Humanities Press, 1924.

184. Tinbergen, N. *The study of instinct.* London: Oxford Univer. Press, 1951.

185. Tissot, R., & Monnier, M. Dualité du système thalamique de projection diffuse. *EEG clin. Neurophysiol.,* 1959, 11, 675–686.

186. Tolman, E. C. *Purposive behavior in animals and men.* New York: Appleton-Century-Crofts, 1932.

187. Vinogradova, O. S. [The role of the orientation reflex in the process of establishing conditioned connections in man.] In E. N. Sokolov (Ed.), *Orientirovochny refleks i voprosy vysshei nervnoi deiatel'nosti.* [The orientation reflex and questions of higher nervous activity.] Moscow: Acad. Pedag. Sci., 1959.

188. Vinogradova, O. S. *Orientirovochny refleks i ego neirofiziologicheskie mekhanizmy.* [The orientation reflex and its neurophysiological mechanisms.] Moscow: Acad. Pedag. Sci., 1961.

189. Vinogradova, O. S., & Sokolov, E. N. [On the dependence of the orient-

ing reflex on the strength of the stimulus.] *Vop. Psikhol.*, 1955, **1**, (2), 85–89.

190. Voronin, L. A., & Sokolov, E. N. Cortical mechanisms of the orienting reflex and its relation to the conditioned reflex. *EEG clin. Neurophysiol.*, 1960 (Suppl. 13), 335–346. Amsterdam: Elsevier Publishing Company.

191. Wald, A. *Statistical decision functions.* New York: Wiley, 1950.

192. Weiner, H. Effects of unwanted signals and dextro-amphetamine sulfate upon instrumental observer responses. Univer. of Maryland, *Lab. Neuropharmacol. Rep.*, 1959, 60–21.

193. Wickens, D. D., Gehman, R. S., & Sullivan, S. A. The effect of differential onset on the conditioned response strength to elements of a stimulus complex. *J. exp. Psychol.*, 1959, **58**, 58–93.

194. Worrell, L., & Castaneda, D. Response to conflict as a function of response-defined anxiety. *J. Pers.*, 1961, **24**, 10–29.

195. Wyckoff, L. B. The role of observing responses in discrimination learning. I. *Psychol. Rev.*, 1952, **59**, 431–442.

196. Zajonc, R. B., & Morrissette, R. The role of uncertainty in cognitive change. *J. abnorm. soc. Psychol.*, 1960, **61**, 168–175.

197. Zaporozhets, A. V. *Razvitie proizvol'nykh dvizhenii.* [The development of voluntary movements.] Moscow: Acad. Pedag. Sci., 1960.

198. Zeleny, G. P. [The orientation of the dog in the domain of sound.] *Proc. Russ. Soc. Physicians*, 1906, **73**.

199. Zimbardo, P. G., & Miller, N. E. Facilitation of exploration by hunger in rats. *J. comp. physiol. Psychol.*, 1958, **51**, 43–46.

LEARNING AND THE FIELDS OF PERCEPTION, MOTIVATION, AND PERSONALITY

ROBERT W. LEEPER
Department of Psychology
University of Oregon

Introduction 366
Theoretical Orientation and Influences 368
Some Heuristic Rules about Abstract Thinking in Psychology 373
   The need to avoid overgeneralizations 373
   The need to avoid being intimidated by incomplete physiological knowledge 375
Our Main Sources of Ideas about Learning and Related Areas. 376
   Broad biological background 377
   Anatomical and physiological studies 378
   Anthropological data 378
   More purely psychological data 379
Major Background Hypotheses Suggested by the Several Fields on Which
Psychology Depends 384
The Setting of Learning in Relation to Other Functioning 391
   Learning as accessory to other functioning 391
   Two main nonmediational theories of the setting of learning . . . 393
   Two main mediational but noncognitive formulations of the setting of
   learning 395
   The setting of learning as interpreted by cognitive theory. 401
   The relation between central processes and organism-environment inter-
   actions 401
   Sensory organizations, representations, and motor-discharge organizations 402
   Properties in common of representational and sensory-organizational
   processes 412
   Motivation as a type of perceptual activity 418
   The relations between processes and structures 425
   Relations between habits and innate mechanisms 431
Main Principles Regarding Learning as Such 434
   General relations between learning, habits, and transitory processes . . 434
   Main types of habits to be accounted for 436

Over-all principles regarding perceptual learning 438
The more particular factors in perceptual learning 443
    Factors that tend to produce organizations and reorganizations . . . 444
    Factors that tend to prevent perceptual reorganizations 449
    Factors that tend to produce enduring residues from perceptual processes 451
The learning of motor-integration habits 454
Interrelations of Personality and Other Areas Discussed 456
    Areas of agreement between cognitive personality theory and psychoanalysis 462
    Broadened concepts of the proper method of studying human life . . 462
    Broadened concepts of the kinds of psychological processes 462
    Increased realization of the importance of motivation 463
    Identification of major techniques used in handling inner motivational
      conflicts 463
    Appreciation of the high substitutability of different expressions of motives 463
    Points of disagreement between cognitive personality theory and psycho-
      analysis 465
    Areas of agreement between cognitive and S-R personality theories . . . 468
    Areas of disagreement between cognitive and S-R personality theories . . 468
    The problem of changing personality habits 470
    The role of idiographic study. 472
Summary 473
References. 475

INTRODUCTION

This paper will deal with the psychology of learning as its "field of primary reference," but the mode of treatment will place almost as much emphasis, and in some respects perhaps more, on the related fields of perception, motivation (especially of emotional sorts), and personality.

The paper will not attempt any *comprehensive* survey of these fields and their interrelations as conventionally developed. Moreover, it will contain little or no reference to many concepts that have been historically significant. Early in the work on this paper, I became convinced that it would be more interesting to proceed idiosyncratically, instead, and aim for the outlines of a conceptual synthesis of the fields at issue via a selection of ideas that impressed me as unusually promising.

It has been a rare privilege to have had the chance to work on this paper and to have had, at times, the gentle prodding of the Editor to keep working and, on occasion, to dig more deeply than I might otherwise have done. My interest has been spurred by the fact that there has been a tremendous freeing of thought, not only in scientific work generally, but specifically within psychology. Though I think that psychology has been less imaginative and revolutionary in this last dozen years than, say, the fields of neurology, genetics, chemistry, molecular biology, and industrial technology, psychology too has seen some remarkable developments of thought and research technique. It has been stimulating to have had the occasion to attempt a more systematic consideration of these developments than might otherwise have been possible.

Personally, I have considerable respect for the proposition in James Conant's little volume *On understanding science* [42] that the basic distinction between a science and a technology is the greater interest of sciences in highly abstract formulations drawn from wide ranges of seemingly unrelated phenomena. I am impressed, too, by his argument that the advantages of such relatively abstract thought are not merely those of economy of statement, important though such economy is for efficient retention of scientific findings and for easy transmission of scientific knowledge. Even more important are the heuristic advantages that come from understanding phenomena in abstract terms which encompass vast ranges of phenomena and which consequently make possible the use of concrete phenomena having great strategic advantages for scientific discovery, just as Lavoisier's work with phosphorus gave him clearer data with which to reconsider the phlogiston hypothesis than other workers had when they studied the smelting of iron and tin. Psychology has an exceedingly difficult subject matter, and the chances are that we, similarly, cannot make the progress we should unless we use as wide a range of phenomena as we can. Admittedly, any such proposal is out of keeping with the popularity of "miniature models" (that is, of miniature areas of research) with some psychologists. There are some special values which have been served by that strategy of research and of theoretical interpretation, but basically it is not the type of approach which has seemed most fruitful in the sciences.

A great part of the work of a science, of course, is the gathering of data. The ultimate source of knowledge in psychology and in other sciences is empirical observation. But, at the same time, it also seems true that the most crucial empirical data often are not gathered unless some shrewd preliminary observations and some imaginative, far-ranging inter-relational thinking have first indicated where some data should be sought.

When Inhelder and Piaget [95] studied the thought processes of children, one of the problems they used, partly by means of little demonstrations, was "Why does this thing float?" (or sink, as the case might be). They found that, at about a certain age, children would explain the floating of a little chip of wood by saying that the chip was "light." Shown how needles and pins would sink rather than float, the children explained this by saying that these things sank because they were made of metal. In some earlier work by Piaget, when children were asked why battleships float, the explanation given was that battleships are strong, as though the thought was that big ships could hold themselves up.

Now, if any child had attempted to do systematic research on this problem, taking measurements of the weight of a long series of objects and noting for each object whether it would float or sink, he would not end up with any clear answer to his puzzle. His measurements almost certainly would not have included data on the relative bulk or displacement of each object observed. Hence, even if the child measured thousands of objects, and with great precision, his data would lead nowhere. So, even though the explanations which these children used demonstrated that they were thinking abstractly, the fact remains that they were dealing in terms of relatively easy abstractions. In the history of mankind, the answer to the question about why things float had to come from seeking some much more difficult abstraction that could be suggested only by puzzling over much rougher data about things which superficially seemed quite different. A major part of the work of science, as Robert Oppenheimer once phrased the thought when he addressed the APA in 1955, is the work of finding " . . . something worthy of which to enquire whether it is right . . . " [178, p. 135].

At any rate, this is the sort of background faith that has gone into this paper. It is not that I am unimpressed with empirical data. Rather, it is that I have little interest in empirical data and elaborate formulas which are valid only in some tiny territory. I see little interest in measurements which concern some effect that results from a number of influences that ought to be dissected out and studied separately but which, instead, are thrown together in an undetermined and sometimes unspecifiable proportion. Since psychology is a field having an almost infinitely varied raw material which it must try to understand and since this raw material is so complex, we have particular need for all the advantages we can get from broad interrelational thinking. We have probably had ten thousand experimental studies in the field of learning alone. We have apparently had plenty of energy for gathering facts. But it seems less sure whether we have used an adequate breadth of knowledge to help us frame the tentative hypotheses which would have brought as much gain from these experiments as we might wish.

THEORETICAL ORIENTATION AND INFLUENCES

To help readers use the material which follows, I ought to indicate the sources of my major concepts. The indebtedness is to no one person, even though, if I had to select merely one person, I have come to realize lately that it is Lashley [19] to whom I am perhaps most indebted, with Köhler [116, 117, 118, 119, 121, 122, 123, 124] and Tolman [228, 229,

230] as close seconds. I have certainly depended greatly upon a host of others, however, such as—from the experimental field—Osgood, Woodworth, Klein, Lorenz, Scott, Harlow, Hebb, Bartlett, Beach, Lewin, McDougall, Maier, Klüver, Bruner, Brunswik, and Krech. Among the important workers in the field of personality upon whom I have depended are, especially, Adler, Sullivan, Horney, Rogers, and Diamond.

Those familiar with the fields of learning and personality will at once recognize these names as predominantly those of workers presenting a "cognitive theory" of learning and personality. May I make clear, however, that the term "cognitive theory" makes me shrink every time I hear it, because it carries connotations for most psychologists which I do not believe are appropriate when we speak of the work of such persons as I have named. The term "cognitive" is a heritage from an early day when "mental processes" were understood as having three aspects—cognitive, conative, and affective. This old classification, which was accepted, for instance, by Immanuel Kant, still plagues psychology, even though we may think we have sloughed it off. Our present idea of that old tripartite division is that it implied that whatever is labeled "cognitive" is to be seen as purely intellectual or rational—something to be contrasted with motivational and emotional phenomena. Furthermore, the term "cognitive," to many psychologists, tends to recall the subjective orientation of the psychology of the time when this term was emphasized—a subjective orientation which suggested that all the aspects of "mental processes" are to be studied either exclusively or at least mainly by subjective observation and that they ought not to be confused with physiological processes. Consequently, when the term "cognitive theory" is used nowadays, it still tends to be understood by most psychologists as a type of theory which is basically nonbiological or even antiphysiological in orientation, which lacks any adequate appreciation of motivational factors, and which generally longs for the good old days when man was understood as a rational being with a good, honest soul.

However, even the older work of psychology, as I tried to indicate in my chapter on *Cognitive processes* in Stevens's *Handbook of experimental psychology* [147], did not suggest that all cognitive processes are conscious processes. From about 1900 on, the work of Ach, Watt, and Woodworth demonstrated that "mental sets" remain effective even when they "drop out of consciousness." The work of Maier [163, 164] showed the influence of "unconscious directions" in problem-solving thinking, and certainly there has been abundant use of the idea of unconscious concept formation.

In the second place, the actual fact seems to be that the "cognitive theorists," rather than being antiphysiological, have characteristically been engaged in actual neuropsychological research to a greater extent than have S-R psychologists—note the work by Lashley, Köhler, Klüver, Pribram, Hebb, Clifford Morgan, Maier, Goldstein, and Krech. Even Woodworth started as a physiologist with Sherrington.

In the third place, as will be proposed later, a closer examination of cognitive processes and of motives perhaps will show that these ought not to be seen as two different sorts of influences, except in the sense that the term "cognitive processes" (or, as I would prefer to phrase it, "perceptual processes") ought to be seen as a more inclusive term. The term should include motivational processes as part of the larger continuum, with "motivational processes" serving as itself a somewhat inclusive term covering both what we might call "physiologically based motives" and what we might call "emotional motives" or "emotional processes." This proposal is controversial. But, at any rate, when this paper explores what many psychologists would classify as a "cognitive" type of approach, I trust that it will be seen as an approach which is physiologically oriented, which puts stress on motivational factors, and which, partly because it defines perceptual processes and emotional processes as being either conscious or unconscious processes, also puts emphasis on the value, and even in some ways the primacy, of behavioral research in psychology.

Why build the discussion around this type of concept? Let me speak first of several secondary reasons. (1) Many important concepts from such workers as Lashley and Köhler have been neglected or poorly understood. (2) On some points, the concepts of cognitive theory have been poorly presented in the first place (as, in Lashley's case, sometimes with overstatements) and need restatement in more careful form. (3) The various cognitive theorists, although they have often expressed hearty respect for one another's work, have not made much attempt to integrate their ideas. Tolman and Köhler, for instance, have made little use of each other's work. It ought to be possible to get an integrated statement which would indicate a lot of potentialities not previously apparent. (4) There are perhaps a number of points where amendments or extensions might be made which would be valuable in rounding out the set of notions available previously. There may be some such extensions in what follows, but actually I think I can trace virtually every point to previous writers, even though sometimes they have been almost isolated voices. If this paper has some contribution, it will primarily be an integrative and interpretive contribution.

These four considerations, however, are not a sufficient reason for devoting the present chapter to the sorts of concepts developed by "cognitive theory"—particularly since, admittedly, this type of approach has been favored by only a minority of psychologists. Neither I nor most other psychologists have sufficient interest in the history of psychology to be willing to take time to explore some set of notions merely because they have been summarized previously in some less adequate fashion than they might have been. There have been frequent instances in science, however, where a viewpoint which was distinctly a minority viewpoint eventually proved to have major potentialities as additional research yielded support for what had rested on very tenuous foundations to begin with. My own feeling is that this is the case with the sort of conceptualization of psychological phenomena which will be described in the following pages and that a careful presentation is needed to make progress along a very promising road for further research in psychology. There are considerable possibilities, too, that this type of approach may give a useful conceptual framework for related technical fields like anthropology (as in the case of Barnett's *Innovation: the basis of cultural change* [13]), sociology, psychiatry, and education, not to mention the fact that some more adequate concepts about psychological phenomena need to be assimilated into our everyday thought in the same way that many basic ideas about geology or about bacteria and viruses are being thus assimilated and used.

A word of warning needs to be sounded to the effect that a number of key terms will be used with more or less seriously altered meanings in the following pages. Mention has already been made that the term "cognitive theory" will be used as carrying different connotations from those now carried for most psychologists. Particularly will the terms "perception" and "perceptual process" be expanded to cover a great deal more than these terms generally have covered, even though a number have shifted to a much broader usage than prevailed earlier.

This redefining of terms creates some risks of confusion, but there is no good means of avoiding such risks. Any term in psychology is almost certain to be a relatively abstract term. Even terms like "maze" and "reversible figure" are moderately abstract terms, referring to any of a diversity of items, and such terms as "perceptual organization," "learning," and "motive" are highly abstract, even though less so than "psychological phenomenon."

There are many criteria for judging the value of abstract terms in different contexts; but in a science, where the aim is to develop the means of identifying and predicting, there is a consequent criterion of the value of abstract terms and of the definitions which go with them. In a science, each term should group together those things that have some important body of functional similarities. Each term should group those things which, on some important scores, obey certain principles that hold true within that group but not outside it. Consequently, even though a science may set up some definitions in a tentative way when there is very little empirical knowledge in the area in question, these definitions must rest on guesses about functional similarities, and the definitions (or classifications) must often change as new empirical knowledge is gained.

Particularly in a young field like psychology, where huge parts of a very difficult territory have as yet been inadequately explored, many of the definitions now rest on very sketchy and tentative indications of functional similarity. Our definitions reflect tentative hypotheses, rather than richly documented knowledge about the cause-and-effect relationships and other functional relationships included under, or implied by, those definitions.

Sometimes psychologists feel that it should be possible to get theoretically neutral definitions for the various abstract terms that they use. "We should stick closely to directly observable factors; then we won't confuse factual observations with uncertain theoretical interpretations." But, instead, the "factual observations" of scientists also have to depend on abstract terms and abstract concepts, and it is better to see that the very warp and woof of scientific observation and thought are in terms of tentative hypotheses about functional similarities and that the meaning of scientific terms often will need to be changed as new knowledge is gained.

The view here expressed is, of course, fundamentally different from that which has been urged by Cattell [39], Eysenck [59] and Guilford [74] with reference to personality. These men have urged that science normally proceeds by clearing up taxonomic or classificatory problems, identifying crucial variables, *before* attempting to determine functional relationships. The view here expressed is the reverse of this. It is the view that progress in studying the functional relationships of concrete materials must be the chief means by which progress on taxonomic problems is made.

When a need for new meanings or groupings is felt, the view is often expressed that we ought to invent new terms to carry the new meanings. This, however, can lead to confusion. We keep our old terms, such as brain, cortex, and dendrite, even though recent research is showing that we must drastically change our conceptions about what these terms refer to. In the same way, as additional research reveals new facts about psychological phenomena, we must expect that our psychological terms will similarly take on new meanings. As Köhler phrased the matter when I once asked him what definition he would regard as appropriate for the term "perception": "That's an empirical question!"

As a concluding note on the theoretical orientation of this paper, let me say that, even though I shall use mainly a type of material that psychologists would tend to see as that of "cognitive theory," there will of course be no attempt to choose material on the basis of some arbitrary criterion that "what is related to cognitive theory is what should be included." The paper will try to deal with basic concepts of the interrelated fields of learning, perception, motivation, and personality. The concepts that will be emphasized are those that seem to me to have most value, regardless of the sources from which they come.

SOME HEURISTIC RULES ABOUT ABSTRACT THINKING IN PSYCHOLOGY

There is a real possibility that psychologists could do more successful building of hypotheses from empirical data if it were recognized that psychology deals with especially complex material and that, in consequence, there might be some explicit rules developed about how to proceed in this work. Some of the principles of statistics are essentially such rules. Thus, one of the rather tricky points of statistics is the distinction between alpha and beta errors (or Type I and Type II errors). Even though the logical point involved is often disregarded, despite the clear explicit formulation of it, it may nevertheless be that this explicit formulation has cut down the frequency of such statements as this: "We found no statistically significant difference between Group *A* and Group *B;* therefore we need not hereafter try to keep constant the factor which differentiated those two groups, since we here proved that it does not make a difference." My own inclination is to believe that any rules of skillful thought will have to be developed by actual practice in thinking and that abstract formulations cannot be of very much help. However, I would like to preface the following sections of the paper with a brief mention of two points.

The Need to Avoid Overgeneralizations

One of the important needs in abstract thinking is to determine carefully what generalization actually can be derived from the data available and to take care not to overgeneralize. As was stated earlier, referring to Conant's discussion of the history of science [42], a distinguishing feature of science is its search for very abstract principles which can encompass great ranges of seemingly diverse things. Since this is the aim in scientific work, it is understandable that psychologists should want to make sweeping generalizations from their observations. But, it is exceedingly important to recognize what generalizations actually are suggested or supported by the evidence available. Psychological principles sometimes are presented which would not have been proposed if the relation between evidence and conclusion had been examined more carefully.

An unusually clear instance of this is the article of James and Eleanor Gibson [71] in which they proposed that perceptual learning is merely a matter of learning to differentiate actual qualities of the present objective stimulation acting on the organism, and not a matter of enrichment of perceptions from earlier training. They would have been on more tenable ground if they had simply said, "We define perceptual learning as what depends exclusively on learning to differentiate various aspects of present stimulation." If they had proceeded in that way, it would have been irrelevant for them to do an experiment on the subject. But the article sought to establish their principle by presenting an experimental demonstration of the fact that human subjects can learn to differentiate stimulus aspects which they did not differentiate at first. It is an interesting experiment; but it is the grossest overgeneralization to propose that any such experiment could prove that all (or even "most" or even "some substantial part") of perceptual learning is differentiation rather than enrichment. To argue in that way is like making a painstaking study of how the nests of meadow larks are built on the ground and then to propose that "Our painstaking study of this bird gives some new reason to believe that possibly all birds build their nests on the ground." In fact, even if one conducted painstaking studies of several hundred species of birds that build their nests on the ground, since people familiar with birds know that there are many species that build nests in trees, one ought not to draw any conclusion more sweeping than that "There is at least a considerable number of birds which nest on the ground."

Similarly, if a person wants to make the sweeping statement "All habit formation requires positive reinforcements," he has a terrific job on his hands. Even if he wishes to draw merely the more modest conclusion that "Most learning depends on factor so and so," he has a major responsibility to make sure that he has canvassed a representative sampling of the whole range of "learning." As Egon Brunswik says [32], we have fairly well learned the lesson that we must have some adequate statistical sampling when we want to make some generalization about the effects that might be seen in some larger population of *individuals* in the same test situation, but we hardly have taken seriously, as yet, our obligation similarly to get a representative sample of whatever larger domain of *situations* or *phenomena* we attempt to describe by our generalizations.

As offering tentative hypotheses, suited for the guidance of further exploration of empirical material, we can risk tentative statements on some very slight grounds, sometimes even proceeding from rather indirect deductive arguments or, as Oppenheimer proposed in his address to the APA on *Analogy in science* [178], using frankly analogical thinking to get hypotheses which might guide the setting up of experiments. But we must be very clear about the fact that, until such deductions have been checked empirically, they are merely the most tentative of hypotheses and that, even after a few tests have been made, the conclusion that can be drawn still must not be a sweeping one. For example, the earlier work on the all-or-none law of nervous impulses was based merely on observations of axones, but it was treated as though it presumably applied also to dendrites; whereas direct studies of dendrites in the cortex are yielding quite a different picture [186]. In psychology, similarly, we have probably hidden a lot of important research questions from ourselves by failing clearly to recognize what generalizations actually could be made from the data used.

The Need to Avoid Being Intimidated by Incomplete Physiological Knowledge

Psychologists ought not to neglect phenomena, nor hesitate to develop psychological principles, merely because there are no known physiological mechanisms which could account for them. On this score, I think that psychologists frequently have been more overawed by physiological and biological criteria than have biologists and physiologists themselves. For example, there has been a tremendous body of work in biology on temporal cycles of biological activity [7, 79]. With every species of animal investigated thus far—and this work now has covered a great range of phylogenetic forms—it has been found that there are diurnal cycles of behavior and of metabolic activity which are approximately 24 hours long and that these occur even under conditions of as nearly completely constant illumination, temperature, and sound as can be secured.

Biologists have been baffled to account for these phenomena. The period of the cycles is not affected when, as with cockroaches, the animals' body temperature is raised or lowered considerably, which seems to rule out the possibility that the cycles are controlled by some single chemical process. The fact that the cycles are not exactly 24-hour cycles unless paced by light is something that rules out some other possible hypotheses —one hamster, under the constant conditions, picks up each day's cycle of activity after about 23.5 hours, another hamster in the same laboratory seems naturally to operate on a 25-hour cycle, etc. [27, 184]. But, this lack of knowledge of how the effect could be accomplished has not been seen by the biologists as something that should lead them to turn from this problem as though it would contaminate them. Their view has been, instead, that purely behavioral studies can be the means of exploring phenomena which then might lead to some most interesting anatomical and physiological discoveries which otherwise they could not possibly make.

Let me add another example or two. With the larvae of *Drosophila*, it has been found by C. S. Pittendrigh [184] that the setting of such 24-hour cycles could be accomplished by exposing the fruitfly larvae to a flash of light of less than a second's duration. After such a single flash of light, the fruitflies later emerge from the pupal stage at some point which is roughly a multiple of 24 hours later—an effect which, under natural conditions, would help to secure this emerging in the early morning, which is favorable to survival of the new winged form. Chrysanthemums, on the other hand, blossom on the basis of the *length* of the day. Birds that migrate by the stars apparently have some mechanism within them which permits them to make allowance for the shifts of the constellations of stars during the night [202, 203]. On all such matters, biologists are interested in exploring such phenomena and have amassed an enormous wealth of data even though they cannot specify, for the time being, how such effects can be produced.

Psychologists need to have the same basic view. As I have urged previously, I think it is a good thing for psychology to be biologically oriented. In the next sections of this paper there will be an attempt to spell out some of the implications of such a biological approach. But if we really are to be "biologically oriented" in the sense of sharing the same basic approach that biology has used, we must guard against tailoring our psychological hypotheses to fit the very incomplete knowledge of biological mechanisms which is now available. It is pseudoscience, for instance, to define motives as very strong stimuli when we do not know whether the stimulation of receptors is actually as strong as from other nonmotivating stimuli or whether the effect comes more from neural mechanisms which give some powerful amplification to afferent input from certain types of stimuli. It is pseudoscience to talk about incipient chewing movements as powerful secondary reinforcers when all rough observations indicate that gum-chewing students do not learn any more than non-gum-chewing students. The contributions of neurology and physiology to psychology are important, but we need to treat psychological data with as much respect as physiologists and neurologists accord to them. To do otherwise is to use biological data, not for generalizations, but for overgeneralizations.

OUR MAIN SOURCES OF IDEAS ABOUT LEARNING AND RELATED AREAS

Before we go on to consider what main principles ought to be recognized as contributing to fruitful interrelationships between such fields as learning, perception, motivation, and personality, it may be best to indicate the main kinds of material and main fields of study which seem especially important for the development of adequate psychological concepts. The discussion of this topic too will follow the type of thought which has been characteristic of the so-called cognitive theorists—that is, of such persons as Lashley, Köhler, Woodworth, Tolman, Osgood, Adler, Horney, and Lewin. Different cognitive theorists have of course emphasized different parts of the types of material discussed below, but the principles of the cognitive approach, in general, call for as wide a use as possible of these sources of empirical knowledge.

Broad Biological Background

More specifically, this includes:

1. The knowledge that we have of the long evolutionary background of man and other animals—knowledge such as that summarized in the splendid volumes edited by Roe and Simpson [195] and by Tax [222]. Any adequate psychology will not be merely a knowledge of human psychology, but will use the vastly broader picture that has developed, especially in the century and more since Darwin published his *The origin of species* in 1859. The concepts of evolutionary biology help us to see, much more adequately, the relations of man and other animals and give a much more long-time picture of all of life.

2. Field studies of present animal forms and of their adaptative activities under natural conditions. As contrasted with physiologists, who more basically take "parts" of the organism as the object of study and who seek the advantages of studying such parts under more restrictive and controllable laboratory conditions, the work that is more expressive of the genius of biology has been work done under natural field conditions— work which, if it used experimental settings, introduced these into this more complex natural background of animal life.

There are certain sorts of data that can be secured only by such means. A good instance is the contrast between the earlier study of the behavior of baboons by Zuckermann [247] on the basis of observations of baboons in a small outdoor area in the London zoo and, on the other hand, the recent observations of Sherwood Washburn and his students [235, 236] on troops of baboons in their natural habitat in Africa. Zuckermann's observations suggested a picture of these primates as almost incredibly savage and aggressive in their relations to one another, with frequent deadly combat, killing of young baboons, and so on. In contrast, the work of Washburn revealed that, under natural conditions, where the troop could spread out in the more natural way consistent with the hierarchies of social dominance, these troops were marked by very little violent behavior. Even in the play of the young, if a smaller animal's cries indicated that it was being roughly treated, the older males would move in and firmly stop the play and keep things more peaceful. Apparently, with baboons, there are factors of actual physical distance which must be respected if the natural social pattern is to be observed. The artificial conditions of the zoo were not revealing at all the very stable and effective social organization which the baboon troops naturally display under the conditions for which they have been adapted to survive.

The work of the ethologists [54, 88, 154, 204, 223, 225] has given a lot of other rich material to show the fruitfulness of both observational and experimental studies in the complex setting in which wild animals normally live.

Anatomical and Physiological Studies

Among anatomical and physiological studies of the mechanisms and detailed processes involved in the more complete life activities of organisms, one type of study is the obviously and directly relevant work of neurologists on such problems as the functioning of the brain stem reticular formation [201] and studies of the development of functioning throughout the embryological period [97]. Another type of study which has become increasingly important as a source of ideas both to neurology and to psychology has been work with complex physical systems which are possibly analogous to the organism in some respects. I refer here to work on automatic control systems in industry, communication systems, and electronic computers. The decade and more since 1950 has certainly seen profound contributions of a basic theoretical value from such other fields.

Anthropological Data

These include broad cultural studies providing, along a different dimension, somewhat the same type of perspective that evolutionary biology has given. Psychology is not interested in describing human life merely in terms that may be restricted to the particular cultural setting under which psychologists normally operate, and the "experiments of nature" that are available partly from records of the past, but even more richly from the diversity of cultural groups now extant, are indispensable for psychologists as well as for anthropologists.

An interesting example of such material is given in a brief article by Colin M. Turnbull [231], reporting some observations on the Pygmy people of Africa. These people live in dense tropical forest which seldom permits vision for more than a few yards, so that even much of the hunting is guided by sound rather than by vision. One of the men of this group traveled with Turnbull to an adjoining area where trees were scarce. In this setting, the Pygmy displayed a lack of size constancy with distant objects which was really extreme. Thus:

Kenge looked over the plains and down to where a herd of about a hundred buffalo were grazing some miles away. He asked me what kind of insects they were, and I told him they were buffalo, twice as big as the forest buffalo known to him. He laughed loudly and told me not to tell such stupid stories, and asked me again what kind of insects they were. He then talked to himself, for want of more intelligent company, and tried to liken the buffalo to the various beetles and ants with which he was familiar.

He was still doing this when we got into the car and drove down to where the animals were grazing. He watched them getting larger and larger, and though he was as courageous as any Pygmy, he moved over and sat close to me and muttered that it was witchcraft. (Witchcraft, incidentally, is known to the BaMbuti only through association with the Bantu. They have no similar concept of the supernormal.) Finally, when he realized that they were real buffalo he was no longer afraid, but what puzzled him still was why they had been so small, and whether they *really* had been small and had suddenly grown larger, or whether it had been some kind of trickery [231, p. 305].

To learn whether the ordinary size-constancy effect in human beings is a consequence of previous perceptual learning, one might dream of raising some human subjects under very unusual conditions of stimulation. This obviously is not possible, but the variations of natural conditions under which these people had lived provided the equivalent of such an experiment. So also do Turnbull's observations bear on the question of whether number concepts can be developed without words to designate more than just the smallest numbers. In this same tribe there were no words for numbering more than four items. But, they gave striking examples of skill in the quick perception of larger quantities of items. A game played by them with seeds or pebbles requires the player to make a quick estimate of whether 0, 1, 2, or 3 additional items would be required to bring to some multiple of 4 the group of seeds tossed out on the ground. Even with up to about 40 items, these players could supply the needed number of additional items before the tossed-out seeds had stopped rolling.

Not only on such particular perceptual skills but also on complex phenomena of outlook, motivation, and personality patterns is it found that anthropological material can add data of tremendous value to our knowledge gained with our own cultural group.

More Purely Psychological Data

These are derived from relatively intensive psychological studies such as are possible especially with human beings in our own cultural group and with animals available for intensive laboratory study.

Included in this category are, of course, the objective or behavioral studies which are so much emphasized in modern psychology. There is no argument about that. But there is a question about whether all the important and even indispensable data of psychology are objective data or whether subjective data also are important.

For a good many years, there has been a strong tendency [now diminishing; see 113, pp. 766–769] to think of psychology as properly only a "behavioral science" and to say that all the "raw data" are merely objective data, even if perhaps they are data about the verbal reports of other human beings. Thus, in the opening sentence of his extremely interesting paper on *A behavioristic analysis of perception and language as cognitive phenomena,* Osgood said, "Psychologists, when they are behaving like psychologists, limit themselves to observing what goes into the organism (stimuli) and what comes out (responses). Between . . . lies a Great Unknown, the nervous system. . . . 'a little black box.' . . . psychological theory, as distinct from psychological observation, is made up of hunches about what goes on in this little black box" [179, p. 75].

Now, this may be right. Perhaps it is true that this is actually the way that psychologists function when they behave "like psychologists." This may be the way that fruitful empirical observations are always made, and this may be an accurate description of the content of all psychological principles. Our field may be concerned solely with objective observations of stimulus conditions, effector responses, physiological conditions, and behavior products, and it may be true that the mediating processes between stimulus situations and overt behavior can be known only as "inferred behavior determinants," to use Tolman's expression. There have been some rather persuasive philosophical arguments to the effect that psychological observation and psychological knowledge must be of this limited sort.

However, there is an alternative to this. A person might maintain the following: (1) The "dependent variable" which people sometimes want to be able to predict and control is not overt behavior but is subjective experience within either themselves or other persons. A person with intractable pain from neuralgia is not concerned primarily with whether he expresses this pain in overt behavior and whether it could be inferred from objective evidence; he is concerned with the fact that the pain exists as a subjective fact. The person with a great deal of discomfort from a neurotic condition or from recurrent psychotic episodes is not concerned exclusively with the fact that he tends to act overtly in unjustified ways but also with the fact that his conscious experience is so far from what he would like it to be. (2) The "independent variable" from which people make predictions in everyday life frequently is not objectively observable facts but is some aspect or other of subjective experience. For example, a person says, "I'd better not try that, because I'm tired" or "This irritates me more than I think it should; there must be something in this situation beyond what I have been able to recognize." (3) It is possible for a person to formulate and test hypotheses which relate various objective and subjective facts within his own life.

For example, I remember how, when Norman Munn and I were very new graduate students, we were fooling around with a rotating color mixer and, for some reason or other, tried out the condition of rotating a combined black and white disk at various slow speeds. We were surprised to find that, at certain speeds, the black came to be edged with bluish purple and that the white sector became blurred with a sort of dirty yellow and then that, at somewhat higher speeds, the whole surface became a shimmering mass of bright orange and green. I remember the comment from one of the older graduate students, Frank Geldard, when we announced our discovery to him: "Yes, yes, Fechner's colors, discovered back in . . . ." In the same way, a person might discover that certain scintillating patterns of light come before migraine headaches; he might find that such and such a program of training enables him to enjoy music which he could not enjoy previously; he might find that, when he is tired, he tends to be irritable in his overt behavior toward others. In all such cases, he is discovering and testing functional relationships which enable him to make predictions which he otherwise would not have made— either predictions from objective data to subjective effects or predictions from subjective data to other subjective data or to overt behavior on his own part. (4) Apparently the knowledge of such functional relationships can be communicated effectively from person to person, so that the second person can anticipate or predict certain effects within himself which he otherwise would not have expected from the specified type of stimulus conditions [as with Fechner's colors, 40] or the specified chemical factor, as with the various effects which come from lysergic acid, or type of training. Apparently we are able to establish a fairly common intersubjective meaning for various words by the training we receive in relatively simpler and more easily controlled situations, and then we can use these same words as aids to thought and as means of communication in other situations where the causal factors are much more complex or ungovernable. Or, at least this is the claim of this alternative to the behavioristic account of psychology. The claim is that, when Purkinje was walking in the flower garden in the evening and noted that the relative brightness of different blossoms seemed different from what prevailed during the daytime, he was not taking note of the verbal reactions of another person nor even of his own verbal responses but was observing some effects within himself which he then tried to represent by verbal means.

There are, therefore, two possible views that can be argued regarding the question of whether the raw data from which psychology can work are merely objective data or whether they also include subjective data (and whether, if also the latter, these add anything of real value so that a psychologist should be ready to use both types of information).

Going at this problem from the standpoint of philosophical considerations, psychologists and philosophers have expended a great amount of energy in arguing the case. All of this argument has seemed inconclusive, however, when approached in this way. Even some of the outstanding logical positivists, despite the fact that they originally argued for merely physicalistic descriptions, have come to see subjective observation as altogether legitimate and valuable [60]. But other philosophers and philosophically minded psychologists still feel that the only logically tenable viewpoint is that of behaviorism.

In this situation, it would seem better for psychologists to approach this issue, not by premises about the nature of reality and the means of communication, but by a technique more suited to their discipline— namely, by treating this as a pragmatic, empirical question. That is, perhaps it would be best to ask what discoveries and hypotheses have come from those workers who have favored solely a behavioristic view- point and what from those who have been willing to use both behavioral and subjective data. From this we might try to judge, as an empirical question, which type of approach has been unusually fruitful and whether perhaps each approach has something to contribute that the other probably would not have contributed. This would not prove that either approach *has* to lead to the sort of conclusion that it does but neverthe- less would fit the scientific tradition that it is worth knowing about some relationships even when we cannot explain why they exist.

I am stressing this point at some length because there seem to be good reasons for saying that what tends to determine whether a relatively simple psychological interpretation of an S-R type will be produced or a more complex mediational theory of a cognitive type is the decision that a psychologist makes about whether he will restrict himself, as much as he can, to strictly objective data or whether he will be willing and even eager to use subjective data as well. I think the basic point is that, when we utilize subjective data as well, we get richer and more complete material. Even if we do not feel happy until the phenomenon has been translated into purely physiological terms, as has been possible now with physiological preparations which illustrate the Purkinje phenomenon, our original formulations often are greatly facilitated by subjective observa- tions.

Thus, despite his behavioristic protestation, quoted above, the same paper by Osgood included the following statement:

We refer to "closure" when actual stimulus events, as independently measured, correspond to what is perceived, but the same tendency toward completion of an integrational unit lies at the base of many perceptual illusions, where the actual stimulus events do *not* correspond to what is integrated. I have an electric clock at home which can't be reset after the current has gone off briefly; I have to stop it and wait a day until time catches up. Every once in a while I glance up to find the time, and momentarily I see the sweep-second hand moving! [179, p. 82.]

The phenomenon Osgood describes can be checked by objective means, as by finding whether persons (or animals) are unable to discriminate under some conditions between actually moving and actually motionless second hands. The phenomenon might even have been discovered in the first place by some chance variation of objective conditions and behavioral observations. But, *pragmatically speaking,* most phenomena of this sort have been discovered originally by less objective means. In still other cases, the perceptual effect is no such stereotyped, duplicatable perception, and could hardly have been discovered without subjective observation. Thus, the following is reported by Woodburn Heron regarding the experiments on sensory deprivation at McGill University:

The subjects reported something else to which we at first paid no particular attention, but which was to emerge as the most striking result of the experiments. Many of them, after long isolation, began to see "images." One man repeatedly saw a vision of a rock shaded by a tree; another kept on seeing pictures of babies and could not get rid of them. Several subjects seemed to be "having dreams" while they were awake. *Not until one of the experimenters himself went through the isolation experience for a long period did we realize the power and strangeness of the phenomenon* [Italics mine]. . . .

Our subjects' hallucinations usually began with simple forms. They might start to "see" dots of light, lines or simple geometrical patterns. Then the visions became more complex, with abstract patterns repeated like a design on wallpaper, or recognizable figures, such as rows of little yellow men with black caps on and their mouths open. Finally there were integrated scenes: e.g., a procession of squirrels with sacks over their shoulders marching "purposefully" across the visual field, prehistoric animals walking about in a jungle, processions of eyeglasses marching down a street. . . . Usually the subjects were at first surprised and amused by these phenomena, looked forward eagerly to see what was going to happen next. . . . But after a while the pictures became disturbing, and so vivid that they interfered with sleep. . . . The subjects had little control over the content of the hallucinations. Some kept seeing the same type of picture no matter how hard they tried to change it" [86, p. 15; see also 61, 87].

Admittedly, these were extraordinary conditions which produced such effects. But, it may very well be that such extraordinary conditions and such extraordinary effects may have extraordinary value as means of revealing some of the most fundamental processes by which the brain operates. The ultimate question, as suggested above, is the heuristic value of different sorts of data. And, if subjective data help us to move ahead more rapidly on some problems than we could have moved without such material, we cannot afford to neglect such data because of any philosophical presuppositions. Of course, we also find that subjective observation cannot reveal certain phenomena, such as the word habits and phrase habits which Bryan and Harter [34] long ago discovered in telegraphic habits, or such as the unconscious concept formation revealed by Hull [93] and by subsequent experimenters like Hanfmann [78], Bouthilet [147, p. 745], Rees and Israel [190], and Manis and Barnes [165], or such as the unconscious motives which seem to be demonstrated by much of psychotherapeutic work. This negative finding also is important, however, from a subjective point of view, because it gives empirical evidence that cognitive processes are more complex than can be revealed by subjective observation. In either case, the use of subjective data seems to give us some additional understanding of the functional relationships which exist in human life.

In summary, let us note that this section has devoted space quite unevenly to several different problems. The additional exploration of certain sorts of material has been intended merely to clear up certain accessory points of considerable importance. The main point of the section has been that the principles of psychology need to be derived from a considerably broader background of knowledge than the layman often realizes that psychologists employ. What I have argued is that the proper data are not merely those from objective behavioral studies but the following broader array: (1) broad biological materials, (2) sources of physiological knowledge, both from direct physiological research and from work on analogous physical systems, (3) data on human beings under some great diversity of cultural conditions, and (4) more narrowly psychological data, including not only behavioral data but also subjective data such as an experimenter can secure, sometimes, only by serving as one of the subjects of an experiment.

MAJOR BACKGROUND HYPOTHESES SUGGESTED BY THE SEVERAL FIELDS ON WHICH PSYCHOLOGY DEPENDS

In the following sections of the paper it is necessary to turn to the more particular hypotheses and principles which come from the four main sources of empirical data which we outlined in the preceding section. In these later sections we will need to indicate more fully the kinds of data by which these more particular principles have been tested. I think there are some advantages, however, in working from some extremely broad propositions first to see what hypotheses we can derive from these. Particularly from evolutionary background, physiological observations, and certain parts of psychological observation, the following principles seem to be indicated:

1. The physical materials of the world were such as would tend, over very long periods of time, to take more and more complex forms. It is not merely that there have been potentialities for more complex chemical compounds than existed originally, and it is not merely that the originally simpler chemical materials became synthesized into the more complex compounds which produced living organisms. In addition, there were the potentialities which have found expression in greater and greater diversity and complexity of anatomical structure, physiological activities, behavior, and conscious experience.

2. In the long course of this evolutionary development, extreme competition for survival has been the general rule. This, combined with the influence of mutations and new environmental conditions, has led to the realization of a great range of the potentialities for different biological forms from which evolutionary selection might be made, as Calvin Stone has sketched in his notable APA presidential address on "Multiply, vary, let the strongest survive and the weakest die—Charles Darwin" [219].

3. The conditions or environmental niches to which adaptation had to be made and under which new forms might survive have constantly changed, too. Land plants developed, for example, permitting animals to find food on land. The appearance of mammals spelled the doom of the diverse dinosaur types, which were like the mammalian forms but more slow-witted and more sluggish in low temperatures. When early human forms reached the stage where they would use language and carry sharp-edged stones for digging food and for use as weapons, reaching a stage which other primates have never reached even though their anatomy (except for their brains) would have permitted this, a powerful new selective influence came in, as Sahlins [200] and Washburn [235] have emphasized, and the further evolution of man probably occurred a lot more rapidly than would have been seen without these new cultural conditions.

4. As a consequence of the severe struggle for existence and of the frequency of hereditary variations, even though each form may not have been pushed to the absolute limits of efficiency of its type of possible development, still it is true that the general tendency has been for the development of amazingly complex, precise, and delicate mechanisms of adjustment. Evolution has seen the development of extraordinarily effective means of sensing the environment, processing the information from the environment, and dealing with the environment to produce changes in it. Such developments have reached virtually the limits of what apparently could be achieved by any physical system which had to be not too specialized along merely one line or another. That is, admittedly, we cannot compete with electronic computers for some purposes nor with

automobiles nor radar devices for other purposes, but animals had to be constituted for a vastly wider range of functions than such specialized devices are designed for. For example, our sensitivity to faint amounts of light is so great that a change of a single molecule in each of not more than about ten retinal cells by a single quantum of light reaching each retinal cell can permit us to discriminate such a stimulation [183]. Bats can guide their flight by sonar devices even when thousands of other bats are flying around in the same cave, each emitting its own cries to guide it to some nesting place [158]. Bloodhounds can follow the odor trail from a particular person, even a day or so after the trail was laid down. A phase difference of only about 1/25,000 of a second between the sound waves reaching the two eardrums of a human being can produce a perception that a source of sound is slightly off center. Such accomplishments do not need to be thought of as miracles. But they do illustrate the point that the long span of evolutionary development has produced some amazingly complex and delicate mechanisms.

5. Although we cannot deduce with any assurance that a particular capacity or type of process will be found in any particular species, we can get a good many fruitful hypotheses from a consideration of such principles as the above. For example, when it was known that bats catch insects primarily by echoes from the high-pitched intermittent tones which the bats produce in flight, it was a good bet that some species of moth would have some auditory mechanism for sensing the approach of bats, so that they could initiate evasive maneuvers which bats, with their larger size, could not exactly copy. This finding has, indeed, been borne out [196]. When it was noted that male birds commonly have brightly colored plumage, rather than protective coloration, the suggestion from this was that birds probably possess good color vision, so that this plumage would have advantages in sexual selection. One of the early studies by Lashley demonstrated this [130]. The existence of lavish colors on blossoms suggested, similarly, something about the color vision of bees, and their capacity is now well established [65]. As an aid for developing hypotheses, the evolutionary concept has had tremendous value.

6. Different mechanisms, however, have been developed for accomplishing the same general results in different species. Evolutionary development has been a matter of branching from more generalized earlier forms, in line with present concepts of stochastic processes. This is obvious in comparative anatomy, as with the contrast between those animals which developed external skeletons, such as crayfish and grasshoppers, and animals which developed the vertebral pattern of an internal skeleton. The multiple-facet eye of dragonflies and bees has achieved the possibility of remarkably good form discrimination, and yet it is basically different from the visual system of the vertebrates and,

oddly, from that of the octopus [52]. The innate equipment, even of closely related forms, often is significantly different—the imprinting which occurs in the young of one species of geese depends chiefly on visual stimuli, for example, but in another species of geese mainly on auditory stimulation. Even though imprinting is so important in many birds, it is not powerful in cuckoos and cowbirds, which deposit their eggs in the nests of other birds [205]. What is innately given in one species has to be a matter of learning in another species. So, while the method of arguing from broad evolutionary principles is a valuable means of getting many hypotheses, the actual characteristics of different types of animal can be known with assurance only by specific study of those types of animals, and great diversities must be recognized whereby analogous effects are secured.

7. One very general consequence of evolutionary development, however, can be stated as follows: the course of evolutionary development generally has given rise to forms which are able to maintain their character and survive successfully despite more or less wide changes in their environments, and despite the fact that their environments frequently are less complex than they are. Various parasitic forms, of course, have become very specialized in what they depend on, and there are a great many examples of complex symbiotic relationships within animal life, as between certain larger species of fish and certain smaller ones that serve as cleaners or groomers [152]. Generally, however, as one goes up the evolutionary scale, there is an increasing degree of independence of the *immediate* environment, at least, for restricted periods of time. What has been attained is a greater stability of functioning than the variations of the immediate environment might have led one to expect. Birds and mammals, for instance, keep a fairly constant optimal temperature despite changes of environmental temperatures which would be fatal to snakes, insects, and bacteria. Land animals have no need for continuing contact with water. Some special food materials, such as iodine and some vitamins, can be stored over long periods of time.

8. Two of the important means by which animals achieve this relative independence of their immediate environments are these: their very fine distance receptors and their highly developed central nervous systems (especially with regard to the potentialities of these for complex perceptual organizations and complex learning). By virtue of these, the relatively more complex animals can detect food or prey or other objects at great distances and on the basis of a great diversity of cues, whereas otherwise such stimulation would be far too slight to be effective.

9. To serve this same need for stability, or for relative independence of the immediate environment, the animals which possess fine distance receptors also have needed neural mechanisms which would yield rela-

tively stable effects out of the kaleidoscopically changing stimulation which they receive. Such phenomena as those of form constancy, color constancy, size constancy, and object constancy or pattern perception [206] are fairly basic biological phenomena, regardless of whether or not they are products of learning or of innate development in any given species. The higher animals also have developed the capacity to maintain longer-sustained sets without any continuing support from relevant environmental stimulation. Thus, when a cat waits on one side of a hole and a mouse on the other, with auditory cues removed, with olfactory cues adapting out, and with nothing but a continuing set from earlier stimulation from the other animal to bridge the time interval, the reason that cats survive is that they can maintain their sets over longer periods of time.

10. To get the versatility that is involved in this relative independence of the immediate environment, what has been particularly important has been the development of cybernetic mechanisms which can control other processes within the organism. Not only on the side of physiological processes is this the rule, as in matters of temperature control and body chemistry (witness recent research indicating that an increase of about 0.1 degree centigrade in the temperature of the blood in the human brain starts the cooling reflexes operating [20]), but these cybernetic mechanisms also are of absolutely fundamental importance for the understanding of the *behavior* of animals. In most situations, for example, what is learned by animals is not some neural mechanism which will produce a particular set of movements regardless of details of the situation where the habit is used, but is a perceptual mechanism which can guide the movements of the organism in some very flexible and appropriately directed fashion. As Ellson has said:

> We know . . . that a man can steer a bicycle down a curved path with his hands on the grips . . . at the ends of the handle bars or . . . near the steering column, which implies different input-output amplitude ratios in each case . . . He can also ride a bicycle with his arms crossed, i.e., with his right hand on the left grip and left hand on the right one, in which case if output is measured as right-hand movement the *sign* of the transform is changed. It is clear therefore that . . . man . . . is obviously a complex system in which many possible transforms are available, these being selected by means of variables other than the immediate single-dimension characteristic of a stimulus arbitrarily called "the" input for purposes of a given system or experiment [55, pp. 653, 656].

Nor is this true merely of man. There is a substantial block of experiments which show that, when some change of a marked sort is introduced into a familiar situation, as through surgical damage to the spinal cord [136], to the cerebellum [137], or to motor areas of the brain [131], the monkeys or rats that have been given previous training when they could use movements of a normal sort can accurately thread their way through mazes or operate other devices with the changed movements they now have to employ [see also 110, 111, 116, 161, 171, 173]. This is, of course, a familiar observation from everyday life: the dog that has cut its foot and now hobbles on three legs still has no difficulties in following learned routes, and the same also is the case with the human being who has to shift to crutches or who shifts from walking to roller skating or bicycle riding.

We cannot, therefore, understand the behavior of an organism by comparing it to a model that represents *one-phase* or unregulated physical systems such as a typewriter or telephone. Instead, the organism must be understood in terms of some model which refers to such *two-phase* systems as incubators or guided missiles or automated industrial devices, where there is one mechanism which executes the orders and another mechanism which serves as a steering or governing mechanism [168]. Except for the influence of such cybernetic devices, there could not possibly be biological systems which are so much more complex than their surroundings and which keep their constant character despite such wide changes in their environments.

11. If behavior is to be governed cybernetically, this means that there have to be guiding processes that are primarily *perceptual* in character —that is, processes which can specify whether or not a required environmental effect has been achieved—rather than mechanisms that are oriented merely toward the performance of some response of an overt sort. Just as with a thermostat, the crucial consideration in a cybernetically governed system is not the performance of any particular motor act, but the attainment of the proper sensory input. A chief contribution of the development of either instinctive mechanisms or learned habits is the provision of norms or specifications of what is to be achieved, so that a spider will try to build a web of a certain sort, the oriole will act so as to achieve its hanging nest, or the small child will try to pronounce words with the dialect of his region.

12. Among the most important cybernetic mechanisms, as far as psychology is concerned, are motivational mechanisms and processes. These are devices, as it were, for tending to guarantee that the organisms will not overdo this matter of independence of environmental conditions but will recurrently seek out what is necessary for individual survival and species survival. A land animal does not have to keep breathing all the time, for instance, but there must be mechanisms which will coerce breathing before the body is dangerously short of breath. The land animal does not need to have a steady intake of water like a plant, but still there must be motivational mechanisms that will coerce it toward

getting water at sufficiently frequent intervals that the *milieu interne* will keep the remarkable stability that Walter B. Cannon emphasized in his concept of homeostatic phenomena [35].

13. We must expect, particularly with the most developed forms of animals, that there will be adaptive mechanisms which possess survival value in general but which sometimes create goals beyond those directly relevant to species survival and sometimes even inimical to such. The play activity of otters, big-horn sheep, chimpanzees, and dolphins [157] seems to produce much activity which is not essential to survival; but still it is probably safe to say that the exploratory interest which finds expression in such play activity is of major value in the lives of animals that depend so greatly on their highly developed brains.

14. Among living organisms, human beings have proved adaptable to living under a greater diversity of circumstances than any other animal. This is true on the side of bodily mechanisms. Only a very small percentage of all the species of animals is larger or more powerful. The diet that man can use is more diversified than the diet of almost any other animal. His longer life span gives man more opportunity to benefit by his great learning ability [41]. Furthermore, man can adapt his motivation and his skills to a much greater range of social settings and types of activity than can other animals. Any investigation of human beings, therefore, must give particular emphasis to the mechanisms and processes by which this relatively great independence of the environment has been achieved in human life.

15. One of the chief means by which adaptations are secured in animals is by the assignment of some relatively stereotyped functions to innate mechanisms and the assignment of other functions to learning and the operation of habits. Except probably in the very simplest organisms, both sources of behavior exist. And, as Attneave says:

> The informational capacity of the germ cell is not indefinitely great, as McCulloch . . . has pointed out; accordingly, it appears likely that competition exists even among desirable traits for representation in the hereditary substance. It may be, therefore, that the blueprint for man's complex and versatile cognitive machinery is transmitted at the expense of blueprints for more specific mechanisms that must be regained by learning [10, p. 647].

Even in the same total activity, some phases of activity will rest on innate mechanisms and some others on learning. Thus, from innate mechanisms it may be predicted that salmon will migrate to the ocean and later up some stream to spawning grounds. But only by knowing the route that had been taken by the young salmon going downstream can it be predicted what choices it will make of streams and of branches of streams when it migrates back again [82]. Furthermore, we must not expect that any given neural mechanism will be either innate or learned. Probably virtually all innate mechanisms get more or less modified by learning; and, on the other hand, a great portion of the habits of organisms, or perhaps all, ought to be thought of as "more or less modified innate mechanisms" [21, Chap. 4; 27, 132, 166, 218].

Various points in the above series will need to be elaborated in what follows. For example, one of the points which will be proposed is that in creatures which have such fine distance receptors as the higher mammals and such high learning capacity as they have, it is particularly to be expected that some of the most important parts of their motivation would be of a type that can be touched off by very slight stimulation and that is especially subject to modification by learning. From this, it will be suggested in turn that one of the most important sorts of motivation in higher animals is emotional motivation, and that the widespread presence of emotional processes in higher animals cannot be understood except by assuming that emotional processes, in the main, have important adaptive or survival value, rather than being basically disruptive or disorganizing in the organism's life.

In various other respects, as well, a lot of details will have to be spelled out. The foregoing principles, however, set the general framework within which, I believe, our more specific principles will have to be developed.

THE SETTING OF LEARNING IN RELATION TO OTHER FUNCTIONING

Learning as Accessory to Other Functioning

As I have said in the previous discussion, learning and the use of habits are particularly important phenomena in the higher animals. They are the two chief means whereby the higher organisms achieve their great flexibility of adaptation. They are the chief means by which organisms are able to deal with environmental situations, not merely in terms of what is directly contacted at the moment, but also in terms of what is remote in space and/or time.

It might seem from these statements that the phenomena of learning should be the primary frame of reference for discussions of psychology—at least of the higher organisms. There has been a strong tendency, especially for some decades in American experimental psychology, to see psychology in just these terms.

However, in a more careful analysis we can see that learning is merely accessory to other functioning of organisms. This fact is suggested by the kind of statement that we make when we try to define learning. For example, we might say that learning is a production of relatively enduring changes within the organism—changes of such a sort that the later functioning of the organism in the same or similar situations will tend to be different from what otherwise would have been seen if it had not been for the earlier learning situation. When we make a statement like this, we are in effect saying that our primary frame of reference needs to be these other modes of functioning which are likely to be changed as a consequence of learning. Learning does not exist merely in itself—any more than a Cheshire cat's grin can persist in any place other than Alice's wonderland. As something that changes other modes of functioning, learning presumably needs to be studied in the larger context of what these other modes of functioning are.

This same point is apparent when we consider the problem of methodology. Learning can be studied only through studies of something else. Even if we define learning as a change in behavior that comes from reinforcements or instruction, as Skinner does, the *behavior* needs to be our primary object of study. If we define learning as something that we *infer* from behavior, the fact remains that learning is something we can study only from changes in other phases of the functioning of the organism.

Even subjectively a person cannot tell that he is "learning." Thus, for example, a person can tell that he has found the solution for some problem that had baffled him previously, but whether this reorganization of his understanding of the problem will have left some enduring change within him which will make it easier for him to solve the same problem or similar problems in later situations—that is something he can judge only from the future or from prior experience with analogous instances in the past.

This conception of learning as a secondary phenomenon is further implied by the fact that in the great majority of learning situations the individual is not attempting to learn anything—even if he has the sophisticated concept that such a phenomenon as learning exists! Probably all animal learning, for instance, is accomplished without any intent to learn. What an animal is doing is merely trying to escape from some enemy, capture some food, find a place where it will be more comfortable, or outdo another animal in some play activity. Learning, if it occurs, comes as an unintended by-product. The same is probably true of learning in infants and small children. Even in human adults a great portion of learning occurs in this way. Yet human beings can learn very important things without any realization that learning is occurring. Probably most of the development of and changes in personality, for example, occurs in this fashion.

In fact, even when a sophisticated human being does set out to learn something, he has to seek to achieve some other objective so that learning will occur incidentally. For example, when he wants to learn to type-write, he sets himself to typewrite pages of material with as much speed and accuracy as possible. The typewritten pages need not in themselves have any importance, but he has to treat them as though it were important for him to produce them. Another example is learning by listening to a discussion and trying to understand it. Still another is learning to speak a foreign language by trying to produce actual sounds in the immediate present occasion. In all these instances, learning is something that comes incidentally in the situation.

Since this is the case, we must try to get a good concept of what learning is related to before we attempt to analyze it.

Two main nonmediational theories of the setting of learning. One theoretical formulation which I believe ought to have received much more attention in psychology is the formulation by Kantor [102] which he has spoken of as an "interbehavioral psychology." His main principle is that psychological events are not basically events within the organism, but interactions between the organism and the stimulus objects or stimulus situations with which the organism is dealing. Another main conviction of Kantor has been that learning and other psychological problems should *not* be studied, even in part, by asking about the physiological mechanisms and processes involved in such interactions, or about any inferentially known psychological processes within the organism, but should be described solely in terms of objectively observable changes of interactions.

Obviously there is much to favor the idea that organisms do interact significantly with their environments and that the unit of study might well be such organism-environment interactions. However, it seems that Kantor unnecessarily handicapped his proposal by his opposition to any analysis of the means within the organism whereby some of the main properties of such interactions are determined. If Kantor's best insights are to be used, or rediscovered, as by the transactionalists [36, 96, 106] and some others, it seems that this will need to be accomplished by psychologists who are interested in using the more efficient and broadly based concepts of mediational or inferential theory.

Brunswik has made a similar call for a merely descriptive rather than inferential approach, as has Skinner [209]. In most of their writings, these men have described the problems of psychology as problems of determining the functional relationships between the objective situation to which the organism is responding and the effect produced by those responses on the environment.

Thus, Brunswik [185, pp. 511–515] proposed that the organism ought to be understood in terms of a "lens model." By this, he meant that there are equivalent processes in the organism which can produce the same end result. The process used is a matter of relative indifference, just as different parts of a camera lens may be covered and yet the lens may produce the same image on the film. Skinner expressed the same idea when he said that the term "response" ought to be used as a class term which would designate any of the different muscular performances which would accomplish the same behavior product [208].

This conception of psychological functioning has advantages of simplicity; it is unquestionably suitable for some purposes, particularly when the investigator's objective is relatively practical, rather than obtaining the means of making relatively precise predictions for very diverse conditions. For example, in industrial engineering, it is valuable to find out that workers in a cotton factory will produce more cloth if the air is kept relatively warm and humid. This information is valuable even if there is no knowledge of why the relationship exists. A recent article on toads gives another curious example. Toads ordinarily will snap up bits of food only if the food object is moving, as when a caterpillar moves on some grass nearby. Trying to find some efficient means of feeding toads in captivity, Kaess and Kaess [101] found that the toads would flip out their tongues and take bits of hamburger from a rotating cafeteria platform with equal readiness. Later they found that not even this movement of the food was required. Toads sitting at the middle of a round platform would snap up bits of meat from the surface around them even if nothing was moving except the wall of their circular cage.

However, it is interesting that Brunswik fundamentally repudiated his earlier methodological formulation in one of his later papers [33]. I remember this well, because I had a paper in the same symposium at the 1954 International Congress of Psychology and I remember how drastically I had to rewrite my paper [148] at virtually the last moment because of Brunswik's insistence that—though he had previously advocated dealing with psychological problems in terms of "distal-distal relationships"—he now viewed this primarily as a means of preliminary identification of relationships and phenomena which should then be studied more intensively.

To illustrate the reasons for making such a different methodological pronouncement from what is usually associated with his name, Brunswik cited an experiment he had performed in which subjects were asked to make a size judgment [185, pp. 544–547]. Some subjects, doing this as a relatively simple perceptual judgment, almost always made errors of a systematic sort, but never more than rather small errors. Other subjects, given additional data which enabled them to use arithmetical calculations, commonly made an exact estimate, but in some cases made occasional wild errors, which subjects making perceptual judgments never did.

Much experimental material—particularly material from concept-formation experiments—supports Brunswik's final viewpoint. It has usually followed the model of Hull's [92] original experiment, presenting stimulus materials which could be handled more abstractly, but presenting them as though involving merely a rote-memory task. As Wertheimer [238], Snygg [212], Hanfmann [78], Spence [216, 147, pp. 738–739] and others have demonstrated, several scores—length of retention, ability to transfer to new situations, and types of errors—differ, depending on whether the subject attacks the problem as a conceptual or a memorizing task. Even when he sees it as a conceptual task, it makes a significant difference if he attacks the work with one type of strategy rather than another, as Bruner, Goodnow, and Austin have demonstrated [31, 68].

Skinner has not modified his earlier proposals as drastically as Brunswik, but even his emphasis on "shaping of behavior" by reinforcement of "successive approximations" is in the same direction. In this, he recognizes that, for more precise work, attention *does* need to be paid to things that come between the objective stimulus situation and the final behavior product [210].

Two main mediational but noncognitive formulations of the setting of learning.   Most psychologists have used mediational theories in talking about psychological phenomena. They have placed greatest emphasis on constructs about processes within the organism, in some instances developing their interpretations on the basis of both objective and subjective data, in other instances trying to work by inferring solely from phenomena which are objectively observable. Let us characterize briefly some examples of these approaches.

1. *The traditional functionalist approach.* In considering psychological functioning, men such as James, Dewey, Angell, and Carr held the following five beliefs: (*a*) Objects need to be sensed; (*b*) the sensory material needs to be used in perceptions, defined as awarenesses of present objects or events; (*c*) these perceptions in some cases lead on to meanings or thoughts; (*d*) motivational processes also need to be recognized as arising either from internal tissue states or from external stimulation as of electric shock; and (*e*) these preceding psychological processes tend to express themselves in motor behavior or action.

2. *The S-R analysis of such workers as Hull and Guthrie.* The functionalist analysis did, of course, provide a conceptual framework for the consideration of learning, and the functionalists did place a great deal of emphasis on learning. However, the framework seemed unsatisfactory to many psychologists for a number of reasons, and a number of basic

modifications were attempted. One was the proposing that the neural processes from stimulation to final behavior should not be broken up into a series of steps such as sensing, perceiving, apprehending, and action, but that the neural processes should be regarded merely as connections or links from stimulus to response. The S-R theory of Hull [93] and Guthrie [75, 76] was urging, one might say, that the hyphen between stimulation and muscular reaction ought not to be fractionated into some smaller phases of the transmission of excitation from S to R. Thus, unlearned behavior was portrayed by Hull as due to innate connections from S to R; learning as establishing other connections; extinction training as building up other S-R linkages which would be prepotent over the habits linked to the same Rs. The essence of this older type of S-R concept is this: The linkage from receptor stimulation to motor response is a functional unit which should not be analyzed further, even though study of the problems of the formation of such linkages and the interactions between different linkages certainly would be profitable.

Objections to the older functionalist formulation. There has been one main sort of objection to picturing psychological processes mainly in terms of conscious processes. This old formulation tended to hamper the extension of psychological research into comparative and developmental psychology. It tended to pose unnecessary difficulties even in the study of intelligent adult human beings. For instance, it is simple to arrange conditions so that we know quite certainly that a person has guided his behavior by a brain process dependent on the phase differences of sound waves reaching his two ears—and consequently we know something about the complex organizing process which occurred in his brain. But it may be much harder to determine whether he guided his behavior consciously. In animal research, we are not concerned with such questions. In a completely darkened room, an owl can swoop down from its perch and grab a small roll of paper which has been dragged through dry leaves on the ground by a string, although it always starts this swoop after the rustling of leaves *stops* [182]. Small children, as mentioned later, extrapolate regular verb endings to words which others around them use in the irregular form. We cannot determine whether they form and use such linguistic principles consciously. But even if such processes in owls and children are unconscious, they have a great deal in common with other sensory and representational processes which are clearly conscious. Consequently, even when psychologists have not felt inclined to cast their thought in behavioristic terms, they have come increasingly to want to frame their definitions of perception, concept formation, and other psychological processes in ways which would make room—and perhaps main room—for the use of behavioral data as a means of getting light on such processes.

Another difficulty with the traditional formulations regarding psychological processes is that the distinction between perception and thought was obscure and uncertain. When we say that a perception is an awareness of present objects and events, we are covering a large area. According to this definition, the taste of food is a perception. So is hearing a sound as coming from a certain direction, hearing one tone as louder than another, and smelling a disagreeable odor. Phenomena of size constancy, apparent movement, visual illusions, and reversible perspective are matters of perception. So is the perceptual process that occurs when a trained musician listens to some very complex music. Another instance is that of a person who *perceives* a funnel-shaped cloud as an approaching tornado. According to such a conception, we would say that the paleontologist Roy Chapman Andrews *perceived* some chunks of rock in the deserts of Outer Mongolia as fossil remains of dinosaur eggs.

This is a huge range of types of process. Part of the range seems very much like the process that occurs when we think about something in the absence of the physical stimulation which originally gave the basis for that thinking. Thus, after Roy Chapman Andrews had had the "perceptual experience" of viewing what he thought might be dinosaur eggs, broken the rocks, and found the fossilized remains of embryonic dinosaurs which never had seen the light of day, it is safe to say that he continued to think about those eggs with a process much like his original perception even after he had laid the rocks carefully away. Indeed, his original perception would have been so little determined by the physical properties of the object before him that, even though there was some present stimulation which helped shape that perception, most of the character of that perception would have to be traced to his long background of training. Nevertheless, if he wanted to check on some detail of the skeletons to see whether there was some detail he had failed to note, he had to get the eggs out and look at them. So, in a measure, even such an exceedingly complex perceptual process would rest on sensory stimulation.

Furthermore, it seems that the same learning which modifies perceptions, as traditionally defined, also modifies the thought processes which go on in the absence of stimulation. A very clear instance of this is seen when people acquire a faulty sense of geographical direction through some faulty clue. In Eugene, Oregon, for instance, many newcomers get their directions twisted by 90 degrees because they take their original orientation from the part of the railroad that goes through town. They fail to note that the railroad leaves its predominantly north-south course and goes east and west through town. It may be only a few days before they realize that the Coast range must be west of town, since the sun is setting behind it, rather than north of town, as they feel it to be. Once established, however, such a faulty orientation persists. But—and this is our present interest—this faulty orientation does not operate merely when the person actually is looking at some spot in the town. When he is away from the city and merely trying to visualize the place, the same difficulty arises. If he succeeds in getting the town turned around by an elaborate thought process, visualizing the larger relationships of different parts of the city, this same activity—though accomplished in any location—will help him when he actually sees the region again.

Still another indication of similarity is this: Effects which come merely from anticipatory representational processes can be indistinguishable from perceptual effects of actually present physical stimuli. Osgood's example of the decrepit clock that he has tolerated is a clear example. Ordinarily we would assume that the perception of a slowly moving second hand is a sensory perception. But Osgood found that the stimulation-supported process was momentarily indistinguishable from his redintegratively given representational process. In fact, this and similar examples suggest that we ordinarily credit to sensory organization much more than we should. When we pick up an empty bucket which we thought was filled with water, it seems almost to shoot into the air. If the bucket had been full, therefore, our response to it would not have been due merely to tactual and kinesthetic stimulation from the pressure of the handle on our hand. Instead, we apparently "order" beforehand some muscular reactions approximately adapted to the weight that will be met; the actual physical stimulations merely bring about some minor changes in the representational process which already has been under way.

In the traditional functionalist portrayal of psychological processes, a third main difficulty was that the place of motives in the whole picture was obscure.

There were additional difficulties in the traditional functionalist view. It was natural, therefore, that there were attempts to overhaul the preconceptions of this view in quite fundamental ways.

Objections to the S-R modification of the functionalist theory. As we have mentioned, one lusty and vigorous rebellion against the functional type of thinking was that of behavioristic thought—more specifically, the S-R formulations of behavioristic thought by Watson, Guthrie, and Hull.

The S-R formulations certainly had the advantage of making a place for behavioral data and for generalizations and inferences from behavioral data. This had a tremendously important emancipating effect on psychology, even though the use of behavioral data by no means started with the behaviorists, but was the natural medium of Ebbinghaus,

Hobhouse, Thorndike, Yerkes, McDougall, Bryan and Harter, Binet, and many other workers on human and animal learning. Even granting this earlier widespread use, we still can appreciate the fact that there was considerable intellectual gain in the behaviorists' clear formulation that psychological processes could be studied as "inferred behavior determinants," to use Tolman's expression. Hull's [92] pioneer objective study of concept formation, for example, certainly made a major change in studies in that field. Watson's pioneer laboratory studies with human infants certainly opened up new fields in developmental psychology. We ought not to lose sight, therefore, of some fairly real gains that come from S-R foundations.

However, even though S-R formulations clearly have had values on some scores, it remains open to question whether it is best to think of the habits formed by learning as something that connects stimuli and responses by hyphens that we cannot profitably fractionate. Whether we remain satisfied with S-R theory on this score probably depends on whether we keep our attention focused on experiments where learners are tested in almost exactly the same experimental situations where the learning has occurred. This is the course of least resistance in experimental work. But it is *not* an adequate method for experimental purposes. Over and over again, experimenters have made valuable discoveries simply by not keeping conditions too constant. Thus, in contrast with Thorndike, who kept his animals equally hungry all through the work and gave reinforcements on every trial, Tolman clarified the distinction between learning and performance by varying such motivational conditions [228, 230]. Pavlov [181] tested his dogs without continuing to give the original reinforcements and discovered the extinction phenomenon. Still further, by testing with altered signals, he discovered the phenomenon of initial generalization. The same point could be made using many other examples.

The question of what happens when tests are made for transfer to new situations after ordinary types of extinction training is particularly relevant for our present problem.

Suppose, for example, that a child has learned to walk or to roller-skate, having repeatedly used skates to go across a large room to secure some reward at a certain spot. Suppose the reward is discontinued, so that after some trials the child no longer walks or roller-skates to that spot. The child's "habit" has been "extinguished," we say. But *what* habit has been extinguished? Will the child be at all hampered in walking or roller skating in other new situations? Or does it seem that what happened in the earlier situation included the development of a motor skill which has been untouched by the extinction training and can now be transferred into new settings as though it were an interchangeable part? The larger experimental situation enables us to make a distinction between one habit—a tool skill—and another habit which had more of the character of a belief that such and such a reward could be secured in such and such a place.

As a matter of fact, Hull's concept of the learning of fractional antedating goal responses [93, chap. 7] was definitely moving in the direction of just such a distinction between one type of habit which would be changed by extinction and another which could readily be transferred. What we are proposing here is not something on which cognitive theory and Hullian theory have entirely differed, but something where there is a difference in amount of use of this distinction and in the interpretation of the nature of the two types of habits.

In much the same way, we can ask whether learning also can produce skills of sensory organization. As Hebb [83] has reported, the person who begins to do experimental work with chimpanzees has difficulty in distinguishing them by appearance. "All chimpanzees look alike!" But as he has more experience, he sees that faces of animals in the colony become quite as distinctive as human faces, and he also finds it increasingly easy to see new faces immediately in this more skillful fashion when new chimpanzees are added to the colony.

Similarly, as Osgood [179] has said, the language learning of a small child involves learning to make some very fine distinctions—between *d* and *t*, *t* and *th*, or *r* and *l*, for example—which will come to seem quite distinctive to him but which will not seem distinguishable to persons from certain other linguistic backgrounds. The child distinguishes these sounds, not merely in the words and in the behavioral contexts where he learned to use them to help guide his behavior, but in quite different contexts as well. This is a part of the "hyphen," therefore, which we can recognize as something relatively independent in the whole transmission of neural excitation from S to R in the original learning situations where he mastered these sounds.

Similarly, when we study the speech of a three- or four-year-old child, we see that he transfers training over to new materials and invents words that he never heard used. Having heard people use words such as *walked, slowest, raining,* and *unfasten,* the child not merely learns to use these particular words in the settings where they are appropriate; he also learns some more generalized habits which produce new expressions like *eated, drinked, goodest, pianoing, higher* (as a verb), and *Let me unkey the door.*

Such examples illustrate the facts which require us to clarify our notions of the different psychological processes we need to study before developing our principles about learning and habit. It seems important for us to develop a picture of the particular functions which can be changed by learning.

The Setting of Learning as Interpreted by Cognitive Theory

I indicated earlier that cognitive theory is the type of psychological theory which seems most promising to me. I have felt that insufficient effort has been made to integrate and extend the contributions of such workers as Lashley, Tolman, Köhler, Woodworth, Osgood, and George Klein and that there are considerable resources in the ideas of cognitive theorists which would greatly reward our exploration. Consequently, although I have indicated some other thinking about the relation of learning to its setting in other modes of functioning of the organisms, I have discussed only the larger aspects of these theories. Now I will aim to carefully explore this subject in terms of thinking which most psychologists would call "cognitive theory." We will discuss half a dozen main concepts about the larger setting which is provided for learning by other phases of the life of the organism. With the groundwork thus laid, we will turn to the question of processes and factors involved in learning itself.

The relation between central processes and organism-environment interactions. One characteristic methodological concept of cognitive psychologists is that research should deal with large functional units as well as with relatively segregated subwholes. This is often described as the "field" concept: the concept that properties are not properties of things as such, but properties, e.g., of organisms in situations. From such principles, one might well expect that cognitive theorists would have given a great deal of attention to the problems which Kantor was emphasizing—the problems of the interacting of organisms with their environments.

There have been some such efforts among cognitive psychologists. This sort of interest has been prominent in the personality theories of Sullivan [174], Adler [6], and Rogers [197]. There has been notable work on this sort of phenomenon in comparative psychology, especially in various phases of the social psychology of animals, as in studies of social hierarchies, territoriality, and conflict, as in studies of baboons (see pp. 377–378). Lewin's influence in social psychology has contributed to research on interactions of person and environment.

However, cognitive theorists do not seem to have taken as much interest in the problems which Kantor urged as we might have expected. What research there has been on this sort of problem seems to have come from other viewpoints as naturally and extensively as from cognitive theory. This seems to be a case where the natural logic of a point of view has not been developed. Perhaps the main trouble has been the difficulties of studying such complex units as Kantor refers to. These difficulties probably will clear up with time. In the meanwhile, we may simply note that this is a type of problem with which cognitive theorists presumably ought to feel at home, but which they have developed only in small part.

In some major respects—as the following discussion will indicate—cognitive psychology has been analytical or reductive in its thinking, trying to understand the processes and mechanisms *involved in* these more complex wholes, rather than taking these larger molar units as objects of study. In so far as cognitive psychology can make contributions to psychology at the present time, most of them are contributions to our understanding of the processes and mechanisms within the organism which may help to explain the larger processes which Kantor and Sullivan have been concerned with. Therefore, we need to turn to the cognitive interpretation of the processes and mechanisms within the organism.

Sensory organizations, representations, and motor-discharge organizations. The main framework has been provided by a threefold analysis of central nervous processes into processes of sensory organization, representation, and motor discharge. This analysis has been implicit, at least, in most of cognitive theory. Its clearest statement was given by Osgood [179] in 1955 at the Colorado Symposium on Contemporary Approaches to Cognition. The following discussion draws heavily on his work.

Let us illustrate, first, what the three phases are. In some respects, the first phase of psychological activity is the organization of afferent neural material into sensory organizations or sensory perceptions. Two spots of light, shown alternately with certain time gaps between them, are seen as a spot of light moving back and forth between two locations. Because of phase difference and/or intensity differences at the two ears, sounds are heard as coming from one direction or another, rather than just as sound. Rather closely similar speech sounds, as mentioned on p. 400, are clearly distinguished by the individual.

In other words, much of what tends to be discussed in textbooks on the "psychology of perception" is what we are calling sensory-organization processes (or what Osgood called "sensory integrations"). The phenomena of figure-ground organization, the perceptual constancies, grouping, and visual illusions are larger subclasses of sensory organizations.

These are processes which have some heavy dependence on more or less closely preceding receptor stimulations. With these processes, the factor of time relationships between different parts of the stimulation is frequently crucial. In vision, for instance, the stimuli for apparent movement must be separated by no more than about one-twentieth of a second, else apparent movement does not occur. The positive afterimage can have an even briefer temporal character, so that a marked flicker will appear on a movie screen before the speed is reduced to the point where the apparent movement stops. In some other phenomena, sensory-organization effects involve much longer intervals. The adaptation level of the person [Helson, 85] can cover longer intervals of time and yet can involve sensory organizations, as when one hears a second tone as louder or softer, lower or higher, than the first. The chances are, therefore, that what we call "sensory-organization processes" actually is a very heterogeneous class and that precise research will reveal a whole series of significant subclasses within it.

The second main type of central processes might be spoken of as representational processes or matters of meaning. Some of the examples of this class would fall under traditional definitions of perception, because they are processes where there is some degree of dependence on immediately preceding or very recent stimulation. For example, a person hears a sound as that of a passing car or a helicopter or a jackhammer— not just as a pattern of sound. A person hears a word or sentence as having a certain meaning. One rooster in the flock perceives another rooster as one which it can dominate or to which it must be submissive. A rat perceives one route in a maze as a route to water, another as the path to food.

Other instances of representational processes, however, have no such close relationship to present receptor stimulations. When a person tries to develop an experimental technique, it is not necessary for him to view any apparatus. When a musician composes a piece of music, he does not need to have any instruments or even scratch pads. When a person thinks about any of the hundreds of thousands of things that we think about, he can do a great deal without external objects or events to help him at the moment. He is dealing in terms of processes which have been enriched through previous perceptual processes which were dependent on definite stimulation, but he has carried over some altered neural mechanisms which now make it possible for him to have such present representational processes in relative independence of environmental stimulation. It may still be that the individual will want to use external stimulation to help these representational processes. Architects prefer to make sketches and build models rather than merely think about possible plans. Writers prefer to make outlines rather than plan articles in their heads.

A main contribution of these representational processes is that they frequently have a very important role as steering or cybernetic processes. They provide the template, as it were, against which the individual matches his behavior products to see whether he has achieved what he was motivated to achieve. The transactionalists have had a valuable point here [36, 96, 106]. They have stressed the point that, when we have talked about perception, our examples have usually been unrepresentative because (and again for reasons of experimental convenience) we have lifted such perceptual processes out of the larger processes in which they usually are found. Perceptions typically are a part of a larger purposive and goal-directed activity. They typically have a future reference or are expectations. They frequently are hypotheses as to what will be met as a consequence of the organism's actions in the given external situation. We can study part perceptions within such larger wholes, but such part perceptions are determined partly by these larger wholes of which they are a part. Cantril [36] has made a good point in saying that the gestaltists have paid too little attention to this consideration and that, in consequence, their treatment of perception has neglected some of their own broader principles in some respects.

The preceding paragraph has stated the main transactionalist principle in somewhat more guarded terms than the transactionalists themselves use; they seem to say "always" or to assume "always" rather than "typically." Personally, I doubt the value of saying that perceptions *always* have a future reference. But, even if we speak guardedly, it still is most important that most of activity must be understood as goal-directed activity governed by what I am here speaking of as perceptual processes, as has been emphasized many times [e.g., Miller, Galanter, and Pribram, 168; Adler, 6; McDougall, 160; Tolman, 228, 229; Woodworth, 245; Lewin, 38]. As Miller, Galanter, and Pribram phrase it, the perceptual process—"plan," to use their words—provides the template against which the organism makes a test to see whether it has attained what it sought to achieve either as a small step in some larger unit or as a final goal.

The templates which the representational processes provide are important, however, in contexts other than cases where the organism is merely trying to achieve some effect. They also provide the templates which the organism uses when it is merely observing events in the environment. A person who knows tennis, for example, expects certain things to happen when he sees certain strokes made. As the ball travels, he corrects his anticipation of the path it will follow and the behavior the other player will use to try to return the ball. But these corrections are only within narrow limits. He would be greatly surprised if the subsequent events did not take *approximately* the course that he represents beforehand.

Much of what is attributed to motor habits is actually a matter of such representational habits and sensory-organization habits, rather than what we will describe as "motor-discharge habits." For example, when a person learns to swim the crawl stroke, part of what he learns is skill in perceiving when his mouth is sufficiently out of water to permit safe breathing. The perceptual skill can be transferred to any other stroke. The football player is learning to perceive what is occurring on complex plays. This skill is one which he can then carry over into another behavioral area as an official in football games.

In fact, many types of learned activity that involve motor activity have little or no development of new motor-coordination habits as a part of what is learned. For instance, it is doubtful that maze learning or learning in a lever-pulling experiment is a matter of new motor skills to any very significant degree. More probably, these are merely cases where new representational habits are developed and govern the use of already acquired motor skills. A person who learns to walk over the necessary routes in a new town is not learning new movement patterns of walking. He is merely learning representational habits which, having been learned with reference to walking, could easily be transferred to bicycle riding or rollerskating.

All such considerations help to explain why cognitive psychologists have been so dissatisfied with the proposition that habits are linkages between stimuli and effector responses. Maybe the whole point can be summed up by saying that movements often are like symbols or actually are symbols. Their significance is determined by the relations of those movements to a larger context of the situation. A person blows on his hands to warm them, he blows on his soup to cool it. He runs as a part of some game, to catch a bus, to escape an angry dog, or to get out of the rain. He sometimes says "No" to indicate acquiescence, as in response to the query "Would you mind if . . . ?"

Particularly in the highest organisms, it seems that a great portion of what has been made possible by the increase of learning capacity has been the increase in capacity for such representational processes. The higher animals live in a vastly more complex world than the lower animals. The difference does not come solely from their finer distance receptors. It comes more because of the capacity to carry over from the past some neural mechanisms which permit much more complex neural processes than would be possible otherwise.

However, with all due respect to sensory-organization processes and representational processes, the fact remains that the organism does have to deal with a physical environment at intervals. It has to use its muscular equipment, frequently in rather complex ways, to try to produce desired effects. Furthermore, even though these movements can be guided to some extent by some informative feedback of a perceptual sort as the movement proceeds, there needs to be some very precise organizations of motor discharge from the brain which will produce successive phases of each response more quickly than can be corrected or supported by such feedback. This is a point which Lashley first emphasized in 1917, illustrating his point by reference to the movements of the violinist, pianist, or person who is speaking [134; see also Woodworth, 245; Osgood, 179; Pribram, 186]. In rapid performances in these fields, there simply is not sufficient time for any kinesthetic or auditory report of one phase of the overt behavior to get back to the brain before the motor discharge for the next phase has to be initiated. The principle of cybernetic control of muscular activity is not sufficient, therefore, to account for all of the properties of muscular response.

Other evidence of the importance of motor-organization processes is research indicating that organisms are equipped through physiological development with a number of neural centers that produce biologically adaptive rhythmic discharges—even though the neural or other stimulation of such centers has no rhythm that corresponds with this discharge. In humans there are neural centers for the coordinated rhythmic discharges involved in laughing, sobbing, sneezing, breathing, uterine contraction, sucking, swallowing, walking movements in newborn infants, sleeping, and other activities. Perhaps the most surprising of all is the rhythmic activity which has been demonstrated [153] with unsuspecting soldiers. They were living under conditions of continual winter darkness in Arctic posts and they had been given watches that were adjusted so that the time cycle of apparently twenty-four hours was actually several hours less. Even though the subjects typically were able to make adjustments of many other phases of their activity, certain cycles of body chemistry still followed more nearly the real 24-hour rhythm, revealing the same basic diurnal rhythm that has been found in every other animal species.

My own attention was drawn to this phenomenon in 1932. At that time, I gave a paper entitled "The Evidence for a Theory of Neurological Maintenance of States of Emotional Motivation" [142], using some material from Walter B. Cannon. Lashley lent support to my proposals by citing Adrian's recent study, which showed that when the brain stem of goldfish was separated from all afferent connections, the center for governing gill movements still continued to send out the usual rhythmic discharges. Since then, Lashley has called attention to a similar, but still earlier, study by Graham Brown.

In the following three decades, many studies have established the same principle—many phases of complex overt response depend not on learned neural mechanisms, but on intrinsic neural centers which provide for the details of coordinated muscular responses. It seems that the function of the higher centers of the brain is primarily to touch off or (very significantly) to terminate or more or less completely inhibit such motor-discharge processes. Thus, to quote the neurologist Paul Weiss:

Intrinsic automatic rhythms have been shown, for instance, by Adrian in the brain stem of the goldfish and in insect ganglia; by Prosser in other arthropods; by Bremer and von Holst in the spinal cord; and by Bethe in jellyfish. I have shown experimentally that any group of bulbar or spinal nerve cells taken from the vertebrates, if deprived of their structural bonds of restraining influences and allowed to undergo a certain degree of degradation, will display permanent automatic, rhythmic, synchronized activity of remarkable regularity. Rhythmic activity, therefore, seems a basic property of pools of nervous elements [97, p. 141].

And, earlier on the same page:

> Moreover, coordinate motor functions of limbs and other parts develop even if these parts have been experimentally prevented from ever becoming innervated by sensory fibers [97, p. 141] . . . The patterns of motor coordination are not replicas, as it were, of the sensory input patterns. The character and structure of the motor output is determined by the intrinsic properties of the organized response system and not by the set of stimuli that are fed into it from the environment or the surrounding body [97, p. 91]. . . . Most of the basic motor patterns of behavior are developed within the nervous system by virtue of the laws of its own embryonic differentiation without the aid of, and prior to the appearance of, a sensory input from the outside world. The basic configuration of the motor patterns, therefore, cannot possibly be a direct product of the patterns of the sensory input. A study of the nervous system and of behavior forces us to consider the output of the nervous system and its patterns as primarily preformed within the nervous system and ready for use, requiring the sensory input for release, facilitation, and modification, but not for its primary shaping [97, p. 73].

In addition, however, to such innately given processes, a great portion of the coordinated motor activities of the higher animals—especially human beings—must be made possible by learning. Therefore, our discussion needs to include a consideration of what Osgood so aptly termed the learning of "motor skill components."

The role of representational processes. The concept which has been presented above does not include some of the most important considerations regarding representational processes and their relationships to sensory-organization processes and motor-integration processes. In good part, the preceding discussion indicated that psychological processes are rather short-term and have three phases—first some organization of the incoming afferent material into sensory-perceptual processes, then perhaps a further arousal of representational processes, and then perhaps a further phase of organization of the nervous activity for discharge to the effectors.

The great importance of representational processes, however, comes from the fact that they have a much more complex character and frequently a much more enduring operation than any such concept suggests. Apparently representational processes are not merely short-lived events of a second or so. Psychological functioning depends very heavily on a stream—perhaps several different concurrent streams—of background representational processes of a long-sustained sort. Psychological activity is *not* something that perpetually springs afresh from peripheral stimulation and that would not exist if there were no specifically adapted peripheral stimulations to support the representational activity that is going on. It is something that comes mainly from the long-continuing representational processes of the organism. This is what Woodworth proposed in his article "Situation-and-goal Set" [245]. The view has been becoming increasingly convincing as psychological and neurological knowledge has developed.

When we speak of such long-sustained representation processes, we need not assume that brain processes are completely independent of peripheral contributions to keep them going and to help keep their character. Indeed, the testimony regarding hallucinations in the McGill studies of sensory deprivation (see p. 383), seems to indicate that some appreciable external stimulation has to keep feeding into the brain to prevent it from going off on tangents of its own, with long-sustained processes that come from who knows what chance influences. The trouble that the McGill subjects had was not that their brains were not active, but that they did not have the sort of stimulation which would have brought that continuing activity under some more useful controls. However, the stimulation required for more effectively organized activity does not have to be some peripheral stimulation that possesses elaborate points of contact with the long-sustained processes of the individual. Suppose that a person has been told by his physician, "These symptoms may indicate a serious cancer, but there is only a minor chance of this. We will do a biopsy next week. In the meantime, don't you worry, but just go about your usual business." The person who has received such an unexpected warning may try to do what he has been told. He may try to avoid all "stimuli" which would remind him of how he now represents his situation. But a long-sustained representational process will continue, changing the significance of almost everything that he meets. This is perhaps a rather melodramatic example, but the phenomenon seems to be a general one.

We can entertain this view of psychological processes more easily now that we have quite a different background of knowledge of the brain than we had during the early part of this century. Earlier, most of psychology was dominated by the view that the nervous system was constructed in a way that would permit virtually only the one-way transmission of nervous impulses from the point of entry into the brain to the point of motor discharge to the effectors. The brain was pictured as a relatively static organ except as afferent impulses came into it to produce some rather quick-fading activity that would quickly pass through to effector discharge.

In contrast, what is now known [97, 186] is that (*a*) the brain anatomically has a great deal of provision for reverberatory loops, particularly between the cortex and subcortical centers; (*b*) cortical tissue, even separated from any possibility of repeated afferent stimulation, can remain active for considerable periods (e.g., an hour) after merely brief stimulations; (*c*) even in the absence of definite external stimulation, the various receptor cells have a good deal of spontaneous firing of impulses to the central nervous system, so that this also helps the brain to remain continually active. The possible picture—in view of present anatomical and neurophysiological evidence—is well expressed by the statement we often make: "When you talk with him, you'll have to *keep in mind* that . . . "

Therefore, the concept that seems possible is the one presented in Lashley's most important paper [134]. His key idea is this: There is always a larger matrix for the organism's more specific and readily identified activities—a matrix consisting of a stream of background representational processes, the content of which changes somewhat (but usually only in accessory ways) because of the afferent neural material from the immediate peripheral stimulations. These long-continuing processes give a much more comprehensive background process than most of our psychological theories have envisaged. The main life of the individual—his main psychological functioning—is this larger set of continuing representations of the nature of different parts of his life situation.

What is the relation between such long-sustained representational processes and the briefer sensory-organization processes and the briefer representational processes that are more or less constantly being stirred up by receptor stimulations? We need to picture a two-way influence. In one direction, the peripherally supported processes bring changes in the long-sustained processes. The individual anticipates approximately the course of future events, but the current stimulation corrects these representational processes, which are derived primarily from still earlier stimulation. The person finds that the object which he picks up does not weigh quite as much as he expected, that his soup is hotter than he expected, or that a lecturer is not developing the line of thought that he expected. Sometimes these corrections are drastic. In any case, one very important part of the organism's life is the stimulation that ordinarily is pouring in constantly to support that background stream of representational processes or to deflect and reshape the stream to some degree.

The other main relation operates in the other direction, with the background representational processes doing a good deal to determine the character of the shorter-phase reactions to current stimulation. This is a point which Osgood [179] has emphasized, speaking of it as a matter of the "predictive relationships" which are involved in some operations of habits. He has supported his point with some very impressive research by himself and his students. As he has shown, for example, sensory thresholds for the perception of words are markedly lower when the words dovetail meaningfully with other words which have just preceded, as from such a prior sequence as "The fox slowly ⎯." Also, perceptions can be correct even when there is a great deal of irrelevant stimulation or "noise." On the other hand, short-range perceptions are often distorted by inappropriate background representations.

These influences of background representational processes are so important—but so seldom emphasized—in current psychology that it is worthwhile to quote a statement by Lashley in his last paper. He summarized his view as follows:

The theory of cerebral organization that I have dreamed up in the course of years . . . involves several postulates about integrative mechanisms.

1. The billions of neurons in the cerebral network are organized into a large number of systems. Each system consists of the traces of a number of habits or memories. Knowledge of the moves and games of chess would constitute one such system; memories of neural anatomy another; and so on through all of the individual's varied interests. The traces or engramata in any system are more closely connected with one another than with other systems. The systems are not anatomically separate, and the same neurons, in different permutations, may participate in many systems. For brevity I shall call these "trace systems."

2. Such a trace system may be thrown into a state of tonic activity by an external stimulus which activates one set of traces within it. In the tonic state the traces of the system are readily excitable and available to recall. Other systems are in abeyance. Thus when one plays chess, the Evans gambit or Philodor's defense may be readily recalled. But if the player is interrupted by the question, "Who won the pennant last year?", he will take some time to "collect his thoughts"; that is, to organize the baseball trace system. Such a general tonic activation seems a plausible explanation of concentration upon a particular subject, limiting associations to that subject. Questions of preparatory adjustment, organization of purposive activities, and the like can be formulated in such terms. . . . Grammatical structure and other ordered activities imply some sorting or arranging mechanism, active before the words reach overt speech or silent thought. The relations in thought structure are antecedent to consciousness. . . .

3. A system in tonic activity dominates the brain field, limiting the organization of other systems. It is relatively impervious to unrelated excitations. An intense stimulus, or an emotionally charged one, such as the sound of one's name, may break in, but the great mass of afferent excitations is excluded. This blocking might be either an active inhibition or

the preemption of neurons which might otherwise be included in the blocked system. . . .

4. The neurons in a trace system, under tonic activation, exert some mutual facilitation. The tonic state of the whole system is thus built up and maintained. This was the only sort of explanation that I could find for the reduction in efficiency of behavior in proportion to the extent of brain damage. . . .

5. The level of tonus in the partially activated system may vary. Circuits which have just been fully activated may retain a high level of subthreshold activity and thus contribute to the temporal organization evident in the memory span.

6. Fixation in memory is generally possible only when the remembered material forms part of such a dominant system. . . . We remember the content of a book, not in the author's words but in meanings which fit into previous knowledge of the subject. During the reading the meanings are not necessarily formulated clearly in verbal or other thought forms, but they may be so formulated later. That is, associations may be formed during reading with traces in the system which are not activated above tonic levels during learning. . . .

Such a system of low level tonic excitation in a system of memory traces would provide a basis for many of the characteristics of mental organization. The circuits of the trace system which are actively firing at levels sufficient to excite other traces would constitute the content of experience, limited and changing from moment to moment. The background of tonic activity would determine the direction of attention and of the flow of thought, restricting it to related associations. It would provide the binding force that holds together the temporal sequences through memory span and more permanent associations. Reduction in the tonic level of the system, as in sleep or under anesthetics, or violent invasion, as in a convulsive seizure, would destroy the organization necessary for memory and the continuity of the conscious state. Partial incomplete disorganization in sleep would permit interaction of different partial systems with the bizarre contaminations that occur in dreams.

These assumptions . . . are, of course, purely speculative and mainly inferences from psychological events. There is no present direct evidence from physiology in support of them. However, they are not inconsistent with what is now known of the physiology of the brain, and I believe that some such mechanism . . . of associated neurons excited at subthreshold levels seems not only a reasonable but an almost necessary consequence of the structure and known physiological properties of the cerebral cortex [135, pp. 6–9].

This discussion, which suggests that habit systems may have states of tonic activity and which speaks about neurons excited at subthreshold values, does not correspond, of course, with our older concept of all-or-none functioning of neurons. However, the all-or-none principle was derived solely from studies on axones in peripheral parts of the nervous system. More recent work, as Pribram has noted in his extremely valuable 1958 review [186], has indicated that the cerebral cortex is heavily dendritic in character and that, furthermore, the dendrites of neurons work in a graded fashion which seems fundamentally different from the operation of axones. (It will be remembered, incidentally, that the long fibers that run from the neurons in the spinal ganglia to the cutaneous receptors and kinesthetic receptors are branches of axones from unipolar cells —not dendrites.) It would be a rash person who would insist now that the neurophysiology of such "trace systems in a state of tonus" is one type of phenomenon rather than another. However, it seems essential for us to hypothesize that one phase of psychological functioning is a matter of "representational processes" which are distinguishably different from "sensory perceptual processes" and from "'motor discharge processes." It also seems important for us to conceive of these representational processes as having a far more complex and frequently a far more temporally extended character than most psychological theorizing has assumed.

Properties in common of representational and sensory-organizational processes. Up to this point, we have emphasized some of the differences between representational and sensory-organizational processes. We have stressed particularly the dependence of sensory-organizational processes on more or less immediately preceding stimulation—as contrasted with the long-sustained functioning which can characterize representational processes. There are enough differences so that it probably is worthwhile to regard these two kinds of processes as belonging to two different categories or ranged along some continuum from perceptual processes that are highly stimulus-dependent to processes that are relatively independent of specific afferent support.

There are five important respects in which both of these types of process are similar, however. Let us review them briefly before we turn to a more detailed consideration of two especially noteworthy respects.

1. *It seems important to define these processes in the case of both types without reference to whether they are conscious or unconscious.* As was said above, we can readily arrange conditions so that we can be sure that a person had a certain mental set or a certain "direction" in his thinking, but we still may have great difficulty in determining whether this was conscious. In the case of animal research, it is possible to demonstrate the operation of various sensory-organizational and representational processes, but there is little to be gained by talking about possible conscious properties. I do not want to suggest that the distinctions between conscious, less clearly conscious, and unconscious processes are unworthy of careful research. On the contrary, I think

this may be one of the important problems that we have been neglecting recently. Nevertheless, as I argued in Stevens's *Handbook of experimental psychology* [147], it seems to me that all such terms as "perception," "concept," "motivation," and "representational process" should be defined without reference to considerations of conscious qualities. If we have evidence that a perceptual process was conscious in a certain case and if we want to indicate this fact, we can add the adjective to indicate that we are speaking about a conscious perceptual process. But the functional similarities between conscious perceptual processes and unconscious perceptual processes are so numerous and important that we ought not bring into our definitions any such features as appeared in the traditional definition of perceptions as "an awareness of present objects or events."

2. *Both types of process may fall anywhere along a continuum from motivationally neutral processes to an extreme of very powerful motivational processes.* Ordinarily when we think of perceptual research, we think of experiments with motivationally neutral stimulations. Subjects are put at tasks of judging distances or directions, length of lines, brightnesses of colors, and so on. This is the most convenient sort of experiment to conduct in the field of perception. It is much easier to get and keep subjects in such experiments than it would be in experiments where persons had to compare the painfulness of different electric shocks. It is hard to provide situations that are really strongly rewarding to laboratory subjects. But these are questions just of expediency of research, and we ought not to be allowing considerations of experimenters' expediency to shape our basic concepts. After all, when a person tastes a very bitter substance or smells a terribly foul odor, this is just as truly a perceptual experience as is the perceiving of a light pressure on the skin. The same thing is true of very complex representational processes. When a person realizes that he has made a terrible mistake, or when he realizes that he has accomplished something really important, these are truly representational processes, even though they also are powerful processes from a motivational point of view.

This question of the relation of motivational and cognitive processes is such an important one that we will come back to it for more extended analysis. I also include it here to round out our general picture of cognitive processes.

3. *It is quite possible for a person to persist in some process which is quite incompatible with some other clear process, even when he knows that the one or the other of the conflicting processes is quite unjustified.* One may know how the Ames distorted room is built and why it yields the effects that it does, and yet he still gets the illusory effect. The same sort of clash can occur within relatively complex repre-

sentational processes. I have already referred to the fact that people can develop a wrong geographical orientation in a region and that such misorientations can persist despite strong efforts of the individual to correct them. The same sort of thing may be true when a person is traveling by train through mountainous country. The train may take a long switchback to gain altitude. The person suddenly notices that the sunlight, which formerly was slanting in through the left windows of the train, is slanting in through the right-hand windows, and he knows that the train must be traveling east rather than west. Even though he knows what must have happened, he has great difficulty in bringing his two representational processes into harmony. Many more complicated examples might be cited. It seems quite apparent, therefore, that an individual does not necessarily function as a unified whole in his cognitive processes and that cognitive processes are not always matters of what the person knows or believes.

Therefore, a cognitive interpretation of representational processes is not an interpretation in terms of our ordinary ideas of knowledge and intellectual processes. Rather, it is a basically biological type of theory; when a person is able to use intellectual evidence to change a previous belief quickly, a cognitive theorist would see this as a special limiting case—one that could occur only under unusual conditions—rather than the paradigm for all perceptual activity.

4. *Not only sensory-organizational processes, but also representational processes may rest on innate mechanisms as well as on past learning.* Köhler, of course, has stressed the autochthonous or innate factors in sensory organization and has tended to play down whatever evidence tended to indicate that sensory organizations could be changed by learning. Rather ironically, however, some of the best evidence we now have of such modification is his own research on figural aftereffects [120, 121, 122, 123, 124, 217], which we will describe later. It is easy to sympathize with Köhler's feeling that the associationists and "neo-associationists" tended to insist—though with too little interest in submitting evidence—that all perceptual organization must be a product of learning. But on the other hand, I can see no reason why the basic gestalt principles should be understood as excluding the possibility that profound modifications are made by learning, especially in the more complex sensory organizations. In fact, as I shall develop later, I see this principle as indispensable for rounding out the gestalt type of thought, rather than contradictory to it.

On the other hand, we need to recognize that innate factors can produce surprisingly complex perceptual processes. Research by Sauer [203] has proved that warblers guide their migrations by the constellations of stars, as indicated experimentally by their reactions in a planetarium where the constellations could be presented incorrectly in relation to North, East, and so on. The work of von Frisch [65] has demonstrated the surprising phenomenon of the responses of bees to the "honey dance," by which bees returning from some rich find of blossoms can communicate to other bees both the *direction* and the *approximate distance.*

Furthermore, innate processes are frequently functionally equivalent to complex learned representations. We emphasized above the role of representational processes as cybernetic mechanisms with reference to overt behavior. But the same sort of cybernetic control exerted by learned "representational processes" is exerted also where there is no sufficient knowledge derived from previous learning and the response has to depend on instinctive mechanisms. When an oriole builds its nest for the first time, when a cliff swallow builds its mud gourd-shaped nest, or when a trap-door spider builds its abode and makes a hinged lid that fits tightly enough to exclude water washing over the ground, no stereotyped series of movements is made in the course of such construction. Overt behavior is continued—with adaptations and repetitions—until the possibly recalcitrant materials yield the species-characteristic effect. We need not propose that the organism visualizes beforehand what is to be achieved—we are merely saying that there is some guiding process (or "plan," in the Miller-Galanter-Pribram sense) which operates cybernetically to control a flexible process aimed at the achievement of some goal.

This problem of the relations of learning and innate mechanisms is a rather complex one, as is the problem of the relation of perceptual processes and motivation. We will return to it also in a later section.

5. *The learning which produces changes either in sensory-organizational processes or in representational processes tends to produce changes in the other sort of process as well.* At least, this is the case in many instances which we can recognize. Suppose a person is shown some incomplete figure which is quite difficult to reorganize perceptually so that it will look like something meaningful. When he is given some information—even just highly abstract information about what class of object is represented by the incomplete figure—the representational process aroused by this information helps him achieve the requisite sensory organization from actual stimulation by the figure. Contrariwise, if he succeeds in reorganizing the fragmented drawing, his later efforts to visualize the figure will take the form of the learned pattern, rather than referring to the meaningless patches of black which otherwise he would visualize.

This may suggest that we do not have one sort of habits that we might call "sensory-organizational habits" and a different sort of habits that we might call "representational habits"—even though we may want to use these two concepts until we get more adequate evidence—but that sensory-organizational processes and representational processes are sometimes distinguishably different only because of different supporting factors. The neural mechanisms in the two cases may have a great deal in common, but the neural mechanisms are working under different conditions in both cases, with much more adequate and steady support in the one case than in the other. This proposal ties in with some modes of thinking which are very characteristic of cognitive theory with regard to this distinction between "processes" and "mechanisms." This distinction is not so important in S-R thought, where the tendency would be to say that a process is merely a mechanism in operation, but where the hidden presupposition is that there can be little variability in processes, just as there can be little variability in the ways that the parts of a machine operate. What may be true, however, is that ordinary machines are poor models of the mechanisms involved in psychological processes and that some other type of physical system would provide a more illuminating model for conceiving of the differences between mechanisms and processes. This is another complex point for a later section.

6. *Both sensory-organizational and representational processes have some other similarities as abstractive or selective and as dynamically organized processes.* When we think of sensory-organizational processes, we have some tendency to think of them as utilizing the full array of available stimulation and afferent material. Even though there are "gating mechanisms" [30] which can reduce the sensory input from some kinds of peripheral stimulation, it still seems plausible that the sensory-organizational processes would reflect all of the readily distinguishable features of the peripheral stimulation or the afferent input from it at least. Such was the view which Hull proposed with regard to learning. He summed up his view in these words:

According to the "law of reinforcement" . . . every one of the receptor discharges and receptor-discharge perseverations active at the time that the to-be-conditioned reaction occurs must acquire an increment of habit strength. . . . [93, p. 206; see also pp. 205–207, 258, 386.]

If sensory-organizational processes had this character, this certainly would be different from conceptual forms of representational process. The essence of conceptual activity seems to be that it abstracts or selects some phases of complex material for representation and disregards others.

However, a closer examination of sensory-organizational processes does not support the idea that they indiscriminately reflect all the properties of the current stimulation. The three papers by Bruner in 1955 and 1957 [28, 29, 30] are magnificent discussions of this selective character of perception and of what he calls the "inferential" character of perceptions, even though he shies away from drawing the conclusion that the term "perception" should be extended to cover conceptual activities. His argument for being hesitant about this, however, rests on selecting a few examples and disregarding a host of others. His argument for distinguishing "perceptual and more conceptual inferences" was this:

> The former appear to be notably less docile or reversible than the latter. I may know that the Ames distorted room that looks so rectangular is indeed distorted, but unless conflicting cues are put into the situation . . . the room still looks rectangular. So too with such compelling illusions as the Müller-Lyer: in spite of knowledge to the contrary, the line with the extended arrowheads looks longer than the equal-length one with those inclined inward [29, p. 124].

But, if we take other examples, this distinction disappears. It is odd that, speaking about reversibility, Bruner made no mention of reversible figures and of research with incomplete figures. With incomplete figures, knowing what to look for *does* help in the reorganization of such figures into well-organized perceptions [144]. With reversible figures, the attainment of a second organization by no means handicaps a return to the first organization. But on the other hand, we can find a great lack of reversibility in many cases of conceptual inference. With a very difficult conceptual task, a subject may labor for hours and become convinced that the task is utterly impossible; later, after he discovers the solution, there is no possibility of his reverting to his previous conception of the puzzle as insolvable.

I would not urge, any more than Bruner does, some "utter indistinguishability" of the simpler sensory-perceptual processes and the more complex conceptual processes. But we will need to search further than Bruner did—or Piaget, whose argument Bruner probably was relying on —to find the distinction. For the present, though, let me stress merely what Bruner was mainly concerned with—the simpler perceptual processes still do not by any means utilize all the qualities of receptor stimulation; they selectively emphasize only one or a few properties and disregard various others. The brain operates essentially as if it were a radio, a device which has to amplify what typically is rather weak afferent neural material and which, to be efficient, selects one phase or another of the afferent material for such amplification. When he tested rats on jumping apparatus for transfer of their discrimination habits to other stimulus cards, Lashley [133] found that different rats sometimes seized on different properties as defining the difference between the positive and negative cards; some rats would transfer easily to one new pair of test cards, while others would transfer only to other test cards. The differences were not explainable in terms of different parts of the cards that the rats had fixated visually.

In other words, there are numerous functional similarities between what psychologists would have traditionally called perceptions and what traditionally would have been called thinking or ideational activity outside the perceptual sphere. There would be some advantages in having one term under which we might group representational processes —of whatever degree of complexity—as well as the sensory-organizational processes. I believe that there is considerable justification for extending the term "perceptual process" to cover this very broad area and keeping the qualified "sensory-perceptual process" or "sensory-organizational process" to refer more narrowly to processes which have some heavy dependence on current receptor stimulations. This usage is coming to be more and more common in psychology. This is a moot point, however. It seems clear that the old boundaries for the phenomena of perception were placed at a poor point. We have moved the boundary stakes in a number of ways. Whether the territory for the term "perception" should be extended to include all representational processes or all cognitive processes is a very controversial (and perhaps relatively unimportant) question. The important thing is to recognize some major changes, such as have been outlined above, that we apparently need to introduce into our discussions of these various processes.

In order not to lose our grasp of the relationships of various main points, we have postponed a more intensive discussion of several major points involved in consideration of processes which set the stage for learning processes. Let us now return to three of these problems.

Motivation as a type of perceptual activity. In the discussion thus far, we have made little reference to phenomena of motivation except in incidental ways. This does not mean, however, that phenomena of motivation, including phenomena of reward and punishment, are unimportant for an approach which stresses perceptual phenomena. Thus, mentioning first some historical examples, we may note the emphasis of McDougall [160], Köhler [116], and Adler [6] on the goal-directedness of behavior, the interest of Tolman in the way in which active motives govern performance [228, 229, 230], the interest of Lewin in conflict situations and other motivational phenomena [38, 145], and the interest which I myself have had in the interpretation of emotional processes as motives [142, 146, 150].

Speaking of this problem in theoretical terms, the main point is this: Among the representational processes discussed above, there are processes which represent that "If that were done, such and such would probably follow"; there are also processes which put the organism under pressure to do such "that's." This does not mean that all representational processes are motives. But it does mean that a perceptual type of approach—as well as an S-R or a Freudian one—needs to take major interest in processes that "arouse, sustain, and direct activity," as Shaffer so aptly expressed the matter. The differences among these three types of approach, therefore, lie in the question of *what* principles they emphasize to interpret motivation, rather than in any difference of degree of emphasis on motivation.

Emphasis on perceptual phenomena in our approach tends to lead to five distinctive concepts concerning motivation:

1. *Motivation is not simply something that has arousal value, as mentioned above, and as Judson Brown has proposed in his recent book* [26]; *it is something that steers or directs activity or gives it a goal-directed character.* Brown urged that motives or drives ought not to be thought of as having a directing or steering influence; he said that habits have such an influence and, if drives also direct behavior, there would be no difference between the two terms. One would be superfluous. We can sympathize with Brown's idea that, if we are to have two terms like "drive" and "habit" (or "motive" and "perceptual process"), there must be some difference of reference between them. But Brown was reasoning as though he thought that two categories in psychology must either overlap entirely or else be coordinate. He was disregarding the fact that different scientific constructs often have a hierarchical relationship, as when we say that "vertebrate" is a more inclusive term than "mammal" and that both are indispensable. It is perfectly possible for us to hold—and this would be basic in a perceptual type of approach—that only a fraction of representational processes in the organism's life—but a very important fraction—put the organism under pressure to exhibit goal-directed activity.

2. *Motivation is not merely a matter of "physiologically based motives," processes that partially depend on bodily states and certain kinds of strong external stimulation, but is also a matter of emotional motives, particularly in the higher organisms.* Most human activity is not based directly on such things as hunger, thirst, cold, or pain from wounds. Most activity is based on other factors—the person enjoys the work he does and feels it is significant; he enjoys the companionship of other persons; he wants to acquire the physical necessities for his later life; he wants to escape a situation that he sees as dangerous; he enjoys music or fishing or other aesthetically significant experiences; he wants to ease his sense of guilt.

Such emotional processes are, as P. T. Young has said in his recent book *Motivation and emotion*, "processes which originate in a psychological situation" [246, p. 352]. They depend for their arousal on very slight cues or on relatively very complex constellations of stimulation.

Thus, goslings investigated by Tinbergen [225] responded with hiding when a cardboard silhouette suggestive of a hawk was passed over their pen; they did not hide when the same silhouette was turned around, so that its pattern was more like a goose or duck. Konrad Lorenz found that, as long as the baby jackdaws had not developed black pin-feathers, the parent birds did not attack him for approaching the nests and taking the young in his hands. However, even though these particular birds were quite tame in their relation to him, they attacked him savagely when he tried to handle young jackdaws that had become covered with black feathers and also when they saw him with some fluttering black paper or cloth in his hand [154]. These particular examples illustrate the point that some emotional processes are instinctively given. Others are made possible by learning. Lorenz observed that young jackdaws show no fear of cats or dogs. He observed one young jackdaw fly down and land on the head of a mongrel dog of the neighborhood. But young jackdaws acquire an appropriate fear because the older jackdaws set up a terrific scolding when a cat or dog appears. The young jackdaws, without experiencing attacks from such animals, acquire the emotional response that they need. Certainly in human life there are no instincts that make a person afraid of dental drills, proud of a car, or anxious to help solve some complex social problem. All these are cases, however—as with the jackdaws who saw someone holding a fluttering black object—where the processes aroused have a double character; they are subtle perceptual processes as well as motivational processes.

The widespread influence of emotional processes as motives fits in with the fact that the higher organisms are distinguished particularly by their excellent distance receptors, their high perceptual capacities, their great learning ability, and their high intelligence. The full biological advantages of these characteristics can be secured only when there are emotional mechanisms which can cause the organism to become powerfully motivated as a consequence of what it can perceive by virtue of them. A baboon must be motivated to get access to a tree not only when it is bitten or clawed by a lion but when it sees or smells a lion at a distance, although, interestingly enough, baboons show no marked concern at the sight of a lion if his belly is pendant with food. The animals that have great learning capacity can realize this asset fully only if, in addition to being spurred to explore situations when they are motivated by bodily needs like hunger, they also are motivated by a need for the satisfaction of doing things and perceiving things [note particularly the observations of McBride and Hebb on dolphins, 157].

Of course, emotional processes sometimes work to prevent adaptations that might otherwise be made. There is nothing peculiar about emotional processes in this fact, however. The mechanisms for breathing are basically adaptive. Nevertheless, drowning sometimes occurs because the mechanism for breathing forces a breathing response before the body actually is desperately short of oxygen. The hunger motive may cause excessive eating. The sex motive may lead to such overpopulation that extreme social difficulties may occur. The fine learning ability of human beings leads to neuroses as well as to realistic habits.

The basic question, therefore, is not whether any biological mechanism is adaptive under *all* circumstances, but whether it has adaptive value *in general*. If we do not examine some sampling of human and animal life which is dictated by the a priori proposition that emotional processes are disorganizing or some sample dictated by the interests of psychopathologists—if we select instead a sample which seeks to get some ecologic validity as a cross section of the life of animals and human beings—we find most of the goal-directed activity of higher organisms to be a matter of emotional processes rather than physiologically based motives.

3. *Emotional motives must be seen, however, as part of a continuum which runs from the clearest examples of emotional motivation to the clearest examples of physiologically based motivation.* It is not possible to find any clear line or gap between the two, any more than it is possible to find a clear dividing line along any of the other continua with which psychology deals. For convenience, we often use dichotomous terms to refer to the two ends of such continua, just as we use such terms as "blond" and "brunette" even though we realize that there is an obvious continuum in hair colors.

A particularly instructive example is the sex motive. There is no question but that it is physiologically based in part. Witness its onset or great increase with the endocrine changes of adolescence and witness the relation of sexual motivation to cycles of ovulation in the female in subhumans. But comparative psychology shows that the sex motive is not merely a function of internal physiological conditions and simple external stimulations. Frank Beach [17] has gathered a fascinating body of material indicating that the sexual arousal of many animals is a matter partly of perception of "appropriate" environmental conditions. Catfish do not breed in aquariums unless plants and rocks are placed in the water. The sex motive of many birds depends on elaborate mating rituals. Crossbreeding between domestic cattle and the American bison can occur only if the bison has been raised from birth among such cattle. In fact, most species are kept distinct from one another not because there is no interspecies fertility, as was formerly believed, but because sexual arousal occurs only with other organisms that have the exact appearance or mode of behavior or even the song of the "own" species [205].

The sex motive, therefore, beautifully illustrates the point that there can be motives which come partly from internal chemical factors and partly from the subtle perceptual discriminations which we mentioned above as characteristic of the emotional processes.

4. *All motives, whether emotional or physiologically based, operate as full perceptual processes.* We do not mean merely processes that are conscious or that have been learned or that occur in close temporal proximity to external stimulation to which they refer. By "perceptual processes," we mean complex, organized neural processes which would include, in the intact organism, the participation of cortical mechanisms. They are matters of the organism's experience—not necessarily conscious —of its situation. They are processes that are able to operate in the sense of the "plans" hypothesized by Miller, Galanter, and Pribram [168] as governing the other activities of the organism.

This is not to deny that, for many motives, there are identifiable subcortical centers that are significantly involved. But the point is this: When these subcortical centers operate in the larger process or motive in the intact organism, the larger neurological process has some quite different properties from those exhibited when such subcortical centers are aroused by artificially segregated stimulation.

At the second Josiah Macy, Jr. Foundation Conference on the Central Nervous System and Behavior in 1959, John C. Lilly reported the behavior of a monkey in which an electrode had been implanted in a subcortical center involved in sexual motivation as evidenced by a sexual reflex when the electric stimulation was switched on:

> If we allow the animal thus to start very long trains of stimuli and start his own erection, the erection builds up over the few seconds period of the train and, when the machine shuts off the train, the penis slowly collapses. Under these conditions, the animal will start an erection, wait 30 to 60 seconds, and repeat his performance. He will continue to do this at about the same rate for 24 hours a day for 2 days without any sleep. It is important to remember that this is his choice, not ours; he starts the trains [of electric stimulation] and all we do is to be sure that the apparatus shuts it off after 10 seconds. We have not prolonged such experiments beyond 48 hours because we do not want to lose a valuable animal [25, p. 79].

In the intact organism, the processes which involve such subcortical mechanisms are by no means so stereotyped. The motive with which this fact has been studied most extensively has been pain, partly because of the medical significance of this process. Pain seemed to fit the concept that physiologically based motives are almost entirely explainable on the basis of strong peripheral stimulation and of subcortical centers for amplifying the effects from such stimulation. And, of course, some specialized neural mechanisms (special pathways, special subcortical centers) have been found for pain [167]. But as the research has proceeded both with animals and with human subjects, it has become more and more apparent that what operates in the organism as a painful experience—a wound or electric shock or dental drilling—is a complex perceptual process. The situation is not a simple one in which the strength of activity of subcortical "pain centers" depends solely on the strength of the peripheral stimulations. Nor is it one in which the processes in the cortex are governed solely by the activity of these centers. There is an influence in that direction, but the activity of cortical areas can increase or decrease the frequency and duration of afferent impulses even at the level of the spinal cord, let alone at a number of other junctions where nerve impulses are relayed to the highest areas of the brain.

Hence in the intact organism there is no simple and standard "biological effect" from a given stimulation that is supposedly "pain arousing." What exists, instead, is a complex perceptual experience, the character of which is determined by the diversity of sorts of influences that we have learned to expect with reference to other perceptual processes. Melzack tells of the observations of H. K. Beecher in World War II:

He was astonished to find that when the wounded were carried into combat hospitals, only one out of three complained of enough pain to require morphine. Most of the soldiers either denied having pain from their extensive wounds or had so little that they did not want any medication to relieve it. These men . . . were not . . . unable to feel pain, for they complained as vigorously as normal men at an inept vein puncture [167, p. 42].

In contrast, studies of surgical patients in civilian life who had incisions similar to such wounds showed that about 80 per cent of such patients "claimed they were in severe pain and pleaded for a morphine injection" [167, p. 42]. Melzack quotes Beecher's interpretation as follows:

There is no simple direct relationship between the wound per se and the pain experienced. The pain is in very large part determined by other factors, and of great importance here is the significance of the wound. . . . In the wounded soldier [the response to injury] was relief, thankfulness at his escape alive from the battlefield, even euphoria; to the civilian, his major surgery was a depressing, calamitous event [167, p. 42].

Melzack cites a great range of evidence, not only from physiological recordings, but also from both behavioral and introspective observations to support his

. . . view of pain as a perceptual experience whose quality and intensity is influenced by the unique past history of the individual, by the meaning he gives to the pain-producing situation and by his "state of mind" at the moment. We believe that all these factors play a role in determining the actual patterns of nerve impulses ascending to the brain and traveling within the brain itself. In this way pain becomes a function of the whole individual, including his present thoughts and fears as well as his hopes for the future [167, p. 49].

I believe that this discussion, together with the fascinating analysis which George Klein previously had given as a consequence of his own efforts to relate concepts of motivation to concepts of cognitive processes [108; see also 125], means that the problems of motivation, even on the side of so-called bodily drives, belong much more clearly within the province of perceptual phenomena than was apparent earlier.

5. *The recognition of the perceptual character of motivational processes has one more very important implication.* Many older interpretations of motivation took for granted the view that drives or motives—as states of tissue need or whatever—are virtually unmodifiable by learning. This was the view held by such different workers as McDougall [160], Floyd Allport [2], J. B. Watson and most other S-R psychologists, and the Freudians. Different terms were used—"instinctive propensities," "prepotent reflexes," "drives," and "instincts"—but the common assumption was that motives were some hard core of biologically given mechanisms or processes which might get linked to new stimuli which could activate them and to new motor responses which might express them, but that the central motivational part itself remains unaltered. According to that view, there may be "acquired drives," but the acquired drive is merely the biologically given process which—either in its entirety or in some fractional part (as incipient chewing movements)—has been tied to some new stimulation. According to this mode of thought, the problem in motivational learning is merely one of discovering the "biologically adequate stimulus" and getting it presented so that it will activate the drive mechanism which is already there. The Freudian view of motivation is essentially the same. Thus Anna Freud stated in 1950:

A great variety of ego mechanisms is brought into action to deal with a comparatively small range of component instincts. . . . Investigation of individuals by analysis demonstrates that the differences between their id strivings are negligible. It is the difference in ego and superego structure which accounts for the infinite variety of human personalities and clinical pictures [63, p. 490].

As opposed to such a view, the natural implication from viewing motives as perceptual processes is that we may expect motives to resemble other perceptual phenomena in being enormously modifiable by learning and by the particular "field conditions" under which they operate in any given situation. Admittedly, some motives work under more of a structural constraint than do other perceptual processes because of the inclusion of subcortical centers such as we have discussed above. But as we have seen, these still permit wide variations even in such a motive as pain. In the case of the more strongly emotional motives, there would be less of such biologically given constraint. Hence, just as we would expect perceptual skills to vary enormously according to whether the person is a primitive hunter, a musician, a football coach, a physician, or a geologist, so we ought also to expect that the neurological processes which we speak of as "actively functioning motives" would be drastically different from one person to another, even within the same general social culture.

If this is true, it still may also be true that there is some value in classifications of types of motive in human life. However, we must expect that such classifications will be merely devices of convenience, not something corresponding to any breaks in the infinitely varied array of motivational processes.

The relations between processes and structures. The preceding sections have implied that there are important differences between the enduring *structural* changes which psychologists generally assume are produced by learning and the *processes* that occur at any given point in the organism's life. Whether this distinction seems to deserve much attention probably depends on different psychologists' background assumptions regarding the nature of the nervous system. Different psychologists use two models. One emphasizes the enduring structures of the nervous system as determining psychological functioning in each moment of the organism's life. One corollary to this is as follows: When a habit is used, if there is some variation from the conditions which existed when the habit was established, it should operate with less efficiency or strength than would have been the case under a closer duplication of the original conditions of stimulation. In other words, there will necessarily be some gradient of stimulus generalization. Fully effective functioning can be expected only with a repetition of the exact conditions which operated when the habits (the enduring structures) were established. In research and theorizing, the main interest is centered on learning (on the establishment of enduring structures).

The other type of model that some psychologists have used to help them organize their knowledge is one that has put emphasis on the idea of processes as well as on the construct of habit structures.

To help explain this latter view, let me first quote Heinrich Klüver's description of a more extreme view, which sees all psychological phenomena as explainable without assuming that learning produces enduring structural changes. In his discussion of Lashley's last paper, quoted above, Klüver said:

> . . . it seems pertinent to remind engineers as well as neurologists and psychologists that there are memory theories, in fact, very elaborate and closely reasoned theories of memory which require no storage, no

"engrams," no "traces" or "residua" in the brain. Special mention should be made of the Hungarian investigator, Julius Pikler, who proposed such a theory a few decades ago. In the sequence of psychological activities constantly directed towards a future that is realized in a present turning into a past, there are never-ending cycles of coiling and uncoiling, folding and unfolding, attachment and detachment, tension and relaxation of tension, but there are, according to this theory, nowhere any "traces" of this flow of activities and adjustments [112, p. 15].

I will not try to summarize the type of experiments [e.g., 5] that have been conducted as attempts to refute this type of theory. I will take for granted—as most other psychologists seem inclined to do—that the terrific volume and diversity of what is learned and retained can hardly be accounted for without assuming that static structural changes are responsible for most of the bridging between original learning situations and those later occasions when memory traces are activated again.

But even if this assumption proves valid, I want to suggest that we cannot successfully account for a great many psychological phenomena without assuming that there are many types of "processes" which we must study and come to understand *as processes.*

For example, the theory of sound waves depends partly on the assumption that the molecules of air are in virtually constant motion, colliding with one another after little journeys of different distances, moving more rapidly when the air is "warmer," and so on. To talk about the propagation of sound waves, however, we need to go beyond this matter of chance collisions between individual molecules and describe the larger statistical picture of what happens when there is some vibrating body which starts a series of compressions and rarefactions which travel at such and such rates. The movement of such sound waves in a room cannot, of course, be adequately described without taking into account the structure of the room in which the sound waves travel. Adding acoustical tile to the walls will change the amount of reverberation. Any object standing in the room will have "sound shadows" behind it. Even a grill made of narrow wooden strips would make an elaborate sound-shadow pattern; it would preserve faintly the design details of that grill—even though the details would be lost within a short distance. The sound waves in such a room, even though affected by the physical structure of the room, are basically self-sustained processes. All their wealth of precise details, sufficient to carry an elaborate symphony concert, is carried by merely transient processes which will leave the air molecules bouncing around in the same unstructured ways as before the sound waves were started.

To illustrate what we mean by "processes," other models would be the transmission of electrons through a complex electric circuit, the establishment and operation of magnetic fields, and the control of shapes of drops of liquid by the forces of surface tension. All such cases illustrate processes which have to be understood partly in terms of the structural conditions under which they occur and partly in terms of the laws of sound waves, magnetic fields, surface tension, etc.

Now is there any real correspondence between such examples and the psychological processes of perception, motivation, and conceptual activity? It is notable that in the Hixon symposium [97] a number of the speakers (Paul Weiss, K. S. Lashley, W. S. McCulloch, and Linus Pauling) stressed this distinction between process and structure. Pauling recently has returned to this problem in a paper analyzing the chemical mode of operation of different anesthetics. He speaks about a type of evidence which, if borne out, would be one of the most striking arguments for distinguishing between "processes" and "structures." He says:

During the last twenty years much progress has been made in the . . . understanding of biological phenomena in terms of the structure of molecules and their interaction with one another. The progress that has been made in the field of molecular biology during this period has related in the main to somatic and genetic aspects of physiology, rather than to psychic. We may now have reached the time when a successful molecular attack on psychobiology, including the nature of encephalonic mechanisms, consciousness, memory, narcosis, sedation, and similar phenomena, can be initiated. . . .

It is likely that consciousness and ephemeral memory (reverberatory memory) involve electric oscillations in the brain, and that permanent memory involves a material pattern in the brain, in part inherited by the organism (instinct) and in part transferred to the material brain from the electric pattern of the ephemeral memory. . . .

It has been noted that unconsciousness produced by a blow to the head or electric shock often has caused complete loss of memory of the events experienced during the period of 10 or 15 minutes before the blow or shock to the brain. Moreover, when the formation of new permanent memories is interfered with by the decreased ability of the brain to carry on metabolic processes involving proteins, as in old age or Korsakoff's syndrome (alcoholism, protein starvation, thiamine deficiency), the memory continues for a period of 10 or 15 minutes, but usually not much longer; the memory seems to persist only so long as conscious attention is directed to it [180, p. 15; see also 66, 94].

In the earlier discussion in the 1948 Hixon symposium (published in 1951), McCulloch had called attention to the fact that the symptoms which are sometimes seen in old age constitute almost an experimental separation between transitory psychological processes (what he called "reverberatory memory" and what Pauling called "ephemeral memory") and the registering of effects from those transitory processes so that there can be some use of the memory later. Thus a very elderly person may inquire why some relative has not come to visit him. The explanation is given that the person in question died some months ago and hence could not come. For the time being the elderly person shows marked signs of grief and discusses intelligently and apparently with some adequate temporary understanding the circumstances of the person's death and various memories regarding the person. But, half an hour later, the elderly person asks all over again why this relative did not come to visit him.

It seems worthwhile to propose that there are two aspects of brain functioning: self-sustained temporary processes—comparable to the propagation of sound waves in a room—and the depositing of structural changes which, with a normal brain, will persist and influence the way that transitory processes operate on subsequent occasions. *It also seems probable that the transitory processes are very important just in their own right and that a fair portion of our psychological principles and psychological research ought to be concerned with them.*

I am assuming that these transient processes are not always conscious processes. I assume further that many of them are conscious only as exceedingly brief processes and cannot leave any habit residues after them. Their effects are as ephemeral as are the sound shadows beyond a narrow obstruction. But a person nevertheless can note that certain transient conscious effects do occur, as in the readily observed experience of the great amount of detail of which one can be transiently conscious when watching the movements of a tree in the breeze. Many other transitory processes leave enough of habit residues for retrospective descriptions or redintegrative images of such past experiences to be secured afterward. The properties of such transitory processes also can be inferred more indirectly from objective "behavioral" data. As a pragmatic matter, it seems that the psychologists who have chosen to work exclusively or almost exclusively from objective data, as even a cognitive theorist like Tolman, have ended up with merely a few rough propositions regarding such transitory processes. I am holding out for—and I do not think it is weakly conservative to do so—the use of a combination of objective and subjective data, without philosophical precommitment that only one type or the other covers the legitimate "observables" from which a psychologist can work. My thoughts still go back, for instance, to the little laboratory incident where Norman Munn and I "discovered Fechner's colors" and to the instance when the McGill investigators, serving as subjects in their own sensory-deprivation experiment, came for the first time to realize how powerful and striking were the phenomena of hallucinatory experiences. One might, somehow or other, have discovered such relationships by objective research even with animals. But as a practical matter, such discoveries have come much more richly and expeditiously through a willingness to use subjective as well as objective data!

If we hypothesize such transitory, self-sustained responses, thinking of them in terms of some model like that of sound waves or surface tension, there are a number of expectations which might come from this. For one thing, it would be expected that *when a habit is used with somewhat different objective stimulation than was involved in the preceding learning situation, this would not necessarily mean that the "learned perceptual response" would be the same in all respects as the previous process, nor that it would be less efficient than the previous process.* For example, suppose a person has heard a certain piece of music played repeatedly on the violin and thereby has learned to hear it more adequately. When he then hears it played with a clarinet or oboe, he will not hear the violin sound, but the present clarinet or oboe sound—and he will hear it with the more adequate grasp of the theme which he carries over from the preceding performances. Similarly, in many situations where a subject would be tested for transposition, there should be no impairment at all. With a tune played in a different key, he will hear it differently because, if asked to continue it by humming or whistling, he will continue in the new key, without even realizing that he is making a change, but he will recognize the tune just as readily as though it were played in the familiar key. I am depending here on a report by Leeper and Leeper on "An Experimental Study of Equivalent Stimulation in Human Learning" [149]. I realize that there have been transposition experiments which indicated that there was impairment when the test material deviated quite markedly from the original training material. Such experiments have neglected Riley's [192] point that learners depend partly on relationships between test designs and background factors. We cannot accept any experimental method which assumes that the relationships which have been perceived are—by some miracle—merely those between the stimulus aspects which the experimenter has chosen as his object of interest.

Beyond the potentialities for transposition are all the other qualities of dynamic organization which the gestalt group have tried to describe by saying that perceptual processes have to be understood in terms of "field concepts" [115, 117, 118]. One of the most fascinating recent experiments has been reported by Pritchard, Heron, and Hebb [187, 188] with stabilized retinal images, using the technique of a reflecting system attached to a corneal lens so that, even when tremor movements occur, the projected image on the retina remains almost exactly the same. This experiment succeeded in using larger and more complex visual designs than those employed in previous studies. What was found, as in earlier studies [191], is that satiation processes were apparently extraordinarily rapid. However, these satiation effects did not prove to be all-or-none affairs, which had previously seemed to be the case where the vision was merely one of straight lines or arcs. Instead, there were rapidly shifting blockings out of different parts of the figures seen—never merely of parts of continuous lines, but an elimination of all but two adjacent lines or two parallel lines of a square, for example. With figures that potentially could be seen as three dimensional rather than two dimensional, the perceptual organization often shifted from one to another three-dimensional pattern, but used the two-dimensional organizations much less than would have been the case under conditions of normal vision. As the writers say, the data gave what seemed to them like a surprising number of confirmations of gestalt principles regarding sensory organization. (The data, furthermore, thoroughly dispose of claims that such shifts occur because of changes of stimulation with shift of fixation from one spot of such designs to another.) This same experiment, though, illustrates a point that Köhler [117, pp. 208–209] has tended to wave aside—that such sensory-perceptual effects also depend

Fig. 1. A figure which, under the conditions of stabilized retinal images [188, p. 71, Fig. 14], showed the influences of sensory-organizational habits.

on the past learning of the individual. The design in Figure 1 could have been disintegrated either into the familiar design of B or 3 or 4 or into various meaningless combinations of lines, but the alternations tended to be between the functional units favored by habit [188, p. 73].

To summarize this picture of transitory processes, let us say the following: To serve the needs of effective evolutionary adaptation with the higher animals, there needed to be a neural mechanism which would create various widespread *equivalence effects,* so that the kaleidoscopic changes of stimulation from one situation to another, with hosts of changes of absolute properties, would still permit *neural processes which would be just as efficient as though such changes of stimulation had not occurred.* It has been very difficult to devise electronic devices which could show this same capacity to deal with patterns. Selfridge and Neisser [206] report on the difficulties met in developing an electronic device which could distinguish as many as 10 letters of the alphabet when they were presented with really very few of the variations that manuscript printing and writing actually include. There need be no suggestion that physical devices cannot conceivably be developed to do this; I am merely saying that the physiological mechanisms developed in the course of evolution have reached virtually the limit of what can be conceived as the maximum sensitivity and stability possible in a physical system that would have to do as great a diversity of things as the biological organism does. In summary, one of the fundamental means whereby the organism can adapt effectively to life situations is through dynamically organized self-sustained processes which temporarily represent the environmental situation in far more detail than can be stored—or needs to be stored—as enduring habits or memory traces in the nervous system.

Even if psychologists are interested almost exclusively in behavioral studies of learning, the problem of properties and laws of these transient processes still must be of great concern—provided the major hypothesis of this section of the paper proves to be valid. If what we have considered proves to be the case, it follows that there are more detailed and complex processes out of which learning sometimes results and that the influence of habits is expressed through processes that are powerfully shaped by other influences, in addition to the habit structures themselves. Even if we should want to reexpress Koffka's ideas in different language, therefore, I believe we are likely to find it necessary to go back to certain major concepts discussed in his *Principles of gestalt psychology* [115]. These were problems that concerned him, and he discussed them with extraordinary ability.

Relations between habits and innate mechanisms.   It is easy to slip into the practice of speaking of habits as "neural structures which result from learning." This sort of expression tended to be used in the 1920s particularly. In that period there were very strong tendencies to exclude the concept of innate mechanisms from psychology or to assume that, insofar as there are any, innate mechanisms may be described as chains of very simple reflex connections from stimuli to specific responses. These conclusions did not rest on any intensive research on possible innate functions, however. The assumption was made—virtually without attempt at validation—that any hypotheses about instinctive processes necessarily were blanket explanations which would choke off empirical research on the phenomena in question.

In the years since then, a tremendous wealth of research material has been developed regarding instinctive processes, especially through the efforts of biologists and neurologists. In contrast with what so many psychologists asserted in the 1920s, we now realize that instinctive mechanisms in different species are very diverse and that these mechanisms often help produce instinctive processes which are so complex that we would have to regard them as really remarkable achievements of training [54, 204, 223] if they were products of learning. There is no means, therefore, of drawing a line on the basis of degree of complexity between what has been learned and what is innate. In fact, as the neurologist R. W. Sperry has said:

The patterning of refined and precisely adapted behavioral patterns has been shown in these studies to be developmentally controlled, and in some cases the experiments yield information about the nature of the growth forces involved. . . . In general the developmental mechanisms, as we now picture them, appear to be of sufficient specificity and elaboration that one need not hesitate, on the basis of complexity alone, to ascribe to inheritance any behavior pattern found among subhuman vertebrates. One gets the impression that no vertebrate behavior pattern, excepting perhaps language and certain other of the more complicated human activities, is too complex to be built into the nervous system so far as the proficiency of the developmental and genetic mechanisms is concerned. Where the behavior pattern is acquired by learning instead of being handled through inheritance, one may assume this to be a result of other factors rather than a limitation in developmental capacity. These changes in neuroembryological theory have profound implications for the evolution of behavior and for all concepts relating to the role of inheritance in behavior [195, pp. 131–132].

Furthermore, the research on instinctive processes has brought a new concept of the relations between habits and innate mechanisms. During the 1920s, the argument generally was that (1) if any process is dependent on a mechanism which has been modified at all by learning, it cannot then any longer be said to be purely innate and hence must be described as "learned" or as dependent on habits; and (2) since it is virtually impossible to rule out all possibility of learning in any given case, it is safest to assume that practically all responses are "learned responses" and to study them merely as such.

At present, instead of using such "either-or" thinking, we might well say that any particular functioning of the organism is a product of "more or less modified innate mechanisms." Thus, the biologists' work on diurnal rhythms (see pp. 406–407) has shown that the cycle of twenty-four hours is basically a biologically given phenomenon and that learning and even the immediate external stimulation (alternate light and dark periods of eleven rather than twelve hours each) can change the pace only if the change is not too drastic. Research on the song of birds shows that it can be modified to some extent—but that certain species-characteristic features still exist [18]. Hoarding of food rests partly on innate mechanisms, but partly also on learning [21, chap. 4; 218]. So our speaking of a particular instance as an "instinct" or as a "habit" cannot be dependent on demonstrations that the functioning in question is purely innate or purely learned. In fact, from what we know now, we might expect that nothing may be purely one or purely the other. Behavior whose source is primarily innate may be spoken of as instinctive, even though it might also be profitable to study how the shadings of such performance come through learning. Other instances may be spoken of as matters of habit because the contributions of learning have been so marked. Even here, our view should be that habits are more or less modified innate mechanisms; to be understood fully, they should be investigated from the standpoint of what innate mechanisms existed as structures which were molded and changed by learning.

It is interesting that this was the concept in which Piaget and Lorenz were able to find a common mode of thought. In *Discussions on child development,* Piaget made this comment:

> As regards Lorenz, I would recall the moment . . . where he discovered with surprise that I was by no means an empiricist (in the sense of explaining development and learning by experience alone) and where he briefly described what he termed his "dynamic apriorism." Lorenz's dynamic apriorism, i.e., the concept of an internal activity of the organism developing in constant interplay with acquired experience, is not very far from development through constant interaction of internal and external factors which we ourselves describe as a continuous formation of structure by successive equilibrations [221, pp. 4–5].

In this type of thought, it no longer seems plausible to say that the problem in controlling learning is one of "finding the biologically adequate stimulus for some response and pairing that stimulus with some other stimulus which then will serve as a conditioned stimulus." With certain limited situations, this statement is a useful rule. But in the case of all three types of habits which we have hypothesized, there typically are no biologically adequate stimuli which can produce the process in question. For example, when a person finally learns to follow complex music in a highly skilled fashion, there has been no biologically adequate stimulus which could originally call out this process. When a person looks at some huge basalt crystals along the Hudson River and recognizes that they must have been formed by the cooling of lava deep under the earth's surface, there has been no biologically adequate stimulus which could evoke this representational process—unless we change the meaning of "stimulus" and discard the original significance of the proposition by saying that the biologically adequate stimulus was a prolonged training period which gradually reshaped the innate neural mechanisms into the complexly altered structures which finally exist.

It seems to me that it is through a recognition of this principle that we may resolve the conflict about which Koch [114] has expressed his concern—a conflict between humanistic interests and scientific interpretations of human life. We could well understand the inevitability of such conflict if the evidence of psychological research could be understood as demanding that the psychological process mediating any particular motor act is as relatively simple a process as S-R or conditioning theory has typically asserted. The indications are, however, that psychological processes are very complex events—even more than can be indicated by introspective evidence—and that they can be tremendously developed and elaborated in the course of learning. We should keep trying to identify the neurological and other physiological mechanisms of these processes; but I do not think we need be in conflict with the humanists if we follow the attitude demonstrated by the biologists in their research on diurnal rhythms—a willingness to regard data as primary and not to see theoretical hypotheses as a basis for saying what can or cannot be true.

MAIN PRINCIPLES REGARDING LEARNING AS SUCH

So far, we have been talking about psychological phenomena mostly with regard to processes of a more or less transitory sort. Only incidentally have we spoken about the hypothesized "habit structures" which are assumed to help shape these processes and which, in some cases, are assumed to result from them. We have talked only incidentally about learning (i.e., about the production of such habit structures). However, there are relationships of fundamental sorts between habits and perceptual processes. We need now to explore the nature of those interrelationships, first in general terms, then in more detail.

General Relations between Learning, Habits, and Transitory Processes

It may be that our discussion is assuming more distinction between learning, habit, and transitory processes than actually exists. It may be that, whenever a perceptual process occurs, there will be some degree of learning from it. However, when we consider the tens or hundreds of thousands of separate perceptual details that are involved in any ordinary day, it seems doubtful that the storage capacity of the brain can be so enormous as to encompass all this. It seems doubtful whether there would be sufficient survival value in such indiscriminate storage that we should expect it from general evolutionary principles. Or, more pragmatically, we can be confident of this: Even if all transitory processes leave corresponding habit structures, most of the habit structures thus created are not demonstrable in practical ways; so our main problem is to find out why some transitory processes leave usable residues which bridge between one occasion and another and why others seemingly do not.

Actually, the great majority of psychologists assume this basic idea of a distinction between learning and passing processes, even though they may not employ such terms. The distinction is assumed by the large group of psychologists who accept S-R-reinforcement theory in one form or another. The assumption they make is that a great deal of behavior fails to result in learning because the Rs are not followed by reinforcement.

The present discussion is in agreement with S-R-reinforcement theory in the proposal that not all psychological processes result in learning. As will be seen later, there is also agreement on the proposition that rewards are very important in determining that some situations will produce learning and a depositing of habit structures. But beyond that, the agreement begins to diminish. There is divergence because of these views in cognitive theory: There are a number of important factors which affect learning but which are not recognized by S-R-reinforcement theories— factors which produce learning even when rewards are not operating. Where the factors emphasized by such reinforcement theory operate, we can find some more adequate statement as to why they have the significance that they do.

I put more emphasis on transitory processes than behavior theorists do because—as I have explained earlier—I am assuming that the transitory processes are much more complex than most psychologists believe. First of all, we have pictured psychological activity as a long-term continuing stream of representational processes and trace systems in a state of tonus. Our proposal is that they give a much more complex neural activity than can possibly be expressed by the overt reactions of the organism, especially at any one moment. Second, we have pictured psychological activity as a matter of sensory-organizational activities processing the afferent neural material which is feeding constantly into the central nervous system and which sometimes then produces changes in the representational processes of the organism. Third, we have pictured psychological activity as a matter of motor-discharge processes which transform the preceding perceptual activity into muscular or glandular reactions.

All three types of transitory processes, we assume, can occur without any practically demonstrable learning. Thus, in line with earlier discussion, it is quite possible for a senile person to have very clear-cut perceptual processes without forming any corresponding memory traces or even without being able to use many habits formed within recent decades. I have been told of one elderly man who used to wander away from his house and later ask, "Who was that nice young woman who just brought me home?" He was told over and over again, "That's your son's wife, Phyllis." And when he was introduced to her over and over again, he would say, "I'm glad to meet you, Phyllis." But these temporary perceptual and motor activities did not seem to leave any residue that he could use the next time. So, even if we cannot ordinarily make a distinction between learning and the perceptual and motor processes from which the learning comes, this unusual situation gives us a basis for viewing learning and transitory processes as two separable phenomena. In addition, we have proposed that this distinction is not merely one that comes with impaired body chemistry, but that it is important on two further scores:

1. Where such transitory psychological processes occur, they cannot be understood merely in terms of the enduring neuropsychological structures of the organism. The *enduring* structures are *part* of what governs the process, just as we said earlier that the structures in a room help us to predict the play of sound waves within it.

But the *temporary* causal factors are important also, just as it is true that we must have information about the stimulation producing the sound waves and knowledge about how sound waves are carried (e.g., that they travel more rapidly in warmer air) if we want to understand the sound-wave activity. In the same way, the laws of dynamic organization of perceptual processes are not reducible to laws of learning and of habit structures, but are laws about the transitory processes dependent on *both* habit structures and other factors.

2. The transitory processes do—at least under some conditions—leave changed structures in the brain. To put it more simply, they leave habits, memory traces, associations, reintegrative mechanisms—or whatever we prefer to call them. This fact becomes of increasing significance as we go higher in the evolutionary series, but it is important even in such animals as bees, the octopus, and fish. Therefore, even from the broader standpoint of biology—let alone from the standpoint of psychology and the social sciences—it is very important to seek an understanding of habits and the learning which produces them.

Main Types of Habits to Be Accounted For

From time to time, we have mentioned the three main types of habits which we believe need to be accounted for by the psychology of learning—sensory-organizational habits, representational habits, and motor-discharge or motor-integration habits. Sensory-organizational habits, we have said, are involved where some altered and frequently more finely differentiated mechanisms are built up for perceptual processes that are heavily dependent on current stimulation. Examples are the skills involved in hearing separate voices in a quartet, in seeing the differences between one type of fir tree and another, and in tasting the differences between different types of coffee.

Representational habits constitute a huge and very heterogeneous collection. Most experiments on learning—maze learning, conditioning, memorizing, problem-solving learning, or concept formation—are concerned with the development of representational habits. These are habits where the psychological processes are not so much concerned with producing perceptual patterns which will reflect features of the present stimulation. Instead, they serve to bring into the situation some factors experienced in earlier situations.

Motor-discharge habits or motor-integration habits permit coordinated muscular responses of which the organism otherwise would have not been capable—or which would not have been under very ready control. Good examples are seen in motor coordinations in various speech sounds and in the skilled movements involved in music, sports, and some manual occupations. The complex skills involved, e.g., in tennis or violin playing are partly sensory-organizational and representational habits. Even excluding such elements, however, there remain many important motor-integration habits in such complex habit systems.

In the following discussion, I will include sensory-organizational habits and representational habits in one common group, "perceptual habits." I am not implying that there are no differences in the principles needed to account for learning of the two subtypes of perceptual habits. However, I am impressed with the great number of principles which they seem to have in common; I even have some doubts as to whether there are differences between two types of perceptual habits. It may be that the differences between visualizing something and seeing it directly come merely from the differences in amount of peripheral support for the habit mechanisms common to both processes. Any such suggestion is quite speculative, however. My main reason for grouping so much together here is a practical consideration—most of the principles that I can recognize seem to hold for the learning of both kinds of habits.

Obviously, as I am using the word, "perception" covers a vast domain that ranges from recognizing differences between sounds and tastes to recognizing differences in social philosophies. Furthermore, the term "perception" is understood as covering whatever motivational processes there are. The enjoyment of food by a hungry person and the terror and pain of a trapped animal are just as truly perceptual processes as are other perceptions, such as seeing apparent movement from two dots of light.

I ought also to stress that many representational processes are action-oriented processes. They are perceptions that such and such objectives might be attained and that such and such actions would lead to their attainment. I mention this because I have realized that my chief terms do not intrinsically suggest this action-oriented quality, as does the term "plan" of Miller, Galanter, and Pribram [168]. I would shift to their term except for the fact that I want to analyze the principles involved in a more inclusive class than their term suggests—just as I previously objected to the transactionalists' interpretation of perception as not inclusive enough. I hope that the reader will keep this in mind, however, and not interpret the following outline as reflecting a picture of life as merely a contemplative activity. Any such view certainly would be inappropriate in cognitive theory rooted in evolutionary concepts.

Over-all Principles regarding Perceptual Learning

To think and speak economically about the development of perceptual habits, we need to use some very general hypotheses about the fundamental character and mode of functioning of the organism—more especially, the brain. To provide such hypotheses, I find myself constrained to speak of psychological processes in terms of the analogy between organisms and electronic computers. I hesitate to speak in this way because this is virtually a faddish thing to do. Furthermore, the analogy certainly is inadequate in many ways. However, there may be real values in the analogy. So let me proceed in this vein—perhaps talking in terms of "psychotronic" rather than electronic computers so that we can deviate from the analogy when we need to do so.

Some key notions from this approach would be as follows: The organism cannot possibly have stored in it the neural mechanisms for handling each specific pattern of stimulation and for making the appropriate effector responses to such stimulation on a concrete basis. The organism has to be built so that it can utilize—to some extent and in some ways—the specific details of current stimulation. However, it must do this by using more generalized stored mechanisms or programs for processing the specific details or raw data of each successive moment. Some programs are given innately (e.g., roosters have a program with regard to what to expect and what to do when they see another rooster dart quickly toward them). Others have to be built up by experience. What is stored from learning is not exclusively concrete memories— perhaps none of what is stored is really concrete—but more generalized mechanisms which then can be used to deal with particular concrete materials. The small child does not remember all the specific words that were used as means of indicating past actions, for example. He does not remember "turned," "walked," "ate," "flew," "broke," and so on— except that he apparently does have the means of understanding what is meant by adults who use such terms! Instead, the child stores a program of such a kind that, when he needs to indicate past action, he says "eated," "drinked," and the like.

Some of these stored generalized mechanisms or programs permit more accurate sensory perceptions—as we have already said, the individual can learn to hear quite clearly the difference between closely allied speech sounds which seem indistinguishable to persons from another culture. Some of these programs are even more restricted in generality—a person learns what another person looks like, for example, and can recognize him easily even though he also has the basis for say-ing, "You look a lot older than when I saw you twenty years ago!" Apparently the brain constantly is building up new programs of smaller or larger scope.

A great portion of psychological activity, however, does not necessarily establish any new programs (enduring neural mechanisms), but is merely a matter of using programs plus the immediately given raw data—just as most of the work of a computer is not a storing of programs but merely using them to handle concrete problems.

In this use of programs, the organism gives much more simplicity and stability to its perception of its situation than otherwise might be expected. When a person looks at a table from different directions, he does not see the corners of the table shifting from one size of angle to another. Instead, he somehow takes into account the considerations of perspective, etc., and sees the square corners as square corners. When he shifts his visual fixation from one spot to another, he does not see the room swirling around him—as he would if he kept his eyes motionless and somehow received the same retinal stimulation that he gets with his changes of fixation. Instead, he integrates the material related to eye movement and the material from retinal stimulation so that he per-ceives a motionless objective environment which he is examining visually.

The organism achieves this relative simplicity and stability in process-ing afferent material by disregarding many aspects of that material. It deals with the material selectively and abstractively—just as an electronic computer does. Furthermore, it combines the material into dynamically organized patterns (being a psychotronic computer rather than an electronic computer) and then deals with dynamically organized proc-esses as its functional units.

In this abstractive and organizing activity, using its stored programs, the organism tends to gloss over minor variations in the material, espe-cially if it is not currently set to look for them. It is as though a computer were constituted so that—even though it could develop new programs from the material with which it operates—it had a tendency to develop no more programs than necessary. It is as though the computer were built to work for maximum gain—not necessarily for highest accuracy, but for the best results when taking into account both the results achieved and the costs of achieving them. Exceptions may be tolerated, inconsist-encies glossed over, and so on. Frequently, therefore, the programs are used in situations where—except for the prior development of those pro-grams—the organism would have developed some program other than that which it carries over from its past.

In response to what is fed into it, however, the psychotronic com-puter sometimes finds that it is confronted with input material which is very ill adapted to its present programs. Rather than glossing over its failures, the organism tends to search for some new program that can be used with more effectiveness in such cases. In such search for new programs, the psychotronic computer may be helped by several types of factors. For one thing, the psychotronic computer is likely to go out on some exploratory ventures and try to get some more data—particularly if it is strongly motivated (has another strong program) to get a better program for that type of situation. For another thing, the psychotronic computer, when it is processing material, tends to develop stresses and strains within itself, particularly if the programs are not very economical programs for the data being dealt with, and tends to organize alternative programs. Sometimes, it will end up with two or more programs for processing the same material in different ways and may alternate between them, as though having no basis for saying that one program is more applicable than the other. On the other hand, new programs sometimes are so much better adapted to the materials than former programs were that the new programs are used exclusively—or almost exclusively—even though the old program apparently still remains stored and can be used under some extraordinary circumstances.

The establishment of a new program is partly a matter of producing a new mode of functioning of the psychotronic computer. Often this is very difficult. A number of factors tend to obstruct the production of new types of process from which new programs might be deposited.

However, even when a new process has been produced momentarily, it is not necessarily sufficient for storing a corresponding program. To change our analogy somewhat—we might say that the storage problem is somewhat analogous to the production of chemical changes on the photographic plate in a camera. For the production of demonstrable chemical effects, it is not sufficient that an image of *some* degree of brightness be focused on the plate, but it is important that the focusing should be rather intense; or longer in duration, or repeated. Or demonstrable deposits might be made if earlier focusing of images already had established some residues which now could be built up further. Or— here our second analogy is quite weak—establishing a new program may be made possible because previous activity has established a lot of other programs (complex trace systems) which are congruent with the new one and lend it support. In fact, some new program may provide so simply for what previously had been registered with several poorly related programs that the new program can be quite firmly established with only minimal contributions from the other factors that normally are required for the effective storing of new programs.

To make more clear what is meant by this series of propositions, let me relate them to a few examples of learning.

The first example involves the two drawings in Fig. 2, which gives two adaptations of the Boring wife–and–mother-in-law figure which I employed in an experiment on sensory-organizational learning [144]. When subjects were given no particular prior preparation regarding the figure, about two thirds of the subjects saw the first figure as representing a rather pert young woman, turned so far to the side that her mouth was hidden. The other third saw a hawk-nosed old woman in full profile. However, when the drawing at the right was shown first to other subjects—even though it is different from the first one in many details—none saw the old woman in the composite, but only the figure from

Fɪɢ. 2. Two adaptations of the Boring wife–and–mother-in-law figure which demonstrate very rapid learning and alternatability of use of habits [144, p. 62, part of Fig. 6].

the other previously seen drawing. When shown a drawing that accentuated the features of the old woman, that pattern prevailed with the composite.

Is this to be spoken of as the development and storing of a program? I realize that this does not conform to what some psychologists might understand by the terms. However, this helps to illustrate what I meant above. What we have here is the establishment—very quickly and easily and with no original groping around and choosing between alternatives—of a *somewhat* generalized mechanism which will help determine the processing of particular afferent materials received later. I use this case for another reason, too. It illustrates a type of situation where the individual—after he has built up a program for each of the possible alternative organizations—cannot stare at the composite without having his perceptual pattern shift back and forth from one alternative to the other. This suggests that building one perceptual habit does not "unlearn" the previous one in cases where there are markedly different alternative organizations, but that a second mechanism gets built along-side the other. If one program is used consistently thereafter, there must be special factors of advantage which account for its predominance. We cannot assume that the unused habit has been erased or lost. The learning of a second language does not mean that the first language is unlearned. Alternative habit systems can be related to different types of situations.

A second example would illustrate the point that a second perceptual organization may be very difficult to achieve originally but that, after it has been achieved through some influence or other, it is very unlikely

FIG. 3. An "incomplete figure" which demonstrates difficulty of perceptual reorganization but efficient creation of habit mecha-nisms from the reorganized perception [170, p. 132, Fig. 4].

that the first perceptual organization will recur. When a person looks at Fig. 3, this is apt to look like just chaotic black marks. But, even though a well-unified organization is difficult to achieve—most readers can demonstrate this for themselves by working at this before reading further—the perceptions can hardly return to their former chaotic character once one has seen the little boy and girl stooping down picking a flower.

Here again, the perceptual habit that is learned may seem to many psychologists too simple to be spoken of as a "program." Usually this term refers to rules or procedures which call for some obvious succession of stages in processing of material. I am suggesting that programs include what can be used almost instaneously and that their key feature is the idea that, because of limitations of storage capacity, the organism tends to store somewhat generalized mechanisms rather than highly specific ones. Just as with Fig. 2, so we can make many variations in Fig. 3, yet the individual who has built up the requisite perceptual mechanism will be able to process any of a considerable range of variations without difficulty.

Other examples of programs extend over into very complex problems, as in the field of personality, where we note that each person develops a number of basic programs with reference to how to handle his interpersonal relationships, for example.

Maybe it would be better to express all this by saying that the individual learns concepts, sensory-organizational habits, personality habits, and so on. We need to examine these phenomena of program development and use in more detailed psychological terms too. Ultimately we will need to try to translate these rather global terms into some series of neurophysiological principles. However, there seem to be some important functional similarities between the whole range of instances of learning in all such areas. In a number of respects, the principles we have been stating in terms of programs, etc., seem well designed to call attention to these common features. They may well have some of the heuristic value that we seek in highly abstract formulations.

The More Particular Factors in Perceptual Learning

The basic principle expressed here is that a major part of learning is the production of perceptual organizations. It is as though we were saying that the first part of the business of taking a good photograph is getting a pattern of light focused on the photographic film—e.g., it is a question of what to point the camera at, what filters to use, what focal length to employ, and so on. Then, provided certain other conditions prevail—proper chemicals on the photographic film and sufficient strength of the light that is focused—the film will be left with a pattern of chemical changes which will not correspond to the pattern of light rays that came to the camera, but to the filtered and perhaps somewhat distorted or altered pattern of light rays focused on the film. Putting this in psychological terms, what we may say is that what gets registered is a reflection of what is experienced in the situation by the individual. Thus with the composite in Fig. 2—if a person sees this as the old woman, the perceptual habit that will tend to result from this perceptual activity will subsequently favor further perceptions of the old woman and will tend to prevent an achieving of the second possible organization. Hence, a cognitive interpretation of learning is definitely not an S-S theory—that is, not a theory that "learning produces linkages between stimuli" or that learning can be predicted in anything more than a rough way from what peripheral stimulation is given. Instead, the theory proposes that, provided certain conditions are present—e.g., perhaps ones of intensity, duration, relevance to previous mechanisms, and goodness of pattern of the perceptual process— the fundamental factor required for learning is merely the production of a perceptual process. The production of a perceptual process (not necessarily conscious) is an indispensable condition for the establishment of a corresponding type of neural mechanism.

When we ask what conditions govern the production of perceptual processes, we need to make a distinction between the factors that exert an immediate influence and the factors that operate indirectly. The factors that operate immediately, for instance, include factors of patterning of the external stimulation reaching the organism, the momentary set of the organism, and the particular conditions of satiation of the relevant neural mechanisms. Other factors, however, have to be taken into account; they help to determine what these more immediate factors will be. For example, exploratory activity is of fundamental importance in determining how the organism will be stimulated. In many respects, a situation cannot stimulate the organism unless the organism explores the situation—pushes down a lever, tastes some food given it, changes its position relative to some objects, puts objects into certain relationships to each other, and so on. Back of this, motivation plays a very important role in many learning situations. Unless the organism is strongly motivated in appropriate ways, it will not explore the situation vigorously and persistently, it will not respond to certain stimulations with any strong perceptual processes, and it will not continue to ruminate on certain things that were encountered. The stimulations that are encountered may be arranged by some independent agent, of course. Therefore, some of the practical problems of the psychology of learning are questions about how a teacher or trainer ought to structure situations so that the external conditions provided would be as effective as possible in producing the desired development of perceptual processes.

Factors that tend to produce organizations and reorganizations. We will not try to be comprehensive in our analysis of the factors determining perceptual organizations, but let us mention some main types of influences:

1. *Innate factors sometimes determine perceptual organizations.* Examples have been mentioned from Tinbergen and Lorenz. Studies on imprinting provide some particularly interesting examples of innate predisposing factors.

2. *The general state and completeness of the nervous system, as contrasted with impairment from cerebral injuries, unusual chemical states, or the like, will help to determine perceptual organizations.* Beach [16], for example, demonstrated that cortical injuries tend to impair the efficiency of instinctive maternal behavior in female rats—not altogether preventing

retrieving of the young that wandered from the nest, for example, but leading to much less efficient performances [see also 132].

3. *Differences of intelligence or level of ability of different species are another factor.* Witness, for example, the great superiority of rats over mice and lions over domestic cats, despite the basic similarities of body build. Various observations in recent years testify to the remarkable abilities of dolphins, despite the limitations of their manipulatory organs. For instance, John C. Lilly has reported:

One of the important differences we found in the bottle-nosed dolphin with a 1600-gm. brain is the speed of learning. One can teach a dolphin to push a lever to start or to stop stimuli, *i.e.*, to self-stimulate or to avoid noxious stimuli. The speed with which they learn to do this is amazing. For example, a female dolphin learned to shut off stimulation in her thalamus with one or two so-called trials. A monkey may engage in 100 trials or more, getting his lever by chance, more or less. A porpoise, on the other hand, is immediately interested in his lever and pushes it experimentally the instant you place it in the tank. He will use his beak to push it up, push it down, push it to the right, and push it to the left. He finds in pushing it that he gets the effect that he wants, so he pushes it up repeatedly. There is none of the random effect seen with the monkey at all. In watching such a performance, one has a feeling of purposefulness and speed which are extremely surprising [25, p. 80].

4. *Previously acquired habits or trace systems of the organism can be powerful factors in determining perceptual organizations.* Witness the "learning set" experiments of Harlow [80, 81] which showed that, with training on several hundreds of discrimination problems, monkeys could be brought to the point where further problems could be mastered in a single trial, even if that first trial was an error that the animal was not allowed to correct.

5. *The temporal and spatial patterning of stimulation is often crucial in determining perceptual organizations.* Hull's theory did well to emphasize the temporal relationship between the signal and the unconditioned stimulus in conditioning situations, and the temporal relations between motor responses and rewards in trial-and-error situations [93]. Skinner [210] has emphasized the same factor in his "successive approximation" method of training, where he uses a clicker to bring the arbitrary signal of food into closer temporal relationship to an act than could be accomplished by presentation of the food itself.

6. *Some other extraordinary arrangements of stimulation are sometimes needed for arousing certain perceptual organizations.* In many difficult learning situations, it seems as though something is needed to help the organism to get the idea. After a perceptual organization has been formed with the aid of rather extreme conditions, this then can help

produce corresponding perceptual processes in other situations where the latter could not have been developed. This principle could be illustrated by examples of how a considerable number of scientific discoveries have been made. It also can be illustrated by work with dogs by Pavlov [181] with reference to establishing fine differentiations in conditioning and by Douglas Lawrence in the field of discrimination learning with rats [138, 139].

7. *Temporary states of satiation which have developed before a stimulus configuration is met can determine the perceptual organization.* It is difficult to experiment on this, but an ingenious example of it is possible with Fig. 4, which Krech and Crutchfield [126] use slightly redrawn from Boring, Langfeld, and Weld's *Foundations of Psychology* [23, pp. 227–228; see also 37, 89]. In the case of this particular set of drawings, if one stares fixedly at either *a* or *c* and then quickly shifts

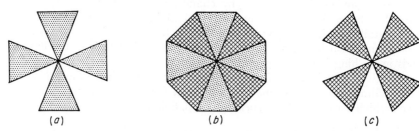

    (*a*)   (*b*)   (*c*)

FIG. 4. Figures that illustrate the effect of satiation in determining original perceptual organization [23, pp. 227–228, Figs. 89, 90; 126, p. 109, Fig. 43].

to *b*, one will not perceive the organization which corresponds to what one previously perceived, but the alternative to it. One could hardly find a better illustration of satiation as a determinant of an original perception of a visual pattern. The same phenomenon ought to be investigated with reference to much more complex stimulus situations.

8. *States of satiation which seem to develop within the nervous system with the continued use of any perceptual mechanism, even when the resulting behavior is definitely rewarded, are of great theoretical interest as another factor in determining perceptual organizations.* In fact, sometimes this influence may be the only means by which to secure some of the possible perceptions of the stimulus situation. For example, a person might be told that Fig. 5 is an unusually complex reversible illusion, with a dozen or more possible patterns, including some three-dimensional organizations which ultimately might be more stable than the more easily seen two-dimensional ones. But if a person is to achieve these various perceptual organizations, he has to stare at this figure long enough for states of satiation to occur which eventually will produce organizations he could not secure at first.

Such changes cannot be understood as consequences of "reactive inhibition" in Hull's sense of muscular fatigue [93] or as consequences of shifts of fixation point, even though both factors have certain influences in some situations. Especially relevant are the findings from the experiment on stabilized retinal images by Pritchard, Heron, and Hebb [187, 188]. Five of the designs they used are shown in Fig. 6. With the ingenious reflecting device which has been developed for keeping the

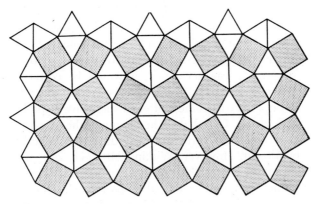

Fɪɢ. 5. A relatively complex reversible figure [67, p. 170].

Fɪɢ. 6. Five designs used in studies of perceptual reorganizations under conditions of stabilized retinal images [188, p. 71, Figs. 9–13].

retinal stimulation almost invariable, despite inevitable tremor movements of the eyes, they found with these figures that a curved-line figure, such as the two left-hand items in Fig. 6,

. . . is relatively stable and quiet, whereas [an angular figure like the third or fourth] . . . is quite unstable and likely to produce an effect of violent motion, as the separate parts appear and disappear in rapid succession. . . . The difference between smoothness and jaggedness appears dramatically in a single pattern such as [the design at the right], in which the angular parts are likely to be active and unpredictable and the rounded parts to form a more stable unit or part figure [188, p. 73].

Such reversals from neural satiation occur also with more complex representations. A substantial number of experiments [46, 47] have now followed up the original experiment by Dashiell [44] and the demonstration by Dennis [48] that rats, run in successive trials through a maze which contains two or more equally economical routes to the goal box at each choice point, have a marked tendency, not necessarily to alternate on successive units, but to alternate in each unit from what was chosen on that unit in the preceding run.

Krechevsky [127, 128, 129] still earlier had demonstrated a tendency for rats not only to develop systematic modes of response but also to shift from some first one to another in much larger sequences of trials in a four-unit-choice apparatus where conditions were varied so that no matter what systematic rule a rat developed, it would be correct on only 50 per cent of the choices. Krechevsky proposed that the rats alternated because of the imperfect usefulness of each successive hypothesis. He was arguing partly from the fact that, if he arranged the apparatus so that a rat would be correct with further use of the same hypothesis, the rat would not abandon it. However, Witkin [240, 241, 242] used an essentially similar situation except that, as in Dennis's situation, the rats were never turned back, no matter on what basis each choice was made. During long training, he found that his rats showed the same effects as Krechevsky's—developing "hypotheses" and also shifting from one systematic type of behavior to another. The satiation factor was probably the key in Krechevsky's experiment, and it is probable—though it ought to be checked—that the only reason Krechevsky's rats continued the same hypothesis when it was made correct is that they made occasional errors which taught them to avoid alternatives to which otherwise they might have shifted.

9. *Repeated stimulation seems to have some possibilities of inducing differentiations, however, which seem explainable neither by satiation nor by feedback of information.* Thus, perhaps the earliest laboratory study of learning is that published by Volkmann in 1858 on the two-point tactual threshold. What he found, as Eleanor Gibson [69] has noted and documented as a frequent subsequent finding, was that the subjects gradually improve in such experiments even when they are not told whether their judgments are correct or not.

Furthermore, these improvements come even where the subject cannot originally make a discrimination at all. Thus, Heinz Werner reports on some of his work:

If, for example, two tones separated by only a few vibrations are presented in succession, at first neither of the tones is definitely distinguishable. Many of our experimental subjects say that both tones are completely ambiguous in their quality. Gradually, often only after repeated hearings, the "contour" of each tone becomes clearly defined and achieves a specific, fixed quality. The tones at first appear approximately on the same uncertain level, but after a time become perceptually separate. . . . The tonal interval actually *stretches out,* and the gap between the two tones widens [237, p. 102].

It seems very probable that something like this is a background development in learning experiments with complex new materials—that the perceptual mechanisms are being developed and elaborated in ways which prepare the organism for much more complex perceptions of many features of the situation than were originally possible.

Factors that tend to prevent perceptual reorganizations.   Our hopes of making good predictions in learning situations depend not only on our ability to recognize factors which tend to favor new organizations, but also on our ability to appreciate factors that make it difficult to replace one perceptual organization with another. This problem is of major practical as well as basic theoretical significance in the field of personality, because a person may realize very strongly that it would be good if he could change his personality habits in certain ways, but may find doing this extremely difficult.

There is, of course, some value in this rough statement: Whatever perceptual organization occurs first will tend to continue on subsequent presentations of the same general situation. Thus, various tachistoscopic experiments have noted that, when a person somehow comes to perceive a picture in some oddly structured way, the faulty perception will tend to continue into later exposures when the length of exposure is such that he ordinarily would have had no difficulty in perceiving the picture correctly [51]. Actuarially, this is a good statement. But, it is only roughly true. It is desirable and possible to analyze the factors which tend to obstruct perceptual reorganizations. As such factors, at least the following can be identified:

1. *Factors which tended originally to bring the first organization into existence will tend still to favor the original organization.* For example, if innate factors favored a certain initial organization, they are apt to do the same later. What was favored by some strong habit originally will thus still be favored. Things that were grouped together because of relative proximity, similarity, congruity, and good form still will tend to remain grouped in the same ways for the same reasons.

2. *Habit mechanisms may have been established in the original situation which now tend to carry over into subsequent situations.* As noted earlier, a person may not realize that he is learning anything when he looks at an ambiguous drawing like the Boring figure and perceives what seems to him like the only natural organization from that. Nevertheless, there still may be a production of factors within him

that will tend later to prevent his shift to other organizations. Any full understanding of this principle needs to go back to other principles as to what produces habits; in itself, it does not take us very far.

3. *The original habit persists because, in some situations, it will have been used not merely as that one specific habit, but as the basis for build-up a larger trace system such as Lashley proposed* (see pp. 410–411). The person, for example, who has established a faulty geographical orientation in a town will have developed analogous orientation habits with reference to innumerable features of the region. Therefore, when he later tries to change his perception to what is factually indicated, this partially activated larger trace system—according to Lashley's hypothesis [135]—will tend to prevent the production of the new and inconsistent perception. Similarly, the individual who built up a conception of himself as handicapped in winning the affection and companionship of others as a child will have learned to perceive countless personal and social situations in the same way. A lot of the stability of personality characteristics probably comes from this.

4. *In some types of situation, the organism is likely to avoid exploration of the situation in ways that might actually lead to changed perceptions.* The experiment by Solomon, Kamin, and Wynne [213, 214, 215] put dogs in a situation where, after the sounding of a signal, they would receive a shock before jumping over a low barrier from one compartment to another. No dog had more than 13 shocks before it began to jump before the signaled shock actually arrived. But further training, with the shocks discontinued, never eliminated this avoidance response, even with a few dogs trained up to 600 trials, 10 trials a day. Some dogs were forced to remain in the compartment by a glass partition over the hurdle. This compulsory "reexploring" of the original situation brought markedly fearful responses at first. These fear reactions subsided as such trials were continued; but when crossing the hurdle was made possible again, most dogs returned to their earlier invariable avoidance behavior under that particular arrangement of the situation. It is easy to see analogies between this and much more complex social and personality situations.

This same refusal to engage in adequate exploratory activity may occur in situations where some positive rewards have been secured, but with less efficiency than might have marked alternative methods. Barnett [12] found that Indian women skilled in the use of digging sticks would not shift from them to steel shovels, even though their husbands, who formerly did no agricultural work, found the shovels more efficient. (Admittedly, this involves complex factors of other sorts, including complex concepts of sex roles, etc.).

5. *Irregularities in the previous relationships of environmental factors may handicap the organism in recognizing any change of such relation-*

ships. Animals that have been rewarded for some given action only irregularly tend to continue the same behavior longer during extinction training than animals that have received invariable rewards. Skinner, especially, has given dramatic illustrations of this phenomenon and has made it a key point in his principles of learning [211]. Pavlov previously had noted the effect in conditioning situations [181]. Particularly the "game-theory" type of approach to learning is exploring many complex instances which ought to be related to such earlier work on the effects of different "schedules of reinforcement" [53, 155, 224]. The principle ought not to be thought of, however, as applicable only to the difficulties that come from irregular rewards or punishments. Other types of expectation habits also are harder to change if the earlier associations of the items in question have been more or less irregular.

6. *Reorganized perceptions may be obstructed because the evidence in later situations is ambiguous and the organism tends to read into the situation the effects it previously learned to expect there.* Particularly in matters of personality is this an important factor. In their social inter-actions, people tend to show so much stereotyped or conventionalized behavior—rather than to frankly express their thoughts and feelings—that an adult cannot easily learn whether his behavior really is pleasing or offending other persons. It is quite easy for an individual, therefore, to keep reading into each present situation the sorts of effects which were demonstrated in more unmistakable form to him by the family group that surrounded him in his childhood.

7. *Reorganized perceptions may be difficult to secure because the individual acts in ways which tend to produce from his environment what he expects to meet.* This probably occurs even in some situations of inter-action with the physical environment, but it is especially important in interactions between complex organisms. Horses are notorious for quick sensing and exploiting of inexperience and timidity on the part of new riders. Animals that have earlier achieved positions of dominance in social hierarchies tend to keep that dominance by confidently assertive behavior which does not any longer match the realities of their relative strength and vigor as compared with that of other animals in the hierarchy. This factor also has tremendous significance in the field of personality.

Factors that tend to produce enduring residues from perceptual processes. We have suggested at various points that only a portion of the huge number of transitory processes in an organism's life leave some enduring habit structures in their wake.

This has been of much concern to S-R-reinforcement theorists, of course. Their general tendency is to say that only those S-R processes that are followed by *rewards*—either of a primary of a secondary sort—will leave increments of habit strength.

We can grant that rewards do seem to be powerful factors in determining what perceptual processes will leave enduring residues. What seems to be the case, however, is that the influence of rewards comes within the range of principles that we already have spoken of. To wit, provided the organism has the relevant motivational condition, some external rewarding factor will tend to produce much more intense or vivid perceptual processes than would otherwise have occurred. Instead of being distracted to other possible perceptual activities, the organism remains preoccupied with the reward and tends to form also a larger perceptual organization of the reward in relation to the means or circumstances that led up to it. Such conditions must produce more extensive and intense brain activity than would have occurred otherwise in the same situation. It seems that the recording of neural changes is to some extent a consequence of *vigorous* perceptual processes rather than very slight processes that have such small motivational quality that they vanish from the brain almost as quickly as they occur.

However, there seems to be every reason for saying that punishments operate in the same way that rewards do, except for the indirect influence that punishments have in producing a search for alternative reactions to the situation. Punishments are suited as naturally to help in the establishment of punishment-expectation habits as rewards are suited to help in the establishment of reward-expectation habits, and for the same reasons. Punishments do not stamp out neural connections; they operate like rewards to stamp in neural mechanisms which reflect the perceptual processes that have occurred—in this case, perceptions that such and such acts or conditions were ones which prefaced such and such painful effects.

Let me quote a concrete example to illustrate the effective learning that punishment sometimes produces. The account is from Madison [150, pp. 311–312]. The child whom he observed was less than a year old at the time of the original incident.

When good weather came and she began to be outdoors . . . her parents had a good opportunity to note that, originally, she was devoid of fear of small crawling or flying insects. She was utterly fascinated by even a tiny ant crawling across the terrace and would follow it with her finger a few inches behind it, "talking" excitedly. She had the same absorbing interest in anything that crawled or flew.

One day she came out on the terrace barefoot and accidentally stepped on a brown honey bee that promptly stung her. She lifted her foot with a scream and saw the bee clinging to the sole of her foot before it flew away. Very soon thereafter, any flying creature—even a housefly—aroused an intense screaming reaction. If she were outdoors and a flying bug came near, she would immediately start crying for protection.

The fear of flying insects continued for years. If a housefly was in her room, she would call a parent and wouldn't play there unless the fly was killed. She collected ladybugs and . . . sowbugs, but didn't like to handle them directly.

Even when she was eight years old, the girl still behaved guardedly with reference to flying insects. Thus, during a vacation trip:

When the family stopped in a cabin full of flying moths, all three children helped clear the cabin by catching them and putting them outdoors. Susan was careful, however, to use a paper napkin to catch them with, never touching them with her hands as the others did freely.

There were various conditions in this case which tended to make it optimal for rapid learning. Thus there was the background of previous attention to insects and the development of perceptual habits with reference to them. The learning situation presented the crucial stimulations with very close temporal and spatial proximity. Yet the role of the factor of punishment in this example hardly can be denied. There should be no neglecting of motivational factors by any perceptual theory of learning.

However, before we decide that the depositing of enduring neural structures can come only through either rewards or punishments, it is worth searching to see whether there are some instances of learning in situations where the influences of rewards and punishments are very slight, if involved at all. I refer to experiments on figural aftereffects, a phenomenon which James Gibson reintroduced to psychologists in 1937 [70]. The perceptions involved in these experiments have no apparent motivational properties except for those required in the background representational processes if a person is to stare fixedly at some simple visual design. For example, in the study of Deatherage and Bitterman [45], the subject simply had to stare at a dot in the center of a circle on a screen before him, then continue to stare at that spot and give a report of the "apparent movement" he saw as a consequence of stimulation which ordinarily would have led him to see a spot of light moving up and down in a straight line somewhat to the left of where the circle had been. After such prior stimulation, the path of the moving patch of light was bowed out to the left, as though avoiding the area where the circle had been.

Do such experiments yield enduring habits, or do they involve merely temporary and completely reversible effects? Köhler and Wallach [124] expected the latter. However, as Köhler and his coworkers continued, they were forced to recognize that the effects looked more and more like learning. The effects developed more strikingly with spaced "practice" than with massing of one long inspection period. (In fact, eight years before Gibson's article, an experiment by Crosland, Taylor, and Newsom

[43] had demonstrated a marked reduction in the Müller-Lyer illusion with merely one brief "trial" each day for thirty days, and with no control of fixation point such as Köhler later assumed would be needed with this same figure.) Furthermore, Köhler and his coworkers finally demonstrated that such figural aftereffects persisted over no-practice periods of two to three months [121, 122, 123; see also 239]. These results do not occur because the subjects are sophisticated and know that they are working with illusory figures. Most of the figural-aftereffect experiments produce unmistakable distortions which did not exist before.

Köhler [123] has been unwilling to speak of these experiments as ones which involve learning, but I see no grounds for excluding them from this field. What is demonstrated in these experiments is the creating of rather enduring effects which come from earlier psychological processes and which help to determine the psychological functioning that will be seen in later presentations of the same or similar situations. That sounds like learning. In fact, I think that Köhler ought to take pride in having demonstrated what is perhaps the most primitive and simple learning situation which has been devised.

But if this is learning, what does it show about the conditions requisite for learning? Here the motivational factors are near the vanishing point. What seems sufficient for learning, therefore, is that there should be some *quantity* of a perceptual process. It seems that this is something like the Roscoe-Bunsen law in vision—*within certain lower limits* the effect of a brief light depends on "intensity times duration" rather than on either alone. What is suggested is that, most basically, learning occurs merely because a perceptual process (of not too slight a sort) takes place.

We need to explore additional factors to see what further conditions must be specified. For example, it may be that learning depends on some possible period of central perseveration or consolidation after the more manifest phase of the perceptual activity has ceased [73, 48a]. Perhaps the factor of "good form" in what is perceived—hard though this factor is to define—may mean that much less intensity of perceptual activity and much less time for consolidation may be required with "good" than with perceptually poorer materials [119]. It may be, as Irvin Rock [193, 194] and W. K. Estes [57, 58] have been proposing, with some new evidence regarding memorizing, that learning occurs in a very discontinuous fashion even when the subjects inspect the same learning materials on every trial.

The Learning of Motor-integration Habits

Even if most research on learning has concerned the development of representational habits, the fact remains that a somewhat distinct type of habit is found in what Osgood [179] has spoken of as "motor skill components." Within many languages, for example, there are special speech sounds which seem very easy to people within the given cultural group, but which are difficult or impossible for persons who have not learned that language in early childhood. These motor-integration habits or motor-skill components seem to depend on the development of neural mechanisms which will produce the proper pattern of efferent discharge from the brain. New functional units for such efferent discharge have to be developed. Even in successive parts of such acts, the timing of successive phases is so close that there is no opportunity for proprioceptive or exteroceptive feedback to govern the immediately following phases of discharge. Furthermore, in addition to such sequential programming, many skilled acts call for a coordinate discharge to many different muscles.

Osgood has given what seems to me like an unusually valuable description of the development of such motor-skill components:

I think that three stages in skill formation could be traced: (1) a very slow and uncertain patterning or ordering of responses on the basis of exteroceptive controls, as in imitating the seen movements of another person; this makes possible (2) a transfer gradually to proprioceptive controls (feedback), accompanied by considerably increased speed of execution; and this more rapid and stable organization in turn makes possible (3) a transfer to central programing in the integrational motor system which we are discussing [179, pp. 83–84].

To this description by Osgood, there are only two points that I would like to add. In the first place, we need to note that in some cases the difficulty in such learning is partly one of being able to produce the requisite muscular responses a first time. Learning to make special speech sounds often involves this problem. Learning to use the muscles again after an attack of poliomyelitis offers another example. Osgood, on the other hand, was speaking about cases where the separate features of the muscular reaction are originally under voluntary control.

In the second place, it is worth noting that there is a certain effect in such motor learning which is much like an effect that is seen in some examples of perceptual learning. I refer to the fact that apparently there is sometimes a need of special means to bring each of two different processes into some longer and stronger state and closer temporal juxtaposition so that there can be some interaction between the two. In the use of complex motor coordinations, there is a first phase that might be described as the choosing and ordering of movements. There is a sense, for instance, in which a typist chooses what keys to strike and how hard to strike each key. He chooses the movement and orders it done. In some cases, however, when the typist inspects what he has typed, he sees that there are certain letters that he did not type hard enough. This perception is so separated in time from the movement-choosing and movement-ordering process, however, that there is little possibility of correcting such faulty habits by this sort of informative feedback. Nor does it seem to be efficient merely to bring the informative feedback into very close time relationships to the performance of a movement if the movement was performed in a highly automatic fashion. With a new typewriter, for example, a typist may continue for quite a time to hit the back-space key because it is located where the tabulator key had been located on his previous machine. He cannot help but note almost instantly that he did not secure the effect he intended. Yet this close succession of action and noting of effects does not prove a sufficient condition for altering the habit. It is as though some neural mechanisms can have such an extremely transient active state that there is no opportunity for the feedback of information to affect them. In such a case, the person may accelerate his learning a good deal by making his choosing and ordering of movements a much more deliberate and emphatic process, as by trying consciously to reach for a certain key and by trying to bring this conscious perception of the action into a unified perception that "*this* action produces *this* effect." If phenomena like this are really important in learning motor-integration habits, it may be that there are some important points in common between motor-integration learning and perceptual learning even if there are some special features in the development of motor-integration habits on many other scores.

INTERRELATIONS OF PERSONALITY AND OTHER AREAS DISCUSSED

In the preceding sections, we have talked mainly about phenomena studied by experimental psychologists. These phenomena have been less complex, typically, than those of personality. As a conceptual framework for the findings from such experimental work, we have discussed mainly a cognitive type of theory such as can be developed from the ideas of experimentalists like Köhler, Lashley, Tolman, Woodworth, Osgood, Bruner, and Lorenz.

In the present section, we need to consider whether this same conceptual framework would be useful also in the field of personality, and, if so, what typical concepts it would suggest. The field of personality is so important, both for theoretical and for practical reasons, that we need to find whether the generalized principles developed in experimental psychology apply also to this more complex field where most of the work of identifying variables and causal relationships has had to depend on other types of investigation, rather than on laboratory research. In an abstract sense, it certainly seems that many phenomena of personality are matters of learning, many other phenomena of personality are matters of perception, and so on. Accordingly, we might well expect that the principles which have been developed through the study of simpler phenomena by experimental research might also apply to this much more complex material of personality, suggesting some hypotheses regarding personality which could not be developed in the field of personality originally but which perhaps can be checked there and found applicable. In addition, there may be heuristic contributions in the other direction. Psychologists may find that the special materials and perspectives of studies of personality may suggest some valuable hypotheses for other portions of psychology as well. So if there are some gains that can be anticipated from comparisons of fields of work which superficially look markedly different from one another, it should be rewarding to try to interrelate what we know about personality and what we know about the simpler processes that can be subjected to laboratory investigation.

To deal with this problem, we must first stake out what we mean by personality. This is not easy. Probably because the phenomena of personality are so complex and, in many respects, so subtle, psychologists have been unable to get any generally accepted formal definitions of personality, and it often happens that the definition an author gives is demonstrably inconsistent with what he includes in a chapter or textbook about personality. Nevertheless, psychologists do show substantial agreement in what they write about when they write about personality, what they select when they plan research on personality, and what they refer to when they construct tests which they speak of as personality tests. Therefore, perhaps the best way to stake out our territory is to cite some examples representative of these "ostensive" definitions of personality and then to say that personality is whatever class of phenomena is functionally equivalent to such examples.

Some typical concrete material would be as follows: In virtually the same objective situation, when three different persons are given some important and useful criticisms of their work, one person responds with caustic attacks on the person providing the criticisms, another person feels grateful for the helpful suggestions and perhaps also expresses this gratitude, and the third person feels devastated because he has "again produced a hopelessly inadequate product." As members of a committee, one person is tactful and persuasive, another person is too submissive, and a third person, although independent in his thinking, is too uncommunicative to be useful. In their recreational life, one person has few interests outside of his professional activities, another person has a great diversity of interests, many of which he enjoys regardless of whether or not he has a chance to share the activity with another person, and a third individual feels restless and dissatisfied unless he has an opportunity to spend almost all his leisure time in the company of other persons. Some other characteristic material of the field of personality might be suggested by mentioning the kinds of problems dealt with by psychotherapists. Still other material might be illustrated by describing some characteristics of small children, as by noting the petulance and demanding behavior of one small child and the happy, outgoing tendencies of another.

Such examples certainly involve phenomena of motivation, especially of emotional sorts. Even though it is incomplete, one can sympathize with the sort of definition given by those who say that personality is a matter of emotional tensions and means of handling them. In contrast, the phenomena studied by laboratory research on perception have involved almost exclusively those effects which are motivationally neutral. There are marked differences, too, between the kind of learning studied in the laboratory and the kind of learning typically involved in personality. For one thing, it seems that people have great difficulties in changing any of their personality habits (assuming we may use this term). Even when they find that they desperately want to make some such changes because of the suffering that their personality characteristics are bringing to themselves and to other persons, they find it extremely difficult, if not impossible. In contrast, the phenomena of learning which are studied in laboratories are in fields where habits can be learned and unlearned within relatively brief periods of time.

It seems no wonder, therefore, that a large portion of the work of development of ideas about personality has been accomplished by workers who believed that experimental psychology would have very little relevance to their work. The separation between experimental psychology and the psychology of personality has resulted also from the fact that much of the development of concepts about personality has come from psychiatrists. The most notable names in the psychology of personality have been such as Pierre Janet, Sigmund Freud, Alfred Adler, Carl Jung, Karen Horney, Harry Stack Sullivan, and Frederick Allen. The background of training and knowledge of such persons gave them little contact with experimental psychology. It is true, too, that in earlier periods psychology itself was much less adequately developed and was not ready to contribute to interrelational thinking in the way that it can now. At the present time, however, the psychology of personality is an area of major interest to psychologists. Part of the reason for this is the extensive development of clinical and counseling psychology, where a knowledge of personality is one of the tools of the trade. Beyond this, however, mainly as a result of the growing capacity of psychological research to handle more and more complex phenomena, the psychology of personality is an important field in its own right.

Technical work on personality has followed one or another of five major types of approach. These are the factor-analytic approach, the psychoanalytic or Freudian approach, the S-R type (in some ways we should say "types") of approach, the cognitive type of approach, and the idiographic type of approach advocated by Gordon Allport [4] and a number of earlier psychologists and philosophers [243, pp. 397–406]. The following discussion will focus most heavily on cognitive interpretations of personality. Some discussion of the other approaches is also needed, however, to show the relationships of this one mode of conceptualization to the other four.

At first thought, the factor-analytic and the idiographic approaches might seem closely related. Both of them place great emphasis on the idea that what is important in personality are the *differences* between persons. Except on this very general point, however, these two approaches are almost diametrically opposite each other. The idiographic approach calls for intensive studies of particular individuals, and it proposes that the important explanatory concepts that might be developed are ones which would apply solely to the given individual. The factor-analytic approach attempts to define dimensions that may be applied to people generally. This approach, because of its particular methods, has to rely on data that can be secured on very large numbers of individuals. Hence it has to rely on data which can be secured by relatively brief observation or testing or questionnaire responses of each person. One is tempted to add that these two approaches differ also in that the factor-analytic method emphasizes statistical analysis of data whereas the idiographic approach typically relies on the psychological processes of the investigator to do the analyzing. This difference is not basic, however. Intensive studies of individuals, attempting to develop "individual-specific laws," might similarly use statistical analyses of data collected on any given individual. The main difference—and it is a profound one—is the difference between the attempt to identify common qualities through analysis of relatively superficial measurements on large hosts of persons and the attempt, on the other hand, to penetrate to terms and laws that would apply only to the given individual.

I have tried to state this matter with some care, chiefly because there has been a tendency to believe that cognitive personality theory is essentially and basically idiographic. This is the verdict that A. R. Jensen [99] expressed in his review of the book on personality by Peter Madison and myself [150], which approached personality in terms of the sorts of concept presented throughout the present paper. Let me return to this matter at the conclusion of this section. In the meantime, I will say merely two things: First, the whole question of idiographic study needs to be restated. Second, although idiographic work (as thus reconceived) is more closely related to cognitive personality theory than to any other type of personality theory, the main reason why cognitive theorists are interested in intensive studies of individual cases is that these studies are a valuable means of identifying some variables and relationships which are important more generally, rather than unique to the individual under investigation. The objective of cognitive personality theory is to develop abstract terms and abstract principles that will help us to understand (e.g., to make predictions regarding) any given individual by carrying over what has been learned from studying other individuals. Cognitive personality theory, as such, is not interested in what is really unique.

Let me consider, next, the factor-analytic type of work. The advocates of it make strong claims. Judging by what they say [39, 59, 74] one might conclude that factor analysis is the method *par excellence* for identifying the fundamental variables involved in personality or even that the factor analysts are the only personality psychologists occupied with trying to identify such fundamental variables. Actually, of course, the factor-analytic type of work is merely one of several methods of attempting to identify the fundamental variables involved in differences of personality. Virtually all research on personality and virtually all other psychological research is an attempt to identify fundamental variables and to determine the functional relationships between such variables. The fundamental issue between factor analysts and other workers in the psychology of personality is not, therefore, the question of whether research on personality ought to "analyze factors" that lie back of the superficially diverse or phenotypical material with which any research starts. Instead, it is the question of how this analysis may most profitably be attempted. The criticism from other types of approach is that the factor-analytic method, because of its having to rely on data on large numbers of persons and hence on relatively superficial data, is seriously limited in what it can discover. This is not to deny that factor-analytic work has importance for some purposes, such as the selection of personnel for certain types of jobs, where it is not important whether the "fundamental factors" identified have any validity other than their efficiency for practical predictions with the particular population to which they are applied. For other purposes, however, the usefulness of factor-analytic work is very limited.

Fundamentally, I can see no reason why research in the field of personality should be expected to have a different basic character from research in any other scientific area. Work in other areas indicates that factor analysts have given a reversed picture of how scientific work proceeds. We do not identify fundamental factors first and then investigate functional relationships; rather, it is the study of functional relationships that leads to the identification of significant variables. Furthermore, most of this work cannot proceed through some blind quantitative analysis of the kinds of data which the field already knows how to recognize; it has more of the character of a sleuthing expedition in which all sorts of clues have to be used to get ideas about what to single out for more intensive observation. Take research on nutrition, for example. This has given us some tremendously useful knowledge about the fundamental factors in diet. This research often started with shrewd field observations, as with the observation that sailors who ate limes did not develop scurvy, that chickens that happened to be fed on polished rice developed symptoms that looked like the symptoms of people with beriberi, that people who lived in certain mountain regions tended to develop goiters, and that people who grew up in certain small areas in the United States tended not to have dental caries even though their teeth sometimes were a bit discolored. Starting with such clues, nutritional research has used laboratory methods, broad field studies, and so on—but primarily has isolated and perhaps intensified the influence of selected factors to see whether the hypothesized functional relationships would be established and thereby lead to certain new classifications of foods. It has been the same in other fields. As far as I can see, in no other sciences are there methods analogous to factor-analytic methods as used in psychology. Nor does it seem likely that, for basic scientific purposes, the factor-analytic approach will have any reason to claim that personality is a peculiar exception.

The most important means of trying to understand personality therefore seem to be the group of approaches which use methods fundamentally analogous to those used in nutrition research, comparative psychology, and the psychology of learning. This basic methodological orientation is shared by psychoanalytic, S-R, and cognitive approaches to personality, despite important differences between these approaches on many other scores. The following discussion, therefore, will be concerned with them. Continuing the exploration undertaken in the earlier parts of this paper, this discussion will place greatest emphasis on a cognitive type of approach to personality. The discussion will proceed, however, by describing some main points of agreement and disagreement, first between psychoanalytic and cognitive theories and then between S-R and cognitive personality theories.[1]

[1] As summaries of psychoanalytic theory, the most useful references, I believe, are Freud's *Civilization and its discontents* [64], Anna Freud's address [63] at Clark University in 1950, Ernest Jones's biography of Freud [100], Erikson's presentation of relatively recent Freudian thinking [56], Madison's careful review, *Freud's concept of repression and defense* [162], and the survey discussions by Monroe [169a] and Progoff [189]. The outstanding presentation of S-R theory in general is Kimble's [107]. As presentations of S-R personality theory, main references are Dollard and Miller [50], Bandura [11], Shaffer and Shoben [207], Rotter [199], Wolpe [244], and Lundin [156]. The references on cognitive theory

Within this discussion, we can indicate only in broad strokes the differences between these three types of personality theory. As a matter of fact, even with reference to cognitive theory we can indicate only some major interrelations between personality psychology and the more general phenomena of learning and perception. The whole body of main principles in the preceding sections of the paper apply as significantly to personality as to other aspects of life. In fact, as probably is apparent, part of the reason for the particular character of the preceding account is the fact, mentioned on p. 369, that the data and hypotheses which have interested me have come not merely from experimentalists such as Lashley, Köhler, and Tolman but also from personality theorists. Hence, the preceding sections have already been presenting interpretations which have been suggested by trying to interrelate a rather broader array of fields than many psychologists have felt it profitable to work with. Even in a short section, however, we can indicate some main theoretical issues which suggest that some heuristic values might come through relating personality with experimental work on learning and other topics.

Areas of Agreement between Cognitive Personality Theory and Psychoanalysis

The following are some main contributions from psychoanalysis which cognitive personality theorists generally accept as important and valid contributions to their own thought:

1. Broadened concepts of the proper method of studying human life. The psychoanalysts have called for methods of study that are more complex than either the old-style introspective observations or the typical behavioral methods of experimental laboratories. They call for long, intensive studies of particular individuals under conditions which might at least partially free the individual from repressive influences which otherwise would prevent his communicating, or even himself being cognizant of, some of his own behavior and inner processes.

2. Broadened concepts of the kinds of psychological processes. Psychoanalysts have given convincing evidence of the existence of repressed

---

fall in two groups: on the one hand are the writings of psychotherapists such as Adler, Horney, Fromm, Jung, Sullivan, Rogers, and George Kelly; on the other hand are the writings of cognitive personality theorists whose thinking has developed more from the side of experimental psychology. For the psychotherapists, valuable summary discussions are those by Hall and Lindzey [77], Ansbacher [6], and Progoff [189], and other typical references are books by Bottome [24], Horney [91], Mullahy [174] on Sullivan, Gerhard Adler [1] on Jung (see also Neumann [176]), Rogers [197, 198], and Kelly [103]. On the side of experimentally oriented cognitivists, mention may be made especially of Murphy [175], Lecky [141], Lewin [38], Diamond [49], Leeper and Madison [150], McCurdy [159], and Gordon Allport [4].

unconscious processes. They have indicated, furthermore, that repressed processes are not merely relatively primitive impulses and thoughts but also highly critical "superego-type" processes and, in addition, defensive processes which the main operating self of the person uses against what it sees as threatening occurrences of these two other types of processes. Cognitive psychologists, although making certain changes of interpretation, have found value in these points, as well as in the proposal from psychoanalysis that there are long-sustained streams of representational processes of a multilevel sort [109]. The psychoanalytic work, even after one does some skeptical culling, also gives a lot of indication of highly bizarre psychological content.

3. Increased realization of the importance of motivation. Academic psychology has tended to deal either with motivationally neutral processes (as in most of perceptual research) or with physiologically based motives (as in most work with animals). The psychoanalysts, on the other hand, have dealt with more complex material which illustrates the great importance of emotional motives. The psychoanalytic inventory of types of motive may be more limited than it should be, but there is no doubt that the psychoanalysts have led to the discovery and honest facing of some facts about the strength that sexual and destructive motivation may have in human life and about the potentially great strength of anxiety and fear. Their work has done a great deal to show that the motivational aspect of psychological activity is much more powerful in determining psychological processes than was realized previously.

4. Identification of major techniques used in handling inner motivational conflicts. Other psychologists may regret the almost exclusive preoccupation of psychoanalysts with methods of handling intrapsychic conflicts as contrasted with interpersonal relationships of various sorts. Nevertheless, these psychologists generally agree that some very important strategies which are developed by the individual are those for handling emotional conflicts within himself, and they borrow heavily from the psychoanalytic contributions on this topic.

5. Appreciation of the high substitutability of different expressions of motives. The psychoanalytic treatment of this problem has not followed exactly the same line of thought which would be natural in cognitive theory, which would relate substitutions to goal directedness of activity. The Freudian theory views motivation as similar to steam pressure which, if blocked from escape at other points, will keep on building up until it finds some means of bursting through the containing structures at some other and perhaps unexpected point. But still, as compared with the general neglect by S-R psychologists of the phenomena of response generalization or response equivalence, the efforts of psychoanalysts have provided a wealth of clinical data showing that strongly motivated behavior and thought may have some very indirect expressions. It is an important concept, for example, that the content of compulsive and obsessive tendencies does not usually reflect directly the motivational sources from which these symptoms come but serves as a substitute for what is more threatening to the individual.

These contributions of psychoanalytic theory have been more thoroughly used by cognitive personality theory than sometimes is asserted. A quite inaccurate picture on this score has been given by the influential and generally very capable book on *Theories of personality* by Hall and Lindzey. Speaking of "the conception of man evolved by Adler, Fromm, and Karen Horney," Hall and Lindzey said:

In a world which has been torn apart by two great wars and the threat of a third one, not to mention the many other forms of violence and irrationality that men display, the picture of a rational, self-conscious, socialized man strikes one as being singularly inappropriate and invalid. One can of course blame society and not man for this deplorable state of affairs, and this is what these theorists do. But . . . If man is so self-conscious, so rational, and so social, why has he evolved so many imperfect social system? [77, p. 154].

Later, speaking about Carl Roger's ideas, they said similarly:

The self-as-object . . . is consciously experienced and these experiences it is assumed can be directly communicated to the investigator. The concept of unconscious motivation plays virtually no part in Rogers' thinking. The person is pretty much what he says he is [pp. 497–498].

Now, admittedly, Rogers has believed that, as a matter of therapeutic procedure, a therapist should focus on trying to understand the client's conscious perceptions of each successive moment. But this has not meant, at all, that Rogers has believed that "the person is pretty much what he says he is"! As a matter of fact, Hall and Lindzey should have gone back to an earlier page of their own, where their characterization ran as follows:

Rogers points out that people will often stoutly maintain and enhance a self-picture that is completely at variance with reality. The person who feels that he is worthless will exclude from awareness evidence that contradicts this picture or he will reinterpret the evidence to make it congruent with his sense of worthlessness. . . . Rogers says that there are levels of discrimination below the level of conscious recognition, and that the threatening object may be unconsciously perceived [77, p. 485].

Similarly, they should have said that, although Adler attached great importance to the person's conscious memories of the earliest vivid experiences he could recall and although Adler believed these were especially instructive as indicators of the basic "life style" of the individual, this did not mean that Adler felt that any person ordinarily could realize the implications of such early memories [6, 24]. On the contrary, Adler maintained that the person almost never is conscious of the more generalized meaning of such early memories in his life and is very resistant to any efforts to explain the meaning of such memories. Instead, he sees them as oddities.

With most cognitive theorists, therefore, there is major acceptance of Freud's concept that the person tends to repress what he sees as threatening to his personality organization and that repressed processes, though unconscious, can exert very important influences.

Points of Disagreement between Cognitive Personality Theory and Psychoanalysis

Cognitive personality theorists see psychoanalytic interpretations as overconstitutionalistic, even though they themselves would emphasize that the organism must be understood as an exceedingly complex ongoing system which has to maintain itself in an environment which, at any given moment, may be giving it only relatively simple physical or chemical support. The cognitive theorists agree that the organism needs a number of innately given motivational mechanisms to produce the goal-directed activity likely to favor the biological survival of the individual or at least the species. They propose, however, that these motivational mechanisms must include not merely such physiologically based motives as hunger, thirst, sex, and discomfort from excessive heat or cold, but also some emotional motives such as the gregarious urges in certain species and the exploratory tendencies which are prominent in highly complex animals. However, the cognitive theorists would also insist that we need to realize that the organism is not a real unity in itself. It is made to function in an environment. Not only does it use that environment in some immediate way, but the organism needs to be shaped and remade in some respects by that environment so that the organism will be adapted to survive in a variety of situations, rather than restricted merely to some particular environmental niche. The organism accordingly has to have perceptual processes which will produce profoundly different effects in different situations. The organism also must be able to carry over, through learning, some effects from what has been encountered in earlier situations.

As the cognitive theorists view things, therefore, the requirements of motivational theory cannot be met just by instinctive forces which well up from inner constitutional sources, according to the psychoanalytic theory of instincts. Even though some human motivation must be of this intrinsic sort, there must be other motivational potentialities which will develop differently under different circumstances, just as the potentiality for tanning of the skin gets utilized more in some environments than in others. Innately, according to cognitive personality theorists, there exist the *beginnings* of social feeling, affection, exploratory interest, intellectual interests, and enjoyment of muscular activities. But these initial potentialities must be greatly developed by learning before the adult can possess the kinds of motivation that are highly desirable for him. Similarly, the hostility and exaggerated erotic motivation seen in some persons are not to be viewed as revealing what would appear also in other persons if it were not for their "mechanisms of defense" but represent either the development of some other motivational potentialities in these areas or represent, as Horney has suggested, particularly with reference to sex motivation, the displacement of other motives into these other areas. This concept of the need for development of emotional potentialities is not the whole of what Gordon Allport has urged with his concept of the functional autonomy of motives [3, 4] but is a main consequence of his concept that the motives which operate in adults are not the same motives which were present innately in infants but are the "oak trees" which have developed by learning from the "acorns" present then.

This charge that psychoanalysis is overconstitutionalistic would doubtless be denied by psychoanalysts. They would point to the fact that Freud's case histories often describe environmental situations which produced such and such neurotic effects. They would emphasize Freud's general idea that the ego is a system of processes for recognizing environmental realities and for trying to guide the rest of personality functioning so as to take environmental realities into account. But, nonetheless, Freud spoke mostly about inner constitutional factors. He gave little attention to the problems of how the ego is developed. He emphasized motivational forces that existed innately in the id and which, as he saw them, were virtually unmodifiable by learning and were determined in their quantitative aspects by constitutional factors rather than by learning and by current situational factors. In the discussion of early childhood, his emphasis was on constitutionally given stages of maturation and their influences, rather than on what life situations might, for example, make the inevitable Oedipus conflict more or less severe than it otherwise would be.

It is of course true that the psychoanalysts have said that the means of expression of motivation may be changed by learning. But the hypothesis regarding the basic motivational forces themselves has been that they are virtually unmodifiable. Let me quote, for instance, from a paper given by an important psychoanalytic theorist, Merton Gill, at a symposium on psychoanalytic theory at the annual meeting of the AAAS in 1954:

Psychoanalysis still adheres to a view of motivation as built on powerful drives rooted in the biology of the organism. However much derived motivations are recognized, psychoanalytic theory still views behavior as essentially motivated by and occurring in the context of bodily drives. Drives for security, success, prestige, status, seem, relative to these basic drives, "superficial" to the psychoanalyst. He thinks rather of castration fear, oedipal wishes, cannibalistic impulses, homosexuality, or a drive to rend and destroy. It is often said that the analyst's preoccupation with these primitive impulses stems from his almost exclusive concern with disturbed personalities. But the analyst believes that the normal person, too, is occupied with dealing with such impulses. The *difference* between the normal and the neurotic he sees, not in the root of the tree of the motivational hierarchy, but much closer to its crown [72, p. 7].

The most natural and satisfying expression of such motives, Freud said, was hardly adapted to the needs of complex society. It is not surprising that Freud drew the conclusion that, even if we keep on having civilization, it will be *Civilization and its discontents* [64].

Behind the other differences mentioned above, perhaps the most important difference between cognitive personality theory and psychoanalytic theory is the following: Psychoanalysts have assumed that psychological processes should be conceived of as separable into two distinct types. Some psychological processes (ego processes) are primarily intellectual or rational and nonmotivational in character. Some other psychological processes (id processes), rather than being *both* intellectual and motivational in character, are solely motivational or solely energizing. As I understand cognitive theory, it needs to be stated, instead, in terms of the proposition that all the processes the analysts refer to when speaking about the functioning of the id are perceptual or cognitive processes in just as true a sense as are the ego processes. Let us assume that there are crude, selfish, and sometimes brutal processes in human beings, such as one's consciously or unconsciously wishing that he could smear feces over himself, that he could flush his baby brother down the toilet, that he is in danger of having his penis cut off because he would like to do the same to his father, and so on. But if and when such psychological processes exist, they are perceptual processes. They are processes with definite and rather specific intellectual content to them, even if this be unconscious. They are processes which portray that "such things will tend to happen if I act in this situation in such and such ways." So, actually, if we take from psychoanalytic writings not the highly abstract statements about the id as merely a repository of energies but the more particular statements about specific phenomena attributed to the id, we find no basis for the psychoanalytic tendency to characterize id processes in purely motivational terms.

As has been said, the cognitive theorists doubt that the psychoanalysts have given an altogether valid picture of the innate motives of human life. But a more important criticism that cognitive theorists would make of psychoanalytic theory is this: There is no such *qualitative* distinction between id processes and ego processes as Freud assumed. There are merely psychological processes—perceptual processes, if you will—and the "id processes" are as truly situation-representing processes as are some of the motivationally neutral processes which we often refer to when we want to speak about intellectual processes. According to cognitive personality theory, we might, if we wished, say that the id is whatever set of processes are socially disapproved in a given culture or family group, so that the individual therefore comes to see them as threatening, but that they are not inherently and qualitatively different from other processes ("ego processes") which are approved by the given social group. This proposal will fit in with a lot of anthropological knowledge. But it would be a really drastic change from the rather central psychoanalytic hypothesis of the differences between id and ego as they use these terms.

Areas of Agreement between Cognitive and S-R Personality Theories

There are various concepts which cognitive theories share with S-R theories and, in some cases, have derived from them. Both theories agree that a great portion of motivation is a function of current stimulation and past training, rather than just welling up from constitutional sources. Both theories attach great importance to rewards and punishments and even to symbolic or secondary rewards and punishments. Both theories find a natural place (in fact, it seems sometimes that cognitive theory can find a more natural place) for the S-R evidence that highly irregular reinforcements produce extreme resistance to extinction. Both theories welcome the evidence that personality habits sometimes are hard to change because the organism has learned avoidance tendencies which prevent the appearance of exploratory behavior which could lead to some new learning. Both theories accept many other principles in common. In his 1943 *Principles of behavior* [93], for instance, Hull made major use of Tolman's 1932 concept [228] that a major distinction needs to be drawn between learning and performance. Many other examples could be given.

Areas of Disagreement between Cognitive and S-R Personality Theories

From the standpoint of methodology, the fundamental criticism directed against S-R thinking by cognitive theorists is that S-R psychologists do not develop their concepts of mediating variables by using a wide diversity of situations to provide data from which to develop inferences. The S-R psychologists (except Skinnerians) agree that "learning," "habits," and similar terms are names for inferred variables. But though recognizing this, they do not also recognize that an adequate concept about any such not directly observed entity can come only through giving that inferred entity an opportunity to demonstrate what it would yield under a really wide range of conditions. They proceed too much, instead, as a physicist might proceed if he concluded that all that could be learned about the structure of a protein molecule would be revealed by one X-ray diffraction photograph of a protein crystal, rather than hypothesizing that protein molecules might have enormous complexity of structure which could be revealed only by integrating the data from some tremendous number of such photographs [105].

For instance, S-R psychologists depend a great deal on the concept that hunger for food is a significant factor in animal behavior. They tend to equate this with some general condition which comes from physiological deficits. Sometimes they speak about the demand for food as a matter of incipient chewing movements. But S-R psychologists tend not to give due weight to the experiments by Tinklepaugh [226, 227] in which he showed that monkeys and chimpanzees, if they have previously seen a preferred food hidden under a cup during trials for delayed-reaction capacities, will show marked signs of frustration and refuse to eat what they find if the preferred food is secretly replaced with a less preferred food during the interval between the point at which they see the food hidden and the point at which they lift the cup and uncover the food. In these experiments, the animals would readily eat less preferred food (lettuce) if they had seen lettuce hidden; but when grapes or bananas were what they had seen hidden and then, in their absence from the room, this food was replaced with lettuce, they acted as though their behavior was affected not merely by a general food need nor by some nondescript chewing movements but by a more differentiated process somewhat specific to the *kind* of food.

Using such broader ranges of data, the cognitive theorists believe, as explained before, that motives are perceptual processes, that learning results in the development sometimes of very complex processes that mediate between stimuli and overt responses, that learning sometimes comes by slow, cumulative changes of basic patterns which already have been established and sometimes by dramatic reorganizations of such patterns, and that learning cannot be predicted in any simple way from relative numbers of reinforcements and nonreinforcements (unless one is speaking, as in genetics, about statistical outcomes rather than what will occur in specific cases).

Similarly, to the cognitive theorists, the factors that produce learning are by no means the relatively few factors emphasized in reinforcement theories. For example, the small child may acquire personality habits partly by having perceptual norms established in him even by persons whom he does not admire or wish to imitate. Or as Adler [6, 24] proposed, a small child may develop his basic personal constructs or "life style" partly by taking stock of what life strategies are employed with outstanding success by a close sibling—not by copying this but by choosing some strategy markedly different from a strategy seen as giving him no grounds for successful competition. The experiments on sensory perception indicate that every stimulus situation is more or less an ambiguous or *vieldeutig* situation and that in such situations perceptual processes may produce quite different perceptual organizations. Carrying this over into their interpretation of learning situations, the cognitive theorists hypothesize that quite different habits might be established in different learners in what is, as near as can be produced, the same objective stimulus situation.

In the course of time, such concepts may get thoroughly absorbed into S-R theory, just as in his concept of reaction potential [93, chap. 14] Hull absorbed the concept that there can be a motivational control of the utilization of habits [143]. But, until a considerable number of such concepts are absorbed (or disproved and dropped from cognitive personality theories), there will be a number of major differences between cognitive and S-R theories, and not mere differences of terminology.

The Problem of Changing Personality Habits

As a means of making a final comparison between the three types of approach to personality, we might consider why personality habits are so hard to change even when a person wants to do this, and what factors permit such changes when they occur.

The psychoanalytic hypothesis on this problem includes two main points: First, the individual has difficulty in changing any crucial features of his personality because the important factors are repressed and unconscious; second, the unalterable impulses of the id are not very palatable or useful impulses anyway, even if they could be faced, and consequently there are some inherent and inevitable difficulties in trying to mold human personality into a form suited to cooperative, disciplined, altruistic living.

S-R personality theorists sometimes accept these same points, as in the case of Dollard and Miller [50]. S-R psychologists are apt to add a number of other points as well. Thus, first, many habits are hard to change because the habit was acquired under conditions of intermittent or irregular reward or punishment. Second, many personality habits produce avoidant reactions, and the individual refuses to reexplore some situations or types of behavior which were punished previously, as in the case of the dogs studied by Solomon and his associates [213, 214, 215].

Third, the environment of the individual usually continues much the same, and it operates to keep training the individual to use the habits which he already has established. Fourth, the individual does not encounter any conditions which evoke some new and appropriate response and provide rewards for it. Fifth, even if the individual does not obtain any external rewards by his habitual behavior, he typically is obtaining some secondary reward, such as some reduction of an acquired drive of fear within himself, and this serves to maintain the strength of the faulty habit.

A cognitive personality theory, I believe, would accept all the above concepts except the psychoanalytic verdict about the inherently unsuitable nature of basic human motivation. But in addition to sharing these points with the two other theories, a cognitive personality theory would add several additional points, as follows: First, personality habits are hard to change partly because, as factors that help to determine perceptual processes in objective situations, they lead different individuals to experience quite different things in the same objective situation. The activity of the individual is affected not by what is objectively present in the stimulus situations he meets but by the perceptual organization which that objective stimulation helps to stir up. Second, personality habits are hard to change because they typically get built into massive trace systems such as Lashley has hypothesized (see pp. 410–411). Third, personality habits typically are hard to change because it is so difficult for the individual, even from a strictly intellectual point of view, to identify what pattern of experience he now uses or to conceive of a pattern of experience and a strategy of life which would be different from what he already employs. This difficulty does not come solely from repressions and resistances, though they complicate the problem. Fourth, the individual has difficulty in changing his personality partly because he tends to act in such a fashion as to create the effects which his personality makes him anticipate, even when these are effects which he deplores. The person who feels that others are indifferent to him tends to make other people indifferent; the person who feels that others are hostile tends to make other people hostile; the person who feels that others are likely to be sympathetic and helpful tends to make them so [140, 174].

Where personality habits are changed, the psychoanalysts point to those influences that have helped the person become conscious of what had previously been repressed. S-R psychologists point to the evocation of new (particularly overt) responses and the prompt provision of reinforcements for those. A cognitive theorist, I believe, would say that the fundamental factor involved in personality change is the production of a new and emotionally powerful organization which will give some more satisfactory framework for certain facts which the individual would be unable to forget or lay aside—an organization which takes cognizance of such realities, but gives them a new meaning. There are other points as well which Madison and I tried to cover in the last main chapter of the book previously mentioned [150]. All of them are related to the basic hypothesis of cognitive theory that, especially for such complex phenomena as are relevant to personality functioning, the mediating processes between "stimulus" and "response" are highly organized and very complex perceptual processes which can be profoundly different in different persons who, in many respects, go through the same outward movements in their everyday lives.

The Role of Idiographic Study

Obviously, since cognitive theory stresses so heavily the complexity of personality and the profound differences that may be developed between one person and another, there are some important respects in which such principles seem related to Gordon Allport's [4] continued insistence that investigations of personality should often be of an idiographic sort, attempting to describe single individuals and to establish the laws which hold true only for each given person.

Even so, I am inclined to believe that the main implications of cognitive theory suggest a conception of idiographic study which is different from Allport's. In the first place, the study of any individual personality must use concepts and perceptual skills developed in good part through experience with other persons. Consequently, idiographic study, for the most part, does not deal with truly "unique" characteristics.

Second, a main purpose of much of idiographic work is the purpose of serving particular practical needs. With any type of complex system, it usually is impossible to make all the important practical predictions which are needed just by measuring the general factors from which predictions might be made. It is for this reason that meteorologists try to learn the rules of weather in particular areas; geologists seek to predict from past earthquake records what may be expected in a given region; physicians try to learn how to predict from past health records of their particular patients, and they know that such predictions are helpful even when they cannot say what abstract laws are involved.

In the third place, from the standpoint of the psychology of personality, the greatest significance of idiographic research arises not because it tells us about unique characteristics but because it is one of our most valuable means of learning about general factors and general laws. The intensive study of individual persons is one of the indispensable means of getting ideas about important dependent and independent variables. It is an indispensable means of developing new abstract hypotheses about cause-and-effect relationships in human life. Therefore there is nothing peculiar to personality or to psychology in such studies. When geologists have a chance to make an intensive study of the development of a new volcano, such as the Paricutin volcano which started to develop in a Mexican cornfield in 1943, they regard it as highly important to make what might be called an idiographic study. Essentially the same thing is involved in the field of comparative psychology in the study of species-specific behavior [18]. The comparative psychologist would prefer to be able to identify and measure, in more generalized terms, the factors which produce such species-specific behavior, and they hope ultimately to know much more about the general causes of such behavior than they do now. However, the point is that the idiographic study of species is a necessary means whereby they can make progress toward that more abstract type of understanding. It is not intended as a substitute for it. In the same way, although the cognitive theory indicates a greater need for idiographic study than is suggested by other theories of personality which do not picture personality as taking such complex and distinctive forms, this fact still does not suggest that cognitive theory is trying to encompass what are really *unique* characteristics. It is merely following the same basic approach that has been helpful in so many other scientific fields.

In conclusion, let me reiterate my conviction that when we are trying to understand the phenomena of learning, perception, motivation, instinctive functions, and personality, we are dealing with almost incredibly complex material. We cannot expect at all that we will get an adequate understanding of this material by using merely miniature-area types of approach. Nor can we stick to our traditional hypotheses. The new work in related fields like neurology, microbiology, biochemistry, and computer theory is challenging us to get some really ingenious and resourceful new approaches to the study of psychological phenomena, both on the side of research techniques and on the side of theoretical developments from our factual data. In this future work, it may be that many of the concepts which have been explored in the present paper will prove mistaken or too simple. But, there has been a tremendous amount of thought and research activity poured into the development of psychological knowledge by workers in psychology, biology, and psychiatry. It may be, therefore, that part of our means of moving toward a more adequate science of human activity can come through asking, as this paper has attempted to do, whether there are some common principles that account both for the floating of chips and the floating of battleships.

SUMMARY

All sciences need the heuristic gains which come from working with as broad an area as possible. Psychology ought, therefore, to explore the interrelations of many different fields. The quest for highly abstract principles should not lead to generalizations not legitimately drawn from available data. Nevertheless, psychologists should not hesitate to use empirical data to develop hypotheses which they could not derive from known biological facts, even though psychology ought to make great use of evolutionary concepts, biological field studies, and physiological data as well as anthropological and more purely psychological data. Psychological data ought to include subjective data as well as behavioral data. Subjective variables are part of the body of dependent variables we want to predict, and they are directly observable variables which have helped in the development of many crucial psychological principles.

Data from these sources suggest particularly that evolutionary development has produced organisms marked by the use of fine distance receptors, motives, perceptual processes, and learning to achieve stable functioning in relative independence of their immediate environments.

Learning needs to be approached by a prior clarification of the several phases of psychological functioning into which psychological processes need to be analyzed. Studies of extinction and of transfer of training show that the "hyphen" of S-R theory needs to be fractionated into sensory-organizational or sensory-perceptual processes, representational processes, and motor-discharge processes. Vastly more detail is processed in sensory perceptions than can be reflected in the longer-continuing representational processes which serve as the main steering processes relative to overt behavior. These cybernetic processes are not generally representations of what motor responses need to be made but of what environmental effects need to be produced. Separable habits are built up in all three phases. Activity is not mainly a succession of processes from receptor stimulation to effector response—the afferent material and sensory-organizational processes of any given moment are likely to be important mostly as merely shaping or qualifying a much more massive and long-continuing stream of representational processes.

Both the sensory-perceptual and the representational processes have so many properties in common that much care should be taken to develop principles regarding these common functional properties. Furthermore, these properties are also exhibited in examples covered by traditional classifications of perception. Hence, it seems advantageous to group the two classes of sensory perceptions and of representational processes under a broadened term of "perceptual processes." Study of motivational processes indicates that these also are a part of the larger continuum of perceptual processes. Within the area of motivational processes, we can distinguish a further continuum which involves physiologically based motives and emotional motives. We need a system of hierarchical concepts, therefore, about different sorts of psychological process.

Perceptual processes and motor-discharge processes may both be regarded as "transitory processes"—not in a sense which rejects the hypothesis that representational processes may continue for hours or longer but in the sense that transitory processes may be analogous to sound waves in the possibility that they may be richly detailed processes which will continue for some time but not leave enduring structural changes which would cause them to have an influence on later functioning.

Our analysis of most of learning ought to explore, first, the factors which determine what perceptual processes are brought into existence. The study of these factors needs to recognize (1) factors which produce certain perceptual organizations in the first place in a given type of situation, (2) factors which will tend to obstruct any changes in that first organization, and (3) factors which will tend to cause changes in the perceptual organization. The analysis of learning calls, further, for a consideration of what factors are responsible for the depositing of habits or memory traces from these perceptual processes. The implanting of habits seems to come particularly from factors that give motivational character to perceptual processes. Rewards and punishments both have the same basic influences in this respect. A depositing of habits also occurs where perceptual processes are relatively colorless, motivationally speaking, as in the figural-aftereffect experiments. In such cases, other factors, such as long or repeated use of the same perceptual process, may be more important, or perhaps other influences such as factors of Prägnanz or relationship to some already established large trace system.

The psychology of personality, although it calls for some distinctive principles not needed elsewhere in psychology, needs to be approached primarily in terms of principles of learning, motivation, and perception which hold outside the field of personality as well as within it. It is another area which should benefit by more extensive efforts to interrelate data and hypotheses from many different parts of psychology.

REFERENCES

1. Adler, G. *Studies in analytical psychology.* New York: Norton, 1948.
2. Allport, F. H. *Social psychology.* Boston: Houghton Mifflin, 1924.
3. Allport, G. W. The functional autonomy of motives. *Amer. J. Psychol.,* 1937, **50,** 141–156.
4. Allport, G. W. *Pattern and growth in personality.* New York: Holt, Rinehart & Winston, 1961.
5. Andjus, R. K., Knoepfelmacher, F., Russell, R. W., & Smith, A. U. Some effects of severe hypothermia on learning and retention. *Quart. J. exp. Psychol.,* 1956, **8,** 15–23.
6. Ansbacher, H. L., & Ansbacher, Rowena (Eds.) *The individual psychology of Alfred Adler.* New York: Basic Books, 1956.

7. Aschoff, J., et al. Report of symposium on "biological clocks." *Cold Spring Harbor Sympos. quant. Biol.*, 1960, **25**, 1–524.

8. Attneave, F. Some informational aspects of visual perception. *Psychol. Rev.*, 1954, **61**, 183–193.

9. Attneave, F. Symmetry, information, and memory for patterns. *Amer. J. Psychol.*, 1955, **78**, 209–222.

10. Attneave, F. Perception and related areas. In S. Koch (Ed.), *Psychology: a study of a science*. Vol. 4. New York: McGraw-Hill, 1962. Pp. 619–659.

11. Bandura, A. Psychotherapy as a learning process. *Psychol. Bull.*, 1961, **58**, 143–159.

12. Barnett, H. G. Culture processes. *Amer. Anthrop.*, 1940, **42**, 21–48.

13. Barnett, H. G. *Innovation: the basis of cultural change*. New York: McGraw-Hill, 1953.

14. Bartlett, F. C. *Remembering*. New York: Cambridge, 1932.

15. Bartlett, F. C. *Thinking*. New York: Basic Books, 1958.

16. Beach, F. A. The neural basis of innate behavior: II. Relative effects of partial decortication in adulthood and infancy upon the maternal behavior of the primiparous rat. *J. genet. Psychol.*, 1938, **53**, 109–148.

17. Beach, F. A. Instinctive behavior: reproductive activities. In S. S. Stevens (Ed.), *Handbook of experimental psychology*. New York: Wiley, 1951. Pp. 387–434.

18. Beach, F. A. Experimental investigations of species-specific behavior. *Amer. Psychologist*, 1960, **15**, 1–18.

19. Beach, F. A., Hebb, D. O., Morgan, C. T., & Nissen, H. W. (Eds.) *The neuropsychology of Lashley*. New York: McGraw-Hill, 1960.

20. Benzinger, T. H. The human thermostat. *Scient. Amer.*, 1961, **204**, (1), 134–147.

21. Bindra, D. *Motivation*. New York: Ronald, 1959.

22. Blake, R. R., & Vanderplas, J. M. The effect of precognition hypotheses on veridical recognition thresholds in auditory perception. *J. Pers.*, 1950, **19**, 95–115.

23. Boring, E. G., Langfeld, H. S., & Weld, H. P. (Eds.) *Foundations of psychology*. New York: Wiley, 1948.

24. Bottome, Phyllis. *Alfred Adler: a biography*. New York: Putnam, 1939.

25. Brazier, Mary A. (Ed.) *The central nervous system and behavior: transactions of the second conference*. New York: Josiah Macy, Jr. Foundation, 1959.

26. Brown, J. S. *The motivation of behavior*. New York: McGraw-Hill, 1961.

27. Bruce, V. G. Environmental entrainment of circadian rhythms. *Cold Spring Harbor Symp. on quant. Biol.*, 1960, **25**, 29–48.

28. Bruner, J. S. Going beyond the information given. In J. S. Bruner et al., *Contemporary approaches to cognition: a symposium held at the University of Colorado*. Cambridge, Mass.: Harvard Univer. Press, 1957. Pp. 41–69.

29. Bruner, J. S. On perceptual readiness. *Psychol. Rev.,* 1957, **64,** 123–152.

30. Bruner, J. S. Neural mechanisms in perception. *Psychol. Rev.,* 1957, **64,** 340–358.

31. Bruner, J. S., Goodnow, J. J., & Austin, G. A. *A study of thinking.* New York: Wiley, 1956.

32. Brunswik, E. *Perception and the representative design of psychological experiments.* Berkeley, Calif.: Univer. Calif. Press, 1956.

33. Brunswik, E. *"Ratiomorphic" models of perception and thinking.* In K. Hammond (Ed.), *Probabilistic functionalism: Egon Brunswik's psychology.* Berkeley, Calif.: Univer. Calif. Press, in press.

34. Bryan, W. L., & Harter, N. Studies in the physiology and psychology of the telegraphic language. *Psychol. Rev.,* 1897, **4,** 27–53; 1899, **6,** 345–357.

35. Cannon, W. B. *Wisdom of the body.* New York: Norton, 1932.

36. Cantril, H. The nature of social perception. *Trans. N. Y. Acad. Sci.,* 1948, **10,** 142–153.

37. Carlson, V. R. Satiation in a reversible perspective figure. *J. exp. Psychol.,* 1953, **45,** 442–448.

38. Cartwright, D. Lewinian theory as a contemporary systematic framework. In S. Koch (Ed.), *Psychology: a study of a science.* Vol. 2. New York: McGraw-Hill, 1959. Pp. 7–91.

39. Cattell, R. B. Personality theory growing from multivariate quantitative research. In S. Koch (Ed.), *Psychology: a study of a science.* Vol. 3. New York: McGraw-Hill, 1959. Pp. 257–327.

40. Cohen, J., & Gordon, D. A. The Prevost-Fechner-Benham subjective colors. *Psychol. Bull.,* 1949, **46,** 79–136.

41. Comfort, A. The life span of animals. *Scient. Amer.,* 1961, **205,** (2), 108–119.

42. Conant, J. B. *On understanding science.* New Haven, Conn.: Yale Univer. Press, 1947.

43. Crosland, H. R., Taylor, H. R., & Newsom, S. J. Practice and improvability in the Müller-Lyer illusion in relation to intelligence. *J. gen. Psychol.,* 1929, **2,** 290–306.

44. Dashiell, J. F. Direction orientation in maze running by the white rat. *Comp. Psychol. Monogr.,* 1930, **7,** No. 32.

45. Deatherage, B. H., & Bitterman, M. E. The effect of satiation on stroboscopic movement. *Amer. J. Psychol.,* 1951, **65,** 108–109.

46. Dember, W. N. Alternation behavior. In D. W. Fiske & S. Maddi (Eds.), *Functions of varied experience.* Homewood, Ill.: Dorsey Press, 1961. Chap. 8.

47. Dember, W. N., & Fowler, H. Spontaneous alternation behavior. *Psychol. Bull.,* 1958, **55,** 412–428.

48. Dennis, W. Spontaneous alternation in rats as an indicator of the persistence of stimulus effects. *J. comp. Psychol.,* 1939, **28,** 305–312.

48a. Deutsch, J. A. Higher nervous function: the physiological bases of memory. *Annu. Rev. Physiol.,* 1962, **24,** 259–286.

49. Diamond, S. *Personality and temperament.* New York: McGraw-Hill, 1957.

50. Dollard, J., & Miller, N. E. *Personality and psychotherapy.* New York: McGraw-Hill, 1950.

51. Douglas, Anna G. A tachistoscopic study of the order of emergence in the process of perception. *Psychol. Monogr.,* 1947, **61,** No. 287.

52. Duke-Elder, S. The emergence of vision in the animal world. *Amer. J. Ophthalmology,* 1958, **46,** 447–463.

53. Edwards, W. Behavioral decision theory. *Annu. Rev. Psychol.,* 1961, **12,** 473–498.

54. Eible-Eibesfeldt, I. The fighting behavior of animals. *Scient. Amer.,* 1961, **205,** (6), 112–122.

55. Ellson, D. G. Linear frequency theory as behavior theory. In S. Koch (Ed.), *Psychology: a study of a science.* Vol. 2. New York: McGraw-Hill, 1959. Pp. 637–662.

56. Erikson, E. H. *Childhood and society.* New York: Norton, 1950.

57. Estes, W. K. Learning theory and the new "mental chemistry." *Psychol. Rev.,* 1960, **65,** 207–223.

58. Estes, W. K., Hopkins, B. L., & Crothers, E. J. All-or-none and conservation effects in the learning and retention of paired associates. *J. exp. Psychol.,* 1960, **60,** 329–339.

59. Eysenck, H. J. *The structure of human personality.* New York: Wiley, 1953.

60. Feigl, H. Some major issues and developments in the philosophy of science of logical empiricism. In H. Feigl & M. Scriven (Eds.), *Minnesota studies in the philosophy of science.* Vol. 1. Minneapolis, Minn.: Univer. Minn. Press, 1956. Pp. 3–37.

61. Fiske, D. W. Effects of monotonous and restricted stimulation. In D. W. Fiske & S. Maddi (Eds.), *Functions of varied experience.* Homewood, Ill.: Dorsey Press, 1961. Pp. 106–144.

62. Flavell, J. H., & Draguns, J. A microgenetic approach to perception and thought. *Psychol. Bull.,* 1957, **54,** 197–217.

63. Freud, Anna. The contributions of psychoanalysis to genetic psychology. *Amer. J. Orthopsychiat.,* 1951, **21,** 476–497.

64. Freud, S. *Civilization and its discontents.* London: Hogarth, 1930.

65. Frisch, K. von. *Bees: their vision, chemical senses, and language.* Ithaca, N.Y.: Cornell Univer. Press, 1950. (See also K. von Frisch. Dialects in the language of bees. *Scient. Amer.,* 1962, **207,** (2), 78–87.)

66. Gaito, J. A biochemical approach to learning and memory. *Psychol. Rev.,* 1961, **68,** 288–292.

67. Gardner, M. Review of H. S. M. Coxeter's *Introduction to geometry. Scient. Amer.,* 1961, **204,** (4), 164–175.

68. Gardner, W., Holzman, P. S., Klein, G. S., Linton, Harriet, & Spence, D. P. Cognitive control: a study of individual consistencies in cognitive behavior. *Psychol. Issues,* 1959, **1,** No. 4.

69. Gibson, Eleanor J. Improvement in perceptual judgments as a function of controlled practice or training. *Psychol. Bull.,* 1953, **50,** 401–431.

70. Gibson, J. J. Adaptation with negative after-effect. *Psychol. Rev.*, 1937, **44**, 222–243.
71. Gibson, J. J., & Gibson, Eleanor J. Perceptual learning: differentiation or enrichment. *Psychol. Rev.*, 1955, **62**, 32–41.
72. Gill, M. The present state of psychoanalytic theory. *J. abnorm. soc. Psychol.*, 1959, **58**, 1–8.
73. Glickman, S. E. Perseverative neural processes and consolidation of the memory traces. *Psychol. Bull.*, 1961, **58**, 218–233.
74. Guilford, J. P. *Personality.* New York: McGraw-Hill, 1959.
75. Guthrie, E. R. Psychological facts and psychological theory. *Psychol. Bull.*, 1946, **43**, 1–20.
76. Guthrie, E. R. Association by contiguity. In S. Koch (Ed.), *Psychology: a study of a science.* Vol. 2. New York: McGraw-Hill, 1959. Pp. 158–195.
77. Hall, C. S., & Lindzey, G. *Theories of personality.* New York: Wiley, 1957.
78. Hanfmann, Eugenia. A study of personal patterns in an intellectual performance. *Charact. & Pers.*, 1941, **9**, 315–325.
79. Harker, Janet E. Diurnal rhythms in the animal kingdom. *Biol. Revs. Cambr. Phil. Soc.*, 1958, **33**, 1–52.
80. Harlow, H. F. The formation of learning sets. *Psychol. Rev.*, 1949, **56**, 51–65.
81. Harlow, H. F. Learning set and error factor theory. In S. Koch (Ed.), *Psychology: a study of a science.* Vol. 2. New York: McGraw-Hill, 1959. Pp. 492–537.
82. Hasler, A. D., & Larsen, J. A. The homing salmon. *Scient. Amer.*, 1955, **193**, (2), 72–76.
83. Hebb, D. O. *The organization of behavior.* New York: Wiley, 1949.
84. Heidbreder, Edna. An experimental study of thinking. *Arch. Psychol.*, 1924, **11**, (73), 1–175.
85. Helson, H. Adaptation level theory. In S. Koch (Ed.), *Psychology: a study of a science.* Vol. 1. New York: McGraw-Hill, 1959. Pp. 565–621.
86. Heron, W. The pathology of boredom. *Scient. Amer.*, 1957, **196**, (1), 52–56.
87. Heron, W., Doane, B. K., & Scott, T. H. Visual disturbances after prolonged perceptual isolation. *Canad. J. Psychol.*, 1956, **10**, 13–18.
88. Hinde, R. A. Some recent trends in ethology. In S. Koch (Ed.), *Psychology: a study of a science.* Vol. 2. New York: McGraw-Hill, 1959. Pp. 561–610.
89. Hochberg, J. E. Figure-ground reversal as a function of visual satiation. *J. exp. Psychol.*, 1950, **40**, 682–686.
90. Hochberg, J. E., & McAlister, E. A quantitative approach to figural "goodness." *J. exp. Psychol.*, 1953, **46**, 361–364.
91. Horney, Karen. *Neurosis and human growth.* New York: Norton, 1950.

92. Hull, C. L. Quantitative aspects of the evolution of concepts: an experimental study. *Psychol. Monogr.*, 1920, **28**, No. 123.
93. Hull, C. L. *Principles of behavior.* New York: Appleton-Century-Crofts, Inc., 1943. Copyright © 1943, Appleton-Century-Crofts, Inc. Reprinted by permission of the publishers.
94. Hydén, H. Satellite cells in the nervous system. *Scient. Amer.*, 1961, **205**, (6), 62–70.
95. Inhelder, Bärbel, & Piaget, J. *The growth of logical thinking.* New York: Basic Books, 1958.
96. Ittelson, W. H. Perception and transactional psychology. In S. Koch (Ed.), *Psychology: a study of a science.* Vol. 4. New York: McGraw-Hill, 1962. Pp. 660–704.
97. Jeffress, L. A. (Ed.) *Cerebral mechanisms in behavior: the Hixon symposium.* New York: Wiley, 1951.
98. Jenkins, W. O., & Stanley, J. C. Partial reinforcement: a review and critique. *Psychol. Bull.*, 1950, **47**, 193–234.
99. Jensen, A. R. Review of Leeper & Madison's Toward Understanding Human Personalities. *Contemp. Psychol.*, 1960, **5**, 353–355.
100. Jones, E. *The life and work of Sigmund Freud.* New York: Basic Books, 1953, 1955, 1957. 3 vols.
101. Kaess, W., & Kaess, F. Perception of apparent motion in the common toad. *Science*, 1960, **132**, 953.
102. Kantor, J. R. *Principles of psychology.* Bloomington, Ind.: Principia Press, 1924. 1926. 2 vols.
103. Kelly, G. A. *The psychology of personal constructs.* New York: Norton, 1955. 2 vols.
104. Kendler, Tracy S. Concept formation. *Annu. Rev. Psychol.*, 1961, **12**, 447–472.
105. Kendrew, J. C. The three-dimensional structure of a protein molecule. *Scient. Amer.*, 1961, **205**, (6), 96–110.
106. Kilpatrick, F. P. Personality in transactional psychology. *J. indiv. Psychol.*, 1961, **17**, 12–19.
107. Kimble, G. A. *Hilgard and Marquis' conditioning and learning.* New York: Appleton-Century-Crofts, 1961.
108. Klein, G. S. Cognitive control and motivation. In G. Lindzey (Ed.), *The assessment of human motives.* New York: Rinehart, 1958. Pp. 87–118.
109. Kleitman, N. Patterns of dreaming. *Scient. Amer.*, 1960, **203**, (5), 82–88.
110. Klüver, H. *Behavior mechanisms in monkeys.* Chicago: Univer. Chicago Press, 1933.
111. Klüver, H. Re-examination of implement-using behavior in a Cebus monkey after an interval of three years. *Acta Psychol.*, 1937, **2**, 347–397.
112. Klüver, H. Discussion of Lashley's paper on cerebral organization and behavior. In *The brain and human behavior, Res. Publ. Ass. nerv. ment. Dis.*, 1958, **36**, 14–16.

113. Koch, S. Epilogue. In S. Koch (Ed.), *Psychology: a study of a science.* Vol. 3. New York: McGraw-Hill, 1959. Pp. 729–788.

114. Koch, S. Psychological science versus the science-humanism antinomy: intimations of a significant science of man. *Amer. Psychologist*, 1961, **16**, 629–639.

115. Koffka, K. *Principles of gestalt psychology.* New York: Harcourt, Brace, 1935.

116. Köhler, W. *The mentality of apes.* F. Winter (Trans.). New York: Harcourt, Brace, 1925.

117. Köhler, W. *Gestalt psychology.* New York: Liveright, 1929.

118. Köhler, W. *Dynamics in psychology.* New York: Liveright, 1940.

119. Köhler, W. On the nature of associations. *Proc. Amer. Phil. Soc.*, 1941, **84**, 489–502.

120. Köhler, W., & Adams, P. A. Perception and attention. *Amer. J. Psychol.*, 1958, **71**, 489–503.

121. Köhler, W., & Dinnerstein, D. Figural after-effects in kinesthesis. In *Miscellanea Psychologica Albert Michotte.* Louvain: Institut Supérieur de Philosophie, 1947. Pp. 196–220.

122. Köhler, W., & Fishback, Julia. The destruction of the Müller-Lyer illusion in repeated trials: I. An examination of two theories. *J. exp. Psychol.*, 1950, **40**, 267–281.

123. Köhler, W., & Fishback, Julia. The destruction of the Müller-Lyer illusion in repeated trials: II. Satiation patterns and memory traces. *J. exp. Psychol.*, 1950, **40**, 398–410.

124. Köhler, W., & Wallach, H. Figural after-effects. *Proc. Amer. Phil. Soc.*, 1944, **88**, 269–357.

125. Krech, D. Cognition and motivation in psychological theory. In W. Dennis et al., *Current trends in psychological theory.* Pittsburgh, Pa.: Univer. Pittsburgh Press, 1951.

126. Krech, D., & Crutchfield, R. *Elements of psychology.* New York: Knopf, 1958.

127. Krechevsky, I. "Hypotheses" vs. "chance" in the pre-solution period in sensory discrimination. *Univer. Calif. Publ. Psychol.*, 1932, **6**, 27–44.

128. Krechevsky, I. The genesis of "hypotheses" in rats. *Univer. Calif. Publ. Psychol.*, 1932, **6**, 45–64.

129. Krechevsky, I. Brain mechanisms and "hypotheses." *J. comp. Psychol.*, 1935, **19**, 425–468.

130. Lashley, K. S. The color vision of birds. I. The spectrum of the domestic fowl. *J. Animal Behav.*, 1916, **6**, 1–26.

131. Lashley, K. S. Basic neural mechanisms in behavior. *Psychol. Rev.*, 1930, **37**, 1–24.

132. Lashley, K. S. Experimental analysis of instinctive behavior. *Psychol. Rev.*, 1938, **45**, 445–471.

133. Lashley, K. S. The mechanism of vision: XV. Preliminary studies of the rat's capacity for detail vision. *J. gen. Psychol.*, 1938, **18**, 123–193.

134. Lashley, K. S. The problem of serial order in behavior. In L. A.

Jeffress (Ed.), *Cerebral mechanisms in behavior: the Hixon symposium.* New York: Wiley, 1951.

135. Lashley, K. S. Cerebral organization and behavior. In *The brain and human behavior, Res. Publ. Ass. nerv. and ment. Dis.,* 1958, 36, 1–14. Reprinted in F. Beach et al. (Eds.), *The neuropsychology of Lashley.* New York: McGraw-Hill, 1960. Pp. 529–543.

136. Lashley, K. S., & Ball, Josephine. Spinal conduction and kinesthetic sensitivity in the maze habit. *J. comp. Psychol.,* 1929, 9, 71–105.

137. Lashley, K. S., & McCarthy, Dorothea A.. The survival of the maze habit after cerebellar injuries. *J. comp. Psychol.,* 1926, 6, 423–433.

138. Lawrence, D. H. The transfer of a discrimination along a continuum. *J. comp. physiol. Psychol.,* 1952, 45, 111–116.

139. Lawrence, D. H. The applicability of generalization gradients to the transfer of a discrimination. *J. gen. Psychol.,* 1955, 52, 37–48.

140. Leary, T. *Interpersonal diagnosis of personality.* New York: Ronald, 1956.

141. Lecky, P. *Self-consistency: a theory of personality.* New York: Island Press, 1945.

142. Leeper, R. W. The evidence for a theory of neurological maintenance of states of emotional motivation. *Psychol. Bull.,* 1932, 29, 571.

143. Leeper, R. W. The role of motivation in learning: a study of the phenomenon of differential motivational control of the utilization of habits. *J. genet. Psychol.,* 1935, 46, 3–40.

144. Leeper, R. W. A study of a neglected portion of the field of learning—the development of sensory organization. *J. genet. Psychol.,* 1935, 46, 41–75.

145. Leeper, R. W. *Lewin's topological and vector psychology.* Eugene, Ore.: Univer. Ore. Press, 1943.

146. Leeper, R. W. A motivational theory of emotion to replace "emotion as disorganized response." *Psychol. Rev.,* 1948, 55, 5–21.

147. Leeper, R. W. Cognitive processes. In S. S. Stevens (Ed.), *Handbook of experimental psychology.* New York: Wiley, 1951. Pp. 730–757.

148. Leeper, R. W. A critical discussion of Egon Brunswik's probabilistic functionalism. In K. Hammond (Ed.), *Probalistic functionalism: Egon Brunswik's psychology.* Berkeley, Calif.: Univer. Calif. Press, in press.

149. Leeper, R. W., & Leeper, Dorothy O. An experimental study of equivalent stimulation in human learning. *J. gen. Psychol.,* 1932, 6, 344–376.

150. Leeper, R. W., & Madison, P. *Toward understanding human personalities.* New York: Copyright © 1959, Appleton-Century-Crofts, Inc. Reprinted by permission of the publishers.

151. Lewis, E. J. Partial reinforcement: a selective review of the literature since 1950. *Psychol. Bull.,* 1960, 57, 1–28.

152. Limbaugh, C. Cleaning symbiosis. *Scient. Amer.,* 1961, 205, (2), 42–49.

153. Lobban, M. C. The entrainment of circadian rhythms in man. *Cold Spring Harbor Symp. quant. Biol.,* 1960, 25, 325–332.

154. Lorenz, K. *King Solomon's ring.* New York: Crowell, 1952.

155. Luce, R. D., & Raiffa, H. *Games and decisions.* New York: Wiley, 1957.

156. Lundin, R. W. *Personality: an experimental approach.* New York: Macmillan, 1961.

157. McBride, A. F., & Hebb, D. O. Behavior of the captive bottle-nose dolphin, Tursiops truncatus. *J. comp. physiol. Psychol.,* 1948, **41,** 111–123.

158. McCue, J. J. G. How bats hunt with sound. *National Geographic,* 1961, **119,** 570–578.

159. McCurdy, H. G. *The personal world.* New York: Harcourt, Brace, 1961.

160. McDougall, W. *The energies of men.* New York: Scribner's, 1932.

161. Macfarlane, D. A. The role of kinesthesis in maze learning. *Univer. Calif. Publ. Psychol.,* 1930, **4,** 277–305.

162. Madison, P. *Freud's concept of repression and defense, its theoretical and observational language.* Minneapolis, Minn.: Univer. Minn. Press, 1961.

163. Maier, N. R. F. Reasoning in humans. I. On direction. *J. comp. Psychol.,* 1930, **10,** 115–143.

164. Maier, N. R. F. Reasoning in humans. II. The solution of a problem and its appearance in consciousness. *J. comp. Psychol.,* 1931, **12,** 181–194.

165. Manis, M., & Barnes, E. J. Learning without awareness and mediated generalization. *Amer. J. Psychol.,* 1961, **74,** 425–432.

166. Maslow, A. S. The instinctoid nature of basic needs. *J. Pers.,* 1954, **22,** 326–347.

167. Melzack, R. The perception of pain. *Scient. Amer.,* 1961, **204,** (2), 41–49.

168. Miller, G. A., Galanter, E., & Pribram, K. H. *Plans and the structure of behavior.* New York: Holt, 1960.

169. Miller, N. E. Liberalization of basic S-R concepts: extensions to conflict behavior, motivation, and social learning. In S. Koch (Ed.), *Psychology: a study of a science.* Vol. 2. New York: McGraw-Hill, 1959. Pp. 196–292.

169a. Monroe, Ruth L. *Schools of psychoanalytic thought.* New York: Dryden, 1955.

170. Mooney, C. M., & Ferguson, G. A. A new closure test. *Canad. J. Psychol.,* 1951, **5,** 129–133.

171. Muenzinger, K. F. Plasticity and mechanization of the problem box habit in guinea pigs. *J. comp. Psychol.,* 1928, **8,** 45–69.

172. Muenzinger, K. F., & Fletcher, F. J. Motivation in learning. VII. The effect of an enforced delay at the point of choice in the visual discrimination habit. *J. comp. Psychol.,* 1937, **23,** 383–392.

173. Muenzinger, K. F., Koerner, L., & Irey, E. Variability in an habitual movement in guinea pigs. *J. comp. Psychol.,* 1929, **9,** 425–436.

174. Mullahy, P. (Ed.) *The contributions of Harry Stack Sullivan.* New York: Hermitage, 1952.

175. Murphy, G. *Personality.* New York: Harper, 1947.

176. Neumann, E. *The origins and history of consciousness.* New York: Pantheon Books, 1954.

177. Oldfield, R. C.. Memory mechanisms and the theory of schemata. *Brit. J. Psychol.*, 1954, 45, 14–23.
178. Oppenheimer, R. Analogy in science. *Amer. Psychologist*, 1956, 11, 127–135.
179. Osgood, C. E.. A behavioristic analysis of perception and language as cognitive phenomena. In J. Bruner et al., *Contemporary approaches to cognition: a symposium held at the University of Colorado.* Cambridge, Mass.: Harvard Univer. Press, 1957.
180. Pauling, L. A molecular theory of general anesthesia. *Science*, 1961, 134, 15–21.
181. Pavlov, I. P. *Conditioned reflexes.* New York: Oxford Univer. Press, 1927.
182. Payne, R. S., & Drury, W. H. Tyto Alba: Marksman of the darkness. *Natural History*, 1958, 67, 316–323.
183. Pirenne, M. H., & Marriott, F. H. C. The quantum theory of light and the psycho-physiology of vision. In S. Koch (Ed.), *Psychology: a study of a science.* Vol. 1. New York: McGraw-Hill, 1959. Pp. 288–361.
184. Pittendrigh, C. S. Circadian rhythms and the circadian organization of living systems. *Cold Spring Harbor Symp. quant. Biol.*, 1960, 25, 159–184.
185. Postman, L., & Tolman, E. C. Brunswik's probabilistic functionalism. In S. Koch (Ed.), *Psychology: a study of a science.* Vol. 1. New York: McGraw-Hill, 1959. Pp. 502–564.
186. Pribram, K. H. A review of theory in physiological psychology. *Annu. Rev. Psychol.*, 1960, 11, 1–40.
187. Pritchard, R. M. Stabilized images on the retina. *Scient. Amer.*, 1961, 204, (6), 72–78.
188. Pritchard, R. M., Heron, W., & Hebb, D. O. Visual perception approached by the method of stabilized images. *Canad. J. Psychol.*, 1960, 14, 67–77.
189. Progoff, I. *The death and rebirth of psychology.* New York: Julian Press, 1956.
190. Rees, H. J., & Israel, H. E. An investigation of the establishment and operation of mental sets. *Psychol. Monogr.*, 1935, 46, No. 210.
191. Riggs, L. A., Ratliff, F., Cornsweet, J. C., & Cornsweet, T. H. The disappearance of steadily fixated visual test objects. *J. Opt. Soc. Amer.*, 1953, 43, 495–501.
192. Riley, D. A. The nature of the effective stimulus in animal discrimination learning: transposition reconsidered. *Psychol. Rev.*, 1958, 65, 1–7.
193. Rock, I. The role of repetition in associative learning. *Amer. J. Psychol.*, 1957, 70, 186–193.
194. Rock, I., & Heimer, W. Further evidence of one-trial associative learning. *Amer. J. Psychol.*, 1959, 72, 1–16.
195. Roe, Anne, & Simpson, G. G. (Eds.) *Behavior and evolution.* New Haven, Conn.: Yale Univer. Press, 1958.
196. Roeder, K. D., & Treat, A. E. The detection and evasion of bats by moths. *Amer. Scientist*, 1961, 49, 135–148.

197. Rogers, C. R. A theory of therapy, personality, and interpersonal relationships, as developed in the client-centered framework. In S. Koch (Ed.), *Psychology: a study of a science*. Vol. 3. New York: McGraw-Hill, 1959. Pp. 184–256.

198. Rogers, C. R. *On becoming a person: a therapist's view of psychotherapy*. Boston: Houghton Mifflin, 1961.

199. Rotter, J. B. *Social learning and clinical psychology*. Englewood Cliffs, N.J.: Prentice-Hall, 1954.

200. Sahlins, M. D. The origin of society. *Scient. Amer.*, 1960, **203**, (3), 76–87.

201. Samuels, Ina. Reticular mechanisms and behavior. *Psychol. Bull.*, 1959, **56**, 1–25.

202. Sauer, E. G. F. Celestial navigation by birds. *Scient. Amer.*, 1958, **199**, (2), 42–47.

203. Sauer, E. G. F., & Sauer, Eleanore M. Star navigation of nocturnal migrating birds. *Cold Spring Harbor Symp. quant. Biol.*, 1960, **25**, 463–473.

204. Schiller, Claire H. (Ed.) *Instinctive behavior*. New York: International Universities Press, 1957.

205. Scott, J. P. *Animal behavior*. Chicago: Univer. Chicago Press, 1958.

206. Selfridge, O. G., & Neisser, U. Pattern recognition. *Scient. Amer.*, 1960, **203**, (2), 60–68.

207. Shaffer, L. F., & Shoben, E. J. *Psychology of adjustment*. (2nd ed.) Boston: Houghton Mifflin, 1956.

208. Skinner, B. F. The generic nature of the concepts of stimulus and response. *J. gen. Psychol.*, 1935, **12**, 40–65.

209. Skinner, B. F. Are theories of learning necessary? *Psychol. Rev.*, 1950, **57**, 193–216.

210. Skinner, B. F. How to teach animals. *Scient. Amer.*, 1951, **185**, (6), 26–29.

211. Skinner, B. F. The experimental analysis of behavior. *Amer. Scientist*, 1957, **45**, 343–371.

212. Snygg, D. The relative difficulty of mechanically equivalent tasks. I. Human learning. *J. genet. Psychol.*, 1935, **47**, 299–320.

213. Solomon, R. L., Kamin, L. J., & Wynne, L. C. Traumatic avoidance learning: the outcome of several extinction procedures with dogs. *J. abnorm. soc. Psychol.*, 1953, **48**, 291–302.

214. Solomon, R. L., & Wynne, L. C. Traumatic avoidance learning: acquisition in normal dogs. *Psychol. Monogr.*, 1953, **67**, No. 354.

215. Solomon, R. L., & Wynne, L. C. Traumatic avoidance learning: the principles of anxiety conservation and partial irreversibility. *Psychol. Rev.*, 1954, **61**, 353–385.

216. Spence, K. W. The solution of multiple-choice problems by chimpanzees. *Comp. Psychol. Monogr.*, 1939, **15**, No. 75.

217. Spitz, H. H. The present status of the Köhler-Wallach theory of satiation. *Psychol. Bull.*, 1958, **55**, 1–28.

218. Stamm, J. S. Hoarding. In E. Hutchings, Jr. (Ed.), *Frontiers in science*. New York: Basic Books, 1958. Pp. 61–69.

219. Stone, C. P. Multiply, vary, let the strongest live and the weakest die —Charles Darwin. *Psychol. Bull.*, 1943, **40**, 1–24.

220. Story, Anne. Figural after-effects as a function of the perceived characteristics of the inspection-figure. *Amer. J. Psychol.*, 1959, **72**, 46–56.

221. Tanner, J. M., & Inhelder, B. (Eds.) *Discussions on child development.* Vol. 4. London: Tavistock, 1960.

222. Tax, S. (Ed.) *Evolution after Darwin.* New York: Basic Books, 1961.

223. Thorpe, W. H. *Learning and instinct in animals.* Cambridge, Mass.: Harvard Univer. Press, 1956.

224. Thrall, R. M., Coombs, C. H., & Davis, R. L. (Eds.) *Decision processes.* New York: Wiley, 1954.

225. Tinbergen, N. *The study of instinct.* London: Oxford Univer. Press, 1951.

226. Tinklepaugh, O. L. An experimental study of representative factors in monkeys. *J. comp. Psychol.*, 1928, **8**, 197–236.

227. Tinklepaugh, O. L. Multiple delayed reactions with chimpanzees and monkeys. *J. comp. Psychol.*, 1932, **13**, 207–243.

228. Tolman, E. C. *Purposive behavior in animals and men.* New York: Century, 1932.

229. Tolman, E. C. Cognitive maps in rats and men. *Psychol. Rev.*, 1948, **55**, 189–208.

230. Tolman, E. C. Principles of purposive behavior. In S. Koch (Ed.), *Psychology: a study of a science.* Vol. 2. New York: McGraw-Hill, 1959. Pp. 92–157.

231. Turnbull, C. M. Some observations regarding the experiences and behavior of BaMbuti pygmies. *Amer. J. Psychol.*, 1961, **74**, 304–308.

232. Warren, R. M. Illusory changes of distinct speech upon repetition— the verbal transformation effect. *Brit. J. Psychol.*, 1961, **52**, 249–258.

233. Warren, R. M. Illusory changes in repeated words: differences between young adults and the aged. *Amer. J. Psychol.*, 1961, **74**, 506–516.

234. Warren, R. M., & Gregory, R. L. An auditory analogue of the visual reversible figure. *Amer. J. Psychol.*, 1958, **71**, 612–613.

235. Washburn, S. L. Tools and human evolution. *Scient. Amer.*, 1960, **203**, (3), 62–75.

236. Washburn, S. L., & DeVore, I. The social life of baboons. *Scient. Amer.*, 1961, **204**, (6), 62–71.

237. Werner, H. *Comparative psychology of mental development.* (2nd ed.) New York: International Universities Press, 1948.

238. Wertheimer, Max. *Productive thinking.* New York: Harper, 1959.

239. Wertheimer, Michael, & Leventhal, C. M. "Permanent" satiation phenomena with kinesthetic figural aftereffects. *J. exp. Psychol.*, 1958, **55**, 255–257.

240. Witkin, H. A. "Hypotheses" in rats: an experimental critique. I. The genesis of systematic behavior in linear situations. *J. comp. Psychol.*, 1940, **30**, 457–482.

241. Witkin, H. A. "Hypotheses" in rats: an experimental critique. II. The

displacement of responses and behavior variability in linear situations. *J. comp. Psychol.*, 1941, **31**, 303–336.

242. Witkin, H. A. "Hypotheses" in rats: an experimental critique. III. Summary evaluation of the hypothesis concept. *Psychol. Rev.*, 1942, **49**, 541–568.

243. Wolman, B. B. *Contemporary theories and systems in psychology.* New York: Harper, 1960.

244. Wolpe, J. *Psychotherapy by reciprocal inhibition.* Stanford, Calif.: Stanford Univer. Press, 1958.

245. Woodworth, R. S. Situation-and-goal set. *Amer. J. Psychol.*, 1937, **50**, 130–140.

246. Young, P. T. *Motivation and emotion.* New York: Wiley, 1961.

247. Zuckermann, S. *The social life of monkeys and apes.* New York: Harcourt, Brace, 1932.

PERSONALITY: ITS PLACE IN PSYCHOLOGY

NEVITT SANFORD
Department of Psychology
Stanford University

Introduction	489
The Problem of Definition	491
The Substance of Personality	498
The search for elements	498
Allport's 1937 survey	501
Some developments since 1937	501
Considerations other than theoretical ones influencing the conceptualization of elements of personality	514
Summary	518
The structure of personality	520
Dynamic organization	522
The action frame of reference	522
Reduction of drive-reduction theory	523
Nature versus nurture	526
Organization inside versus organization outside	528
Unconscious processes	532
Personality as a whole	536
Mechanisms as variables of personality	538
Summary	538
Personality and the dimension of time	540
The momentary personality	541
Persistence and change	544
The problem of uniqueness	547
Boundaries of Personality	550
Behavior	550
The effects of behavior	553
The environment	553
Physical structure and physiological processes	557
Character, temperament, intelligence	558
Personality as a Field of Inquiry	559
Subdivisions of the field	559
Subdivision according to method	559

Differences in perspective and in general direction of approach . . . 560
Personality in relation to other orders of phenomena 562
Subdivision according to theoretical structure 563
Personality and general psychology 564
Historical note 564
New thinking about boundary problems 566
The general psychological approach to personality 566
The personality approach to general psychology 568
The situation at the present time 570
A view of the future 573
References 579

INTRODUCTION

This essay[1] is a sketch for a broad overview of the present status of theory and research in the field of personality. What I have done was suggested by the Editor's outline. My assignment was to write about personality with special attention to variables, relationships among variables, boundaries, and relations with variables in other fields. Each of these areas contains problems or issues that have concerned the student of personality for a long time and still concern him. As the essay took shape, attention was focused more and more upon some of these issues. The essay's organization, however, still conforms rather closely to the outline.

I have assumed—in company, I believe, with most theorists in this field—that personality exists as an organized whole (system), that is constituted of parts or elements (subsystems), and separated somehow from an environment with which it interacts. Thus we can see that fundamental questions for the theorist have had to do with the nature of the elements (theoretical variables); with principles of organization (interrelationships among variables); with delimitation, that is, how personality is to be separated conceptually from other phenomena such as behavior or the environment (boundaries); and with relations between personality and other phenomena. These are the major kinds of problems or issues discussed here. They all concern the conceptualization of personality, its theoretical substance, boundaries, and transactions.

[1] I want to thank the following friends and colleagues who read the manuscript and made helpful suggestions: Donald Brown, Mervin Freedman, Walter Gruen, Richard Jung, Daniel Miller, Harvey Nash, David Rapaport, Milton Rokeach, Ephraim Rosen, Brewster Smith, Silvan Tomkins. Warm thanks go also to the members of Psychology 248E at Berkeley in the spring of 1958; they helped to clarify the issues discussed here.

The essay was completed while the author was a Fellow at the Center for Advanced Study in the Behavioral Sciences.

Other issues concern personality as a field of inquiry. During the past thirty years there has developed and been established within our universities a broad field of research and teaching that is called "personality." Attention may be given to theoretical and practical subdivisions of the field and to overlapping and interaction with other areas of inquiry. I turn to these matters in the end, after discussing theoretical issues of the kinds indicated above. When it comes to the relations between personality and other fields of inquiry, however, I confine myself to the relations of personality and general psychology. It would be highly interesting to go into the relations of personality to social psychology, to sociology and anthropology, not to mention abnormal psychology and clinical psychology. But time and space are limited. I am satisfied that, in dealing with the relations of personality and general psychology, I have at least touched upon issues that are important and controversial.

Each of the major areas of theoretical dispute—elements, organization (including its temporal aspects and the problem of uniqueness), boundaries, and transactions—is approached in the same general way. I first define some major issues and then consider proposals that have been made by psychologists of different theoretical positions. This offers an opportunity to compare some major theories of personality. Then I note trends of thought and research in the area under consideration, going back over approximately the past three decades, and looking ahead to the future. In discussing trends, I take the view that producing theories and deciding what research to do by what methods are forms of behavior that have determinants other than and in addition to scientific enlightenment. It is suggested that choices respecting theory, problems, and methods depend upon fundamental decisions concerning the nature and functions of science and the goals and prospects of psychology. These decisions, in their turn, are influenced by processes in the society and culture in which the psychologist lives. The creator of theories is to some extent a product of his times; and a full understanding of what has happened in the field of personality during the past thirty years requires that this period be viewed in a much longer time perspective.

I regret that lack of information and of the time to acquire it have prevented me from going into developments abroad; I have had to restrict myself almost exclusively to activities in the United States and Canada.

The section on the search for elements runs to greater length than the others. This is not because the problems in this area seem most important; rather it is because it is necessary to introduce in this early section the theoretical orientations that are referred to throughout the essay, because I try to develop here the points of view and the mode of analysis that are utilized—but taken for granted—later on.

Naturally I have had misgivings about attempting to present an overview of theory and research in the whole field of personality. The field is vast and complex; it has expanded very rapidly in recent years and continues to do so. In order to bring the whole into view, it is necessary to back off from it or, even better, to take a position above it—the bird's-eye view. This kind of perspective is attained at the expense of clear perception of details. In many instances I have merely broached or sketchily outlined issues that deserve to be treated at length, for some important movements in the field become visible only when one views the whole.

Having taken a position outside the field, I have felt that setting forth my own orientation and preferences in respect to theory would be inappropriate. My present and former students will no doubt conclude that my treatment of psychoanalytic concepts and theories—which I prefer, when choices are necessary—has been rather skimpy. Perhaps I have bent over backward. I have not hesitated, however, to express opinions of other people's work or to judge the significance of ideas or findings. The reader will have no trouble in identifying my biases. Still, when I speak of trends or connections among events I am not being arbitrary; for the most part, I am talking about facts of recent and current history—facts that are unmistakable and significant for any estimate of progress in the field of personality.

THE PROBLEM OF DEFINITION

Donald Adams [1] introduces his book *The Anatomy of Personality* by pointing out that all definitions of personality use terms that require definition; sooner or later one must point to or exhibit that to which he is referring. On the basis that it is easier to point to personality than to the terms used in its definitions, Adams writes: "By the term *personality* I shall mean an entity of the sort you are referring to when you use the first personal pronoun." This gets the discussion going.

The discussion may be started here by the suggestion that what many psychologists today mean by personality is implied in a statement by Schjelderup which is taken from a follow-up study of people whom he had psychoanalyzed twenty to twenty-five years before.

Rather too briefly, but on the whole fitly, and in accordance with the results of this follow-up study, the personality changes effected by a successful analysis can be summed up in some such way as this: The more the neurotic inhibitions are dispelled and anxiety is extirpated, the more does natural self-consciousness emerge and the less stiff and cramped are the attitudes of the personality. The field of experience is enlarged, the attitude toward work and toward other people becomes more open and natural—without too much dependence, without exaggerated demands, but also without exaggerated modesty.

If the personality-changing aims of analysis were to be summed up in a simple formula, it might perhaps be Ibsen's: To be one's self. Or, to put it in other words: Analysis makes possible a higher degree of personality integration [232, p. 118].

Professor Schjelderup may or may not have defined all the terms he employs; he may or may not have offered sufficient evidence for the propositions stated; the concern here is with what he assumes that his readers—psychologists, psychiatrists, social scientists—understand and take for granted respecting personality. The following thoughts are implicit in his statement.

1. Personality is a whole, embracing parts or elements. (Neurotic inhibitions, anxiety, self-consciousness, attitudes are *of* the personality.)

2. One may remark on the state of the whole (personality exhibits degrees of integration) and of particular parts (attitudes of the personality may be more or less stiff and cramped).

3. The parts or elements of personality, apparently, are numerous and varied: neurotic inhibitions, anxiety, self-consciousness, attitudes, field of experience, dependence, demands, modesty.

4. The same kind of part may be differentiated according to specific *contents*—an attitude toward work and an attitude toward other people, for example.

5. Parts may vary in amount; neurotic inhibitions may be more or less dispelled, anxiety more or less extirpated.

6. Parts, like the whole, may vary in structure. Attitudes may be stiff and cramped or open and natural, the field of experience may be large or small, and so on.

7. Parts of the personality are related one to another formally. Elements may or may not be included in the field of experience, depending upon how large it is.

8. Parts of the personality are related dynamically in the sense that a change in one will bring changes in others. As anxiety is extirpated, natural self-consciousness emerges, for example.

9. Structural aspects of the whole and the parts are mutually related; for instance, in an integrated personality, attitudes are not stiff and cramped. "Integration" is one of those words that will have to be defined; but we may assume for the moment that Professor Schjelderup is using the term in its common meaning of "bringing together of parts." Where there is maximum togetherness or connectedness of parts, they have characteristic features: they are open and natural rather than stiff and cramped.

10. Function is prior to structure. Features of parts and of the whole

and formal relationships among parts depend upon dynamic relationships among the parts. It is because of neurotic inhibition and anxiety that natural self-consciousness is submerged, attitudes are stiff and cramped, the field of experience is narrowed, and the personality as a whole is not integrated.

11. Personality is a more or less stable or enduring structure. Were this not so, we could not speak of "the changes effected by a successful analysis."

12. Personality—in whole and in part—interacts with an environment. Attitudes of personality are *toward* work and *toward* people; successful analysis and the use of verbal techniques in other forms of social interaction effect changes in personality—apparently by working directly upon neurotic inhibitions and anxiety.

13. To list the kinds of changes that may occur is to sum up what has been said about the ways in which personality or its parts may vary in the structure of the whole, in the structure of parts, in the quantities of parts, and in dynamic relationships among parts.

14. Not mentioned by Professor Schjelderup—but implied by his statement as a whole—is the existence of *mechanisms* by which neurotic inhibitions are dispelled and anxiety extirpated, and by which changes in attitude and in the field of experience are induced.

15. The functioning of personality as a whole and the functioning of its parts may be evaluated according to some criteria or other. A high degree of personality integration, apparently, is a good thing—presumably because this is a healthy condition. The functioning of parts is good or bad according to whether it favors the integration of the whole. "Too much dependence," "exaggerated demands," "exaggerated modesty" ought to be changed not so much because they are socially troublesome, but because these tendencies are not "open" and "natural"; they are "stiff" and "cramped" and hence do not connect with other parts of the personality to make for its integration.

16. All Schjelderup's statements about personality are *general*. They are statements about personality in general, about "the" personality— any and all personalities.

These assumptions seem to be fairly neutral with respect to current theory of personality. No doubt this has much to do with the generality of the statement—it is so general that it is true of any system, or, perhaps, better, it would be true if stated with sufficient precision. But clearly, Schjelderup is talking about the psychological processes of persons; even so, it is doubtful that many current theorists would find much to object to here.

Some psychologists might object to the holistic orientation of the statement; but this would be not so much on principle as on the ground that such an orientation is rather idealistic and not conducive to research. By "holistic orientation" I mean the disposition to view the personality as a whole, and to consider that behavior can be fully understood only in the context of this whole. This position is considered in some detail later. Some presentations of a holistic point of view imply that the whole personality, or whole parts of it, are not susceptible to techniques of analysis. Holism does not necessarily have this implication. The essential idea is that living systems (e.g., cells, organs, attitudes, the ego, and personality) function as units. Any act or performance of such systems involves system-wide processes; therefore, the functioning of any part or subsystem depends in some degree upon the functioning of the whole. This is far from saying that wholes, such as the personality, cannot be analyzed; it is saying that analysis should include the exposition of the relations of parts to the whole. This kind of holistic orientation does not even imply that part functions might not be studied more or less by themselves; but it implies that the psychologist who would isolate such a function for intensive study should realize that he is abstracting a part from the whole. (The "organismic point of view," to which reference is occasionally made here, is essentially the same thing as "holistic orientation." The term "organismic" seems to be preferred by writers with backgrounds in biology or writers who like to include physiological processes in their schemes of things.) The point is this: Theoretical controversy concerns the nature of the elements of personality, the mechanisms of their interaction and of the transactions between personality and the environment, rather than broad assumptions such as those stated earlier.

Actually, the same kind of analysis that was made of the Schjelderup statement could be made of many contemporary statements *about* personality in which the authors have permitted themselves to write at length and without defining their terms. For example, in writing about the implications of their research for the study of personality, Smith, Bruner, and White [251] made use of all the concepts and assumptions that have been set down above. The same might be said about most contemporary case studies.

Our concern is not to argue for the implicit communality in current views, but to introduce terms that have a place in discussions of how personality should be defined. We may now examine some more or less formal definitions and see if the terms already introduced are not the most important ones.

The following definitions, or conceptions, seem to be more or less representative. We may take them in the order in which they have been introduced into the literature of psychology. It is conventional nowadays to begin with Allport's 1937 definition. "Personality is the dynamic organization within the individual of those psychophysical systems that determine his unique adjustments to his environment" [6, p. 48]. It should be noted, however, that in 1932 Murphy and Jensen defined personality as the "whole dynamic system of tendencies which differentiate one person from another" [179, p. v].

Murray did not offer a single definition of personality in his earlier writings; rather, he considered personological phenomena in different contexts and proposed different definitions of personality at different times. But by bringing together several statements from *Explorations in Personality,* it is possible to see what he meant by "personology."

We were accustomed to conceive of personality as a temporal integrate of mutually dependent processes developing in time . . . Personality is at all times an integral whole . . . The constituent processes are functionally inseparable [181, pp. ix–x]. . . .

Since all complex adaptive behavior is evidently coordinated by excitations in the brain, the unity of the organism's development and behavior can be explained only by referring to organizations occurring in this region [181, p. 45]. . . .

Personalities constitute the subject matter of psychology. . . . Personology, then, is the science of men, taken as gross units . . . . Since it (personology) has to do with the life histories of individuals (the largest unit) it must be most inclusive, other types of psychology being specialties or branches of it [181, p. 4]. . . .

Because of the meaningful connection of sequences, the life cycle should be taken as a unit, *the long unit* for psychology . . . the history of the organism *is* the organism [181, p. 39].

Another organismic, or holistic, conception of personality and one that is at the same time field-theoretical is that of Angyal.

Personality . . . defined, dynamically, as the processes of living [9, p. 374].

The life process does not take place within the body alone, but includes the intrasomatic and extrasomatic happenings. . . . The realm in which the life process takes place has been called the "biosphere." . . . The biosphere is roughly differentiated into subject (organism) and object (environment) [9, p. 123]. . . .

we propose to study life as a unitary whole and endeavor to describe the *organization and dynamics of the biosphere* [9, p. 100]. . . .

Personality can be regarded as a hierarchy of systems. In the larger personality organization the significant positions are occupied by constituents which themselves are also systems [9, p. 186].

Lewin did not offer a formal definition of personality; rather, his conception emerges from his various writings.

Bronfenbrenner offers a useful summary:

Lewin conceives of personality as a "differentiated region of the life space," a "more or less unitary and more or less closed" organization of interrelated psychical systems. Although he never formally defines the last concept, it is readily apparent from his discussion that the psychical system denotes a disposition to respond in a particular way to selective aspects of the psychical field [32, p. 212].

Linton's definition is brief and inclusive. Personality is taken to mean

The organized aggregate of psychological processes and states pertaining to the individual [148, p. 84].

Krech and Crutchfield say:

Characteristic modes of tension reduction are learned by the individual as a function of his past experiences of success or failure with them and of the opportunity for employment of them within the confines of his particular culture. *Personality* may be described as the pattern of relative importance of these various modes of adjustment to tension which uniquely characterizes the individual [137, p. 73].

Newcomb states:

Now personality, as I am sure we are all agreed, is known only as we observe individual behavior. (I am using the term "personality," by the way, in the inclusive sense of referring to the individual's organization of predispositions to behavior.) What I want to suggest is that the *kind* of behavior from which we can learn most about personality is role behavior. By observing John Doe in such capacities as husband, host, employee, and employer, we can discover those kinds of order and regularity in his behavior which are the goal of the student of personality [186, p. 277].

Cattell makes the point that, at this stage of our knowledge, only a denotative definition of personality is possible.

For this reason we may say: *Personality is that which permits a prediction of what a person will do in a given situation.* . . . Personality is . . . concerned with *all* the behavior of the individual, both overt and under the skin [48, pp. 2–3].

For McClelland personality is—

The most adequate conceptualization of a person's behavior in all its detail that a scientist can give at a moment in time [151, p. 69].

Eysenck's definition follows rather closely that of Allport:

Personality is the more or less stable and enduring organization of a person's character, temperament, intellect and physique, which determines his unique adjustment to his environment [67, p. 2].

And in Hilgard we find the same influence. Personality is—

. . . the sum total of individual characteristics and ways of behaving which in their organization or patterning describe an individual's unique adjustment to his environment [109, p. 407].

Von Bertalanffy, the general systems theorist, offers "a tentative definition of the living organism."

A living organism is a hierarchy of open systems maintaining itself in a steady state due to its inherent system conditions. . . . It appears that a corresponding definition could be applied as a general model of personality [278, p. 37].

Sullivan notes—

. . . the relatively enduring pattern of recurrent interpersonal situations which characterize a human life [261, p. 111].

Finally, we may consider a contemporary definition based on an attempted integration of the most important theories of personality. Bronfenbrenner offers—

A conception of personality as a system of relatively enduring dispositions to experience, discriminate, or manipulate actual or perceived aspects of the individual's environment (including himself) [32, p. 158].

It may be noted that no definitions by psychoanalysts have been offered here. It seems that psychoanalytic writers from Freud [84] on have conceived of personality as synonymous with the psyche, and their theories of personality have been general psychological theories. Thus for Freud in his later, functionalist phase [81, 82, 83], the personality is made up of the three major systems, the *id,* the *ego,* and the *superego,* the interactions of which determine behavior. For Jung [119] also, the personality is made up of interacting systems, the principal ones being the *ego,* the *personal unconscious,* and the *shadow.*

For Fairbairn [69], a British psychoanalyst in the tradition of Melanie Klein, personality is a system comprising the *ego* and *internalized objects.*

Without unfairly or incorrectly committing any of the above writers to holistic views it is possible to say that for all of them personality is something, usually a very inclusive or comprehensive something, embracing parts or elements—processes, subsystems, characteristics—which are organized or patterned. (As for what the elements are—how they are to be conceptualized and how they are organized—that is another story.)

There is less agreement concerning the time perspective in which personality is seen. Some writers accent the organization of processes at a given moment, others accent the organization or patterning of sequences of events over long periods. This, however, does not seem to be a matter for any theoretical controversy; writers who are concerned about the organization of life cycles are not inclined to slight organization as of any given moment, and writers who focus upon the personality of the moment are not inclined to deny that this personality is lawfully related to its past and future.

There is also lack of agreement respecting the uniqueness of each personality and of its adjustments to its environment. Some writers seem to consider it important to mention this aspect (or supposed aspect) of personality, and others do not. This, as we shall see, is a controversial matter.

We may also note differences in the way writers delimit personality. Although the brief definitions given above cannot be said to represent the writers' total views on this matter, it does seem that we have to deal with different conceptions of the boundaries of personality. Does it or does it not include overt behavior, the products of behavior, some parts or features of an environment, physique and physiological functioning, character, temperament, and intelligence?

These, then, are the topics that must be discussed here: kinds of elements and the manner of their organization, personality in the perspective of time, the question of uniqueness, and the problem of boundaries.

THE SUBSTANCE OF PERSONALITY

The term "substance" is used here to refer to parts *and* how they are put together.

The undeveloped state of the field of personality psychology becomes apparent as soon as we turn to the ways in which psychologists have conceptualized the elements—the processes, the subsystems—that make up personality. Here variety and differences of opinion are the rule. This is not surprising when we consider that personality is an abstraction, a construction of the theorist; although related to empirical facts, it is not merely a summary of such facts. Thus it is that the elements of personality are ascribed by the theorist, and this in accordance with his preferences. For this reason, it is impossible at this stage to achieve an agreed definition of personality in terms of its substance.

The Search for Elements

Proposals of units into which personality might be analyzed have been many and varied during the course of the history of psychology. Many proposals are still in good standing. It is our task here to discuss the nature of the problem of analysis, to offer a brief survey of the proposals, to point out some considerations other than purely theoretical ones that have shaped the conceptualization of elements and, to note if possible, any trends in theory and in research.

Angyal [9] has pointed out that there are four possible ways to divide for purposes of study, a whole object, such as an animal, a plant, or a building. One can make random "cuts" and obtain a number of *fragments;* one can divide the whole according to a certain previously fixed principle which does not take into account the intrinsic nature of the whole (like dividing a tree into inch cubes); one can "divide" by abstraction, resolving the object into a number of distinguishable properties or features; finally, one can divide the whole according to its structural articulation, the lines of division being prescribed by the structure of the whole itself.

All of the ways of dividing personality have been attempted by psychologists.

The practice of making arbitrary cuts is a common one that has certain obvious advantages. For example, certain dispositions in the person might be chosen for investigation or assessment because of their practical importance. As in the case of the OSS assessment work [192], psychologists of quite different theoretical orientations can cooperate in the assessment of such dispositions and in investigations of their value as predictors of future performances—because no one is required to commit himself to a theory concerning the determinants of such dispositions or their relations one to another in the personality. The same can be said for the development, by strictly empirical means, of tests to predict socially relevant kinds of behavior—a type of enterprise that is still flourishing [18, 19, 20, 91, 101, 280]. Such proceedings are theoretically quite neutral; all that need be assumed is that personality has certain regularities of functioning that express themselves in consistent behavior and make prediction possible. Facts obtained in this empirical way are not to be despised; apart from their possible practical usefulness, they may later find a place in a theoretical formulation of personality—*if* the means by which they were obtained were indeed strictly empirical.

The practice of dividing personality in accordance with an irrelevant fixed principle is rarely—if ever—encountered in pure form in contemporary psychology of personality. The older stimulus-response psychology—according to which the basic unit for psychology was the stimulus-response connection and personality was simply the sum total of such connections—and the older faculty and factorial approaches to personality were pretty good examples of the present mode of dividing an object. Modern stimulus-response theory [58, 172, 174, 190, 191, 236, 237, 241] shows much awareness of the complexity of personality and has been concerned to introduce concepts to explain how stimulus-response elements are built up into larger wholes. Similarly, modern factor analysis [49, 65, 95] goes forward in accordance with some kind of conceptual model of personality functioning.

Abstracted features of the whole personality (e.g., soundness, stability, maturity, harmoniousness) are often used as variables. Indeed, the literature seems to show that students of personality can hardly do without such concepts; they creep almost inevitably into the discussion as soon as one devotes particular attention to any one individual. The use of such variables usually involves no commitment to any theoretical position; psychologists can agree to use the variables while differing in their formulations of the states, processes, and relationships that give rise to them. Such variables are also usually measured poorly, if at all. To appraise such features of a personality as soundness or stability obviously requires a pretty thoroughgoing understanding of that personality, such as could be attained only by intensive study over time. Psychologists have not studied personalities in this way very often, but—unable to make sense without reference to abstracted features of the whole—they have made do with ratings of them.

Psychologists have rarely undertaken to derive elements in accordance with the principle of structural articulation; that is, they have not often started with a conception of the whole personality and then sought to divide it along lines suggested by a theory of its organization. The most common practice has been to start with a general theory of behavior and then simply to transpose to personality whatever units of analysis had been adopted—"habits" for stimulus response theories [58, 174], "needs" for functionalist theories [181, 164, 181], "regions" for gestalt theories [47, 144], for example. Sears [235] considers this sound practice, while Allport [6] has considered it "wholly unsuitable." One might ask whether this practice is not in actuality an example of division according to an irrelevant fixed principle. I think this is not often clearly the case; as suggested above, most contemporary personality theorists who employ units of this kind show concern about the functional roles of these units in the organization of personality. Whether or not there is division according to an irrelevant fixed principle would have to be shown on the basis of careful analysis of particular cases. The fact remains, however, that starting with the whole is not the American way; a serious attempt to derive elements by taking the intrinsic nature of the whole into account would run headlong into the prevailing accent on the measurability of personality variables and on the prediction of behavior in concrete situations. For the best examples of division by structural articulation, it seems that we have to go back to the psychoanalytic theories of Freud

[81] and of Jung [119]. Each of these psychologists divided the psyche into several major systems; and propounded theory, according to which the nature of the whole was expressed in the interactions among these systems. Thus, none of Freud's three major systems—id, superego, ego—can be defined without reference to the others and to the whole personality. That these crude notions have persisted over the years seems to be largely due to the fact that psychologists do have occasion, particularly in clinical practice, to conceive of whole personalities, and for this purpose, better concepts than those of Freud have not as yet come along.

Allport's 1937 survey. Writing in 1937, G. W. Allport [6], grouped the proposals for the analysis of personality that had been made up to that time in the following way:

1. Practical and a priori classifications. These proposals would correspond in a general way to the random cuts and abstracted features mentioned above.

2. Uniform (nomothetic) elements, including faculties, elements of general psychology, such as habits, or images, or feelings, and dynamic elements of the nomothetic order such as Murray's *needs*.

3. Stimulus-response elements.

Allport was critical of all these kinds of elements; of those in the first group because they were of no theoretical interest or significance; of those in the second group because they were not distinctly *personal*, i.e., unique to the individual; and of those in the last group because they made insufficient allowance for the generality and complexity of personal dispositions. As his idea of a suitable element for the analysis of personality, he introduced the concept of trait, a biophysical, generalized, functionally autonomous, concrete, and personal determining tendency.

Some developments since 1937. In psychology a great deal of history has been made in the last twenty years. The search for elements of personality has continued apace, and although the dilemmas confronting the theorist seem to be about the same now as then, it seems possible to detect some trends in thought and in research.

For one thing, theorists seem to be considerably more aware of each other today than they were twenty years ago or earlier. Allport could point to various schemes for the analysis of the total personality and note that they scarcely overlapped. Today there is much more overlapping. The contemporary writer—even though he may be primarily an exponent of one of the classical theories of personality such as the stimulus-response, psychoanalytic, and field theoretical ones—is very likely to try to show that his scheme may be reconciled with other schemes, or that it takes into account or thoroughly embraces their important features. To be sure, a certain amount of theoretical imperialism persists, and a writer may implicitly invite others to share his assumption that his scheme is a better formulation of what the others are getting at, but even here there seems to be very considerable awareness of other approaches.

An aspect of this increase in mutual awareness among theorists is the tendency of each to strive for comprehensiveness—to include in his scheme the products of other people's thought and research. Murray, for example, in his most recent contribution to theory [183], acknowledges his indebtedness to colleagues in sociology and anthropology for helping him to bring his theory into line with current thinking about man in society. Again, Cattell [49] is best known as a "trait psychologist" or "factor theorist," but he seems to have no difficulty in including conceptions from dynamics psychology and psychoanalysis in his scheme.

Consistent with this there is perhaps an *increased sense of the complexity of personality.* Or perhaps there is a more widespread perception of the relative newness of this field and an increased sense of modesty about what we can hope to accomplish in the immediate future. Great minds have labored and left us not a general scheme that all can tentatively accept, but a variety of competing schemes which all seem to have some merit. Every day there is a fresh call for a general theory of personality, but not many psychologists seem willing to take on the task of creating one. There is much discussion and much disagreement concerning the kind of theory or, more particularly, the kind of conceptual model that we ought to have [30, 66, 72, 127, 150, 160, 161, 196, 209, 254, 278]. This increases our sophistication about theory making, but perhaps at the same time our cautiousness about offering anything more than a preliminary or tentative outline or sketch also increases. It is not that eclecticism is particularly valued; on the contrary, "having a theory" or "starting with a theory" seems very much the favored thing; it is rather that psychologists seem somewhat humbled and frustrated before the vastness of the problem. Happily, this state of affairs does not seem to have put any brakes upon research in the field. It is possible operationally to define innumerable variables of personality in terms of consistency in behavior, hypothesizing some underlying regularity of functioning, and, to state some theory in accordance with which one can predict certain relationships with fair accuracy. One cannot study everything at once in any case, and one may hope that facts discovered in this way may some day find a place within an over-all formulation.

Dynamic elements of the nomothetic order have continued to be the most typical variables of personality. Personality theorists traditionally have preferred a functionalist point of view or "action frame of reference" [Parsons, 195, 196], that is, a way of looking at behavior that gives a central place to strivings that are important to the survival, growth, and identity of the organism [34, 79, 126, 154, 155, 181, 209]. To accomplish these purposes in the complex and changing environment that is every person's lot involves the setting and the achievement of diverse goals. Modes of striving, that is, the kinds of goals and techniques that are successful in reducing tension, removing stress, or maintaining equilibrium are learned and become more or less characteristic of the individual. Thus all theories of personality posit a multiplicity of *motives* as more or less durable attributes of the person. There are differences of views concerning the fundamental nature of striving, the number of different motives that should be conceptualized, the manner in which they are learned, the degree of their generality, and the nature of their relations one to another—but there does not seem to be much doubt that motives exist as elements of personality.

The functional point of view has a great many immediate implications. The conception of an organism striving in a complex environment and learning in accordance with experiences of success and failure is actually the basis for the formulation of a great many variables of personality. It is common to distinguish *goal states* (conditions of reduced tension, or equilibrium with concomitant gratification) from *goal objects* (objects—to use the broadest sense of the term—that become important because of their role in attaining goal states) and to distinguish both goal states and goal objects from instrumentalities, techniques, or devices calculated to further the attainment of goals. This differentiation becomes the basis for three broad classes of personality variables: motives (needs, impulses, drive states); motive-object combinations (sentiments, object relations, attitudes, values—in certain common senses of these words); and instrumental traits (modes, style).

This breakdown does not meet with universal approval. Opinions differ as to which of the above terms are to be preferred and how they should be defined. And more than this, clearly the same phenomena may be dealt with on different levels of analysis; for example, *habits* might be identified in each of the three areas. But this will have to suffice as a rough statement about some of the major kinds of elements of personality that proceed from the prevailing functionalist point of view.

In recent years the accent upon motives has decreased and the accent upon cognitive variables of personality has increased. According to the functionalist point of view, the cognitive processes of a person are in the service of his adaptive needs. There is a long tradition of personality research that has attempted to show the influence of motivational factors, such as needs, sentiments, attitudes, and values, upon various kinds of cognitive functions, ranging from the perception of differences among weights to the building of systems of belief [2, 36, 78, 128, 180, 201, 203, 207, 215, 220, 225, 251, 288]. The numerous cognitive variables of personality that have been posited—ideologies, belief systems, cognitive structures—have been seen as having a functional role in the over-all adjustment of the individual.

This frame of reference in psychology, though it has long had its exponents within academic psychology [e.g., W. McDougall, 154, 155], has been most characteristically the psychology of the clinic; its rise to influence in the general field of psychology is a part of the history of clinical psychology. In the thirties and forties, the efforts of the functionalists to put across their point of view was a source of considerable excitement within the ranks of academic psychologists. Today the functionalists' struggle seems largely to have been won; they have been able to relax, even to inquire whether cognitive functions did not deserve more attention as variables in their own right, as variables having perhaps a certain independence of motives. In these circumstances, the long-time experts in cognition [e.g., 10, 35, 104, 149, 242, 279] have, of course, come in for their innings.

Cognition comes in for fresh attention in two ways: first, as a motive in its own right; and second, as a function independent of motive, having its own laws and developmental history and possibly interacting with motive.

The need to know, to find meaning, to achieve some kind of structure in the world that one perceives, first brought into prominence by Bartlett [22] and reemphasized by Tolman [272], has recently been used by G. Kelly [122] as the fundamental postulate in a whole system of psychology. In Kelly's system, the cognitive process of anticipating events —far from being merely in the service of more fundamental needs—is itself a disposition so fundamental that many of the so-called "basic psychological needs" may operate in *its* service—for example, aggression may be understood as an effort to force events to go according to one's expectations.

To put so much emphasis on the striving aspect of cognition is different from merely saying that to cognize is in the nature of the beast or saying, with Krech and Crutchfield [137], that "man is an organizing animal as far as his perceptions are concerned." From this point of view, it is not so much that cognition alone may determine molar behavior as that cognition enters into the determination of all behavior, and that cognition and the products of past cognition may set the limits within which motivations may operate. If what a man knows depends on what he needs, so may his needs depend on what he knows or believes or expects. If man cannot help but cognize and if, through cognizing, he builds up a fund of experience, then it may be said that what he knows, believes, and expects at any given time depends heavily upon what his environment has chanced to put in his way.

Thus an accent on cognition usually goes with an accent on the environment rather than personality needs as a determinant of behavior. And if a man sets his goals in accordance with his experience, then clearly many of his motives will depend upon his past or present cognitive functioning. Consequently, an accent on cognition tends to accompany an accent on conscious—as opposed to unconscious—processes and, with respect to the life history of the individual, an accent on later rather than on earlier events in explaining the development of personality.

Interestingly, there is also a new willingness to give cognitive processes their due—perhaps more than their due—in psychoanalysis, perhaps the most functionalist or action-oriented of all functionalist psychologies, as well as in psychology generally. This is seen in the contemporary pre-occupation of American writers with what the psychoanalysts call "ego psychology" [88, 98, 208]. The new ego psychology, set forth by Hartmann, Kris, and Lowenstein [98], argues that the ego, which embraces diverse cognitive functions, does not emerge from the id, but has its own independent origins and course of development.

This is not the place to go into the theoretical issues involved. The main point here is that virtually all personality theorists today are at considerable pains to conceptualize cognitive variables of personality— cognitive habits, cognitive structures, cognitive systems, cognitive maps; beliefs, opinions, expectations, conceptions, ideologies, and so on. And owing to the new inclination to assign these cognitive variables varying amounts of autonomy or even the status of determinants of goals, there is a fresh appreciation of the complexity of the relationships within the personality.

The accent on cognitive variables, though it has its own independent history, may be viewed as *a part of a larger current emphasis on the higher mental processes and upon the distinctively human (as opposed to animal) in man.* This trend may be most readily identified by contrasting it with behaviorism and psychoanalysis, against which it, in large part, is a reaction. If these two schools of thought have emphasized such "low" things as instincts and impulses and automatic conditioning, the new trend accents man's "higher" nature, his rationality, his self-consciousness. Here the influence of gestalt psychology has been strong: It states that the "higher processes" are usually "larger wholes" which are considered to have as much "reality" as the elementary processes to which psycho-analysis and behaviorism would "reduce" all phenomena.

This trend of thought has been supported by certain trends in research and practice, even as it has helped to stimulate them. Of great importance has been the intensive study of normal—and superior—people, with the use of methods and concepts derived primarily from the clinic [21, 111, 121, 150, 157, 163, 181, 224, 259, 267, 268]. Murray's early work at the Harvard Psychological Clinic [181] was the beginning. This was pure research into the functioning of the normal personality as a whole. Personality assessment in more recent years, beginning with the OSS venture [192], has usually had a practical orientation—to select individuals for social roles in which they might be "effective," a proceeding which put the accent on "positive" competencies, virtues, resources, and the like.

Paralleling this development has been the spread of the notion, in America, that psychotherapy is not merely a means for treating ailments or relieving suffering but a positive good that might well be made available to everybody. The rise of clinical psychology and its interest in defining a distinctive role for itself has combined with and been nurtured by the traditional American interest in self-improvement. The result has been a climate in which the aims of psychotherapy and the goals of personality development are matters of lively concern [13, 21, 63, 115, 116, 163, 178, 229, 233, 240, 250, 265, 284, 287].

A means for defining such objectives has been found in the idea of growth [63, 284]. Sometimes growth toward such objectives as autonomy, stable self-identity, and integration is regarded as "natural" [White, 284, Erikson, 62, 63, 64]; sometimes it is regarded merely as change—under the impact of culture—in directions that are valued in this particular society. In either case, the psychotherapist has found himself allied with developmental psychologists and specialists in child training and education whose chief concern is with the conditions favoring or hampering this or that developmental desideratum.

Psychoanalysts and behaviorists of thirty years ago would probably have been horrified to be told that they were reducing the image of man and showing a woeful disregard for his potentialities. They would have been justified in thinking that by attending to neglected aspects of man's nature and contributing facts and theories that explained his behavior they were at long last offering that noble creature some means for controlling himself. Psychologists identified with these schools of thought today might well deny that their schemes are essentially nonhumanistic or inadequate to deal with man's "higher" functions, or they might argue that the whole issue of "higher" versus "lower" is, in the context of science, meaningless. But the fact remains that their critics [e.g., 8, 10, 122, 164, 212] have gone on to conceptualize variables of personality that are designed to deal with the more social, the more mature, the more rational aspects of man—all of which had small place in the older scheme.

The differences in general outlook with which we are concerned here are reflected in differences in theory; in their turn, these have led to some differences in the conceptualization affecting all the kinds of variables of personality. Thus if we are to follow Maslow [165], we have to posit not only the usual drive-reduction (*deficit*) motives, but *growth* motives as well; if we are to follow the modern trend in cognitive psychology, we must put the accent not so much on illusions, projections, and other need-driven distortions of reality as on the self-active processes of perception and on the more mature, more rational, and more complicated cognitive structures; and if we are to follow one of the main streams in modern dynamic theory of personality, we must put relatively less emphasis upon the defensive activities of the ego and relatively more emphasis upon its constructive, positively adaptive functions.

When our concern is with the conceptualization of variables of personality, this fact is particularly important: Where the accent is on the positive, the healthy, the mature, the socially valuable, and so on, it is necessary to speak of features of the whole personality. By observing the whole person engaged in transactions with his environment, we are able to appraise his efficiency, creativity, autonomy, and the like; by regarding the whole person as a system, we are able to gain some appreciation of his differentiation, integration, flexibility, resilience, soundness, and breadth.

Psychologists who accent higher mental processes seem to give larger place in their scheme of things to the concept of self. In the recent literature of research and theory, this concept seems to have attained very considerable prominence [7, 26, 51, 108, 211, 212, 230, 246, 249, 253, 258, 263, 283].

In much of this literature self and ego are discussed together. Sometimes the two terms are regarded as synonymous; sometimes they are used to refer to different phenomena, with sometimes the one and sometimes the other term being used to stand for the same phenomenon. Writers who employ both self and ego as different concepts usually consider the two to be related—with different degrees of intimacy. Some writers get by with only one of these concepts; in this case, the one embraces much the same phenomena that other writers treat with the use of both concepts.

Perhaps the present state of affairs is not quite so hopelessly confused as this. Two quite different trends in personality theory seem to have converged, and the process of sorting out the contributions of the two has not yet been completed. Psychologists of the functionalist persuasion, who have conceived of the personality as embodying a multiplicity of strivings, have always recognized the likelihood of conflict—among the strivings and between the strivings and the environment—hence, they have found it necessary to conceive of mechanisms or processes in accordance with which the activities of the person were regulated. The regulating functions—inhibition, scheduling, reality testing, decision making, and the like—have usually been thought to be related, constituting a system, in other words. Hence, the ego in psychoanalysis and in modern dynamic theory of personality.

At the same time, awareness of oneself has long been regarded as a particularly salient aspect of human experience. Psychologists who have been focused upon experience have been interested to explore the dimensions and the conditions of this salient feature. Apparently there is a great deal to be explored. As Adams [1] pointed out, an individual can get a good preliminary idea of what is meant by personality itself by examining what he means when he uses the pronoun "I."

But neither Adams nor many other writers wish to argue that this content of awareness is all there is to personality, or even that all the regulatory processes often called "ego" necessarily find their way into awareness. Thus we may note in much contemporary writing two conceptions that are clearly distinct: (1) a group of processes usually called "ego functions," and (2) a content of awareness that the perceiving individual refers to as his "self."

Each of these conceptions supplies the basis for numerous variables of personality. Various so-called "ego functions" have been distinguished [80, 185, 209, 222, 262], and these are considered to vary in prominence and effectiveness from one individual to another. To the long list of psychoanalytic mechanisms, as we have seen, academic psychologists have been wont to add various more constructive, integrative, or fundamentally more adaptive functions. More than this, it is common to conceive of the ego as a system in some sense of this term, perhaps usually as a set of related variables. This has meant that one could ascribe to the ego all the properties and the attributes that could be ascribed to any system.

With respect to the experience of self, it has been possible to distinguish numerous variables of content and organization—what features are ascribed, how are they patterned, how is this pattern valued, how consistent is it over time, and so on. Actually, the self of experience has also been conceived as a system, embracing subsystems, and hence variables on the order of differentiation, integration, breadth, and rigidity.

If the self of awareness, the perceived or conceived self, or the phenomenal self or the self image is strictly a matter of individual experience, then it seems proper enough to ask—as many psychologists have done—what processes underlie this experience or other experiences. And it seems proper to go ahead and make inferences concerning these processes—hence, the inferred self [Hilgard, 108], a complex structure or structures. More variables. This would be the "real" self, the one that the psychologist can study by appropriate techniques. And if he should succeed in getting a grip upon it, he would be in a position to appraise the discrepancies between what is really there and what the subject experiences.

In the common view, there is considerable affinity between the self of awareness and the processes usually ascribed to the ego. In the classical psychoanalytic view, the ego is the part of the personality that is closest to consciousness and in closest touch with the external world. Some of its major functions, such as intending and decision making, are well calculated to give the individual the impression that his self is determining what he will do. More than this, processes that are not of the ego, in the psychoanalytic view (e.g., primitive impulses, or readinesses to respond automatically to threats of punishment) are likely to be excluded by the individual from his conception of himself. This certainly argues for considerable overlap between conscious ego processes and the self of awareness.

On the other hand, no writer who makes systematic use of ego as regulative processes considers that all these processes are represented in awareness. Nor is it usually held that the processes underlying the phenomenal self are limited to the so-called "ego processes."

Thus there emerge four major conceptions that have some currency and respectability: (1) regulative processes and mechanisms, often considered to be related and to constitute an ego system; (2) the self of awareness or phenomenal self; (3) regulative processes and mechanisms that enter into awareness and become candidates for inclusion in the phenomenal self; and (4) the inferred self, the aggregate of processes underlying the phenomenal self.

Obviously, none of the first three of these conceptions is coterminous with personality itself, and none is so considered. Rather, they are parts or elements of the whole—but they are complex parts and may be "divided" by analysis according to some theory of their structure and functioning or by abstracting some of their features. The inferred self would appear to come close to being the same thing as personality. It seems, at any rate, that anything about the personality might conceivably be incorporated by the individual into his phenomenal self. On the other hand, he might make similar use of some things that are not in his personality—his body or certain features of his environment, perhaps what others mistakenly attribute to him or what he mistakenly appropriates, for example.

This brief account, focused as it is upon candidates for the status of element of personality, rather bypasses the lively theoretical controversy that marks the whole area of the self and the ego. Much of the controversy concerns the origins and determinants of the self and the ego and their relations to the rest of the personality and hence is not particularly relevant to a survey of elements. One of the main differences of opinion has to do with the question of how many of the functions that psychoanalysts and psychoanalytically oriented psychologists attribute to the ego might more properly be attributed to the phenomenal self. In general, of course, writers who emphasize what we have called the higher things are inclined to attach more importance to the phenomenal self. Here, as much as in any area of personality psychology, controversy and confusion flourish in the absence of suitable objective indexes of the hypothetical constructs with which we are concerned. If there were sufficient methodological access to the ego and to the inferred self, theoretical issues could be turned quickly into empirical questions.

An interesting feature of contemporary writing about the self and about the ego is its holistic orientation. This orientation, as we have seen, has been with us for a long time; for an equally long time psychologists have been put off by the implications of unanalyzability contained in the term "whole personality" and have tended to scoff at the idea of actually studying anything so "global" [66]. To judge by recent writings, there is less objection to conceiving of or studying the whole self or the whole ego by empirical means. More than this, approaches to the study of these hypothetical subsystems have been rather strictly holistic in that the whole and its parts have been seen as mutually related, changes in a part being capable of affecting the whole and the functioning of the whole being capable of determining what happens in the parts.

Holism was the core principle in the views of Lecky, one of the early important contributors to the theory of the phenomenal self.

The point is that all of an individual's ideas are organized into a single system, whose preservation is essential. In order to be immediately assimilated the idea found as the result of a new experience must be felt to be consistent with the ideas already present in the system. . . . The nucleus of the system, around which the rest of the system revolves, is the individual's idea or conception of himself [141, p. 150].

Rogers [212] and other writers who have been more or less identified with his school of "client-centered" psychotherapy—Snygg and Combs [253], for example—are in Lecky's tradition. It is a fact of considerable importance for developments in personality psychology that Rogers and his students and associates have not merely adopted holism as a comfortable philosophy, but have made it the cornerstone of their psychotherapeutic work and research. With the phenomenal self as the nucleus of the personality organization, the holistic view dictates that the way to change the individual's behavior is to change his conception of himself, and this is the major task in client-centered psychotherapy. Where the concern is with research on the processes and effects of psychotherapy or on personality growth—and this has long been a major concern of Rogers and his associates—the procedure is to explore the phenomenal self directly by a variety of techniques involving self reports, to study diverse patterns of behavior in relation to the phenomenal self, and to see how this self changes with varying conditions. Recent years have seen an outpouring of research in these areas [e.g., 33, 206, 213, 218, 238]. Whereas psychologists differ with respect to the role and functions of the phenomenal self, not many deny that such a self exists or that studies of its contents and vicissitudes are useful.

The same holistic orientation may be found in other contemporary writers of quite different theoretical points of view. G. Klein, for example, works with a psychoanalytic conception of ego and, with a great deal of research to go on, has been a particularly effective spokesman for holism.

Our target is a theory which would lead to laws of *perceivers*, not laws of perception, a theory which would be not so much concerned with linking generalized field conditions or states of motivation to perception in general as with linking them with the organization of people. . . . The placating formula which a person develops—his equilibrating mechanisms—are his *ego-control system* . . . if analyses of perception are to have any relevance to personality theory, they must disclose how the control principles, the equilibrating mechanisms appear *in* and *through* its functioning [125, pp. 328–330].

Again Hilgard has written that—

All the (Freudian) mechanisms imply a self-reference, and . . . the mechanisms are not understandable unless we adopt a concept of the self [108, p. 376].

The concept of the self that Hilgard prefers is that of the inferred self. The chief point is that the functioning of any one of the mechanisms—what can be observed about it—depends upon the activities and states of the inferred self.

There is, of course, little here that cannot be found in the works of the older holistic or organismic writers [e.g., 9, 89, 141, 210, 252, 282]. The point is that this general orientation gains increasingly wide acceptance and plays an increasingly important role in the design of research.

The holistic or organismic orientation that is apparent in contemporary discussions of the self and the ego would appear to be part of a larger trend toward increasing acceptance and utilization of ideas from gestalt psychology [134, 135, 144], the organismic view in biology [210, 219], and general-systems theory [4, 94, 170, 171, 277, 278].

Allport [6] could remark in 1937 that certain conceptions drawn from gestalt psychology, such for example, as Wertheimer's *radix*, Koffka's *ego-systems*, Lewin's *regions*, *tension-systems*, *inner-personal strata* and the like "were helpful." MacKinnon [158] called for an integration of Lewin's "topological psychology" and the kind of dynamic psychology represented by Murray. And Rapaport—according to Hall and Lindzey [97]—when reviewing H. Werner's *Comparative Psychology of Mental Development* [281] in 1940, could point out that this systematic treatment of development from the gestalt point of view was not in reality a theory of development and that what was needed was an integration of gestalt psychology and psychoanalysis.

The intervening years seem not to have brought any new over-all syntheses embodying both a more or less complete gestalt or systems theory and a thoroughgoing functionalist or behavior theory, but there has been a steady increase in the use of gestalt and "systems-theoretical" concepts by most writers. Sometimes it seems that the concepts have crept in as they have gradually become a part of the general culture of psychology; sometimes they seem to have been deliberately adopted as a means for supplementing an existing theoretical structure. The quotation from Schjelderup with which we began seems to be an example of the latter. The gestalt or general-systems concepts are used to build a kind of formal model of the personality, the parts or regions then being filled in with more specific contents and the whole thing set in motion with the use of the psychoanalytic mechanisms.

For a long time the common reaction of American researchers to the gestalt and general-systems imports was that there was nothing wrong with the new concepts except that there was no way to obtain measures of them—nothing wrong, in other words, except that they were useless. However, as abstracted features of the whole personality (integration, adaptability) and the properties of subsystems (breadth, complexity, rigidity, isolation) have become household words among writers, there has been increasingly wide recognition that one *has* to have objective indexes of these things. Accordingly, researchers have been getting down to the serious business of supplying operational definitions. Hence there has been a great increase in the number and variety of personality variables treated in research reports, the increment being made up in large part of measures pertaining to the properties of subsystems or the whole personality system.

If personality is more of a whole than it used to be, it seems also to be more "social." As we have seen, the major accent of the traditional functionalists was on strivings, the organism's *own* strivings, rather than on its responsiveness to the environmental stimuli of that moment. To clinch the argument for strivings, the usual recourse was to biology, to man's kinship with the lower animals, at least in this respect. It must have seemed obvious to Freud and McDougall, who were in the tradition of Darwin, that the needs to survive and to perpetuate the species were fundamental to all human activity. More modern psychologists, aware of their own purposes, have examined the rat to see if he was not governed in the same way, and this agreeable creature has obliged by confirming most of the hypotheses of purposivism. Meanwhile, with the development of anthropology and sociology, evidence that virtually all the distinguishable features of personality are correlated with features of the cultural or of the social environment of the individual's remote or recent past has gradually accumulated and become rather overwhelming. Thus one of the major problems of gamesmanship among the personality psychologists of the functionalist point of view has been how to become more "social" without really changing. They were able to point out that their systems had always made place for learning in the social environment. However, the fact remains that during the past twenty-five years there has been a steady increase in the number and variety of personality variables representing what has been learned or internalized through interaction with the social environment, e.g., "role dispositions," "interpersonal reaction systems," "social values," and so on [143, 186, 187].

A final trend in theory making may be noted. Twenty years ago, the personality theorist went to considerable pains to marshal the arguments and the evidence in favor of the *generality* of his major personality variables—the traits or needs or attitudes that were his units of analysis. For example, G. Allport [6] agreed that honesty was a general trait in the sense that honest behavior was evoked by a wide variety of situations, and Murray [181] agreed that "needs" were general in the sense that directed striving was evoked by a kind of stimulus situation and persisted —with variations in instrumental behavior—until a kind of end situation was reached. At the time, such conceptions had to be defended against the prevalent "habit psychology," which argued that particular responses were learned in particular situations and that specific stimulus-response connections were the essential elements of personality [99, 100]. The controversy was a lively one for a number of years, but today it seems to have receded into the background—though it may be becoming salient again [45, 124]. This would appear to be one of those instances in which a problem more or less disappears—not because it is solved, but because it is replaced by other more pressing problems. At any rate, almost all of the kinds of elements of personality that have been considered in this essay have been conceived as having some generality. Undoubtedly, enough evidence from research has been accumulated so that the authors or defenders of generalized traits, needs, attitudes, or systems feel some security. Yet it is likely that no one would care to argue that specificity of habit or of fixation does not also exist in nature. And the processes of generalization or fixation seem to be just about as obscure as ever. Most students of personality seem willing to consider that man is both a generalizing and a fixating animal and that how much generality or specificity will characterize a given disposition of a person is an empirical question.

Considerations other than theoretical ones influencing the conceptualization of elements of personality. The discussion thus far seems to have shown clearly enough that the kinds of elements into which personality is analyzed proceed from the kinds of general theories with which different writers approach the field. Also, the kinds of elements preferred and the ways in which they are conceptualized appear to depend to some extent upon a worker's orientation with respect to method of approach and with respect to the kind of problem he has set himself.

We have already seen, for example, that workers concerned with practical problems—personality assessment or the development of useful tests, for example—may get by with a minimum of theory or make use of elements that are theoretically neutral. When the psychologist addresses himself to these or other practical problems involving people, he is very likely to use categories that are at once coarser and less abstract than the categories that would appeal to the experimentalist or to the devotee of elegant theory. For example, the psychotherapist, faced with the task of making sense of vast quantities of verbal material, has no alternative but to employ gross units of analysis; faced with the task of taking action, often on short notice, he has to deal with the relatively concrete and particular—without stopping to translate his thoughts into the terms of a general theoretical system. Much the same considerations hold in the case of a psychologist who wishes to develop a test that will be predictive of behavior in some practical situation.

Differences among psychologists in respect to preferred size of analytic categories and preferred level of abstraction often seem to be mistaken for differences in fundamental theory or orientation, and communication among workers having these different preferences increases very slowly— if at all. One could not, of course, ask the practical worker to use finer categories or less concrete conceptions than are suited to his purpose; one could ask only that he use concepts that lend themselves to reduction and systematic treatment. And one could ask the general theorist, who would clear up fine points of his scheme by experimentation, to consider occasionally what his fine units might add up to in the way of molar behavior and how his general scheme might be filled in with contents familiar to the practical worker.

Related to molarity of elements and abstractness of concepts is the matter of *observability of the variables of personality.* Strictly speaking, no elements of personality are observable with perfect directness; all are *inferred* from behavioral indexes. But there is wide variation in the degree of directness or explicitness with which the inferences may be made [23, 25, 168]. This is a matter about which students of personality still differ widely. Some prefer to stick close to the facts of observation and to treat manifest behavior characteristics as the elements of personality; others permit themselves the use of hypothetical constructs, such as unconscious hostility toward one's father, which have highly indirect ties to what is observable.

The issue involved here has a long history. The early psychology of personality, particularly aspects stemming from the clinic, made free and sometimes freewheeling use of hypothetical constructs. For many critics, this was "mysticism" that had no place in "scientific psychology." The scientific psychology of the time was mainly a kind of know-nothing behaviorism whose stock in trade was objectivity. To these critics of personality theory, the discovery of Bridgman's operationism [31] was a great boon. It became something of a fashion to reject—as being outside of science—concepts that could not be "defined operationally," that is, in terms of steps taken to obtain an objective index of a given concept. It had always been possible to stall a conversation with a personality theorist by asking him to define his terms; now, by asking him to define his terms operationally, one could make him wish that he had remained silent from the beginning. But the personality theorists, exhibiting their characteristic adaptability—according to which they are always changing while always remaining essentially the same—continued to do what they were doing, but somewhat more cautiously and with somewhat more attention to conceptual clarity and to objective indicators of their hypothetical constructs and theoretical statements.

The personality theorists have been vindicated to a considerable extent. Today it is possible to say that "operationism in psychology" has changed, while the constructs that came under its strongest attack are very much alive and kicking. A great deal of discussion—philosophers of science have been influential participants [24, 70, 71, 73, 105, 234]—has led to the fairly generally accepted conclusion that the radical operationism of Bridgman is not the best guide in psychological theory making. Today it is pretty generally recognized that there are practically no theoretical statements that can be completely and directly verified by observation and that hypothetical constructs are not only necessary to the activity of the human intellect, but have led to the best success in predicting and explaining behavior. Modern operationism does not require that every concept be defined in terms of operations, but only that it be somehow connectable, however indirectly, with some kind of observable. Thus the "operational reformulation of psychoanalysis," as Ellis [61] has shown, does not mean replacing psychoanalytic concepts and theories with something entirely different—not many of them, at any rate—but showing how they may be stated in molar terms at the level of intervening variables so that they may be confirmed or disproved by observation.

Constructs to stand for processes central to or "deep within" the personality have as good standing as they ever did—perhaps better. But this does not mean that all theorists feel free to use such constructs. After all, a bias in favor of the objective, the tangible, and the immediately observable existed long before operationism was invented; so did a bias in favor of the vaguely all-inclusive, intangible, and difficult to observe or unobservable. Psychologists still locate themselves at different places on the scale extending from one of these extreme positions [87, 248] (the objectivist) to the other [183, 209, 274]. And this is to some extent independent of general theoretical position. A strictly operationalistic psychology would have to be behavioristic, but modern behaviorists divide rather sharply on the issue of hypothetical constructs. And among personality theorists and clinical psychologists who prefer the vague but inclusive dynamic concepts, some are far more concerned about verifiability than others.

In general, it seems that the issue—free use of hypothetical constructs versus accent on observability—is not so sharply drawn as it used to be. Although the situation at this moment is somewhat obscure, a consideration of the past twenty-five or thirty years shows a slow but steady movement in the direction of greater accent upon and greater acceptance of the more intangible in personality theory. Psychologists of the more hardheaded variety have discovered that they may look into some of the more interesting and dubious conceptualizations of the personologists without loss of scientific respectability, and personality and clinical psychologists, whose stock in trade would naturally be—by virtue of their upbringing—the dynamic theories of personality, psychoanalytic or other, have grown in methodological sophistication.

To some extent, preference respecting elements for the analysis of personality seems to be associated with *preferences for certain methods of investigation*. The psychologist with a strong attachment to the experimental method must, of course, limit himself to variables that can be manipulated experimentally. But in one view—perhaps the most common one—there are aspects of personality that cannot be experimented upon in the usual laboratory situation. This may be either because of their nature (e.g., things that are apparent only when the person is observed in numerous varied situations or things whose meaning cannot be detected unless they are seen in a very broad context) or because of the present technical difficulties (e.g., arousing in a laboratory guilt feelings equal in quality and intensity to those in the clinician's scheme of things). In the circumstances, it is natural for the convinced experimentalist not only to set problems for which his method is suited, but actually to conceive of personality as made up of elements of the sort that he can get hold of, as it were. Hence a tendency to regard personality as an aggregate of measurable performances; hence a tendency to treat measures as elements of personality rather than indexes (of dubious validity) of true elements which are capable of manifesting themselves in various other measurable performances. Such method-centeredness [162] naturally makes for superficiality. And it permits the experimentalist to be easier on himself than is healthy. If our gifted experimentalists would spend less time in trying to cut personality to fit the pattern of tried and true methodology and more time in devising techniques for studying what the dynamic theorist or common sense itself regards as elements of personality, both our experimental methodology and our knowledge of personality functioning would probably advance more rapidly.

Another example of method-centeredness is the tendency found among experts in objective personality testing by verbal means to over-accent the consistent and the common—to the neglect of the inconsistent and the rare, which may be even more significant. Again, there seems to be a tendency among devotees of projective tests to conceive of a personality as an organization of fantasies and defense mechanisms whose overt behavior—difficult to predict from projective tests—does not matter very much.

Probably most psychologists would agree, when not forced to defend their favored method, that personality is complicated enough to require study by all existing psychological methods and some that have not yet been invented.

Some students of personality are interested primarily in differences among people, others in differences in the same person at different times. In other words, some are interested in durable attributes with respect to which individuals clearly differ, which are predictive of behavior in varied situations, and which provide meaningful and practically useful bases for sorting people out [e.g., 65, 91, 101, 243]. Others are interested in personality change [e.g., 54, 56, 157, 231]. This makes a difference in the kinds of elements that are conceived or preferred. The investigator of individual differences is likely to concentrate upon attributes (e.g., abilities, temperamental traits) or tendencies (e.g., introversion-extroversion, neuroticism, delinquency, masculinity-femininity) which have presumed correlates in the soma or the genes or which on empirical ground appear to be highly generalized and pervasive. On the other hand, students of change prefer elements that, according to theory, have their major correlates in experience, e.g., social attitudes, values, opinions, and dispositions in respect to interpersonal relationships. This last constitutes at least one respect in which experimentalists and psychotherapists belong together and separate from the inveterate mental tester.

It would naturally occur to someone concerned to survey psychologists' proposals for elements of personality to consider that perhaps the psychology of personality is what personality psychologists do, that the essential or important elements are the most persistently investigated. This would be a losing game so far as American psychology is concerned. One's conception of the substance of personality would depend upon the date of the work used as a sample. The fact is that personality research in this country—thanks to our ability and our desire to communicate and our higher regard for facts than for theories—is highly susceptible to trends and fashions. One year it will be "values" that occupy the center of the stage; another year, "anxiety" or "cognitive structures" or "authoritarianism" or the "achievement motive." This is not to suggest that the fashionable life is bad; on the contrary, it is interesting and, in a way, productive. It does suggest that attention to what investigators happen to be doing at a particular time is a poor guide to an understanding of the substance of personality.

Summary.   Personality is always conceived of as a whole, requiring analysis into parts or elements. The logically possible ways of dividing a whole—by random cuts, in accordance with a fixed principle, by abstracting features of the whole, in accordance with some theory concerning its structural articulation—all have been used by psychologists in their efforts to find suitable elements. Allport, in his 1937 survey [6], found all these practices, but noted that the most significant and important proposals proceeded from some general theory of personality or of the mental life. Hence (1) uniform elements, including faculties, elements from general psychology, dynamic elements of the nomothetic order, and factors, (2) stimulus-response elements; and (3) Allport's own concept of *trait*.

The dilemmas confronting the personality theorist today seem in a number of basic ways the same as they were in 1937, but a study of the last twenty years reveals significant trends in thought and research. Theorists seem to be more aware of each other and frequently more willing to include other people's contributions in their own hopefully comprehensive schemes. There is an increased sense of the complexity of personality, which manifests itself in repeated calls for a general theory and a cautious modesty about presuming to offer one.

Dynamic elements of the nomothetic order—needs, motives, and strivings, with their related goal states, goal objects, and instrumentalities (the essential conceptions of the functionalist point of view)—have generally improved their position so that they have a rather commanding place among the personality variables. But in recent years particularly there has been a decreasing accent on motives and a rather sharply increased accent on variables of cognition. This seems to be a part of a larger movement in the direction of "thinking about higher things," a movement that seems to be largely a reaction against the biological and clinical emphasis of the older functionalist theories, including psychoanalytic theories. Another part of this movement seems to be the greatly increased interest in the self or ego, part systems of the personality in whose functioning the more highly developed—the healthier, the more mature, productive, and efficient—aspects of personality come into their own.

Contemporary thinking about the functioning of the self or of the ego shows a strong holistic or organismic orientation. This seems to be an aspect of another general trend—the increasing acceptance and utilization of ideas from gestalt psychology, general-systems theory, and the organismic point of view in biology. The role of these ideas has been not so much to modify existing theoretical schemes as to supplement them; but in performing this function they have led to the conceptualization of numerous new variables of personality, particularly variables pertaining to the formal properties of subsystems and the whole personality.

If personality is more of a whole than it used to be, it is also more social than it used to be. Developments in sociology and anthropology have been accompanied by a steady increase in the number and variety of personality variables representing what has been learned in the social or cultural environment. The old argument about the generality versus the specificity of personality elements seems to have died down; other issues seem to have replaced this one, and until it again comes to the fore, most psychologists seem willing to give some place to both generality and specificity.

But considerations other than theoretical ones or commitments to particular theoretical systems have seemed to influence the conceptualization of elements of personality.

Psychologists who are concerned with practical problems perforce use categories of analysis that are coarser and less abstract than those which appeal to the experimentalist or devotee of elegant theory. This is a continuing source of misunderstanding and failure in communication. Psychologists also differ in the degree of their regard for hypothetical constructs or, more particularly, in the degree of indirectness or implicitness in the relationship between construct and observable that they are willing to tolerate. Understanding of the problems involved here has increased greatly in the past twenty years, and the trend during this period has been toward wider as well as more sophisticated use of hypothetical constructs.

Some psychologists are particularly interested in persistent differences among people, others in how the same person changes. The former prefer to investigate variables that are presumably genetically or somatically linked or at least highly generalized and pervasive; the latter put the accent on variables supposed to be correlated with experience.

Method-centeredness and the tendency to follow fashion in research are still fairly prominent features of the American psychological scene. They help to determine at a particular time what elements of personality seem generally to be preferred. These tendencies favor the production of factual knowledge, but they contribute nothing to advances in theory and, unless seen in a broad perspective, they give a misleading impression of the state of affairs on the theoretical front.

The Structure of Personality

How structure is conceived and explained is even closer to the heart of a theory of personality than is the choice of elements, and one could hardly do justice to the theorists who have attacked this problem without setting forth their systems in some detail. Since this is not the place for such a survey, the present treatment may be limited to a few salient issues and trends. More than this, there is some affinity between kinds of elements and organizing principles that are conceptualized; hence we may avoid some repetition by merely referring to theoretical positions that have already been touched upon.

Almost all our definitions of personality mention or imply organization or patterning of its elements. But there general agreement ends.

What does structure of personality mean? The term "structure" is used here as a more inclusive term than "organization"; it refers to *all* the relationships in personality—to formal relationships (e.g., inclusion) as well as to functional relationships. Organization is a structure of functional relationships. Thus it is not limited to harmonious arrangements or to states of affairs marked by freedom from conflict or inconsistency.

What is structured? It makes a big difference whether we are talking about a "life cycle"—one conception of personality—or about something that exists for a moment or a relatively short span of time; whether we are talking about the structure of a "field" that embraces both a person and his actual environment, or about a personality that interacts with an environment. It is too bad that when our concern is personality we cannot talk about everything at once. Actually, it seems necessary to give special treatment to the problems touched on here—personality in the perspective of time and the problem of the "boundaries" of personality—and this will be done later. Here we may get on with a consideration of general principles by regarding personality as a more or less stable structure that endures long enough for studies to be made. We may leave until later the organization of sequences of changes that occur during the course of an individual's life. Also, we may do well to follow most contemporary writers in regarding personality as a "system," a set of related variables. This system is no doubt usually a part of some more inclusive system, but this does not prevent us from concentrating for the moment upon what F. H. Allport [4] calls its "inside structuring."

The language of personality theory is replete with terms referring to purely formal—as opposed to functional or dynamic—relations among the parts. The earlier quotation from Schjelderup was intended to illustrate this point. The use of such terms continues, regardless of whether or not they are elevated to the status of concepts. And such usage persists more or less independently of what model of personality functioning one adopts—whether one thinks of personality as being like a machine, a brain, an animal, a building, or a system of a more general sort. In most instances, one is dealing with something that is conceived as existing in space; hence, one possibility of order or patterning lies in the use of spatial metaphors to describe arrangements of parts and whole. This is a possibility that no theorist fails to avail himself of.

As we have seen, a great many proposed variables pertain to formal aspects of the whole personality or its parts—to features such as size, number of parts, number of different parts, connectedness of parts, and so on. Other variables pertain to formal relationships among the parts and to their arrangement or distribution with respect to the whole. Thus two or more parts may be related by similarity, proximity, inclusion, and so on; while a given part in its relations to the whole may be described as being central (i.e., connected with many other parts) or peripheral (isolated), outer (i.e., in direct relationship with the environment) or inner.

Although the kinds of formal relationships that a theorist accents depend to some extent upon the particular model of personality that he adopts, these are rarely matters for theoretical dispute. All personality theorists are concerned primarily with *dynamic organization,* that is, the interaction of processes. Differences have to do mainly with the nature of the processes—with the *content* of the parts or subsystems, as we saw in our consideration of elements—and with the nature of their interaction. Thus everybody will agree that personality is more or less differentiated; but what the differentiated parts are, why and how differentiation occurs —these are matters for some debate. In general, the analysis of personality into states, conditions, arrangements—supposing that these can be observed or more or less accurately inferred—prepares the way for explanation in terms of dynamic theory.

It may also be remarked that there are certain kinds of functional relationships that apparently obtain in any kind of operating totality and, like formal relationships, may be regarded as neutral as far as personality theory is concerned. In machines as well as in organisms, there may be subordination and superordination, means-end relations, or mere coordination [12]. Differences in theory do not become apparent—assuming that all theorists are using an operating totality as a model— until one begins filling in these abstractions with particular kinds of contents. For example, there may be a hierarchy of "habits" as well as a hierarchy of "needs" or "values."

Dynamic organization. Personality is universally conceived as a going concern. Either it is busily adapting itself to forces from outside or initiating activities of its own or both. In either case, energy and/or information are distributed and redistributed between the personality and its environment and within the personality. If one concentrates on the personality system by itself, one seeks lawful transactions among the parts and lawful transformations of particular parts.

The action frame of reference. According to the point of view of functionalism or action theory, which is traditional and widely accepted among personality theorists, the fundamental organizing principle is striving. Goals are set, and such resources as are necessary for the attainment of these goals are mobilized. At any moment of a person's existence, at least one need or drive is active, and diverse other processes are being organized in its service.

The action point of view permits wide variation in the way the striving itself is conceived. Striving may be occasioned by a physiological drive and take the direction of reducing the tension induced by that drive; it may be in the service of some lofty purpose, a conscious intention involving a complicated program of action.

American psychologists have always been hardheaded about teleology, unwilling to attribute events in an organism to final causes, but it has long been more or less generally agreed that directed striving is simply a fact of observation and so can find a place in diverse theoretical systems. As for the "why" of directed striving—a minimum conception that could be widely accepted is that the striving is to reduce tension or to restore equilibrium. This notion could be utilized by psychologists who differed widely about how many and what kinds of man's susceptibilities to tension were native and how many acquired and, for that matter, about how many of the acquired ones were merely derivations from the native ones.

Psychologists using the disequilibrium-equilibrium formula, whether borrowing the physiological principle of homeostasis [167, 239, 256, 257] or utilizing a formal model, could also differ with respect to the size and complexity of the system or subsystem which they believe actually exists or which is appropriate for analysis—as indeed they do. Some prefer to focus upon the tension that is generated in some particular region of the organism by a particular drive state and reduced by a particular response. Others are more interested in larger systems, such as the ego, which have their own problems of maintaining themselves in a steady state, whatever their origins. However molecular or however molar one may prefer to be, if one uses the concept of system and the disequilibrium-equilibrium formula, one must conceive of equilibrating mechanisms.

This is the ground in which personality theory flourishes most luxuriantly. Psychologists have produced a great diversity of equilibrating mechanisms. These range all the way from the stimulus → response → reduction-of-tension formula to the "ego's mechanisms of defense." The major theoretical issue here probably has to do with which are to be preferred—gestalt principles such as closure, dynamic self-distribution, *pragnanz,* or the associationistic principles of behaviorism. There is little to indicate an early resolution of this issue.

Equilibrating mechanisms are major organizing principles where one's focus is upon the single system. But in the view of most writers, personality comprises numerous systems, and theory must take account of their interactions. Obviously, the same system may be viewed with attention to its inside structuring or to its relations with other systems or to the relations of the two. Where the larger system is the chief object of concern, subsystems enter into the formulas of equilibrating mechanisms. Of particular importance here is the means-end relationship or, rather, a series of these relationships, a program in which immediate goals are means for attaining more distant ones. Or subsystems may be simply coordinated, existing side by side, as it were, or one may be a specification or concretization of another, e.g., if a person has a generalized attitude of hostility toward the Church, responses of rejection may be elicited by a great many religion items in a test.

In this connection, the most widely used conception is probably that of hierarchy. In stimulus-response theory, for example, habits are said to be arranged in a hierarchy in this sense: When a given stimulus is presented, there is some one response that is most likely to occur—and so on for a number of responses. This is true whether one is speaking of the state of affairs existing at the time of birth or after experience and learning. Similarly, if one speaks in more general terms, as Krech and Crutchfield [137] do, of "various modes of adjustment to tension," one may go on to consider the "priorities and hierarchies of importance among them," which constitute the major feature of personality organization for these writers. Among the major functions of personality, Murray and Kluckhohn [185] include *scheduling,* which lessens or resolves conflict by permitting "the execution of as many aims as possible one after the other" [185, p. 38].

Reduction of drive-reduction theory. Despite its central place in traditional personality theory and in much other psychological theory, the drive-reduction hypothesis (the homeostatic principle) has in recent years come in for some hard knocks or well-calculated neglect, at least. With the new emphasis on the "normal" and the "higher," one hears less about the individual's "adustments" or "adaptations" and more about his "self-activity" and "natural growth tendencies"; in addition, dissatisfaction with the disequilibrium-equilibrium formula has been expressed by a variety of psychologists, including some of the more hard-headed ones, especially when this formula purports to be the principle underlying all motivation.

Objections seem to be essentially of two sorts. One is that the disequilibrium-equilibrium formula is too simple; the other is that organisms —particularly humans—do other things besides seek ways and means to reduce tension or restore equilibrium.

Some of the older tension-reduction theories seem to have been based on analogies to simple physical systems or certain physiological systems in which the final state of equilibrium was the same as that which existed before the disequilibrating circumstances arose. Nowadays it is frequently pointed out that the final and the initial states of equilibrium are very apt to be different, that the condition attained after striving is a new state of equilibrium. This is explained by the fact that organisms grow and develop; the equilibrium that they attain must somehow take account of their increased size and complexity. As C. Bühler [41] has put it, "The individual tries to maintain equilibrium at the same time that he expands." One could still say that the individual *tends* to recapture his earlier states of equilibrium but that he cannot; the world being what it is, the individual has to change in order to maintain the same level of stability that he enjoyed before. Thus—within limits—the stable states of the individual must be on progressively higher levels. Probably this general view of the matter does not encounter strong objections among personality theorists today.

More controversial is the view that equilibrium—however new or however high its level—is not enough. C. Bühler [41], for example, starts with the notion that life's basic tendency is toward expansion (growth and reproduction) and then argues that this larger process utilizes homeostatic mechanisms or else that it is a process of which only one aspect is homeostasis. She quotes W. B. Cannon on the point that homeostasis frees the organism for more complicated social tasks and aligns herself with Goldstein [89], whose "self-actualization" is the drive that carries the organism on to activity after equilibrium has been reached.

Bühler cites with approval Fenichel's [74] conception of homeostasis as a process having the aim of maintaining a level of tension that is characteristic for the organism, rather than abolishing tension altogether. This is in keeping with Goldstein's [89] notion that the healthy organism maintains a level of tension adequate to enable it to intiate further activity. Thus it is the nature of organisms to raise tension levels that are too low and to lower levels that are too high. Murray and Kluckhohn [185] list the "generation of tension" among the major functions of personality. Taking issue with Freud, as they say, they go on to argue that it is not a tensionless state which is generally most satisfying to a healthy organism, but the process of reducing tension—hence people will see to it that they have tensions to reduce. In the same vein, Mowrer has distinguished what he regards as two fundamentally different learning processes, *solution learning* and *sign learning.* "Solution learning is problem solving, drive reducing, pleasure giving; whereas sign learning, or conditioning, is often—perhaps always—*problem making*" [174, p. 5; italics mine].

This is reminiscent of Maslow's [164] distinction between *coping behavior* and *expressive behavior.* But here a new conception appears. Organisms or personalities not only do things *in order* to further some objective or other—to reduce tension or to raise it—they just do things —period. Murray and Kluckhohn, after calling self-expression a function of personality, go on to say:

> More basic and elementary than integrated goal-directed activities are the somewhat anarchic, unco-ordinated medley of tentative, short-lived mental processes which characterize the stream of consciousness during periods of rest and day dreaming, at one extreme, and during periods of intense emotional excitement or lunacy, at the other. For these spontaneous, random, ungoverned, but yet expressive cacophonies of energy we have proposed the term "process activity." This is pure Being, a state in which the mind moves in its own inherent manner for its own intrinsic pleasure [185, p. 37].

These processes do become "shaped into effective or aesthetic patterns—telling gestures, ritual dances, songs, dramas—which are more perfectly expressive of emotion or of valuations." All this, of course, is much like K. Bühler's [42] conception of "function pleasure."

Murray and Kluckhohn, in the systematic statement from which the above quotation was taken, devote about as much space to process activity and the generation of tension as to the reduction of tension. Again, the critique of drive reduction and the presentation of alternative processes take up a great deal of space in recent literature on motivation and personality theory. A student unversed in history and inexperienced in the game of trying to induce changes in behavior or personality might easily conceive the notion that tension reduction is of no special importance and is, perhaps, on the way out. The fact is that this conception is of enormous importance and still very much with us. It was the tension-reduction hypothesis that got personality theory off the ground and made clear to the literate public that there was going to be a scientific psychology that meant business. The hypothesis had to be fought for and defended, for it was far less palatable to man thinking about himself than notions like self-expression or self-initiated activity. Today the central importance of tension reduction is—long since—so well established that its proponents can relax and give due attention to other matters; positive enthusiasts for these other matters are assured a wider hearing than before. As a result, a kind of balance is being restored; certain previously neglected processes or features of the person are being given due attention. More than this, the criticisms of drive-reduction theory by such writers as McClelland [152, 153], Olds [189], Koch [132], Hebb [102, 103], and White [286], in addition to those mentioned above, have been effective enough to make clear the necessity for development of a more general theory of human motivation. Among promising efforts in this direction are those of Koch, who has distinguished between "intrinsic" and "extrinsic" motivation; of Mowrer [176], who has recently stressed the importance of affects in accounting for anticipatory behavior; and particularly those of Tomkins [276], who regards the affective system as primary (in the sense that affects do not require concurrent amplification from the drive system) and as more general than the drive system (in the sense that affects may be triggered by a greater variety of activators and give rise to a greater variety of behavior). It seems safe to say, however, that the satisfactory general theory to be evolved will give place to the idea of tension reduction.

Nature versus nurture. To get away from the tension-reduction formula is, apparently, to take a more optimistic view of man's nature. It is to prefer processes that are less mechanical, to consider that man does more than just adapt, to assume that his potential for higher levels of functioning is there from the beginning. It is to be in what Allport [8] calls "the Leibnitzian tradition," or to share the philosophical view of the Ancients that the development of a thing depends upon its nature.

It is not that all critics of tension reduction are properly called "nativistic." Rather, there is a general nativistic position, according to which organizing tendencies are simply a part of man's nature, and from this position tension reduction is consistently attacked. Allport is right when he says that the issue is basically a philosophical one and puts behaviorism and classical psychoanalysis in the Lockeian tradition. Adherents of this tradition would put a minimum into personality at the beginning and accent the building up of things.

The Leibnitzian tradition has been gaining ground of late. Most of the modifications of classical psychoanalysis that have been wrought on American soil, e.g., by Fromm [86], Horney [112, 113], Sullivan [261], and Szasz [264], have indicated that personality is from the beginning more organized and organizing than Freud supposed, and may be regarded as aspects of this same general trend. Official psychoanalysis itself seems at last to have heard the voice of Leibnitz [88, 205, 208]. The "autonomous ego" of Hartmann, Kris, and Loewenstein [98] blesses man from the beginning with organizing powers; he is spared the necessity of deriving them from his id in the interests of survival. This, of course, serves to bring psychoanalysis into closer relationship with classical nonfunctional general psychology, according to which mechanisms of perceiving, learning, and thinking were aspects of man's nature.

The nativism with which we are here concerned is not nativism of a general sort, which would attribute more of everything to human nature; rather, it is a selective nativism which would attribute more that is potentially "high" or complicated or "good" to man's nature—shades of Rousseau. Matters used to be the other way around. Instincts, with all their capacity for evil, were the major features of man's native endowment; an optimist was a man who—like Freud and the behaviorists—believed that man could nonetheless learn, however painfully, from his experience and so attain a measure of freedom.

No doubt, this whole issue—with its philosophical roots and ideological foliage—should be seen in the light of history and world conditions. Such a perspective might reveal that the Lockeian tradition opened the way to the scientific study of man's mind and, by its accent on the possibilities of change through experience, prepared the way for the revolutionary changes in social institutions that began in Britain and were even more marked in America and in France. Our American distaste for "bad" nativism has certainly persisted, as witness the fact that Kleinian psychoanalysis [129], the most potent school of psychoanalytic thought in Britain, does not flourish here. Since the Kleinian brand is distinguished mainly by its nativist bias—the instinctual nature of aggression, the universality of stages of development, and the like—it seems reasonable to conclude that it is because of this bias that it is excluded. But apparently our hopeful outlook has rendered us unable to resist suggestions about man's native goodness—particularly since this is not a time for change or revolution.

On the other hand, remarks about American optimism may be wearing a bit thin. After all, save for the case of Melanie Klein, we have found a place for virtually all the European and British trends of psychological thought, and that great "pessimist," S. Freud, won much greater acceptance in America than among British and Continental psychologists. (At the Salzburg Seminar in American Studies in 1952, the writer lectured mainly on Freud. This was new and pretty unpalatable stuff to most of the young Continental social scientists. Again, a quick reading of the symposium on European and American personality theory held at the International Congress of Psychology in Montreal [202] fails to reveal any mention of Freud by the Continental theorists. No doubt, this has much to do with the virtual absence of clinical psychology in Europe, but one would find far greater acceptance of Freud by American psychiatrists than by European ones.)

European-American comparisons—always difficult enough owing to the diversity existing in both places—have been rendered almost impossible by the past twenty-five years's immigration of so many of the greatest and most influential European psychologists. If, however, we are to remark on American optimism, it is only fair to take note of European pessimism. This is something that the Continental intellectual has for many years worn like a badge. But since World War II, something has been added: Man is not so much evil as he is unfortunate. He is here "as upon a darkening plain," etc., etc. He has an infinite capacity for suffering; but this is not so bad; he has to undergo the final indignity of having his responses conditioned. The American's answer to all this is, of course, "So what?" He is thus spared envelopment in that romanticism which has so long cumbered Continental thought and action and which is still, apparently, a real danger.

Whatever its major geographical locus, the new nativism has perhaps been carried far enough to restore the balance that was upset by the upsurge of behaviorism and psychoanalysis. Man may indeed turn out to be from the beginning more worthy than he appeared from these two points of view. But it would be a shame if he escaped investigation for that reason. The great danger in putting too much into the personality at the start is that one may thus dodge the difficulties of looking into origins. Stimulus-response psychology may have erred in giving man so few native endowments, but at least it has faced up to the task of explaining how things get built up.

Of course, the present excursion into the sociology of knowledge should not be permitted to obscure the fact that the nature-nurture question is still fundamentally an empirical one. Ideology flourishes in the absence of solid fact about man's native endowments. Actually, it must be admitted that recent developments in neurophysiological and biopsychological knowledge have been favorable to the more "optimistic" of the positions described above. Current models of the nervous system [e.g., 12] are far more differentiated than those employed by classical stimulus-response psychology, and there is evidence that man comes into the world with more complex capacities for function than was commonly supposed even fifteen years ago [92, 197, 198]. This, however, does not diminish the importance of learning or suggest that there might be some let-up in investigations of the early development of personality. Rather, it suggests that learning is a more subtle and complicated business than it is often taken to be and that a fresh approach to learning in the framework of the new neurophysiological models might permit us to come to grips with the complexity of personality at last.

Organization inside versus organization outside. If behaviorism and psychoanalysis put little into the personality to begin with and concentrate on what is built up, there is another school of thought which says that there never is very much in the personality, as far as organization is concerned. According to this point of view, a great deal—perhaps most—of the consistency and order that we observe in behavior is to be attributed to regularities in the surrounding social and cultural environment. And the reference here is to the contemporary environment, the situation in which the behavior occurs, rather than the environment of the past.

Starting with the indisputable fact that all behavior depends upon the individual's situation (the constellation of environmental stimuli, usually social) as well as upon factors within him, the "situationist" chooses to accent the former and to minimize the latter. If he is interested in a kind of behavior, he is inclined to seek its correlates in the situation—the individual's group memberships or social role, for example. If he is interested in a kind of situation he places many individuals in the situation and notes the similarities in their responses. These are major, and, of course, legitimate concerns of social psychology. What makes the personality psychologist anxious is the inclination of some social psychologists [e.g., 46, 246] to overaccent the presumed similarities among all people and to suppose that the universal human endowment consists mainly of a few dispositions—to imitate social norms, to conform with the requirements of social roles, and the like —which serve to make people more adaptable to their society and culture. Society and culture thus become the sovereign organizers of human behavior and human life, and the personality psychologist is left with nothing to do.

Field theory, in the hands of many of its adherents, often adds up to about the same thing. Lewin's field theory started out as a purely psychological theory. Behavior was to be understood as a result of the interplay among factors in the person and in the psychological environment. But much of the experimental work that has proceeded from this orientation has tended to smudge over the boundaries between the psychological and the objective or nonpsychological environments or to assume that the relations between them were one to one. In addition, since factors in the objective environment were much easier to get hold of than those in the person, the experimental work has tended to accent the former and neglect the latter, sometimes even reducing the person to a "point region." In field theory, it is the field that is organized—and if the field is to comprise environmental forces overwhelmingly, there is obviously little need for a psychology of personality.

And then there is the view that the personality—as it has been traditionally conceived—is not a suitable unit for psychological study. Since the individual is always enmeshed in a network of interrelationships with other individuals and since nothing about his behavior can be fully understood apart from this context, one should not focus on relationships within an individual (*his* organization), but on "interpersonal relationships" [Sullivan, 261]—not on the "monadic unit" as Sears [236] calls the single individual, but on "dyadic units," i.e., aggregations of two or more individuals.

These developments have not caught the traditional personality psychologist unprepared. His answer to the situationist seems to have been somewhat as follows: "You are interested in situations; I am interested in persons. You are interested in behavior per se; I am interested in behavior because it is the only means I have for finding out about the dispositions of people and about how they are organized. You proceed by subjecting many individuals to the same situation and noting the communalities in their responses; I proceed by observing the same individual in a variety of situations and noting his persistent tendencies."

The answer to the field theorists in the tradition of Lewin has been less sharp. As pointed out earlier, personality theorists of the functionalist or action orientation have been generally receptive to topological and gestalt psychology; they have addressed themselves to the Lewinian experimentalists in terms of sorrow more than reproach. "It is too bad that you seem unable or unwilling to conceive and to measure variables in the person, or to put a little content into the regions and systems which you suppose to exist there. If you did, your understanding of people would be deeper and your predictions of behavior more accurate."

Preference for certain units of analysis is, of course, an arbitrary matter that need not involve theoretical controversy. If a personality theorist complains that Sullivan's or Sear's units are too large, he must be prepared for the same complaint from psychologists who believe that subsystems—needs or habits, for example—are about as large as anyone could hope to investigate thoroughly. Still—if only for sentimental reasons—there will probably always be people who want to focus on the individual himself, rather than on some of his parts or the social systems of which he is a unit. Since man the individual—not groups or psychical subsystems—knows joy and suffering and bears moral responsibility, he will probably always be the object of a certain amount of sympathetic curiosity.

Of course, a focusing on a given unit of analysis is likely to have some basis in theory, and this seems to be the case with Sullivan and Sears. In Sullivan's view, the person—the other person—is the most important source of stimuli for the developing individual. Sullivan's exclusion of stimuli arising in certain zones of the body (accented in Freudian psychoanalysis) and those arising in the "part-objects" (e.g., the breast, accented in Kleinian psychoanalysis) appears to be quite arbitrary. However, in the present state of our knowledge, such choices of what to emphasize and what to leave out are not only possible, but actually correlates of successful theory making. Sears [236] is primarily interested in predicting overt behavior. In proposing the dyadic unit, he takes the position of the social psychologist, whose concern is with *all* the correlates of a given kind of behavior. Undoubtedly one may hope to account for more of the variance in the aggressive behavior of children by taking account of variables in them and in the people with whom they are close, for example. This is all very well, but it is not a particular concern of the student of personality.

The personality theorist may have answers for the situationist and the cultural determinist—this is not to say that he has not been influenced by them through the years. Personality psychology has become more social not only with respect to elements, but also with respect to the locus of organizing principles. There is certainly an increased sense of the relatedness of personality structure—not just behavior—and structure in the social environment. Increasingly we realize that we do not detract from such favorite concepts as the superego, ego identity, or self-concept by supposing that—despite their relative stability and autonomy—they have had to be to some degree sustained by forces in the social environment and may be altered radically by extreme social change. Indeed, such realization has been furthered by certain observations [27, 221, 227] of how shifts in the pattern of the individual's social environment may penetrate effectively his "deeper" or more central regions.

This line of thought has suggested some extremely interesting hypotheses, for example, Werner's [281] notion that the degree of differentiation of personalities in a society depends on the degree of functional differentiation in that society. Studies of authoritarianism in the United States and in Arab states [204, 226] suggest the hypothesis that the more structuration or integration in a culture, the less internal integration an individual needs.

Clearly, at this stage in the development of personality psychology, nothing more is to be gained by opposing personality factors and the social system and asking which is the more important. Nor is anything to be gained by conceiving global constellations of field forces in which the individual is somehow enmeshed. What is needed is more knowledge of the articulation of personality systems and social systems. This requires more rather than less attention to the relatively autonomous personality structures and more searching analysis of social structures in terms that are psychologically relevant. The student of personality will still be focused upon the internal structuring of personality, but he will realize that his hypothetical subsystems are not fully understood unless the conditions of their change can be specified.

Unconscious processes. Few, if any, personality theorists today appear to believe that a person is aware of all the processes determining his behavior at any particular time. Murray and Kluckhohn have proposed using the adjective "regnant" to stand for "the momentarily governing processes at the superordinate [regnant] level of integration in the brain-field" [185, p. 7]. Conscious processes are regnant, but not all regnant processes are conscious.

In such a view as this, consciousness is functional in the sense that it furthers activities that are advantageous to the person. Linton has elaborated this point and clarified a well-known and important principle of personality organization—one set forth by William James [117]. Linton distinguishes between "emergent" and "esablished" responses; the former grade into the latter, but the polar positions in the series seem clear enough.

At the emergent end of the scale we have those behaviors which are evoked by new and unfamiliar situations. . . . At the established end of the scale we have those behaviors which are evoked by familiar situations. Such behaviors are thoroughly organized and patterned. While the emergent responses always involve some degree of consciousness of the situation and of effort to solve the problem which it presents, established responses are automatic and can be produced without either the registry of the situation or the associated behavior attaining a conscious level.

The responses which any individual is capable of making extend over the full range represented by this scale, but their distribution in the scale is far from uniform. . . . It is easier to live by habit than by conscious intent, and most of us do live by habit most of the time. . . . The fact that we can carry on most of our activities at the habitual level serves to conserve energy and to provide the surplus vigor required to develop new forms of behavior as the need for them arises. . . . we may picture the personality as consisting of an organized relatively persistent core of habits surrounded by a fluid zone of behavioral responses which are in process of reduction to habitual terms [148, pp. 93–95].

Processes may be conscious or unconscious, then, depending upon the situation and needs of the organism. They are likely to be unconscious if there is no need for their conscious activity, if other processes occupy the center of the stage, or if their being unconscious is favorable to the economy of the organism's over-all functioning. But presumably such processes are capable of becoming conscious; and they do, if the light shifts in their direction as it were, or if a new situation requires that they be reviewed. They are not forcibly prevented from becoming conscious by the operation of other factors in the personality. Processes which *are* so barred from access to awareness are unconscious in Freud's [84] original meaning of this term. It is "the unconscious" (i.e., those processes which are unconscious) in this sense that plays the crucial role in the psychoanalytic theory of neurosis and is the cornerstone of the dynamic theory of personality that prevails among clinical psychologists today.

According to action theory, processes are made unconscious or debarred from consciousness when this serves some need—usually a rather intense need—of the personality (e.g., to resolve a conflict, to reduce anxiety, to preserve self-esteem, to remove a sense of threat to the integrity of the personality). The "repression" of psychological contents and the maintenance of barriers to their again becoming conscious are thus adaptive strategems or mechanisms. But clearly they can be so only in some limited or temporary way for, as we have seen, consciousness is itself adaptive and unquestionably this state characterizes the highest adaptive powers of the personality. The organized, conscious parts of the personality do not—if they can help it—turn over to their major competitor the functions that keep them in business. But they cannot always help it, and this is a crucial point. Repression is a reaction to crisis; it is resorted to when the strains upon the personality are greater than can be managed by the more differentiated, the more refined and elegant, the more flexible—all of which is to say conscious— systems that have developed. What happens is a function both of the intensity of the strain and the adequacy of the conscious systems. In childhood, the conscious controlling systems are weak—relative to those in adulthood—and strains are as great as at any time; hence childhood is preeminently the time for repression. (Freudian theory cannot be understood apart from the context of a developmental psychology.)

Unfortunately, adaptations made under conditions of extreme strain cannot be easily reversed; this is particularly true if, as is so often the case, strains are continuing. It is likely that adaptations resorted to in the face of one strain will be generalized to others. The personality, meanwhile, keeps growing—not just by undoing its early adaptations, but by incorporating them into its larger structures. The early adaptations remain like wounds in the trunk of the tree; though they may be to some extent encapsulated, all future growth is somehow congruent with their existence. More than this, as old wounds, they are susceptible to reopening or, perhaps more aptly, as lines of stress, they continue to invite the channelization of strains.

One need not seek far for the implications of this formulation for personality organization. Unconscious structures have their own distinctive response characteristics and their own laws of functioning

[138, 169]. And they are related dynamically to the conscious processes of the personality. Indeed, a vast amount of personality theory, particularly that which is influenced by Freudian psychoanalysis, is taken up with just this matter—with how unconscious processes are "reflected" in consciousness, or transformed or disguised in such a way as to make them compatible with conscious aspirations and with how the more conscious, "controlling" systems of the personality ward off, defend themselves against, manage, or integrate unconscious processes.

The place of the unconscious in what is nowadays called "stratification theory" or theory according to which personality is organized in levels, is a highly complicated matter. It has long been common practice among personality theorists to speak of unconscious processes as being on a deeper level than conscious ones. In his early work, Freud divided the psyche into the conscious, the preconscious, and the unconscious, a topography that has not been challenged in psychoanalytic thinking. It has commonly been considered that the unconscious was at the deepest level, the conscious at the most superficial. In more recent personality theory, however, it is clear that the surface-depth dimension has been conceived in quite different ways. The present writer has attempted to summarize the major trends of thought on this problem [225], noting that the adjective "deeper" has been used in diverse ways—to refer to processes that were less available to consciousness or to the motoric; to processes that were laid down earlier in the individual's development; to biological as opposed to learned responses; to the neurologically lower; to the determining or ruling rather than to the determined or ruled or instrumental; to processes that are "inner" in the sense of not being dependent upon immediate field conditions; to processes that are relatively resistant to change; and finally, to processes that are relatively hidden from observation. Each of these conceptions is accompanied by theory concerning the determinants of relationships between processes on the deeper levels and processes on more superficial ones. Processes that are unconscious in Freud's sense may have any or all of the characteristics just listed, but none of these characteristics applies only to such unconscious processes. These processes have to be distinguished by their own special dynamics, a matter that has been the chief concern of a vast quantity of psychoanalytic observation and theory. Unconscious motives are commonly said to be marked primarily by insatiability and resistance to modification through experience, being unresponsive to pleasure or pain, rewards or punishments, logic or argument. Behavior that proceeds from unconscious motives is automatic, inflexible, repetitive in disregard of consequences.

The study of these unconscious processes may proceed in the same way as does the investigation of any other processes of personality; they are hypothetical constructs which, as parts of a theoretical system, are retained or rejected according to their success in ordering or explaining observations or in forming the basis for predictions of behavior. The fact that they are not conscious is only one of their manifest features, and a rather negative one at that. And, as we have seen, other processes of personality have this characteristic. It seems, however, that the investigator who would make inferences about unconscious dynamics by making observations of behavior would be foolish to neglect what his subjects can and cannot report.

Unconscious processes in Freud's system were strictly psychological, and his followers have continued to speak of these processes in the language of psychology—"unconscious perception," "unconscious feeling," "unconscious fantasy," and so on. The older introspectionist psychology used to say "unconscious and therefore physiological." Present-day phenomenologists seem to take this same view of the matter, arguing that the conception of unconscious psychological processes is a contradiction in terms. Angyal [9] has urged that unconscious processes be regarded as psychophysiologically neutral. They, like other hypothetical constructs in personality theory, should be given a place in a formal model of personality functioning and assigned such attributes as are most helpful in predicting behavior. This general approach to the problem seems to be winning increasing favor among personality theorists [2, 79, 126, 183, 209].

The status of unconscious processes of the Freudian variety in personality theory today seems to parallel that of action theory in general. If one considers the last twenty-five or thirty years, it is apparent that acceptance of unconscious processes as determinants of behavior has steadily increased; yet at the present time they appear to be undergoing a certain deemphasis. Psychologists who have long taken these processes for granted seem to have been showing interest in a "more balanced view," and this falls into line with the current accent on the normal or the higher. Writers who have been identified with this latter trend, such as Allport [8], Goldstein [89], and Rogers [212], do not deny the validity of the Freudian dynamics so much as suppose that they have an important place only in the determination of abnormal behavior. Psychoanalytic theorists have perhaps encouraged this view by stressing for so long the crucial role of unconscious dynamics in symptom formation; but they have consistently refused to accept any categorical distinction between the normal and the abnormal and, moreover, they have conceived of unconscious processes as motivating forces in creative and socially constructive activity. At the same time, however, they have argued that, in the interests of personality integration, it were better that the unconscious be made conscious—in so far as this is possible. "In so far as possible"—this is a rather typical phrase in psychoanalytic writing. The point of view it expresses is strongly implicit in all drive-reduction theory. The individual does not easily reverse or even alter fundamentally his early adaptations; rather, he has to make the most of them. Differences among personality theorists respecting unconscious dynamics are mainly differences in emphasis, but variations are wide, and most writers are to be found at one extreme or the other. This is because what is involved here is not a matter of arbitrary preference, but two contrasting views of the nature of life.

Personality as a whole. When we speak of the organization of personality, we are referring to the whole personality; we mean that *all* of its parts are functionally related one to another and to the whole. Earlier in this paper, concern was expressed lest certain writers be unfairly committed to a holistic or organismic orientation. This was perhaps overcautious. As Hall and Lindzey [97] point out, all personality theorists are holistic. Naturally they do not wish merely to breathe the word "whole" and mean thereby something that could only be spoiled by analysis. But if personality is conceived as anything more than a mere enumeration of things, if the parts of personality are related by any operation other than mere addition, then holism is necessarily implied. Indeed, even the conception of a sum has holistic implication; the psychologist who wanted to make sure that he had nothing to do with holism would have to restrict himself to enumeration or avoid the idea of personality altogether.

Of course, some psychologists have done and are doing this last. It is possible to study some part function of people without considering its relations to other part functions. For example, one may concentrate on the relations of a response to external stimuli without paying any attention to the place of that response in a context of personality functioning, or one may develop a test of some performance, focusing on relations between test responses and an external criterion without troubling about the personal meaning of those responses. But these activities have nothing to do with the psychology of personality, nor do the workers who carry them out consider themselves to be personality psychologists. When students of personality engage in these types of research activity, they are usually careful to say that they are abstracting part functions from the whole to which they naturally belong and that they are proceeding in this way because they must in order to obtain exact information.

It used to be considered virtuous when a thoroughgoing holist— Murray [181], for example—showed a willingness to perform the analysis and to make the abstractions necessary to the performance of research. Nowadays such analysis and abstraction are taken for granted, and have become second nature to the researcher in personality. All contemporary holists deny that they were ever opposed to analysis in the first place; they were only concerned that it be performed in the right way. For some time now, there have been questions: Is the business of abstraction being carried out too readily or too easily? Are investigators forgetting to think of their variables in terms of their meaning in relation to larger wholes? Are they too easily satisfied with the, say, 25 per cent of the variance in some performance that could be accounted for by reference to situational factors and to one or two diagnosed traits of personality?

It was stated in an earlier section that the holistic orientation was being increasingly accepted and utilized in research design. The main point was that more contemporary theorists and researchers—such as Rogers [211], Klein [125], and Hilgard [108]—were taking seriously or insisting on their obligations under a holistic frame of reference and finding new approaches to the study of relationships lying on what Klein [125] has called the "vertical dimension," that is, relationships between part functions (e.g., a characteristic of perception) and a whole (e.g., the ego system). Studies of the self and of the ego were offered as examples.

Apparently it is very difficult to concentrate upon the inside structuring of a particular whole, such as the phenomenal self or the ego, and at the same time give adequate attention to the transactions between this whole and the larger one in which it has a place. Thus, it is probably no accident that at the time of increased accent upon the ego as organizer, a whole that influences the functioning of all its parts, there is also increased accent upon the autonomy of the ego. Some writers apparently think that the ego has its own history and its own absolute strength; it is like a rock upon which waves of id impulses or waves of scrupulosity from the superego are broken. This view is less holistic than that of classical psychoanalysis, which always considered that ego strength was relative to the tasks that it had to perform and that one could not make any complete statements about ego functioning without taking into account what was going on in the superego and the id. Of course, the new conception of the ego at least partly represents an effort to get away from the older and less optimistic picture of the ego as the rider of a runaway horse—a picture which is imputed to Freud. This picture, though no doubt somewhat unnerving, is at least as holistic as anyone could wish. It ought to be possible to construct in theoretical terms an ego that is independent of the optimism-pessimism scale, that is at least as complicated as the modern autonomous ego, and that can be seen in the context of its functional relationships with other large subsystems and the whole personality.

Mechanisms as variables of personality. It goes without saying that individuals differ with respect to all the organizing principles that have been touched upon here. For example, one person may have been far more successful than another in getting his tendencies to response arranged in a hierarchy or in setting up a schedule that minimizes conflicts and allows adequate gratification of a variety of needs. By paying attention to organizing activities, it is possible to define a great many personality variables and this has been done, of course. Thus elements of personality as discussed above are by no means the only variables that we have. Elements interact with others and are transformed in accordance with dynamic principles. The interaction processes and equilibrating mechanisms, considered by themselves, have quantitative aspects. We may ask how frequently they are employed, how much energy is channeled through them, how much strain is required before they are called into play, how important they are relative to other processes and mechanisms, and so on. Does the individual, for example, delay gratification of one need in order to attain more gratification of this or other needs later on? How effectively does he do this? How regularly? Under what degrees of intensity of the original need?

It is possible to define other variables by considering certain mechanisms in relation to certain elements. Of course, as soon as we specify a few elements and say what their mode of interaction is with certain other specified ones we have to deal with something very complicated indeed. Yet such patterns—or syndromes as they are sometimes called— do not altogether defy description or even certain crude forms of quantification. "Authoritarianism" as this word is ordinarily understood [225] is a pattern of dynamic relationships among elements. It seems to take quite similar forms in different individuals and to vary in respect to quantity; it has seemed possible to speak of the amount of an individual's authoritarianism, or of the degree of his readiness to permit his authoritarian pattern to go into action. Much the same thing might be said of other patterns of personality, such as compulsiveness, narcissism, overcompensatory dependence, that are too large and complicated to be regarded merely as traits but nonetheless have quantitative aspects.

Summary. Personality is usually conceived of as a more or less stable structure that endures long enough for studies to be made. It exists always as a subsystem in larger social systems, but it is possible to concentrate for the moment upon its inside structuring.

The term "structure" is used here to refer to *all* the relationships within personality, while the term "organization" applies only to functional relationships. One way of finding order or patterning in personality is by using a spatial model to describe features of parts and their arrangement in relation to each other and the whole. Such analysis may prepare the way for explanation in dynamic terms, that is to say, in terms of lawful transformations of parts and transactions among parts.

According to the prevailing action frame of reference, the major organizing principle is that of striving to reduce tension or to restore equilibrium. Diverse resources are mobilized and organized as equilibrating mechanisms. This general formula holds for any subsystem of the personality that has been the object of tension-producing stimulation. But personality, in the minds of most theorists, consists of very numerous subsystems, and many of them are subjected to some strain at the same time; hence the necessity for organization on a larger scale, e.g., for coordination, scheduling, establishing hierarchies of importance.

The tension-reduction formula has been the object of much criticism in recent years. One line of criticism has led to general agreement that the states of equilibrium existing before and after striving are not usually the same since individuals change in the course of their strivings, so their stable states have to be on progressively higher levels. Another line of criticism is simply that the tension-reduction formula is not enough to account for all the activities of the organism; there is also tension generation, self-expression, and the triggering of affects by a variety of stimuli. This line of criticism has been sufficiently effective so that a more general theory of human motivation now seems called for and is being sought energetically.

In considering the sources of organizing tendencies in behavior and personality, some theorists accent the original nature of man; others accent what is developed during the individual's life; still others accent the regularities in the contemporary social and cultural environment. The view that personality is from the beginning more organized and organizing than behaviorism or psychoanalysis have traditionally supposed has been gaining ground in recent years. Some writers accent natural growth trends and the autonomous ego, others stick to the tension-reduction formula. The issue may be illuminated to some extent by viewing it in a social-historical context, but it remains most essentially an empirical one.

Situationism, certain tendencies in field theory, and modern theories of interpersonal relations have minimized organization in the individual personality and accented the social group and the culture as the organizers of human behavior and human life. In the face of arguments from these schools of thought, the student of personality has usually stood his ground, reiterating his preference for studying the individual human whose organized dispositions structure the situations he encounters. Nevertheless, here as in the case of elements, personality theory has gradually become more "social"; there is more concern about the articulation of personality systems and social systems, about how the more or less autonomous structures of the personality are sustained by surrounding social forces.

The literature on personality often differentiates among processes that are conscious, processes that are not conscious but capable of becoming so, and processes that are forcibly prevented from becoming conscious. Activities directed to the management of a new stimulus or problem are considered most likely to be conscious, while habitual responses or devices for automatic adjustment are not. "The unconscious," in the Freudian sense, refers to processes that have been rendered unconscious, usually in childhood, because this was the only available means for adapting to severe strains. Adaptations of this kind are not easily reversed; they tend to persist, to function in accordance with their own special dynamics, to enter into diverse functional relationships with other structures of the personality. The Freudian view of the unconscious has gradually won wide acceptance among psychologists, particularly during the last twenty-five years, but it is undergoing a certain deemphasis at the present time—an aspect, as it seems, of the current preoccupation with the "normal" and the "higher."

When psychologists speak of the organization of personality, they are almost always referring to the *whole* personality. All personality psychologists are holistic in the sense of believing that all particular response characteristics have functional roles in the operations of the whole. The most common practice has been to abstract part functions from their natural place in the whole to study them more closely. This has become so routine that one wonders whether many personality psychologists have not forgotten their true holistic position. Recent years, however, have witnessed a fresh impulse to take holism seriously, and to deliberately design researches to reveal the significance of part functions in larger totalities. This has been best exemplified by work on the ego and the self. One might hope that concentration on the inside structuring of these large elements of personality might be sustained even while their dependence upon the functioning of the whole that included them was given the attention it deserves.

Interaction processes and equilibrating mechanisms, like the elements of personality discussed earlier, have quantitative aspects and may be treated as variables of personality. These processes and mechanisms, when taken in combination with the particular elements that they affect, yield patterns or syndromes of personality which also have their quantitative aspects.

Personality and the Dimension of Time

As we have seen, most theorists and researchers regard personality as a more or less stable structure that endures long enough for studies of it to be made. One may speak of the organization existing now, at the time of this experimental session, or during the course of this three-day assessment. It seems generally agreed, however, that personality changes in lawful ways, that the succession of events in time exhibits patterns that can be studied. Holistic writers, such as Murray [183] and Angyal [9] have insisted that the life cycle of the individual is a whole, a temporal gestalt, and thus a natural unit for analysis and study. They readily agree, however, that it is very difficult to study a whole life and that it is not inappropriate to abstract short units for intensive investigation. This, of course, is what is done in practice, the short units ranging in length from the single experimental session to the period of childhood or that of old age.

The momentary personality. When the psychologist speaks of a personality organization existing for a moment, he usually has in mind the *psychological present,* a time in which all the factors necessary to predict behavior may be said to be operating. He is concerned, in other words, with *systematic causation* of personality functioning. This is contrasted with *historical causation,* in which factors operating in the present are understood as traces or consequences of past events. The distinction is usually associated with the name of Kurt Lewin. In one of his early works, Lewin made clear his intention to supply concepts and methods that would make it possible for "the experimental method to press on beyond the psychology of perception and memory to such vital problems as those with which psychoanalysis was concerned" [144, p. v]. His efforts have met with very considerable success. Numerous experimental studies [14, 57, 106, 107, 136, 145, 146, 289] have shown that phenomena such as regression, identification, or aggression, which have always had historical connotations in psychoanalytic literature, can be explained in the terms of systematic laws. Indeed, if historical causes are to be of any account at all, there must be traces or consequences of past events persisting in the present and finding some place in the mechanisms that lead from causes to effects. But events of the past *do* leave traces or consequences that operate potently in the present, and the systematic exploration of a present behavior that does not take them into account, while it may be accurate, is incomplete.

The development of systematic or ahistorical psychology has not only stimulated experimental studies of personality; it has had important effects upon the practice of psychotherapy. It is a far cry from present-day methods to the apparent concern of the older psychoanalysis with "uncovering the patient's past." Psychotherapy undertakes to change people; to this end it must confine itself to the manipulation of factors that are operating in the present, since it cannot change the past. Psychoanalysis assumes that important experiences from the past are *transferred* to the present and that present insight into present emotional relationships permit an individual to recall and understand his past.

The dethronement of the past in psychoanalytic and psychotherapeutic practice is not necessarily related to the recent accent on the contemporary social situation or on events of the recent past as determinants of neurotic difficulties. The questions of what the historical causative factors in personality are and whether they are inside the personality or in the social situation are quite different from the question of how one deals with the matter of systematic causation. Thus, Ezriel [68] has urged that in psychoanalysis of individuals and groups *all* interpretations should be transference interpretations, directed to events of the "here and now." He acknowledged the influence of Lewin upon his thinking, yet he belongs mainly to the Kleinian school of psychoanalysis, according to which the events that are most important in the history of neurosis happen in the first year of life.

To find the past in the present is not the only task of the researcher or psychotherapist who wishes to understand personality in accordance with systematic laws. He must also find something of the future in the present. If personality is, as Murray and Kluckhohn [184] say, "an ongoing manifold of structured processes," then some, perhaps many, of the processes that we may observe right now have functional roles in the promotion of long-range objectives, and thus are to be fully revealed only when these objectives have been appreciated. Obviously one cannot always tell where a person is going just by noting the direction in which he is headed; one may have to follow him a way in order to form a reasonable hypothesis. (And this is to say nothing of whether or not he actually reaches his destination.) Similarly, finding the past in the present is not, as Chein [52] has pointed out, just a matter of detecting traces of remote events; it is often a matter of noting "unfinished business," unresolved conflicts or unfulfilled needs, initiated some days or weeks or years ago but still organizing many of the present observable processes.

It is primarily considerations of this kind that have led personality theorists to say that one can study short periods of personal life only by abstracting a part from the whole. Researchers on personality—however self-conscious they may have been about the process of abstraction —have considered that although one could not tell all about a process without seeing it in the context of larger temporal wholes, one could nevertheless tell something, and they have proceeded to do the best they could.

But another issue is involved here. How long is the present? What is the relation of systematic causation to the length of time during which we observe our subjects? If we are to see the present as partly organized by long-range objectives and if we predict the future from the present on this basis, we have only systematic principles to guide us. And, presumably, the unfinished business that organizes present processes is carried forward in accordance with the same dynamic laws that hold for strivings in general. This means that one could investigate a temporal unit of behavior that lasted a week or longer and still stay within the framework of systematic causation. Certain variables that were operating at the beginning would be measured, and the final state of affairs would be predicted according to some dynamic hypothesis. For example, one might predict that a humiliating experience experimentally induced would be recalled better after a week or a month than after an hour, and tests would be made at the stated times. But the same period could be studied with attention to historical causation, by surveying the major events of the period and noting which had left traces at the end, or taking a sample of the subject's verbal responses—some dreams or a word-association test—and noting which ones could be traced to the events of the preceding week or months. As a matter of fact, the investigator who performed the experiment on remembered humiliation would be likely to supplement his systematic study with a historical one; he would explore the possibility that a knowledge of intervening events might help explain some of the exceptions to his rule.

If one can make a systematic investigation over a period of a month, there appears to be no reason the same could not be done for a longer period. The general procedure would be the same. Naturally, as the time span increases, the intervention of factors not taken into account at the beginning is very likely to increase also. The task of controlling these factors becomes very difficult. One may either concentrate on one or a very few cases and try to keep a record of all important happenings or use many subjects, hoping to cancel out enough of the "accidental" factors. In work of this kind, a concern with historical factors is a concern with "individual differences." The early experimental work of Lewin and his associates was concerned with the pure case or the general law. As in much present-day animal experimentation, it was permissible to throw out cases that varied so greatly from the group in some particular that they did not fulfill the conditions of the experiment. Nowadays the researcher in personality often combines systematic and historical modes of investigation in accordance with the focus of his interest. The trend probably is toward increasing use of the historical method in an effort to identify and measure more of the factors operating in the present and thus discover laws of greater generality.

This approach ordinarily involves fairly large blocks of time. To observe the consistency in behavior that is the basis for inferring factors of personality, the subject must be seen in varied situations—a time-consuming process. If subjects are "known" through clinical studies or surveys of their characteristic responses, they may be placed in laboratory situations for intensive investigation of particular processes. One may either control the personality factors while concentrating on the effects of a particular situation [e.g., 54, 56, 60] or direct attention to the role of personality factors in the determination of some particular kind of behavior [e.g., 28, 75, 110, 214]. This approach seems to be preferred by personality psychologists today; it stands in contrast to Lewin's earlier approach, which tended to ignore individual differences, and the more traditional approach of experimental psychology, which sought to rule them out by the use of many subjects.

With increased understanding of systematic and historical causation and the relations between them, there has developed an increased willingness to investigate by experimental methods processes that in their nature take time. Studies of the effects of psychotherapy [e.g., 213, 217], of the conditions of changes of attitudes [e.g., 55, 120, 188, 231], and of the relations of present personality organization to future performance [e.g., 76, 111, 121] belong here. Whereas such studies may cover time spans roughly corresponding to periods of life—the four years of college, for example—they are still systematic as long as they are focused upon the effects of conditions determined at the beginning.

Persistence and change. Personality psychologists of the action frame of reference have favored the historical study of factors in the person because they have been impressed by the durability of these factors. They have been most concerned with tendencies in the person which persist through time and enter into the determination of behavior in diverse situations. Lewin and his early associates could neglect historical causation because they considered that the apparent persistence of tendencies was really due to the persistence of field conditions. These conditions turned out to be, as we have seen, mainly a matter of what was going on in the objective environment. If personality depended on field conditions and changed as they changed, obviously there was little point in making case studies to discover what differences in readiness to respond the individuals brought to the experimental situation.

This is a way of stating a general issue in personality theory, the issue of persistence versus change. All theorists conceive of a more or less stable structure, but some seem to accent the "more" and some the "less"; some are inclined to stress the apparent fixity of inner structures and the continuity of the past and the present, while others stress change with circumstances and the possibility of new beginnings.

The issue—one might call it the contrasting views of man—has loomed rather large in the history of thought. Perhaps the contrast has been sharpest in the philosophies of Nazism and Marxism, the former holding that an individual is totally determined once and for all by his "blood" or "race," the latter that personality is merely a reflection of the social-economic system in which the individual lives. In common sense and in folklore the two views seem to have competed on more or less even terms.

The theories of psychoanalysis [84, 129, 209], with their heavy emphasis upon childhood traumata and repression, have been pre-eminently theories of persistence. Stimulus-response theories have had much this same aspect, though they offer explanations for change as well as for persistence; their accent on the continuity of the past and the present has justified their being classed with theories that stress the importance of early events in the determination of personality and later behavior [58, 237]. Both psychoanalysis and behaviorism, as we have seen, are heavily environmentalistic in stressing experience rather than genetic factors to account for individual differences in personality, but the emphasis is on the environment of the past rather than the present and on the persistence of structures, once developed, into the present. The contrast is with situationism [245], field theory [144], and certain cognitive theories [e.g., 10] which generally accent the possibilities of change through responsiveness to changing situations or through bringing to bear the cognitive abilities that have been developed.

However, few psychologists today seem disposed to state the issue in such general terms or to take a position on one side or the other. All theorists recognize the necessity for dealing with both persistence and change and show a tendency to do so in a differentiated way, with attention to different kinds of structure, different kinds of change, different conditions and mechanisms of change [50, 120, 123, 231]. Points of view are expressions of the general theoretical positions, since a theory of how structures change has to be consistent with a theory of their determination and functioning.

The divisions here are along lines that we have previously noted. Theorists who put little structure into the personality have little difficulty in accounting for change. Personality changes as the social situation or the social-field conditions change. For that matter, these theorists have a ready explanation of persistence too, for the social and cultural structures that are supposed to determine the organization of personality are often very durable.

Theorists who concentrate on the building up of structures during the early years are not inclined to suppose that these structures will yield to change without a struggle. According to psychoanalytic theory and probably action theory in general, the most durable structures of the personality do not change essentially unless their unconscious sources are made conscious to the subject. Stimulus-response psychology, of course, attempts to bring change as well as persistence under the same set of general principles; thus, for example, a response will not persist unless it is reinforced, but the possible reinforcing agencies in the person become in time very numerous and very complicated.

The theorists of this group do not deny that personality can and does change as a result of interactions with the environment, but they insist that these changes are consistent with the individual's past and with his presently operating tendencies. In general, these theorists proceed in accordance with the tension-reduction principle: The personality system or any subsystem of it will change when it encounters strain of such quality and intensity that old adaptive responses will not suffice and new ones have to be improvised; the system will handle the strain in the way that involves the least general disturbance to itself; and the particular adaptive responses elicited will depend upon the state and developmental status of the system.

Writers who do not restrict themselves to the principle of homeostasis sometimes accent the individual's potential for change and sometimes his capacity for self-consistency despite radically changing circumstances. The fact is that these writers [e.g., 8, 164, 116] are not so much concerned with the persistence-change dimension as they are with the "higher" versus the "lower." If a situational determinist should present his views, these writers would reply by calling attention to the individual's capacity to carry out long-term programs of rational action, to maintain a stable self-conception, to act in accordance with a consistent system of values. If, on the other hand, an individual presents a fixed pattern of behavior—presumably based on personality structures —that has endured for years, these writers are likely to consider with hope the prospects of change after a few hours of therapy devoted to bringing about cognitive restructuring or changes in the conception of the self. (Such a case might lead a psychoanalyst to think of a two-year course of treatment and a behaviorist of a rigorous program of deconditioning.) More than this, the fact that changes do occur under these circumstances has led these writers to conclude that the psychoanalytic and behaviorist theories of determination must be wrong. Representatives of these latter views reply, of course, that the changes under consideration are superficial or temporary.

These contrasting views are not so much in conflict as they often appear to be. Sometimes different writers are talking about different things, different kinds of structures in the personality. Not only are there different mechanisms of change and different determinants of consistency, but some seem more applicable than others to certain kinds of personality structures. We have seen that there are several theoretically more or less neutral ways of classifying the structures of personality—the outer and the inner, the central and the peripheral, the phenotypic and the genotypic, the conscious and the unconscious. There would appear to be little objection to saying that subsystems of any of these groupings might be momentary, temporary, or enduring. If this is so, then different hypotheses are required to explain the different states of the different subsystems.

The Problem of Uniqueness

Although several of the above authors have included the idea of uniqueness or "unique adjustments" in their definitions of personality, the argument for the uniqueness of each personality and the plea for the study of the single case have been put most forcibly and most persistently by G. Allport. He stated his general position in 1937 [6], and in 1955 [8] we find him sticking to his guns.

By and large, psychologists seem to have been rather unimpressed by Allport's argument and plea. Many have taken the trouble to answer him by pointing out that every entity in nature—each part or feature of a person, each event—is unique and that science can proceed only by noting uniformities; that all laws of nature are essentially of a statistical character, being statements about the average of a number of events; that if we can average the responses of a single individual, we may do the same with the responses of many individuals; that the uniqueness of a given personality may be set forth by specifying his position with respect to a number—and not necessarily a very large number—of nomothetic variables.

Nevertheless, the notion has persisted that the study of personality is or should be primarily concerned with the individual, what differentiates him from other individuals, and the ways in which he is rare, if not unique. What is general belongs to general psychology, what is left over—individual differences, unique organizations, the rare, the special—may be claimed by personality psychology. Rather curiously, on this point certain general psychologists have made common cause with Allport, with whom they otherwise seem to have little in common.

Meanwhile, psychologists who have been most intimately involved with the study of individual personalities—in personality assessment [e.g., 159, 181, 192, 259, 284], clinical diagnostic studies [e.g., 44, 130, 199, 275], and psychotherapeutic work [e.g., 45, 85, 93, 175]—have acted as if they had never heard of Allport or the recommendation that they concentrate on individual differences or unique organizations. They have generalized. They have supposed that their statements about relationships in the personalities they studied—how tensions are managed, defenses maintained, new experiences assimilated, and the like—were quite generally true. Indeed, they have supposed that their formulations of individual cases also had some generality, that the pattern of dynamic relationships found to characterize a given individual was very similar to patterns that could be found in other— perhaps many other—individuals. From a methodological point of view, the major criticism of these students of personality has been that they tend to *overgeneralize,* to suppose that what is true of neurotics is true of people in general or that what is found in Western cultures will be found universally, for example. The uniqueness of the individual, then, has not been the foremost or even an important concern of psychologists who have been most taken up with the study of individuals.

Allport says: "Strictly speaking every adjustment of every person is unique, in time and place, and in quality. In a sense, therefore, this criterion seems redundant. It becomes important, however, in our later discussions of the problem of *quantitative* variation among individuals in respect to the so-called common traits . . . and is therefore emphasized in the definition" [6, p. 49]. Clearly Allport does not mean that personality determines the individual's unique adjustments, while adjustments that are not unique are determined by something else, or some other conditions. Since all adjustments of all individuals are unique, it is indeed redundant to say "unique adjustments." Allport, as he says, is preparing the ground for his critique of "common traits" and for his accent on the concept of ideographic trait. (But since all manifestations of all traits are unique, one can make statements about traits only on the basis of uniformities and averages of numerous responses. Most psychologists would probably agree that not all traits exist in all people, that some are far more common than others, and that some are rare.) All this is as plain to Allport as it is to anybody else. The way to understand his position is to put the accent not on uniqueness, but on holism. What Allport most wants to do, as he makes clear in *Becoming* [8], is to understand the "Johnian" quality of John's behavior. The way to accomplish this is not to study a thousand other people in order to show how unlike them John is; rather, one would study each aspect of John in relation to his whole personality to see if something of John himself is expressed in each segment of his behavior. This is the holistic approach, and a study of Allport's methodological recommendations shows that all of them are consistent with it. His complaints about the usual approach of clinical psychology were boiled down to two in 1955: (1) The universal dimensions employed in the study of personality may be irrelevant to John's personality; and (2) the study of the interrelations of the dimensions has not been carried far enough. Most clinical psychologists, while taking a far less pessimistic view with respect to the possibilities of common traits, would agree that John might have some exceedingly rare traits. As for the second criticism, they would admit it with enthusiasm, urging that the study of the inter-relations of dimensions of the person is the most important—and the most difficult—task of psychology.

But—and this is a crucial point—to expose the Johnian quality of John's behavior or to state one's understanding of the vast and complicated structure of his personality is not to say that the Johnian quality of John is not very much like the Willian quality of Will or that certain scientific and practical purposes are not best served by grouping the two individuals. And we say this while granting that John is unique and Will is unique—like everybody else—and that each is uniquely valuable.

Kluckhohn and Murray [131, p. 35] have neatly stated:

Every man is in some respects
1. like all other men
2. like some other men
3. like no other man

Psychology has so far been almost entirely concerned with *2*—with the discovery of the ways in which a man or a group of men is like some other men. Of course, we would like to know the ways in which all men are psychologically alike, but obstacles to sampling the whole human race have so far proved insuperable. And in the highly differentiated and complex Western societies in which most psychological research is carried on, differences by age, sex, social class, and sub-culture loom very large indeed. Still, we can say that among normal adults in Western societies there are modes of behavior that seem to have considerable generality and that a given man is in some respect like a great many other men. This holds for what is ordinarily called "personality functioning" as well as for the familiar processes of perception and learning. Obviously, if one wished to know what to expect under some condition from the whole population of the United States or how to influence that population, as advertisers and propagandists often do, one would do best to use averages.

Much psychological work aimed at the control of behavior is directed to distinctive subgroups of the population. The more humanistic applications of psychology—psychotherapy and counseling, education and correctional work, and child training—are always concerned with the individual. Here the psychologist is guided mainly by knowledge of ways in which the individual is like some others, and the most general principles are not the most helpful ones. Many of them are taken for granted as general rules, of which the given individual's functioning is a special case. But each individual is a special case, and a little study shows that—whatever else he might be—he is not average. His differences from others in particular functions usually have to be referred to larger organizations in his personality. This organization is, of course, unique. But there is nothing to do about uniqueness—except admire it or perhaps understand and manipulate the conditions that favor it. Any action must be based on knowledge of the conditions under which a given action will produce a given effect. The conditions that the psychotherapist or educator primarily deals with are to be found in the individual's organized states and processes, which have some generality —this is what makes practical work with individuals possible.

BOUNDARIES OF PERSONALITY

The foregoing discussion has been concerned with the essential nature of personality, i.e., with its elements and their organization. A complete definition of personality, however, must deal with the problem of delimitation: It must say what is excluded and how personality is to be distinguished from the phenomena that are closely related to it.

The view that personality is to be distinguished from overt behavior and from the environment with which it interacts has been expressed. Here I will suggest that personality should also be distinguished from the effects of the individual's behavior upon his environment, social or other, and from the physical structure and physiological processes of the individual. It is to be noted, however, that each of these excluded orders of phenomena is actually included in one or more of the definitions presented at the beginning of this essay. The whole problem of boundaries is difficult and controversial, and at present one's position with respect to this problem is bound to involve some commitment to a particular theoretical approach and, probably, a degree of arbitrariness.

Behavior

Allport has stated as explicitly as anyone that personality is not the same thing as behavior or activity. "It is what lies *behind* specific acts and *within* the individual" [6, p. 218]. "The systems that constitute personality are in every sense *determining tendencies,* and when aroused by suitable stimuli provoke those adjustive and expressive acts by which the personality comes to be known" [6, p. 49]. White [285, p. 96] gives a contemporary expression of the same point of view: "To say that we measure the achievement motive is metaphorical, not literal. Our measures give us but hints of what lies hidden in the person being tested. . . . the index has something to do with achievement motivation" [285, p. 97].

In the 1937 statement just quoted, Allport was taking a position in opposition to the then current trend in behavioristic theory to contrive a psychology without an organism, i.e., to consider that the subject matter of psychology consisted in relationships between objectively observable stimuli and objectively observable responses. In so far as personality existed for writers who expressed this view, it had to consist of "behavior," observable stimulus-response relationships—for this was all that existed for the psychologist. Undoubtedly all personality theorists preferring the action frame of reference agreed and would agree with Allport today.

But modern S-R theory—at least where it is directed to the phenomena of personality—does not presume to get along without any hypothetical constructs at all. Indeed, the "stimulus" itself is often necessarily hypothetical [96]. When it is assumed that all responses are instigated by stimuli, the problem is often to find the stimuli that are provoking observed responses. While the investigator is conducting his quest for the stimulus, it exists, we may suppose, in his mind's eye. Similarly, "habit," which in S-R theory is used to stand for any stable or enduring characteristic of a person, would appear to be a hypothetical construct. Not all the habits that an individual has learned, which together make up his personality, can possibly be observed at any one time, yet they exist somewhere in the structure of the person. They may be theoretically observable, when our techniques of observation become sufficiently advanced. In the meanwhile, there is at least some gap between what is observed and what is conceived to exist—presumably in the functioning of the individual's nervous system.

The most characteristic feature of modern S-R theory is not that it dispenses with hypothetical constructs altogether, but that it strives to use no more of such concepts than are absolutely necessary and to maintain the closest possible ties between what is conceived and what is observed.

Modern S-R theory is reflected in the definitions of personality by McClelland [151, p. 9] and Hilgard [109] which were quoted earlier. These definitions, more than any of the others quoted, strive to keep *behavior*—rather than systems, processes, or dispositions—in the focus of attention. For McClelland, personality is the "conceptualization of a person's *behavior*" (italics mine). Note that personality is a conceptualization and not a description. For Hilgard, personality is "the sum total of individual characteristics and *ways of behaving* which in their organization or patterning describe an individual's unique adjustment to his environment" (italics mine). It is interesting to note here that while Allport speaks of personality as "determining the individual's unique adjustments," Hilgard says "describe." This would appear to be another expression of the S-R theorist's tendency to be cautious and objective and to ascribe no more to the "insides" of the person than is necessary.

In the quotation just cited, White [285, p. 97] is suggesting that this is precisely the tendency that sometimes leads the S-R psychologist into serious error. So eager is he to keep concepts and observables closely tied together that he sometimes mistakes the latter for the former. Even when he is far from claiming that personality is embraced by overt behavior, he nonetheless tends to act as if this were so because, as it seems, overt behavior is relatively easy to get hold of.

The idea of relatively loose or remote and complicated relationships between measures of overt behavior and "what lies hidden in the person being tested"—the absence of one-to-one correlation in any population of subjects—is surely one of the most cherished ideas in the dynamic theorist's scheme of things. The same or very similar measured behavior may be ascribed to different processes in the personality in different individuals or in the same individual at different times. And the same personality process may express itself in different observable ways. The beauty of a concept like "achievement motive" is not that it can be measured by a simple operation in a laboratory situation, but that it can help explain a consistent trend of behavior in a variety of situations— the congruence, one might say, of a variety of measures. And when brought into relation with other concepts in theoretical formulations, the achievement motive can help explain the more complex phenomena of everyday behavior. One must proceed, of course, by measuring what can be measured and by demonstrating relationships among measures. But personality processes themselves are not measured; they are invoked to explain observed relationships and to predict relationships that will be observed under specified conditions. This use of personality concepts and theory is not, as we have seen, a departure from operationism so long as the concepts are tied to something that can be observed; it is the means by which the personality theorist maintains his freedom to think about his material.

In an essential way, then, the distinction between personality and behavior is the distinction between the concept and that which is observable. But one might ask how the matter should be handled if it turned out that what was once conceived could now be observed directly —if, for example, someone should contrive an instrument from which we could read directly variations that until now we had imagined occurring in some component of personality. There are two answers to this question. One is that the possibilities of ever finding such perfect indexes of personality variables are remote—and seem to be becoming more so. When Tolman [270, 271] and later Hull [114] and their numerous followers worked with "intervening variables" in the 1930s, the hope and expectation was that means of linking inferred explanatory concepts un-equivocally to observables would be found. As Koch [133] has recently pointed out, this quest has been virtually abandoned. Not only did Tolman [273, 274] change his mind about the possibility of measuring intervening variables by "defining experiments," but there seems to be widespread and increasing agreement with Lazarsfeld's [140] argument that, for any intervening variable, a variety of indicators will correspond. Lazarsfeld believes his argument holds—even for animal experimenta-tion. When we come to the human personality, the discovery of specific indicators of theoretical variables seems to be virtually out of the question.

The other answer to the question is based on simple logic. If per-sonality is defined as something that, among other things, helps to de-termine observed behavior, then it cannot be at the same time observed behavior. If one can observe it, then it is not personality! Of course, it is possible to imagine that we might some day observe phenomena that have been generated solely by personality processes—conceivably this might be done by getting at the brain directly. But these phenomena would certainly not be behavior in the usual sense of responses or acts of people.

The Effects of Behavior

The effects of a person's behavior upon others, his "social stimulus" value, is often very impressive. In the past, some writers were so struck by these effects that they were led to regard them as the chief data or even as the defining substance of personality. If, however, we are to sep-arate personality and behavior, it seems that we must separate personality and the effects of behavior by the same logic. The relationship of the two is like that of a factory to its products. The typical effects of a per-son's behavior—not only his influence upon other people, but his crea-tions, constructions, and achievements—are expressive of his personality and important sources of inferences about it. But such "effects" as we are able to observe usually have other determinants besides personality, and there is more to personality than can ever be perceived in its effects.

The Environment

Although personality and the effects of personality in action are dif-ferent things, they may nevertheless be parts of the same person-environ-ment system. The individual and his social environment constitute a dynamic configuration whose parts are so closely related that drawing lines of demarcation is often very difficult. Some theorists prefer to make this configuration rather than personality itself the unit for study; others emphasize factors in the "field" surrounding the individual so much that the concept of personality barely retains its integrity. The view here is that in a universe of related events it is necessary to be arbitrary to some extent and that we do well to study one order of events without studying all the other orders to which it is related. Thus we may separate personality and the environment conceptually and study any interesting relations between them.

But this does not say just how the boundary lines are to be drawn. One's approach to this problem seems to depend on what conceptual model of personality functioning one adopts. One conception is the common-sense one that a man's personality is somewhere inside of him, "under his skin," and that, as his body carries this structure into different environments, it somehow remains much the same or at least maintains some consistency with itself. Personality according to this view must be located in nature. Sophisticated versions of this conception take into account what we know about bodily functioning and without hesitation place the seat of personality in the brain. It is only to activities of the brain, the conserver of experience and the integrator of processes, that we may ascribe the *organization* that is the most essential feature of the personality. Personality is thus postafferent and preefferent. The task of distinguishing between personality and the environment from this point of view is no different from that of distinguishing between, say, a memory image and the physical stimulus that gave rise to it. Processes involving a change in the form of energy intervene between the two.

Not all the processes of personality that we may infer from the observation of behavior have any known correlates in brain functioning as yet. Supposing, as we must, that such correlates may ultimately be discovered, we are free to conceptualize brain processes to explain our observations, taking care that our conceptualizations do not contradict what is known about brain functioning. This would be using a "physiological model" of personality processes.

The other main type of model of personality is the "formal" model. Personality is represented as an open system with inputs and outputs. A circle or an ellipse or some such figure represents the personality and since all systems, with the exception of the universe, have environments, the area outside but adjacent to the figure is referred to as the environment. The two areas, the personality and the environment, are filled in with the subsystems that must be conceptualized. What separates personality from the environment is the boundary, and this has whatever properties the theorist thinks he should ascribe to it. (We assume, of course, that what the theorist does is in accordance with known facts and hope that it will aid the discovery of new ones.) This is the way Lewin [144] proceeded in distinguishing between the *person* and the *psychological environment,* and between the *life space*—which embraced both person and psychological environment—and the *nonpsychological environment.* Boundaries between these regions were endowed with the property of *permeability,* and they were conceived in dynamic terms as regions that offered resistance to exchange of energy between neighboring systems. Miller [170], in presenting what he calls "general behavior systems theory, a subcategory of general systems theory," points out that the boundaries of systems—such as personality—are not always clear-cut, that a given individual or behaving subsystem may be a part of several systems, and that the essential fact about a boundary is that any exchange of energy across it leads to some change in the energy form.

Proceeding in this general way, clearly we may conceptualize as many systems and subsystems as we like and define their boundaries in theoretical terms. But finding empirical support for these conceptualizations or showing that one of them fits the facts better than some other is a different matter. It is sometimes very difficult to say whether a given variable is in the personality or the environment. Perhaps, as Miller suggests, it is in both. Certainly we may observe personality-environment relationships that seem just as "bounded" as does the personality itself. However, we are not without guides to the location of variables. For example, there is the purely formal criterion: A variable is the personality system if the operations of that variable can be deduced from personality processes. Or we may view the matter in probabilistic terms: A unit may be said to be incorporated by personality in so far as the variance due to personality is greater than the variance due to the environment. And again, we may make use of a homeostatic model and consider that personality imposes limits on the range of variation in behavior that can be elicited by the environment.

The great benefit of formal models is that they suggest what to look for—in particular, they direct our attention to areas that might otherwise be neglected. In this respect, Lewin's conception of the psychological environment has been a contribution of great importance. In the early thirties, when Lewin's views were just beginning to have an impact in this country, American psychologists—except where psychoanalysis was influential—were largely involved in attempting to construct an objective S-R psychology and were seriously neglecting the organism. The psychological environment called proper attention to the world in which the individual actually lives, the world of his experience, his hopes and aspirations, his fears—thus it made inroads into the then current trend.

Murray, with his concept of "beta press" [181], Rogers with his "phenomenology" [211], and psychoanalysis with its "inner world"—all were soon to ensure the psychological environment of an adequate place in personality theory. In other fields of psychology, gestalt theory, phenomenology, and cognitive theory have been sufficiently potent forces.

Today, the psychological environment or some very similar conception has a very important place in the thinking of most personality theorists, and there is flourishing research on relationships involving the individual's cognitions, interpretations, constructions, and the like. Indeed, Lewin and Rogers, like the psychoanalysts before them, have been accused of paying far too little attention to the world of reality. The same criticism will undoubtedly be directed to the recent work of G. Kelly [122].

From the point of view of common sense and the physiological model, the psychological environment is inside the personality. Although there is no question that individuals respond to a *feeling* of being rejected or to a *sense* of lowered self-esteem, these phenomena are clearly post-afferent. Clearly, they are also correlated with events in the physical (geographical) environment—either that of the present or that of the past. Theorists may differ in the importance that they attach to this environment, but none can justify its complete neglect. Happily, there is no reason in theory why a psychologist cannot be interested in both the geographical and the psychological environments, in their interrelationships, and in the relations of each or both in the functioning of the person. But he must recognize that, if he is to study relationships involving the "real" (geographical) environment, he must specify its stimuli without benefit of a subject's perception of it. This is no easy matter, particularly in the case of the all-important social environment. One can learn a great deal about an individual's psychological environment by the relatively comfortable procedure of listening to him talk about himself or by the highly respectable procedure of placing him in a number of carefully controlled experimental situations. But to characterize the real environment in which he lives from day to day requires special methods and techniques—and a great deal of legwork. In clinical practice, for example, psychotherapy is the preferred method for understanding and treating the disturbed individual, but it is commonly agreed that where time is limited and action is called for there is no substitute for visits to the patient's home and/or interviews with members of his family—and possibly other relevant people—by a trained social worker. Again, in the earliest attempts at personality assessment, the aim was to predict the individual's future behavior on the basis of intensive studies of him in a "living-in" situation. This procedure persisted long after it was generally recognized that tests and interviews with the individual ought to be supplemented by visits to the home, interviews with the spouse, observation of the subject on the job, and the study of other institutions within which he performed in social roles; the difficulties and expense of such investigation seemed too great. But in more recent assessment studies, such as those of Stern, Stein, and Bloom [259], efforts have been made to formulate the demands of the subject's situation and to obtain measures of them—the requirements of his roles and the values and practices of the institution in which he works, for example. Other examples of special studies of the environment are the work of Pace and Stern [194] in devising a special instrument for studying the characteristics of colleges; other work [77, 269] that has sought to improve prediction of students' performance and to enlarge our understanding of personality development in college by specifying relevant features of the institutional setting; the well-known ecological studies of Barker and Wright [16, 17]; and the investigations by Elizabeth Bott [29] of the individual in his family and "social network."

Physical Structure and Physiological Processes

The reasons for studying the organism as a whole, for regarding all the biological and psychological processes that take place under a person's skin as parts of a single system, are at least as cogent as the reasons for regarding the individual and his environment as a system. The question is whether we should equate personality and organism as a whole as some writers [e.g., Eysenck, 67] have done or regard personality as a separate system that interacts with other systems of the organism. The matter is particularly complicated if we regard personality as an organization of processes in the brain and thus can make no categorical distinction between personality functioning and other biological events.

Yet it would be inconsistent with this essay not to prefer to distinguish personality from the constitution and to study the relations between the two. Indeed, this seems to be the most common practice among personality theorists.

In research in this field, sometimes the bodily process and sometimes the personality function is treated as the independent variable. The former proceeding is illustrated by studies of the effects of damage to the brain on personality [90] or by studies in which gross variations in bodily form or function are considered to be perceived by the individual and responded to in accordance with his needs and values—as would be the case in physical handicap, for example [139]. Research in which the personality process is treated as the independent variable is illustrated by studies which indicate that prolonged psychological disturbances lead to changes in organ systems—ulcers of the stomach, for example [173]. However, research is commonly directed to producing correlations between physical and physiological variables on the one hand and personality variables on the other—explanation then being sought in terms of complex interactions between the two sets of variables. This is true, for example, of studies stimulated by Sheldon's [243, 244] classic and influential work on physique and personality. Sheldon, of course, emphasizes the biological basis of his "somatotypes" and has offered hypotheses to explain how the individual's bodily constitution helps to determine some of his characteristic behavior. Sheldon admits, however, that the somatotypes might change under the impact of nutritional or other environmental changes, and other psychologists [97, 223] have been ready with hypotheses to explain how personality processes might influence physique.

Although literature on the relations between bodily processes and psychological factors is vast [15, 59, 247], this whole area has been rather neglected by personality psychologists. This might be attributed to our American cultural history—we are optimistic environmentalists. It might also be attributed to the way the scientific disciplines are organized—"psychosomatic" relationships have been more or less effectively claimed by the medical profession. Unquestionably, the varied and complicated relationships between personality and bodily processes constitute a rich and relatively unexplored field for investigation. But if personality psychologists regard other things as more important and sufficiently engrossing, it is difficult to see how they can be reproached. Probably they have the right instinct. On the other hand, these psychologists often seem to regard the investigation of bodily processes as at least important enough to "let George do it." They do not mind suggesting that physiological psychologists ought to study other physiological things in addition to the central nervous system. Personality psychologists, of course, would like someone to study the bodily processes in which personality seems to have a determining role. They will probably have to do it themselves. The physiological psychologist typically is after bigger game—the processes underlying the functioning of personality itself. One can only wish him luck, however much a conservative man might marvel at such ambition.

Character, Temperament, Intelligence

"Character" and "temperament" seem to have virtually disappeared from the literature as technical terms. It used to be that phenomena brought under these headings were regarded by some theorists as something different from personality (Allport defined character as "personality evaluated") or as something to be included within personality ("Temperament refers to the characteristic phenomena of an individual's emotional nature . . . these phenomena being regarded as dependent upon constitutional make-up and therefore largely hereditary in origin") [6, p. 54]. Thus it was necessary for surveyors of the field, such as MacKinnon [158], to discuss the boundary problems thus posed. Today we are spared this necessity because character and temperament have simply been absorbed into that vast domain called "variables of personality." The question of whether there are clusters or syndromes that deserve one or the other of these names is usually regarded as an empirical rather than a theoretical one. Psychoanalytic theory and practice still make some systematic use of the concept of character, but the typical personality psychologist—if he is interested in such matters—is likely to consider any of the observables here involved under the general heading of "ego functioning."

Intelligence is a more complicated matter. From the point of view of organismic theory of personality, intellectual performance would be regarded in the same way as any other. One would observe consistencies in behavior and hypothesize underlying regularities of functioning in the personality. One could refer to these regularities as intelligence. On the other hand, in our society much interest attaches to intelligent *behavior,* and usually we are interested in *all* of its correlates, some of which are certainly not in the personality. Probably for some time to come, there will be a continuation of the present practice of measuring and evaluating intellectual performances and then seeking, among other things, their "personality correlates." How these correlates are to be conceptualized seems an open question. It may be that there are identifiable subsystems that have special roles in intellectual functioning, or it may be that we have to deal here with certain features of the personality organizations as a whole.

PERSONALITY AS A FIELD OF INQUIRY

Subdivisions of the Field

The field of personality, considered as a domain of research and teaching, has expanded and developed at a phenomenal rate during the past twenty years. In one psychology department—and this is probably not atypical—the first course entitled "Personality" was introduced in 1940; now there are seven courses in the "personality area," not including abnormal psychology, individual differences, motivation, or clinical psychology. The movement that has generated this elaboration may be slowing down, but it shows no signs of coming to a halt. Moreover, it seems well understood that the content of courses must change fairly rapidly in order to keep pace with developments in the field.

Subdivision according to method. Most of the courses that have been added in recent years have centered either upon some method for investigating personality or upon the relations of personality to some other field or order of phenomena. This way of organizing teaching corresponds generally to the prevailing organization of research activity; and, whereas the addition of a new course is usually an expression of the interests of a particular member of a department, the expansion of teaching over the years tends to keep pace with research. Theoretical work has likewise flourished, but in teaching it seems that the effort is usually to order developments to the basic course in theories of personality. Sometimes the attempt is made—as in the present essay—to organize a course around theoretical issues, bringing the contributions of various writers to bear upon them. Any attempt to subdivide the field along lines prescribed by the theoretical structure of personality itself is rarely observed.

It seems that the older courses in the psychology departments were, with respect to method, quite catholic; they made use of such investigations as were available—case studies, researches involving objective tests of personality, experiments. As the field has expanded and researches have multiplied, it has seemed natural—given the methodological orientation of American psychologists—that we should have courses in the case study, personality testing, personality assessment, and experimental psychodynamics. An examination of university departmental offerings will also usually reveal courses in projective techniques and, very likely, courses concerned with particular techniques, such as the Rorschach test. But these will usually be called "clinical courses." This raises the question of where the personality field stops and clinical psychology begins. This is a difficult matter. It is perhaps enough to suggest that in clinical courses the technique and training in the use of the techniques are accentuated, whereas in personality the accent is on the substantive aspects of investigations, the line between the two rarely being very clearly drawn. The point for us here is that one way of subdividing the field of personality—a fairly noncontroversial way—is according to the method by which data or research results are obtained. How far subdivision and specialization along this line can be carried without resulting in a lamentable fragmentation of the field is a matter for debate. Perhaps the limit has already been reached.

Differences in perspective and in general direction of approach. Earlier in this essay, we had occasion to observe that preference for a given method tends to be associated with preference for a given type of theory concerning the nature of personality. For example, case studies are favored by organismic theorists. But the relationship is by no means one to one. Some organismic theorists might prefer experiments in lifelike situations. Similarly, there are certain perspectives in which personality may be viewed and certain general approaches to its study which, though they have implications for methodology, are not tied to any particular method. Nor are they bound to any particular theory.

If one thinks of personality as an organization that exhibits some continuity even as it changes throughout the individual's life span, then one may, as we have seen, concentrate on (1) different time spans or periods of the personality's existence, (2) on its changing aspects or on its more enduring features, and (3) on systematic or on historical approaches to explaining its functioning. Divisions of labor according to these several emphases may be noted in teaching and research.

The whole life span is sometimes regarded as a suitable unit for study [40, 142, 156, 157, 182, 216, 268]. According to White [284], the "study of lives" has been the major concern of the Harvard Psychological Clinic. Courses in biography or personality as biography sometimes appear among the departmental offerings. More commonly, of course, certain more or less ill-defined periods of life, such as adolescence or later maturity, are chosen for special attention. Courses or investigations that go under these latter names may or may not be concerned primarily with personality. Instead, they may be directed to the various determinants of certain kinds of behavior or to the effects of environmental factors that become prominent at particular times of life. It seems, however, that one could quite logically abstract a certain segment of the life span and study the organization of personality in both its changing and enduring aspects during that period. In contrast to investigations or courses directed to the life span or large segments of it, there are the usual inquiries, of course. These are directed to organization in general as it is found at the time of an experiment or during the course of, say, a three-day assessment period.

One sometimes encounters nowadays a course in "personality change," which attempts to bring together materials from psychotherapy, experiments, and longitudinal studies of development. The central concern is with the conditions and processes of changes in personality organization. A vast array of empirical studies have been directed to these latter problems. The contrast is with the theme in research and teaching that accents the prediction (forecasting) of future performances from measures of the presumably more durable traits or features of the personality. This has been a traditional concern of "the psychology of individual differences." Individual differences include more than differences in personality, but personality may be taught—just as it may be investigated—from the individual-differences point of view. The great difficulty with change versus enduringness as the basis for a division in the field of personality is that there seems to be no good reason why any subsystem of the personality should not be observed with attention both to change and permanence. On the other hand, one might say that in a department in which the substantive aspects of personality were taught only from the individual-differences point of view, there would seem to be room for a course in personality change.

Courses or texts dealing with personality development appear to be highly varied. Such a course or text might be concerned primarily with major theories of personality, such as S-R theory, psychoanalysis, or gestalt theory and with their influence on developmental change—or it may be primarily a course in one or another of these theories. Such a course might be organized around different periods of life or stages of development, or around different processes or determinants of change; it might accent continuity with the past (enduringness) or new beginnings (change); finally, it might more or less limit itself to historical or systematic causation. This last distinction has been maintained not only in different approaches to development, but in divisions of the field as a whole. Experimental psychodynamics, which took its major inspiration from K. Lewin's exposition of systematic causation [144], was one of the first additions to course offerings in personality. It stood in contrast to the conventional course, which concerned itself primarily with consistency in behavior and the diagnosis of persisting tendencies and assumed that what was present in the personality had been learned as a result of past experience. Although courses on experimental psychodynamics accented the results of controlled investigations, other sources of information were commonly utilized. Time was taken to familiarize the student with such phenomena as substitution, repression, regression, and so on. The division of labor along the line of systematic versus historical causation has been a useful one. And it still makes sense. Today, however, much of the material that used to belong to experimental psychodynamics and personality has been brought into the standard course on motivation, and most students of personality are concerned with both the systematic and the historical causes of the phenomena they observe.

Personality in relation to other orders of phenomena. Here belong the "personality and . . . " courses that have become a familiar feature of the psychology department and are to be encountered in sociology, anthropology, and social welfare departments as well. The relations of personality to each of the groups of phenomena that were excluded from the earlier definition of personality have been the object of such study, and a very considerable body of fact and theory has been accumulated.

In one group of relationships, personality variables are usually in the dependent role. Kluckhohn and Murray [131] refer to society, culture, and constitution as *determinants* of personality, and probably not many psychologists would offer serious objections. The student of personality may display the banner before the "and" in the title of his course in "personality and culture" instead of "culture and personality," as the anthropologist would have it or "personality and social role" instead of "role determinants of personality," as the sociologist would have it. When one says "personality and physique" or "personality and bodily changes," he suggests that personality may be the independent variable or that the influences of the two domains are mutual at the least. Indeed, the *interaction* of personality and its social environment is usually assumed also. However, there is no denying that in the vast array of studies of personality in relation to cultural, social, physical, and physiological factors, personality is more determined than determining.

But there is another group of "personality and . . . " courses or investigations in which personality is rather clearly the determinant. Here the relationship is between personality and some form of behavior or effect of behavior—personality and opinion, personality and prejudice, and conformity, and delinquency, and leadership, and so on.

Specialization according to the type of phenomenon with which personality is related is undoubtedly here to stay. It is a way of proceeding that arouses little controversy. The possibilities of differentiation within the domains to which personality is related seem very great. We may anticipate further expansion along this line.

Subdivision according to theoretical structure. In the organization of research activity, the investigator inevitably limits himself to one or a few conceptually distinct elements or subsystems of the personality. Some of these have achieved sufficient status so that the researcher may identify his activity by reference to a domain to which it belongs, e.g., researches on ego functioning, the self-concept, cognitive structures, or mechanisms of defense. In teaching, however, it is extremely rare to divide the labor in this way in the academic departments. We do not find, for example, one course on "the self concept" and another on "conscience and its vicissitudes."

The contrast with the state of affairs in psychoanalytic institutes is striking. Here the curriculum is designed largely in accordance with the psychoanalytic theory of personality; hence, one usually finds courses on the libido theory, dreams, the mechanisms of defense, the superego, and so on.

As suggested above, something of this tendency crept into the psychology department under the guise of experimental psychodynamics, where the emphasis was often upon mechanisms rather than upon the traditional contents—needs, attitudes, and the like—but this was usually not a frank division according to theoretical structure. The course in psychology of the unconscious may have something of this same aspect, giving special attention to certain hypothetical subsystems (e.g., complexes, insatiable needs, unconscious fantasies) that are rarely treated fully in the standard course on personality. On the other hand, such a course may be taught from the point of view of general psychology or may occupy itself with an aggregate of isolated abnormal phenomena and not be a course in personality at all.

Resistance in the psychology departments to dividing the teaching of personality according to a theoretical scheme seems to be in part an expression of devotion to the prevailing organismic point of view. When one undertakes to present the "basic facts and theories of personality," he is likely to experience a strong impulse to deal with the whole thing or to concentrate upon its salient feature, which turns out to be organization. If he takes up theories of personality in turn, it soon appears that each is an effort to conceptualize the whole—the elements and their organization. The present writer has taught a course in personality regularly since 1940. Looking back, it appears that this course has changed a great deal. At first it was organized around Murray's "need scheme," then it came under the sway of a psychoanalytic frame of reference, and in more recent years there has been experimentation with a general-systems approach. But at all times there was an effort to give a course in *personality* rather than in some part or subsystem thereof. Probably this type of resistance to fragmentation is widespread among personality psychologists.

Perhaps even more important has been the reluctance among academic psychologists to make the necessary commitment to a general theoretical scheme and, when such commitment has been made, their inability to achieve the agreement necessary to the planning of teaching. This is striking testimony to the relative lack of theoretical development of personality as a field; and it poses a persistent dilemma as to how that development is to be achieved. There are obvious advantages to proceeding as the psychoanalysts have done, and the appeal of the psychoanalytic frame of reference, with its rational basis for subdividing the whole personality, has been very strong. But the wariness of many personality psychologists about "premature structuration," with its threats to objectivity and freedom in interpreting events, has not been altogether misplaced. On the other hand, delay of the development of an acceptable general theory involves grave danger; in the absence of such a theory, the present tendency to organize the field according to methods or relations with other fields will result in serious fragmentation and watering down.

Personality and General Psychology

Historical note. Thirty-five years ago it would have been fairly easy to differentiate between personality and general psychology. At that time general psychology was still concerned with laboratory studies of the generalized adult mind, abstracting part processes such as learning or perception and studying them in many subjects. It was guided by the waning classical introspectionism or by the still fairly new behaviorism. The whole vast area of molar behavior, particularly motivation, and the personality processes brought over from the clinic—complexes, mechanisms of defense, and the like—were left to the personality psychologists.

Problems of definition were actually as acute then as now, but nobody was troubled about his identity as either a personality psychologist or a general psychologist. Each had his own concepts, methods, and assumptions, and the two had very little in common.

In the intervening years, things have changed radically. For one thing, the concepts and theories from the dynamic psychology of personality have won wide acceptance. And this includes the concepts and theories of psychoanalysis and psychoanalytic psychologies. It has become apparent that motivational phenomena and the relations of motivation to other processes, even repression, are just as general as the more familiar phenomena of learning or perception; hence they are worthy of attention from psychologists in general [118, 147].

Thus Hilgard stated, in his presidential address before the American Psychological Association in 1949: "The problems of human motivation and personality belong to all psychologists. The problems of the self-concept are general problems of psychological science" [108, p. 380].

During the same period, developments in general psychology gave rise to the hope that we were about to achieve a general theory adequate to deal with the whole range of behavior, including the functioning of the personality, of course. Theories developed and elaborated on the basis of the intensive study of particular areas of subject matter could be generalized to all behavior. Major examples are Hull's theory [114], springing mainly from studies of learning, and gestalt theories, springing mainly from the study of perception [134, 135].

Of particular significance has been the field theory of Kurt Lewin. His *Dynamic Theory of Personality* [144] appeared in 1933. Allport could call this a misnomer, on the ground that it appeared to be straight general psychology. Allport was most struck, of course, by the absence of any reference to individual differences and of any means for depicting the uniqueness of the individual. Personality psychologists working in the functionalist or "action" tradition could well wonder what had happened to their familiar variables of personality—instincts, needs, traits, complexes, and the like—which they were in the habit of relating to the past history of the individual. For Lewin, behavior was to be explained systematically, that is, by reference to a field that contained variables in the person and forces in the psychological environment. He wrote that his psychology was deliberately conceived to bring the experimental method to bear upon "such vital problems as those with which psychoanalysis was concerned." There is no question but that he was effective. He and his associates and followers have produced much research on such problems as anger, altruism, regression, frustration, substitution, and level of aspiration [14, 57, 106, 107, 145, 146, 193, 289, 290].

The point for us here is not only that the "laws" of behavior, for Lewin, were *general*—thus paying no attention to individual differences —but that the accent on the *field* had the effect of smudging over the traditional boundaries between personality and the environment. This has meant that contemporary gestalt psychologists investigate problems from the erstwhile private preserves of personality psychology without feeling any need to mention personality or individual differences at all.

If general psychology has thus been stretching itself to embrace more and more of what used to belong to the personality field, so has research in personality—most of it informed by the prevailing action and organismic point of view—served to bring "variables of personality" to an increasingly prominent place in the attention of the experimentalist in general psychology. There have been literally hundreds of researches undertaken by personality psychologists and devoted to showing that variables of personality were predictive of individual differences in the performance of laboratory tasks. In recent years, general psychologists have often used the same design; witness a succession of experiments in which scores on the Taylor Anxiety Scale [266] have been related to conditioning.

Such work has served to increase the doubt that there are any general laws that hold in any detailed way for all people—regardless of age, sex, culture, social class, and personality. The theory and experimental work of Egon Brunswik [37, 39], with its assumption of the probabilistic aspect of perceiving, has further cast doubt on the generalizability of our nomothetic laboratory-derived laws.

New thinking about boundary problems. The developments mentioned above have certainly brought personality and general psychology closer together and exposed a great deal of overlapping of the two areas. Many psychologists, unable to enjoy any longer the splendid isolation of the past, have been facing up to the problem of definition.

But with their usual flair for disagreement, psychologists have succeeded in taking up positions about as far apart as they could get. Some view general psychology as one of several sciences that are propaedeutic to personology, the central science of man. There is the opposite view—that personality psychology is a branch of general psychology, the more complex phenomena of personality being ultimately reduceable to general psychological laws.

Each of these views is worthy of some discussion.

The general psychological approach to personality. A statement in favor of the general psychological approach to personality is that of Child:

The writer has no interest in helping to preserve the integrity of personality study as an isolated entity, welcoming instead the fact that as general psychology becomes more adequate to deal with the whole range of human behavior there is ever less occasion to recognize personality study in the traditional sense as a discipline in any way distinct [53, p. 149].

Again, note Hilgard:

Personality is saved from being synonymous with general psychology because its reference is to the single individual and to the unique organization of the traits that characterize him and his activity [109, p. 407].

These writers are expressing a view that has a long history in psychology. Psychology is the study of behavior, and personality is the learned behavior of people. Personality is the result of the way in which individuals have adjusted to the world about them; the study of personality is the study of how people come to be what they are. Of course, people differ widely in what they have learned; each person is indeed unique. But all have learned in accordance with the same general laws. This point of view puts the accent on what has been learned; but presumably the functioning or behaving of the personality right now—the assimilation of new experiences, the management of conflicting tensions, and the like—is in accordance with the general laws of psychology. The essential point is that there are no laws of personality functioning apart from the laws of general psychology.

But personality is "saved" from being synonymous with general psychology because of its concern with individual differences and the uniqueness of each person. Thus its natural concern is with the measurement of the learned characteristics of the person, its units of analysis being taken most appropriately from general psychology—motives, perceptions, emotional reactions, and so on. The characteristics are organized in the person in accordance with general psychological laws, but each individual is uniquely organized, and this is the special concern of the personality psychologist.

The point of view expressed here is perhaps most closely associated with representatives of Hull's learning theory. In addition to Child and Hilgard, there are Dollard and Miller [58] and Mowrer [174]. The viewpoint is also expressed by writers not so identified, e.g., Stagner [255].

In a curious way, this point of view gains strength from Allport's position. He, as we have seen, has been at pains to stress individuality, the "unique," as the special province of personality study. Writers of the present tradition have been happy to say, "All right, you can have it," and to cite him in support of their view that general psychology is responsible for the bulk of psychological knowledge, while personality is a kind of fringe domain. This is despite Allport's views that most so-called "general psychology" is off the track and can contribute little or nothing to the kind of individuality he means. (Of course, Allport himself has contributed to the general psychology of personality development, most notably with his doctrine of "functional autonomy" [6]).

We have seen also that classical gestalt psychology and the topological psychology of Kurt Lewin have also supposed that their general laws were adequate to the whole range of psychological phenomena and that individual differences hardly mattered.

It seems that writers who stress the general-psychological approach to personality usually tend to regard psychology as a relatively advanced science and seem optimistic about the possibilities of developing, perhaps soon, a general theory "adequate to deal with the whole range of human behavior." It is probably no accident that staunch supporters of this view have usually been identified with some particular theoretical system and have perhaps been led to overestimate its potency.

The personality approach to general psychology. If the essence of the point of view just described is that there are no laws of personality functioning apart from the laws of general psychology, the essence of the present view is that there are no general psychological laws that do not take personality processes into account. Cattell [48] gives a strong statement of this position. Not only is study of the total personality necessary for applications in industrial, educational, and clinical psychology—the *individual* being the same whether he appears in factory, school, or clinic —but—

. . . this mandate from applied psychology is less imperative than the corresponding demand from pure psychology for founding all progress in particular fields upon a study of personality. We do not deal with a "perception" or an "emotion" or a "conditioned reflex" but with an organism perceiving or acquiring a conditioned reflex, as part of some large pattern or purpose. . . . It is essential to bring fine laboratory instruments to bear in experiments on behavior; but it is a mistake to suppose that laws of learning, or of perception and emotion, can be found that do not take into account the total personality. The study of the total personality is thus the hub from which radiate all more specialized studies and it is only by turning on this center that they make progress [48, p. 2].

Equally strong statements are those by Klein [125, 126, 128], citing research that provides—

. . . ample evidence that purposes, aims, intentions, suffuse the very act of perceiving. All this work challenges the idea of "internal requiredness" or autochthony in the stimulus field, of "field structures" which are so compelling as to have a predestined and universal effect independent of personal intent. It has also helped to bury the older conception of an autonomous perceptual system which is capable of study apart from the larger context of the total system of the person, an idea born out of a myopia to personality theory [125, p. 328].

Perhaps the most widely quoted recent statement of this general point of view is that of Klein and Krech:

The kind of theory we are advocating is one which views all behavior within the context of the total organism. This is another way of saying that all the processes within the organism are "adaptive"; each function or behavior serves an *organismic purpose* [127, p. 11].

And in another place they write "an adequate personality theory must be a thoroughgoing behavior theory and all theories of behavior must be personality theories" [127, p. 11].

Part of the interest attaching to these statements springs from the fact that Klein and Krech strike many psychologists, as they do this one, as strange bedfellows. Klein has long been identified with personality research, particularly with the kind of investigation that relates individual differences in laboratory performances to the functioning of personality, while Krech is a general psychologist, long an exponent of gestalt psychology and, more recently, of a general-systems theory. It is as if Krech were saying, "An adequate personality theory must be a thorough-going behavior theory," and Klein were completing the sentence with "and all theories of behavior must be personality theories." It is a nice expression of the new closeness of personality and general psychology.

Although the general psychological approach to personality is represented in the views of these writers, particularly in what was just ascribed to Krech, it is clear that the general intent of their paper is to support the organismic point of view as against classical reductionism. These writers are frankly and warmly holistic, quoting with approval Bertalanffy on the point that an enormous preponderance of vital processes and mechanisms have a whole-maintaining character.

Perhaps I should point out that on the battleground of holism versus reductionism, Klein and Krech are late arrivals and, in a sense, replacements. Among psychologists, probably the most important exponent of the organismic point of view is Murray. Many psychologists have flirted with the organismic outlook—as many still do—but Murray has been married to it. Not only has he stated the position consistently for thirty years, but he organized large-scale researches in accordance with it and devised a methodology which, more than any other yet devised, had some promise of dealing adequately with its implications.

This is not intended to belittle the general importance of gestalt psychology or of the holistic thinkers who carry on in the tradition of European thought [Angyal, 9; Goldstein, 89; Stern, 5, 260]. It is rather to stress the fact that Murray, unlike most of the holists, was willing to separate parts from the whole by abstraction and get on with the business of investigation—and thus his importance for American psychology. Gestalt psychology has rarely been concerned in intensive investigations of personality. Psychoanalysis, particularly in its European versions, has been implicitly holistic all the time, but it seems that its spokesmen have not made systematic statements of this position, or if they have, they have not had much influence on psychologists.

Murray's statement of the organismic point of view follows:

The organism is from the beginning a whole, from which the parts are derived by self-differentiation. The whole and its parts are mutually related; the whole being as essential to an understanding of the parts as the parts are to an understanding of the whole. (This is a statement of the organismal theory.) Theoretically it should be possible to formulate for any moment the "wholeness" of an organism; or in other words, to state in what respect it is acting as a unit [181, p. 39].

Murray says he takes his wording from E. S. Russel [219] who in turn has stated the organismal viewpoint of W. E. Ritter [210]. He goes on:

We were accustomed to conceive of personality as a temporal integrate of mutually dependent processes (variables) developing in time, and from this conception it follows that a large number of determining variables as well as their relations must be recognized, and approximately measured, if one is to give an adequate interpretation—analysis and synthesis—of a single human event . . . This conclusion led to our first important decision, which was: that all experimenters should use one and the same group of subjects. Each worker continued as before with his own problem, but under the new plan he had the findings of other observers to aid him in the interpretation of his results [181, p. ix].

"His own problem" often included the experimental attack on some general psychological problem, e.g., emotional conditioning, sensorimotor learning, repression, cheating, reaction to frustration.

This general approach is being followed by Holt, Klein, and others at the New York University Research Center for Mental Health and at the Institute of Personality Assessment and Research at the University of California under the direction of D. W. MacKinnon.

The situation at the present time. If personality and general psychology are so largely overlapping as the above discussion would seem to indicate, we have to face the question of whether they are to be separated at all and, if so, in accordance with what principles.

We must not, however, cross too many bridges before we come to them. The above statements about the generality of psychological laws or about the inclusiveness of the organismic point of view are hopefully programmatic; they are considerably at odds with what seems to be the present state of affairs in psychology.

The accomplishments of general psychology, measured against the task of dealing scientifically with the whole range of human behavior, are not impressive. General psychology can predict, to a degree somewhat better than chance, what will be the average response of a group of individuals to a variety of stimuli or situations, but it is pretty far from being able to predict what any one individual will do. General psychologists seem often to mistake intentions for accomplishments and the capacity to lecture on what science is or ought to be for the capacity to produce scientific knowledge. The plain fact is that when it comes to slightly complicated practical problems, general psychology has but rarely got beyond common sense. The gap between the academic psychology of the laboratory and the practical psychology of psychotherapy is still so large that workers in the two fields seem to be in different realms of discourse. It is well for all psychologists to remember the remark of I. A. Richards that psychology had so far managed to say vaguely and obscurely what everybody knew already. But he added that here and there new light had crept in. It continues to creep in occasionally. But scientific general psychology with a bearing on human behavior is mainly a promise—a bright and hopeful promise, but little more. Advances in general psychology have been expressed most clearly in the increased willingness of general psychologists to attack more complicated problems. But the effects of these advances have not as yet been very sharply reflected in the teaching of general psychology.

As for the organismic point of view—it wins its way slowly. The 1951 paper by Klein and Krech was certainly evidence that this point of view has made headway since Murray wrote in 1938. But their clarion call for radical revisions in general psychological research and teaching seems largely to have fallen upon deaf ears. Psychologists have kept on doing what they were doing.

For one thing, the whole organismic approach still encounters direct opposition. For example, one of the outstanding researches expressing the new upsurge of the organismic point of view is *Personality through Perception* by Witkin et al. [288]. Gardner Murphy [177] thought this work "an extraordinary achievement" in the direction of bringing the process of perception into relation with the entire personality of the perceiver, but it was severely criticized by Postman [200]. Not only was Postman inclined to throw out the whole thing on methodological ground, but he objected rather strenuously to the whole approach, urging that his fellow academic psychologists forget such morbid personality stuff and concentrate on something fundamental, i.e., the mechanism of perception. There is no doubt that Postman speaks here for a great many academic psychologists—perhaps the majority.

Again, the realistic supporters of the organismic view have had to admit the necessity of abstracting parts from the whole, even the necessity of studying part functions in relative isolation; they have been able only to urge, as did Murray, that the psychologist in his experimental work "recognize that he is observing merely a part of an operating totality and that this totality, in turn, is but a small temporal segment of a personality" [181, p. 4]. Psychologists have been realistic enough to make a virtue of a necessity; after a virtuous nod in the direction of totality, they have gone on doing what they found interesting and rewarding.

Interestingly enough, the personality psychologists themselves have not in recent years been very organismic as far as their researches have been concerned. They have usually been content to use a few variables of personality as predictors of performance in some situations and, like the general psychologist, have been happy if they could get statistically significant relationships between averages for groups.

It is only fair to say, however, that limitations upon this kind of research have been largely dictated by circumstances. Projects such as that which issued in *Personality through Perception* are expensive and difficult to organize. The lone researcher, or the graduate student looking for a thesis problem is in a poor position to manage more than a handful of personality variables, and he is almost bound to settle for a design that resembles the traditional academic experimental one more than anything truly organismic.

And more than this, the "experimental" approach still carries such prestige—is so often regarded as the only road to salvation—in psychology that many workers who might otherwise probe deeply into personality choose the method rather than the problem, and thus seem more at home with their general psychological colleagues than with the honor-bright personologists. Promotions in the university departments depend upon publications; and the psychological journals are geared to this circumstance. A short paper based on the experimental manipulation of two or three variables is the most practical vehicle of communication—that or a textbook or compilation that accords with the prevailing views of what is sound. Only the most secure older psychologist is in a position to embark on a project that might involve two or three years without publication. Many clinical students have been badgered enough by the academic psychologists of the departments—and attracted enough by the rewards of their internships—so that they spend as little time as possible in the department and more time in the clinic, where they fraternize with psychiatrists and become increasingly alienated from academic psychology. They do not live in a setting or life space that is well calculated to inspire or stimulate research.

Thus a merger of personality and general psychology does not seem really imminent. Despite an unmistakable trend toward greater closeness and integration, the traditional separateness in respect to concepts, methods, points of view and interests is still very much with us. Still, the trend toward integration promises to continue by fits and starts, and it is appropriate to try and look into the future in a paper of this sort. More than this, the recent thinking about the general psychological approach to personality and the personological approach to general psychology is sufficiently advanced so that the question of how the two fields should be related in an ideal world is an intellectually intriguing one.

A view of the future.   The central question is what would or should be the relations of general psychology and personality psychology once the organismic point of view came to be universally held. According to the above statements of this point of view, it would no longer be possible to say that one kind of psychology was more general than the other or that they differed with respect to the kinds of behavior that they studied. There would be just one psychology, a psychology of persons; and personality psychologists and general psychologists would perform the same kinds of researches, those directed to exposing the mutual relations of part and whole processes and to the formulation of organismic laws.

The teaching of psychology would also have to be profoundly modified. It might well be modeled after clinical teaching in medicine in which the focus is upon the patient rather than upon particular organ systems taken singly and in turn. Students would be introduced to psychology by means of the case study; all would study cases in which all, or as many as possible, of the person's processes had already been studied by appropriate techniques, and the focus would be upon the integration of the whole. At the next stage, the students and their instructors would actually engage in research, all hands studying the same group of subjects throughout the several years of a graduate course. Students would take turns with different procedures or methods —those most appropriate to the study of different processes—while all seminars would be in the nature of staff conferences.

What is wrong with this picture? Perhaps nothing is wrong essentially, but it invites the same response as do all holistic schemes, that is, this is all very well but there must be analysis, there must be concentration on complicated part processes, and hence there must be divisions of labor. The most that we may hope to gain from starting with a holistic orientation is some increase in the rationality or some decrease in the arbitrariness with which we cut the pie. But cut the pie we must; when this is done, it becomes apparent that whereas general psychology and personality psychology cannot be separated categorically, neither has to worry about the scope or distinctiveness of its domain.

The organismic point of view does not say merely that part functions such as learning or perception depend upon the larger personality systems within which they are embedded; it says that parts and wholes are *mutually* related. This means that a student of ego functioning, let us say, must not only consider how such functioning depends upon the organization of the whole personality, but he must analyze ego functioning in terms of processes operating at a lower level.

This way of approaching psychological problems becomes clear enough to the personologist when he is called upon to explain the functioning of social groups. Here he will be inclined to favor analysis in terms of the personality types of the group's constituent members, but if he is a true holist he will not be surprised or put off if a social theorist reminds him that there are things about personality that do not become apparent until the individual is seen in the context of the social group.

It seems that although classical reductionism would allow no place for holistic laws, the thing does not work the other way around; the holistic orientation does not eliminate the necessity for certain kinds of reductive activity. We may still approach the explanation of complex phenomena by reference to interactions of processes at the next lower level. Thus, for example, we may go from the behavior of social organizations to the personality types of the constituent members, from personality to motives and emotions, from motives and emotions to conditioning, and from conditioning to phenomena of isolated nerve fibers. From this point of view, it is hard to see how analysis at one level could be regarded as more legitimate than analysis at the others. The student of conditioning who was somewhat contemptuous of the vague globalism of the student of emotion could be regarded in the same way by students of the action of the nervous system. The scientist who preferred a given level of analysis should use concepts that are consistent with what is known at lower levels, but he should remember that the object of reduction is to make a better synthesis possible, that is, to increase our understanding of the wholes that are just as "real" as their parts.

It is difficult to meet these requirements, but the direction of progress seems clear enough. Personality psychology traditionally has maintained a certain separateness by concerning itself primarily with relatively gross units of analysis—traits, motives, attitudes, complexes, and the like. Its inferences concerning these "psychophysical systems" in the individual have been based primarily upon the observation of molar behavior. It is difficult to see how personality psychology can do without units of analysis as gross as those mentioned—certainly not so long as it is concerned with the whole person or with a person's life during some fairly long span of time or, for that matter, with the development of a humanistic or practically useful psychology. One might hope, however, that personality psychology will eventually develop a set of terms that is more adequate than the present ones, that is, terms that are at once more consistent with the psychology of conditioning, perception, emotion, and the like and more appropriate to a consideration of the individual as a unit in the social system.

The general psychologist most characteristically devotes himself to a level of analysis somewhere between nervous functioning and the gross units of the personality psychologist, trying to find general laws to which complex phenomena may be reduced and trying to maintain his independence of physiology.

It may be anticipated that the trend in general psychology toward concern with more complex phenomena and the use of larger analytic categories will be continued. In this case, we should expect the personality psychologist to make room by moving a few steps further to the left. If general psychologists, following Hilgard's recommendation [108], are going to study the Freudian mechanisms in relation to the self, we should expect the personality psychologist happily to study the self in relation to still larger subsystems of the personality.

And similarly with respect to the time span covered by the behavior under study. If general psychologists are going to study the achievement drive in relation to performance in a series of experimental tasks lasting, say, a week, they have to take but a step in order to study the achievement drive in relation to performances in natural situations lasting through several years of school. In this case, we should expect the personality psychologist to direct his attention to still larger intervals of time, even to the whole life span.

In short, it is impossible to see how differences in levels of analysis are to be dispensed with or why there should not be divisions of labor determined along this line. Such divisions of labor are bound to involve differences in method. If the personality psychologist should insist on covering more ground, on working to embrace the true totality of the personality of the moment or of the life span, he would of course have to rely, as in the past, upon the case history and upon such procedures as the interview and projective techniques, which aim at comprehensiveness. The psychologist—in search of detailed information about some particular function which he had abstracted from the whole and would analyze with the use of finer categories—might be able to limit himself to rigorous tests and experimental procedures. Thus we are bound to have specialists, and—given the inclination of American psychologists to become attached to their methods—we should expect something less than perfect understanding among the specialists working at different levels and in various subregions.

As for the kinds of things that the general psychologist might single out for intensive study, perhaps we should not expect or desire any complete break with tradition. It has been stated that personality and general psychology cannot be separated on the basis of the kinds of behavior that they study. This is not to say that they may not concentrate upon different kinds of *relationships*.

When the present writer was a graduate student in 1930, he was presented with the following schema in a psychophysics course.

S stood for stimulus, NS for nervous system, C for consciousness, and B for behavior. These were the kinds of data available to the psychologist, and his proper study was the relationships among them. Each of these domains of data obviously covers a great deal of territory, and one could study relationships obtaining within each—although in this case he would have to limit himself to consciousness and behavior in order to remain within the realm of psychology. For that matter one could, following Brunswik [39], divide the stimulus and the behavior domains into their proximal and distal and their molecular and molar aspects and proceed with the study of relationships in which these subdivisions had a place. Psychology has come a long way since 1930, but we could hardly claim that we know as much about such relationships as we would like or that further information about them might not be obtained by the traditional procedure of abstracting them from their organismic context. The kind of psychology that attends to such matters may not be very "general," but it is certainly not personality psychology.

Another way of regarding the matter is to consider that from time to time interest attaches to a particular variable within one or another of the domains just indicated and to the discovery of *all* of its correlates. If, for example, we are interested in all the correlates of a certain kind of perceiving behavior, we will of course study this behavior in relation to numerous variables of personality—attitudes, motives, types of ego organization, and the like—but we would also look for correlates in the stimulus field, in the nervous system, in the cultural background of the subject, and so on. In these latter cases, we would most certainly be outside the field of personality psychology. Investigations of this kind are common in social psychology. For example, in work that makes no mention of personality, conforming behavior has been shown to be related to a variety of situational, social, and cultural factors [3, 11, 188, 245]. In addition, interest often centers quite legitimately upon all the kinds of response or upon the most common response in a given population or, hopefully, in people in general to some particular stimulus or stimulus situation. Information of these kinds is certainly not to be despised.

The great difficulty for general psychology is that the "general" laws so much admired and so eagerly sought are never very general. On the contrary, they are usually quite specific. The experimentalist, acting in accordance with his ideal of exactitude and limiting himself to variables that can be measured with precision, ignores or controls so many other relevant variables that his final result—a statistically significant relationship between factor A and factor B—is usually of extremely limited generality. To take an example, it is now well known that there are sex differences in the mechanisms of perceiving [288]. Where the experimentalist on perception ignores this fact, as he has usually done in the past, and averages the responses of males and females, the only thing we can be sure of is that no subject responds as the average says. If, on the other hand, the experimenter takes account of sex differences and limits himself to subjects of one sex or the other, the generality of his findings declines sharply. We have every reason to believe that what is true of sex is also true of various other factors in the individual—in his social-group memberships and in his culture, as well as in his personality—so that all we can say for most of our so-called "general psychological propositions" is that they are probably true of some people. The dilemma is compounded by the fact that the highest degrees of generality tend to go with the "lowest" level of analysis. Indeed, the bulk of our most cherished general laws are not truly psychological at all, but rather psychophysiological, and there is still a tendency for the psychologist who feels he must do something "basic" to move ever closer to physiology. When this is done without attention to how these basic things articulate with processes on higher levels, it amounts to a flight from the persistent problems of psychology.

Our consideration of the relations of personality and general psychology has led to the conclusion that these two fields do not differ essentially with respect to the kinds of behavior that they study or the generality of the propositions they seek to demonstrate. Both are properly interested in general laws governing the relations of behavior and the organization of personality. But so vast and complex are the phenomena embraced by this last that we cannot hope to avoid analysis on different levels or the singling out of particular processes for intensive study; some of these processes involve relationships other than those of the behavior-personality variety and as such fall well outside of any psychology of personality. Attention to different levels of analysis and concentration upon particular processes or relationships naturally requires much differentiation and specialization in method.

The question that naturally arises, then, concerns the possibilities of increased understanding and perhaps increased coordination of effort among psychologists in general. As we have seen, a natural methodological consequence of the organismic point of view would seem to be, as Murray [181] proposed, that all experimenters—within a given institute or department—should employ the same group of subjects, each observer using the findings of the others to aid him in the interpretation of his results.

This suggestion was offered in 1938, and it had been acted upon at the Harvard Psychological Clinic for some years before that. It was clear from the start that the kinds of techniques that could be brought within this general methodological scheme varied all the way from the most open-ended psychodiagnostic devices to rigorous experimental procedures. Yet the suggestion has rarely been acted upon. Why? The reasons would seem to have as much to do with the social psychology of the profession—with attitudes and values and traditions—as with fundamental differences in theory.

A study of our professional behavior might well reveal as one of its most troublesome features the utopianism of so many of our experimentalists and general theorists. It is a paradox, as ingenious as one might hope to find, that while our so-called "hardheaded psychologists" were terrorizing the clinicians and personality researchers by their righteous insistence upon exactitude, experimental rigor, and the like, they themselves were moved by the wildest dreams of all-embracing theoretical structures or general laws that would hold for all animals in all times and places. "Utopian" is the word because so far all such schemes and most such general laws have fallen to pieces as soon as they were confronted with the realities of human life, their adherents being the while precisely in the position of those social reformers who are forever concocting plans for saving humanity but who do not like "folks." It would be a considerable aid to understanding if these zealots did not put forward their particular schemes and ways of doing things as if they were science itself and did not act as if what circumstances forced them to do was a chosen path to salvation instead.

Personality psychology, by no means free of the strains that beset psychology in general, has for some time tended to split into a "rigorous experimental branch" and a sort of clinical, holistic branch. In the former, there seems often to be an inclination to win acceptance by imitating the prevalent; in the latter, there seems often to be an element of defensive withdrawal and a too hasty conclusion that academic psychology has nothing to offer. One might hope that personality psychologists who are tempted by the first alternative will do a better job of sticking to their guns, and that those of the latter inclination will realize that there is no way to do without basic psychology. None of the fundamental courses of the graduate curriculum can be left out of the training of the personality psychologist. Where the effort has been made to offer training in clinical psychology or in "personality and social" by offering only courses at the level of gross categories of analysis, it has been discovered that the traditional academic courses had to be reinserted, or the result was a rather hopeless lack of discipline. Still the record shows that clinical and personality psychologists have generally and rather uncomplainingly gone through the whole general psychological curriculum. One of the best things that could happen in psychology would be the introduction by the departments of the requirement that all students take courses in clinical or personality psychology, or at least that they perform a case study. This would be sound evidence that the organismic point of view was taken seriously; it would not mean that either personality psychology or general psychology was about to disappear into the other, but only that the stage had been set for a genuine integration of effort.

REFERENCES

1. Adams, D. *The anatomy of personality*. New York: Doubleday, 1954.
2. Adorno, T. W., Frenkel-Brunswik, Else, Levinson, D. J., & Sanford, R. N. *The authoritarian personality*. New York: Harper, 1950.
3. Allport, F. H. The j-curve hypothesis of conforming behavior. *J. soc. Psychol.*, 134, **5**, 141–183.
4. Allport, F. H. *Theories of perception and the concept of structure*. New York: Wiley, 1955.
5. Allport, G. W. The personalistic psychology of William Stern. *Charact. & Pers.*, 1937, **5**, 231–246.
6. Allport, G. W. *Personality: a psychological interpretation*. New York: Holt, Rinehart & Winston, 1937.
7. Allport, G. W. The ego in contemporary psychology. *Psychol. Rev.*, 1943, **50**, 451–478.
8. Allport, G. W. *Becoming*. New Haven, Conn.: Yale Univer. Press, 1955.
9. Angyal, A. Foundations for a science of personality. New York and Cambridge: The Commonwealth Fund and the Harvard Univer. Press, 1941.
10. Asch, S. E. *Social psychology*. Englewood Cliffs, N.J.: Prentice-Hall, 1952.
11. Asch, S. E. Studies of independence and submission to group pressure: I. A minority of one against a unanimous majority. *Psychol. Monogr.* 1956, **70**, No. 416.
12. Ashby, R. W. *Design for a brain*. New York: Wiley, 1952.
13. Balint, M. On genital love. *Int. J. Psychoanal.*, 1948, **29**, 34–40.
14. Barker, R. G., Dembo, T., & Lewin, K. Frustration and regression: an experiment with young children. *Univer. Iowa Stud. Child Welf.*, 1941, **18**, No. 1.

15. Barker, R. G., Wright, B. A., & Gonick, M. R. *Adjustment to physical handicap and illness: a survey of the social psychology of physique and disability.* New York: Social Science Research Council, 1946.

16. Barker, R. G., & Wright, H. F. Psychological ecology and the problem of psychosocial development. *Child. Develpm.*, 1949, **20**, 131–143.

17. Barker, R. G., & Wright, H. F. *Midwest and its children: the psychological ecology of an American town.* Evanston, Ill.: Row, Peterson, 1955.

18. Barron, F. Complexity-simplicity as a personality dimension. *J. abnorm. soc. Psychol.*, 1953, **48**, 163–172.

19. Barron, F. An ego-strength scale which predicts response to psychotherapy. *J. consult. Psychol.*, 1953, **17**, 327–333.

20. Barron, F. Some personality correlates of independence of judgment. *J. Pers.*, 1953, **21**, 287–297.

21. Barron, F. *Personal soundness in university graduate students.* Berkeley, Calif.: Univer. Calif. Press, 1954.

22. Bartlett, F. C. *Remembering.* New York: Cambridge, 1932.

23. Bergmann, G. Theoretical psychology. In C. P. Stone (Ed.), *Annual review of psychology.* Stanford, Calif.: Annual Reviews, 1953.

24. Bergmann, G. *Philosophy of science.* Madison, Wis.: Univer. Wis. Press, 1957.

25. Bergmann, G., & Spence, K. W. Operationism and theory construction. In M. H. Marx (Ed.), *Psychological theory.* New York: Macmillan, 1951.

26. Bertocci, P. A. The psychological self, the ego and personality. *Psychol. Rev.*, 1945, **52**, 91–99.

27. Bettelheim, B. Individual and mass behavior in extreme situations. *J. abnorm. soc. Psychol.*, 1943, **38**, 417–425.

28. Block, J., & Block, J. An investigation of the relationship between intolerance of ambiguity and ethnocentrism. *J. Pers.*, 1951, **19**, 303–311.

29. Bott, E. *Family and social network.* London: Tavistock, 1957.

30. Brand, H. The contemporary status of the study of personality. In H. Brand (Ed.), *The study of personality.* New York: Wiley, 1954.

31. Bridgman, P. W. *The logic of modern physics.* New York: Macmillan, 1927.

32. Bronfenbrenner, U. Toward an integrated theory of personality. In R. R. Blake & G. V. Ramsey (Eds.), *Perception: an approach to personality.* New York: Ronald, 1951.

33. Brownfain, J. J. Stability of the self concept as a dimension of personality. *J. abnorm. soc. Psychol.*, 1952, **47**, 597–606.

34. Bruner, J. S. Personality dynamics and the process of perceiving. In R. R. Blake & G. V. Ramsey (Eds.), *Perception: an approach to personality.* New York: Ronald, 1951.

35. Bruner, J. S., et al. *Contemporary approaches to cognition.* Cambridge, Mass.: Harvard Univer. Press, 1957.

36. Bruner, J. S., & Goodman, C. Value and need as organizing factors in perception. *J. abnorm. soc. Psychol.*, 1947, **42**, 33–44.

37. Brunswik, E. Organismic achievement and environmental probability. *Psychol. Rev.,* 1943, **50**, 255–272.
38. Brunswik, E. *Systematic and representative design of psychological experiments.* Berkeley, Calif.: Univer. Calif. Press, 1947.
39. Brunswik, E. The conceptual framework of psychology. *Int. Encyc. Unif. Sci.* Vol. I. Chicago: Univer. Chicago Press, 1950.
40. Bühler, C. The curve of life as studied in biographies. *J. appl. Psychol.,* 1935, **19**, 405–409.
41. Bühler, C. Maturation and motivation. *Personality: symposia on topical issues,* 1951, **1**, 184–211.
42. Bühler, K. *Die geistige Entwicklung des Kindes.* (4th ed.) Jena: Gustav Fischer, 1924.
43. Bullard, D. M. (Ed.) *Psychoanalysis and psychotherapy: selected papers of Frieda Fromm-Reichmann.* Chicago: Univer. Chicago Press, 1959.
44. Burton, A., & Harris, R. E. (Eds.) Case histories in clinical and abnormal personality. *Clinical studies of personality.* Vol. II. New York: Harper, 1955.
45. Burwen, L. S., & Campbell, D. T. The generality of attitudes toward authority and nonauthority figures. *J. abnorm. soc. Psychol.,* 1957, **54**, 24–31.
46. Cantril, H. The place of personality in social psychology. *J. Psychol.,* 1947, **24**, 19–56.
47. Cartwright, D. Lewinian theory as a contemporary systematic framework. In S. Koch (Ed.), *Psychology: a study of a science.* Vol. 2. New York: McGraw-Hill, 1959.
48. Cattell, R. B. *Personality.* New York: McGraw-Hill, 1950.
49. Cattell, R. B. Personality theory growing from multivariate quantitative research. In S. Koch (Ed.), *Psychology: a study of a science.* Vol. 3. New York: McGraw-Hill, 1959.
50. Cattell, R. B., & Cross, P. Comparison of the ergic and self-sentiment structures found in dynamic traits by R- and P-techniques. *J. Pers.,* 1952, **21**, 250–270.
51. Chein, I. The awareness of self and the structure of the ego. *Psychol. Rev.,* 1944, **51**, 304–314.
52. Chein, I. The genetic factor in ahistorical psychology. *J. gen. Psychol.,* 1947, **36**, 151–172.
53. Child, I. Personality. In C. P. Stone & L. McNemar (Eds.), *Annual review of psychology.* Vol. 5. Stanford, Calif.: Annual Reviews, 1954.
54. Christie, R. Changes in authoritarianism as related to situational factors. *Amer. Psychologist,* 1952, **7**, 307–308. (Abstract)
55. Coch, L., & French, J. R. P. Overcoming resistance to change. *Hum. Relat.,* 1948, **1**, 512–532.
56. Cowen, E. J., Landes, J., & Schaet, D. E. The effects of mild frustration on the expression of prejudiced attitudes. *J. abnorm. soc. Psychol.,* 1959, **58**, 33–39.
57. Dembo, T. Der Aeger als dynamisches problem. *Psychol. Forsch.,* 1931, **15**, 1–144.

58. Dollard, J., & Miller, N. E. *Personality and psychotherapy.* New York: McGraw-Hill, 1950.
59. Dunbar, F. *Emotions and bodily changes.* New York: Columbia Univer. Press, 1938.
60. Eager, J., & Smith, M. B. A note on the validity of Sanford's authoritarian-equalitarian scale. *J. abnorm. soc. Psychol.,* 1952, **47,** 265–267.
61. Ellis, A. An operational reformulation of some of the basic principles of psychoanalysis. In H. Feigl & M. Scriven (Eds.), *Minnesota studies in the philosophy of science.* Vol. I. Minneapolis, Minn: Univer. Minn. Press, 1956.
62. Erikson, E. H. *Childhood and society.* New York: Norton, 1950.
63. Erikson, E. H. Growth and crises of the "healthy personality." In C. Kluckhohn, H. A. Murray, & D. M. Schneider (Eds.), *Personality in nature, society and culture.* (2nd ed.) New York: Knopf, 1955.
64. Erikson, E. H. Identity and the life cycle: selected papers. *Psychological Issues.* Vol. I. New York: International Universities Press, 1959.
65. Eysenck, H. *Dimensions of personality.* London: Routledge, 1947.
66. Eysenck, H. *The scientific study of personality.* London: Routledge, 1952.
67. Eysenck, H. *The structure of human personality.* London: Methuen, 1953.
68. Ezriel, H. Experimentation within the psychoanalytic session. *Brit. J. Phil. Sci.,* 1956, **1,** 29–48.
69. Fairbairn, W. R. D. *Psychoanalytic studies of the personality.* London: Tavistock, 1952.
70. Feigl, H. Operationism and scientific method. *Psychol. Rev.,* 1945, **52,** 250–259.
71. Feigl, H., & Brodbeck, M. *Readings in the philosophy of science.* New York: Appleton-Century-Crofts, 1953.
72. Feigl, H., & Scriven, M. (Eds.) *Minnesota studies in the philosophy of science.* Vol. I. Minneapolis, Minn.: Univer. Minn. Press, 1956.
73. Feigl, H., & Sellers, W. (Eds.) *Readings in philosophical analysis.* New York: Appleton-Century-Crofts, 1949.
74. Fenichel, O. *The psychoanalytic theory of neurosis.* New York: Norton, 1945.
75. Fisher, J. The memory process and certain psychosocial attitudes with special reference to the law of Pragnanz. *J. Pers.,* 1951, **19,** 406–420.
76. Fishman, J. A. Non-intellective factors as predictors, as criteria, and as contingencies in selection and guidance. In T. R. McConnell (Ed.), *Selection and educational differentiation.* Berkeley, Calif.: Univer. Calif., Field Service Center and Center for the Study of Higher Education, 1960.
77. Freedman, M. B. The passage through college. In N. Sanford (Ed.), Personality development during the college years. *J. soc. issues,* 1956, **12,** No. 4.
78. Frenkel-Brunswik, E. Intolerance of ambiguity as an emotional and perceptual personality variable. *J. Pers.,* 1949, **18,** 108–143.

79. Frenkel-Brunswik, E. Personality theory and perception. In R. R. Blake & G. V. Ramsey (Eds.), *Perception: an approach to personality*. New York: Ronald, 1951.

80. Freud, A. *The ego and the mechanisms of defense*. London: Hogarth, 1937.

81. Freud, S. *The ego and the id*. London: Hogarth, 1927.

82. Freud, S. *Civilization and its discontents*. London: Hogarth, 1930.

83. Freud, S. *Inhibitions, symptoms and anxiety*. London: Hogarth, 1936.

84. Freud, S. The interpretation of dreams. In *The basic writings of Sigmund Freud*. New York: Random House, 1938. (First German edition, 1900.)

85. Freud, S. *Collected papers*. Vol. II. New York: Basic Books, 1959.

86. Fromm, E. *Man for himself*. New York: Holt, Rinehart & Winston, 1947.

87. Gibson, J. J. Perception as a function of stimulation. In S. Koch (Ed.) *Psychology: a study of a science*. Vol 1. New York: McGraw-Hill, 1959.

88. Gill, M. The present state of psychoanalytic theory. *J. abnorm. soc. Psychol.*, 1959, **58**, 1–9.

89. Goldstein, K. *The organism*. New York: American Book, 1939.

90. Goldstein, K. Functional disturbances in brain damage. In S. Ariete (Ed.), *American handbook of psychiatry*. New York: Basic Books, 1959.

91. Gough, H. G. *California psychological inventory manual*. Palo Alto, Calif.: Consulting Psychologists Press, 1957.

92. Granit, R. *Receptors and sensory perception*. New Haven, Conn.: Yale Univer. Press, 1955.

93. Greenson, R. R. The classic psychoanalytic approach. In S. Ariete (Ed.), *American handbook of psychiatry*. New York: Basic Books, 1959.

94. Grinker, R. (Ed.) *Toward a unified theory of human behavior*. New York: Basic Books, 1956.

95. Guilford, J. P. *Personality*. New York: McGraw-Hill, 1959.

96. Guthrie, E. R. *The psychology of learning*. (Rev. ed.) New York: Harper, 1952.

97. Hall, C., & Lindzey, G. *Theories of personality*. New York: Wiley, 1957.

98. Hartmann, H., Kris, E., & Loewenstein, R. Comments on the formation of psychic structure. In T. French et al. (Eds.), *The psychoanalytic study of the child*. Vol. 2. New York: International Univer. Press, 1947.

99. Hartshorne, H., & May, M. *Studies in deceit*. New York: Macmillan, 1928.

100. Hartshorne, H., & May, M. *Studies in the organization of character*. New York: Macmillan, 1930.

101. Hathaway, S. R., & McKinley, I. C. *The Minnesota multiphasic per-*

sonality inventory. (Rev. ed.) New York: Psychological Corporation, 1943.

102. Hebb, D. O. *The organization of behavior.* New York: Wiley, 1949.

103. Hebb, D. O. Alice in Wonderland or psychology among the biological sciences. In H. F. Harlow & C. N. Woolsey (Eds.), *Biological and biochemical bases of behavior.* Madison, Wis.: Univer. Wis. Press, 1958.

104. Heider, F. *The psychology of interpersonal relations.* New York: Wiley, 1958.

105. Hempel, C. G. A logical appraisal of operationalism. *Scient. mon.,* 1954, **79,** 215–223.

106. Henle, M. An experimental investigation of dynamic and structural determinants of substitution. *Contr. psychol. Theory,* 1942, **2,** No. 7.

107. Henle, M. The influence of valence upon substitution. *J. Psychol.,* 1944, **17,** 11–19.

108. Hilgard, E. R. Human motives and the concept of the self. *Amer. Psychologist,* 1949, **4,** 374–382.

109. Hilgard, E. R. *Introduction to psychology.* New York: Harcourt, Brace, 1953.

110. Hollander, E. P. Authoritarianism and leadership choice in a military setting. *Amer. Psychologist,* 1953, **8,** 368–369.

111. Holt, R., & Luborsky, L., et al. *Personality patterns of psychiatrists.* Vols. I and II. Topeka, Kan.: Menninger Foundation, 1958.

112. Horney, K. *The neurotic personality of our time.* New York: Norton, 1937.

113. Horney, K. *New ways in psychoanalysis.* New York: Norton, 1939.

114. Hull, C. L. *Principles of behavior.* New York: Appleton-Century-Crofts, 1943.

115. Jahoda, M. Toward a social psychology of mental health. In M. J. E. Senn (Ed.), *Symposium on the healthy personality.* New York: Josiah Macy, Jr. Foundation, 1950.

116. Jahoda, M. *Current concepts of positive mental health.* New York: Basic Books, 1958.

117. James, W. *The principles of psychology.* Vol. I. New York: Holt, Rinehart & Winston, 1890.

118. Jones, M. R. (Ed.) *Current theory and research in motivation.* Vol. V. Lincoln, Neb.: Univer. Neb. Press, 1957.

119. Jung, C. G. *Collected works.* Vol. 9. *Archetypes and the collective unconscious.* New York: Pantheon, 1954.

120. Katz, D., & Stotland, E. A preliminary statement to a theory of attitude structure and change. In S. Koch (Ed.), *Psychology: a study of a science.* Vol. 3. New York: McGraw-Hill, 1959.

121. Kelly, E. L., & Fiske, D. W. *The prediction of performance in clinical psychology.* Ann Arbor, Mich.: Univer. Mich. Press, 1951.

122. Kelly, G. *The psychology of personal constructs.* Vol. I. New York: Norton, 1953.

123. Kelman, H. C., & Cohler, J. Reactions to persuasive communication

as a function of cognitive needs and styles. Paper read at Eastern Psychol. Ass., April, 1959. *Amer. Psychologist*, 1959, **14,** 571. (Abstract)

124. Kenny, D. T., & Ginsberg, R. The specificity of intolerance of ambiguity measures. *J. abnorm. soc. Psychol.*, 1958, **56,** 300–305.

125. Klein, G. S. The personal world through perception. In R. R. Blake & G. V. Ramsey (Eds.), *Perception: an approach to personality.* New York: Ronald, 1951.

126. Klein, G. S. Perception, motives and personality. In J. L. McCary (Ed.), *Psychology of personality.* New York: Logos, 1956.

127. Klein, G. S., & Krech, D. The problem of personality and its theory. *J. Pers.*, 1951, **20,** 2–23.

128. Klein, G. S., & Schlesinger, H. J. Where is the perceiver in perceptual theory? *J. Pers.*, 1949, **18,** 32–47.

129. Klein, M. *Contributions to psychoanalysis, 1921–1948.* London: Hogarth, 1948.

130. Klopfer, B., & Kelley, D. M. *The Rorschach technique.* Yonkers-on-Hudson, N.Y.: World, 1946.

131. Kluckhohn, C., & Murray, H. A. Personality formation: the determinants. In C. Kluckhohn & H. A. Murray (Eds.), *Personality in nature, society, and culture.* New York: Knopf, 1948.

132. Koch, S. Behavior as "intrinsically" regulated: work notes toward a pre-theory of phenomena called "motivational." In M. R. Jones (Ed.), *Current theory and research in motivation.* Vol. IV. Lincoln, Neb.: Univer. Neb. Press, 1956.

133. Koch, S. Epilogue. In S. Koch (Ed.), *Psychology: a study of a science.* Vol. 3. New York: McGraw-Hill, 1959.

134. Koffa, K. *Principles of gestalt psychology.* New York: Harcourt, Brace, 1935.

135. Kohler, W. *Gestalt psychology.* New York: Liveright, 1929.

136. Kounin, J. Experimental studies of rigidity. *Charact. & Pers.*, 1941, **9,** 251–282.

137. Krech, D., & Crutchfield, R. *Theory and problems of social psychology.* New York: McGraw-Hill, 1948.

138. Kubie, L. The fundamental nature of the distinction between normality and neurosis. *Psychoanal. Quart.*, 1954, **23,** 167–204.

139. Landis, C., & Bolles, M. *Personality and sexuality in the physically handicapped woman.* New York: Hoeber, 1942.

140. Lazarsfeld, P. F. Latent structure analysis. In S. Koch (Ed.), *Psychology: a study of a science.* Vol. 3. New York: McGraw-Hill, 1959.

141. Lecky, P. *Self-consistency.* New York: Island Press Co-operative, Inc., 1945.

142. Lehman, H. G. The creative years in science and literature. *Scient. mon.* 1936, **43,** 151–162.

143. Levinson, D. J. Role, personality and social structure in the organizational setting. *J. abnorm. soc. Psychol.*, 1959, **58,** 170–181.

144. Lewin, K. *Dynamic theory of personality.* New York: McGraw-Hill, 1935.

145. Lewin, K., Dembo, T., Festinger, L., & Sears, R. R. Level of aspiration. In J. McV. Hunt (Ed.), *Personality and the behavior disorders.* Vol. I. New York: Ronald, 1944.

146. Lewin, K., Lippitt, R., & White, R. Patterns of aggressive behavior in experimentally created social climates. *J. soc. Psychol.,* 1939, **10**, 271–299.

147. Lindzey, G. *Assessment of human motives.* New York: Holt, Rinehart & Winston, 1958.

148. Linton, R. *The cultural background of personality.* New York: Appleton-Century-Crofts, 1945.

149. Luchins, A. An evaluation of some current criticisms of gestalt psychological work on perception. *Psychol. Rev.,* 1951, **58**, 69–95.

150. McCary, J. L. (Ed.) *Psychology of personality.* New York:Logos, 1956.

151. McClelland, D. C. *Personality.* New York: Sloane, 1951.

152. McClelland, D. C. Notes for a revised theory of motivation. In D. C. McClelland (Ed.), *Studies in motivation.* New York: Appleton-Century-Crofts, 1955.

153. McClelland, D. C., Atkinson, J. W., Clarke, R. A., & Lowell, E. J. *The achievement motive.* New York: Appleton-Century-Crofts, 1953.

154. McDougall, W. *Introduction to social psychology.* London: Methuen, 1908.

155. McDougall, W. *The energies of men.* London: Methuen, 1932.

156. Macfarlane, Jean W. The life-career approach to the study of personality development: some findings from a thirty-year longitudinal study. Berkeley, Calif.: Institute of Human Development, 1960. (Mimeographed)

157. Macfarlane, Jean W., Allen, L., & Honzik, M. P. A developmental study of the behavior problems of normal children between twenty-one months and fourteen years. *Univer. Calif. Publ. Child Develpm.,* 1954.

158. MacKinnon, D. W. The structure of personality, In J. McV. Hunt (Ed.), *Personality and the behavior disorders.* New York: Ronald, 1944.

159. MacKinnon, D. W. Applications of clinical psychology to assessment. In D. Brower & L. E. Abt (Eds.), *Progress in clinical psychology.* New York: Grune & Stratton, 1952.

160. MacKinnon, D. W. Fact and fancy in personality research. *Amer. Psychologist,* 1953, **8**, 138–146.

161. MacKinnon, D. W., & Maslow, A. H. Personality. In H. Helson (Ed.), *Theoretical foundations of psychology.* New York: Van Nostrand, 1951.

162. Maslow, A. H. Problem-centering vs. means-centering in science. *Phil. Sci.,* 1946, **13**, 326–331.

163. Maslow, A. H. Self-actualizing people: a study of psychological health. *Personality: symposia on topical issues,* 1950, No. 1.

164. Maslow, A. H. *Motivation and personality.* New York: Harper, 1954.

165. Maslow, A. H. Deficiency motivation and growth motivation. In M. R.

Jones (Ed.), *Current theory and research in motivation.* Vol. III. Lincoln, Neb.: Univer. Neb. Press, 1955.

166. May, R. The existential approach. In S. Ariete (Ed.), *American handbook of psychiatry.* New York: Basic Books, 1959.

167. Maze, J. R. On some corruptions of the doctrine of homeostasis. *Psychol. Rev.,* 1953, **60**, 405–412.

168. Meehl, P. E., & MacCorquodale, K. On a distinction between hypothetical constructs and intervening variables. *Psychol. Rev.,* 1948, **55**, 95–107.

169. Miller, J. G. Unconscious processes and perception. In R. R. Blake & G. V. Ramsey (Eds.), *Perception: an approach to personality.* New York: Ronald, 1951.

170. Miller, J. G. Toward a general theory for the behavioral sciences. *Amer. Psychologist,* 1955, **10**, 513–531.

171. Miller, J. G. Information input overload and psychopathology. *Amer. J. Psychiatry,* 1960, **116**, 695–704.

172. Miller, N. E. Liberalization of basic S-R concepts: extensions to conflict behavior, motivation and social learning. In S. Koch (Ed.), *Psychology: a study of a science.* Vol. 2. New York: McGraw-Hill, 1959.

173. Mittelman, B., Wolff, H. G., & Schorf, M. Emotions and gastroduodenal functions. *Psychosom. Med.,* 1942, **4**, 5–61.

174. Mowrer, O. H. *Learning theory and personality dynamics.* New York: Ronald, 1950.

175. Mowrer, O. H. *Psychotherapy: theory and research.* New York: Ronald, 1953.

176. Mowrer, O. H. *Learning theory and behavior.* New York: Wiley, 1960.

177. Murphy, G. Introduction. In H. A. Witkin et al., *Personality through perception.* New York: Harper, 1953.

178. Murphy, G. *Human potentialities.* New York: Basic Books, 1958.

179. Murphy, G., & Jensen, F. *Approaches to personality.* New York: Harper, 1932.

180. Murray, H. A. The effects of fear upon estimates of the maliciousness of other personalities. *J. soc. Psychol.,* 1933, **4**, 310–329.

181. Murray, H. A. *Explorations in personality.* New York:, Oxford, 1938.

182. Murray, H. A. Introduction to Melville's "Pierre." In Herman Melville, *Pierre.* New York: Farrar Straus, 1949.

183. Murray, H. A. Preparations for the scaffold of a comprehensive system. In S. Koch (Ed.), *Psychology: a study of a science.* Vol. 3. New York: McGraw-Hill, 1959.

184. Murray, H. A., & Kluckhohn, C. Outline of a conception of personality. In C. Kluckhohn & H. A. Murray (Eds.), *Personality in nature, society, and culture.* New York: Knopf, 1948.

185. Murray, H. A., & Kluckhohn, C. Outline of a conception of personality. In C. Kluckhohn, H. A. Murray, & D. M. Schneider (Eds.), *Person-*

ality in nature, society, and culture. (2nd ed.) New York: Knopf, 1955.

186. Newcomb, T. M. Role behavior in the study of individual personality and of groups. *J. Pers.,* 1950, **18,** 273–290.

187. Newcomb, T. M. *Social psychology.* New York: Dryden, 1950.

188. Newcomb, T. M. Attitude development as a function of reference groups: the Bennington study. In E. Maccoby, T. M. Newcomb, & E. J. Hartley (Eds.), *Readings in social psychology.* New York: Holt, Rinehart & Winston, 1958.

189. Olds, J. A physiological study of reward. In D. McClelland (Ed.), *Studies in motivation.* New York: Appleton-Century-Crofts, 1955.

190. Osgood, C. E. Behavior theory and the social sciences. *Behav. Sci.,* 1956, **1,** 167–185.

191. Osgood, C. E. Motivational dynamics of language behavior. In M. R. Jones (Ed.), *Current theory and research in motivation.* Vol. V. Lincoln, Neb.: Univer. Neb. Press, 1957.

192. OSS Assessment Staff. *Assessment of men.* New York: Holt, Rinehart & Winston, 1948.

193. Ovsiankina, Maria. Die Wiederaufnahme von unterbrochener Handlungen. *Psychol. Forsch.,* 1928, **11,** 302–382.

194. Pace, C. R., & Stern, G. An approach to the measurement of the psychological characteristics of college environments. *J. educ. Psychol.,* 1958, **49,** 269–277.

195. Parsons, T., Bales, R. F., & Shils, E. A. *Working papers in the theory of action.* Glencoe, Ill.: Free Press, 1953.

196. Parsons, T., & Shils, E. A. (Eds.) *Toward a general theory of action.* Cambridge, Mass.: Harvard Univer. Press, 1952.

197. Penfield, W. The permanent record of the stream of consciousness. *Proceedings of the Fourteenth International Congress of Psychology,* Amsterdam: North Holland, 1955.

198. Penfield, W., & Jasper, A. *Epilepsy and the functional anatomy of the human brain.* Boston: Little, Brown, 1954.

199. Phillipson, H. *The object relations technique (with tests).* Glencoe, Ill.: Free Press, 1956.

200. Postman, L. Personality through perception. Review of Witken, H. A., et al. *Psychol. Bull.,* 1955, **52,** 79–83.

201. Postman, L., Bruner, J. S., & McGinnies, E. Personal values as selective factors in perception. *J. abnorm. soc. Psychol.,* 1948, **43,** 142–154.

202. *Proceedings of the Fourteenth International Congress of Psychology.* Amsterdam: North Holland, 1954.

203. Proshansky, H., & Murphy, G. The effects of reward and punishment on perception. *J. Psychol.,* 1942, **13,** 295–305.

204. Prothro, E. T., & Melikian, L. The California Public Opinion Scale in an authoritarian culture. *Publ. Opin. quart.,* 1953, **17,** 353–362.

205. Pumpian-Mindlin, E. Propositions concerning energic-economic aspects of libido theory. In L. Bellak (Ed.), Conceptual and methodological problems in psychoanalysis. *Ann. N. Y. Acad. Sci.,* 1959, **76,** Art 4.

206. Raimy, V. C. Self-reference in counseling interviews. *J. consult. Psychol.,* 1948, **12,** 153–163.

207. Rapaport, D. *Emotions and memory.* Baltimore: Williams & Wilkins, 1942.

208. Rapaport, D. The theory of ego autonomy: a generalization. *Bull. Menn. Clin.,* 1958, **22,** 13–35.

209. Rapaport, D. The structure of psychoanalytic theory: a systematizing attempt. In S. Koch (Ed.). *Psychology: a study of a science.* Vol. 3. New York: McGraw-Hill, 1959.

210. Ritter, W. E. *The unity of the organism.* Boston: Badger, 1919.

211. Rogers, C. R. *Client-centered therapy: its current practice, implications, and theory.* Boston: Houghton Mifflin, 1951.

212. Rogers, C. R. A theory of therapy, personality, and interpersonal relationships, as developed in the client-centered framework. In S. Koch (Ed.), *Psychology: a study of a science.* Vol. 3. New York: McGraw-Hill, 1959.

213. Rogers, C. R., & Dymond, R. (Eds.) *Psychotherapy and personality change.* Chicago: Univer. Chicago Press, 1954.

214. Rokeach, M. Generalized mental rigidity as a factor in ethnocentrism. *J. abnorm. soc. Psychol.,* 1948, **43,** 259–278.

215. Rokeach, M. *The open and closed mind.* New York: Basic Books, 1960.

216. Rosenzweig, S. The ghost of Henry James: a study in thematic apperception. In C. Kluckhorn, H. A. Murray, & D. M. Schneider (Eds.), *Personality in nature, society, and culture.* (2nd ed.) New York: Knopf, 1955.

217. Rubinstein, E. A., & Parloff, M. B. (Eds.) *Research in psychotherapy.* Washington, D.C.: American Psychological Association, 1959.

218. Rudikoff, E. C. A comparative study of the changes in the concepts of the self, the ordinary person, and the ideal in eight cases. In C. R. Rogers & R. F. Dymond (Eds.), *Psychotherapy and personality change.* Chicago: Univer. Chicago Press, 1954.

219. Russel, E. S. *Form and function.* London: Murray, 1916.

220. Sanford, N. The effects of abstinence from food upon imaginal processes: a preliminary experiment. *J. Psychol.,* 1937, **3,** 145–159.

221. Sanford, N. Individual and social change in a community under pressure: the oath controversy. *J. soc. Issues,* 1953, **9,** 25–42.

222. Sanford, N. The dynamics of identification. *Psychol. Rev.,* 1955, **62,** 106–118.

223. Sanford, N. Surface and depth in the individual personality. *Psychol. Rev.* 1956, **63,** 349–359.

224. Sanford, N. (Ed.) Personality development during the college years. *J. soc. Issues,* 1956, **4,** 3–70.

225. Sanford, N. The approach of "The authoritarian personality." In J. L. McCary (Ed.), *The psychology of personality.* New York: Logos, 1956.

226. Sanford, N. Our students today: individualists or conformers. Berkeley,

Calif.: Univer. of Calif., Institute of Personality Assessment and Research, 1957. (Mimeographed)

227. Sanford, N. The impact of a woman's college on its students. In A. E. Traxler (Ed.), *Long-range planning for education*. Washington, D.C.: American Council on Education, 1958.

228. Sanford, N., et al. Physique, personality and scholarship. *Monogr. Soc. Res. Child Develpm.*, 1943, **8**, No. 1.

229. Sanford, N., et al. The findings of the Commission in Psychology. *Ann. N. Y. Acad. Sci.*, 1955, **63**, 341–364.

230. Sarbin, T. R. A preface to a psychological analysis of the self. *Psychol. Rev.*, 1952, **59**, 11–22.

231. Sarnoff, I., & Katz, D. The motivational basis of attitude change. *J. abnorm. soc. Psychol.*, 1954, **49**, 115–124.

232. Schjelderup, H. Lasting effects of psychoanalytic treatment. *Psychiatry*, 1955, **18**, 109–133.

233. Scott, W. A. Research definitions of mental health and mental illness. *Psychol. Bull.*, 1958, **55**, 67–87.

234. Scriven, M. A study of radical behaviorism. In H. Feigl & M. Scriven (Eds.), *Minnesota studies in the philosophy of science*. Vol. I. Minneapolis, Minn: Univer. Minn. Press, 1956.

235. Sears, R. R. Personality. In C. P. Stone (Ed.), *Annual Review of Psychology*. Stanford, Calif.: Annual Reviews, 1950.

236. Sears, R. R. Social behavior and personality development. In T. Parsons & E. A. Shils (Eds.), *Toward a general theory of action*. Cambridge, Mass.: Harvard Univer. Press, 1951.

237. Sears, R. R. A theoretical framework for personality and social behavior. *Amer. Psychologist*, 1951, **6**, 476–482.

238. Seeman, J., & Raskin, N. J. Research perspectives in client-centered therapy. In O. H. Mowrer (Ed.), *Psychotherapy: theory and research*. New York: Ronald, 1953.

239. Selye, H. The general adaptation syndrome and the diseases of adaptation. *J. clin. Endocrin.*, 1946, **2**, 117–230.

240. Senn, M. J. E. (Ed.) *Symposium on the healthy personality*. New York: Josiah Macy, Jr. Foundation, 1950.

241. Shaffer, L. F., & Shohen, E. J. *Psychology of adjustment*. (2nd ed.) Boston: Houghton Mifflin, 1956.

242. Sheerer, M. Cognitive theory. In G. Lindzey (Ed.), *Handbook of social psychology*. Cambridge, Mass.: Addison-Wesley, 1954.

243. Sheldon, W. *The varieties of human physique: an introduction to constitutional psychology*. New York: Harper, 1940.

244. Sheldon, W. (with C. W. Dupertius & E. McDermott). *Atlas of men: a guide for somatotyping the adult male at all ages*. New York: Harper, 1954.

245. Sherif, M. *The psychology of social norms*. New York: Harper, 1936.

246. Sherif, M., & Cantril, H. *The psychology of ego-involvements*. New York: Wiley, 1947.

247. Shock, N. Physiological factors in behavior. In J. McV. Hunt (Ed.),

Personality and the behavior disorders. Vol. I. New York: Ronald, 1944.

248. Skinner, B. F. Are theories of learning necessary? *Psychol. Rev.,* 1950, **57,** 193–216.

249. Smith, M. B. The phenomenological approach in personality theory: come critical remarks. *J. abnorm. soc. Psychol.,* 1950, **45,** 516–522.

250. Smith, M. B. Research strategies toward a conception of positive mental health. *Amer. Psychologist,* 1959, **14,** 673–681.

251. Smith, M. B., Bruner, J., & White, R. W. *Opinions and personality.* New York, Wiley, 1956.

252. Smuts, F. C. *Holism and evolution.* New York: Macmillan, 1926.

253. Snygg, D., & Combs, A. *Individual behavior: a new frame of reference for psychology.* New York: Harper, 1949.

254. Spence, K. W. The nature of theory construction in contemporary psychology. *Psychol. Rev.,* 1944, **57,** 47–68.

255. Stagner, R. *Psychology of personality.* New York: McGraw-Hill, 1948.

256. Stagner, R. Homeostasis as a unifying concept in personality theory. *Psychol. Rev.,* 1951, **58,** 5–17.

257. Stagner, R. Homeostasis: corruptions or misconceptions?—a reply. *Psychol. Rev.,* 1954, **61,** 205–208.

258. Stephenson, W. *The study of behavior.* Chicago: Univer. Chicago Press, 1953.

259. Stern, G. S., Stein, M., & Bloom, B. S. *Methods in personality assessment.* Glencoe, Ill.: Free Press, 1956.

260. Stern, W. *General psychology from the personalistic standpoint.* New York: Macmillan, 1938.

261. Sullivan, H. S. *The interpersonal theory of psychiatry.* New York: Norton, 1953.

262. Symonds, P. M. *The dynamics of human adjustment.* New York: Appleton-Century-Crofts, 1946.

263. Symonds, P. M. *The ego and the self.* New York: Appleton-Century-Crofts, 1951.

264. Szasz, T. S. A critical analysis of some aspects of the libido theory. In L. Bellack (Ed.), Conceptual and methodological problems in psychoanalysis. *Ann. N. Y. Acad. Sci.,* 1959, **76,** Art. 4.

265. Szasz, T. S. The myth of mental illness. *Amer. Psychologist,* 1960, **15,** 113–118.

266. Taylor, J. A. The relationship of anxiety to the conditioned eyelid response. *J. exp. Psychol.,* 1951, **41,** 81–92.

267. Terman, L. M., & Oden, M. H. *The gifted child grows up.* Stanford, Calif.: Stanford Univer. Press, 1947.

268. Terman, L. M., & Oden, M. H. *The gifted group at mid-life: thirty-five years' follow-up of the superior child.* Stanford, Calif.: Stanford Univer. Press, 1959.

269. Thistlethwait, D. College environments and the development of talent. *Science,* 1959, **130,** 71–76.

270. Tolman, E. C. Operational behaviorism and current trends in psy-

chology. *Proceedings Twenty-fifth Anniversary Celebration Inaugural Graduate Studies.* Los Angeles: Univer. S. Calif. Press, 1936.

271. Tolman, E. C. The determiners of behavior at a choice point. *Psychol. Rev.,* 1938, **45,** 1–41.

272. Tolman, E. C. Cognitive maps in rats and men. *Psychol. Rev.,* 1948, **55,** 189–208.

273. Tolman, E. C. A psychological model. In T. Parsons & E. A. Shils (Eds.), *Toward a general theory of action.* Cambridge, Mass.: Harvard Univer. Press, 1951.

274. Tolman, E. C. Principles of purposive behavior. In S. Koch (Ed.), *Psychology: a study of a science.* Vol. 2. New York: McGraw-Hill, 1959.

275. Tomkins, S. S. *The thematic apperception test: the theory and technique of interpretation.* New York: Grune & Stratton, 1947.

276. Tomkins, S . S. *Consciousness, imagery, and affect.* New York: Springer, 1961.

277. von Bertalanffy, L. An outline of general systems theory. *Brit. J. phil. Sci.,* 1950, **1,** 134–165.

278. von Bertalanffy, L. Theoretical models in biology and psychology. *J. Pers.* 1951, **20,** 24–38.

279. Wallach, H. Some considerations concerning the relation between perception and cognition. *J. Pers.,* 1949, **18,** 6–13.

280. Webster, H., & Heist, P. *Construction of a multiple trait personality test for use with college populations.* Univer. of Calif., Center for the Study of Higher Education, 1959. (Mimeographed)

281. Werner, H. *Comparative psychology of mental development.* (Rev. ed.) Chicago: Follett, 1948.

282. Wheeler, R. H. *The science of psychology.* (2nd ed.) New York: Crowell, 1940.

283. White, R. W. *The abnormal personality.* New York: Ronald, 1948.

284. White, R. W. *Lives in progress.* New York: Dryden, 1952.

285. White, R. W. The achievement motive. Review of D. C. McClelland, J. W. Atkinson, R. A. Clark, & E. J. Lowell. *Psychol. Bull.,* 1955, **52,** 95–97.

286. White, R. W. Motivation reconsidered: the concept of competence. *Psychol. Rev.,* 1959, **66,** 297–333.

287. Whitehorn, J. C. Goals of psychotherapy. In E. A. Rubinstein & M. B. Parloff (Eds.), *Research in psychotherapy.* Washington, D.C.: American Psychological Association, 1959.

288. Witkin, H. A., et al. *Personality through perception.* New York: Harper, 1953.

289. Wright, B. A. Altruism in children and the perceived conduct of others. *J. abnorm. soc. Psychol.,* 1942, **37,** 218–233.

290. Zeignarnik, B. Über das Behalten von erledigten und unerledigten Handlungen. *Psychol. Forsch.,* 1927, **9,** 1–85.

PROBLEMS OF PERSONALITY AND SOME RELATIONS TO ANTHROPOLOGY AND SOCIOLOGY

IRVIN L. CHILD
Department of Psychology
Yale University

Definition of the Study of Personality 593
Major Problems in Personality Study 594
Examples of Relatively Isolated Personality Research 598
    The breadth of consistencies 598
    The importance of consistencies 608
    The origins of consistencies 612
Some Relations to Anthropology and Sociology 615
    Universality of phenomena of personality 615
    Social dimensions suggesting personality dimensions 623
    Role and personality 628
References 632

DEFINITION OF THE STUDY OF PERSONALITY

Personality is not a topic of inquiry for which there is a definition to which all psychologists adhere. For the present discussion, personality will be defined as comprising consistencies of individual differences in behavior which are internally determined. In substance, this agrees with much recent usage, such as that of Allport [1] and Eysenck [42].

This definition excludes consistencies of behavior which are universal—for example, a universal tendency for loud and sudden noises to evoke a startle response. The definition also excludes consistencies which can be attributed entirely to the situation. Thus if the high degree of aggression characteristic of a person can be shown to be entirely a function of his being in extremely frustrating circumstances, he will not be described as having a highly aggressive personality. But of course, the requirement of internal determination refers only to present functioning, not to past origin. If a person is highly aggressive now in a variety of situations because in the past his situation was consistently frustrating, then the present consistency is immediately determined by internal residues and is to be included under the label "personality."

Such a definition obviously does not refer to any separable part of the functioning of an individual. Consistencies may function according to much the same kinds of laws, regardless of whether they are universal or vary from one person to another. Nor does a person shift from one kind of functioning to another as he moves from situations distinctive of him to situations he shares with other people but responds to distinctively. Thus this definition of personality does not purport to isolate a particular kind of entity or process within the person. It is intended merely to direct attention to a set of problems. An important part of people's variation in behavior lies in consistencies which distinguish them from other people and which are attributable to the internal effects of previous experience or to organismic characteristics. Personality study is directed to the understanding of those consistencies.

MAJOR PROBLEMS IN PERSONALITY STUDY

This definition leads readily to three general problems or questions with which students of personality have been primarily concerned.

The first has to do with the extent of consistency in individual differences. The meaning of this question can be introduced by reference to two unrealistic extremes. On the one hand, it is imaginable that there might be no truly internally determined differences among people in their behavioral consistencies—that the apparent differences in personality among individuals might be due entirely to variation in the situations in which they find themselves and to which they are responding. At the other extreme, it might conceivably be argued that every element in a person's behavior is to some extent dependent upon a single overriding strand of consistency which unites all his behavior at a moment and the sequence of his behavior through the days and years.

While no one is likely to espouse either of these extreme views, there is ample room for disagreement on the question of whether the general degree of consistency in personality approaches more nearly the one or the other extreme. This sort of general question has been debated by writers on personality. At present, the orientation of psychology and personality study is increasingly empirical, so general debate on a question so unlikely to be settled by observation in the near future is not likely to arouse great interest.

In more specific form, however, this first problem remains of great and often unnoted importance. Given the demonstration of any consistency in individual differences, the extent to which this particular consistency holds true becomes a very important question. Does it represent a consistency observable only under laboratory conditions, only when measurement is made with a particular kind of technique, only for aspects of behavior under conscious control, and not for aspects of behavior influenced by unconscious motivation? Is the particular dimension of consistency relevant to understanding all personalities, or is it a dimension useful only in understanding the personalities of certain individuals? In such forms as these, the question of the extent of consistency is bound to remain important.

The second problem has to do with the identification of major consistencies. It will doubtless be granted by everyone that individuals may differ from each other in an infinity of ways. So long as the student of personality attempts to deal with this infinity of possible consistencies of behavior, the contribution of science would seem to be restricted to the development of techniques useful in identifying the perhaps unique consistencies of each individual. Indeed, Allport [2] has argued for this as a major function of personality study. Most students of personality, however, seem to believe either explicitly or implicitly that more than techniques of inquiry is of general utility in understanding different individuals. Regardless of the uniqueness of each individual, it seems useful to deal with individuals in terms of a limited number of abstract dimensions. But what should these dimensions be?

Much that has been written on personality is centered directly on this one question. One author argues for the importance of one dimension, a second author wishes to supplement it with two other dimensions, and a third argues that none of those dimensions is truly appropriate or fundamental and that still other dimensions must be substituted. Lying behind such controversy and often not brought out into the open is the basic question of the criteria that are appropriate for deciding on the relative importance of various dimensions along which personality differences might be ordered.

The third question has to do with the origins of individual differences in personality. Given the fact that two individuals differ in the degree or mode of aggression that is consistently represented in their behavior or in the extent to which aggression of any sort is a consistent characteristic of their behavior, how do these differences come about? To most psychologists, this question—being the one that most obviously refers to empirical relationships among variables—is so clearly of importance as to need no justification or elucidation. To many psychologists outside personality study, however, it might come as a surprise to discover how little of the writing on personality is actually concerned in any way with this third question.

Stated thus in general terms, these three questions may seem inextricably mixed. The extent of consistency must vary from one dimen-

sion of personality to another, so that one can hardly expect a meaningful discussion of how much consistency there is unless the kind of
consistency one is talking about is specified—and does anyone normally
bother to talk about a kind of consistency unless he believes it to be
in some way important? Surely, too, the extent to which consistency is
found will be a function of the causal influences which produce consistencies and will vary from one set of causal conditions to another.
Most important of all, each of the various consistencies in behavior is
doubtless produced by a different set of causal factors—sometimes
entirely unknown, sometimes reasonably well identified—and many
psychologists would hold that those dimensions of consistency for
which we have the best hope of establishing a definite relationship
with some set of causal factors are the ones most worth studying.

Yet it is a fact that these three questions have to a great extent
been considered independently. This is less true of the first question
than of the others, although there has even been abstract discussion
of the extent of consistency in personality in general. The other two
questions have often been considered quite independently. Most of
the argument for the importance of one or another dimension of
variation has been completely devoid of any consideration of the
probable causal influences. In addition, a great deal more discussion
of the importance of a particular dimension has been accompanied only
by a vague argument—unsupported by any specific reference to facts—
for a genetic kind of influence. In writings focused on the origins of
consistency in personality, the theoretical aspect has not generally
been divorced from consideration of what are important dimensions
of personality. The writer who is discussing in the abstract the origins
of aggression, achievement motivation, neuroticism, and the like, is
usually clearly implying that the characteristic he is discussing is a
general one of importance for understanding or dealing with variations
in personality. But when it comes to the empirical side of the studies
concerned with origins of consistency, there appears to be lack of any
real attention to whether the dimension involved is truly important
or whether the consistency is of a magnitude sufficient to justify the
theoretical interpretation offered. Thus a study of the origins of some
personality variable—approached theoretically in terms which suggest
a very broad and in many ways important dimension of common
variation in the behavior of an individual—may actually refer empirically only to questionnaire answers, only to doll play, or only to
stories told in the Thematic Apperception Test. To be sure, these
measurements may turn out to be representative of a broad consistency
in behavior and to merit an important sounding label. An equally
possible outcome is that much effort will have been wasted in studying

the causal antecedents of an isolated triviality. One of the weaknesses of personality study thus far has been precisely this—studies identifying consistencies and testing their generality have been carried on largely in the absence of concern for their possible origins, and studies of causal origins of personality characteristics have been carried on largely in the absence of real concern for their generality.

A fourth problem has often been considered as falling in the province of personality study. This is the study of psychodynamics or the mechanisms of adjustment. Though this is more difficult than the first three problems to phrase as a question, it might be expressed in this way: What are the mechanisms or processes that intervene between the original instigation to action and the final action or lack of action which results? This would include, for example, the experimental study of identification, regression, and displacement in which attention is focused on universal laws of dynamics of behavior, not on the development of consistent characteristics of the individual. One may wonder at first whether there is any justification—other than the accidents of history—for such a concern to have been classified under personality study, since it seems unrelated to the study of individual differences, which is often taken as the essential characteristic of personality study.

There is certainly this justification at least: This is an aspect of general psychology which bears most directly and intimately upon the concerns of personality study. For the processes underlying individual positions on a dimension of personality may in considerable part be found to consist of the operation of universal principles of psychodynamics. For example, if people differ in the consistency and strength of their hostility toward strangers, the present internal nature of these consistencies or lack of them in each person might be expressed in terms of a general theory of displacement of aggression.

Then too, a theory of psychodynamics is bound up with any attempt to account for the origins of consistencies of behavior. If a person arrives at a consistency of behavior as a cumulative result of his interaction with the social environment, then we may expect that the consistency is built up through a series of episodes—each of which could be accounted for in terms of a theory of psychodynamics, just as the psychic residues of the series must be accounted for by a theory of learning. The very study of psychodynamics, moreover, may often make use of the material and methods of personality study in the sense in which we have defined it here. Thus in studying the resolution of conflict about aggression, it may be difficult to control experimentally the strength of anxiety about aggression and more convenient to locate groups of subjects who already differ in the extent of their anxiety about aggression. And even where such a study is focused upon the psychodynamic process rather than on understanding individual differences, it inevitably throws light upon individual differences in personalities by showing the possibility of restatement or explanation in terms of psychodynamic process. Yet for the sake of coherence and in order to permit a more integrated discussion, this paper will not be explicitly concerned with the problem of psychodynamics, but will focus on personality study as the study of consistencies in individual differences.

EXAMPLES OF RELATIVELY ISOLATED PERSONALITY RESEARCH

The nature of these three major problems may be further explicated by examples of relatively isolated research concerned with each of them. These are examples of personality research which is isolated simply in the sense of depending little on other fields of knowledge. It is difficult to find pure examples, so steadily has personality study been influenced by other fields of knowledge; and relation to other fields of knowledge will be avoided in the discussion here more than it was by the original authors. Discussion of even relatively pure cases may help prepare for illustrating the interrelations of personality study and other fields of knowledge, such as anthropology and sociology, as will be done later in this chapter.

The Breadth of Consistencies

For the first problem, the extent of consistency in personality, a most important and relatively pure instance is provided by the studies of moral character—a classic in the history of personality research—by Hartshorne, May, and Shuttleworth [56]. In this research, a number of ingenious tests were devised to measure honesty, helpfulness, inhibition, and persistence. The three-volume report is devoted very largely to the problem of how much consistency there is in these aspects of personality. The consistency is certainly much lower than would have been expected from many common-sense notions about character. For its overwhelming accumulation of evidence to this effect, the research stands as a permanent and important addition to knowledge on the general problem of extent of consistency. The relation of this research to theories about consistency is less clear, however. The authors regarded their findings as incompatible with a notion of "'traits' or fundamental unified faculties of personality." Whether there was at that time an extreme view of trait consistency which would be disproved by the findings is a historical problem which we will not deal with here. Certainly it is doubtful whether any psychologists today would have such extreme notions of trait consistency that they would be discomfited by the degree of specificity found by Hartshorne, May, and Shuttleworth. Most attempts at theoretical understanding of human behavior would lead one to expect some intermediate degree of consistency in personality—neither complete determination by variables in the momentary situation nor complete absence of determination by them. The student of personality, then, may regard as a part of his task the assessment of the degree of consistency actually found. For the particular aspects of personality dealt with, the possibility of working effectively toward such an assessment is well illustrated by the work of Hartshorne, May, and Shuttleworth.

Difficulties in arriving at such an assessment may also be illustrated by the same study. Such ingenuity in the invention of personality measures as was shown by these investigators is not easily found. The generalizability of findings from one set of measures to the whole of everyday behavior of people remains always a problem. Appropriate mathematical skills are needed for the analysis of data, though these are easier for the psychologist to obtain now than they were a generation ago. Perhaps the most important difficulty is the fundamental question of how far such a method of study really goes toward assessing the true degree of consistency in personality. This is the question which Allport poses in his critical discussion [1, pp. 250–255] of this research. A person may be consistent within himself in a variety of ways. The correlational method of analysis ordinarily gets at only the particular ways of being consistent that tend to be bases of consistency throughout the sample and fails altogether to identify consistencies that are unique to the individual. Hence the answer given by the usual correlational approach to the question of how much consistency really is just the statement of a lower limit of consistency. Or, to put it another way, this approach indicates how much consistency there is by one criterion—a criterion which is perhaps a good deal more important than Allport wished to recognize in his critical argument, yet not all-important. If we could segregate groups of subjects in whom the bases of consistency were somewhat different—cultural groups, for example, or groups distinguished by dominant motive—and applied ordinary correlational methods to each group separately, the degree of consistency arrived at should be closer to the self-consistency which Allport seems to consider most important to assess. Yet any such procedure always leaves open the possibility of choosing other procedures instead. The question of how much consistency is a more complicated one than first appears, even when considered as a rather isolated problem of personality study alone.

Recognition that the truest statement is the one which takes account of the individual's unique forms of consistency may prompt some to suppose that literary methods are more apt than scientific methods. This supposition seems to result from a confusion about the aims of science and art, a confusion which is encouraged by the fact that intensive study of consistencies within a single individual occurs most often in a clinical setting where aims of science, art, and practice are blended in a single effort. But where an assessment of consistencies within the single individual has occurred under the influence of the generalizing and objectifying aims so characteristic of science, it has been clear that the usual scientific methods are highly useful and indeed indispensable for dealing here as elsewhere with scientific questions. A nice demonstration was provided by Baldwin's [10] statistical treatment of consistencies in letters written by a single person. More recently, the techniques of factor analysis have been applied by Cattell to consistencies in the day-to-day variations in psychological measurements of the single individual [25, and other research summarized in 26].

The question of how much consistency has continued to be asked primarily with respect to differences among individuals, however. Whether there is any completely general consistency influencing every act of a person has remained a topic for speculation—and usually not explicitly stated in so extreme a form. This speculative question is raised at least by implication in attempts at schematic pictures of the hierarchical organization of personality. A good example is provided by Eysenck's review of theories of personality organization [42, chap. 1]. Here Eysenck argues that the most appropriate use of the term "type"— appropriate in being the general usage of the Continental scholars who have contributed most to the development of this construct—is to apply it to consistencies of a very general nature. This use of "type"—as a term akin to habit or trait, but applied to consistencies far above these in the hierarchical organization of internal consistencies—is, of course, entirely different from the use of the same term by many American psychologists to refer to categorization as distinguished from quantitative measurement, a use recently exemplified by Humphreys [58]. Guilford [55] also uses the term "type" for consistencies of the most general character, and again the picture of hierarchical organization by implication raises the questions: How complete is the hierarchical organization? Is there a level at which we may usefully recognize types so general that they to some extent determine every act of the person?

These speculations about hierarchical organization suggest that their authors believe that a high degree of consistency will be found. The view that consistencies are instead likely to be limited is also very much alive and may be illustrated by Rotter's *Social Learning and Clinical Psychology* [92]. Rotter's presentation, like those of Eysenck and Guilford, is highly sophisticated from the point of view of scientific method and not directed at taking a definite position on this undecidable issue and arguing for it as anything like a validated finding. His thesis seems to be rather of a heuristic sort—an argument that science and practice will be more rapidly advanced by concentration on the study of variations in consistency, on the failure of consistency, rather than on a quest for even the little bit of consistency that may still persist despite variation. But the assumption underlying this very reasonable argument is the very general one being considered here—the assumption that internally determined consistencies of behavior are extremely limited. He says, for example:

There is relatively low predictive value to a measure of how much aggression a person has in terms of a percentile score (which does not tell when the person will be aggressive and when he will not be aggressive). The psychologist needs to know what kinds of stimuli or what kinds of situations result in aggressive behavior, so that he may make more individualized predictions or have a better understanding of how the subject has been affected by previous experience [92, p. 260].

Generalizing later the view exemplified here, he says that present personality tests are "attempts to do too much with too little. What is needed are many more specific tests to measure specific things" [92, p. 334]. With this orientation, his survey of existing personality tests tends to be highly critical, emphasizing the lowness of their validity rather than the point that they do have some validity which might make them of real use for many purposes. Clearly his position on the question of how much consistency is to be found in personality—though not dogmatically stated—is an important determinant of the tone and impact of the whole book.

Awareness of the value of an emphasis on specificity of test to situation is not confined to those who share Rotter's particular theoretical approach. In a very different context, for example, Mandler and Sarason [80] and Sarason et al. [94], intending to study the effects of anxiety on test performance, have begun by constructing instruments designed to measure tendency to be anxious in test situations rather than being content with more readily available instruments for measuring tendency to be anxious in a variety of situations. An interesting confirmation of the value of Sarason and Mandler's situation-specific questionnaire on anxiety is the finding by Raphelson [89] that it was more predictive of a physiological index of anxiety arousal in a test situation than was a questionnaire on general anxiety.

In certain kinds of instances, on the other hand, improved knowledge of the relations between measured personality traits and specific performances opens up the possibility that some of these relations may be expressed in general principles of behavior, with a single personality characteristic being predictive perhaps of opposite effects on different performances as a result of a difference in the way general principles apply to the two different situations. Such efforts have been made by Spence [99, chaps. 6, 7], for example, in predicting that general anxiety as measured by the Taylor questionnaire [101] would facilitate the rate of simple conditioning and interfere with performance on certain more complex tasks. Similarly, Sarason et al. [94] study various predictions about the relation of test anxiety to performance, basing their work on a theory of the effects of anxiety and hypotheses about the behavioral processes involved in good or bad performance on each test. For some tests, high anxiety was expected to facilitate performance, for some it was expected to interfere with performance—on the whole, the expectations were confirmed. In somewhat parallel fashion, Broverman and Lazarus [24] show that the direction of maximum interference between two simultaneous tasks is affected by the relative compatibility of the two tasks with the person's general cognitive style. In the broader framework of viewing personality as the study of internally determined consistencies, such developments contribute toward establishing just what dimension of a particular performance is relevant to any particular larger consistency.

Perhaps all students of personality are likely to tentatively adopt and be influenced by some view on this very general question of the extent of consistency through personality as a whole. And, one would gather from their activities, most of them seem to judge that greater consistency will be found than Rotter's statement seems to indicate. But such judgments are not often expressed. The question: How much consistency? has been more often asked, and tentatively answered, with reference to something far less than the whole domain of personality. The concern that Hartshorne, May, and Shuttleworth had for asking this question about moral character, other psychologists have continued to have for other limited areas of behavior. A few examples will illustrate how frequent and how important this concern is.

First consider an example that will illustrate the relevance of this concern to the practical uses of personality measurement. One of the variables in Rorschach response to which clinicians give attention is relative responsiveness to color versus form as a determinant of perception of the ink blots. One's judgment of how to interpret a person's position on this variable (as for any other) surely ought to be influenced by knowledge of how broad a consistency it is a part of and what other specific variables form a part of that consistency. A study by Keehn [67, 68] indicated that research does not necessarily lead to a confirmation of the obvious—and it is the experience of many researchers in personality that confirmation of the obvious in such matters is so rare as to be very surprising—[see Wolff, 113, on the generality of certainty as a dimension of personality; or Forster, Vinacke, and Digman, 46, on the generality of flexibility in problem situations]. Keehn constructed a battery of many tests which had been or might be assumed to measure relative responsiveness to color versus form. He found that there was a consistency which could be appropriately labeled in this way. But the color-form variable on the Rorschach was not a part of it. The inclusion of several tests which seemed to be related to whole versus part perception enabled Keehn to make the tentative generalization that color-form responsiveness in the Rorschach is probably related to such a dimension instead—that is, the responsiveness to color on Rorschach cards is, on the whole, indicative of ability to assimilate this element as well as form into the perception. Such knowledge—about just what other measures a given variable is and is not consistent with—is obviously necessary for that variable to be assigned its proper meaning in practical use.

A second kind of illustration concerns the permanence of personality characteristics—their consistency through time. On intelligence-test performance, data on long-range consistency have been explored for some time [e.g., Anastasi, 6, pp. 231–238]. The same is true for certain personality questionnaires that have been available in a constant form for many years; Kelly [69] provides a notable example of such research. But attention has recently been given to the long-range consistency of other variables too. For example, Kagan and Moss [63] report a degree of consistency for the presence of achievement themes on the Thematic Apperception Test which is statistically significant through almost six years of later childhood and adolescence. While the consistency is not very great, the internal consistency of the measure is probably too low for it to be otherwise. Dennis [40] has extended the period for which consistency can be measured by selecting a particular variable which, in a small group of people, can be measured over a span of approximately sixty years. This variable is the average sentence length in the letters of long-lived persons whose letters have been published. He finds sentence length in the third decade of life to be consistent with sentence length in the eighth decade of life, to the extent indicated by a correlation coefficient of .78. Dennis [35, 37] has also studied consistency in the productivity of scientists through their professional life; there, too, he finds a very high degree of consistency. With the accumulation of data by research institutes that have started longitudinal studies or preserved the data of cross-sectional studies, later generations of psychologists may be able to extend such knowledge of long-range consistency. This will obviously be of special interest in connection with hypotheses about basic and permanent effects of either hereditary endowment or early experience. But it might be very challenging to theoretical understanding even in a case where no persuasive explanatory hypothesis is immediately apparent, as seems to be true of the Dennis findings.

A third illustration is testing whether a given consistency holds true for all kinds of persons or for given persons at all stages of development. Examples are numerous, and each might well point toward a whole range of possible research on the conditions giving rise to consistencies. For example, is a given consistency found at all ages? If not, just how does it vary with age? This question, asked earlier of cognitive abilities [cf. Anastasi, 6, pp. 357–360], is now being asked about other consistencies, too, as may be exemplified in research by Cattell [27]. Do men and women show the same consistencies? Examples of interesting differences between the sexes are provided by various findings on projective-test measurement of achievement orientation, summarized by McClelland et al. [78, pp. 175–176] and McClelland [77, pp. 37–38] and by the research of Bieri, Bradburn, and Galinsky [21] on perceptual performances, where the difference in pattern between the sexes helps sharpen the conception of the nature of the consistencies within each sex. In quite another area, that of motor skills, Fleishman [45] has studied variations in the factorial composition of a skill (in relation to a number of reference tests) as a function of amount of training the subject has had. This research provides a paradigm which might be useful in studying the effects on motivational and stylistic consistencies of less controllable experiences, such as psychotherapy or exposure to various life crises. It might be applied to studying variations in whatever stable characteristics of personality the degree of anxiety is related to—as this relationship changes during psychotherapy. Or if the other relevant measures are also likely to be changing, the paradigm could be altered by separately analyzing the interrelations of a battery of measures applied before therapy and again after termination.

Another general problem with which personality study has been much concerned recently—since the publications by Murray et al. [85] and Sanford et al. [93]—has to do with the relation between various spheres or types of behavioral data. One may make, for example, a three-fold distinction: (1) observational records of a person's overt behavior (of other kinds than those in the following two categories); (2) records of a person's statements about his own behavior and feelings; and (3) records of a person's fantasy or imaginative productions. One problem that may then be posed is this: If consistencies are sought for separately within each of these three spheres of behavioral data, will parallel consistencies be found in the three spheres? For example, if a factor labeled "introversion-extroversion" appears as a broad consistency in people's statements about themselves, will a factor identifiable with this also appear as a broad consistency in observations of overt behavior? Answers to this kind of question are a major concern of recent books by Cattell [26] and Eysenck [42]. So far, the outside spectator is impressed by the difficulty of arriving at a conclusive answer on the basis of the very complicated similarities and differences among analyses of very different bodies of data. But there appears no reason to doubt that clear agreement will eventually be reached.

Rather a larger number of psychologists have been concerned with a different kind of question about the relation between different spheres of behavioral data. Typically, the question has been asked about consistencies of somewhat lesser breadth than those usually appearing in discussion of the previous problem. It is the question of whether a variable found in one sphere will be correlated with a variable of apparently similar nature found in another sphere. For example, if strength of aggressive tendency is a strand of some consistency in overt behavior, will people who are high in overt aggression also describe themselves as aggressive or produce fantasies with aggressive content? The consistency between overt behavior and self-descriptive statements may be viewed as a problem of the validity of self-descriptive statements (only for statements which refer to or suggest implications for overt behavior as defined here) and thus of the validity of measuring techniques which make use of self-description. Understood in this way, testing such consistency has been a recurrent concern in the attempt to validate various questionnaires intended to measure personality. This problem does not seem to have aroused great theoretical interest, though its relevance to the general problem of the self-conception and its challenge to any general treatment of human processing of information should eventually guarantee it such a treatment. So far, the consistency between fantasy and overt behavior and between fantasy and self-description have more regularly aroused an interest which goes beyond the very important—but methodological rather than substantive—concern with the validity of measuring devices.

Substantive concern with the relation between overt behavior and fantasy is readily illustrated with the problem of aggression. "Overt behavior" will include ratings of overt aggression by a person's associates (the method most frequently used here), as well as observations by an investigator. The relation between aggression in fantasy and overt behavior has been found to be positive, negative, and absent in different studies, as is indicated in the excellent brief reviews included in research articles by Kagan [62] and Lesser [74]. Such discrepancies clearly challenge understanding, and these two studies are among those which attempt to meet the challenge. Kagan's study makes two important points:

1. Positive correlation between aggression in overt behavior and fantasy is greatly increased if the definition of aggression in fantasy is narrowed down to the definition used for overt behavior, thus suggesting that part of the previous inconsistency was due to failure to compare really parallel measures (and perhaps to use on the fantasy side of a measure that is not itself internally consistent).

2. So far as theory conceives the source of consistency to be common inhibition of overt behavior and fantasy by anxiety, then consistency should be increased by measuring fantasy under conditions most apt to arouse aggressive thoughts which then may or may not be inhibited by anxiety. A different prediction might be made from the assumption that consistency between overt behavior and fantasy results principally from the common influence of strength of a generalized aggressive drive, and clearly research testing the two predictions is relevant to basic problems in personality study.

Lesser [74] uses the concept of conflict to clarify the relation between aggression in overt behavior and fantasy. He shows that by selecting groups of boys whose mothers are relatively encouraging or discouraging of their son's aggression, the relation between the two measures of aggressive tendency may be made positive or negative, respectively—a difference that seems predictable from an analysis of aggressive behavior as an outcome of conflict between aggressive tendency and anxiety evoked by this tendency. Conflict theory attempts to take into account positive drive and anxiety, and their interaction, in predicting what relation between overt behavior and fantasy will be found under each of various sets of conditions. In a later study, Lesser [75] derives several specific predictions from such an analysis and finds confirmatory evidence. For example, overt aggression is more accurately predicted from a combination of its positive correlation with fantasied aggression and its negative correlation with fantasy evidence of aggression anxiety than from either measure separately. Thus a theory about multiple influences on a behavioral tendency may reveal consistencies which a common-sense approach of looking for apparent similarities might miss altogether.

Such an outcome is not restricted to phenomena of aggression, which have received special attention. This may be illustrated by a study by Fitzgerald [44] on dependency. His finding is very different from Lesser's, but the theoretical significance he gives it is similar. He finds that dependency themes in fantasy are not dependably associated with amount of dependency in overt behavior, but with evidence of conflict about dependency (this measure being derived from an interview). There have been attempts to investigate the relation between fantasy and overt expressions of achievement striving as a consistency which varies under different conditions and in ways related to general psychological theory. Illustrations are recent studies by Lazarus et al. [72], and Reitman [90] and various earlier studies described in Atkinson [8].

The consistency between apparently similar variables in fantasy and self-descriptive statements (or other verbal techniques, such as agreement with sentiments) has been investigated to a slight extent for a number of variables [e.g., Sanford et al., 93; Child, Frank, and Storm, 31]. The most striking finding has been lack of consistency or uniform direction of consistency. This lack is very disturbing since investigators frequently depend on one or the other of these measures as an index of motive strength, without adequate validation of the particular measure used. De Charms et al. [34] have begun to compare the separate correlates of these two kinds of measures in achievement orientation. Davids and Pildner [33] have shown that the consistency between self-descriptions and projective tests (as well as the consistency within each type) varies greatly with testing conditions in the case of alienation. While their study deals with effects of having subjects see their test performance as a contribution to science rather than as a screening for employment and is thus most obviously related to problems of practical prediction, they also relate their findings to Allport's theoretical views [3] on consistency between types of personality measures as a function of maturity and integration. Studies on the relation between fantasy and self-descriptions have not thus far been as productive—in relation to general theory—as the corresponding attempt to study the relation between fantasy and overt behavior, but these excellent beginnings should be followed up.

A realization of the limitations and restrictions of the usual way of measuring behavioral consistencies—(i.e., by determining the correlation coefficient for a pair of variables) has arisen, especially in the study of fantasy or imaginative production in relation to other spheres of behavior. The first study by Lesser [74] illustrates the limitation. For his entire sample of boys, the correlation between overt and fantasy aggression was close to zero. Only when the sample was broken into two groups according to maternal attitude toward aggression did there appear any evidence of a correlation between overt and fantasy aggression—a correlation of opposite direction in the two groups. Clearly, some of the most exciting discoveries of behavioral consistencies will be made only when appropriate sets of variables are studied with an eye to such complex relationships. Wallach and Gahm [103] have recently studied graphic expansiveness-constrictiveness in the drawing of abstract designs, viewing this as a possible symbolic expression of thoughts about social relationships. Their hypotheses led them to study this variable in relation to extroversion and anxiety; the expectation that the relation between graphic expansiveness and extroversion would differ according to degree of anxiety was confirmed. The rather impressive relationship between the amount of paper a person uses and the degree of extroversion was confirmed by Wallach et al. [104] in a subsequent study using grade school girls instead of college women, drawings made under different circumstances, and an overt rather than a questionnaire measure of extroversion. But clearly the relationship was not likely to be seen at all—and certainly would not have been seen so adequately—without the idea that the consistency might be present in some circumstances and absent or reversed in others and without the prior identification and measurement of the relevant circumstances. Such findings reinforce the already present scepticism, about the ultimate value of the relatively nontheoretical quest for consistencies in whatever has been measured that for so long characterized much empirical work in personality study. They also reinforce the widespread feeling that greater progress may come from intensive study of more limited areas of behavioral consistency in which some sort of theory provides a guide for directing inquiry. In relation to the broad question of how much consistency there is—this development implies that quantitative methods of interindividual research can show much more consistency than the first and simplest applications might indicate.

The Importance of Consistencies

Let us turn to the second problem: identifying which dimensions of consistency in personality are important. The best examples of personality study relatively uninfluenced by other areas are found in the most empirical studies, which attempt to survey a given field of trait variation and then determine what the consistencies are. The argument is that the finding of a consistency under such circumstances is a testimony to its importance. A particularly good example is Cattell's attempt [cf. 26, pp. 71–73, and the references given there] to sample personality traits which are represented by words in the English vocabulary, then measure individuals with respect to those traits and study the intercorrelations to determine clusters and eventually factors. He started with Allport and Odbert's [4] list of trait names in the English language, though computational restrictions unfortunately necessitated reducing the sample to a smaller size than might be hoped for. The origin of the trait names—in the folk wisdom embodied in language, rather than in the history of psychological testing—gives this research a special importance in Cattell's attempt to synthesize the results of his various studies dealing with the identification of major dimensions of consistency in personality.

Some attempt at systematic coverage of the field of behavior is seen also in *Explorations in Personality,* by Murray and his collaborators [85]. An effort was made here to construct a natural history of the motivational variables in a small group of college students who were intensively studied. To be sure, there is more evidence here than in Cattell's study of influence from a professional tradition outside psychology—in this case, psychiatry—but the influence is not as sharp as it is in studies focused on a specific variable suggested by psychiatric thought. Both studies indicate that the student of personality may simply take observable variations in personality among individuals, assigning himself the descriptive task of identifying simple observable dimensions and the organizational task of making a simpler or more coherent picture of the broader consistencies uniting these observable dimensions. Factor analysis is an ideal technique for the latter task, but Murray's work illustrates the possibility of making a useful contribution to this aspect of natural history by more informal methods.

A somewhat similar argument—one which is likely to be made in general accounts of personality rather than in specific research studies —is this: Consistencies of great breadth have an outstanding importance simply because of their breadth. This seems to be the assumption made in prescientific characterology and in psychiatric typology such as that of Jung [61]. It is the assumption of recent writers [e.g., Eysenck, 42] in their portrayals of the hierarchical organization of behavior, which we referred to earlier. When adequately tested, this standard of great breadth will obviously be a significant one. However, one must guard against the belief that it is the only standard for judging the importance of a consistency in personality. Even if most aspects of our behavior are slightly correlated in a way describable as introversion-extroversion, the contribution of this factor to any one aspect might still be very slight indeed. The mistake of overstress on the standard of breadth is probably most likely to be made by laymen, as can be seen from the exaggerated importance given to the concept of general intelligence in popular thinking.

In the absence of adequate evidence for assessing the breadth of such apparently broad consistencies as introversion-extroversion, a substitute standard lies in the regularity with which similar consistencies emerge in different research studies or in interpretations of research by different people. Attempts have been made in recent years [Cattell, 26; Eysenck, 42; French, 49; Guilford, 55] to summarize and compare large segments of the research on consistencies, primarily the research using factor analysis as a technique. Anyone reading these surveys and judging the importance of various consistencies in personality must be influenced by his impressions of the regularity with which they appear to turn up. Most research has been so unsystematically varied in choice of subjects, measuring techniques, methods of analysis, and so forth, that only a limited amount of agreement in such judgments can be expected.

The standards considered thus far for judging importance all tend to fuse the first and second problems of personality study. They all take the breadth of a consistency—in one sense or another of "breadth" —as itself determining the importance of the consistency. But other standards separate the problem of breadth from that of importance more clearly, for they do not stress the breadth of the consistency but its specific nature.

One of these standards is practical importance. A measured personality variable is often found to be predictive of something in people's lives that it would be useful to predict; usually, of course, this is the outcome of a deliberate search for successful methods of prediction. For example, Barron [14] has constructed a questionnaire which he finds to be predictive of the outcome of psychotherapy. For what is measured by any such tests, one may claim the degree and kind of importance which is justified by its consistency with—and thus prediction of— some variable of practical consequence. Of course, other consistencies are predictive in ways not likely to be of great practical value because their practical predictive use—in contrast to their research use—would be in a situation where people would be motivated to respond in a way that would yield favorable predictions for them, and they would probably be able to do so. This would seem to be true, for example, of Gough's [54] personality scale to predict scholastic achievement. The importance of such variables must, on the whole, rest on other grounds.

This practical basis for judging the importance of a personality variable corresponds to the concept of criterion validity for a test. These two uses of the same facts are not, however, equivalent. A test is valid for predicting any criterion variable to the extent that it does predict that criterion variable. The practical importance of the criterion variable has no bearing on the judgment of validity. But what is measured by a test has importance (by this standard) only to the extent that prediction of the criterion variable is important. A test predicting which people would be horrified and which people would be intrigued by the unexpected sight of a wild rat would have little practical importance in a country where the unexpected sight of wild rats is rare—though it might turn out to be an important test for other reasons.

Another standard for judging the importance of a personality variable is the extent to which it shows with other variables consistencies predicted from a theory of some importance. This is related to one aspect of what has come to be called "construct validity," following the suggestion of Cronbach and Meehl [32]. As in the case of criterion validity, however, the fact of validity is not the same as the judgment of importance. For a personality variable to fit beautifully into a network of variables as predicted by an isolated and completely trivial theory would not give it any importance—at least, not immediately. Perhaps such an outcome would justify an expectation that in the long run the theory would not turn out to be really trivial.

Many claims—stated or implied—for the importance of various personality variables consist largely of an appeal to this standard. Thus the argument by Gardner et al. [50] for the importance of a number of consistencies among perceptual tests is based principally on the considerable degree of harmony between the pattern of consistencies and the pattern which was expected, according to the theory of cognitive styles which guided the research. One can, of course, bring such an argument to data after the fact. Armed with an analysis of cognitive styles, such as that provided by Gardner et al., one may turn back to Thurstone's strictly empirical study [102] of consistencies among perceptual performances and judge certain findings important for present research because they fit the analysis to some degree.

Another standard relies upon the relation of the consistency to some variable which can be identified as a causal influence on it. Psychology is directed largely—some might say entirely—to learning about the causes of behavior. Thus any consistencies for which we have some knowledge of the causes will assume an importance which consistencies having unknown causes do not have. To some extent, this importance may be attached to a mere assignment of causal influences to one or another large category—e.g., biological vs. social—or to an assessment of the relative dominance of various categories of influence. Thus if Cattell [28] is able to persuade his fellow psychologists that the relative influence of nature and nurture on certain personality variables can be assessed with an accuracy justifying the labor, then the variables for which the most competent and varied assessments have been made have a special importance.

More obvious, however, is the importance of consistencies about whose origins there is some more specific knowledge. Sometimes this knowledge is more or less exclusively of empirical origin; sometimes it is more theoretical. Sometimes a consistency is important because there is an interesting theory about its origins, even though the theory may not have been tested in these respects. This has been the status, for instance, of Freudian character-type variables as they have most frequently appeared in psychological research. Sears [97, pp. 67–70] reviews some early research on anal character which falls into this pattern. Later research on Freudian character types, mostly falling into the same pattern, has been reviewed by Blum [22] and by Child [30].

This standard of judging the importance of a consistency by knowledge about its origins corresponds to another aspect of what, with reference to measuring techniques, is called "construct validity." The same is true of a final standard to be considered—the significance of a consistency as cause, rather than effect. Like the other standards, this involves a still broader consistency as the basis for judging the importance of a somewhat narrower consistency. But again, it is the particular character of this broader consistency—its being related to a theory about cause and effect—rather than its mere breadth, that justifies the judgment of importance.

This final standard has been especially conspicuous in personality research in the last few years. For example, anxiety has been a concept of special importance in recent research. It has entered into theoretical predictions about variations in performance resulting from different levels of anxiety, and techniques of measuring anxiety as a consistent individual difference have permitted the test of these predictions [e.g., Spence, 99; Taylor, 101; Sarason et al., 94]. Similar evidence has appeared for other personality consistencies having a causal significance in relation to performance. These have included habitual tendency to make task-interfering responses to frustration [Waterhouse and Child, 105; Williams, 111], ego strength [Alper, 5], and certain aspects of cognitive style [Broverman and Lazarus, 24]. This standard links personality study directly wtih the general study of psychodynamics. The theory that predicts some effect of anxiety as a personality consistency may also predict the same effect resulting from anxiety produced as a purely temporary condition by external pressures. The distinctive characteristics of personality study lose their relevance at this point, and thus, as indicated earlier, psychodynamics is not here considered as a branch of personality study. However, it may turn out that an adequate account of psychodynamics must depend on knowledge of personality, since the effects of single variables may vary according to the personality structure in which they are embedded. Such an assumption would seem to be a part of Alper's [5] reason for using the term "ego strength" for a set of variables which might instead have been described in motivational terms, for example.

The Origins of Consistencies

Research on the third general problem, the origins of consistencies, has a very insistent tendency to relate itself immediately and obviously to other areas of knowledge. Indeed, it is apparent from the preceding section that the problem of importance also inevitably touches on other areas of knowledge. It would not be easy—and perhaps it would not be profitable—to assemble here many studies as pure or isolated as some of those cited in the previous section.

An excellent example of such a study, however, is provided by the research on parental behavior and its effects, begun by Champney [29] and continued by Baldwin and others [11, 12] at the Fels Research Institute. This work was partly directed at understanding parent behavior for its own sake. In addition, it was directed at relating parent behavior, as one set of causal influences, to child personality, as effect. It is this aspect of the work that is relevant here. A set of possible causal influences are approached with the descriptive and classificatory eye of natural history. The variables selected for initial study and the rationale for deciding upon them are discussed by Champney in an article [29] which is of great interest as an example of thoughtful, self-conscious planning of the natural history of such a set of possible causes. The variables and the methods used in assessing them are presented more fully by Baldwin and others [11]. The same authors, in another monograph [12], discuss the simplified description of these variables through cluster analysis. By this procedure—akin in its aim to factor analysis—they arrive at a few general dimensions which summarize much of the consistency in the large number of variables used in gathering the data. These dimensions—comparable to those which might emerge from a factor analysis—are then studied in relation to variables of child personality.

These studies illustrate the possibility of an approach to causal study of personality by direct confrontation with data on personality and probable influences, little guided by other specific areas of knowledge. That is, rather than drawing upon a preexisting systematization about the causal variables developed in some other field of knowledge, the student of personality could make a natural-history approach to a new identification of them. But this has not been done often.

In this Fels research, the authors were interested in identifying consistencies in parent behavior, as well as in considering them as causal influences on child personality. This is a good place, however, to consider an important point: When variables are being measured only for study as possible causal influences on behavior, the logic of investigation does not demand that these causal variables represent consistencies in the way that we expect personality variables to represent consistencies.

The way in which we expect personality variables to represent consistencies may be referred to as "correlational consistency"; that is, the various items or parts or instances which are put together to form the variable are correlated with each other in their occurrence. This is the meaning of consistency that is involved in the concept of reliability and in relevant aspects of the concept of validity. The knowledge that a purported measure of a particular psychological variable has good reliability constitutes evidence that this variable as so measured has correlational consistency. As we pointed out earlier, some of the consistencies may involve much more complicated relationships than simply linear correlations among a group of variables. But still, correlation in some sense is expected; a set of randomly related variables do not form a consistency of personality.

Where a variable is measured to study the effects of the degree to which it is present on other people, however, it need not be a consistency in this sense. For example, if a person has a typical chronic degree of self-confidence, which is a sum or mean of degrees of self-confidence in several areas—occupational success, sexual status, emotional relations, conformity to a moral ideal, for example—the various components do not need to be correlated for us to have some characteristic average stimulus value for other persons in frequent and varied interaction with him. General self-confidence would not be of interest as a consistency of personality if these components were uncorrelated, except for the interest in knowing that no such consistency exists. But a general measure of a person's self-confidence might still be extremely useful in testing predictions about the effect of his mean level of self-confidence on his children or other close associates.

An example from economics may make this argument clearer. The total amount of money a person receives during a year is an important fact for predicting his economic relations with others. This is the case, regardless of whether components which might be separately measured—income from salary, hourly wages, own business, investments, gifts, etc.—are positively or negatively correlated or not correlated at all. Whether many psychological characteristics significant for a person's stimulus value to others would in fact fail to be correlational consistencies may be doubtful. But to take correlational consistency as a requirement for measuring a variable for such a purpose is surely to risk error by extending the methods of personality study to an area where they are inappropriate. All that is needed here to justify assembling components into a larger variable is that they be logically consistent with respect to the purpose for which they are being assembled—that is, that theory indicate that the same effects are to be expected from the several components. Indeed, the same considerations seem to apply to a variable which is being measured for the purpose of studying the effect a person's standing on it may have on himself, in view of its self-stimulus value.

Research on the origins of consistencies was illustrated in the previous section, where knowledge about origins was seen as one standard for judging the importance of consistencies. It will also be illustrated in the following sections on relations to anthropology and sociology. Moreover, research on the origins of personality consistencies follows a general paradigm so familiar in psychology that it seems unnecessary to illustrate it further here.

SOME RELATIONS TO ANTHROPOLOGY AND SOCIOLOGY

Universality of Phenomena of Personality

A major influence of anthropology on personality study, one that seems likely to be of increasing importance, grows directly out of its orientation toward the study of human cultures all over the world. Potentially, of course, anthropology supplies data immediately relevant to personality study from a diversity of cultures—to some extent it already provides such data. Beyond this, anthropology's orientation toward study of all mankind and awareness of potential variations between cultures exert a healthy influence on the research worker who probably studies only people who share his cultural tradition. This is highly relevant to the three basic problems reviewed above.

There is little need to be concerned with questions of universality or cultural variation in certain areas of personality study. When the purpose of identifying a consistency and judging the extent to which it holds true is solely to make a practical application of this knowledge to personality variations among members of our own society, the immediately relevant information is naturally about variations within our own society. But as soon as any interest arises in drawing a conclusion about personality variations among human beings in general, no conclusion can be justified unless there is reason to believe that the same phenomena would be duplicated in individuals reared in very different cultural settings.

The possible bearing of data from other societies on questions about breadth and importance of consistencies may be illustrated at a further extreme by Diamond's [41] comparative account of personality and temperament. His comparison is not primarily among human societies, however, but between man and other species. In a review of relevant research about dimensions of behavioral variation in other species, he finds pervasive evidence that four dimensions are important: tendencies toward affiliative, fearful, aggressive, and impulsive behavior. He then argues that this reinforces the other reasons—already present from the study of man—for believing that these variables have an especially fundamental importance in the study of consistencies of human personality.

There seems not to have been any very systematic attempt to use existing anthropological data for this sort of purpose. Some tentative conclusions may be justified by the work of Whiting and Child [108] and Barry, Bacon, and Child [17]. The former authors analyzed the child training practices of a number of preliterate societies with respect to oral behavior, excretion, sex, dependence, and aggression. The universal relevance of the first three is guaranteed by the nature of the human body. It might be reasonable, however, to doubt the universal relevance of dependence and aggression; in that event, it is significant that the analysts do not seem to have been unable to evaluate these variables in any society because of irrelevance to a sizable body of data about personal interactions (though they were sometimes unable to for lack of information). But the analysts were not especially instructed to watch for this problem. In the work of Barry, Bacon, and Child, the analysis was done by two psychologists who were alert to this problem. In analyzing child training practices with respect to achievement striving, self-reliance, nurturance, obedience, and responsibility, they did not feel these concepts to be irrelevant to the behavior described for any of the societies for which reasonably full descriptions were available. Of course, these studies only tell us whether an observer from our society can use these concepts in discriminating among societies with repect to customary behavior; they do not tell us whether they would appear as consistencies in an analysis of interindividual differences within any of these societies.

When the question of origin of personality consistencies arises, information about other cultural settings may become quite crucial. Thus it is sometimes argued that any broad consistency such as emerges in second-order factor analysis must be very fundamental and essentially biological in origin. This suggests that the same higher-order factors should emerge from a study of individual differences in any other cultural group. Whether this is so cannot be known until it is tested. Until then, it remains perfectly possible that even the broadest consistency found in our society is somehow the result of particular social conditions influencing personality development here. The needed information cannot be supplied merely by a finding of similar factors in individuals who have developed in various European countries. Certainly, cultural conditions in all European countries are extremely similar, in comparison with the range of cultural variations found in mankind as a whole.

The problem of the origin of sex differences in personality offers another example here. When sex differences are observed only within our society, one possible hypothesis is that they are consequences of arbitrarily chosen customs of our particular cultural tradition. When cross-cultural study of sex differences in socialization by Barry, Bacon, and Child [17] shows that a similar pattern of sex differences is extremely widespread in independent cultural traditions, this hypothesis becomes untenable. To what extent our sex differences in personality are more or less direct consequences of biological differences and to what extent they result from a common but not necessary cultural adaptation to biological differences remains uncertain. But the possible origins are narrowed down by exclusion of the hypothesis of near irrelevance of biological differences.

The outcome of a search for consistencies in other cultures may be relevant even for purposes for which one would not ordinarily think cultural variation to be significant. Thus if certain consistencies are considered of biological origin because of their fundamental character in our own society, then—in such practical concerns as psychotherapy, for example—a person's position on such a dimension may be taken as a fact about his nature and unalterable. On the other hand, if comparative study casts doubt on the biological origins of this variable, then much more attention may be given to possible modification of a person's position on it in psychotherapy.

Quantitative research of this sort, permitting the comparison of consistency of various dimensions in different cultural settings, does not seem to have been undertaken in anthropological research. To be sure, the Rorschach test has been given in various cultural groups—and possibly to a sufficient number of subjects so that the data might be used in this way. References to a number of studies reporting Rorschach data from other cultures are given by Henry and Spiro [57]. In this research, individual scores are more likely to be published than in most psychological research; Kaplan [64] includes in his study scores of 123 persons of four Southwestern cultures on 25 Rorschach variables. In addition, Kaplan [65, 66] has made a very substantial beginning toward assembling fieldworkers' actual protocols of projective test responses for later researchers. But anthropological use of the Rorschach has not been accompanied by an interest in measuring consistencies within the responses to the instrument. Indeed, this interest has been rare in the use of the Rorschach in Western culture. For examples of research on consistencies in Rorschach responses, see the references by Wittenborn [112] to his own work and that of others, and also Keehn [67]. Application in other cultures of additional techniques sufficiently standardized for comparative study of consistencies has also begun. Leblanc [73], for example, describes an application of the Thematic Apperception Test and of the Sentence Completion Test to groups in Katanga; for the Thematic Apperception Test, she is able to refer to a number of previous applications in various non-Western cultures. Even though the pictures used as test stimuli are varied from one society to another, consistencies of response could be reasonably compared. A number of techniques have been used in a six-culture study directed by Whiting, Lambert and Child, which is not yet published. Of special interest is the use of systematic observation of behavior. Problems in the application of this method and a conceptual analysis which may be useful in obtaining cross-cultural comparability of data have been presented by Lambert [70]. The techniques used in the six-culture study are outlined by Whiting et al. [109] in the guide prepared in advance of the field work.

Up to the present, the best examples of cross-cultural comparison of consistencies are comparisons among complex societies. Angelini [7], for example, has applied the Thematic Apperception Test as used by McClelland et al. [78] to men in a Brazilian university, and also tested Brazilian university women with special pictures of women which resembled those of men in being suggestive of achievement. For a group of 30 men and a group of 40 women, he found extremely high correlations between amount of concern with achievement expressed in an individual's TAT stories and performance on three intellectual tasks (anagrams, coding, and decoding). The correlations are so high as to suggest much greater individual consistency in these dimensions among university students in Brazil than among university students in the United States.

A more extensive comparison of university students in different countries on other aspects of personality is available in the comparative studies of value preference by Morris [83], partly in collaboration with Jones [84]. A description of 13 ways of life drawn from philosophical and religious traditions was translated from English into several other languages and presented to university students with the instruction to rate each according to their personal preference. For three national samples of university students from the United States, India, and China. intercorrelations were calculated and factor analyses were done. In general, the factor patterns were similar for the three national groups, and the major discrepancies seemed to be partly accounted for by an inappropriate translation of one of the ways of life into Chinese. Taking degree of preference for any single way of life as an observed personality characteristic, we have evidence that the organization of such preferences in respect to individual differences is relatively constant for these three groups of widely different cultures. It is not perfectly clear just what interpretation is to be put upon this fact. To what extent is the similarity of consistencies among cultures to be considered a necessary consequence of similarity of meaning structures? To what extent as a similarity in an aspect of personality structure which might have been found to vary despite a constancy of meaning structure? Fascinating problems may be worked out in connection with cross-cultural comparisons of meaning structures. Such work has been begun by Osgood and others [86, pp. 170–176]. In any event, Morris's findings do indicate a very significant consistency that could not have been known for certain in advance. Morris's research cannot be extended to the general population of primitive groups, as the instrument requires a degree of education and intellectual sophistication such as university students possess. The general pattern of his research would be applicable to data obtained through different measuring instruments, however, and could be directed at measurement of other traits.

The consistencies considered here so far concern the way individuals differ from each other in a single group, with the consistencies compared between different groups. Another approach which is also suggested by anthropology is the direct measurement of consistency in cross-cultural variation and the comparison of this with consistency in interindividual variation in any cultural group. This requires treating the culture of the individual group as in some way comparable to the personality of the individual. There is certainly no equation here; the culture of a group is not equivalent to the personality of the typical individual *in toto*. Yet for some aspects of culture, the determinants may lie in personality processes of the typical group member to a sufficient degree so that a genuine contribution to understanding can be obtained. In that event, study of cultural consistency—ordinarily considered relevant only to anthropology—may become directly relevant to the interests of personality research. A study of the culture may be to some degree a study of typical personality, and comparative study of a number of cultures may to the same degree permit transcultural test of hypotheses about personality. An example of such research, which considers cultural consistencies in relation to a theory about personality consistencies, is the cross-cultural study of Whiting and Child [108]. Especially relevant here is a factor analysis of some of their data by Prothro [88]. Considering together ratings provided by Whiting and Child on a number of variables of child training and adult culture, Prothro analyzes the intercorrelations among these variables for a sample of primitive societies. The factor analysis yields several patterns of consistency of great interest; thus discovered as consistencies of cultural variation, they immediately suggest the possibility of similar patterns of consistency to be explored in individual variation.

Overenthusiasm about what is shown by such studies could readily lead to mistaken judgments about the uniformity of personality among the members of a society. The danger is especially great in the case of complex societies, as is pointed out by Inkeles and Levinson [59] in their excellent general analysis of the concept of national character. But it is present also in the case of simpler societies, and Dennis has presented some apt examples. The customary emphasis on cooperation rather than competition among the Hopi, he points out, might well lead to a characterization of the Hopi as relatively lacking in competitive wishes or attitudes. Yet he finds that in certain test situations, Hopi children respond even more competitively than some white American children [36]. In another paper [39], Dennis points out that the characteristics of Bedouin drawings, which might readily be given a hypothetical significance for modal personality, seem explicable by reference to their culturally determined experience with art. Of course, as he points out, the analysis of a single instance such as this yields no definitive conclusion, but it suggests caution in drawing specific inferences from the findings of cross-cultural research.

One way out of some of these conceptual difficulties may be found by taking as data not cultural facts, but actual modal measurements of behavioral characteristics for the members of a group. It is such data, of course, that Dennis supplies in the studies just cited. His other recent work [38] suggests the wealth of data relevant to hypotheses about culture and personality that may be obtained when ingenious methods are devised. He has asked children in several cultural groups questions of this form: What is so-and-so for? Why does a person do so-and-so? Classifying responses into the categories of benevolent, malevolent, hedonistic, and religious, he finds tremendous differences in the frequency distribution of these categories in the various cultural groups studied.

Such data obtained on individuals in different cultural groups are conceivably of value not only as a check on the correspondence between individual behavior and cultural norm, but even as a means for studying consistencies on a transcultural basis. Thus if a standard measuring instrument has been applied to a small sample in a number of cultural communities, the sample in any one community may be too small to justify doing a factor analysis with respect to individual differences within the community. But at the same time, the sample may be large enough to provide a fairly stable estimate of the median or modal position of individuals in the sample on each variable measured. Thus cross-cultural variations, using the median or modal score on each variable within a cultural group as the original datum, could be intercorrelated and subjected to factor analysis. This procedure has apparently not been applied at all as yet, though the data which would permit it to be done may already be available, at least for the Rorschach test.

The special value of the anthropological approach, through its contribution to questions of universality, is most important in connection with the problem of origins of personality characteristics. Here too, the immediate practical interest of the clinician may not seem to be served by such inquiries. If the causal influences on a personality variable are thoroughly understood for our own society, then this is all the practitioner needs to know in dealing with his patient. But such knowledge is all too imperfect. An attempt to check on the presence in other cultures of causal sequences supposedly known in ours may lead to a greatly improved understanding of the causal mechanisms really operating within our own society. For many a student of personality, moreover, the investigation of universality or variation of causal mechanisms in various cultural settings has a great interest of its own which needs no justification by relevance to immediate practical needs.

An example might be provided by the psychoanalytic hypothesis of oral fixation—the hypothesis that certain continuations of oral interest and their indirect consequences may be produced by oral frustration in infancy, such as severe procedures in weaning or weaning at particular times. A study of individual differences in European society which apparently yields some degree of confirmation of the hypothesis is provided by Goldman-Eisler [53]. It reports a significant correlation between certain personality characteristics which psychoanalytic theory might hold to be products of oral fixation (measured in young adults by questionnaires) and age of weaning (as reported retrospectively by the subjects' mothers). Even if, through repeated and varied studies, such findings were widely confirmed for our society, we might not be able to feel that the conditions responsible for fixation were thoroughly understood. Does harsh or early weaning, for example, have to be combined with certain other uniform characteristics—a rather compulsive and exaggerated interest in problems of child rearing, for example—in order to bring about oral fixation? By parallel studies on individual differences in very different communities, we could possibly determine whether the sole causal factors had been properly identified by these studies in our own society.

As for the problem of identifying consistencies, research on the problem of origins may take the culture rather than the individual as a unit. One part of the study by Whiting and Child [108], for example, illustrates the possibility that the causal processes referred to as oral fixation can be confirmed in the study of cultural consistencies. They find that whether societies have oral explanations of sickness (explanations which consider the sickness to result from oral actions) is highly correlated with the severity of weaning. In addition to oral fixation, other hypotheses about the effects of early childhood experience were tested. The general reasoning is this: The customary modes of child training would produce a tendency for adults to have the personality characteristics resulting from such upbringing, and these personality tendencies would then influence the aspects of the adult culture which are least subject to reality testing and most subject to motivational influence. The index of such projective tendencies in adult culture used by Whiting and Child was provided by customary explanations and treatments of illness. Cross-cultural correlations, then, between variables of child training and response to illness permit a test of specific hypotheses about the influence of child training on personality. In its bearing on knowledge of origins of personality, this sort of test is more indirect than interindividual correlations, but the evidence yielded is universal or transcultural. The results of this and a number of later studies, as reviewed by Whiting [107], indicate that this is a very fruitful mode of attack on the study of culture integration and on the transcultural test of hypotheses about the origins of personality. However, for a causal hypothesis to have universal validity with respect to individual differences, it does not necessarily have to be valid for cultural differences as well. Certainly many other processes influence culture integration, in addition to personality processes of a typical individual.

These comments have been expressed in terms of a search for universalities. This orientation is to some extent justified by the fact that many statements about personality are couched as though they referred to mankind in general, although the data are actually drawn only from individuals within our society. Thus a special function of the anthropological approach here might be to test the underlying assumption of universality, and a confirmation of this assumption would justify the particular importance attached to those statements by those who make them. On the other hand, we should not overlook the fact that a failure to confirm the universal validity of the statements might be of equal—though different—interest. In finding that intercorrelations among behavior traits are differently organized in different cultural groups, for example, we will already seem to have excluded a simple biological interpretation of the organization found among us, and in investigation of the several cultural settings we may gain clues to its proper explanation. Similarly, if an apparent causal sequence—discovered in our own society but couched in universal terms—fails to hold true in other cultural settings, then we have learned that our initial statement of the relationship was probably at fault and we may find clues which will permit us to make a revised and better statement. Thus a finding of cultural relativity, whether in the existence or importance of consistencies or in their origins, is quite as positive an outcome as a finding of universality.

Another specific and relevant topic of anthropological origin is ethnopsychology. The term has come to be used for the concepts and hypotheses of a psychological nature which are current in a particular culture. It is parallel to such terms as "ethnobotany" or "ethnozoology."

Relevant here is the fact that the concepts about dimensions of personality which are explicit or implicit in any culture's terms and discourse about people may give a view of what dimensions of personality have been traditionally isolated for recognition. A systematic comparison of the dimensions recognized in various cultural traditions would be of interest and might reveal a basic resemblance or differentiations that are understandable in relation to other aspects of the cultures. For nations of Western European tradition, similarities in ethnopsychology might well be traceable simply to their common history. However, comparison of the ethnopsychology of various more nearly independent traditions for which written documents dealing explicitly with personality differences are available might be of some value. For one example of such a document, see Shryock's edition [98] of an ancient Chinese work on human personality. Of even greater interest—and greater certainty of independence—would be an analysis of psychological conceptions of isolated primitive groups whose conceptions have not originated in any of the major traditions of civilizations. It is doubtful whether data adequate for this purpose have been gathered as a part of general ethnographic work, but special efforts to obtain such data might be extremely rewarding. An illustration of the potentialities is afforded incidentally in a study of ethnophilosophy by Brandt [23]. Investigating the ethical attitudes of the Hopi to clarify the general nature of ethical attitudes and their causal origins, Brandt was led to a brief treatment of Hopi conceptions of personality traits. While fully aware of the uncertainties of translation, he tentatively concludes that some common American trait concepts are quite absent among the Hopi, and vice versa. Obviously, there would be a great interest in understanding the bases for such variation in a number of societies and in knowing what trait concepts (if any) remain approximately constant through all cultural variations.

Social Dimensions Suggesting Personality Dimensions

Another possible relation of personality study to anthropology and sociology is this: The analysis of culture or social structure may call attention to kinds of variation which may be significantly reflected in individual personalities. Some significant behavioral variation among social groups may be the origin of the hypothesis that a corresponding variation will be significant among individuals. This seems to have been an important influence on the definition of personality dimensions in a prescientific era. Such terms as "Latin temperament" seem to illustrate just such a transferral to individual personality of a supposedly important difference between groups. Examples of such an influence or potential influence of anthropology and sociology will be discussed here without any attempt to evaluate their role exactly. In any of these cases, what has been done by the researcher is obviously a joint product of many strands in intellectual history, and in these examples, the strand of anthropology or sociology is important.

One possibility is that comparison of various primitive societies with respect to their general ethos might yield dimensions of variation among cultures which would also be significant for personality variation in a single society. The possibility is illustrated, for example, by Ruth Benedict's book *Patterns of Culture* [20], even though the particular dimensions she selects seem to be based on traditional European conceptions of variation in individual temperament, rather than emerging from consideration of the cultures themselves.

A more directly pertinent example is provided by the Whiting and Child study [108] already mentioned. Seeking for a cultural index of worried preoccupation with one or another basic motivational theme such as orality, sexuality, or aggression, they selected customary reactions to illness. This is a relatively obvious index to choose in studying nonliterate cultures because of the great diversity of therapeutic techniques and explanations of illness and the relative absence of realistic bases for them. But once a cross-cultural comparison has directed attention to this dimension of variation, the less obvious variations along this dimension among individuals in our society may then be noted. Despite the relatively great degree of scientific realism with which we deal with disease, people do still differ in their reactions and in ways which may well form consistencies parallel to those found in the cross-cultural study. In explaining one's own illness by reference to contagion, for instance, there is the opportunity to emphasize either that one probably swallowed the germs, or that one got too close to other people, or that other people maliciously sneezed, and so on. If consistencies in such behavior are found in the future, it is because the much greater variation among cultures first called attention to this aspect of behavior.

A similar instance is provided by studies of supernatural beliefs done by Spiro and D'Andrade [100], by Lambert, Triandis, and Wolf [71], and by Whiting [106]. Variations among supernatural beliefs are much greater among different societies than among individuals within one society. Examination of the more general personality consistencies of which supernatural beliefs may be a part is therefore readily made in cross-cultural study. For example, once cross-cultural evidence has been found that degree of malevolence in the customary conception of the deity is related to the degree to which child training produces anxiety and conflict [71], then the possibility arises that the lesser variations in personal conceptions among members of a single church might have a similar relation to motivational consistencies.

Art style or design preference is another aspect of behavior for which cross-cultural variations are very great, so that exploration of consistencies with other behavioral variables is facilitated. Barry [16] has made such an exploration. For a sample of primitive societies, he rated a number of separate features of art style and found a consistency to which he gave the label "complexity versus simplicity." There is a possible relation here to dimensions of variation in individual preferences for visual designs. Barron [13, 15] has investigated a dimension to which he has applied the same label of "complexity versus simplicity"; and Potanin [87] has investigated a dimension to which the same label might have been applied. So far the intercultural and the interindividual studies have been done independently; whether there is much real similarity in the consistencies investigated in the several studies is not clear. But it is noteworthy that the intercultural study rather leads the way here in analysis of various specific components which might or might not participate in a consistency of complex versus simple. (This is partly because such an analysis was less relevant to the purposes of the interindividual investigators, but perhaps it is also partly because the very great intercultural variation makes an impressive impact on anyone who attends to it.) All three studies provide evidence that the dimension being dealt with is related to motivational aspects of personality. Though this aspect of the research does not indicate whether the several studies are dealing with a variable that is at all similar, it clearly illustrates that comparable kinds of relationship between motivation and artistic preferences can be investigated by either method.

Sometimes what is specifically contributed by cross-cultural investigation is the variable viewed as a cause, rather than the personality consistency itself. This is true of a study which Fischer [43] has recently made, in which he uses Barry's ratings [16] of various specific variables in art style. He extracts for special attention the variable of relative predominance of straight versus curved lines, which seem likely to symbolize masculinity and femininity respectively. He finds a relation between this variable and features of social organization which might lead to a relatively greater security or power of men or of women as against the other sex. For example, curved lines tend to characterize the art of patrilocal societies, in which the men living in a household are blood relatives, while the women are generally unrelated. Straight lines tend to characterize the art of matrilocal societies, in which the opposite is true. Fischer's interpretation is that when either sex has relatively greater solidarity—hence power and security—its members will be free to enjoy in fantasy symbolism of the opposite sex. When a sex group is less secure, its members will tend to seek fantasy symbolism of their own sex as a model or source of reassurance. This interpretation is consistent with his findings, regardless of whether art style is considered to be determined primarily by men or by women. It appears, moreover, to be consistent with some findings on individual differences in sex-symbol preferences as a function of sexual maturity in the United States and Scotland [47, 79], if maturity is thought of as another determinant of security in one's sex role. At least in part, it seems to be consistent with the findings of a comparative individual difference study [60] made in Ghana, using the procedures of the Scottish study. The variable of relative power of one sex as against the other as an influence on expression or liking of sexual symbolism, however, seems to emerge distinctively from the cross-cultural study because variations among societies in this respect are so great. A similar general variable has been made use of by Whiting [106] in cross-cultural study of identification. He postulates that the power position of the father will be one determinant of the child's identification with him. Once one sees a variable clearly as a result of looking at the very great variations among cultures, one is prepared to see it possibly functioning within a narrower but still important range for individual differences in our society.

Another example of a causal variable which may stand out more clearly in cross-cultural research because of the greater variation is the character of the food-getting economy. Barry, Child, and Bacon [18] find consistencies in socialization behavior to be related to a distinction between economies of high food accumulation (in which food is produced seasonally and stored for later consumption, and child training stresses responsibility and obedience) and economies of low food accumulation (in which food is sought from nature each day and cannot be stored, and child training stresses self-reliance and achievement). While this exact economic variation would not be found within a complex society such as ours, rather similar causal variables might be found. Indeed, a very similar one has been identified by Miller and Swanson [81]. Their distinction between entrepreneurial and bureaucratic economic relations seems to have something important in common with the cross-cultural variable in representing parallel pressures toward risk assumption as against rule conformity. Their distinction seems to represent an influence of sociology rather than anthropology, and the simultaneous appearance of somewhat similar developments in personality study under these two influences illustrates a convergence that may be expected even more frequently in the future.

Social class is, of course, another concept in sociology which is relevant to personality study. Auld [9] has reviewed earlier studies on social-class differences in personality-test measurements. These studies simply check on whether class groups do differ, on the average, in any measurement which happens to have been made. Later studies, more relevant here, use the concept of social class as a basis for formulating the kinds of differences that might be expected. In the research on child training and personality recently published by Miller, Swanson, et al. [81, 82], social class has this place as one of the basic concepts used in planning the research.

A sociological and anthropological influence with a historical slant is found in Riesman's suggestion of a dimension of inner-directedness versus other-directedness [91]. This dimension seems to be developed to characterize two general modes of social functioning—a supposed other-directedness of contemporary American society and a supposed inner-directedness of American society of several generations ago. Riesman, in the course of his discussion, really implies a variation among individuals at the present time in the extent to which they approach the one or the other extreme. Sofer [98a, 19] has shown that a questionnaire can be devised which will measure individuals' positions along such a dimension of personality variation. If this dimension should turn out to be significant, underlying a considerable consistency in individual variation, then it would appear to be an example of a dimension whose original definition came out of an essentially sociological or anthropological comparison of social groups. That it may well turn out to be significant, either in itself or as a part of some larger consistency, is suggested by the finding that scores on the Sofer questionnaire are related to persuasibility in response to propagandistic communications [Linton and Graham, 76].

In general, then, to the extent that people of different status within a complex society such as ours seem to have differing values or patterns of social interaction, these differences may suggest significant dimensions of individual personality variation. Such an origin for conceptions of personality dimensions may have special value in that a dimension then carries with it from its origin some tentative hypothesis about causal influences on individual position along it. There is, of course, the danger that dimensional concepts with such an origin will be misused as stereotypes—that basing a dimensional concept on the typical characteristics of a group will lead to the mistaken notion that those characteristics are shared by all members of that group. At least, this is much less likely to occur when such concepts develop in a context of personality research. The assumption, moreover, that personality varies at least somewhat dependably with status group—the assumption is suggested by such phrases as "middle-class morality" or "proletariat ideol-

ogy," which have arisen in contexts remote from personality research—
might then come to be subjected to the test of evidence.

The relation between social and personality dimensions which has
been presented is primarily one of suggestion. Social differences of
obvious importance in everyday life—expressed in concepts which have
been clarified by the work of sociologists and anthropologists—may
suggest similar concepts important for analysis of personality differences
among individuals. Social analysis, that is, may play a constructive role
in bringing about the discovery of important kinds of consistency in
personality, and in a way that carries with it strong suggestions about
where to look for an understanding of the origins of these particular
consistencies. There is, however, another side to this relation which
needs to be mentioned. It is that relevance to social variations may
usefully serve as one criterion for the importance of any dimension
of personality, whether its discovery has come as a result of social
analysis or some quite different means. Thus if a particular personality
test yields 50 different measures, and 3 of them regularly show large
differences among the means of various social groups, those three
should be looked at with special interest. Obviously, this would not be
acceptable as the sole criterion for the importance of a dimension of
personality. But as one among several criteria, it may be a useful guide
and, for limited purposes, it might be the most significant one.

Role and Personality

Among the influences of anthropology and sociology on social psychology, one of the most significant has been the analysis of social
structure into statuses with their accompanying roles. *Status* is a defined
position in a social structure, such as father, daughter, minister, judge,
friend. *Role* is the customary pattern of behavior expected of a person
when he is occupying a particular status. The relevance of this analysis
for personality has already been discussed by various writers, but the
effect on research has not yet been as great in personality study as in
other aspects of social psychology. Much of the personality research
influenced by this analysis is reviewed by Sarbin [95] in a more general
discussion of the implications of the concept of role for social psychology.
It must be said that the role concept is also influenced directly by the
theatrical background of the concept, and "role-playing" is sometimes
applied by psychologists to behavior imitative of an individual rather
than behavior conforming to role expectations in the cultural sense
(a distinction that is in practice not a clear-cut one).

One possible effect of the status and role analysis is on research on
origins of personality consistencies, by providing an appropriate con-

ceptual framework in which to express a number of influences on personality. A number of hypotheses about influences on personality may be seen as having to do with possible generalized effects of conformity to a particular role. Thus if a successful marriage has a stabilizing influence on personality, this would seem to be expressible in part as an influence of behavior at certain times of the day, in performance of the role of husband or wife, upon behavior at other times of the day when one's behavior is not immediately dominated by this role. Of greater theoretical interest, however, since the role of husband or wife is to some extent immediately present even in interaction with other people than the spouse, is the question of the maintenance of certain effects on behavior after the role is terminated. For example, consider the lasting effects on personality of successful marriages which are terminated early by the death of one partner. Though the surviving partner's behavior may be expected to be in part an adjustment to the new situation created by being widowed, still a lasting effect of the modification of behavior involved in performing the role of spouse may be one important influence. Similarly, for the possible influence of occupation on personality. At the time one is functioning in the occupation, the possible influence of a most direct nature is the generalization of behavior on the job to behavior off the job. Possible continuation of effects after one is no longer in the occupation would represent a continuation, after abandoning a role, of behavior appropriate to the role.

The concept of role thus brings out possible similarities in the processes involved in such diverse influences on personality as those of being married and occupying a particular job. Moreover, the concept of role helps call attention to the possibility that there may be no such influence here as is so commonly supposed—that the responses appropriate to a role are performed while functioning in the role and are not generalized to other situations either at the time or later.

Of special importance here is the fact that role terminology can be appropriately applied to the phenomena dealt with in psychoanalytical theory of psychosexual development. The possible lasting effects of fixation at a particular period of psychosexual development may be seen to be a special case of broad generalization and long continuation of role behavior after one has ceased playing that role. Such a view may be useful in setting psychoanalytical theory of psychosexual development in a framework of general psychology and in formulating appropriate research relating to it. An example is to be found in the work of Whiting, Kluckhohn, and Anthony [110] on the function of male initiation ceremonies at puberty. The ceremonies are seen as facilitating a difficult transition in role and therefore as needed most in societies where the pattern of child training is such that the boy's earlier identification with the female role is relatively strong and the transition to adult male role involves an especially radical change.

Implicit in what has already been said about the conception of role is that it calls attention to possible additional consistencies in personality. In this respect, its influence is similar to that of cross-cultural comparisons in suggesting personality variables. One such consistency which is being explored is role-taking aptitude. Though Sarbin and Jones [96], in describing their development of a measure of this variable, do not particularly stress the anthropological and sociological influences on their thought, the measure they use is one which they might well have developed out of those influences alone. The subject is asked to describe how his life would have been different if he had been (1) born into the opposite sex, and (2) born a Russian. Two measures of the fullness or adequacy of the answers are used and found to be related to adequacy of actual role-enacting behavior. Of special interest —as indicating that this role-taking aptitude is a part of some larger personality consistency—is the finding that it has a substantial correlation with Barron's [14] questionnaire measure of "ego strength."

Another consistency suggested by the concept of role is the extent to which a person's being in a situation of role conflict produces a persistent or important state of psychological conflict. This variable may well be related to the role-taking aptitude just considered, but it has thus far not been considered with it as a part of the same study. Getzels and Guba have measured extent of psychological conflict about role conflict in a group of people in approximately the same role-conflict situation—career Air Force officers assigned as instructors in Air University and thus engaged simultaneously in two occupational roles markedly different in many respects. Their questionnaire measure of self-rated concern about various specific elements of this role conflict not only was internally consistent [51], but was related to a number of more general personality measures, including questionnaires described as measuring intolerance of ambiguity [52]. It seems reasonable to conjecture that the conflict measure, while taken with respect to a single major conflict, might be consistent with a general pattern of disturbance by any conflict of role, and that this may be part of a more general consistency of personality. If so, one may see the concept of role as suggesting ways in which general dimensional concepts in personality may be found useful in understanding social phenomena such as those of group conflict.

Other consistencies to which the concept of role may usefully direct attention are those which may result from participation in a particular role. Such consistencies have already been mentioned above in connection with the value of the role concept in studying the origins of consistencies. Of special importance in connection with the problem of the breadth and importance of consistencies, however, is the fact that the concept of role directs attention to the possibility that many consistencies may be much narrower and perhaps less important than they at first sight appear.

Certain consistencies in an individual's observed behavior, that is, may turn out to be consistencies which are dictated by conformity to the requirements of a role and are not displayed when the person is not acting in that role. Awareness of this may lead to the discovery that certain consistencies are not as broad as at first supposed, that the behavior observations on which they were based were all made on persons who were at the moment playing a particular role and that the consistencies found do not carry over into their behavior in other roles. This may even apply to personality data which consist of a person's responses to a questionnaire or other individual diagnostic instrument. Here the tester is likely to hope that the individual subject as a total person is responding in a sharply focused manner to the standardized stimuli supplied by the questionnaire. But in fact, the person may be responding also to stimuli much more diffuse—including the social situation in which he is being tested—and be responding essentially in his capacity as occupant of a particular status. Of course, in the conspicuous case of a person whose status is that of an applicant, this possibility does not go unnoticed, and questionnaires calling for self-evaluations are thus not ordinarily regarded as useful instruments for measuring differences among applicants for a position. But the same thing may be true in more subtle ways. To what extent, for example, are the personality questionnaires filled out by college students as research subjects, filled out somewhat distinctively in their roles as students? To what extent would their responses be different—even the intercorrelations among their responses altered—if the data were collected in a social situation where they occupied a very different status, such as that of church member or lover?

In more general form, this question applies not only to specific roles occupied by a person within his society, but also to his entire role as a member of his society. This has an important bearing on the question of national character or basic personality type. Where members of different cultural groups are found to differ in personality characteristics, to what extent does this indicate genuine differences in personality as it has been defined here? To what extent does it represent differences in behavior more externally determined by response to the social surroundings in which people are functioning? Here, at least for the future, is a special relevance of studies of personality during acculturation. When knowledge of national character has advanced far enough so that it is possible to assess the extent to which an individual's personality corresponds to a national-character type appropriate to his background, it will be important to study the modification of this measure in adults undergoing acculturation. When an adult is suddenly transported from one cultural setting to another, do the national-character aspects of his functioning disappear rather abruptly because of removal from the setting which would evoke them? Or are they retained with great persistence in a new social setting? An experiment by French and Zajonc [48] illustrates the possibility of applying psychological techniques to this question. They studied students from India in an American university, experimentally varying the extent to which situational cues tended to make their role as Indian students or their role as American students more salient, and observed effects on their deference toward a professor. The effects were in the direction of shift in behavior appropriate to intended role salience, but not of overwhelming size or consistency. If deference toward professors in Indian culture may be thought of as part of some more general trait of Indian national character—this was not the intent of French and Zajonc—then these results might lead one to doubt whether this whole pattern of consistency is readily altered with a shift in situation.

REFERENCES

1. Allport, G. W. *Personality.* New York: Holt, Rinehart, & Winston, 1937.
2. Allport, G. W. The use of personal documents in psychological science. New York: Social Science Research Council, 1942. (Social Science Research Council Bulletin No. 49.)
3. Allport, G. W. The trend in motivational theory. *Amer. J. Orthopsychiat.,* 1953, **23,** 107–119.
4. Allport, G. W., & Odbert, H. S. Trait-names: a psycho-lexical study. *Psychol. Monogr.,* 1936, **47,** No. 1.
5. Alper, Thelma G. Predicting the direction of selective recall: its relation to ego strength and N achievement. *J. abnorm. soc. Psychol.,* 1957, **55,** 149–165.
6. Anastasi, Anne. *Differential psychology.* (3rd ed.) New York: Macmillan, 1958.
7. Angelini, A. L. Um novo método para avaliar a motivação humana: estudo do motivo de realização. São Paulo: Univer. de São Paulo, 1955. (Univ. de São Paulo, Faculdade de Filosofia, Ciências e Letras, Boletim No. 207.)
8. Atkinson, J. W. (Ed.). *Motives in fantasy, action, and society.* Princeton, N.J.: Van Nostrand, 1958.
9. Auld, F., Jr. Influence of social class on personality test responses. *Psychol. Bull.,* 1952, **49,** 318–332.
10. Baldwin, A. L. Personal structure analysis: a statistical method for

investigating the single personality. *J. abnorm. soc. Psychol.*, 1942, **37**, 163–183.

11. Baldwin, A. L., Kalhorn, Joan, & Breese, Fay Huffman. Patterns of parent behavior. *Psychol. Monogr.*, 1945, **58**, (3).

12. Baldwin, A. L., Kalhorn, Joan, & Breese, Fay Huffman. The appraisal of parent behavior. *Psychol. Monogr.*, 1949, **63**, (4).

13. Barron, F. Personality style and perceptual choice. *J. Pers.*, 1952, **20**, 385–401.

14. Barron, F. An ego-strength scale which predicts response to psycho-therapy. *J. consult. Psychol.*, 1953, **17**, 327–333.

15. Barron, F. Complexity-simplicity as a personality dimension. *J. abnorm. soc. Psychol.*, 1953, **48**, 163–172.

16. Barry, III, H. Relationships between child training and the pictorial arts. *J. abnorm. soc. Psychol.*, 1957, **54**, 380–383.

17. Barry, III, H., Bacon, Margaret K., & Child, I. L. A cross-cultural survey of some sex differences in socialization. *J. abnorm. soc. Psychol.*, 1957, **55**, 327–332.

18. Barry, III, H., Child, I. L., & Bacon, Margaret K. Relation of child training to subsistence economy. *Amer. Anthrop.*, 1959, **61**, 51–63.

19. Bell, Elaine G. Inner-directed and other-directed attitudes. Unpublished doctor's dissertation, Yale Univer., 1955.

20. Benedict, Ruth. *Patterns of culture.* Boston: Houghton Mifflin, 1934.

21. Bieri, J., Bradburn, W. M., & Galinsky, M. D. Sex differences in perceptual behavior. *J. Pers.*, 1958, **26**, 1–12.

22. Blum, G. S. *Psychoanalytic theories of personality.* New York: McGraw-Hill, 1953.

23. Brandt, R. B. *Hopi ethics.* Chicago: Univer. Chicago Press, 1954.

24. Broverman, D. M., & Lazarus, R. S. Individual differences in task performance under conditions of cognitive interference. *J. Pers.*, 1958, **26**, 94–105.

25. Cattell, R. B. The chief invariant psychological and psychophysiological functional unities found by P-technique. *J. clin. Psychol.*, 1955, **7**, 319–343.

26. Cattell, R. B. *Personality and motivation structure and measurement.* Yonkers-on-Hudson, N.Y.: World, 1957.

27. Cattell, R. B. Anxiety, extraversion, and other second-order personality factors in children. *J. Pers.*, 1959, **27**, 464–476.

28. Cattell, R. B. The multiple abstract variance analysis equations and solutions: for nature-nurture research on continuous variables. *Psychol. Rev.*, 1960, **67**, 353–372.

29. Champney, H. The variables of parent behavior. *J. abnorm. soc. Psychol.*, 1941, **36**, 525–542.

30. Child, I. L. Socialization. In G. Lindzey (Ed.), *Handbook of social psychology.* Vol. 2. Cambridge, Mass.: Addison-Wesley, 1954. Pp. 655–692.

31. Child, I. L., Frank, Kitty F., & Storm, T. Self-ratings and TAT: their

relations to each other and to childhood background. *J. Pers.*, 1956, **25**, 96–114.

32. Cronbach, L. J., & Meehl, P. E. Construct validity in psychological tests. *Psychol. Bull.*, 1955, **52**, 281–302.

33. Davids, A., & Pildner, Jr., H. Comparison of direct and projective methods of personality assessment under different conditions of motivation. *Psychol. Monogr.*, 1958, **72**, (11).

34. de Charms, R., Morrison, H. W., Reitman, W., & McClelland, D. C. Behavioral correlates of directly and indirectly measured achievement motivation. In D. C. McClelland (Ed.), *Studies in motivation.* New York: Appleton-Century-Crofts, 1955. Pp. 414–423.

35. Dennis, W. Predicting scientific productivity in later maturity from records of earlier decades. *J. Geront.*, 1954, **9**, 465–467.

36. Dennis, W. Are Hopi children noncompetitive? *J. abnorm. soc. Psychol.*, 1955, **50**, 99–100.

37. Dennis, D. Age and productivity among scientists. *Science*, 1956, **123**, 724–725.

38. Dennis, W. Arab and United States children: some psychological comparisons. *Trans. N.Y. Acad. Sci.*, 1960, **22**, (Ser. II), 589–605.

39. Dennis, W. The human figure drawings of Bedouins. *J. soc. Psychol.*, 1960, **52**, 209–219.

40. Dennis, W. The long-term constancy of behavior: sentence length. *J. Geront.*, 1960, **15**, 195–196.

41. Diamond, S. *Personality and temperament.* New York: Harper, 1957.

42. Eysenck, H. J. *The structure of human personality.* London: Methuen, 1953.

43. Fischer, J. L. Art styles as cultural cognitive maps. *Amer. Anthrop.* 1961, **63**, 79–93.

44. Fitzgerald, B. J. Some relationships among projective test, interview, and sociometric measures of dependent behavior. *J. abnorm. soc. Psychol.*, 1958, **56**, 199–203.

45. Fleishman, E. A. Abilities at different stages of practice in rotary pursuit performance. *J. exp. Psychol.*, 1960, **60**, 162–171.

46. Forster, Nora C., Vinacke, W. E., & Digman, J. M. Flexibility and rigidity in a variety of problem situations. *J. abnorm. soc. Psychol.*, 1955, **50**, 211–216.

47. Franck, Kate. Preference for sex symbols and their personality correlates. *Genet. Psychol. Monogr.*, 1946, **33**, 73–123.

48. French, J. R. P., & Zajonc, R. B. An experimental study of cross-cultural norm conflict. *J. abnorm. soc. Psychol.*, 1957, **54**, 218–224.

49. French, J. W. *The description of personality measurements in terms of rotated factors.* Princeton, N.J.: Educational Testing Service, 1953.

50. Gardner, R. W., Holzman, P. S., Klein, G. S., Linton, Harriet B., & Spence, D. P. Cognitive control: a study of individual consistencies in cognitive behavior. *Psychol. Issues*, 1959, **1**, No. 4.

51. Getzels, J. W., & Guba, E. G. Role, role conflict, and effectiveness: an empirical study. *Amer. sociol. Rev.*, 1954, **19**, 164–175.

52. Getzels, J. W., & Guba, E. G. Role conflict and personality. *J. Pers.,* 1955, **24,** 74–85.
53. Goldman-Eisler, Frieda. Breastfeeding and character formation. In C. Kluckhohn, H. A. Murray, & D. M. Schneider (Eds.), *Personality in nature, society, and culture.* New York: Knopf, 1954. Pp. 146–184. (Reprinted from *J. Pers.,* 1948, **17,** 83–103; 1950, **19,** 189–196; *J. ment. Sci.,* 1951, **97,** 765–782.)
54. Gough, H. G. The construction of a personality scale to predict scholastic achievement. *J. appl. Psychol.,* 1953, **37,** 361–366.
55. Guilford, J. P. *Personality.* New York: McGraw-Hill, 1959.
56. Hartshorne, H., May, M. A., & Shuttleworth, F. K. (for Vol. III) *Studies in the nature of character.* New York: Macmillan, 1928–1930. 3 vols. Vol. I, *Studies in deceit,* 1928; Vol. II, *Studies in service and self-control,* 1929; Vol. III, *Studies in the organization of character,* 1930.
57. Henry, J., & Spiro, M. E. Psychological techniques: projective tests in field work. In A. L. Kroeber (Ed.), *Anthropology today.* Chicago: Univer. Chicago Press, 1953. Pp. 417–429.
58. Humphreys, L. G. Characteristics of type concepts with special reference to Sheldon's typology. *Psychol. Bull.,* 1957, **54,** 218–228.
59. Inkeles, A., & Levinson, D. J. National character. In G. Lindzey (Ed.), *Handbook of social psychology.* Vol. 2. Cambridge, Mass.: Addison-Wesley, 1954. Pp. 977–1020.
60. Jahoda, G. Sex differences in preferences for shapes: a cross-cultural replication. *Brit. J. Psychol.,* 1956, **47,** 126–132.
61. Jung, C. G. *Psychological types.* New York: Harcourt, Brace, 1923.
62. Kagan, J. The measurement of overt aggression from fantasy. *J. abnorm. soc. Psychol.,* 1956, **52,** 390–393.
63. Kagan, J., & Moss, H. A. Stability and validity of achievement fantasy. *J. abnorm. soc. Psychol.,* 1959, **58,** 357–364.
64. Kaplan, B. A study of Rorschach responses in four cultures. *Papers Peabody Mus. Amer. Arch. & Ethnol., Harvard Univer.,* 1954, **42,** No. 2.
65. Kaplan, B. (Ed.). *Primary records in culture and personality.* Vol. I. Madison, Wis.: Microcard Foundation, 1956. See also *Psychol. Abstr.,* 1957, **31.** (Abstract 7849.)
66. Kaplan, B. (ed.). *Primary records in culture and personality.* Vol. II. Madison, Wisc.: Microcard Foundation, 1957. See also *Psychol. Abstr.,* 1959, **33.** (Abstract 3622.)
67. Keehn, J. D. Rorschach validation. III: An examination of the role of colour as a determinant in the Rorschach test. *J. ment. Sci.,* 1953, **99,** 410–438.
68. Keehn, J. D. A factorial study of tests of color-form attitudes. *J. Pers.,* 1955, **23,** 295–307.
69. Kelly, E. L. Consistency of the adult personality. *Amer. Psychologist,* 1955, **10,** 659–681.
70. Lambert, W. W. Interpersonal behavior. In P. H. Mussen, *Handbook*

of research methods in child development. New York: Wiley, 1960. Pp. 854–917.

71. Lambert, W. W., Triandis, Leigh M., & Wolf, Margery. Some correlates of beliefs in the malevolence and benevolence of supernatural beings: a cross-societal study. *J. abnorm. soc. Psychol.*, 1959, **58**, 162–169.

72. Lazarus, R. S., Barker, R. W., Broverman, D. M., & Mayer, J. Personality and psychological stress. *J. Pers.*, 1957, **25**, 559–577.

73. Leblanc, M. *Personnalité de la femme Katangaise: contribution à l'étude de son acculturation.* Louvain: Publications Universitaires, 1960.

74. Lesser, G. S. The relationship between overt and fantasy aggression as a function of maternal response to aggression. *J. abnorm. soc. Psychol.*, 1957, **55**, 218–221.

75. Lesser, G. S. Conflict analysis of fantasy aggression. *J. Pers.*, 1958, **26**, 29–41.

76. Linton, Harriet, & Graham, Elaine. Personality correlates of persuasibility. In I. L. Janis, et al., *Personality and persuasibility.* New Haven, Conn.: Yale Univer. Press, 1959. Pp. 69–101.

77. McClelland, D. C. Methods of measuring human motivation. In J. W. Atkinson (Ed.), *Motives in fantasy, action, and society.* Princeton, N.J.: Van Nostrand, 1958. Pp. 7–42.

78. McClelland, D. C., Atkinson, J. W., Clark, R. A., & Lowell, E. L. *The achievement motive.* New York: Appleton-Century-Crofts, 1953.

79. McElroy, W. A. A sex difference in preferences for shapes. *Brit. J. Psychol.*, 1954, **45**, 209–216.

80. Mandler, G., & Sarason, S. B. A study of anxiety and learning. *J. abnorm. soc. Psychol.*, 1952, **47**, 166–173.

81. Miller, D. R., & Swanson, G. E. *The changing American parent.* New York: Wiley, 1958.

82. Miller, D. R., & Swanson, G. E., with W. Allinsmith, E. B. McNeil, Beverly B. Allinsmith, J. Aronfreed, Betty J. Beardslee, and L. M. Lansky. *Inner conflict and defense.* New York: Holt, Rinehart & Winston, 1960.

83. Morris, C. *Varieties of human value.* Chicago: Univer. Chicago Press, 1956.

84. Morris, C., & Jones, L. V. Value scales and dimensions. *J. abnorm. soc. Psychol.*, 1955, **51**, 523–535.

85. Murray, H. A., et al. *Explorations in personality.* New York: Oxford, 1938.

86. Osgood, C. E., Suci, G. J., & Tannenbaum, P. H. *The measurement of meaning.* Urbana, Ill.; Univer. Ill. Press, 1957.

87. Potanin, Natalia. Perceptual preferences as a function of personality variables under normal and stressful conditions. *J. abnorm. soc. Psychol.*, 1959, **59**, 108–113.

88. Prothro, E. T. Patterns of permissiveness among preliterate people. *J. abnorm. soc. Psychol.*, 1960, **61**, 151–154.

89. Raphelson, A. C. The relationships among imaginative, direct verbal,

and physiological measures of anxiety in an achievement situation. *J. abnorm. soc. Psychol.,* 1957, **54**, 13–18.

90. Reitman, W. R. Motivational induction and the behavioral correlates of the achievement and affiliation motives. *J. abnorm. soc. Psychol.,* 1960, **60**, 8–13.

91. Riesman, D. *The lonely crowd.* New Haven, Conn.: Yale Univer. Press, 1950.

92. Rotter, J. B. *Social learning and clinical psychology.* Englewood Cliffs, N.J.: Prentice-Hall, 1954.

93. Sanford, R. N., Adkins, Margaret M., Miller, R. B., & Cobb, Elizabeth A. Physique, personality and scholarship. *Monogr. Soc. Res. Child Developm.,* 1943, **8**, No. 1.

94. Sarason, S. B., Davidson, K. S., Lighthall, F. F., Waite, R. R., & Ruebush, B. K. *Anxiety in elementary school children.* New York: Wiley, 1960.

95. Sarbin, T. R. Role theory. In G. Lindzey (Ed.), *Handbook of social psychology.* Vol 1. Cambridge, Mass.: Addison-Wesley, 1954. Pp. 223–258.

96. Sarbin, T. R., & Jones, D. S. An experimental analysis of role behavior. *J. abnorm. soc. Psychol.,* 1955, **51**, 236–241.

97. Sears, R. R. Survey of objective studies of psychoanalytic concepts. New York: Social Science Research Council, 1943. (Social Science Research Council Bulletin No. 51.)

98. Shryock, J. K. *The study of human abilities: the Jen wu chih of Liu Shao.* (American Oriental Series, Vol. 11.) New Haven, Conn.: American Oriental Society, 1937.

98a. Sofer, Elaine G. Inner-direction, other-direction, and autonomy: a study of college students. In S. M. Lipset & L. Lowenthal (eds.), *Culture and social character: the work of David Riesman reviewed.* Glencoe, Ill.: Free Press, 1961. Pp. 316–348.

99. Spence, K. W. *Behavior theory and conditioning.* New Haven, Conn.: Yale Univer. Press, 1956.

100. Spiro, M. E., & D'Andrade, R. G. A cross-cultural study of some supernatural beliefs. *Amer. Anthrop.,* 1958, **60**, 456–466.

101. Taylor, Janet A. Drive theory and manifest anxiety. *Psychol. Bull.,* 1956, **53**, 303–320.

102. Thurstone, L. L. *A factorial study of perception.* Chicago: Univer. Chicago Press, 1944. (Psychometric Monograph No. 4.)

103. Wallach, M. A., & Gahm, Ruthellen C. Personality functions of graphic constriction and expansiveness. *J. Pers.,* 1960, **28**, 73–88.

104. Wallach, M. A., Green, L. R., Lipsitt, P. D., & Minehart, Jean B. Contradiction between overt and projective personality indicators as a function of defensiveness. *Psychol. Monogr.,* 1962, **76**, (1).

105. Waterhouse, I. K., & Child, I. L. Frustration and the quality of performance: III. An experimental study. *J. Pers.,* 1953, **21**, 298–311.

106. Whiting, J. W. M. Sorcery, sin, and the superego: a cross-cultural study of some mechanisms of social control. In M. R. Jones (Ed.),

Nebraska Symposium on Motivation. Vol. 7. Lincoln, Nebr.: Univer. of Nebr. Press, 1959. Pp. 174–195.

107. Whiting, J. W. M. Socialization process and personality: personality as a mediator in the patterning of culture. In F. L. K. Hsu (Ed.), *Psychological anthropology.* Homewood, Ill.: Dorsey Press, 1961. Pp. 355–380.

108. Whiting, J. W. M., & Child, I. L. *Child training and personality: a cross-cultural study.* New Haven, Conn.: Yale Univer. Press, 1953.

109. Whiting, J. W. M., et al. *Field guide for a study of socialization in five societies.* Cambridge, Mass.: Harvard Univer., Laboratory of Human Development, 1954.

110. Whiting, J. W. M., Kluckhohn, R., & Anthony, A. S. The function of male initiation ceremonies at puberty. In Eleanor E. Maccoby, T. Newcomb, & E. Hartley (Eds.), *Readings in social psychology.* New York: Holt, Rinehart & Winston, 1958. Pp. 359–370.

111. Williams, J. E. Mode of failure, interference tendencies, and achievement imagery. *J. abnorm. soc. Psychol.,* 1955, **51,** 573–580.

112. Wittenborn, J. R. Some comments on confounded correlations among Rorschach scores. *J. consult. Psychol.,* 1959, **23,** 75–77.

113. Wolff, W. M. Certainty: generality and relation to manifest anxiety. *J. abnorm. soc. Psychol.,* 1955, **50,** 59–64.

THE STUDY OF SOCIAL RELATIONSHIPS: SITUATION, IDENTITY, AND SOCIAL INTERACTION[1]

DANIEL R. MILLER

*Department of Psychology
University of Michigan*

Introduction 641
  Intrapersonal and interpersonal viewpoints . . . 641
  Primary components of interpersonal systems 642
  The phrasing of problems 645
Psychological Analysis of the Situation 646
  The subject's perception of the total situation 647
  Classifying specific features of situations 648
  Need-oriented conceptions of the situation 649
  Research on behavior settings 650
  Research on atmospheres and climates 652
Analysis of the Situation in Terms of the Properties of Groups 653
  Objective characteristics of groups 653
  Some basic principles pertaining to social structure 655
  Reference groups 662
Analysis of the Situation: Relevance of Social Structure and Personality . . 667
Identity 670
  Frequently mentioned characteristics of self 670
Types of Identity and Their Structures 673
  Public identity and self-identity 673
  Structure of identity 674
  Dimensions and traits 676
  Values and moral standards 677
The Appraisal of Identity 679
  Self-appraisal: actual, potential, and ideal identities 679

[1] The manuscript benefited greatly from critical readings of the original draft by D. F. Aberle, J. R. P. French, Jr., and H. L. Wilensky. Many valuable contributions to the section on identity were made by J. R. P. French, Jr., and the members of a seminar with which he and I were associated.

Self-realization 680
Public esteem and self-esteem 681
Dynamics of Esteem 683
    Set and discrepancy 683
    Variables related to fluctuations in esteem 684
    Receptiveness to information bearing on self-esteem 687
Methods of Investigating Self-identity 688
    Objective self-description 688
    The semantic differential 691
    The repertory test 691
    Relatively unstructed techniques 692
Identity and Society: Some Over-all Impressions 692
    The masculine subidentity: an illustration 692
    Limits of the concepts of public and self-identity 694
    Identity and the relations between social structure and personality . . . 694
    Public identities as sources of situational pressure 695
    Identity as a product of striving for consistency . . . 696
The Study of Social Interaction 698
Bases of Social Relationships 699
    Interpersonal communication 699
    Background, experience, and skill 699
    Attitudes, interests, values 700
    Roles and subidentities 701
    Mechanisms of defense 702
Classification of Needs 703
    Murray's system 703
    Other systems 704
Classification of Action 705
    Problem solving in small groups 705
    Action 706
    Combinations of action and value 707
    Action modes 707
    Systems designed to classify special kinds of action 708
Patterns of Interaction 709
    Matching of the individual characteristics of participants 709
    Characteristics of interpersonal systems 711
Methods of Studying Social Interaction 713
    Units of behavior 713
    Sources of data 715
Systems for Classifying Interaction: Some Over-all Impressions 717
    Common denominators among the systems for classifying needs 717
    A provisional system for classifying needs 718
    Some components of a provisional interpersonal system 720

Concluding Comments on the Study of Social Relationships 723

References. 727

INTRODUCTION

The social relationship is a new and very popular topic—one of the most mentioned subjects in journals of personality, social psychology, sociology, and psychiatry, and so new that it is more easily identified by illustration than by definition. The disagreement even about the term "relationship" is not surprising in view of investigators' disparate backgrounds. The field represents a coalescence of theories in three disciplines—on self and social communication in sociology, on identity and interpersonal relationships in psychoanalysis, on motivation, perception and small groups in psychology. Even within a discipline, theoretical statements are often hard to compare because they reflect the viewpoints of particular schools. This chapter attempts to summarize and evaluate different positions, to indicate points of agreement and disagreement, to introduce infrequently discussed but pertinent topics, and to use some current concepts and principles in the formulation of testable hypotheses.

Intrapersonal and Interpersonal Viewpoints

Psychologists have traditionally limited themselves to the individual, engaging in a quest for "genetypic" traits which provide the basis for predicting the subject's behavior with many kinds of people in many situations. For example, the predisposition to anxiety has been considered a general trait. Scores on anxiety tests have been used to predict the capacities for achievement in school, for getting along socially, and for controlling physical movements. This emphasis on internal disposition distinguishes psychological principles from the interpersonal conceptions of other disciplines, but it is being changed by the increasing interest in social interaction. Although there are similarities in the interests and methods of investigators with these two viewpoints, there are important differences between their objects of study and their methods.

Susanne Langer has observed that "the way a question is asked limits and disposes the ways in which any answer to it—right or wrong— may be given" [118, p. 1]. Some of the most fundamental differences between intrapersonal and interpersonal conceptions originate in the questions asked. In a study of friendship, for example, the investigator who prefers intrapersonal concepts studies traits of the subject that may affect his capacity to make friends—his tolerance of frustration, his passivity, his sensitivity to another's feelings, and his hostility; he anticipates that the more the subject's traits approximate an ideal pattern— tolerance, low passivity, high sensitivity, low hostility—the more likely he is to make friends easily. Sociometric measurement often indicates significant association between such variables and popularity. Interpersonal phrasing also requires information about individual dispositions, but the information is used to throw light on the relationships between certain types of people in particular types of situations. The question thus shifts from "How will a person with these traits be accepted by his peers?" to "How well will this particular combination of people get along?" The investigator studies a particular friendship, not one person's adjustments to friends in general; the compatibility of a particular couple, not one man's promise of realizing a successful marriage; the ways in which a son and father behave toward one another, not the boy's general adjustment.

What is gained from shifting attention from individual traits to interactions among people? Students of interaction would probably claim that it is necessary for understanding much of the behavior that interests the psychologist. Murray [150] thinks that the representation of the great bulk of human reactions requires the analysis of verbal and physical reactions of two interacting people. While disagreeing with Sullivan's effort to restrict psychology to interpersonal relationships, Murray states, "I use dyadic interactions as a test of every formulation or theoretical system I find in the literature."

This does not require redefinitions of all issues of personality in interpersonal language; many problems are best phrased with reference to one man's psyche. It seems safe to assume, however, that the fruitfulness of many principles will ultimately depend on their contribution to the understanding of human relationships and that many problems are best phrased in interpersonal terms. Some specific advantages in the study of interaction —the phrasing of significant new problems, the definition of relations between concepts now considered parts of different systems, and the probable improvement in predictions, for example—will emerge in the summary of empirical work presented here.

It is first necessary to define two terms which are given differing meaning by various theorists, "interaction" and "relationship." As used here interaction is "the reciprocal influence of individuals upon one another's actions when in one another's immediate physical presence" [75, p. 15]. Relationship is a pattern of specific, recurrent interactions performed in the service of individual or group goals.

Primary Components of Interpersonal Systems

In the analysis of an interpersonal system, problems may be grouped into three areas of discourse: the situation, the identities of participants, and the pattern of interaction.

1. The situation. Too often psychologists pay attention to the situation in which events take place solely because it constitutes an annoying source of variance which must be controlled if the investigator is to have any confidence in his interpretation of the experimental results. According to Peak [160] investigators are often insensitive to the required situational controls and negligent in describing the experimental situation. As a rule, psychologists only control a few features of the situation, such as instructions and time limits. Peak feels that the relative indifference to the significance of the situation derives from the implicit assumption that the processes being studied are "independent of most variables and therefore relatively static and stable, an assumption which is clearly false for such processes as attitudes, needs, adjustment mechanisms, interactions and other group phenomena" [160, p. 247]. She also observes that few studies fulfill one of the basic requirements of objective measurement—a statement about the conditions of observation, including a complete description of the total situation.

The literature abounds with research on individual variation where the situation is held constant; increasingly, there are studies on the effects of different situations where individual differences are held constant. Few studies have involved interrelations between variations in behavior and different situations. Until recently psychologists have been indifferent to the problem of defining categories for classifying different parts of a situation and different kinds of situations. Murphy [148] notes that no book has been written in English on the systematic study of environments. Presumably he refers to psychological publications, for much sociological literature can be viewed as an effort to describe social environments.

In contrast, most sociologists feel that individual dispositions vary greatly with the situation. In fact, many [31, 62] define dispositions in terms of situationally defined roles, rejecting as reifications the postulated internal tendencies which are presumed to be independent of situations. To point up these conflicting emphases, Cottrell [48] asked a class to rate the personalities of children described in two case studies. One child was uncooperative at home, where he sulked and bullied younger children; the second was a daydreamer in class, timid, and bullied by his schoolmates. Cottrell's students rated the first boy high and the second boy low on the traits of aggressiveness, hostility, and stubbornness. The two studies referred to the same child. It is not surprising that sociologists and anthropologists, primarily interested in explaining regularities in the social behavior of groups, have devoted considerable thought to the classification of situations and their components. Some psychotherapists [2, 49, 193] find that these classifications clarify some of the discrepant reactions of patients in different situations.

A few psychologists have concerned themselves with the nature of situations—theorists who specialize in the person's perceptions of his physical and social environment. Brunswik [34, 35] advocates sampling situations as a required coordinate to sampling persons. Lewin [129] proposes a system of categories to analyze situations, and Barker and his associates [11, 12] have developed criteria for identifying specific "behavior settings."

2. Self and other as perceived objects. Social psychologists [48] typically picture each person in an interaction as experiencing a relation between two selves, his and another's. Hallowell [83] notes that the participants' conceptions of themselves define their degree of personal adjustment in the linguistic and cultural terms of their society. The actions of both are scrutinized by both in the light of the values and goals of particular groups. An individual is inclined to see himself and the other person as he thinks he is seen by people whose esteem he values. When the behavior of either participant stands out—exceeding or falling below some group norm—the group may evaluate not only his action, but also his self. If the group is important to him, he accepts their evaluation. To protect his self-esteem the average person controls his behavior so that he is acceptable to different groups. Appraisal of oneself and of the other person is thus phrased in such terms as "can" and "cannot," "will" and "will not," "should" and "should not" [171, p. 80].

Psychotherapists are interested in self-esteem because it illuminates conditions which evoke certain perceptual distortions—phenomena like guilt and shame, and pathologies like obsessive-compulsive neurosis and depression. Some psychologists [133], too, view social behavior in the context of an organized perceptual field in which the points of reference are selves (subjects) and others (objects). Psychological research has used the concept of self to clarify many aspects of social behavior, such as motives to conform to the group's standards, levels of self-esteem, and conditions under which defense mechanisms are employed.

3. Patterns of interaction. The sociologist, the psychotherapist, and the perceptual theorist are also interested in another major area, the patterns of interaction between people. Representative of a commonly held sociological point of view is Parsons's [158] conception of relationships as irreducible social systems involving interactions of personalities. Among the psychotherapists Freud [68] comments on the difficulties of differentiating between individual and group psychology; Bion observes that "no individual, however isolated in time and space, can be regarded as outside a group or lacking in active manifestations of group psychology" [20, p. 224], and Sullivan [204] explains behavior in terms of "me-you patterns." The interest of psychotherapists in social phenomena has undoubtedly been stimulated not only by concern with the social context of behavior, but also by the mutuality of feelings in the relationship between therapist and patient in treatment. Far from being a dispassionate observer, the therapist reacts emotionally as well as cognitively to the emotions and cognitions of his patient.

Psychologists who specialize in perception describe interaction in terms similar to those used by sociologists. Heider [87] states that interpersonal events are represented psychologically in each participant: each refers his action to the other and the other's action to himself. Similarly, Scheerer [181] observes that each person perceives psychological facts as shared by both. The type of interaction depends on the similarity of the context for both participants and on the awareness by each of their mutual perceptions and attitudes.

The Phrasing of Problems

The nature of the situation, the mutual perception and evaluation of identity, the pattern of interaction between participants—these are the general areas into which various theories and studies of interpersonal relations will be divided. The examination of each area inevitably involves a number of generic positions which usually distinguish the formulation of interpersonal problems from that typically found in studies of individual dispositions.

First, most investigators stress the individual's perceptual organization of his world. They assume that the ways in which he discriminates, classifies, and conceives various objects, situations, and relationships provide the keys to much of his social behavior. As Ruesch and Bateson put it, "Man lives by those propositions whose validity is a function of his belief in them" [177, p. 212]. They cite the example of the paranoiac, who distrusts every man, acts on the distrust, and finds that people tend to be untrustworthy. Hallowell [83] states that in some societies witchcraft is as real—as pertinent to social behavior—as are the moral values of the "good life."

Second, an interest in the theory of systems characterizes much of the thinking about social interaction; it has been motivated partly by the shift from complex intrapersonal systems to even more complicated interpersonal systems entailing the interacting perceptions of participants. The present vogue of systems theory [176] is reflected by the marked similarities in Lewin's "lifespace" [128, 129], Sullivan's interpersonal situation [204], Zelditch's formalization [223] of Parson's system of action, Spiegel's conceptualizational process [192], and Ruesch and Bateson's social interaction [177]. These views postulate a dynamic, self-regulating system in equilibrium, which varies with respect to such properties as flexibility of adjustment in the face of external pressure and degrees of integration and differentiation. Internal structure is typically described by such concepts as position, force, region, boundary, distance, direction, value, and interchange process [85, 129, 161, 177]; all parts of the internal structure are viewed as standing in temporal and spatial relations to each other, the space being conceived in psychological and social terms. Social interaction is occasionally pictured by a spatial diagram which contains two circles (the participants) connected by arrows going in opposite directions (action and reaction) and surrounded by an ellipse (the boundary) that defines the limits of the social situation. Sometimes the two circles are elaborated to indicate the psychological structures of participants [203, 223].

Third, investigators are much intrigued by the phrasing of relations between social and psychological structures. Many psychological processes are inseparable from their social origins and content; thus it is hard to account for the perpetuation of a relationship without taking into account such social elements as values, roles, and the organization of groups. Understanding what keeps a husband and wife bound to each other, for example, requires information about their conception of obligations to each other and their children and about the important "reference groups" for each.

The chapter will consider theoretical positions and empirical findings pertaining to situation, definition of self, and social interaction. An attempt will be made to describe methods of measuring certain proposed variables and to review some unresolved questions. A concluding section summarizes the primary reasons for studying interpersonal relationships and lists a number of the pressing theoretical and methodological problems.

PSYCHOLOGICAL ANALYSIS OF THE SITUATION

A cogent demonstration of behavioral variations in different situations has been provided by Block and Bennett, who obtained a woman's Q-sorts of her interactions with 23 individuals. When subjected to factor analysis, the results reveal considerable differences in her behavior and feelings, depending on whether she is with friends or neighbors, colleagues or superiors, relatives—such as the husband and mother—or patients. With close friends and neighbors, she feels at ease—she trusts and confides in them, and tries to please and impress them. With colleagues and superiors, she feels uneasy, inhibited, awkward, inadequate, resentful and guilty, and she acts in a guarded manner. Her friends' evaluations of her social behavior coincide with her own; colleagues' evaluations do not. This suggests conflict over and perceptual distortions of professional relationships. The investigators conclude:

"Traitology" continues to prosper in psychology as witnessed by the plethora of "personality dimensions" that continue to be offered. But the hierarchical ordering of these dimensions and the ways in which they may be connected to particular contexts tend to be unspecified. A considerable advance in prediction will be achieved only when we begin to understand the relationships between personality and social situation [24, p. 324].

It is one thing to agree that different situations affect the ways in which internal dispositions are expressed—quite another to develop a language for analyzing them. Only rudimentary steps have been taken in this direction. Of the two approaches to be considered, one is predominantly psychological and usually aimed at describing the subject's perception of the situation; another is more concerned with objective group pressures. Most papers have been devoted to classification for its own sake rather than subsequent theoretical applications of the system.

The Subject's Perception of the Total Situation

The theorists whose work will be mentioned here have devoted their attention primarily to the development of terminology. Of the three general systems that will be described, only Lewin's system has been employed in a significant number of empirical studies; the two others will be summarized to suggest the kinds of concepts which seem important to various workers.

Lewin's topological system has been covered in detail in previous publications [128, 129] and will not be detailed here. It is interesting to note that self and social situation were two of his primary interests at the time when he developed his analysis of the life space. Of particular relevance to the social situation are his concepts of region and subregion, direction, psychological distance, relative degree of cognitive structure, extent of overlap, consonance, potency, and valence.

The systems of Bateson [14] and Chien [43] owe much to the work of Lewin and Tolman. Bateson proposes three types of category: global characteristics, such as the properties of the geobehavioral environment and the degree of organization; components of the situation, such as available objects and the supports and constraints affecting the expression of particular motives; and perceptual characteristics which affect a person's view of his environment, such as misperceptions caused by various traits such as low intelligence, perceptual habits, and personal standards.

Chein's analysis of situation examines the distribution of such items as goals, which can serve as need satisfiers, supports, constraints, and means-end parts. Objects are analyzed in terms of discriminada, cues, manipulanda, and unpleasant and pleasant properties. Chein is particularly interested in directors, the environmental features which tend to induce specific directions in people's behavior. Among his directors are the spatiotemporal patterning of stimuli, goals, supports, constraints, and normative factors which delimit behavior.

Classifying Specific Features of Situations

Behavior settings.   Working in the tradition of Lewin, Barker [11, 12] has developed the creative approach of analyzing situations into "behavior settings." Barker and Wright have studied such phenomenal features of a town as a baseball game in progress, a Latin class, a Rotary club. Barker notes that the organization of most social activities is independent of the participation of particular persons and that the laws of operation of most settings consequently are not the laws of individual psychology. What can be termed "behavior settings" can be identified by such criteria as the participants, kinds of power figures, physical space, time, objects like chairs and typewriters, molar-action units, and behavioral mechanisms. Each setting is analyzed in terms of participation, which is described by means of such concepts as tempo, intensity, gross motor activity, talking, manipulation, thinking, and affective behavior; richness, which refers to the variety of possible responses, and is described in terms of population, pattern of action, and mechanisms; centrality, which defines the degree of interdependence with other settings in the town; and similarity to other settings, which is analyzed with reference to pattern of action, mechanisms, locus, and objects.

Settings are viewed as homeostatic systems. They normally exhibit a characteristic level of functioning produced by a balance of influences from three sources—the larger community, specific influences, and influences from the individuals involved. Like social roles, which will be discussed below, behavior settings impose obligations on their occupants and can satisfy a number of personal motives.

Codes designed for specific settings.   A number of studies analyzed the situation using concepts like those of Barker, but containing specific content. The work of Gump, Sutton-Smith, and Redl [80] and Gump and Sutton-Smith [81] illustrates such a special system for coding settings. A study performed in a summer camp for disturbed preadolescent boys was devoted to "activity settings" and the limits they set on behavior. Data gathered from interviews with campers and counselors and from observations of the campers' behavior identified the settings, which were named "swimming," "crafts," etc., and rated with respect to such variables as prescriptiveness of pattern, available props, provision for physical locomotion, bodily movements, the competence required, and degree of institutional control. Ratings of swimming were low for prescriptiveness, high for the number of available props, and very high for physical locomotion.

Gump and his associates also compared activity settings with respect to attractions and frustrations, the limits they imposed on various kinds of behavior, and their characteristic interactions and types of individual acts.

For swimming, the attractions that the children listed most frequently were analyzed in terms of such categories as opportunity for locomotion, satisfaction with developing skills, and passive pleasures. Common frustrations included being prevented from entering the water and failing to get or keep the ball while in the water.

Among the categories of interaction were solo play, adult-related solo play, peer-related solo play, sharing play, competitive play, and combative play. Contacts among children were coded with respect to such acts as helping or attacking. Swimming was characterized by more social asserting and attacking and less helping than crafts, for example.

Regions for self-presentation. In his analysis of self-presentation, Goffman [75] divides the behavioral environment into regions which he regards as synonymous with Barker's settings. Various groups have built up expectations about the appropriateness to a region of different kinds of conduct for each of them. Goffman uses dramaturgical terms to analyze the ways in which the self is presented. The performance is given in the "front region," where the performer has to comport himself in accordance with the moral and instrumental standards set by the audience. To illustrate one front region, Goffman quotes De Beauvoir's description of a woman's play acting in the presence of a masculine audience—she presents herself as "an imaginary personage through mimicry, costumery, studied phrases." The performance is prepared in the "back region," where the performer can relax and knowingly contradict the impression fostered by her performance before the audience. "With other women, a woman is behind the scenes; she is polishing her equipment but not in battle . . ." Barriers between the two regions, and between them and the "outside," prevent the audience and outsiders, such as children, from entering forbidden regions and spoiling the performance.

To account for relationships such as those between the physician and patient, between girls and boys on dates, and between teachers when students are and are not present, Goffman uses information about the accessibility of regions, tasks performed, and people's skills. Like Lewin and Barker, he assumes that barriers can vary in permeability and that regions and their functions can be reconstituted.

Need-oriented Conceptions of the Situation

In developing categories, some investigators—concerned with the connections between personality and motivation—have concentrated on incentives and the attainment of goals. Like Lewin, Murray is interested in both the objective and perceived features of the situation, which he defines in terms of three different kinds of effect, or "press," that they exert or may exert on the subject. Situations can provide actual and potential press, "benefits" or satisfying press, and "harms" or dissatisfying press. Harms are further subdivided into active types, lacks, and barriers. In an early list [151], Murray included press created by the others' motivations, such as dominance and nurturance, and by events in the subject's life, such as illness and birth. More recently [149], he has restricted press to the need-aim of another individual—an individual's need for dominance creates a press which impels the subject to behave in a conforming manner. This definition precludes events that do not represent the needs of others.

Rotter [175] also feels that situational pressures are best categorized in terms parallel to the actor's needs. He identifies situations by the reinforcements they are most likely to provide. The reinforcements are described in the language of cultural meanings. He is convinced that the perceived situation affects a person's behavior as profoundly as the actual situation does. He therefore stresses the importance of the subject's anticipations of reinforcement, anticipations which are complex results of objective probability, generalization, patterning, past experience, and the ambiguity of cues. Some reinforcements are identified with people. Examples are "authority-figure situations" and "heterosexual situations," terms which imply relationships with particular kinds of individuals. Other reinforcements are identified with roles; the person assumes that certain actions are appropriate to the expectations of people in complementary roles. The probability of reinforcement is related to "freedom of movement," the mean expectancy of obtaining satisfactions after engaging in acts directed toward the accomplishment of related goals. High freedom of movement implies an expectation of success for many different acts in different situations. Low freedom of movement implies expectation of success for only a few acts in different situations. Depending upon their probability, Rotter classifies reinforcements as "dominant," "most likely to occur," "mixed," "unstructured," or "unfamiliar." Since the cues are not readily identified in the latter two cases, it is hard for the subject to estimate the probabilities of various responses.

A subject's reactions to a situation partly depend on his anticipation of gratification; in turn, this is related to his standards of gratification and the available rewards. To analyze the subject's standards, Rotter employs the "minimal goal level," the lowest goal in a continum of potential reinforcements that would be considered satisfying in particular situations.

Research on Behavior Settings

Some of the theoretical potential of the concept of "behavior setting" is suggested by two of Barker's studies [11] in which he compared behavior in both sufficiently populated and undermanned settings. One study was designed to test the assumption that the larger the size of a setting, the smaller its coercive power over individuals. This assumption was confirmed by analyses of absenteeism. The trend was the same in factories, coal pits, the textile industry, Rotary clubs, churches, and music festivals —the larger the organization, the higher the rate of absenteeism.

Having observed that settings provide opportunities and impose obligations, Barker asked himself how these would change if the number of people was decreased enough to interfere with a setting's functions. Obviously, there would be an increased claim upon the remaining persons. As the number declined, he reasoned, the forces acting upon each person would be stronger, and their range would be greater. Specifically, the individual would be called upon to undertake more difficult and more important tasks; he would feel more insecure because of the increased threat of failure; the group would be less sensitive to differences between people; there would be a reduction in the maximal performance of tasks, a greater frequency of success and failure.

In a second investigation, Barker tested some of his hypotheses by surveying the demands of settings in an undermanned American town and in an adequately populated English town which were comparable in all other respects. As anticipated, the American example exceeded the English one in proportion of responsible positions, amount of time spent in the setting, and range of age groups. Barker also inferred that the operations of a significantly greater number of American than English settings would be seriously crippled if they had to do without adolescents.

In a study of hyperaggressive children in residential treatment, Raush, Dittmann, and Taylor [167] selected six settings for observation: breakfast, other meals, organized games, unorganized group activities, arts and crafts, and snacks at bedtime. They were interested in finding out how relationships between children and staff varied in different settings. The reasons behind the choice of settings reveal a sensitivity to the issues that concerned Lewin, Barker, and Gump—gratification, like the association of eating and security with meals; adaptation to limits set by the expectations of others, like the kind of rules in games; and opportunity for social interaction, like that afforded by unorganized activity in groups.

The data reveal significant differences in the behavior the children displayed in various settings. Children are more friendly toward each other at breakfast than at other meals for example. The competitive games with clearly defined rules elicit more aggressive behavior toward other children than do arts and crafts. More important, there is an interaction between situational and psychological variables—situations have different meanings for different children, and individual differences among children vary with the situation.

Research on Atmospheres and Climates

Lewin, Lippitt, and White's early study of "social climates" or "social atmospheres" [130] has stimulated many subsequent investigations. In the original research, investigators coached leaders of boys' groups to use an authoritarian, democratic, or *laissez-faire* approach. The authoritarian leader determined practically all policies concerning club activities. The democratic leader made policies a matter of group decision and encouraged the boys to conduct discussions and to allocate the responsibilities for various jobs. The leader with the *laissez-faire* approach was passive in social participation, left all decisions about procedure and activity to the group, supplied help when asked, but unlike the other leaders, provided no evaluations.

Leaders' actions, combined with the experiences of the groups, established different means of expression of group responses to frustration. The patterns were labeled "social atmospheres." The "aggressive autocracies" were more ready than other groups to express their frustrations in interclub wars, the "apathetic autocracies" internalized aggression, and the groups with atmospheres labeled "democratic" and *"laissez-faire"* took practical steps to eliminate the sources of frustration. In relating to authoritarian leaders, boys in some clubs found that the required dependency was quite compatible with the group's goals; boys in other clubs displayed a frustrated hopelessness in the face of overwhelming power. When leaders came late, the "autocracies" continued with started work, but showed no initiative in beginning new activities, whereas the "democracies" continued to begin things on their own, and the *"laissez-faire* groups" managed to be active, though not productive.

Many subsequent investigations have been made of the atmospheres leading to group or to leader-centered decisions. Bovard [30] observed communication of feeling, identification, and clinical insight in small face-to-face groups which actually were classes in elementary psychology. Verbal exchange was maximized in the case of group-centered communication, and held to a minimum in that of leader-centered communication. After thirty-nine hours of classes, students were asked to discuss a problem in human relations presented in a film. The group-centered class exceeded the leader-centered class in communication of feeling, identification with characters in the film, and understanding of dynamics.

Gibb [73] and his associates have found that "defensive" atmospheres are distinguished by expressions of powerlessness and unpredictability, mutual attack, and poorly integrated sequences of group efforts, whereas "supportive" atmospheres produce feelings of ability to exert legitimate influence, comfort with the group's decision, conflict directed toward problem solving, considerable mutual support, integrated sequences of mutual activity, and acceptance of deviant opinion. Defensiveness is increased by induced polarization, instructional sets, increased size of the group, and violations of role expectations; supportiveness is increased by feeling-oriented reports, group discussions of negative self-perception and role expectation, informality of group atmosphere, and sustained permissive leadership.

Barker and Wright's "social weather" [12] refers to conditions surrounding an individual and is identified by the social responses he elicits from his associates. To study the social weather of children, Barker and Wright used the Fels Parent Behavior Rating Scales to rate each subject on the nine dimensions of approval, affectionateness, acceptance, attention, assistance, communication, adaptation, privilege, and choice.

ANALYSIS OF THE SITUATION IN TERMS OF THE PROPERTIES OF GROUPS

A division of social relationships into situation, identity, and pattern of mutual responses provides a convenient framework for surveying the field but must be supplemented by information about relationships among the three. Hence, this section which deals with aspects of social interaction that reflect pressures created by group membership, introduces a topic which recurs frequently in other parts of the chapter.

Objective Characteristics of Groups

Ecology. It is generally taken for granted that ecological conditions have profound effects on psychological dispositions and social interaction although there is little empirical evidence to support this assumption. The significance of ecology for personality is suggested by Barnouw's observations [13] of the extreme individualism and lack of cooperativeness among the Chippewa, who feel it is preferable to get along on one's own in a hard world than to trust others who will not be available when needed. Barnouw attributes their suspiciousness and their self-dependence and self-control to their geographical isolation, particularly in winter, when they must face hardships without the community's help.

Clarity of the situation. Experiments have revealed that social relationships vary with other features of the situation, such as strangeness, clarity, the size of the group, and its pressures to conform. When children one to three years old were placed by Arsenian [7] in a strange playroom for five minutes, their rated security varied with the familiarity of the situation and the presence of the mother. Cohen [45] found that when a group of adults performed a task involving vague and unfamiliar pictures, uncommon words, and the presentation of cues in an arbitrary order, they expressed more aggression than when they had familiar pictures, commonly understood words, and repeated single cues. Ambiguity also played a significant part in Sherif's research [184]. In an ambiguous situation, the individual conformed to group standards when provided a frame of reference for perceiving the task.

Size of the group.   According to Simmel [221], the type of pressure exerted by the situation varies considerably with the group's size. He notes that relationships in the dyad are more intimate than those in larger groups; each person knows he can depend on himself and only one other. The affective structure depends primarily on what each shows or gives to the other person; it cannot be ameliorated—as it might be in a larger group—by a third party or by a delegation of duties to an impersonal organization. In contrast, any member of a triad can be the intermediary who unites or separates the other two. The third man can be nonpartisan, mediator, indirect bond, or the one who divides and rules by exploiting the quarrels of the others.

Some of Simmel's observations are supported by the behavior which Bales and Borgatta [10] observed in problem-solving groups of different sizes. Two-man groups were low in disagreement and high in manifestation of tension, volunteered suggestions, and requests for opinions and orientation. Members of dyads seem more concerned with avoiding severe disagreement than members of larger groups. Each participant in the dyad is eager to learn about the other's opinions and becomes anxious when there is a danger of aggression or even disagreement.

The group's pressures to conform.   Some well-known studies have provided evidence of certain pressures inherent in group organization. According to Festinger [59] conformity is motivated largely by cohesiveness, or attraction to the group or to its members. A study by Bovard [29] indicates that the more cohesive the group, the more quickly it determines a "zone of conformity" which defines the range of issues in which conformity is expected. According to Back's research [8] prominent motives for conformity are the desire for prestige, involvement in group tasks, and attraction to other members. Back found that subjects' behavior reflected their motivation for entering the group. Some were concerned primarily with the task and paid little attention to the reactions of others; others viewed their performance as a means of attracting other members, made a personal effort, and felt resentful if they did not succeed. Frequent attempts by subjects to influence others were associated with high, rather than low, cohesiveness. The gangs that Whyte [218] studied punished deviation viciously, and Schacter's groups [180] enforced conformity by arousing fear of punishment, ridicule, and rejection.

Some Basic Principles Pertaining to Social Structure

Terminology. Some concepts pertaining to social roles and reference groups will next be viewed in the context of a social structure, some in the context of the individual's position in a society. For readers who are not familiar with concepts commonly used to analyze social structure, we present a survey of some basic sociological principles here.

Each theorist writing on society differs in some significant degree from others. The position taken here resembles most closely the viewpoints of Marion J. Levy [126] and Leslie A. White [217]—although these two theorists also differ at points.

A social system can be divided according to three different principles. The most familiar is a division into various types of organized social units, such as the family, factory, church, and club, and unorganized but recognized social catgories, such as men, women, Negroes, and people in the working class. A system of relationships can also be analyzed with respect to its fundamental structure, which includes economic, political, religious, and educational aspects. Economic features —those referring to the allocation of goods and services, for example— might be observed in concrete structures such as the government, business enterprises, and the family. Finally, any membership unit can be analyzed ultimately as a set of social positions. A family may be divided into the positions of father, mother, husband, wife, son, daughter, brother, sister; a factory into manual workers, clerical staff, administrative personnel.

Social roles. The mutual responses of two people can often be explained more readily by their shared conceptions about the behavior appropriate to their two *roles* than by their psychological characteristics or the unique qualities of the social interaction. When roles are the primary determinants of behavior, various pairs of people having different psychological characteristics and styles of reciprocal action may give similar responses. In a study of psychotherapeutic sessions, Lennard and Bernstein [124] found patterns characteristic of all therapist-patient pairs—patterns independent of techniques and personalities. On the average, the patients produced four times as much verbal material as the therapists did, but asked one-seventh as many questions. As time passed, each pair increased references to feelings and established a rate of interaction from which they varied very little. The therapists gradually decreased their explanations of the conditions of therapy and increased their evaluations of patients' behavior.

Herbst's investigation of marital roles [89] reveals a shared hierarchy of expectations about the husband's obligations. In descending order of frequency, he is expected to participate in the economic and social activities of the family, to perform his own household duties, to care for children, and sometimes to participate in the wife's household duties. Universal requisites for the wife are household and social activities and the care of children. She may also participate in the common work of the household, in economic activities, and in the performance of her husband's tasks, in that order of frequency. Such expectations represent social pressures on a wife, and throw light on her behavior.

Most sociologists and anthropologists concentrate on the differential influence of situations and minimize the influence of internal dispositions. Thomas [209] maintains that a man responds as the situation requires him to respond. When the situation changes, his role changes, and he manifests a changed personality. In the opinion of Thomas and Znaniecki [210], values and attitudes provide keys to the meaning of a situation. Impressed by the extent to which values are applied to patterns of mutual expectations among related participants, sociologists have developed the conception of "role" to account for the translation of values into patterns of action. To trace connections between social situations and behavior it is necessary to start with the concept of "social position." Sociologists are no more inclined than personality theorists to agree on definition of terms—as used here, social position overlaps with Linton's status [131] and Levy's role [126]. Each position has rights and obligations and can be occupied only by a person with the requisite qualifications. An individual finds himself in a number of positions and categories; he is a lawyer, father, Catholic, and member of the Junior Chamber of Commerce. In each position or category he plays a number of roles. A public school teacher, for example, may have relationships with his pupils, his colleagues, the school principal, and the superintendent of schools. Merton [142] has labeled as "role-set" the complement of an individual's role relationships resulting from his social position or social category.

By definition, the rights and obligations of a position are reciprocal with the rights and obligations of other positions. One person can have a right only if another person is responsible for its satisfaction. No position can be defined independently of another position. If a father does not provide sufficient nourishment, his offspring may be removed by a court because the offspring has the right to be fed and the father has the obligation to provide the food.

The concepts of rights and obligations are norms which specify expected and preferred behaviors. The normative aspect of roles is stressed in most definitions. Linton [131] conceives of roles as actions performed by persons to validate their occupancies of positions. Merton

[142] stresses both the normative and reciprocal aspects of role relationships. Role partners act on reciprocal expectations regarding each other's behavior. These reciprocal expectations define the nature of a role.

Even the casual student of social roles must conclude that they may curtail people's social behavior. The reasons for, and the relative inflexibility of, some of the limits begin to make sense when the role is viewed as a unit of a concrete social structure. If the social structure is to carry out its functions, it must limit the behavior of individuals who occupy positions in it.[2] A man finds that he is under pressure to act in accordance with the expectations of other members of the organization and that they have definite ideas about the behavior appropriate to a person in his position. He cannot regard roles merely as rules of the game which he can change when he has the whim.

The fact that structures are interlocked within the society makes constraints even greater. Thus the modern family is responsible for the care, feeding, and socialization of immature children; no other structures in the society can completely take over these functions for intact families. Consequently, a woman who has young children and wants to work full time may face the antagonism of her husband and such simple obstacles as the unavailability of baby sitters, the lack of nurseries for children under three, and the part-time schedule of most nurseries. Thus, it is only by personal attention that a woman can fulfill her obligations to her children.

Roles versus dispositions. The definition of roles raises a crucial problem for the personality theorist. To what extent is social behavior affected by the roles people assume? Can they account for most of the variance that psychologists explain by postulating various internal dispositions? Theoretical positions vary from complete reliance on the properties of roles to complete reliance on the properties of dispositions.

Brim is at one extreme, claiming that "the learned repertoire of roles is the personality. There *is* nothing else. There is no core personality 'underneath' the behavior and feelings." Contradicting psychologists who conceive of the adult personality in terms of general characteristics, Brim says it is difficult to see evidence of general traits in people's behavior. He is more struck by—

. . . the great variation of the individual's behavior from one situation to another during the course of the day . . . What should capture the interest of the student of personality . . . is not the consistency of individual

---

[2] It is not implied here that the functions of any given social unit are totally beneficial for the society as a whole; rather, the implication is that the total set of structures found in any given society is likely to have a preponderance of adaptive over maladaptive functions—otherwise the society would not long survive.

differences. . . . Rather it is the great adaptability, the truly impressive variation in response to situational demands, which characterizes man as he moves from one situation to another [31, p. 137].

But what about the self? As far as Brim is concerned, it is an awareness of one's roles. But does one not have a conception of a core self? He agrees that one does, but denies that it is anything more than a reflection of one's actions in the most salient roles. And what about the consistency in behavior across situations? Brim has four answers. First, available data on consistency reveal weak trends. Second, for traits like "sociability," which "tend to be functionally unimportant . . . because the expression of these characteristics is less regulated by situational norms," there may be a greater consistency than for other traits. (Goffman [75] and Simmel [221] assume that sociability is important and highly regulated.) Third, the characteristics of some individuals are consistent because of a generalization of responses from one salient role to others. Finally, Brim thinks the inadequately socialized person may behave consistently because he is unable to discriminate between roles and lacks the skills for meeting role requirements in certain situations.

In restricting social relationships to the pressures of roles, Brim tries to shut the door on the personality theorist, but Sargent [179] pries it open, stressing the extent to which playing roles depends on the perception and interpretation of expectations. Sargent views a person's role as "a pattern or type of social behavior which seems situationally appropriate to him in terms of the demands and expectations of those in his group." To play a role, a person must take and maintain a "mental set." A set prevents the guest at a polite dinner party from telling a dirty joke and the man in church from lighting a cigarette. The significance of values and perception is emphasized by sociologists such as Wilensky [219] and Reissman [170], who distinguish between the objective role and the meanings a man assigns to it—his conceptions of what it is, what it should be, and what it might become. Once the playing of roles is viewed in terms of communication between people, principles of perception and perceptual distortion become relevant to the study of the responses of people to one another.

Rommetveit [173] introduces psychological issues when he analyzes roles in terms of the concepts of "norm sender" (the person who exerts social pressure by communicating his expectations) and "norm receiver" (the person playing the role). The receiver's behavior may vary with his perceptions and definitions of the sender's purposes, messages, and pressures, and with his anticipations of the sender's standards and sanctions.

Even when interpreted in the same way, a message may have different effects on two receivers—depending on their reference groups.

Merton [142] advocates research on the reasons why certain groups are more influential than others in forming individuals' frames of reference and on the conditions under which various reference groups are invoked.

A number of psychotherapists [2, 49, 191] have attempted to analyze simultaneously both roles and the dynamics of personality. Spiegel [192] has done the most systematic thinking on the problem. He regards the social role as the basis upon which family action is integrated. Hence, he uses the degrees and kinds of conflict between social roles as indications of the amounts and types of strain in systems of values, relations between people, and even intrapsychic processes. He analyzes the events within families on three levels: cultural-value orientations, social roles and resolution of conflicts between them, and internal psychodynamics as seen from the psychoanalytic standpoint.

Undeniably the idea that roles serve as important constraints deserves serious study—study which may throw light on individual behavior. The psychologist can contribute to the explanation of role playing, since psychological phenomena are involved in the understanding of behavior appropriate to a situation, the maintenance of sets, the perception of social pressures, the communication and interpretation, in fairly ambiguous situations, of norms, some of which are poorly defined and some conflicting. Most psychologists who have concerned themselves with roles and the social situation would agree with Murphy:

We cannot define the situation operationally except in reference to the specific organism which is involved; we cannot define the organism operationally in such a way as to obtain predictive power for behavior, except in reference to the situation. Each serves to define the other; they are definable operationally while in the organism-situation field [148, p. 891].

Types and components of roles. Despite widespread interest in roles, few attempts have been made to classify them. Of the categories that have been proposed, few have been used in systematic research and it is difficult to estimate their fruitfulness. Rommetveit [173], Sargent [179], and Stouffer and Toby [196] have suggested a differentiation between cultural and personal roles. The former means behavior expected of an individual in a particular social position; the latter means the expectations concerning an individual's unique ways of relating to others in informal cliques. (When a situation is informal and vaguely defined, a person's skills and dispositions may influence his roles considerably.)

Gibb's investigations of constraints [73] have led him to coin the term "role boundary," which refers to the inclusive and exclusive limits imposed by the group: the range of behavior to which the group responds favorably as well as the range of proscribed acts. Members may be conscious or unconscious of the imposition and acceptance of this boundary. When a member violates his role boundary, others may respond by inattention, self-deception about the meaning of his action, or open condemnation. Role boundaries may be either formal or informal. The informal is often as commanding as the formal, but tends to be less controllable. Comparisons of norm sending and receiving in groups revealed the existence of many misinterpretations by norm receivers of messages about informal role boundaries.

Gibb's concept of "role repertoire" seems very similar to Benne and Sheats's [16] "role flexibility." Role repertoire is defined as the range and adequacy of a person's behavior in the role, and role flexibility is defined as skill and security in a wide range of roles. Group members displayed individual variation in role repertoires, that is, people differed in their skills with particular roles, in the number of roles attempted, in their awareness of limitations of roles, and the ratio between roles attempted and roles taken well. Gibb found that repertoires could be influenced considerably by training in the understanding and skill required to take particular roles.

Hartley and Hartley [85] propose that roles be analyzed with reference to such dimensions as pervasive versus limited, imposed versus achieved, clarity, congruence, or the degree to which roles can be combined into clusters, and the extent to which the attitude and action is public rather than private. Sargent [179] suggests specificity, extensiveness, continuity over time, degree of prestige, difficulty in fulfillment, conflict among roles, and relative consciousness of the role. Benne and Sheats [16], who have concentrated on the efficiency of groups, analyze behavior in terms of task roles. These include initiator, information seeker, and coordinator; group-building and maintenance roles, such as harmonizer, expediter, and standard setter; and roles such as aggressor, blocker, and self-confessor.

Studying roles. More thought has been given to the theoretical significance of roles than to methods of identifying them. Their complexity emerges when one attempts to devise a code for the communication between norm sender and norm receiver. There is seldom complete agreement within a group about the standards which apply to a particular role, and there is some question about the way in which the different messages and the amount of agreement should be conceptualized. Even if the norm senders agree, they often differ in the pressure they exert or in their means of exerting it. And norm receivers can be distinguished by the selective attention they give to different messages and by their acceptance of pressure.

The interactions between norms and other variables suggest the need of classifying norms in terms of range of activities and contexts. The same pressure may vary in meaning, depending upon whether it defines a role in the family, on the job, or in the general society. Serious thinking about both theory and empirical investigations is needed to establish the basis for dimensions on which most investigators can agree.

Although the study of roles is relatively new, some progress has been made in the exploration of techniques. To measure dimensions of roles based on Parsons's pattern variables [157], Stouffer and Toby [196] and Laulict [119] employed Guttman's method to construct a number of scales, but their validity is questionable because they were based on the subjects' responses to paper-and-pencil tests describing role conflicts in hypothetical situations. In a study of actual roles, Rommetveit [173] considered the sender's perception of pressure, the receiver's experience of actual and potential pressure, and the investigator's observations of overt to covert pressure applied by the sender. Each of these variables can be investigated for both approved and disapproved behavior. Newcomb [152] has proposed that the concept of expectations be elaborated by asking respondents about behavior that is demanded, permitted, and forbidden to the role player. Each type can be placed on a continuum in accordance with the percentage of agreement. Jacobson, Charters, and Liebermann [100] found that expectations about a role differed depending upon whether the respondents were in the role, functionally related to someone in the role, or remotely related to him. Evidently separate continua need to be defined for different "criterion populations."

Gross, Mason, and McEachern [79] analyzed the picture that school superintendents and school board members had of their roles. Superintendents and school board members had significantly different expectations on all items of a test pertaining to "division of labor." Significant differences were also found in expectations of superintendents' attributes and of performance of both superintendents and board members.

Some examples of the sources of disagreement point to types of variables which may require control in investigations of roles. The illustrations are phrased in the investigators' language. More responsibility was assigned to a position by its incumbents than by the incumbents of other positions. The more the incumbents of two positions agreed in their definitions of each other's roles, the more highly they rated one another's performance. In specifying the obligations of a man in position A to a man in position B, people in the same organization differed, depending on how much contact they had had with the incumbent of position B—if they knew him well, and were presumably identified with him, they assigned many obligations to the person in the complementary position.

The agreement among school board members was positively related to such variables as the frequency of previous contacts, religious homogeneity, concern with civic duty and "representing some group," similarity in education and in political values, and the proportion of women. Agreement was negatively related to the size of school boards. The findings may be summarized: Consensus in the expectations of role senders is influenced by involvement in one's own position, conflicting interests of people in different positions, liking for or identification with the man playing the role, the point of view the norm sender has developed as a result of occupying his own position, his previous experience with the position and the incumbent, and similarity in the backgrounds and values of norm senders.

Reference Groups

Both the communicators of expectations and the players of roles define their expectations in accordance with the norms of specific reference groups. These concepts are best introduced by some examples.

Requested by Blake, Rosenbaum, and Duryea [23] to contribute to a worthwhile fund, people asked, "What is expected of me?" "How much do you need?" and particularly "How much are others giving?" Such inquiries were intended to identify a particular group's standards concerning contributions. With reference to the norms of that group, a refusal would have meant risking rejection.

Wilensky's study of intellectuals in labor unions [219] provides some vivid illustrations of different reference groups. The "missionary type" of intellectual acts with respect to the norms of a political or religious group outside the union; the mission often comes into conflict with the requirements of his job and the values of officials in the union. The "professional service expert" conforms to the standards of an outside professional group in performing his job. Concerned with the concept of the ideal staff expert, the research product, and the elimination of frustrations of the job, he is often torn between practical compromises and his desire to render competent, efficient, objective, technical service of which professional colleagues outside the union would approve. Wilensky also describes the "union politico," who seeks influence and power as ends in themselves, and the "careerist," who is motivated primarily by income, promotion, and security, has the mobility strivings of people for whom the middle class is a reference group, is intensely identified with the union and untroubled by ideological motivation or the norms of outside professional groups.

A reference group is one with which the individual feels identified, either positively or negatively. The group may be an attractive one or an unattractive one, having characteristics opposite to those toward which the individual strives. As Newcomb [152] observes: "It is possible to avoid a particular value or act because it characterizes a group to which one is violently opposed." A person may even find it necessary to acquire the characteristics of a group that he feels is generally unacceptable because becoming "somebody bad" is preferable to his only other alternative, being "not quite somebody" [53].

Membership groups and reference groups often coincide, but one does not have to belong to a group to use its norms as a frame of reference. One may use an unorganized category—adolescents, the working class, even a nonexistent group like pre-Civil War Southern plantation owners or the gods on Mount Olympus.

Reactions to both negative and positive reference categories are illustrated by the aspirations of middle-class fathers concerning their sons' future jobs. Although few of the twenty fathers who were interviewed by Aberle and Naegele (1) had made specific occupational plans for their sons, most expressed disapproval of working-class occupations. The respondents even found some professional jobs unacceptable, particularly academic ones.

Most regarded their children's current problems as auguries for adulthood. The most frequently mentioned problems were poor grades in school, excessive passivity, athletic incompetence, overconformity, and excitability—all difficulties that would be handicapping in jobs requiring advanced training, initiative, and self-control. Skills and values mentioned as desirable would be assets to professional men, executives, and owners of small businesses. The evaluations of traits as problems or assets probably depended on norms derived from the social class with which the fathers identified.

Of the various kinds of norms [5], "directives" [115] are probably most relevant to behavior guided by reference groups. Directives pertain to standards which influence selection of modes, means, and ends of action, and they are particularly relevant to choices faced in commonly recognized and recurrent situations [145, 173]. A directive refers to expected or preferred action. The person is expected to do something or to avoid doing it. Like all norms, the directive is enforced by some kind of sanction [173]—violations are punished and conformity is rewarded.

A reference group can have different functions. The ones cited thus far illustrate what Kelley [110] calls the "normative" function—providing rewards and punishments for conformity—or lack of conformity—to its standards. In its "comparison" function, the group provides comparison points—the traits of its members—which a person uses to make evaluations. When asking psychology students for their levels of aspiration on a test of literary information, Chapman and Volkmann [40] told three groups the average scores attained by authors and critics, psychology students, or unselected WPA workers. Obviously, responding to the normative functions of these reference groups, subjects set their mean levels of aspiration lower than the average attained by the critics, similar to the average of the psychologists, and above that of the WPA workers.

Is there a common core of social positions and categories to which most people turn for frames of reference? Evidence summarized by Katz and Lazarsfeld [109] reveals that the reference group selected varies with the issue, the person's background and his specific attitudes and needs. Knowing that certain people are Catholics, for instance, one can predict their politics with confidence, but not their attitudes toward birth control. Another illustration is provided by Shipton's analysis [186] of the sources of public opinion. From qualitative interviews with inhabitants of an industrial city of 45,000 people, he derived 24 potential sources of influence on public opinion. Then citing a school issue which was the subject of a referendum and about which most people were poorly informed, he asked a random sample of 902 respondents to name the three groups which were most helpful in forming an opinion. The number of social positions and categories is small—families, ethnic groups, occupational organizations, groups in the same social class, and fraternal and veteran's organizations. Colleagues, neighbors, and coworkers were not mentioned.

Even if the reference group's implications for action were crystal clear—and often they are not—there would sometimes be conflict between standards of different reference groups or between reference and membership groups. Kahl's research [107] on fathers' ambitions for their sons provides some good examples. The boys were all above average in intelligence and came from the lower middle class or the working class. An unusually high proportion planned to go to college. The fathers who urged their sons to go to college usually deplored their own failure to obtain degrees, which might have opened the gate to professional positions. These parents were actually members of the lower middle or working class, but their reference group was the upper middle class. The men who did not exert pressure on their sons were more worried about getting by than getting ahead. Only for the fathers who accepted their social status did membership and reference groups coincide.

In addition to the attendant conflicts, the use of reference groups is frequently complicated by their vagueness. When Bott [27] inquired into the standards of British families, she found considerable variation in conceptions of social class, which she explained by the lack of objective criteria for identifying it. As a reference group, social class was used more often by economically mobile than by stable individuals. When it was invoked, the norms were often applied inconsistently and mostly in connection with special topics, such as classification of strangers, discussion of the total society, and making decisions about behavior in unfamiliar situations. Bott thinks the vagueness is an asset since it permits flexible action in different circumstances.

Internalized objects. The malleability of standards may be attributed even more to the fact that most of a person's reference groups are not present when he employs their norms as a basis for action; such groups may not even exist except in his mind. He reacts not only to people in the immediate situation, but to friends, relatives, authorities, and heroes, some of whom he has never seen, some long since dead, some legends or myths. They constitute what psychoanalysts have called his "internal objects" or his "internal society." Freud [67] developed the conception of internalized objects as a result of his observations of depression, the symptoms of which became clear when he assumed that the patient had "internalized" a significant figure with whom an ambivalent relationship had developed and that the struggle was continuing. Freud views the superego as a product of this introjection and interprets the existence of the superego as evidence that everyone internalizes certain individuals who have been partners in significant earlier relationships.

The current generation of psychoanalysts has extended the theory of object relationships, postulating the internalization of objects during different stages of psychosexual development [54, 114]. Stress on perception makes it possible to postulate such phenomena as the introjection of a part object like the breast during the earliest days of development and the separate internalization of different facets of the same person, such as his good and bad self, insofar as they are perceived by the young child as separate identities. According to the theory, the same physical mother may be internalized as a group of different mothers because her standards and behaviors change as she assumes different identities during various stages of the child's development. Each internalized object has its unique relationship with a separate aspect of the self. The young infant behaves dependently with his succorant mother; the rebellious two-year old is ambivalent to his demanding and punishing mother and his loving supportive mother; the ascetic adolescent is independent and distant with his solicitous mother. Such relationships provide reference individuals who affect adult behavior.

The earlier internalized relationships tend to be nonlogical, unverbalized, and sometimes sources of shame, and many tend to be repressed. They are useful in explaining irrational, rejected, and sometimes tyrannical, personal values which affect behavior in many situations, and with many significant people. They may explain why an employee reacts defensively to a friendly superior, as though he were a hostile father; why a husband makes passive appeals to his wife, as though he were a little child who was seeking his mother's support; why an adult woman sometimes provokes her husband to attack her, as though she were a guilty daughter.

These observations may be summarized by a statement that would probably be acceptable to many sociologists [46, 159] and psychoanalysts [20, 54, 114]: People do not internalize abstract norms, but images of themselves in concrete relationships with specific people or groups. A person probably abstracts a principle only after he has internalized a specific relationship with a reference object or group.

The ways in which people are influenced by their reference groups are illuminated by a series of studies initiated by Sherif's investigation of the autokinetic phenomenon. Sherif [184] asked each subject to estimate the movement of a point of light in a dark room, then permitted him to learn about another person's judgment; the subject typically modified his norms so that they tended to approximate those of the other person. Bovard [28] has demonstrated that norms established in the autokinetic situation are maintained with considerable accuracy over a period of a month. Shonbar [187] added many perceptual cues to the autokinetic phenomenon, but individual norms still showed significant convergences in the group. When two subjects made judgments, both responded in a manner that was more characteristic of the group than of either individual. Such assimilation, however, does not occur automatically. According to Maussner's findings [136, 137], it varies with reinforcement of the original estimate. If the reinforcement was positive when the subjects were alone, they were disinclined to change; if the reinforcement was negative, they were more ready to alter their original estimates. Degree of assimilation was also positively related to the success of the other person, who was a confederate in this study, and to his relative status.

This research suggests variables that may contribute to what French and Zajonc [65] have described as the "situational potency" of a subject's membership, "the degree to which a group membership is aroused in a particular situation relative to the degree to which his membership in other groups is aroused." Evidence concerning the autokinetic phenomenon suggests separate potencies for one's own norms, the norms of another person, especially if his efforts have been successful or his status is high, and the norms of the group.

French and Zajonc varied the situational potencies of Indian students in the United States by having them perform one task under the direction of an Indian "professor," another under the direction of an American "professor." Charters and Newcomb [42] used a similar technique. Different groups of students, each group having the same religious faith, were gathered in separate rooms and told that they were to help in the construction of a questionnaire on religious beliefs. The leaders then conducted noncontroversial discussions of the basic assumptions underlying the opinions of all people of that particular faith. In their answers to a questionnaire, Catholic subjects more closely approximate the orthodox religious position than did members of the same faith in a control group whose awareness of membership was not increased. For Catholics, the situation had apparently increased the situational potency of their religious reference group.

ANALYSIS OF THE SITUATION: RELEVANCE OF SOCIAL STRUCTURE AND PERSONALITY

Only a beginning has been made in the analysis of situations. Psychologists and sociologists have devoted most of their efforts to developing a descriptive language, which is usually abstract because it is designed to describe a complete system such as a total society or everything the person can perceive. Social scientists have found such terms as "boundary," "behavior setting," "role-set," and "social category" helpful in planning research. Since these terms are so abstract, they have been supplemented by additional concepts when applied to concrete situations. The incompleteness of current systems has not prevented many investigators from using the concepts and testing some of their implied relationships. Manipulating situations with respect to such variables as clarity, incentives, and restrictiveness of leadership has not been difficult, and some studies have yielded results that will be used in constructing theories.

Much attention has been devoted above to the sociological concepts of reference group and role. Because many psychologists are disinclined to use roles in their thinking about personality and socialization some evaluation of the term seems appropriate here. It is all to easy to pick out the weaknesses in a developing set of principles, to stress the lack of consensus concerning even the basic meaning of a term such as "role," to point out how vague and all-embracing it has become, so that it has been applied by different theorists to a range of behaviors that virtually encompasses most of psychology and sociology. While valid, such criticisms should not lead one to overlook the potential value of the issues summarized by the term "role."

The most frequent mentioned asset of role is that it serves as a needed bridge between theories of social structure and personality. An understanding of the restraints of roles requires the study of their location in the structure of society; an understanding of the perception and learning of roles and their effects on behavior requires the study of the psychological characteristics of role senders and role receivers and the means of communication between them.

A characteristic that has particular relevance to the study of social interaction is built into the concept of role. Definitions of role require the assumption of reciprocal expectations. The rights and obligations of one role are meaningless without reference to the rights and obligations of some other role; the concept of a norm sender requires the complementary concept of a norm receiver. Traditional intrapersonal concepts which assume the completeness of Leibnitz's monads are not sufficient to describe the reciprocal pressures and actions in social behavior.

Further differences between the two kinds of terms emerge when one attempts to substitute for roles such psychological concepts as expectation, interaction, and communication. The replacement is possible for some questions, particularly those which can be answered in terms of abstract general principles, but the concept of role is needed for questions which require information about the content of specific norms, a person's obligations to others in a specific social group, the sources of the values and perspectives that influence his social behavior.

The research on roles raises many problems interesting to both the psychologist and sociologist, problems which might be attacked cooperatively by workers in both fields. Conflict is such a field; the promising skeletal theory provided by such abstract psychological concepts as "strength of need" and "approach-avoidance" can be clothed with flesh and blood social roles. The literature on roles suggests a differentiation between various types of conflicts—between the incompatible standards of people who disagree about the same role; between incompatible standards pertaining to different but simultaneous roles; between incompatible standards within the same reference group or different reference groups; between incompatible pressures within one's membership group or one's role and one's psychological traits; between different instrumental methods for carrying through a role. Research on such specific problems usually leads to concern with the social origins of conflict, and prompts the investigation of topics like acculturation, social mobility, assimilation, and membership groups with contradictory norms.

The interrelation of social and psychological forces is revealed in a number of studies. In discussing conflict between roles, Bronfenbrenner, Harding, and Gallwey [32] report evidence of blind spots in the perception of contradictory expectations, suggesting that they may be distorted by the same mechanisms that are used to resolve other kinds of conflict. A study of student nurses by Menzies [140] shows how the definition of a role can result in the recruitment of candidates with specific kinds of defense mechanisms. A job analysis revealed the existence of many conflicting sources of pressure. Nurses were shifted frequently from one ward to another, with the result that the girls were often confused about some of their responsibilities. Several nurses were usually assigned to the same set of patients, so that the care of any one patient was divided among a number of students. Nurses were not allowed to perform any tasks that required decisions. It was clearly conveyed to each nurse that she was expected to avoid emotional involvement with patients and to keep a stiff upper lip concerning her feelings. Often the students had nothing to do because an excessive number of candidates was hired and attempts were not always made to schedule their time. The result of this was selection of nurses with pathological defenses that made easier an adjustment to the impersonal relationships with patients, the extirpartion of feelings, the breakdowns in services for patients which resulted from sudden changes in assignments, the diffusion of responsibility, and the guilt created by the underemployment of candidates. Among the student nurses who completed training, a high proportion had strong propensities for such "psychotic" defenses as denial and projection.

Ecology also provides clues about the meaning of situations and lends itself to interdisciplinary research. Barker and Wright's attempts [12] at systematic analysis have opened up an important new field for psychologists—one that would benefit from the exploration of unstated assumptions about forces very similar to role expectations. This seems to be a propitious time for increased communication between certain ecologists, psychologists, and specialists in social structure—all of whom are investigating a core of similar problems. Heretofore, most specialists in social structure have been disinclined to state their basic assumptions about ecology. Certain studies of industrial sociology are an exception. Facts about the layout of a plant, for example, are too critical for the analysis of social relationships to be slighted by merely implicit description. The influence of systematic ecological concepts is apparently spreading to other areas. An appreciation of the significance of ecological structure for face-to-face relationships induced Goffman [75] to categorize this topic along some of the lines proposed by Barker and Wright.

Psychologists can make many contributions to the solution of problems that have arisen in the study of roles and reference groups. Consider the earlier example of fathers who are identified with a category (the middle class) to which they have never belonged and who apply the norms of this reference group to themselves and project them to their sons. How does one conceptualize the meaning of a social category to a man? Is the category an abstraction, or is it defined by images of significant people? In what way does it affect his behavior? How does he conceive of its norms? Just how does a person identify with a reference group? These and many other questions are within the province of current theories of learning and personality and can be studied by techniques that psychologists can employ most proficiently. Such research may contribute significantly to an understanding of the relations between social structure and many phenomena now being studied by personality psychologists and social psychologists.

IDENTITY

The growing literature on the connections between the self and social behavior testifies to the significance of the topic of self in current psychological, sociological, and psychiatric thinking. Theoretical developments are still rudimentary. In fact, there is still no consensus about the definition of self. There are, however, a number of findings which suggest the possible outlines of ultimate theory. This section lists characteristics of self that have been mentioned frequently by various investigators, continues with the writer's tentative system of categories for analyzing phenomena often related to the self, and concludes with a few hypotheses about the operations of the self, particularly the process of self-appraisal during inner conflict.

Frequently Mentioned Characteristics of Self

Object of awareness. One sense of the concept is an object of awareness that identifies the person to himself and to those who know him; moreover, it has continuity over time [53, 101] so that the person feels that he is the same self today that he was yesterday.

Name. A person's self is identified socially by his name. Strauss [197] notes that everyone is known by a name and that a name signifies much more than a person's label. Quoting Dewey, Strauss says that naming identifies an object as a member of some category. By implication, the classification relates the object to others in the same and different categories. A name indicates a person's sex, for example, and often provides clues to his ethnic background, his religion, his generation, and his race. Classification thus provides clues to the types of activity in which a person may become involved.

Bodily feelings. One's body and its functions provide the locus for the sense of a continuing self with a name. In James's [101] opinion, the nucleus of the "me" is the bodily existence felt at the present time. According to a basic assumption of psychosexual theory, the body is the locus of the child's most important experiences during the first few years of life. Schilder [182] thinks that many bodily feelings represent projections of the self-feelings as they are experienced in the course of one's encounters with others, and Symonds [205] adds that the body becomes the "core of later self-value" because it is a source of pleasure and pain and a useful instrument for satisfying many social goals.

Axis of meaning. Many theorists regard the self as point of reference for establishing the meaning of different objects in our world. Boas [26] long ago commented on the universality of the pronouns "I," "thou," and "he," and said that they provide man with a linguistic means of distinguishing between himself, the person addressed, and the object of the conversation. MacLeod observes:

No object-organization can exist without a self as a point of reference, and . . . no feelings of selfhood can be maintained without at least some degree of organization in the area of the nonself. Self and object have many characteristics in common. Each constitutes a segregated entity in the same perceptual field, oriented and extended in space, persisting in time, maintaining its identity in spite of the changes in the field [133, pp. 200–201].

The self is thus the axis of a world view in which the properties of existence are distributed with respect to self and nonself [168].

Some theorists [114, 139] think that once the self is established it can be used as a device for learning about the properties of other people. One projects what one would feel if one were someone else and then identifies with him, putting oneself in his place and sensing how the projected traits fit him. By this procedure, one can tell whether "he is more or less like me, another self who has traits, can initiate action, can be kindly or cruel, praised or blamed for what he does" [133].

Control of activity. Each person thinks of himself as an "I," an active self with awareness and control of his actions. The self is experienced as doing the intending and the acting. In May's phrase [138], "The self is not the sum of the roles you play, but your capacity to know that you are the one playing these roles."

The self in social relationships. A person's picture of himself is indissolubly linked with his experiences in social relationships. Like Mead [139], Hilgard [92] is of the opinion that "the self, as a social product, has full meaning only when expressed in social interaction," and conversely, Cottrell [48] feels that social behavior can be understood only if it is seen in the context of the reciprocal influences that people exert on each other in face-to-face relationships. As pictured by Cooley [46], Mead [139], Sullivan [203], and Heider [87], the act of either participant is the product of an almost inconceivably complex interplay of acts and perceptions. Consider a meeting between two boys. At any moment, each boy responds not only to the other's previous act or series of acts, but also to anticipations of his reactions to possible acts by either boy. Because of his anticipations, each boy often inhibits his first impulse and considers the possible results of various acts in deciding how he will behave. Once he does act, his behavior enables the other boy to find out whether his anticipations were correct and elicits new impulses in him— impulses which he may inhibit or express. During this process, each participant is aware of himself and his meaning for the other, each judges the adequacy of his own and the other's behavior, each gets an impression of the evaluations of the other participant—and each takes all these judgments into account in his subsequent action.

Responsibility and the appraisal of self.   A man's self may be defined in terms of his unique manner of playing his roles. In fulfilling his minimal level of obligations, each person develops his own unique pattern of characteristics, a pattern that is evident in different areas of endeavor and over some period of time. Two teachers may both honor their responsibilities to their students, but in very different ways. One teacher is distant, whereas the other is warm; one covers the details of lessons compulsively, the other slights them in favor of grand theoretical schemes; one teacher is matter of fact, the other enthusiastic. Each becomes known to his students by the pattern of such traits, and the pattern describes his manner of expressing his "inner solidarity with [the] group's ideals and identity" [53].

Each member of a group has a vested interest in the performances of the others because the rights of his position are the responsibilities of another person and because most people in an organization are concerned with its welfare. Everyone is inevitably aware of everyone else's style of meeting obligations, and every member evaluates the others in terms of the adequacy with which they meet them. Often the evaluation of a particular skill is generalized to a man's total self. If a teacher gives boring lectures, his students may come to think of him as a poor teacher even though he covers the materials creatively.

The group's picture of a person's self determines their reactions to him. Goffman [75] observes that high esteem enables a group member to manipulate others to his own advantage—a fact that motivates most people to present themselves to others in the best possible light. Pepitone [163] has found that a person's attractiveness to others varies with their perceptions of his degree of responsibility, the goodness of his intentions, and the justifiability of his positive and negative acts. Such pressures reinforce conformity to norms and their internalization. Many anthropologists believe that the universal internalization of some norms is necessary for the survival of social systems. According to Wallace [213] the "regulation of patterned behavior" depends on the ability of people to act autonomously in accordance with the necessities of the social system. Therefore, each person must have an image of the society and of his own behavioral regularities to act in ways that reduce stress on all levels of the system. Hallowell [83] says that self-awareness is necessary for the working of the human social order, and that the self must be so organized as to facilitate relationships in a society.

TYPES OF IDENTITY AND THEIR STRUCTURES

Public Identity and Self-identity

In further references to the phenomena just listed, the generic term "self" will be replaced by "identity," which has two connotations: The pattern of observable or inferable attributes "identifies" a person to himself and others; his identity is a socially labeled object which is of great concern and frequently reevaluated both by the person and others in groups in which he is a member. Identity will be divided first into types and then into their components. Concepts within these categories were defined by the writer [143] as a prelude to the study of self-appraisal and the stability of social relationships.

In time, the members of a social group develop a detailed picture of each individual, his *public identity*. They conceive of this identity in terms of the characteristics which are most relevant to the group's norms and which therefore have the greatest effect on his relationships with others. Each man has as many public identities as he has associations in his various social groups and with people in different social categories. As James [101] puts it, " A man has as many social selves as there are individuals (or groups) who recognize him." The *objective public identity* is a person's pattern of traits as they appear to members of the groups; the *subjective public identity* is his perception of his appearance to the group. *Self-identity,* the person's private version of his pattern of traits, is similar to the more common "self-concept"—except that self-concept sometimes lacks the connotation that the self is a social object. Subjective public identity exerts a considerable influence on self-identity. In great part, "the individual experiences himself as such, not directly, but . . . indirectly, from the particular standpoints of other individual members of the same social group, or from the generalized standpoint of the social group as a whole to which he belongs" [139, p. 215]. Cooley's "looking-glass self" is similar to the present conception of public identity. To explain its development, he postulates the following sequence of events: "the imagination of our appearance to the other person, the imagination of his judgment of that appearance, and some sort of self-feeling, such as pride or mortification" [46, p. 183]. Of course, the judgments of others are not the only source of information about oneself. Once a person has internalized certain relationships, he interprets and evaluates himself independently. Internalization helps him evolve a self-identity which he views within the same rubric of meanings and values that he uses to conceive of the public identities of himself and others. There are not many references to public identity in the literature [53], but quite a few to self-identity.

Murphy [148] comments on the "self-observers," and Rogers [172] and many others have studied the "self-concept."

Structure of Identity

The building of theory requires, in addition to a classification of identities into types, a standard language for describing the components of each type and some of their interrelationships. The term "structure" refers to a "system of relationships between identifiable parts. It is . . . inferred from events observed under specified conditions and [it provides] . . . the basis for predicting behavior on subsequent occasions when there are reasons to believe that the system of relations has not changed" [162, p. 325]. Psychological structures can be described in terms of the spatial and temporal relations of their parts, the space being conceived in psychological terms. Viewed in spatial terms, the total identity can be divided into three general regions, the *core, subidentities,* and *persona.* The core may be viewed as the organizing part of the identity is that its traits interact with all the other traits outside the core. Symonds uses the term "core" when he discusses "concepts" which are usually "formed earliest, lie closest to the center of the personality, and hence are the most difficult to change" [205, pp. 118–119]. Among the examples he gives are sexual identity and one's identity as an only child in the family. Dai's [49] "primary self" is analogous to the core, as is James's [101] "truest, strongest, deepest self." Observing that each person has a hierarchical organization of selves, Dai notes that the first and most basic is acquired in the family. The primary self delimits the definitions of life goals and of behavior in secondary groups, sets in motion the basic self-defending and self-enhancing mechanisms, and is the major object of self-appraisal.

Some components of the core are suggested by the previously cited list of frequently mentioned characteristics of self. Wherever a man goes or whatever he does, his reactions involve his body and its sensations, his awareness and evaluation of self, his feelings of intentionality and control, and his sense of responsibility. It is probable that the core also includes identities developed while playing early roles in the family.

A peripheral region, the part of identity that is exhibited to the world, has been characterized by Jung as the persona [105] and by Goffman as the "presented self" [75]. The persona is modeled after the ideal identity and represents a compromise between characteristics of the actual self-identity and the pressures of the social situation.

Most traits of an identity may be found in the area between the periphery and the core, an area occupied by subidentities [143] or "secondary selves" [49]. Dai states that these tend to be restricted by characteristics of the primary selves, are learned later, and vary more with immediate situations.

Each man has quite a number of subidentities. Most of the more important ones are delimited by the boundaries of specific roles. Some are the individual's own creations. In discussing the life of G. B. Shaw, Erikson [53] discerns such unique subidentities as the snob, the noisemaker, and the diabolical one. A man has both the roles and subidentities of lawyer, father, and friend. Role and subidentity are similar in that both have attributes which are interpreted in terms of the group's norms. Role and subidentity also differ in a number of ways. Role refers to the minimum of attitudes and behavior required for participation in the overt expression of the social position [131]. A subidentity represents a cluster of all the attributes manifested by a person, not the minimal requirements for a position. A role can usually be played by a number of people; a subidentity, like a fingerprint, is unique to one individual.

There are further differences. A role designates pressures on an individual from people in complementary positions and describes what is required, expected, or tolerated by others. A subidentity consists of a person's traits and describes what he is like and how he does things. A subidentity indicates the kind of lawyer a man is, the kind of father he is. Finally, a role tends to be defined in terms of fewer standards than a subidentity, which is defined exhaustively by all the traits a particular person manifests in playing the role. Much more detail is required to depict a person's subidentity than to define his role.

Since a subidentity is delimited by the boundaries of a role, it is possible to evaluate compatibilities between the two. In general, the more the traits of a man's subidentity permit him to express himself within the limits of the role, the more compatible the role is with the subidentity. The incompatibilities between role and subidentity highlight the differences between the two. An illustration is provided by the man who became a laboratory technician because he did not earn good enough grades in school to qualify as a bacteriologist. As a laboratory technician he more than satisfies the expectations of the people with whom he has social relationships, so he is playing his role well. However, he is very unhappy because many aspects of his subidentity are more appropriate to the occupation he chose initially than the one he has.

The compatibility between role and subidentity has begun to interest sociologists. In a recent symposium Inkeles [96] observes that people who are recruited for some jobs tend to have personal characteristics which are not directly related to the roles, but have substantial effects on their adjustments to the roles. He feels that the personal characteristics ultimately affect the general quality of the institution's functions. In the same publication, Gouldner takes organizational theorists to task because they have not yet "incorporated into their theoretical models a systematic concern with the way in which the diverse social identities that people bring into the organization affect organizational behavior" [76, p. 412]. Aspects of identity which, in Gouldner's opinion, may affect organizational behavior even though they may seem irrelevant to the social role are sex, ethnic membership, special talents, and a self-image as a competent professional.

Dimensions and Traits

An understanding of the appraisal of identity requires information about the nature of a man's specific traits. Among others, Gerard [71] has observed that a social group often defines traits with respect to single dimensions. A *dimension* will be viewed here as a set of alternative attributes or traits which are treated by the group as having a common core of meaning and as constituting a roughly linear scale. Each trait thus has a *location* on the dimension. Locations on a specific dimension usually constitute only a partially ordered set, since they usually cannot be assigned precise numerical values.

Dimensions of identity may refer to qualities, such as kinds of physical traits; to possessions, such as a bank account; to social categories, such as race and religion; to skills such as the ability to play baseball; to impulses; to beliefs; to acts. Appraisal focuses attention on traits which reflect style of action; actions seem to have the most significance for evaluation of identity both by the public and the individual. An individual's act which is condemned by most people tends to shift him toward devalued locations on dimensions affected by that act. An approved act earns more coveted locations. If the act is ideal, the individual may be publicly recognized as an exceptionally good person.

Dimensions vary in degree of abstraction. Some dimensions, such as degree of activity or physical height, refer to observable characteristics. Some represent the group's deductions from observed behavior. From a man's degree of activity in a threatening situation, an observer may infer the directness of his aggression—the more active he is, the more aggressive they think he is. Some dimensions are defined at even higher levels of abstraction. From the directness of aggression and other traits, an observer may make inferences about a man's relative courage. From relative courage and other traits, the observer may infer a man's capacity for leadership. Various dimensions may thus be affected by the same action.

Identity dimensions are frequently bipolar, and the extremes are regarded as complements or opposites. Locations on two typical dimensions vary between dominant and submissive, courageous and cowardly.

The units are maximal at each end of the scale and decrease toward zero, which is at the midpoint. This conception of dimensions is contained in the work of Simmel [221], who contends that a statement and its negation do not define a dimension, since the negation states only nonoccurrence. It is the converse or, more precisely, the complement of a concept which completes the dimension. Simmel finds that what he calls a "social form" is usually near the midpoint of a scalable bipolar dimension. Social forms are simply the ways in which patterns of social action manifest themselves repeatedly. They are modal responses.

The meanings of dimensions may be clarified by examples taken from research on conflict and its resolution. A specific impulse is experienced in terms of four general categories of dimensions [145] which refer to the agent, the nature of the intended act, the kind of affect, and the potential object. Each category subsumes a number of dimensions, and various combinations of attributes from the four dimensions can express the original need with differing degrees of directness. To resolve conflict about an impulse, the person can shift his unacceptable location on any dimension to one he considers more acceptable. He can relinquish an impulse to attack in favor of verbal criticism. He can resolve his conflict about a hostile impulse to a relative or a good friend by substituting a more remote object. Anna Freud [66] describes a girl who could not tolerate her anger to her mother, deflected it to a number of other females, and finally attacked herself.

Conflicts about needs can also be resolved by substituting or redefining goals. Interviews with policemen reveal that they may feel guilty if they think they are inflicting pain on a suspect for sadistic reasons, but not if they view the same act as a means of obtaining evidence which will protect the community [216]. The act is made acceptable by redefining the aggressive goal as one of public service.

Values and Moral Standards

Depending on his frame of reference, an individual assigns particular *values* to each location on a dimension of attributes; associated with each dimension of attributes is a dimension of values. In terms of the dimension of values, one can distinguish at least one threshold in terms of which the distribution of attributes can be divided into segments. The dimension of courage may be divided into an ideal segment with locations characterized by great tenacity in the face of stress, a segment of acceptable locations entailing the ability to hold one's own against some opposition, and a segment with unacceptable locations entailing fear and lack of resolution.

Depending on the nature of the attributes and values, there can be marked differences in the ranges, numbers, and orders of segments. In evaluating some dimensions—cleanliness, for example—most people discriminate only two segments. Dirtiness is disapproved, cleanliness is acceptable but not idealized. Members of certain groups, however, have values which do idealize cleanliness, defining it as next to godliness.

Other dimensions may be evaluated in terms of two categories, but an ideal segment is substituted for the negatively evaluated one. If a woman volunteers her time to work in a hospital, her action is often considered exemplary; if she does not, the action—or lack of action— is not considered evil.

Ideal and unacceptable attributes are often located at the opposite extremes of a dimension, but there are many exceptions. On the dimension of courage, for example, both extremes may be unacceptable—one because locations are determined by actions the group considers cowardly, the other because locations are earned by actions the group considers foolhardy. Unlike some other dimensions, the idealized segment for degree of courage is next to one of the negatively evaluated segments.

Some dimensions are evaluated in moral terms and some are not. What is the difference between a moral and nonmoral standard? To have moral implications, a dimension must have three characteristics according to Miller and Swanson [145]. A location must be determined by specific acts, the acts must reflect the actor's intentions, and the alternatives must either hinder or help the ultimate goals of the community or one of its subgroups. Mistreating children is an action of concern to the community and is considered immoral when done deliberately. Failure to achieve an occupational goal is usually not a moral issue, except in the case of some ambitious families in the middle class; failure is not chosen, and it affects the ultimate good of one person, not the community.

There tends to be consensus in groups about meaning and value; people could not communicate without common definitions. Dimensions, which provide the frame for categorizing meaning and value, are continually reinforced by conversations, reading, and common experiences. Some experiences, like playing lacrosse, are so specialized that their meanings and values are unique to particular groups; other experiences, like being the object of physical attack, have such universal significance that they are interpreted in similar ways in a large number of societies.

Different social positions and categories can produce contrasting ways of perceiving and judging the same thing. Studies [107, 144, 218] of perception and socioeconomic status in American society suggest that there are greater differences in values than meanings. Boys in two social classes probably relate the stealing of valuable property to the dimension of courage, but differ in their evaluation of the act. Most likely, a lawyer's son would view the act as foolhardy, while the truckdriver's son would regard it as courageous.

Even dimensions of meaning can differ considerably with socio-economic status. This is partly because working-class Americans are less inclined to use concepts or to visualize abstract relationships than middle-class Americans [145]. Comparisons of people in different societies disclose even greater contrasts in dimensions of meanings. Lee's analysis [123] of the Trobriand Islanders' language reveals an interest in things or acts, but not in relationships. The Trobriander rarely makes comparisons, he passes no judgments, and he offers no motives for acts. His dimensions of meaning and value are obviously fewer and less elaborate than those of the middle-class American.

THE APPRAISAL OF IDENTITY

Much of the terminology introduced thus far points to some primary topics in studies of identity: discrepancies between standards and one's identity, self-realization, the process of self-appraisal. The appraisal of self is ubiquitous and continuous, part of all one's social interactions. Group members are usually very sensitive to dimensions which are subject to commonly accepted norms or which affect the attainment of the group's goals. Goffman (75) points out that groups are organized on the principle that any individual possessing certain social characteristics has a right to expect others to respond appropriately. In other words, most people act on the premise that anyone who, in his approach to others, signifies the possession of certain traits ought to have this claim honored. But he has the moral obligation to be what he claims he is. To protect the interest of the group, the other members subject his attempts to validate his claims to continual surveillance. Even in the case of a newcomer, it is not long before the group has a fairly clear picture of his social positions and categories, his roles, and the details of his public identity. From this picture the group makes inferences about his potential and evaluates him on a dimension of public esteem.

Self-appraisal: Actual, Potential, and Ideal Identities

To analyze the process of appraisal, various investigators have made comparisons between three identities: what the individual is like at a particular point in time, what he would be like if he achieved his potential, and what he would be like if he realized all his ideals about himself. These three are labeled here *actual identity, potential identity,* and *ideal identity,* and they can be seen as components of either the public identity or the self-identity.

The actual public identity is the pattern of current traits by which a person is known in a specific group. The actual self-identity is his conception of what he is really like. Each person and his public also have impressions of his potential identity which are based on their conceptions of his unrealized capacities. Sometimes the potential represents an aspired self, a "self to be realized [95, 148]; sometimes the concept has the quality of perfection that makes it virtually indistinguishable from the ideal. Some of the concepts which have this idealized quality are Jung's [106] archetype of selfhood, Adler's [4] "creative self," Rank's [165] "true self," and Maslow's [135] "actualized self." Seldom is the nature of the potential defined in other than general terms.

Every group has a conception of what an ideal member is like; in these terms, it may formulate the ideal public identity of a particular member. In adapting the group's ideal to his own potential, an individual develops an ideal self-identity. Horney [95] speaks of the ideal self, and Rogers [172] has investigated the self-concept that an individual would most like to possess. Murray [151] describes the "idealized picture of the self" as a set of ambitions leading to a goal conceived by the person as himself at "his highest hope." For Erikson [53], the "ego ideal" is "a set of to-be-strived-for but forever not-quite-attainable ideal goals for the self." According to Allport [6], the ideal self defines one's goals for the future: "Every mature personality may be said to travel toward a port of destination, selected in advance, or to several related ports in succession, their ideal always serving to hold the course in view."

Self-realization

Because a group takes for granted a man's volitional control, they hold each member responsible for his conformity to commonly accepted norms; his success in meeting his obligations is the subject of frequent appraisal by him and by the group. In part, they judge his success by the discrepancies between his actual and either his potential or his ideal identities. The sizes of his discrepancies are then used as indexes of what has been described in such terms as "self-realization" [95], "self-actualization" [135], and "self-determination" [165].

The complexity of appraisal is indicated by the different kinds of discrepancies and the extent of their interaction with other variables. The meanings of the discrepancies, for example, are complicated by the various estimates people have of their own potentials. A man usually conceives of at least two levels—the level he can reach if he uses all his time efficiently and the level he can reach if he develops his unrealized capacities and improves his skills. If a man visualizes these two types of potential, he is faced with two discrepancies between actual and potential locations on dimensions of his self-identity—and two additional ones for his public identity if his two conceptions of his potential are shared by his membership group.

It is also possible to conceive of a discrepancy between potential and ideal levels. Adler [4] concentrated on the problems of the physically handicapped who must learn to tolerate large discrepancies between potential and ideal identities. If a man and his group have two definitions of his potential and these are applied to both his public identity and his self-identity, he can have four different discrepancies between his four pairs of potential and ideal identities. Appraisal is even more complicated than has been suggested. Each of the eight discrepancies just listed can occur separately within any of a man's subidentities.

Thus far, the discussion of appraisal has proceeded on the assumption—frequently stated in the literature—that it is the identities which are seen as being discrepant. Yet in judging themselves and each other, people often think more in terms of specific traits than identities. A football player carrying the ball would like to feel less frightened when he is running into a group of tacklers. His dissatisfaction with himself is created by a discrepancy between actual and potential locations on a dimension of courage. If his fear affects his play, he may become known as a timorous football player or even a poor football player, but the generalizations which lead to these public subidentities are derived from discrepancies between specific traits.

Public Esteem and Self-esteem

For the study of self-appraisal, the analysis of identity requires some additional structural concepts. Dimensions of the total public identity can be ranked in terms of degree of *salience* [71], their significance in light of the group's values. To a football team, skill in running is more salient than cleanliness, for example. The greater the dimension's salience, the more effect fluctuation in location is likely to have on a person's status in the group. And, of course, the height of an individual's location affects his *public esteem*, a dimension on which the group judges the worth of his public subidentity. One may hypothesize, then, that public esteem varies directly with the salience of the dimension and the height of the individual's location.

Just as salience indicates the significance of dimensions for a group, *self-involvement* concerns the significance of dimensions according to a person's values; and just as public esteem is the group's evaluation of a person's public subidentity, his self-esteem is his own evaluation of his subidentity. One may postulate that the more a person is identified with his group, the higher the correlation between what is salient to them and what is self-involving to him. Another hypothesis parallels the association of public esteem with salience and the public's estimate of a man's location; self-esteem probably varies with self-involvement and the person's estimate of his location.

Estimates of location are often complicated by the person's need to maintain a minimal level of self-esteem, and by inevitable comparisons with locations on related dimensions. Benoit-Smullyan [17] postulates a trend toward "status equilibration," a tendency for locations on different dimensions to reach a common level. If an individual's locations on two different dimensions—prestige and political power, for example—are incommensurate, he will be impelled to bring them into line, preferably by raising his lowest location. Fenchel, Monderer, and Hartley [56] asked college students to rate their statuses in five different reference groups. All the ratings of an individual tended to approach a common high anchorage level, but the trend was relatively weak when the subjects attached little importance to their standings. These results suggest the following hypothesis: The accuracy with which a person estimates his location varies inversely with both his self-involvement in the dimension and the differences in valuation of the location and others on dimensions in which self-involvement is high.

Another aspect of structure, *centrality*, refers to the interdependence between one dimension and others [12]. Centrality and salience are sometimes regarded as synonyms. An illustration from Pepitone's analysis of the attribution of causality [163] points up the difference between the terms as they are used here. A person's attractiveness varied with his locations on such dimensions as degree of responsibility and goodness of intentions. These dimensions were *salient* to the group, but not necessarily *central;* their salience was unrelated to their interdependence with other dimensions. More central was social status, which interacted with some of the more salient dimensions. The higher a person's social status, the more the subjects justified any of his behavior which was relevant to status dimensions. If he seemed to be an important person, for example, the group showed a strong tendency to rate him high on the dimension of goodness of intentions. Harvey [86] has reported a similar phenomenon. The higher a child's sociometric status, the more his peers tended to overestimate his future performance in a test of level of aspiration; the lower his status, the lower was the estimate of his probable performance by his peers.

Salience and centrality may be applied to the analysis of total subidentities in addition to dimensions. A vocational subidentity is usually more salient than an avocational one; a sexual subidentity is usually more central than a recreational one.

Integration, differentiation, and *complexity* are three further dimensions of structure which are relevant to the resolution of conflicts resulting from low esteem. The dimension of integration may be divided into such segments as well-integrated, split, diffuse, and disintegrated. A split [67, 114] is created by a barrier to awareness of parts of the identity. The larger the number of barriers the less able the person is to integrate the functions of the divided parts. According to Erikson [53] diffusion is a common problem of adolescents, who have not quite given up the identities of childhood and have not yet quite mastered the identities of adulthood. The disintegration of an identity has been used by Federn [55] to explain many of the symptoms of psychosis.

Differentiation refers to the number of dimensions in a subidentity; the larger the number, the greater the differentiation. Complexity refers to the number of different categories, or clusters, into which dimensions can be grouped. Psychosexual theory [57] provides some examples. At each state of development a child is required to master a group of skills. In that a mature person can employ the clusters of skills at all psychosexual levels, he may be said to have a more complex subidentity than that of a fixated person who is proficient only with the clusters of the earlier levels.

DYNAMICS OF ESTEEM

Set and Discrepancy

The average person maintains a fairly stable self-identity by a routine set of activities with his family, his colleagues, his friends and neighbors. In his relationships with them, he anticipates responses appropriate to a person like him. These responses, which signify an acceptable level of public esteem, reaffirm his self-identity and maintain his self-esteem. Consequently he approaches others with a certain *set*.

The meaning of set may be illustrated by some hypothetical encounters. Two men meeting for the first time are prepared for certain events—an older man meeting a youth anticipates some expression of respect, for example. If the two are complete strangers, each anticipates a certain amount of formality. A homeowner expects a breezy informality or a mask of sincere warmth from a door-to-door salesman. Each person's set is in line with his self-identity and the public identity of the other person. Set is not a conscious expectation that a particular event will happen; it is a state of readiness, often unverbalized, referring not to any single event but to a range of probabilities. Any number of events may be congruent with the public and self-identities of the participants; it makes sense that they should occur to such a pair.

A man usually becomes aware of his sets when they are contradicted by events, revealing a discrepancy between his public and self-identities. If the group's perception suggests that he has underrated himself, he may find the fact difficult to assimilate but still he will probably make the necessary correction without much difficulty, particularly if his self-involvement in the dimension it not too intense. But what if the dimension matters deeply to him? An individual "must learn to be most sure of himself where he means most to others—those others, to be sure, who have come to mean the most to him" [53, p. 57]. "Any value entering the system which is inconsistent with the individual's valuation of himself cannot be assimilated; it meets with resistance and is likely, unless a general reorganization occurs, to be rejected" [121, p. 89]. In other words, it is difficult for anyone to accept what is incompatible with his sets, especially when it requires a shift from an approved to a morally unacceptable picture of himself.

A man's public identity may also be defined as the sets that his group has toward his behavior. Sets increase a group's stability by helping the members to anticipate each other's behavior, so both groups and individuals are likely to be conservative about changing their estimates of an object's esteem. Even when faced with evidence that contradicts their sets toward an accepted member, the group tends to resist change, particularly if the evidence bears on salient dimensions.

Variables Related to Fluctuations in Esteem

The definitions of public esteem and self-esteem can be used as a basis for defining additional testable hypotheses pertaining to the forces affecting the maintenance and reduction of discrepancies. It is hypothesized that public esteem varies as a function of four variables. One is the group's conception of the discrepancy between a man's potential and his actual locations. The discrepancy can be positive or negative, positive if the potential location is higher than the actual one. Two is the value of the man's actual location on a dimension. The more disapproved the attribute, or the larger the discrepancy (providing it is positive), the lower the public esteem. Three is the centrality of the dimension, and four is its salience. The more salient it is for the group, the greater will be the fluctuations in public esteem for the same shifts in location.

It may be postulated that self-esteem varies with the size of the discrepancy between potential and actual locations, the value segment of the actual location, the centrality of the dimension, and the person's self-involvement in it. All these variables are defined by the individual's perceptions, not those of this group.

Self-esteem is probably related to three additional variables, the *communicated public identity*, the discrepancy between public and self-esteem, and the weight of the reference group. The more specific and frequent are the group's communications about a member's public identity, the more cognizant he becomes of low public esteem and incorrect conceptions of his identity; the greater the discrepancy between his

public and self-esteem the more difficulty he has in fulfilling the obligations of his role; the more inclined he is to use the group's frame of
reference in evaluating himself and others, the more his level of self-
esteem corresponds to the level of his public esteem.

Given a particular discrepancy between public and self-esteem,
one can visualize forces which maintain the discrepancy and forces which
work toward a closing of the gap. The forces vary for discrepancies
differing in direction, which will be discussed in turn.

Consider a discrepancy in which public esteem is lower than self-
esteem. The individual has violated a norm, and the group has signified
its disapproval by lowering his public esteem. He can reduce the discrepancy by lowering his self-esteem or raising his public esteem. He
can maintain the discrepancy because he disagrees with the group's
judgments or rejects the group's frame of reference.

There will be external pressures to reduce the discrepancy by lowering
self-esteem. Group pressure to conform begins when public esteem falls
below a particular level and can become every coercive for salient and
central dimensions. The emotional effects of such disapproval have been
colorfully depicted by William James:

> In what capacity is it that I claim and demand a respectful greeting
> from you instead of this expression of disdain? It is not as being a bare I
> that I claim it; it is as being an I who has always been treated with respect,
> who belongs to a certain family and "set," who has certain powers, posses-
> sions, and public functions, sensibilities, duties, and purposes, and merits
> and deserts. All this is what your disdain negates and contradicts; this is
> "the thing inside me" whose changed treatment I feel the shame about;
> this that was lusty, and now, in consequence of your conduct, is collapsed
> [101, p. 322].

The description suggests that an individual will respond to a group's
pressure except when it is based on an intolerably low level of public
esteem. Hallowell [83] notes that the self is a primary object and that
positive self-evaluation is at the heart of a man's motivation. Sullivan
[204] observes that any event which may seriously disturb evaluation
of self-identity elicits marked anxiety because of the threatened change
in the established pattern of relating to others. The anxiety calls forth
the "security operations" which are intended to restore the level of
self-esteem.

Rogers [172] and Horney [95] feel that low self-esteem creates
great anxiety, interferes with behavior, and is a source of pathology.
Goffman [75] fills in the picture: Most people attempt to create an ideal
impression of themselves by their behavior. Anything incompatible with
the impression an individual has created brings the relationship to a

halt—the mutual definition is no longer valid, and the participants do not know how to act. The disruption raises questions about his capacities and lowers his public esteem. It is very difficult for the person unmasked to assign meanings to objects, to accept responsibility for his behavior, and to organize his actions toward others, since his self, which underlies his activities, is discredited.

The average individual will go to any lengths to prevent his self-identity from being so much demeaned that he cannot carry on his daily round. He may even adopt defenses which lead him into psychosis [55]. Epstein's study [52] of reactions to one's own expressive behavior reveals the conscious and unconscious self-deception that both normal and psychotic people use when evaluating themselves. Each subject indicated his preferences for samples of vocal expression, handwriting, and drawing. The samples included one by the subject—thoroughly disguised. Although the disguise was effective, all subjects rated their own samples most favorably. The schizophrenics, however, rated themselves much lower than when they recognized the samples as their own.

The more a person subscribes to the group's values, the more he inclines to agree with group judgment. If his membership group is also his reference group, he values their approval. When their disapproval contradicts his conception of himself he is inclined to change the level of his self-esteem to that of his public esteem—providing it is not too low.

Reducing a discrepancy may be accomplished by actual self-improvement that raises public esteem. For example, if an individual is considered too passive, he may learn to take initiative so that he can earn the respect of the group. But what if his standing is based on traits over which he has no power, such as insufficient intelligence? He must then find other methods of reducing anxiety, such as denial of the facts or joining another group.

The discrepancy between high public esteem and lower self-esteem creates its own set of problems. Gratification from high public esteem is very seductive, of course. From his high standing, a man can infer that his contributions are valued by the group and that he will probably have their support in future endeavors. The less he subscribes to the group's values, the easier it is for him to maintain the discrepancy. If they are a negative reference group, he may even be gratified by his success in deceiving them about his true capabilities. But what if he subscribes to group values? One way he can reduce the discrepancy is to lower his public esteem by revealing his inadequacies, but the potential penalties, particularly for unacceptable locations, tend to inhibit his impulse to expose his faults. More probably he will do everything he can to improve the basis for his self-esteem so that he will merit his public esteem.

Receptiveness to Information Bearing on Self-esteem

How will a person respond to information which may affect his self-esteem? Five general factors probably affect his reactions. One pertains to the clarity of the information—the less clear or the more inconsistent it is, the more readily it may be ignored or distorted. The content and its implications also effect receptivity to information. A man will probably be less receptive to evidence that his location on a dimension is lower than he thinks than to evidence that it is the same or higher. His receptivity will probably vary with the amount of the discrepancy, his degree of self-involvement in the dimension, and its salience for his social group.

The group's pressure on the individual is the third factor. The more salient the dimension, the more pressure the group will probably exert on a member with an unacceptable location. And the more potent the group is to an individual's frame of reference, the more compelled he is to act in accordance with the information.

The possibilities of changing one's location on a salient dimension or substituting an acceptable attribute on another dimension constitute a fourth group of factors. The more optimistic a person can be about improving his standing, the more he will be inclined to accept information about his unacceptable attributes without distortion. Even if he cannot improve his location, he can lower his self-involvement and transfer it to another dimension. The puny boy who dreams of being a football hero sometimes shifts his aim to a scholarly career in which he can find his ultimate gratification.

The possibilities of substitution vary with the dimension. Consider a core dimension—initiative is a good example, salient for many groups, an object of self-involvement early in the lives of most people, and high in centrality. If his location is unacceptably low, a man, particularly one in the middle class, cannot shift his involvement to another dimension; there are no alternatives which permit him to relinquish initiative and still maintain his self-esteem. He is forced to deceive himself about his self-identity or his perceived public identity. Substitution is most feasible when a dimension is neither central nor part of a man's core self-identity—a matter of choosing a sport in which he can excel, for example.

A person's manner of perceiving and resolving emotional problems constitutes a fifth group of influences. Given a low level of public esteem which he cannot change, a man can solve his problem by altering the information about his relative standing, his definition of the dimension, or his valuation of various locations. He can also attempt to manipulate his location, his self-involvement in the dimension, its salience for the group, or its centrality for him or the group. Or he can decrease his identification with the group, even give up his membership. In accomplishing each of these changes, he can be realistic or unrealistic. He can acknowledge the inadequacies underlying low public esteem and make practical efforts to improve, or he can deceive himself by employing defense mechanisms such as denial and repression. He can reexamine the values of his reference group and conclude rationally that they are unacceptable, or he can project his hostilities on his reference group and feel that even though he accepts their values they are persecuting him. If his public esteem is erroneously high, he can attempt to improve the performance which causes his low self-esteem, or reduce the discrepancy by a splitting of the self [113]. Once he has redefined the locations causing his low self-esteem as part of the "not me" [204], he can erroneously appraise himself as having the traits that the group attributes to him.

METHODS OF INVESTIGATING SELF-IDENTITY

Which dimensions are pertinent to a particular identity? How does one learn the characteristics of a specific dimension? How does one investigate perceptual distortions aimed at bolstering a sagging self-esteem? Research on identity is so new that these questions can be answered only tentatively.

Objective Self-description

Answers to objective tests provide the most common source of information about self-identity. Bill's Index of Adjustment and Values [19], one of the better known questionnaires, contains 49 of Allport's 124 trait names that had the greatest test-retest reliability in a pilot study. A subject answers three questions about each trait: How often are you this sort of person? How do you feel about being this way? How much of the time would you like this trait to be characteristic of you? The sum of all answers to the first question provides a description of actual self. The sum of answers to the second question is an index of the subject's self-acceptance or self-esteem. The sum of differences between the first and third questions is viewed as the discrepancy between actual and ideal selves. The subject may also answer the questions with reference to some peer group.

To measure some of the variables in Leary's method of coding interpersonal relationships [120], LaForge and Suczek [116] constructed their Interpersonal Check List, a test with 128 items, 8 for each of Leary's 16 variables. The subject checks adjectives that apply to him, depicting his actual and ideal selves. Brownfain's subjects [33] rate themselves on 25 items—most favorable or positive realistic self-concept; most unfavorable, or negative realistic self-concept; realistic private self-concept, and the most accurate estimate of oneself as seen by the group.

The Q-sort, one of the most popular methods of investigating the self, requires the subject to divide statements about himself into stacks. Fiedler and Senior [61] gave subjects 76 descriptive statements taken from Murray's research [151], and asked that they be sorted into eight categories, containing 1, 5, 12, 20, 20, 12, 5, and 1 statements in that order. The best description of him was to be placed at one extreme, the poorest was to go at the other. By requiring a specified number of statements in each pile, the investigators forced the subjects to create a normal distribution of their sortings.

Investigators have often assumed that the size of the discrepancy between actual and potential self is related to emotional disturbance. Turner and Vanderlippe [212] compared adjustment-test scores of Oberlin seniors in the high and low quartiles of a distribution of congruence. There were significant positive correlations between the congruence of actual and potential self and scores on the Guilford-Zimmerman Temperament Survey scales for ascendance sociability, stability, activity, and thoughtfulness.

Problems of validity. Studies of objective self-reports have revealed some serious limitations in the method—limitations which also apply to most paper-and-pencil personality tests. The subjects' cooperation is required and only conscious reactions can be elicited. The same item must be interpreted in the same way by all subjects; they may not consistently over- or underestimate themselves, nor may they distort responses to appear well adjusted.

Evidence indicates that the validity of self-reports varies with the subjects' self-involvement, the social desirability of the traits, and the content of items. According to Gerard [72], subjects who were given instructions calculated to elicit deep self-involvement ranked themselves higher than they were ranked by others and overestimated the rank they would get from others. Edwards [51] obtained a correlation of .85 between the mean Q-sort and his scale of social desirability. To eliminate this source of error, he has paired items by desirability and requested a choice between them. Jourard and Laskow's study [104] shows self-disclosure to vary with the topic. Subjects revealed much more about attitudes, interests, and work than about personality, the body, and money.

Few investigators have reported on their selection of items for the Q-sort or other methods of self-report. It is often implied that the same results would have been obtained had the items been different, but evidence is not produced in support of this assumption. Sometimes items lack uniformity of content; some are timeless, for example, while others specify frequency. Usually all items are added together and thus weighed equally. There is seldom an analysis of the relations between items and self-identity, and it is difficult to know whether the reported results apply to all dimensions or to only a very few.

Many investigators assume that self-reports are valid, but the results of three studies indicate the advisability of testing validity. Block and Thomas [25] report a significant relation between self-acceptance and the denial scale of the Minnesota Multiphasic Personality Inventory. Smith [188] found no significant associations between the degree of emotional disturbance in a group of patients and various techniques for obtaining the self-concept. Chance [39] found that patients' self-ratings agreed with their most acceptable self-pictures as rated by the therapists, but were unrelated to their references to themselves in therapy. Furthermore, attempts to validate a self-report by an objective criterion are sometimes complicated by response sets. A correlation between reported self-acceptance and a test of personal adjustment may be spuriously high because the subjects tend to react in the same way to socially desirable items in the two instruments.

Interpretation of self-reports raises three basic questions. Does high self-acceptance necessarily indicate high self-esteem? Some investigators assume it does, and ignore the possibility that high acceptance may simply mean that a person has recognized his limitations and is reconciled to them. Second, does a significant association between self-acceptance and an index of social effectiveness like sociometric status indicate that the former caused the latter? Some investigators are inclined to answer this question affirmatively despite the possibility that a third variable, such as high social status, may earn high sociometric ratings and result in development of a sense of self-acceptance. Third, does a discrepancy between reported actual and ideal selves reflect adequate statistical discrimination of subjects on both variables? Most investigations proceed on this assumption. In Rosen's study [174] descriptions of the ideal self varied very little, thus affording poor discriminations among the subjects. Other investigations reveal the same lack of variation. Correlations between criteria of maladjustment and discrepancy scores are usually no higher than those between the criteria and simple reports of self-acceptance. Such results make it seem probable that the ratings of ideal self contribute nothing to the variance of discrepancies between actual and ideal self.

Studies of self-acceptance suggest the advisability of controlling such variables as sex, education [82], pathology [69], and social class [112]. In view of some of the relations postulated in this chapter, an investigator should select items from clearly defined dimensions and should find out whether the items which belong to different dimensions should be combined in one score. Discrepancy scores would be interpreted more easily if information were provided about dimensions from which items were selected, the subjects' actual as well as perceived locations, the centrality of dimensions, and the subjects' self-involvement.

The Semantic Differential

One technique with considerable promise for eliciting information about self-identity, the semantic differential [156], studies the meanings of words for the subject. He is asked to locate a group of concepts on each of a series of seven-point scales whose extremes are such polar adjectives as "good" and "bad." The scales were derived by a factor analysis of ratings by 100 subjects of 20 words on 76 scales. Osgood analyzes the meanings of ratings by projecting them on factors labeled "evaluative," "potency," and "activation" and defines differences in terms of distances in n-dimensional space. In different studies Osgood has changed the concepts in accordance with the topic. In an investigation of a therapeutic case [155], the patient was asked to rank fifteen concepts on ten scales. The concepts, describing the major persons and problems involved in therapy, included such terms as "me," "my mother," "my job," and "sex."

The semantic differential has much to commend it. It is objective. It permits scaling and mapping concepts, so it is suitable to the diagramming of the total identity. The ratings permit inferences about unconscious aspects of the subject's identity. The disadvantage is that both concepts and scales are selected by the experimenter. The subjects can only rate the given words on the given scales—and they do not necessarily include the dimensions and values that the subjects use to view themselves. There is an encouraging similarity in the factors obtained from different subjects, but there is some question whether other techniques—projective tests, for instance—might not produce other factors.

The Repertory Test

In Kelly's opinion, if a subject uses a construct to compare other people, he must also view himself in its terms. "When . . . a client describes the other people who populate his intimate world, he is essentially stating the coordinate axes with reference to which he must plot his own behavior" [111, p. 132]. Kelly's Repertory Test [111] requires the subject to think about people he has known—a favorite teacher, his wife, a neighbor, a colleague. The original test presents twenty such roles, each on a separate card. The subject writes the name of the person he has known who was most appropriate for the role on each card. Then the examiner presents the cards in combinations of three and asks, "In what important way are two alike, but different from the third?" The answers define a construct. The word "myself" may be written on one of the cards to see how well the constructs apply to the self-identity. From various sortings, different constructs are obtained.

The test has an important asset: The subject, not the examiner, produces the attributes of a construct and then develops the structure. However, the test is limited by the list of roles. Thus far, the list has not been constructed in the light of a systematic consideration of social structure, but this is easily remedied. There are serious questions about the subjects' cooperativeness and accuracy. Kelly says it is necessary to assume that the subjects respond in terms of their more crucial constructs, they have insight into their reactions, and possess the language to describe them accurately. Such assumptions may be warranted with some subjects, but not with those who have limited education or intelligence or feel very threatened.

Relatively Unstructured Techniques

McLeod [133] stresses the importance of obtaining the subject's view of his world. He suggests the intensive interview because it gives the subject leeway to order his perceptions in his own way. Hilgard [92], concerned with the unconscious parts of the self, advocates using projective techniques and clinical interviews. The present writer and his colleagues have investigated self-identity by the use of subjects' self-ratings and references to themselves in projective tests and recorded interviews, and independent ratings of subjects based on analyses of behavior during recorded interviews. From such data, it is possible to develop indexes of objective and subjective public subidentities and of conscious and unconscious parts of the self-identity in a manner described by Leary [120] and by Chance [39].

IDENTITY AND SOCIETY: SOME OVER-ALL IMPRESSIONS

The Masculine Subidentity: An Illustration

The concept of subidentity represents a special way of grouping phenomena which are often classified in other ways. One example, the masculine subidentity, will now be discussed in order to illustrate some of the forces which mold dimensions, the nature of some of the dimensions, and how the concept of identity facilitates the phrasing of relationships between the structure of society and the individual's psychological characteristics.

The male has a social obligation to propagate the species. Attributes which interfere with this function—impotence, sterility, and homosexuality —are regarded as nonmasculine and may even make a man an object of pity or ridicule.

Dimensions of the body image, and the part of the masculine subidentity, are salient for most groups. "Physical attractiveness" is a label for a cluster of locations on some dimensions of the body image, dimensions in which there is much self-involvement. The meanings of this cluster are socially shared and high in centrality, and a man's traits can have profound effects on many social relationships as well as sexual ones. The significance for self-esteem of unacceptable locations on physical dimensions is illustrated in Levy's [125] interviews with twenty boys. All but two revealed sensitivity to variations from the group's norms. All were concerned with physical prowess, and boys who were weak, short, or thin were very anxious about these attributes. Deviant characteristics of the nipples or genitals created severe doubts about the masculine subidentity. The most frequently mentioned sources of standards were peers' criticism and parents' disapproval or anxiety about disfigurements and malfunctions.

Probably because of their economic and military consequences, physical strength and skill have always defined some dimensions of masculinity. Boys' games are designed to develop these qualities. It is worth noting that girls' contests are not so rough and do not require as much aggressiveness or strength. Thus girls do not threaten the dominance of males, which is important to both sexes.

It is not possible to consider masculine subidentity without taking occupational subidentity into account. A boy is compelled to make his way in the economic system, which has traditionally been entrepreneurial and contains many specialized occupations that are hierarchically ordered with respect to status. Theoretically, anyone is qualified for positions with high status; they are achieved, not inherited. In addition to his opportunities, the male has definite responsibilities. He is usually the breadwinner. Before the days of bureaucratization, this meant taking risks to realize occupational goals, taking initiative, persisting, being aggressive and competing in accordance with accepted rules. When necessary he was a good loser [44].

Sex differences are very significant in traits relevant to occupational success. Men are more interested than women in mechanical skills and information [199], for example. Men, particularly those in the working class, are more centrifugal than women in style of physical expression [145], which may be attributed to the fact that men are more accustomed than women to using their large muscles. On attitude tests men get lower scores than women for expressions of passivity, sensitivity, and compassionateness [207], traits appropriate to the feminine subidentity.

A listing of some dimensions of the masculine public subidentity illustrates how closely the most salient ones are related to a man's social positions and categories. With reference to their economic positions, men are assigned locations on dimensions such as the capacity to take risks, amount of mechanical aptitude, and directness of aggression. With reference to their social position as husband and their sexual category, men are assigned locations on dimensions such as the desire for hetero-sexual objects, potency, and fertility. Dimensions of body image are also included—height, strength, physical skills and physical attractiveness. Most of these traits are part of the core, as are dominance and initiative. Of course the ways these traits are evaluated, and the resulting levels of public esteem, depend in great part on a man's reference group: physical strength and mechanical interest are more important for status among laborers than among the rather sedentary members of the middle class.

Limits of the Concepts of Public and Self-Identity

How does identity differ from the rest of personality as it is usually conceived by the psychologists? Identity is everything which the individual regards as being part of his self or someone else's self. All his other perceptions are excluded. Also excluded are the phenomena inferred by the investigator—the capacities, the dispositions, the structures and processes—which are the subject matter of most theories of personality. Some of them are memory, defense mechanisms, mobility, thinking, and intelligence. These concepts are part of the language of the investigator, not the layman. Some of these concepts, such as defense mechanisms, are, by definition, unknowable to an individual when he uses them.

Identity and the Relations Between Social Structure and Personality

Social positions and categories have been examined for the light they might throw on the origins of subidentity and ultimately, on certain dimensions of personality. As has been noted, an individual in a social position seeks to have his rights honored and to fulfill his obligations to people in related positions. The group communicates its norms about these relationships in the form of expectations about roles. For effective communication, everyone in a group must have the same frame of reference; without shared meaning and values, people could not anticipate the form and nature of events, and social behavior could be neither initiated nor sustained.

People develop many subidentities in the course of occupying social positions and playing the appropriate roles. If a man fulfills his obligations and honors the rights and privileges of people in related positions, he earns a high level of public esteem and the group bestows appropriate rewards. If he does not fulfill his obligations and violates the rights and privileges of people, he earns a low level of public esteem and the group expresses its disapproval. The group's reactions undoubtedly reinforce his learning of the social norms and the meanings of various dimensions of public identity.

The concept of identity seems essential to the study of relations between social structure and personality. Inkeles and Levinson [97] feel that research on personality development has underrated the relevance of adult roles, the stages of socialization, and the child's environment. The use of principles pertaining to subidentities and their development avoids this tendency. In the course of learning to relate to significant people, an individual acquires different subidentities at each stage of development. The patterning of a subidentity during any stage is a product of traits learned in previous stages and roles played in relationships with significant individuals. The subidentities of one stage may or may not be integrated with those of the next, depending upon the similarities in the stages—people with whom the individual relates, types of relationship, and the subidentities themselves. The practices of significant adults thus represent only one of a number of factors which may affect a child's subidentity; early events—viewed in the contexts of social relationships—are components in a sequence. not "causes" of the adult's subidentity.

Public Identities as Sources of Situational Pressure

Role expectations and behavior settings have been named earlier as two primary sources of situational pressures. Two additional sources are public identity and public esteem. Once a person develops a public identity, the group has its sets concerning his behavior in most situations and assigns him responsibilities in terms of its conceptions of his locations on salient dimensions. For a member to participate in group endeavors, others must know what to anticipate from him, and he must act in accordance with their anticipations.

From these observations it is inferred that most groups resist change in the identities of their members; the greater the change, the more marked the resistance. Of course, this varies with time and the nature of the change. Group recognition of change may require the time it takes to reorganize, and improvement is usually recognized before a deficiency. Groups are probably more conservative than individuals in recognizing change; thus a man's self-esteem fluctuates more rapidly than his public esteem.

The group's power rests largely in its capacity to define the level of a member's public esteem. The more identified he is with the group, the more he evaluates himself as they evaluate him. In other words, the greater their weight as a reference group, the closer the public esteem is to the self-esteem, and the more motivated the member is to conform to the group's pressures. The extent of his conformity probably varies with additional variables such as the strengths of boundaries which keep him in the group, the strengths of needs gratified by active relations within the group, and the exclusiveness of the group in satisfying his needs.

Identity as a Product of Striving for Consistency

The individual's inclination to reduce discrepancies between public identity and his self-identity, the principle of status equilibration, the creation of a false impression of compatibility between different parts of the self-identity by defensive distortions—these postulates can be explained by the assumption of a striving toward consistency, which, in much of the literature on perception, is taken as inherent in man. Lecky [121] states that man is "a unit in himself, a system which operates as a whole" and continually strives for one goal, the "maintenance of a unified organization." Lecky uses the concept of consistency in two senses. First, a person's interpretations of events must be consistent with his experiences for him to be at "harmony with the environment." Second, his interpretations of events must be internally consistent for him to maintain his "individuality." Like Lecky, Rogers [172] and Snygg and Combs [190] accept a striving toward consistency as an organizing principle.

Heider [88] postulates a force toward "balance"—one example of which is the condition in which a man's attitudes toward an individual or event are all negative. When some attitudes are positive and others are negative, the resultant tension creates a state of imbalance which continues until there is a cognitive reorganization. Festinger's "dissonance" is similar—he considers it a kind of relationship among cognitions. As he defines it, "Two opinions or beliefs, or kinds of knowledge are dissonant with each other if they do not fit together—that is, if they are inconsistent, or if, considering only the particular two items, one does not follow from the other" [60, p. 13].

Dictionaries commonly use the synonyms "agreement" and "congruence" for "consistency." To the logician, consistency signifies that two propositions are neither contrary nor contradictory. In some of the literature, consistency is virtually equated with "comprehensibility"; people are described as behaving consistently, having consistent attitudes, and looking for consistency in the behavior of others and in events. Consistency appears to be defined in more than one way, but is probably used most often to mean absence of contradiction.

Psychotherapists and perceptual psychologists are interested in consistency because it is a requisite for rational action. Locations on dimensions which are inconsistent with a man's norms make it difficult for him to know how to act. Defense mechanisms help him to become unaware of contradictions between parts of his subidentity and give him the false assurance that he is acting consistently. Once he learns that consistency makes action possible, he looks for it in new situations. He may then become anxious when events seem inconsistent because he has learned that without a "scheme of understanding and prediction" [111], he cannot anticipate them. The recognition of predictable events and the capacity to behave consistently are learned in many social settings with different types and degrees of reinforcement; thus people differ considerably in their notions of consistency, their capacity to recognize it, and their striving for it.

Freud [67], Ferenczi [58], and Werner [215] supply ample evidence that the power to perceive certain fundamental physical principles does not exist at birth and is often developed with difficulty. Even the bases for discriminating between objects in the environment and in fantasy must be learned. It takes months to learn the cues that provide a consistent sense of distance, years to get a consistent picture of causation or time. Under stress even the normal adult can lose his capacity to discriminate cues of distance or of real versus imaginary objects within a very few hours [18]. Some symptoms of personality disorder reflect the abandonment of the more mature, consistent responses in favor of others entailing confusions of internal and external events or between contiguity and causality [55]. Even such regressive reactions may be interpreted as having a kind of consistency, but it is a kind which entails very different principles from those characteristic of more mature reactions.

Certain types of behavior show no sign of consistency as it is interpreted here. If an infant's experiences are not ordered in some way he can understand, his behavior will not be guided by a general striving for compatibility between perceptions. The world of an infant may be so lacking in predictable events that he never even learns the simplest perceptual constancies; he is said to have "marasmus" [194], and he usually dies.

Lack of consistency may also characterize the behavior of adolescents and adults. When a society creates many stresses, the incomprehensibility of events and the resultant frustrations may discourage members from seeking consistent methods of adjustment. Some investigators use this explanation to account for the unwillingness of delinquents to make an adequate adjustment to the adult world. It is possible to imagine a society in which the relationships in some major organizations are so poorly organized that impulsive, nonrational reactions are the rule [50]. If this drift toward inconsistent behavior goes too far, the society ultimately perishes.

It seems prudent to regard consistency as a group of phenomena, not as an explanatory principle. To say that someone does something because he is trying to be consistent only suggests a probable range of explanations, the details of which are being studied by such investigators as Heider [88], Cartwright and Harary [38], Newcomb [153], and others.

THE STUDY OF SOCIAL INTERACTION

Investigators have three general reasons for studying social interaction: to explain the sources of people's attraction to and rejection of each other; to analyze the patterns of reciprocal social behavior; and to measure the forces and barriers which contribute to the strengths and weaknesses of relationships. To answer the first question, social scientists find people who have chosen, rejected, or ignored each other and compare them with respect to variables which, according to some theoretical principle, may have contributed to the mutual reactions. Among the variables which have been studied are similarity of interests and compatibility of defenses.

Patterns of reciprocal behavior can be investigated whether or not the subjects have chosen each other. Teachers decide on their students' seating arrangements; hospitals assign patients to rooms. While people who have not chosen to share an activity do not, at first, have a relationship, their behavior can be explained by some of the principles that bear on the patterning of interaction.

To find out why people stay together or drift apart, investigators have observed subjects in relationships characterized by different degrees of stability or different patterns of mutual adjustment. Queries have focused on the forces and barriers, conscious and unconscious, external and internal, which account for spouses or friends or co-workers staying with each other and maintaining effective relationships or separating.

Although lacking controls and objective techniques, psychotherapeutic case studies contain a wealth of material on the conditions which help or hinder people's attempts to get along with each other. Controlled empirical studies have not been numerous; researchers have apparently been discouraged by the heterogeneity of the variables which may affect the stability of relationships. Acceptable basic categories for classifying action, identifying and measuring needs, and analyzing changes in relationships over time are still to be developed.

There is little agreement about definitions of interaction and relationship. The definitions of "interpersonal behavior" used by Leary [120] and Schutz [183], for example, refer to what many people would regard as intrapersonal traits. Leary considers an individual's behavior as interpersonal if he is related overtly, consciously, ethically, or symbolically to another human being. Schutz considers behavior interpersonal if the individual takes a second person into account in making a particular decision during a particular interval of time.

In contrast, other investigators emphasize the mutuality of interactions. In Heider's [87] version of full-fledged interaction, each participant must be able to represent to himself the situation that includes himself and others and the fact that the others possess a corresponding view of the situation. Interaction thus requires similar and mutually relevant representations. Parsons [158] conceives of a relationship as a social system involving an interaction of personalities, each of which is an object to the other in a cognitive, cathectic, and evaluative sense. Given such differences in definitions, one cannot expect investigators to agree on a common set of problems. The object of this survey is to summarize the questions that have been raised and some of the more promising methods.

BASES OF SOCIAL RELATIONSHIPS

Interpersonal Communication

Some theorists emphasize communication as necessary for social interaction; in most cases, they have added mutual awareness as a subsidiary condition. For Rogers (172), the "least minimal experience" is a social contact in which each participant makes a perceived or subceived difference in the experience field of the other. Ruesch and Bateson [178] consider a relationship to be a system of communication which requires shared cultural premises and the participants' mutual recognition that each has entered into the perceptual field of the other. Lippitt's [132] analysis of social interaction invokes each person's perceptions and evaluations of the expectations, evaluations, and behavior both by himself and the other participant. Block and Bennett [24] suggest that social interaction be analyzed in terms of combinations of effective and ineffective senders and receivers of communications.

Background, Experience, and Skill

Much of the sociological literature supports the principle that people are attracted to others with similar or complementary backgrounds and skills. Winch's [220] review of the research on marriage shows that compared to people not married to each other or to the chance distributions of traits, husbands and wives are significantly more alike in age, race, religious affiliation, ethnic origin, location of residence at the time of marriage, socioeconomic status, amount of formal education, and previous marital status. Spouses also show marked resemblances in intelligence, neurotic tendency, and temperament. He is inclined to reject the assumption that these similarities provide the basis for marital compatibility and considers them important primarily because they provide social access to potential spouses. Within the field of choice, each person then selects the one who gives the greatest promise of gratifying his or her basic needs—not necessarily the most similar person. While Winch has provided evidence that spouses gratify each other's needs, he has not investigated the claim that similarities in such variables as intelligence and economic status only provide social access and do not contribute to the strength of the marriage.

Studies reveal that skills developed by participation in certain relationships may affect the choice of partners and the stability of their relationship. Gilchrist [74] asked members of social groups to work together on tasks and arranged to have some people succeed and some fail. When requested to choose members of new groups to engage in an activity requiring the same skills, most subjects wanted to be with people who had succeeded. The same trend continued in further regrouping. In short, people selected each other on the basis of relative skill in the field of endeavor.

Toman [211] found that marital compatibility varied with patterns of sex and order of birth in the spouses' families. The marriage between the older brother of a sister and the younger sister of a brother tended to be the most successful. Both partners were used to getting along with a sibling of the opposite sex. Both were untroubled by conflicts of rank, since the husband had been accustomed to living with a younger female, and the wife had been accustomed to living with an older male. The marriage between the younger brother of a brother and the younger sister of a sister tended to be least successful. Being younger siblings, both husband and wife had come to rely on the support of an older person. In some cases each partner tried to transform the other into a senior on whom he or she could depend. Neither person had lived with a sibling of the opposite sex, so that marriage required many novel adjustments.

Attitudes, Interests, Values

Winch [220] lists studies relating marital compatibility to similarity of religious, esthetic, and political interests and of attitudes to such topics as birth control and communism. The reported associations [93] between frequency of social contact and increasing similarity of orientation and between mutual interests and friendship are consistent with these findings. Newcomb [153] found that when a group had lived in a cooperative residence for approximately three months, mutual liking was associated with agreements in attitudes toward specified objects and rank-ordered scores on the Allport-Vernon-Lindzey Study of Values. The population of seventeen students broke into rather cohesive subgroups that could have been predicted on the basis of common interests.

Spiegel and Kluckhohn's research [193] on conflict in immigrant families revealed two sources of strain in "cultural-value orientations." One was the lack of fit among some values of the original culture; the second was incongruity between original values and the dominant American values. Conflicts of values were, for the most part, denied.

Roles and Subidentities

It is often claimed—although seldom supported—that adequacy of social interaction depends on the compatibility of the participants' roles. Spiegel [192] reports that the expectations communicated by each participant lead the other to fall in line, providing there is a "complementarity" or "matching of roles." Discrepant expectations create a tension which participants attempt to reduce by persuasion. Among the causes of discrepancies are ignorance of one's role, and disagreements between role partners about common goals, methods of playing a role, cultural values, and one's rights to take a role.

Sullivan [203] may be alluding to either roles or subidentities when he refers to "each 'me' and its appropriate 'you'" as aspects of configurations that recur in the relationsips between husband and wife over a period of years. In another publication [204], however, Sullivan emphasizes that a relationship requires an integration of complementary needs and reciprocal patterns of activity, terms which seem more relevant to subidentities than to roles. Sullivan adds that some needs and styles of behavior—particularly those reflecting anxiety about relationships with others—are organized as part of the self system.

In the view of Ruesch and Bateson [177, 178] roles provide a code for interpreting the significant rules that govern the situation and communication. These investigators use the rules to analyze a system of interrelating selves. Miller [143] has proposed an analysis of relationships in terms of subidentities whose interaction is partly constrained by the norms relevant to the participants' roles.

Social role is the primary unit that Ackerman [2] uses to analyze interaction. By equating social role with the social self, however, he seems to be referring to what is called "public identity" in this chapter. He discriminates between the social self and the "inner self," and apparently overlooks the sociologists' concepts of social position and social role.

Herbst [89, 90] asked a group of children to name the people in the family who performed various tasks and the people who decided on the assignments. He also asked whether there were disagreements about the assignments. From the data he drew inferences about the structures of roles within the family, the sources, degrees, and directions of power relationships, and the resulting degrees of tension.

One of Herbst's primary interests was identifying external and internal pressures that prompt a child to perform household tasks. To this end he developed indexes of the different pressures bearing on a task. One is the ratio of external pressure to internal attraction—parental expectation versus liking for the task. Others are the ratios of external pressure to internal pressure, and of attraction to internal pressure. A sense of obligation is an example of an internal pressure. From answers to the questionnaire Herbst also derived various patterns of external pressure. One is the coalition, a subset of persons in a group which exerts pressure toward the attainment of a specific end—father and mother together exert pressure on the son to take responsibility for keeping the drive free of snow.

Mechanisms of Defense

Clinicians frequently assume, in their interpretations of cases, that hierarchies of defense mechanisms impose limits on the kinds of relationships that are possible between people. Johnson's [102] picture of the complementary defenses of parents and children throws light on the origins of children's symptoms, such as phobias, transvestism, and soiling. The parents can use defenses that facilitate control and unawareness of their forbidden impulses only so long as these impulses are gratified vicariously through the children's behavior. To retain their vicarious gratifications, the parents unconsciously encourage their children not to change, even to the point of providing rewards for the continuation of the symptoms. The children are motivated by the rewards and by identification with the parents to retain the symptoms and to remain unaware of the underlying conflicts.

The literature on psychotherapy contains many examples of symptoms which reflect the complementary defense mechanisms used by pairs of people. Weiss [214] describes a man who—defending himself against castration threat by avoidance of sexual relationships—had a stable marriage with an infantile woman who achieved an indifference toward sex by repression and regression. Jacobson [99] reports the marriage between a schizophrenic man and a rigid, compulsive woman whose predictable behavior helped him to strengthen his own defenses against the threat of a breakdown. Menzies [140] has shown how group members who differ in status and are under pressure use projection to stabilize their relationships. The employee in the senior position attributes irresponsible parts of himself to his junior, and the junior projects harsh disciplinary impulses on his senior.

Cohen [44] conducted a controlled investigation of the association between subjects' social compatibility and their hierarchy of defenses. The subjects were college students with common psychosexual disturbances, which he aroused in order to elicit defenses. The Blacky Pictures and the auxiliary technique, the Defense Preference Inquiry, were employed to study the psychosexual dimensions of oral sadism, anal expulsiveness, oedipal intensity, castration anxiety, and sibling rivalry, and the defenses of projection, avoidance, regression, reaction formation, and intellectualization. Cohen paired his subjects on the basis of preferred defense and intensity of psychosexual disturbance. When the pairs of subjects performed a task that aroused the common psychosexual disturbance, subjects with predilections for projection were more negative to each other than were subjects with other kinds of defenses. When both projectors were high in a common area of conflict, their comments about each other were more negative than when only one projector was high. The unfavorable reactions to social contact were not characteristic of people with any other common defenses.

CLASSIFICATION OF NEEDS

Most research on social interaction has concentrated on compatibility between the needs of participants, the actions of participants, and the actions of one participant and the needs of the other. Consensus about terminology is still lacking, but there are some similarities in the systems of classification employed by certain investigators. The similarities, the significance of some of the obtained associations, the possibility of comparing the results of different studies—all these lend promise to the field of research and even suggest the outlines of a future theoretical system concerning social interaction.

Murray's System

Many studies have made use of Murray's list [151]. Of the original group of 20 items which were proposed after an intensive study of a few subjects, the needs for achievement, affiliation, aggression, and dominance have been used most frequently in empirical research.

In a further classification Murray [149] suggests such dichotomies as primary or viscerogenic and secondary or psychogenic; overt or manifest, and covert or latent; focal with specificity for classes of objects, and diffuse or general. In addition there are proactive needs, which are largely determined from within; reactive needs, which are elicited by external events; effect needs, which lead to some desire or goal state; process activity needs, which are aimed at "sheer function pleasure"; motile needs, which are aimed at perfection in an activity.

Murray [149] has also proposed that needs be viewed in terms of initiating inner states, external situations, and imagined situations which are accepted as future possibilities. The classification also includes categories for directions of movements and words, kinds of aim and effects produced, and the activities, effects, or situations with which a need is associated.

Investigators of social relationships have made use only of Murray's original lists of needs. Winch [220] compared husbands and wives on 12 of Murray's needs and the three additional traits of anxiety, emotionality, and vicarious gratification. His predictions concerning the complementary matching of needs in marital partners were supported by the results. Factor analyses of subjects and variables produced the same trends. A bipolar dimension varying from "assertive" to "receptive" is common to the variables most important for marital compatibility; assertive people tend to marry receptive ones, and vice versa. Some of the obtained factors are dominance versus submission, succorance versus nurturance, independence versus succorance, yielding dependency, and hostile dominance.

Gardner and Thompson [70] selected 12 needs from Murray's list to investigate "social harmony" among undergraduate residents of fraternities. On each scale, a subject estimated the potentialities of others in his fraternity for satisfying several of his psychological needs, such as affiliation, succorance, and achievement. Various indexes of social compatibility derived from the scales were significantly related to good morale, as indicated by pleasant associations to fraternity life, essays written in defense of fraternities, and ratings of the group's effectiveness. Associations between indexes of compatibility derived from the scales and actual accomplishments of fraternities were not very high.

Other Systems

Stock and Thelen [195] constructed the Reactions to Group Situations Test to measure Bion's [20] four valences, fight, flight, pairing, and dependency. Subjects completed 44 stories with themes of pairing, fight, dependency, flight, and mixed or ambiguous situations. Endings were analyzed to determine the subjects' acceptance or rejection of their covert and overt expressions of valences and the extent to which action, inhibited action, and ideation were favored. In a study of the classification system, the subjects' self-descriptions were obtained by Q-sorts of 60 statements concerned with such themes as the four valences, counterpairing, and counterdependency. The results revealed needs to take a directive role, establish intimate relationships, seek directive aggressive outlets, retain status, and avoid dissension.

Schutz [183] thinks that interaction is prompted by three needs—for inclusion, control, and affection. The first is the need to establish and maintain satisfactory interaction and association with people. The second is the need to establish and maintain satisfactory relationships in positions of control and power. The third is the need to establish close personal feelings with another. Each need is analyzed in terms of its typical action, feeling, and directionality, as well as its forms—desired, ideal, anxious, and pathological. In applying the forms to the need for inclusion, Schutz proposes this list: oversocial, social, undersocial, and psychotic, particularly schizophrenic.

Jones and Thibaut [103] reject the usual list of needs in favor of "intermediate action goals." The first is the gaining of cognitive clarity about a shared event; each participant takes an informational orientation and uses the other as an extension of his own perceptual reality testing. The second is the attainment of consensual validity; each participant tries to get the other's support for his own values, attitudes, and aspirations. The third is the maximizing of beneficent social responses; a person acts to elicit positive, affective evaluation from other participants, regardless of their values or beliefs. His action is motivated by a desire for increased power over others or for reassurance of his own worth. The fourth goal is achieved by some external means; one participant may try to influence the other by providing access to particular activities or people or the support to attain the group's goal.

CLASSIFICATION OF ACTION

Problem Solving in Small Groups

Probably the most generic system for classifying action has been proposed by Bales [9], who developed 12 categories by studying problem solving in small groups, hoping that they would be relevant to the dynamics of larger social systems. A subject can show solidarity or tension release, agree, give suggestions, opinion, or orientation; he can also ask for orientation, opinion, or suggestions; and he can disagree, show tension or antagonism. These abstract categories pertain only to processes; the system is not pertinent to substantive problems.

Bales's categories can be subdivided in a number of ways. In one classification the 12 are reduced to the 6 primary dimensions of orientation, evaluation, control, arriving at decisions, tension management, and integration. Another division produces 6 positive actions and 6 which vary from neutral to negative with reference to the solution of systemic problems. Still another division yields 6 which are most relevant to problems of adaptation and instrumental control, and 6 which are pertinent to expressions of emotional reactions, tensions, and the maintenance of an integrated group. Finally, the twelve categories may be divided into positive reactions, attempted answers, questions, and negative reactions.

Strupp [200, 201] considers Bales's variables overinclusive and general and does not find them helpful in making detailed analyses of therapists' actions. However, Strodtbeck [198] and Lennard and Bernstein [124] found them very helpful in answering quite different questions. Strodtbeck coded discussions of families who were trying to settle disagreements and computed the extent to which each person supported every other person. Lennard and Bernstein employed a condensation of Bales's system to analyze the mutual reaction of therapists and patients. The categories were reduced to three types—descriptive propositions, requests for or offers of information, and evaluative propositions. Unlike Strupp, Strodtbeck and Lennard and Bernstein were concerned with the uniformities of behavior that stem from particular roles; their results would probably be equally applicable to the role aspects of helping relationships —lawyer and client, physician and patient, teacher and student.

Action

Leary and his associates [64, 120] analyzed the mutual responses of people in terms of the two basic bipolar dimensions of power and affiliation. For power, the extremes are dominance and submission; for affiliation, the extremes are hostility and affection. By plotting the two basic dimensions in geometric space and developing new points by combining extremes of adjacent dimensions, Leary created a circular grid with 16 segments. Seeking respect and being softhearted, for example, are combinations of dominant and affectionate behavior. Acting hurt and provoking punishment are combinations of passive and hostile behavior. Exhibitionism and exploitation are combinations of dominant and aggressive behavior. The titles Leary gives the segments are managerial, autocratic, responsible, hypernormal, overconventional, cooperative, dependent, docile, masochistic, self-effacing, distrustful, rebellious, aggressive, sadistic, competitive, and narcissistic. Each segment is divided into three sections: one describes the socially acceptable action, a second describes the behavior provoked by the action; a third describes the pathological version of the trait. The arrangement of the 16 variables on the grid represents a circular continuum; the rating of any kind of behavior defines it with reference to its ordinal distance from other variables.

Leary cites no evidence for his organization or the conceptual or empirical independence of the variables—nor does he attempt to justify the omission of variables included in other systems. He does claim that "extensive validation" has shown that the order of his 16 units represents the empirical facts.

In a study of the relationships between therapists and patients, Chance [39] assigned Leary's two basic dimensions the more neutral labels "positive-negative" and "active-passive," and combined the two variables into four categories: negative and active, positive and active, negative and passive, and positive and passive. Characteristic of negative and active relationships are dictating, rebelling, rejecting, threatening, and disapproving actions. Actions typical of positive and active relationships include directing, teaching, supporting, and loving. Characteristic of negative and passive relationships are passive criticism, lack of appreciation, complaint, distrust, apology, retreat, cowed obedience, obeying feared authority, and submission. Common to positive and passive relationships are seeking love and praise, cooperating, trusting, admiring, conforming and obeying. Information was obtained from patients' self-reports, patients' references to themselves in therapy, responses to semi-structured interviews, and therapists' ratings.

Raush, Dittmann, and Taylor [166, 167] employed four categories, derived from Leary's code, to analyze the therapeutic progress made by six "hyperaggressive" boys in a residential institution. Involvement and appropriateness of behavior were added to Leary's basic dimensions of hostility-friendliness and dominance-passivity. Two behavioral analyses—separated by a year and a half—revealed a decrease in the children's hostile-dominant behavior toward adults, and an increase in friendly-passive behavior toward both peers and adults. Changes in patterns of behavior were usually accompanied by reciprocal changes in the behaviors of both children and adults.

Combinations of Action and Value

Murray [149] and Barker and Wright [12] recently proposed two systems which merit description because of their sophisticated approaches to the analysis of social action. Murray suggests separate analyses of 12 vectors, or action tendencies, and 14 values. Some of the action tendencies are renunciation, acquisition, bestowal, retention, and avoidance. Among the values are knowledge, beauty, sex, and authority. The primary asset of the system is the descriptive richness provided by combinations of vectors and values, such as the renunciation of the intellectual life, the acquisition of knowledge, and the avoidance of people and situations which may lead to the weakening of one's beliefs.

Action Modes

Barker and Wright [12] classify behavior in terms of "action modes," which are analogues of Murray's needs. There are seven modes, each of which is rated on a four-point scale from zero to 3. The categories are dominance, with the goal of ascendance over the other person; aggression, with the purpose of making the other person suffer; resistance, aimed at withstanding cohesive social influence or warding off harm; submission, designed to eliminate or meliorate stressful interaction; nurturance, with the goal of meeting or ratifying the other person's needs; appeal, intended to obtain gratification of one's own needs by sympathetic action of the other person; and avoidance, which is aimed at retreat from the dissatisfying effects of the other's company, behavior, or some aspect of the situation.

In the description of each action mode, Barker and Wright list the end sought, label the mode as "spontaneous" or "reactive" or both, and give examples of common variants, motor indexes, verbal indexes, common descriptive terms, emotional concomitants, and illustrative episodes. In addition, the authors describe each mode in terms of "action attributes," including the degree of pressure, amount of affection, mood, and evaluation.

Systems Designed to Classify Special Kinds of Action

To study specific theoretical problems, some investigators have constructed codes for circumscribed kinds of behavior. To depict the influence that a mother might have on her child, Bishop [21] observed the pair for two half-hour sessions, and tabulated the type of behavior every five seconds using separate notational systems for the mother and the child. Some of the categories in the mother's code were: makes contact, either verbal or physical or both; helps child physically; structures to stimulate independent thinking; leaves responsibility of decision to the child; interferes to stop activity. Among the items in the children's code were: seeks help, seeks praise, and indicates anxiety. To determine the mothers' influence on their children, Bishop correlated the proportions of different kinds of behavior manifested by the pairs. Maternal acts such as directing, interfering, criticizing, and strong stimulation related positively to the children's noncooperation, inhibition, and reluctant cooperation; the correlations varied between .45 and .71. Directing, interfering, criticizing, and lack of contact correlated positively with noncooperation, inhibited, and reluctant cooperation; the coefficients varied between .42 and .62.

Smith [189] employed some of Bishop's categories to study the dependency expressed by preschool children toward their mothers. Using Bishop's categories as a point of departure, Moustakas, Sigel, and Schalock [147] constructed a scale which embraces a much broader range of behavior than was coded by either Bishop or Smith. Some of Bishop's items were refined, her definitions clarified, and many categories were added, as well as a scale of anxiety and hostility. The final system—the scale, 89 categories for the adult, and 82 categories for the child—is devoted to verbal and social behavior, but the investigators think that postural signals and facial expressions could be the subjects of further categorization. The recording procedure is modeled after that of Bishop. (Depending on the subjects' behaviors, the observers put the appropriate symbols on printed squares, each signifying a five-second interval. The location of a symbol in a square is determined by the identity of the individual who initiated the behavior.)

To study "interpersonal anger" in children, Kaplan and Goodrich [108] developed a specialized set of categories: provocation, which could be direct with intent, indirect with intent, or misperceived; phases of anger, which were cognitive, physiological, emotional, and conative; reevaluaton, and action, which consisted of warning, fantasy punishment, displaced retaliation in time, displaced retaliation to another, and immediate revenge. The account of the coding system does not indicate the conditions of its use or the results.

A number of systems have been constructed for coding the behavior of psychotherapists. Strupp's [200, 201] major categories are facilitation, exploratory operations, clarification, interpretive operations, structuring, direct guidance, and irrelevant activity. The code lists specific instances for each category. Silence and passive acceptance are subcategories of facilitating communication; greetings and small talk are examples of irrelevant activity. In addition, Strupp rates such variables as directedness, which varies on a five-point scale from noninferential to highly inferential; dynamic focus, which varies on a five-point scale and pertains to the introduction of new frames of reference; and therapeutic climate, which varies on a five-point scale from cold to warm.

PATTERNS OF INTERACTION

Why is it that some pairs of people are indifferent to each other, some feel mutually repelled, and some act as though they were made for each other? Investigators have taken two approaches: One concentrates on the characteristics of each participant and then tests compatibility in social interaction; the other focuses on types of interpersonal systems.

Matching of the Individual Characteristics of Participants

Similarities. The most frequent explanation of mutual liking is similarity of traits. By itself, however, similarity is not sufficient. It is often stated or implied that the partners must also be high on the dimension on which they are similar and that they must have at least a moderate amount of self-involvement. People are more likely to get together because they are both skilled artists than because they lack artistic talent, for example. Being at the opposite ends of such a dimension often creates a basis for mutual indifference or mutual rejection.

Research on similarity reveals four subtypes, the simplest of which is homogamous matching. Two people are alike and feel comfortable with each other because of their likeness. Izard [98] found that friends are more alike than randomly selected subjects in deference, exhibition-ism, and endurance, as measured by Edwards' Personal Preference Schedule. These similarities of personality were interpreted as facilitators of positive mutual feeling. An investigation of marital compatibility by Corsini [47] revealed that similarity of the self-percepts of husbands and wives is significantly associated with the marital happiness reported on Burgess and Wallin's test.

A second type of similarity applies to traits, like interests, attitudes, and talents, which facilitate endeavors to attain a common goal. According to Burgess and Cottrell [36], agreement between spouses on such matters as handling family finances, ways of relating to in-laws, and recreational preferences is significantly related to reported marital happiness.

A third type of similarity pertains to the capacity of participants to gratify the same needs in each other. In the investigation of Gardner and Thompson [70], two individuals were described as being high in "social harmony" if each indicated that his social need could be fulfilled by the other. The high evaluation did not require a similarity in the locations of participants on the same dimension. The affiliative need of each member, for instance, could be gratified by different attributes in the other person; the two subjects might both have high, low, or dissimilar locations on the dimension.

A final type of similarity involves the possession of mutually valued emotional commodities. According to Schutz's [183] findings, mutual attraction can be based on the high interchange of such characteristics as power and affection—provided that the participants have similar preferences for the shared characteristics. In Beisser's [15] sample of disorganized families, ineffectual, detached people were attracted to each other because the ineffectual nature of one participant was not threatening to the detachment of the other.

Opposites. Some investigators have worked on the assumption that opposites attract. Winch [220] cites a number of dimensions—dominance, nurturance, and achievement-oriented independence, for example—on which the tendencies of husbands and wives to be at opposite poles ex-ceded the proportions expected by chance.

Complementary matching. Complementary traits on different dimensions afford a third basis for compatibility. Investigators usually assume that traits on different dimensions are complementary if they facilitate mutual gratification of the participants. According to Winch [220], needs X and Y of people A and B are complementary when A's behavior, which is motivated by A's need X, gratifies B's need Y, and B's behavior, which is motivated by B's need Y, gratifies A's need X. Winch reports significant associations between pairs of complementary needs; between secure nurturance and high need for approval, for example, and between hostile dominance and yielding dependence. Complementary traits may explain the stability of some of the marriages described by Beisser [15]—between a controlling and belittling female and a vulnerable, susceptible man; between a pain-seeking, long-suffering man and a troublesome, ineffectual woman; between an anxious, adequate woman and a passive, dependent man.

Characteristics of Interpersonal Systems

Some investigators have proposed methods of analysis which are truly interpersonal in that they describe patterns of mutual reaction within a system containing two or more people, not a system restricted to the traits of an individual. The concept of cooperation, for example, makes sense only when it is applied to reciprocal responses.

Reciprocality. Jones and Thibaut [103] propose that interactions be classified in three ways, depending upon type of reciprocality. In "noncontingent interaction" a participant's behavior is affected solely by the prescriptions of his role. In fact, the participants are not really interacting —relationships among behaviors result from simple synchronization. Formalized ceremonies and the contacts of detached schizophrenics are examples.

"Asymmetrically contingent interactions" may be illustrated by the contacts of an interviewer and a respondent. The reactions of one, the respondent, are fully contingent on the behavior of the other, the interviewer, which is independently determined. Or the asymmetrically contingent interaction may occur because one participant is highly restricted by the norms of his role, and the other is less restricted and more open to interpersonal influence. Such systems tend to be unstable; either the less restricted participant stops listening or, more frequently, the interaction becomes reciprocally contingent.

Most social interaction is "reciprocally contingent." Each participant is continuously sensitive to the behavior of the other, interprets its meaning, and tries to judge the most socially appropriate response.

Interplay variables. The most detailed systems for classifying interpersonal patterns has been proposed by Barker and Wright [12]. Their "interplay variables" describe the organization of mutual social behavior with respect to participants' goals, and are defined in terms of six basic categories—compatible, incompatible, competitive, mutually opposed, and mutually supporting. Actions are compatible when the behavior of each participant is consistent with the goal of the other, incompatible when the behavior of each participant is inconsistent with the goals of the other. The behavior of each participant hinders or counteracts the behavior of the other in the case of mutually opposed actions; one strikes and the other defends by striking back, so the conflict represents mutual opposition and incompatibility. Competitive actions, which may be incompatible or compatible, result when both participants elect to do the same things and each attempts to outdo the other. Actions are mutually supportive when both do the same thing, and each tries to facilitate the attempts of the other to attain the common goal.

Barker and Wright's interplay variables are conflict, disjunction, unfriendly rivalry, cooperation, conjunction, friendly rivalry, and juxtaposition. Conflict occurs when actions are incompatible and mutually opposed. In disjunction, they are incompatible without being incongruent in any other way. In unfriendly rivalry, the actions are incompatible and competitive. In cooperation, they are compatible and mutually supporting. In conjunction, they are compatible but do not have to be facilitative or mutually supporting. In friendly rivalry, actions are compatible and competitive. In juxtaposition, they are divergent; neither participant responds in relation to the other.

Barker and Wright's variables can be divided into two genetic categories when viewed in terms of participants' goals: The acts of each participant are either consistent or inconsistent with the goals of the other participant; the acts are mutually supporting or mutually hindering. The other variables represent combinations and special instances of these basic categories.

Responsibility. Herbst [89] developed a system of classification to analyze the way power is used in family roles. His code seems applicable to relationships in other kinds of social units. Eight categories concern who decides about a task and who performs it. The first two categories, autonomy of husband or of wife, entail an avoidance of interaction; one person decides about an activity and performs it by himself. The next two categories represent leadership by husband or by wife; the leader makes the decision and both perform the task. In two types of autocracy, one spouse decides and the other does the work. Syncratic cooperation requires a mutual decision and sharing the work. Syncratic division of functions also begins with a mutual decision by husband and wife, but then either one or the other performs the task.

METHODS OF STUDYING SOCIAL INTERACTION

Units of Behavior

Basic units. From the flow of events within the period of social interaction, the investigator must select analytic units appropriate to the purposes of his research. Lennard and Bernstein [124], who studied verbal communication in psychotherapy, analyzed "propositions." These are verbalizations, each containing a subject and predicate, either expressed or implied. In their code, a "statement" consists of an uninterrupted sequence of propositions; an exchange or "interaction" consists of two statements in sequence, one by each participant. They tabulated the number of propositions in a statement and the rate of interaction, which is the number of exchanges either in one hour or on one transcribed page.

Murray [150] has proposed the "interpersonal proceeding" as a unit of interaction. One proceeding includes the movements and words of the actor and the reaction of the other person. Directionally organized, intermittent successions of proceedings are "serials"—exemplified by friendship, marriage, and careers in business.

In Barker and Wright's [12] system the "action circuit" must be closed for an interaction to occur—the two participants must be acting in relationship with each other. If they do, the simplest unit that can be used to analyze the flow of events is the "action sequence"; participant S initiates the action, and participant A responds. This unit is the same as Murray's interpersonal proceeding and similar to Lennard and Bernstein's "interaction." If A initiates the action, the sequence is described as A-S. A more complex event, the "cycle," consists of an initiating action, a reaction, and at least one subsequent action by the initiating participant. The action sequence is thus coded in terms of order of actions and complexity of interaction.

Molar units. An "episode" is a longer molar unit. It depicts behavior and situation, mediates and determines superordinate trains of action, and is the arena for a face-to-face social interaction [12]. In terms of a person's present position relative to a goal, an episode has constancy and direction. Sometimes it is the longest action that a child can name when asked what he is doing. Barker and Wright classify episodes in terms of their issues or their psychological significance at the point of termination. Examples of issues are "success," which is the attainment of the goal after overcoming much resistance; "nonattainment," which is a relinquishment of the goal after encountering much resistance but without blaming anyone; and "gratification," which is the attribution of credit for the result to someone else or to circumstances. Episodes are also classified in terms of length in minutes, extent and type of overlap, relative weight, and form of transition.

Thibaut and Kelley's [208] "behavior sequence" consists of a number of specific motor and verbal acts, organized sequentially and directed to the attainment of some immediate end state. According to them, everyone evaluates the outcomes of behavior sequences in terms of his comparison level—what he feels he deserves. A comparison level of alternatives is the lowest level of outcomes that a person accepts in the light of the alternative opportunities that are available. The attraction of a person to the dyad is determined by the discrepancy between the outcomes attained and the comparison level of alternatives. The terminology is intended to stress the investigators' basic assumption, which is derived from game theory: A person enters and stays in a relationship only as long as it provides him with sufficient rewards and the costs are not too high.

Miller [143] has noted that the "chain of reactions"—a term comparable to "behavior sequence"—can be quite lengthy, is sometimes organized in terms of the participants' social roles, can have a unique structure for a particular pair of people, and tends to be repeated in its entirety whenever it occurs. The length of the sequence is a function of the goals of participants. Miller has pointed out that some of the actions in these sequences may have unconscious components; in this case they are not very amenable to personal control. Probably the larger the number of unconscious links in a chain of reactions, the more automatically the chain is followed.

Adams and Romney's [3] analysis of one chain of reactions, the "authority sequence," throws light on some aspects of its structure. The writers consider a simple sequence of acts: A makes an unpleasant noise; B says, "Keep quiet!" in a threatening voice; A stops the noise; the threat is withdrawn. B's authority is reinforced by A's compliance and A's compliance is reinforced by the withdrawal of threat. The probability that the sequence tends to continue until it is complete is proportional to the amount of previous reinforcement. The authors provide illustrations of other sequences; in each of them, the pattern of reinforcement tends to create what other writers have called a "molar unit."

Omitted from Adams and Romney's analysis, which was inspired by Skinner's work, are the meanings and values underlying the actions in the authority sequence. Suppose one asks why the person in authority makes the initial coercive request. An interview might reveal that he fears he will lose face as a father if he does not exert his authority or that he cannot concentrate on his homework because of the noise. Such findings would help to concretize and amplify their analysis by providing specific motives and their connections with the participants' social positions. Such findings would also indicate that a sequence has meaning as a totality because it reflects the temporal dimension of a mutual task with shared meanings and evaluations. The fact that Barker and Wright [12] stress meanings and values may be inferred from their codification of the issue of each episode. Presumably the episode continues until the issue is decided one way or another.

Special units. A special type of episode—Horney [94] once called it the "vicious circle"—consists of the reinforcement by interaction with other people of a socially handicapping reaction. In Horney's example, a person with an excessive need for affection is inclined to demand exclusive and unconditional love and feels rebuffed if he does not get it. Yet he must repress the intense hostility aroused by the presumed rebuff for fear he will lose all affection. Because he cannot face his feelings, he becomes increasingly anxious, a fact that further intensifies his excessive need for affection.

Vicious circles characterize some of the intrafamilial disturbances which prompt people to seek psychotherapy. Mittelmann [146] describes a circle which begins with parents disagreeing and quarreling in their child's presence. Because of the child's conflicting identifications with the disputants and his fears of abandonment, he becomes very anxious. This makes the parents anxious, and they become more combative—and the child becomes even more disturbed.

Lippitt [132] has noted that circles may be benign as well as vicious; socially acceptable responses may also be reinforced in a social interaction. He has investigated the mutual responses of preadolescents and found that an outgoing child who accepts himself finds it easy to be cooperative in the group, act in a friendly manner, and influence other children without being pushy. In turn, the other children regard him as a warm and competent person who respects their opinions and has friendly intentions. They consequently indicate their liking and acceptance of him by accepting his suggestions, a response that confirms his feelings about himself and reinforces his outgoing behavior.

Sources of Data

Psychotherapy. Sullivan [203] and Bion [20] are two of many psychoanalysts who have used therapeutic experiences as a source of information about interaction between family members or between psychotherapists and patients. Spiegel and Kluckhohn [193] obtained their information about families from weekly psychotherapy sessions with the mother, father, child, and other members of the family and from visits to homes. The simultaneous contacts permitted comparisons of the mutual perceptions and interpersonal behaviors of various members of the family. The present writer, in association with J. Westman and staff, has been conducting simultaneous interviews with both parents, a procedure that is valuable in highlighting the mechanisms either person uses to maintain the stability of the relationship.

Subjects' reports. Using 45 open-ended questions to initiate conversation about topics relevant to needs, Winch [220] followed up each answer with further questions until the subject had no further associations. A subject might be asked how he felt when he was in line in a crowded restaurant and someone stepped in front of him or how he felt when he saw his name in print. Interviews were recorded, transcribed, and rated on five-point scales. He also obtained subjects' histories by interviews and administered the Thematic Apperception Test to gain information relevant to covert motivation. Data obtained by means of the test provided fewer significant associations for the same hypotheses than did data from the interviews.

Schutz [183] studied interpersonal behavior by means of a verbal inventory requiring the subjects to check one of six categories ranging from "usually" to "never." Some typical items were "I try to be with people." "I try to include other people in my plans." "I like people to invite me to things." Chance [39] and Fiedler and Senior [61] asked pairs of patients and therapists for self-ratings and mutual ratings of actual and ideal selves, and Gardner and Thompson [70] requested fraternity members to consider twelve of their needs in turn and to rate the others with respect to their capacities to satisfy them.

On going situations. Sometimes social interaction can be studied in functioning organizations. Raush, Dittmann, and Taylor [166] observed disturbed preadolescents in a residential treatment center. Gump, Sutton-Smith, and Redl [80] coded the behavior of preadolescent boys in a summer camp. The subjects in both studies tended to have the same types of problems, were engaged in standard activities which were planned for different times of the day and week, and were in the care of professionally trained adults whose behavior was predictably consistent and benign. Such settings provide the possibility of controlling variables which can affect the experimental results.

Gardner and Thompson [70] took advantage of previously established groups, college fraternities, in a study of social compatibility. Others [153, 185] have participated in the organization of new groups because this enabled them to create special opportunities for observing, testing, and interviewing subjects.

Contrived situations. Temporary groups have often been created solely for the purpose of performing tasks pertinent to the investigators' hypotheses. Bales and Borgatta [10] organized groups to solve problems; Bovard [30] organized groups to learn about psychology. Special tasks have been created even more frequently than special groups. Strodtbeck

[198] has devised an ingenious technique to study the resolution of disagreements in families. From attitudes in which self-involvement is high, he selects a number about which there is disagreement and asks the family to discuss them with a view to coming to an agreement.

Investigators have also selected different combinations of subjects— families [198], parent and child together [21], child alone [7], and subject and investigator's confederate [130]. Behavior is typically analyzed by ratings or tabulations. Detailed descriptions of sources of data, various kinds of situations, problems which have been studied by observations of different types of subjects, and methods of coding data are contained in the surveys of Hare, Borgatta, and Bales [84], Heyns and Lippitt [91], and Lambert [117].

SYSTEMS FOR CLASSIFYING INTERACTION: SOME OVER-ALL IMPRESSIONS

Common Denominators among the Systems for Classifying Needs

The different needs and actions proposed in various theories reflect the terminological chaos characteristic of the field of personality, a fact that makes it difficult to compare the findings of different studies. Dominance, for example, is viewed by some investigators as a need, by others as an act. It has even been regarded as a general style: one can help or hinder in a dominant way.

Many popular concepts seem excessively complex. Some commonly used labels apply to actions alone, others to combinations of actions and objects. Examples of terms connoting objects are the need for "nurturance," which is defined as giving sympathy and gratifying the needs of a helpless object, and the need for "infavoidance," which refers to the avoidance of conditions or situations which may lead to belittlement, embarrassment, scorn, and the like [148]. The analyses of acts and objects by themselves seem sufficiently complex to warrant separate codes.

Many systems seem to have been designed for very different purposes. Similarities need not be expected among codes of problem solving in groups, the actions of therapists, and mothers' influence on children. Differences among systems have probably been increased by the variety of theoretical viewpoints. The code for problem solving in groups is applicable only to processes and was deliberately made sufficiently general to cover other kinds of social systems. The code for therapists is very specific and restricted to action in the therapeutic relationship. The codes for mothers and children were designed for a specific kind of situation, and their contents were greatly influenced by the investigator's concern with objectivity. There are greater similarities among the more exhaustive systems, but some of them seem to be as alien as different languages. Theorists have obviously not even concurred on definitions of terms. For Leary [120], "affiliation" refers to acts, and is defined by the dimension of hostility-affection; for Murray [151], the term "affiliation" is a need to draw near and enjoyably cooperate or reciprocate with an "allied other."

Despite the considerable differences, there is a surprising consensus in the choice of some variables. Both dominance and submission are included in the systems of Barker and Wright, Beisser, Chance, Gardner, Leary, Murray, Schutz, Thompson, and Winch. Aggression or hostility may be found in the codes of Barker and Wright, Beisser, Bion, Chance, Leary, and Murray; affiliation may be found in the codes of Bion, Chance, Gardner and Thompson, Leary, Murray, and Schutz. Avoidance may be found in the systems of Barker and Wright, Bion, Murray, and Schutz; nurturance in the systems of Barker and Wright, Murray, and Winch. The inclination to seek the active support to another appears as passivity, dependency, and succorance in the codes of Barker and Wright, Beisser, Bion, Chance, Gardner and Thompson, Leary, and Murray.

"Infavoidance" and "managerial," "inclusion" and "flight," "deference" and "passivity"—this is just a sample of the variety of concepts used to classify needs or actions. Can one have any hope of finding common denominators in variables that seem so heterogeneous? Are these the best variables for the job of analyzing interaction? The suitability of items can be judged only with reference to the purposes of the research. Interaction has been analyzed in the study of many types of problems; the ultimate evaluation of any code will be determined by empirically established results. Despite the variety of purposes, a general system of classification that would be most fruitful for a large number of problems could probably be developed. A number of investigators, some with very dissimilar goals, have begun to examine some common variables which point to the possible dimensions of a general system.

A Provisional System for Classifying Needs

A perusal of the different coding systems suggests that a considerable number of interpersonal acts can be classified in terms of four generic dimensions, three of which were suggested by Freud [67] in "Instincts and Their Vicissitudes." In interpreting the various ways in which motives could be expressed, he used three bipolar dimensions: activity-passivity, friendliness-hostility, and self-other. A fourth, called "approach-avoidance" in American psychology, was independently employed by Lewin [127] and by Reich [169] and Horney [95] in the psychoanalytic group.

Part of a coding system for action that the writer has been evolving employs the same four variables—in addition to a number of others. The variables are used to describe the primary dimensions of acts [145], which include action, affect, object, agent, and goal state. Each action is categorized on the scales of approach-avoidance, initiative-passivity, and direct-indirect; affect is rated on a scale of pleasant-unpleasant. Agents and objects are coded with respect to such variables as generation, sex, kinship, and occupational role. Goal states are assigned many of the common labels of needs, such as sex, hostility, and achievement, and dichotomized in terms of the person's aim to be either an agent or an object. The classification of a response on the relevant dimensions produces results like these: a preadolescent boy (agent) actively approaches (action) his younger sister (object) to help her (goal state); a child in kindergarten (agent) passively avoids cooperation (action) with a teacher (object) because he seeks to be hurt (goal state).

The code can be used to classify a great variety of responses because it permits the selection of intermediate points on various dimensions. Mild resistance, slow retreat, and headlong flight are three types of passive avoidance, for instance, which differ in degree of avoidance and amount of passivity.

An examination of the proposed dimensions suggests two reasons why it is often hard to compare subjects with respect to commonly labeled needs such as dominance, affiliation, deference, and autonomy: They differ markedly in their generality, and they cannot always be compared on the same dimensions. Deference is an example of a need that is defined only by a goal, to acquiesce to someone else's pressures, which is associated with pleasant or unpleasant affect, and can be expressed by any kind of action, active or passive, hostile or friendly, approaching or avoiding. Dominance is somewhat more specific, requiring active approaches in addition to the goal of being the agent of someone else's actions. Heterosexuality is even more specific, since it refers to particular categories of acts, affects, and objects in addition to goal states.

Comparability of concepts requires definition by the same dimensions. It seems reasonable to compare the relative strengths of a person's needs for dominance and succorance, which can be analyzed in terms of the same dimensions—actions and goal states. Other needs—change, which refers to a goal state, and abasement, which refers to acts and objects, for example—are defined in terms of such different dimensions that their comparison is not meaningful. It is often possible to describe an act such as helping a child to read, in terms of a large group of needs—dominance, affiliation, nurturance, intraception, change, and endurance—which differ in generality and are defined in terms of different dimensions.

The description may be accurate, but difficult to understand until it is placed in the context of a more general system with comparable dimensions of responses.

Some Components of a Provisional Interpersonal System

Basic concepts. Exploratory research of the conditions under which families are bound together or drift apart has moved this writer to define some fundamental variables that bear on the stability of small face-to-face groups [143]. Some of the variables represent extensions of the ones in the systems for classifying needs. *Stability* is the resistance of the system to forces creating change. In accounting for it, investigators have proposed a large number of seemingly relevant concepts. People are not inclined to seek each other out or to live together unless they have similar backgrounds, skills, attitudes, values and interests, compatible roles and subidentities, and matching needs and defenses. The multiplicity of concepts makes it apparent that terms like "role" and "identity" and "attitude," which represent different theoretical traditions, have to be rephrased and integrated as part of the same system. One way of doing this is by concepts patterned after those used by Lewin [129]. Three kinds of concepts seem particularly fruitful to the description of interpersonal systems: *valences,* or forces which attract one person to another; *aversions,* or forces which cause one participant to avoid the other; and *permeabilities* of the *barriers* to particular kinds of action. All three vary in strength.

"Valence" has been substituted for "cathexis," a previously used concept [143] which requires questionable assumptions about energy. Lewin [129] conceives of a valence as the value of a region for a person. He conceives of the value as being positive or negative, but it is used here only in the positive sense. According to Herbst [90], valence is a reaction to a person's activity-related-to-an-object. The agent, act, affect, and object form an indissoluble unit of meaning. The person's attraction to the activity with the object may be conceived as a disposition with particular strength which is aimed at the reinstating, when feasible, of the total relationship with the object. Since one can engage in many different activities with the same object, it can become the focus of many valences differing in strength.

A mutual valence is a *bond,* a disposition of two or more people to engage in a specific kind of reciprocal action. Presumably, the disposition has been reinforced by previous mutual gratifications. The same two people can share in many kinds of activities, and can, therefore, have many bonds.

Aversions or negative valences, and *divergences* or mutual aversions are the negative counterparts of valences and bonds. A person is often aversive to an object with respect to an activity that has led to unpleasant consequences: the shared activity may have served as the barrier to one of his goals or may have provided no gratifications. The aversion is thus a disposition to avoid a specific kind of interaction with the object. In the case of a divergence, both participants are disposed to avoid the specific interaction.

Implicit in the terms just cited is another aspect of the code: the act may be associated with a pleasant or unpleasant emotional state. The code thus permits the classification of reciprocal responses in terms of approach-avoidance, pleasant and unpleasant affect, and specific acts, agents, and objects. Other combinations of these dimensions are *facilitative aversion,* in which the agent enjoys avoiding a particular act with the object, usually because it helps him, *conflict,* in which each participant engages in action calculated to block the other's goal, and the various *incongruences,* which involve discrepancies in the affective states of participants: one enjoys the particular kind of encounter and the other dislikes it, so their actions are aimed at discrepant goals.

A barrier defines the penalties of particular actions either with the partner or with people outside the relationship. All relationships are protected from dissolution by barriers, which vary in permeability. Because an impermeable barrier is created by her religion, a Catholic woman who is unhappily married must remain committed to her marital relationship even though her aversions are stronger than her valences.

Some possible predictions. The proposed set of categories is designed to identify and measure variables which affect the stability of the interpersonal system, be it a single impersonal encounter, such as that between a storekeeper and a customer, or an enduring relationship, such as that between lifelong friends. Using the language of the proposed concepts, one may hypothesize that stability is augmented by valences, bonds, and relatively impermeable barriers, and decreased by aversions, incongruences, and conflicts. Valences and bonds make people want to share in gratifying activities, and impermeable barriers prevent the participants from drifting apart, even when there are few bonds. Aversions lead to disengagement, incongruences create frustration, and conflicts create new aversions and reinforce old ones.

The quantities for each of the terms in the equation are estimated on the basis of the type of variable used to analyze identity and interaction. The strength of one participant's valence, for instance, varies with the extent to which one of his aims is furthered by the other person's specific attributes. The attributes frequently refer to action, but they may also be physical traits or even possessions.

To assess the valence for A of B's trait, the observer must estimate its significance for such variables as A's self-esteem and public esteem.

The valence for A is likely to be a function of such variables as the discrepancy between A's actual location on a dimension, and the location A can attain by virtue of B's trait, the value segment of A's actual location, A's self-involvement in the dimension, and the salience of the dimension for A's social group. In other words, the attractiveness of a pretty girl to the man who hopes to increase his social status varies directly with the extent to which his social status can be increased by marriage to her, the degree to which he judges himself in terms of his social status, and the importance of social status in his group; the girl's attractiveness varies inversely with the man's current level of social status.

Implicit in the emphasis on the realization of goals as the basis of relationships is a presumed association between the affective change resulting from their attainment and the reinforcement of social bonds. The gratification afforded by attaining a goal reinforces the attachment to the partner sharing the endeavors; conversely, the frustration of failure, weakens the attachments. According to this position, which is related to those of Thibaut and Kelley [208] and Winch [220], similar or complementary traits are necessary but not sufficient to create positive valences or to forge bonds; the creation of a relationship also requires that each person's goals by made achieveable by the traits of the other person. The effective results of the mutual action provide the forces binding the participants together.

Aversions and divergences may develop because the goals of one person are hindered by the other's traits—a husband is eager to save enough money to increase his social status, but his wife is a spendthrift. Aversions and divergences may also arise because of incongruencies, conflict, or the lack of the necessary conditions for a relationship: The participants have no common interest—one loves music, the other is bored by it; the participants behave incompatibly—one approaches to be helped, the other approaches to hurt; they favor defenses leading to conflict—both use the other as an object upon which to project hostility.

Relationships vary in flexibility as well as in stability. *Flexibility* refers to a system's capacity to retain its original coherence by adjustment to changing external pressures. An inflexible system might be rather stable in the absence of change, but may collapse when new developments alter the bases of the participants' bonds and barriers. Such a system is exemplified by the stable marriage which is dissolved after the birth of a child. Another marriage is less stable, but shows more flexibility when modifications are required.

Flexibility probably varies with a number of factors, one of which is the extent to which valences, bonds, aversions, and divergences are conscious or unconscious. The more unconscious the components are, the less available they are to deliberate action and the harder they are to change. One may also postulate that flexibility is directly related to the maturity of defenses [145], which is estimated from the degree of distorted perception, the social handicap resulting from their use, their specificity to particular kinds of conflict, and the extent to which their acquisition requires the previous learning of other skills.

According to another hypothesis, flexibility varies directly with the permeability of external barriers. The greater the permeability, the less difficulty there is for the individuals to establish relationships with new people when earlier bonds have been dissolved by such changes as the children's leaving home or the spouse going to work.

Some predictions pertain to both stability and flexibility. For example, the more impermeable the barriers or the stronger or more numerous the valences or bonds, the more incongruency and conflict the system can tolerate before reaching the point of dissolution. A couple who share many pleasant activities or fear that a separation may hurt the children will tolerate more friction and unpleasant changes than a couple with fewer gratifications or without children. Also, the more the action in a relationship is restricted by role pressures to specific and codified forms, the less will stability and flexibility vary with conscious and unconscious components of the relationship or with the maturity of the participants' defense mechanisms. On the other hand, the more diffuse the relationship, the greater the probability that stability and flexibility will be affected by the unconscious components and the maturity of defenses. The dynamics of participants' personalities will have less effect on the efficiency of work partners in highly organized jobs than on the fortunes of a marriage.

CONCLUDING COMMENTS ON THE STUDY OF SOCIAL RELATIONSHIPS

This chapter has been devoted to the problems of a developing field of study which is anchored in the theories of current psychology and sociology and is applying them to problems pertaining to the social situation, public identity and self-identity, and social interaction and the social relationship. This final section is concerned with moot questions and unsolved problems.

Why study interpersonal relationships? Generally speaking, they play a major part, usually an implicit one, in most theories of personality, developmental psychology, and social psychology. Still another answer is required if the question implies that only disposition need be considered in predicting behavior and that the import of situation and social interaction can be safely ignored once they have been controlled in the experimental design. An individual's dispositions often cast considerable light on his behavior, but their expression is contingent on the norms of the situation, the dynamics of the other person, and the bonds and barriers of the relationship. The investigator who dismisses such variables as sources of error is assuming an excessive handicap in explaining behavior. Just how much he is sacrificing is suggested by Raush, Dittmann and Taylor's study [167] of hyperaggressive children. The social behavior of the children varied significantly with their traits, the settings, the time phase, and the identity of the other person—whether he was with a peer or an adult. Moreover, these variables interacted to a considerable extent. There was a substantial multiple interaction among the variables of setting, aggression, and time phase. Had the analysis of independent variables been restricted to individual differences among the children, the investigators would have sacrificed most of the variance. The setting accounted for as much of the variance as individual differences; the statistical interaction between setting and individual differences accounted for more variance than the sum of their independent effects.

The vagueness of many of the papers on self and identity might prompt the skeptic to question the value of these terms. What does one gain, he might ask, by organizing under the omnibus term "identity" such concepts as traits and values, which are already in common use by psychologists? The answer is: Identity is recognized universally, is labeled by appropriate nouns and pronouns, is viewed in every society as having properties such as control of impulse and social responsibility, and is a highly prized object. Identities are significant both socially and psychologically. Public evaluation of a man's identity enables societies to enforce their norms. The effort to maintain adequate levels of public esteem and self-esteem provides man with some of his strongest motives. As indicated by studies cited here, identity is so basic to all social relationships that it has to be taken into account in studying such fundamental topics as the association between social structure and personality, the socialization of the child, the nature of social perception, the dynamics of social motives, and the resolution of inner conflict.

If one accepts these answers and starts to plan research, he will find himself beset with methodological and theoretical problems which are common to most psychological research on personality and social behavior, but which are particularly significant in building interpersonal theory. The two most urgent problems are the definition and measurement of dimensions and norms. The disagreement among investigators on such fundamental questions as whether or not dimensions are bipolar has already been mentioned. This disagreement results partly from an unsolved methodological problem—the identification of dimensions as they are perceived by subjects. In most research, the subjects' perceptions of dimensions are prejudged by the investigators. When subjects are allowed to provide their own dimensions, they are often distorted if they concern objects of high self-involvement. Parts or even total dimensions may be given special meanings, exaggerated, or repressed, depending on whether they are sources of high or low self-esteem. Significant contributions to methods of eliciting the subjects' actual perceptions are being made in current linguistic research by Zajonc [222], Osgood [156], and others. Special investigations are required of the perception of dimensions salient to various groups and will probably employ recordings of spontaneous conversations and independent ratings based on the raters' interpretations of the subjects' unconscious and conscious reactions.

Norms are inseparable from the dimensions of objects and acts to which they apply, so that some of the research on meaning and norms will have to go ahead simultaneously. The complexity of norms is indicated by the fact that they vary in degree of generality, consistency, explicitness, clarity, and the intensity of the shame and guilt which follow their violation [145]. Measurement of these variations is required to investigate topics such as conditions for maintaining self-esteem, sources of shame and guilt, and the stability of social relationships.

Meanings and value are both prominent in the analysis of social perception, a topic which has received the increasing attention of psychologists in recent years [22, 206]. The topic of perception has been prominent throughout this chapter, particularly in the references to research on self-identity. It has been assumed that self-identity is perceived in terms of the same system of meanings used to perceive people generally; indeed, the same system must be used for all persons, since one learns about oneself from the reactions of others and projects one's own dimensions in attempting to determine what other people are like. It has also been assumed that each person uses a slightly different system of values for judging himself than he uses to judge others—he is kinder to himself than to others because of the necessity of maintaining an adequate level of self-esteem. Further empirical research is needed, not only on these hypotheses, but on the nature of balance [38], the ways in which combinations of traits are perceived [206], and the bases for liking and rejecting people [154].

Internalization is relevant to self-esteem and to social interaction, yet it has been studied very little. There is little evidence about the process of internalization, and even less on the nature of the content internalized. Here it has been assumed that what gets internalized is a total relationship, including a specific subidentity, specific objects, and mutual acts. It is often claimed that only objects get internalized; sometimes it is assumed that only standards get internalized. There are many descriptions of groups being internalized as well as individuals —one identifies with one's school or one's neighborhood. Various people probably perceive the same group in different ways, but what are these perceptions like? Is a group seen as some vague, generalized "other," as an organization chart, as a cluster of faceless beings surrounding significant individuals, as the embodiment of an ideal or a symbol, as a vehicle for expressing certain functions?

The welter of terms with varying and overlapping meanings and the variety of measuring techniques sometimes make it very difficult to compare studies of what is—or seems to be—the same phenomenon. In research on motivation and action, for example, definitions of terms such as "affiliation" and "aggression" differ, and the methods for identifying the reactions to which the terms refer vary so much in the degree of inference permitted the observer that what some investigators call "acts" would be called "needs" by others. Psychologists need to compile a handbook with arbitrary definitions and descriptions of standard methods.

A final group of problems concerns compatibility. People are presumed to be compatible because of complementary traits, but how can the observer know when traits are complementary? The concept implies that each member of a pair supplies a lack in the other; in the literature the term is often used for dissimilar traits—despite the fact that its literal meaning is not violated by similar traits. Are similarity and certain kinds of dissimilarity sufficient to explain the fact that two people choose to share particular activities? Foote [62] wonders why similar past experiences may not make a relationship boring and tend to weaken it. Analogous questions can be raised about dissimilar traits. Are not relationships in which one participant always contributes, and the other always receives, likely to create irritation and boredom because of repetitiousness and inequity? The answers to both questions are affirmative for some types of people, some variables, and some situations. How are they to be identified? Complicating the problem of definition is the fact that so many variables enter into a relationship—interests, attitudes, habits, skills, values, needs, expressive styles, defenses, roles, subidentities, acts. Do all of them affect the stability and flexibility of relationship? To what degree and under what conditions?

Only tentative answers to these questions have been suggested here. Judging from the increase in empirical studies of social interaction, social roles, and self-identity, and the high level of competence of the investigators, much fruitful research on the theory of interpersonal relationships can be expected in the near future.

REFERENCES

1. Aberle, D. F., & Naegele, K. D. Middle-class fathers' occupational roles and attitudes toward children. *Amer. J. Orthopsychiat.*, 1952, **22**, 366–378.
2. Ackerman, N. W. *The psychodynamics of family life.* New York: Basic Books, 1958.
3. Adams, J. S., & Romney, A. K. A functional analysis of authority. *Psychol. Rev.*, 1959, **66**, 234–251.
4. Adler, A. *Social interest.* London: Faber, 1938.
5. Albert, Ethel M. The classification of values: a method and illustration. *Amer. Anthrop.*, 1956, **58**, 221–248.
6. Allport, G. W. *Personality: a psychological interpretation.* New York: Holt, 1937.
7. Arsenian, Jean M. Young children in an insecure situation. *J. abnorm. soc. Psychol.*, 1943, **38**, 225–249.
8. Back, K. Influence through social communication. *J. abnorm. soc. Psychol.*, 1951, **46**, 9–23.
9. Bales, R. F. *Interaction process analysis.* Reading, Mass.: Addison-Wesley, 1951.
10. Bales, R. F., & Borgatta, E. F. Size of groups as a factor in the interaction profile. In A. Hare, E. F. Borgatta, & R. F. Bales (Eds.), *Small groups.* New York: Wiley, 1955. Pp. 396–413.
11. Barker, R. G. Ecology and motivation. In M. R. Jones (Ed.), *Nebraska symposium on motivation, 1960.* Lincoln, Neb.: Univer. Neb. Press, 1960. Pp. 1–49.
12. Barker, R. G., & Wright, H. F. *Midwest and its children; the psychological ecology of an American town.* Evanston, Ill.: Row, Peterson, 1954.
13. Barnouw, V. Acculturation and personality among the Wisconsin Chippewa. *Mem. Amer. Anthrop. Ass.*, 1950, No. 72.
14. Bateson, G. Morale and national character. In G. Watson (Ed.), *Civilian morale.* Boston: Houghton Mifflin, 1942. Pp. 71–91.
15. Beisser, P. T., et al. *Classification of disorganized families for use in family oriented diagnosis and treatment.* New York: Community Research Associates, 1953.
16. Benne, K. D., & Sheats, P. Functional roles of group members. *J. soc. Issues*, 1948, **4**, 41–49.
17. Benoit-Smullyan, E. Status types and status inter-relations. *Amer. sociol. Rev.*, 1944, **9**, 151–161.
18. Bexton, W. H., Heron, W., & Scott, T. H. Effects of decreased variation in the sensory environment. *Canad. J. Psychol.*, 1954, **8**, 70–76.
19. Bills, R. E., Vance, E. L., & McLean, O. S. An index of adjustment and values. *J. consult. Psychol.*, 1951, **15**, 257–261.
20. Bion, W. R. Experiences in groups: VII. *Hum. Relat.*, 1951, **4**, 221–227.

21. Bishop, Barbara M. Mother-child interaction and the social behavior of children. *Psychol. Monogr.*, 1951, **65**, No. 11 (Whole No. 328).
22. Blake, R. R., & Ramsey, G. V. (Eds.). *Perception: an approach to personality.* New York: Ronald, 1951.
23. Blake, R. R., Rosenbaum, M., & Duryea, R. Gift-giving as a function of group standards. *Hum. Relat.*, 1955, **8**, 61–73.
24. Block, J., & Bennett, Lillian. The assessment of communication. *Hum. Relat.*, 1955, **8**, 317–325.
25. Block, J., & Thomas, H. Is satisfaction with self a measure of adjustment? *J. abnorm. soc. Psychol.*, 1955, **51**, 254–259.
26. Boas, F. *Mind of primitive man.* New York: Macmillan, 1938.
27. Bott, Elizabeth. *Family and social network.* London: Tavistock, 1957.
28. Bovard, E. W. Social norms and the individual. *J. abnorm. soc. Psychol.*, 1948, **43**, 62–69.
29. Bovard, E. W. Group structure and perception. *J. abnorm. soc. Psychol.*, 1951, **46**, 398–405.
30. Bovard, E. W. Clinical insight as a function of group process. *J. abnorm. soc. Psychol.*, 1952, **47**, 534–539.
31. Brim, O. G. Personality development as role learning. In I. Iscoe & H. Stevenson (Eds.), *Personality development in children.* Austin, Tex.: Univer. Tex. Press, 1960. Pp. 127–159.
32. Bronfenbrenner, U., Harding, J., & Gallwey, Mary O. *The measurement of skill in social perception.* Princeton, N.J.: Van Nostrand, 1958.
33. Brownfain, J. J. Stability of the self concept as a dimension of personality. *J. abnorm. soc. Psychol.*, 1952, **47**, 597–606.
34. Brunswick, E. *Perception and the representative design of psychological experiments.* Berkeley, Calif.: Univer. Calif. Press, 1956.
35. Brunswick, E. Representative design and probabilistic theory in a functional psychology. *Psychol. Rev.*, 1955, **62**, 193–218.
36. Burgess, E. W., & Cottrell, L. S. *Predicting success or failure in marriage.* Englewood Cliffs, N.J.: Prentice-Hall, 1939.
37. Cameron, N. Deterioration and regression in schizophrenic thinking. *J. abnorm. soc. Psychol.*, 1939, **34**, 265–270.
38. Cartwright, D., & Harary, F. Structural balance: a generalization of Heider's theory. *Psychol. Rev.*, 1956, **63**, 277–293.
39. Chance, Erika. *Families in treatment.* New York: Basic Books, 1959.
40. Chapman, D. W., & Volkmann, J. A social determinant of the level of aspiration. *J. abnorm. soc. Psychol.*, 1939, **34**, 225–238.
41. Chapple, E. D. Measuring human relations: an introduction to the study of the interaction of individuals. *Genet. Psychol. Monogr.*, 1940, **22**, 1–147.
42. Charters, W. W., & Newcomb, T. M. Some attitudinal effects of experimentally increased salience of a membership group. In G. E. Swanson, T. M. Newcomb, & E. L. Hartley (Eds.), *Readings in social psychology.* New York: Holt, 1952. Pp. 415–419.
43. Chein, I. The environment as a determinant of behavior. *J. soc. Psychol.*, 1954, **39**, 115–127.

44. Cohen, A. R. Experimental effects of ego-defense preference on interpersonal relations. *J. abnorm. soc. Psychol.*, 1956, **52**, 19–27.

45. Cohen, A. R. Situational structure, self-esteem, and threat-oriented reactions to power. In E. Cartwright (Ed.), *Studies in social power.* Ann Arbor, Mich.: Univer. Mich., 1959. Pp. 35–52.

46. Cooley, C. H. *Human nature and the social order.* New York: Scribner, 1922.

47. Corsini, R. J. Understanding and similarity in marriage. *J. abnorm. soc. Psychol.*, 1956, **52**, 327–332.

48. Cottrell, L. S. The analysis of situational fields in social psychology. *Amer. sociol. Rev.*, 1942, **7**, 370–382.

49. Dai, B. A socio-psychiatric approach to personality organization. *Amer. sociol. Rev.*, 1952, **17**, 44–49.

50. Dubois, Cora A. *The people of Alor.* Minneapolis, Minn.: Univer. Minn. Press, 1944.

51. Edwards, A. L. Social desirability and personality test construction. In B. M. Bass & I. A. Berg (Eds.), *Objective approaches to personality assessment.* Princeton, N.J.: Van Nostrand, 1959. Pp. 100–118.

52. Epstein, S. Unconscious self-evaluation in a normal and a schizophrenic group. *J. abnorm. soc. Psychol.*, 1955, **50**, 65–70.

53. Erikson, E. H. The problem of ego identity. *J. Amer. psychoanal. Ass.*, 1956, **4**, 56–121.

54. Fairbairn, W. R. D. *An object-relations theory of the personality.* New York: Basic Books, 1954.

55. Federn, P. *Ego psychology and the psychoses.* New York: Basic Books, 1952.

56. Fenchel, G. E., Monderer, J. H., & Hartley, E. L. Subjective status and the equilibration hypothesis. *J. abnorm. soc. Psychol.*, 1951, **46**, 476–479.

57. Fenichel, O. *The psychoanalytic theory of neurosis.* New York: Norton, 1945.

58. Ferenczi, S. Stages in the development of a sense of reality. In *Sex in psychoanalysis.* New York: Bruner, 1950.

59. Festinger, L. Informal social communication. *Psychol. Rev.*, 1950, **57**, 271–282.

60. Festinger, L. *A theory of cognitive dissonance.* Evanston, Ill.: Row, Peterson, 1957.

61. Fiedler, F. E., & Senior, Kate. An exploratory study of unconscious feeling reactions in fifteen patient-therapist pairs. *J. abnorm. soc. Psychol.*, 1952, **47**, 446–453.

62. Foote, N. N. Identification as the basis for a theory of motivation. *Amer. sociol. Rev.*, 1951, **16**, 14–21.

63. Foote, N. N. Matching of husband and wife in phases of development. Chicago: Univer. of Chicago, Family Study Center (Reprint No. 7), 1956.

64. Freedman, M. B., Leary, T. F., Ossorio, A. G., & Coffey, H. S. The interpersonal dimension of personality. *J. Pers.*, 1951, **20**, 143–161.

65. French, J. R. P., & Zajonc, R. B. An experimental study of cross-cultural norm conflict. *J. abnorm. soc. Psychol.*, 1957, 54, 218–224.

66. Freud, Anna. *The ego and the mechanisms of defense.* New York: International Universities Press, 1946.

67. Freud, S. *Collected papers.* London: Hogarth, 1949.

68. Freud, S. *Group psychology and the analysis of the ego.* New York: Bantam, 1960.

69. Friedman, I. Phenomenal, ideal, and projected conceptions of self. *J. abnorm. soc. Psychol.*, 1955, 51, 611–615.

70. Gardner, E. F., & Thompson, G. G. *Social relations and morale in small groups.* New York: Appleton-Century-Crofts, 1956.

71. Gerard, H. B. The effect of different dimensions of disagreement on the communication process in small groups. Unpublished doctor's dissertation, Univer. of Mich., 1951.

72. Gerard, H. B. Some effects of involvement upon evaluation. *J. abnorm. soc. Psychol.*, 1958, 57, 118–128.

73. Gibb, J. R. Defense level and influence potential in small groups. Research Reprint Series, No. 3. Washington, D.C.: National Training Laboratories, 1960.

74. Gilchrist, J. C. The formation of social groups under conditions of success and failure. *J. abnorm. soc. Psychol.*, 1952, 47, 174–187.

75. Goffman, E. *The presentation of self in everyday life.* New York: Doubleday, 1959.

76. Gouldner, A. W. Organizational analysis. In R. K. Merton, L. Broom, & L. S. Cottrell (Eds.), *Sociology today.* New York: Basic Books, 1959. Pp. 400–428.

77. Gray, H. Psychological types in married people. *J. soc. Psychol.*, 1949, 29, 189–200.

78. Greenacre, Phyllis (Ed.). *Affective disorders.* New York: International Universities Press, 1953.

79. Gross, H., Mason, W. S., & McEachern, A. W. *Explorations in role analysis.* New York: Wiley, 1958.

80. Gump, P., Sutton-Smith, B., & Redl, F. Influence of camp activities upon camper behavior. Unpublished paper.

81. Gump, P., & Sutton-Smith, B. Activity setting and social interaction: a field study. *Amer. J. Orthopsychiat.*, 1955, 25, 755–761.

82. Gurin, G., Veroff, J., & Feld, Shiela. *Americans view their mental health.* New York: Basic Books, 1960.

83. Hallowell, A. I. *Culture and experience.* Phila, Pa.: Univer. Pa. Press, 1955.

84. Hare, A., Borgatta, E. F., & Bales, R. F. (Eds.). *Small groups.* New York: Wiley, 1953.

85. Hartley, E. L., & Hartley, Ruth E. *Fundamentals of social psychology.* New York: Knopf, 1952.

86. Harvey, O. J. An experimental approach to the study of status relations in informal groups. *Amer. sociol. Rev.*, 1953., 18, 357–367.

87. Heider, F. Consciousness, the perceptual world, and communications

with others. In R. Tagiuri & L. Petrullo (Eds.), *Person, perception, and interpersonal behavior.* Stanford, Calif.: Stanford Univer. Press, 1958. Pp. 27–32.

88. Heider, F. *The psychology of interpersonal relations.* New York: Wiley, 1958.

89. Herbst, P. G. The measurement of family relationships. *Hum. Relat.,* 1952, **5,** 3–35.

90. Herbst, P. G. Analysis and measurement of a situation: the child in the family. *Hum. Relat.,* 1953, **6,** 113–140.

91. Heyns, R. W., & Lippitt, R. Systematic observational techniques. In G. Lindzey (Ed.), *Handbook of social psychology.* Cambridge, Mass.: Addison-Wesley, 1954. Pp. 370–404.

92. Hilgard, E. R. Human motives and the concept of the self. *Amer. Psychologist,* 1944, **4,** 374–382.

93. Homans, G. C. *The human group.* New York: Harcourt, Brace, 1950.

94. Horney, Karen. *The neurotic personality of our time.* New York: Norton, 1937.

95. Horney, Karen. *Neurosis and human growth.* New York: Norton, 1950.

96. Inkeles, A. Personality and social structure. In R. K. Merton, L. Broom, & L. S. Cottrell (Eds.), *Sociology today.* New York: Basic Books, 1959. Pp. 249–276.

97. Inkeles, A., & Levinson, D. J. National character: the study of modal personality and sociocultural systems. In G. Lindzey (Ed.), *Handbook of social psychology.* Vol. II. Reading, Mass.: Addison-Wesley, 1954. Pp. 977–1020.

98. Izard, C. E. Personality similarity and friendship. *J. abnorm. soc. Psychol.,* 1960, **61,** 47–51.

99. Jacobson, Edith. Manic-depressive partners. In V. S. Eisenstein (Ed.), *Neurotic interaction in marriage.* New York: Basic Books, 1956. Pp. 125–134.

100. Jacobson, E., Charters, W. W., & Liebermann, S. The use of the role concept in the study of complex organizations. *J. soc. Issues,* 1951, **7,** 18–27.

101. James, W. *The principles of psychology,* Vol. I. New York: Holt, 1890.

102. Johnson, Adelaide M. Factors in the etiology of fixations and symptom choice. *Psychoanal. Quart.,* 1953, **22,** 475–496.

103. Jones, E. E., & Thibaut, J. W. Interaction goals as bases of inference in interpersonal perception. In R. Tagiuri & L. Petrullo (Eds.), *Person, perception, and interpersonal behavior.* Stanford, Calif.: Stanford Univer. Press, 1958. Pp. 151–178.

104. Jourard, S. M., & Laskow, P. Some factors in self-disclosure. *J. abnorm. soc. Psychol.,* 1958, **56,** 91–98.

105. Jung, C. G. *The development of personality.* New York: Pantheon, 1953.

106. Jung, C. G. *Two essays on analytical psychology.* London: Routledge, 1953.

107. Kahl, J. A. Education and occupational aspirations of "common man" boys. *Harvard educ. Rev.*, 1953, **23**, 186–203.
108. Kaplan, D. M., & Goodrich, D. W. A formulation for interpersonal anger. *Amer. J. Orthopsychiat.*, 1957, **27**, 387–395.
109. Katz, E., & Lazarsfeld, P. F. *Personal influence.* Glencoe, Ill.: Free Press, 1955.
110. Kelley, H. H. Two functions of reference groups. In G. E. Swanson, T. M. Newcomb, & E. L. Hartley (Eds.), *Readings in social psychology.* New York: Holt, 1952. Pp. 410–414.
111. Kelly, G. A. *The psychology of personal constructs.* New York: Norton, 1955.
112. Klauser, S. Z. Social class and the self-concept. *J. soc. Psychol.*, 1953, **38**, 201–205.
113. Klein, Melanie. On the development of mental functioning. *Int. J. Psychoanal.*, 1958, **39**, 84–90.
114. Klein, Melanie, et al. (Eds.). *Developments in psychoanalysis.* London: Hogarth, 1952.
115. Kluckhohn, C. Values and value-orientation in the theory of action. In T. Parsons, E. A. Shils, et al., *Toward a general theory of action.* Cambridge, Mass.: Harvard Univer. Press, 1951. Pp. 388–433.
116. LaForge, R., & Suczek, R. The interpersonal dimension of personality: III. An interpersonal check list. *J. Pers.*, 1955, **24**, 94–112.
117. Lambert, W. W. Interpersonal behavior. In P. H. Mussen (Ed.), *Handbook of research methods in child development.* New York: Wiley, 1960. Pp. 854–917.
118. Langer, Susanne K. *Philosophy in a new key.* Cambridge, Mass.: Harvard Univer. Press, 1948.
119. Laulict, J. Role conflict, the pattern variable theory, and scalogram analysis. *Soc. Forces*, 1955, **33**, 250–254.
120. Leary, T. *Interpersonal diagnosis of personality.* New York: Ronald, 1957.
121. Lecky, P. *Self-consistency: a theory of personality.* New York: Island Press Co-operative, Inc., 1951.
122. Lecky, P. The personality. In C. E. Moustakas (Ed.), *The self.* New York: Harper, 1956. Pp. 86–97.
123. Lee, Dorothy P. A primitive system of values. *Phil. Sci.*, 1940, **7**, 355–365.
124. Lennard, H. L., & Bernstein, A. *The anatomy of psychotherapy.* New York: Columbia Univer. Press, 1960.
125. Levy, D. W. Body interest in children and hypochrondriacs. *Amer. J. Psychiat.*, 1932, **12**, 295–315.
126. Levy, M. J. *The structure of society.* Princeton, N.J.: Princeton Univer. Press, 1952.
127. Lewin, K. Environmental forces in child behavior and development. In C. A. Murchison (Ed.), *A handbook of child psychology.* Worchester, Mass.: Clark Univer. Press, 1931. Pp. 94–127.
128. Lewin, K. *Resolving social conflicts.* New York: Harper, 1951.

129. Lewin, K. *Field theory in social science.* New York: Harper, 1951.
130. Lewin, K., Lippitt, R., & White, R. K. Patterns of aggressive behavior in experimentally created "social climates." *J. soc. Psychol.,* 1939, **10,** 271–299.
131. Linton, R. *The study of man.* New York: Appleton-Century-Crofts, 1936.
132. Lippitt, R. *A theoretical model for observing and interpreting group social interaction and social structure,* Publ. 121-NTL, Univer. of Michigan, Inst. Soc. Res., 1960.
133. MacLeod, R. B. The phenomenological approach to social psychology. *Psychol. Rev.,* 1947, **54,** 193–210.
134. Manis, M. Social interaction and the self concept. *J. abnorm. soc. Psychol.,* 1955, **51,** 362–370.
135. Maslow, A. H. Self-actualizing people. In C. E. Moustakas (Ed.), *The self.* New York: Harper, 1956. Pp. 160–194.
136. Maussner, B. Studies in social interaction, III. *J. appl. Psychol.,* 1953, **37,** 391–393.
137. Maussner, B. The effect of prior reinforcement on the interaction of observer pairs. *J. abnorm. soc. Psychol.,* 1954, **45,** 65–68.
138. May, R. (Ed.). *Existence: a new dimension in psychiatry and psychology.* New York: Basic Books, 1956.
139. Mead, G. H. *The social psychology of George Herbert Mead.* Chicago: Univer. Chicago Press, 1956.
140. Menzies, Isabel E. P. A case-study in the functioning of social systems as a defence against anxiety. *Hum. Relat.,* 1960, **13,** 95–121.
141. Menzies, Isabel E. P. *Some psychological factors involved in marriage.* London: Tavistock Publ., 1960.
142. Merton, R. K. *Social theory and social structure.* Glencoe, Ill.: Free Press, 1957.
143. Miller, D. R. Personality and social interaction. In B. Kaplan (Ed.), *Studying personality cross-culturally.* Evanston, Ill.: Row, Peterson, 1961. Pp. 271–300.
144. Miller, D. R., & Swanson, G. E. *The changing American parent.* New York: Wiley, 1958.
145. Miller, D. R., & Swanson, G. E. *Inner conflict and defense.* New York: Holt, 1960.
146. Mittelmann, B. Analysis of reciprocal neurotic patterns in family relationships. In V. W. Eisenstein (Ed.), *Neurotic interaction in marriage.* New York: Basic Books, 1956. Pp. 81–100.
147. Moustakas, C. E., Sigel, I. E., & Schalock, H. D. An objective method for the measurement and analysis of child-adult interaction. *Child Developm.,* 1956, **27,** 19–134.
148. Murphy, G. *Personality: a biosocial approach to origins and structure.* New York: Harper, 1947.
149. Murray, H. A. Toward a classification of interactions. In T. Parsons, E. A. Shils, et al., *Toward a general theory of action.* Cambridge, Mass.: Harvard Univer. Press, 1951. Pp. 434–464.

150. Murray, H. A. Preparations for the scaffold of a comprehensive system. In S. Koch (Ed.), *Psychology: a study of a science*. Vol. 3. New York: McGraw-Hill, 1959, Pp. 7–54.

151. Murray, H. A., et al. *Explorations in personality*. New York: Oxford, 1938.

152. Newcomb, T. M. *Social psychology*. New York: Dryden, 1950.

153. Newcomb, T. M. An approach to the study of communicative acts. *Psychol. Rev.*, 1953, **60**, 393–404.

154. Newcomb, T. M. Varieties of interpersonal attraction. In D. Cartwright & A. Zander (Eds.), *Group dynamics*. Evanston, Ill.: Row, Peterson, 1960. Pp. 104–119.

155. Osgood, C. E., & Luria, Zella. A blind analysis of a case of multiple personality using the semantic differential. *J. abnorm. soc. Psychol.*, 1954, **49**, 579–591.

156. Osgood, C. E., Suci, G. J., & Tannenbaum, P. H. *The measurement of meaning*. Urbana, Ill.: Univer. Ill. Press, 1957.

157. Parsons, T. *The social system*. Glencoe, Ill.: Free Press, 1951.

158. Parsons, T. The superego and the theory of social systems. *Psychiatry*, 1952, **15**, 15–26.

159. Parsons, T., & Bales, R. F. *Family, socialization, and interaction process*. Glencoe, Ill.: Free Press, 1955.

160. Peak, Helen. Problems of objective observation. In D. Katz & L. Festinger (Eds.), *Research methods in the behavioral sciences*. New York: Dryden, 1953. Pp. 243–300.

161. Peak, Helen. Attitude and motivation. In M. R. Jones (Ed.), *Nebraska symposium on motivation, 1955*. Lincoln, Neb.: Univer. Neb. Press, 1955. Pp. 149–188.

162. Peak, Helen. Psychological structure and psychological activity. *Psychol. Rev.*, 1958, **65**, 325–347.

163. Pepitone, A. Attributions of causality, social attitudes, and cognitive matching processes. In R. Tagiuri & L. Petrullo (Eds.), *Person, perception, and interpersonal behavior*. Stanford, Calif.: Stanford Univer. Press, 1958. Pp. 258–276.

164. Pepitone, A., & Wilpizeski, E. Some consequences of experimental rejection. *J. abnorm. soc. Psychol.*, 1960, **60**, 359–364.

165. Rank, O. *Will therapy, truth and reality*. New York: Knopf, 1945.

166. Raush, H. L., Dittmann, A. T., & Taylor, T. J. The interpersonal behavior of children in residential treatment. *J. abnorm. soc. Psychol.*, 1959, **58**, 9–26.

167. Raush, H. L., Dittmann, A. T., & Taylor, T. J. Person, setting, and change in social interaction. *Hum. Relat.*, 1959, **12**, 361–378.

168. Redfield, R. The primitive world view. *Proc. Amer. Phil. Soc.*, 1952, **96**, 30–36.

169. Reich, W. *Character analysis*. New York: Orgone Press, 1949.

170. Reissman, L. A study of role conceptions in bureaucracy. *Soc. Forces*, 1949, **27**, 305–310.

171. Riezler, K. *Man: mutable and immutable*. Chicago: Regnery, 1950.

172. Rogers, C. R. A theory of therapy, personality, and interpersonal relationships as developed in the client-centered framework. In S. Koch (Ed.), *Psychology: a study of a science.* Vol. 3. New York: McGraw-Hill, 1959. Pp. 184–256.

173. Rommetveit, R. *Social norms and roles.* Minneapolis, Minn.: Univer. Minn. Press, 1955.

174. Rosen, E. Self-appraisal and perceived desirability of MMPI personality traits. *J. counsel. Psychol.,* 1956, **3**, 44–51.

175. Rotter, J. B. *Social learning and clinical psychology.* Englewood Cliffs, N.J.: Prentice-Hall, 1954.

176. Ruesch, J. Analysis of various types of boundaries. In R. R. Grinker (Ed.), *Toward a unified theory of human behavior.* New York: Basic Books, 1956. Pp. 340–361.

177. Ruesch, J., & Bateson, G. Structure and process in social relations. *Psychiatry,* 1949, **12**, 105–124.

178. Ruesch, J., & Bateson, G. *Communication.* New York: Norton, 1951.

179. Sargent, S. S. Conceptions of role and ego in contemporary psychology. In J. H. Rohrer & M. Sherif (Eds.), *Social psychology at the crossroads.* New York; Harper, 1951. Pp. 355–370.

180. Schachter, S. Deviation, rejection, and communication. *J. abnorm. soc. Psychol.,* 1951, **46**, 190–207.

181. Scheerer, M. Cognitive theory. In G. Lindzey (Ed.), *Handbook of social psychology.* Reading, Mass.: Addison-Wesley, 1954. Pp. 91–142.

182. Schilder, P. *The image and appearance of the human body.* Psyche Monog., No. 6. London: Kegan Paul, Trench, Trubner & Co., 1935.

183. Schutz, W. C. *FIRO-B: a three-dimensional theory of interpersonal behavior.* New York: Rinehart, 1958.

184. Sherif, M. *The psychology of social norms.* New York: Harper, 1936.

185. Sherif, M. A preliminary experimental study of inter-group relations. In J. H. Rohrer & M. Sherif (Eds.), *Social psychology at the crossroads.* New York: Harper, 1951. Pp. 388–424.

186. Shipton, L. Reference groups in the formation of public opinion. Unpublished doctor's dissertation, Harvard Univer., 1955.

187. Shonbar, R. A. The interaction of observer pairs in judging visual extent and movement. *Arch. Psychol.,* Vol. 41, No. 299. New York: Columbia Univer. Press, 1945.

188. Smith, A. The discrepancy in the meaning of self in a multilevel personality system and emotional disturbance. *Dissertation Abstr.,* 1958, **19**, 1120.

189. Smith, Henrietta. A comparison of interview and observation measures of mother behavior. *J. abnorm. soc. Psychol.,* 1958, **57**, 278–282.

190. Snygg, D., & Combs, A. W. *Individual behavior.* New York: Harper, 1949.

191. Spiegel, J. P. The resolution of role conflict within the family. *Psychiatry,* 1957, **20**, 1–16.

192. Spiegel, J. P. Interpersonal influences within the family. In B.

Schaffner (Ed.), *Group processes*. Transactions of the Third Conference. New York: Josiah Macy, Jr. Foundation, 1957. Pp. 23–115.

193. Spiegel, J. P., & Kluckhohn, Florence R. *Integration and conflict in the family*, Behavior Report 27, Group for the Advancement of Psychiatry, Topeka, Kan., 1956.

194. Spitz, P. Hospitalism. In Anna Freud, et al. (Eds.), *Psychoanalytic study of the child*. Vol. I. New York: International Universities Press, 1945. Pp. 53–74.

195. Stock, Dorothy, & Thelen, H. A. *Emotional dynamics and group culture*. Washington, D.C.: National Training Laboratories, 1958.

196. Stouffer, S., & Toby, J. Role conflict and personality. *Amer. J. Sociol.*, 1951, **56**, 395–406.

197. Strauss, A. L. *Mirrors and masks*. Glencoe, Ill.: Free Press, 1959.

198. Strodtbeck, F. L. Husband-wife interaction over revealed differences. *Amer. sociol. Rev.*, 1951, **16**, 468–473.

199. Strong, E. K. *Vocational interests of men and women*. Stanford, Calif.: Stanford Univer. Press, 1943.

200. Strupp, H. H. A multidimensional analysis of techniques in brief psychotherapy. *Psychiatry*, 1957, **20**, 387–397.

201. Strupp, H. H. A multidimensional comparison of therapist activity in analytic and client-centered therapy. *J. consult. Psychol.*, 1957, **21**, 301–308.

202. Strupp, H. H. A multidimensional system for analyzing psychotherapeutic techniques. *Psychiatry*, 1957, **20**, 293–306.

203. Sullivan, H. S. Psychiatry: an introduction to the study of interpersonal relations. In P. Mullahy (Ed.), *A study of interpersonal relations*. New York: Hermitage, 1949. Pp. 98–121.

204. Sullivan, H. S. *The interpersonal theory of psychiatry*. New York: Norton, 1953.

205. Symonds, P. M. *The ego and the self*. New York: Appleton-Century-Crofts, 1951.

206. Tagiuri, R., & Petrullo, L. (Eds.). *Person, perception, and interpersonal behavior*. Stanford, Calif.: Stanford Univer. Press, 1958.

207. Terman, L. M., & Miles, Catherine C. *Sex and personality*. New York: McGraw-Hill, 1936.

208. Thibaut, J. W., & Kelley, H. H. *The social psychology of groups*. New York: Wiley, 1959.

209. Thomas, W. I. The behavior pattern and the situation. *Publ. Amer. Sociol. Soc.*, 1928, **22**, 1–13.

210. Thomas, W. I., & Znaniecki. *The Polish peasant in America*. New York: Knopf, 1927.

211. Toman, W. Family constellation as a character and marriage determinant. *Int. J. Psychoanal.*, 1959, **40**, 316–319.

212. Turner, R. H., & Vanderlippe, R. H. Self-ideal congruence as an index of adjustment. *J. abnorm. soc. Psychol.*, 1958, **57**, 202–206.

213. Wallace, A. F. C. Revitalization movements. *Amer. Anthrop.*, 1956, **58**, 264–281.

214. Weiss, E. *Principles of psychodynamics*. New York: Grune & Stratton, 1950.

215. Werner, H. *Comparative psychology of mental development*. Chicago: Follett, 1948.

216. Westley, W. A. Violence and the police. *Amer. J. Sociol.*, 1953, **59,** 34–41.

217. White, L. A. *The science of culture*. New York: Farrar & Straus, 1949.

218. Whyte, W. F. *Street-corner society*. Chicago: Univer. Chicago Press, 1943.

219. Wilensky, H. L. *Intellectuals in labor unions*. Glencoe, Ill.: Free Press, 1956.

220. Winch, R. F. *Mate-selection; a study of complementary needs*. New York: Harper, 1958.

221. Wolff, K. H. (Ed.). *The sociology of George Simmel*. Glencoe, Ill.: Free Press, 1950.

222. Zajonc, R. B. *Cognitive structure and cognitive tuning*. Ann Arbor, Mich.: University Microfilms, 1955.

223. Zelditch, M. A note on the analysis of equilibrium systems. In T. Parsons & R. F. Bales (Eds.), *Family, socialization, and interaction process*. Glencoe, Ill.: Free Press, 1955. Pp. 401–408.

CLINICAL PSYCHOLOGY, PSYCHO-PATHOLOGY, AND RESEARCH ON SCHIZOPHRENIA[1]

ELIOT H. RODNICK
University of California
Los Angeles

Introduction 739
Clinical Psychology as a Field of Reference 740
  Clinical psychology and psychopathology 740
The Interrelationship of Sciences in Research on Schizophrenia 742
The Broad Field of Primary Reference. 747
  Etiological considerations 747
Delimitation of the Primary Field of Reference 752
Schizophrenia from the Viewpoint of Psychological Variables 755
Delineation of Interrelations between the Fields of Reference with Respect to
  Motivational Factors in Schizophrenic Performance 757
  Bridging principles between fields of reference 762
  Speculations regarding major variables with promise for "bridging" relation-
    ships 763
    Developmental factors 763
    Psychoanalytic propositions 765
    Psychological mechanisms underlying the syndrome 766
    Psychophysiological factors 766
Methodological Interrelationships 766
Collaborative, Administrative, and Educational Mechanisms 768
  Problems of collaborative research in psychopathology 768
  Administrative and technical problems 769
  Some conditions of research settings 769
    Choice of research problem 770
    Intercommunication among fields of psychology 771
    Administrative considerations 772
    The psychopathology laboratory as an integral part of psychology labo-
      ratories 772
Concluding Remarks 774
References 775

[1] The research reported in this paper has been supported by a U.S. Public Health Service research grant (M-629) from the National Institute of Mental Health.

INTRODUCTION

The consideration of the various patterns of empirical and conceptual interrelations among fields bearing on the clinical applications of psychology—including those which fall within and outside current conceptions of what constitutes psychological science—would involve a far more ambitious analysis than is possible here. Such an analysis of the historical developments which have shaped clinical psychology and the conceptualizations underlying the variables in its domain can be best undertaken by considering the various groupings of variable and field relationships in the areas with which clinical psychology is concerned. Such groupings would be too large for more than a superficial cataloguing of research issues, and they would be highly arbitrary. For one thing, the field of application is not entirely clear. When problems of extreme behavioral disturbance are under consideration there is less disagreement. But then other fields—medicine and the cognate sciences on which it is based, for example—become equally concerned with the problem for research inquiry as well as for clinical practice. Problems of overlap between disciplines arise. Can the essential variables in such instances be treated as falling primarily within psychology or—for purposes of analysis— should they be treated from the outset as falling within the broader domain of general biological science? This choice of conceptual domain has implications for specific research strategies and for the fields of reference from which the variables will be considered. In fact, in actual investigations—even within a single area of psychopathology—both types of considerations have been made.

When activity moves away from primary preoccupation with extreme deviance of behavior, which may often be accompanied by somatic dysfunction, there is more disagreement. Does clinical practice and research fall within a specific subarea of psychology? Or is all psychology, including various subareas, the field of primary reference? Clinical psychology then becomes the field of secondary reference. To complicate matters still further, there is often confusion between the *practice* of psychology in clinical settings (including the more focused research on which it is based) and the *systematic research* in psychopathology, which may provide the basic science underpinnings for some segment of the practice of clinical psychology. But in the domain of psychopathology, psychology is only one of several fields of reference.

Therefore it did not seem profitable to map the conceptual and empirical variables across the various fields of reference in either clinical psychology or psychopathology. Analysis limited to a single problem area, such as schizophrenia, appeared somewhat more workable. But even here the research clusters comprising what appears to be a specifically narrow focus are extensive and heterogeneous and cut across many scientific domains; the mapping of interrelationships cannot be much more than a superficial analysis. Therefore, this paper does not undertake an analysis of the various empirical and theoretical variables which research on the psychopathology of schizophrenia attempts to explain; it concerns primarily the conditions and attributes of research which seem pertinent to an examination of interrelationships between fields in only one aspect of the psychopathology of schizophrenia.

CLINICAL PSYCHOLOGY AS A FIELD OF REFERENCE

Clinical psychology has recently emerged as the area of psychology which is concerned with using general psychological science in understanding, diagnosing, and treating behavioral maladjustment, disability, and anomalies of adjustment. To the extent to which these disabilities and anomalies are a function of developmental and adjustment factors which follow principles isolated through research, and to the extent to which they can be modified by techniques derived from such research, the clinical psychologist can function as a relatively autonomous investigator and professional. But some problems with which he is concerned are related to attributes about which he professes to have no special competence—attributes which are also the concern of investigators and professionals in other fields. Thus, the clinical psychologist must frequently function as a member of a group, bringing the pertinent techniques and knowledge of psychology to bear on problems which transcend his specialized concerns.

The range of behavioral characteristics included within these behavioral anomalies extends widely across the broad spectrum of psychological science. Therefore much of the knowledge and many of the techniques of basic psychological science are pertinent—either directly or indirectly—to clinical psychology. When the clinical psychologist works in fields such as psychopathology, he can apply the techniques and data of other areas of psychology to only a limited extent; frequently he must consider new research approaches which are more specifically relevant to psychopathology. For these reasons, one can question whether—at its present stage of development—clinical psychology in its generic sense should be considered a field of applied psychology.

Clinical Psychology and Psychopathology

The psychologist in psychopathology finds that conceptualizations based on research in general psychology are frequently inadequate for investigating extreme deviations of behavioral adjustment. He must therefore undertake developmental research to obtain basic data for his research. These have at least the potentiality of making a major impact on research and development of theory in general psychology. The relationship between psychoanalysis and general psychology is a convenient illustration of this point. The development of research and theory in the psychoanalytic movements can be viewed as an attempt at psychological research in psychopathology—research which has implications for understanding normal behavior. The difficulties engendered by its isolation from general psychology need not detract from the originality and the basic nature of its contributions to general psychological science [12, p. 706 ff.].

Let us consider only the relationships between clinical psychology and other areas of psychology. Obviously, clinical psychologists are faced with the Herculean task of mastering and using relevant contributions from various areas. Other investigators in psychological science do not often have such a task; they can limit themselves to an intensive examination of a specific problem involving a much narrower segment of psychological knowledge. It is understandable why so much investigative effort in clinical psychology has gone into the assessment and diagnosis, with a limited set of psychological instruments, of a narrow range of clinical conditions and on a few techniques for modifying behavior—techniques which were derived primarily from the classical remediation procedures of general psychiatry and psychoanalysis.

Relatively little of the psychologists' effort has gone into intensive basic research on the psychopathological conditions themselves. Clinical psychology has depended heavily on the extensive descriptive and research contributions of clinical psychiatry and psychoanalysis. Of recent years, psychopathology's research base derived from general psychology has been extremely limited in both amount and significance.

If one also considers that many aspects of psychopathological investigation that are relevant to clinical psychology require extensive formal knowledge of other fields—the physiological sciences, neuroanatomy, various areas of medicine, anthropology, sociology, public health, etc.—the relationships of clinical psychology with other areas of science seem extensive indeed.

A discussion of the emergence of clinical psychology as a profession based on the development of psychological science is beyond the scope of this paper. Yet the issues are relevant; the practicing clinical psychologist's need for basic knowledge required for functioning as a diagnostician and therapist who is acquainted with psychopathology has affected his training, background, and research interests. Background and experience have frequently been introduced at the expense of the intensive literature and research experience which would equip the clinical psychologist for research in depth and breadth on psychopathological conditions. In addition, such research is often not included in the research activities of the psychology laboratory where he is trained—often his teachers, with whom he could serve as apprentice, do not carry on such research [74]. The reason why basic research in psychopathology has not had widespread interest in psychology until recently is clear. Where such research has been carried out in university laboratories, it has often involved setting up simple analogs of psychopathological conditions based on clinical reports in the psychiatric literature. The investigators frequently have lacked the contact with the psychopathological behavior which would equip them with sufficient background to develop new ways of exploring the phenomena. Because of the need for familiarity and direct experience in the settings in which conditions occur, most university training for research in psychopathology is conducted in the training program for clinical psychologists, which has limited training opportunities for nonprofessionally oriented psychologists. The clinical psychology graduate student must have a broad curriculum to equip him for a range of professional clinical activities. Thus it is often difficult to include research training that is sufficiently specialized for some aspects of psychopathology research. The recent increase in interest of nonclinically trained psychologists in research on psychopathology may permit more differentiation in training in the future. Modifying the training program by reducing the breadth of clinical training and concentrating only on limited aspects of the clinical field would make possible more intensive research training. Such a trend may have a bearing on the level of sophistication of the research by psychologists specializing in psychopathology.

THE INTERRELATIONSHIP OF SCIENCES IN RESEARCH ON SCHIZOPHRENIA

The remainder of this paper will consider the interrelationship issue from the viewpoint of investigations on the psychopathology of schizophrenia. The reasons for this choice are as follows:

1. It is the research area in psychopathology with which the author is most intimately acquainted.

2. The symptoms of schizophrenia are relatively dramatic and can therefore be more readily differentiated from behavioral attributes of normally functioning persons; the behavioral deviations are more generalized and involve much of his psychological functioning. They are therefore particularly puzzling and not readily accounted for by a simple application of a few known psychological principles.

3. The breadth of somatic deviations, their similarity to other forms of psychopathology involving known or suspected lesions, and the relatively systematic onset and course of the disorder—all have often

intrigued investigators from other biological fields who consider the disorder to be as much somatic as psychological.

4. The nature of the symptoms themselves raises basic questions regarding the interrelationship between somatic and psychological functioning.

5. The history of research interest in schizophrenia is long and permits an analysis of research trends and fashions as a function of the state of development of the various sciences.

6. There appears to have been more systematic and extensive support for program research in this field than for any other research area in psychopathology.

The investigation of schizophrenia presents the scientist-investigator, as well as the systematic theorist, with a problem area of enormous complexity. As well as any other area in psychopathology, it illustrates the interrelatedness of the various areas of scientific inquiry, as well as the difficulties inherent in a sectarian approach to science. At the outset, let us point out that the *scope* of the phenomena is in itself a major issue. The attributes of the identifiable phenomena appear to fall within a broad segment of cognate basic and applied sciences. Even before the investigator can profitably attempt to isolate attributes of schizophrenic behavior which appear to be susceptible to systematic inquiry, he is faced with an overwhelming accumulation of contributions by investigators with widely differing backgrounds, acquaintance with the problem area, interests, orientations, language, theoretical positions, standards of investigation, and general sophistication in the basic attributes of scientific inquiry. Furthermore, the variation in the ethos of their various disciplines makes for difficulties in communicating effectively about past research.

Problems of this type are not unique in medicine, which has made increasingly productive use of contributions of basic and applied science which appear to be directly relevant to the investigation, solution, and handling of human somatic disability. Progress in making effective use of the contributions of psychological, behavioral, and social science has been less smooth, however, even when the interrelationships with behavioral variables may have significant implications for treatment and remediation, although the somatic aspects are paramount. An example of this is the difficulty with which systematic behavioral science research is incorporated in the fields of medical rehabilitation, geriatrics, and pharmacology.

As a branch of medicine, psychiatry has had much more difficulty in utilizing the various sciences bearing on the disabilities with which it is concerned. Historically, it has evolved as a branch of medicine which attempts to cope with psychological and behavioral disabilities. Some of these disabilities appear to be directly comparable to the somatic dysfunctions with which medicine is clearly concerned; but others may appear to bear only a superficial resemblance to classical somatic dysfunctions. In attempting to delineate its area of concern, modern psychiatry has been hard pressed in developing conceptual frameworks and models within which psychiatric disabilities might be placed.

Largely because of its historical roots in classical medicine and the fact that training of practitioners was typically limited to the medical field, psychiatry has always attempted to adopt physical disease and somatic disability as its working model and to keep its field firmly anchored in general medicine. The concepts, nosologies, modes of research inquiry, and theoretical conceptualizations in psychiatry are intimately derived from medicine. The institutional settings in which psychiatry functioned were shaped to conform with the attributes of the hospital and medical out-patient clinic. This was a perfectly natural evolution, since many of the severe disabilities with which it was concerned were either obvious somatic dysfunctions or could be so considered. Differential diagnosis from other known somatic disorders required extensive training in medical diagnosis; the care and treatment of the disabilities—even prior to an understanding of etiology—could be based upon the utilization of therapeutic practices of general medicine. The consideration of these disabilities as illnesses and diseases represented a major social advance in their identification, care, and treatment, for it provided a familiar institutional framework which society could accept. It made available a professional manpower pool with a training and treatment philosophy, as well as the potentiality of a research-based orientation toward the nature of psychiatric disability. It led to intensive observation and description of various psychiatric conditions appearing in hospital and clinic settings, as well as in individual practice, and culminated in the development of a widely accepted and useful descriptive classification of psychiatric conditions which has survived for over sixty years [3]. For psychiatric conditions directly resulting from a somatic lesion, the identification of the disability and research leading to effective treatment could be related to advances in particular fields of medicine or its related sciences. Successful research of this sort is typified by the work on paresis, which was shown to be a consequence of central nervous system lesion resulting from syphilitic infection. Noguchi and Moore's 1913 research [57] demonstrating this relationship led ultimately to the utilization of specific modes of therapy for bacterial infections, and this has brought the disorder under control in recent years. The understanding of *how* such lesions lead to thought and behavioral disturbances is, however, only poorly understood and awaits further progress in such fields as physiology and psychology.

But in other psychiatric conditions in which a somatic lesion was not as apparent, there has been more difficulty in using advances in other pertinent areas for understanding the condition or in developing sophisticated methods of research inquiry which would lead to systematic data on which potentially fruitful hypotheses could be based. For years, the contributions of psychoanalytic psychiatrists were poorly coordinated with those of conventional institutional psychiatry. The latter were related more directly to the research orientations and techniques of the preclinical sciences and clinical medical fields represented in medical school curricula. Psychoanalytic psychiatrists evolved their own specialized training centers outside the standard medical schools—in most cases, outside of university research centers. But psychoanalytic theory and research, based as they were on direct concern with the phenomena of psychopathology, provided psychiatry with what was essentially a most fruitful model of psychological theory for both conceptualization and research. The conflicts of an earlier day between a conventional medical approach to the phenomena of psychopathology and the psychoanalytic point of view has largely disappeared in recent years.

The dilemma it has inherited, however, by assimilating psychoanalysis as its basic field is inherent in the attributes of psychoanalysis which resulted from its long isolation from research in the other biological, psychological, and social sciences. The point is this: The phenomena of severe psychopathology have been largely the concern of psychiatric investigators working primarily in medical settings and having the basic orientations of either conventional medical practice or psychoanalytic theory. To be sure, they utilized specific techniques, research approaches, and—in some limited instances—conceptual contributions of psychological, anthropological, and sociological science, when these could be drawn upon to identify, describe, and understand particular phenomena of psychopathology. But these contributions were adapted to the original frames of reference of psychiatry. Until quite recently, the contributions of these nonmedical disciplines have not had a major impact on shaping psychiatry as a field, although they have influenced individual theorists and investigators, such as Meyer [56], Alexander and French [1], Goldstein [34], Rorschach [66], and Benjamin [9].

This state of affairs may be partly a function of the illness and disease model of psychopathology to which psychiatry has adhered through its development as a branch of medicine, as has been discussed recently by Szasz [73]. Its heavy reliance on psychoanalysis as its basic field has tended to keep psychiatry isolated from other areas of psychological and behavioral sciences—except through the common ground of psychoanalysis. Another contributing factor which should not be minimized is this: Psychological science has not been overly successful in making the necessary theoretical and methodological data bridges with the phenomena of psychopathology as seen in the psychiatric setting because of its concern with behavior which could be studied in limited university laboratories. Investigators have relied heavily on analogs of attributes of psychopathology as described by psychiatric clinicians which could be established in the laboratory. Too often these have been inadequate—central components of the variables were missing, and hence only limited contributions to understanding were made (e.g., the research on experimental neuroses). In other instances, the techniques of psychological science which were developed for another purpose have been utilized by psychologists for comparing psychopathological conditions with "normal" behavior—as manifested in the laboratory. The investigator's inexperience with psychopathological phenomena, his frequent inability to carry out controls which would make a comparison interpretable, and the lag in developing appropriate research methods may have limited the contributions of psychological science to psychopathology.

There are some notable exceptions. The development of the psychometric area led to the significant and fruitful utilization of test instruments for assessing and diagnosing psychopathological conditions. Perhaps more than any other single factor, this contribution is responsible for the recent widespread acceptance of clinical psychology as one of the basic professions in the mental health area.

The role of the psychological investigator as research methodologist has recently helped in introducing more sophisticated and scientifically more acceptable research techniques. The research psychologist, functioning as methodologist, has served as a translator of mathematicostatistical procedures for coding and manipulating data in forms suitable for clinical investigations, which made more systematic tests of the tenability of clinically based hypotheses possible. In this role, he also introduced procedures derived from general psychology, such as the control and manipulation of variables for assessing the attributes and extent of behavioral change. A recent development which can serve as an illustration is the utilization of psychological methods for assessing the behavioral effects of drugs [75]. Other contributions of experimental psychological science to psychopathology could be enumerated.

Psychopathology covers a broad range of conditions and is of specific interest to a number of scientific disciplines besides psychiatry, which has generally had the primary responsibility for the management and treatment of the more incapacitating conditions. It would be futile to attempt to summarize even superficially the contributions of the various sciences which have been involved in research in psychopathology. A meaningful discussion of all the contributions of psychology alone is beyond the scope of this paper.

Our topic is the interrelationship between aspects of psychological science and an illustrative problem area—psychopathology. Although the field has been identified historically with medicine in general and psychiatry in particular, it is pertinent to ask why general psychology has had such limited impact on shaping the commonly used theoretical conceptions and the clinical investigative procedures of psychopathology. The more obvious factors are related to the isolation of psychiatric medicine from psychology during most of its development. Consequently, its concepts and modes of research made for communication difficulties with general psychological science. In turn, the parallel historical isolation of general psychological science, with some exceptions, from the systematic investigation of the phenomena of psychopathology limited the usefulness of its research and theoretical contributions to an understanding of psychopathological conditions. But current trends in both psychology and psychiatry indicate that this state of affairs is rapidly changing.

THE BROAD FIELD OF PRIMARY REFERENCE

Research in schizophrenia has ranged across many scientific fields, and each has at times tended to consider itself the primary field of investigation. The early clinical descriptions recognized the variegation in clinical patterns included within the concept of schizophrenia. Beginning with the descriptive classifications suggested by Kraepelin, the range of symptom or reaction types subsumed under the rubric of schizophrenia has been assumed by many investigators to be the consequence of common pathological processes. Others have taken the position that—despite some similarities in reaction pattern—this is not a common disorder, but a heterogeneous set of conditions which stem from a variety of etiological factors.

In 1911, Bleuler [11] described schizophrenia as a gradually progressive deterioration of the entire personality which expressed itself in disorders of feeling, thought, and conduct and frequently included a tendency to withdraw from reality. The basic symptoms are primarily manifested in psychological terms, such as disturbances in (1) associations and thought processes, (2) affect, (3) adaptive capacity to social reality, (4) sense of reality, (5) drive and emotional control, and (6) object relations. Within the psychoanalytic framework these have been considered as manifestations of disturbances in ego control [7, 8]. Yet many of these symptoms are seen in other organic reaction types as well, particularly in acute and chronic brain syndromes, although usually with different patterning [36].

Etiological Considerations

The research used to support conflicting notions as to possible etiology come from a variety of sources including biochemistry [37, 48,

49], genetics [43, 45], physiology [27, 38, 39], psychology [47, 61, 77, 78, 79], psychiatry [26, 46, 51, 72], and sociology [18]. Bellak in 1958 attempted to reconcile the disparate views regarding possible genetic, physiological, psychological, and social etiological factors into what he called "an integrative view" which would take into consideration the various research studies which, on face value, appeared to be in conflict with one another:

The concept of the schizophrenias as disorders of many different etiologies but with a shared final common path of ego disturbance leads quite logically to the concept that the diagnosis of schizophrenia at present can best be made on the basis of the degree of ego disturbance in a given patient. It also follows that the degree of ego disturbance we are willing to term "schizophrenia" is based on an arbitrary decision. Quite understandably, the literature abounds with divergent opinions on diagnostic concepts [6, p. 52].

The field of primary research reference in investigating the behavioral disturbances comprising the set of symptoms which can—with some arbitrariness—be called schizophrenia has been a subject of controversy almost from the beginning of systematic research on the condition. The puzzling nature of the symptoms—some appear to be extreme variations of commonly observed behavior in nonpathological states, and others are bizarre and clearly pathological—has presented investigators and theorists with a basic dilemma. Even with the inefficient and admittedly crude investigative techniques, theoretical models, and concepts of psychological functioning that are available, can these behavioral anomalies be accounted for in terms of purely psychological conceptions? For some aspects, the research evidence and common sense supported this position, even though the characteristics of possible psychological, developmental, or interpersonal etiological factors and the nature of the mediating mechanisms were not at all understood. But when other characteristics of the condition are considered, a plausible case can be made for viewing the behavioral characteristics as a consequence of more basic genetic, biochemical, or neurophysiological attributes which, when identified, would account for the deviance in behavior in terms of somatic components.

These conflicting positions of extreme somatotropic versus psychotropic models represent another form of the mind-body problem not as a philosophical issue, but as one which has direct implications for research on a common problem which could be viewed from one of several facets. Hoskins [39], in summarizing some twenty years of research effort by the Worcester State Hospital group, attempted a not particularly successful reconciliation through the formulation of a general biological model. More recently, Jackson, in discussing various research strategies and conceptual views regarding schizophrenia, remarks that "although the most ardent biochemist agrees that there are psychological consequences for the processes he describes and the most convinced psychologist is prepared to admit the biochemical nature of the intermediate processes involved, yet they are scarcely able to communicate their findings to one another, let alone relate them in any meaningful fashion" [42, p. 4].

Despite attempts to develop a more adequate psychosomatic model which would provide a framework for interrelating efforts in the various fields, the research clusters have had essentially parallel developments, even though much of the research effort has been through interdisciplinary teams. Each field has tended to use variables drawn from its own field as the primary point of reference *variable* and those of other fields as the secondary field of reference. But since information indicates that one or more of the "secondary" fields may be primary for some aspects of the disorder, the more commonly held views are those involving multiple causation or conjectures regarding the interrelationships among variables, the nature of which is only dimly apprehended even in a general way.

Even a brief overview of the characteristics of the interrelationships among research efforts is a monumental task. One can select only a few attributes to illustrate characteristic trends, but in doing so other contributions which are significant exceptions will inevitably be bypassed. At an operational level, the research clusters generally either basically ignored the contributions of other clusters or drew on them primarily for their utility as a source of quantitative indexes of the attributes of the subject populations with which the data obtained in the primary reference field could be related. Thus, in the research on possible genetic factors, the psychiatric contributions of clinical descriptions have been employed casually to identify the population to be used in statistical analysis of proband trends [45]. A recent exception is Rosenthal's study [67]. He applied Phillips's [59] premorbid rating scale to a reassessment of Slater's data [71] on psychotic twins and was able to demonstrate that premorbid level of behavioral adjustment was a significant factor in reducing the variance of the schizophrenic subject population for which possible genetic explanations were tenable.

In biochemical-physiological investigations, psychological measurement devices have been used frequently to furnish a more objective and quantitative way of characterizing either the subject populations or the behavioral attributes to which the biochemical or physiological variables are to be related. The converse has characterized much of the research in which psychological research is the field of primary reference.

The difficulties inherent in interrelating a diversity of fields—each having its own languages, frames of reference, limitations in point of view, styles of research strategy, standards of research evidence, and conceptual rigor—are illustrated in Luszki's report of a series of conferences of psychopathology investigators who all had had extensive research experience with investigators of other disciplines [52]. The problems reported largely result from the fact that the techniques and concepts used in such research tend to be discipline-centered, rather than problem-oriented. Frequently methods were selected by chance or because of their availability, rather than for their relevance to the problem.

It would be hazardous to attempt now to characterize the main independent and dependent variables of schizophrenia which have emerged after some sixty years of intensive research effort. Although the literature on physiological and biochemical differences between schizophrenics and nonschizophrenics is extensive, very few differences have been consistently corroborated when investigator, technique, or laboratory has been varied or when proper experimental controls were instituted [37, 48]. With continuing investigation and replication, earlier differences tend to drop out, and new ones appear. Questions have been raised whether even these few differences will hold under closer experimental scrutiny; be that as it may, even the particular differences for which a relatively adequate case be made point toward a psychosomatic type of relationship. At present, it is impossible to indicate whether somatic or behavioral variables are of primary or secondary significance. The difficulty with attempting to consider the essential interrelationship among these classes of variables is that the analysis must be made in terms of past research on biochemical and physiological factors in etiology, which have turned out to be negative on the whole. Yet the characteristics of the phenomena point toward the plausibility of implicating biochemical and physiological factors directly. In a field where the nature of such etiological factors is unknown, one significant positive contribution may suddenly change the whole pattern of research and the conceptual framework on which it is based.

Paraphrasing Jackson [42], research clusters (with interrelationships among them) can be categorized according to their definitions of schizophrenia:

1. A disease in the classical medical sense, which may be either genetically or constitutionally determined, but with a time factor which determines the developmental stage at which it is manifested.

2. With or without some external invading agent as a precipitating factor, it is a disease involving either a biochemical or physiological dysfunction.

3. A biological disorder which predisposes the individual to inadequate resources in coping with psychological adjustment stresses or physiological dysfunctions.

4. A disorder involving anomalies of development in which the

psychological and physiological resources needed for adjustment fail to develop adequately. Some of the psychosomatic views of an interrelationship between somatic and psychological variables can be included in this cluster.

5. The disorder may be viewed in developmental terms in which the factors influencing development are psychological and/or interpersonal.

6. The disorder may be viewed in terms of the operation of psychological principles such as drive, anxiety, and regression, in which prior experience and learning may influence the nature of the response. Much research is concerned with the application of general principles of behavior which might account for the occurrence of the disorder, its attributes, and its course of development.

7. The disorder may be considered in terms of interpersonal influence, the role of membership in particular family groups, or social class and societal ecological factors.

These research clusters are not necessarily independent; many studies are concerned with interrelationships among them. Ignoring the classical mind-body problem even in its modern version and avoiding any judgment on the evidence regarding genetic, biochemical, or physiological variables as primary independent variables, research clearly indicates that psychological factors contribute heavily to the variance of behavioral anomalies.

Because schizophrenia has important personal and social implications, the pressures for ameliorating its symptoms have forced premature attempts at therapy before research has suggested scientific courses of action. The sense of urgency for developing workable therapy and preventive techniques has shaped research and theoretical contributions and forced premature and unsubstantiated speculation about the nature of the condition, the variables involved, and the ways in which they might be interrelated. Research-based data have too frequently been cast into poorly defined and articulated theoretical models which make their retrieval by other investigators difficult—if not impossible. The implications of observations and data are often readily overgeneralized, without adequate specification of conditions, techniques, or attention to critical controls. For these reasons, the lack of suitable corroborative studies persists. Apart from the inevitability of an inadequate level of sophistication and elegance of research in such a complex and difficult area, the consequences of the pressure for obtaining findings which have immediate preventive and therapeutic utility should not be minimized in determining the choice of variable to be investigated and shaping the characteristics of the research. The data which permit a charting of the problem area in relatively neutral theoretical terms are sparse; with all too few exceptions, they have been only a fortuitous by-product of the research.

DELIMITATION OF THE PRIMARY FIELD OF REFERENCE

A more profitable way of considering the interrelationships is to limit the analysis to a more manageable set of relationships centering around a specific subproblem area which illustrates the issues involved in a productive research strategy in more concrete fashion. The editor of this series has permitted me to approach the topic from the standpoint of personal research experiences.

Garmezy and I [64] reported research on motivational factors in schizophrenia and indicated that we were concerned with the interrelationship between two fields: dynamic psychiatry and experimental psychology. From the former, we derived the possible significance of social censure as an independent variable in our experiments for an understanding of the principles involved in the occurrence of psychological deficits in schizophrenia. Our choice of the censure variable was partly dictated by extensive clinical reports on the schizophrenic's withdrawal as a defense response to failure and criticism. We were also mindful of the fact that this withdrawal response was often quite variable and inconsistent. The variability and inconsistency of the deficit and the withdrawal in a number of psychological functions had led some observers to hypothesize that motivational variables might be implicated [40, 41]. From a more experimentally oriented psychology, we selected dependent variables regarding deficit performance which could be specified with more precision and employed in a wide variety of experimental situations. We attempted to control in a standardized fashion the instigating conditions of censure and to manipulate them in a specified and systematized way. A major purpose was to develop objective and quantitative ways of estimating the deficit performance and to exert reasonable control over the contaminating variables which make an interpretation of the relationships between dependent and independent variables precarious. At the same time, to identify the characteristics of the subjects for replicability and to reduce the heterogeneity of variance which has plagued much research, we sharply delimited the permissible range of attributes of our subject groups.

In 1957, we presented a fairly representative series of quotations from both the clinical and experimental literature which seemed to illustrate how clinical descriptions of schizophrenic behavior could be translated into variables which could be investigated [64]. Our own research investigated the functional relationships between social censure as a stimulus variable and behavioral deficits as response variables in a wide variety of experimentally controlled tasks. These included discrimination of neutral and affectively relevant stimuli under censure and noncensure conditions, verbal learning and recall, size estimation, concept formation, and semantic meanings of words which appeared to have personal relevance for schizophrenics. The left-hand column below represents clinical discussions of the stimulus or cue conditions and the right-hand column represents the response measures of an experimentally oriented view:

The Clinical View

What does the schizophrenic patient see as he sits before the therapist? Primarily, he sees threat, every human relationship means threat to the schizophrenic person, whether threat of physical or sexual assault, rejection, seduction, misunderstanding, depreciation or great expectation—each human contact is frightening in the schizophrenic isolation. . . . Those who work with schizophrenic patients often note the sensitivity so many of them possess! Undoubtedly this sensitive awareness of another person is a defensive necessity for living in a world seen as threatening [16, p. 240].

Dementia praecox is a defensive reaction in a sensitive human being to a feeling of personal failure. . . . Fundamental to the psychosis is an intolerable loss of self-respect [38, p. 1210].

Schizoid withdrawal frequently begins in childhood, and appears typically to bear some relation to the character of the parent-child and child-parent relationship.

While examination of the literature for description of the typical parent-child relations in the background of schizophrenia reveal some range of description, the descriptions of various investigators seem to agree in giving a picture of a parent overpowering to a child, a parent with whom it would be more than usually difficult for the child to establish his individuality, his selfhood, without doing so through

The Experimental View

The disturbance in psychological function, which is quite widespread, does not seem to be at the level of organization represented by the patellar tendon reflex or even that of sensory phenomena. It appears where perceptual organization and voluntary behavior play a role. With respect to the latter it emerges especially in new situations where an adaptive difficulty is strikingly in evidence [69, p. 59].

The lessening of interaction between the person and his environment in schizophrenia becomes particularly evident when he is exposed to various stimuli. The reduction of responses to stimuli emanating from the physical and social environment is well known in the psychology of schizophrenia [4, p. 622].

It is interesting to relate the size of the differences in reaction-time found for schizophrenics and controls to the complexity of the task involved. . . . For reflex time, the simplest level, the means for the two groups are essentially identical. For simple reaction-time, the differences between the groups are fairly marked and are statistically significant. . . . For the simplest of choice reactions involving a simple visual discrimination another marked increment in the differences between the groups appears. The reactions of patients have been found to average much slower than normal for still more complicated activities: for various types of choice-reaction, for word

The Clinical View (Cont.)

negativism or schizoid withdrawal [44, p. 739].

Since the child is in constant expectancy of disapproval, and tries desperately to anticipate possibilities of disapproval in the futile attempt to avoid them, he becomes sensitive to the slightest sign of the oncoming reproach. Thus the preschizophrenic develops the sensitive personality which has been described by many authors. This sensitivity to disapproval persists until it is covered by other defenses. The preschizophrenic is never able to tolerate even minor frustrations, because frustrations mean disapproval from other human beings [5, p. 56].

The first type (of schizophrenogenic mother), which occurs relatively infrequently, is the overtly rejecting mother. Such a mother has usually conceived unwillingly and is rejecting of the child from birth onwards. She is cold and sadistically critical of her offspring, insists that the patient meet her excessive demands for neatness and cleanliness, for politeness and observance of social forms, or for fulfillment of her own unfulfilled ambitions. At the same time she destroys the patient's self-confidence by her constant nagging, disapproval, and complete nonacceptance of him—or her—as a person. Such a mother frequently describes the patient as a difficult, ungrateful, unresponsive, stubborn child who has been a chore and a burden, until finally he has added to the mother's discomfiture by developing a mental illness! . . .

We may designate the second type of mother as the covertly rejecting mother. She exerts an equally malignant influence on her child's

The Experimental View (Cont.)

associations, for reactions on a substitution-test, for many of the standard tests [40, p. 996].

The ability of normal and schizophrenic Ss to deal with information involving human and non-human stimuli was compared. When Ss were matched on the basis of ability to utilize information about non-human stimuli, it was found that the problem-solving behavior of schizophrenics was significantly disrupted by the presence of human stimuli in the test situation. When the same populations were matched for ability to solve problems involving human stimuli, no significant differences were found in their capacity to deal with information involving non-human stimuli [20, p. 128].

Our data do not support the contention that the chronic schizophrenic is generally characterized by low physiological responsiveness. . . .

One clear instance of low responsiveness in the chronic schizophrenic group was noted in the Pain-Stress Test. The schizophrenics did not press the button to signal pain as often as did the normal controls. Here it is tempting to conclude that pain stimulation was less stressful for the schizophrenics. But this explanation fails to account for the higher level of muscular tension in the right arm, the higher heart rate and higher diastolic blood pressure which the schizophrenics showed in comparison with normal controls. . . .

Our data thus indicate that in schizophrenia those aspects of responsiveness which are associated with emotional arousal may remain

The Clinical View (Cont.)

mental development, but in a much more subtle way. She is just as dominating as the sadistically hostile mother, but her domination takes the form of overprotectiveness— probably a reaction formation against unconscious hostility—of such an extreme degree as to merit the appellation of "smother love." This pattern is most frequently found in infantile, egocentric mothers who fatten parasitically on their children and who aim, through babying them, to prevent them from ever becoming independent. . . . The patient is not fooled, however, and when asked about his feelings never fails to indicate that he was not loved as a child. This is by far the most common pattern of parent-child relationships in schizophrenia [60, pp. 251–252].

The Experimental View (Cont.)

intact, while the mechanisms underlying overt, "purposive" acts may be defective or inoperative. This conclusion is counter to the traditional view that "affect is flat" in chronic schizophrenia. Typically, the run-of-the-mine chronic schizophrenic appears emotionally unresponsive to the observer (e.g., in a psychiatric interview).

But this observation may be due more to lack of "purposive" response to the questions of the examiner than to any general decrease in affectivity. Our chronic schizophrenic group, it should be emphasized, would similarly have been judged as unresponsive, had only measures of response to the specific painful stimuli been available. However, measures reflecting general level of activity suggested the opposite—that the chronic schizophrenic was quite "responsive." It is also important to consider that in some cases this responsiveness may have had determinants which were largely independent of any easily denotable aspects of the situation.

The thought processes of the patients could be one such determinant [53, pp. 370–372].

SCHIZOPHRENIA FROM THE VIEWPOINT OF PSYCHOLOGICAL VARIABLES

Psychological investigations of the schizophrenic process have drawn extensively from a broad range of psychological fields. Significant researches which have contributed conceptual models, theoretical formulations, research techniques, and important data to the current psychological knowledge about schizophrenia have come from such diverse fields as neuropsychology and physiological psychology, learning, perception, motivation, psychometrics and individual differences, genetic and developmental psychology, personality, social psychology, intellectual functioning, and psycholinguistics. Even such a partial catalogue points to the difficulty of identifying the research issues in investigating schizophrenia with just the professional aspects of clinical psychology.

A dilemma arises when a research area is arbitrarily identified with a field of psychological science which is largely concerned with the *practice* of psychology. On the one hand, coping with research problems in psychopathology requires first-hand familiarity with and apprehension of the phenomena. The investigator cannot depend on the selective observations, generalizations, or inferences presented by other practitioners. These have been screened and abstracted through the cerebral cortices of persons—no matter how capable—who have different apperceptive masses influencing their perceptions. The investigator must check the fit of his colleagues' contributions with the attributes of the phenomena as he perceives them. Significant features may have been overlooked or ignored because the original observers could make no sense of them. The observations and inferences may have been unduly distorted; they may have been communicated in forms which are not meaningful to the investigator working from a different conceptual or theoretical framework. Or apprehension of the phenomena may require specialized training for appreciation of their significance. Regardless of the reason, psychological investigators in psychopathology need to work in settings in which they can have direct contact with the conditions they intend to research. In so doing, they need direct access to all relevant phenomena. Effective work with schizophrenics places a special premium on specialized training and experience in working with psychotics. The investigator should be familiar with previous research and clinical observations and the specialized techniques for obtaining relevant data. Recently established university training programs in clinical psychology strive for more effective training of investigators through the integration of clinical experience with the formal courses. Clinical psychologists have developed specialized techniques which coordinate well with those of their nonpsychological colleagues, and the researcher should be familiar with them when they are pertinent to his work. For such reasons, research in psychopathology has been identified with clinical psychology. Although psychopathology is one of the fundamental research and theoretical areas on which the practice of clinical psychology is based, the two fields are interdependent, although they do not necessarily have a shared identity.

The other horn of the dilemma is this: At this stage, we can hardly guess which areas of research in psychology may make the most effective contributions in advancing psychopathology. Who can tell whether the next major advance will come as a consequence of new developments in learning? Operant behavior? Group processes? Computor technology applied to behavior? Neuropsychology? Cognition? General behavior theory? The analysis of motivational mechanisms? Psychometrics? Or perhaps none of these? The relevant variables are broadly based in the total science of psychology. This dilemma of trying to delimit clinical psychology and psychopathology causes much of the universities' difficulty in developing a realistic and reasonable curriculum for clinical psychologists.

Therefore, the traditional lines of demarcation of fields relevant to psychological research in schizophrenia do not appear to be particularly fruitful either for specifying the significant secondary fields of reference or identifying the more crucial variables to be investigated. Even with the limited advances made to date, the potentially fruitful variables and interrelationships cut across too many traditional fields to make specifying some of them particularly meaningful.

DELINEATION OF INTERRELATIONS BETWEEN THE FIELDS OF REFERENCE WITH RESPECT TO MOTIVATIONAL FACTORS IN SCHIZOPHRENIC PERFORMANCE

Even a problem such as the analysis of psychological factors in schizophrenia is too broad a frame of reference for considering interrelationships between fields of research in psychopathology. A sharper delineation may serve as a more satisfactory illustration. I can accomplish this best by an account of research with which my colleagues and I were engaged at Duke University over a ten-year period.[2]

We were first interested in investigating factors which might be implicated in the widespread occurrence of psychological deficit in various psychological functions and in bringing greater specificity to the proposition that schizophrenic patients exhibit psychological deficit in a wide variety of tasks. The inconsistency of this deficit and our investigations of the schizophrenic's response to stress with the Worcester, Massachusetts, group suggested the possible fruitfulness of investigating deficit performance as a function of motivational factors. I had reported that Garmezy and I were impressed with the fact that the clinical observations of sensitivity to criticism on the part of schizophrenic patients might be reformulated into an experimental paradigm in which the independent variable could be censure. We were not attempting to validate any particular theory or point of view. We were interested in seeing whether—at a behavioral level—it would be possible in investigations of schizophrenia to manipulate a limited number of variables in a systematic manner. We chose a few functions, including learning, perceptual,

[2] Much of the ensuing summary of these researches is included in our reports to the National Institute of Mental Health for U.S. Public Health Service Grant M-629 [65].

and language behavior, to explore the deficit in attributes that were roughly analogous to those observed clinically. The evidence obtained in these investigations appeared to support the proposition that psychological factors play a significant role in the disorder. Any theory of schizophrenia must ultimately account for these findings [31, 64, 65].

Our research began with certain observations made of the performances of schizophrenics under stressful and nonstressful conditions. For example, in an unpublished study of motor learning it was found that, even in a quite complex task based on learning to operate a realistic airplane-type pursuitmeter, schizophrenics under nonstress conditions were able to learn at essentially the same rate and level as did their normal controls [68]. On the basis of other researches, the mere presence of the psychosis might have been expected to interfere with efficiency. This did not occur, however, when the conditions facilitated a high interest level, but did appear under an anxiety-stress situation, which occurred when they made errors. Garmezy [30] undertook an experiment on learned discrimination in which the behavior and the conditions of stress could be more adequately controlled. He found that under conditions in which only social reward (a "right" signal) was operative, as well as when there was suitably high motivation, schizophrenics were able to learn the discrimination and to perform as well as the normal subjects. The differences appeared when criticism (a "wrong" signal) was introduced for errors in discrimination. The choice of these experimental variables was not happenstance. The schizophrenic's hypersensitivity to criticism had been observed and reported extensively in many clinical studies. In an earlier report, Garmezy and I cited the contributions of a few psychiatric observers making this point [5, 15, 29]. The results of the Garmezy experiment, we believed, served as an experimental confirmation of the hypothesis.

Our subsequent research at Duke University was directed toward trying to relate *presumed* life history experiences of the patients to contemporary motive and habit structures in an effort to isolate some of the variance in deficit behavior. Therefore, we chose either experimenter-induced censure or figural representations of parental censuring figures as independent variables in learning [10], concept-formation [50, 76], perceptual discrimination, size discrimination, preference judgments [2, 17, 19, 21, 22, 35, 80], etc. Dunn [22] was able to show that the patient reacts differentially to cues in which censure is an attribute of the stimulus material (a picture of a mother scolding a child), even though it is not directed at or referable to him, for he is in no way criticized for his performance. In this task, schizophrenics were able to make as satisfactory complex discriminations as could the normal subjects for the various pictorial materials, with the exception of the scene of the mother scolding a boy. It is particularly noteworthy that Dunn found that the poorest discriminators of the scolding scene were those who had more traumatic relationships with the mother as reported in their case histories.

In addition to these findings of the potent role played by censure, we found that the male schizophrenics used in our studies could not be considered as a homogeneous group with respect to these effects. Our group showed that the level of adequacy of social and sexual *premorbid* adjustment of the schizophrenic subjects, as determined by a scale devised by Phillips [59], is a significant factor in determining response to various experimental tasks involving criticism. For example, poor premorbid subjects appear to be significantly more hypersensitive than schizophrenics having a more adequate level of premorbid adjustment. They show greater performance deficits and are more avoidant in response to criticism. The sex of the parent represented as the criticizing figure is important. The poor premorbid schizophrenics have greater difficulty with tasks involving concept formation and visual discrimination when the mother is the censuring figure in the task; good premorbid patients show a comparable type of difficulty with paternal censure materials. Both groups differ from normal subjects [22, 50]. Furthermore, these differential effects for good and poor premorbid subjects are reflected in differences in perceptions regarding the child-rearing attitudes of the mothers and fathers [33]. These attitudinal views, in turn, appear to be consonant with the behavior of the parents themselves when the parents of good and poor premorbid subjects are compared with those of matched normal subjects [24].

Englehart [23] has shown that the hypersensitivity to criticism extends even to the semantic meanings of language. Using Osgood's Semantic Differential Technique [58], he found that schizophrenic and normal subjects differ significantly in the potency and activity factors involved in semantic meanings of word concepts concerning criticizing, rejection, and domination—*bossy, demanding, neglecting, ignoring, scolding, punishing,* etc. No differences were found among the subject groups for these word concepts on the evaluation factor, nor for any of the three factors on positive affectional words—*sympathetic, affectionate, loving,* and *protecting.* In view of the clinical importance attached to association processes, it is particularly noteworthy that these commonly used words referring to motivational relationships with both parents, which our other experimental studies had shown to be significant, had different semantic associations for schizophrenic subjects than for their normal controls. Furthermore, the semantic associations varied according to differential life history experiences as reflected in the Phillips rating of premorbid level. Our interpretation of the lack of differences in the evaluative factor was that schizophrenics were able to react to those concepts in a manner which was culturally appropriate, whereas the potency and activity factors were more adequate reflections of their personally individualized responses. It is of particular interest that Phillips's rating of premorbid adjustment has been shown to be significantly related to the prognosis of schizophrenics, despite information on behavior antedating the onset of the psychosis, upon which the rating is based [25, 59].

Finally, our earlier studies of purported child-rearing practices arose from the clinical hypothesis that the roots of the patient's sensitivity to criticism could be found in the pattern of early relationships with the mother. Using scales of child-rearing practices that were based upon modifications of the Shoben and Mark scales [54, 70], Harris [35] found significant differences in the practices each group ascribes to the mother. Poor premorbid schizophrenic subjects tended to see their mothers as more dominating, rejecting, and overprotective in comparison with good premorbid schizophrenic and normal subjects. Although the latter two groups were able to express disapproval of these attributes of many of the maternal child-rearing practices, the poor premorbid schizophrenics were able to express disapproval of the rejecting attitudes only. Confirmation of these differences among groups was reported recently by Garmezy, Clarke, and Stockner [33], who found that all three groups differed in the attitudinal ascriptions assigned to their mothers and fathers. The two schizophrenic groups tended to place greater emphasis on dominance and ignoring behaviors, with the poor premorbid subjects tending to assign higher scores to their mothers and the good premorbid subjects to their fathers.

Since such retrospective reports of child rearing are open to considerable criticism [32], our group attempted to investigate more specifically the differential responsivity of schizophrenic subjects as a function of their premorbid level of adjustment. The basic hypothesis was that these two groups may have differed in the home authority relations, with resulting differential effects on the identification process and the self-concept of the child who ultimately develops schizophrenia. These early experiences may have influenced the development of the resources and coping behaviors of the patient in some way. We recognized the problems inherent in adducing complex familial interactions from laboratory situations which have been simplified to bring the psychological processes in schizophrenia under systematic and orderly appraisal. Such complexities are deduced most effectively out of clinically sophisticated controlled investigations of interaction. However, our laboratory findings are congruent with extensive reports [42] and are based upon data which are derived from both patients and their parents.

Just *how* early experience may facilitate or retard the faulty resources and coping behaviors cannot be drawn from our data. Nor is this paper the place to speculate about the mechanisms. However, the following points may serve to illustrate briefly the direction of our thinking: If the fathers of good premorbid patients act in a more assertive manner, participate actively in decision making, and in general manifest greater adequacy—despite the pathology in the family interaction—these patterns of paternal behavior may indicate a relatively more adequate interparental interaction in the patient's family group. Such patterns may have permitted more adequate resources to develop in the patient (as reflected in a more satisfactory level of premorbid adjustment). Such fathers may also have served as models for male identification (however faulty and fragile) and thereby facilitated greater social and sexual adequacy. On the other hand, the peripheral and ineffectual nature of fathers of the poor premorbid patients could provide only a model of submission to a powerful, autocratic, interpersonally insensitive mother— a model which may predispose the patient toward the childhood acquisition of patterns of avoidance, withdrawal, and compliance in the face of multiple frustrations originating in the mother-child relationship. In the former case, more adequate coping resources might have more opportunity to develop, since both parents are interacting with the patient. Even a passive and compliant mother might tend to counteract the overly dominating father. In the latter case, the father's passive role may make the mother's behavior particularly potent as a contributor to the later inadequacy of social and psychological adjustment. The particular constellation of factors may be such that they have their crucial impact very early in the life of the child, and somehow affect his subsequent personality patterns and other aspects of his development as well.

Our effort to carry out a test of the tenability of such a hypothesis is illustrated by two recent unpublished experiments. In both, the adult schizophrenic is required to react to stimulus materials of a mother scolding a boy and a father scolding a boy. Results of both experiments confirm the fact that good and poor premorbid schizophrenics react differentially, depending upon which parent is doing the scolding. Both groups differ from normal subjects. Kreinik [50] found that poor premorbid schizophrenics tended to show greater conceptual thinking disturbance when the stimulus materials reflect the mother scolding the boy, whereas the good premorbid patients do so if the parent represented is the father. Comparable results occurred in another experiment by Dunham [21] involving perceptual discrimination of contentual material. He repeated Dunn's [22] technique of having the subject detect minor variations in pictorial material presented tachistoscopically. Again, the poor premorbid schizophrenics showed their maximum deficit in pictures of a mother scolding a boy, whereas the good premorbid subjects tended to show greater deficit if the scolding figure was the father.

Finally, in an experiment with the parents of good and poor premorbid adult schizophrenics, Farina [24] found marked differences in the attributes of both parents in a situation requiring an interpersonal interaction in order to report jointly on their methods of handling a series of hypothetical child-rearing problems. An analysis of taped recordings of actual verbal behavior showed that the mothers of the poor premorbid patients were more dominating and less yielding than their spouses. This was in marked contrast with the behavior of the parents of the good premorbid patients. In that group, the fathers showed marked dominance, exceeding the pattern exhibited by either of the normal control subjects. An even more striking difference was found in the measures of conflict behavior of the parents in the interaction. The conflict was significantly greater for the parents of the poor premorbid group, with the "good premorbid" parents being intermediate, and virtually no conflict at all for the parents of the normal group. The schizophrenic ascribes different traits and child-rearing practices to his parents, and Farina has shown conclusively that the mothers and fathers differ in an experimental task. They do so in a way which is wholly congruent with the experimental data obtained from the patients themselves. Both patients and parents differ from their matched normal control.

Bridging Principles between Fields of Reference

Only the highlights which illustrate the interpenetration of the various psychological and psychiatric fields in a specific research area are described above. We had chosen to stay within as neutral as possible a theoretical framework, although obviously basic theoretical considerations did help to determine both the choice of variable and the modes of investigative procedure. The findings indicated that deficit behavior in schizophrenics is cue-specific and occurs in a lawful fashion, that the patterns bear some relationship to behavior antedating the onset of the psychosis, and that the pattern of early family experience is probably a very significant contributor to the variance of both such cue-specific deficit behavior and the occurrence and prognosis of schizophrenic behavior. Our research was concerned with only one aspect of the cue characteristics which we could manipulate in experimental situations— we do not know whether it is a crucial aspect or only one attribute of a more complex pattern of cue characteristics. Much was left out and needs to be done before a more definitive theory of schizophrenia can be developed. But this is not the proper time or context in which to discuss these issues. It is inexpedient to discuss here either the relationships between our findings and the research of others which impinges at various points on our own research or the preliminary attempts we have made to determine whether our findings are specific for schizophrenia rather than for psychopathological behavior in general.

But I have presented enough to illustrate the nature of the main "bridging laws" with which our research was concerned. They are concerned with the following:

1. The relationship between clinical manifestations of the disorder and specific aspects of psychological function

2. The relationship between motivational variables and specific attributes of deficit behavior in various areas of psychological function

3. The relationship between motivational variables and the cue specificity of the stimuli to which the schizophrenic is responding

4. The relationship of these motivational variables and cue-specific stimuli to premorbid patterns of adjustment

5. The relationships of such premorbid patterns of adjustment to early experiences in interfamilial influence, particularly interparental interaction with the child, which may predispose the child to adopting schizophrenic modes of response in later adulthood

6. The relationship between such early child parental interactions to the cue-specific deficit behavior which the adult schizophrenic manifests

Any elucidation of these interrelations clearly cuts across a number of psychological fields of inquiry; they are interdependent with methodological and theoretical advances in those fields.

Speculations Regarding Major Variables with Promise for "Bridging" Relationships

Developmental factors. Any speculation regarding the potential fruitfulness of the choice of particular variables is always hazardous unless they follow as essential corollaries from a rigorous theoretical analysis. Any reasonably adequate general theoretical formulation of the complex behavior of schizophrenia is at this time premature—although it is possible to test the tenability of a particular working hypothesis regarding specific attributes. There are examples of varying degrees of theoretical specificity and experimental rigor of this sort—Mednick's hypothesis of deficit on the basis of an S-R theory of anxiety [55] or the Broen-Storms [13, 14] hypothesis of deficit in terms of Hull-Spence drive theory. But since these formulations select the aspects they wish to account for and ignore other essential features which the hypothesis would have difficulty in handling, I shall confine the discussion to empirical variables and leave out discussion of the role of systematic theoretical variables in psychological research on the psychopathology of schizophrenia.

At this stage in the development of psychological research on psychopathology, there is a pressing need for a mapping of schizophrenic behavior in terms of empirical psychological variables. One great handicap to productive theorizing is the paucity of substantiated data from well-controlled systematic psychological research on the attributes of more than the simplest functions of schizophrenic behavior which could serve as a data base for more sophisticated hypotheses and which, in turn, could be subjected to experimental verification.

Perhaps my main point is that establishing empirical variables which can be systematically manipulated in experiments with schizophernic subjects is desirable. The general clinical descriptions of schizophrenic behavior—although an indispensable first step in facilitating the identification of essential features of the schizophrenic process—are too difficult to handle experimentally because of their complexity, vagueness, and contamination with uncontrolled variables. But systematic research with particular variables adduced from these clinical descriptions is possible, as I have attempted to show earlier describing our research. In many respects, this is not so much a cross-translation of variables from one field to another as it is a redefinition of the variable to a form which permits either a manipulation of the variable or a more adequate identification of a suitable index of the variable described in some quantitative mensurational form. The primary virtue is that it permits an advance from generalized qualitative description to a more specific quantitative form. This makes possible the experimental manipulations which can question or disprove particular working hypotheses.

In our research, the most promising variables are probably those concerned with the early familial and interparental influence on the child and their impact on the child's coping behavior which appears comparable to that of the adult schizophrenic. We were forced to conjecture regarding the parental influence in the schizophrenic's early experience. Having to work with symbolic representations of parent-child interaction limited severely the potency of the cue stimuli we used with our schizophrenic subjects. One can, of course, reformulate the variable so that it will be more appropriate for the adult schizophrenic. (This we attempted to do in a limited fashion in the earlier studies involving censure.)

But if adult schizophrenic behavior is partly a function of behavior patterns having their roots in the coping mechanisms of early childhood, more specific and concrete evidence of continuities of behavior patterns is needed. Furthermore, it would seem more efficient to explore the cue stimuli and the patterns of response to such stimuli in children in schizophrenogenic-prone families. The choice of such families need not be random, since there is now a growing literature regarding the possible characteristics of such families [42].

It is pertinent to ask what factors would make some children prone to develop schizophrenic behavior, while their siblings show no evidence of the disorder. Any hypothesis that considers these interpersonal and familial patterns of reinforcement significant must account—at least partially—for this variance if it is to have much validity. The difficulty with current formulations is their highly general nature. Hence they are unable to account satisfactorily for the differences between siblings. Systematic research on this stage of development of the child may supply the data for more specific hypotheses and theoretical formulations.

We felt that an analysis of such cue stimuli (and responses) in children in these families would provide a better base for determining the cue stimuli which might be appropriate for demonstrating the attributes of psychological deficit in the adult schizophrenic.

An analysis of such interrelationships in developmental terms clearly places such research squarely in the field of developmental psychology, in terms of both empirical and theoretical variables. It is perhaps self-evident that any advance in the analysis of behavioral development should have direct implications for research on developmental factors in psychopathology. The tenability of the converse of this proposition should also be obvious.

Psychoanalytic propositions. The hypothesis that schizophrenia is based on libidinal and ego regression is an old one in psychoanalytic thinking, dating back to at least Freud's analysis of the Schreber case [8, 28]. Psychoanalytic research and theory has provided the most fruitful and consistent framework for viewing the phenomena of schizophrenic behavior in psychodynamic terms. It has also been productive in formulating hypotheses regarding the nature of the psychopathological mechanisms involved in the development of symptoms. But their effective use for systematic psychological research requires a reformulation of such psychoanalytic conceptions into a form which facilitates the manipulation of isolatable variables in experimental research. Such reformulations presupposes a reciprocal effort by an experimentally oriented psychology to utilize psychoanalytic contributions (or derivatives suitably systematized for use in controlled research) as a source for hypotheses in experimental psychopathology. Cross-translations of psychoanalytic theory into the terms of another psychological theory which may have been developed to account for a different segment of behavior is not sufficient; bridges through common empirical variables may in the long run prove more profitable.

We have not made any direct utilization of psychoanalytic theory or research approaches because of our interest in remaining within the framework of easily objectified empirical variables. However, we were constantly aware of the limitations this placed on the aspects of the schizophrenic process we were able to study. Developments resulting in a more effective bridging between psychoanalytic contributions and an experimentally oriented psychology should raise the level of sophistication of experimental psychological research in schizophrenia.

Psychological mechanisms underlying the syndrome. A whole field of research endeavor lies in elucidating the mechanisms involved in the occurrence of the specific symptoms of the schizophrenic syndrome. Most of this research lies in the psychoanalytic literature. Systematic and imaginative research is needed to make the bridges with the conceptualizations growing out of general experimental psychology. We were not directly concerned with the symptom syndromes of our patients; any attempt to draw inferences from our data regarding implications for mechanisms involved in the occurrence of schizophrenic symptoms can be only speculative. Despite many attempts, a psychology based on its experimental science aspects has not been particularly productive in elucidating the nature and function of the mediating mechanisms involved in the production of schizophrenic symptoms. The schizophrenic subject—because of the dramatic deviance of his behavior—might be expected to be an excellent setting in which to investigate the interrelationships between personality, learning, motivational, perceptual, and neuropsychological mechanisms. But our lack of clarity as to how mechanisms in these areas of function interrelate has undoubtedly served as a major barrier to sophisticated experimental research. We have thus far been more successful in utilizing *techniques* developed for research in the various areas than in utilizing the *theoretical conceptions* concerning likely mediating mechanisms. I indicated earlier that there have been some recent attempts to utilize drive theory to account for particular aspects of schizophrenic behavior—but until more empirical research shows their fruitfulness, assessment of the ultimate importance of these contributions appears premature.

Psychophysiological factors. I have avoided reference to variables which might be considered as falling in physiological psychology and neuropsychology. This has not been because of an attempt to minimize the obvious importance of these variables in understanding the schizophrenic process; rather it is because any discussion of this area—if it is to serve as more than a superficial skimming of the terrain—requires a more extensive presentation than is possible here. It also requires the skillful hand of someone more sophisticated with research and conceptualizations in these fields. I have therefore chosen to commit an error of omission, rather than one of commission.

METHODOLOGICAL INTERRELATIONSHIPS

Because clinical psychology has always been identified with the use of psychological techniques in the clinic, it has been identified with psychological testing and treatment procedures. The development of practicable tests of intellectual function at verbal and nonverbal levels had immediate applicability in clinical conditions. The practical development in using these and other devices for evaluating interferences with intellective functioning in psychopathology was a logical development; it paved the way for the psychologist's current role as a diagnostician. The usefulness of projective test techniques for assessing psychodynamic factors has made them an almost indispensable part of the diagnostic process. The psychologist's familiarity with psychodynamic mechanisms—necessary for meaningful interpretation of test findings— opened the way for the acceptance of the psychologist as a therapist, even in psychiatric settings.

Psychological test techniques have been widely accepted for the assessment of dependent variables in psychopathological research, particularly because of their relatively objective and quantitative characteristics. But other techniques of general experimental psychology which are less specifically identified with clinical psychology have been used in a limited fashion for the measurement and control of specific psychological variables such as reaction time, learning, perception, etc. Despite the restrictions in the way they were employed, however, the use of these procedures has nevertheless had a considerable impact on psychiatric research, and the research-trained psychologist has become a central member of the interdisciplinary research team.

The psychologist has influenced psychiatric research not only through the introduction of more sophisticated instrumental techniques for the measurement of variables, but through his role as the research-design and statistical methodologist as well. The concept of experimental testing of working hypotheses, the isolation of critical variables through the sophisticated use of controls, the application of more elegant research design and statistical procedures for obtaining an assessment of variance—all have had their impact and have become widely accepted in psychiatric research, which earlier had relied on psychiatric clinical case descriptions.

I shall not restate the effect of interrelationships stemming from clinical psychiatry—particularly psychoanalysis—on the extensive shaping of clinical psychology both methodologically and conceptually. These influences have raised problems for clinical psychology, which has recently found itself the field of conflict between an experimentally grounded psychology and a clinically oriented psychiatry. The advocacy of objectivity in mensuration, isolation of individual variables through experimental manipulation and control, verifiability of hypotheses, and operational definability of many of its terms—all have frequently been difficult to reconcile at an operational level with the clinical utility of description, assessments, and judgments, which place more reliance on maturity of experience than on explicitness of terms. Whether these conflicts lessen as the maturing psychological science permits the application of a more sophisticated psychological science to the clinical aspects of psychopathology remains for the future to determine.

COLLABORATIVE, ADMINISTRATIVE, AND EDUCATIONAL MECHANISMS

Problems of Collaborative Research in Psychopathology

Luszki [52] presents an excellent discussion of the problems of interdisciplinary team research, based on a series of conferences. Participants were experienced investigators in anthropology, psychiatry, psychology, and sociology—and all had participated in interdisciplinary research groups working on mental health research. Her report also includes an extensive bibliography.

Under certain circumstances, there are obvious advantages to collaborative research in borderline areas, particularly when investigators interact as colleagues and share common approaches and evaluation of data. In such cases, they are able to establish common frames of reference, despite differences in disciplines. Even when working on the same problem, they need not necessarily make common assumptions, but the interaction becomes more fruitful when each is able to appreciate how the assumptions and working hypotheses grow out of differences in orientation and supporting data in the separate fields. Collaborators working together in this fashion often find cross-translations of terms from one field into another most profitable; thus each is better able to bring to bear the most relevant techniques of his field on a common problem. In many aspects, the primary advantage of large interdisciplinary organizations is the opportunity provided for the spontaneous development of small groups who can work together on particular joint problems.

Handicaps interfering with fruitful interdisciplinary research are well documented in the Luszki report. The primary difficulty is the restriction on the freedom of the investigator, who often finds himself working on the least common denominator of a problem, where he is unable to use the full ingenuity and creative power provided by his background. Once the research is under way, it is difficult to follow up new leads or to change research objectives when the emerging data indicate the desirability of doing so. Unevenness in competence and differences in research and conceptual style may compound difficulties of communication in assessing the assumptions or inferences from data which make cross-translations profitable.

Where such conditions prevail, interdisciplinary collaboration frequently becomes little more than either research consultation or a resource for techniques from fields with which the primary investigators may be unfamiliar. The effective utilization of secondary scientific fields is often severely limited.

Administrative and Technical Problems

For the psychologist working as a research investigator in clinical settings, there are often additional problems in the way of effective deployment as a psychological scientist. The usual methods and standards of control are difficult to achieve in clinical settings—even under the best of circumstances. But when the research is dominated by administrative considerations which are insensitive to reasonably adequate conditions for psychological research, the psychologist often finds that his activity is limited to utilizing available psychological tests and ratings as an adjunct to clinical observation. He is often handicapped in selecting procedures and a research design which would be pertinent to a more significant research question. This point need not be belabored beyond the direct statement that productive research on psychopathology requires meeting the canons of good science with ingenuity. The administrative requirements of such research frequently involve modification of the usual clinical procedures to permit adequate control of the research conditions. Implementation of such modifications—if the research is to be more than an incidental by-product of the usual clinical activity—often requires that the investigator be a full member of the clinical team, with a voice in determining the research conditions he needs.

This takes on special importance when the characteristics of the clinical and control populations become critical conditions of the research. For example, Garmezy and I described elsewhere [64] some of the methodological considerations which we deemed important for our own research, but which we believed were too often minimized in research on psychopathology. The response heterogeneity and variability of schizophrenics is often accentuated in research investigations by inappropriate selection of experimental groups of schizophrenic patients as subjects. The research literature is replete with studies in which a schizophrenic sample has included male-female, acutely disturbed-chronic, cooperative-recalcitrant, and medicated-nonmedicated patients who may vary widely in educational and socioeconomic classes. Our research showed how a consideration of premorbid level alone had marked affects on reducing the heterogeneity of performance of our patients.

Some Conditions of Research Settings

The discussion above has been concerned with the cross-discipline aspects of research settings, particularly those involving collaboration in medically oriented clinics in which the administrative control of the setting is often in the hands of clinicians who have had limited training or experience in the attributes of good research methods.

For the remainder of this paper, I should like to consider the conditions of the research setting which appear to have been major influences in shaping the character of psychological research in psychopathology. The frame of reference for this discussion is primarily the interrelations—across fields of psychology—which are pertinent to research issues in psychopathology. One of the most serious limitations has been the widespread divorcement of psychopathology research laboratories from the university psychological laboratories. With a few partial exceptions, departmental psychology laboratories are not particularly well suited for research training in psychopathology. There is recognition of this problem in a few universities, where good research centers are available nearby for the research training of psychologists in psychopathology, but the training which does occur there is too frequently poorly coordinated with that in the departmental laboratories. Some of the factors contributing to this state of affairs have been discussed elsewhere [62, 63].

The characteristic research training efforts of many universities which do not incorporate reasonably adequate clinical research facilities in their laboratory structure appear to be based on the assumption that research training in psychological areas represented in their laboratories can transfer to later research activities in the clinic. This is a questionable assumption which is not frequently made for research training in other areas of psychology. Training in the scholarship and general scientific research methods undertaken in one area of psychology undoubtedly has some generalization to research activity in other areas. If this were not so, much of the framework of educational curricula could be questioned. But the prospective researcher needs experience and training in the specific techniques, research strategies, and problem formulation of his specialized field of research early in his training. A forceful case can be made for the proposition that research competence can be *taught* only when the student serves as apprentice to teachers who are themselves productive researchers in the field [74]. The common lack of a suitable teaching-research laboratory closely associated with psychology departments has implications for the quality of research in psychopathology in both the choice of the problem and research technique as well as the degree of communication across fields of psychology. Such conditions might be modified if there were more extensive changes in the research laboratory structure for psychology, some of which will be discussed below.

Choice of research problem. When the student has had his basic research training in areas other than psychopathology, he may be predisposed to formulate problems in terms of areas of psychology which are represented in the psychology laboratory, rather than the requirements of the problem. Thus his research may be essentially an extension of a problem in general psychology adapted for work with a psychopathological population. The primary point of reference is basically determined by a question arising in general psychology, rather than psychopathology. The techniques he may plan to use in learning, perception, thinking, etc., may have been developed specifically for other populations and may be poorly suited to the problems and clinical populations on which the research is to be carried out. Critical conditions which may determine the suitability of the procedure may not be met. For example, the classical memory-drum techniques for presenting stimulus materials to cooperative college students in research on learning are quite unsuited for research with schizophrenics. Poor performance of schizophrenic patients may lead to incorrect inferences regarding the nature of the learning deficits, which more suitable procedures and more direct familiarity with research techniques might obviate [cf. 64, pp. 165–171]. Training in research involves much more than familiarity with particular techniques and procedures; the most essential aspects should be in imaginative but critical thinking in identifying research questions amenable to systematic scientific inquiry. Such skills can be sharpened best in supervised research experiences on the problems and with the populations to be researched. Although training programs in clinical psychology—with which psychological research in psychopathology is commonly identified—are organized around the use of clinical settings for clinical teaching, university departments have not been very concerned with the effective use of these settings for research training as an integral part of the graduate curriculum. The graduate student too frequently finds himself confronted for the first time with responsibility for carrying out competent research in a complex area with little preparation or training. The choice of problem is therefore too often dictated either by his familiarity with clinical assessment and therapeutic procedures or by the easier recourse of working with an inadequate analog to the psychopathological condition in the departmental psychology laboratory. The same conditions can also affect the choice of problem for departmental staff members, who supply much of the senior manpower for research in psychopathology, when the difficulties of carrying out well-designed research in an inconvenient or remote clinical setting make the alternative of a more easily manipulable situation appear particularly attractive.

Intercommunication among fields of psychology. The relative isolation of psychopathology research laboratories from the departmental psychology laboratories tends to perpetuate the communication barriers between clinical and nonclinical staff members in the same department. This reduces the likelihood of nonclinical psychologists bringing their more sophisticated skills to bear on research issues pertinent to psychopathology. The widespread trend in medical centers of adding psychologists who are trained in various fields of psychology to their research staffs is in response to the recognition that research problems in psychopathology need the specialized skills and viewpoints of a broad range of psychological fields. However, this is only a partial solution, unless such research-staff members are able to continue in close communication with the university's psychology departments in both research and graduate teaching. Insufficient appreciation of the importance of close liaison has sometimes forced psychology departments in medical centers—in the interests of more effective research and research teaching—to establish independently a broadly based psychology staff which parallels that of the university psychology department in many respects.

Administrative considerations. One component in facilitating more effective use of psychological science in psychopathology research is an administrative framework for the clinical research laboratory which recognizes the need for appropriate conditions for psychological research. This can be a serious matter, particularly in clinical research laboratories in medical settings, but it may also exist as a problem in psychology department clinics as well. Where such research is interdisciplinary, compromises may be necessary to find the best common denominator. But for psychological researches which need not adapt to such restrictions, the conditions for creative and original research by psychologists may require control over both the choice of the problem and the details of the research—when these are not controverted by the needs for good clinical practice in the care of the patient. Such conditions are not apt to be optimal for effective psychological research when decisions as to choice of problem or technique are controlled by persons in another field than the investigator's or when the independent research interests of the psychologist are not respected.

The psychopathology laboratory as an integral part of psychology laboratories. Many psychological problems in psychopathology— particularly those involving close collaboration with medically based sciences—can be investigated most effectively in well-equipped, well-staffed laboratories in psychiatric installations. Where there is close liaison, such laboratories can be considered as extensions of the main psychology laboratories for both teaching and research. But for many aspects of research relevant to psychopathology, such an arrangement is not as appropriate as a clinical research laboratory which is more integral with the main psychology laboratories. Psychological analysis has been severely handicapped by too sharp a division between "pathology" and the general behavioral mechanisms of "normal" people. The lack of a suitable research laboratory for investigating the milder aspects of behavioral deviation in the context of investigating normal behavior may be at least partially responsible for perpetuating this trend. Research on the bridging variables between normal behavioral mechanisms and those in psychopathology requires empirical investigation with appropriate subject populations. These can be carried out more effectively in psychology laboratories where there is a reasonable likelihood that proper conditions can be maintained, and where colleagues in related fields are close at hand to participate in sharpening relevant research issues. Such a laboratory could be based on a research-oriented clinic which was maintained as a part of the laboratory to ensure the availability of suitable subject populations under proper clinical conditions.

The potential utility of such clinic-laboratory arrangements can be illustrated by reference to our research. One implication is the possibility that some aspects of deficit behavior to cue-specific responses are related to premorbid adjustment, as well as to factors in the childhood intrafamilial situation. We were confronted with having to draw inferences retrospectively about early developmental factors from the behavior of adult schizophrenics. A profitable field for investigating these adduced relationships would be the systematic investigation of the relation among familial attributes, cue stimuli, and the milder manifestations of behavioral disturbance in children and adolescents which have some comparability to the premorbid behavior of schizophrenics. This is particularly difficult to carry out now, since clinics tend to provide neither the proper populations nor appropriate conditions for systematic psychological research when the needs of this research require some modification of clinic policy.

The further development of psychological laboratories specifically designed for research in psychopathology and coordinated with other psychology laboratories should affect the general level of sophistication and elegance of research in those particular areas of psychological science by helping overcome some of the critical deficiencies which characterize much of the current research in psychopathology. Some of these laboratories will undoubtedly serve as stable independent organizations specially designed and maintained as concentrated research centers for the intensive investigation of specific areas of psychopathology. This would be a logical continuation of the historical development of large-scale efforts in establishing appropriate research conditions for investigation of psychopathology.

If the university psychology laboratories are not expanded along comparable lines, much of the training of psychological investigators equipped to investigate significant problems in psychopathology will have to be carried out, perhaps postdoctorally, in such independent specialized research centers. Such a development might continue the isolation of university departments from an intensive consideration of psychological factors in psychopathology as an aspect of general psychology. A suitable training laboratory structure within graduate departments of psychology would also go a long way toward facilitating the proper development of clinical psychology as an integral part of the general field of psychological science.

CONCLUDING REMARKS

It is difficult—even in a sketchy overview of some of the interrelationship aspects of psychological research in psychopathology—to avoid being harshly critical of many trends of research effort in this field—even though one can appreciate the complexity of the factors which have contributed to this state of affairs. The observer is left with the conviction that research has not exploited effectively either the potentialities of current knowledge of psychology or the significance such research has for the development of general psychological science. Many research issues in psychopathology are interdependent with many other areas of psychology. Significant advances in any of these fields—either empirically or with respect to theory development—may have immediate consequences for the others in research strategy and the more adequate interpretation of poorly explained data which may be too difficult to handle in the framework of current theoretical conceptualizations.

Such issues are particularly apparent when the focus of inquiry is narrowed to the consideration of only a few rather limited aspects of the psychopathology of schizophrenia. Even though—for purposes of a first order of approximation—the particular research inquiry is kept within manageable limits by considering only the fields of reference in psychology, it is apparent that even the empirical variables cannot be conveniently contained within any specific area of psychology. The fields of primary and secondary reference become arbitrary assignments, depending upon which facet of the problem is being examined empirically at the moment. Any major advance at a theoretical level which can account for the central phenomena with even *reasonable* effectiveness will—in all probability—be interdependent with advances in general psychology. For this reason, an analysis of the appropriate conditions for effective intercourse between research efforts in psychopathology and those in pertinent related areas of psychology becomes particularly relevant. Suitable conditions for serious research inquiry (and the related training for research) have direct implications for both the rate of advance in psychological research in psychopathology and its character.

Despite the fact that current research on psychological factors in schizophrenia point to the high probability that factors affecting psychological development are involved in the etiology of schizophrenia, a significant amount of the variance may very well be contributed by biochemical and physiological variables. The case has yet to be established empirically, however, as to the extent of such variance, the nature of the mediating mechanisms, and how they may interrelate with the significant psychological variables. Any analysis at this level clearly cuts across a number of scientific fields which cannot long continue their research efforts in conceptual isolation. A suitable theoretical model which would permit coordinated empirical research among these various fields has yet to be developed, however.

REFERENCES

1. Alexander, F., & French, T. M. *Psychoanalytic therapy.* New York: Ronald, 1946.
2. Alvarez, R. R. A comparison of the preferences of schizophrenic and normal subjects for rewarded and punished stimuli. Unpublished doctoral dissertation, Duke Univer., 1957.
3. American Psychiatric Association, Committee on Nomenclature and Statistics. *Diagnostic and statistical manual for mental disorders.* Washington: 1952.
4. Angyal, A., Freeman, H., & Hoskins, R. G. Physiologic aspects of schizophrenic withdrawal. *Arch. Neurol. Psychiat.,* 1940, **44,** 621–626.
5. Arieti, S. *Interpretation of schizophrenia.* New York: Brunner, 1955.
6. Bellak, L. (Ed.). *Schizophrenia, a review of the syndrome.* New York: Logos Press, 1958.
7. Bellak, L. The schizophrenic syndrome. In L. Bellak (Ed.), *Schizophrenia, a review of the syndrome.* New York: Logos Press, 1958. Pp. 3–63.
8. Bellak, L. & Blaustein, A. B. Psychoanalytic aspects of schizophrenia. In L. Bellak (Ed.), *Schizophrenia, a review of the syndrome.* New York: Logos Press, 1958. Pp. 279–335.
9. Benjamin, J. D. Directions and problems in psychiatric research. *Psychosom. Med.,* 1952, **14,** 1–9.
10. Bleke, R. C. Reward and punishment as determiners of reminiscence effects in schizophrenic and normal subjects. *J. Pers.,* 1955, **23,** 479–498.
11. Bleuler, E. *Dementia praecox or the group of schizophrenias.* New York: International University Press, 1950.
12. Boring, E. G. *A history of experimental psychology.* (2nd ed.) New York: Appleton-Century-Crofts, 1950.

13. Broen, W. E., Jr., & Storms, L. H. A reaction potential ceiling and response decrements in complex situations. *Psychol. Rev.*, 1961, **68**, 405–415.

14. Broen, W. E., Jr., Storms, L. H., & Schenck, H. U., Jr. Inappropriate behavior as a function of the energizing effect of drive. *J. Pers.*, 1961, **29**, 489–498.

15. Cameron, N. *The psychology of behavior disorders.* Boston: Houghton Mifflin, 1947.

16. Cholden, L. Observations on psychotherapy of schizophrenia. In Frieda Fromm-Reichmann & J. L. Moreno (Eds.), *Progress in psychotherapy.* New York: Grune & Stratton, 1956. Pp. 239–247.

17. Clarke, A. R. Conformity behavior of schizophrenic subjects to maternal figures. Unpublished doctoral dissertation, Duke Univer., 1961.

18. Clausen, J. A., & Kohn, M. L. Social relations and schizophrenia: a research report and a perspective. In D. D. Jackson (Ed.), *The etiology of schizophrenia.* New York: Basic Books, 1960. Pp. 295–320.

19. Culver, C. M. The effect of cue value on size estimation in schizophrenic subjects. Unpublished doctoral dissertation, Duke Univer., 1961.

20. Davis, R. H., & Harrington, R. W. The effect of stimulus class on the problem-solving behavior of schizophrenics and normals. *J. abnorm. soc. Psychol.*, 1957, **54**, 126–128.

21. Dunham, R. M. Sensitivity of schizophrenics to parental censure. Unpublished doctoral dissertation, Duke Univer., 1959.

22. Dunn, W. L., Jr. Visual discrimination of schizophrenic subjects as a function of stimulus meaning. *J. Pers.*, 1954, **23**, 48–64.

23. Englehart, R. C. Semantic correlates of interpersonal and parental attributes in schizophrenia. Unpublished doctoral dissertation. Duke Univer., 1959. Also, *Amer. Psychol.*, 1959, **14**, 403.

24. Farina, A. Patterns of role dominance and conflict in parents of schizophrenic patients. *J. abn. soc. Psychol.*, 1960, **61**, 31–38.

25. Farina, A., & Webb, W. W. Premorbid adjustment and subsequent discharge. *J. nerv. ment. Dis.* 1956, **124**, 612–613.

26. Fenichel, O. *The psychoanalytic theory of neurosis.* New York: Norton, 1945.

27. Freeman, H. Physiological studies. In L. Bellak (Ed.), *Schizophrenia, a review of the syndrome.* New York: Logos Press, 1958, Pp. 174–215.

28. Freud, S., Psychoanalytic notes upon an autobiographical account of a case of paranoia (Dementia Paranoides). In *Collected papers of.* . . . Vol. 3. London: Hogarth, 1957. Pp. 387–470.

29. Fromm-Reichmann, Frieda, *Principles of intensive psychotherapy.* Chicago: Univer. Chicago Press, 1950.

30. Garmezy, N. Approach and stimulus differentiation by schizophrenic and normal subjects under conditions of reward and punishment. *J. Pers.*, 1952, **21**, 253–276.

31. Garmezy, N., & Rodnick, E. H. Premorbid adjustment and performance in schizophrenia: implications for interpreting heterogeneity in schizophrenia, *J. nerv. ment. Dis.*, 1959, **129**, 450–466.

32. Garmezy, N., Farina, A., & Rodnick, E. H. The structured situational test: a method for studying family interaction in schizophrenia. *Amer. J. Orthopsychiat.*, 1960, **30**, 445–452.

33. Garmezy, N., Clarke, A. R., & Stockner, Carol. Child rearing attitudes of mothers and fathers as reported by schizophrenic and normal patients. *J. abn. soc. Psychol.*, 1961, **63**, 176–182.

34. Goldstein, K. *Human nature in the light of psychopathology.* Cambridge: Harvard Univer. Press, 1940.

35. Harris, J. G., Jr. Size estimation of pictures as a function of thematic content for schizophrenic and normal subjects. *J. Pers.*, 1957, **25**, 651–671.

36. Hinsie, L. E., & Campbell, R. J. *Psychiatric dictionary.* (3rd ed.) New York: Oxford, 1960.

37. Horwitt, M. K. Fact and artifact in the biology of schizophrenia. *Science,* 1956, **124**, 429–430.

38. Hoskins, R. G. Dementia praecox: a simplified formulation. *J. Amer. Med. Ass.*, 1931, **96**, 1209–1212.

39. Hoskins, R. G. *The biology of schizophrenia.* New York: Norton, 1946.

40. Hunt, J. McV., & Cofer, C. N. Psychological deficit. In J. McV. Hunt (Ed.), *Personality and the behavior disorders.* New York: Ronald, 1944. Pp. 971–1032.

41. Huston, P. E., and Shakow, D. Learning in schizophrenia: I. Pursuit learning. *J. Pers.*, 1948, **17**, 52–74.

42. Jackson, D. D. (Ed.). *The etiology of schizophrenia.* New York: Basic Books, 1960.

43. Jackson, D. D. A critique of the literature on the genetics of schizophrenia. In D. D. Jackson (Ed.), *The etiology of schizophrenia.* New York: Basic Books, 1960. Pp. 37–87.

44. Jenkins, R. L. The schizophrenic sequence: withdrawal, disorganization, psychotic reorganization. *Amer. J. Orthopsychiat.*, 1952, **22**, 738–748.

45. Kallman, F. J. *The genetics of schizophrenia.* New York: Augustin, 1938.

46. Kant, O. Differential diagnosis of schizophrenia in light of a concept of personality stratification. *Amer. J. Psychiat.*, 1940, **97**, 342–357.

47. Kantor, R. E., Wallner, J. M., & Winder, C. L. Process and reactive schizophrenia. *J. consult. Psychol.*, 1953, **17**, 157–162.

48. Kety, S. Biochemical theories of schizophrenia. *Science,* 1959, **129**, 1528–1532; 1590–1596.

49. Kety, S. Recent biochemical theories of schizophrenia. In D. D. Jackson (Ed.), *The etiology of schizophrenia.* New York: Basic Books, 1960, Pp. 120–145.

50. Kreinik, P. S. Parent-child themas and concept attainment in schizophrenia. Unpublished doctoral dissertation, Duke Univer., 1959.

51. Longfeldt, G. The prognosis in schizophrenia. *Acta Psychiatrica et Neurologica, Scandinavica Supplementum 110.* Copenhagen: Ejnar Munksgaard, 1956.

52. Luszki, Margaret B. *Interdisciplinary team research methods and problems.* Washington: National Training Laboratories, 1958.
53. Malmo, R. B., Shagass, C., & Smith, A. A. Responsiveness in chronic schizophrenia. *J. Pers.*, 1951, **19**, 359–375.
54. Mark, J. C. The attitudes of the mothers of male schizophrenics toward child behavior. *J. abnorm. soc. Psychol.*, 1953, **48**, 185–189.
55. Mednick, S. A learning theory approach to schizophrenia. *Psychol. Bull.*, 1958, **55**, 316–327.
56. Meyer, A. Collected papers. Baltimore, Md.: Johns Hopkins Press, 1952. 4 vols.
57. Noguchi, H., & Moore, J. W. A demonstration of Treponema Pallidum in the brain of cases of general paralysis. *J. exp. Med.*, 1913, **17**, 232–238.
58. Osgood, C. E., Suci, G., & Tannenbaum, P. *The measurement of meaning.* Urbana, Ill.: Univer. Ill. Press, 1957.
59. Phillips, L. Case history data and prognosis in schizophrenia. *J. nerv. ment. Dis.*, 1953, **117**, 515–525.
60. Reichard, Suzanne, & Tillman, C. Patterns of parent-child relationships in schizophrenia. *Psychiatry*, 1950, **13**, 247–257.
61. Rodnick, E. H. The effect of metrazol shock upon habit systems. *J. abnorm. soc. Psychol.*, 1943, **37**, 560–565.
62. Rodnick, E. H. Some problems of research in clinical psychology. *Amer. J. Orthopsychiat.*, 1953, **23**, 307–314.
63. Rodnick, E. H. Training for research in the mental health field. In C. R. Strother (Ed.), *Psychology and mental health.* Washington: American Psychological Association, 1956. Pp. 93–109.
64. Rodnick, E. H., & Garmezy, N. An experimental approach to the study of motivation in schizophrenia. In M. R. Jones (Ed.), *Nebraska Symposium on Motivation.* Lincoln, Neb.: Univer. Neb. Press, 1957. Pp. 109–184.
65. Rodnick, E. H., & Garmezy, N. Motivational factors in the production of psychological deficits in schizophrenia. Unpublished progress reports, National Institute of Mental Health (Grant No. M-629), 1954, 1955, 1962.
66. Rorschach, H. *Psychodiagnostik.* Leipzig: Ernst Bircher Verlag, 1921.
67. Rosenthal, D. Some factors associated with concordance and discordance with respect to schizophrenia in monozygotic twins. *J. nerv. ment. Dis.*, 1959, **129**, 1–10.
68. Sands, S. L., & Rodnick, E. H. Concept and experimental design in the study of stress and personality. *Amer. J. Psychiat.*, 1950, **106**, 673–679.
69. Shakow, D. The nature of deterioration in schizophrenic conditions, *Nerv. ment. Dis. Monogr.*, 1946, No. 70.
70. Shoben, E. J., Jr. The assessment of parental attitudes in relation to child adjustment. *Genet. Psychol. Monogr.*, 1949, **39**, 103–148.
71. Slater, E., with the assistance of James Shields. *Psychotic and neurotic illnesses in twins.* London: H. M. Stationery Office, 1953.

72. Sullivan, H. S. Conceptions of modern psychiatry. *Psychiatry*, 1940, **3**, 1–117.
73. Szasz, T. S. The myth of mental illness. *Amer. Psychol.*, 1960, **15**, 113–118.
74. Taylor, D. W. (Ed.) Education for research in pyschology. Report of an *ad hoc* committee of the Education and Training Board, American Psychological Association. *Amer. Psychol.*, 1959, **14**, 167–179.
75. Uhr, L., & Miller, J. G. *Drugs and behavior.* New York: Wiley, 1960.
76. Webb, W. W. Conceptual ability of schizophrenics as a function of threat of failure. *J. abn. soc. Psychol.*, 1955, **50**, 221–224.
77. Winder, C. L. Some psychological studies of schizophrenics. In D. D. Jackson (Ed.), *The etiology of schizophrenia.* New York: Basic Books, 1960. Pp. 191–247.
78. Wittman, M. Phyllis. An evaluation of opposed theories concerning the etiology of so-called "dementia" in dementia praecox. *Amer. J. Psychiat.*, 1937, **93**, 1363–1377.
79. Wittman, M. Phyllis, & Steinberg, D. L. Prodromal factors in schizophrenia. *Amer. J. Psychiat.*, 1944, **100**, 811–816.
80. Zahn, T. P. Acquired and symbolic affective value as determinants of size estimation in schizophrenic and normal subjects. *J. abnorm. soc. Psychol.*, 1959, **58**, 39–47.

A HISTORICAL AND THEORETICAL ANALYSIS OF SOME BROAD TRENDS IN CLINICAL PSYCHOLOGY[1]

JULIAN B. ROTTER
*Department of Psychology
The Ohio State University*

Introduction 780
Historical Trends 782
The Measurement of Intelligence 786
    Intelligence estimates from projective tests 791
    The current situation 791
Diagnosis 793
    The source of concepts for personality diagnosis 793
    Measures of personality 800
        Projective techniques 801
        Personality questionnaires 804
        Structured vs. unstructured tests 805
        Summary of personality tests 808
    The diagnosis of brain damage 809
        Tests of brain damage 810
Psychotherapy 810
    Early trends and psychoanalytic influences 810
    The Rankian movement 813
    Learning theory approaches 816
    Group psychotherapy 818
    Psychotherapy and the clinical psychologist's values 819
    Research in psychotherapy 821
    Psychotherapy—summary 821
An Overview 822
References 824

INTRODUCTION

A quarter of a century has passed since the publication of C. M. Louttit's *Clinical Psychology* [79] in 1936. Louttit's book is considered

[1] I am greatly indebted to Dr. June E. Chance and Dr. Richard Jessor for their many helpful suggestions following their critical reading of this manuscript.

by many to be one of the earliest major attempts to present a standard text of a broad field of psychological application which has been called "clinical psychology." Where previous articles and volumes had dealt specifically with mental tests, special disorders, abnormal psychology, etc., Louttit attempted to relate and describe systematically a field of application which had been formalized only a few years before, over some objections, in the organization of a clinical section of the American Psychological Association.

A comparison of Louttit's book with the treatises on clinical psychology published recently indicates that a tremendous change has taken place in the activities, interests, and ideas of the people who now consider themselves clinical psychologists. It is quite clear from a review of the intermediate years that the period of change is not over, but that clinical psychology is currently in an extremely active period of growth and change.

In order to determine the sources of these changes as well as their nature and interrelationship with other fields, an historical analysis seems most appropriate. A science of practice accumulates methods to meet contemporary challenges and sometimes maintains them long past their period of immediate usefulness. As a result, an examination of the theoretical, cultural, and socioeconomic influences on the behavior, ideas, and practices of clinical psychologists over the course of time appears to provide the best approach to understanding the present status and underlying bases of current clinical psychological study.

To define or delimit clinical psychology on either logical or practical grounds is to attempt a task which would be likely to please very few, if any. A narrow logical definition would be rejected by many clinical psychologists. A broad but loose definition would overlap heavily with such fields as educational psychology, social psychology, counseling psychology, psychiatry, and industrial psychology. On the other hand, a definition of clinical psychology in terms of what it is that people who call themselves clinical psychologists actually do would probably overlap with all the fields of psychology—applied and theoretical. No attempt will be made, therefore, to provide a neat, logical definition of clinical psychology which adequately differentiates it from all other applied fields in psychology or other sciences.

Possibly the most general definition of what the clinical psychologist is concerned with can be broadly described as "the psychological adjustment of individuals." The interest in the individual's adjustment includes two general functions, the first of which could be called "assessment" or "description" and sometimes is referred to as "diagnosis," and the second is one of therapy or management.

The extensive changes in clinical psychological practice in the last twenty years have involved changes in methods. Perhaps more importantly, they have been changes in emphasis on the age and types of patients dealt with under these two general functions and in the relative importance attached to treatment as compared to diagnosis. A brief overview of these historical trends will help orient the reader to the sections that follow.

HISTORICAL TRENDS

During the 1930s and prior to World War II, the larger proportion of psychologists who identified themselves as clinical psychologists worked primarily with children's problems. They did so in settings such as university clinics, community clinics, traveling clinics operated by state departments of public welfare and sometimes by state departments of education, as well as in institutions for the feebleminded, clinics for the physically handicapped, speech pathology clinics, and institutions for the delinquent or predelinquent. Their major job was psychological testing with a great emphasis on intellectual ability and deficit. In many instances, rather thorough case studies were obtained, utilizing either their own or social workers' case materials in addition to tests. The information obtained was used to make recommendations —usually to teachers, parents, therapists involved in some special handicap training, referring physicians, and juvenile authorities. The university training of most of the clinicians tended to be limited to courses on group testing, the Stanford-Binet, abnormal psychology, and perhaps child psychology or child development. Most of the training in practical clinical skills was obtained as field experience on the job or, in some rare instances, as genuine internship [Shakow, 125].

Rarely did the clinical psychologist do extensive face-to-face therapy with children. In a few instances [Louttit, 80], such therapy was carried out in community clinics and was limited primarily to a rather eclectic approach to play therapy. Occasionally something approaching psychotherapy was carried out by clinical psychologists working with adolescent delinquents and persons having speech problems, particularly stutterers.

Work with adults was distinctly less common than work with children. Primarily, clinical psychologists working with adults had some institutional placement, usually a state psychiatric hospital in which their primary job was giving tests to aid the psychiatrist in making a diagnosis. Other positions were in prison systems where the psychologist combined the functions of classification and clinical assessment of inmates. Prison psychologists occasionally did individual or group psychotherapy. In the psychiatric hospital, individual or group psychotherapy tended to be rare; if present at all, it was only a minor aspect of the psychologist's job. Psychologists in institutional positions frequently found themselves involved in problems of selection of attendants, aides, or other personnel, with particular emphasis placed upon the personality adjustment or emotional stability of the applicants.

Toward the latter thirties, emphasis on personality testing, particularly with adults in mental hospitals, began to increase, but it was still heavily outweighed by the emphasis on tests for ability and deficiency, tests purporting to determine the presence of deterioration, brain damage, or disabilities, and tests for special skills. Most books published in this period in the general area of clinical psychology were test manuals. Extensive reports of the diagnostic value of some tests of intellectual functioning appeared later. Psychologists rarely were involved in the publication of descriptions of methods of face-to-face treatment.

The advent of World War II, the war itself, and its aftermath—all of these produced important changes in the practices of clinical psychologists. One of the important early effects resulted from a large migration in the late thirties of both psychologists and psychiatrists, many of whom were escaping the totalitarian regimes. Several of this group had psychoanalytic interests and training (Freudian, Adlerian, Jungian). Although they did not initiate psychoanalytic thinking in this country, their activities and writings led to an increased interest in personality and personality development in general and psychoanalytic concepts in particular. Individual personality tests such as the Rorschach also were reintroduced to psychologists and psychiatrists in this period and some of the German and Austrian psychologists brought in a German characterological approach to personality. The general effect on the clinical psychologists and psychiatrists with whom they came in contact was to reduce the emphasis on intelligence, deficit or ability testing and to increase the emphasis on personality development, dynamics, and description.

The war itself led to an increased interest in clinical psychology and in the potential contribution of clinical psychologists to the treatment of mental patients. The large number of rejections in the draft for reasons of instability and intellectual deficiency created a national concern with the general problem of prevention and amelioration. After the war, this concern led to a greatly enlarged budget for the Institute of Public Health. Psychologists made a strong impression on people working in the mental health field because of their techniques, which could be used for selection, and because of their general knowledge of research methods. The U.S. Public Health Department, in making grants during the postwar period and advising the states on the use of these grants, placed great stress upon hiring clinical psychologists for both clinical and research purposes.

Within the Armed Forces, a large number of psychological breakdowns preceding or during combat found the medical services inadequately equipped to deal with the problem. Psychiatrists were few; consequently, both psychiatrists and clinical psychologists were trained in short courses to deal with the problem. Again the psychologist, with his selection techniques and his knowledge of research methods, created a strong impression on the people working in this field. Plans for an expanded program for the care and treatment of veterans included substantial sums for the training and hiring of clinical psychologists.

Support for training of clinical psychologists, both from the U.S. Public Health Service and from the Veterans Administration, went to universities which undertook an extensive program at the Ph.D. level for training clinical psychologists. Many of the students supported themselves—through the Veterans Administration—by working in Veterans Administration facilities which were scattered throughout the states. As their clinical material, these students had adults who had been psychologically incapacitated to some extent by their Army experience. Since the Veterans Administration training program was the largest program supporting the training of clinical psychologists, a major trend after the war was toward an interest in the personality problems of adults. The Veterans Administration was willing to hire the psychologists who finished in approved programs at salaries which generally exceeded those obtainable in schools, prisons, or community centers. Consequently, there was a marked increase in interest and training for working with adults who had personality breakdowns or problems in the postwar period.

During the war, the practical necessity of returning as many men as possible to combat led to a number of expedient attempts to do psychotherapy on patients. When clinical psychologists were available, they were frequently pressed into group psychotherapy [Bijou, 15] and, in some cases, individual therapy in the Army setting.

The work of Carl Rogers [108] during and immediately following the war in the field of psychotherapy—particularly his emphasis on publishing actual therapy protocols—created widespread interest. The somewhat sterile approach to diagnosis yielded—at least for many psychologists—to a strong desire to do therapy and to do something which could be immediately seen as helpful to the patient. This interest in adult psychotherapy, stimulated by new translations of European writings and by the presence of lay and medically trained analysts from the Continent, opened up the area of long-term face-to-face treatment of adults for clinical psychologists. This was a province of practice which previously was almost the exclusive domain of a few psychoanalytically trained psychiatrists. That one had neither to be psychoanalyzed, nor psychoanalytically oriented, nor have an M.D. in order to do such treatment was readily accepted by clinical psychologists.

The U.S. Public Health Service supported a conference on the training of clinical psychologists at Boulder, Colorado, in 1949 [Raimy, 104]. This conference resulted in a number of general agreements, one of which was to try to make the Ph.D. a minimum requirement for an individual calling himself a clinical psychologist. Thus, the Ph.D. began to be required, either formally or informally, for clinical psychologists in universities and in all kinds of practical settings. Many of the universities lost interest in training clinical psychologists below the Ph.D. level. Due to the large number of openings available, it was natural that most clinical psychologists, with their greater investment in training, would enter the positions with the best economic future. Since these did not include community clinics, prison systems, school systems, clinics for the physically handicapped, etc., a general drift began toward work with adults and adult problems. More and more clinical psychologists accepted positions in the Veterans Administration, state hospitals, universities, university medical schools, private practice, and industrial consulting firms which emphasized the individual adjustment of executives.

In summary, then, since the early thirties, a general shift took place (1) away from a major emphasis on children's problems and handicaps to problems of adult adjustment, (2) away from a strong emphasis in intelligence testing, testing for psychological deficits and interference in intellectual functioning to an interest in testing for personality description and adjustment, and (3) away from an interest in diagnosis and description with an emphasis on the psychologist's function as a tester to an interest in psychotherapy and the actual management of cases.

Of course, each new emphasis in clinical interest resulted in a revised approach to older methods. For example, in the period between 1945 and 1950, literally scores of studies were done with intelligence tests such as the Wechsler-Bellevue Scale [Rabin and Guertin, 102], attempting to use these tests for purposes of diagnosis or personality assessment, thus indicating a markedly revised interest in intelligence testing.

In discussing the source and nature of the theory and research currently being applied by clinical psychologists, it is both logically and historically appropriate that we consider this theory under three large headings: (1) intelligence testing, (2) personality measurement and description, and (3) psychotherapy. Not only does this trichotomy provide some convenience in organizing this chapter, but the theory itself which is utilized in these three areas of application reflects differences which are understandable in light of social forces present at the different times at which they became the focus of interest for clinical psychologists.

An assessment of the major trends in clinical psychology both as to the techniques in use and the source of concepts employed by clinical psychologists in one brief chapter requires the neglect of many aspects of both practice and theory. Consequently, it is difficult to justify the selection of both the techniques and the ideas which will be surveyed and the selection of influences which have had a major effect on clinical psychological practices and theory. The following discussions deal with general trends, not including all important concerns of clinical psychologists; the more specific topics should be regarded as examples of these trends rather than descriptions of the most important developments in clinical psychology.

THE MEASUREMENT OF INTELLIGENCE

The earliest phase of the applied movement which now is known as clinical psychology was concerned primarily with the measurement of intelligence for purposes of studying individual adjustment. Although psychologists had earlier been concerned with the measurement of individual differences on a variety of mental, sensory, and motor tests, clinical psychology in this country is usually considered to have begun with Lightner Witmer's establishment, in 1896, of a clinic to deal with the adjustment problems of children. The major concern of this clinic and succeeding ones was handicapped children—the deaf, the blind, the mentally defective, and the physically handicapped. With the advent of intelligence testing, particularly the Binet-Simon method, the role of the psychologist in the clinic clearly became one of measurement of intellectual capacities and potentialities. The earliest employment of clinical psychologists was in university clinics, institutions for the feebleminded, child guidance clinics, and the like. Somewhat later, psychologists found jobs testing individual patients in mental hospitals. Although clinical psychologists performed functions other than ability testing, mental testing dominated the majority of their practice and almost all of the books published in this area before 1930 were essentially manuals of tests such as those of Whipple in 1910 [151], Terman in 1916 [141], Pintner and Paterson in 1917 [99], Goodenough in 1926 [35], Wells in 1927 [150], and Bronner, Healy, Lowe, and Shimberg in 1927 [19]. In work with adult mental patients, some use was being made of inventories and the word-association method, but there was relatively little testing of personality characteristics for purposes of individual case study.

Although the prediction of individual "mental capacity" is still an important area of practice for the clinical psychologist, the purpose of giving tests has expanded to a considerable extent during the last thirty years. The early theory of intelligence and mental abilities, however, has persisted to a large degree in current thinking, and the understanding of current conceptions requires some knowledge of the *theory* of the early mental testing movement.

There seems to be general agreement that the early work on the measurement of mental abilities stems from the German, Scottish, French, and English "faculty" psychologists. What the tests intended to measure were faculties of the mind, sometimes conceived in some over-all fashion as the intellectual faculties, including judgment, reasoning, memory, discrimination, etc., and sometimes conceived of as relatively specific characteristics. These were thought to be innate in character but affected by experience to some extent, particularly by central nervous system and sensory disorders. Strangely enough, Binet and Simon, although referring to intelligence as a "faculty," frequently made reference to the fact that they did not believe that this ability was entirely a matter of inheritance but that it also reflected training and opportunity. Peterson [96], in his early book on intelligence, referred somewhat skeptically to statements made by Binet regarding the intellectual gains of presumably feebleminded children being trained by Binet. However, Binet's feeling that this innate capacity was subject to training had little effect and essentially was neglected until later developments in American psychology.

Referring to intelligence as an innate faculty of the mind does not necessarily include the notion of a faculty as a kind of force impelling the individual to action, as some writers thought. Rather, we are using the term to describe a presumed inherent characteristic of the "mind," a built-in way of perceiving and reacting which defined not only what the individual would do, but also what he could not do on a genetic and neurological basis. This early conception contained the notion that there are other faculties such as emotions and will, and their relative strength in any given individual affected the intellectual faculties by domination and inhibition. For example, intellectual functioning was affected in mental disorders because of the domination of emotional faculties or deterioration of the will (motivation). In general, there was more reliance on the idea that the emotions, or lack or disintegration of the will interfered with the expression of the intellect and intellectual faculties and abilities that there was on the conception that the individual's life experience determined the kind and degree of development of a variety of skills.

In his early work, Binet needed to use some measure of serious retardation in intellectual functioning. He arbitrarily selected two mental age years as a criterion of such retardation [Stoddard, 137]. It was soon apparent that such a criterion would be differential at different age levels; to correct this, Stern [136] suggested dividing the mental age by the chronological age and so gave birth to the IQ. It is Stoddard's opinion, probably well founded, that Stern's "innocent contribution" has created much more difficulty in the area of mental testing than could have been foretold at the time of its inception.

A rather active controversy was carried out in the late twenties and early thirties regarding the nature of intelligence. Was it made up of specific abilities [Thurstone, 144; Thorndike, 143] or was it determined largely by a general factor [Spearman, 135]? This discussion, as far as clinical psychology is concerned, was relatively academic because general intelligence and the IQ were by this time "entitized" and reified to a considerable extent, and the conception of some general over-all faculty was implicitly accepted, as indicated by the actual practice of clinical and educational psychologists. Although it was believed that general intelligence was made up of different, highly correlated specific abilities, it was also widely believed that under normal conditions some general factor or trait adequately described the individual's potential to learn.

Once the IQ was reified, discussion did not center around whether or not this was a useful construct, but around what intelligence *really* was, and every psychologist had his own private meaning for the term. This situation led Johnson to write:

Thus, the word *intelligence* has been used—and is currently used—to refer to a bewildering variety of activities and assumed qualities. Discussion about intelligence, therefore, drips with controversy, invective, and obfuscation: animals have intelligence; animals cannot have intelligence; intelligence is hereditary; it is environmentally determined; the rate of mental growth is increased in an enriched environment, decreased in an impoverished one; it is not; intelligence is comprised of a general factor together with a number of specific factors; it consists of specific factors only; it is mainly a verbal affair; its verbal aspects are relatively unimportant, etc. [56, p. 115].

Not only was it thought that the IQ of an individual was a meaningful and useful construct, it was also accepted that—barring the advent of some kind of "physical" or "mental" pathology—the IQ should remain constant. Although such constancy was difficult to empirically demonstrate [Bayley, 11; Sontag, Baker, and Nelson, 134], the "ideal" instruments were constructed and refined in such a way as to not *test* this assumption but to *build* it into each scale. In this way, a test was considered to be better, more valid, and more acceptable if it could demonstrate such constancy over long periods of time. Tests were devised not so much to obtain an adequate sample of what the child could do or what he had learned, but presumably (although this now seems a little ridiculous) to measure his really true innate capacity and, if possible, to minimize the aspects of experience and training.

Of course, the next step in such reasoning was to assume that if the individual did not function as well in life situations—in school, on the job, etc.—as he should according to his innate ability, then he was a victim of some kind of mental or physical pathology. If it could be demonstrated or assumed that his functioning relative to others at one time was higher than it was currently, he was likewise the victim of pathology. The concept of intelligence being made up of specific abilities also has its place here, since it was conceivable that under different kinds of pathology, different kinds of specific abilities would be more affected than others. The pattern of different abilities (i.e., verbal versus performance, new memory versus old memory, concrete versus abstract, etc.) could be used not only to indicate the presence of pathology, but also to indicate the specific nature of the pathology so that particular diagnostic groups presumably would show a specific pattern of discrepancies.

It is on these two basic principles that much of the work of the clinical psychologist concerned with adjustment was based. Of course, there were applications in addition to those seeking to "diagnose" pathology or maladjustment. For example, tests were devised to measure presumed innate capacity for individuals with various language, physical, and sensory limitation in order to make predictions about educability.

The foregoing analysis is to some extent an oversimplification. The notion of specificity was more accepted by some, and many of the omnibus-type tests were analyzed for special abilities and tests were created to measure specific abilities, for example, sensori-motor functions, memory, judgment, verbal ability, etc. The profile of these various abilities was used for the purpose of indicating particular kinds of pathology, and also for the purpose of making predictions and suggestions about training, education, placement, and other forms of management of individuals.

Psychology, like the other social sciences, frequently reflects the social and political thought of the times. The concept of intelligence was no exception to this. The idea of innate unchanging characteristics (the constant IQ) was not consistent with the social and political thought of the thirties, and it was attacked by both sociologists and psychologists. Early studies on racial differences in intelligence yielded to studies on changes in intelligence as a function of education and other environmental changes. Particularly influential in changing attitudes were the studies on changes in the intelligence of Negroes moving from the South to the North [Klineberg, 65]. Within psychology this emphasis was crystallized into "the nature-nurture controversy" [Skeels, 131].

A group of investigators at the Iowa Child Welfare Station (B. Wellman, H. Skeels, M. Shodak, G. Stoddard, R. Updegraff, H. Williams, and others) completed a number of studies demonstrating an increase in IQ as a result of early stimulation by foster parents or preschool attendance. These studies made a considerable dent on belief in both the constancy of the IQ and the innate nature of intelligence.

Along with the studies of the Iowa group, a new look was taken at the previously convincing studies of the Jukes and the Kallikaks [Louttit, 79]. They were now regarded as very flimsy evidence for the inheritance of feeblemindedness. Later studies such as those of Schmidt [122] and Axline [8], although themselves heavily criticized, emphasized that many of the so-called "mentally deficient" were in reality "emotionally blocked." Controversies about the inheritance of feeblemindedness where there is no known organic pathology and the total influence of heredity in intelligence are still going on, but the earlier concepts of the innateness and constancy of the IQ have been severely shaken. In current clinical practice, there is a general acceptance of the idea that training and the environment have a large influence on development of the ability to score on intelligence tests. However, it is also generally believed that the influence of environment is maximum in the early years and minimum by the time adolescence appears.

In the forties, the sociologists and social psychologists continued to emphasize the importance of cultural influence on intelligence and attempted the development of "culture-free intelligence tests" [Eells, Davis, Havighurst, Herrick, and Tyler, 25]. Actually, these tests were apparently no more successful than others in providing materials which equalized or controlled previous experience. It is somewhat surprising that the emphasis on culture and training did not result in a discarding of the notion of over-all intelligence and the IQ in favor of a clear understanding of the value of varied tests in assessing what has been learned and what each test can predict. Rather, the early trend to entitize and reify the IQ continued. *That is, it is surprising that the pressure from sociology and from the social-political thought of the times was to break down the emphasis on the innateness of intelligence, but not to reject the concept of general intelligence itself or its constancy for the later years of development.*

A strong indication of dissatisfaction with this older conception of intelligence can be seen in a recent article by Liverant [77]. He summarizes his penetrating reexamination by concluding that the genetic model representing the antecedent conditions of intelligence is essentially untestable and not in accord with recent conceptual advances in both genetics and psychology. Liverant also states that the majority of the evidence indicates that the concept is not capable of subsuming the great variety of behaviors now assumed to be related to intelligence. He feels that the behavior realm typically ascribed to intelligence should be incorporated into a social learning theory with a focus of interest on the situational conditions which facilitate or hinder the acquisition of various problem-solving skills and the conditions which hinder or facilitate the performance of these skills.

Intelligence Estimates from Projective Tests

The advent of projective tests for the assessment of personality and for the purposes of diagnosis did result in some change or addition to the prevailing concepts of intelligence for many clinicians. However, these changes seemed to reintroduce more strongly the old faculty psychology. Although estimates were made from projective tests purporting to approximate the scores that might be obtained from tests such as the Stanford-Binet or Wechsler-Bellevue Intelligence Scale, it was generally assumed that such approximations were not substitutes for the formal tests already in widespread use. However, going back to the older faculty ideas, a reintroduction was made of the concepts of imagination, emotions, and will or drive as separate faculties. Presumably, some projective tests, particularly the Rorschach, are able to assess both present functioning and "true limits of capacity," with an emphasis on imaginative and integrative ability [Klopfer, Ainsworth, Klopfer, and Holt, 66, chap. 12]. These true limits may not be reached by the individual because of his lack of drive (will), lack of control of emotions, or lack of contact with reality. The typical intelligence test is seen by some clinicians as measuring efficiency rather than true capacity. The projective tests then were included in the testing battery of these psychologists not only for an assessment of personality deviations, but also for an assessment of intellectual dysfunction or loss as a result of some pathological condition and as a method of assessing "true intellectual capacity."

The Current Situation

Although the assessment of intelligence of individuals for the purpose of predicting their education or occupational achievement is still part of the function of the clinical psychologist, it no longer is his major interest. The latter emphases on dynamics, adjustment, and psychopathology has led to (1) the widespread use of intelligence tests as indicators of the extent or nature of the maladjustment or to explain the reason for some problems of adjustment, (2) the analysis of test profiles to relate specific disabilities to specific diagnoses, including whether or not low-level functioning is a true feeblemindedness or a functional limitation imposed because of an emotional disorder, and (3) the development of tests based on the work of neurologists and physiological psychologists and purporting to indicate damage to the brain.

The tests of brain damage are in part based on theories of brain functioning but, to a large extent, they have been accepted on rather shaky empirical grounds. These measures will be discussed briefly in the section on diagnosis. The many studies attempting to relate patterns of performance on point scales, such as the Wechsler-Bellevue, to diagnoses are almost purely empirical in nature and have usually failed to cross-validate on repeated tests with new populations.

One result of this interest in profiles or patterns for measuring pathology has been the greater reliance in clinical practice on point scales. Point scales such as the Wechsler Adult Intelligence Scale [148] and Wechsler Intelligence Scale for Children [147] are supplanting age scales such as the Stanford-Binet because of the greater conveniences in analyzing and comparing subtests.

The tendency in recent research is to avoid or neglect explicit theory in justifying the method of measurement of intellectual dysfunction psychologically or neurologically described. Empirical findings are reported but turn out to be nonsubstantial on repeated and careful objective testing. The methodologies of research are probably less at fault in this failure to cross-validate instruments than the concepts of pathology (i.e., treating brain damage as if it were some type of entity with similar characteristics, regardless of the individual or the locus, or the extent or nature of the brain pathology) and diagnosis (Kraepelinian), which are unreliable and do not actually abstract pathological behavior in a useful way for prediction.

In general, theorizing in the area of intellectual performance has remained relatively isolated and sluggish, and it seems that theories of intelligence have changed little in fifty years. Anastasi [6] has carefully argued that genetic determinants have at best only a distant relationship to complex intellectual behavior. However, we still seem primarily to measure faculties, innate in origin and general in nature, except that two additions to this theory have been accepted in the last thirty years. First, the specifics which make up the general characteristics of intellectual ability are differently affected in different kinds of psychopathology or psychophysiological pathology. Second, innate ability can be affected—sometimes considerably affected—by environment or culture, particularly in the early years.

Little use has been made of constructing tests specifically to measure variables of an intellectual nature which could be deductively arrived at from logical, systematic analyses of the theories of brain functioning or newer theories of psychological dysfunction. This is probably because logical and systematic theories in these areas are scarce.

As to the measurement of intellectual ability itself, surprisingly little use has been made of the tremendous body of knowledge accumulated by psychologists in the area of learning. Although the tests presumably measure the ability to learn, they almost always measure what *has been learned* rather than measuring or observing the individual in the process of learning. Only a few tests of "recent memory" and some problem-solving items that are really novel provide measures of the ability to learn some new material during the test itself. Tests for higher-level learning skills, such as those suggested by Harlow [41] and Schroder and Rotter [123] have not been made. Nor has there been attempt to break through the rigid categories of faculty psychology and devise constructs and tests which conceptualize the individual as solving problems in a variety of situations—without theoretical bias toward generality or innate limitations.

DIAGNOSIS

The clinical psychologist has met the problem of diagnosis with a set of personality variables and with an armamentarium of tests. Until recently, however, the tests he used were not clearly developed as operations for explicit theoretical variables. When they were so developed, they were often used for purposes different from those for which they were intended, accruing a variety of nonsystematically related concepts. Although it will result in some overlap, the following sections will discuss the source and nature of the concepts involved in personality tests separately from a discussion of the kinds of instruments in current practice. A final brief section will deal with concepts and tests utilized in the diagnosis of brain damage.

The Source of Concepts for Personality Diagnosis

While the early work in intelligence testing was rooted in faculty psychology, the problem of diagnosis—even in its beginnings—appeared to draw on medicine or medical pathology for its orientation. The clinical psychologist was initially concerned with using his tests of intelligence and abilities, verbal and nonverbal, to discriminate the feebleminded (i.e., pathological individuals who could not be expected to benefit from normal educational or training procedures) and the more educable individuals (i.e., the blind or partially sighted, the deaf or partially deaf, the crippled, etc.) from those with less potential. Although the problems themselves were drawn from the medical approach to treating illness, the early work was oriented toward application in the field of education and training. Later on, when intelligence tests were beginning to be widely accepted, the clinical psychologist became involved in some problems of selection. With the growth of universal education and changing philosophies of education, his tests were also used to "diagnose" the superior child or the genius. The superior child was studied since he, too, required a special kind of handling or training in the school system.

With wider and wider acceptance of intelligence testing, clinical psychologists began to be hired in both institutions for the feebleminded and clinics and schools to make objective appraisals of abilities. Once hired, the clinical psychologist found himself being called on not merely to provide estimates of intelligence, but also to help make so-called "differential diagnoses." Was the limitation on ability permanent or temporary? Was the limitation on ability a result of a pathology or disease which was considered to be mental rather than physical, or "functionally psychotic" rather than "organic"?

In order to answer these questions, the clinical psychologist began to study the profile of responses to different kinds of test items, performance as compared to verbal, old memory to new learning, abstract to concrete, perception of form relationships compared to rate of manipulation. Tests were devised to sample the learning potential of individuals handicapped in hearing instructions, understanding English, seeing stimulus materials, manipulating form boards, etc. The standard intelligence tests gave way to a large variety of verbal and performance tests and the compilation of manuals for intelligence testing cited earlier.

As the clinical psychologist began the attempt to differentiate the source or kind of pathology from the patterning of intellectual tests, he also became involved in discovering limitations of performance resulting from functional conditions such as emotional inhibitions, psychoneurosis, and psychosis. It was a short step from here into positions in the mental hospitals to aid the psychiatrist in the diagnosis of patients.

Some psychologists worked in penal institutions, where they weeded out the individuals who belonged in either mental hospitals or institutions for the feebleminded and selected those most able to profit from education and training.

In this new diagnostic function, the clinical psychologist not only drew his problems from the fields of pathology and medicine, but made his application in the same field. For the most part, his function was to help the psychiatrist or another physician diagnose the patient's disease (sometimes this resulted in differential administrative management but rarely in differential face-to-face psychotherapy). In doing so, he took on the terminology and the concepts of psychiatry which had changed little since the middle of the nineteenth century and, in the opinion of some [Lewin, 75; Kantor, 59; Rotter, 115], he made a step in a direction which would limit his contributions for some time to come. That is, by accepting the disease-entity approach to behavior and tailoring his own tests and thinking to these concepts, the clinical psychologist may well have become involved in a relatively fruitless area of investigation and application.

The disease-entity approach to personality description is a true carryover of medical thinking into the psychological realm. Basically, the disease-entity approach in medicine deals with assumed specific diseases with regular symptom patterns caused by foreign organisms or resulting from specific structural defects. Applied to mental disorders or psychologically deviant behavior, it is assumed that a person so afflicted is a victim also of a disease in a literal sense. The disease might be inherited, based on a genetic weakness or some exogenous factor affecting the nervous system, or it might possibly be partially the result of early traumatic experience. It was made manifest by a constellation of symptoms which might be overlapping, as in the case of measles and scarlet fever, and making a differential diagnosis—particularly in an early stage of the disorder—was consequently a highly subjective "art."

The failure really to understand and develop methods of treating these "diseases" led to the substitute activity of classifying them for a long period of time. Here the psychologist could find a function. Was a disorder a true split from reality, genetically based and presumably of lifetime duration—or was it temporary and within the normal range, although extreme? Was it a side effect of structural attack on the nervous system, malingering, or what? Was the apparent depression, although cyclical, a true depression which reflected extreme personality deviation of lifelong duration—or was it merely the apathy of an individual whose interests in the outside world disintegrated as his disease advanced? Was the patient's refusal to communicate related to a deep depression, stuporous withdrawal, or major damage to the brain resulting in total aphasia?

The problem presented by the psychiatrist, in which he asked the help of the psychologist, was to identify the true underlying disease. Since the textbook-defined cases were quite rare, the method was to describe the many symptoms and hopefully to arrive at a best guess of the "true diagnosis." In the late thirties and early forties, these were the major concepts with which the clinical psychologist worked. His traits were the symptoms of the various disorders of the psychiatric diagnostic schema. These included the nonpsychotic classifications of the hysterical, obsessive, neurasthenic, and psychasthenic neurosis, and various classifications of psychopathic deviate. The present method of classifying psychopathological behavior is considered to have originated with Kraepelin [68] in the late nineteenth century. Zilboorg and Henry [154] have shown that Kraepelin's diagnostic schema was a natural outgrowth of work in the preceding century. To the many classifications of mental disorder extent at the time and based largely on symptomatology, Kraeplin added the principle of classification by prognosis. Following Moebius [Rosanoff, 112], he stressed division of mental disorders into exogenous and endogenous categories and leaned heavily on the concept that mental abnormalities were disease entities. This latter concept had been a part of lay and learned thinking, at least since the time that mentally disturbed people were considered to be possessed by devils. Symptom, etiology, and prognosis were combined, not in any systematic way, but largely following the mode of the times. Kraepelin believed strongly that dementia praecox was an organic or endogenous disease and was incurable. Additions to and reinterpretations of the Kraepelinian system have been made from time to time, but the method of classification has changed little. The formulation of the nature of dementia praecox was changed considerably by Bleuler [Zilboorg and Henry, 154], and the "disease" was renamed "schizophrenia." Zilboorg and Henry in explaining the success of the Kraepelinian system state:

The Kraepelinian system was a true triumph of a settled question. Historically and psychologically the triumph was very great because it brought about, in textbooks at least, the fulfillment of the age-long ambition of bringing mental disease into medicine, carrying it through the front door, so to speak, bringing about a complete union of psychiatry and medicine.

It is easy to think in terms of categories and entities; now that the nosological approach to psychological abnormality has been incorporated into the textbooks of medicine, psychiatry, and abnormal and clinical psychology, getting rid of it is extremely difficult.

A second source of concepts came from the influence of psychoanalysis, which was becoming stronger in the thirties and became prominent after World War II. Of course, from a much earlier time, the concepts of Adler [1], particularly as applied in child guidance clinics, and the concepts of Freud, particularly applied to work with adults, were being utilized by psychologists operating in the field of adjustment and treatment. Some techniques for measuring the kinds of variables involved in the Adlerian and Freudian formulations had been developed [Symonds, 139]. The technique perhaps most frequently used and specifically developed to describe variables peculiarly psychoanalytic was the word-association technique. It was developed by Jung to discover the presence of specific "complexes" postulated in the psychoanalytic conception of maladjustment. Interestingly enough, the same technique was more widely used [Kent and Rosanoff, 63] as a tool to aid in the diagnosis of schizophrenia.

The influx of psychoanalysts from Central Europe as a result of Nazi persecution had a profound effect on psychiatry and, through psychiatry, on clinical psychology. As a result of this influence, psychiatrists could be graded on a continuum from those who used purely the psychiatric diagnostic schema and its lists of symptoms as their conceptual tools to those who used purely a description of psychoanalytic dynamics for their description and understanding of mental abnormality. The presumed problems, as viewed from the psychoanalytic point of view, lay in the unconscious and were not readily amenable to interview techniques, questionnaires, etc. The psychologist had no way to get at these unconscious attitudes until the development of a new mode of testing—now known as projective tests—presented an opportunity which was enthusiastically accepted. The development of the projective technique did provide the psychologist with a set of tools to use for the description of personality from a psychoanalytic point of view, as well as new tools to deal with the older psychopathological concepts.

Two other general sources of concepts for the measurement of personality should be mentioned, although they have been less popular and less influential in general, except as they have been incorporated either into the psychoanalytic or psychiatric nosological approach. One of these may be called "trait theory" which, in its most limited aspect, involves typological conceptions. The description of traits of character, which historically also has its roots in faculty psychology, has been of interest in the general field of personality theory for some time. However, clinical psychology, with its origin in medical and educational problems of pathology, had no ready utility for lists of traits, except as they related to various disease entities or reflected the internal dynamics of the psychoanalyst. Because of this, rather elaborate schemata such as those provided by Allport [5], Cattell [21], and the personalistic psychology of Stern [136] did not lead to the development of special diagnostic tools widely used by the clinical psychologist.

The early descriptions of mental diseases probably were partially influenced by some of the general typological thinking of the nineteenth century; in this sense, they are incorporated in the disease-entity approach.

Although typologies have flourished from the time of the early Greeks, present-day typological concepts in psychology are predominantly influenced by the French school, represented by the work of Rostan in 1828, and by the German school of Kretschmer [Sheldon, 128], whose typology followed closely that of Rostan. Rostan categorized into a digestive type, a muscular type, a respiratory type, and a cerebral type. These types correspond rather closely to Kretschmer's "pyknic," "athletic," "athletic-asthenic," and "asthenic types." Even when the typology has a more-or-less quality, so that a given person may be thought of as having a place on the continuum of a single trait or as having various degrees of characteristics of several types, one is still faced with a narrow, limited, and crude method of describing human behavior.

The present-day development of the Rostan and Kretschmer typology is best exhibited in the work of Sheldon [128, 129]. Although Sheldon has worked out one of the most elaborate typological systems and has fitted it out with the most objective referents for classification purposes, his typology remains subject to the usual criticisms.

Jung's [57] typology of extrovert and introvert is based primarily on psychological rather than constitutional determinants, in contrast to the typologies discussed above. It overlaps heavily, nevertheless, with the description of the psychological characteristics of the constitutional types.

Another classification schema has been developed based on the typing of individuals for their predominant sensory imagery. In modern times, this development traces back to the work of Galton [29], published in 1907. People who tended to image things predominantly in one sensory modality were classified into types such as: a visual imagery type, an auditory imagery type, a kinesthetic imagery type, etc. Rorschach [111], who was influenced both by the Jungian introvert-extrovert typology (which he called "introversive" and "extratensive") and by the imagery psychology popular in this time, combined the two and oriented his tests around the primary and basic characteristics of the *Erlebnistypus:* Testees on the Rorschach who tended to see things in movement (kinaesthesis) were considered to be introversive; those who tended to see percepts on the cards utilizing color were extratensive. The balance of these factors was the major descriptive variable of the test.

These general types found their way into abnormal psychology via Kraepelin [68] in 1913 and Kretschmer [70] in 1925. The asthenic or leptosomic body build was associated with the potential for dementia praecox, and pyknic body build was associated with the tendency toward manic depressive psychosis. Body type itself became one of the characteristics of the "disease" and often helped establish a differential diagnosis in difficult cases. For the most part, typological thinking represents only a minor trend in present-day psychology. It still, however, has a basic influence in traditional abnormal psychology and in the area of psychiatric diagnosis.

Psychoanalysis has also developed its types (oral character, anal character, etc.), which are based on the individual's early experiences.

For the most part, the typological thinking of importance to clinical psychologists has come from the disease-entity and psychoanalytic approaches to deviant behavior.

Mention should be made of the application of learning theory to problems of psychopathology or of the attempt to understand stable personality characteristics as a result of learning. The works of Mowrer [88] and Dollard and Miller [23] are perhaps best known in this connection. There have been many attempts to describe specific abnormal behaviors as a result of conditioning or association processes, but in general, these attempts provided no new concepts for describing personality. Rather they provided a description of the process involved in the development of the abnormal behavior as conceived in psychiatric terms, psychoanalytic terms, or both.

Of growing interest, but still considerably limited in actual clinical application, is a conception of personality in terms of needs or goal-directed responses [Murray, 91; Rotter, 115]. Although these theories undoubtedly originated in part in the psychoanalytic movement (including the Adlerian and Rankian conceptions), they have achieved a relative independence of specific analytic concepts and have developed some measures for their basic constructs. Partly as a result of the influence of Kantor [59], Lewin [75], Adler [2], and role-theory conceptions of sociology such as those of Thomas [142], the problem of pathology is not approached in terms of the diseases of the psychiatric diagnostic schema or the internal conflicts of analysis, but in terms of the interactions of the individual and his social field. The problem of maladjustment and adjustment does not involve merely a search for causes within the individual; there is a search for explanation in the individual's interaction with his particular social field or life space.

Other conceptions of personality are relatively recent—at least in their details of development. The Rankian movement, including Frederick Allen, Carl Rogers, and others, provides examples but such influence has been felt more in the development of therapeutic technique than in the development of diagnostic tools.

In general, the major influence on the concepts which the clinical psychologist used in differential diagnosis or in testing for descriptive purposes has come from the people who hired him to do the job, that is, from medically trained individuals with or without psychiatric training. These physicians were concerned for the most part with the classification or identification of the particular illness from which the patient was suffering. The psychoanalytically trained psychiatrist was interested in identifying the conflict, fixation, or instinctual anomaly from which the patient was suffering. Although the psychologist has added conceptual tools from other sources to some extent, these have not been the dominating ones in his repertoire. There are current signs, however, that the psychologist, by his own research tools and training in theoretical systematization, is beginning to bring to bear concepts of his own to deal with the problem of describing relatively stable behavioral characteristics of individuals. Examples of the building of test instruments around such concepts are the Level of Aspiration tests [Rotter, 114; Escalona, 26], originating in the work of Lewin, and the Edwards Personal Preference Schedule [24], originating in Murray's personality theory. A partial step in this direction is the attempt of some psychologists to statistically purify psychiatric concepts by factor analysis of clinical descriptions [Wittenborn, 152] and to develop tests such as the Minnesota Multiphasic Personality Inventory (MMPI) [Hathaway, 44], which are ultimately aimed at substituting for subjective psychiatric diagnoses rather than merely predicting them.

Measures of Personality

In his earlier operations, the clinical psychologist's interest in personality was secondary to his work in assessment of ability. He paralleled the psychiatrist in the use of case history material and the interview as his source of information regarding the personality (the relatively stable characteristics other than intellectual) of his patients. Some techniques for evaluation of personality were developed quite early, but these were the tools of the psychologist concerned with research and selection (as in the case of the Woodworth-House questionnaire in World War I) more than they were tools for the clinical psychologist in his individual casework. Some questionnaires were, however, adapted for the clinic. A description of these tests is provided in Symonds [139]. One of these techniques, the Pressey X-O Test [101] was a forerunner of some of the later projective techniques.

As the clinical psychologist's interest began to turn toward differential diagnosis of functional disorders, new instruments were needed. One of the first widely used methods was the word-association technique. Symond's chapter on this test is still a standard reference. Naturally, the first attempts to widen the psychologist's diagnostic potential came from the reanalysis of techniques he used for intellectual assessment. The studies of Roe and Shakow [107] and Babcock [10] on analysis of the Stanford-Binet with pathological cases and of Jastak [52] and Bijou [14] on profile analysis of behavior problems are classical illustrations of this trend. Application of some of the work of physiologists and psychologists in the realm of emotions was tried out experimentally. These experimental procedures were not widely used as regular clinical techniques. The adjustment questionnaires obviously had their limitations. It was hardly worthwhile for the clinical psychologist to discover that the case already in the hospital or clinic was maladjusted, and he could make no particular use of the fact that the maladjustment score was 10 percentiles higher or lower than that of another patient. For feeble-minded and psychotic patients, the questionnaire technique did not seem particularly applicable and so-called "psychopaths" could not be relied upon to tell the truth. As clinical psychologists became more and more involved in the problems of diagnosis of psychiatric groups or in assessing the analytic dynamics of a patient, a vacuum developed in their repertoire of measurement techniques which was filled, in part, by the development and wider use of what has come to be called "projective tests."

Projective techniques. The term "projective test" is loosely applied to a variety of tests which are differentiated from other personality tests by all, some, or one of the following characteristics: (1) disguised purpose, (2) freedom of response, (3) global nature, usually encompassing a large number of specific variables, and (4) absence of detailed explicit norms and subjective scoring and interpretation.

The early forerunner of these tests was the previously cited word-association method. The Rorschach test, developed by a Swiss psychiatrist and introduced in this country through the writing of David Levy, Emil Oberholser, and Samuel Beck [Krugman, 71], was the instrument on which many of the more widely used current tests were modeled. Through courses by Samuel Beck and later Bruno Klopfer and Marguerite Hertz, clinical psychologists became acquainted with this instrument in the later thirties. During the war, it was taught to clinical psychologists in training in the Army and immediately following the war, it became a standard part of the clinical psychologist's techniques and training.

Work involving the use of inkblots to study personality antedates the development of the Rorschach test by many years. However, Rorschach was the first to develop an instrument specifically developed for clinical purposes. Rorschach was a psychiatrist who was interested in the problem of diagnosis of mental disease. He tried to construct an instrument that could be used to differentiate various kinds of mental disorders, ranging from organic brain disease to neurosis and including all of the so-called "functional psychoses," epilepsy, and feeblemindedness. Most of this work was done around 1916, and the theoretical concepts employed by Rorschach were the theoretical concepts current in Europe at that time. Although Rorschach makes some reference to psychoanalysis, he was predominantly influenced by the approach to mental disorder of Kraepelin, as somewhat revised by Bleuler. He conceived of the various mental disorders as disease entities, some functional and some organic in origin. The functional disorders were largely predetermined by constitution and inheritance, and each disease or disorder was so global in its nature that all of the affected person's activities were in part a reflection of its all-pervasiveness. Along with this adherence to disease-entity thinking was an implicit acceptance of faculty psychology current in his day and still relatively influential in present-day psychology. He speaks of the will, the emotions, the intellect, and the imagination as separate aspects or faculties of the organism that are sometimes struggling within the individual for dominance.

The dynamic aspect of Rorschach's theory is not the dynamics of the psychoanalyst or the dynamics of the field theorist, but the dynamics of the internal struggle among faculties and the attempt to describe behavior in terms of the relationships among faculties. A third source from which Rorschach drew his theories was that of the typologies referred to earlier. For the most part, however, Rorschach's "theory" (as it is sometimes referred to) is more a conglomerate than a systematic approach to personality. Certainly, it was less of a theory than that being developed by Freud or Adler around the same time.

In the late thirties, L. K. Frank [27] wrote an article on the new procedures, which he called "projective techniques." This label is now generally regarded as a misnomer. Along with the Rorschach test and some play techniques developing out of child therapy, he included some new tests developed by Henry A. Murray and his co-workers. Murray was developing a personality theory based on psychoanalysis but differing in its systematization. In 1935, Morgan and Murray [87] published a description of the Thematic Apperception Test; in 1937, Murray [90] described a variety of methods for the purpose of eliciting fantasies. Murray's goal was to obtain the same kind of material which appeared in dreams and presumably gave more ready access to unconscious ideation. One of these in particular, the Thematic Apperception Test, caught on and led to the development of a variety of other projective techniques which were mainly concerned with discovering the content of the subject's deeper or less obvious motivations.

Immediately following World War II, with the impetus of the Veterans Administration training program and its concern with serious problems of adjustment in adults, these methods achieved a high degree of popularity; the clinical psychologist could be as easily identified by his Rorschach or Thematic Apperception Test cards as he could by the Stanford-Binet or Wechsler-Bellevue Intelligence Scales. During this time, a large number of new projective tests were constructed and manuals written—usually following the two trends we have already outlined. They were either primarily concerned with obtaining information about unconscious motivation ("He has strong, passive, dependent needs," for example) or they were concerned with determining diagnoses, helping in the problem of making differential diagnoses, or describing the traits considered to be important for making psychiatric diagnoses. In a crude way, these two purposes have been systematized as dealing with the structure (diagnostic category) of personality or the content (psychoanalytic conflicts) of personality. The joint use of the Rorschach test to obtain structural information and the Thematic Apperception Test or a similar instrument to obtain content material was suggested by Harrison [42] and later by others.

For the most part, the universities rejected psychoanalysis and the projective techniques when they first made their appearance. This rejection in part accounts for the fact that the concepts and tools of the clinical psychologist came largely from psychiatry, medicine, and neurology, rather than from psychological theories of learning or perception. However, with the support for clinical psychology coming from the Veterans Administration and the U.S. Public Health Service, the large universities began to develop major training programs in clinical psychology. For the most part, earlier clinical psychologists did their research in traditional problems of psychology—then went out and practiced clinical psychology, which apparently bore little relationship to the research they had done at the university. The students in these new programs were able to do research with their own techniques and concepts. The projective tests were subjected to a great deal of testing at about the same time these methods were at the height of popularity. Most of the carefully done validation research resulted in relatively negative findings. However, with the typical cultural lag which takes place between research and application, it was still several years before a more skeptical and conservative attitude began to be taken toward the projective methods. As a result of the negative findings, clinical psychologists began to turn to other techniques. Particularly for research purposes they made increased use of techniques [Incomplete Sentences Blank of Rotter and Rafferty, 119]; Blum's Blacky Test, 16; Rosenzweig's Picture Frustration Test, 113] which were considered to have some of the advantages of projective instruments, but were capable of objective scoring.

The decline in the widespread enthusiasm for projective tests coincided with the increasing interest of clinical psychologists in psychotherapy. The over-all result has been not so much a rejection of projective tests and search for new methods as it has been a decline in the general concern and interest with diagnostic testing and a greater concern and interest with the problems of psychotherapy.

The effects of operationism in psychology and of the appearance of systematic behavior theories, such as those of Lewin and Hull, had their indirect effect on the clinician's attitude toward personality tests. This was more apparent for the more recently trained clinicians.

Many of these clinical psychologists began to look for more explicit operational variables and theories with which to conceptualize their problem and to regard tests as operations for systematic variables. A general orientation toward regarding tests as referents or operations for theoretical constructs has been emphasized by Cronbach and Meehl [22] and Rotter [115, chap. 8].

Personality questionnaires. Along with the development of projective tests, more refined and clinically oriented questionnaire methods were devised. An outstanding example of this is the MMPI [Hathaway, 44]. This method, borrowing again from the psychiatric diagnostic schema, set up nine empirically derived scales on the basis of psychiatric classification of patients at the University of Minnesota Hospital. Additional scales were set up to measure the consistency and honesty of the respondent. Although it was a somewhat lengthy test, it did have the advantage of dealing specifically with the categories or concepts in which the psychiatrist was interested. The difficulty with this and other similar scales lies in the unreliability of the criteria on which they were developed. Numerous studies demonstrating this limitation have been made [Rotter, 115, chap. 2] and cross validation of these scales on different populations usually resulted in inconsistent findings. Humm and Wadsworth [48] developed a similar scale for use in industrial selection, based on Rosanoff's psychiatric classification of types; the Guilford-Martin Test [38], based on a factor analysis and a trait approach, was also used in some clinics for high school children.

A more recent development in personality questionnaire tests is that of Gordon [36], Edwards, [24], and Liverant [76], who tried to avoid the problem of a respondent giving the answer which they felt to be most socially acceptable by developing a forced-choice questionnaire in which the choices are presumably of equal social desirability. The Edwards scale attempted measurement of some of Murray's list of needs. Liverant measured some need constructs from social-learning theory, and Gordon based his on a factor analysis of empirically derived items. In general, the evolution of forced-choice questionnaires in the personality realm is relatively new, but it appears to be a promising trend.

Another recent development is that of behavioral tests, for the most part instigated by the work of Lewin and his students. The best known of these is the level-of-aspiration technique, which is used to some extent in practical clinical situations. Behavioral tests are essentially work sample tests. They place the subject in a situation involving self-evaluation or frustration, and observations are made of his behavior in that situation rather than from his verbal statements about his feelings and attitudes or from his imaginative productions. The novelty of some of these instruments partly accounts for their lack of general popularity. However, their less general use in clinical practice also stems from the fact that they are relatively specific in nature and not simply relatable to the more generally used psychiatric and psychoanalytic concepts.

Structured versus unstructured tests. At the present time, some controversy continues between the advocates of projective tests and advocates of questionnaire methods. The controversy has two aspects, although they are often confused. One is the relative merit of subjective "clinical" versus actuarial or statistical [Meehl, 84] scoring and interpretation. The second is the relative merit of the structured direct test as compared to the indirect or unstructured test.

The categorization of structured and unstructured tests is somewhat confusing, and it would be better to substitute some other terms. The Stanford-Binet and the Rorschach can be regarded either as structured or unstructured, depending on how they are used. It appears that the difference lies in the degree of ambiguity of the instructions or the task presented to the subject and whether or not the method of scoring and interpretation is objective or subjective rather than the test materials.

For example, if one should ask a subject to count the Rorschach cards, one has an unambiguous test; if one should hand a subject the MMPI cards and ask him to put together the ones that he thinks should go together, one has an ambiguous test. Obviously, combinations of ambiguity and objectivity are possible—as are unambiguous and subjective interpretations.

The major differences between ambiguous and unambiguous tests can be regarded as twofold. The first of these is disguise of purpose. In some instances it is, of course, of value to hide the purpose of the test so that the subject cannot consciously or without awareness try to create some definite impression of himself. Numerous studies indicate that conscious control is a matter of degree, and subjects can change their responses in a specific direction in both objective and projective kinds of tests.

Along with the possible gain from disguise of purpose is a loss which may well outweigh the gain. Some studies suggest very strongly that the subject does not take an ambiguous test passively. He attributes some purpose to the test, and the purpose he attributes to it may well hinge on odd bits of information, the setting of the test, differential emphasis on the words in the same instructions, and so forth. In fact, it is just because the subject is not sure of the purpose of the test that his own hypotheses hinge on minor clues, frequently ones of which the examiner is not aware. In short, as is strongly suggested by the study of Henry and Rotter [46], these tests may be much more susceptible to slight differences in the conditions of testing than structured tests, and their utility may be sharply curtailed if the individuals using them are not aware of this susceptibility.

This suggests that these tests are dangerous tools to use in selection and in research where they are presumed to be valid instruments measuring one or more personality variables. However, they may be ideally suited to research on the influence of the psychological situation on test responses and to some research relating various experimental conditions to perception.

The second characteristic of many of these tests is their omnibus quality. That is, instead of measuring a single or a few specific variables, these tests can produce responses which allow the subject to be placed in some rough high or low positions on a great many variables.

While it seems obvious that the ambiguous test cannot compete with carefully constructed unambiguous tests in measuring some clear and simple criterion for which the unambiguous test has been constructed, such a test can be of great value for the clinician, particularly one who is involved in some general assessment of the subject's personality. The clinician does not have available one test to measure the subject's hostility toward father, another for hostility toward mother, one for dependence on wife, another for anxiety over masculinity, etc. Even if he did have such tests available, he would never have the time to give them all. He relies instead on the hypothesis—which should be tested with each instrument—that what the subject *does* in a free choice situation reveals the variables on which he is most different from others. However, since the responses of subjects can be so different and scored on so many different variables and since criteria for the things he is interested in are so difficult to obtain, validation of his judgments are hard to come by. Properly used, these instruments have value at the present time in providing the clinician with hypotheses—leads for further investigation. Such leads can be tracked down through additional testing, sometimes with more specific tests and with case history material. At least for some kinds of therapy, they may be invaluable to the psychotherapist in increasing the efficiency of his treatment.

In regard to actuarial versus clinical interpretation and scoring, both the evidence and logic argue for the fact that when one is predicting some specific, measurable criterion and has previous data on test responses and the criterion from a truly representative sample of a relatively homogeneous population, then a multiple correlation, regression equation, or other statistical device will predict the same criterion from another representative sample better than will subjective judgment—if the same conditions of testing hold.

In most practical testing situations, however, one rarely finds these conditions, namely, a specific, easily measured criterion, available or easily obtainable data and norms, a population on which norms have been obtained that is truly representative of the population they will be applied to, a relatively homogeneous population, and identical conditions of testing. Consequently, it is possible that there are practical testing situations in which the clinical or subjective method may be superior for certain purposes. Obviously, whether the clinical method is superior in any specific instance is at least partially dependent on the clinician.

What makes for a good clinician is not, however, a matter of general agreement or even of much discussion, although the study of Kelly and Fiske [61] made one empirical approach to the problem. It seems to this writer that, in theory, a "good" clinician has at least two frequently neglected advantages over the regression equation or multiple correlation. In practice, however, he is not very often specifically trained to make use of these advantages.

The first advantage is that he supplies informal or implicit norms from his experience that the objective scoring fails to supply. For example, let us take a personality questionnaire used to predict success at college. Where the test supplies different norms for men and women and possibly for age, he may consider differences in the meaning of a particular response for students from rural versus urban homes, for wealthy versus poor, for high school athletes versus nonathletes, for students of Italian versus Jewish extraction, for a single individual who went to the university school and probably had taken the same test before versus all the rest, etc. It can be argued, of course, that all these things can be done—by the accumulation of more norms or scores, feeding them into the multiple correlation, etc.—except that they are neither practical nor economical. In many instances, the number of cases in any group would be too small to develop meaningful statistical norms. However, the clinician can bring his experience to bear with variables that he has obtained from other groups and from his reading and general scientific knowledge.

The second major skill the clinician may add is the interpretation of the effects on response resulting from differences in testing conditions. A recent trend in validity testing indicates that a great variety of situational factors will significantly affect test responses [Lord, 78; Sarason, 121; Gibby, Miller, and Walker, 31; Mussen and Scodel, 92; Rotter, 116; Phares and Rotter, 97; Masling, 82]. These conditions include not only many characteristics of the examiner, the place, and the time of testing, etc., but the set, attitude, previous knowledge, etc., of the subject toward the test. For example, he can estimate for one subgroup or an individual the effect of an examiner who is likely to create hostility, the effect of time of administration (i.e., early Monday morning, just before lunch, late in the afternoon), or even the effects of recent changes in the draft law on the motivation of draftable college students. In general, such considerations give him information about the amount of effort and cooperation of the subject and, perhaps more important, the subject's purposes in taking the test. Again, many of these factors could be entered into an equation if enough data were gathered, but again, it would not be practical or economical in many cases. Quantification is always superior to no quantification if it is practical and economical, but the interpretation of or prediction from quantified scores and variables in many practical situations can be improved upon by a good clinician.

For both types of tests, a serious theoretical gap has been noted by several authors [Peak, 93; Butler, 20; Jessor and Hammond, 55] between the actual behavior of subjects taking tests and the inferences made from such behavior. Considering this problem in a recent analysis of the failure to predict goal-directed life behavior from personality tests, Rotter [118] has stressed the failure to apply our theories and knowledge about behavior in general to the test-taking behavior of subjects, as well as to the variables presumably being measured. The analysis emphasizes the failure to systematically differentiate expectancy for reinforcement from reinforcement, reward, or incentive value as *test constructs* and as influences on behavior in the testing situation. Current testing and prediction procedures also fail to recognize the major importance of the psychological situation both in analyzing the meaning or significance of test behavior and in determining what are the life situations to which prediction can be reasonably anticipated.

Summary of personality tests. Most of the tests mentioned in the foregoing sections have failed to establish themselves as having high utility or validity for practical prediction. This is partly the result of the fact that so many of them have been developed against the criteria of psychiatric diagnoses which themselves have poor reliability, and serious doubts have been raised about the value of these psychiatric concepts. Some have failed to demonstrate experimental validity because they have been developed in an attempt to discover unconscious motivations and "deeper" conflicts. For such instruments, the problems of finding adequate criteria are so great that they have rarely been surmounted. Some new trends have appeared in testing—tests are being developed for the measurement of less global or complex concepts than schizophrenia or anxiety, and there are promising studies in objective scoring of some projective tests, in the forced-choice personality questionnaire, and in behavioral testing. The projective tests should not be written off, however, as useless. Although they have limited value as instruments of known validity for research purposes, they can be extremely useful when the clinician regards his findings from these instruments as hypotheses for purposes of further exploration, rather than as independent and objective indications of generalized character traits residing within the individual.

Perhaps the greatest promise for the future of personality tests lies in the variety of criticisms on theoretical grounds of present procedures and the application of psychological principles of behavior to test construction. While new advances in statistics and test construction procedures can be of considerable value, they cannot supplant an adequate theory of complex social behavior applied to the test-taking behavior itself.

The Diagnosis of Brain Damage

In the realm of brain damage, the clinical psychologist's concepts also developed from a medical orientation. However, his concepts came from the neurologist rather than the psychiatrist. Hypotheses on the psychological effect of brain damage were formulated by such men as Jackson [51], Kleist [64], and Head [45], among the important early workers, and by Goldstein [32] and Weisenberg, together with the psychologist Katherine McBride [149] in the thirties. The concepts which these neurologists applied basically involved the same general faculty approach that was being applied in the area of intellectual abilities. Abstract reasoning, form perception, verbal ability, judgment, memory, etc., were the characteristics which would or would not be affected by particular kinds of damage to the brain. The early trend was toward strict localization, and the kind of intellectual dysfunction presumably revealed the localization of the damage. In addition to these concepts, the work of the gestalt psychologists introduced concepts such as disorders in figure-ground relationships, disintegration of gestalt images, distortions of figures, and abstract versus concrete reasonings.

Lashley's [72] doctrine of "equipotentiality" and Goldstein's [33] gestalt approach reduced some of the emphasis on strict localization of mental functions. Coupled with the additional influence of the psychiatric classificatory approach, this led to a generalizing of the nature of any damage to the brain. In consequence, brain damage is commonly regarded in practice as another kind of disease. This trend took place, although the work of Weisenberg and McBride [149] appears to have established the relevance of the distinction of dominant vs. nondominant hemisphere, as well as the relevance of broad concepts of localization, particularly whether or not the damage was anterior or posterior to the Rolandic fissure. As a result of this generalized view, numerous studies by psychologists have recently compared brain-damaged patients to patients with neurological disorders, making the assumption that brain damage, like schizophrenia, is an entity. The brain-damaged patients are expected to have some characteristic way of behaving, regardless of the nature, size, or location of the damage. The greater part of the evidence does not support this generalized view of the effect of malfunctioning of parts of the cerebral cortex.

Tests of brain damage. With the extreme difficulty of making neurological studies of the brain, the neurologist and psychiatrist turned to the psychologist for help, at least in the preliminary diagnosis of brain disorders. Since the intelligence testing movement had already developed some considerable diversification in terms of measuring specific abilities and disabilities, the items of standard intellectual tests were broken down into groupings so that memory functioning could be separated from new learning, language ability from performance, etc. Separate scales for memory function, such as the Wells Memory Scale [150] were developed and later revised by Wechsler [146]. Special tests developed by neurologists, particularly in the field of aphasia, were adapted by psychologists [Halstead, 39], and techniques like the Vigotsky Test [Hanfmann and Kasanin, 40] and the BRL Sorting Test [Bolles, Rosen, and Landis, 17] were in occasional use to study the possible loss of the higher processes of abstracting. More recently, specific tests were devised applying some of the work in experimental psychology [Hunt, 49] in the general field of perception and concept formation and many of them were largely influenced by gestalt psychology and the principle of isomorphism [Goldstein and Sheerer, 34]. Tests utilizing memory for designs seemed to be particularly useful, and the work of Bender [12] was extended in the development of a test instrument, the Bender-Gestalt. Graham and Kendall [37] have also devised such an instrument. Projective tests, such as the Rorschach, have been adopted to this diagnostic problem [Piotrowski, 100; Harrower-Erikson, 43], but these attempts have not stood up well on cross validation.

The validation of all these instruments for diagnosing brain damage has been badly handicapped by the difficulty of establishing criteria. The absence of a useful schema for delimiting different kinds of brain dysfunctioning and the difficulty of obtaining comparable control groups or accurate predamage data for patient groups are two of the major obstacles.

PSYCHOTHERAPY

Early Trends and Psychoanalytic Influences

The earliest form of psychotherapy in which psychologists regularly were involved might best be called the "management of children." The early child guidance clinic was involved with problems of intellectual ability and concerned with advising parents and teachers and suggesting placements. The clinicians relied primarily on what might be called "common-sense principles." Gradually the ideas of Freud and Adler began to infiltrate into the guidance clinics. Particularly in the psychological clinics offering advice and recommendations, the ideas of Adler [1] seemed to hold more sway in dealing with children. By 1931, Woodworth could write:

However true and adequate Adler's psychology may or may not be in the ultimate sense, it certainly embodies much proximate truth that is immediately applicable to life. One might say that his conceptions are easier than Freud's, easier to grasp and easier to apply. Especially in assisting children to master their problems, Adler's line of approach has proved its value, so that he has already won a position of influence in the educational field [153, p. 168].

However, in face-to-face treatment of children, Freudian-trained psychiatrists were beginning to adapt the techniques of Anna Freud and Melanie Klein, and play therapy with children was begun by psychologists working in child guidance clinics. The rather extreme approach involved in a more literal translation of psychoanalytic methods to children was not immediately popular, and play therapy with children varied considerably in the degree of conformity to the Freudian technique advocated by Melanie Klein and Anna Freud. Adler contributed concepts such as style of life, position in the family, sibling rivalry, inadequacy, inferiority, or insecurity feelings, displacement by other siblings, pampering, overprotection, cooperation, responsibility, and social interest. The Freudians contributed concepts such as catharsis, castration, transference, resolution of the Oedipus complex, and repressed hostility in dealing with children's problems.

Of particular importance was the notion of catharsis and repressed hostility. Many of the techniques relied heavily on expressive methods in which it was assumed that improvement would follow from the catharsis of repressed hostility [Levy, 74; Shaw, 126; Solomon, 133; Bender and Woltmann, 13]. Such catharsis was accomplished through finger painting, breaking balloons, playing in sand and mud, watching puppet shows, venting aggression against doll figures, etc.

For the most part, the treatment of children has not changed greatly in the last fifteen years, with the exception of the addition of new techniques which are derived from the Rankian group and which will be discussed below. Techniques vary from complete emphasis on treatment of parents with little face-to-face therapy with children, perhaps typified mostly by the Adlerian group, to extensive long-term

child analyses with or without extensive treatment of parents, typified
by the more orthodox psychoanalytic school. In between these extremes
are all varieties of treatment methods, many of them borrowing from
psychoanalysis, with particular emphasis on catharsis. It is interesting
that many of the neo-Freudians and Freud himself began to reject the
importance of catharsis. Alexander and French [3] and Dollard and
Miller [23] raised the question of whether expression of "repressed"
feeling actually follows, rather than leads to improvement. These
writers place greater emphasis on insight and attribute to catharsis only
the role of leading to the potential for insight. In spite of the rejection
of the importance of catharsis by some leaders of the analytic movement, much of the face-to-face therapy with children still relies heavily
on catharsis itself as a major treatment concept.

Psychotherapeutic work with adults was more rarely attempted by
clinical psychologists in the early development of this applied field.
With few exceptions, psychotherapy with adults was practiced only by
psychiatrists and a few lay analysts until the late thirties in this country.[2]
Treatment by hypnosis, originating in work of the French school and
via Freud's early work, was occasionally practiced by psychologists, but
it never got a strong foothold. It is only rarely relied upon at the present
time, although an upsurge of such treatment methods occurred during
World War II, particularly in reference to the treatment of soldiers
who experienced traumatic combat conditions [Brenman and Gill, 18].
In most cases, such hypnotic treatment was applied as a short method
for speeding up the process of catharsis. In some cases, catharsis was
the goal of the treatment itself, in others it was the first step leading to
interpretation and attempts to accomplish insight.

The influx of both medically trained and lay analysts to this country
in the thirties resulted in the treatment of didactic analyses of a number
of psychologists, some of whom began to practice some form of analytic
therapy. A multiplicity of schools of neo-Freudians developed. Ansbacher
[7] has perhaps more aptly designated members as "neo-Adlerians."
Horney, [47], Fromm, [28], Kardiner, [60] and Sullivan [138] were
included in these schools. For the most part, these writers broke off
from traditional psychoanalysis by placing less emphasis on the importance of cleaning out the unconscious and by the rejection of the theory
of instincts and by the rejection of a sexual basis for all motivation. They

[2] It is significant that in the two-volume handbook *Personality and the
Behavior Disorders,* edited by Hunt [50], which was the standard source book in
the training of clinical psychologists immediately after the war, only 1 chapter out
of 35 was concerned with psychotherapy. This chapter was entitled "Psychiatric
Treatment" and it was written by a psychiatrist. Recent texts in clinical psychology by psychologists such as Pennington and Berg [94], Wallen [145], and
Garfield [30] devote about one-quarter of the text, on the average, to psychotherapy.

did rely on some version of Adler's concept of inferiority, usually in terms of security, and in some concept like Adler's "social interest," usually in terms of love for others. Clinical psychologists in contact with these various schools, either through their own analyses or professional association, developed all varieties and shades of psychoanalytic methods. The advent of World War II resulted in an increased interest in psychotherapy, and the writings of Carl Rogers were very influential in getting many psychologists involved in the actual practice of psychotherapy. Conceptually, Rogers seems to fit into a general movement stemming from Rank, which will be discussed below.

The Rankian Movement

Like most of the others who broke away from Freudian psychoanalysis, Rank [105] objected to the primacy of sexual drive as a basic explanation of motivated behavior in humans. He also, like Adler, tended to reject importance of the unconscious as a storehouse of energy and the cleaning out of the unconscious as a first step in psychotherapy. For Adler, this meant more direct dealing with the patient at what the psychoanalyst would call the "ego level," consequently, there was more direct interpretation and shorter psychotherapy. Rank carried these ideas even further.

From the point of view of the sociology of knowledge, it is interesting to note that when Rank came to this country he had considerable contact with schools of social work. Here his task was to advise on teaching social workers who were working with indigent families how to deal with the personal problems of their clients. Orthodox analysis was obviously highly inappropriate, and the major problem many of these patients faced could be conceptualized as one of dependency. The social workers themselves did not have the time for extensive training in psychodynamics, and any methods they employed would have to be suitable to the level of training and knowledge they had in this area. It is not surprising, therefore, that Rank's ideas began more and more to be directed toward a method which did not involve complex analysis of unconsicous motivation and past experience.

Rank asserted that delving into the past served no useful purpose, but fixated the patient in the painful situations of the past, leaving him powerless to deal constructively with his current problems. He therefore rejected not only catharsis, but insight into the origin of current conflicts, feeling that they were neither necessary nor particularly useful in accomplishing change in the client. It was also clear to Rank that it would be hard to break off therapy with highly dependent individuals involved in the typical analytic "transference" and to get them to stand on their own feet. He felt that the relationship between the patient and the therapist from the very beginning should be one which stimulated the patient toward independence.

Rank's method of therapy, as it gradually evolved, placed great emphasis on a discussion of the relationship between the patient and the therapist with a partial rejection by the therapist of the patient's attempts to lean on him. Content centered around the analysis of current problems rather than analysis of the past. Without catharsis and insight, however, to explain why people should get better, Rank utilized the concept of will power, a prevalent concept in Europe at the time. His concept of will was conceived as another human faculty explaining man's efforts toward the obtaining of his goals. He felt that everyone had such a faculty and that if it were directed into constructive channels, it would allow him to make a better solution of his problems. He therefore considered the purpose of therapy to be awakening the patient's "constructive will" by the therapist's role as a "counter will." Rank's work was translated by Jessie Taft, a social worker who wrote *The Dynamics of Therapy* [140], in which she described Rank's ideas and applied them to social work. She introduced the term "relationship therapy" to describe this method.

Rank and Taft's work apparently had some influence on Carl Rogers and on Frederick Allen [4], a young psychiatrist who applied Rank's ideas to play therapy with children. The term "constructive will," however, was not an acceptable one in American psychology, and Allen essentially substituted a "creative acceptance" of oneself. Such acceptance was accomplished by freeing the individual of "anxiety" and "disorganized feelings" and through a generalization of the relationship achieved by the therapist in play therapy. Allen drew an analogy from the biology that the growth process is one of differentiation and integration and that before psychological growth could proceed, it was first necessary for the client to differentiate himself from others, particularly the adults controlling his environment.

Carl Rogers [108, 109], essentially in the Rankian tradition, accepted the general principle that therapy could proceed—without an analysis of the past—through the client's ability to solve his problems as he saw more deeply into them as a result of the therapist's reflection of his feelings. Inherently, Roger's conception still emphasized the dependent nature of the client and the importance of the client's differentiating himself from others. Like Rank and Allen, he explained the basis for change as the freeing of the patient's "growth potential." Later he dropped this term in favor of "self integration" to describe the internal process which accounts for the patient's getting better as a result of therapy. The notion of the self he uses can be related to Jung [58], Lecky [73] and Raimy [103]. Rogers carried the rejection of the importance of the past further than the relationship therapists did. He not only felt that the therapist need not explore the past for the patient's benefit, but that it served no useful purpose for the therapist. In fact, a diagnostic orientation on the part of the therapist would interfere with his intuitive understanding of the patient's feelings, which he should reflect back to the patient. It is apparent that such a view of therapy required an attitude and frame of mind or particular kind of personality on the part of the therapist more than some form of special training. Rogers's approach to therapy opened the way for people of many disciplines to engage in treatment without a long training program, personal analysis, or medical background. His early book *Counseling and Psychotherapy* [108], published a few years prior to the rapid growth of clinical psychology after World War II, was widely read. Rogers also brought the psychologists' interest in research and research orientation into the field of therapy, and his published use of recorded therapy interviews opened the door to psychologists to do research in this area.

One interesting side effect of the Rogerian movement was the denial of the necessity for diagnosis or even description of the individual's personal characteristics. The more a clinical psychologist accepted Rogers's orientation, the less he was concerned with or interested in diagnostic methods. In addition, the gradual disillusionment with the validity of techniques in common practice resulted in greater and greater interest in psychotherapeutic techniques, particularly in the settings where psychotherapy was possible.

Although Rogers's work led many psychologists to feel that psychotherapy was a legitimate field for them, they often differed strongly with Rogers's methods and the more complete phenomenological theoretical formulations [110] which he gradually evolved. As a result, other therapeutic approaches were also more widely explored. Frequently without the requirement of didactic and control analysis, many clinical psychologists began to practice and teach some self-understood version of one of the psychoanalytic techniques. Sometimes these methods followed classical lines, sometimes a rather personal version of the methods of Freud, Adler, Horney, Sullivan, Jung, and others.

One rather different orientation is that of G. A. Kelly, who has some theoretical commonality with the Rankian school. Kelly [62] has lately published a personality theory which is based, like that of Rogers, on a phenomenological approach. Both Rogers and Kelly stress that the true concern of psychology is the internal perceptions of the subject, his internal frames of reference, or his subjective constructions of events, not prediction of behavior stemming from external stimuli. Where Rogers emphasizes feelings, Kelly is concerned with the subject's "personal constructs" or verbal and preverbal abstractions. He also has much in common with semanticists such as Korzybski [67]. Interestingly enough, Kelly's orientation to therapy involves the restructuring by the therapist of the patient's roles, following a study of the nature and content of the patient's personal constructs. The directiveness and methods of the therapist are quite different from those of Rogers, although both apparently start with much common theoretical ground.

The presumed difference between an S-R (objective- or stimulus-orientated psychology) and a phenomenological (experience- or subjective-orientated psychology) approach is being used increasingly as a basis for justifying different therapeutic techniques, although Jessor [53] has argued quite convincingly that the two theoretical approaches are much less different in operation than is usually believed.

Within the past few years, several American clinical psychologists have become interested in the variety of therapy methods, mostly originating on the Continent, which are loosely categorized as "existential analysis" [May, Angel, and Ellenberger, 83]. The general orientation has much in common with phenomenological approaches, although many variants deal with the unconscious life and use historical techniques. Such methods are based on the writings of continental philosophers such as Kierkegaard, Heidegger, and Nietzsche. It is difficult, however, to determine what many of these methods have in common—each borrows from different aspects of different writers—and most of the theoretical justification for the approach is obscure and laden with value terms. Perhaps the common ground for these approaches is the primary emphasis on the inner experiencing of the patient and a rejection of stereotyped approaches, "canned" interpretations, and psychiatric labels.

Learning Theory Approaches

Particularly in the areas of diagnosis and psychotherapy, the conceptual thinking of the clinical psychologist has been borrowed, for the most part, from psychiatry and psychoanalysis. However, as psychologists became more involved in psychotherapy, the possibilities of more strictly psychological approaches began to appear since the process of psychotherapy itself can so readily be understood as a learning process. It is not surprising that the beginning writings in this area take psychoanalysis as a point of departure. Two major contributors of this kind were Mowrer [89] and Dollard and Miller [23].

Although Mowrer started with psychoanalysis, he rejected the notion that the problem in psychoneurosis was one of an overly strong superego leading to excessive repressions; rather, he felt that neurotics had "learned" social taboos but not assimilated them. The psychopath or criminal presumably has neither learned nor assimilated social taboos. Exactly what the distinction between learning and assimilation is or how it can be predicted it is not clear. Nevertheless, Mowrer's theorizing has brought him to the conclusion that the problem of psychotherapy was not one of weakening the superego but strengthening it; consequently, his method of therapy is more directive. It is, in many ways, closer to that of Adler, who felt that the patient had to give up his struggle for superiority in favor of interest in society.

Dollard and Miller have attempted to reinterpret much of psychoanalysis, using concepts derived primarily from Hull's learning theory. To do so, it was necessary to reject some of the notions of Freud, particularly the emphasis on instincts as differentiated from drives and, to some extent, the importance of catharsis. Primarily, their contribution was one of reinterpreting psychoanalysis in learning terms, but in discussing psychotherapy, they placed much more emphasis on its problem-solving character.

In a later development, Rotter [115] described a social-learning theory and its implications for psychotherapy, but formulated no extensive descriptions of specific psychotherapeutic techniques. This theory utilizes an expectancy and a reinforcement principle, but accepts an empirical law of effect rather than drive reduction. Behavior potential, expectancy, reinforcement value, and the psychological situation are the four basic descriptive variables.

From this point of view, the patient's maladjustment does not lie within him, but in his relationship to the social environment. Potentially, the problem can be approached both through changes in the patient's attitudes and behavior and through changes in the attitudes and behavior of the people around him. This emphasis leads to implications regarding the treatment of other individuals in the patient's environment, such as the teacher, parents, wives, husbands, etc. In individual face-to-face psychotherapy with adults, there is an increased emphasis on an understanding of the consequences of behavior, particularly so that delayed negative reinforcements or dissatisfaction and pain can be related to their logical source. There are also attempts to achieve insight into the origin of maladaptive behaviors. One implication of social-learning theory is that psychotherapy must include considerably more discussion of alternative methods of dealing with life's problems leading to the patient's trying out new behavioral solutions to his problems, including the development of "higher level" problem solving skills. Relatively less stress is placed on how the problems arose and the reduction of internal conflict through cartharsis and insight. The latter is considered important only as the understanding of origins and motivations helps the particular patient achieve a position where he is more willing and ready to change his own behavior. If the patient can be helped to see and try out new solutions in his daily living, then he can determine for himself which changes will provide him with more satisfaction in the long run. Although this view of therapy has not been extensively tested, a number of laboratory studies [Rotter, 115, chaps. 5, 6] have dealt with principles which appear to be logically related to the therapeutic methods.

A recent book of Phillips [98] describes an approach to psychotherapy rejecting Freud's depth theory and drawing on "conflict theory." Phillips places great importance on the role of the therapist in helping the patient to structure the assumptions implicit in his behavior and to resolve his own conflict through the investigation of alternative methods of behaving. Although differing from social-learning theory on many points, Phillips, like Rotter, has attempted to build psychotherapeutic implications out of a human learning model rather than to reinterpret other methods by loosely translating them into learning terms. Shaffer [124], Shaw [126], and Shoben [130] have also urged the greater application of human learning principles to psychotherapy and H. B. Pepinsky and P. N. Pepinsky [95] have more extensively applied an anxiety-drive model to counseling.

Group Psychotherapy

One of the consequences of World War II was that clinical psychologists in military settings were asked primarily because of lack of other personnel, to conduct group psychotherapy. Such groups were formed in prisons, convalescent centers, hospitals, and training centers. For the most part, these meetings were referred to as "gripe sessions"; more than anything else, it was assumed that if the patients could get rid of suppressed hostilities, express them, or talk them out, they would generally be less hostile to or more understanding of the authority demands of their situations. Although the success of these sessions has been questioned (some observers felt they did more to increase hostilities than to dissipate them), they served to introduce many clinical psychologists into the practice of group psychotherapy. Since World War II, they have continued to function rather broadly, working with both children and adults.

It is not possible to discuss here the great variety of techniques and concepts employed in group psychotherapy. In addition to the application of individual psychotherapy concepts such as Slavson's [132] application of psychoanalysis and Axline's [8] application of Rogers's methods to a group situation, concepts and techniques were borrowed from many sources. Moreno's [86] psychodrama technique and various derivatives of it are widely used, as well as principles of leadership and group interaction derived from sociology, social psychology, sociometry, and group dynamics.

Although the principles have not been clearly formulated, there has been an increasing trend to focus on group psychotherapy as a kind of therapy which provides special opportunities. The tendency is no longer to regard group therapy as a kind of mass situation with the same goals as individual psychotherapy. Rather it is regarded as a special situation where the patient has the opportunity to learn group norms, where he can be reinforced for social interest, and where he is able to learn about other's reactions to his own social behavior.

Psychotherapy and the Clinical Psychologist's Values

Although it is not customary, any general survey of psychotherapy should include reference to the values inherent in current practices. If the psychologist is to treat individuals, he must first decide what maladjustment and adjustment are. In other words, who should be treated, and what is the goal of treatment?

There is no logical or systematic way of determining the nature of maladjustment from theories of behavior. What behavior or which people we would call "maladjusted" or "adjusted" depends primarily upon value judgments (judgments of good and bad), at least at some level of theorizing. To state that something requires a value judgment is not to imply that it may be avoided. The clinical psychologist must make such a value judgment for himself. Do we consider as maladjusted the nonconformist who has few or no friends but writes excellent poetry, the man who is caught in the illegal act of putting a slug in the subway, the apparently self-accepting homosexual, or the patient in a mental hospital who, though confused from an outsider's point of view, seems to be happy and relaxed after years of hospitalization? Our answer will depend upon our basic value judgments on the nature of adjustment. Of course, there is an implication here that maladjustment represents more than a label. The judgment implies that someone should do something about it, that society or the clinical psychologist operating as an individual should make some attempt to change the person. Were we to assume that nobody should attempt to change someone else unless that person seeks the change, then we could get rid of the concept of maladjustment entirely and empty a large portion of our mental hospitals.

With some exceptions, psychologists (and certainly society in general) do believe that they have a responsibility to try to help people, or at least to help them discover that they would be better off with some changes. In addition to the people who seek psychological help, there are many others who would benefit from it, for example, the mother who is overprotecting her child; the person who is a danger to himself or to others; the only child, happy as the center of attention of indulgent parents and grandparents, who is heading for difficulties later in life; and the expressly miserable adult who is apparently convinced that his difficulties are physical and seeks no help of a psychological nature. If we equate maladjustment or the concept of maladjustment with the concept of those who need to be treated, helped, or changed, we must determine the kinds of behavior or people we would include in this category.

With the exception of Rogers and some of the followers of Adler, most clinical psychologists have avoided the problem of defining their own values. Instead, they rely on the concept of disease borrowed from medicine. By some ultimate criterion not made explicit, specific behaviors or constellations of behaviors are indications of disease, and anyone having a specific disease needs treatment. Therefore, we have the illnesses of the psychopath, immature personality, nervous disposition, psychotic, compulsive neurotic, and the rest. Diseases themselves are identified by authorities and may be found described in certain textbooks.

The importance of psychologists becoming more explicit about their values has been recently discussed by Jessor [54]. The three value concepts broadly conceived which appear to be *implicit* in the practice of psychotherapy might be called the "conformity approach," the "self-centered approach" and the "social-centered approach."

The conformity criteria for adjustment implies that a man should accept the values of his culture and that he is maladjusted when he fails to accept the mores, the goals, and the beliefs of his society. Although few clinical psychologists would admit to such a belief themselves, like others in our society,[3] they may frequently rely on conformity as the criterion of adjustment in the absence of other explicit value concepts.

The self-centered approach holds that the internal feelings of happiness, well-being, harmony, and freedom from pain and internal conflict are the criteria for adjustment. The person who feels more unhappy is more maladjusted, the behavior that results in the feeling of unhappiness or lack of well-being is the maladjusted behavior. The psychoanalytic and client-centered approaches to psychotherapy have emphasized these criteria by implication if not by overt statement.

The social-centered point of view stresses the social contribution of the person and his behavior. Does the person contribute to the welfare of others, to society as a whole? Does he fulfill some useful function in society? The same criterion can be applied to some specific behavior. Is it, in a broad sense, contributive to the society the person lives in? This was the emphasis of Alfred Adler and his concept of social interest. Adler [2] felt that the problem of treatment or psychotherapy was one of building social interest in the patient, and Sullivan [138] and Mowrer

[3] Mills [85] and Reisman [106] have described such conformity trends among American social scientists.

[89] have also by implication accepted the same value conception. Sullivan did this by relating adjustment to the ability to love others; Mowrer did so by relating adjustment to the acceptance of social responsibility.

Although these value concepts are more frequently complementary than incompatible, as good social scientists clinical psychologists still need to explore more thoroughly both their own value systems and the implications of these value systems for the practice of psychotherapy.

Research in Psychotherapy

Although many of the concepts and methods of clinical psychology have been borrowed from other disciplines, clinical psychologists have contributed the major effort and methodology to research on the effectiveness of psychotherapy and the nature of the process. The problems and limitations of this research have been described in the *Annual Review of Psychology* for 1960 [117] and in previous issues and in a recent symposium of the conference on psychotherapy published by the American Psychological Association [Rubenstein and Parloff, 120].

Such research on therapist variables, patient variables, process variables, treatment outcomes, and criteria for improvement is proceeding vigorously, and many dissertations which would have been concerned with projective tests in an earlier period now deal with some aspect of psychotherapy. Particularly favored are studies varying therapist characteristics and laboratory analogs to psychotherapy, since these areas of investigation are more amenable to inexpensive short-term research. In the latter category are studies of verbal conditioning, an application of Skinner's work on instrumental conditioning, recently reviewed by Krasner [69]. These investigators have been particularly effective in demonstrating possible subtle effects of therapist behavior.

Psychotherapy—Summary

Although most of the specific techniques used in psychotherapy stem from Freud, the general trend is toward the development of less time-consuming and presumably more efficient techniques and methods than classical psychoanalysis. The general over-all trend is toward less emphasis on investigation of the past and interpretation of symbolic manifestations of the unconscious and more emphasis on dealing with the present, using the patient's relationship to the therapist in therapy as a source of learning. More recently, there has been increased interest in conceiving of the patient's difficulties in terms of inadequate solution of problems. Sullivan and Rotter place particular emphasis—possibly derived originally from

Adler, Lewin, and Kantor—on viewing the patient's difficulty in terms of his relationships with others and seeing maladjustment as lying not necessarily so much inside the patient as in his relationship with others.

At any rate, it is clear that clinical psychologists are beginning to feel some security in this general area and to contribute ideas that are more strictly psychological in nature. They seem ready to tamper with some of the highly valued taboos that derive from Freudian psychoanalysis.

One of the striking aspects of most of the psychotherapeutic techniques in common usage is their relatively loose relationship to theory. Although two or more psychoanalytically oriented therapists can argue from the same theory, they can emerge with considerably different techniques. The situation is similar for the more nonanalytic approaches, as illustrated by the considerably different emphasis in treatment of Kelly and Rogers, both of whom start their theorizing from a somewhat extreme phenomenological point of view. Although learning theory and perception theory are likewise beginning to lead to formulations of new or revised techniques of psychotherapy, it is probably safe to say that none of the theories of the nature of personality and its development are at this time so carefully structured and systematized that their implications for psychotherapy may be regarded as purely logical deductions from the theory.

Many of the recent attempts to reconceptualize the variables of therapy appear to have little as a goal other than the justification of previously learned techniques by using more widely accepted psychological concepts. However, they are also beginning to lead to new methods. The reconceptualization itself in many cases has the salutary effect of suggesting methodology for the validation of the principles of psychotherapy, either directly with patients as subjects or through laboratory experiments which provide "near analogies" to the psychotherapeutic situation.

AN OVERVIEW

The field of clinical psychology has changed considerably in its short history, and it appears that the change itself has been rapidly accelerated since World War II. Changes reflect the effects of such broad cultural conditions as wars at home and abroad, economic conditions, the broad trends of professionalization in psychology as a whole, the degree of interest of the university in training for a relatively new profession, and the kind of support government is giving the university. The issue of whether or not clinical psychologists are primarily practitioners or scholars and researchers is still an open one. The development of the profession also reflects the changing culture concepts regarding education, psychological disorders, and treatment.

It appears to this writer that psychiatry and psychoanalysis and its schools have played a much heavier role than traditional psychology in providing the practicing clinical psychologist with his conceptual tools. It should be remembered, however, that the university has been interested in training clinical psychologists only for a very short period of time. Prior to World War II, except for work in intelligence testing, the university provided the clinical psychologist with very little training for the practical jobs he was to do. Since he obtained his training in the clinical setting, he assimilated also the concepts of the people who had been working in that setting for a longer period of time.

The contributions of experimental and theoretical psychology, however, have not been negligible. The work in psychophysics has contributed heavily to the development of testing procedures and methods of measurement—for the more standardized tests in particular. The gestalt work in perception was a major source of theory and research in the development of tests for brain damage and also exerted a strong influence in the development of some of the projective techniques. More recently psychologists have been going both to learning theory and to perception theory to find a logical or sounder theoretical basis for their personality theories and psychotherapeutic techniques. Particularly promising is the fact that they are beginning not merely to look for justification for techniques and theories which have been previously accepted on an authoritative and subjective basis but also to derive new methods of treatment and new concepts from preexisting theory and research.

We have not discussed in any detail the actual established validity of the clinical psychologist's practices in the field of intelligence testing, diagnosis, and psychotherapy. In the latter two fields, it is hard to establish what this may be, but attempts to validate instruments in common use, for the most part, have been only slightly successful. Experimentally established validities—when they occur—are generally at such a low level as to hardly warrant their use in individual predictions. As for the field of psychotherapy, research itself has been so difficult that there are available neither sufficient data as to its effectiveness, nor established principles which have been tested independently in the laboratory and which can be logically and confidently applied to the complex psychotherapeutic situation.

The over-all picture, however, is not necessarily discouraging. To some extent, progress has been limited by the inadequacy of the constructs or conceptual tools with which the clinical psychologist has been working in the past and only recently has begun to challenge. New conceptual tools may bring new methods, and both may bring higher validities and greater utility. In any case, the more thorough training now required of clinical psychologists and some of the recent attempts to carry basic theory and research into the area of application under complex conditions may hold considerable promise for the future.

REFERENCES

1. Adler, A. *Guiding the child on the principles of individual psychology.* New York: Greenberg, 1930.
2. Adler, A. *Social interest: a challenge to mankind.* New York: Putnam, 1939.
3. Alexander, F., & French, T. M. *Psychoanalytic therapy.* New York: Ronald, 1946.
4. Allen, F. *Psychotherapy with children.* New York: Norton, 1942.
5. Allport, G. W. *Personality: a psychological interpretation.* New York: Holt, Rinehart, & Winston, 1937.
6. Anastasi, Anne. Heredity, environment and the question "how?" *Psychol. Rev.,* 1958, **65,** 197–208.
7. Ansbacher, H. L. "Neo Freudian" or "Neo Adlerian"? Report on a survey conducted among members of the American Psychoanalytic Association. *Amer. Psychologist,* 1953, **8,** 165–166.
8. Axline, V. *Play therapy.* Boston: Houghton Mifflin, 1947.
9. Axline, V. Mental deficiency—symptom or disease? *J. consult. Psychol.,* 1949, **13,** 313–327.
10. Babcock, H. *Time and the mind.* Cambridge, Mass.: Sci-Art, 1941.
11. Bayley, Nancy. On the growth of intelligence. *Amer. Psychologist,* 1955, **10,** 805–818.
12. Bender, L. A visual motor gestalt test and its clinical use. *Res. Monogr. Amer. Orthopsychiat. Ass.,* 1938, No. 3.
13. Bender, L., & Woltmann, A. Use of puppet shows as a therapeutic method. *Amer. J. Orthopsychiat.,* 1936, **6,** 341–354.
14. Bijou, S. W. Behavior efficiency as a determining factor in the social adjustment of mentally retarded young men. *J. genet. Psychol.,* 1944, **65,** 133–145.
15. Bijou, S. W. *The psychological program in AAF convalescent hospitals.* U.S. Army Air Force Aviation Psychology Program Research Reports, 1947, No. 15.
16. Blum, G. S. A study of the psychoanalytic theory of psychosexual development. *Genet. Psychol. Monogr.,* 1949, **39,** 3–99.
17. Bolles, M. M., Rosen, G. P., & Landis, C. Psychological performance tests as prognostic agents for the efficacy of insulin therapy in schizophrenia. *Psychiat. quart.,* 1938, **12,** 733–737.
18. Brenman, M., & Gill, M. M. *Hypnotherapy.* New York: Josiah Macy, Jr. Foundation, 1944.
19. Bronner, A. F., Healy, W., Lowe, G. C., & Shimberg, M. E. *A manual of individual mental tests and testing.* Boston: Little, Brown, 1927.
20. Butler, J. M. The use of a psychological model in personality testing. *Educ. psychol. Measmt.,* 1954, **14,** 77–89.

21. Cattell, R. B. *Personality: a systematic theoretical and factual study.* New York: McGraw-Hill, 1950.
22. Cronbach, L. J., & Meehl, P. E. Construct validity in psychological tests. *Psychol. Bull.,* 1955, **52**, 281–302.
23. Dollard, J., & Miller, N. E. *Personality and psychotherapy: an analysis in terms of learning, thinking, and culture.* New York: McGraw-Hill, 1950.
24. Edwards, A. *Personal preference schedule.* New York: Psychological Corp., 1954.
25. Eells, K., Davis, A., Havighurst, R. J., Herrick, E., & Tyler, R. *Intelligence and cultural differences.* Chicago: Univer. Chicago Press, 1951.
26. Escalona, S. K. *An application of the level of aspiration experiment to the study of personality.* New York: Teachers Coll., Columbia Univer., Bureau of Publications, 1948.
27. Frank, L. K. Projective methods for the study of personality. *J. Psychol.,* 1939, **8**, 389–413.
28. Fromm, E. *Man for himself.* New York: Holt, Rinehart, & Winston, 1947.
29. Galton, F., *Inquiries into human faculty and its development.* New York: Dutton, 1907.
30. Garfield, S. L. *Introductory clinical psychology.* New York: Macmillan, 1957.
31. Gibby, R. G., Miller, D. R., & Walker, E. L. The examiner's influence on the Rorschach protocol. *J. consult. Psychol.,* 1953, **17**, 425–428.
32. Goldstein, K. The significance of the frontal lobe for mental performance. *J. neurol. Psychopath.,* 1936, **17**, 27–40.
33. Goldstein, K. *The organism.* New York: American Book, 1939.
34. Goldstein, K., & Sheerer, M. Abstract and concrete behavior: an experimental study with special tests. *Psychol. Monogr.,* 1941, **33**, No. 239.
35. Goodenough, F. *Measurement of intelligence by drawing.* Yonkers, N.Y.: World, 1926.
36. Gordon, L. V. *Gordon personal profile.* Yonkers, N.Y.: World, 1951.
37. Graham, F. K., & Kendall, B. S. Performance of brain damaged cases on a memory-for-designs test. *J. abnorm. soc. Psychol.,* 1946, **41**, 303–314.
38. Guilford, J. P., & Martin, H. G. *The Guilford-Martin Personnel Inventory.* Beverly Hills, Calif.: Sheridan Supply Co., 1943.
39. Halstead, W. C. Preliminary analysis of grouping behavior in patients with cerebral injury. *Amer. J. Psychiat.,* 1940, **96**, 1263–1294.
40. Hanfmann, E., & Kasanin, J. Conceptual thinking in schizophrenia. *Nerv. Ment. Dis. Monogr.,* 1942, No. 67.
41. Harlow, H. F. The formation of learning sets. *Psychol. Rev.,* 1949, **56**, 51–65.
42. Harrison, R. The thematic apperception and Rorschach methods of personality investigation in clinical practice. *J. Psychol.,* 1943, **15**, 49–74.

43. Harrower-Erikson, M. R. Personality changes accompanying cerebral lesions. I. Rorschach studies of patients with cerebral tumors. *Arch. Neurol. Psychiat.*, 1940, **43**, 859–890.
44. Hathaway, S. R. *The Minnesota Multiphasic Personality Inventory.* Minneapolis, Minn.: Univer. Minn. Press, 1943.
45. Head, H. *Aphasia and kindred speech disorders.* Vols. I & II. New York: Macmillan, 1926.
46. Henry, E. M., & Rotter, J. B. Situational influences on Rorschach responses. *J. consult. Psychol.*, 1956, **20**, 457–462.
47. Horney, K. *New ways in psychoanalysis.* New York: Norton, 1939.
48. Humm, D. G., & Wadsworth, G. W. The Humm-Wadsworth temperament scale. *Personnel J.*, 1934, **12**, 314–323.
49. Hunt, H. F. *The Hunt-Minnesota Test For Organic Brain Damage.* Minneapolis, Minn.: Univer. Minn. Press, 1943.
50. Hunt, J. McV. *Personality and the behavior disorders.* Vols. I & II. New York: Ronald, 1944.
51. Jackson, J. H. *Selected writing of Hughlings Jackson.* James Taylor (Ed.). London: Hodder, 1932.
52. Jastak, J. School test patterns of clinic children. *Del. State med. J.,* 1939, **11**, 114–119.
53. Jessor, R. Phenomenological personality theories and the data language of psychology. *Psychol. Rev.*, 1956, **63**, 173–180.
54. Jessor, R. Social values and psychotherapy. *J. consult. Psychol.*, 1956, **20**, 264–266.
55. Jessor, R., & Hammond, K. R. Construct validity and the Taylor Anxiety Scale. *Psychol. Bull.*, 1957, **54**, 161–170.
56. Johnson, W. *People in quandaries.* New York: Harper, 1946.
57. Jung, C. G. *Psychological types.* New York: Harcourt, Brace, 1923.
58. Jung, C. G. *Modern man in search of a soul.* New York: Harcourt, Brace, 1933.
59. Kantor, J. R. *Principles of psychology.* Vols. I & II. New York: Knopf, 1924.
60. Kardiner, A. *The psychological frontiers of society.* New York: Columbia Univer. Press, 1945.
61. Kelly, E. L., & Fiske, D. W. *The prediction of performance in clinical psychology.* Ann Arbor, Mich.: Univer. Mich. Press, 1951.
62. Kelly, G. A. *The psychology of personal constructs.* Vols. I & II. New York: Norton, 1955.
63. Kent, G. H., & Rosanoff, A. J. A study of association in insanity. *Amer. J. Insanity,* 1910, **67**, 37–126.
64. Kleist, K. Gehirnpathologische und lokalisatorische Ergebnisse uber Horstrorungen. Gerquschtaubheiten und Anusion. *Mach. f. Psychiat. u. Neuro.,* 1928, **68**, 853–860.
65. Klineberg, O. Cultural factors in intelligence test performance. *J. Negro Educ.,* 1934, **3**, 478–483.
66. Klopfer, B., Ainsworth, M. D., Klopfer, W. G., & Holt, R. R. *Developments in the Rorschach Technique.* Yonkers, N.Y.: World, 1954.

67. Korzybski, A. *Science and sanity.* (2nd ed.) New York: International Non-Aristotelian Library, 1941.
68. Kraepelin, E. *Lectures on clinical psychiatry.* London: Baillière, 1913.
69. Krasner, L. Studies of the conditioning of verbal behavior. *Psychol. Bull.,* 1958, **55**, 148–170.
70. Kretschmer, E. *Physique and character.* London: Routledge, 1925.
71. Krugman, M. Out of the inkwell: the Rorschach method. *Charact. & Pers.,* 1940, **9**, 91–110.
72. Lashley, K. S. *Brain mechanisms and intelligence: a quantitative study of injuries to the brain.* Chicago: Univer. Chicago Press, 1929.
73. Lecky, P. *Self-consistency; a theory of personality.* New York: Island Press Co-operative, Inc., 1945.
74. Levy, D. Trends in therapy—release therapy. *Amer. J. Orthopsychiat.,* 1939, **9**, 713–736.
75. Lewin, K. *A dynamic theory of personality.* New York: McGraw-Hill, 1935.
76. Liverant, S. The use of Rotter's social learning theory in the development of a personality inventory. *Psychol. Monogr.,* 1958, **72** (Whole No. 445).
77. Liverant, S. Intelligence: a concept in need of re-examination. *J. consult. Psychol.* 1960, **24**, 101–110.
78. Lord, E. E. Experimentally induced variations in Rorschach performance. *Psychol. Monogr.,* 1950, **64**, No. 10.
79. Louttit, C. M. *Clinical psychology.* New York: Harper, 1936.
80. Louttit, C. M. The nature of clinical psychology. *Psychol. Bull.,* 1939, **36**, 361–389.
81. Louttit, C. M. *Clinical psychology of exceptional children.* New York: Harper, 1957.
82. Masling, J. The influence of situational and interpersonal variables in projective testing. *Psychol. Bull.,* 1960, **57**, 65–85.
83. May, R., Angel, E., & Ellenberger, H. F. (Eds.) *Existence.* New York: Basic Books, 1958.
84. Meehl, P. E. *Clinical vs. statistical prediction.* Minneapolis, Minn.: Univer. Minn. Press, 1954.
85. Mills, C. W. *White collar: the American middle class.* New York: Oxford, 1951.
86. Moreno, J. L. Psychodrama and psychopathology of interpersonal relations. *Psychodrama Monogr.,* 1945, No. 16.
87. Morgan, D., & Murray, H. A. A method for investigating phantasies: the Thematic Apperception Test. *Arch. Neurol. Psychiat.* 1935, **34**, 289–306.
88. Mowrer, O. H. *Learning theory and personality dynamics.* New York: Ronald, 1950.
89. Mowrer, O. H. (Ed.) *Psychotherapy: theory and research.* New York: McGraw-Hill, 1953.
90. Murray, H. A. Techniques for a systematic investigation of fantasy. *J. Psychol.,* 1937, **3**, 115–145.

91. Murray, H. A. Toward a theory of interaction. In T. Parsons & E. A. Shils (Eds.), *Toward a general theory of action*. Cambridge, Mass.: Harvard Univer. Press, 1952.

92. Mussen, P. H., & Scodel, A. The effects of sexual stimulation under varying conditions on TAT sexual responsiveness. *J. consult. Psychol.*, 1955, **19**, 90.

93. Peak, Helen. Problems of objective observation. In L. Festinger & D. Katz (Eds.), *Research methods in the behavioral sciences*. New York: Dryden, 1953.

94. Pennington, L. A., & Berg, I. A. (Eds.) *An introduction to clinical psychology*. (2nd ed.) New York: Ronald, 1954.

95. Pepinsky, H. B., & Pepinsky, P. N. *Counseling theory and practice*. New York: Ronald, 1954.

96. Peterson, J. *Early conceptions and tests of intelligence*. Yonkers, N.Y.: World, 1925.

97. Phares, E. J., & Rotter, J. B. An effect of the situation on psychological testing. *J. consult. Psychol.* 1956, **20**, 291–293.

98. Phillips, E. L. *Psychotherapy: a modern theory and practice*. Englewood Cliffs, N.J.: Prentice-Hall, 1956.

99. Pintner, R., & Paterson, D. *A scale of performance tests*. New York: Appleton-Century-Crofts, 1917.

100. Piotrowski, Z. A. The Rorschach ink-blot method in organic disturbances of the central nervous system. *J. nerv. ment. Dis.* 1937, **86**, 525–537.

101. Pressey, S. L. A group scale for investigating the emotions. *J. abnorm. soc. Psychol.*, 1921, **16**, 55–64.

102. Rabin, A. I., & Guertin, W. H. Research with the Wechsler-Bellevue test, 1945–1950. *Psychol. Bull.*, 1951, **48**, 211–248.

103. Raimy, V. C. Self reference in counseling interviews. *J. consult. Psychol.* 1948, **12**, 153–163.

104. Raimy, V. C. (Ed.) *Training in clinical psychology*. Englewood Cliffs, N.J.: Prentice-Hall, 1950.

105. Rank, O. *Will therapy*. New York: Knopf, 1936.

106. Reisman, D. *Individualism reconsidered*. Glencoe, Ill.: Free Press, 1954.

107. Roe, A., & Shakow, D. Intelligence in mental disorder. *Ann. N.Y. Acad. Sci.*, 1942, **12**, 361–390.

108. Rogers, C. R. *Counseling and psychotherapy*. Boston: Houghton Mifflin, 1951.

109. Rogers, C. R. *Client-centered therapy, its current practice, implications, and theory*. Boston: Houghton Mifflin, 1951.

110. Rogers, C. R. A process conception of psychotherapy. *Amer. Psychologist*, 1958, **13**, 142–149.

111. Rorschach, H. *Psychodiagnostics*. W. Morganthaler (Ed.). New York: Grune & Stratton, 1942.

112. Rosanoff, A. J. *Manual of psychiatry and mental hygiene*. (7th ed.) New York: Wiley, 1938.

113. Rosenzweig, S. The picture association and its application in a study of reaction to frustration. *J. Pers.*, 1945, **14**, 3–23.

114. Rotter, J. B. Level of aspiration as a method of studying personality. II. Development and evaluation of a controlled method. *J. exp. Psychol.*, 1942, **31**, 410–422.

115. Rotter, J. B. *Social learning and clinical psychology.* Englewood Cliffs, N.J.: Prentice-Hall, 1954.

116. Rotter, J. B. The role of the psychological situation in determining the direction of human behavior. In M. R. Jones (Ed.), *Nebraska symposium on motivation.* Lincoln, Neb.: Univer. Neb. Press, 1955.

117. Rotter, J. B. Psychotherapy. In P. R. Farnsworth & Q. McNemar (Eds.), *Ann. Rev. Psychol.*, **11**, Palo Alto, Calif.: Annual Review Inc., 1960, 381–414.

118. Rotter, J. B. Some implications of a social learning theory for the prediction of goal directed behavior from testing procedures. *Psychol. Rev.*, 1960, **67**, 301–316.

119. Rotter, J. B., & Rafferty, J. E. *Manual for the Rotter Incomplete Sentences Blank, college form.* New York: Psychological Corp., 1950.

120. Rubenstein, E. A., & Parloff, M. B. (Eds.) *Research in psychotherapy.* Washington, D.C.: American Psychological Association, 1959.

121. Sarason, S. The test situation and the problem of prediction. *J. clin. Psychol.*, 1950, **6**, 387–392.

122. Schmidt, B. G. Changes in personal, social and intellectual behavior of children originally classified as feebleminded. *Psychol. Monogr.*, 1946, **60**, No. 5.

123. Schroder, H. M., & Rotter, J. B. Rigidity as learned behavior. *J. exp. Psychol.*, 1952, **44**, 141–150.

124. Shaffer, L. F. The problem of psychotherapy. *Amer. Psychologist*, 1947, **2**, 459–467.

125. Shakow, D. An internship year for psychologists (with special reference to psychiatric hospitals). *J. consult. Psychol.*, 1938, **2**, 73–76.

126. Shaw, F. J. Some postulates concerning psychotherapy. *J. consult. Psychol.*, 1948, **12**, 426–431.

127. Shaw, R. F. *Finger painting.* Boston: Little, Brown, 1934.

128. Sheldon, W. H. *The varieties of human physique: an introduction to constitutional psychology.* New York: Harper, 1940.

129. Sheldon, W. H. *The varieties of temperament: a psychology of constitutional differences.* New York: Harper, 1942.

130. Shoben, E. J. Some observations on psychotherapy and the learning process. In O. H. Mowrer (Ed.), *Psychotherapy: theory and research.* New York: Ronald, 1953.

131. Skeels, H. M. Some Iowa studies of the mental growth of children in relation to differentials of the environment: a summary. *The thirty-ninth yearbook of the National Society for the Study of Education. Intelligence: its nature and nurture.* Bloomington, Ill.: Public School, 1940.

132. Slavson, S. R. *An introduction to group therapy.* New York: Commonwealth Fund, 1943.
133. Solomon, J. C. Active play therapy. *Amer. J. Orthopsychiat.,* 1938, **8,** 479–498.
134. Sontag, L. W., Baker, C. T., & Nelson, Virginia L. Mental growth and personality development: a longitudinal study. *Monogr. Soc. Res. Child Develpm.,* 1958, **23,** No. 68.
135. Spearman, C. *The abilities of man.* New York: Macmillan, 1927.
136. Stern, W. *General psychology from the personalistic point of view.* New York: Macmillan, 1938.
137. Stoddard, G. D. *The meaning of intelligence.* New York: Macmillan, 1943.
138. Sullivan, H. S. *The interpersonal theory of psychiatry.* New York: Norton, 1953.
139. Symonds, P. M. *Diagnosing personality and conduct.* New York: Appleton-Century-Crofts, 1931.
140. Taft, J. *The dynamics of therapy.* New York: Macmillan, 1933.
141. Terman, L. M. *The measurement of intelligence.* Boston: Houghton Mifflin, 1916.
142. Thomas, W. I. *Social behavior and personality.* E. H. Volkert (Ed.). New York: Social Science Research Council, 1951.
143. Thorndike, E. L., et al. *The measurement of intelligence.* New York: Teachers Coll., Columbia Univer., Bureau of Publications, 1927.
144. Thurstone, L. L. *The nature of intelligence.* New York: Harcourt, Brace, 1926.
145. Wallen, R. W. *Clinical psychology.* New York: McGraw-Hill, 1956.
146. Wechsler, D. *The Wechsler Memory Scale.* New York: Psychological Corp., 1945.
147. Wechsler, D. *Wechsler Intelligence Scale for Children.* New York: Psychological Corp., 1949.
148. Wechsler, D. *Manual for the Wechsler Adult Intelligence Scale.* New York: Psychological Corp., 1955.
149. Weisenberg, T., & McBride, K. E. *Aphasia.* New York: Commonwealth Fund, 1935.
150. Wells, F. L. *Mental tests in clinical practice.* Yonkers, N.Y.: World, 1927.
151. Whipple, G. M. *Manual of mental and physical tests.* Baltimore, Md.: Warwick and York, 1910.
152. Wittenborn, J. R. Symptom patterns in a group of mental hospital patients. *J. consult. Psychol.,* 1951, **15,** 290–302.
153. Woodworth, R. J. *Contemporary schools of psychology.* New York: Ronald, 1931.
154. Zilboorg, G., & Henry, G. W. *A history of medical psychology.* New York: Norton, 1941.

HUMAN ENGINEERING AND PSYCHOLOGY

FRANKLIN V. TAYLOR[1]
Engineering Psychology Branch
Applications Research Division
U.S. Naval Research Laboratory

I. The Field of Human Engineering 833

Introduction. 833

Definition 834

Engineering Psychology 837

Area 1. Display requirements—man as a receiver 838

Detectability 839

Identification 839

Area 2. Control requirements—man as an emitter 841

Force and time configurations of response 842

Efficiency of different responses 842

Area 3. Displays, controls, and system dynamics—man as an information

processor 843

Decision making 843

Continuous control 847

Area 4. Effects of continued performance and environmental stress on

data processing 848

Vigilance 848

Environmental stress 849

Area 5. Man-machine systems evaluation 850

Human Engineering Design 851

[1] The editor regretfully records Dr. Taylor's death on March 12, 1960. The manuscript for this essay was received in December, 1957. Other authors who had submitted early manuscripts had the opportunity to revise and update their contributions shortly before Study II went to press. Despite advances in the field of human engineering since this essay was completed, it will be evident that Dr. Taylor's brilliant organization of the field and his discussion of methodic underpinnings and relationships will long remain viable.

We are much indebted to Dr. George E. Briggs of The Ohio State University, who inserted recent references to update the manuscript and was also kind enough to read proof.

Equipment design 851
Human engineering guides 852
II. Interrelationships between Psychology and Human Engineering . . . 853
Goals 853
  Knowledge 854
  Actions 855
Subject Matter 856
  Component behavior. 856
    The human element 856
    Mechanical elements 859
    Comparison of human and mechanical elements 859
  System performance 859
Methology 860
  Engineering psychology 860
  Man-machine system technology 863
    Subsystems versus total systems 864
Variables. 865
  Area 4 866
  Area 5 866
    Independent variables 867
    Dependent variables 870
  Areas 1, 2, and 3 872
Concepts 874
  Two types of models 874
  Relationship between empirical and systematic variables 876
  Use of engineering models 877
III. Long-term Contributions of Human Engineering to Psychology . . . 879
Methods 879
Subject Matter 880
Concepts 880
  The system concept 880
  A continuous model of human behavior 883
  Scientific metalanguage 886
IV. Collaborative, Administrative, and Educational Mechanisms 888
A Unified Human Factors Approach 889
Administration of Human Engineering 891
  Training 892
  Technology 893
  Science 893
Education 895
  The two training programs 895
  The human factors core 896
References 897

I. The Field of Human Engineering

INTRODUCTION

"Human engineering" is a vague and imprecise name for a variety of activities relating to the adjustment of the human to his surroundings. At one time, although probably not originally [163], the term referred to the selection and training of men to take their proper place in industry and society. In a figurative sense, humans were "engineered" to fit their social and physical environment in order to make them happier and more productive. It also has a second, and entirely different, meaning. In the most frequently accepted current use, the term "human engineering" refers to efforts to design man's surroundings to accord with his capacities and limitations—the environment is "engineered" to fit the man. A still different usage combines both meanings; the term refers indiscriminately to the selection and training of men and the design of their environment. (To add to the confusion, there is by no means universal agreement as to the precise meaning of the word "environment.")

Some have sought to define the term in the broadest sense possible and to include attempts to change the form of a government or to alter the climate of a continent. Others have been somewhat more restrictive and have limited human engineering to activities devoted to modifying man's immediate physical environment in the effort to improve safety, comfort, or the general effectiveness of the man in his routine functions. Such usage would include research and development relating to food, clothing, heating, lighting, and housing as human engineering activities. The design of gas masks, body armor, space suits, and research in many areas of environmental medicine and industrial psychology would also be incorporated into human engineering under this definition.

Still others restrict the environment, which they regard as the fit object of human engineering modification, to machines with which men interact from time to time. For those who accept this restriction and do not include selection and training within the definition, human engineering becomes research and development aimed at the design of better man-operated equipment. The term will be used in this sense here.

In employing "human engineering" for this limited activity, we are helping to perpetuate a misnomer, for it is the machine—not the human—which one seeks to "engineer." The fundamental aims of this new discipline are no different from those of engineering proper; both seek to create better mechanisms. The difference, of course, lies in the extent to which the human's biological and psychological characteristics are taken into account. What is needed, but is not at hand, is a term which connotes in a neat fashion the emphatic human reference or human orientation of this new variety of engineering as it contrasts with the older and more conventional forms. Lacking such a happily descriptive term, however, one is forced to accept, although not necessarily condone, the use of "human engineering" for the discipline or portion thereof to be discussed in this study.

The justification for restricting this analysis to the design of machines, rather than the rest of the physical environment, is this: The preponderant effort has been directed to this circumscribed area, and we believe that this field of human engineering at the present time promises most in the way of eventual unification. Admittedly, this restriction excludes much interesting research and development which is often included by the current broad definitions of the field. Certainly, there is no intention to minimize the importance of this work, nor should the limitation on material be viewed as an attempt to preempt the term "human engineering" for a single aspect of the whole field. We simply feel that it is more profitable to limit the discussion to a segment of human engineering where the facts and principles are cohesive and where a start toward formalization has been made. In the same way, the exclusion of selection and training procedures from human engineering is based upon general current usage and the desire to retain manageability—not on any doubt of the validity and importance of those proven human factors approaches (see recommendations in Sec. IV). The reader should, however, constantly bear these restrictions in mind.

DEFINITION

Human engineering is one of the newest developments in applied psychology. It began during World War II when psychologists acquired an interest in the design of radars, sonars, fire control systems, aircraft displays and controls, and other similar devices. Hitherto, the design of mechanical or electronic equipment was the undisputed province of the engineer, and the contributions of the psychologist were confined to the conduct of research and giving advice on the selection and training of the operators. However, it very early became apparent that attempts to fit the man to the machine were not enough to cope with the multiplicity of mechanisms, the bewildering speed with which modified equipments succeeded one another, and the complexity of performance demanded of the human operators. Therefore, efforts were made by the psychologists to assist the engineers in improving their designs to reduce the operator load and the selection and training requirements, while at the same time enhancing the performance of the mechanisms. Sufficient success was achieved during the war to encourage the development of this endeavor on an expanding scale during the postwar years. Today, human engineering is a well-recognized and burgeoning activity.

Fundamental to this new field is the concept of the man-machine system, wherein the human operator and the mechanical device are both considered as elements in one over-all complex. In this view, the man is a highly flexible organic component inserted in series between mechanical or electronic elements in a single information-processing system. When the man is considered in this fashion, it immediately becomes obvious that, in order to design the mechanical components properly, his characteristics must be taken into full account. Human engineering seeks to do this. It may be defined as (1) the study of the behavioral properties of (*a*) man in interaction with machines, and (*b*) total man-machine systems; and (2) the structuring of the latter to enhance system performance.

This complex definition implies several things. First of all, it is evident that human engineering is more than psychology. Although it is fair to say that psychologists were instrumental in starting human engineering and played a major role in its development, it would be quite wrong to attempt to characterize the whole field as a psychological science. Rather, it is more correct to say that psychology is one of several disciplines which together make up human engineering. The fact that it deals with the behavior of both men and man-machine systems indicates at the outset that engineering and physical science are involved in the new discipline. Furthermore, very early in the development of man-oriented engineering, the psychologists and engineers were joined by physiologists, anatomists, and anthropologists, who were also interested in helping develop better human-operated equipment. Time-and-motion specialists, operations analysts, and, later, systems analysts also contributed concepts and methods.

Second, the definition given above makes it clear that human engineering has both scientific and technological aspects [30]. The study of the behavior of men or of systems is a scientific undertaking, whether it is done in a human engineering establishment or in academic surroundings. Human engineering research differs in no fudamental way from any other kind of research; its aim is understanding, its goal is knowledge. However, quite different from this is the attitude of the human engineering technologist who seeks to apply the knowledge which he or others have gained. His aim is the translation of scientific findings into electronic circuits and "black boxes" which will compensate for the human's limitations or complement his abilities in specific situations. He is primarily intent upon designing better performing man-machine systems, regardless of the scientific value of his developments. Generally, he seeks to achieve pragmatic results, and understanding has value only to the extent that it assists his practice.

This duality of goals can make for considerable confusion unless it is fully comprehended. In human engineering, it would be much less troublesome if this polarization in interests occurred between different subdisciplines rather than within any one. Thus, if the engineers were always the human engineering technologists and the psychologists sought only to contribute as research scientists, it would not be difficult to minimize the clash of the two somewhat incompatible viewpoints, and the analysis of the relationship between psychology and human engineering would be a simpler task.

As it is, however, the science-technology cleavage does not occur strictly along the boundaries between disciplines. Although it is true that the majority of engineers who interest themselves in human engineering cast their lot on the side of technology, not all of them do. Furthermore, many psychologists and, to a lesser extent, physiologists and other biologists who entered human engineering as research scientists have unconsciously or deliberately breached the attitudinal boundary between science and applied engineering; they have expanded their frames of reference to include the goals and many of the interests of the engineering technologist. In the early days of the close association, the members of each discipline served more or less within the confines of their own profession as classically defined; now the interdisciplinary distinctions have begun to blur, and some of each profession have begun to act less like themselves and more like those in other professions. Among the psychologists who consider themselves to be human engineers, some are still experimental psychologists in the traditional sense, others spend part of their time on research and part on application, and still others are full-time technologists, with attitudes and goals more typical of engineering than psychology.

Thus it is necessary to separate the aims, methods, and contributions of the psychologists by their roles—as research scientists or technologists. We shall use the term *engineering psychology* to describe the experimental research aspects of human engineering; the term *human engineering design* will be employed when we are referring to the non-experimental technological aspects of the subject, whether carried out by engineers or psychologists.

The fact that human engineering involves considerations of the man as a machine operator might lead to its classification as a branch of industrial psychology. Apart from the fact that human engineering includes more than psychology, as has already been mentioned, there can be no real objection to this so long as the differences between the approaches of human engineering and traditional industrial psychology are kept in mind. Industrial psychologists have usually concentrated upon the proper selection and training of operators and upon social factors. Human engineers, on the other hand, tend to leave the man alone and to redesign the machine. Industrial psychologists deal with the wide variety of repetitive tasks found in modern industry; human engineers customarily work with tasks such as controlling, monitoring, and decision making, which require a high information-transmission rate. Finally, industrial psychology tends to be operator-oriented, whereas human engineering is oriented to the man-machine system.

This last fact emphasizes the important point that—whatever else it may be considered to be—human engineering is most certainly a part of the new subject of "systems research and design." A good case can be presented for the statement that human engineering is actually the best developed field in a "systems" domain which covers not only man-machine systems, but man-man and machine-machine systems as well. This broad new area of research, enlisting investigators and theorists from the biological, psychological, physical, and engineering sciences, seeks for general principles relating to the combination of elements within an interacting complex. However, with the exception of the work on man-machine systems, too little effort has been devoted to the systems field to warrant an evaluation at the present time.

ENGINEERING PSYCHOLOGY

The current experimental research in human engineering can be classified fairly neatly into five categories. Four represent research domains which are organized around the central concept of the man as an information-processing link in a man-machine system. The fifth category contains all engineering psychology studies carried out with the intent of evaluating existing systems or system components.

The idea of the man as an information channel arises naturally from a consideration of the human's role in operating a mechanism such as a gun-aiming system. Information concerning the location of the target relative to the position of the gun is presented to the operator on some variety of display. He reads off this information, processes it in some way so as to reach decisions as to what to do, and makes appropriate responses by applying force to one or another type of control. Since the target is moving, the operator must carry out these processes continuously so that the system will follow.

In other types of devices, the man performs similar functions. In piloting a plane, listening on sonar, controlling the depth of a submarine, operating a radar, plotting the position of targets, navigating a ship, or monitoring instruments in a control room, the operator takes in information, processes it, and emits it in the form of some response either continuously or in occasional bursts. Operator behavior, then, can be described as the reception, processing, and emission of information. The relative importance of the three functions, of course, varies from task to task, and there are many situations in daily life where one or even two of them may drop out for extended periods of time. This, however, in no way diminishes the general usefulness of the concepts as foci of research in engineering psychology.

The practical contributions of human engineering are achieved when the mechanical portions of a man-machine system are designed to fit in with operator requirements as they relate to the transmission of information through the human link. First of all, the displays, controls, and dynamic properties of the system must be designed to set the proper task. In addition, they must be built to optimize his performance in extracting information from the machine, processing it, and reinserting it into the mechanism. A large part of engineering psychology consists of research aimed at discovering the principal factors involved in achieving these optimizations. Studies may be grouped naturally into three clusters: (1) display requirements in relation to the human as a receiver, (2) control requirements relative to man as an emitter, and (3) displays, controls, and system dynamics as related to the operator, who is considered as an information-processing device. A fourth research area completes the coverage of engineering psychology not involving system evaluations. This consists of work on the effects of fatigue, vigilance, and environmental stress upon the transmission properties of the human operator.

Area 1. Display Requirements—Man as a Receiver

The studies falling under this heading deal with the problem of transferring information from the machine into the man. Here the attention is on factors making for a good man-machine information couple rather than upon the meaning, appropriateness, or relevancy of the information transferred from the machine to the human.

Although these studies deal primarily with sensory processes, it should be recognized that motor responses are also frequently involved. Reading displays, for example, usually requires eye movements, and tactual and kinesthetic information concerning the location and status of a control can be obtained only through making reaching and grasping responses. Thus, considering the man as an information receiver is not tantamount to regarding him as a passive sensing device. Rather, the research in this area of engineering psychology deals with sensorimotor processes, but only those in which the primary function is the extraction of information from the mechanical portions of the man-machine system.

At the very outset, then, one may note a difference in breakdown between engineering psychology and traditional experimental psychology. Whereas classically the sensory processes are regarded as a field of research apart from response, the two are much more intimately linked in engineering psychology. Not only is it true that both sensory and motor processes are involved in receiving information from the environment, but the same is equally true when we turn to consider human information processing and emission. In all human engineering research, it appears more fruitful to consider the operator from the point of view of the totality of his various processes rather than taking these processes piecemeal, as is often done in experimental psychology.

The research on the receiver characteristics of the man divides conveniently into two topics, detectability and identification. Several research clusters may be distinguished under both.

Detectability. A considerable amount of effort has been devoted to experimentation on the factors which are important in the detection of radar and sonar echoes on cathode ray displays [60, 139]. In some instances, the tests have been conducted with simulated targets appearing against uniform backgrounds. In these cases, the detection problem involves only the sensing of the presence of a stimulus. Other tests have required the operator to detect the target against a pattern of random brightness variations on the tube face, representing real or simulated radar noise. Under these conditions, signal detection involves not only the factor of visibility, but pattern discrimination as well. The effects on detectability of variations in target size, brightness, and contrast produced by alterations in a variety of radar parameters have been more or less systematically explored, as have the effects of variables such as viewing distance and angle, scope size, visual search area, target location, and level of ambient illumination. Theoretical models have been developed for the human detection process, and a recent report by Swets, Tanner, and Birdsall [167] provides a clear introduction to this work.

Several studies relevant to the auditory detection of sonar echoes have been carried out, although not many have been reported in the psychological literature. Detectability has been studied relative to signal duration [139, p. 224], monaural versus binaural listening [158; 164, pp. 87, 141–142], interaural phase relations [91, 92, 93], and to the presence or absence of a coincident visual signal [154].

Identification. The detection of a target requires only the discrimination of the presence or absence of an information-carrying signal against either a uniform or randomly distributed energy background.

Identification, however, requires the extraction of further information from the spatial or temporal pattern of the stimuli presented in addition.

Visual pattern recognition. Employing figures constructed by rule, investigations have been made of stimulus variables which are important in the perception, identification, and recall of visual patterns of the type which might appear upon radar or television screens [1, 3, 5, 63]. Such factors as orientation, symmetry, and degree of randomness are considered, and recent work emphasizes the importance of quantitative specification of pattern shapes.

Perception of velocity and acceleration. Many of the tasks encountered in human engineering require that the operator respond not only to the location of a target, but also to the manner in which its position is changing. Therefore, studies have been undertaken on the subject's ability to perceive velocity and the rate of change of velocity under a variety of conditions [32, 79].

Legibility. The factors underlying the legibility of numbers, letters, and display indicators have been extensively studied by engineering psychologists. Reviews of these studies are to be found in several reference works [35, 60, 139]. Among others, the following variables have been investigated: the size and form of numerals and letters; foreground and background color and brightness; the nature of illumination and the effects of glare; the viewing angle and distance; the spacing between letters; the size and shape of displays; the size, number, and spacing of scale marks; the shape and size of indicator pointers; and the configuration of reference grids and overlays. Many of these factors have been found to interact, and different recommendations sometimes result when performance criteria are altered.

Multidimensional cues. Information can be displayed to the operator through variations along a single stimulus dimension, such as hue, or through altering the stimulus in several dimensions, such as hue brightness and saturation. Recently, several experiments have been carried out on the effects of compounding stimulus dimensions on such tasks as the location of items in a display, learning to assign arbitrary labels to visual forms, and the absolute judgment of stimuli. The effects of compounding dimensions appear to depend upon the nature of the subject's task [58], although more information is generally transmitted to the human through multicoordinate than single coordinate displays [142].

Warning signals. To be effective, a warning signal must intrude into whatever task the operator is performing and elicit immediate attention. Studies have been undertaken [77, 160] to determine the attentional value of various types of warning lights which vary in their color, location, and flash rate.

The discrimination of auditory, tactual, and kinesthetic cues. The human operator receives information relevant to the control of machines through sense modalities other than vision. Consequently, some attention has been paid by human engineers to auditory, tactual, and kinesthetic discriminations as they apply to human engineering. One practical problem involving hearing which was extensively investigated during the war centered on the pilot's ability to maintain aircraft heading under the guidance furnished by radio range signals [65]. These were so presented that the pilot heard a steady tone in his earphones when the plane was in the center of the flight path, but the signal changed into a Morse code A or N when he deviated too far to one side or the other. The ability of subjects to make the required auditory discrimination was studied with varying factors, such as type of earphone, signal intensity, signal-to-noise ratio, auditory signal pattern, and presence or absence of selective filters.

Investigations of the tactual-kinesthetic appreciation of shape have been conducted with reference to obtaining easily distinguished knobs for control handles [100]. The ability of the operator to discriminate forces and displacements which he applies to a control column has also been studied [99; 121, chap. 11] with a view to recommending the best means of providing "artificial feel" for the controls of modern high-speed aircraft.

The hearing of speech. The field of speech communications is a large and important area of research in its own right [114], involving many considerations other than those of human engineering. Nevertheless, much research in this area may be classified as engineering psychology, as it has led to recommendations for the design of electronic speech-filtering networks, earphones, annunciators, and others.

Area 2. Control Requirements—Man as an Emitter

By applying force to handwheels, levers, switches, control columns, and other controls, the human inserts informational signals into the machine which he is operating. The nature of these emitted signals depends to some extent upon the part of the body supplying the force and the characteristics of the control used. Research here is directed toward discovering how the operator configures his responses and how response efficiency is altered by variations in control parameters and changes in the type of control. The aim is to recommend control design which will assure the optimum transmission of information from the man into the machine.

The manipulation of controls is not to be regarded as a purely motor process any more than the reception of information is entirely a matter of sensing. All human responses involve proprioceptive feedback; many controlling actions are cued exteroceptively as well—when the operator relies upon vision to guide him in grasping one control after releasing another, for example. Thus we repeat that human engineering research almost invariably deals with behavioral processes which involve all parts of the affector–central-nervous-system–effector loop to an important extent, even though the different research domains emphasize different functional aspects of the total activity.

Force and time configurations of response. Investigations of the manner in which operators apply and remove force when moving a control have been carried out for a variety of conditions [60]. The temporal pattern of the control displacements has been recorded; in at least one study [171], actual velocities, accelerations, and rates of change of acceleration were obtained directly. In all of the studies, the amplitude of the required movements was altered, although the experiments have differed in the way the information concerning the appropriateness of the response has been fed back to the operator.

Sequential responses, such as those required by many industrial tasks, have also been timed by a variety of means. The earlier work which was carried out by time-and-motion engineers led to the conclusion that the different components of a sequential operation were independent of one another [13]. However, recent experiments [85], some of which have not reached publication, suggest that this conclusion is open to question for at least some types of tasks.

Sometimes minor alterations in equipment will effect important changes in the speed of performing a sequential response. It has been shown that the addition of reference dots centered within each of the 10 finger holes on a modern dial telephone speeds up the dialing of a seven-digit number by 0.5 second.[2] Although it is only a 5 per cent saving, it represents a staggering figure when it is applied to all calls made in a single day.

Efficiency of different responses. Considerable attention has been devoted by engineering psychologists to the effectiveness with which different types of responses can be made by subjects working with a wide variety of controls. The tasks studied have included reaching for controls without the use of vision [59]; cranking handwheels of different diameters in different positions and orientations against varying amounts of friction and inertia [89, 144, 145, 146]; rapid movements with different body members [60, pp. 1319–1326]; slow and quick straight-line displacements of light controls in different directions relative to the body and joints of the limb [60, pp. 1331–1333]; and patterned control column movements with varying amounts of spring centering, viscous damping, and inertia [6, 7]. A variety of performance criteria have been employed included smoothness of force application, amount of oscillation upon ter-

---

[2] Verbal communication with John Karlin, Bell Telephone Laboratories, Murray Hill, N.J.

mination of a movement, maximal and average force exerted, maximal frequency of oscillatory movements, speed of response, and accuracy of movement. In one recent study [61] employing reciprocal tapping and disk and pin transfer between two positions, the capacity of the human response system has been assessed in terms derived from information theory.

Area 3. Displays, Controls, and System Dynamics—Man as an Information Processor

Studies previously described have centered on the problems involved in getting information from the machine into the man or from the man into the machine; studies to be dealt with under this rubric involve information processing on the part of the man himself. Here we are concerned with what the operator must do to transform the data he receives from his displays into appropriate responses. Consequently, experiments emphasize the manner in which the displayed information is coded, the nature and complexity of what must be done with it, and the relevance of the response to the processing task required. In this category, the meaningfulness of a display is taken into consideration. The relative merits of control actions are also considered in relation to the particular sequence of events which lead to these actions.

The work falls into two broad classes—one centers on discrete decision-making tasks, the other on continuous data processing such as that required when the operator acts as an element in a tracking or control loop. Some research in both areas is directed toward specifying the characteristics of the data-transformation process itself; other investigations are more concerned with the influence of display and control factors on the complexity of this process.

Decision making. *Capacity.* A very simple variety of decision making is encountered in reaction-time studies. There has recently been a revival in interest in this classical field of research stimulated by information theory and nourished by the hope that reaction-time measures will provide psychologists with an index of the human's capacity to transmit information. Earlier studies have been reviewed in the new context, and numerous experiments have recently been devised and performed wherein quantitative information measures have been applied [2, 135, 148]. Welford [183] has provided a detailed discussion of such measurement in relatively simple skill tasks. Although many of the recent investigations have utilized the disjunctive reaction-time experiment in its standard form, others have employed tachistoscopic presentations [104], serial reaction times [105] and card-sorting techniques [46, 110] as methods for obtaining their basic data. Still others [148, pp. 341–349] have dispensed with controlled experimentation almost entirely and substituted the observation of highly practiced sequential psychomotor skills as a basis for making determinations of human channel capacity.

Other reaction-time research projects involve the much contested "psychological refractory phase" [182]. A number of findings suggest that when two stimuli, both of which call for a response, are presented in close succession, the response to the second will be delayed by a psychological refractory period set up in the nervous system by the first stimulus-response process. Such a result would imply a discontinuous functioning of the human as a data-processing channel. However, there is some dispute as to the nature and length of the refractory phase [47, 51] and, indeed, as to its actual existence [52].

A different approach to determining the factors involved in the human's information-processing capacity is taken in experiments where the subject is required to respond to signals presented by several simultaneously active input channels. In studies employing visual inputs [41, 42, 126, 131], both the number of active channels and the average signal frequency in any one channel have been varied. As the operator load is increased by upping either the number of channels or the signal frequency, performance falls—but it falls more rapidly with channel load than with frequency load. Many studies have been performed recently on multiple-channel listening, where the subject is called upon to comprehend several simultaneous messages [29, 137]. Although information is always lost under these circumstances, the loss has been shown to vary widely with conditions, and under certain circumstances, the amount of information dissipated can be minimized through the use of special techniques. Most of these investigations shed light upon the operator's limited capacity, and some of them point to certain of the factors which define this limit.

Display coding. The complexity of the data-processing task of the human when he is acting as transmission link between a machine's displays and controls is very directly affected by the way information is presented or "coded," to adopt the jargon of information theory. If it is properly coded, relatively little processing is required, for the information will be in a form in which it can be used immediately. However, the same information, improperly coded, will necessitate some type of operation by the subject to translate it into a form on which his decisions can be based. Since this recoding process will presumably consume time and provide opportunities for errors, it will have the effect of degrading the operator's performance. Consequently, a major research effort has developed around display coding, and a variety of informational displays have been studied from this point of view. In this section, only displays used in making discrete decisions will be treated. Later the coding of displays employed in tracking and other continuous control processes will be discussed.

If numerical data are to be read directly, coding considerations would favor the use of counters, rather than movable pointer dials [60, p. 1302]. From the point of view of coding, numbering scales by 1's, 10's, or 100's has been found to be superior to the use of a modulus of 2 or 20 [60, p. 1302]. The direction in which the scale values increase has also been found to be important in dial reading [60, p. 1302]. Studies have been made of various ways of presenting scalar information which is required in precise form over a very wide range of values [60, p. 1303]. The relative usefulness of tables or graphs [60, p. 1304], the precision of use of navigation plotters of various designs [59, pp. 73–90], and the speed of interpreting dials with moving pointers and moving scales [60, p. 1310] has also been investigated. Interpolation between range rings of different values on polar coordinate plots [60, p. 1302] and between modulus points on scales has been investigated [60, pp. 1305–1306] in the effort to get at factors inducing confusion.

If many dials are being scanned in the effort to detect significant departures from desired values, it has been found that the speed of detecting deviations is increased by aligning the pointers of all the dials so that they form horizontal patterns when they are all indicating the desired reading [60, p. 1300].

Considerable choice may be exercised in displaying spatial information obtained by radar. It may be presented in linear or nonlinear, Cartesian, or polar coordinates and the view may be stabilized with reference to the vehicle carrying it or to external space (say true north). Investigations of these different displays [23; 59, pp. 159–170; 71] suggest that their relative virtues are, at least in part, determined by the use to which the information read from them is put.

In addition to visual displays, auditory [114] and vibratory [76] displays also have been tested relative to coding.

The relationship between display coding and control coding. If the dimensions of the display are isomorphic with those of the control, a condition of "stimulus-response compatibility" is said to exist. Reduced isomorphism is referred to in terms of the "degree" of incompatibility. If the display and associated control have the same "sense" (e.g., a movement to the right of the one being associated with a right movement of the other), the arrangement is said to be in harmony with a "population stereotype." The stereotype is violated and compatibility is reduced when the sense of the display is different from that of the control.

Both of these factors have been investigated experimentally [60, pp. 1306–1309; 72, 106, 148, pp. 316–341] and have been shown to be of considerable importance in governing the speed and accuracy of operator performance. The degree of isomorphism between the display and control has been demonstrated, under some conditions, to override the intrinsic excellence of the coding of the display or control when either is considered in isolation.

The greater the display-control compatibility, the more pronounced is the disturbance caused by violations of a population stereotype; it is to be expected that direction-of-motion preferences would weaken almost to the point of extinction when the display and control parameters were entirely unrelated. The findings of all studies of coding compatibility are consistent with the interpretation that the number and complexity of the operator's data-processing steps are of critical importance in his transmission of information; the more they can be reduced, the higher will be his transmission rate [148, pp. 316–341].

Decision-making in probabilistic situations. In the majority of tasks considered by the human engineer, the responses called for are entirely determined by the immediately preceding events. In a reaction-time experiment, the correct response is directly specified by the stimulus, considered in relation to the instructions stored by the subject. In this case, the "decision" consists merely in recalling the response previously assigned to the stimulus and choosing it from among the other response alternatives. In other man-machine systems, the situation is somewhat more complex, but still highly determinate. In some tracking tasks, for example, the decision as to what response to emit must take into account not only the information presented on the tracking display, but kinesthetic information concerning the status of the control as well. Still, although the decision here involves the comparison of different sorts of information, the appropriate response bears an invariant relationship to the spatiotemporal structure of the stimulus pattern.

In many life situations, however, this direct relationship does not obtain, for the required response is related to preceding events only statistically. In these cases, the probabilities of outcomes and possibly their relative values must be taken into account in order to arrive at a decision as to what actions to take. Many of the decisions confronting aircraft pilots and other commanding officers, where imponderables must be considered, are of this class.

Although very little research on this variety of complex decision making has been done in engineering psychology, the subject will undoubtedly receive considerable attention in the future, as the role of the human operator as a decision maker becomes more fully appreciated. Some preliminary work has been carried out under the aegis of systems research, and the subject has undergone considerable development in the hands of sociologists and experimental psychologists [49, 50].

Continuous control. In many man-machine systems, the operator acts as an integral part of a continuous control loop. He plays such a role in piloting aircraft, steering ships, diving submarines, driving tanks and automobiles, and in tracking with gun and missile control directors. The primary variables affecting the data-processing behavior of the human operator in a continuous control loop relate to display coding, control coding, and the dynamic properties of the system through which he is acting. Variations in any of these may have important effects upon the nature of the operator's task and the precision with which he and the over-all system perform.

Display coding. Whatever the human controller must do, he requires information properly presented so that a minimum amount of recoding is necessitated. Experiments have been carried out with attention to display variables.

Tracking performance has been compared with reference to the sense modality employed. Auditory tracking has been compared with visual tracking [95, 96, 97], and several varieties of auditory display have been used together in providing signals for simultaneous control in several coordinates [67].

Because of their flexibility, visual displays are more widely used in tracking than are displays employing other modalities, and they have been studied from the point of view of coding. Pursuit displays, which present separate indications of target and follower motion, are generally found to be superior to compensatory displays, which show only tracking error [52, 143, 157]. Under some circumstances, however, a compensatory indicator permits greater tracking precision than does a pursuit display [38]; in other cases, no differences are found [37]. Unconventional forms of indication, such as the phase-plane display [141], have been shown to be effective in certain tracking situations. Evidence [150, 151] indicates that not all of the cues contained within the normal unrestricted view of the runway are necessarily required by a pilot in landing an airplane. Instruments designed so that the moving parts represent the aircraft attitude as referred to a fixed horizon line produce fewer confusions among novices than displays which operate the other way round [60, p. 1309; 134, pp. 76–77]. The proper integration of aircraft-type displays has been shown to be an important factor in pilot performance [161, 165].

Control coding. Tracking has been studied in terms of the efficiency of response of different parts of the body employed [60, p. 1331], in respect to handedness [80, 162] and in relation to the required force application [18; 22; 60, pp. 1331–1333; 78].

System dynamics. The tracking precision of a man-machine system is, to an important extent, a function of the dynamic properties of the elements of the system. Investigations have been carried out to determine how alterations in the dynamics of the nonhuman components affect performance. Included in these are tracking studies which investigate the effects of varying such parameters as display gain [15, 24, 86, 88], display-control gain [60, pp. 1325–1326; 86, 88], display-control sense [64, 83, 84], target width and brightness [82, 116, 178], frequency of target illumination [14, 102], input frequency [37, 38, 86, 138], input amplitude [24, 86, 115, 140], input intricacy [52; 62, pp. 125–141; 86; 179], amount, nature, and locus of delays in the tracking system [40, 111, 166, 180, 181], and the extent and nature of aided tracking [38, 88, 115, 140, 156]. Special engineering techniques for overcoming the deleterious effects of lags and phase shifts such as "display quickening" have been experimentally validated in applications to simulated submarines, gunfire control systems, and fixed- and rotary-wing aircraft [9, 19, 21, 22, 149, 152, 165, 170, 172]. Positive transfer of training has been demonstrated when going both ways between quickened and unquickened systems [94], and the quickening procedure has been shown to permit the operator to increase the number of control tasks which he can handle simultaneously [20, 170].

In some experiments, the data have been collected in such a way that it has been possible to compute autocorrelations, cross-correlations, spectral density functions, or to represent human performance in terms of such engineering criteria as are provided by the Nyquist diagram [52, 54, 62, 108, 109, 123, 153, 179]. Several investigators have sought to use these or other techniques to derive mathematical expressions of the human operator's behavioral properties in terms of linear differential equations [53; 60, pp. 1327–1331; 107; 108; 109; 176] or quasi-linear models [52, 132].

Area 4. Effects of Continued Performance and Environmental Stress on Data Processing

The research so far described has dealt with the various aspects of information transmission by the human operator when working under ideal conditions. However, a knowledge of the way in which human behavior changes with prolonged periods of activity and in response to abnormal environmental conditions is often of considerable value to the human engineer. Consequently, studies of environmental effects which utilize data-processing-type tasks are regarded as forming a fourth research area in engineering psychology.

Vigilance. When the human operator is called upon to perform some information-transmission task over an extended period of time, his speed and accuracy often change. This change—usually, although not always, downward—is called a "vigilance effect" if relatively little muscular activity is involved [127]. Otherwise it is considered to be an effect of fatigue. In either case, the human engineer must know the amount and direction of the change and the parameters which affect it. Consequently, several types of performance have been tested under a variety of conditions. Unclassified studies deal with such tasks as making visual-scale settings [155], continuous controlling [69, 87, 159], watching lights, dials, and indicators for sudden signals [93, 128], and detecting targets on cathode ray tubes [45, 117]. The findings suggest that the subject's expectancy concerning the arrival of signals is an important variable and that performance falls off with time if his expectancy is low, whereas it remains constant, or actually rises, when this expectancy is high [48].

Several techniques which may reduce the performance decrement usually found in vigilance tasks have been studied. These include techniques to bias the subject's search behavior [11], the use of efficient information encoding on the display [70], and the use of artificial signals inserted among the infrequent "true" signals [75].

Environmental stress. The effects of sleep deprivation upon human information processing have been investigated, and the results suggest that lack of sleep most affects tasks in which the rate of information transmission is low.[3] Serial reaction time [68] and pursuit tracking[4] have been studied while the subjects worked in high temperatures. The effects of cold have been assessed relative to finger numbness [129, 130] and the dexterity exhibited in loading and firing a rifle and assembling a Bren gun while wearing different types of gloves [103]. Performance under noisy conditions has been extensively studied, with the finding that a decrement due to noise is most easily demonstrated with tasks which require long periods of continuous alertness [26, 27, 28]. Experiments have also been carried out on the effects of vibration [118, 119], anoxia [122], and increased G-forces [31] upon human performance.

In a recent study [69], subjects performed tracking tasks varying in mathematical complexity under vigilance conditions while simultaneously carrying out secondary tasks. The stress produced by the necessity of performing continuously for a relatively long period and by the requirement that two tasks be performed at once had a greater adverse effect upon the mathematically more complex tracking than upon the simple.

[3] Verbal communication with Robert Wilkinson, Applied Psychology Research Unit, 15 Chaucer Rd., Cambridge, England.

[4] Verbal communication with Richard Pepler, Applied Psychology Research Unit, 15 Chaucer Rd., Cambridge, England.

In a study of direct relevance for engineering psychology, Garvey and Taylor [74] compared three ways of reducing stress effects: by selecting "stress-resistant" subjects, by training subjects, and by a human engineering modification (quickening) of the information display. The application of a human engineering principle far surpassed the selection and the training techniques in ameliorating stress effects on tracking performance.

Area 5. Man-Machine Systems Evaluation

The major portion of engineering psychology research has been discussed previously under one or another of four research areas. All of this work has been aimed at clarifying the operator's role in man-machine systems, discovering important environmental effects on human performance, and specifying the display, control, and dynamic variables which are of predominant importance for human engineering. One may regard this research as providing the psychological core of human engineering.

In the next part of this section, the technological aspects of human engineering will be described. However, before leaving engineering psychology research, one additional type of investigation must be noted. This falls in between strictly technological undertakings and the type of research previously covered. It is comprised of comparative tests of experimental, prototype, or operational man-machine systems, where the emphasis is on the evaluation of the system relative to some other system or to itself modified in some way. Here experimental methods are employed to determine how system variables affect performance. Often the results are specific to the devices employed, and frequently they do not permit of scientific generalization.

Because of this and also because many of the evaluative studies are carried out under a security classification, little of this work is available in published form. Yet it is an important part of human engineering and it is often the most costly research carried out in this field, both in terms of money and manpower.

Evaluative studies have been performed on headphones, range finders, gun sights, fire control and missile-control systems, aircraft instruments, radar sets, information plotting systems, CIC lighting systems, target-designation equipment, combat information centers, and airplane control rooms, to name but a few. In some instances, the tests are performed in the laboratory with system inputs being simulated; in other cases, they are carried out in the field. But in both situations, the attendant complexities and difficulties of control make this necessary variety of research as trying as any in which psychologists are likely to participate.

HUMAN ENGINEERING DESIGN

Our definition of human engineering pointed up the fact that this new discipline has a technological as well as a scientific side. Actually it is the former—here called "human engineering design" which is the *raison d'être* of engineering psychology, since the need for better information about how men read displays and operate controls first stimulated psychologists to carry out research in the man-machine system context. Certainly the practice of human engineering long antedated its emergence as a science. Design engineers have been considering human requirements for as long as they have been developing man-operated equipment, and in many instances, their efforts have left little to be desired. Our household appliances, motor cars, and transport vehicles are quite satisfactory devices, and they have been developed with but little help from engineering psychologists or others who are professionally identified with human engineering.

Possibly human engineering would not have emerged as a formal discipline involving psychologists if it had not been for an evolution of man-machine systems from those which made only slight demands on the operator to others which tax the human element to near its upper limit. Increased vehicular speeds, the multiplication of data for decisions produced by developments in sensing, storing, and collating information, and the necessity for increased system-operating precision—all requiring higher rates of information processing—have necessitated modern human engineering.

Today the development of machines has reached a point where special knowledge and skill are required to understand how and when to insert the man in order to ensure enhanced, rather than reduced, system performance. In the years ahead, it will become increasingly necessary for technologists to take human characteristics into account. As untrained laymen come to deal more and more intimately with machines, it may become an economic necessity to devise the quickest, least demanding, and most foolproof means by which they can communicate with their mechanisms. Hence the present and future need for formalized human engineering on both a scientific and technological level!

Equipment Design

The human engineering technologist contributes to system development at three levels of complexity. At the simplest level, he participates in the design of individual displays, controls, and dynamic mechanical or electronic arrangements. At a somewhat more complex level, he contributes to the design of operating consoles, which are groups of displays and controls. In both cases, he is working with system components. He also plays an important role at a still higher level of complexity; here he assists in structuring complex systems that are composed of several human and mechanical elements. In this capacity, he helps to distribute subtasks among men and machines and to determine the configuration of the system.

At all three levels, his goal is a high over-all probability of task accomplishment of the final system. He must design not only with a view to optimized peak performance, but also for reliability, ease of maintenance, and reduced operator selection and training requirements.

The technological effort in human engineering is very extensive. Certainly it is much greater than is commonly appreciated by psychologists who are not closely identified with the field. Literally hundreds of devices and systems have been affected to a greater or less extent during the last ten years by human engineering considerations. Psychologists have assisted in the design of many types of displays, including those used with sonars, radars, gunfire control devices, missile launching and controlling equipment, and information-processing systems. These displays have included optical and infrared telescopes, periscopes, CRT displays, battle plan indicators, auditory listening systems, plotting boards, submarine "Christmas trees," and a wide variety of aircraft-, surface ship-, and submarine-indicating instruments. Human engineering designers have also helped with such controls as control columns, handgrips, keysets, instrument knobs, and artificial limbs, and they have played an important role in "aiding" or quickening such control systems as are involved in theodolites, radar-gunfire control systems, missile control devices, optical gun sights, aircraft and drone landing systems, and submarine diving displays.

Human engineers have also assisted with the layout of consoles or instrument complexes for devices such as gunfire control systems, radars, sonars, target-designation devices, missile systems, a large variety of ground, air, and sea vehicles, a variety of industrial machines, an atomic reactor, and test equipment for an earth satellite. Finally, human engineering technologists have participated in the planning and layout of such complex multiman-machine systems as those represented by a task force command ship combat information center, an air-borne CIC, a ship-borne electronic data-processing system, numerous special-purpose weapons-control centers, an Army antiaircraft missile-control station, ship-borne missile-control devices, aircraft-control towers, and bomber aircraft crew stations.

Human Engineering Guides

In addition to participating in the design of specific equipment, the human engineering designer has sought to contribute to technology by writing handbooks, texts, and special articles to provide information which will be useful to anyone designing man-machine systems. The Tufts University *Handbook of Human Engineering Data* [175] and the *Human Engineering Guide for Equipment Designers* by Woodson [185] are the first general-purpose guides so far published, but a major effort is now being devoted by the three military services toward writing a new and more comprehensive human engineering handbook. Several chapters have already been published in preliminary form [12, 55, 56, 57, 173].

Special-purpose guides have also been prepared for the assistance of equipment designers. These include *Guide to Design of Electronic Equipment for Maintainability* [66], *Handbook on Training and Training Equipment Design* [136], *Human Engineering Principles for Mine Test Design* [147], and *Procedures for Including Human Engineering Factors in the Development of Weapon Systems* [177]. Information of value to the human engineering designer is also contained in *Human Factors in Air Transport Design* [122], *Applied Experimental Psychology* [35], *A Human Engineering Bibliography* [120], *The Design and Conduct of Human Engineering Studies* [33], *Human Factors in Undersea Warfare* [139], "Engineering Psychology and Equipment Design" in the *Handbook of Experimental Psychology* [60], *Human Engineering* [121], and *Research Techniques in Human Engineering* [34].

II. Interrelationships between Psychology and Human Engineering

In the preceding section, the scientific and technological activities of human engineering have been described. It should be apparent that human engineering is, in very essence, a bridging discipline between psychology and engineering. It will now be of interest to explore this relationship further and to contrast and interrelate psychology, as it is embodied in human engineering, with the older parent subject from which, in part, it took its origin. To this end, the goals, subject matter, methods, variables, and concepts of human engineering will be discussed in some detail.

GOALS

The general aims of human engineering have been described previously, but it seems worthwhile to reaffirm them, to analyze them with greater care, and to place them in juxtaposition with the aims of psychology.

Human psychology is regarded in this essay as the science directed toward the comprehension of man's behavior relative to his physical and social environment. In contrast, human engineering has been defined as a discipline whose ultimate purposes are the comprehension and design of man-machine systems. Clearly, the goals of these two fields differ significantly both in the type of knowledge sought after and the manner in which the knowledge is utilized.

Knowledge

Psychology aims at acquiring, through scientific means, a broad understanding of all types of the human's reaction to all aspects of his surroundings. It is often held that this knowledge is sought in order to predict and control behavior; however, attempts to perform the latter are often conceded to provide tests of the accuracy of the psychological knowledge rather than justifications of the science. Thus understanding man's behavior is—for the majority of "pure" psychologists—a goal unto itself, requiring no ulterior projection. For them, the test of psychological knowledge is the accuracy and comprehensiveness of the existing anthroponomic laws.

Psychology may be defined negatively, as well. Although it is a science of behavior, its interests extend only to the reactions of living creatures; if it is human psychology, to the behavior of men. In spite of the fact that some have pleaded against it [17, 98], the psychologist usually limits his interests to the behavior which he considers as taking place within the human individual. All behavior outside of this—external to the man-environment interface—is considered taboo for psychology, since it is within the preserves of other sciences.

However, such is not the case for human engineering. Since the aim in this field is to understand and structure anthropomechanical complexes, the knowledge required relates to the behavior of machines as well as men. For the practicing human engineer, the response characteristics of electronic circuits and mechanical arrangements are just as relevant as the behavioral properties of the man.

Nevertheless, if human engineering is broader than psychology, in encompassing the behavior of machines as well as men, it is more limited in what it asks about the man. Academic psychology embraces all manner of human action; engineering psychology fixes its focus only upon system-relevant behaviors. In other words, the human engineer is not interested in human behavior in general, but in the aspects of behavior which might be classed as the engineering properties of the man. The engineering psychologist is not tested for comprehensive understanding of all human behavior, but for his power to make more effective systems with more restricted psychological knowledge. For this reason, it is to be anticipated that human engineering can contribute only in a modest way to the facts and principles of general psychology.

Actions

The goals of human engineering differ from those of conventional psychology. The nature of the knowledge sought is different, and the actions taken or not taken on the basis of this knowledge are different. The classical psychologist—or any other classical scientist, for that matter—seeks only to know and communicate his knowledge. The human engineer seeks to *do* as well as to *know*. Thus human engineering is doubly an applied science; not only does it strive for applicable knowledge, it includes the actual application.

Such is also true, of course, of all fields of applied psychology. The training specialist not only performs research on learning, he also builds trainers and works out training programs intended to ensure more rapid acquisition of subject matter or skill. The selection specialist tries to refine his test methods; but he also develops particular tests to select the intelligent and the skillful for advanced education or for the jobs which call for unusual abilities. Similarly, the clinical, the industrial, and the applied social psychologists seek for a better understanding of their sciences; they also *use* their sciences to alter the nature of the world they live in.

On the surface, then, it would appear that human engineering is but another variety of applied psychology. Certainly in respect to its "psychological knowledge aspects," this is precisely what it is. Yet when the nature of its "practice" is examined, human engineering may be distinguished from the other fields of applied psychology in two very important ways:

1. Whereas all the other applied psychologies seek to control and influence *people,* human engineering technologists direct their efforts toward modifying systems made up of both *men and machines.* Since this is the case, a second difference has to follow.

2. In all the older fields of applied psychology, the practitioner is still a psychologist when he leaves off research and turns to application. However, when the human engineer starts to practice, he becomes an engineer in fact, for he participates in the design of mechanical or electronic equipment. The structuring of systems is certainly an extra-psychological activity, regardless of who does it or the extent of interest in human behavior on the part of the designer.

In summary, the goals of human engineering, relating to both knowledge and action, provide an avenue connecting the biological and psychological sciences with the applied physical sciences. At the same time, the very fact that human engineering is the product of these cross-disciplinary aims makes it clearly evident that this new field differs significantly from other areas of applied psychology, in which both knowledge and the actions taken upon the knowledge fall within the confines of psychology as it is classically defined. The physical science aspects of the new discipline exert a pull upon the interests and actions of human engineers which is centripetal to engineering and centrifugal to the orthodox anthropocentrism of psychology.

SUBJECT MATTER

Two classes of subject matter are distinguishable in human engineering. These relate to (1) the behavior of the human and nonhuman components of man-machine systems, and (2) over-all system performance.

Component Behavior

The human element.   Engineering psychology is concentrated primarily on specifying the characteristics of human behavior which are relevant when men operate machines under both "normal" conditions and conditions of environmental stress. The studies which lead to this type of knowledge fall under the first four of the five broad research areas described in the first section of this report. There they were categorized as dealing with the characteristics of the man as an information channel or processing device. The behavior involved would probably fall under the classical psychological categories of sensory, motor, and psychomotor responses. Furthermore, as a previous analysis [169] has suggested, the psychomotor behaviors of greatest interest to the human engineer are (1) voluntary, (2) almost exclusively in response to visual and auditory inputs, (3) mediated through contractions of the striate muscles, and (4) of the type in which the output is imitative of certain characteristics of the input.

If the writer's definition of human engineering is used, the psychological subject matter of this discipline is restricted to a small part of psychology proper. Actually, however, the assumptions which have been made by the majority of workers in this field have limited it even further. Most studies in engineering psychology to date have assumed that the subjects were arrested at some fixed level of learning, that their motivation was optimal, that their responses were uninfluenced by social factors, and that they were all "average" men. In short, engineering psychology has placed very little stress upon interhuman or intrahuman factors which are known to be important in much of human behavior. It is true that attempts are often made to control the effects of motivation, learning, individual differences, and social relationships, but these factors are seldom systematically varied in engineering psychology. In some of the work it has been tacitly assumed —and occasionally openly stated—that the psychomotor processes under investigation were so fundamental and basic to the man that most of the "psychological" variables could be neglected.

There is no denying that some of the display and control variables are very powerful in altering performance and in overriding effects of training, selection, and social factors—there is evidence to support this fact. It is just as true, however, that learning and individual differences sometimes bring about greater changes in operator behavior than do the variables which are preferred by the present-day human engineer. If the engineering psychologist broadened his investigations to include a more deliberate study of social, motivational, individual-difference, and learning factors on psychomotor processes, the goal of proper man-machine system design might be served better. If this were done, conceivably interactions of great importance in optimizing systems—and no less important for psychological theory—would be discovered.

It also seems likely that human engineering would profit if the making of decisions that are considerably more probabilistic and complex than those studied today became a topic of research. As has already been pointed out, a large part of engineering psychology deals with the information-transmission type of human behavior, where the output follows or patterns the input. In such situations, the specifications for the required response are contained within the stimulus configuration or its history. The subject merely has the task of "reading" the input signals, "recalling" the rules imposed by the situation, and "deciding" to give the indicated response. Although the reading and recalling may, at times, be extremely complex and difficult operations, the "decision process" itself would appear to be so simple that it is hardly worthy of this designation.

In contrast, many decisions faced by a ship's captain or an airline pilot are of quite a different order. Usually there are many pieces of information to which probabilities and values must be assigned; events and rules must be remembered, and possible outcomes must be weighed before the appropriate action is decided upon. When one considers the vast amount of information which must sometimes be taken into account in order to reach a "yes-no" decision in combat or in daily life, it would seem more appropriate to characterize the process as "information reduction" rather than "information transmission."

Nowadays complex decisions must often be made by operators of machines. Available evidence suggests that even if decision frequency does not increase in the future, the time stress on decisions and the seriousness of mistakes most certainly will increase. The rapid evolution of machines in the direction of fantastic aircraft speeds and full factory automation, to choose but two examples, is forcing out the human as a controller; at the same time, it is making his decision functions more critical. With the advent of space flight and the increased mechanization of factory control processes, a faulty decision by the monitor-controller in an emergency might spell personal or economic disaster. It would seem desirable, therefore, for engineering psychologists to undertake studies of complex decision making as it might occur in such man-machine situations. If this were done, human engineering could well be in a position to answer—with experimental data rather than guesswork—many of the questions which will be posed ten to twenty years hence.

Engineering psychology must also work toward determining the best ways for ordinary laymen to insert information into and extract information from machines. Except for a few devices such as the dial telephone and household appliances, the mechanisms of modern life are operated by selected and trained personnel; even automobile drivers must pass tests. However, it is likely that consumer-operated machines will play an increasingly important role in our civilization. Consequently, these machines will have to be designed so that an average person with no special training will be able to operate them with dispatch, with only occasional error, and without undue physiological or mental stress. Clearly, much research is needed if economically and socially disastrous design errors are to be avoided.

When one considers the subject matter so far discussed, it should be evident that there is a substantial overlap—although much of this area is relatively undeveloped—between engineering psychology and conventional psychology. Much of the research which has recently been performed with a view to the improvement of man-operated mechanisms has its parallel in the work of many "pure" experimental psychologists. Fundamental sensory, motor, and psychomotor research is often indistinguishable from that carried on under the aegis of human engineering.

But the overlap between experimental and engineering psychology is not complete, nor are extensive data from experimental psychology directly applicable to the design of systems. As we mentioned earlier, the engineering psychologist seeks for system-relevant facts concerning human behavior, and it must be emphasized that not all facts, even though they concern psychomotor performance, can meet this criterion. As a result, much of the knowledge collected by the fundamental research worker is of no direct use to the human engineering technologist for, whereas it is relevant to psychology, it is not in the proper form for application to the design of machines.

The overlap in the area of the effects of environmental stress and continued performance on behavior would become much greater if our definition of human engineering were broadened to include the design of all of man's surroundings. Furthermore, if human behavior other than sensory, motor, and psychomotor reactions were included in engineering psychology, there would be opportunity for many more knowledge interactions between stress and vigilance studies by experimental psychologists, physiologists, and medical men and by experimenting human engineers. There can certainly be no quarrel with those who may wish to expand the coverage of human engineering in this fashion, although the writer prefers the more limited definition for the reasons given earlier.

Mechanical elements. It should be apparent that the human engineering technologist needs information about the mechanical and electronic system components, as well as knowledge of man. Fortunately, most of this information about mechanical elements is already available in engineering or physics texts, so that research is not necessary. True, new mechanisms and circuits are constantly being designed by engineers, and these do require testing. But, compared to our knowledge of the engineering properties of man, the information available concerning electronics and mechanics is extensive. The human engineering designer merely has to reach up on the shelf to obtain the physical components with which to structure his systems.

Comparison of human and mechanical elements. In order to design effective man-machine devices, it is necessary to know the relative performance characteristics of men and mechanisms in carrying out the same system tasks. To obtain this information, the psychologist must be sufficiently familiar with the functional properties of the physical components to run off the appropriate comparisons on the man. Thus a working knowledge of electronic and mechanical elements is a necessity for the human engineering technologist and for the engineering psychologist as well.

Although very little direct cross-comparison has yet been made, it is recognized as a field of investigation which requires extensive development. Because so little has been done, this "comparative dynamology" of men and machines did not appear in the first section of this report as a separate research domain. For the same reason, there can be relatively little overlap in subject matter between conventional psychology and this new area of human engineering.

System Performance

The human engineer involves himself directly with man-machine systems when he serves as a technologist helping to design systems and when he participates in experimental tests intended to evaluate them. In respect to the latter, it will be recalled that systems evaluation was earlier designated as the fifth and final research domain of engineering psychology. This is an important research area in human engineering which has received little attention from psychologists outside of the field.

Although they were initially drawn into this systems work primarily because they possessed techniques for dealing with human variability, many psychologists have now acquired a scientific interest in the field. Whenever a man is inserted in series with physical components, the performance of the total complex is a function of human behavior and also, quite obviously, of the performance of the nonhuman components. The laws by which men and physical components combine and interact dynamically to produce a system output are not yet established; it is the hope of determining these invariant relationships which has fired engineering psychologists to start research on systems per se. Some of them believe that this research adumbrates a new and independent subarea of science—neither psychology nor engineering, but an interdisciplinary combination.

METHODOLOGY

In discussing the methodological interrelationships between psychology and human engineering, a clear separation must be made between the research and technological aspects of the latter. Most research methods of engineering psychology are drawn without modification from the parent field. Man-machine system technology, however, borrows very little from psychology in the way of method.

Engineering Psychology

Apart from general attitude and point of view, perhaps the major contribution of psychology to human engineering research is in methodology. Without question, the vast majority of engineering psychology studies employ instrumental methods and techniques of data analysis which are identical with those of academic psychology [33, 34]. Also, in very many instances, the organization and systematization of the findings follow lines which are very similar to those of conventional experimental psychology.

In a few instances, however, research methods and techniques of systematization which were developed by engineers have been appropriated and put to use. Two general methodologies have been taken over from applied physical science, one stemming from what has come to be called "communication theory" or "information theory" [4, 39], the other from "servo theory" [174]. The former is also arousing widespread interest among experimental psychologists, for it is particularly suited to the discrete signals so often employed in psychological research. Although it provides no novel instrumental techniques, information theory does make the derivation of a new index of human performance possible. This measure of the information content of behavior has great generality in that it applies to a wide variety of materials, to many aspects of human data processing, and to the activities of both living creatures and inanimate objects. Thus, it is possible to compute the amount of information contained in various written and spoken messages, television pictures, display configurations, and decision situations, to mention but a few examples. The information-handling capacity of the various sensory modalities can be measured and compared, the response mechanisms can be assessed in the same terms, and the transmission properties of the complete human input-"throughout"-output channel can be calculated and related to those of mechanical and electronic systems.

Servo theory, which was developed for handling continuously acting systems, provides both instrumental procedures for collecting data and techniques for analyzing and organizing results obtained in tracking and control experiments [53]. The theory—it is still developing the field to which it is indigenous—was intended to help engineers determine and specify the response properties of open- and closed-loop servo systems. At the present stage of its development, it can deal most adequately with linear systems—and man is most certainly *not* representative of this class [52, 168]. For this reason, nonlinear procedures of transient and steady-state analysis, which are used in engineering [43], appear to be of considerable use also in engineering psychology.

Many of the methods which have been created by mathematicians for dealing with continuous performance data have found direct application in engineering psychology. Human tracking responses have been subjected to various frequency analysis techniques and auto-, cross- and multivariate-correlation procedures [52, 62, 107, 123, 179]. Human transfer functions are developed and stated as differential equations [108, 109, 176, 179] or graphed as Bode plots [52, 54] or Nyquist diagrams [153]. Although it is too soon to appraise the value of these methods for engineering psychology, there are high hopes for payoff among the more mathematically inclined human engineers [132].

The use of complex analog and digital computers must also be mentioned as an important instrumental procedure taken over from engineering. Analog computers have two principal uses in engineering psychology research: (1) to simulate the dynamics of man-operated control systems in aircraft, submarines, missile guidance systems, and the like; and (2) to imitate the behavioral properties of the man.

The use of computers as dynamic simulators is necessary because we must obtain information about the human's response characteristics in situations where there are lags and phase shifts in the loop which he is closing and where direct test would be prohibitively dangerous or costly. The procedure is to give the subject displays and controls which are tied into the computer, to set up the precise equation of the control system being simulated, and then to energize the computer, letting the human subject control as he would in the actual device [165]. By recording system performance and by altering simulated display and control parameters and system dynamics, a considerable amount of information may be obtained quickly and at relatively low cost.

Analog computers are also used in engineering psychology as robots which imitate the man. The idea is to simulate human performance as closely as possible, then to use the parametric settings on the computer to characterize the operator's performance [133]. One begins by making an educated guess as to the transfer function which will best represent the operator's performance in the particular control loop chosen for the test. This equation is then set into the computer, along with that which represents the control system dynamics. The simulated man then tracks a course through the simulated system, and the performance of the robot is recorded for subsequent comparison with the performance of the man as he works through the same dynamics. Discrepancies are gradually teased down through trial-and-error adjustments of the computer until a satisfactory match is obtained. Since at this point the man and his simulacrum perform alike, readings of the computer settings provide the dimensional constants of the human transfer function.

Digital computers are just coming into use in engineering psychology. Although they have been employed up to now chiefly for computing tables and higher order correlations, they are beginning to be used to generate complex visual patterns which—either photographed and projected or viewed directly—constitute inputs to the subject in a variety of studies of displays. In one example cited by Green [81], a high-speed digital computer was used to generate a series of simulated radar views of a target moving through a field of random noise. The noise spots appeared in different places on each "sweep," but a single target dot advanced through a succession of positions in the way in which a "real" target would move across the face of the radar scope. Tests were run with varying amounts of noise and different blip/scan ratios.

An attempt to synthesize the display manually would have required hundreds of separate views, one for each frame, and each would have had to be worked out, painted or constructed in some other way, and photographed. This would have taken so much time and effort that the test would probably never have been undertaken in the first place. In contrast, once the digital computer was programed—a matter of a few hours—each filmstrip of 40 frames was generated and photographed in about twenty seconds.

Other simulated display situations have been created through the use of digital computers. These include (1) presentations of highly realistic enemy aircraft raids as affected by randomizing factors imitating those of real life, (2) two-dimensional line figures which can be "rotated" as if in three or more dimensions, and (3) randomly generated dot patterns through which the perception of form may be studied by altering the probability of occurrence of the dots in different regions of the pattern [81].

Man-machine System Technology

In contrast with engineering psychology research, human engineering design is carried out with methods which owe very little to experimental psychology. Essentially, there are three basic methods of getting information which have been adopted by practicing human engineers when they are setting out to redesign an existing system. These consist of (1) asking opinions of the operators, (2) measuring elements of system performance through time and motion, micromotion, link, or other activity analysis, and (3) analyzing accidents [33].

Since, however, human engineers usually must work with systems which have not yet been built but are only in the process of design, they have had to develop further techniques of their own. In most instances, these turn out to be time-and-motion analyses on blueprints or other simplified representations of the intended device [90]. At the outset, the purpose and informational requirements of the projected system are considered, the processes which must be performed are identified, and possible component configurations are delineated. After drawing up alternative system designs—block diagrams, flow charts, or designs in some other form—precise and detailed procedural analyses are made of the hypothetical response sequences called for. Move for move, every action from beginning to end of the anticipated operating routine is described, either verbally or through the use of notational conventions or time charts. A study of these sequences often reveals operational bottlenecks in certain of them and points up advantages in the design features predicated by others.

When time and circumstance permit, mock-ups may be constructed so that either primitive—though actual—time-and-motion or link analyses can be performed or at least the system configuration can better be appreciated. In the case of projected control systems, analog computers are used to create the dynamic situations which will confront the operator when the systems have been built. With human subjects actually in the control loop, gain factors or other mechanism parameters are adjusted to achieve optimum system performance.

Sometimes the gains are set in the absence of any operator. In these cases, a computer analog of the man is inserted in the human's place, and the tests are run with the robot closing the loop on the system. Such a substitution is permissible only when the minimal transfer function required of the man can be specified, as in the case of quickening. The procedure is then to set this "rock-bottom" transfer function into the computer in the man's place and to adjust the loop gains to optimize system performance under these conditions. When this is carried out properly, it may be expected that—if the actual transfer properties of the operator of the projected system are no less complex than those simulated—the system will perform in an optimum fashion. This technique permits much more extensive and rapid exploration of parametric values than could ever be accomplished if human subjects had to be employed. Furthermore, the utilization of a robot makes working in "fast time" entirely feasible—speeding up the whole control problem many times over, while keeping the temporal relationships of the control sequence unchanged—thus further facilitating the processes involved in control design.

It may be remarked parenthetically that much of today's empirical testing, employing computer techniques, would not be necessary if completely adequate system mathematics were at hand. The difficulty is that the man is nonlinear and nonstationary [52, 168], and there are no simple paper-and-pencil methods for dealing with this class of system components. Undoubtedly, the greatest need today in man-machine system technology is the development of a convenient nonlinear mathematics.

Subsystems versus total systems. Closely related to methodology is one's general approach to his job. Although psychologists began to assist actively in the design of machines less than twenty years ago, a broadening in the human engineer's conception of his task is evident. At the outset, he made no effort to specify what role the human operator would play in the system, regarding this as the prerogative of the engineer. Rather he devoted his full attention to seeing to it that the role—whatever it might be—was played to perfection, or as near to perfection as possible.

Thus, once the engineer had specified that the man was to track, the human factors technologist merely did his best to select the displays and controls which would make for the best tracking. He did not consider that the question of whether tracking was an appropriate task was within his purview. Similarly, if the engineer stated that a pilot needed a fuel gauge, the human engineer immediately set to work to assist in producing one which was legible at a glance and configured in such a way as to reduce confusion. He did not challenge the engineer's original decision. Had he done so, he might have discovered that the pilot required no fuel gauge at all, but rather an instrument which displayed time and distance of flight remaining.

In short, the first approach adopted by the human engineering designer would now be described as subsystem-oriented. However, the shortcomings of this limited attack very soon became apparent, and many of the human engineering technologists began to take a much broader view of their mission. Today when they are called upon to furnish design suggestions intended to optimize the operator's performance of a particular data-processing task, they seek first to determine precisely what this task should be [90, 177].

To do this, it is necessary to consider the purpose of the over-all system and the presumed effectiveness of various alternative subsystems which might be employed to achieve this purpose. This broad overview often indicates ways in which the operator's task can be redesigned to require less in the way of analog computation or other forms of complex data handling. Frequently the deliberate substitution of one data-processing task for another (one subsystem for another) brings about improvements in system performance which are considerably more striking than those which can be realized through working with any one subsystem alone. Examples of this include the significance enhancement in controlling accuracy produced by quickening and aiding man-machine follow-up devices.

It is now recognized by the enlightened human engineering designer that both the system and subsystem approaches are valid and that they must be used together if high-performance man-machine systems are to be built. More than that, the viewpoints now constitute the two fundamental and complementary approaches of human engineering technology.

VARIABLES

Since the subject matter of engineering psychology includes human psychomotor behavior under both normal and abnormal environments and, in addition, the over-all performance of man-machine systems, many diverse types of variable and variable relationship may be expected within the different research domains. Of the five areas delineated in Sec. I, it is in the fourth, which deals with the effects of continued performance and environmental stress, that the variables utilized are most similar to those of orthodox psychology.

Area 4

In this research field, the independent variables are either correlates of the state of the organism or involve dimensionally simple physical parameters. Thus the number of hours spent by the subject without sleep, the length of time since the start of a continuous performance, the rate at which target signals are introduced, the temperature of the skin, the ambient noise level, the amplitude and frequency of bodily vibration, or the amount, direction, and duration of applied G-forces, and other independent variables are manipulated. On the other hand, the dependent variables are usually fairly unambiguous measures of human performance, such as the number of targets overlooked, the number of mental arithmetic problems completed in a fixed time, the length of the reaction time, the speed of card sorting, or the time needed to learn a list of nonsense syllables by rote.

The variables of area 4 are rather conventional. Those encountered in the remaining research clusters, areas 1, 2, 3, and 5, are far more complex and confounded than those generally met in psychology. Because the manipulation of such complex sets of parameters so typifies engineering psychology and because this complexity is so little understood, the discussion to follow will deal exclusively with them, and no further mention will be made of the variables in area 4.

Area 5

In area 5, *Man-machine Systems Evaluation*, the complexity and contamination of both the independent and dependent variables are most clearly and dramatically illustrated. Therefore, we will deal with this area first and at some length. The unusual characteristics of the quantities which we will call "system variables" can best be illustrated by example. Consider a test to compare two hypothetical data-processing systems that might be developed for use aboard ship. Both are radar devices which sense and track aircraft targets, either manually or automatically, and then synthetically display them to an operator on a polar coordinate plot. The principal task of the operator is to call out the bearing and range of the target which most threatens his own ship. He will, of course, have other duties, but these will not concern us, nor will we consider what is done with the information his "decisions" and reports provide.

Let us rig the example so that the two systems differ markedly and yet plausibly. In both, all the targets are displayed; in one, a symbol beside each target designates its course and speed and thereby furnishes a basis for the operator to compute threat, relative to time of arrival. In the other system, the targets appear without symbols, but a marker circle circumscribes the most threatening target. This circle is generated by a "threat computer" inserted ahead of the display. It is built to accept the target information provided by the tracking mechanism, store appropriate quantities, utilize the same rules and criteria as the man, and compute, at very high speed, relative threat to own ship. We may require that the threat computation be a repetitive process so that, in both systems, as soon as the most pressing target is signaled, the next most threatening must be determined, and so on, until all have been evaluated.

Now there can be very little doubt about the outcome of a run-off between these two man-machine devices. Although the over-all data-processing task of the two systems is the same, the human plays the role of a computer in one, but not in the other. Assuming that the mechanical or electronic component which calculates the threat in the "better" system is reliable and rapid, one would anticipate that the performance scores of the two systems under heavy load would differ by at least an order of magnitude.

However, the interest now is not in the size of this difference, but in the nature of the variables involved in this evaluation. In this example, the dependent variable is clearly a measure of human performance. The speed and accuracy with which threat is reported by the operator is the empirical variable, and it quite obviously reflects the man's behavior. It is interesting to note, however, that the same variable becomes a system dependent variable when the performance is related to the system input rather than to that of the man. Thus, by changing reference, the dependent variable can become a measure of performance of either the man alone or the total man-machine system. As a psychological dependent variable, it measures only the performance of the human element in extracting information from the displays, processing this information, and reading out target position. However, as a system variable, it reflects the activity of all the system components, animate and mechanical, which act in series to store, compute, read out, and emit bearing and range.

The fact that the human is the output element in the illustrative system permits us to derive either a system or human performance score from the same responses. As will be shown later, in systems where the human responds through mechanical or electronic components—where the man is not the final link in the system chain—one does not have the same freedom with dependent variables. There, relevant, pure, human performance variables are often unavailable, and only system performance measures can be obtained.

Independent variables. The characteristics of the independent system variables are most effectively illuminated by our first example. Taking a quick view of the hypothetical experiment, we find that only one independent variable is involved, i.e., the structure of the system inserted ahead of the man. However, a more careful look reveals that the variable actually consists of two basic components and that both are being varied qualitatively rather than quantitatively.

As to the first point, when the systems are switched, not only are the components ahead of the man altered, but so is the psychomotor task of the operator. With one of the systems, he merely has to scan the display, locate the circled target, and read off its range and bearing. No threat computation is required of him, nor could he perform it even if he wished to do so, since insufficient information is supplied. However, with the other system, he must first determine which target is the most threatening and then call off its range and bearing. The threat is estimated by (1) choosing a target on the display, (2) reading off its course and speed from the associated symbol, (3) calculating mentally how close the target will come to the ship and how soon, (4) storing this information while repeating the whole calculation and storage process for every target on the plot, and (5) comparing the stored threat values of all targets in order to select the most dangerous.

Clearly, the psychomotor tasks posed by the two systems are very different. Furthermore, since both the display and the behavioral task differ, the basic logic of experiment is so violated that it is impossible to judge the precise effects of either component upon the performance of the system or the man. It is like setting out to compare human performance with two different types of numerical display by requiring the operator to perform entirely different tasks with them. If he added digits from left to right and called off the sum with one and if he merely read them off as they appeared with the other, obviously little would be learned either about the displays or the mental processing tasks.

Normally, if one set out to measure behavior change induced by controlled sensory variations, one would expect to work within the same psychomotor task continuum throughout the experiment, regardless of the values assumed by the independent variable. Thus if one were studying the reaction time to two intensities of a light, the behavior measured when the stimulus was weak would be assumed to be the same general kind of behavior as that observed when the intensity was high—in other words, one would assume that it was voluntary reaction time throughout the experiment, and not reaction time to low intensities and startle reflex to high, for example.

The psychological "experiments" provided ready-made in systems tests often do not provide such consistency, as we have pointed out. In many practical systems studies, there is a serious confounding of physical with operator task variables. Sometimes the psychomotor task component of the independent variable shifts simultaneously with only one physical component, such as the display mode in our earlier example. In other instances, however, the confounding is compounded, with as many as four sets of parameters varying simultaneously and correlatively. Thus, in comparing two man-vehicle systems—two types of aircraft, for example—it is common to encounter marked differences in (1) displays, (2) controls, (3) system dynamics, and (4) the nature of the operator's psychomotor task. Clearly, all that one can know from such a systems test is that one complete system is better than another. This lets one decide between systems, but it is hardly an example of enriched psychological research.

The second characteristic of the independent system variable, illustrated in the example, is its qualitative nature. An analysis of the two components of the variable shows that both are multidimensional and that dimensional discontinuities are encountered in passing from one of the system modes to the other.

Consider first the dimensions within the displays. Both plots show the same number of targets in the same way. In one, coded symbols are displayed alongside each target; in the other, this type of symbol does not appear, but a circle surrounds the target which is to be reported. Symbol shape and number constitute two independent dimensions along which variations occur in one of the displays but not in the other; the threat marker on the display associated with the computer is always a circle, and only one such marker ever appears at a time. Thus when display mode is altered, dimensions drop out or are added. In some experiments, it is not only the number of dimensions which change, as in this instance, but one whole set of dimensions may be substituted for another when the mode is altered. In either case, this is what is meant by saying that the display mode variable is qualitative rather than quantitative.

Dimensional discontinuities may also be observed in the psychomotor task component of the independent variable. When the operator shifts from computing threat and reading off the position of the most dangerous target in one system to merely detecting the encircled target and calling its position in the other, he drops out a whole set of task dimensions. Patently, the two psychomotor tasks are qualitatively different. The same is true of very many actual systems evaluations. One system may require the operator to act analogously to a complex differential equation solver; another may call for nothing more than proportional responding. Or one information-transmission system may require the human to transform data presented in Cartesian coordinates into a polar coordinate plot; another might require only a very simple linear translation. Probably in the majority of systems experiments, the operator's task is a qualitatively changing component of the independent variable.

Although conventional psychologists must occasionally work with qualitative variables, they tend to avoid them whenever possible because of their scientific inelegance. Rarely, if ever, would the academician deliberately set out to compare two qualitatively different psychomotor tasks of the type found in systems tests. Since the two behaviors could not be located on the same continuum, they would appear to differ so grossly that the psychologist would see little purpose in comparing them. Certainly, the student whose interest was centered on establishing the laws of human behavior would not consider it profitable to compare the speed of running with that of swimming, or the ability to multiply in one's head with that of multiplying on a slide rule, or a housewife's skill in washing clothes with a scrubbing board with that of operating an automatic washer. Although this kind of comparison would interest the system designer, they would hardly be revealing to the psychologist.

Dependent variables. Thus, the independent variables of systems experiments stand indicted on the two counts of component confounding and qualitative, rather than quantitative, variation. But it is not only the characteristics of the independent variable which cause difficulty in drawing meaningful psychological inferences from systems experiments; the dependent variable is often equally troublesome. True, in the one example cited, the dependent variable is a direct and unambiguous measure of human performance. But in many, perhaps most, systems tests, the dependent variable is a measure of system performance, not human performance. In all cases where the man operates upon the world through mechanical or electronic portions of the system, the dependent variable must reflect the performance of the human operator as well as that of the components through which he works.

In an earlier paper by the author [169], an instructive, although absurd, illustration of this was provided by a hypothetical race between a boy on a bicycle and another on a pogo stick. Considering this as an experiment, the independent variable is clearly the nature of the boy-vehicle system, and the dependent variable is some measure of speed. There is little doubt as to the outcome of such a race—or the fact that one could infer very little about human psychomotor performance from the outcome. It is perfectly apparent that the fact that the boy on bicycle travels faster than the boy on pogo stick does not imply that the winner is doing a better job of bicycle riding than the loser is of pogo-stick hopping. Actually, the contrary might be true—if there were some means available of assessing both performances on an absolute basis. As long as one is dealing with a system performance variable—as is the case here and in many actual systems evaluations—the behavior of the human in the system can only be inferred, and often this inference is hazardous indeed.

Of course, this would not be a serious matter if it were always possible in systems tests to select some other dependent variable which did directly reflect human behavior. But in many studies there is no meaningful, uncontaminated psychomotor performance variable. Whenever the human responds through some variety of control, his response is inextricably involved with the physical properties of the control itself. Thus—as in our example—it is not possible to measure human hopping behavior independently of the characteristics of the thing hopped on or to measure pedaling in the absence of pedals.

Or consider the more sensible case of two control columns, one spring-restrained, the other unsprung but viscously damped. If the operator moved both at the same constant velocity, it could not be concluded that his behavior was the same in the two situations. The physical relationships are such that to move the viscously damped control at a constant rate, a constant force is required from the operator, whereas to achieve the same constant movement with the spring-restrained control, a constantly *increasing* force must be supplied [21]. Thus, in this case, what the man does with his hand is just as much a function of the properties of the control as it is of the properties of his muscles; the same behavior can represent very many different muscle response/control dynamics combinations. Because of this, it is often fruitless to expect to achieve, or even to seek for, "pure" measures of human behavior.

The fundamental dynamic inseparability of men (and other creatures) from their physical environments has, of course, been recognized for a long time. Philosophers and psychologists have often pointed out that behavior is an interaction among things and that it is arbitrary and misleading to single out the animate ones as doing all the behaving while the others are regarded as making up the environment. Actually, it is the system which behaves, not the individual components.

The systems concept, as here used, has arisen only recently; early writers who bothered with this problem worked out different ways of conceptualizing behavior and of identifying the "meta-thing" which does the behaving. Although the views of Kantor [101] and Lewin [112] may have been somewhat similar to those expressed here, Hunter [98] and A. F. Bentley [17] certainly betrayed an anthropocentrism which the concept of the man-environment system now calls into question. Bentley would deal with the matter by creating a conceptual behavior space centered around the man and extending from him out into the physical environment. Whereas the skin is the boundary of the man as an object, his behavior extends *transdermally* to a behavioral *superfice* which, like an amoeba, alters its shape with the action, but always includes the objects with which the man is in dynamic interaction. Hunter's view appears to be rather similar and equally man-centered.

It should be clear from this that recognition of the confounding of human behavior with that of the physical elements of the environment is nothing new. It should be equally clear that neither this confounding nor the various views which emphasize it is of the least practical consequence to scientific psychology as long as one deals only with situations in which the portions of the human's environment through which he acts are linear and remain constant during an experiment. If, in a tracking study, the independent variables are something other than the nature of the control or system dynamics—if the subject always uses the same control device with the same physical properties, and if the output of the control always bears a one-to-one relationship with the output of the man—it matters not the least that the behavior measured is that of the man–control-stick system and not that of the human alone. Since the contribution of the part of the system through which the man is working is unaltered, any changes in the response of the system resulting from variations in the parameters under investigation can be attributed to the man. Thus they become directly relevant to psychology.

But let the properties of the components through which the human is operating be varied, and it becomes vital to recognize the contaminated nature of the performance measure. Change the control from spring-restrained to damped, and the alteration in behavior is a composite of direct physical effects and adjustments in human performance. In this type of confounding, what actually happens is that the *independent* variable includes a component of the so-called *dependent* variable. One is directly manipulating an element of the very thing which is used as an index of performance. Furthermore, the roles of the mutually contaminated elements of the variable are not always obvious, so that further research is often needed to disentangle the psychology from the physics. Certainly, if the confounding is not recognized and the behavioral changes are attributed exclusively to the man, a scientific blunder is committed.

Areas 1, 2, and 3

Having described the variables encountered in the evaluation of man-machine systems, those met with in the first three research areas of human engineering will now be discussed. These remaining research clusters comprise the majority of the experiments in engineering psychology and include rather extensive studies of displays, controls, and display-control relationships.

There is no sharp distinction between tests of systems and the engineering psychology experiments carried out in the laboratory. The studies of area 5 stand at one end of a continuous spectrum of human engineering investigation. Close to this end are the experiments done with simulated systems or system components. Many controlling and tracking studies belong here, as do studies of multidimensional displays and controls. In fact, most of the investigations within clusters 2 and 3 lie at this end of the continuum; the independent variables are often qualitative, frequently confounded, and invariably complex, while the dependent variables represent the performance of systems rather than men more often than not.

At the other end of the scale are experimental investigations included in engineering psychology because they shed light upon human information-processing characteristics, but are otherwise indistinguishable from conventional psychophysical studies or experiments in sensory or motor physiology. These undertakings are set apart by the simplicity and purity of the variables and the low relevance of the findings to the problems of system design.

In the middle falls the rather small remainder of research on the engineering properties of the man. Most of this is found in area 1 and deals with display considerations, although a few experiments in 2 and 3 fit into this middle category. Independent variables are often qualitative here, but to an important extent they are less complex and confounded than those of out-and-out systems studies. Moreover, the dependent variables in most cases are either unadultered human performance measures or indexes of system behavior with the contaminating physical elements in the variable held constant.

In this group are studies involving the manipulation of such engineering parameters as radar scope gain, signal-to-noise level, the nature and amount of speech filtering, the length and spacing of scale markings, the number and variety of coordinates in a visual indicator, and the amount of information in a figure. The measures taken are such things as the time to report seeing a target, the number of words repeated correctly, the length of time to read a scale and the number of errors made, the number of identifying features reported, and the speed and accuracy of figure identification.

Note that only the studies in this last category illustrate a clear bridging relationship between engineering and psychology at the level of variables. Here engineering variables are systematically manipulated, while measures of human performance are recorded. For the rest of engineering psychology research, the bridging either takes place at another level or *among the components within a variable,* as has been so clearly illustrated in the case of evaluative studies of man-machine systems.

CONCEPTS

Two Types of Models

As we turn from consideration of empirical variables to concepts, we can distinguish two schools of engineering psychologists. The conservative school employs traditional psychological constructs and models to describe the performance of the human element in the system and reserves the language of physical science and engineering for discussing the behavior of the mechanical or electronic components. The engineering or mechanical-model school uses essentially the same physical science concepts to describe the actions of both the man and the mechanism.

For the conservatives, engineering psychology is still very much like other forms of psychology. To be sure, the subject matter is more limited, as we have seen, but otherwise it is very much the orthodox anthropocentric psychology of the past thirty years. To describe human behavior, the conservative modelers customarily employ such terms as *stimulus, response, sensation, perception, understanding, meaning, attention, expectancy, drive, fatigue,* and *skill.*

To the psychologist, such concepts are meaningful and serviceable in designing conventional experiments, but they possess the disadvantage of being entirely different in both vocabulary and syntax from the engineering terms used to describe mechanical or electronic devices. Because of this, the human engineer who employs psychological constructs in dealing with the operator's behavior must abruptly switch languages when he considers the behavior of the machine elements. The transition from one construct language to the other is not easily made, and exact translation is often impossible because of the complete lack of overlap between the two sets of concepts. As a result, engineers and dyed-in-the-wool psychologists frequently find communication difficult, and engineers have sometimes complained that the construct barrier has reduced the relevancy to engineering of the human factor data which the psychologist supplied.

An obvious way out of this enforced scientific bilingualism is to adopt a metalanguage which is appropriate to all system components, whether human or inanimate. A start has been made by the mechanical-model school of engineering psychology. For this school, human behavior is a matter of inputs, outputs, coding, storage, information transmission, stability, transfer function, and bandpass. Some members of the "new" school derive their basic concepts from information theory; others have been more influenced by the servo approach. But whichever model is preferred, it is being applied throughout the anthropomechanical system, so that it is not necessary for the avant-garde engineering psychologist to switch constructs at the man-machine interface.

It would be quite wrong to think that the difference between the two groups of engineering psychologists is merely a matter of words. True, they speak different languages—more important, they carry out different research. Today engineering modelers are asking questions about human behavior which were literally inconceivable a few years ago. Yet systems engineers require answers to precisely this kind of question. How well can the man act as the analog of an amplifier, integrator, or differentiator? How good is he as a surrogate for different kinds of computers? Is his gain fixed or variable? If the latter, how does it change with alterations in the system dynamics? How linear is the man under different circumstances? What is his ultimate bandwidth; how does his bandpass change with circumstances? Is he more like a single or multichannel transmission device? What is his channel capacity? These are a few of the questions which arise when the man is held up to an engineering model; they are questions to which answers are now being sought in the laboratories of engineering psychology.

When these and other similar queries about the engineering properties of the man have been answered, it may be possible to develop true system design principles which will be dependent upon both psychology and engineering but which will be neither, strictly speaking. One of the first of such nondenominational principles to emerge in human engineering employs the system concepts of "unburdening" and quickening [22] and advocates that continuous control systems should be so designed that the operator can behave in a fashion no more complex that that which is analogous to simple amplification. Other such principles will undoubtedly soon be developed, but it would seem to be a safe bet to suggest that they will occur most readily to engineering psychologists who adopt a system-centered point of view and dispassionately model the man in terms of engineering processes.

It must not be supposed that, because it is possible to identify two different ways of conceptualizing the man and describing his behavior, all engineering psychologists fit neatly and completely into one school or the other. In fact, the majority of experimenting human engineers, although leaning more in one direction than the other, utilize both types of constructs and language systems, either at different times or concurrently. It is not at all unusual to find descriptions of behavior in engineering psychology articles in which both psychological and engineering constructs are used indiscriminately. Thus, Chernikoff and Taylor [38] employ engineering independent variables in a tracking study, measure system performance, and draw inferences about human behavior. Part of the time these inferences are couched in the construct language of psychology as, for example, when they speak of stimulus, response, target course difficulty, motor-task complexity, inference, attention, and knowledge of results. In the same discussion, however, they also use such concepts as human "noise," output force, information channels, unburdening, damping, and aided tracking. Likewise, Deininger and Fitts [148, pp. 316–341], in discussing several related studies, deliberately reformulate many of the older psychological constructs in information-theory terms. Similarly, Birmingham and Taylor [22] manage, within a single theoretical article, to juggle two different models and the three construct languages of psychology, engineering, and man-machine system design. Many other examples of this willingness to shift back and forth between anthropomorphic and mechanomorphic constructs could be cited—in fact, it is hard to avoid such examples—but these will suffice.

There is certainly no intent to imply that anything is wrong with thus mixing one's models. In fact, it is inevitable that both construct languages will exist in engineering psychology side by side for some time, with neither sufficiently well developed to entirely supersede the other. If the conservatives are right, and the new models prove sterile, or if they are quite wrong, and the engineering concepts turn out to be fruitful, one or the other construct language may die out. But until that happens, most engineering psychologists will use both, in proportions suitable to their scientific tastes and their research problems.

Relationship between Empirical and Systematic Variables

Both the experimental variables and theoretical constructs of human engineering have been considered; a word concerning their relationship is now in order. The maturity of a science can be judged from the nature of this relationship, for the more highly developed the field, the more rigorous the connection between the variables and the concepts. In physics the two are most intimately associated, with the variables acting as fundamental elements of the defining operations of the constructs. It is well recognized that some of the concepts of psychology are less precisely defined, so that confusion and disagreement occasionally arise as to which empirical variables are associated with precisely what constructs (or systematic variables). In its short history, engineering psychology has certainly not outgrown this limitation of its parent. Although hopes are high, the concepts of experimental human engineering have not yet achieved a precision significantly different from those of academic experimental psychology.

An illustration of this is furnished by the notion of "task difficulty." This is one of the most widely employed concepts in the field of human engineering, yet it is so ill defined as to be of dubious value. The difficulty of a tracking task has been varied by numerous manipulations, including target-course amplitude, frequency, randomness; the qualitative nature of the display and its magnification; the number of coordinates controlled; the type of control and its physical properties; the directional and sensitivity relationship between the control and the display; the nature of the tracking system dynamics; the sense modality involved in "reading" the display; and the part of the body doing the responding.

Widely different experimental results are obtained, depending upon which of these empirical variables are used. For example, the optimum aided-tracking time constant shifts upward if task difficulty is upped by increasing target-course frequency [38]. However, the optimum shifts downward if task difficulty is increased by increasing course amplitude while holding frequency constant [140]. In the same way, the more difficult of two tracking tasks (as judged by a systems score) is found to be *more* sensitive to stress if the difficulty is varied through altering system dynamics, but *less* sensitive if it is changed by modifying display gain [69].[5] Indisputably, the construct of task difficulty is so vague that it is of little value in furthering scientific understanding or guiding an engineer in designing better systems.

Those who defend the use of engineering models and a physico-mathematical construct language contend that the emerging concepts possess, among other virtues, a definitional purity which is not characteristic of all the systematic variables of psychology proper. However, although the new constructs may be intrinsically cleaner and therefore capable of more discriminative definition, the point has not yet been fully demonstrated, but only alleged. Certainly, there is not yet universal agreement concerning the particular empirical variables through which such concepts as human gain, available bandwidth, or amount of information processed are actualized. Most definitely, the continuing responsibility of remaining alert to the possibility of a low correlation between what one does and what one thinks he is doing is shared by both the conservative engineering psychologists and the members of the new school.

Use of Engineering Models

Before concluding the discussion of constructs and models, a little more should be said about the way in which those derived from engineering are used. It has been argued that when the human engineer employs the models and concepts of physical science, he does so primarily because he believes that they will help him make a better contribution

[5] Verbal communication with William Garvey, U.S. Naval Research Laboratory, Washington 25, D.C.

to the design of man-machine systems. Also, some psychologists consider that there is an outside chance that modeling human psychomotor behavior in terms of mechanical processes will stimulate new lines of psychological research, provide new knowledge, and furnish a means of establishing more elegant relationships among the facts already known.

But whatever the purpose of holding the man up to computers or servo motors or communications systems may be, it is not to seek in the one a reductive explanation of the other. Often one science seeks to reduce its molar facts to the molecular structures of another "more fundamental" science, e.g., psychologists sometimes seek to explain human behavior in terms of physiology. Certainly most present-day engineering psychologists who use a construct language of applied physical science do not expect to find in it an explanation of their psychological facts in this sense. Just as the engineer does not try to give a psychological account of the operation of his servos and computers, so the human engineer is scarcely more likely to accept the workings of a servo motor or computer as a veridical representation of the operation of the mind. He may expect that some of the laws of servo behavior will have their parallels in human response, so he may study the machine first in order to study the man better. But he would not anticipate that the parallels would be exact, if pursued down to the level of microstructure; even if they did prove to be exact in some few cases, he would be certain that further probing would reveal important differences in the dynamic substrata of the two.

The engineering psychologist regards the man as being many times more complicated than existing servos or digital computers. Even when the human is acting like the machines, the similarity is assumed to be the result of a kind of natural hoax, perpetrated through event trains quite different from those underlying the mechanical behaviors reproduced. In short, although many human engineers expect their engineering models to illuminate human behavior, few expect them to provide a reductive explanation of it.

Certainly some engineering psychologists consider that the models do furnish an explanation of a different type. Many regard explanation as nothing more than description—and the more precise and complete the description, the better the explanation becomes. For them, the engineering models do furnish explanations of human response; in serving as interpretive schema, they provide a neat and compact description of some aspects of man's behavior. The servo, the information channel, the computer, and the physical processes which underlie them are working models of behavior, so to speak. They represent sets of dynamic configurations, logically ordered, so that a knowledge of a few of the processes permits others to be deduced.

To the extent that these interpretive models are congruent with human behavior, they may be said to explain it for the theoretically sophisticated psychologist. For him, the search for explanation consists of identifying elements of human behavior with those of the model, deducing new functional relationships in reference to the model, translating these back into human behavior, and finally testing for these predicted behavioral relationships through psychological experiment. Thus, explanation improves for him as more and more functional relationships deduced from the model are identified in human behavior.

In summing up, it is evident that the engineering models either do or do not explain—depending on one's view of what constitutes proper explanation. But for all who utilize them, they serve as fructuous schema for suggesting system-relevant and technologically important research.

III. Long-term Contributions of Human Engineering to Psychology

In the preceding sections, we have compared and contrasted human engineering and psychology. Although opinion and bias have undoubtedly reduced the objectivity, the effort has been to report what human engineers have been up to during the first few years of their professional existence and to analyze their ventures relative to those of their colleagues in academic psychology. However, in this section, we shall prognosticate lines of influence; in the next, we shall advocate specific courses of action. Clearly, prejudice is bound to enter—the pages ahead must be read with this caveat in mind and with the full expectation that another writer might foresee quite different directions of development and plead for educational and administrative programs other than those recommended here.

As long as human engineering continues to evolve along present lines, it will indubitably exert influences upon psychology. We may expect to see psychology affected by its offspring in regard to methods, subject matter, and concepts.

METHODS

Relatively few new instrumental procedures have been developed in engineering psychology, so that the contribution in this realm has been small. However, the use of analog and digital computers and such techniques as frequency analysis, cross-correlation, and autocorrelation might very profitably be extended into motor skills, learning, and other basic areas of psychological research. Furthermore, we expect that new methods will constantly be developed in human engineering and that they will have value for academic as well as engineering psychology.

SUBJECT MATTER

Very similar statements may be made about subject matter. Engineering psychology is such a new field that it has developed very little subject matter of its own, but what it has already acquired and what it will acquire in the future in the way of data on psychomotor behavior will, of course, be of direct interest to academic psychology.

Less of the systems material will interest the fundamental research worker, but the findings in this field are well worthy of note by applied psychologists who work in selection and training. For example, it is becoming increasingly clear [20, 69, 170, 172] that there is an important relationship between the operator's precise role in the man-machine system and the amount of benefit which may be expected from selecting operators and training them. In some instances, proper attention to human-engineering the sytsem has greatly reduced the requirements for selection and training. Preliminary evidence [69, 74] also points to the conclusion that sometimes human engineering considerations are more important than considerations of adjusting the operator to the machine in immunizing system performance against the effects of task-induced stress. Such studies are little more than suggestive since they merely scratch the surface of a big applied-problem area. Nevertheless, they are certainly worth following up and illustrate subject-matter contributions of human engineering to other areas of applied psychology.

CONCEPTS

The System Concept

If any one thing epitomizes human engineering and sets it apart from its parent subject, it is the concept of the man-machine system. This system concept is, of course, quite foreign to anthropocentric psychology, since it places the mechanism on a par with the man who controls it and creates a new unit which is hierarchically superior to both. However, if the concept is broadened to include creatures other than men and physical objects and events other than those narrowly defined as machines, it is pertinent to much that is dealt with in psychology.

Almost without exception, psychological experiments are systems experiments. In the last analysis, the behavior of a creature—or any physical object, for that matter—cannot be measured except through its effect on something else. In this sense, every measurement involves a system. But in a much more obvious way, many psychological investigations encapsulate the subject within a multicomponent physical system and measure the performance of the system, rather than that of the man or animal alone.

In a simple auditory-reaction-time experiment, for example, some physical device delivers a signal (say, a tone) and starts a clock. The sound waves are conducted through the air and through the mechanisms of the ear to take an effect upon the receptors. After the impulses have passed through the nervous system, the subject responds by applying force to a key. The key closes and stops the clock. The time from the initiation of the signal at the front end of the system to making of an electrical connection on the other end is recorded. Very little time is consumed in the conduction of the sound waves through the air and the mechanical portions of the ear and in physically displacing the key from full-open to closed position. Thus there can be no serious practical objection to regarding the time for the complete system to operate as the subject's reaction time. Nevertheless, a change in the spring tension of the key or the distance of travel before closing may alter reaction time and this will reflect no change whatsoever in the subject, but a change in the mechanical response of the system. The manner in which the tone comes on may also be quite important in this system measure. If it comes on gradually, it may not reach a threshold value until several milliseconds after the clock has been started. Thus it will add to the difference between recorded response time and the actual reaction time of the subject (if the latter could be measured independently of the rest of the system).

In the great majority of psychological experiments which are actually systems studies, the subject's contribution to system performance so overwhelms that of the other components that they are customarily neglected. However, although it would certainly be pedantic to insist that one must always formally acknowledge the contribution of the nonanimate components, it would seem prudent to keep the possibility of this type of confounding in mind and to note its effect when it becomes more than trivial.

It is most certainly not trivial in the field of motor skills. Many of the athletic, industrial, and military skills studied by psychologists involve humans performing as elements in man-machine systems. Moreover, the measures used to index the skills are frequently system scores which reflect both the behavior of the man and the physics of the situation. And often the physical relationships are just as important as the psychology. In a sailing race, the characteristics of the sailboat have a very great deal to do with who wins. Furthermore, there is no way of measuring a sailor's skill without having him actually sail a boat or use some kind of dynamic simulator. In the same way, bowling skill can be assessed only by having the bowler bowl balls down an alley at pins and counting the number that are knocked down. Obviously, the physical characteristics of the bowling gear are reflected in the skill measure.

This suggests that it is entirely arbitrary to think of sailing and bowling as *human skills* when they are more properly regarded as *man-mechanism system skills*. Flying, driving, skating, and fencing also fall into this category as do all sports with bats, balls, rackets, cues, bows, arrows, mallets, etc., and forms of work involving grasping, transporting, placing, cranking, and pounding objects—to list but a few. In fact, all skills in which the human participates, but which are assessed in terms of a system score, fall into this category. This includes most psychomotor actions.

Thus the fact that the systems concept can be extended into psychology and fitted to a new research area is of very little moment. But the potential value of the application is raised from the level of a mere conceptual curiosity to that of an important contribution to behavioral science because this concept permits the human's role to differ in significance from one skill to the next. Analysis suggests that the relative contributions of the man and the mechanism to the over-all score have much to do with the way the skill measure responds to learning, individual differences, and environmental stress.

Oversimplifying for the sake of exposition, we can distinguish two types of man-mechanism skill. In one, the performance of the system faithfully reflects the behavior of the man; his score and the system score are one and the same. Running and skating are examples of this kind of skill. A great deal of physics is involved in both and special equipment is required for the skater, but still—relative to other skills—it is all pretty much up to the man. When his performance changes, the score reflects it directly and linearly.

In the second type of skill, the behavior of the system is less directly related to that of the man. In some instances, the system performance measure is insensitive to changes in the human's precision. To choose a ridiculous example, the amount of money that a man makes in playing a slot machine bears very little relationship to the way he pulls the handle. The mechanism dynamics are the important things in this system "skill," and the human's contribution is very small indeed. Similarly, with quickening, the performance of a control system becomes relatively unresponsive to changes in the level of the operator's performance; an untrained man, for example, does as well as a practiced operator [20, 170].

A different nonlinear relationship between the behavior of the man and the over-all system obtains when the system is marginally stable. In many circus-type balancing skills and in a variety of industrial and military tasks in which lags are encountered in a control loop, a very slight decrease in the level of precision of the human's performance may result in a much more profound change in the behavior of the system. In this type of skill, variations in the proficiency of the man are distorted and magnified nonlinearly by the mechanism dynamics so that measures of system performance are likely to give a false impression of the course of any changes in human behavior.

Thus it seems perfectly possible that the same independent variable might appear to have no effect on one man-mechanism skill, a slight effect on another, and a marked effect on a third—while actually human proficiency had altered by the same amount in each case. It is evident that precise conclusions about the effects of learning [8], abnormal environments, and all other independent variables upon the behavior of the man may be safely drawn only when the research is carried out on behaviors wherein the human and the system performance scores are linearly related. With all other skills—especially when interskill comparisons are involved—inferences about human activity from over-all measures are dangerous unless the precise nature of the relationship between the performance of the man and the system is known.

Because the system approach is new to this field, very little is known of how the measures of different skills relate to the behavior of the performers. How much more important is the role of the man in archery than in rifle shooting? How will a given increase in the variance of human performance affect an automobile-driving score in comparison with pursuit-rotor performance? How do different systems distort the shape of the learning curve of the man in the system? These are the kinds of questions which are raised when the human engineer applies his viewpoint to problems of skill. One or two relevant studies have been carried out to date [8, 69], but the great majority have yet to be conceived and performed.

To sum up, we suggest that when the concept of the man-machine system is extended from human engineering into the basic research area of motor skills, dimensions which hitherto have received very little attention are revealed. The degree of fidelity with which the system proficiency measure reflects human performance and the nature of the transformations of man's behavior wrought by different systems may someday be recognized as considerations of fundamental importance to psychology.

A Continuous Model of Human Behavior

Another possible contribution of engineering psychology to the concepts of the parent field may stem from an essentially negative point of view. Most human engineers who are working in the field of continuous control and tracking have become singularly disenchanted with the concepts of stimulus and response and are seeking for fruitful substitutes. A basic difficulty arises from the fact that both concepts indicate that the mainsprings of behavior are discontinuous energy changes. Typically, a stimulus is something which comes on, stays on for a while, and then goes off; usually it has a beginning, a duration, and an end. Similarly, a response is regarded as occurring at a certain time. This certainly implies that it is not occurring the rest of the time.

Thus the concepts of stimulus and response have tended to favor a kind of on-or-off notion of behavior. Of course, some modern psychologists have reacted against this "quantum-like" interpretation of S-R concepts and have taken pains to redefine the terms to circumvent their all-or-none implications. Yet in spite of these efforts, the discrete notion of stimulus and response still colors the thinking of at least a minority of psychologists. Furthermore, although it certainly does not follow logically from the stimulus-response model, the idea has gradually developed in some areas of psychology—perhaps as the result of implicit analogous inference—that the man is fundamentally a discontinuous performer. Information theory of the Shannon type has—superficially, at least—seemed to lend credence to this view, as has the established physiological fact of the discrete nature of the nervous impulse.

It cannot be denied, of course, that often the human does act intermittently. In fact, in the majority of psychological experiments, the human is plied with what are essentially discrete step-function signals, and he responds with corresponding step-function responses. For such behavior, the concept of an on-or-off-type stimulus and response may be quite fruitful, and the model of the response mechanism as a discontinuously operating device may do no harm. It should be pointed out, however, that the fact that discrete responses are evoked by discrete inputs does not necessitate a discontinuously operating mechanism. An analog computer, set up to track, gives essentially step-function outputs when subjected to step-function inputs, but this does not gainsay the fact that the computer is operating continuously and will follow a sine wave when required to do so, for example.

Other difficulties with the concepts of stimulus and response have been frequently noted. They include the frequent definition of stimulus in terms of a creature's response to it and the notion, now admittedly passé, that behavior is entirely stimulus-driven. However, a much more serious problem involves the utilization of the two concepts in engineering psychology research. The difficulty becomes apparent when the precise stimuli and responses involved in a continuous tracking task of several minutes' duration must be identified. Since the signal energy to which the subject is responding is altering continuously, there are no convenient points to reference the transition from one "stimulus" to another. Likewise, it is extremely difficult to distinguish separate responses in the subject's unceasing behavior. One could, of course, take care of this by arbitrarily defining "responding" as moving the control, but this would be most unsatisfactory with some tracking devices. With a spring-restrained control, for example, the definition would exclude all constant applications of force by the operator as responses, since they would result in no control motion. Other defining conventions would prove to be equally unsatisfactory. One is forced to conclude either that a series of unspecifiable stimuli and responses underlie the behavior, or that the whole tracking task involves but one colossal stimulus and one enduring response. Either way, the precise signals for action remain a scientific mystery.

Unfortunately, the human engineers have not found an entirely satisfactory substitute for the concepts which their work—along with the work of others—has called into question. Had they done so, the news would not require comment here, for it would hardly have escaped the notice of what would certainly be a most grateful profession. However, some engineering psychologists feel that an ultimate solution may be along the lines of the development of a complex feedback servo theory. Admittedly, the present-day model is too limited to provide much help in understanding most of the psychomotor behaviors dealt with in human engineering. Yet even in its primitive form, it does possess two virtues which recommend it to the attention of the behavior theorist.

First, if all inputs and outputs are placed on quantitative scales with zero representing the complete absence of the quantity, they can be dealt with on a continuous basis. Second, the servo model introduces the very important concept of the output being a function, not of the input alone, but of the difference between the input and some other quantity which reflects the state of the system. In the simplest cases, the input is compared with some direct function of the output, but other comparisons which are somewhat more analogous to the responding man are made in more complex systems.

The essential point, however, is this: The model accommodates one of the cardinal facts of human behavior, i.e., response is initiated and controlled, not by external energies, but rather by "mismatches" [124, 125] between the input and the expected or desired function of that input. In tracking, for example, the subject makes no effort to correct errors which are within his tolerance level. Likewise, he does not respond to an error if he predicts from its rate and acceleration that it will have dropped close to zero in a reaction time. In daily life, he takes action only when the existing state of events, as determined through sensory inputs, is out of harmony with events as anticipated or desired.

Admittedly, the primitive feedback servo schema is not yet ready to supplant diagrams of the S-O-R type which are at the heart of psychology. Yet one cannot help feeling that the concepts of stimulus and response must soon be replaced by more fruitful constructs in at least some fields of psychology and that possibly some elaborations of the continuous follow-up model will be acceptable. No matter how skeptical one may be about the applicability of servo theory to human behavior, one must admit that the servo language has an enriched mathematical syntax and describes the behavior of manlike servos very adequately without recourse to the concepts of stimulus and response. Perhaps someday a development of the theory will help psychologists do the same for men. If this does come about, it is to be expected that the servo approach will be most fruitful in the areas of psychomotor response and motor skill, although there are indications [73] that the continuous model may also be of value in describing changes in behavior which occur in the course of learning.

Scientific Metalanguage

The entire construct language which is being developed by the "new" school of engineering psychology is by all odds the most exciting contribution of human engineering to psychology and science in general— far more important than any specific finding, method, or concept. As we have pointed out, engineering or physical-process models are being held up to the man in order to extract behavioral relationships which are both system-relevant and expressible in physicomathematical terms. In doing so, they may be performing the very important function of destroying the barrier which has always stood between the physical and psychological sciences [169].

For reasons too complicated to discuss in detail here, psychology has developed concepts which tend to be untranslatable into the construct languages of the other sciences. This has placed us in the position of having to describe the actions of living creatures with one language and the behavior of physical objects in the environment with another. It has also walled off psychology from the other scientific disciplines and forced psychologists into the position where they could communicate freely only with one another. This has encouraged a kind of conceptual inbreeding which has operated against the development of an altogether vigorous construct language. Although psychology has become more and more scientific over the years as far as its methods and instrumental procedures are concerned, its concepts have not kept up. Today, human mind and behavior are thought about in essentially the same ways in which they have been conceptualized for years. New words are used, and the definitions are more rigorous and operational, yet that which is being specified is very much the same old type of syntactically impoverished construct.

A universal language of action which applies to all behaving things, animate or inanimate, may overcome the problem of interscience translation and at the same time eliminate psychology's conceptual endogamy. If this can be done and if the construct language has a rich and provocative syntax, all science should benefit.

Norbert Wiener and his associates [184] have, of course, pointed the way. In setting forth the idea of a construct metalanguage of control, the cyberneticists have taken an exceedingly bold and long first step. The start which they have made is being followed up in many sciences other than psychology and by many psychologists other than those in human engineering. Yet we contend that the engineering psychologists' role in the development of the new approach has been one of leadership, and that it derived, in part, from their pragmatic interests. Because they were trying to help design man-machine systems, many of them recognized early the vital necessity of using the same models and constructs to describe the behavior of both human and inanimate components.

Support for their venture was drawn from two corollaries of the systems viewpoint. One of these emphasized the dynamic inextricability of the behaving man and those elements of the environment to and through which he was responding. This interactional, or transactional, confounding of men and machines certainly argues against maintaining separate construct languages for the two system components. So does the hypothesis, which has already received experimental corroboration, that human and mechanical processes, although often unequal in precision, are frequently interchangeable. The system designer often has the option of using men or circuits to perform a given type of computation; either can do the job—although the circuits may be faster and more accurate, yet less reliable and more costly. This ability of the man to act as surrogate for mechanical and electronic processes—or, if one prefers, the ease with which machines can be built to simulate the man—provides a compelling argument for describing the basic response processes of both in the same terms.

The engineering psychologists have also been encouraged in their efforts by occasional success in improving the performance of actual systems, achieved through new models and constructs. In this regard, they have been more fortunate than like-minded academic psychologists who are also working with information theory and other mathematico-physical models. For them, the only tests of the value of the new ways of thinking about human behavior have been estimates of their scientific fruitfulness and the theoretical elegance of their generalizations. In contrast, the human engineer could see his success as well as estimate it.

Of course, the merest start toward the new set of universal constructs has been made. At present, the engineering models are far too simple to be used effectively with any but the most primitive of man's behaviors. Perhaps both information and servo theory will have to be discarded and new and completely different complex models developed before really important results can be achieved. Furthermore, much research will have to be done on the engineering properties of human behavior before an adequate construct vocabulary can be built up. What has been developed to date is more in the nature of a conceptual lingua franca—a pidgin engineering, as it were—by which engineers and psychologists are beginning to communicate, rather than a true scientific metalanguage.

But the start has been made, and that is the important thing. In this modest beginning may be perceived, for the first time, a reasonable hope that an interscience language of behavior will be developed in the years ahead. If this does sometime come about, engineering psychologists will be able to claim at least part of the credit.

IV. Collaborative, Administrative, and Educational Mechanisms

In this final section, recommendations will be made concerning organizational and educational arrangements for human engineering. These recommendations represent the opinion of one man and therefore must be received with caution. There are other reasons for being chary of accepting any detailed administrative proposals relative to this new field. The first is the very fact that it is a new field which is rapidly changing, growing, and developing. To saddle the burgeoning discipline with a rigid curriculum and an inflexible professional ethos would be to restrict it and thus do it and society an injustice.

But human engineering is not only young, it is unconventional, drawing as it does upon engineers' concepts of what they want from psychology and psychologists' notions of what constitutes proper engineering. Its vigor stems from the very incongruity of its parent disciplines; it could have developed only as a result of different professions attempting to cope with subject matters foreign to them. Had psychologists and engineers stuck to their own fields—as, no doubt, the conservatives in both professions might have preferred—human engineering could not have been born. By the same token, a too enthusiastic effort to organize, regularize, and institutionalize human engineering—to make a discipline out of what is, by its very nature, an interdiscipline—may cripple it. For example, any attempt to set precise standards for education or experience or to license engineering psychologists would be premature and dangerous at the present time.

But if overspecification is a hazard to a new field, so is the failure to plan at all or to make an effort to provide support and guidance when necessary. For this reason, we conclude with some general remarks concerning directions which we feel administrative and educational policy should take relative to human engineering.

A UNIFIED HUMAN FACTORS APPROACH

Today the human engineering approach to man-machine systems is split off from that of the psychologists, who attempt to improve system performance through selecting and training the human operators. Furthermore, many human engineers have become so preoccupied with machines that they have forgotten that the well-being of the human component is a *sine qua non* for system effectiveness. This has forced the physiologists, environmental medical specialists, and habitability experts into developing their own approaches to equipment design. Thus we find a plethora of human factor specialties, each claiming to supply a vital service to the engineer. Small wonder that the layman—and often the expert—is bewildered and confused as to what *the* spokesman for the man in the machine is really trying to say, since he speaks in many tongues and gives many different and often conflicting sets of directions.

Why such a multiplicity of human factor approaches have emerged is quite understandable, of course. The man is an extremely complicated organism; he can play a tremendous variety of roles and is subject to an infinity of influences. Since human behavior is a function of so many things, specialties which emphasize limited classes of influences and neglect others will naturally develop. Soon these narrow fields of concentration generate individual points of view, construct languages, and subject matters which form the basis of little subsciences, each seeming warped and esoteric to the others but entirely adequate to itself.

However, the time may now have arrived to begin to interrelate these human factor specialties and to substitute collaboration for competition among the proponents of the different points of view. To this end, three suggestions are offered:

1. Various actions could be taken to acquaint different human factors specialists with other approaches to the design and use of man-machine systems. Experts from the fields of selection, training, human engineering, environmental physiology, etc., could discuss, in reports and symposia, their various ways of improving the performance of aircraft, submarines, information-processing systems, and other man-operated devices. Although somewhat similar attempts have been made in the past,

they have suffered from a lack of specific and common referents. The different specialists have always been free to choose their own examples, which has meant that it has not been possible to assess the nature and degree of overlap between the approaches. The selection people might discuss their success or failure in selecting riflemen; the training experts, the ways of teaching Morse code; the physiologists, the design of a lightweight helmet; and the human engineers, the design of a synthetic informational display. The end products are so entirely different that it is impossible to achieve any appreciation of what the different approaches could accomplish for a given man-machine system.

Obviously, discussions directed to specific and common systems are needed. Instead of generalized topics such as "What can selection, training, human engineering, etc., do for the military man?" there should be discussions of what these and the other human factor fields can contribute to the performance of such specific man-machine devices as certain aircraft control loops, particular navigational systems, driver-automobile combinations, the pilot in his space suit, air-traffic control systems, etc. In many instances, of course, a particular approach will have no contribution to make, but this is precisely the kind of thing one wants to know. Only by getting the proponents of the different human factor viewpoints to become specific about the same end products can commensurability be achieved. Without this, it is difficult to begin to estimate the help which the various approaches can provide for the system planner.

Industrial psychology would seem to be in a position to make a contribution to the development of a unified human factors attack on systems. Many feel that it already embraces at least portions of the various subdisciplines which together make up the applied human factors area [44]. If the industrial psychologist would broaden his field to include the man-machine systems view and if he would incorporate the new developments in human engineering and environmental medicine, he could be a powerful key figure in laying the groundwork for the ultimate emergence of a much more consistent and unified human-referenced engineering.

2. Government and some industrial human engineering laboratories could employ several types of human factors specialists to make a joint approach to system design problems. It would certainly be feasible and useful in large laboratories to bring engineers, physiologists, and environmental medical experts together with human engineers to deal with problems involving the design of such complex systems as aircraft, tanks, and ships. This is now being done to a limited extent, but a more deliberate effort to broaden the technological aspects of human factors approach would be desirable.

However, it must be confessed that there are at present insuperable administrative difficulties in the way of combining the selection and training approaches with that of the human engineer. The foremost obstacle is provided by the fact that three entirely different organizations may be charged with the responsibility for the design of operational systems, the selection of operators, and operator training, respectively— at least in some branches of the government. In such services, a laboratory under the aegis of one organization has available only mechanisms to implement recommendations concerning its own area of responsibility. It would be to little avail, therefore, for a human engineering laboratory to attempt to lay out a training program for the operators of a system on which it was working, for example, or to suggest the criteria which might be employed in their selection. Although a limited human factor team approach is possible, it will not be complete until there are some rather fundamental administrative changes.

3. Joint research by the different human factor specialists would seem to be a good way to integrate the fields. This research should be system-oriented rather than man-oriented and should explore thoroughly the interrelationships among the factors relative to learning, individual differences, the effects of stress, and the nature of the human tasks. The few pilot studies already undertaken [20, 69, 74] suggest that some very important interactions between the type of performance required of the operator by the mechanics of the system and the other three human factor variables will be found. Once the nature and extent of these interrelationships are known, plans for the design and use of man-machine systems can be made with far more assurance than at present.

If the administrative difficulties in the way of truly collaborative interspecialty research prove serious, the actual experimentation could be done by specialists from one area who would consult with their colleagues in the other areas. Although any of the specialists could take the major responsibility, the human engineering laboratories might be best equipped to perform the systems research which the approach requires.

If a full-blown interhuman factor research program appears too ambitious, a useful contribution to unification would be made by having training and selection groups adopt the systems viewpoint, choose several system-relevant human tasks, and carry out their research on these particular psychomotor processes. Were this done systematically, the information obtained would fit in with that derived from engineering psychology to provide the basis for a broad and truly useful human factors science and technology.

ADMINISTRATION OF HUMAN ENGINEERING

There are five types of organization which are currently involved in some way or other with human engineering. It is instructive to consider the roles which these groups are playing today and to suggest courses of action aimed at enhancing their contributions to the new field. The organizations to be considered are as follows:

1. University departments of psychology and physiology
2. University departments or subdepartments of (*a*) human engineering, engineering psychology, aviation psychology, applied experimental psychology, industrial psychology (in some instances), and (*b*) engineering
3. Service-sponsored laboratories staffed by government employees or government contractors
4. Commercial human engineering consulting organizations
5. Human factors groups and engineering departments in electronic, aircraft, and other equipment industries

Together, these five groups are responsible for all aspects of human engineering. This means that, in addition to conducting engineering psychology research and practicing human engineering design, they must also provide for the training of all human engineers. The responsibilities are, of course, not shared equally but assumed in proportions largely determined by the nature of the institution and the available facilities. For example, universities are, or will be, far more able to perform the educative function than departments in industrial organizations; the latter are better equipped to discharge technological responsibility. All five types have been involved in each of the three functions; it is important to make this explicit and to plan to eventually bring about some division of labor.

Training

At present, the training of engineering psychology research workers is the undisputed province of the first and second groups listed above, whereas the training of human engineering technologists—to the extent that they are taught at all—is going on in all organizations except the first group. In the last four groups, the technological education is usually informal and imparted through the apprenticeship system, although formal courses are now beginning to be taught in such places as some university human engineering departments, the Bell Telephone Laboratories, and the Navy Bureau of Ships. In addition, one- or two-week human engineering summer courses are now being offered occasionally to engineers in the Armed Forces and industry by universities, government contract organizations, and commercial consulting firms.

It would seem desirable that training should eventually be assumed almost entirely by the universities. However, before they can undertake training of the human engineering technologists, the other institutions will have to provide the substance of the technological courses to be taught, write many of the textbooks, and supply some of the teachers. In order to move as rapidly as possible toward the day when the universities will shoulder the full training load, easy communication between university departments and outside organizations should be encouraged. Specifically, the actual interchange of personnel by universities and government, commercial, and industrial laboratories for periods up to a year would be very desirable. So would the development and teaching of more formal technological courses by nonuniversity groups to pre- and postdoctoral trainees. Finally, one or more journals which would accept technological contributions would be a great boon to all attempting to establish training programs, as well as to technologists.

Technology

Although all five types of institutions have been involved to a degree in human engineering design, obviously a group's technological contribution should be in proportion to its physical and intellectual propinquity to the systems being designed. By this criterion, an organization's technological responsibility would increase, the further down it appears on the listing given earlier. Certainly it would seem generally desirable to free university scientists and teachers from design, which could be done more effectively by human engineers in commerce and industry. As time goes on, the responsibility for active human engineering application will probably fall more and more heavily upon the commercial and industrial organizations, while the first three groups are increasingly freed to develop the scientific side of the new field. Of course, there will always be a need for consultation and advice from outstanding scientists and technologists, regardless of whether they are employed by universities, government, or industry, so it is not likely that any of the five groups will ever completely withdraw from practice. Nevertheless, the trend toward increased technological responsibility on the part of organizations low on the list seems both apparent and desirable, and it probably should be encouraged.

Science

It is reasonable to suppose that the responsibility for the scientific functions of human engineering will continue to be divided for years among all five varieties of institutions, just as it is today. The changes which may be predicted relative to (1) the distribution of effort as applied to science versus technology, and (2) an increasing division of labor as to the type of scientific pursuit indulged in within the different classes of organizations.

As one moves down the list of institutional types, one draws ever nearer to a specific end product. If we convert this into a research continuum, we note an increasing directedness or end-product orientation as we move down the list. Although this trend is certainly discernible, it is not as clear today as it probably will be in a few years, and it was by no means as apparent in the past as it is right now.

When human engineering started during World War II, the only psychological institutions which could be called upon were university departments of psychology and a few industrial psychology groups in certain universities [25]. In short, if applied human engineering research were to be done, the experimental psychologists would have to do it, either at home laboratories or in the field. And do it they did—with the result that engineering psychology got its start.

However, as government laboratories and commercial consulting firms came into being, they took over some of the product-oriented work and thus began to free the university psychologists for more basic science. In the last few years, the industrial concerns have set about establishing their own laboratories. It is to be expected that they will ultimately take on more and more of the highly applied research, relaxing the pressure on the service-supported laboratories as well as the universities. This would seem to be a desirable trend which should be encouraged by the agencies which are responsible for underwriting system developments.

Another influence which is now reducing the specific product orientation of research in the first three groups is the developing awareness of the desirability and feasibility of establishing rather fundamental human engineering principles. At the start of the venture, all human engineering experimentation was *ad hoc* in nature. Today there is a growing belief that engineering psychology theory may be developed to a point where it will serve both science and technology far more effectively than purely empirical practical research ever could. This belief is leading many experimenting human engineers to bend every effort to substitute basic human engineering research programs for programs concerning specific devices whenever possible.

The degree to which a group's research is basic or directed is not the only thing which distinguishes the group or its research; the scientific concepts and subject matter may also vary. The first group consists of psychology and physiology departments in which research is expected to be directly relevant to the one field or the other. However, an interesting development in human engineering is the emergence of the concept of the man-machine system and the beginning of systems research. It is the essence of this new research that interest is on the system as a whole—either as a product being evaluated or as a new scientific unit—rather than on the man. In a very real sense, systems research represents a young scientific field whose boundaries are by no means coincident with those of psychology, but include parts of other sciences as well.

Because of this, we might anticipate that it would be rather difficult for the university departments of physiology and psychology to accommodate this new discipline, both administratively and in terms of scientific mission. On the other hand, since the other organizations are in no way bound to confine themselves to any one of the orthodox sciences, they are free to develop systems considerations to whatever extent it is felt to be profitable. As time goes on, one would expect a greater differentiation in the nature of scientific contributions by university basic science departments, and government and industrial research groups. The university departments of applied psychology and engineering will probably fall in between the two, with some individual departments leaning further toward the systems approach than others. Thus we suggest that the ordering of institutions in terms of their proximity to a specific end product reveals another roughly scaled research dimension along which differentiation is beginning to take place.

Among the nonuniversity institutions—all of which probably are equally advanced in the development of the systems viewpoint—another division of scientific labor may soon be expected. This relates to the performance of evaluative tests on operational man-machine systems developed by industry. Because of the impropriety of industrial human engineering groups evaluating their own products, service-sponsored laboratories and perhaps commercial consulting organizations will be called on increasingly to participate in appraising the contractors' efforts. Thus, in addition to a large scientific and small technological function, the service-sponsored laboratories may soon acquire an evaluative responsibility which will distinguish them from the university departments and the industrial human engineering laboratories.

EDUCATION

The Two Training Programs

It has been made clear that the human engineering technologist has one set of aims, interests, and methods, and the engineering psychologist has another. It is recommended that, in the future, the differences between these two kinds of human engineer be recognized by the establishment of two distinctly different university training programs [30]. In brief, the technologist should be trained as an engineer who specializes in human factors, while the research-oriented human engineer should be trained as a psychologist or physiologist, with a minor in man-machine systems engineering. The two specialists would thus have entirely different educational backgrounds, except for a small area of overlap in which human factors considerations were combined with those of engineering.

The idea would be to have the human engineering practitioner of the future study for a B.S. in engineering—hopefully a B.S. in human engineering or system engineering. The first two years of his training would probably be identical with the first two years of any other engineer. However, during his third and fourth years, he would specialize in human engineering by taking courses in industrial or systems engineering, a course in psychology for engineers, and one or more courses in human engineering [16, 44]. In order to accommodate these studies within an already crowded curriculum, it would be necessary to substitute them for less appropriate conventional courses. Although the B.S. would generally be the highest degree sought, as is now the case in other types of engineering, Ph.D.'s would occasionally be granted in the new engineering specialty.

In contrast to the technologist, the human engineering scientist would generally study for an advanced degree in engineering psychology or physiology, although many might stop short of a Ph.D. Except for the special courses to be described, the program for a degree in engineering psychology would be the same as that for experimental psychology. The recommended courses which would be taken by a student specializing in the new experimental field would include the same core human engineering studies offered to the technologist, a course in engineering, adapted for psychologists, and either physics, advanced mathematics, or computer techniques [10]. As is the case with the proposed engineering degree for the technologist, the addition of the new course requirements for the degree in engineering psychology would necessitate dropping certain studies now often taken by the candidate in experimental psychology.

The Human Factors Core

An important element in the proposed curriculum for both the human engineering scientist and the technologist is the core program in human engineering. This course, or series of courses, should be very broad in its coverage; it should include the material customarily associated with human engineering within its narrowest definition and, in addition, selection, training, and other human factor considerations. Furthermore, it is most important that the subject matter should be selected for its system relevance and presented so that it leads directly—and without a great deal of reinterpretation—to systems-oriented thinking. The realization of such a course is many years off, but the type of course and topics envisaged are as follows:

1. *The Concept of the Man-machine System.*
   System properties peculiar to combinations of men and machines. Learning, individual differences, stress effects relative to system performance.

2. *The Engineering Properties of the Man.*
   a. Mechanical properties. Anthropometry. Upper and lower limits of applied force. Vibratory properties of human mass.
   b. Transduction across the man-machine interface. Informational properties of different displays and controls. Informational properties of receptors and effectors. Coding. Speech communications. Communication with machines.
   c. Information and storage capacity of human. Maximum information transmitted under different conditions. Information processing. Span of perception. Memory. Decision making.
   d. Linear properties of the man. Analog processes such as integration and differentiation. Linear approximations of the human transfer function.
   e. Nonlinear and nonstationary properties of the man. Surrogate digital computer functions of the human. Time delays. Learning, relative to gain, transfer function, informational capacity, etc. Individual differences relative to same. Effects of environmental stress and prolonged activity upon the same characteristics.

3. *System Analysis.*
   Experimental methods applied to man-machine systems. Operator opinion sampling. Activity analysis. Operations analysis. Accident analysis. Computer techniques.

4. *System Synthesis.*
   System planning methods. Assignment of roles to human and mechanical components (precomputation, quickening, unburdening). Adjusting the mechanism to the man (designing displays, controls). Utilizing handbooks.

5. *System Optimization.*
   a. Design of operating procedures. Selection of "best" ways of interacting with machines.
   b. Selection of operators. Tests and procedures.
   c. Training of operators. Training methods, devices.
   d. Engineering of the environment to reduce stress and to enhance stable performance. Habitability. Safeguarding against deleterious environments. Morale.

REFERENCES

1. Adams, O. S., et al. Relations among some measures of pattern discriminability. *J. exp. Psychol.*, 1954, **48**, 81–88.
2. Alluisi, E. A. Conditions affecting the amount of information in absolute judgments. *Psychol. Bull.*, 1957, **64**, 97–103.

3. Attneave, F. Physical determinants of the judged complexity of shapes. *J. exp. Psychol.*, 1957, **53**, 221–227.

4. Attneave, F. *Applications of information theory to psychology: a summary of basic concepts, methods, and results.* New York: Holt, Rinehart & Winston, 1959.

5. Attneave, F., & Arnoult, M. D. The quantitative study of shape and pattern perception. *Psychol. Bull.*, 1956, **53**, 452–471.

6. Bahrick, H. P. Accuracy of positioning responses as a function of spring loading in a control. *J. exp. Psychol.*, 1955, **49**, 437–444.

7. Bahrick, H. P., et al. Reproduction of simple movements as a function of factors influencing proprioceptive feedback. *J. exp. Psychol.*, 1955, **49**, 445–454.

8. Bahrick, H. P., et al. Learning curves—facts or artifacts? *Psychol. Bull.*, 1957, **54**, 256–268.

9. Bailey, A. W., & Sweeney, J. S. *Preliminary study of helicopter attitude display systems.* U.S. Naval Res. Lab. Memo Report 451, 1955.

10. Baker, C. H. Mathematical training for applied experimental psychology. *Canad. J. Psychol.*, 1953, **7**, 183–191.

11. Baker, C. H. Attention to visual displays during a vigilance task: I. Biasing attention. *Brit. J. Psychol.*, 1958, **49**, 279–288.

12. Baker, C. H., & Grether, W. F. Visual presentation of information. In *Joint services human engineering guide to equipment design,* Wright Air Develp. Center Tech. Report 54-160, 1954. Chap. II.

13. Barnes, R. M. *Motion and time study.* (2nd ed.) New York: Wiley, 1940.

14. Battig, W. F., et al. Effect of frequency of target intermittence upon tracking. *J. exp. Psychol.*, 1955, **49**, 244–248.

15. Battig, W. F., et al. The effects of error-magnification and marker size on bidimensional compensatory tracking. *Amer. J. Psychol.*, 1955, **48**, 585–594.

16. Bauer, H. J. Another course in human engineering. *Amer. Psychologist,* 1957, **12**, 226.

17. Bentley, A. F. The behavioral superfice. *Psychol. Rev.*, 1941, **48**, 39–59.

18. Birmingham, H. P. *Comparison of a pressure and moving joystick.* U.S. Naval Res. Lab. Interim Letter Report 3600-330/50, 1950.

19. Birmingham, H. P., & Conklin, J. E. *A proposed method for improving spot-scope tracking of radar information.* U.S. Naval Res. Lab. Letter Report C-3600-96A/52, 1952.

20. Birmingham, H. P., et al. *A demonstration of the effects of quickening in multiple-coordinate control tasks.* U.S. Naval Res. Lab. Report 4380, 1954.

21. Birmingham, H. P., & Taylor, F. V. A design philosophy for man-machine control systems. *Proc. IRE*, 1954, **42**, 1748–1758.

22. Birmingham, H. P., & Taylor, F. V. *A human engineering approach to the design of man-operated continuous control systems.* U.S. Naval Res. Lab. Report 4333, 1954.

23. Bowen, H. M., & Woodhead, M. M. Estimation of track targets after preview. *Canad. J. Psychol.*, 1955, **9**, 239–246.

24. Bowen, J. H., & Chernikoff, R. *The relationship between magnification and course frequency in compensatory aided tracking.* U.S. Naval Res. Lab. Report 4913, 1957.

25. Bray, C. W. *Psychology and military proficiency.* Princeton, N.J.: Princeton Univer. Press, 1948.

26. Broadbent, D. E. Noise, paced performance and vigilance tasks. *Brit. J. Psychol.*, 1953, **44**, 295–303.

27. Broadbent, D. E. Some effects of noise on visual performance. *Quart. J. exp. Psychol.*, 1954, **6**, 1–5.

28. Broadbent, D. E. Noise: its effect on behavior. *Royal Soc. Health J.*, 1955, **75**, 541–545.

29. Broadbent, D. E. *Perception and communication.* New York: Pergamon Press, 1958.

30. Bromiley, R. B. Human engineering-psychophysiology or engineering. *J. Aviation Med.*, 1956, **27**, 231–235.

31. Brown, J. L., & Lechner, Marian. *Acceleration and human performance: a survey of research.* Naval Air Develpm. Center Report NADA-MA-5503(1), 1955.

32. Brown, R. H. The effect of extent on the intensity-time relation for the visual discrimination of movement. *J. comp. physiol. Psychol.*, 1957, **50**, 109–114.

33. Chapanis, A. *The design and conduct of human engineering studies.* San Diego, Calif.: San Diego State College Foundation, 1956.

34. Chapanis, A. *Research techniques in human engineering.* Baltimore, Md.: Johns Hopkins Press, 1959.

35. Chapanis, A., et al. *Applied experimental psychology.* New York: Wiley, 1949.

36. Chernikoff, R., et al. A comparison of pursuit and compensatory tracking under conditions of aiding and no aiding. *J. exp. Psychol.*, 1955, **49**, 55–59.

37. Chernikoff, R., et al. A comparison of pursuit and compensatory tracking in a simulated aircraft control loop. *J. appl. Psychol.*, 1956, **40**, 47–52.

38. Chernikoff, R., & Taylor, F. V. Effects of course frequency and aided time constant on pursuit and compensatory tracking. *J. exp. Psychol.*, 1957, **53**, 285–292.

39. Cherry, C. *On human communication.* New York: Technology Press and Wiley, 1957.

40. Conklin, J. E. Effect of control lag on performance in a tracking task. *J. exp. Psychol.*, 1957, **53**, 261–268.

41. Conrad, R. Speed and load stress in a sensorimotor skill. *Brit. J. industr. Med.*, 1951, **8**, 1–7.

42. Conrad, R. Some effects on performance of changes in perceptual load. *J. exp. Psychol.*, 1955, **49**, 313–322.

43. Cosgriff, R. L. *Nonlinear control systems.* New York: McGraw-Hill, 1958.

44. Coyer, R. A. A course in human engineering. *Amer. Psychologist,* 1956, **11**, 241–243.

45. Craik, K. J. W., & MacPherson, S. J. *The effect of certain operating conditions on the visibility of P.P.I. radar echoes.* Med. Res. Counc. APU 16, 1945.

46. Crossman, E. R. F. W. Entropy and choice time: the effect of frequency unbalance on choice response. *Quart. J. exp. Psychol.,* 1953, **5**, 41–51.

47. Davis, R. The limits of the psychological refractory period. *Quart. J. exp. Psychol.,* 1956, **8**, 24–38.

48. Deese, J. Some problems in the theory of vigilance. *Psychol. Rev.,* 1955, **62**, 359–368.

49. Edwards, W. The theory of decision making. *Psychol. Bull.,* 1954, **51**, 380–417.

50. Edwards, W. Behavioral decision theory. *Annu. Rev. Psychol.,* 1961, **12**, 473–498.

51. Elithorn, A., & Lawrence, C. Central inhibition: some refractory observations. *Quart. J. exp. Psychol.,* 1955, **7**, 36–57.

52. Elkind, J. I. *Characteristics of simple manual control systems.* MIT, Lincoln Lab. Tech. Report 111, April, 1956.

53. Ellson, D. G. The application of operational analysis to human motor behavior. *Psychol. Rev.,* 1949, **56**, 9–17.

54. Ellson, D. G., & Gray, Florence E. *Frequency responses of human operators following a sine wave input.* U.S. Air Force, Air Materiel Command Memo Report MCREXD-694-2N, 1948.

55. Ely, J. H., Bowen, H. M., & Orlansky, J. Man-machine dynamics. In *Joint services human engineering guide to equipment design,* Wright Air Develpm. Center Tech. Report 57-582, 1957. Chap. VII.

56. Ely, J. H., Thomson, R. M., & Orlansky, J. Design of controls. In *Joint services human engineering guide to equipment design,* Wright Air Develpm. Center Tech. Report 56-172, 1956. Chap. VI.

57. Ely, J. H., Thomson, R. M., & Orlansky, J. Layout of work places. In *Joint services human engineering guide to equipment design,* Wright Air Develpm. Center Tech. Report 56-171, 1956. Chap. V.

58. Erikson, C. W., & Hake, H. W. Multidimensional stimulus differences and accuracy of discrimination. *J. exp. Psychol.,* 1955, **50**, 153–160.

59. Fitts, P. M. (Ed.) *Psychological research on equipment design.* Washington: U.S. Government Printing Office, 1947.

60. Fitts, P. M. Engineering psychology and equipment design. In S. S. Stevens (Ed.), *Handbook of experimental psychology.* New York: Wiley, 1951.

61. Fitts, P. M. The information capacity of the human motor system in controlling the amplitude of movement. *J. exp. Psychol.,* 1954, **47**, 381–391.

62. Fitts, P. M., et al. Application of auto-correlation and cross-correla-

tion analysis to the study of tracking behavior. In *Air Force human engineering, personnel, and training research.* Air Res. Develpm. Command Tech. Report 56-8, 1955.

63. Fitts, P. M., et al. Stimulus correlates of visual pattern recognition: a probability approach. *J. exp. Psychol.,* 1956, **51**, 1–11.

64. Fitts, P. M., & Simon, C. W. *The arrangement of instruments and the position of instrument pointers as determinants of performance in an eye-hand coordination task.* U.S. Air Force, Air Materiel Command Tech. Report 3832, 1950.

65. Flynn, J. P., et al. *Auditory factors in the discrimination of radio range signals: collected informal reports.* Off. Sci. Res. Develpm. Report 6292, Psycho-acoustic Lab., Harvard Univer., 1945.

66. Folley, J. D., Jr., & Altman, J. W. *Guide to design of electronic equipment for maintainability.* Pittsburgh, Pa.: American Institute for Research, 1956.

67. Forbes, T. W. Auditory signals for instrument flying. *J. Aero. Sci.,* 1946, **13**, 255–258.

68. Fraser, D. C., & Jackson, R. F. Effect of heat stress on serial reaction time in man. *Nature,* 1955, **176**, 976–977.

69. Garvey, W. D. *The effects of "task-induced stress" on man-machine system performance.* U.S. Naval Res. Lab. Report 5015, 1957.

70. Garvey, W. D. Operator performance as a function of the statistical encoding of stimuli. *J. exp. Psychol.,* 1957, **54**, 109–114.

71. Garvey, W. D., et al. Prediction of future position of a target track on four types of displays. *Canad. J. Psychol.,* 1957, **11**, 93–103.

72. Garvey, W. D., & Knowles, W. B. Response time patterns associated with several display-control combinations. *J. exp. Psychol.,* 1954, **47**, 315–322.

73. Garvey, W. D., & Mitnick, L. L. An analysis of tracking behavior in terms of lead-lag errors. *J. exp. Psychol.,* 1957, **53**, 372–378.

74. Garvey, W. D., & Taylor, F. V. Interactions among operator variables, system dynamics, and task-induced stress. *J. appl. Psychol.,* 1959, **43**, 79–85.

75. Garvey, W. D., Taylor, F. V., & Newlin, E. P. *The use of "artificial signals" to enhance monitoring performance.* U.S. Naval Res. Lab. Report 5269, 1959.

76. Geldard, F. A. Adventures in tactile literacy. *Amer. Psychologist,* 1957, **12**, 115–124.

77. Gerathewohl, S. J. Conspicuity of flashing light signals of different frequency and duration. *J. exp. Psychol.,* 1954, **48**, 247–251.

78. Gibbs, C. B., & Clutton-Baker, J. *Pressure operated manual control levers.* Med. Res. Counc. Gr. Brit., R.N.P.R.C., Operational Efficiency Sub-committee Report No. 200, 1951.

79. Gottsdanker, R. M. The ability of human operators to detect acceleration. *Psychol. Bull.,* 1956, **53**, 477–487.

80. Grant, D. A., & Kaestner, N. F. Constant velocity tracking as a

function of S's handedness and the rate and direction of target course. *J. exp. Psychol.*, 1955, **49**, 203–208.

81. Green, B. F. The use of high speed digital computers in studies of form perception. In *Academy of Sciences, N.R.C. Vision Committee, Proceedings of Tufts Univer. Symposium on Form Discrimination*, Publication 561, 1957, 65–75.

82. Green, R. F. Transfer of skill on a following tracking task as a function of task difficulty (target size). *J. Psychol.*, 1955, **39**, 355–370.

83. Green, R. F., et al. Performance on a following task as a function of the continuity of the plane and direction of movement of the control cranks and target follower. *J. Psychol.*, 1955, **40**, 403–410.

84. Green, R. F., et al. Compensatory tracking performance as a function of the directions and planes of movement of the control cranks relative to the movement of the target. *J. Psychol.*, 1955, **40**, 411–420.

85. Hall, N. B., Jr. Internal relations of elemental motions within a task. *J. appl. Psychol.*, 1956, **40**, 91–95.

86. Hartman, B. O., & Fitts, P. M. Relation of stimulus and response amplitude to tracking performance. *J. exp. Psychol.*, 1955, **49**, 82–92.

87. Hauty, G. T., & Payne, R. B. Fatigue and the perceptual field of work. *J. appl. Psychol.*, 1956, **40**, 40–46.

88. Helson, H. Design of equipment and optimal human operation. *Amer. J. Psychol.*, 1949, **62**, 473–497.

89. Helson, H., & Howe, W. H. *A study of factors determining accuracy of tracking by means of handwheel control.* Off. Sci. Res. Develpm. Report 3451, The Foxboro Co., 1942.

90. Hill, J. H. Procedural analysis in the design of display and control panels. *Off. Naval Res., Res. Rev.,* ONR, 18–24, July, 1957.

91. Hirsh, I. J. Binaural summation and interaural inhibition as a function of the level of masking noise. *Amer. J. Psychol.*, 1948, **61**, 205–213.

92. Hirsh, I. J. The influence of interaural phase on interaural summation and inhibition. *J. acoust. Soc. Amer.*, 1948, **20**, 536–544.

93. Holland, J. G. Technique for behavioral analysis of human observing. *Science*, 1957, **125**, 348–350.

94. Holland, J. G., & Henson, Jean B. Transfer of training between quickened and unquickened tracking systems. *J. appl. Psychol.*, 1956, **40**, 362–366.

95. Humphrey, C. E. *Auditory displays. I. Spatial orientation by means of auditory signals, an exploratory study.* Johns Hopkins Univer., Appl. Physics Lab. APL/JHU TG-122, 1952.

96. Humphrey, C. E., & Thompson, J. E. *Auditory displays. II. Comparison of auditory and visual tracking in one dimension, (A) discontinuous signals, simple course.* Johns Hopkins Univer., Appl. Physics Lab. APL/JHU TG-146, 1952.

97. Humphrey, C. E., & Thompson, J. E. *Auditory displays. II. Comparison of auditory tracking with visual tracking in one dimension, (B) discontinuous signals, complex course.* Johns Hopkins Univer., Appl. Physics Lab. APL/JHU TG-147, 1952.

98. Hunter, W. S. The psychological study of behavior. *Psychol. Rev.,* 1932, **39**, 1–24.

99. Jenkins, W. O. The discrimination and reproduction of motor adjustments with various types of aircraft controls. *Amer. J. Psychol.,* 1947, **60**, 397–406.

100. Jenkins, W. O. Tactual discrimination of shapes for coding aircraft-type controls. In P. M. Fitts (Ed.), *Psychological research on equipment design.* Washington: U.S. Government Printing Office, 1947.

101. Kantor, J. R. *Principles of psychology.* Vols. 1 and 2. New York: Knopf, 1924, 1926.

102. Katz, M. S., & Spragg, S. D. S. Tracking performance as a function of frequency of course illumination. *J. Psychol.,* 1955, **40**, 181–191.

103. Kenchington, K. W. L., & Draper, J. *Trials at low temperatures of gloves, cold/wet.* Ministry of Supply, Directorate of Physiological and Biological Res., C.E.P.R.E., 1956.

104. Klemmer, E. T., & Frick, F. C. Assimilation of information from dot and matrix patterns. *J. exp. Psychol.,* 1953, **45**, 15–19.

105. Klemmer, E. T., & Muller, P. F., Jr. *The rate of handling information: key pressing responses to light patterns.* U.S. Air Force, Human Factors Operations Res. Lab. Memo Report 34, March, 1953.

106. Knowles, W. B., et al. The effect of speed and load on display-control relationships. *J. exp. Psychol.,* 1953, **46**, 65–75.

107. Knowles, W. B., et. al. A correlational analysis of tracking behavior. *Psychometrika,* 1957, **22**, 275–287.

108. Krendel, E. S. *The spectral density of tracking performance.* Part I. *The effect of instructions.* Wright Air Developm. Center Tech. Report 52-11(1), 1952.

109. Krendel, E. S. *The spectral density of tracking performance.* Part II. *The effects of input amplitude and practice.* Wright Air Develpm. Center, Tech. Report 52-11(2), 1952.

110. Krulee, G. K., & Sinclair, E. J. *Some behavioral implications of information theory.* U.S. Naval Res. Lab. Report 4119, 1953.

111. Levine, M. *Tracking performance as a function of exponential delay between the control and display.* U.S. Air Force, Wright Air Develpm. Center, Tech. Report 53-236, 1953.

112. Lewin, K. *Principles of topological psychology.* New York: McGraw-Hill, 1936.

113. Licklider, J. C. R. The influence of interaural phase relations upon the masking of speech by white noise. *J. acoust. Soc. Amer.,* 1948, **20**, 150.

114. Licklider, J. C. R., & Miller, G. A. The perception of speech. In S. S. Stevens (Ed.), *Handbook of experimental psychology.* New York: Wiley, 1951.

115. Lincoln, R. S., & Smith, K. U. Systematic analysis of factors determining accuracy in visual tracking. *Science,* 1952, **116**, 183–187.

116. Lincoln, R. S., & Smith, K. U. Visual tracking. II. Effects of brightness and width of target. *J. appl. Psychol.,* 1952, **36**, 417–421.

117. Lindsley, D. B., et al. *Radar operator "fatigue": the effect of length and repetition of operating period on efficiency of performance.* Off. Sci. Res. Dev. 3334, Res. Report No. 6, Publ. Bd. No. 18366, U.S. Dept. of Commerce.

118. Loeb, M., et al. *A preliminary investigation of the effects of whole-body vibration and noise.* Army Med. Res. Lab. Report 145, 1954.

119. Loeb, M., et al. *A further investigation of the influence of whole-body vibration and noise on tremor and visual acuity.* Army Med. Res. Lab. Report 165, 1954.

120. McCollom, I. N., & Chapanis, A. *A human engineering bibliography.* San Diego, Calif.: San Diego State College Foundation, 1956.

121. McCormick, E. J. *Human engineering.* New York: McGraw-Hill, 1957.

122. McFarland, R. A. *Human factors in air transport design.* New York: McGraw-Hill, 1946.

123. McGill, W. Multivariate information transmission. *Psychometrika,* 1954, **19**, 97–116.

124. MacKay, D. M. Mentality in machines III. *Proc. Arist. Soc. Suppl.,* 1952, 61–86.

125. MacKay, D. M. Operational aspects of some fundamental concepts of human communication. *Synthese,* 1954, **9**, 182–198.

126. Mackworth, J. F., & Mackworth, N. H. The overlapping of signals for decisions. *Amer. J. Psychol.,* 1956, **69**, 26–47.

127. Mackworth, N. H. The breakdown of vigilance during prolonged visual search. *Quart. J. exp. Psychol.,* 1948, **1**, 6–21.

128. Mackworth, N. H. *Researches on the measurement of human perform-ance.* Med. Res. Counc. Spec. Report 268. London: H. M. Stationery Office, 1950.

129. Mackworth, N. H. Finger numbness in very cold winds. *J. appl. Physiol.,* 1953, **5**, 533–543.

130. Mackworth, N. H. Cold acclimatization and finger numbness. *Proc. Royal Soc.,* B, 1955, **143**, 392–407.

131. Mackworth, N. H., & Mackworth, J. F. *Searching for a series of decisions.* Medical Res. Counc. Gr. Brit., APU Report 234/56, 1956.

132. McRuer, D. T., & Krendel, E. S. *Dynamic response of human opera-tors.* Wright Air Develpm. Center Tech. Report 56-524, 1957.

133. Mead, R. J., & Diamantides, N. *Application of GEDA to human dynamics studies.* Goodyear Aircraft Corp., Akron, Ohio, GER-6608, 1955.

134. Melton, A. W., & Briggs, G. E. Engineering psychology. *Annu. Rev. Psychol.,* 1960, **11**, 71–98.

135. Miller, G. A. The magical number seven, plus or minus two: some limits on our capacity for processing information. *Psychol. Rev.,* 1956, **56**, 81–97.

136. Miller, R. B. *Handbook on training and training equipment design.* Wright Air Develpm. Center Tech. Report 53-136, 1953.

137. Mowbray, G. H., & Gebhard, J. *Comparison and interaction among*

sensory input channels. Johns Hopkins Univer., Appl. Physics Lab. TG-264, 1956.

138. Noble, M., et al. The frequency response of skilled subjects in a pursuit tracking task. *J. exp. Psychol.,* 1955, **49**, 249–256.

139. Panel on Psychology and Physiology. *Human factors in undersea warfare.* Washington, D.C.: National Research Council, Committee on Undersea Warfare, 1949.

140. Pearl, B. E., et al. Visual tracking. IV. Interrelations of target speed and aided-tracking ratio in defining tracking accuracy. *J. appl. Psychol.,* 1955, **39**, 209–214.

141. Platzer, H. L. *A non-linear approach to human tracking.* Franklin Inst., Interim Tech. Report No. I-2490-1, 1955.

142. Pollack, I., and Ficks, L. Information of elementary multidimensional auditory displays. *J. acoust. Soc. Amer.,* 1954, **26**, 155–158.

143. Poulton, E. C. Perceptual anticipation in tracking with two-pointer and one-pointer displays. *Brit. J. Psychol.,* 1952, **43**, 222–229.

144. Provins, K. A. Effect of limb position on the forces exerted about the elbow and shoulder joints on the two sides simultaneously. *J. appl. Physiol.,* 1955, **7**, 387–389.

145. Provins, K. A. Maximum forces exerted about the elbow and shoulder joints on each side separately and simultaneously. *J. appl. Physiol.,* 1955, **7**, 390–392.

146. Provins, K. A., & Salter, Nancy. Maximum torque exerted about the elbow joint. *J. appl. Physiol.,* 1955, **7**, 393–398.

147. Psychological Research Associates. *Human engineering principles for mine test design.* U.S. Navy, Bureau of Ordnance, NAVORD Report 5339, 1956.

148. Quastler, H. (Ed.) *Information theory in psychology.* Glencoe, Ill.: Free Press, 1955.

149. Ritchie, M. L., & Bamford, H. E., Jr. *The effect upon the output of a complex man-machine system of quickening and damping a derivative feedback display.* Wright Air Develpm. Center Tech. Report 57-103, 1957.

150. Roscoe, S. N. The effects of eliminating binocular and peripheral monocular visual cues upon pilot performance in landing. *J. appl. Psychol.,* 1948, **32**, 649–662.

151. Roscoe, S. N. Flight by periscope (1) performing an instrument flight pattern; the influence of screen size and image magnification. *Univer. Ill. Bull.,* 1951, **48**(55), 1–46.

152. Rund, Patricia A., et al. *The utility of quickening techniques in improving tracking performance with a binary display.* U.S. Naval Res. Lab. Report 5013, 1957.

153. Russell, L. Characteristics of the human as a linear servo-element. Unpublished master's thesis, MIT, Servomechanisms Lab., 1951.

154. Ryan, T. A. Interrelations of the sensory systems in perception. *Psychol. Bull.,* 1940, **37**, 659–698.

155. Saldanha, E. L. *An investigation into the effects of prolonged and exacting visual work.* Med. Res. Counc. Gr. Brit., APU 243/55, 1955.

156. Searle, L. V. *Psychological studies of tracking behavior. Part IV. The intermittency hypothesis as a basis for predicting optimum aided-tracking time constants.* U.S. Naval Res. Lab. Report 3872, 1951.

157. Senders, J. W., & Cruzen, M. *Tracking performance on combined compensatory and pursuit tasks.* U.S. Air Force, Wright Air Develpm. Center Tech. Report 52-39, 1952.

158. Shaw, W. A., et al. The difference between monaural and binaural thresholds. *J. exp. Psychol.,* 1947, **37,** 229–242.

159. Siddall, G. J., & Anderson, D. M. Fatigue during prolonged performance on a simple compensatory tracking task. *Quart. J. exp. Psychol.,* 1955, **7,** 159–165.

160. Siegel, A. I., & Stirner, F. W. *Caution and warning light indicators for Naval aircraft: VII. The effects of color contrast, brightness contrast, and mode of legend presentation on the attention intruding value of peripherally positioned light indicators.* U.S. Navy, NAMC-ACEL-369, 1958.

161. Simon, C. W. *Altimetry studies: (2) A comparison of integrated vs. separated, linear vs. circular, and spatial vs. numerical displays.* Hughes Aircraft Co., W.S.D.L. Tech. Memo 435, 1956.

162. Simon, J. R., et al. Effects of handedness on tracking accuracy. *Percept. mot. Skills Res. Exch.,* 1952, **4,** 53–57.

163. Stevens, S. S. Human engineering. *Amer. Psychologist,* 1957, **12,** 222.

164. Stevens, S. S., & Davis, H. *Hearing.* New York: Wiley, 1938.

165. Sweeney, J. S., et al. *Comparative evaluation of three approaches to helicopter instrumentation for hovering flight.* U.S. Naval Res. Lab. Report 4954, 1957.

166. Sweeney, J. S., et al. *A study of the effects of filtering on the performance of a manual compensatory tracking task.* U.S. Naval Res. Lab. Report 5205, 1958.

167. Swets, J. A., Tanner, W. P., Jr., & Birdsall, T. G. Decision processes in perception. *Psychol. Rev.,* 1961, **68,** 301–340.

168. Taylor, F. V. *Nonlinearity in human response.* U.S. Naval Res. Lab. Progr. Report, 8-14, November, 1949.

169. Taylor, F. V. Psychology and the design of machines. *Amer. Psychologist,* 1957, **12,** 249–258.

170. Taylor, F. V. Simplifying the controller's task through display quickening. *Occup. Psychol.,* 1957, **21,** 120–125.

171. Taylor, F. V., & Birmingham, H. P. Studies of tracking behavior. (II) The acceleration pattern of quick manual corrective responses. *J. exp. Psychol.,* 1948, **38,** 783–795.

172. Taylor, F. V., & Birmingham, H. P. Simplifying the pilot's task through display quickening. *J. aviat. Med.,* 1956, **27,** 27–31.

173. Thomson, R. M., Cooner, B. J., Jacobs, H. H., & Orlansky, J. Arrangement of groups of men and machines. In *Joint services human engineer-*

ing guide to equipment design, Off. Naval Res. Report ACR-33, 1958. Chap. VIII.

174. Truxal, J. G. *Automatic feedback control system synthesis.* New York: McGraw-Hill, 1955.

175. Tufts College, Institute of Applied Experimental Psychology. *Handbook of human engineering data.* U.S. Navy Special Devices Center 199-1-2, 1951.

176. Tustin, A. The nature of the operator's response in manual control and its implications for controller design. *J. Inst. Elec. Eng.,* 1947, **94**, 190-202.

177. Van Cott, H. P., & Altman, J. W. *Procedures for including human engineering factors in the development of weapon systems.* Wright Air Develpm. Center Tech. Report 56-488, AD-97305, 1956.

178. Voss, J. F. Effect of target brightness and target speed upon tracking proficiency. *J. exp. Psychol.,* 1955, **49**, 237–243.

179. Walston, C. E., & Warren, C. E. *A mathematical analysis of the human operator in a closed-loop control system.* U.S. Air Force Personn. Train. Res. Cent. Res. Bull. 54–96, 1954.

180. Warrick, M. J. *Effect of transmission type control lags on tracking accuracy.* U.S. Air Force, Air Materiel Command Tech. Report 5916, 1949.

181. Warrick, M. J. Effect of controller lag, gear ratio, frequency of pointer oscillation and their interaction in compensatory tracking. (mimeo.) Aero Med. Lab., Wright Field Air Force Base, Dayton, Ohio, 1950.

182. Welford, A. T. The psychological refractory period and the timing of high-speed performance—a review and a theory. *Brit. J. Psychol.,* 1952, **43**, 2–19.

183. Welford, A. T. The measurement of sensory-motor performance: survey and reappraisal of twelve years' progress. *Ergonomics,* 1960, **3**, 189–229.

184. Wiener, N. *Cybernetics.* New York: Wiley, 1949.

185. Woodson, W. E. *Human engineering guide for equipment designers.* Berkeley, Calif.: Univer. Calif. Press, 1954.

ENGINEERING PSYCHOLOGY

PAUL M. FITTS
Department of Psychology
University of Michigan

Introduction 909
Variables of Interest for Engineering Psychology 910
Dependent variables 910
Efficiency 910
Reliability 911
Ease of learning and degree of retention 911
Safety and habitability 911
Preference factors 911
Consideration of individual differences and population resources. . . . 912
Relations among dependent variables: "trade-off" functions 913
Independent variables. 914
Joint Objectives of the Fields Involved in Human Factors Engineering . . 916
Related scientific fields. 916
Related professional fields. 917
Engineering psychology and the system concept 918
The Content of Engineering Psychology 919
Relevance of existing psychological facts and theories for engineering design. 919
Relation of human performance theory to other theoretical areas in psy-
chology 920
Detection and discrimination capacities 920
Perceptual capacities 921
Motor capacities 921
Learning, memory, problem solving, and concept formation 922
Decision processes 923
Social processes and communications 923
Motivation and preference 923
Physiological processes 924
Other areas of psychology 924
Mathematical models 925
Information theory 925
Feedback (servo) theory 925

Computer theory 925
Operations research 926
The Methodology of Engineering Psychology 926
The research setting 926
The study of information-handling processes 927
The study of response processes 928
The study of stimulus-response interactions 928
The study of judgmental and decision-making processes 929
Systems research methods 929
Efficient test methods 930
Task taxonomy 930
Summary and Forecast 931
References 932

INTRODUCTION

Engineering psychology seeks to understand how human performance is related to task variables (especially engineering design variables) and to formulate theory and principles of human performance that can be applied to the design of human tasks, human-operated equipment, and man-machine systems.

On the scientific side, the engineering psychologist is interested in areas of research that contribute facts, principles, or theories relating directly to an understanding of human performance characteristics. He is also interested in parameters that influence the relations between task variables and performance, such as individual differences, motivation, and level of training. Thus engineering psychology draws its basic facts and theories widely from many areas of psychological research. Experimental psychology, with its emphasis on psychological processes, has the closest overlap with engineering psychology. It is important to recognize such overlap. It should be noted at the same time, however, that much psychological data and many psychological theories are of little or no value to engineering psychology in that they cannot be applied to the design of tasks, equipment, or systems. This will become clearer later in the discussion.

On the professional side, engineering psychology is but one of several biological and social sciences that support an applied specialty which has recently come to be called "human factors engineering." Human factors engineering aims to ensure that the tools and machines that man uses, the tasks he is asked to perform, and the roles assigned to him in man-machine systems are congruent with his characteristics, capabilities, and preferences. The importance of such objectives has long been recognized by engineers. For example, in 1828 civil engineering was initially defined as the "art of directing the great sources of power in nature for the use and convenience of man" [8, p. 443]. With the rapid growth in technological progress that has occurred in recent years, human factor problems have multiplied. As a result, efforts to design machines so as to optimize over-all man-machine system effectiveness have become increasingly important.

Psychologists who specialize in the professional aspects of human factors engineering usually find that they must work closely with engineers if they hope to see behavioral data applied to specific design problems. If such psychologists work as part of an interdisciplinary team, they usually preserve their professional identities and gain recognition as specialists in human factor problems. If they take on actual design responsibilities, they should realize, as F. V. Taylor [19] pointed out, that they are now functioning as human factors engineers. These specialists may some day be required to meet engineering certification standards.

In summary, an engineering psychologist either attempts to extend the frontiers of knowledge in the area of human performance theory or serves as a specialist or human factors consultant in connection with engineering design or testing. Often he does both.

VARIABLES OF INTEREST FOR ENGINEERING PSYCHOLOGY

The area covered by engineering psychology is best specified by the dependent variables that the field attempts to predict or to optimize and by the independent variables that it attempts to manipulate. For the present, reference is made to empirical rather than to systematic variables; the systematic or theoretical areas of engineering psychology cannot be neatly defined by listing the independent and dependent variables that are studied since theory consists in part of conceptualization of intervening variables.

Dependent Variables

Efficiency. Improved efficiency is probably the most commonly sought objective in the application of psychological data in engineering design, and speed of performance is the most common measure of efficiency. Precision is another measure.

The prediction of efficiency is based on the study of variables affecting the speed and precision of performance in many types of tasks, such as reading, computing, controlling, checking, etc. The ultimate goal is to predict not only the superiority of one task design over another, but the time required for different response processes and the distribution of measures of the precision of responses.

Reliability. Uniformity of performance under both normal and stressful circumstances, infrequency of complete failure or breakdown, and absence of gross errors are of importance as a criterion of effective performance. This is equally true whether system functions are performed by a man or by mechanical elements that are manufactured, calibrated, and maintained by men. The goal of increased reliability includes the reduction of all types of error—both gross and precision errors—made by human operators in using equipment. [For a discussion of types of human error, see 10.]

Human performance often is least reliable under conditions of information overload (when a person is given more than he can do) or information underload (when the level of activity in a task falls below the minimum required to maintain alertness). It sometimes is possible to extend the range of effective performance or to obtain greater precision and reliability in a given environment through engineering design. Thus it is important that data on the precision and reliability of behavior be obtained from research that covers wide ranges of task conditions with respect to stress and load.

Ease of learning and degree of retention. One of the goals of engineering psychology is to find ways of designing new tasks so that (1) the total training time required to reach some desired level of proficiency is reduced and (2) the level of proficiency will be maintained after the initial training period is over.

These two objectives depend upon knowledge of population stereotypes—the well-established habits which most people bring to a new task—and upon knowledge of transfer and interference effects from previous learning.

Safety and habitability. It is important that tasks, tools, and man-machine systems be designed so that the likelihood of harmful side effects is minimized and performance of the task can be maintained over long periods of time in the job environment. This design objective covers the effects of extrinsic (environmental) factors, such as lighting, plus intrinsic (task) characteristics, such as information overload. It also covers the reduction of accidents.

In some instances, it is unavoidable that men undergo severe stress in performing a particular task. The acceleration, deceleration, and confinement attendant on space travel are examples of such stressful factors. It is highly desirable for machines and equipment to be designed on the basis of accurate information regarding man's ability to work under these stresses and with precise knowledge of the degree of degradation in his performance that will result from their presence.

Preference factors. People do not always prefer conditions or items which maximize efficiency, reliability, safety, or ease of learning. Yet individual preference is often of major concern to the designer and must be added to our list of primary dependent variables. This is especially true in the design of consumer goods, personal equipment, homes, automobiles, hand tools, and other items which are purchased by individuals for their own use.

In addition, however, jobs often can be made interesting, dull or ugly surroundings made aesthetically pleasing, uncomfortable or annoying environments made tolerable, and job enhancement employed as a means of reducing absenteeism and labor turnover. Thus preference has many secondary effects which are directly and indirectly related to performance. Therefore an important objective of engineering psychology research is the measurement and prediction of preferences and the understanding of the widespread secondary effects which may occur because of differences in motivation, attitudes, and human satisfactions. It is not the aim of the engineering psychologists to change man's preferences, motivations, or aesthetic experiences; instead he treats these factors as intervening or dependent variables and attempts to optimize them through the manipulation of engineering design variables.

Consideration of Individual Differences and Population Resources

It has occasionally been said—by persons who fail to understand the goals of engineering psychology—that this area neglects individual differences and considers only the typical or average man. This is far from true in a general sense. Examples of engineering application of data regarding individual differences can be found in the work of specialists who devise sensory aids (eyeglasses and hearing aids, for example) and prosthetic devices, analyze new military weapon systems for qualitative personnel requirements, and design jobs appropriate for older workers. In the design of such items as clothing and protective equipment, an attempt is made to accommodate all types (sizes, etc.) of people. In other instances, the characteristics of some particular strata of the population may dictate the design. The assumption may be made, for example, that equipment must be designed so that even the least intelligent can use it with no special training; at the other extreme, the assumption may be made that only people with unusual aptitudes and a great deal of special training will ever use the equipment.

From a broader viewpoint, it is also desirable to match job characteristics to population resources, available skills, etc. Thus jobs would be designed so that job requirements matched available population resources. It seems highly unlikely that this could ever be accomplished except in the most general way, however.

An aim of engineering psychology research relating to the accommodation of individual differences is to obtain data on performance both at asymptotic levels of training and at intermediate levels. Such studies are especially laborious since they involve the experimental training of groups of people for long periods of time in various types of tasks, and information in this area is incomplete.

Relations among Dependent Variables: "Trade-off" Functions

The classes of dependent variables listed above are based on a systematic analysis of human factor objectives in engineering design. Such an analysis is only a first step in the development of satisfactory criteria, however. The relations among different criterion measures must also be considered. This is especially important in cases where it is not possible to maximize all dependent measures and where a compromise must be sought among several correlated criteria.

Unfortunately, few objective analyses that are of interest for engineering psychology have been made of the relations between the dependent variables. Relatively little is known, for example, about the relation between preferences for different tasks and performance levels in tasks or even about the correlation of speed and reliability measures for different tasks. It is a good guess that most of the classes of variables listed above are not independent and that some are negatively correlated. Thus, it may not be possible to optimize certain task characteristics without sacrificing other desirable characteristics.

In applying human performance data to the design of complex man-machine systems, it is also important to note that a man's proficiency may be secondary in importance to the proficiency of the entire system; system output often may be increased not so much by improving man's performance of some particular function as by changing the functions that he is required to perform. Man's role in a complex man-machine system is thus determined in part by how his characteristics compare with those of existing machines; his role often represents a compromise that is best from the viewpoint of the performance of the over-all system. Thus a man may sometimes be asked to perform a function that he does slowly and with difficulty because of general system considerations [9a].

The optimum compromise among several human performance criteria often is dictated by system considerations. Optimization of any one criterion, such as speed, may be undesirable if the means taken to achieve this serve to degrade some other aspect of system performance. These qualifications are equally true for all the criteria listed in the preceding section.

Another system consideration, not heretofore mentioned, is growth potential. Systems and the roles and functions of men in systems are often determined by the possibility of growth, adaptation, or change in the man-machine system. At times this consideration may outweigh the advantages of adding some feature that would add short-term efficiency. Man, of course, is far more adaptable than a machine; thus, one reason for assigning system functions to a man is the added adaptability or growth potential which he brings to the man-machine system.

Independent Variables

As stated earlier, engineering psychology will not be identified in this discussion by its theoretical position so much as by the types of variables it considers. Whereas engineering psychology shares an interest in the dependent variables described earlier with other applied psychology fields, such as personnel and training, it is interested in optimizing these variables through the manipulation of a relatively unique set of independent variables. These can be called "engineering design variables" or, more broadly, "task variables."

A task variable is an intrinsic characteristic of a task or the immediate environment in which it is performed whose manipulation affects an individual's performance. The information available in a choice situation, the way this information is displayed, and the information-processing functions that must be performed by the operator are examples of task variables.

Although organismic and procedural variables may usually be distinguished from task variables, it is obvious that all three classes of variables often interact. Thus, the engineering psychologist should always be aware of the types of people who will perform a particular task and the level of their training—even though he may be primarily interested in studying performance as a function of the nature of the task.

Not all task variables can be manipulated by the design engineer (or the engineering psychologist). The input or load which defines the nature of a task often must be accepted in whatever form it happens to take. As an illustration, accuracy in transcribing dictation is dependent on the speaking rate and diction of the speaker (two characteristics of the source of information), as well as on the particular set of response symbols used in transcription (longhand, shorthand, stenotypy, etc.). From the viewpoint of the person transcribing the dictation, both the nature of the stimulus and the coding of the response are task variables, since both influence the effectiveness of transcription; however, only the second can be considered an engineering design variable in this instance.

From one viewpoint, the attempt to distinguish among areas of psychology in terms of the types of independent variables that are manipulated to reach common goals is arbitrary and violates the common-sense notion that the nature of a problem should dictate the means taken to solve it. The latter view calls for choice of the most efficient route— if a particular goal can be reached by more than one, e.g., by manipulating different classes of variables. To use a familiar example—if one is ill, he first wants the services of a general diagnostician, not a specialist who can treat only one type of illness. It can be argued that any professional specialization which limits the psychologist to the use of any subset of the several available methodologies and techniques is arbitrarily restrictive; attempts to compartmentalize areas of psychology in terms of the independent variables manipulated by each area can be viewed as similarly restrictive. This is especially true in the manipulation of task, organismic, or procedural variables to improve the performance of a task.

From another viewpoint, however, there are practical as well as scientific considerations which support the proposal that engineering psychology be distinguished from other areas of psychology in terms of the types of independent variables manipulated. One such consideration is this: Two broad and easily recognized classes of independent variables which can be manipulated by psychologists are (1) those involving the possibilities for modifying tasks so that they are more suitable for people, and (2) those involving the possibilities of modifying or selecting people so that they are better adapted to particular tasks. These two types of applications are attempted at different times and places in the everyday world, are controlled by different administrative agencies, and require specialized knowledge of rather different sorts.

Since the engineering psychologist engages in research that he hopes may some day contribute to the design of new tasks, machines, and systems, he should be able to make his findings available prior to the creation of new products or systems and understand enough of engineering methods and the problems faced by design engineers so that he can communicate his findings to them. In a similar manner, personnel and training specialists, who contribute primarily to the selection (or guidance) and subsequent preparation of people to perform different specialized tasks, must work closely with the individuals who direct personnel and training programs and should understand their professional problems. However, wherever the emphasis is on personnel and training problems of future rather than existing systems (i.e., wherever qualitative personnel requirements are recognized as an important factor in determining the original design of new systems), the administrative distinctions between engineering, personnel, and training psychology largely disappear and people who are broadly trained in all of these areas are needed.

It should be noted in passing that several early publications in the field of psychology [e.g., 16] emphasized that there are two avenues through which psychology can contribute to human productivity. Somehow this twofold approach has not been emphasized. As an illustration, although industrial psychologists have given some attention to environmental factors (lighting, ventilation, music, humidity, etc.) and methods of work, they have devoted their efforts chiefly to personnel problems and have generally not concerned themselves with the manipulation of engineering design (task) variables.

In view of these considerations, the position, stated earlier, that engineering psychology is presently identified partially by the independent variables it studies appears to be defensible. This is especially true since the customary administrative distinction between the two broad avenues for improving performance will apparently persist for some time to come. The writer accepts this dichotomy with reluctance and hopes that the distinction becomes less important as time goes on. However, as Cronbach [7] has pointed out and as we emphasize elsewhere in this chapter, the scientific work which supports engineering psychology will profit from greater emphasis on individual differences and skill levels as these interact with task variables.

JOINT OBJECTIVES OF THE FIELDS INVOLVED IN HUMAN FACTORS ENGINEERING

Several scientific and professional fields have important contributions to make to human factors engineering. Some relations among these fields will now be considered with particular reference to engineering psychology, first in terms of aims and objectives and then in terms of subject matter and methodological relations.

Related Scientific Fields

Physiologists, anatomists, and physical anthropologists are feeling the demands of design engineers for data on people's physical and physiological characteristics—body size, endurance, and requirements for life-support systems. Biophysicists, environmental physiologists, and radiobiologists are being asked a host of questions regarding human tolerances for noise, vibration, high and low temperatures, radiation, and gravitational forces other than the normal level of one g. The biological sciences, therefore, share with psychology an interest in research relating to several engineering design objectives, especially safety and habitability.

The social sciences—economics, sociology, business and industrial administration, and social psychology, for example—have recently felt the demand for facts and principles relating to group-performance capabilities in situations requiring teamwork, such as large man-machine systems. Engineers need guiding concepts in designing communication networks, allocating responsibilities among different members of work teams, and devising workplace layouts for groups of people. Problems of team effectiveness become even more acute in stressful environments. Thus the social sciences are coming to share with psychology and the biological sciences an interest in certain performance objectives which can be influenced by the designs of man-machine systems.

Related Professional Fields

Almost all engineering specialties have a stake in human factors engineering, since most engineering products are built and/or used by people. The systems engineer has perhaps the most direct interest in the objectives of this area, since he often deals with man-machine systems. Several specialties, such as communication and illuminating engineering, are built upon the application of certain kinds of human factors data, such as those relating to vision, hearing, and body size, to problems in particular areas of engineering. The industrial engineer and the operations research specialist are vitally concerned with the proper utilization of people in new systems. Architects and industrial designers are intimately concerned with questions of human aesthetics and functional requirements. Other types of engineers also encounter human factor design problems, but perhaps less frequently than the ones mentioned above.

Preventive medicine, including industrial medicine, is concerned with reducing accidental trauma and in applying corrective measures wherever special hazards to health and safety arise. Such work by the medical profession is usually done in collaboration with safety engineers, and is one part of the broad field of human factors engineering.

Men in the many professions that share an interest in human factors engineering objectives have found that collaboration is one of the ways to ensure achievement. The typical physiologist, sociologist, economist, or psychologist, having agreed to serve in a professional capacity as a member of a team working on an engineering design problem, will frequently recognize that he knows very little about engineering, just as the typical design engineer who is faced with complex human factor problems will realize that he has had little or no formal introduction to human factor data and theory. Starting with mutual respect for the special competencies of men in other areas, many effective professional teams have been formed in which engineers and behavioral scientists have worked in close cooperation. In general, this sort of teamwork appears to be a good solution to the problem of designing complex man-machine systems.

The role of the psychologist on such an engineering design team is usually one of supplying and interpreting human factor data. Another important contribution of the professionally oriented engineering psychologist has been the compilation of handbook-type data—the summarization of psychological data and principles in a form which can be readily applied to engineering design problems.

Engineering Psychology and the System Concept

The design and development of complex man-machine systems has been profoundly influenced in recent years by what is generally called the "system concept" [10a]. For the present purposes, a system can be defined as an assemblage of elements characterized by a common purpose and tied together by an information-flow network, the interactions of the elements being of such complexity that prediction of system performance from an analysis of the properties of isolated elements is very difficult. We are interested here in man-machine systems, but the definition holds equally well for other types of systems, from the circulatory and respiratory systems of the physiologist to the planetary systems of the astronomer.

In a complex man-machine system, the human operator may receive feedback from various intermediate processes or machine components, interact with other human operators, and be able to observe and react to the final output. If each human and machine element has its own dynamic characteristics (i.e., lags, resonancies, nonlinearities, filtering properties, etc.) and if the input to each element is partially determined by feedback of outputs from other elements, some of the difficulties in predicting over-all system dynamics can be seen at once. The necessity for studying the entire system in dynamic operation is evident.

The system concept influences the research role of the engineering psychologist in several ways. As a minimum, it may simply lead an experimenter who is studying some specific aspect of a task (such as a specific display problem) to consider more carefully how that aspect of the task relates to total man-machine system performance. For example, as Alphonse Chapanis pointed out some years ago, since uncorrelated errors in a system accumulate as the sum of their separate variances, the reduction of many small sources of error may result in very little improvement in over-all system output, whereas the reduction of a single large source of error may result in a surprisingly large system improvement. At most, the system concept may lead engineering psychologists to build complex machine simulators (such as aircraft simulators) and to undertake experiments on large man-machine system interactions.

The system concept also has important implications for the professional role of the engineering psychologist. System designers must think in broad terms and be able to deal with very complex interrelations, rather than become engrossed with the details of component design. But few young engineers are adequately trained to deal with broad problems, especially problems that include human factor considerations. In fact, the engineering psychologist may be fully as well prepared as the engineer to take a truly system approach to design problems. Man is a highly complex system; training in engineering psychology, including training in the methodology of research on multiple-variable problems, may be an excellent preparation for work on complex man-machine system problems. As a consequence, one of the important professional areas now opening up to engineering psychologists is management of systems research and development activities and participation in the planning and staff functions relating to the creation of new man-machine systems and their associated personnel subsystems.

Professional activities relating to systems research and development include analyses of the requirements for new systems, specification of system output criteria, and consultation regarding the roles to be assigned to people in future systems. F. V. Taylor once called the psychologist who engages in this kind of work a high-level "human engineering technologist." Such a person, he stated, contributes to system development at three levels:

At the simplest, he designs individual displays, controls, or display-control relationships. At a somewhat more complex level, [he] contributes to the design of consoles and instrument panels. At the highest level of complexity, he assists in structuring large systems composed of many mechanical elements and frequently several human beings. In this capacity he helps to determine what information must flow through the system, how it must be processed, how many men are required, what tasks they will perform, and what type of information each one will need. In short, the engineering psychologist helps at this level to determine the configuration of the system [19, p. 251].

Taylor also pointed out that such a professional person may also participate in man-machine system evaluation and suitability testing.

THE CONTENT OF ENGINEERING PSYCHOLOGY

The content of engineering psychology overlaps that of many other fields of psychology, especially experimental psychology. This does not mean, however, that all psychological experiments produce data of equal value for engineering design. As a matter of fact, a relatively small amount of the data in published reports of psychological research is of direct interest for engineering psychology, i.e., deals quantitatively with relationships among task variables and human performance characteristics.

Relevance of Existing Psychological Facts and Theories for Engineering Design

Any theoretically oriented research in psychology may have relevance for human factors engineering applications, of course. The extent to which it does have relevance to the problems of engineering design appears to depend on three considerations:

1. *Relevant independent variables.* Can the independent variables (of which the data are a function) be manipulated in or have some relevance for the design of tasks, machines, or man-machine systems, i.e., do the data relate to the manipulation of what we have defined as engineering design variables?

2. *System relevance.* Do the general conditions of the experiment, including features of the task which are treated as parameters and those treated as random variables, have system relevance? In other words, is it possible to generalize the experimental data to particular classes of systems and system environments?

3. *Relevant performance measures.* Are the dependent variables measured in quantitative physical units or capable of being converted to such units, i.e., is it possible to specify how much effect task variables will have on performance in terms of meaningful physical units such as time, weight, bandwidth, bits, or RMS error in volts?

The last criterion is important because in engineering design planning it is impossible to determine whether or not a design feature is worth what it will cost or to make compromises on a rational basis unless quantitative physical measures of the relevant dependent variables are available. In the case of certain dependent measures, such as subjective preference, meeting this criterion is especially difficult. However, some notable successes have been achieved even here. As an illustration, comparative determinations have been made of the direct saving in bandwidth resulting from an optimum weighting and an equal weighting of the three primary colors used to produce TV pictures of a specified subjective quality [4].

With these three criteria in mind, we may now consider further the content of engineering psychology and how it interrelates to the subject matter of other areas of psychology. The author proposes to consider several other subject-matter areas, pointing out some of the empirical findings and systematic ideas that are most and least relevant for engineering psychology.

"The psychology of human performance" is the most general description of the subject matter that is of interest for the present topic. We shall be concerned especially with theory and empirical data that specify quantitatively the levels of performance that can be expected under various conditions, including the task conditions that result in maximum performance levels.

Relation of Human Performance Theory to Other Theoretical Areas in Psychology

Detection and discrimination capacities. The study of discrimination capacities provides a good starting point for a psychology of human performance. The capacity for differentiation among motor responses, based on proprioceptive feedback, as well as capacities for visual, auditory, tactual, and other discriminations, is highly relevant. We find a great wealth of factual data and well-established theory relating to these topics, and much of it is highly relevant for engineering psychology.

In most tasks and systems, information (stimuli, signals, etc.) must be responded to on an absolute basis rather than a comparative basis. Information-handling rate (identification of and response to signals) under speeded conditions is often much more important than capacity under nonspeeded conditions. However, most of the data on human discrimination capacities relates to comparative judgments made under nonspeeded conditions. As a result, it is often impossible to make predictions from discrimination data to performance in system tasks. Questions pertaining to probability of identifying signals in normal working environments, ability to identify symbols rapidly, or ability to select relevant from among irrelevant signals often cannot be answered from the data taken in highly controlled experimental situations.

In short, the demands of engineering psychology are primarily for data regarding absolute (rather than comparative) discrimination, the effects of speed stress on sensory processes, and the identification of "signal in noise," i.e., for data on the probabilities of detection and identification of signals under system-relevant conditions.

Perceptual capacities. Perception is another area in which much empirical data and many theories are available. The data and theory most relevant to engineering psychology deal with complex pattern perception, such as the specification of ability to recognize complex patterns in (visual or auditory) noise and to estimate the statistical parameters of stochastic processes. For example, speech production and perception need to be understood to the extent required to permit the design of speech-recognition machines, and visual-pattern recognition needs to be understood to the extent necessary to predict the performance of photo interpreters.

Most of the problems of display design (design of instruments, radar and sonar displays, signs, and symbols) can be formulated as general perceptual problems. Such formulations indicate that most of the display design problems of engineering psychology can be placed somewhere within the existing framework of experimental psychology, but that most of the existing experimental data are not relevant to system problems.

Motor capacities. Psychologists have conducted a good deal of recent research on psychomotor performance and aspects of skill. Research in this area, after a promising start in the decades from 1890 to 1910, became a neglected topic until revived by the problems encountered during World War II. The present writer would not go quite as far as

Taylor [19, p. 256] in subsuming most of the subject matter of engineering psychology under the category of sensorimotor or psychomotor behavior, but he agrees that a large proportion of directly relevant material is found here.

The major reason why relatively more facts and theories regarding skilled performance are directly relevant may be that feedback theories have dominated thinking in this area for a long time. Such theories [e.g., 2] are compatible with the systems viewpoint and with the types of engineering models (feedback control systems, etc.) commonly used by current systematic formulations in engineering psychology.

Learning, memory, problem solving, and concept formation. Among the wealth of factual and theoretical material regarding learning and related behavioral processes, we find some that is directly relevant to problems of engineering and some that is not. Animal learning is generally of less interest than human learning. Studies of paired-associate learning and rote learning are of less interest than studies of skill learning; long-term skill learning is especially important. Long-term retention and recall is as important as short-term or immediate memory. Environmental and task conditions that stimulate creativity, as shown in reasoning processes and the formation of new concepts, are especially important for engineering psychology.

Design specialists are frequently faced with the question of how to devise a new task (item of equipment, system, etc.) so that a required level of proficiency can be attained after a minimum amount of new learning. The answer to such a question requires knowledge of the task variables that determine learning difficulty and the amount of positive transfer than can be expected from old to new tasks. It is not sufficient to invoke generalizations stated in terms of the "similarity of tasks"; one must specify exactly how similarity is to be measured and what degree of similarity will produce what level of performance. These are difficult questions—questions which learning theory is not yet ready to handle.

Another frequent type of question met by engineering psychology concerns man's absolute performance capabilities in memory and problem-solving tasks. How much can a man remember, and at what rate can he solve problems? Many such questions cannot be answered satisfactorily today. In particular, theories are needed that specify determinants of difficulty in learning, the time (how many trials, etc.) required to reach proficiency, and the levels at which improvement essentially ceases.

The design of training equipment is also an area of interest for engineering psychology. Although training equipment is in one sense part and parcel of training procedures, the problems of designing such equipment, particularly complex system-simulation devices, are very similar to other equipment design problems—and hence they are of interest for engineering psychology. Training equipment design and utilization is obviously a subject-matter area in which a close interrelationship exists among several areas of psychology.

Decision processes. At the system design level, one of the most important and most frequently encountered issues is the proper use of man for judgmental and decision processes, as against the use of automata (based on preprogramed computers, fixed strategies, etc.) for performing similar functions. Data-processing machines can carry out very long and sometimes moderately complex operations, but every minute step must be specified in the instructions; people are ingenious in devising their own methods and can handle some very complex problems. In order to compare human versus machine capacities, however, we need better data on the former.

Related issues are man's abilities in estimating probabilities and establishing the relative values of alternatives in the context of some system activity. Increasing pressure for this type of information is probably contributing to the considerable increase in psychological research on decision-making and higher mental processes. Until recently this was an area in which relatively little theory of any sort was available; however, it is now a very active area and should make important contributions to engineering psychology in the future.

Social processes and communications. Large systems usually include several people who cooperate in the accomplishment of over-all system objectives. Social psychology certainly has a stake in the engineering design characteristics of such systems, especially in so far as they affect the relations among the people who comprise the system team. Although much of the subject matter of social psychology deals neither with engineering design variables nor with measures of human productivity in system-relevant tasks, interest in the latter topics may be expected to increase and proportionally more theories in this area may become relevant to system design. The effects of automation on the worker and the role of management in supervising technological change are issues of joint interest to the industrial social psychologist and the engineering psychologist [e.g., 15].

Motivation and preference. From the viewpoint of intrinsic job satisfaction and the relation of preference to performance, human motivation is another somewhat neglected area as far as engineering psychology is concerned. Since the beginning of the industrial revolution, jobs have been tending to become less and less intrinsically motivating. Yet relatively few psychological studies have been directed at the question of how to make them more interesting. Fortunately, some important principles are already available. The study of group dynamics and interpersonal relations among team members has led to numerous generalizations that can guide the system engineer in planning communication systems, the arrangement of work groups, and the role of people in future systems. The work of B. F. Skinner and others in regard to the use of reinforcement (or feedback) schedules to shape performance provides another theoretical basis for designing more rewarding tasks.

Experimental aesthetics is still another dormant area of psychology in which there are strong demands for data from designers. In such applied areas as product design, styling, decorating, and architecture, there is great interest in the effects of light, color, shape, and form, texture, acoustic qualities, space, etc., on man's aesthetic experiences. One of the intriguing questions is the relation between preference and function.

The study of preferences and demands for products has generally been associated with marketing and advertising. However, questions about consumer behavior frequently arise in product design. In particular, the degree of consumer or user acceptance of a new (and often functionally better) item is a very important consideration in its development, and the prediction of future demands for new products is needed to guide research on the creation of new devices and systems.

Physiological processes. The key to the solution of many problems of human factor engineering is held by physiological psychology. The understanding of man's elemental capacities for the discrimination, identification, and processing of signals, for short-term memory, for patterned movements, for reaction time, etc., which are the foundation stones of performance theory, rest heavily on physiological psychology at a basic level. At a more applied level, the alleviation of environmental stresses, the design of protective equipment, the planning of optimal cycles of work and rest, and the solution of many special problems relating to the design of seats, lighting systems, and safety devices often require extensive data of a sort which the physiological psychologist is most likely to possess.

The greatest gap in the physiological area, from the viewpoint of engineering psychology, is the lack of theory or empirical data relating physiological variables to performance data. Valid physiological correlates of alertness, fatigue, stress, work load, and the like would be particularly useful in the design of man-machine systems.

Other areas of psychology. Other areas of psychology which have not been singled out for special discussion—psychotherapy, personality, counseling or vocational guidance—undoubtedly have some subject-matter overlap with engineering psychology. In general, however, the most important areas of overlap are those discussed above.

Mathematical Models

At a theoretical level, efforts to specify human performance capabilities and limitations have been greatly stimulated by recent developments in applied mathematics, developments often first applied to problems in the analysis and synthesis of electronic and physical systems.

Information theory. Shannon [18], in his original publications on information theory, dealt with the measurement of the information content of English-language communications and included other facets of human behavior by implication. Psychologists were not long in following up on such suggestions and in exploring the utility of information measures for the study of many topics [see 3, 10b, 13, 17]. Engineering psychologists have relied heavily on this theoretical approach, since the study of human information processing provides data that are of immediate interest for human factors engineering. Theories that look on man as a communication or data-processing system offer considerable promise for the extension of human performance theory.

Feedback (servo) theory. The regulation of homeostatic behavior by feedback mechanism has long been under study. However, the recent rapid development of an applied mathematics dealing specifically with feedback systems, the growth of a professional area known as control engineering, and the attention attracted by the theory of cybernetics [see 2, 22] have stimulated new efforts to study human performance. No single feedback model, simple or complex, provides a complete model of human behavior in control tasks. Man has great capacity for adapting his behavior to maximize the output of whatever system he is asked to control and can, in fact, assume the characteristics of many different control devices. In servo terminology, he is a highly nonlinear device, one that cannot be specified by a simple mathematical model. The feedback model, however, has been a starting point for the development of a promising set of theoretical formulations regarding human control processes [5, 14]. Some of this theoretical work has been contributed by engineering psychologists and has both general and applied implications. The analog computer has proved to be an invaluable aid to research in this area.

Computer theory. The high-speed digital computer and data-processing machine, in addition to replacing man in the performance of many computational and other tasks, offers many interesting possibilities for research, especially as it stimulates theory building and research on human performance characteristics. It is interesting to note that some of the most important theoretical contributions in this area have come, not from psychologists, but from the engineers and mathematicians who were first interested in computers [e.g., 20]. Current work on artificial intelligence, on "problem-oriented" machine languages, on computer programing, particularly on heuristic programs, are examples of research trends of great interest and importance for human performance theory [11a, 21].

Operations research. Various mathematical and physical models, in addition to the ones mentioned above—cueing theory, game theory, decision theory, operational gaming, and linear programming, for example—are being used extensively to solve applied problems arising from the management and operation of man-machine systems [1, 12]. These problems include topics as varied as the management of a hospital, the logistic support of an Army division, the operation of a mail-order firm, and the scheduling of production. The interesting aspect of operations research, for the present topic, is the possibility of developing general theories of individual, group, and man-machine performance that are based upon precise physical or mathematical models. The area is one in which engineering psychologists find much of common interest with engineers and applied mathematicians.

THE METHODOLOGY OF ENGINEERING PSYCHOLOGY

Since engineering psychology represents a somewhat new research emphasis for psychology, examining the principal methodologies that it has developed or borrowed from older areas of research in psychology will be of special interest. At the present time, engineering psychology is primarily an empirical science. When faced with demand for new knowledge or the solution of a new problem, the engineering psychologist usually turns for an answer, not to a formal (mathematical or theoretical) model, but to some form of empirical research. Theories such as those derived from feedback and information theory may provide tentative answers to human factor design questions when empirical data are lacking; more often they serve as guidelines for research. Engineering psychology is largely dependent, therefore, on its empirical methodology.

In reviewing the methodology of engineering psychology and its relations to the methodology used in other areas of psychology, we shall consider some general aspects first, then proceed to the methodology of more specific types of studies.

The research setting. An important general consideration is whether the research is to be conducted under laboratory or field conditions. Both settings are now used. The methods employed in field studies include interviews (e.g., critical-incident studies of errors in equipment use), statistical analysis of existing data (e.g., data from accident records), and direct observation (e.g., the recording and subsequent content analysis of voice communications). These methods have been taken over from older areas of psychology for the most part. Surveys of design problems are often made as part of a comprehensive survey of some operational problem that encompasses an area larger than that of engineering psychology—as part of a study of accidents, for example.

Usually a field setting is chosen when interest centers on the identification of aspects of a system or operation that are critical from the human viewpoint or on the testing or validation of the results of applying a principle derived from laboratory studies. Survey methods, both oral and written, have proved very useful as a means of identifying critical aspects of operations or analyzing criterion problems, for example. Here the engineering psychologist leans heavily on the techniques developed in industrial, personality, social, counseling, and clinical psychology. Field tests or experiments may sometimes be arranged, although it is often difficult to provide suitable conditions for field testing.

A laboratory setting is usually chosen if the problem is sufficiently well defined and understood so that critical aspects can be abstracted and studied under controlled conditions and if a long-term approach can be taken. Complex system-simulation facilities, using computers as a basis for much of the simulation, are also coming into more general use. Thus the laboratory setting provides a close tie with the classical topics studied by experimental psychology, whereas the field setting provides opportunity for identifying important real-life problems and for validating generalizations obtained in the laboratory.

To understand the relation of the laboratory methodologies used by engineering psychologists to those employed in other experimental studies, it is necessary to reemphasize engineering psychology's interest in predicting—and often in discovering how to optimize—some aspect of performance. This interest in performance dictates much of what goes on in the engineering psychology laboratory. It guides the engineering psychologist in the selection of experimental methods, apparatus, and tasks. This interest in predicting system-relevant performance is nowhere illustrated more clearly than in the study of problems relating to the optimization of stimuli (display devices). Stimuli must be optimized in relation to the performance of some particular task and in some particular system context. In other words, the use to which stimulus information is to be put and the task environment in which it is to be used must be specified before valid methodology can be developed for studying display problems.

The study of information-handling processes. Stimulus information is frequently utilized by a man at work in complicated tasks that require him to process large amounts of information under speed stress. Such tasks frequently involve the use of information acquired from several different sources. Furthermore, the outcomes of alternative decisions are not always predictable on a deterministic basis; alternative actions must therefore be considered in relation to the degree of confidence to be placed in the stimulus information and the values attached to different alternative outcomes. In order of complexity, the questions asked about stimulus information involve (1) detection (visibility, audibility, etc.), (2) legibility or intelligibility, and (3) interpretability. Study of each of these questions requires a different methodology.

Classical work on sensory discrimination provides well-tested methods for the study of stimulus detection. The study of absolute discrimination and the scaling of stimuli with respect to equal discriminability can be accomplished with few modifications of standard and long-used methods.

Much of the methodology needed to study legibility and intelligibility of displays has had to be developed specifically for this purpose by engineering psychologists. This topic also is a relatively old one, but a number of recent innovations in methodology have been introduced [6, 9]. The study of display interpretability, however, calls for special new methodology almost exclusively. Thus, as the problems of stimulus optimization become more complex and increasingly important for engineering psychology, research methodology becomes more specific to this field.

The study of response processes.   Methods employed in this area include the study of single discrete responses, serial discrete responses, and continuous motor behavior (21a). Classical psychophysical methods can be applied to the study of simple movement processes. Electrical recordings of muscle activity offer one avenue for the analytic study of response processes. A direct means for detailed response analysis is the use of special transducers and electronic equipment for recording movement rates and accelerations, the forces involved in movements. Techniques for frequency analysis, borrowed largely from electrical engineering, are available for determining response bandwidth, resonance, etc. As the motor tasks in which the experimenter is interested become more complex, however, new and rather specialized methods of analysis are required.

The study of stimulus-response interactions.   Engineering psychology is coming increasingly to emphasize, not stimulus or response processes alone, but the interrelations of the two, i.e., the optimization of stimulus-response processes. From a methodological viewpoint, the only unique aspect of this approach is the requirement for concurrent analysis of both stimulus and response variables in the same experiment in order to discover principles for selecting optimum S-R combinations. In the study of simple tasks, this requires no special innovations of apparatus or methods. In studying complex tasks, however, where man's responses act on (or through) an external physical system and where stimuli include feedback signals from the machine, newer experimental methods and apparatus are required.

One of the characteristics of most human tasks in a system context is the requirement of time sharing—the alternation between different aspects of a complex task. Therefore, one of the important classes of interaction that must be studied is the interaction between different aspects of complex tasks.

The study of judgmental and decision-making processes. Most research on problem solving, decision making, and other intellectual activities has used methodology that may place serious limitations on generalizing findings to decision making in real man-machine systems. For one thing, much of the methodology has used static tasks in which the individual "solves" a specific (static) problem, but does not suffer the consequences of failures or find that the situation changes as soon as he takes any action. Improved methodology and models for studying more complex decision tasks are needed here, as in many other areas (7a).

Systems research methods. The implication of the systems concept for psychology has already been discussed. To conduct research on man-machine systems, actual or simulated machine subsystems must be brought into the laboratory. The usual procedure is to rely on simulation of the machine components in order to provide realistic stimulus and control functions (input and output devices).

One of the simplest man-machine systems which has had extensive laboratory study is a control system such as that used in an airplane, a submarine, or an automobile. The dynamics of the machine components are faithfully represented by some analog device such as a computer. Space does not permit a description of the methods used in analyzing system characteristics and simulating them in the laboratory. However, descriptions of such methods have been published elsewhere [11, 18a]. Interestingly, the techniques of analysis and synthesis of machine components have been borrowed primarily from control engineering. One important benefit of using the engineering approach to system analysis and synthesis is that the results of such research can easily be communicated to engineers, and thus the appreciation of research findings is greatly facilitated. It is also an easy matter for one researcher to duplicate the facilities and apparatus used by another investigator.

System research methodology depends heavily on the possibility of constructing an adequate mathematical model so that machine elements can be represented by an analog such as a computer. In the example given above, the psychologist utilizes aerodynamics or other theory in creating an analog of vehicle dynamics. In the study of logistic, communication, management, and other types of systems, the mathematical models developed by specialists in operations research are utilized in a similar manner.

System simulation techniques are just beginning to be understood well enough to be exploited by engineering psychologists. They are likely to be used increasingly in the future and offer promise for the study of human performance capabilities in the most complex and important types of tasks of interest for engineering psychology. [10a].

Efficient test methods. The engineering psychologist, trained in the experimental laboratory, often is not prepared to deal with the exigencies of field tests and evaluation studies. Given sufficient time, equipment, etc., he knows how to bring experimental methodology to bear on problems. However, in the short time periods available for designing, developing, and testing new man-machine systems, these methods are impractical; therefore many very important decisions are made on the basis of inappropriate theory, inadequate data, or relatively unreliable personal opinions. Under these circumstances, the applied engineering psychologist has a great need for methods that are much more efficient—even if less powerful—than classical laboratory methods.

One of the greatest needs in engineering psychology is for rapid and efficient test methods that can be used to fill the void between precise, conservative, traditional laboratory methods and the procedures that are actually followed in answering the most important system design issues. The scientific psychologist must, of course, continue to insist on high standards of methodological rigor for theoretical research; he can, nevertheless, make a very important contribution to human factors engineering practice by research which has as its aim the development of more efficient, even if less reliable, methods for answering certain types of applied problems. Methods based on observation, rather than measurement, and on the collection and use of samples of expert opinion might be a possibility.

Task taxonomy. In the last analysis, the success of efforts to build a foundation of scientific psychology on which an applied science of human factors engineering can rest will depend on the ease with which psychological theory, principles, and facts can be used by design engineers and on the soundness of the interpretations which they make of the scientific data. The challenge to psychology is to produce theory which is sound and which can guide the practical decisions and actions of men in another profession. A uniform *task taxonomy* is one of the necessary ingredients of such a theoretical foundation. From the very first conception of a new system and the roles men will play in it to the final field testing, the meaning of terms used to specify roles, tasks, and job functions must be unambiguous. The identification of relevant facts, the application of theory, the selection of appropriate tests, the simulation of real or proposed systems in the laboratory are all steps in which taxonomy forms the bridge between theory and application.

Fortunately, there is wide interest in task taxonomy today, and a substantial amount of relevant literature has developed. Job analysis was early recognized as important in industrial psychology. The analysis and measurement of factors in individual differences provide much relevant theory. And the emphasis on operational definitions in fields such as learning and perception has helped to establish the validity of generalizations from theory to specific tasks and the appropriateness of alternative methods for problem-oriented research.

SUMMARY AND FORECAST

Engineering psychology is a scientific and research area which contributes to the broader professional area of human factors engineering. The central scientific topic of engineering psychology is human performance theory, prediction of the performance levels of different types of people in different types of tasks and at various levels of training. The central professional topic is the application of performance and preference data to the design of tasks, machines, and man-machine systems.

Historically and logically, human performance research is closely related to experimental psychology. However, the types of variables it considers, the settings in which it is conducted, the concepts it employs, and the uses to which its findings are put are also sufficiently distinctive to give it a somewhat separate identity.

The training of an engineering psychologist should prepare him primarily for a scientific career in basic or problem-oriented research. He should also be prepared to act as an expert adviser regarding human factor aspects of systems. His training should emphasize related scientific areas, such as mathematics and physics, which form a background for human performance theory and a basis for better understanding of engineering problems [see 1*a*]. Such broad scientific training, together with practical experience, also prepares him for professional work as a specialist on an engineering design team, as a man-machine systems expert, and as a consultant on human factor problems in engineering.

In engineering, there is every indication of steadily increasing support for human factors work. It is likely that the undergraduate engineering curriculum, in spite of its present course overload, may come to include emphasis on psychology. Such added emphasis, it should be noted, could actually mean a considerable broadening of undergraduate engineering training. At the graduate level, it is likely that an increasing number of engineers may elect to spend a year in the study of psychology, not with the purpose of shifting fields, but in order to prepare for work as a human factors engineer. Thus there should be increasing application of psychology to the design and development aspects of a constantly changing technology through the work of engineers as well as psychologists.

On the theoretical side, the contact with physical scientists and engineers, the work on complex new computer, communication, data-processing, and control systems, and the ready access to new developments in mathematics and in engineering will stimulate new types of research in engineering psychology. In turn, engineering psychology will provide several invigorating influences on its parent field of psychology. It will add to the pressure that is moving psychological theory nearer to mathematics and the physical sciences. It will encourage the more frequent formulation of psychological theory in a metalanguage that is more readily understandable to other scientists. And it will offer a much needed stimulus to an old, a broad, an important, but a somewhat neglected area of psychological theory—the study of human performance.

REFERENCES

1. Ackoff, R. L. The development of operations research as a science. *Oper. Res.,* 1956, **4,** 265–295.
1a. American Psychological Assn., Division 21 Committee on Training. Training in engineering psychology. *Amer. Psychol.,* 1961, **16,** 171–177.
2. Ashby, W. R. *An introduction to cybernetics.* New York: Wiley, 1956.
3. Attneave, F. *Applications of information theory to psychology.* New York: Holt-Dryden, 1959.
4. Baldwin, M. W., & Nielsen, G. Subjective sharpness of simulated color television pictures. *J. Opt. Soc. Amer.,* 1956, **46,** 681–685.
5. Birmingham, H. P., & Taylor, F. V. *A human engineering approach to the design of man-operated continuous control systems.* U.S. Naval Res. Lab. Report No. 4333, 1954.
6. Chapanis, A. *Research techniques in engineering psychology.* Baltimore, Md.: Johns Hopkins Press, 1959.
7. Cronbach, L. J. The two disciplines of scientific psychology. *Amer. Psychologist,* 1957, **12,** 671–684.
7a. Edwards, W. Dynamic decision theory and probabilistic information processing. *Human Factors,* 1962, **4,** 59–73.
8. *Encyclopaedia Britannica.* Vol 8. Chicago: Encyclopaedia Britannica, 1949. Section on civil engineering.
9. Fitts, P. M. Engineering psychology and equipment design. In S. S.

Stevens (Ed.), *Handbook of experimental psychology*. New York: Wiley, 1951. Pp. 1287–1340.

9a.Fitts, P. M. Functions of man in complex systems. *Aerospace Engng.*, 1962, **21**, 34–39.

10. Ford, A. Types of errors in location judgments on scaled surfaces. II. Random and systematic errors. *J. appl. Psychol.*, 1949, **33**, 382–394.

10a.Gagme, R. M. (Ed.) *Psychological principles in system development*. New York: Holt, Rinehart, & Winston, 1962.

10b.Garner, W. R. *Uncertainty and structure as psychological concepts*. New York: Wiley, 1962.

11. Harter, G. A., & Fitts, P. M. *The functional stimulating of complex systems by means of an analog computer*. Air Force Pers. Training Res. Center, San Antonio, Tex., Report No. TN-56-133, 1956.

11a.Licklider, J. C. R., & Clark, W. E. On-line man-computer communication. *Amer. Fed. Information Processing Soc., Proceedings of the Spring Joint Computer Conference*, 1962, **21**, 113–128.

12. McCloskey, J. F., & Trefethen, F. N. *Operations research for management*. Baltimore, Md.: Johns Hopkins Press, 1954.

13. McMillan, B., et al. *Current trends in information theory*. Pittsburgh, Pa.: Univer. Pittsburgh Press, 1954.

14. McRuer, D. T., & Krendal, E. A. *Dynamic responses of human operators*. U.S. Air Force, Wright Air Develpm. Center Tech. Report No. 56-524, October, 1957.

15. Mann, F. C., & Hoffman, L. R. *Automation and the worker*. New York: Holt-Dryden, 1960.

16. Münsterberg, H. *Psychology and industrial efficiency*. Boston: Houghton Mifflin, 1913.

17. Quastler, H. *Information theory in psychology*. Glencoe, Ill.: Free Press, 1955.

18. Shannon, C. E., & Weaver, W. *The mathematical theory of communication*. Urbana, Ill.: Univer. Ill. Press, 1949.

18a.Sinaiko, H. W. *Selected papers on human factors in the design and use of control systems*. New York: Dover, 1961.

19. Taylor, F. V. Psychology and the design of machines. *Amer. Psychologist,* 1957, **12**, 249–258.

20. Von Neuman, J. *The computer and the brain*. New Haven, Conn.: Yale Univer, Press, 1958.

21. Warren, N. D. Automation, human engineering, and psychology. *Amer. Psychologist*, 1956, **11**, 531–536.

21a.Welford, A. T. The measurement of sensori-motor performance. *Ergonomics*, 1960, **3**, 189–229.

22. Wiener, N. *Cybernetics*. New York: Wiley, 1948.

NAME INDEX

Page numbers in **boldface** type indicate bibliography references; *n.* indicates footnote references.

Aberle, D. F., 639*n.*, 663, **727**
Abt, L. E., **586**
Ach, N., 369
Ackerman, N. W., 701, **727**
Ackoff, R. L., **932**
Adams, D., 491, 508, **579**
Adams, J. S., 714, **727**
Adams, O. S., **897**
Adams, P. A., **481**
Adamson, J. F., **109**
Adis-Castro, G., 100, **111**
Adkins, M. M., **637**
Adler, A., 369, 376, 401, 404, 418, 458, 462*n.*, 464, 465, 470, 680, 681, **727**, 796, 799, 802, 811, 813, 815, 817, 820, 822, **824**
Adler, G., 462*n.*, **475**
Adorno, T. W., **579**
Adrian, E. D., 406
Ainsworth, M. D., 791, **826**
Albert, E. M., **727**
Alexander, F., 745, **775**, 812, **824**
Allen, F., 458, 799, 814, **824**
Allen, L., **586**
Allinsmith, B. B., **636**
Allinsmith, W., **636**
Allport, F. H., 52, **103**, 214, 215, **250**, 424, **475**, 520, **579**
Allport, G. W., 263, **279**, 459, 462*n.*, 466, 472, **475**, 488, 494, 496, 500, 501, 511, 513, 518, 526, 535, 547, 548, 550, 551, 558, 565, 567, **579**, 593, 595, 599, 607, 608, **632**, 680, 688, **727**, 797, **824**
Alluisi, E. A., **897**
Alper, T. G., 612, **632**
Alpert, R., 264, **279**
Altman, J. W., **901**, **907**
Alvarez, R. R., **775**
Amatruda, S., **357**
Ames, A., 46, **103**, 105
Amsel, A., 259, 262, **279**

Anastasi, A., 603, 604, **632**, 792, **824**
Anderson, D. M., **906**
Anderson, E. E., 258, **279**
Anderson, H. H., **281**
Anderson, L. K., **107**
Andjus, R. K., **475**
Andrews, R. C., 397
Angel, E., 816, **827**
Angelini, A. L., 618, **632**
Angell, J. R., 395
Angyal, A., 495, 499, 535, 541, 569, **579**, **775**
Anokhin, P. K., 293, 294, 309, **353**, **354**
Ansbacher, H. L., 462*n.*, **475**, 812, **824**
Ansbacher, R., **475**
Anthony, A. S., 629, **638**
Antonitis, J. J., **359**
Apostel, L., **361**
Arieti, S., **583**, 587, **775**
Aristotle, 151
Armington, J. E., **354**
Armus, H. L., 159, 174
Arnoult, M. D., **103**, **898**
Aronfreed, J., **636**
Arrow, K. J., 24, 27
Arsenian, J. M., 653, **727**
Asch, S. E., **579**
Aschoff, J., **476**
Ashby, R. W., **579**
Ashby, W. R., **932**
Atkinson, J. W., 270, 271, 272, 275, 276, **279**, 281, 360, 586, 607, **632**, 636
Attneave, F., 22, 24, 26, 27, **354**, 390, **476**, **898**, **932**
Auld, F., Jr., **632**
Austin, G. A., 395, **477**
Axline, V., 790, 818, **824**

Babcock, H., 800, **824**
Bachrach, A. J., 213*n.*
Back, K., 654, **727**
Backer, R., 260, **282**

935

Bacon, M. K., 616, 626, **633**
Bahrick, H. P., **898**
Bailey, A. W., **898**
Baker, C. H., **898**
Baker, C. T., 788, **830**
Baker, K. E., **104, 106, 212,** 243, **250**
Baldwin, A. L., 273, 600, 613, **632, 633**
Baldwin, M. W., **932**
Bales, R. F., **588,** 654, 705, 706, 716, 717, **727, 730, 734, 737**
Balint, M., **579**
Ball, J., **482**
Bamford, H. E., Jr., **905**
Bandura, A., 461n., **476**
Barker, R. G., 557, **579, 580,** 644, 648, 649, 650, 651, 653, 669, 707, 708, 711, 712, 713, 715, 718, **727**
Barker, R. W., **636**
Barnes, E. J., 384, **483**
Barnes, R. M., **898**
Barnett, H. G., 371, 450, **476**
Barnouw, V., 653, **727**
Barron, F., **354, 580,** 610, 625, 630, **633**
Barry, H., III, 616, 625, 626, **633**
Bartlett, F. C., 369, **476,** 504, **580**
Bartley, S. H., 42, **104**
Bass, B. M., **729**
Bateson, G., 645, 647, 699, 701, **727, 735**
Battig, W. F., **898**
Bauer, H. J., **898**
Bavelas, A., **112**
Bayer, E., 258, **279**
Bayley, N., 788, **824**
Beach, F. A., 270, 369, 421, 444, **476, 482**
Beardslee, B. J., **636**
Beck, S., **801**
Becker, G. M., 326, **354**
Beecher, H. K., 423
Beer, B., **358**
Beisser, P. T., 710, 711, 718, **727**
Bélanger, D., **354**
Bell, E. G., **633**
Bellak, L., **588, 591,** 748, **775, 776**
Bender, L., 810, 811, **824**
Benedict, R., 624, **633**
Benjamin, J. D., 745, **775**
Benne, K. D., 660, **727**
Bennett, L., 646, 699, **728**
Benoit-Smullyan, E., 682, **727**
Bentley, A. F., 871, **898**
Benzinger, T. H., **476**
Berg, I. A., **729,** 812n., **828**
Berger, H., 306, **354**
Bergman, R., 88, **106**

Bergmann, G., 34, 52, 53, **104,** 271, 272, 275, **279, 580**
Beritov, I. S., 333, **354**
Berlyne, D. E., 24, 26, 27, 61, 85n., **104,** 253n., 259, 274n., **279,** 284, **354, 355**
Bernstein, A., 655, 706, 713, **732**
Bertocci, P. A., **580**
Bethe, A., 406
Bettelheim, B., **580**
Bevan, W., **104**
Bexton, W. H., **104, 727**
Beyrl, F., **104**
Biderman, A. D., **359**
Bieri, J., 604, **633**
Bijou, S. W., 784, **800, 824**
Bills, R. E., 688, **727**
Bilodeau, E. A., **174**
Bindra, D., 261n., 274n., **279,** 296, **355, 476**
Binet, A., 399, 787
Bion, W. R., 644, 704, 715, 718, **727**
Birdsall, T. G., 839, **906**
Birkhoff, G., **355**
Birmingham, H. P., 876, **898, 906, 932**
Bishop, B. M., 708, 709, **728**
Bitterman, M. E., 156, **175,** 453, **477**
Blackwell, H. R., **104**
Blake, R. R., **104, 108, 476, 580, 583, 585, 587,** 662, **728**
Blaustein, A. B., **775**
Bleke, R. C., **775**
Bleuler, E., 747, **775,** 796, 801
Block, Jack, **580,** 646, 690, 699, **728**
Block, Jean, **580**
Bloom, B. S., 556, **591**
Blough, D. S., 141, **175,** 232, **250, 251**
Blum, G. S., 276, **279,** 612, **633,** 803, **824**
Boas, F., 671, **728**
Bolles, M. M., **585,** 810, **824**
Bolles, R. C., 273
Boneau, C. A., **175**
Bonvallet, M., 307, **355**
Borgatta, E. F., 654, 716, 717, **727, 730**
Boring, E. G., 53, 71, **104, 108, 113,** 446, **476, 775**
Borisova, M. N., 362
Bott, E., 557, **580,** 664, **728**
Bottome, P., 462n., **476**
Bouthilet, L., 384
Bovard, E. W., 652, 654, 666, 716, **728**
Bowen, H. M., **899, 900**
Bradburn, W. M., 604, **633**
Braden, I., **359**
Brand, H., **580**
Brandt, R. B., 623, **633**

Bray, C. W., 899
Brazier, M. A., 476
Breese, F. H., 633
Breland, K., 168, 175
Breland, M., 168, 175
Bremer, F., 406
Brenman, M., 812, 824
Bretnall, E. P., 283
Bricker, P. D., 40, 104
Bridgman, P. W., 38, 104, 515, 580
Briggs, G. E., 252, 831n., 904
Brim, O. G., 657, 658, 728
Broadbent, D. E., 899
Brodbeck, M., 582
Broen, W. E., Jr., 763, 776
Brogden, W. J., 250
Bromiley, R. B., 899
Bronfenbrenner, U., 496, 497, 580, 668, 728
Bronner, A. F., 786, 824
Bronson, W. C., 111
Broom, L., 730, 731
Broverman, D. M., 602, 612, 633, 636
Brower, D., 586
Brown, D., 489n.
Brown, G., 406
Brown, J. L., 899
Brown, J. S., 174, 259, 263, 270, 271, 274n., 275, 279, 299, 355, 419, 476
Brown, R. H., 899
Browne, C. T., 250
Brownfain, J. J., 580, 688, 728
Bruce, V. G., 476
Bruner, J. S., 104, 111, 211, 218, 231, 243, 250, 251, 271, 272, 275, 329, 355, 369, 395, 416, 417, 456, 476, 477, 484, 494, 580, 588, 591
Brunswik, E., 45, 46, 47, 49, 89, 90, 104, 105, 369, 374, 393, 394, 395, 477, 566, 576, 581, 644, 728
Brush, E. S., 261n., 267, 270, 282
Bryan, W. L., 384, 399, 477
Bühler, C., 524, 581
Bühler, K., 525, 581
Bullard, D. M., 581
Bullock, D. H., 175
Bunge, M., 350, 355
Burgess, E. W., 710, 728
Burton, A., 581
Burwen, L. S., 581
Buser, P., 355
Bush, R. R., 355
Butcher, J., 177
Butler, J. M., 808, 824
Butler, R. A., 356
Butter, C. M., 175

Caldwell, W. E., 166, 175
Cambell, R. J., 777
Cameron, N., 728, 776
Campbell, B. A., 127, 175, 256, 261, 280, 282
Campbell, D. T., 21, 22, 24, 26, 27, 135n., 175, 581
Cannon, W. B., 390, 406, 477, 524
Cantril, H., 105, 356, 404, 477, 581, 590
Cardo, B., 331, 356
Carlson, V. R., 477
Carr, H. A., 395
Cartwright, D., 477, 581, 698, 728, 729, 734
Castaneda, D., 315, 364
Caton, R., 306
Cattell, J. McK., 231
Cattell, R. B., 273, 346, 356, 372, 477, 496, 502, 568, 581, 600, 604, 605, 608, 609, 611, 633, 797, 825
Champney, H., 613, 633
Chance, E., 690, 692, 707, 716, 718, 728
Chance, J. E., 780n.
Chapanis, A., 40, 104, 899, 904, 918, 932
Chapman, D. W., 105, 663, 728
Chapple, E. D., 728
Charters, W. W., 661, 666, 728, 731
Chein, I., 251, 542, 581, 647, 728
Chernikoff, R., 875, 899
Cherry, C., 899
Child, I. L., 21, 24, 27, 268, 276, 278, 283, 566, 567, 593, 607, 612, 616, 618, 619, 621, 622, 624, 626, 633, 637, 638
Cholden, L., 776
Chow, K. L., 21, 24, 105
Christie, R., 581
Clark, K. E., 5
Clark, R. A., 281, 360, 586, 636
Clark, W. E., 933
Clarke, A. R., 760, 776, 777
Clausen, J. A., 776
Clutton-Baker, J., 901
Cobb, E. A., 637
Coch, L., 581
Cofer, C. N., 274n., 280, 777
Coffey, H. S., 729
Cohen, A. R., 356, 654, 703, 729
Cohen, J., 477
Cohler, J., 584
Cohn, B. N., 94, 95, 105
Coleman, T. B., 141, 176
Coles, D. R., 109
Coles, G. R., 212

Collier, G. H., **112, 175,** 304, **362**
Combs, A., 510, **591, 696, 735**
Comer, P. B., **110**
Comfort, A., **477**
Conant, J. B., 367, 373, **477**
Conger, B., **111**
Conger, J. J., 256, 280
Conklin, J. E., **898, 899**
Conrad, R., **899**
Cooley, C. H., 671, 673, **729**
Coombs, C. H., **486**
Cooner, B. J., **906**
Coons, E., **356, 359**
Cornsweet, J. C., **484**
Cornsweet, T. H., **484**
Corsini, R. J., **710, 729**
Cosgriff, R. L., **900**
Cotton, J. W., **112**
Cottrell, L. S., 643, 671, 710, **728, 729,** 730, 731
Cowen, E. J., **581**
Coyer, R. A., **900**
Craik, K. J. W., **900**
Cronbach, L. J., 611, **634,** 804, **825,** 916, **932**
Crosland, H. R., 453, **477**
Cross, P., **581**
Crossman, E. R. F. W., **900**
Crothers, E. J., **478**
Crowder, T. H., **356**
Crowder, W. F., 304, 305, **356**
Crutchfield, R., 446, 481, 496, 504, 523, 585
Cruzen, M., **906**
Culler, A. J., **250**
Culver, C. M., **776**
Cumming, W. W., 21, 22, 24, 27, 213, 252

Dai, B., 674, **729**
D'Andrade, R. G., 624, **637**
Darrow, C. W., 294, 306, 313, **356**
Darwin, C., 377, 385, 512
Dashiell, J. F., 448, **477**
David, P. R., 21, 24
Davids, A., 607, **634**
Davidson, K. S., **637**
Davis, A., 790, **825**
Davis, H., **906**
Davis, R., **900**
Davis, R. C., 24, 27, 235, 240n., **250,** 310, **356**
Davis, R. H., **776**
Davis, R. L., **486**
Deatherage, B. H., 453, **477**
de Beauvoir, S., 649
de Charms, R., 607, **634**

Deese, J., **211, 900**
Deininger, R. L., **876**
Delafresnaye, J. F., **359**
Dell, P. C., 307, **355, 356**
De Martino, M. F., **283**
Dember, W. N., 297, **356, 477**
Dembo, T., **579, 581, 586**
de Montpellier, G., **357**
Dennis, W., **106,** 448, **477, 481,** 603, 604, 619, 620, **634**
Deutsch, J. A., **477**
Devore, I., **486**
Dewey, J., 288, **356,** 395, 670
Diamantides, N., **904**
Diamond, I. T., 21, 24
Diamond, S., 369, 462n., **478,** 615, **634**
Digman, J. M., 603, **634**
Dinnerstein, D., **481**
Dittmann, A. T., 651, 707, 716, 724, **734**
Djang, S-S., 69, 73, **105**
Doane, B. K., **479**
Dodwell, P. C., 135n., **175**
Dollard, J., 60, 61, 65, **105, 110,** 186, **211,** 259, 268, 276, **280,** 461n., 470, **478,** 567, **582,** 799, 812, 816, 817, **825**
Doob, L. W., **280**
Douglas, A. G., **478**
Draguns, J., **478**
Draper, J., **903**
Drury, M. B., **105**
Drury, W. H., **484**
Dubois, C. A., **729**
Duffy, E., **356**
Dufort, R. H., **175**
Duke-Elder, S., **478**
Dunbar, F., **582**
Dunham, R. M., 761, **776**
Dunhoffer, H., **357**
Dunn, W. L., Jr., 758, 761, **776**
Dupertius, C. W., **590**
Duryea, R., 662, **728**
Dyer, W. R., 305, **356**
Dykman, R. A., **356**
Dymond, R., **589**

Eager, J., **582**
Earl, R. W., 297, **356**
Ebbinghaus, H., **398**
Edwards, A. L., 689, 710, **729,** 804, **825**
Edwards, B. J., 80, **110**
Edwards, W., **478, 900, 932**
Eells, K., 790, **825**
Egger, M., 316, **356**
Ehrenfreund, D., **105**
Ehrlich, S., **357**
Eible-Eibesfeldt, I., **478**

Eisenstein, V. S., **731, 733**
Eissler, K., **105**
Elithorn, A., **900**
Elkind, J. I., **900**
Ellenberger, H. F., 816, **827**
Ellis, A., 515, **582**
Ellis, W. D., **105**
Ellson, D. G., 243, **250**, 388, **478, 900**
Ely, J. H., **900**
Englehart, R. C., 759, **776**
Epstein, S., 686, **729**
Epstein, W., 51n., **105**
Ericksen, S. C., 273
Eriksen, C. W., 38, 39, 40, 42, **105, 106,
    107, 175,** 250, 359, 900
Erikson, E. H., 461n., **478,** 506, **582,**
    675, 680, 683, **729**
Ermolaeva-Tomina, L. B., 362
Escalona, K., 800, **825**
Estes, W. K., 123, 124, 132, 133, 160,
    175, 251, 262, 271, 273, 275, **280,**
    355, 454, **478**
Eysenck, H. J., **356, 372, 478,** 496, 557,
    582, 593, 600, 605, 609, **634**
Ezriel, H., 542, **582**

Fairbairn, W. R. D., 497, **582, 729**
Farber, I. E., 257, 259, 270, 271, 275,
    279, 280, 355
Farina, A., 762, **776, 777**
Farnsworth, P. R., 829
Fechner, G. T., 264, **280, 357,** 381, 428
Federn, P., 683, **729**
Feigl, H., **478, 582, 590**
Feld, S., **730**
Feldman, H., **104**
Fenchel, G. E., 682, **729**
Fenichel, O., 524, **582, 729, 776**
Ferenczi, S., 697, **729**
Ferguson, G. A., **483**
Fessard, M. A., 309, **357**
Festinger, L., 262, 269, 270, 276, **280,
    281,** 586, 654, 696, **729, 734, 828**
Ficks, L., **905**
Fieandt, K. v., **105**
Fiedler, F. E., 689, 716, **729**
Finger, F. W., 160, **175, 361**
Fischer, J. L., 625, **634**
Fishback, J., **481**
Fisher, J., **582**
Fishman, J. A., **582**
Fiske, D. W., 297, 317, **357, 477, 478,**
    584, 807, **826**
Fitts, P. M., 24, 27, 876, **900, 901, 902,
    902,** 908, **932, 933**
Fitzgerald, B. J., 606, **634**
Flavell, J. H., **478**

Fleck, F. S., **111**
Fleishman, E. A., 604, **634**
Fletcher, F. J., **483**
Flynn, J. P., **901**
Folley, J. D., Jr., **901**
Fonda, C. P., **359**
Foote, N. N., 726, **729**
Forbes, T. W., **901**
Ford, A., **933**
Forgays, D. G., **105, 110**
Forgus, R. H., 75, 76, **105, 106**
Forster, N. C., 603, **634**
Foss, B. M., **357, 362**
Fowler, H., **477**
Fox, S. S., 311, **357**
Fraisse, P., **357**
Franck, K., **634**
Frank, K. F., 607, **633**
Frank, L. K., 802, **825**
Franz, S. I., **106**
Fraser, D. C., **901**
Freedman, M. B., 489n., **582, 729**
Freeman, G. L., 181, **211**
Freeman, H., **775, 776**
French, D., 21, 24, 27
French, J. R. P., Jr., 259, **280, 581,** 632,
    634, 639n., 666, **730**
French, J. W., 609, **634**
French, T. M., **583, 745, 775,** 812, **824**
Frenkel-Brunswik, E., **357, 579, 582, 583**
Freud, A., 424, 461n., **478, 583,** 677,
    730, 736, 811
Freud, S., 173, 253, 257, 259, 264, 268,
    271, 272, 275, 276, **280,** 321, 458,
    461n., 465, 466, 467, 468, **478,** 497,
    500, 501, 512, 524, 526, 527, 533,
    534, 535, 537, **583,** 644, 665, 697,
    718, **730,** 765, **776,** 796, 802, 811,
    812, 815, 817, 821
Frick, F. C., **903**
Friedman, I., **730**
Fries, C. C., 226, **250**
Fromm, E., 462n., 464, 526, **583,** 812,
    825
Fromm-Reichmann, F., **776**

Gaffron, M., 22, 24, 26, 27, **178**
Gagné, R. M., **106, 212, 933**
Gahm, R. C., 607, **637**
Gaito, J., **478**
Galambos, R., **357, 358**
Galanter, E., 278, **281,** 404, 415, 422,
    437, **483**
Galbrecht, C. R., **356**
Galinsky, M. D., 604, **633**
Gallwey, M. O., 668, **728**
Galton, F., 798, **825**

Gantt, H., 311, **362**
Ganz, L., 140, 146, **175**
Gardner, E. F., 704, 710, 716, 718, **730**
Gardner, M., **478**
Gardner, R. W., 611, **634**
Gardner, W., **478**
Garfield, S. L., 812n., **825**
Garmezy, N., 273, 752, 757, 758, 760, 769, **776, 777, 778**
Garner, W. R., 38, 39, 40, 42, **106, 175, 933**
Garvey, W. D., **109**, 850, 877n., **901**
Gastaut, H., **357**
Gastaut, M., 309, **357**
Gebhard, J., **904**
Gehman, R. S., **364**
Geldard, F. A., 381, **901**
Gerard, H. B., 676, 689, **730**
Gerathewohl, S. J., **901**
Gershuni, G. V., 311, **357**
Gesell, A., **357**
Getzels, J. W., 630, **634, 635**
Gewirtz, J. L., 342, **357**
Gibb, J. R., 652, 659, 660, **730**
Gibbs, C. B., **901**
Gibby, R. G., 807, **825**
Gibson, E. J., 60, 63, 64, 73, 74, 75, 76, 80, 81, 83, 86, 87, 88, 91, **106, 113, 196, 212**, 373, 448, **478, 479**
Gibson, J. J., 44, 45, 48, 49, 56, 60, 63, 64, 73, **106**, 165, **175**, 187, 196, **212**, 373, 453, **479, 583**
Gilchrist, J. C., 700, **730**
Gilinsky, A. S., 50, **107**
Gill, M., 466, **479, 583**
Gill, M. M., 812, **824**
Ginsberg, R., **585**
Girdner, J. B., **357**
Gladwin, T., **355**
Glanzer, M., 296, **357**
Gleitman, H., 166, **175**
Glickman, S. E., **357, 479**
Goffman, E., 649, 658, 669, 672, 674, 679, 685, **730**
Goldiamond, I., 96, 97, **107**, 213n.
Goldman-Eisler, F., 621, **635**
Goldstein, K., 370, 524, 535, 569, **583**, 745, **777**, 809, 810, **825**
Gonick, M. R., **580**
Goodenough, F., 786, **825**
Goodman, C. C., 218, **250, 580**
Goodnow, J. J., 168, **176**, 395, **477**
Goodrich, D. W., 709, **732**
Goodwin, W. R., 201, **212**
Gordon, D. A., **477**
Gordon, L. V., 804, **825**
Goss, A. E., **107, 112**

Gottschaldt, K., 30, 51n., 67, 68, 69, 70, 73, **107**
Gottsdanker, R. M., **901**
Gouldner, A. W., 676, **730**
Gough, H. G., 583, 610, **635**
Goustard, M., **357**
Graham, C. H., 22, 24, 27, 35, 36, 37, 60, 79, 83, 101, 102, **107**, 180, **212**, **250**
Graham, E., 627, **636**
Graham, F. K., 810, **825**
Granit, R., **583**
Grant, D. A., **901**
Grastyán, E., **357**
Graves, M. E., **357**
Gray, F. E., **900**
Gray, H., **730**
Gray, P. H., **358**
Gréco, P., **357, 358**
Green, B. F., **107**, 862, **902**
Green, L. R., **637**
Green, R. F., **902**
Greenacre, P., **730**
Greenfeld, N., **107**
Greenson, R. R., **583**
Gregg, L. W., **250**
Gregory, R. L., **486**
Grether, W. F., **898**
Grinker, R. R., **583, 735**
Gropper, G. L., **111**
Gross, H., 661, **730**
Gruen, W., 489n.
Guba, E. G., 630, **634, 635**
Guertin, W. H., 785, **828**
Guilford, J. P., **358**, 372, **479, 583**, 600, 609, **635, 825**
Gump, P., 648, 651, 716, **730**
Gurin, G., **730**
Guthrie, E. R., 84, **107**, 151, **176**, 219, 246, **251**, 261, 263, **280**, 395, 396, 398, **479, 583**
Guttman, L., 661
Guttman, N., 21, 22, 27, 114, **175, 176, 177**

Haber, R. N., 264, **280**
Hake, H. W., 38, 39, 40, 42, **106, 107, 175, 900**
Hall, C. S., **283**, 462n., 464, **479**, 511, 536, **583**
Hall, J. F., 274n., **280**
Hall, N. B., Jr., **902**
Hallowell, A. I., 21, 24, 26, 27, 644, 645, 672, 685, **730**
Halstead, W. C., 810, **825**
Hamburg, D. A., 253n.
Hamilton, W. F., 141, **176**

Hammond, K., **477**, **482**, 808, **826**
Hanawalt, N. G., 68, **107**, 218, **251**
Hanfmann, E., 384, 395, **479**, 810, **825**
Hanson, H. M., 154, 155, 157, 158, 159, **176**
Harary, F., 698, **728**
Harding, J., 668, **728**
Hare, A., 717, **727**, **730**
Harker, J. E., **479**
Harlow, H. F., **111**, **176**, 239, **251**, 259, 270, 271, 272, 275, **280**, 343, **356**, **358**, 369, 445, **479**, **584**, 793, **825**
Harrington, R. W., **776**
Harris, J. D., 358
Harris, J. G., Jr., 760, **777**
Harris, R. E., 581
Harrison, R., 803, **825**
Harrison, R. H., 163, **177**
Harrower-Erikson, M. R., 810, **826**
Harter, G. A., **933**
Harter, N., 384, 399, **477**
Hartley, E. L., **588**, **638**, 660, 682, **728**, **729**, **730**, **732**
Hartley, R. E., 660, **730**
Hartman, B. O., **902**
Hartmann, H., 505, 526, 583
Hartshorne, H., **583**, 598, 599, 602, **635**
Harvey, O. J., 682, **730**
Hasler, A. D., **479**
Hastorf, A. H., 105
Hathaway, S. R., **583**, 800, 804, **826**
Hauty, G. T., **902**
Havighurst, J., 790, **825**
Hawkins, W. F., 96, 97, **107**
Hayek, F. A., 135*n*., **176**
Head, H., 809, **826**
Healy, W., 786, **824**
Hearst, E., **176**, 316, **358**
Hebb, D. O., 58, 59, 73, 78, 79, 82, **107**, 135*n*., **176**, 187, 271, 275, 294, 317, 343, **358**, 369, 370, 400, 420, 429, 447, **476**, **479**, **483**, **484**, 526, **584**
Heidbreder, E., **479**
Heidegger, M., 816
Heider, F., **584**, 645, 671, 696, 698, 699, **730**, **731**
Heimer, W., 484
Heinemann, E., 164, **176**
Heise, G. A., **110**
Heist, P., 592
Helmholtz, H. L. F., 46
Helson, H., **176**, 196, 212, 403, **479**, 586, **902**
Hempel, C. G. A., **584**
Henderson, R. L., **358**
Henle, M., 76, 77, **107**, **584**
Henneman, R. H., **109**, **110**, **111**

Henry, E. M., 805, **826**
Henry, G. W., 796, **830**
Henry, J., 617, 635
Henson, J. B., **902**
Herbart, J. F., 328
Herbst, P. G., 655, 702, 712, 720, **731**
Herma, H., 105
Heron, W., 78, **104**, **107**, 383, 429, 447, **479**, **484**, 727
Herrick, E., 790, **825**
Hertz, M., 801
Hess, E. H., 80, 81, **108**, 273
Hess, W. R., 358
Heyns, R. W., 717, **731**
Hiebel, G., 307, **355**
Hilgard, E. R., 24, 54, **108**, 253, **280**, **358**, 497, 508, 511, 537, 551, 565, 567, 575, **584**, 671, 692, **731**
Hill, J. H., **902**
Hill, W. F., 259, **280**
Hinde, R. A., **358**, **479**
Hinsie, L. E., **777**
Hirsh, I., **902**
Hobhouse, L. T., 399
Hochberg, J. E., 41, 42, 72, **108**, **112**, **358**, **479**
Hoffman, L. R., **933**
Holaday, B. E., **108**
Holland, J. G., **902**
Hollander, E. P., **584**
Holt, B. G., 347, **363**
Holt, E. B., 295, **358**
Holt, R., 570, **584**
Holt, R. R., 791, **826**
Holway, A. H., **108**
Holzman, P. S., 478, **634**
Homans, G. C., **731**
Honig, W. K., 152, 153, 154, 155, 156, 158, **176**, **177**
Honzik, C. H., 265, **283**
Honzik, M. P., 586
Hopkins, B. L., 478
Horney, K., 369, 376, 458, 462*n*., 464, 466, **479**, 526, **584**, 680, 685, 715, 718, **731**, 812, 815, **826**
Horwitt, M. K., **777**
Hoskins, R. G., 748, **775**, **777**
Hovland, C. I., **108**, 139, **177**, 313, **358**
Howe, W. H., **902**
Howes, D. H., 41, 100, **108**, **112**, **251**
Hsu, F. L. K., **638**
Hull, C. L., 56, **108**, 123, 124, 126, 136, 139, 148, 149, 160, 164, **177**, **212**, 254, 255, 256, 257, 258, 260, 262, 265, 268, 271, 272, 274, 275, **280**, 384, 395, 396, 398, 399, 400, 416,

Hull, C. L. (*cont.*), 445, 447, 468, 470, **480**, 552, 565, 567, **584**, 763, 803, 817
Humm, D. G., 804, **826**
Humphrey, C. E., **902**
Humphreys, L. G., 262, 600, **635**
Hunt, H. F., 810, **826**
Hunt, J. McV., 360, 586, 590, **777**, 812*n.*, **826**
Hunter, W. S., 220, 871, 782, **903**
Hurwitz, H. M. B., **358**
Huston, P. E., **777**
Hutchings, E., Jr., **485**
Hydén, H., **480**

Inhelder, B., 367, **480**, **486**
Inkeles, A., 24, 27, 619, **635**, 675, 695, **731**
Irey, E., **483**
Irwin, F. W., 274*n.*, **280**, 326, **358**
Iscoe, I., **728**
Israel, H. E., 384, **484**
Ittelson, W. H., 20, 22, 24, 26, **105, 108**, **480**
Izard, C. E., 710, **731**

Jackson, D. D., 748, 750, **776, 777, 779**
Jackson, D. N., **108**
Jackson, J. H., 809, **826**
Jackson, R. F., **901**
Jacobs, H. H., **906**
Jacobson, E., 661, **731**
Jacobson, Edith, 702, **731**
Jahoda, G., **635**
Jahoda, M., **584**
James, H., 341, **358**
James, W., 235, 288, **359**, 395, 532, **584**, 670, 673, 674, 685, **731**
Janet, P., **458**
Janis, I., 273, **636**
Jasper, A., **588**
Jasper, H. H., 309, 315, **359**, **362**
Jastak, J., 800, **826**
Jaworska, K., **363**
Jeffress, L. A., **480**, **482**
Jenkins, H. M., 163, **177**
Jenkins, J. J., **109**
Jenkins, R. L., **777**
Jenkins, W. O., **480**, **903**
Jensen, A. R., 459, **480**
Jensen, F., 495, **587**
Jessor, R., 780*n.*, 808, 816, 820, **826**
John, E. R., 331, **359**
Johnson, A. M., 702, **731**
Johnson, D. M., 85, 86, **108**
Johnson, H. M., **220**
Johnson, W., 788, **826**

Jones, A., 301, **359**
Jones, D. S., 630, **637**
Jones, E., 461*n.*, **480**
Jones, E. E., 705, 711, **731**
Jones, L. V., 618, **636**
Jones, M. R., 110, 269, **281, 282, 283**, 360, 361, **584, 585, 587, 588, 637**, 727, 734, **778, 829**
Jourard, S. M., 689, **731**
Jung, C. G., 458, 462*n.*, 497, 501, **584**, 609, **635**, 674, 680, **731**, 796, 798, 814, 815, **826**
Jung, R., 489*n.*

Kaess, F., 394, **480**
Kaess, W., 394, **480**
Kaestner, N. F., **901**
Kagan, J., 603, 605, **635**
Kahl, J. A., 664, **732**
Kalhorn, J., **633**
Kalish, H. I., 55, **108**, 136, 139, 140, 148, **176, 177**
Kallman, F. J., **777**
Kamin, L. J., 450, **485**
Kanfer, F. H., 62, **109**, 251
Kant, E., 145, 369
Kant, O., **777**
Kantor, J. R., 219, 220, **251**, 393, 401, 402, **480**, 795, 799, 822, **826**, 871, **903**
Kantor, R. E., **777**
Kaplan, B., 617, **635, 733**
Kaplan, D. M., 709, **732**
Kardiner, A., 812, **826**
Karlin, J., 842*n.*
Kasanin, J., 810, **825**
Katona, G., 24, 26, 27
Katz, D., 258, **281**, 584, 590, **734, 828**
Katz, E., 664, **732**
Katz, M. S., **903**
Keehn, J. D., 602, 603, 617, **635**
Keller, F. S., **251**
Kelley, D. M., **585**
Kelley, H. H., 663, 714, 722, **732, 736**
Kelly, E. L., **584**, 603, **635**, 807, **826**
Kelly, G. A., 462*n.*, **480**, 504, 556, **584**, 691, 692, **732**, 815, 816, 822, **826**
Kelman, H. C., **584**
Kenchington, K. W. L., **903**
Kendall, B. S., 810, **825**
Kendler, T. S., **480**
Kendrew, J. C., **480**
Kenny, D. T., **585**
Kent, G. H., 797, **826**
Kessen, M. L., 261, **282**
Kessen, W., **359**
Kety, S., **777**

Kierkegaard, S. A., 816
Killam, K. F., 331, 359
Kilpatrick, F. P., 109, 480
Kimble, G. A., 175, 461n., 480
King, R. A., 160, 177, 178
King-Ellison, P., 109
Kish, G. B., 359
Klauser, S. Z., 732
Klein, G. S., 270, 271, 275, 276, 281, 369, 401, 424, 478, 480, 511, 537, 568, 569, 570, 571, 585, 634
Klein, M., 497, 527, 585, 732, 811
Kleist, K., 809, 826
Kleitman, N., 480
Klemmer, E. T., 903
Klimpfinger, S., 109
Klineberg, O., 789, 826
Klopfer, B., 585, 791, 801, 826
Klopfer, W. G., 791, 826
Kluckhohn, C., 523, 524, 525, 532, 542, 549, 562, 582, 585, 587, 589, 635, 732
Kluckhohn, F. R., 701, 715, 736
Kluckhohn, R., 629, 638
Klüver, H., 135n., 177, 369, 370, 425, 480
Knoepfelmacher, F., 475
Knowles, W. B., 901, 903
Koch, S., 106, 107, 108, 110, 111, 175, 176, 178, 212, 251, 270, 277, 280, 281, 282, 283, 296, 297, 359, 433, 476, 477, 478, 479, 480, 481, 483, 484, 485, 486, 526, 553, 581, 583, 584, 585, 587, 589, 592, 734, 735
Koerner, L., 483
Koffka, K., 109, 217, 249, 251, 359, 431, 481, 511, 585
Köhler, W., 58, 109, 169, 177, 368, 370, 372, 376, 401, 414, 418, 430, 453, 454, 456, 462, 481, 585
Kohn, M. L., 776
Korzybski, A., 816, 827
Kounin, J., 585
Kowalska, M., 363
Kraehenbuehl, D., 356, 359
Kraepelin, E., 747, 796, 798, 801, 827
Krasner, L., 821, 827
Krech, D., 369, 370, 446, 481, 496, 504, 568, 569, 571, 585
Krechevsky, I., 135n., 448, 481
Kreinik, P. S., 761, 777
Krendel, E. S., 903, 904, 933
Kretschmer, E., 797, 798, 827
Kris, E., 505, 526, 583
Kroeber, A. L., 635
Krugman, M., 801, 827
Krulee, G. K., 109, 903

Kubie, L., 585
Kubzanzky, P. E., 310, 359
Külpe, O., 50, 109, 199
Kurke, M. I., 111

LaBerge, D. L., 109, 212
Lacey, O. L., 110
Lacey, O. W., 109
Laffal, J., 314, 359
LaForge, R., 688, 732
Lambert, W. W., 23, 27, 253n., 259, 281, 618, 624, 635, 636, 717, 732
Landes, J., 581
Landis, C., 585, 810, 824
Lane, R. E., 24, 27
Langer, S. K., 641, 732
Langfeld, H. S., 446, 476
Lanier, L. H., 5
Lansky, L. M., 636
Larsen, J. A., 479
Lashley, K. S., 81, 109, 135n., 164, 177, 185, 212, 368, 370, 376, 386, 401, 405, 406, 409, 410, 417, 425, 427, 450, 456, 462, 471, 481, 482, 809, 827
Laskow, P., 689, 731
Lát, J., 285, 312, 345, 359
Laulict, J., 661, 732
Lavoisier, A. L., 367
Lawrence, C., 900
Lawrence, D. H., 21, 22, 24, 27, 51, 78n., 109, 160, 177, 179, 201, 212, 262, 269, 276, 281, 446, 482
Layman, J. D., 106
Lazarsfeld, P. F., 553, 585, 664, 732
Lazarus, R. S., 40, 109, 251, 359, 602, 607, 612, 633, 636
Leary, T. F., 482, 688, 692, 699, 706, 707, 718, 729, 732
Lebedinskaia, E. I., 359
Leblanc, M., 617, 636
Lechner, M., 899
Lecky, P., 462n., 482, 510, 585, 696, 732, 814, 827
Lee, D. P., 679, 732
Leeper, D. O., 429, 482
Leeper, R. W., 21, 22, 24, 26, 27, 71, 72, 73, 109, 365, 429, 462n., 482
Lehman, H. G., 585
Leibnitz, G. W., 526, 668
Lennard, H. L., 655, 706, 713, 732
Leontiev, A. N., 357
Lesser, G. S., 605, 606, 607, 636
Leuba, C., 243, 251
Leventhal, C. M., 486
Levin, H., 273
Levin, M. M., 109

Levine, M., 168, **177, 903**
Levine, R., **251**
Levinson, D. J., **579, 585,** 619, **635,** 695, 731
Levy, D., 801, 811, **827**
Levy, D. W., 693, **732**
Levy, M. J., 655, 656, **732**
Lewin, K., 221, 253, 259, 262, 263, 268, 269, 276, **280,** 369, 376, 401, 404, 418, 462*n.,* 495, 496, 511, 529, 530, 541, 542, 543, 544, 554, 555, 556, 562, 565, 568, **579, 585, 586,** 644, 645, 647, 648, 649, 651, 652, 718, 720, **732, 733,** 795, 799, 800, 803, 804, 822, **827,** 871, **903**
Lewinger, H., **109**
Lewis, E. J., **482**
Lichten, D., **110**
Licklider, J. C. R., **903, 933**
Liebermann, S., 661, **731**
Lighthall, F. F., **637**
Lilly, J. C., 422, 445
Limbaugh, C., **482**
Lincoln, R. S., **903**
Lindsley, D. B., 273, 306, **359, 360, 904**
Lindsley, O. R., 303, **360**
Lindzey, G., **281,** 358, 462*n.,* 464, **479, 480,** 511, 536, 583, 586, 590, **633, 635, 637, 731, 735**
Linton, H., **478,** 627, 634, 636
Linton, R., 496, 532, 586, 656, **733**
Lippitt, R., 265, **283, 586,** 652, 699, 715, 717, **731, 733**
Lipset, S. M., **637**
Lipsitt, P. D., **637**
Lisina, M. I., 336, **360**
Lissák, K., **357**
Littman, R. A., 273
Liverant, S., 790, 804, **827**
Livingston, R. B., 24
Lobban, M. C., **482**
Loeb, M., **904**
Logan, F. A., 262, 274*n.,* **281**
Long, E. R., 51, **109, 110, 111**
Long, J. B., **177**
Longfeldt, G., **777**
Lord, E. E., 807, **827**
Lorenz, K., 369, 420, 433, 444, 456, **482**
Lounsbury, F. G., 26
Louttit, C. M., **780, 781, 782,** 790, 827
Lowe, G. C., **786, 824**
Lowell, E. L., **281,** 315, **360, 586,** 636
Lowenstein, R., 505, 526, **583**
Lowenthal, L., **637**
Luborsky, L., **584**
Lubow, R. E., 331, **360**
Luce, R. D., **482**

Luchins, A. S., 59, **110, 586**
Ludin, R. W., 461*n.,* **483**
Luria, A. R., 335, **360**
Luria, Z., **734**
Luszki, M. B., 750, 768, **778**

McAlister, E., **358, 479**
McBride, A. F., 420, **483**
McBride, K. E., 809, **830**
McCarthy, D. A., **482**
McCary, J. L., **585, 586, 589**
McCleary, R. A., 40, **109, 251**
McClelland, D. C., 263, 264, 268, 270, 271, 272, 275, 276, 278, 279, **281,** 293, **360,** 496, 526, 551, **586, 588,** 604, 618, **634, 636**
McCloskey, J. F., **933**
Maccoby, E. E., **588, 638**
McCollom, I. N., **904**
McConnell, T. R., **582**
McCormick, E. J., **904**
MacCorquodale, K., 52, **110,** 271, 272, 275, **587**
McCracken, W. I., **175**
McCue, J. J. G., **483**
McCulloch, W. S., 390, 427
McCurdy, H. G., 426*n.,* **483**
McDermott, E., **590**
McDougall, W., 263, 266, 298, **360,** 369, 399, 404, 418, 424, **483,** 504, 512, **586**
McEachern, A. W., 661, **730**
McElroy, W. A., **636**
McFarland, R. A., **904**
Macfarlane, D. A., **483**
Macfarlane, J. W., **586**
McGill, W., **904**
McGinnies, E. M., **110,** 231, **251, 588**
Mach, E., **177**
MacKay, D. M., **904**
McKinley, I. C., **583**
MacKinnon, D. W., 511, 558, 570, **586**
Mackintosh, I., 243, 250
Mackworth, J. F., **904**
Mackworth, N. H., **904**
McLean, O. S., **727**
MacLean, P. D., **360**
MacLeod, R. B., 671, 692, **733**
MacLeod, S., **177**
McMillan, B., **933**
McNamara, H. J., 166, **177**
McNeil, E. B., **636**
McNemar, Q., **581, 829**
MacPherson, S. J., **900**
McRuer, D. T., **904, 933**
Madarász, I., **357**
Maddi, S. R., 297, 317, 357, 477, 478

Madison, P., 452, 459, 461n., 462n., 472, 482, 483
Madlafousek, J., 312, 360
Madsen, K. B., 274n., 281
Magoun, H. W., 307, 361
Maier, N. R. F., 369, 370, 483
Mailloux, N., 105
Malmo, R. B., 273, 322, 360, 778
Mandelbrot, B., 361
Mandler, G., 359, 601, 636
Manis, M., 384, 483, 733
Mann, F. C., 933
Mark, J. C., 760, 778
Marquis, D. G., 358
Marriott, F. H. C., 484
Martin, H. G., 825
Marx, M. H., 259, 270, 281, 580
Masling, J., 807, 827
Maslow, A. H., 270, 277, 281, 483, 506, 525, 586, 680, 733
Mason, W. A., 212
Mason, W. S., 661, 730
Matalon, B., 357
Matter, J., 211
Maussner, B., 666, 733
May, M. A., 583, 598, 599, 602, 635
May, R., 281, 587, 671, 733, 816, 827
Mayer, J., 636
Maze, J. R., 587
Mead, G. H., 269, 281, 671, 733
Mead, R. J., 904
Mednick, S., 763, 778
Meehl, P. E., 52, 110, 271, 272, 275, 587, 611, 634, 804, 805, 825, 827
Melikian, L., 588
Mellinger, J. C., 111
Melton, A. W., 904
Melzack, R., 423, 483
Menzies, I. E. P., 668, 703, 733
Merton, R. K., 656, 659, 730, 731, 733
Meryman, J. J., 174
Meyer, A., 745, 778
Meyer, L. B., 360
Miles, C. C., 736
Miller, D. R., 21, 24, 27, 270, 489n., 626, 627, 636, 639, 678, 701, 714, 733, 807, 825
Miller, G. A., 104, 110, 251, 278, 281, 404, 415, 422, 437, 483, 903, 904
Miller, J. G., 555, 587, 779
Miller, M., 110
Miller, N. E., 60, 61, 65, 105, 110, 160, 177, 186, 211, 212, 256, 257, 260, 261, 268, 271, 272, 274, 275, 276, 280, 281, 282, 301, 316, 356, 360, 364, 461n., 470, 478, 483, 567, 582, 587, 799, 812, 816, 817, 825

Miller, R. B., 637, 904
Mills, C. W., 820n., 827
Milner, P., 264, 282
Minehart, J. B., 637
Mishkin, M., 110
Mitnick, L. L., 354, 901
Mittelman, B., 587, 715, 733
Moebius, N., 796
Moltz, H., 341, 342, 360
Monderer, J. H., 682, 729
Monnier, M., 309, 363
Montgomery, K. C., 259, 282
Mooney, C. M., 483
Moore, A. U., 331, 360
Moore, J. W., 744, 778
Moreno, J. L., 776, 818, 827
Morf, A., 360
Morgan, C. T., 273, 360, 370, 476
Morgan, D., 802, 827
Morgan, R. C., 106
Morganthaler, W., 828
Morozova, N. G., 327, 328, 360, 361
Morris, C., 618, 619, 636
Morris, J. B., 305, 356
Morrison, H. W., 634
Morrissette, R., 326, 364
Moruzzi, G., 307, 361
Moss, H. A., 603, 635
Mosteller, F., 355
Mote, F. A., 160, 177, 361
Moustakas, C. E., 708, 732, 733
Mowbray, G. H., 904
Mowrer, O. H., 262, 267, 268, 270, 271, 272, 275, 276, 280, 282, 526, 567, 587, 590, 799, 816, 817, 820, 821, 827, 829
Mueller, C. G., 251
Muenzinger, K. F., 483
Mullahy, P., 462n., 483, 736
Muller, P. F., Jr., 903
Munn, N., 381, 428
Münsterberg, H., 933
Murchison, C. A., 732
Murphy, G., 72, 110, 112, 251, 259, 263, 282, 462n., 483, 495, 571, 587, 588, 643, 659, 674, 733
Murray, H. A., 263, 271, 272, 275, 495, 501, 502, 505, 511, 513, 523, 524, 525, 532, 536, 541, 542, 549, 555, 562, 564, 569, 570, 571, 578, 582, 585, 587, 589, 604, 609, 635, 636, 640, 642, 649, 650, 680, 689, 703, 704, 707, 713, 718, 733, 734, 799, 800, 802, 804, 827, 828
Mussen, P. H., 635, 732, 807, 828

Naegele, K. D., 663, **727**
Nash, H., 489*n*.
Nealy, S. M., 80, **110**
Nebylitsyn, V. D., **361, 362**
Neisser, U., **113**, 430, **485**
Nelson, V. L., 788, **830**
Neumann, E., 462*n*., **483**
Newcomb, T. M., 270, 496, **588, 638,** 661, 663, 666, 698, 701, **728, 732,** **734**
Newlin, E. P., **901**
Newsom, S. J., 453, **477**
Nielsen, G., **932**
Nietzsche, F., 816
Nissen, H. W., **105,** 259, 270, 271, 275, **282, 361, 476**
Noble, M., **905**
Noguchi, H., 744, **778**
North, A. J., 160, **177**
Nowlis, V., 260, 270, **282**

Oberholser, E., 801
Obrist, W. D., **361**
O'Connell, D. N., **113**
Odbert, H. S., 608, **632**
Oden, M. H., **591**
Oldfield, R. C., **484**
Olds, J., 264, 270, 274*n*., **282, 361,** 526, **588**
Oppenheimer, R., 368, 374, **484**
Orbach, J., **110**
Orlansky, J., **900, 906**
Osgood, C. E., 22, 24, 27, **110, 212,** 249, **251,** 273, 369, 376, 380, 382, 383, 398, 400, 401, 402, 405, 407, 409, 454, 455, 456, **484, 588,** 619, **636,** 691, 725, **734,** 759, **778**
Ossorio, A. G., **729**
Ovsiankina, M., **588**

Pace, C. R., 557, **588**
Page, D. L., **328**
Papanek, M. L., **211**
Paramanova, N. B., **363**
Parducci, A., 86, **110**
Parloff, M. B., 589, 592, 821, **829**
Parsons, T., 269, **282,** 502, **588, 590,** **592,** 644, 645, 661, 699, **732, 733,** **734, 737, 828**
Paterson, D., 786, **828**
Pauling, L., 427, **484**
Pavlov, I. P., 148, 151, **177,** 225, 261, **282,** 293, 298, 311, 312, 317, 330, 345, **361,** 399, 446, 451, **484**
Payne, R. B., **902**
Payne, R. S., **484**
Peak, H., 270, **282,** 643, **734,** 808, **828**

Pearl, B. E., **905**
Penfield, W., **588**
Pennington, L. A., 812*n*., **828**
Pepinsky, H. B., 818, **828**
Pepinsky, P. N., 818, **828**
Pepitone, A., 672, 682, **734**
Pepler, R., 849*n*.
Perky, C. W., **251**
Petelina, V. V., **361**
Peterson, J., 787, **828**
Petrullo, L., **731, 734, 736**
Pettigrew, T. F., **176**
Pfafflin, S. M., **110**
Pfaffmann, C., 27
Phares, E. J., 807, **828**
Phillips, E. L., 818, **828**
Phillips, L., 749, 759, 760, **778**
Phillipson, H., **588**
Piaget, J., 338, 339, 340, 341, 350, **355,** 357, 358, **361,** 367, 417, 433, **480**
Pick, H. L., Jr., 106, **113**
Piéron, H., **357**
Pikler, J., 426
Pildner, H., Jr., 607, **634**
Pintner, R., 786, **828**
Piotrowski, Z. A., 810, **828**
Pirenne, M. H., **484**
Pittendrigh, C. S., 375, **484**
Platzer, H. L., **905**
Podell, J. E., **109**
Polezhaev, E. F., 294, **361, 362**
Polikanina, R. I., **362**
Pollack, I., **905**
Polya, G., **328**
Postman, L., 20, 21, 22, 24, 27, 30, 100, **110, 111, 112, 211,** 231, 243, **250,** **251,** 270, 271, 272, 275, **362, 484,** 571, **588**
Potanin, N., 625, **636**
Poulton, E. C., **905**
Pratt, C. C., 48, **111**
Premack, D., 128*n*., 129*n*., **178,** 304, **362**
Prentice, W. C. H., 33, **111**
Pressey, S. L., **828**
Pribram, K. H., 27, 278, **281,** 370, 404, 405, 412, 415, 422, 437, **483, 484**
Pritchard, R. M., 429, 447, **484**
Probatova, L. E., **362**
Progoff, I., 461*n*., 462*n*., **484**
Pronko, N. H., 246, **252**
Proshansky, H., **588**
Prosser, C. L., 406
Prothro, E. T., **588,** 619, **636**
Provins, K. A., **905**
Pumpian-Mindlin, E., **588**
Purkinje, J. E., 381, 382

Quastler, H., 905, 933

Rabin, A. I., 785, 828
Radom, S., 363
Rafferty, J. E., 803, 829
Raiffa, H., 482
Raimy, V. C., 589, 785, 814, 828
Ramsey, G. V., 104, 108, 580, 583, 585, 587, 728
Rank, O., 680, 734, 813, 814, 828
Rapaport, D., 489n., 511, 589
Raphelson, A. C., 601, 636
Rashevski, N., 362
Raskin, N. J., 590
Ratliff, F., 22, 24, 27, 232, 251, 484
Ratoosh, P., 22, 24, 27, 107, 212
Raush, H. L., 651, 707, 716, 724, 734
Razran, G., 330, 362
Redfield, R., 734
Redl, F., 648, 716, 730
Rees, H. J., 384, 484
Reese, W. G., 356
Reich, W., 718, 734
Reichard, S., 778
Reid, L. S., 110, 111, 178
Reisman, D., 820n., 828
Reissman, L., 658, 734
Reitman, W. R., 607, 634, 637
Restle, F., 135n., 178
Reynolds, B., 265, 282
Reynolds, G. S., 362
Rheingold, H. L., 342, 362
Richards, I. A., 571
Riesen, A. H., 111, 175, 218, 251
Riesman, D., 627, 637
Riezler, K., 734
Riggs, L. A., 484
Riley, D. A., 56, 111, 429, 484
Ritchie, B. F., 270
Ritchie, M. L., 905
Ritter, W. E., 570, 589
Robinson, J., 311, 362
Robinson, J. S., 111
Robinson, J. V., 305, 356
Roby, T. B., 260, 261, 282
Rock, I., 51n., 105, 111, 454, 484
Rock, R., 33, 58, 113
Rodnick, E. H., 27, 273, 738, 776, 777, 778
Roe, A., 377, 484, 800, 828
Roeder, K. D., 484
Roger, A. J., 355, 357
Rogers, C. R., 277, 282, 369, 401, 462n., 464, 485, 510, 535, 537, 555, 556, 589, 674, 680, 685, 696, 699, 735, 784, 799, 813, 814, 815, 816, 818, 820, 822, 828

Rohrer, J. H., 110, 735
Roitbak, A. I., 362
Rokeach, M., 489n., 589
Rokotova, N. A., 362
Rommetveit, R., 658, 659, 661, 735
Romney, A. K., 714, 727
Ronco, P. G., 109
Rorschach, H., 745, 778, 798, 801, 802, 828
Rosanoff, A. J., 796, 797, 804, 826, 828
Roscoe, S. N., 905
Rosen, E., 489n., 690, 735
Rosen, G. P., 810, 824
Rosenbaum, M., 662, 728
Rosenblith, W. A., 27
Rosenthal, D., 749, 778
Rosenzweig, M. R., 98, 100, 111, 112
Rosenzweig, S., 589, 803, 829
Rosner, B. S., 24, 27
Rossman, I. L., 112
Rostan, L., 797, 798
Rotter, J. B., 27, 270, 461n., 485, 600, 601, 602, 637, 650, 735, 780, 793, 795, 799, 800, 803, 804, 805, 807, 808, 817, 818, 821, 826, 828, 829
Rousseau, J. J., 527
Roussel, J., 259, 279
Rozhdestvanskaia, V. I., 362
Rubinstein, E. A., 589, 592, 821, 829
Rudikoff, E. C., 589
Rudolph, R. L., 164, 176
Ruebush, B. K., 637
Ruesch, J., 645, 699, 701, 735
Rund, P. A., 905
Russel, E. S., 570, 589
Russell, D. H., 280
Russell, J. T., 81, 109, 112
Russell, L., 905
Russell, R. W., 475
Ryan, T. A., 905

Sahlins, M. D., 385, 485
Saldanha, E. L., 906
Salter, N., 905
Samson, E. W., 362
Samuels, I., 485
Sands, S. L., 778
Sanford, N., 21, 24, 27, 488, 579, 582, 589, 590, 604, 607, 637
Sarason, S. B., 601, 602, 612, 636, 637, 807, 829
Sarbin, T. R., 590, 628, 630, 637
Sargent, S. S., 658, 659, 660, 735
Sarnoff, I., 590
Sauer, E. G. F., 414, 485
Sauer, E. M., 485
Schacter, S., 344, 362, 655, 735

Schaet, D. E., 581
Schafer, R., 72, 112
Schaffner, B., 736
Schalock, H. D., 708, 733
Scheerer, M., 645, 735
Schenk, H. U., Jr., 776
Schilder, P., 670, 735
Schiller, G. H., 485
Schjelderup, H., 491, 492, 493, 494, 512, 521, 590
Schlesinger, H. J., 585
Schlosberg, H., 139, 178
Schmidt, B. G., 790, 829
Schneider, B. M., 111
Schneider, D. M., 582, 587, 589, 635
Schneirla, T., 273
Schoenfeld, W. N., 21, 22, 24, 27, 213, 240n., 251, 252
Schorf, M., 587
Schroder, H. M., 793, 829
Schutz, W. C., 699, 705, 710, 716, 718, 735
Schwartz, C. B., 70, 112
Scodel, A., 807, 828
Scott, J. P., 369, 485
Scott, T. H., 104, 479, 727
Scott, W. A., 590
Scriven, M., 478, 582, 590
Searle, L. V., 906
Sears, P. S., 260, 273, 276, 282
Sears, R. R., 260, 268, 271, 275, 276, 280, 282, 313, 358, 500, 530, 531, 586, 590, 611, 637
Seashore, H., 112
Seeman, J., 590
Selfridge, J. A., 251, 430
Selfridge, O. O., 485
Sellers, W., 582
Selye, H., 590
Senders, J. W., 906
Senior, K., 689, 716, 729
Senn, M. J. E., 584, 590
Seward, J. P., 112, 265, 270, 282, 362
Shaffer, L. F., 419, 461n., 485, 590, 818, 829
Shagass, C., 778
Shakow, D., 777, 778, 782, 800, 828, 829
Shannon, C. E., 362, 925, 933
Sharpless, S., 315, 362
Shaw, F. J., 811, 818, 829
Shaw, R. F., 829
Shaw, W. A., 906
Sheats, P., 660, 727
Sheatz, G., 358
Sheerer, M., 590, 810, 825
Sheffield, F. D., 256, 260, 261, 262, 266, 271, 275, 280, 282

Sheldon, W. H., 557, 558, 590, 797, 798, 829
Shephard, R. N., 178
Sherif, M., 24, 27, 110, 246, 252, 362, 590, 654, 666, 735
Sherrington, C. S., 363, 370
Shields, J., 778
Shils, E. A., 588, 590, 592, 732, 733, 828
Shimberg, M. E., 786, 824
Shipton, L., 664, 735
Shoben, E. J., 461n., 485, 590, 760, 778, 818, 829
Shock, N., 590
Shonbar, R. A., 666, 735
Shryock, J. K., 623, 637
Shuford, E. H., Jr., 178
Shuttleworth, F. K., 598, 599, 602, 635
Sickles, W. R., 363
Siddall, G. J., 906
Sidman, M., 316, 358
Siegel, A. I., 112, 906
Sigel, I. E., 708, 733
Simmel, G., 654, 658, 677
Simon, C. W., 901, 906
Simon, H. A., 24, 27
Simon, J. R., 906
Simon, T., 787
Simpson, G. G., 377, 484
Sinaiko, H. W., 933
Sinclair, E. J., 903
Siskel, M., 157
Skeels, H. M., 789, 790, 829
Skinner, B. F., 119, 121, 123, 132, 136, 137, 138, 139, 164, 167, 178, 209, 212, 219, 220, 225, 226, 230, 232, 240, 252, 263, 343, 363, 392, 393, 394, 395, 445, 451, 485, 591, 714, 924
Skodak, M., 790
Slater, E., 749, 778
Slavson, S. R., 818, 830
Smedslund, J., 135n., 178, 340, 360, 363
Smith, A., 690, 735
Smith, A. A., 778
Smith, A. U., 475
Smith, D. E., 72, 112
Smith, H., 708, 735
Smith, K. U., 903
Smith, M. B., 489n., 494, 582, 591
Smith, W. A. S., 326, 358
Smith, W. C., 175
Smock, C. D., 347, 363
Smuts, F. C., 591
Snyder, F. W., 246, 252
Snyder, L. H., 21, 24
Snygg, D., 395, 485, 510, 591, 696, 735
Sofer, E. G., 627, 637

Sokolov, E. N., 293, 309, **363, 364**
Solomon, J. C., 811, **830**
Solomon, R. L., 41, **108, 112,** 139, **178,** 259, 261*n.,* 267, 270, **281, 282,** 450, 470, **485**
Sołtysik, S., 321, **363**
Sommer, R., **112**
Sontag, L. W., 788, **830**
Spearman, C., 788, **830**
Spence, D. P., **478, 634**
Spence, K. W., 34, 61, **104, 112,** 139, 152, 155, 160, **178,** 258, 264, 265, 271, 272, 273, 274, 275, **283,** 395, **485, 580, 591,** 602, 612, **637,** 763
Sperry, R. W., 431
Spiegel, J. P., 645, 659, 701, 715, **735, 736**
Spindler, G., 24, 27
Spindler, L., 24, 27
Spiro, M. E., 617, 624, **635, 637**
Spitz, H. H., **485**
Spitz, P., **736**
Spragg, S. D. S., **903**
Stacey, C. L., **283**
Stagner, R., 567, **591**
Stamm, J. S., **485**
Stanley, J. C., **480**
Stein, M., 556, **591**
Steinberg, D. L., **779**
Stennett, R. A., **363**
Stephenson, W., **591**
Stern, G. S., 556, 557, 588, **591**
Stern, W., 569, **591,** 788, 797, **830**
Stevens, S. S., 141, **178, 281, 359,** 369, 413, **476, 482, 900, 903, 906, 933**
Stevenson, H., **728**
Stimmel, D. T., 160, **177**
Stirner, F. W., **906**
Stock, D., 704, **736**
Stockner, C., 760, **777**
Stoddard, G. D., 788, 790, **830**
Stone, C. P., 385, **486, 580, 581, 590**
Storm, T., 607, **633**
Storms, L. H., 763, **776**
Story, A., **486**
Stotland, E., **356, 584**
Stouffer, S., 659, 661, **736**
Strachey, J., **280**
Stratton, G. M., 246, 252
Strauss, A. L., 670, **736**
Street, R. F., 71, **112**
Strodtbeck, F. L., 706, 716, **736**
Strong, E. K., **736**
Strother, C. R., **778**
Strupp, H. H., 706, 709, **736**
Sturtevant, E. H., **252**
Sturtevant, W. C., **355**

Suci, G. J., **636, 734, 778**
Suczek, R., 688, **732**
Sullivan, H. S., 369, 401, 402, 458, 462*n.,* 497, 526, 530, **591,** 642, 644, 645, 671, 685, 701, 715, **736, 779,** 812, 815, 820, 821, **830**
Sullivan, S. A., **364**
Sutton-Smith, B., 648, 716, **730**
Swanson, G. E., 270, 626, 627, **636,** 678, **728, 732, 733**
Sweeney, J. S., **898, 906**
Swets, J. A., **839, 906**
Symonds, P. M., **591,** 670, 674, **736,** 796, 800, **830**
Szasz, T. S., 526, **591,** 745, **779**

Taft, J., 814, **830**
Tagiuri, R., 731, 734, **736**
Tannenbaum, P. H., **636, 734, 778**
Tanner, J. M., **486**
Tanner, W. P., Jr., **839, 906**
Tax, S., 377, **486**
Taylor, D. W., **779**
Taylor, F. V., 24, 27, 831, 850, 875, 876, **898, 899, 901, 906,** 910, 919, 922, **932, 933**
Taylor, H. R., 453, **477**
Taylor, J., 826
Taylor, J. A., 279, **283, 591,** 602, 612, **637**
Taylor, J. G., **363**
Taylor, T. J., 651, 707, 716, 724, **734**
Teplov, B. M., 345
Terman, L. M., **591, 736,** 786, **830**
Terrace, H. S., 159, **178**
Tétreau, B., **354**
Thelen, H. A., 704, **736**
Thibaut, J. W., 705, 711, 714, 722, **731, 736**
Thistlethwaite, D., **363, 591**
Thomas, D. R., 158, 160, **177, 178**
Thomas, H., 690, **728**
Thomas, W. I., 656, **736,** 799, **830**
Thomasson, P. J., **356**
Thompson, G. G., 704, 710, 716, 718, **730**
Thompson, J. E., **902**
Thompson, W. R., 343, **358**
Thomson, R. M., **900, 906**
Thorndike, E. L., 261, 399, 788, **830**
Thorpe, W. H., **486**
Thrall, R. M., **486**
Thurstone, L. L., 325, **363, 637,** 788, **830**
Tighe, T. J., **106, 113**
Tillman, C., **778**
Tinbergen, N., **363,** 420, 444, **486**

Tinklepaugh, O. L., 469, **486**
Tissot, R., 309, **363**
Titchener, E. B., **112**, 224, 236
Toby, J., 659, 661, **736**
Tolman, E. C., **111**, **112**, 166, 205, **212**,
  261, 262, 263, 265, 267, 271, 275,
  283, 334, **363**, 368, 370, 376, 380,
  399, 401, 404, 418, 428, 456, 462,
  468, **484**, **486**, 504, 552, 553, **591**,
  592, 647
Toman, W., 700, **736**
Tomkins, S. S., 489n., 526, **592**
Traxler, A. E., **590**
Treat, A. E., **484**
Trefethen, F. N., **933**
Tresselt, M. E., 86, **112**
Triandis, L. M., 624, **636**
Truxal, J. G., **907**
Turnbull, C. M., 378, 379, **486**
Turner, R. H., 689, **736**
Tustin, A., **907**
Tyler, R., 790, **825**

Uhr, L., **779**
Updegraff, R., 790

Vance, E. L., **727**
Van Cott, H. P., **907**
Vanderlippe, R. H., 689, **736**
Vanderplas, J. M., **112**, **476**
Veroff, J., **730**
Verplanck, W. S., **112**
Vidale, E. B., 27
Vinacke, W. E., 603, **634**
Vinh-Bang, **360**
Vinogradova, O. S., **363**
Volkert, E. H., **830**
Volkmann, A. W., 448
Volkmann, J., 663, **728**
Von Bertalanffy, L., 497, 569, **592**
von Bonin, G., 24
von Frisch, K., 415, **478**
Von Holst, E., 169n., **178**, 406
Von Neuman, J., **933**
Von Senden, M., 82, **113**, 218, 252
Voronin, L. A., 293, **359**, **360**, **361**, **362**,
  364
Voss, J. F., **907**
Vurpillot, E., **357**

Wade, M., **177**
Wadsworth, G. W., 804, **826**
Waite, R. R., **637**
Wald, A., **364**
Walk, R. D., 74, 75, 76, 80, 81, **106**, **113**
Walker, E. L., 807, **825**
Wallace, A. F. C., 672, **736**

Wallach, H., **113**, 453, **481**, **592**
Wallach, M. A., 607, 608, **637**
Wallen, R. W., 812n., **830**
Wallin, 710
Wallner, J. M., **777**
Walston, C. E., **907**
Warren, C. E., **907**
Warren, N. D., **933**
Warren, R. M., **486**
Warrick, M. J., **907**
Washburn, S. L., 377, 385, **486**
Waterhouse, I. K., 612, **637**
Watson, G., **727**
Watson, J. B., 220, 398, 399, 424
Watt, H. J., 369
Weaver, W., **362**, **933**
Webb, W. W., **776**, **779**
Webster, H., **592**
Wechsler, D., 810, **830**
Weiner, H., 289, **364**
Weisenberg, T., 809, **830**
Weiss, E., 702, **737**
Weiss, P., 406, 427
Weisz, P., **359**
Weitzenhoffer, A. M., 253n.
Weld, H. P., 446, **476**
Welford, A. T., 843, **907**, **933**
Wellman, B., 790
Wells, F. L., 786, **830**
Welsh, G. S., **354**
Werner, H., 448, **486**, 511, 531, **592**,
  697, **737**
Wertheimer, Max, 59, **113**, 395, **486**,
  511
Wertheimer, Michael, **113**, **486**
Westley, W. A., **737**
Westman, J., 715
Wheeler, R. H., **592**
Whipple, G. M., 786, **830**
White, L. A., 655, **737**
White, R. K., 652, **733**
White, R. W., 277, **283**, 494, 506, 526,
  550, 551, 561, **586**, **591**, **592**
Whitehorn, J. C., **592**
Whiting, J. M. W., 253n., 256n., 260,
  268, 270, 273, 276, 278, **282**, **283**,
  616, 618, 619, 621, 622, 624, 626,
  629, **637**, **638**
Whyte, W. F., 654, **737**
Wickens, D. D., 61, 77, **113**, 252, **364**
Wiener, N., 887, **907**, **933**
Wike, E. L., **177**
Wilensky, H. L., 639n., 658, 662, **737**
Wilkes, W. P., **356**
Wilkinson, H. J., **359**
Wilkinson, R., 849n.
Williams, H., 790

Williams, J. E., 612, **638**
Wilpizeski, E., **734**
Winch, R. F., 699, 700, 704, 710, 711, 716, 718, 722, **737**
Winder, C. L., **777, 779**
Winter, F., **481**
Witkin, H. A., 448, **486, 487,** 571, **587,** **588, 592**
Witmer, L., **786**
Wittenborn, J. R., 273, 617, **638,** 800, **830**
Wittman, M. P., **779**
Wodinsky, J., **175**
Wohlwill, J. F., **360**
Wolf, M., **356,** 624, **636**
Wolff, H. G., **587**
Wolff, K. H., **737**
Wolff, W. M., 603, **638**
Wolfle, D., 5
Wolman, B. B., **487**
Wolpe, J., 253n., 461n., **487**
Woltmann, A., 811, **824**
Wood, P., **177**
Woodhead, M. M., **899**
Woodson, W. E., 853, **907**
Woodworth, R. S., **113,** 214, 215, **252,** 271, 275, 369, 370, 376, 401, 404, 405, 408, 456, **487,** 811, **830**
Woolsey, C. N., **111, 584**
Worrell, L., 315, **364**
Wright, B. A., **580, 592**

Wright, H. F., 557, **580,** 648, 653, 669, 707, 708, 711, 712, 713, 715, 718, **727**
Wulff, J. J., 260, **282**
Wyckoff, L. B., Jr., **113,** 128n., **178,** 238, 252, 316, **364**
Wylie, R. C., **104**
Wynne, L. C., 450, **485**

Yerkes, R., 399
Yokoyama, M., **113**
Young, P. T., 263, 264, 268, 270, 271, 275, **283,** 419, **487**

Zahn, T. P., **779**
Zajonc, R. B., 326, **364,** 632, **634,** 666, 725, **730, 737**
Zander, A., **734**
Zaporozhets, A. V., 335, 336, **364**
Zeigarnik, B., **592**
Zelditch, M., 645, **737**
Zeleny, G. P., 311, **364**
Zener, K. E., 22, 24, 26, 27, **104, 178**
Zilboorg, G., 796, **830**
Zimbardo, P. G., 301, **364**
Zimmer, H., **359**
Zimmerman, C., **104**
Zimmerman, E. R., **358**
Znaniecki, F., 656, **736**
Zuckerman, C. B., 33, 58, **113**
Zuckermann, S., 377, **487**

SUBJECT INDEX

Abilities, general and specific, 788, 799
Absenteeism, 651
Acceleration and velocity perception, 840
Accommodation, 340–341, 350
Acculturation, 631–632
Accuracy and practice, 82ff., 911
  (*See also* Efficiency)
Achievement motivation, 257, 276, 606–607, 618
Action acceptor, 293
Action circuit, 713
Action classification, 705–709, 719
Action modes, 707–708
Action sequence, 713
Activity level and arousal, 307–308
Activity-passivity, 718–719
Activity settings, 648–649
Actual identity, 679–680
Adaptation level, 293, 402–403
Additive hypothesis, 185–186
Adequate stimulus, 236, 433
Adjustment, and discrepancy between actual and potential self, 689, 690
  as general concern of clinical psychologist, 781–782, 789, 791, 819–821
  premorbid, of schizophrenics, 759, 760
Administration of human engineering, 891–895
Aesthetics, 346, 348–349, 924
Affection, 705
Affective arousal, 263–268, 310
Afferent processes and learning theory, 114–174, 183ff., 189, 402–412
Affiliation, 706–707, 718
Aggression, and behavior setting, 651
  and frustration, 259–260
  relations among various measures, 605–606
All-or-none law, 374–375, 411–412
Ambiguity, intolerance of, 346–347, 630
Ambiguous figures, 71–72, 441–442
Ameaningful thinking, 29
American Psychological Association, 5
America's Psychologists, 5

Analog computers, 861–862, 864, 884, 925, 929–930
Analytic vs. naïve attitude, 89–90
Anger, 259–260, 709, 811, 818
Animal psychophysics, 232–233
Anthropological studies, 378–379, 615–632
Anthropology, relations of personality to, 593–632
Anxiety, 257, 261–262, 264, 292, 320, 342, 533, 601, 602, 608, 612, 685, 758
Apperceptive mass, 328
Appetitive motives, 264
Apprehensiveness, 257
  (*See also* Anxiety)
Approach-avoidance, 718–719
Approximation, successive, 209, 395, 445
Aptitude, role-taking, 630
Arousal, and drive, 263–268, 307–310, 419
  and exploratory behavior, 310–316
  mechanism, 257–258, 306–316, 344–345
  potential, 317–321, 351–352
  variations in, 344–345
Arousal jag, 305, 334, 348
Art, 348–350, 600, 625–626
Aspiration level, 663–664, 804
Assimilation, 340–341, 350
Association theory, 63–66, 414
Asthenic body build, 798
Asymmetrically contingent interactions, 711
Atmosphere, social, 652–653
Attensity, 330
Attention, 163–165, 331–332, 334, 336, 840
  and imprinting, 341–342
  (*See also* Vigilance)
Attitude, and psychophysical judgment, 50, 89–90
  and situational meaning, 656
Attributes in coding, 195–197

Auditory cues to control machines, 841
Authoritarian leadership, 652
Authoritarianism, 538
Authority sequence, 714–715
Autokinetic effect, 246, 666
Aversive behavior, 255–260, 265, 293, 310, 720–723

Baboons, observational studies, 377
Barriers, 720–723
Behavior sequence, 714
Behavior settings, 648–651, 723–724
Behavior systems, 278
Behavioral frame of reference, 7–8, 10, 22, 35ff., 118–121, 379–384, 398–400, 428–429, 505
Behavioral tests, 804–805
Binocular vision, 81
Biological-physiological motivation theory, 274–275
Biological sciences, and human factors engineering, 916
and psychology, 8, 375–376, 427, 739
Biosphere, 495
Black box, 380
Blindness, 81–82
(See also Sensory deprivation)
Body image, 693, 694
Body-mind problem, 748
Bond, 720–723
Boredom drive, 304–305
Boulder conference on training of clinical psychologists, 785
Brain damage, diagnosis, 809–810
Bridging problems, 4, 17, 101–103, 763–766

Capacity, information-processing, 843–844
Careerist, 662
Case study, 573, 715–716
Catharsis, 811–812, 814, 817
Cathexis, 720
Causation (see Explanation)
Censure and schizophrenia, 752ff.
Central processes, 60–61, 402–412, 422–424, 427–428, 554
Centrality, 682, 687–688
Chain of responses, 218, 714
Change, in intelligence, 789–791
of personality habits, 470–472, 491–493, 506, 517–518, 544–547, 603–604
in psychotherapy, 817–818
of situation and role, 656
Channel load, 844, 911
Character, 558–559, 598–599

Character, national, 619–620, 631–632
Child training practices, 616, 760–762
Choice, 152–157, 911–912, 923–924
Class, social, and personality, 626–627
and reference groups, 663–665
Classical conditioning, 135ff.
and epistemic behavior, 323–324
and exploratory responses, 301, 329–331
Classification, action, 705–709, 719
needs, 703–705, 717–720
psychiatric disorders, 795–796
tasks, 930–931
Client-centered therapy, 510–511, 784, 814–815
Climate, social, 652–653
Clinical and experimental view of schizophrenia, 753–755
Clinical psychology, 504, 506, 738–775, 780–824
historical and theoretical analysis of some broad trends, 780–824
diagnosis, 793–810
historical trends, 782–786
introduction to article, 780–782
measurement of intelligence, 786–793
overview, 822–824
psychotherapy, 810–822
psychopathology, and research on schizophrenia, 738–775
broad field of primary reference, 747–751
clinical psychology as field of reference, 740–742
collaborative, administrative, and educational mechanisms, 768–774
concluding remarks, 774–775
delimitation of primary field of reference, 752–755
interrelationship of sciences, 742–747
interrelationships, methodological, 766–768
in motivational factors, 757–766
introduction to article, 739–740
schizophrenia from viewpoint of psychological variables, 755–757
training in, 756, 770–774, 782, 784, 785, 803, 823
Closure, 382–383
Cluster analysis, 613
Coding, in continuous tasks, 847–850
in discrete tasks, 844–846
Coding-response hypothesis, 187–198
Cognitive clarity, 344, 705
Cognitive dissonance, 262, 269, 276, 696
Cognitive style, 611

Cognitive theory, 56, 267, 369–370, 376ff., 401–434
of personality, 462–473, 503ff.
Cohesiveness, 654–655
Collative motivation theory, 316–322, 329–338
Collative properties of exploratory behavior, 290–293, 313–315
Common sense, 571, 606, 811
Communicated public identity, 684–685
Communication, in bees, 415
interpersonal, 699, 923
speech, in engineering psychology, 841, 921
Compatibility, 726, 845–846
Compensatory displays, 847
Competition and cooperation, 619–620
Complementary matching of traits, 710–711, 726
Complexity, 291, 292, 297, 321, 625, 682–683
Computers, 439–440, 861–864, 884, 923, 925–926, 929–930
Concept formation, 395, 922–923
Conceptual conflict, 325
Conditioning (see Classical conditioning; Instrumental conditioning; Theory conditioning)
Configuration, 32, 52–54, 291
of response, 842
Conflict, 219, 256, 257, 293–295, 302–303, 314–316, 321, 324ff., 339, 340, 351, 463, 606, 630, 659, 668, 677, 718–719, 721
Conformity, 654–655, 696, 820
Congenital blindness, 81–82
(See also Sensory deprivation)
Conscious processes, 396, 412–413, 427, 464–465, 508, 509, 532–534
Consensual validity, 705
Consistency, 543–544, 593–615, 658, 696–698
Constancy, 48, 50, 89–90, 217, 245–247, 378–379, 388, 439
of IQ, 788–791
Constant error, 87–88
Constrictiveness-expansiveness, 607–608
Construct validity, 611, 612
Consultation, 322
Consumer behavior, 924
Contact comfort, 343
Continuity in learning, 200–202
Control, of behavior, 549–550, 705, 925
continuous, 847–850, 875, 883–886, 928
Control requirements for machines, 841–843

Controls, displays, and system dynamics, 843–850
Converging operations, 37–43
Cooperation and competition, 619–620
Coping behavior, 525, 760, 764
Core, 674, 687
Correlation, 180–183, 224ff., 599
among dependent variables, 913–914
Creative art, 348–350, 625–626
Cross-cultural studies, 615–632
Cross validation, 792
Cues, auditory, tactual, and kinesthetic, discrimination of, 841
monocular, 81
multidimensional, in engineering psychology, 840
response-produced, 60–63, 65, 186–187
Cultural differences, 378–379
Culture-free intelligence tests, 790
Curiosity, 295, 302–304, 323ff.
(See also Exploratory behavior)
Cybernetics (see Feedback)
Cycles, diurnal, 375–376, 406, 432

Data language, 48–49, 101
Decision making, capacity for, 843–844
in probabilistic situations, 846, 857–858, 923
sequential, 326–329, 844, 929
Defense, perceptual, 40–41, 219
(See also Aggression; Repression)
Defense mechanisms, 668–669, 702–703
Defensive atmospheres, 652–653
Deficit, performance, in schizophrenia, 752, 757ff., 762ff.
Democratic leadership, 652–653
Dependency, of preschool children toward mothers, 708–709
and psychotherapy, 813–814
relations among various measures, 606
Depression symptoms, 665
Depression, sensory, 79–82, 317, 383, 408
sleep, 849
Deprivation drives, 256, 265
Depth, kinetic, effect, 59
perception, 80–81
Design, human engineering, 851–853, 914–916
Detectability, 839, 928
Developmental factors in schizophrenia, 762–765
Diagnosis, 793–810, 815
of brain damage, 809–810
measures of personality for, 800–809
source of concepts for, 793–800
Dial reading, 845

Differential training, 67–71
Differentiation, 682–683
Digital computers, 861–863, 925–926
Dimensionality, 144–148, 181, 676–677, 687ff., 724–725
    discontinuity in passing from one system to another, 869–870
Directed acts, 296
Directed thinking, 322, 324, 326–329, 339–340, 367–368
Directives, 663
Directors, 647
Discontinuity of performance, 884
Discrepancy hypothesis, 293
Discrete task performance, 843–846, 884, 928
Discrimination, 224–227
    of auditory, tactual, and kinesthetic cues in control of machines, 841, 920–921
    of complex forms, 34, 67ff., 841, 921
    and generalization, 55, 74ff., 155ff., 205ff., 225–227, 229ff.
    and instruction stimuli, 49–51
    sensory deprivation and, 79–82
    successive, 229ff.
    unconscious, 40–41
    (See also Psychophysics)
Discrimination-reversal studies, 201–202
Discriminative inhibition, 159–161
Disease-entity approach to personality, 795, 820
Disequilibrium, 338–339
Display, coding, 844–847, 914
    control and system dynamics, 843–850
    requirements, 838–841, 921
Dispositions vs. roles, 657–659
Dissonance, cognitive, 262, 269, 276, 696
Distal and proximal stimuli, 45, 49–50, 90–91, 184ff.
Diurnal cycles of behavior, 375–376, 406, 432
Divergences, 720–723
Diversive and specific exploration, 289–290, 302–306
Dolphins, speed of learning in, 445
Dominance, 717, 719
Drive, 254–260, 467, 533
    and arousal, 308, 338
    boredom, 304–305
    frustration-induced, 259–260, 266
    hunger, 258, 469
    and intensity in behavior, 298–299
    reduction, 124–126, 260ff., 323, 338, 506–507, 523–526, 817
    as state, 256–257

Drive, success-induced, 266–267
    (See also Exploratory behavior; Motivation; Needs)
Drive stimuli, 256–257
Dualism, 53, 137n., 173
Dyadic interaction, 530, 642, 654
"Dynamic apriorism," 433
Dynamic organization of personality, 522–523, 597–598, 797

Eagerness, 257
Early learning, 73–76, 338–344, 545, 665–666
Ecological and functional validity, 45–46
Ecology, 653, 669
Economy, food-getting, and socialization, 626
Effect, law of, 84–85, 264, 416, 817
Efficiency, and arousal, 308
    of different responses, 842–843, 910
Ego processes, 467–468, 507ff.
Ego psychology, 505, 507ff.
Ego strength, 612, 630
Electroencephalography, 306–307, 331
Elicitation hypothesis, 128n.–129n.
Emergent responses, 532
Emitter of information in human engineering, 838, 841–843
Emotional development, 342–343, 391
Emotional processes, 418ff., 463ff., 787
Emphasis, 267, 334
Empirical approach, 1ff., 23–25, 51ff., 101–103, 128–129, 367–368, 377ff., 499, 876–877, 926
    to schizophrenia, 763–766
Empty-organism approach, 7–8, 26, 131
Engineering psychology, 831–897, 908–932
    content, 919–926
    introduction to article, 909–910
    joint objectives of fields involved in human factors engineering, 916–919
    methodology, 926–931
    summary and forecast, 931–932
    variables for, 910–916
Enrichment theory, 63–66
Entropy, 292, 294–295, 324
Environment, engineering to fit man, 833–897, 908–932
    and heredity, 526–528, 789–791
    immediate, independence from, 387–391, 403
    viewed as determinant of behavior, 529–532, 553–557, 643, 656
Episode, 713–714

Epistemic and exploratory behavior, motivational problems, 284–353
Equilibration, 338–339, 433, 511, 522–523, 696
Equipment design, 851–852, 915, 922–923
Equipotentiality, 809
Equisection method, 39–40
Error, constant, 87–88
of standard, 339
Established responses, 532
Ethnopsychology, 622–623
Evaluation, man-machine systems, 850, 866–872, 930
Event perception, 161–163
Evolutionary theory, 351, 377, 385ff., 430–431
Excitability, 151, 345–346
Existential analysis, 816
Expansiveness-contrictiveness, 607–608
Expectation, 293, 296, 333, 404, 451, 504, 650, 656–658, 661ff.
contradictory, 668–669
of signals and vigilance, 849
Experience, and perception, 32–35, 57ff.
(*See also* Perception)
Experimental and clinical view of schizophrenia, 753–755
Experimental method, in perception, 35ff., 49ff., 66–91
in personality, 516–517, 571–572
in psychology compared to human engineering, 860ff., 880ff., 919–924, 926–931
in psychopathology, 746, 752ff., 769
in studying social interaction, 716–717
Explanation, 8, 52–54, 127, 129–130, 132, 541–544, 611–612, 878–879
(*See also* Reductionism)
Exploration erg, 346
Exploratory behavior, 444
classification, 288–290
collative motivation and learning, 329–338
definition, 286–288
determinants, 290–295
and epistemic behavior, motivational problems, 284–353
Expressive behavior, 525, 607–608, 625–626
Extinction, 159–161, 242, 262, 330, 399–400
Extrinsic motivation, 277–278, 289, 324–325, 526
Extroversion, 608, 798
Eye movements, 78–79

Facilitative aversion, 721
Factor-analytic approach, 459–461, 500, 600, 609, 613, 616, 620
Facts and laws, 121, 368
Faculty psychology, 787, 802, 809
Family roles, 655–656, 700, 712, 760–762
Fantasy and other behaviors, 604–607
Fear (*see* Anxiety)
Fechner law, 125
Feedback, 335–336, 388–389, 403, 405–406, 415, 861, 885, 887, 925
proprioceptive, 841–842
Field studies, 377–378, 716, 926–927
Fields of psychology, 6, 7, 9, 27–28
Figural aftereffects, 453–454
Figure-ground perception, 72, 247–249
Flexibility, 722–723
Force and time configurations of response, 842
Forced-choice technique, 804
Form perception, 34, 58ff., 66ff., 79ff.
Fractionation method, 39–40
Fragments of personality, 499
Freedom of movement, 650
Friendliness-hostility, 718–719
Frustration and leadership, 652
Frustration-induced drives, 259–260, 266
Function pleasure, 525
Functional autonomy, 567
Functional and ecological validity, 45–46
Functionalism, 395–399, 502–503, 507, 522
probabilistic, 45–46
transactional, 46–47, 513

Gain factors, 864
Gating mechanisms, 416
General intelligence factor, 788
Generalization, 55, 62–63, 74, 77, 84, 144–157, 163–165, 205–211, 225–227, 229ff., 241–244, 429, 513
of personality dimensions (*see* Consistency)
primary, gradient, 139–144, 207–209, 225, 229
across sensory modalities, 98
transposition, 56, 152ff., 202–205, 246–247, 429
Gestalt psychology, 32–35, 43–44, 52–54, 57–60, 66ff., 220, 269, 404, 414, 429–430, 505, 511–512, 809
(*See also* Lewinian theory)
Global characteristics, 647
Goal-directed behavior, 266, 277–278, 404, 418, 419, 522, 649–650, 722, 799
Goal objects, 503, 647

Goal states, 503, 719
Gradient, primary generalization, 139–
    144, 207–209, 225, 229
Graphic expansiveness-constrictiveness,
    607–608
Group psychotherapy, 818–819
Groups, membership, 663, 664
    objective characteristics, 653–655
    reference, 662–667, 695–696
    small, problem solving in, 705–706
    social structure, 655–662
Growth, 506–507, 814, 913–914
Guides for human engineering, 852–853
Guttman's laws of behavior and facts of
    perception, 114–174
    basic concepts of conditioning theory,
        157–170
    behavior kinetics and behavior struc-
        ture, 134–136
    behavior theory as general outlook,
        170–173
    introduction to article, 114–123
    laws of reinforcement, 123–134
    primary generalization gradient, inverse
        hypothesis, 139–144
    problems of generalization and experi-
        ments, 148–157
    reprise, 173–174
    sensory order and generalization, 144–
        148
    stimulus generalization, 136–139

Habitability, 911
Habits and innate mechanisms, 431–434
Habituation, 159
Hallucinations, 383, 408
Historical causation, 541–544
Holistic orientation, 493–494, 510–513,
    536–537, 548–549, 569ff.
Homeostasis, 268, 351, 390, 522, 524–
    526, 546, 648, 925
Hostility, 259–260, 709, 811, 818
Hostility-friendliness, 718–719
Hullian theory (see S-R theory)
Human engineering and psychology, 831–
    897, 908–932
    collaborative, administrative, and edu-
        cational mechanisms, 888–897
    field of human engineering, 833–853
        definition, 834–837
        engineering psychology, 837–850
        human engineering design, 851–853
        introduction to article, 833–834
    interrelationships between, 853–879
    long-term contributions to psychology,
        879–888

Human factors approach, 889–891, 896–
    897, 909–910, 916–919
Humor, 347–348
Hunger drive, 258, 469
Hyperaggressive children, 651
Hypnosis, 812
Hypotheses, building in psychology, 373–
    376
    perceptual, 47–48, 448

Id processes, 467–468
Ideal identity, 679–680
Identification, in engineering psychology,
    839–841, 928
Identity (see Self)
Idiographic approach, 459–460, 472–473,
    530, 547–550
Illness, 621–622, 624, 795, 820
Illusions, 217, 245–247, 339, 382–383,
    402–403, 417, 666
Imagery type, 798
Imprinting, 387
    human, 341–342
Improvement in perceptual judgments,
    82ff., 339–340, 448–449
Incentive-motivation factor, 258
Incidental learning, 94–95, 332–335,
    392–393
Inclusion, 705
Incomplete figures, 71–72, 415, 417, 442–
    443
Incongruency, 721
Individual differences, 344–347, 517–518,
    547–550, 567, 594ff., 724, 912–913
    extent of consistency in, 594–595
Industrial psychology, 836–837, 890
Infavoidance, 717
Inference, 32, 33, 45–48, 57, 79–80, 120,
    165, 339–340, 380ff., 393ff., 417,
    514–517, 550ff., 870–871
Information theory, 200, 291–292, 324,
    837ff., 860–861, 925
Inhibition, discriminative, 159–161
    response, 41, 330
Innate mechanisms, 390–391, 406–407,
    414–415, 424, 431–434, 465–467,
    787
Instruction stimulus, 50–51, 182, 231–
    232, 237–240
Instrumental conditioning, 157ff.
    and epistemic behavior, 323
    and exploratory responses, 302–306,
        329–331
Instrumental traits, 503
Integration, 682–683
Intellectual development, 338–341
Intellectualizers, 346–347

Intellectuals and reference groups, 662
Intelligence, 559, 783, 785
  measurement, 786–793
  and perceptual learning, 445
Intensity in behavior, and drive, 298–299
Intention to learn, 392–393
Interaction, social, 530–531, 639–726
Interbehavioral psychology, 393
Interdisciplinary research, 669, 767–770, 917
Interest, 327–328, 342, 700–701
Intermediate action goals, 705
Intermittent reinforcement, 262
Internalization, 665–667, 672, 725–726
Interpersonal relationships, 530–531, 639–726
Interplay variables, 711–712
Interview for study, of self-identity, 692
  of social interaction, 716
Intolerance of ambiguity, 346–347, 630
Intrapersonal view, 641–642
Intrinsic motivation, 277–278, 289, 324–325, 526
Introjection, 665–667
Introspection, 32ff., 240
  (See also Phenomenology)
Introvert, 798
Intuitive thought, 340
Inverse hypothesis, 139–144
Involuntary behavior, 335–336
IQ, 788–791
Isomorphism, 32, 44, 53–54, 220
  in display and control coding, 845–846

Job analysis, 931

Kinesthetic cues to control machines, 841
Kinetic behavior, 134–136
Kinetic depth effect, 59
Knowledge (epistemic and exploratory behavior), 284–353

Laissez-faire leadership, 652
Language learning, 400
Latency (reaction time), 129, 231, 843–844, 881
Latent learning, 265, 332–335
Lawrence's nature of stimulus, relationships between learning and perception, 179–211
  applications to experimental problems, 198–211
  coding-response hypothesis, 187–192
  implications of coding hypothesis, 192–198
  introduction to article, 179–180

Lawrence's nature of stimulus, relationships between learning and perception, learning-theory approaches to set, 183–187
  psychophysics and learning, 180–183
Laws of psychology, 8, 17, 132, 135, 511, 547, 565ff., 578
  all-or-none, 374–375, 411–412
  emphasis, 267, 334
  and facts of perception, 114–174
  Fechner, 125
  perception vs. learning, 436
  reinforcement, 84–85, 123–134, 264, 416, 817
Leadership and social climate, 652, 653
Learning, 390ff.
  early and adult, 73–76, 338–344
  and epistemic behavior, 323–324
  exploratory behavior, collative, motivation and, 301, 329–338
  imprinting, 341–342, 387
  incidental, 94–95, 332–335, 392–393
  language, 400
  latent, 265, 332–335
  laws (see Laws of psychology)
  and perception, 9–10, 21–22, 30–103, 114–174, 179–211, 338–341, 365–475
    motivation, and personality (Leeper), 365–475
    heuristic rules on abstract thinking, 373–376
    interrelations of personality and other areas, 456–473
    introduction to article, 366–368
    learning in relation to other functioning, 391–434
    main principles, 434–456
    main sources of ideas, 376–384
    major background hypotheses, 384–391
    summary, 473–475
    theoretical orientation and influences, 368–373
  perceptual, 57–66, 338–341, 397–398, 443–454
  rote, 73–74, 395
  sets, 239, 445
  sign and solution, 525
  and species differences, 445
  tests of process, 793
  verbal, 73–74, 91–103, 226–227, 329ff.
Learning curves, 132–133, 135
Learning theory, 54ff., 170–173, 183–187, 200ff.
  afferent processes and, 114–174, 183ff., 402–412

Learning theory, and human engineering, 884–885, 922
 motivation in, 253–279
 and perception, 114–174
 and personality, 799
 and psychotherapy, 816–818
Legibility, 840, 928
Lens model, 394
Level of aspiration, 663–664, 804
Lewinian theory, 269, 276, 496, 529, 530, 541, 543, 544, 554–555, 565–566, 647ff.
 (*See also* Gestalt psychology)
Life space, 496, 554–555, 647
Linearity, 872
Link analysis, 863
Literal perception, 45
Localization of function, 809
Logical thinking, 339–340, 367–368
 (*See also* Thinking)
Longitudinal studies, 575, 603–604
Looking-glass self, 673
Loudness scale, 39–40

Man-machine system, 835–897, 909ff.
Marasmus, 697
Marital roles, 655–656, 700, 712
Marriage, resemblance between partners, 699–700, 710
Masculine subidentity, 692–694
Matching of traits, complementary, 710–711, 726
Meaning, 403
 of form percepts, 34, 57, 59–60
Measurement, cluster analysis, 613
 nonlinear mathematics, 864, 925
 sampling, 374, 644
 (*See also* Correlation; Factor-analytic approach; Methods; Psychophysics; Quantification)
Mediation, 47–48, 61, 62, 186ff., 241–244, 380ff., 393ff.
Medical training, 744–746
Membership groups, 663, 664
Memory, and perceptual experience, 33–34, 40–41, 46, 51*n.*, 58, 91–103
 theories, 425–428
Metalanguage, 35, 37, 874–875, 886–888
Methods, of developing adequate psychological concepts, 376–384
 in engineering psychology, 848, 879–900, 926–931
 experimental, for study of perceptual learning, 66–91
 of measuring recognition of words, 91–103

Methods, pedagogical, 328–329, 559–564, 573–579
 phenomenal, 32–35, 37, 48–49, 53
 psychophysical (*see* Psychophysics)
 of study, of personality, 458–462, 472–473, 499ff., 516–517, 559ff., 573–579, 800–801
  of schizophrenia, 766–768
  of self-identity, 688–692
  of social interaction, 646–647, 713–717
Mind-body problem, 8, 748
Miniature models, 367
Minimal goal level, 650
Mismatches between input and expectation, 885
Missionary type of intellectual, 662
MMPI, 804
Modal personality, 619–620
Models, computer, 438–443, 861–864, 884, 923–926, 929–930
 information theory and servo, in human engineering, 874–879, 883–886, 925–926
 lens, 394
 miniature, 367
 of personality, 521ff., 554–555
 somatotropic vs. psychotropic, of schizophrenia, 748–749
Molar analysis, 401–402, 574–575, 713–715
Molecular biology, 427
Monocular cues, 81
Motion parallax, 80–81
Motivation, achievement, 257, 276, 606–607, 618
 and epistemic and exploratory behavior, 284–353
 extrinsic and intrinsic, 277–278, 289, 324–325, 526
 and job performance, 923–924
 in learning theory (Hilgard), 253–279
  introduction to article, 253–255
  needed revisions in Hullian theory, 255–260
  neohedonism, affective arousal as core of motivation, 263–268
  other sources of motivational psychology, 268–279
  problems of primary and secondary reinforcement, 260–262
 and perception, 40–41, 365–475
 and personality and learning, 365–475, 649–650
 (*See also* Drive; Needs; Reinforcement)
Motivational mechanisms, 389–390, 463

Motivational problems (Berlyne), 284–353
  arousal, 306–316
  collative motivation, 316–322
  epistemic behavior, 322–329
  exploratory behavior, collative motivation, and learning, 329–338
  extensions to other areas, 338–350
  final word, 351–353
  introduction to article, 285–286
  nature and determinants of exploratory behavior, 286–295
  question of exploratory drives, 295–306
Motivational processes, 418–434, 463, 526
  in schizophrenia, 757–766
Motives, 503–504
  appetitive, 264
  deficit and growth, 506–507
  (See also Drives; Motivation; Needs)
Motor-discharge habits, 404ff., 454–456
Motor skills, 454–456, 604, 881–883, 921–922
Müller-Lyer illusion, 246, 417, 454
Multidimensional cues, 840
Music, 349

Naïve observation, 32, 34, 89–90
National character, 619–620, 631–632
National Science Foundation, 5
Naturalistic observation, 377–378, 716
Nature vs. nurture, 526–528, 789–791
Nebraska symposium on motivation, 269–276
Needs, and aversive drives, 255–257, 261ff., 533
  classification, 703–705, 717–720
  for cognition, 346, 504
  (See also Epistemic behavior)
  and personality, 799
  (See also Drive; Motivation; Motives)
Negative affect, 265
Negative transfer effects, 211
Neobehaviorism, 10, 22
Neohedonism, 263–268
Neurosis, 816ff.
Noise and performance decrement, 849
Nomothetic approach, 502–503, 530, 547–550, 566
Noncontingent interaction, 711
Nondirective therapy (client-centered therapy), 510–511, 784, 814–815
Nonlinear mathematics, 864, 925
Norm sender and norm receiver, 658–659
  coding communication between, 660–661
  and role boundaries, 660
Normal personality, 505–506, 523–524

Norms, 343–344, 656–657, 662ff., 724, 725
  developmental, for personality characteristics, 604
Novelty, 290–291, 294, 296, 297, 315, 319, 330–331, 343
Noxious stimulation drives, 256, 265
Null hypothesis and perception, 33, 67–68
Number concepts, 379
Nurses, selection and defense mechanisms, 668–669
Nurturance, 717
Nurture vs. nature, 526–528

Object identification, 198–200
Object language, 34–35, 37
Objective public identity, 673
Objectivity, 32–33, 215–216, 264, 379–384, 428–429, 514–517, 805ff., 816
Observation, epistemic, 322
  naïve, 32, 34, 89–90
  naturalistic vs. laboratory, 377–378, 716–717, 926–927
On understanding science, 367
One-phase system, 389
Operant, 136ff., 169
Operationism, 8, 34–35, 37ff., 53, 219–220, 382, 512, 515, 803–804
Operations research, 926
Oral fixation, 621
Organismic orientation (see Holistic orientation)
Organization, dynamic, of personality, 522–523
  inside vs. outside, 528–532
  perceptual, factors producing and preventing, 444–451
  sensory, 58, 66ff., 71ff., 82, 144–148, 207, 402–412, 435, 436
Orienting reflexes, 296, 311–313, 330, 331, 334, 336
Overgeneralization, 373–375, 548, 751

Pain, 422–424
Parasympathetic response, 258
Parental behavior, 613–614, 664, 708–709; 715
  and schizophrenia, 759–762, 764–765
Paresis, 744
Pattern density, 80–81
Pattern recognition, 840, 921
Patterns of interaction, 644–645, 709–712
Pedagogical methods, 328–329, 559–564, 573–579
Perception, and behavior, 114–174, 213–249

Perception, convergence of interest in, 9–10, 21–22
  development in child, 338–341
  figure-ground, 72, 247–249
  form, 34, 58ff., 66ff., 79ff.
  and learning, 9–10, 21–22, 30–103, 114–174, 179–211, 365–475
    conceptualizations of perceptual learning, 57–66
    definition of learning, 54–57
    definitions of perception, 31–54
    experimental designs, 66–91
    introduction to article (Postman), 31
    and recognition of words, 91–103
  research in engineering psychology, 839ff.
  schematic, 45
  and sensation, 43–44, 57–58, 63, 117, 214–215
Perceptual curiosity, 302ff., 323
Perceptual defense, 40–41, 219
Perceptual function, 36
Perceptual hypotheses, 47–48
Perceptual learning, 57–66, 338–341, 397–398, 443–454
Perceptual process, 397–398, 418ff., 443ff.
Perceptual response disposition, 38
Perceptual system, 42–43, 51, 645
Performance deficit in schizophrenia, 752, 757ff.
Peripheral responses, 60–61
Permeability of barriers, 720–723
Persistence and change as treated, in personality research, 603–604
  in personality theory, 544–547
  (See also Change; Consistency)
Persona, 674
Personality, approaches to study, 458–462, 594–598
  and arousal, 345
  boundaries, 550–559
  change, 470–472, 491–493, 506, 517–518, 544–547
  consistency, 593–615
  courses, 559–564, 573–579
  definition, 494–498, 593–594
  and dimension of time, 540–547, 603–604
  field, subdivisions, 559–564
  fragments, 499
  and general psychology, 564–579, 597
  and learning theory, 799
  mechanisms or processes, 597–598
  modal, 619–620
  and motivation, 365–475, 649–650
  normal, 505–506, 523–524

Personality, perception, motivation, and learning, 365–475
  physique and, 557–558, 798
  place in psychology (Sanford), 488–579
    boundaries, 550–559
    as field of inquiry, 559–579
    introduction to article, 489–491
    problem of definition, 491–498
    substance, 498–550
  relations to anthropology and sociology (Child), 593–632
    examples of relatively isolated research, 598–615
    study of, definition, 593–594
    major problems in, 594–598
  and role (see Role behavior)
  structure, 520–540, 594–598
  syndromes, 278–279
  tests, 517, 601–603, 610, 617–618, 783, 791, 800–809
  traits, 346–347, 501, 513, 548, 598–599, 641–642, 646–647, 657–658, 676–677, 797
    similarity in social interaction, 709–710, 726
  type, 557–558, 600, 797–798, 802
  uniqueness problem, 547–550, 567, 593ff.
  units, 498–520, 604ff.
  viewed as system, 489ff., 507, 520ff.
Personality through Perception, 571, 572
Personality-social orientation and motivation, 270–277
Personality theory, 498ff., 520ff.
Phase sequences, 61
Phenomenology, 32–35, 37, 48–49, 53, 57–60, 101, 119–120, 215, 380ff., 508ff., 535, 555, 815–816
Philosophy of science, 8, 515
Physiological frame of reference, 7–8
Physiological psychology and human factor engineering, 924
Physiology and psychology, relations between, 7–8
Physique and personality, 557–558, 798
Pilot performance, 847
Plans, 422, 437
Play activities, 390
Play therapy, 811, 814
Pleasure-pain theory, 263–268
Point scales, 792
Policy and Planning Board, 5
Population resources, 912–913
Positive affect, 265, 317
Positivism (see Operationism)
Potency, situational, 666–667

Potential identity, 679–680
Power, 706–707, 712
Prediction of behavior, 570–571, 577, 601, 610
Predictive relationships, 409–410
Predifferentiation, stimulus, 62–63, 210–211, 244, 334, 335
Preference, 152–157, 911–912, 923–924
Premorbid adjustment of schizophrenics, 759, 760
Preparatory set, 50–51
Prepotent response theory, 266
Press, 649–650
Primary self, 674
Probabilistic decision making, 846, 857–858
Probabilistic functionalism, 45–46, 89–91
Proband trends, 749
Problem solving in small groups, 705–706
Proceeding, interpersonal, 713
Process and structure, 425–431
  in personality theory, 520–540, 557–558
Process activity, 525
Process-centered approach, 26
"Process fields" of psychology, 6, 7, 27–28
Processor of information in human engineering, 838, 843–850, 914, 927–928
Professional service expert, 662, 917
Professionalization in psychology, 822
Project A, 5
Project B, 5
Projection in group members, 703
Propositions, analysis in psychotherapy, 713
Proximal and distal stimuli, 45, 49–50, 90–91, 184ff.
Pseudoscience, 376
Psychoanalytic theory, 173, 268–269, 276, 424, 462–473, 497, 505, 509, 526–527, 533–536, 541–542, 621, 629–630, 665–666, 745, 765, 796–797, 810ff.
Psychoanalytic training, 745
Psychodrama, 818
Psychology, and biological sciences, 8, 375–376, 427, 739
  goals, 854–856
  and human engineering, 831–897, 908–932
  place of personality in, 488–579
  "process fields," 6, 7, 27–38
  and social sciences, 8–9
  structure of science, 1–29
  subparts, 9, 27–28
Psychology and the Human Agent, 5

Psychopathology, 738–775, 789
Psychophysical parallelism, 53
Psychophysics, 32, 35–37, 39–40, 43–45, 63–67, 84–89, 91ff., 125ff., 139–141, 180–183, 227–233
Psychosexual development, 629–630, 665–666, 683
Psychosis, 686, 738–775
Psychosomatic relationships, 557–558, 749
Psychotherapy, 541–542, 715–716, 782ff., 810–822
  client-centered, 510–511, 784, 814–815
  group, 818–819
  predicting outcome, 610
  psychotherapist behavior, 709, 815–816, 818, 821
  therapist-patient role behaviors, 655, 707, 715
Psychotropic versus somatotropic models of schizophrenia, 748–749
Public esteem, 681–683, 695–696
Public identity and self-identity, 673–674, 679ff.
Public opinion, 664
Punishment, 452–453
Purkinje phenomenon, 381, 382
Purposivism, 512, 522
Pursuit displays, 847
Pyknic body build, 798

Q-sort, of interpersonal relations, 646–647
  for studying self, 689
Qualitative variables, 870
Quantification, of generalization gradient, 139–144
  of human operator's behavioral properties, 848
  in perception, 35ff.
  of personality mechanisms, 538
  of reinforcement, 123ff.
  (*See also* Methods; Psychophysics)
Questionnaire method, for measuring personality, 800–801
  for self-identity studies, 688–691
Quickening, 848, 850, 875

Ratio scales, 39–40
Rational man, 464, 697
Reaction time, 129, 231, 843–844, 881
Reality principle, 321
Recall, 93–95
  (*See also* Memory)
Receiver of information in human engineering, 838–841
Receptivity to information regarding self-esteem, 687–688

Reciprocality, 711
Recognition, and perception, 33–34, 51n., 91–103
  unconscious, 40–41, 46, 219
  visual pattern, 840
Reductionism, 8, 48, 375–376, 569, 574, 878
Redundancy, 200, 292
Reference groups, 662–667, 695–696
Reflection of feelings, 814–815
Reflexes, orienting, 296, 311–313, 330, 331, 334, 336
Refractory phase, 844
Regions, 649, 674
Regnant processes, 532
Reinforcement, and conflict reduction, 315–316, 817–818
  differential, 55, 61, 62, 65, 72, 83, 94–95, 157ff., 225–226
    (See also Discrimination)
  and drive concepts, 299–300
  history of organism, 218, 219, 235–237, 451
  intermittent, 262
  laws, 84–85, 123–124, 264, 416, 817
  primary and secondary, 260–262, 329, 343, 451ff.
  and social situations, 650
  and task performance in engineering psychology, 924
  threshold, 126, 127
  variable, 451
Relationship therapy, 814
Reliability, 911
Repertory test, 691–692
Representational habits, 412–418, 436ff.
Repressers, 346–347
Repression, 533, 816
  of hostility, 811
Response-produced cues, 60–63, 65, 186–187
Response system, 42–43, 51, 95ff., 168–169
Responses, categories, 39–40, 167ff.
  class, 166–170, 223, 394
  coding, 187–198
  definition, 222–224
  different, efficiency of, 842–843, 910
  emergent and established, 532
  force and time configurations, 842
  inhibition, 41, 330
  parasympathetic and sympathetic, 258
  peripheral, 60–61
Responsibility, 672, 712
Retardation, 787–788, 790
Retention (see Memory)
Reticular formation, 307, 308, 309, 321, 331, 378

Reverse afferentation, 293
Reward centers, 321
Rigidity, 347
Role behavior, 496, 628–632, 643, 655–662, 667–702
Role boundary, 659–660, 675
Role flexibility, 660
Role repertoire, 660
Role-set, 656
Role-taking aptitude, 630
Rorschach test, 602–603, 617, 791, 801–803
Rote learning, 73–74, 395

S-R interactions in engineering psychology, 928–929
S-R theory, 32, 35–37, 51, 55, 60–63, 124ff., 148–149, 164, 166, 180, 186–187, 216ff., 254ff., 382, 395–399, 434–435, 468–472, 499–500, 513, 546, 551–552, 567, 816, 884–885
Safety, 911
Salience, 681–682, 687
Sampling, 374, 644
Satiation, stimulus, 296, 429–430, 446–449
Scaling, 35–37, 39–40, 84–89
  (See also Psychophysics)
Scheduling, 523
Schematic perception, 45
Schizophrenia, 738–775
  etiology, 747–751
Schoenfeld and Cumming's behavior and perception, 213–249
  advanced paradigm $S \rightarrow R_1 \cdot R_2$, 233–244
  assessment of representative perceptions, 244–249
  introduction to article, 214
  problem of perception, 214–220
  simple paradigm $S \rightarrow R$, 220–233
  summary, 249
School board members, role, 661–662
School superintendents, roles, 661–662
Science, and art, 349–350, 600
  other, relations to psychology, 1–29
  of practice, 781–782
  and technology, 367, 835–836, 893
  terminology, 371–372
Secondary reinforcement, 260–262, 329, 343, 451ff.
Secondary self, 674–675
Selection and training, 833, 880, 914–916
Selectivity, 417–418
  and arousal, 308–310
Self, actualization, 524, 680–681
  appraisal, 679–683
  characteristics, 670–672

Self, concepts, 277, 507–512, 670–698, 814
  potential, 679–680
  primary, 674
  secondary, 674–675
  types and structures, 673–679
Self-centered approach as value, 820
Self-esteem, 644, 681ff., 688, 690, 725, 760ff.
Self-involvement, 681, 682, 687
Self-other, 718–719
Self-presentation, 649, 672, 674
Semantic differential, 691, 759–760
Sensation, and learning theory, 114–174
  and perception, 43–44, 57–58, 63, 117, 214–215
Sensitivity, to criticism, 752ff.
  to problems, 346
  (*See also* Epistemic behavior)
Sensory deprivation, 79–82, 317, 383, 408
Sensory and motor processes in engineering psychology, 838–839, 920–922
Sensory order, 58, 66ff., 71ff., 82, 144–148, 402–412, 435, 436
Sensory-perceptual process, 418
Sensory preconditioning (*see* Stimulus, predifferentiation)
Sequential decision making, 326–329, 844, 929
Sequential motor responses, 842, 844
Sequential response dependency, 233
Serials, 713
Servo theory (*see* Feedback)
Set, 50–51, 67, 69, 182–187, 238–240, 683–684
  (*See also* Instruction stimulus)
Settings, behavior, 648–651, 723–724
Sex differences, 604, 616–617, 625–626, 693–694
  in perception, 577
Sex drive, 258–259, 421–422
Sexual development and role, 629–630, 665–666, 683
Shaping behavior, 209, 395, 445, 924
Sickness, 621–622, 624, 795, 820
Sign learning, 525
Similarity, stimulus, 205–209
  of traits in social interaction, 709–710, 726
Simplicity-complexity dimension of aesthetic preferences, 346–347, 625
Simulated systems, 862–864, 929–930
Simultaneous discrimination, 229
Situation, 529ff, 553–557, 642–644, 646–670, 723–724
Situation tests, 804–805
Situational potency, 666–667
Size of behavior setting, 650–651, 654

Skills, motor, 454–456, 604, 881–883, 921–922
Sleep deprivation, 849
Small groups, problem solving in, 705–706
Social atmosphere, 652–653
Social censure and schizophrenia, 752ff.
Social-centered approach, 820–821
Social class, and personality, 626–627
  and reference groups, 663–665
Social climate, 652–653
Social desirability, 689
Social form, 677
Social interaction, 698–726
Social norms, 343–344, 656–657, 662ff., 724, 725
Social position, 656–657, 664
Social relationships, situation, identity, and social interaction, 639–726
  bases, 699–703
  classification, of action, 705–709
    of needs, 703–705
    systems, 717–723
  concluding remarks, 723–726
  identity, 670–698
  introduction to article, 641–642
  patterns, 709–712
  primary components of interpersonal systems, 642–646
  situation, 646–670
  study of social interaction, 698–699
    methods, 713–717
Social sciences, and human factors engineering, 916–917
  and psychology, 8–9
Social structure of groups, 655–662
Social weather, 653
Socialization, 341–344
  and food-getting economy, 626
Sociology, and personality, 593–632
  and psychology, 8–9
Solution learning, 525
Somatotropic vs. psychotropic models of schizophrenia, 748–749
Somatotypes, 558, 798
Sound waves, 426
Species differences and learning, 445
Specific abilities, 788, 789
Specific and diverse exploration, 289–290, 302–306
Specificity theory, 63–66
Speech communications in engineering psychology, 841, 921
Stability, 720–723
  of aircraft under radio guidance, 841
Statistics (*see* Measurement)
Status, 628–632, 656, 682
Stereotyped functions, 390–391

Stimulus, adequate, 236, 433
  class, 137, 165–166
  -as-coded, 189ff.
  distal and proximal, 45, 49–50, 90–91,
    184ff.
  generalization, 85–88, 136–139, 163–
    165
  instance, 137, 165
  instruction, 50–51, 182, 231–232, 237–
    240
  nature, 136ff., 179–211, 220–222
  predifferentiation, 62–63, 210–211,
    244, 334–335
  satiation, 296, 429–430, 446–449
Stochastic processes, 386–387
Stratification theory, 534
Stress, and data-processing, in engineer-
    ing psychology, 848–850
  and schizophrenia, 758
Structural behavior, 134–136
Structuralism, 43–44, 60
Structure and process, 425–431
  in personality theory, 520–540, 557–
    558
  in social relationships, 655–662, 674
Study I, 1–3, 6, 13–14, 18, 25
Study II, 1–29
Subception, 40
Subidentities, 674–676, 701–702
Subjective public identity, 673
Subjectivity, 32–33, 101, 119, 379–384,
    428–429, 805ff., 815–816
  (See also Phenomenology)
Substitute-stimulus hypothesis, 186–187,
    206ff.
Success-induced drives, 266–267
Successive approximation, 209, 395, 445
Successive discrimination, 229ff.
Summation, 148–151
Superego, 816–817
Supernatural beliefs, 624–625
Supportive atmospheres, 652–653
Surprising stimulus patterns, 315
Sympathetic system response, 258
Synesthesia, 243–244
Systematic causation, 541–544
Systematic vs. empirical studies, 1ff., 10,
    23–25, 51, 876–877
Systematic formulation, definition of, 2
Systems, dynamics, displays, and controls,
    843–850
  interpersonal, 712
  performance, 859–860, 870–871, 880–
    883
  research and design, 837, 918–919
Systems theory, 645–646

Tact, 226–227, 230
Tactual cues to control machines, 841
Task, continuous and discrete perform-
    ance, 843–850, 875, 883–886, 928
  difficulty, 876–877, 922
  roles, 660
  taxonomy, 930–931
  variables, 914–916
Taxonomy, task, 930–931
Teaching methods, 328–329
  in field of personality, 559–564, 573–
    579
  (See also Training)
Technology, in human engineering, 851–
    853, 863–865
  vs. research, 367, 835–836, 893
Temperament, 558–559, 615
Temperature, high and low, and informa-
    tion processing, 849
Template, 403–404
Tension reduction, 496, 503, 522–526
  (See also Drive)
Test-taking behavior, 808
Tests, of brain damage, 810
  for clinical use, in psychopathology,
    766–767, 783, 791–793
  intelligence, 786–793
  personality, 517, 601–603, 610, 617–
    618, 783, 791, 800–809
Thematic Apperception Test, 802–803
Themes of analysis, 2–3, 16–18
Theoretical vs. empirical studies, 1ff., 10,
    23–25, 129, 514, 763ff., 926
Theory, 54ff., 170–173
  biological-physiological motivation,
    274–275
  of cerebral organization, 410–411
  cognitive (see Cognitive theory)
  collative motivation, 316–322, 329–338
  conditioning, 157–170
  enrichment, 63–66
  general, of psychology, 565
  information, 200, 291–292, 324, 837ff.,
    860–861, 925
  interpersonal, 724–726
  learning (see Learning theory)
  Lewinian (see Lewinian theory)
  of memory, 425–428
  of mental testing movement, 787–793
  personality, 498ff., 520ff.
  prepotent response, 266
  psychoanalytic (see Psychoanalytic
    theory)
  S-R (see S-R theory)
  of schizophrenia, 763–766
  servo, 860–861, 925
  (See also Feedback)

Theory, of sound waves, 426
specificity vs. association, 63–66
stratification, 534
systems, 645–646
Therapy (see Psychoanalytic theory;
Psychotherapy)
Thinking, ameaningful, 29
directed, 322, 324, 326–329, 339–340,
367–368
intuitive, 340
Threat, 533
Time dimension in personality theory,
540–547, 603–604
Time and force configurations of responses, 842
Time-and-motion analysis, 863–864
TOTE, 278
Trace, memory, 58–59, 426
Tracking tasks, 846–848, 861, 864, 877,
883–886
under vigilance conditions, 849–850
Trade-off functions, 913–914
Training, in clinical psychology, 756,
770–774, 782, 784, 785, 803, 823
in human engineering, 892–893, 895–
897, 931–932
medical, 744–746
psychoanalytic, 745
Trait, 346–347, 501, 513, 548, 598–599,
641–642, 646–647, 657–658, 676–
677, 797
similarity in social interaction, 709–
710, 726
Transactional functionalism, 46–47
Transactionalism, 403–404
Transfer, 209–211
(See also Generalization)
Transference, 542, 813
Transforms, 388
Transitory processes, 428ff., 434–436
Transmission of information between
man and machine, 838–843
Transposition, 56, 152ff., 202–205, 246–
247, 429
Twins and schizophrenia, 749
Two-factor theories, 267–268
Two-phase systems, 389
Type, personality, 557–558, 600, 797–
798, 802

Unburdening, 875
Uncertainty (entropy), 292, 294–295,
324
Unconscious processes, 40–41, 46, 57,
412–413, 464–465, 532–536
Union politico, 662
Uniqueness of personality, 547–550,
567, 593ff.

Units, of personality, 498–520, 604ff.
of social interaction, 713–715
Universality of personality phenomena,
615–623
Unlearned responses, 390–391, 406–407,
414–415, 424, 431–434, 465–467,
787
exploratory, 300–301

Valences, 720–723
Validity, consensual, 705
construct, 611, 612
functional and ecological, 45–46
intelligence tests, 788–789, 792, 823
perceptual reports, 32–34, 39, 68, 71,
82, 91ff.
performance, 79–80, 604ff.
personality tests, 601, 604ff., 610–611,
689–691, 803, 823
Values, 276, 277, 297, 618–619, 656,
677–679, 700–701, 707, 819–821
Variables, in definitions of perception,
48–54
dependent, 222–224
empirical, in schizophrenia, 763–766
in engineering psychology, 865–873,
910–916
input and intervening, in Hullian
system, 254–255
interplay, 711–712
qualitative, 870
from which psychology can develop,
380–384
Velocity and acceleration perception, 840
Verbal learning, 73–74, 91–103, 226–227,
329ff.
Verbal report, 716
and experience, 32–33, 68, 71, 219–
220, 240–241
Vexierversuch, 96–98, 236–237
Vicious circle, 715
Vigilance, 848–849
Vision, binocular, 81
Visual cliff, 80–81
Visual pattern recognition, 840
Voluntary behavior, 335–336, 856

Warning signals, 840
Weaning and personality characteristics,
621–622
Will power, 814
Withdrawal in schizophrenia, 752
Word-association technique, 796–797
Word recognition, 91–103

Zone of conformity, 654